Definition of Absolute Value

$$|x| = \begin{cases} x \text{ when } x \geq 0 \\ -x \text{ when } x < 0 \end{cases}$$

Absolute Value Equations

- If $k \geq 0$, then $|x| = k$ is equivalent to $x = k$ or $x = -k$.
- If a and b are algebraic expressions, $|a| = |b|$ is equivalent to $a = b$ or $a = -b$.

Absolute Value Inequalities

- If $k > 0$, then $|x| < k$ is equivalent to $-k < x < k$.
- If $k > 0$, then $|x| > k$ is equivalent to $x > k$ or $x < -k$.

These two properties hold for $\leq$ and $\geq$ also.

Circles

The standard form of an equation of a circle with center (h, k) and radius r:
$$(x - h)^2 + (y - k)^2 = r^2$$

The standard form of an equation of a circle with center $(0, 0)$ and radius r:
$$x^2 + y^2 = r^2$$

Quadratic Functions

A **quadratic function** is a second-degree polynomial function in one variable of the form
$$f(x) = ax^2 + bx + c \text{ or } y = ax^2 + bx + c,$$
where a, b, and c are real numbers and $a \neq 0$.

The graph of a quadratic function of the form
$$f(x) = ax^2 + bx + c \quad (a \neq 0)$$
is a **parabola** with vertex at
$$\left(-\frac{b}{2a}, c - \frac{b^2}{4a}\right)$$

- If $a > 0$, the parabola **opens upward.**
- If $a < 0$, the parabola **opens downward.**

The **standard form of an equation of a quadratic function** is
$$y = f(x) = a(x - h)^2 + k \quad (a \neq 0)$$

The vertex is at (h, k).
- The parabola opens upward when $a > 0$ and downward when $a < 0$.
- The axis of symmetry of the parabola is the vertical line graph of the equation $x = h$.

Tests for Symmetry

Test for x-axis symmetry:
To test for x-axis symmetry, replace y with $-y$. If the resulting equation is equivalent to the original one, the graph is symmetric about the x-axis.

Test for y-axis symmetry:
To test for y-axis symmetry, replace x with $-x$. If the resulting equation is equivalent to the original one, the graph is symmetric about the y-axis.

Test for origin symmetry:
To test for symmetry about the origin, replace x with $-x$ and y with $-y$. If the resulting equation is equivalent to the original one, the graph is symmetric about the origin.

Graphs of Common Functions

Greatest-Integer Function

Interest Formulas

Compound interest formula:
If P dollars are deposited in an account earning interest at an annual rate r, compounded n times each year, the amount A in the account after t years is given by
$$A = P\left(1 + \frac{r}{n}\right)^{nt}$$

Continuous compound interest formula:
If P dollars are deposited in an account earning interest at an annual rate r, compounded continuously, the amount A after t years is given by the formula
$$A = Pe^{rt}$$

College Algebra

MATH 7

11th Edition

R. David Gustafson | Jeff Hughes

CENGAGE
Learning·

Australia • Brazil • Japan • Korea • Mexico • Singapore • Spain • United Kingdom • United States

College Algebra: MATH 7, 11th Edition

College Algebra, 11th Edition
R. David Gustafson | Jeff Hughes

© 2013, 2010 Cengage Learning. All rights reserved.

For product information and technology assistance, contact us at
Cengage Learning Customer & Sales Support, 1-800-354-9706

For permission to use material from this text or product,
submit all requests online at **cengage.com/permissions**
Further permissions questions can be emailed to
permissionrequest@cengage.com

This book contains select works from existing Cengage Learning resources and was produced by Cengage Learning Custom Solutions for collegiate use. As such, those adopting and/or contributing to this work are responsible for editorial content accuracy, continuity and completeness.

Compilation © 2015 Cengage Learning

ISBN: 978-1-305-74749-4

WCN: 01-100-101

Cengage Learning
20 Channel Center Street
Boston, MA 02210
USA

Cengage Learning is a leading provider of customized learning solutions with office locations around the globe, including Singapore, the United Kingdom, Australia, Mexico, Brazil, and Japan. Locate your local office at:
www.international.cengage.com/region.

Cengage Learning products are represented in Canada by Nelson Education, Ltd.

For your lifelong learning solutions, visit **www.cengage.com/custom.**

Visit our corporate website at **www.cengage.com.**

Contents

Equations and Inequalities

CAREERS AND MATHEMATICS: Marketing

People who work in the field of marketing coordinate their companies' market research, marketing strategy, sales, advertising, promotion, pricing, product development, and public relations activities. Advertising managers direct a firm's promotional campaign while marketing managers promote products and services. Promotions managers work on incentives to increase sales while public relations managers plan and direct the public image for the employer. Sales managers plan and direct the distribution of the product to the customer.

Education and Mathematics Required
- For marketing, sales, and promotions management positions, employers often prefer a bachelor's or master's degree in business administration with an emphasis on marketing. For advertising management positions, some employers prefer a bachelor's degree in advertising or journalism. For public relations management positions, some employers prefer a bachelor's or master's degree in public relations or journalism.
- College Algebra, Business Calculus I and II, and Economic Statistics are required.

How Marketing Managers Use Math and Who Employs Them
- Statistics is used for predicting sales and effectiveness of advertising campaigns.
- These managers are found in virtually every industry. They are employed in wholesale trade, retail trade, manufacturing, the finance and insurance industries, as well as professional, scientific, and technical services, public and private educational services, and healthcare.

Career Outlook and Salary
- Overall employment of advertising, marketing, promotions, public relations, and sales managers is expected to increase by 13 percent through 2018.
- The median annual wages in May 2008 were $80,220 for advertising and promotions managers, $108,580 for marketing managers, $97,260 for sales managers, and $89,430 for public relations managers.

For more information see: www.bls.gov/oco

The main topic of this chapter is equations—one of the most important concepts in algebra. Equations are used in almost every academic discipline and especially in chemistry, physics, medicine, computer science, and business.

1.1 Linear Equations and Rational Equations

In this section, we will learn to

1. Use the properties of equality.
2. Solve linear equations.
3. Solve rational equations.
4. Solve formulas for a specific variable.

It's been said that "weddings today are as beautiful as they are expensive." Suppose a couple budgets $3,000 for their wedding reception at a historic home. If $600 is charged for renting the home and there is a $24-per-person fee for food and beverages, how many guests can the couple accommodate at their reception?

If we let the **variable** x represent the number of guests, the expression $600 + 24x$ represents the cost for the reception. That is, $600 for the home rental plus $24 times the number of guests, x. We want to know the value of x that makes the expression equal $3,000.

We can write the statement $600 + 24x = 3000$ to indicate that the two quantities are equal. A statement indicating that two quantities are equal is called an **equation.** In this section, we will review how to solve equations of this type.

If $x = 100$, the equation is true because when we substitute 100 for x, we obtain a true statement.

$$600 + 24(100) = 3000$$
$$600 + 2400 = 3000$$
$$3000 = 3000$$

The couple can accommodate 100 guests at their wedding reception.

An equation can be either true or false. For example, the equation $2 + 2 = 4$ is true, and the equation $2 + 3 = 6$ is false. An equation such as $3x - 2 = 10$ can be true or false depending on the value of x.

If $x = 4$, the equation is true, because 4 satisfies the equation.

$$3x - 2 = 10$$
$$3(4) - 2 \stackrel{?}{=} 10 \qquad \text{Substitute 4 for } x. \text{ Read } \stackrel{?}{=} \text{ as "is possibly equal to."}$$
$$12 - 2 \stackrel{?}{=} 10$$
$$10 = 10$$

This equation is false for all other values of x.

Any number that satisfies an equation is called a **solution** or **root** of the equation. The set of all solutions of an equation is called its **solution set.** We have seen that the solution set of $3x - 2 = 10$ is $\{4\}$. To **solve** an equation means to find its solution set.

There can be restrictions on the values of a variable. For example, in the fraction

$$\frac{x^2 + 4}{x - 2}$$

we cannot replace x with 2, because that would make the denominator equal to 0.

EXAMPLE 1   **Finding the Restrictions on the Values of a Variable**

Find the restrictions on the values of b in the equation: $\dfrac{7b}{b + 6} = \dfrac{2}{b - 1}$.

SOLUTION   For $\frac{7b}{b+6}$ to be a real number, b cannot be -6 because that would make the denominator 0. For $\frac{2}{b-1}$ to be a real number, b cannot be 1 because that would make the denominator 0. Thus, the values of b are restricted to the set of all real numbers except 1 or -6. ∎

Self Check 1   Find the restrictions on a: $\dfrac{5}{a+5} = \dfrac{3a}{a-2}$.

Now Try Exercise 13.

There are three types of equations: identities, contradictions, and conditional equations. These are defined and illustrated in the following table.

Type of Equation	Definition	Example
Identity	Every acceptable real number replacement for the variable is a solution.	$x^2 - 9 = (x+3)(x-3)$ Every real number x is a solution.
Contradiction	No real number is a solution.	$x = x + 1$ The equation has no solution. No real number can be 1 greater than itself.
Conditional Equation	Solution set contains some but not all real numbers.	$3x - 2 = 10$ The equation has one solution, the number 4.

Two equations with the same solution set are called **equivalent equations.**

1. Use the Properties of Equality

There are certain properties of equality that we can use to transform equations into equivalent but less complicated equations. If we use these properties, the resulting equations will be equivalent and will have the same solution set.

Properties of Equality

The Addition and Subtraction Properties
If a, b, and c are real numbers and $a = b$, then

$$a + c = b + c \quad\text{and}\quad a - c = b - c$$

The Multiplication and Division Properties
If a, b, and c are real numbers and $a = b$, then

$$ac = bc \quad\text{and}\quad \frac{a}{c} = \frac{b}{c} \quad (c \neq 0)$$

The Substitution Property
In an equation, a quantity may be substituted for its equal without changing the truth of the equation.

2. Solve Linear Equations

The easiest equations to solve are the **first-degree** or **linear equations.** Since these equations involve first-degree polynomials, they are also called **first-degree polynomial equations.**

Linear Equations

A **linear equation in one variable** (say, x) is any equation that can be written in the form

$$ax + b = 0 \qquad (a \text{ and } b \text{ are real numbers and } a \neq 0)$$

To solve the linear equation $2x + 3 = 0$, we subtract 3 from both sides of the equation and divide both sides by 2.

$$2x + 3 = 0$$

$$2x + 3 - 3 = 0 - 3 \qquad \text{To undo the addition of 3, subtract 3 from both sides.}$$

$$2x = -3$$

$$\frac{2x}{2} = -\frac{3}{2} \qquad \text{To undo the multiplication by 2, divide both sides by 2.}$$

$$x = -\frac{3}{2}$$

To verify that $-\frac{3}{2}$ satisfies the equation, we substitute $-\frac{3}{2}$ for x and simplify:

$$2x + 3 = 0$$

$$2\left(-\frac{3}{2}\right) + 3 \stackrel{?}{=} 0 \qquad \text{Substitute } -\frac{3}{2} \text{ for } x.$$

$$-3 + 3 \stackrel{?}{=} 0 \qquad 2\left(-\frac{3}{2}\right) = -3$$

$$0 = 0$$

Since both sides of the equation are equal, the solution checks.

In Exercise 74, you will be asked to solve the general linear equation $ax + b = 0$ for x, thereby showing that every conditional linear equation has exactly one solution.

EXAMPLE 2   Solving a Linear Equation

Find the solution set: $3(x + 2) = 5x + 2$.

SOLUTION   We proceed as follows:

$$3(x + 2) = 5x + 2$$

$$3x + 6 = 5x + 2 \qquad \text{Use the Distributive Property and remove parentheses.}$$

$$3x + 6 - 3x = 5x - 3x + 2 \qquad \text{Subtract } 3x \text{ from both sides.}$$

$$6 = 2x + 2 \qquad \text{Combine like terms.}$$

$$6 - 2 = 2x + 2 - 2 \qquad \text{Subtract 2 from both sides.}$$

$$4 = 2x \qquad \text{Simplify.}$$

$$\frac{4}{2} = \frac{2x}{2} \qquad \text{Divide both sides by 2.}$$

$$2 = x \qquad \text{Simplify.}$$

Since all of the above equations are equivalent, the solution set of the original equation is $\{2\}$. Verify that 2 satisfies the equation.

Self Check 2   Find the solution set: $4(x - 3) = 7x - 3$.

Now Try Exercise 35.

ACCENT ON TECHNOLOGY   **Checking Solutions to Linear Equations**

Using the table feature on a graphing calculator, we can easily check the solution of a linear equation. We enter each side of the equation into the graph editor; go to the table, and then enter the value of x that we found as the solution. The value of both entries in the table should be the same. These steps are shown in Figure 1-1 below for Example 2. We see that both Y1 and Y2 equal 12 when $x = 2$. This verifies the solution.

Enter each side of the equation.   **Go to the table and enter the value $x = 2$.**

(a)   (b)

FIGURE 1-1

EXAMPLE 3   **Solving a Linear Equation with Fractions**

Find the solution set: $\dfrac{3}{2}y - \dfrac{2}{3} = \dfrac{1}{5}y$.

SOLUTION   To clear the equation of fractions, we multiply both sides by the least common denominator (LCD) of the three fractions and proceed as follows:

$$\frac{3}{2}y - \frac{2}{3} = \frac{1}{5}y$$

$$30\left(\frac{3}{2}y - \frac{2}{3}\right) = 30\left(\frac{1}{5}y\right) \qquad \text{Multiply both sides by 30, the LCD of } \frac{3}{2}, \frac{2}{3}, \text{ and } \frac{1}{5}.$$

$$45y - 20 = 6y \qquad \text{Remove parentheses and simplify.}$$

$$45y - 20 + 20 = 6y + 20 \qquad \text{Add 20 to both sides.}$$

$$45y = 6y + 20 \qquad \text{Simplify.}$$

$$45y - 6y = 6y - 6y + 20 \qquad \text{Subtract } 6y \text{ from both sides.}$$

$$39y = 20 \qquad \text{Combine like terms.}$$

$$\frac{39y}{39} = \frac{20}{39} \qquad \text{Divide both sides by 39.}$$

$$y = \frac{20}{39} \qquad \text{Simplify.}$$

The solution set is $\left\{\dfrac{20}{39}\right\}$. Verify that $\dfrac{20}{39}$ satisfies the equation.

Self Check 3   Find the solution set: $\dfrac{2}{3}p - 3 = \dfrac{p}{6}$.

Now Try Exercise 43.

EXAMPLE 4 **Solving Linear Equations**

Solve: **a.** $3(x + 5) = 3(1 + x)$ **b.** $5 + 5(x + 2) - 2x = 3x + 15$

SOLUTION **a.** $3(x + 5) = 3(1 + x)$

$3x + 15 = 3 + 3x$ Remove parentheses.

$3x - 3x + 15 = 3 + 3x - 3x$ Subtract $3x$ from both sides.

$15 = 3$ Combine like terms.

Since $15 = 3$ is false, the equation has no roots. Its solution set is the empty set, which is denoted as $\varnothing$. This equation is a contradiction.

b. $5 + 5(x + 2) - 2x = 3x + 15$

$5 + 5x + 10 - 2x = 3x + 15$ Remove parentheses.

$3x + 15 = 3x + 15$ Simplify.

Because both sides of the final equation are identical, every value of x will make the equation true. The solution set is the set of all real numbers. This equation is an identity.

■

Self Check 4 Solve: **a.** $-2(x - 4) + 6x = 4(x + 1)$
                              b. $2(x + 1) + 4 = 2(x + 3)$

Now Try Exercise 51.

3. Solve Rational Equations

Rational equations are equations that contain rational expressions. Some examples of rational equations are

$$\frac{2}{x - 3} = 7, \qquad \frac{x + 1}{x - 2} = \frac{3}{x - 2}, \qquad \text{and} \qquad \frac{x + 2}{x + 3} + \frac{1}{x^2 + 2x - 3} = 1$$

When solving these equations, we will multiply both sides by a quantity containing a variable. When we do this, we could inadvertently multiply both sides of an equation by 0 and obtain a solution that makes the denominator of a fraction 0. In this case, we have found a false solution, called an **extraneous solution.** These solutions do not satisfy the equation and must be discarded.

The following equation has an extraneous solution.

$$\frac{x + 1}{x - 2} = \frac{3}{x - 2}$$

$$(x - 2)\left(\frac{x + 1}{x - 2}\right) = (x - 2)\left(\frac{3}{x - 2}\right) \qquad \text{Multiply both sides by } x - 2.$$

$$x + 1 = 3 \qquad \qquad \frac{x - 2}{x - 2} = 1$$

$$x = 2 \qquad \qquad \text{Subtract 1 from both sides.}$$

If we check by substituting 2 for x, we obtain 0's in the denominator. Thus, 2 is not a root. The solution set is $\varnothing$.

EXAMPLE 5 **Solving a Rational Equation**

Solve: $\dfrac{x + 2}{x + 3} + \dfrac{1}{x^2 + 2x - 3} = 1.$

SOLUTION Note that x cannot be -3, because that would cause the denominator of the first fraction to be 0. To find other restrictions, we factor the trinomial in the denominator of the second fraction.

$$x^2 + 2x - 3 = (x + 3)(x - 1)$$

Since the denominator will be 0 when $x = -3$ or $x = 1$, x cannot be -3 or 1.

$$\frac{x + 2}{x + 3} + \frac{1}{x^2 + 2x - 3} = 1$$

$$\frac{x + 2}{x + 3} + \frac{1}{(x + 3)(x - 1)} = 1 \qquad \text{Factor } x^2 + 2x - 3.$$

$$(x + 3)(x - 1)\left[\frac{x + 2}{x + 3} + \frac{1}{(x + 3)(x - 1)}\right] = (x + 3)(x - 1)1 \qquad \text{Multiply both sides by } (x + 3)(x - 1).$$

$$\cancel{(x + 3)}(x - 1)\left(\frac{x + 2}{\cancel{x + 3}}\right) + \cancel{(x + 3)}\cancel{(x - 1)}\frac{1}{\cancel{(x + 3)}\cancel{(x - 1)}} = (x + 3)(x - 1)1 \qquad \text{Remove brackets.}$$

$$(x - 1)(x + 2) + 1 = (x + 3)(x - 1) \qquad \text{Simplify.}$$

$$x^2 + x - 2 + 1 = x^2 + 2x - 3 \qquad \text{Multiply the binomials.}$$

$$x - 1 = 2x - 3 \qquad \begin{array}{l}\text{Subtract } x^2 \text{ from both sides} \\ \text{and combine like terms.}\end{array}$$

$$2 = x \qquad \text{Add 3 and subtract } x \text{ from both sides.}$$

Because 2 is a meaningful replacement for x, it is a root. However, it is a good idea to check it.

$$\frac{x + 2}{x + 3} + \frac{1}{x^2 + 2x - 3} = 1$$

$$\frac{2 + 2}{2 + 3} + \frac{1}{2^2 + 2(2) - 3} \overset{?}{=} 1 \qquad \text{Substitute 2 for } x.$$

$$\frac{4}{5} + \frac{1}{5} \overset{?}{=} 1$$

$$1 = 1$$

Since 2 satisfies the equation, it is a root.

Self Check 5 Solve: $\dfrac{3}{5} + \dfrac{7}{x + 2} = 2$.

Now Try Exercise 61.

4. Solve Formulas for a Specific Variable

Many equations, called **formulas,** contain several variables. For example, the formula that converts degrees Celsius to degrees Fahrenheit is $F = \frac{9}{5}C + 32$. If we want to change a large number of Fahrenheit readings to degrees Celsius, it would be tedious to substitute each value of F into the formula and then repeatedly solve it for C. It is better to solve the formula for C, substitute the values for F, and evaluate C directly.

EXAMPLE 6   Solving a Formula for a Specific Variable

Solve $F = \dfrac{9}{5}C + 32$ for C.

SOLUTION   We use the same methods as for solving linear equations.

$$F = \frac{9}{5}C + 32$$

$$F - 32 = \frac{9}{5}C \qquad \text{Subtract 32 from both sides.}$$

$$\frac{5}{9}(F - 32) = \frac{5}{9}\left(\frac{9}{5}C\right) \qquad \text{Multiply both sides by } \frac{5}{9}.$$

$$\frac{5}{9}(F - 32) = C \qquad \text{Simplify.}$$

This result can also be written in the form $C = \dfrac{5F - 160}{9}$.

Self Check 6   Solve $C = \dfrac{5}{9}(F - 32)$ for F.

Now Try Exercise 79.

EXAMPLE 7   Solving a Formula for a Specific Variable

The formula $A = P + Prt$ is used to find the amount of money in a savings account at the end of a specified time. A represents the amount, P represents the principal (the original deposit), r represents the rate of simple interest per unit of time, and t represents the number of units of time. Solve this formula for P.

SOLUTION   We factor P from both terms on the right side of the equation and proceed as follows:

$$A = P + Prt$$

$$A = P(1 + rt) \qquad \text{Factor out } P.$$

$$\frac{A}{1 + rt} = P \qquad \text{Divide both sides by } 1 + rt.$$

$$P = \frac{A}{1 + rt}$$

Self Check 7   Solve $pq = fq + fp$ for f.

Now Try Exercise 85.

Self Check Answers   1. all real numbers except 2 or -5 2. $\{-3\}$ 3. $\{6\}$
4. **a.** no solution   **b.** all real numbers   5. 3   6. $F = \dfrac{9}{5}C + 32$
7. $f = \dfrac{pq}{q + p}$

Exercises **1.1**

Getting Ready
You should be able to complete these vocabulary and concept statements before you proceed to the practice exercises.

Fill in the blanks.

1. If a number satisfies an equation, it is called a _____ or a _____ of the equation.
2. If an equation is true for all values of its variable, it is called an _____.
3. A contradiction is an equation that is true for _____ values of its variable.
4. A _____ equation is true for some values of its variable and is not true for others.
5. An equation of the form $ax + b = 0$ is called a _____ equation.
6. If an equation contains rational expressions, it is called a _____ equation.
7. A conditional linear equation has _____ root.
8. The _____ of a fraction can never be 0.

Practice
Each quantity represents a real number. Find any restrictions on x.

9. $x + 3 = 1$

10. $\dfrac{1}{2}x - 7 = 14$

11. $\dfrac{1}{x} = 12$

12. $\dfrac{3}{x - 2} = 9x$

13. $\dfrac{8}{x - 3} = \dfrac{5}{x + 2}$

14. $\dfrac{x}{x - 3} = -\dfrac{4}{x + 4}$

15. $\dfrac{1}{x - 3} = \dfrac{5x}{x^2 - 16}$

16. $\dfrac{1}{x^2 - 3x - 4} = \dfrac{5}{x} + 2$

Solve each equation, if possible. Classify each one as an identity, a conditional equation, or a contradiction.

17. $2x + 5 = 15$

18. $3x + 2 = x + 8$

19. $2(n + 2) - 5 = 2n$

20. $3(m + 2) = 2(m + 3) + m$

21. $\dfrac{x + 7}{2} = 7$

22. $\dfrac{x}{2} - 7 = 14$

23. $2(a + 1) = 3(a - 2) - a$

24. $x^2 = (x + 4)(x - 4) + 16$

25. $3(x - 3) = \dfrac{6x - 18}{2}$

26. $x(x + 2) = (x + 1)^2$

27. $\dfrac{3}{b - 3} = 1$

28. $x^2 - 8x + 15 = (x - 3)(x + 5)$

29. $2x^2 + 5x - 3 = (2x - 1)(x + 3)$

30. $2x^2 + 5x - 3 = 2x\left(x + \dfrac{19}{2}\right)$

Solve each equation. If an equation has no solution, so indicate.

31. $2x + 7 = 10 - x$ 32. $9a - 3 = 15 + 3a$

33. $5(x - 2) = 2(x + 4)$ 34. $5(r - 4) = -5(r - 4)$

35. $7(2x + 5) - 6(x + 8) = 7$

36. $6(x - 5) - 4(x + 2) = -1$

37. $\dfrac{5}{3}z - 8 = 7$ 38. $\dfrac{4}{3}y + 12 = -4$

39. $\dfrac{z}{5} + 2 = 4$ 40. $\dfrac{3p}{7} - p = -4$

41. $\dfrac{3x - 2}{3} = 2x + \dfrac{7}{3}$ 42. $\dfrac{7}{2}x + 5 = x + \dfrac{15}{2}$

43. $\dfrac{3x + 1}{20} = \dfrac{1}{2}$ 44. $2x - \dfrac{7}{6} + \dfrac{x}{6} = \dfrac{4x + 3}{6}$

45. $\dfrac{3 + x}{3} + \dfrac{x + 7}{2} = 4x + 1$

46. $2(2x + 1) - \dfrac{3x}{2} = \dfrac{-3(4 + x)}{2}$

47. $\dfrac{3}{2}(3x - 2) - 10x - 4 = 0$

48. $\dfrac{a(a - 3) + 5}{7} = \dfrac{(a - 1)^2}{7}$

49. $\dfrac{(y + 2)^2}{3} = y + 2 + \dfrac{y^2}{3}$

50. $(t + 1)(t - 1) = (t + 2)(t - 3) + 4$

51. $x(x + 2) = (x + 1)^2 - 1$

52. $(x - 2)(x - 3) = (x + 3)(x + 4)$

53. $2(s + 2) + (s + 3)^2 = s(s + 5) + 2\left(\dfrac{17}{2} + s\right)$

54. $\dfrac{3}{x} + \dfrac{1}{2} = \dfrac{4}{x}$

55. $\dfrac{2}{x + 1} + \dfrac{1}{3} = \dfrac{1}{x + 1}$ 56. $\dfrac{3}{x - 2} + \dfrac{1}{x} = \dfrac{3}{x - 2}$

57. $\dfrac{9t + 6}{t(t + 3)} = \dfrac{7}{t + 3}$

58. $x + \dfrac{2(-2x + 1)}{3x + 5} = \dfrac{3x^2}{3x + 5}$

59. $\dfrac{2}{(a - 7)(a + 2)} = \dfrac{4}{(a + 3)(a + 2)}$

60. $\dfrac{2}{n - 2} + \dfrac{1}{n + 1} = \dfrac{1}{n^2 - n - 2}$

61. $\dfrac{2x + 3}{x^2 + 5x + 6} + \dfrac{3x - 2}{x^2 + x - 6} = \dfrac{5x - 2}{x^2 - 4}$

62. $\dfrac{3x}{x^2 + x} - \dfrac{2x}{x^2 + 5x} = \dfrac{x + 2}{x^2 + 6x + 5}$

63. $\dfrac{3x + 5}{x^3 + 8} + \dfrac{3}{x^2 - 4} = \dfrac{2(3x - 2)}{(x - 2)(x^2 - 2x + 4)}$

64. $\dfrac{1}{n + 8} - \dfrac{3n - 4}{5n^2 + 42n + 16} = \dfrac{1}{5n + 2}$

65. $\dfrac{1}{11 - n} - \dfrac{2(3n - 1)}{-7n^2 + 74n + 33} = \dfrac{1}{7n + 3}$

66. $\dfrac{4}{a^2 - 13a - 48} - \dfrac{2}{a^2 - 18a + 32} = \dfrac{1}{a^2 + a - 6}$

67. $\dfrac{5}{y + 4} + \dfrac{2}{y + 2} = \dfrac{6}{y + 2} - \dfrac{1}{y^2 + 6y + 8}$

68. $\dfrac{6}{2a - 6} - \dfrac{3}{3 - 3a} = \dfrac{1}{a^2 - 4a + 3}$

69. $\dfrac{3y}{6 - 3y} + \dfrac{2y}{2y + 4} = \dfrac{8}{4 - y^2}$

70. $\dfrac{3 + 2a}{a^2 + 6 + 5a} - \dfrac{2 - 3a}{a^2 - 6 + a} = \dfrac{5a - 2}{a^2 - 4}$

71. $\dfrac{a}{a + 2} - 1 = -\dfrac{3a + 2}{a^2 + 4a + 4}$

72. $\dfrac{x - 1}{x + 3} + \dfrac{x - 2}{x - 3} = \dfrac{1 - 2x}{3 - x}$

Solve each formula for the specified variable.

73. $k = 2.2p;\ p$

74. $ax + b = 0;\ x$

75. $P = 2l + 2w;\ w$

76. $V = \dfrac{1}{3}\pi r^2 h;\ h$

77. $V = \dfrac{1}{3}\pi r^2 h;\ r^2$

78. $z = \dfrac{x - \mu}{\sigma};\ \mu$

79. $P_n = L + \dfrac{si}{f};\ s$

80. $P_n = L + \dfrac{si}{f};\ f$

81. $F = \dfrac{mMg}{r^2};\ m$

82. $\dfrac{1}{f} = \dfrac{1}{p} + \dfrac{1}{q};\ f$

83. $\dfrac{x}{a} + \dfrac{y}{b} = 1;\ y$

84. $\dfrac{x}{a} - \dfrac{y}{b} = 1;\ a$

85. $\dfrac{1}{r} = \dfrac{1}{r_1} + \dfrac{1}{r_2};\ r$

86. $\dfrac{1}{r} = \dfrac{1}{r_1} + \dfrac{1}{r_2};\ r_1$

87. $l = a + (n - 1)d;\ n$

88. $l = a + (n - 1)d;\ d$

89. $a = (n - 2)\dfrac{180}{n};\ n$

90. $S = \dfrac{a - lr}{1 - r};\ a$

91. $R = \dfrac{1}{\dfrac{1}{r_1} + \dfrac{1}{r_2} + \dfrac{1}{r_3}};\ r_1$

92. $R = \dfrac{1}{\dfrac{1}{r_1} + \dfrac{1}{r_2} + \dfrac{1}{r_3}};\ r_3$

Discovery and Writing

93. Explain why a conditional linear equation always has exactly one root.

94. Define an extraneous solution and explain how such a solution occurs.

Review

Simplify each expression. Use absolute value symbols when necessary.

95. $(25x^2)^{1/2}$

96. $\left(\dfrac{25p^2}{16q^4}\right)^{1/2}$

97. $\left(\dfrac{125x^3}{8y^6}\right)^{-2/3}$

98. $\left(-\dfrac{27y^3}{1{,}000x^6}\right)^{1/3}$

99. $\sqrt{25y^2}$

100. $\sqrt[3]{-125y^9}$

101. $\sqrt[4]{\dfrac{a^4 b^{12}}{z^8}}$

102. $\sqrt[5]{\dfrac{x^{10} y^5}{z^{15}}}$

1.2 Applications of Linear Equations

In this section, we will learn to

1. Solve number problems.
2. Solve geometric problems.
3. Solve investment problems.
4. Solve break-point analysis problems.
5. Solve shared-work problems.
6. Solve mixture problems.
7. Solve uniform motion problems.

John Shearer/WireImage

Tim McGraw is one of the most successful country music singers. He is married to country singer Faith Hill and is the son of former baseball player Tug McGraw. His albums sales have exceeded 40 million copies and his concert tours have been attended by thousands of fans.

Suppose you hear that for one day only Tim McGraw concert tickets can be purchased for 30% off the original price. Knowing this is a bargain, you immediately purchase a ticket for $28, the selling price. Later that day, this question comes to mind: What was the original price of the concert ticket?

A linear equation can be used to model this problem. We can let x represent the original price of the concert ticket and subtract 30% of x (the discount) and we will get the selling price $28. The linear equation is $x - 0.3x = 28$. We can solve this equation to determine the original price of the concert ticket.

$$x - 0.3x = 28$$
$$0.7x = 28 \qquad \text{Combine like terms.}$$
$$x = \frac{28}{0.7} \qquad \text{Divide both sides by 0.7.}$$
$$x = 40$$

The original price of the concert ticket is $40.

In this section, we will use the equation-solving techniques discussed in the previous section to solve applied problems (often called *word problems*). To solve these problems, we must translate the verbal description of the problem into an equation. The process of finding the equation that describes the words of the problem is called **mathematical modeling.** The equation itself is often called a **mathematical model** of the situation described in the word problem.

The following list of steps provides a strategy to follow when we try to find the equation that models an applied problem.

Strategy for Modeling Equations

1. Analyze the problem to see what you are to find. Often, drawing a diagram or making a table will help you visualize the facts.
2. Pick a variable to represent the quantity that is to be found, and write a sentence telling what that variable represents. Express all other quantities mentioned in the problem as expressions involving this single variable.
3. Find a way to express a quantity in two different ways. This might involve a formula from geometry, finance, or physics.
4. Form an equation indicating that the two quantities found in Step 3 are equal.
5. Solve the equation.
6. Answer the questions asked in the problem.
7. Check the answers in the words of the problem.

This list does not apply to all situations, but it can be used for a wide range of problems with only slight modifications.

1. Solve Number Problems

EXAMPLE 1   Solving a Number Problem

A student has scores of 74%, 78%, and 70% on three exams. What score is needed on a fourth exam for the student to earn an average grade of 80%?

SOLUTION   To find an equation that models the problem, we can let x represent the required grade on the fourth exam. The average grade will be one-fourth of the sum of the four grades. We know this average is to be 80.

The average of the four grades	equals	the required average grade.
$\dfrac{74 + 78 + 70 + x}{4}$	$=$	80

We can solve this equation for x.

$$\frac{222 + x}{4} = 80 \qquad \text{\small 74 + 78 + 70 = 222}$$

$$222 + x = 320 \qquad \text{\small Multiply both sides by 4.}$$

$$x = 98 \qquad \text{\small Subtract 222 from both sides.}$$

To earn an average of 80%, the student must score 98% on the fourth exam. ∎

Self Check 1   A student scores 82%, 96%, 91%, and 92% on four college algebra exams. What score is needed on a fifth exam for the student to earn an average grade of 90%?

Now Try Exercise 9.

2. Solve Geometric Problems

EXAMPLE 2   Solving a Geometric Problem

A city ordinance requires a man to install a fence around the swimming pool shown in Figure 1-2. He wants the border around the pool to be of uniform width. If he has 154 feet of fencing, find the width of the border.

FIGURE 1-2

SOLUTION   We can let x represent the width of the border. The distance around the large rectangle, called its **perimeter,** is given by the formula $P = 2l + 2w$, where l is the length, $20 + 2x$, and w is the width, $16 + 2x$. Since the man has 154 feet of fencing, the perimeter will be 154 feet. To find an equation that models the problem, we substitute these values into the formula for perimeter.

$$P = 2l + 2w$$ The formula for the perimeter of a rectangle.

$$154 = 2(20 + 2x) + 2(16 + 2x)$$ Substitute 154 for P, $20 + 2x$ for l, and $16 + 2x$ for w.

$$154 = 40 + 4x + 32 + 4x$$ Use the Distributive Property to remove parentheses.

$$154 = 72 + 8x$$ Combine like terms.

$$82 = 8x$$ Subtract 72 from both sides.

$$10\frac{1}{4} = x$$ Divide both sides by 8.

This border will be $10\frac{1}{4}$ feet wide.

Self Check 2   In Example 2, if 168 feet of fencing is available, find the border's width.

Now Try Exercise 13.

3. Solve Investment Problems

EXAMPLE 3   **Solving an Investment Problem**

A woman invested $10,000, part at 9% and the rest at 14%. If the annual income from these investments is $1,275, how much did she invest at each rate?

SOLUTION   We can let x represent the amount invested at 9%. Then $10,000 - x$ represents the amount invested at 14%. Since the annual income from any investment is the product of the interest rate and the amount invested, we have the following information.

Type of investment	Rate	Amount invested	Interest earned
9% investment	0.09	x	$0.09x$
14% investment	0.14	$10,000 - x$	$0.14(10,000 - x)$

The total income from these two investments can be expressed in two ways: as $1,275 and as the sum of the incomes from the two investments.

The income from the 9% investment	plus	the income from the 14% investment	equals	the total income.
$0.09x$	$+$	$0.14(10,000 - x)$	$=$	$1,275$

We can solve this equation for x.

$$0.09x + 0.14(10,000 - x) = 1,275$$

$$9x + 14(10,000 - x) = 127,500$$ To eliminate the decimal points, multiply both sides by 100.

$$9x + 140,000 - 14x = 127,500$$ Use the Distributive Property to remove parentheses.

$$-5x + 140,000 = 127,500$$ Combine like terms.

$$-5x = -12,500$$ Subtract 140,000 from both sides.

$$x = 2,500$$ Divide both sides by -5.

The amount invested at 9% was $2,500, and the amount invested at 14% was $7,500 ($10,000 - $2,500). These amounts are correct, because 9% of $2,500 is $225, 14% of $7,500 is $1,050, and the sum of these amounts is $1,275.

Self Check 3   A man invests $12,000, part at 7% and the rest at 9%. If the annual income from these investments is $965, how much was invested at each rate?

Now Try Exercise 21.

4. Solve Break-Point Analysis Problems

Running a machine involves two costs—**setup costs** and **unit costs.** Setup costs include the cost of installing a machine and preparing it to do a job. Unit cost is the cost to manufacture one item, which includes the costs of material and labor.

EXAMPLE 4   **Solving a Break-Point Analysis Problem**

Suppose that one machine has a setup cost of $400 and a unit cost of $1.50, and a second machine has a setup cost of $500 and a unit cost of $1.25. Find the **break point** (the number of units manufactured at which the cost on each machine is the same).

SOLUTION   We can let x represent the number of items to be manufactured. The cost C_1 of using machine 1 is

$$C_1 = 400 + 1.5x$$

and the cost C_2 of using machine 2 is

$$C_2 = 500 + 1.25x$$

The break point occurs when these two costs are equal.

The cost of using machine 1	equals	the cost of using machine 2.
$400 + 1.5x$	$=$	$500 + 1.25x$

We can solve this equation for x.

$$400 + 1.5x = 500 + 1.25x$$

$$1.5x = 100 + 1.25x \qquad \text{Subtract 400 from both sides.}$$

$$0.25x = 100 \qquad \text{Subtract } 1.25x \text{ from both sides.}$$

$$x = 400 \qquad \text{Divide both sides by 0.25.}$$

The break point is 400 units. This result is correct, because it will cost the same amount to manufacture 400 units with either machine.

$$C_1 = \$400 + \$1.5(400) = \$1,000 \qquad \text{and} \qquad C_2 = \$500 + \$1.25(400) = \$1,000$$

Self Check 4   An ATM has a setup cost of $3,000 and operating costs averaging $1 per transaction. Another ATM machine has a setup cost of $3,500 and an operating cost of $0.50 per transaction. Find the number of transactions at which the costs for each ATM is the same.

Now Try Exercise 29.

5. Solve Shared-Work Problems

EXAMPLE 5   **Solving a Shared-Work Problem**

The Toll Way Authority needs to pave 100 miles of interstate highway before freezing temperatures come in about 60 days. Sjostrom and Sons has estimated that it can do the job in 110 days. Scandroli and Sons has estimated that it can do the job in 140 days. If the authority hires both contractors, will the job get done in time?

SOLUTION   Since Sjostrom can do the job in 110 days, they can do $\frac{1}{110}$ of the job in one day. Since Scandroli can do the job in 140 days, they can do $\frac{1}{140}$ of the job in one day. If we let n represent the number of days it will take to pave the highway if both contractors work together, they can do $\frac{1}{n}$ of the job in one day. The work that they can do together in one day is the sum of what each can do in one day.

The part Sjostrom can pave in one day	plus	the part Scandroli can pave in one day	equals	the part they can pave together in one day.
$\dfrac{1}{110}$	$+$	$\dfrac{1}{140}$	$=$	$\dfrac{1}{n}$

We can solve this equation for n.

$$\frac{1}{110} + \frac{1}{140} = \frac{1}{n}$$

$$(110)(140)n\left(\frac{1}{110} + \frac{1}{140}\right) = (110)(140)n\left(\frac{1}{n}\right) \qquad \text{Multiply both sides by } (110)(140)n \text{ to eliminate the fractions.}$$

$$\frac{(110)(140)n}{110} + \frac{(110)(140)n}{140} = \frac{(110)(140)n}{n} \qquad \text{Use the Distributive Property to remove parentheses.}$$

$$140n + 110n = 15{,}400 \qquad \frac{110}{110} = 1, \frac{140}{140} = 1, \text{ and } \frac{n}{n} = 1.$$

$$250n = 15{,}400 \qquad \text{Combine like terms.}$$

$$n = 61.6 \qquad \text{Divide both sides by 250.}$$

It will take the contractors about 62 days to pave the highway. With any luck, the job will be done in time. ∎

Self Check 5   John and Eric both work at Firestone Auto Care. John can install a new set of tires in 45 minutes. Eric is faster and can install a set in 30 minutes. If John and Eric work together, how long will it take them to install one set of tires?

Now Try Exercise 33.

6. Solve Mixture Problems

EXAMPLE 6   **Solving a Mixture Problem**

A container is partially filled with 20 liters of whole milk containing 4% butterfat. How much 1% milk must be added to obtain a mixture that is 2% butterfat?

SOLUTION   Since the first container shown in Figure 1-3 contains 20 liters of 4% milk, it contains 0.04(20) liters of butterfat. To this amount, we will add the contents of the second container, which holds 0.01(l) liters of butterfat.

The sum of these two amounts will equal the number of liters of butterfat in the third container, which is 0.02(20 + l) liters of butterfat. This information is presented in table form in Figure 1-4.

FIGURE 1-3

The butterfat in the 4% milk	plus	the butterfat in the 1% milk	equals	the butterfat in the 2% milk.
4% of 20 liters	+	1% of l liters	=	2% of $(20 + l)$ liters

	Percentage of butterfat	·	Amount of milk	=	Amount of butterfat
4 % milk	0.04		20		0.04(20)
1% milk	0.01		l		0.01(l)
2% milk	0.02		$20 + l$		0.02($20 + l$)

FIGURE 1-4

We can solve this equation for l.

$$0.04(20) + 0.01(l) = 0.02(20 + l)$$

$$4(20) + l = 2(20 + l) \qquad \text{Multiply both sides by 100.}$$

$$80 + l = 40 + 2l \qquad \text{Remove parentheses.}$$

$$40 = l \qquad \text{Subtract 40 and l from both sides.}$$

To dilute the 20 liters of 4% milk to a 2% mixture, 40 liters of 1% milk must be added. To check, we note that the final mixture contains $0.02(60) = 1.2$ liters of pure butterfat, and that this is equal to the amount of pure butterfat in the 4% milk and the 1% milk; $0.04(20) + 0.01(40) = 1.2$ liters. ∎

Self Check 6   Milk containing 4% butterfat is mixed with 8 gallons of milk containing 1% butterfat to make a low-fat cottage cheese mixture containing 2% butterfat. How many gallons of the richer milk is used?

Now Try Exercise 39.

7. Solve Uniform Motion Problems

EXAMPLE 7   **Solving a Uniform Motion Problem**

A man leaves home driving his Ford F-150 truck at the rate of 50 mph. When his daughter discovers than he has forgotten his wallet, she drives her Ford Mustang after him at a rate of 65 mph. How long will it take her to catch her dad if he had a 15-minute head start?

SOLUTION   Uniform motion problems are based on the formula $d = rt$, where d is the distance, r is the rate, and t is the time. We can draw a diagram and organize the information given in the problem in a chart as shown in Figures 1-5 and 1-6. In the chart, t represents the number of hours the daughter must drive to overtake her father. Because the father has a 15-minute, or $\frac{1}{4}$ hour, head start, he has been on the road for $\left(t + \frac{1}{4}\right)$ hours.

50 mph

65 mph

FIGURE 1-5

	d	$=$	r	$\cdot$	t
Man	$50\left(t + \frac{1}{4}\right)$		50		$t + \frac{1}{4}$
Daughter	$65t$		65		t

FIGURE 1-6

We can set up the following equation and solve it for t.

The distance the man drives	equals	the distance the daughter drives.

$$50\left(t + \frac{1}{4}\right) \qquad = \qquad 65t$$

We can solve this equation for t.

$$50\left(t + \frac{1}{4}\right) = 65t$$

$$50t + \frac{25}{2} = 65t \qquad \text{Remove parentheses.}$$

$$\frac{25}{2} = 15t \qquad \text{Subtract } 50t \text{ from both sides.}$$

$$\frac{5}{6} = t \qquad \text{Divide both sides by 15 and simplify.}$$

It will take the daughter $\frac{5}{6}$ hour, or 50 minutes, to overtake her dad. ∎

Self Check 7   On a reality television show, an officer traveling in a police cruiser at 90 mph pursues Jennifer who has a 3-minute head start. If the officer overtakes Jennifer in 12 minutes, how fast is Jennifer traveling?

Now Try Exercise 53.

Self Check Answers   **1.** 89   **2.** 12 feet   **3.** \$5,750 at 7%; \$6,250 at 9%   **4.** 1,000   **5.** 18 minutes   **6.** 4   **7.** 72 mph

Exercises **1.2**

Getting Ready
You should be able to complete these vocabulary and concept statements before you proceed to the practice exercises.

Fill in the blanks.

1. To average n scores, _____ the scores and divide by n.

2. The formula for the _____ of a rectangle is $P = 2l + 2w$.

3. The simple annual interest earned on an investment is the product of the interest rate and the _____ invested.

4. The number of units manufactured at which the cost on two machines is equal is called the _____.

5. Distance traveled is the product of the _____ and the _____.

6. 5% of 30 liters is _____ liters.

Practice
Solve each problem.

7. Test scores Tate scored 5 points higher on his midterm and 13 points higher on his final than he did on his first exam. If his mean (average) score was 90, what was his score on the first exam?

8. **Test scores** Courtney took four tests in science class. On each successive test, her score improved by 3 points. If her mean score was 69.5%, what did she score on the first test?

9. **Teacher certification** On the Illinois certification test for teachers specializing in learning disabilities, a teacher earned the scores shown in the accompanying table. What was the teacher's score in program development?

Human development with special needs	82
Assessment	90
Program development and instruction	?
Professional knowledge and legal issues	78
AVERAGE SCORE	86

10. **Golfing** Par on a golf course is 72. If a golfer shot rounds of 76, 68, and 70 in a tournament, what will she need to shoot on the final round to average par?

11. **Replacing locks** A locksmith at Pop-A-Lock charges $40 plus $28 for each lock installed. How many locks can be replaced for $236?

12. **Delivering ads** A University of Florida student earns $20 per day delivering advertising brochures door-to-door, plus 75¢ for each person he interviews. How many people did he interview on a day when he earned $56?

13. **Electronic LED billboard** An electronic LED billboard in Times Square is 26 feet taller than it is wide. If its perimeter is 92 feet, find the dimensions of the billboard.

14. **Hockey rink** A National Hockey League rink is 115 feet longer than it is wide. If the perimeter of the rink is 570 feet, find the dimensions of the rink?

15. **Width of a picture frame** The picture frame with the dimensions shown in the illustration was built with 14 feet of framing material. Find x its width.

$(x + 2)$ ft

x ft

16. **Fencing a garden** If a gardener fences in the total rectangular area shown in the illustration instead of just the square area, he will need twice as much fencing to enclose the garden. How much fencing will he need?

24 ft x ft

x ft

17. **Wading pool dimensions** The area of the triangular swimming pool shown in the illustration is doubled by adding a rectangular wading pool. Find the dimensions of the wading pool. (*Hint:* The area of a triangle $= \frac{1}{2}bh$, and the area of a rectangle $= lw$.)

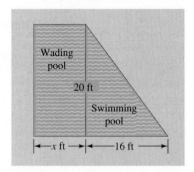

Wading pool

20 ft

Swimming pool

x ft   16 ft

18. **House construction** A builder wants to install a triangular window with the angles shown in the illustration. What angles will he have to cut to make the window fit? (*Hint:* The sum of the angles in a triangle equals 180°.)

$x°$

$(x + 30)°$ $(x + 30)°$

19. **Length of a living room** If a carpenter adds a porch with dimensions shown in the illustration to the living room, the living area will be increased by 50%. Find the length of the living room.

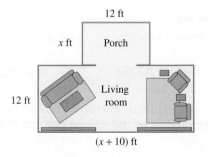

12 ft

x ft   Porch

12 ft   Living room

$(x + 10)$ ft

20. Depth of water in a trough The trough in the illustration has a cross-sectional area of 54 square inches. Find the depth, d, of the trough. (*Hint:* Area of a trapezoid $= \frac{1}{2}h(b_1 + b_2)$.)

21. Investment problem An executive invests $22,000, some at 7% and some at 6% annual interest. If he receives an annual return of $1,420, how much is invested at each rate?

22. Financial planning After inheriting some money, a woman wants to invest enough to have an annual income of $5,000. If she can invest $20,000 at 9% annual interest, how much more will she have to invest at 7% to achieve her goal? (See the table.)

Type	Rate	Amount	Income
9% investment	0.09	20,000	.09(20,000)
7% investment	0.07	x	.07x

23. Investment problem Equal amounts are invested at 6%, 7%, and 8% annual interest. If the three investments yield a total of $2,037 annual interest, find the total investment.

24. Investment problem A woman invests $37,000, part at 8% and the rest at $9\frac{1}{2}$% annual interest. If the $9\frac{1}{2}$% investment provides $452.50 more income than the 8% investment, how much is invested at each rate?

25. Ticket sales A full-price ticket for a college basketball game costs $2.50, and a student ticket costs $1.75. If 585 tickets were sold, and the total receipts were $1,217.25, how many tickets were student tickets?

26. Ticket sales Of the 800 tickets sold to a movie, 480 were full-price tickets costing $7 each. If the gate receipts were $4,960, what did a student ticket cost?

27. Discounts After being discounted 20%, a weather radio sells for $63.96. Find the original price.

28. Markups A merchant increases the wholesale cost of a Maytag washing machine by 30% to determine the selling price. If the washer sells for $588.90, find the wholesale cost.

29. Break-point analysis A machine to mill a brass plate has a setup cost of $600 and a unit cost of $3 for each plate manufactured. A bigger machine has a setup cost of $800 but a unit cost of only $2 for each plate manufactured. Find the break point.

30. Break-point analysis A machine to manufacture fasteners has a setup cost of $1,200 and a unit cost of $0.005 for each fastener manufactured. A newer machine has a setup cost of $1,500 but a unit cost of only $0.0015 for each fastener manufactured. Find the break point.

31. Computer sales A computer store has fixed costs of $8,925 per month and a unit cost of $850 for every computer it sells. If the store can sell all the computers it can get for $1,275 each, how many must be sold for the store to break even? (*Hint:* The break-even point occurs when costs equal income.)

32. Restaurant management A restaurant has fixed costs of $137.50 per day and an average unit cost of $4.75 for each meal served. If a typical meal costs $6, how many customers must eat at the restaurant each day for the owner to break even?

33. Roofing houses Kyle estimates that it will take him 7 days to roof his house. A professional roofer estimates that it will take him 4 days to roof the same house. How long will it take if they work together?

34. Sealing asphalt One crew can seal a parking lot in 8 hours and another in 10 hours. How long will it take to seal the parking lot if the two crews work together?

35. Mowing lawns Julie can mow a lawn with a lawn tractor in 2 hours, and her husband can mow the same lawn with a push mower in 4 hours. How long will it take to mow the lawn if they work together?

36. Filling swimming pools A garden hose can fill a swimming pool in 3 days, and a larger hose can fill the pool in 2 days. How long will it take to fill the pool if both hoses are used?

37. Filling swimming pools An empty swimming pool can be filled in 10 hours. When full, the pool can be drained in 19 hours. How long will it take to fill the empty pool if the drain is left open?

38. Preparing seafood Kevin stuffs shrimp in his job as a seafood chef. He can stuff 1,000 shrimp in 6 hours. When his sister helps him, they can stuff 1,000 shrimp in 4 hours. If Kevin gets sick, how long will it take his sister to stuff 500 shrimp?

39. Diluting solutions How much water should be added to 20 ounces of a 15% solution of alcohol to dilute it to a 10% solution?

40. Increasing concentrations The beaker shown below contains a 2% saltwater solution.
   a. How much water must be boiled away to increase the concentration of the salt solution from 2% to 3%?
   b. Where on the beaker would the new water level be?

41. Winterizing cars A car radiator has a 6-liter capacity. If the liquid in the radiator is 40% antifreeze, how much liquid must be replaced with pure antifreeze to bring the mixture up to a 50% solution?

42. Mixing milk If a bottle holding 3 liters of milk contains $3\frac{1}{2}$% butterfat, how much skimmed milk must be added to dilute the milk to 2% butterfat?

43. Preparing solutions A nurse has 1 liter of a solution that is 20% alcohol. How much pure alcohol must she add to bring the solution up to a 25% concentration?

44. Diluting solutions If there are 400 cubic centimeters of a chemical in 1 liter of solution, how many cubic centimeters of water must be added to dilute it to a 25% solution? (*Hint:* 1,000 cc = 1 liter.)

45. Cleaning swimming pools A swimming pool contains 15,000 gallons of water. How many gallons of chlorine must be added to "shock the pool" and bring the water to a $\frac{3}{100}$% solution?

46. Mixing fuels An automobile engine can run on a mixture of gasoline and a substitute fuel. If gas costs $3.50 per gallon and the substitute fuel costs $2 per gallon, what percent of a mixture must be substitute fuel to bring the cost down to $2.75 per gallon?

47. Evaporation How many liters of water must evaporate to turn 12 liters of a 24% salt solution into a 36% solution?

48. Increasing concentrations A beaker contains 320 ml of a 5% saltwater solution. How much water should be boiled away to increase the concentration to 6%?

49. Lowering fat How many pounds of extra-lean hamburger that is 7% fat must be mixed with 30 pounds of hamburger that is 15% fat to obtain a mixture that is 10% fat?

50. Dairy foods How many gallons of cream that is 22% butterfat must be mixed with milk that is 2% butterfat to get 20 gallons of milk containing 4% butterfat?

51. Mixing solutions How many gallons of a 5% alcohol solution must be mixed with 90 gallons of 1% solution to obtain a 2% solution?

52. Preparing medicines A doctor prescribes an ointment that is 2% hydrocortisone. A pharmacist has 1% and 5% concentrations in stock. How much of each should the pharmacist use to make a 1-ounce tube?

53. Driving rates John drove to Daytona Beach, Florida, in 5 hours. When he returned, there was less traffic, and the trip took only 3 hours. If John averaged 26 mph faster on the return trip, how fast did he drive each way?

54. Distance problem Allison drove home at 60 mph, but her brother Austin, who left at the same time, could drive at only 48 mph. When Allison arrived, Austin still had 60 miles to go. How far did Allison drive?

55. Distance problem Two cars leave Hinds Community College traveling in opposite directions. One car travels at 60 mph and the other at 64 mph. In how many hours will they be 310 miles apart?

56. Bank robbery Some bank robbers leave town, speeding at 70 mph. Ten minutes later, the police give chase, traveling at 78 mph. How long, after the robbery, will it take the police to overtake the robbers?

57. Jogging problem Two Michigan State University cross-country runners are 440 yards apart and are running toward each other, one at 8 mph and the other at 10 mph. In how many seconds will they meet?

58. Driving rates One morning, Justin drove 5 hours before stopping to eat lunch at Pizza Hut. After lunch, he increased his speed by 10 mph. If he completed a 430-mile trip in 8 hours of driving time, how fast did he drive in the morning?

59. Boating problem A Johnson motorboat goes 5 miles upstream in the same time it requires to go 7 miles downstream. If the river flows at 2 mph, find the speed of the boat in still water.

60. Wind velocity A plane can fly 340 mph in still air. If it can fly 200 miles downwind in the same amount of time it can fly 140 miles upwind, find the velocity of the wind.

61. **Feeding cattle** A cattleman wants to mix 2,400 pounds of cattle feed that is to be 14% protein. Barley (11.7% protein) will make up 25% of the mixture. The remaining 75% will be made up of oats (11.8% protein) and soybean meal (44.5% protein). How many pounds of each will he use?

62. **Feeding cattle** If the cattleman in Exercise 61 wants only 20% of the mixture to be barley, how many pounds of each should he use?

Use a calculator to help solve each problem.

63. **Machine tool design** 712.51 cubic millimeters of material was removed by drilling the blind hole as shown in the illustration. Find the depth of the hole. (*Hint:* The volume of a cylinder is given by $V = \pi r^2 h$.)

d mm

9 mm

64. **Architecture** The Norman window with dimensions as shown is a rectangle topped by a semicircle. If the area of the window is 68.2 square feet, find its height h.

h ft

6 ft

Discovery and Writing

65. Consider the strategy you use to solve investment and uniform motion problems. Describe any similarities you observe in these problem types.

66. Which type of application was hardest for you to solve? Why? What strategy or approach works best for you when approaching solving this problem?

Review

Factor each expression.

67. $x^2 - 2x - 63$

68. $2x^2 + 11x - 21$

69. $9x^2 - 12x - 5$

70. $9x^2 - 2x - 7$

71. $x^2 + 6x + 9$

72. $x^2 - 10x + 25$

73. $x^3 + 8$

74. $27a^3 - 64$

1.3 Quadratic Equations

In this section, we will learn to

1. Solve quadratic equations using factoring and the Square Root Property.
2. Solve quadratic equations using completing the square.
3. Solve quadratic equations using the Quadratic Formula.
4. Determine the easiest strategy to use to solve a quadratic equation.
5. Solve formulas for a variable that is squared.
6. Define and use the discriminant.
7. Write rational equations in quadratic form and solve the equations.

Fenway Park, America's most beloved ballpark, is home to the Boston Red Sox baseball club. The park opened in 1912 and is the oldest major league baseball stadium.

In baseball, the distance between home plate and first base is 90 feet and the distance between first base and second base is 90 feet. To find the distance between home plate and second base, we can use the *Pythagorean Theorem*, which states that

The sum of the squares of the two legs of a right triangle is equal to the square of its hypotenuse.

Because home plate, first base, and second base form a right triangle, we can let x represent the distance between home plate and second base (the **hypotenuse** of the right triangle) and 90 feet represent the length of each leg. We can then apply the Pythagorean Theorem and write the equation $90^2 + 90^2 = x^2$. To find the distance between home plate and second base, we must solve this equation.

$$90^2 + 90^2 = x^2$$

$$8{,}100 + 8{,}100 = x^2 \qquad \text{Square 90 two times.}$$

$$16{,}200 = x^2 \qquad \text{Simplify.}$$

To find x, we must determine what positive number squared gives 16,200. From Chapter 0, we know that this number is the square root of 16,200.

$$\sqrt{16{,}200} \approx 127.3 \qquad \text{Use a calculator and round to the nearest tenth.}$$

To the nearest tenth, the distance between home plate and second base is 127.3 feet.

Since this equation contains the term x^2, it is an example of a new type of equation, called a *quadratic* equation. In this section, we will learn several strategies for solving these equations.

1. Solve Quadratic Equations Using Factoring and the Square Root Property

Polynomial equations such as $2x^2 + 11x - 21 = 0$ and $3x^2 - x + 2 = 0$ are called *quadratic* or *second-degree* equations.

Quadratic Equation   A **quadratic equation** is an equation that can be written in the form $ax^2 + bx + c = 0$, where a, b, and c are real numbers and $a \neq 0$.

To solve quadratic equations by factoring, we can use the following theorem.

Zero-Factor Theorem   If a and b are real numbers, and if $ab = 0$, then

$$a = 0 \qquad \text{or} \qquad b = 0$$

PROOF   Suppose that $ab = 0$. If $a = 0$, we are finished, because at least one of a or b is 0.

If $a \neq 0$, then a has a reciprocal $\frac{1}{a}$, and we can multiply both sides of the equation $ab = 0$ by $\frac{1}{a}$ to obtain

$$ab = 0$$

$$\frac{1}{a}(ab) = \frac{1}{a}(0) \qquad \text{Multiply both sides by } \frac{1}{a}.$$

$$\left(\frac{1}{a} \cdot a\right)b = 0 \qquad \text{Use the Associative Property to group } \frac{1}{a} \text{ and } a \text{ together.}$$

$$1b = 0 \qquad \frac{1}{a} \cdot a = 1$$

$$b = 0$$

Thus, if $a \neq 0$, then b must be 0, and the theorem is proved.

EXAMPLE 1   Solving a Quadratic Equation by Factoring

Solve: $2x^2 - 9x - 35 = 0$.

SOLUTION   The left side can be factored and written as

$$(2x + 5)(x - 7) = 0$$

This product can be 0 if and only if one of the factors is 0. So we can use the Zero-Factor Theorem and set each factor equal to 0. We can then solve each equation for x.

$$2x + 5 = 0 \qquad \text{or} \qquad x - 7 = 0$$
$$2x = -5 \qquad\qquad\qquad x = 7$$
$$x = -\frac{5}{2}$$

Because $(2x + 5)(x - 7) = 0$ only if one of its factors is zero, $-\frac{5}{2}$ and 7 are the only solutions of the equation.

Verify that each one satisfies the equation. ∎

Self Check 1   Solve: $6x^2 + 7x - 3 = 0$.

Now Try Exercise 17.

Comment

The Zero-Factor Theorem can be used only when there is a constant term of 0 on the right side of the equation.

In many quadratic equations, the quadratic expression does not factor over the set of integers. For example, the left side of $x^2 - 5x + 3 = 0$ is a prime polynomial and cannot be factored over the set of integers.

To develop a method to solve these equations, we consider the equation $x^2 = c$. If c is positive, it has two real roots that can be found by adding $-c$ to both sides, factoring $x^2 - c$ over the set of real numbers, setting each factor equal to 0, and solving for x.

$$x^2 = c$$
$$x^2 - c = 0 \qquad\qquad\qquad \text{Subtract } c \text{ from both sides.}$$
$$x^2 - \left(\sqrt{c}\right)^2 = 0 \qquad\qquad \left(\sqrt{c}\right)^2 = c$$
$$\left(x - \sqrt{c}\right)\left(x + \sqrt{c}\right) = 0 \qquad \text{Factor the difference of two squares.}$$
$$x - \sqrt{c} = 0 \quad \text{or} \quad x + \sqrt{c} = 0 \qquad \text{Set each factor equal to 0.}$$
$$x = \sqrt{c} \quad \Big| \quad x = -\sqrt{c}$$

The roots of $x^2 = c$ are $x = \sqrt{c}$ and $x = -\sqrt{c}$. This fact is summarized in the **Square Root Property.**

Square Root Property   If $c > 0$, the equation $x^2 = c$ has two real roots:

$$x = \sqrt{c} \qquad \text{or} \qquad x = -\sqrt{c}$$

EXAMPLE 2   Solving a Quadratic Equation by Using the Square Root Property

Solve: $x^2 - 8 = 0$.

SOLUTION   We solve for x^2 and use the Square Root Property.

$$x^2 - 8 = 0$$

$$x^2 = 8$$

$$x = \sqrt{8} \quad \text{or} \quad x = -\sqrt{8}$$

$$x = 2\sqrt{2} \quad \bigg| \quad x = -2\sqrt{2} \qquad \sqrt{8} = \sqrt{4}\sqrt{2} = 2\sqrt{2}$$

Verify that each root satisfies the equation.

Self Check 2   Solve: $x^2 - 12 = 0$.

Now Try Exercise 21.

EXAMPLE 3   Solve: $(x + 4)^2 = 27$.

SOLUTION   Again, we will use the Square Root Property.

$$(x + 4)^2 = 27$$

$$x + 4 = \sqrt{27} \qquad \text{or} \quad x + 4 = -\sqrt{27}$$

$$x + 4 = 3\sqrt{3} \quad \bigg| \quad x + 4 = -3\sqrt{3} \qquad \sqrt{27} = \sqrt{9}\sqrt{3} = 3\sqrt{3}$$

$$x = -4 + 3\sqrt{3} \quad \bigg| \quad x = -4 - 3\sqrt{3}$$

Verify that each root satisfies the equation.

Self Check 3   Solve: $(2x + 5)^2 = 45$.

Now Try Exercise 33.

2. Solve Quadratic Equations Using Completing the Square

Another way to solve quadratic equations is called **completing the square.** This method is based on the following products:

$$x^2 + 2ax + a^2 = (x + a)^2 \qquad \text{and} \qquad x^2 - 2ax + a^2 = (x - a)^2$$

The trinomials $x^2 + 2ax + a^2$ and $x^2 - 2ax + a^2$ are perfect-square trinomials, because each one factors as the square of a binomial. In each case, the coefficient of the first term is 1. If we take one-half of the coefficient of x in the middle term and square it, we obtain the third term.

$$\left[\frac{1}{2}(2a)\right]^2 = a^2 \qquad \text{and} \qquad \left[\frac{1}{2}(-2a)\right]^2 = (-a)^2 = a^2$$

This suggests that to make $x^2 + bx$ a perfect-square trinomial, we find one-half of b, square it, and add the result to the binomial. For example, to make $x^2 + 10x$ a perfect-square trinomial, we find one-half of 10 to get 5, square 5 to get 25, and add 25 to $x^2 + 10x$.

$$x^2 + 10x + \left[\frac{1}{2}(10)\right]^2 = x^2 + 10x + (5)^2$$

$$= x^2 + 10x + 25 \qquad \text{Note that } x^2 + 10x + 25 = (x + 5)^2.$$

To make $x^2 - 11x$ a perfect-square trinomial, we find one-half of -11 to get $-\frac{11}{2}$, square $-\frac{11}{2}$ to get $\frac{121}{4}$, and add $\frac{121}{4}$ to $x^2 - 11x$.

$$x^2 - 11x + \left[\frac{1}{2}(-11)\right]^2 = x^2 - 11x + \left(-\frac{11}{2}\right)^2$$

$$= x^2 - 11x + \frac{121}{4} \qquad \text{Note that } x^2 - 11x + \frac{121}{4} = \left(x - \frac{11}{2}\right)^2.$$

To solve a quadratic equation in x by completing the square, we follow these steps.

Strategy for Completing the Square	**1.** If the coefficient of x^2 is not 1, make it 1 by dividing both sides of the equation by the coefficient of x^2.
	2. If necessary, add a number to both sides of the equation to get the constant on the right side of the equation.
	3. Complete the square on x:
	a. Identify the coefficient of x, take one-half of it, and square the result.
	b. Add the number found in part a to both sides of the equation.
	4. Factor the perfect-square trinomial and combine like terms.
	5. Solve the resulting quadratic equation by using the Square Root Property.

To use completing the square to solve $x^2 - 10x + 24 = 0$, we note that the coefficient of x^2 is 1. We move on to Step 2 and subtract 24 from both sides to get the constant term on the right side of the equal sign.

$$x^2 - 10x = -24$$

We can then complete the square by adding $\left[\frac{1}{2}(-10)\right]^2 = 25$ to both sides.

$$x^2 - 10x + \mathbf{25} = -24 + \mathbf{25}$$

$$x^2 - 10x + 25 = 1 \qquad \text{Simplify on the right side.}$$

We then factor the perfect square trinomial on the left side.

$$(x - 5)^2 = 1$$

Finally, we use the Square Root Property to solve this equation.

$$x - 5 = 1 \quad \text{or} \quad x - 5 = -1$$
$$x = 6 \qquad\qquad x = 4$$

EXAMPLE 4   Solving a Quadratic Equation by Completing the Square

Use completing the square to solve $x^2 + 4x - 6 = 0$.

SOLUTION   Here the coefficient of x^2 is already 1. We move to Step 2 and add 6 to both sides to isolate the binomial $x^2 + 4x$.

$$x^2 + 4x = 6$$

We then find the number to add to both sides by completing the square. Since one-half of 4 (the coefficient of x) is 2 and $2^2 = 4$, we add 4 to both sides.

$$x^2 + 4x + 4 = 6 + 4 \qquad \text{Add 4 to both sides.}$$

$$x^2 + 4x + 4 = 10$$

$$(x + 2)^2 = 10 \qquad \text{Factor } x^2 + 4x + 4.$$

$$x + 2 = \sqrt{10} \qquad \text{or} \quad x + 2 = -\sqrt{10} \qquad \text{Use the Square Root Property.}$$

$$x = -2 + \sqrt{10} \qquad \qquad x = -2 - \sqrt{10}$$

Verify that each root satisfies the original equation.   ■

Self Check 4   Solve: $x^2 - 2x - 9 = 0$.

Now Try Exercise 49.

EXAMPLE 5   **Solving a Quadratic Equation by Completing the Square**

Use completing the square to solve $x(x + 3) = 9$.

SOLUTION   We remove parentheses to get

$$x^2 + 3x = 9$$

Since the coefficient of x^2 is 1 and the constant is on the right side, we move to Step 3 and find the number to be added to both sides to complete the square. Since one-half of 3 (the coefficient of x) is $\frac{3}{2}$ and the square of $\frac{3}{2}$ is $\frac{9}{4}$, we add $\frac{9}{4}$ to both sides.

$$x^2 + 3x + \frac{9}{4} = 9 + \frac{9}{4} \qquad \text{Add } \frac{9}{4} \text{ to both sides.}$$

$$\left(x + \frac{3}{2}\right)^2 = \frac{45}{4} \qquad \text{Factor } x^2 + 3x + \frac{9}{4} \text{ and combine terms on right.}$$

$$x + \frac{3}{2} = \frac{\sqrt{45}}{2} \qquad \text{or} \quad x + \frac{3}{2} = -\frac{\sqrt{45}}{2} \qquad \text{Use the Square Root Property.}$$

$$x + \frac{3}{2} = \frac{3\sqrt{5}}{2} \qquad \text{or} \quad x + \frac{3}{2} = -\frac{3\sqrt{5}}{2} \qquad \sqrt{45} = \sqrt{9}\sqrt{5} = 3\sqrt{5}$$

$$x = \frac{-3 + 3\sqrt{5}}{2} \qquad \qquad x = \frac{-3 - 3\sqrt{5}}{2} \qquad \begin{array}{l}\text{Subtract } \frac{3}{2} \text{ from both sides.} \\ \text{and combine.}\end{array}$$

Verify that each root satisfies the original equation.   ■

Self Check 5   Solve: $x(x + 5) = 1$.

Now Try Exercise 51.

EXAMPLE 6   **Solving a Quadratic Equation by Completing the Square**

Use completing the square to solve $6x^2 + 5x - 6 = 0$.

SOLUTION   We begin by dividing both sides of the equation by 6 to make the coefficient of x^2 equal to 1. Then we proceed as follows:

$$6x^2 + 5x - 6 = 0$$

$$x^2 + \frac{5}{6}x - 1 = 0 \qquad \text{Divide both sides by 6.}$$

$$x^2 + \frac{5}{6}x = 1 \qquad \text{Add 1 to both sides.}$$

$$x^2 + \frac{5}{6}x + \frac{25}{144} = 1 + \frac{25}{144} \qquad \text{Add } \left(\frac{1}{2} \cdot \frac{5}{6}\right)^2, \text{ or } \frac{25}{144}, \text{ to both sides.}$$

$$\left(x + \frac{5}{12}\right)^2 = \frac{169}{144} \qquad \text{Factor } x^2 + \frac{5}{6}x + \frac{25}{144}.$$

We now apply the Square Root Property.

$$x + \frac{5}{12} = \sqrt{\frac{169}{144}} \qquad \text{or} \quad x + \frac{5}{12} = -\sqrt{\frac{169}{144}}$$

$$x + \frac{5}{12} = \frac{13}{12} \qquad\qquad x + \frac{5}{12} = -\frac{13}{12}$$

$$x = \frac{8}{12} \qquad\qquad\qquad x = -\frac{18}{12}$$

$$x = \frac{2}{3} \qquad\qquad\qquad x = -\frac{3}{2}$$

Verify that each root satisfies the original equation.

Self Check 6   Solve: $2x^2 - 5x - 3 = 0$.

Now Try Exercise 57.

3. Solve Quadratic Equations Using the Quadratic Formula

We can solve the equation $ax^2 + bx + c = 0 \ (a \neq 0)$ by completing the square. The result will be a formula that we can use to solve quadratic equations.

$$ax^2 + bx + c = 0$$

$$\frac{ax^2}{a} + \frac{b}{a}x + \frac{c}{a} = \frac{0}{a} \qquad \text{Divide both sides by } a.$$

$$x^2 + \frac{b}{a}x = -\frac{c}{a} \qquad \text{Simplify and subtract } \frac{c}{a} \text{ from both sides.}$$

$$x^2 + \frac{b}{a}x + \frac{b^2}{4a^2} = \frac{b^2}{4a^2} - \frac{4ac}{4aa} \qquad \text{Add } \frac{b^2}{4a^2} \text{ to both sides and multiply the numerator and denominator of } \frac{c}{a} \text{ by } 4a.$$

$$\left(x + \frac{b}{2a}\right)^2 = \frac{b^2 - 4ac}{4a^2} \qquad \text{Factor the left side and add the fractions on the right side.}$$

We can now use the Square Root Property.

$$x + \frac{b}{2a} = \sqrt{\frac{b^2 - 4ac}{4a^2}} \qquad \text{or} \quad x + \frac{b}{2a} = -\sqrt{\frac{b^2 - 4ac}{4a^2}}$$

$$x = -\frac{b}{2a} + \frac{\sqrt{b^2 - 4ac}}{2a} \qquad\qquad x = -\frac{b}{2a} - \frac{\sqrt{b^2 - 4ac}}{2a}$$

$$x = \frac{-b + \sqrt{b^2 - 4ac}}{2a} \qquad\qquad x = \frac{-b - \sqrt{b^2 - 4ac}}{2a}$$

These values of x are the two roots of the equation $ax^2 + bx + c = 0$. They are usually combined into a single expression, called the **Quadratic Formula.**

Quadratic Formula   The solutions of the general quadratic equation, $ax^2 + bx + c = 0$, are

$$x = \frac{-b \pm \sqrt{b^2 - 4ac}}{2a} \quad (a \neq 0)$$

The Quadratic Formula should be read twice, once using the $+$ sign and once using the $-$ sign. The Quadratic Formula implies that

$$x = \frac{-b + \sqrt{b^2 - 4ac}}{2a} \quad \text{or} \quad x = \frac{-b - \sqrt{b^2 - 4ac}}{2a}$$

Caution

Be sure to write the Quadratic Formula correctly. Do **not** write the Quadratic Formula as

$$x = -b \pm \frac{\sqrt{b^2 - 4ac}}{2a}$$

EXAMPLE 7   **Solving a Quadratic Equation Using the Quadratic Formula**

Use the Quadratic Formula to solve $x^2 - 5x + 3 = 0$.

SOLUTION   In this equation $a = 1$, $b = -5$, and $c = 3$. We will substitute these values into the Quadratic Formula.

$$x = \frac{-b \pm \sqrt{b^2 - 4ac}}{2a} \qquad \text{This is the Quadratic Formula.}$$

$$x = \frac{-(-5) \pm \sqrt{(-5)^2 - 4(1)(3)}}{2(1)} \qquad \text{Substitute 1 for } a, -5 \text{ for } b, \text{ and 3 for } c.$$

$$x = \frac{5 \pm \sqrt{13}}{2} \qquad (-5)^2 - 4(1)(3) = 25 - 12 = 13$$

Both values satisfy the original equation.   ∎

Self Check 7   Solve: $3x^2 - 5x + 1 = 0$.

Now Try Exercise 65.

EXAMPLE 8   **Solving a Quadratic Equation Using the Quadratic Formula**

Use the Quadratic Formula to solve $2x^2 + 8x - 7 = 0$.

SOLUTION   In this equation, $a = 2$, $b = 8$, and $c = -7$. We will substitute these values into the Quadratic Formula.

$$x = \frac{-b \pm \sqrt{b^2 - 4ac}}{2a} \qquad \text{This is the Quadratic Formula.}$$

$$x = \frac{-8 \pm \sqrt{8^2 - 4(2)(-7)}}{2(2)} \qquad \text{Substitute 2 for } a, 8 \text{ for } b, \text{ and } -7 \text{ for } c.$$

$$x = \frac{-8 \pm \sqrt{120}}{4} \qquad 8^2 - 4(2)(-7) = 64 + 56 = 120$$

$$x = \frac{-8 \pm 2\sqrt{30}}{4} \qquad \sqrt{120} = \sqrt{4 \cdot 30} = 2\sqrt{30}$$

$$x = \frac{2\left(-4 \pm \sqrt{30}\right)}{4}$$ Factor out 2 in the numerator.

$$x = \frac{-4 \pm \sqrt{30}}{2}$$ Simplify.

Both values satisfy the original equation.

Self Check 8   Solve: $4x^2 + 16x - 13 = 0$.

Now Try Exercise 69.

4. Determine the Easiest Strategy to Use To Solve a Quadratic Equation

So far, we have solved quadratic equations by *factoring*, by the *square root method*, by *completing the square*, and by the *Quadratic Formula*. With so many methods available, it is useful to think about which one will be the easiest way to solve a specific quadratic equation. Although we have used completing the square to develop the Quadratic Formula, it is usually the most complicated way to solve a quadratic equation. Therefore, unless specified, we will usually not use this method. However, we will complete the square again later in the book to write certain equations in specific forms.

The following chart summarizes the different types of quadratic equations that can occur, a suggested method for solving them, and an example.

Type of Quadratic Equation	Easiest Strategy to Solve It	Example
Equations of the form $ax^2 + bx + c = 0$ where the left side factors easily.	Use factoring and the Zero-Factor Theorem.	Solve: $6x^2 - 11x + 3 = 0$ $(2x - 3)(3x - 1) = 0$ $2x - 3 = 0$ or $3x - 1 = 0$ $x = \frac{3}{2}$ $\bigg\vert$ $x = \frac{1}{3}$
Equations of the form $ax^2 + bx = 0$ where the constant term is missing and the left side factors easily.	Use factoring and the Zero-Factor Theorem.	Solve: $9x^2 + 6x = 0$ $3x(3x + 2) = 0$ $3x = 0$ or $3x + 2 = 0$ $x = 0$ $\bigg\vert$ $x = -\frac{2}{3}$
Equations of the form $ax^2 - c = 0$ where the term involving x is missing and the left side factors easily.	Use factoring and the Zero-Factor Theorem.	Solve: $4x^2 - 9 = 0$ $(2x + 3)(2x - 3) = 0$ $2x + 3 = 0$ or $2x - 3 = 0$ $x = -\frac{3}{2}$ $\bigg\vert$ $x = \frac{3}{2}$
Equations of the form $ax^2 - c = 0$ or $x^2 = k$ where k is a contant.	Use the Square Root Property.	Solve: $2x^2 - 5 = 0$ $x^2 = \frac{5}{2}$ $x = \pm\sqrt{\frac{5}{2}}$ $x = \pm\frac{\sqrt{10}}{2}$

(continued)

Type of Quadratic Equation	Easiest Strategy to Solve It	Example
Equations of the form $\quad ax^2 + bx + c = 0$ where the left side cannot be factored easily or cannot be factored at all.	Use the Quadratic Formula.	Solve: $3x^2 - x - 5 = 0$. $x = \dfrac{-b \pm \sqrt{b^2 - 4ac}}{2a}$ $x = \dfrac{-(-1) \pm \sqrt{(-1)^2 - 4(3)(-5)}}{2(3)}$ $\quad \begin{array}{l} a = 3 \\ b = -1 \\ c = -5 \end{array}$ $x = \dfrac{1 \pm \sqrt{1 + 60}}{6}$ $x = \dfrac{1 \pm \sqrt{61}}{6}$

5. Solve Formulas for a Variable That Is Squared

Many formulas involve quadratic equations. For example, if an object is fired straight up into the air with an initial velocity of 88 feet per second, its height is given by the formula $h = 88t - 16t^2$, where h represents its height (in feet) and t represents the elapsed time (in seconds) since it was fired.

To solve this formula for t, we use the Quadratic Formula.

$$h = 88t - 16t^2$$

$$16t^2 - 88t + h = 0 \qquad\qquad \text{Add } 16t^2 \text{ and } -88t \text{ to both sides.}$$

$$t = \frac{-(-88) \pm \sqrt{(-88)^2 - 4(16)(h)}}{2(16)} \qquad \text{Substitute into the Quadratic Formula.}$$

$$t = \frac{88 \pm \sqrt{7,744 - 64h}}{32} \qquad\qquad \text{Simplify.}$$

6. Define and Use the Discriminant

We can predict what type of roots a quadratic equation will have before we solve it. Suppose that the coefficients a, b, and c in the equation $ax^2 + bx + c = 0$ $(a \neq 0)$ are real numbers. Then the two roots of the equation are given by the Quadratic Formula

$$x = \frac{-b \pm \sqrt{b^2 - 4ac}}{2a} \qquad (a \neq 0)$$

The value of $b^2 - 4ac$, called the **discriminant,** determines the nature of the roots. The possibilities are summarized in the table as follows.

Discriminant	Number of Roots and Type of Roots
0	One repeated rational root
Positive and a perfect square	Two different rational roots
Positive and not a perfect square	Two different irrational roots
Negative	No real number roots

EXAMPLE 9   Using the Discriminant to Determine the Number and Type of Roots of a Quadratic Equation

Determine the number and type of roots of $3x^2 + 4x + 1 = 0$.

SOLUTION   We calculate the discriminant $b^2 - 4ac$.

$$b^2 - 4ac = 4^2 - 4(3)(1) \qquad \text{Substitute 4 for } b, 3 \text{ for } a, \text{ and 1 for } c.$$

$$= 16 - 12$$

$$= 4$$

Since a, b, and c are real numbers and the discriminant is positive and a perfect square, there will be two different rational roots. ∎

Self Check 9   Determine the number and type of the roots of $4x^2 - 3x - 2 = 0$.

Now Try Exercise 87.

EXAMPLE 10   **Using the Discriminant to Find the Constant k**

If k is a constant, many quadratic equations are represented by the equation

$$(k - 2)x^2 + (k + 1)x + 4 = 0$$

Find the values of k that will give an equation with roots that are equal rational numbers.

SOLUTION   We calculate the discriminant $b^2 - 4ac$ and set it equal to 0.

$$b^2 - 4ac = (k + 1)^2 - 4(k - 2)(4)$$

$$0 = k^2 + 2k + 1 - 16k + 32$$

$$0 = k^2 - 14k + 33$$

$$0 = (k - 3)(k - 11)$$

$$k - 3 = 0 \quad \text{or} \quad k - 11 = 0$$

$$k = 3 \qquad\qquad k = 11$$

When $k = 3$ or $k = 11$, the equation will have equal roots. As a check, we let $k = 3$ and note that the equation $(k - 2)x^2 + (k + 1)x + 4 = 0$ becomes

$$(3 - 2)x^2 + (3 + 1)x + 4 = 0$$

$$x^2 + 4x + 4 = 0$$

The roots of this equation are equal rational numbers, as expected:

$$x^2 + 4x + 4 = 0$$

$$(x + 2)(x + 2) = 0$$

$$x + 2 = 0 \quad \text{or} \quad x + 2 = 0$$

$$x = -2 \qquad\qquad x = -2$$

Similarly, $k = 11$ will give an equation with equal rational roots. ∎

Self Check 10   Find k such that $(k - 2)x^2 - (k + 3)x + 9 = 0$ will have equal roots.

Now Try Exercise 93.

7. Write Rational Equations in Quadratic Form and Solve the Equations

If an equation can be written in quadratic form, it can be solved with the techniques used for solving quadratic equations.

EXAMPLE 11   **Solving a Rational Equation**

Solve: $\dfrac{1}{x-1} + \dfrac{3}{x+1} = 2.$

SOLUTION   Since neither denominator can be zero, $x \neq 1$ and $x \neq -1$. If either number appears as a root, it must be discarded.

$$\frac{1}{x-1} + \frac{3}{x+1} = 2$$

$$(x-1)(x+1)\left[\frac{1}{x-1} + \frac{3}{x+1}\right] = (x-1)(x+1)2 \qquad \text{Multiply both sides by } (x-1)(x+1).$$

$$(x+1) + 3(x-1) = 2(x^2 - 1) \qquad \text{Remove brackets and simplify.}$$

$$4x - 2 = 2x^2 - 2 \qquad \text{Remove parentheses and simplify.}$$

$$0 = 2x^2 - 4x \qquad \text{Add } 2 - 4x \text{ to both sides.}$$

The resulting equation is a quadratic equation that we can solve by factoring.

$$2x^2 - 4x = 0$$

$$2x(x-2) = 0 \qquad \text{Factor } 2x^2 - 4x.$$

$$2x = 0 \quad \text{or} \quad x - 2 = 0$$

$$x = 0 \quad \Big| \quad x = 2$$

Verify these results by checking each root in the original equation.   ∎

Self Check 11   Solve: $\dfrac{1}{x-1} + \dfrac{2}{x+1} = 1.$

Now Try Exercise 109.

Self Check Answers   1. $\dfrac{1}{3}, -\dfrac{3}{2}$ 2. $2\sqrt{3}, -2\sqrt{3}$ 3. $\dfrac{-5 + 3\sqrt{5}}{2}, \dfrac{-5 - 3\sqrt{5}}{2}$

4. $1 + \sqrt{10}, 1 - \sqrt{10}$ 5. $\dfrac{-5 + \sqrt{29}}{2}, \dfrac{-5 - \sqrt{29}}{2}$ 6. $3, -\dfrac{1}{2}$

7. $\dfrac{5 \pm \sqrt{13}}{6}$ 8. $\dfrac{-4 \pm \sqrt{29}}{2}$ 9. two different irrational roots

10. $3, 27$ 11. $0, 3$

Exercises **1.3**

Getting Ready

You should be able to complete these vocabulary and concept statements before you proceed to the practice exercises.

Fill in the blanks.

1. A quadratic equation is an equation that can be written in the form _____, where $a \neq 0$.

2. If a and b are real numbers and _____, then $a = 0$ or $b = 0$.

3. If $c > 0$, the equation $x^2 = c$ has two roots. They are $x =$ _____ and $x =$ _____.

4. The Quadratic Formula is _____ ($a \neq 0$).

5. If a, b, and c are real numbers and if $b^2 - 4ac = 0$, the two roots of the quadratic equation are repeated _____.

6. If a, b, and c are real numbers and $b^2 - 4ac < 0$, the two roots of the quadratic equation are _____.

Practice

Solve each equation by factoring.

7. $x^2 - x - 6 = 0$

8. $x^2 + 8x + 15 = 0$

9. $x^2 - 144 = 0$

10. $x^2 + 4x = 0$

11. $2x^2 + x - 10 = 0$

12. $3x^2 + 4x - 4 = 0$

13. $5x^2 - 13x + 6 = 0$

14. $2x^2 + 5x - 12 = 0$

15. $15x^2 + 16x = 15$

16. $6x^2 - 25x = -25$

17. $12x^2 + 9 = 24x$

18. $24x^2 + 6 = 24x$

Use the Square Root Property to solve each equation.

19. $x^2 = 9$

20. $x^2 = 64$

21. $y^2 - 50 = 0$

22. $x^2 - 75 = 0$

23. $2x^2 = 40$

24. $5x^2 = 400$

25. $4x^2 = 7$

26. $16x^2 = 11$

27. $2x^2 - 13 = 0$

28. $-3x^2 = -11$

29. $(x - 1)^2 = 4$

30. $(y + 2)^2 - 49 = 0$

31. $(x + 1)^2 - 8 = 0$

32. $(y + 2)^2 - 98 = 0$

33. $(2x + 1)^2 = 27$

34. $(5y + 2)^2 - 48 = 0$

Complete the square to make each a perfect-square trinomial.

35. $x^2 + 6x$

36. $x^2 + 8x$

37. $x^2 - 4x$

38. $x^2 - 12x$

39. $a^2 + 5a$

40. $t^2 + 9t$

41. $r^2 - 11r$

42. $s^2 - 7s$

43. $y^2 + \dfrac{3}{4}y$

44. $p^2 + \dfrac{3}{2}p$

45. $q^2 - \dfrac{1}{5}q$

46. $m^2 - \dfrac{2}{3}m$

Solve each equation by completing the square.

47. $x^2 - 8x + 15 = 0$

48. $x^2 + 10x + 21 = 0$

49. $x^2 + 12x = -8$

50. $x^2 - 6x = -1$

51. $x^2 + 5 = -5x$

52. $x^2 + 1 = -4x$

53. $2x^2 - 20x = -49$

54. $4x^2 + 8x = 7$

55. $3x^2 = 1 - 4x$

56. $3x^2 + 4x = 5$

57. $2x^2 = 3x + 1$

58. $2x^2 + 5x = 14$

Use the Quadratic Formula to solve each equation.

59. $x^2 - 12 = 0$

60. $x^2 - 60 = 0$

61. $x^2 - 25x = 0$

62. $x^2 + x = 0$

63. $2x^2 - x - 15 = 0$

64. $6x^2 + x - 2 = 0$

65. $3x^2 = -5x - 1$

66. $2x^2 = 5x + 11$

67. $x^2 + 1 = -7x$

68. $13x^2 + 1 = -10x$

69. $3x^2 + 6x = -1$

70. $2x(x + 3) = -1$

71. $5x\left(x + \dfrac{1}{5}\right) = 3$

72. $7x^2 = 2x + 2$

Solve each formula for the indicated variable.

73. $h = \dfrac{1}{2}gt^2;\ t$

74. $x^2 + y^2 = r^2;\ x$

75. $h = 64t - 16t^2;\ t$

76. $y = 16x^2 - 4;\ x$

77. $\dfrac{x^2}{a^2} + \dfrac{y^2}{b^2} = 1;\ y$

78. $\dfrac{x^2}{a^2} - \dfrac{y^2}{b^2} = 1;\ x$

79. $\dfrac{x^2}{a^2} - \dfrac{y^2}{b^2} = 1;\ a$

80. $\dfrac{x^2}{a^2} - \dfrac{y^2}{b^2} = 1;\ b$

81. $x^2 + xy - y^2 = 0;\ x$

82. $x^2 - 3xy + y^2 = 0;\ y$

Use the discriminant to determine the number and type of roots. Do not solve the equation.

83. $x^2 + 6x + 9 = 0$

84. $-3x^2 + 2x = 21$

85. $3x^2 - 2x + 5 = 0$

86. $9x^2 + 42x + 49 = 0$

87. $10x^2 + 29x = 21$

88. $10x^2 + x = 21$

89. $x^2 - 5x + 2 = 0$

90. $-8x^2 - 2x = 13$

91. Does $1{,}492x^2 + 1{,}984x - 1{,}776 = 0$ have any roots that are real numbers?

92. Does $2{,}004x^2 + 10x + 1{,}994 = 0$ have any roots that are real numbers?

93. Find two values of k such that $x^2 + kx + 3k - 5 = 0$ will have two roots that are equal.

94. For what value(s) of b will the solutions of $x^2 - 2bx + b^2 = 0$ be equal?

Change each rational equation to quadratic form and solve it by the most efficient method.

95. $x + 1 = \dfrac{12}{x}$

96. $x - 2 = \dfrac{15}{x}$

97. $8x - \dfrac{3}{x} = 10$

98. $15x - \dfrac{4}{x} = 4$

99. $\dfrac{5}{x} = \dfrac{4}{x^2} - 6$

100. $\dfrac{6}{x^2} + \dfrac{1}{x} = 12$

101. $x\left(30 - \dfrac{13}{x}\right) = \dfrac{10}{x}$

102. $x\left(20 - \dfrac{17}{x}\right) = \dfrac{10}{x}$

103. $\dfrac{1}{x} + \dfrac{3}{x + 2} = 2$

104. $\dfrac{1}{x - 1} + \dfrac{1}{x - 4} = \dfrac{5}{4}$

105. $\dfrac{1}{x + 1} + \dfrac{5}{2x - 4} = 1$

106. $\dfrac{x(2x + 1)}{x - 2} = \dfrac{10}{x - 2}$

107. $x + 1 + \dfrac{x + 2}{x - 1} = \dfrac{3}{x - 1}$

108. $\dfrac{1}{4 - y} = \dfrac{1}{4} + \dfrac{1}{y + 2}$

109. $\dfrac{24}{a} - 11 = \dfrac{-12}{a + 1}$

110. $\dfrac{(a - 2)(a + 4)}{10} = \dfrac{a(a - 3)}{5}$

111. $\dfrac{4 + a}{2a} = \dfrac{a - 2}{3}$

112. $\dfrac{36}{b} - 17 = \dfrac{-24}{b + 1}$

Discovery and Writing

113. If r_1 and r_2 are the roots of $ax^2 + bx + c = 0$, show that $r_1 + r_2 = -\dfrac{b}{a}$.

114. If r_1 and r_2 are the roots of $ax^2 + bx + c = 0$, show that $r_1 r_2 = \dfrac{c}{a}$.

In Exercises 115 and 116, a stone is thrown straight upward, higher than the top of a tree. The stone is even with the top of the tree at time t_1 on the way up and at time t_2 on the way down. If the height of the tree is h feet, both t_1 and t_2 are solutions of $h = v_0 t - 16t^2$.

115. Show that the tree is $16t_1 t_2$ feet tall.

116. Show that v_0 is $16(t_1 + t_2)$ feet per second.

117. Explain why the Zero-Factor Theorem is true.

118. Explain how to complete the square on $x^2 - 17x$.

Quadratic equations can be solved automatically by using a computer program, such as Excel.

119. Solve: $2x^2 - 3x - 4 = 0$.

   a. Open an Excel spreadsheet. In cell B1, enter the left side of the equation as

   $= 2{*}A1{\wedge}2 - 3{*}A1 - 4$

   (Cell A1 is reserved for the value of x.)

   b. After pressing ENTER, you will see the number -4 in cell B1. Since cell A1 is empty, its value is considered to be 0 and the value of the quadratic is -4 when $x = 0$.

   c. To solve the equation, enter a guess for the solution in cell A1. To find a positive solution, enter 1 as a guess in cell A1.

   d. Click inside cell B1. On the Menu bar, look under the Tools menu for SOLVER. (If there is no SOLVER, choose Add-Ins and then, inside the dialog box, select Solver Add-In and click OK.) After choosing SOLVER, a parameters window will appear. Inside the window, in front of Equal To, select Value Of, and be sure it is followed by the number 0. In the GUESS box, enter $\$A\$1$. Then click Solve. When the Solver Results dialog box opens, be sure that Keep Solver Solution is selected, and click OK. The solution of the equation appears in cell A1.

   e. Find the negative solution of the equation.

120. Use Excel to solve $6x^2 + 13x - 5 = 0$.

Review

Simplify each expression.

121. $5x(x - 2) - x(3x - 2)$

122. $(x + 3)(x - 9) - x(x - 5)$

123. $(m + 3)^2 - (m - 3)^2$

124. $[(y + z)(y - z)]^2$

125. $\sqrt{50x^3} - x\sqrt{8x}$

126. $\dfrac{2x}{\sqrt{5} - 2}$

1.4 Applications of Quadratic Equations

In this section, we will learn to

1. Solve geometric problems.
2. Solve uniform motion problems.
3. Solve falling body problems.
4. Solve business problems.
5. Solve shared-work problems.

The Grand Canyon Skywalk is a tourist attraction located along the Colorado River in the state of Arizona. The glass walkway is shaped like a horseshoe and is 4,000 feet above the floor of the canyon. The Grand Canyon, known for its overwhelming size and beautiful landscape, is awe-inspiring and one of our nation's most astounding natural wonders.

If a Clif energy bar is accidentally dropped over the side of the skywalk, how long will it take it to hit the canyon floor?

If t represents the time in seconds, the quadratic equation $-16t^2 + 4,000 = 0$ models the time it takes the energy bar to fall to the canyon floor. We can solve this equation by using the Square Root Property

$$-16t^2 + 4,000 = 0$$

$$-16t^2 = -4,000 \qquad \text{Subtract 4,000 from both sides.}$$

$$t^2 = 250 \qquad \text{Divide both sides by } -16.$$

$$t = \pm\sqrt{250} \qquad \text{Use the Square Root Property.}$$

$$t \approx \pm15.8 \qquad \text{Round to the nearest tenth.}$$

Because time cannot be negative, we disregard the negative answer. The time it will take the energy bar to reach the canyon floor is about 15.8 seconds.

As this example illustrates, the solutions of many problems involve quadratic equations.

1. Solve Geometric Problems

EXAMPLE 1   **Solving an Area Problem**

The length of a rectangle exceeds its width by 3 feet. If its area is 40 square feet, find its dimensions.

SOLUTION   To find an equation that models the problem, we can let w represent the width of the rectangle. Then, $w + 3$ will represent its length (see Figure 1-7). Since the formula for the area of a rectangle is $A = lw$ (area = length × width), the area of the rectangle is $(w + 3)w$, which is equal to 40.

w ft

$(w + 3)$ ft

FIGURE 1-7

The length of the rectangle	times	the width of the rectangle	equals	the area of the rectangle.
$(w + 3)$	$\cdot$	w	$=$	40

We can solve this equation for w.

$$(w + 3)w = 40$$

$$w^2 + 3w = 40$$

$$w^2 + 3w - 40 = 0 \qquad \text{Subtract 40 from both sides.}$$

$$(w - 5)(w + 8) = 0 \qquad \text{Factor.}$$

$$w - 5 = 0 \quad \text{or} \quad w + 8 = 0$$

$$w = 5 \qquad \qquad w = -8$$

When $w = 5$, the length is $w + 3 = 8$. The solution -8 must be discarded, because a rectangle cannot have a negative width.

We can verify that this solution is correct by observing that a rectangle with dimensions of 5 feet by 8 feet has an area of 40 square feet. ∎

Self Check 1   The length of a rectangle exceeds its width by 10 feet. If its area is 375 square feet, find its dimensions.

Now Try Exercise 5.

EXAMPLE 2   **Solve a Right Triangle Problem**

On a college campus, a sidewalk 85 meters long (represented by the red lines in Figure 1-8) joins a dormitory building D with the student center C. However, the students prefer to walk directly from D to C. If segment DC is 65 meters long, how long is each piece of the existing sidewalk?

FIGURE 1-8

SOLUTION   We note that the triangle shown in the figure is a right triangle, with a **hypotenuse** that is 65 meters long. If we let the shorter leg of the triangle be l meters long, the length of the longer leg will be $(85 - l)$ meters. By the **Pythagorean Theorem**, we know that the sum of the squares of the two legs of a right triangle is equal to the square of the hypotenuse. Thus, we can form the equation

$$l^2 + (85 - l)^2 = 65^2 \qquad \text{In a right triangle, } a^2 + b^2 = c^2.$$

which we can solve as follows.

$$l^2 + 7{,}225 - 170l + l^2 = 4{,}225 \qquad \text{Expand } (85 - l)^2.$$

$$2l^2 - 170l + 3{,}000 = 0 \qquad \text{Combine like terms and subtract 4,225 from both sides.}$$

$$l^2 - 85l + 1{,}500 = 0 \qquad \text{Divide both sides by 2.}$$

Since the left side is difficult to factor, we will solve this equation using the Quadratic Formula.

$$l = \frac{-b \pm \sqrt{b^2 - 4ac}}{2a}$$

$$l = \frac{-(-85) \pm \sqrt{(-85)^2 - 4(1)(1{,}500)}}{2(1)}$$

$$l = \frac{85 \pm \sqrt{1{,}225}}{2}$$

$$l = \frac{85 \pm 35}{2}$$

$$l = \frac{85 + 35}{2} \quad \text{or} \quad l = \frac{85 - 35}{2}$$
$$= 60 \qquad\qquad\qquad = 25$$

The length of the shorter leg is 25 meters. The length of the longer leg is $(85 - 25)$ meters, or 60 meters.

Self Check 2 The length of a video screen is 21 feet shorter than its height. If the diagonal of the screen is 39 feet, find the height of the screen.

Now Try Exercise 15.

2. Solve Uniform Motion Problems

EXAMPLE 3 **Solving a Uniform Motion Problem**

A man drives 600 miles to a convention. On the return trip, he is able to increase his speed by 10 mph and save 2 hours of driving time. How fast did he drive in each direction?

SOLUTION We can let s represent the car's speed (in mph) driving to the convention. On the return trip, his speed was $s + 10$ mph. Recall that the distance traveled by an object moving at a constant rate for a certain time is given by the formula $d = rt$. If we divide both sides of this formula by r, we will have a formula for time.

$$t = \frac{d}{r}$$

We can organize the information given in this problem as shown in the following table.

	d	$=$	r	$\cdot$	t
Outbound trip	600		s		$\dfrac{600}{s}$
Return trip	600		$s + 10$		$\dfrac{600}{s + 10}$

Although neither the outbound nor the return travel time is given, we know the difference of those times.

The longer time of the outbound trip	minus	the shorter time of the return trip	equals	the difference in travel times.
$\dfrac{600}{s}$	$-$	$\dfrac{600}{s + 10}$	$=$	2

We can solve this equation for s.

$$\frac{600}{s} - \frac{600}{s + 10} = 2$$

$$s(s + 10)\left(\frac{600}{s} - \frac{600}{s + 10}\right) = s(s + 10)(2) \qquad \text{Multiply both sides by } s(s + 10) \text{ to clear the equation of fractions.}$$

$$600(s + 10) - 600s = 2s(s + 10) \qquad \text{Simplify.}$$

$$600s + 6,000 - 600s = 2s^2 + 20s \qquad \text{Remove parentheses.}$$

$$6,000 = 2s^2 + 20s \qquad \text{Combine like terms.}$$

$$0 = 2s^2 + 20s - 6,000 \qquad \text{Subtract 6,000 from both sides.}$$

$$0 = s^2 + 10s - 3,000 \qquad \text{Divide both sides by 2.}$$

$$0 = (s - 50)(s + 60) \qquad \text{Factor.}$$

$$s - 50 = 0 \quad \text{or} \quad s + 60 = 0 \qquad \text{Set each factor equal to 0.}$$

$$s = 50 \qquad \qquad s = -60$$

The solution $s = -60$ must be discarded. The man drove 50 mph to the convention and $50 + 10$, or 60, mph on the return trip.

These answers are correct, because a 600-mile trip at 50 mph would take $\frac{600}{50}$, or 12 hours. At 60 mph, the same trip would take only 10 hours, which is 2 hours less time.

Self Check 3   Terrence drives his motorcycle 600 miles to Key West, Florida. On the return trip, he is able to increase his speed by 10 mph and save 3 hours of driving time. How fast did he drive in each direction?

Now Try Exercise 19.

3. Solve Falling Body Problems

EXAMPLE 4   **Solving a Falling Body Problem**

If an object is thrown straight up into the air with an initial velocity of 144 feet per second, its height is given by the formula $h = 144t - 16t^2$, where h represents its height (in feet) and t represents the time (in seconds) since it was thrown. How long will it take for the object to return to the point from which it was thrown?

SOLUTION   When the object returns to its starting point, its height is again 0. Thus, we can set h equal to 0 and solve for t.

$$h = 144t - 16t^2$$

$$0 = 144t - 16t^2 \qquad \text{Let } h = 0.$$

$$0 = 16t(9 - t) \qquad \text{Factor.}$$

$$16t = 0 \quad \text{or} \quad 9 - t = 0 \qquad \text{Set each factor equal to 0.}$$

$$t = 0 \qquad \qquad t = 9$$

At $t = 0$, the object's height is 0, because it was just released. When $t = 9$, the height is again 0, and the object has returned to its starting point.

Self Check 4   How long does it take the ball in Example 4 to reach a height of 324 feet?

Now Try Exercise 23.

4. Solve Business Problems

EXAMPLE 5   **Solving a Business Problem**

A bus company shuttles 1,120 passengers daily between Rockford, Illinois, and O'Hare Airport. The current one-way fare is $10. For each 25¢ increase in the fare, the company predicts that it will lose 48 passengers. What increase in fare will produce daily revenue of $10,208?

SOLUTION   Let q represent the number of quarters the fare will be increased. Then the new fare will be $(10 + 0.25q)$. Since the company will lose 48 passengers for each 25¢ increase, $48q$ passengers will be lost when the rate increases by q quarters. The passenger load will then be $(1,120 - 48q)$ passengers.

Since the daily revenue of $10,208 will be the product of the rate and the number of passengers, we have

$$(10 + 0.25q)(1,120 - 48q) = 10,208$$

$$11,200 - 480q + 280q - 12q^2 = 10,208 \qquad \text{Remove parentheses.}$$

$$-12q^2 - 200q + 992 = 0 \qquad \text{Combine like terms and subtract 10,208 from both sides.}$$

$$3q^2 + 50q - 248 = 0 \qquad \text{Divide both sides by } -4.$$

Since the left side is difficult to factor, we will solve this equation with the Quadratic Formula.

$$q = \frac{-b \pm \sqrt{b^2 - 4ac}}{2a}$$

$$q = \frac{-50 \pm \sqrt{50^2 - 4(3)(-248)}}{2(3)} \qquad \text{Substitute 3 for } a, \text{ 50 for } b, \text{ and } -248 \text{ for } c.$$

$$q = \frac{-50 \pm \sqrt{2,500 + 2,976}}{6}$$

$$q = \frac{-50 \pm \sqrt{5,476}}{6}$$

$$q = \frac{-50 \pm 74}{6}$$

$$q = \frac{-50 + 74}{6} \quad \text{or} \quad q = \frac{-50 - 74}{6}$$

$$= \frac{24}{6} \qquad\qquad = \frac{-124}{6}$$

$$= 4 \qquad\qquad\quad = -\frac{62}{3}$$

Since the number of riders cannot be negative, the result of $-\frac{62}{3}$ must be discarded. To generate $10,208 in daily revenues, the company should raise the fare by 4 quarters, or $1, to $11.

Self Check 5   A rock band has been drawing average crowds of 400 people. It is projected that for every $1 increase in the $10 ticket price, the average attendance will decrease by 20. At what ticket price will nightly receipts be $4,500?

Now Try Exercise 31.

5. Solve Shared-Work Problems

EXAMPLE 6   **Solving a Shared-Work Problem**

One environmental company can clean up an oil spill on a beach in 2 days less time than its competitor. Working together they were able to clean up the spill in 10 days. How long would it have taken the first company to clean up the spill if it worked alone?

SOLUTION   Suppose the first company can clean up the spill in x days. Then the first company can do $\frac{1}{x}$ of the job each day. Because the first company can do the work in 2 days less than its competitor, it will take the competitor $(x + 2)$ days to clean up the spill. The competitor can do $\frac{1}{x+2}$ of the job each day.

Working together, they can clean up the spill in 10 days. So together they can do $\frac{1}{10}$ of the job each day. The sum of the work each can do in one day is equal to the work that they can do together in one day.

The part the first company can clean up in one day	plus	the part the second company can clean up in one day	equals	the part they can clean up together in one day.
$\dfrac{1}{x}$	$+$	$\dfrac{1}{x+2}$	$=$	$\dfrac{1}{10}$

We can solve this equation for x.

$$\frac{1}{x} + \frac{1}{x+2} = \frac{1}{10}$$

$$10x(x+2)\left(\frac{1}{x} + \frac{1}{x+2}\right) = 10x(x+2)\left(\frac{1}{10}\right) \qquad \text{Multiply both sides by } 10x(x+2) \text{ to eliminate the fractions.}$$

$$\frac{10x(x+2)}{x} + \frac{10x(x+2)}{x+2} = \frac{10x(x+2)}{10} \qquad \text{Distribute the multiplication by } 10x(x+2).$$

$$10(x+2) + 10x = x(x+2) \qquad \frac{x}{x} = 1, \frac{x+2}{x+2} = 1, \text{ and } \frac{10}{10} = 1.$$

$$10x + 20 + 10x = x^2 + 2x \qquad \text{Use the Distributive Property to remove parentheses.}$$

$$0 = x^2 - 18x - 20 \qquad \text{Subtract } 20x \text{ and } 20 \text{ from both sides.}$$

Since the right side cannot be factored over the integers, we will solve the equation with the Quadratic Formula.

$$x = \frac{-b \pm \sqrt{b^2 - 4ac}}{2a}$$

$$x = \frac{-(-18) \pm \sqrt{(-18)^2 - 4(1)(-20)}}{2(1)} \qquad \text{Substitute 1 for } a, -18 \text{ for } b, \text{ and } -20 \text{ for } c.$$

$$x = \frac{18 \pm \sqrt{324 + 80}}{2}$$

$$x = \frac{18 \pm \sqrt{404}}{2}$$

$$x = \frac{18 \pm 20.09975124}{2}$$

$$x = \frac{18 + 20.09975124}{2} \quad \text{or} \quad x = \frac{18 - 20.09975124}{2}$$

$$\approx 19.05 \qquad\qquad\qquad\qquad \approx -1.05$$

Since the work cannot be completed in a negative number of days, we discard the solution of -1.05. Thus, the first company can complete the job working alone in a little over 19 days. ■

Self Check 6   A hose can fill a swimming pool in 7 hours. Another hose needs 2 more hours to fill the pool than the two hoses combined. How long would it take the second hose to fill the pool?

Now Try Exercise 39.

Self Check Answers   **1.** 15 feet by 25 feet   **2.** 36 feet   **3.** 40 mph to Key West and 50 mph returning   **4.** 4.5 seconds   **5.** $15   **6.** ≈4.9 hours

Exercises **1.4**

Getting Ready
You should be able to complete these vocabulary and concept statements before you proceed to the practice exercises.

Fill in the blanks.

1. The formula for the area of a rectangle is _____.

2. The formula that relates distance, rate, and time is

_____.

Practice
Solve each problem.

3. Geometric problem A rectangle is 4 feet longer than it is wide. If its area is 32 square feet, find its dimensions.

4. Geometric problem A rectangle is 5 times as long as it is wide. If the area is 125 square feet, find its perimeter.

5. Dallas Cowboys video screen The Dallas Cowboys stadium has the world's largest video screen. The rectangular screen's length is 88 feet more than its width. If the video screen has an area of 11,520 square feet, find the dimensions of the screen.

Ken Durden/Shutterstock.com

6. IMAX screen A large movie screen is in the Panasonic IMAX theater at Darling Harbor, Sydney, Australia. The rectangular screen has an area of 11,349 square feet. Find the dimensions of the screen if it is 20 feet longer than it is wide.

7. Geometric problem The side of a square is 4 centimeters shorter than the side of a second square. If the sum of their areas is 106 square centimeters, find the length of one side of the larger square.

8. Geometric problem If two opposite sides of a square are increased by 10 meters and the other sides are decreased by 8 meters, the area of the rectangle that is formed is 63 square meters. Find the area of the original square.

9. Flags In 1912, an order by President Taft fixed the width and length of the U.S. flag in the ratio of 1 to 1.9. If 100 square feet of cloth are to be used to make a U.S. flag, estimate its dimensions to the nearest $\frac{1}{4}$ foot.

10. Geometric problem Find the dimensions of a rectangle whose area is 180 cm² and whose perimeter is 54 cm.

11. Metal fabrication A piece of tin, 12 inches on a side, is to have four equal squares cut from its corners, as in the illustration. If the edges are then to be folded up to make a box with a floor area of 64 square inches, find the depth of the box.

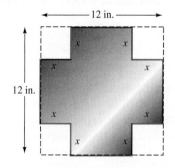

12. Making gutters A piece of sheet metal, 18 inches wide, is bent to form the gutter shown in the illustration. If the cross-sectional area is 36 square inches, find the depth of the gutter.

13. Geometric problem The base of a triangle is one-third as long as its height. If the area of the triangle is 24 square meters, how long is its base?

14. Geometric problem The base of a triangle is one-half as long as its height. If the area of the triangle is 100 square yards, find its height.

15. Right triangle If one leg of a right triangle is 14 meters shorter than the other leg, and the hypotenuse is 26 meters, find the length of the two legs.

16. Right triangle If one leg of a right triangle is five times the other leg, and the hypotenuse is $10\sqrt{26}$ centimeters, find the length of the two legs.

17. Manufacturing A manufacturer of television sets received an order for sets with a 46-inch screen (measured along the diagonal), as shown in the illustration. If the televisions are $17\frac{1}{2}$ inches wider than they are high, find the dimensions of the screen to the nearest tenth of an inch.

18. Finding dimensions An oriental rug is 2 feet longer than it is wide. If the diagonal of the rug is 12 feet, to the nearest tenth of a foot, find its dimensions.

19. Cycling rates A cyclist rides from DeKalb to Rockford, a distance of 40 miles. His return trip takes 2 hours longer, because his speed decreases by 10 mph. How fast does he ride each way?

20. Travel times Jake drives a tractor from one town to another, a distance of 120 kilometers. He drives 10 kilometers per hour faster on the return trip, cutting 1 hour off the time. How fast does he drive each way?

21. Uniform motion problem If the speed were increased by 10 mph, a 420-mile trip would take 1 hour less time. How long will the trip take at the slower speed?

22. Uniform motion problem By increasing her usual speed by 25 kilometers per hour, a bus driver decreases the time on a 25-kilometer trip by 10 minutes. Find the usual speed.

23. Ballistics The height of a projectile fired upward with an initial velocity of 400 feet per second is given by the formula $h = -16t^2 + 400t$, where h is the height in feet and t is the time in seconds. Find the time required for the projectile to return to earth.

24. Ballistics The height of an object tossed upward with an initial velocity of 104 feet per second is given by the formula $h = -16t^2 + 104t$, where h is the height in feet and t is the time in seconds. Find the time required for the object to return to its point of departure.

25. Falling coins An object will fall s feet in t seconds, where $s = 16t^2$. How long will it take for a penny to hit the ground if it is dropped from the top of the Sears Tower in Chicago? (*Hint:* The tower is 1,454 feet tall.)

26. Movie stunts According to the *Guinness Book of World Records, 1998,* stuntman Dan Koko fell a distance of 312 feet into an airbag after jumping from the Vegas World Hotel and Casino. The distance d in feet traveled by a free-falling object in t seconds is given by the formula $d = 16t^2$. To the nearest tenth of a second, how long did the fall last?

27. Accidents The height h (in feet) of an object that is dropped from a height of s feet is given by the formula $h = s - 16t^2$, where t is the time the object has been falling. A 5-foot-tall woman on a sidewalk looks directly overhead and sees a window washer drop a bottle from 4 stories up. How long does she have to get out of the way? Round to the nearest tenth. (A story is 12 feet.)

28. Ballistics The height of an object thrown upward with an initial velocity of 32 feet per second is given by the formula $h = -16t^2 + 32t$, where t is the time in seconds. How long will it take the object to reach a height of 16 feet?

29. Setting fares A bus company has 3,000 passengers daily, paying a 25¢ fare. For each nickel increase in fare, the company projects that it will lose 80 passengers. What fare increase will produce $994 in daily revenue?

30. Jazz concerts A jazz group on tour has been drawing average crowds of 500 persons. It is projected that for every $1 increase in the $12 ticket price, the average attendance will decrease by 50. At what ticket price will nightly receipts be $5,600?

31. Concert receipts Tickets for the annual symphony orchestra pops concert cost $15, and the average attendance at the concerts has been 1,200 persons. Management projects that for each 50¢ decrease in ticket price, 40 more patrons will attend. How many people attended the concert if the receipts were $17,280?

32. Projecting demand The *Vilas County News* earns a profit of $20 per year for each of its 3,000 subscribers. Management projects that the profit per subscriber would increase by 1¢ for each additional subscriber over the current 3,000. How many subscribers are needed to bring a total profit of $120,000?

33. Investment problems Morgan and Chloe each have a bank CD. Morgan's is $1,000 larger than Chloe's, but the interest rate is 1% less. Last year Morgan received interest of $280, and Chloe received $240. Find the rate of interest for each CD.

34. Investment problem Scott and Laura have both invested some money. Scott invested $3,000 more than Laura and at a 2% higher interest rate. If Scott received $800 annual interest and Laura received $400, how much did Scott invest?

35. Buying microwave ovens Some mathematics professors would like to purchase a $150 microwave oven for the department workroom. If four of the professors don't contribute, everyone's share will increase by $10. How many professors are in the department?

36. Digital cameras A merchant could sell one model of digital cameras at list price for $180. If he had three more cameras, he could sell each one for $10 less and still receive $180. Find the list price of each camera.

37. Filling storage tanks Two pipes are used to fill a water storage tank. The first pipe can fill the tank in 4 hours, and the two pipes together can fill the tank in 2 hours less time than the second pipe alone. How long would it take for the second pipe to fill the tank?

38. Filling swimming pools A hose can fill a swimming pool in 6 hours. Another hose needs 3 more hours to fill the pool than the two hoses combined. How long would it take the second hose to fill the pool?

39. Mowing lawns Kristy can mow a lawn in 1 hour less time than her brother Steven. Together they can finish the job in 5 hours. How long would it take Kristy if she worked alone?

40. Cleaning the garage Working together, Sarah and Heidi can clean the garage in 2 hours. If they work alone, it takes Heidi 3 hours longer than it takes Sarah. How long would it take Heidi to clean the garage alone?

41. Planting windscreens A farmer intends to construct a windscreen by planting trees in a quarter-mile row. His daughter points out that 44 fewer trees will be needed if they are planted 1 foot farther apart. If her dad takes her advice, how many trees will be needed? A row starts and ends with a tree. (*Hint:* 1 mile = 5,280 feet.)

42. Angle between spokes If a wagon wheel had 10 more spokes, the angle between spokes would decrease by 6°. How many spokes does the wheel have?

43. Architecture A **golden rectangle** is one of the most visually appealing of all geometric forms. The front of the Parthenon, built in Athens in the 5th century B.C. and shown in the illustration, is a golden rectangle. In a golden rectangle, the length l and the height h of the rectangle must satisfy the following equation. If a rectangular billboard is to have a height of 15 feet, how long should it be if it is to form a golden rectangle? Round to the nearest tenth of a foot.

$$\frac{l}{h} = \frac{h}{l - h}$$

44. Golden ratio Rectangle $ABCD$, shown here, will be a **golden rectangle** if $\frac{AB}{AD} = \frac{BC}{BE}$ where $AE = AD$. Let $AE = 1$ and find the ratio of AB to AD.

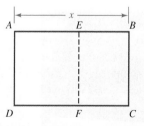

45. Automobile engines As the piston shown moves upward, it pushes a cylinder of a gasoline/air mixture that is ignited by the spark plug. The formula that gives the volume of a cylinder is $V = \pi r^2 h$, where r is the radius and h the height. Find the radius of the piston (to the nearest hundredth of an inch) if it displaces 47.75 cubic inches of gasoline/air mixture as it moves from its lowest to its highest point.

46. History One of the important cities of the ancient world was Babylon. Greek historians wrote that the city was square-shaped. Its area numerically exceeded its perimeter by about 124. Find its dimensions in miles. (Round to the nearest tenth.)

Discovery and Writing

47. Is it possible for a rectangle to have a width that is 3 units shorter than its diagonal and a length that is 4 units longer than its diagonal?

48. Which of the preceding application problems did you find the hardest? Why?

Review

Perform the operations and simplify.

49. $\dfrac{2}{x} - \dfrac{1}{x-3}$

50. $\dfrac{1}{x} \cdot \dfrac{x^2 - 5x}{x-3}$

51. $\dfrac{x+3}{x^2-x-6} \div \dfrac{x^2+3x}{x^2-9}$

52. $\dfrac{\dfrac{1}{x} - \dfrac{1}{2}}{x-2}$

53. $\dfrac{\dfrac{1}{x} + \dfrac{1}{y}}{\dfrac{1}{x} - \dfrac{1}{y}}$

54. $\dfrac{x}{x+1} + \dfrac{x+1}{x} \cdot \dfrac{x^2-x}{3}$

1.5 Complex Numbers

In this section, we will learn to

1. Simplify imaginary numbers.

2. Perform operations on complex numbers.

3. Find powers of i.

4. Determine the absolute value of a complex number.

5. Solve quadratic equations with complex roots.

6. Factor the sum of two squares.

The Blue Man Group is a highly successful group of creative performers who cover themselves in blue grease paint, wear latex bald caps, and dress in black. They combine rock music, comedy, multimedia theatrics, and sophisticated lighting to entertain their audiences.

There are a variety of themes used in Blue Man performances, and the group uses fractals in their shows. Fractals are beautiful art designs that are computer generated from numbers called *complex numbers*. We will study these numbers in this section. A fractal is shown on the next page.

Steven Good/Shutterstock.com

All of the quadratic equations that we considered in Section 1.3 had roots that were real numbers. However, the solutions of many quadratic equations are not real numbers. For example, if we use the Quadratic Formula to solve $x^2 + x + 2 = 0$, we get solutions that are not real.

$$x = \frac{-b \pm \sqrt{b^2 - 4ac}}{2a}$$

$$x = \frac{-1 \pm \sqrt{1^2 - 4(1)(2)}}{2(1)} \qquad \text{Substitute 1 for } a, \text{ 1 for } b, \text{ and 2 for } c.$$

$$x = \frac{-1 \pm \sqrt{1 - 8}}{2}$$

$$x = \frac{-1 \pm \sqrt{-7}}{2}$$

Each solution involves $\sqrt{-7}$. This is not a real number, because the square of no real number is -7.

1. Simplify Imaginary Numbers

For many years, mathematicians considered numbers such as $\sqrt{-1}$, $\sqrt{-5}$ and $\sqrt{-9}$ to make no sense. Sir Isaac Newton (1642–1727) called them "impossible numbers." In the 17th century, these symbols were called **imaginary numbers** by René Descartes. Today, they have important uses, such as describing the behavior of alternating current in electronics. The imaginary numbers are based on the imaginary unit, and the imaginary unit is denoted by the letter i.

Imaginary Unit i   The **imaginary unit** is denoted by the letter i and is defined as

$$i = \sqrt{-1}$$

From the definition it follows that $i^2 = -1$.

Because imaginary numbers follow the rules for exponents, we have

$$(3i)^2 = 3^2 i^2 = 9(-1) = -9$$

Since $(3i)^2 = -9$, $3i$ is the square root of -9, and we can write

$$\sqrt{-9} = \sqrt{(-1)(9)}$$

$$= \sqrt{-1}\sqrt{9} \qquad \sqrt{ab} = \sqrt{a}\sqrt{b}$$

$$= 3i \qquad\qquad \sqrt{-1} = i$$

The Multiplication Property of Radicals can be used to simplify imaginary numbers. Four examples are shown in the table below.

Comment

When $\sqrt{b}i$ and $\sqrt{bi}$ are handwritten, it is easy to confuse them. To avoid confusion, we will write i first so that it is clear that i is not under the radical symbol.

Imaginary Numbers Written in Terms of i

$$\sqrt{-25} = \sqrt{(-1)(25)} = \sqrt{-1}\sqrt{25} = (i)(5) = 5i$$

$$-\sqrt{-169} = -\sqrt{(-1)(169)} = -\sqrt{-1}\sqrt{169} = -(i)(13) = -13i$$

$$\sqrt{-24} = \sqrt{(-1)(24)} = \sqrt{-1}\sqrt{24} = (i)(2\sqrt{6}) = 2\sqrt{6}i \text{ or } 2i\sqrt{6}$$

$$\sqrt{-\frac{8}{49}} = \sqrt{(-1)\left(\frac{8}{49}\right)} = \sqrt{-1}\sqrt{\frac{8}{49}} = (i)\left(\frac{\sqrt{8}}{\sqrt{49}}\right) = (i)\left(\frac{2\sqrt{2}}{7}\right) = \frac{2\sqrt{2}}{7}i \text{ or } \frac{2i\sqrt{2}}{7}$$

Caution

If a and b both are negative, then $\sqrt{ab} \neq \sqrt{a}\sqrt{b}$. For example, the correct simplification of $\sqrt{-16}\sqrt{-4}$ is

$$\sqrt{-16}\sqrt{-4} = (4i)(2i) = 8i^2 = 8(-1) = -8$$

The following simplification is incorrect. Since both numbers are negative, the Multiplication Property of Radicals does not apply.

$$\sqrt{-16}\sqrt{-4} = \sqrt{(-16)(-4)} = \sqrt{64} = 8$$

ACCENT ON TECHNOLOGY   Simplifying Imaginary Numbers

If we place our graphing calculator in $a + bi$ mode, it can be used to simplify many imaginary numbers. Please note that on a graphing calculator i is located above the decimal point key.

In Figure 1-9, we see the graphing calculator results for $\sqrt{-81}$, $\sqrt{-\frac{4}{25}}$, and $\sqrt{-108}$.

```
√(-81)
                9i
√(-4/25)
               .4i
√(-108)
        10.39230485i
```

FIGURE 1-9

2. Perform Operations on Complex Numbers

Numbers that are the sum or difference of a real number and an imaginary number, such as $3 + 4i$, $-5 + 7i$, and $-1 - 9i$, are called *complex numbers*.

Complex Numbers

A **complex number** is a number that can be written in the form $a + bi$, where a and b are real numbers and $i = \sqrt{-1}$.

The number a is called the **real part,** and b is called the **imaginary part.**

If $b = 0$, the complex number $a + bi$ is the real number a. If $a = 0$ and $b \neq 0$, the complex number $a + bi$ is the imaginary number bi. It follows that the set of real numbers and the set of imaginary numbers are subsets of the set of complex numbers. Figure 1-10 illustrates how the various sets of numbers are related.

Complex numbers

Real numbers $a + 0i$	Imaginary numbers $0 + bi$ ($b \neq 0$)
$0, 3, \frac{7}{3}, \pi, 125.3$	$4i, -12i, \sqrt{-4}$

$4 + 7i, \ 5 - 16i, \ \dfrac{1}{32 - 12i}, \ 15 + \sqrt{-26}$

FIGURE 1-10

To determine whether two complex numbers are equal, we can use the following definition.

Equality of Complex Numbers   Two complex numbers are **equal** if their real parts are equal and their imaginary parts are equal. If $a + bi$ and $c + di$ are two complex numbers, then

$$a + bi = c + di \quad \text{if and only if} \quad a = c \quad \text{and} \quad b = d$$

EXAMPLE 1   **Using the Definition of Equality of Complex Numbers**

For what numbers x and y is $3x + 4i = (2y + x) + xi$?

SOLUTION   Since the numbers are equal, their imaginary parts must be equal: $x = 4$. Since their real parts are equal, $3x = 2y + x$. We can solve the system

$$\begin{cases} x = 4 \\ 3x = 2y + x \end{cases}$$

by substituting 4 for x in the second equation and solving for y. We find that $y = 4$. The solution is $x = 4$ and $y = 4$. ■

Self Check 1   Find x: $a + (x + 3)i = a - (2x - 1)i$.

Now Try Exercise 19.

Complex numbers can be added and subtracted as if they were binomials.

Adding and Subtracting Complex Numbers   Two complex numbers such as $a + bi$ and $c + di$ are **added** and **subtracted** as if they were binomials:

$$(a + bi) + (c + di) = (a + c) + (b + d)i$$

$$(a + bi) - (c + di) = (a - c) + (b - d)i$$

Because of the preceding definition, the sum or difference of two complex numbers is another complex number.

EXAMPLE 2   **Adding and Subtracting Complex Numbers**

Simplify: **a.** $(3 + 4i) + (2 + 7i)$ **b.** $(-5 + 8i) - (2 - 12i)$

SOLUTION   **a.** $(3 + 4i) + (2 + 7i) = 3 + 4i + 2 + 7i$
$$= 3 + 2 + 4i + 7i$$
$$= 5 + 11i$$

b. $(-5 + 8i) - (2 - 12i) = -5 + 8i - 2 + 12i$
$$= -5 - 2 + 8i + 12i$$
$$= -7 + 20i$$ ■

Self Check 2   Simplify: **a.** $(5 - 2i) + (-3 + 9i)$ **b.** $(2 + 5i) - (6 + 7i)$

Now Try Exercise 23.

Complex numbers can also be multiplied as if they were binomials.

Multiplying Complex Numbers The numbers $a + bi$ and $c + di$ are **multiplied** as if they were binomials, with $i^2 = -1$:

$$(a + bi)(c + di) = (ac - bd) + (ad + bc)i$$

Because of this definition, the product of two complex numbers is another complex number.

EXAMPLE 3 **Multiplying Complex Numbers**

Multiply: **a.** $(3 + 4i)(2 + 7i)$ **b.** $(5 - 7i)(1 + 3i)$

SOLUTION **a.** $(3 + 4i)(2 + 7i) = 6 + 21i + 8i + 28i^2$

$$= 6 + 21i + 8i + 28(-1) \qquad i^2 = -1$$

$$= 6 - 28 + 29i$$

$$= -22 + 29i$$

b. $(5 - 7i)(1 + 3i) = 5 + 15i - 7i - 21i^2$

$$= 5 + 15i - 7i - 21(-1) \qquad i^2 = -1$$

$$= 5 + 21 + 8i$$

$$= 26 + 8i$$

Self Check 3 Multiply: $(2 - 5i)(3 + 2i)$.

Now Try Exercise 33.

To avoid errors in determining the sign of the result, always express numbers in $a + bi$ form before attempting any algebraic manipulations.

EXAMPLE 4 **Multiplying Complex Numbers**

Multiply: $\left(-2 + \sqrt{-16}\right)\left(4 - \sqrt{-9}\right)$.

SOLUTION We change each number to $a + bi$ form:

$$-2 + \sqrt{-16} = -2 + \sqrt{16}\sqrt{-1} = -2 + 4i$$

$$4 - \sqrt{-9} = 4 - \sqrt{9}\sqrt{-1} = 4 - 3i$$

and then find the product.

$$(-2 + 4i)(4 - 3i) = -8 + 6i + 16i - 12i^2$$

$$= -8 + 6i + 16i - 12(-1) \qquad i^2 = -1$$

$$= -8 + 12 + 22i$$

$$= 4 + 22i$$

Self Check 4 Multiply: $\left(3 + \sqrt{-25}\right)\left(2 - \sqrt{-9}\right)$.

Now Try Exercise 37.

Before we discuss the division of complex numbers, we introduce the concept of a complex conjugate.

Complex Conjugates   The complex numbers $a + bi$ and $a - bi$ are called **complex conjugates** of each other.

For example,

- $2 + 5i$ and $2 - 5i$ are complex conjugates.
- $-\frac{1}{2} + 4i$ and $-\frac{1}{2} - 4i$ are complex conjugates.
- $13i$ and $-13i$ are complex conjugates. That is, the complex conjugate of $0 + 13i$ is $0 - 13i$.

What makes this concept important is the fact that the product of two complex conjugates is always a real number. For example,

$$(2 + 5i)(2 - 5i) = 4 - 10i + 10i - 25i^2$$

$$= 4 - 25(-1) \qquad\qquad i^2 = -1$$

$$= 4 + 25$$

$$= 29$$

In general, we have

$$(a + bi)(a - bi) = a^2 - abi + abi - b^2i^2$$

$$= a^2 - b^2(-1) \qquad\qquad i^2 = -1$$

$$= a^2 + b^2$$

To divide complex numbers, we use the concept of complex conjugates to rationalize the denominator.

EXAMPLE 5   **Dividing Complex Numbers**

Divide and write the result in $a + bi$ form: $\dfrac{3}{2 + i}$.

SOLUTION   To divide, we rationalize the denominator and simplify.

$$\frac{3}{2 + i} = \frac{3(2 - i)}{(2 + i)(2 - i)}$$

To make the denominator a real number, multiply the numerator and denominator by the complex conjugate of $2 + i$, which is $2 - i$.

$$= \frac{6 - 3i}{4 - 2i + 2i - i^2}$$

Multiply.

$$= \frac{6 - 3i}{4 + 1}$$

Simplify the denominator.

$$= \frac{6 - 3i}{5}$$

$$= \frac{6}{5} - \frac{3}{5}i$$

It is common to accept $\frac{6}{5} - \frac{3}{5}i$ as a substitute for $\frac{6}{5} + \left(-\frac{3}{5}\right)i$.

Self Check 5   Divide and write the result in $a + bi$ form: $\dfrac{3}{3 - i}$.

Now Try Exercise 45.

EXAMPLE 6   Dividing Complex Numbers

Divide and write the result in $a + bi$ form: $\dfrac{2 - \sqrt{-16}}{3 + \sqrt{-1}}$.

SOLUTION $\dfrac{2 - \sqrt{-16}}{3 + \sqrt{-1}} = \dfrac{2 - 4i}{3 + i}$ Change each number to $a + bi$ form.

$= \dfrac{(2 - 4i)(3 - i)}{(3 + i)(3 - i)}$ To make the denominator a real number, multiply the numerator and denominator by $3 - i$.

$= \dfrac{6 - 2i - 12i + 4i^2}{9 - 3i + 3i - i^2}$ Remove parentheses.

$= \dfrac{2 - 14i}{9 + 1}$ Combine like terms; $i^2 = -1$.

$= \dfrac{2}{10} - \dfrac{14i}{10}$

$= \dfrac{1}{5} - \dfrac{7}{5}i$

Self Check 6   Divide and write the result in $a + bi$ form: $\dfrac{3 + \sqrt{-25}}{2 - \sqrt{-1}}$.

Now Try Exercise 53.

Examples 5 and 6 illustrate that the quotient of two complex numbers is another complex number.

3. Find Powers of i

The powers of i with natural number exponents produce an interesting pattern as shown in the table.

Comment

i^0 is 1 because any number except 0 raised to the 0th power is 1.

Powers of i	
$i^1 = \sqrt{-1} = i$	$i^5 = i^4 i = 1i = i$
$i^2 = \left(\sqrt{-1}\right)^2 = -1$	$i^6 = i^4 i^2 = 1(-1) = -1$
$i^3 = i^2 i = -1i = -i$	$i^7 = i^4 i^3 = 1(-i) = -i$
$i^4 = i^2 i^2 = (-1)(-1) = 1$	$i^8 = i^4 i^4 = 1(1) = 1$
The pattern continues: $i, -1, -i, 1, \ldots$.	

EXAMPLE 7   Simplifying Powers of i

Simplify: i^{365}.

SOLUTION   Since $i^4 = 1$, each occurrence of i^4 is a factor of 1. To determine how many factors of i^4 are in i^{365}, we divide 365 by 4. The quotient is 91, and the remainder is 1.

$$i^{365} = (i^4)^{91} \cdot i^1$$

$$= 1^{91} \cdot i^1 \qquad i^4 = 1$$

$$= i \qquad\qquad 1^{91} = 1 \text{ and } 1 \cdot i = i$$

■

Self Check 7   Simplify: $i^{1,999}$.

Now Try Exercise 63.

The result of Example 7 illustrates the following theorem.

Powers of i   If n is a natural number that has a remainder of r when divided by 4, then

$$i^n = i^r$$

When n is divisible by 4, the remainder r is 0 and $i^0 = 1$.

We can also simplify powers of i that involve negative integer exponents.

$$i^{-1} = \frac{1}{i} = \frac{1 \cdot i}{i \cdot i} = \frac{i}{-1} = -i \qquad\qquad i^{-2} = \frac{1}{i^2} = \frac{1}{-1} = -1$$

$$i^{-3} = \frac{1}{i^3} = \frac{1 \cdot i}{i^3 \cdot i} = \frac{i}{i^4} = \frac{i}{1} = i \qquad\qquad i^{-4} = \frac{1}{i^4} = \frac{1}{1} = 1$$

ACCENT ON TECHNOLOGY   **Performing Operations on Complex Numbers**

If we place our graphing calculator in $a + bi$ mode we can use it to perform operations on complex numbers. Addition, subtraction, and multiplication of $7 - 2i$ and $2 + i$ are shown in Figure 1-11(a). Division of $7 - 2i$ and $2 + i$ is shown in Figure 1-11(b). We can also find powers of i using our graphing calculator. i^{24} and i^{25} are shown in Figure 1-11(c). Since $4\mathrm{E}^-13i$ can be approximated as 0, $i^{24} = 1$. Since $-5\mathrm{E}^-13$ can be approximated as 0, $i^{25} = i$.

```
(7-2i)+(2+i)
            9-i
(7-2i)-(2+i)
            5-3i
(7-2i)(2+i)
          16+3i
```

(a)

```
(7-2i)/(2+i)
        2.4-2.2i
Ans►Frac
       12/5-11/5i
```

(b)

```
i^24
        1+4E-13i
i^25
       -5E-13+i
```

(c)

FIGURE 1-11

4. Determine the Absolute Value of a Complex Number

Absolute Value of a Complex Number	If $a + bi$ is a complex number, then

$$|a + bi| = \sqrt{a^2 + b^2}$$

Because of the previous definition, the absolute value of a complex number is a real number. For this reason, i does not appear in the result.

EXAMPLE 8 **Determine the Absolute Value of a Complex Number**

Write without absolute value symbols: **a.** $|3 + 4i|$ **b.** $|4 - 6i|$

SOLUTION In each case, we apply the definition of absolute value of a complex number.

a. $|3 + 4i| = \sqrt{3^2 + 4^2}$ **b.** $|4 - 6i| = \sqrt{4^2 + (-6)^2}$
$ = \sqrt{9 + 16}$ $ = \sqrt{16 + 36}$
$ = \sqrt{25}$ $ = \sqrt{52}$
$ = 5$ $ = \sqrt{4 \cdot 13}$
$ = \sqrt{4}\sqrt{13}$
$ = 2\sqrt{13}$

Self Check 8 Write without absolute value symbols: $|2 - 5i|$.

Now Try Exercise 75.

EXAMPLE 9 **Determine the Absolute Value of a Complex Number**

Write without absolute value symbols: **a.** $\left|\dfrac{2i}{3 + i}\right|$ **b.** $|a + 0i|$

SOLUTION **a.** We first write $\frac{2i}{3 + i}$ in $a + bi$ form:

$$\frac{2i}{3 + i} = \frac{2i(3 - i)}{(3 + i)(3 - i)} = \frac{6i - 2i^2}{9 - i^2} = \frac{6i + 2}{10} = \frac{1}{5} + \frac{3}{5}i$$

and then find the absolute value of $\frac{1}{5} + \frac{3}{5}i$.

$$\left|\frac{2i}{3 + i}\right| = \left|\frac{1}{5} + \frac{3}{5}i\right| = \sqrt{\left(\frac{1}{5}\right)^2 + \left(\frac{3}{5}\right)^2} = \sqrt{\frac{10}{25}} = \frac{\sqrt{10}}{5}$$

b. $|a + 0i| = \sqrt{a^2 + 0^2} = \sqrt{a^2} = |a|$

From part b, we see that $|a| = \sqrt{a^2}$.

Self Check 9 Write without absolute value symbols: $\left|\dfrac{3i}{2 - i}\right|$.

Now Try Exercise 85.

5. Solve Quadratic Equations with Complex Roots

The roots of many quadratic equations are complex numbers, as the following example shows.

EXAMPLE 10   **Solving a Quadratic Equation with Complex Roots**

Solve: $x^2 - 4x + 5 = 0$.

SOLUTION   In this equation, $a = 1$, $b = -4$, and $c = 5$.

$$x = \frac{-b \pm \sqrt{b^2 - 4ac}}{2a}$$

$$= \frac{-(-4) \pm \sqrt{(-4)^2 - 4(1)(5)}}{2(1)} \qquad \text{Substitute 1 for } a, -4 \text{ for } b, \text{ and 5 for } c.$$

$$= \frac{4 \pm \sqrt{16 - 20}}{2}$$

$$= \frac{4 \pm \sqrt{-4}}{2}$$

$$= \frac{4 \pm 2i}{2} \qquad\qquad\qquad \sqrt{-4} = \sqrt{4}\sqrt{-1} = 2i$$

$$= 2 \pm i \qquad\qquad\qquad \frac{4 \pm 2i}{2} = \frac{2(2 \pm i)}{2} = 2 \pm i$$

The roots $x = 2 + i$ and $x = 2 - i$ both satisfy the equation. Note that the roots are complex conjugates.

Self Check 10   Solve: $x^2 + 3x + 4 = 0$.

Now Try Exercise 113.

6. Factor the Sum of Two Squares

We have seen that the sum of two squares cannot be factored over the set of integers. However, it is possible to factor the sum of two squares over the set of complex numbers. For example, to factor $9x^2 + 16y^2$ we proceed as follows:

$$9x^2 + 16y^2 = 9x^2 - (-1)16y^2$$

$$= 9x^2 - i^2(16y^2) \qquad\qquad i^2 = -1$$

$$= 9x^2 - 16y^2i^2$$

$$= (3x + 4yi)(3x - 4yi) \qquad \text{Factor the difference of two squares.}$$

EXAMPLE 11   **Factoring the Sum of Two Squares**

Factor: $100x^2 + 144y^2$.

SOLUTION   We will rewrite $100x^2 + 144y^2$ as the difference of two squares and then factor.

$$100x^2 + 144y^2 = 100x^2 - (-1)144y^2$$

$$= 100x^2 - i^2 144y^2 \qquad\qquad i^2 = -1$$

$$= 100x^2 - 144y^2 i^2$$

$$= (10x + 12yi)(10x - 12yi) \qquad \text{Factor the difference of two squares.}$$

Self Check 11   Factor $x^2 + 225y^2$.

Now Try Exercise 121.

Self Check Answers   **1.** $-\dfrac{2}{3}$ **2. a.** $2 + 7i$ **b.** $-4 - 2i$ **3.** $16 - 11i$ **4.** $21 + i$

5. $\dfrac{9}{10} + \dfrac{3}{10}i$ **6.** $\dfrac{1}{5} + \dfrac{13}{5}i$ **7.** $-i$ **8.** $\sqrt{29}$ **9.** $\dfrac{3\sqrt{5}}{5}$

10. $-\dfrac{3}{2} \pm \dfrac{\sqrt{7}}{2}i$ **11.** $(x + 15yi)(x - 15yi)$

Exercises **1.5**

Getting Ready
You should be able to complete these vocabulary and concept statements before you proceed to the practice exercises.

Fill in the blanks.

1. $\sqrt{-3}$, $\sqrt{-9}$, and $\sqrt{-12}$ are examples of _____ numbers.

2. In the complex number $a + bi$, a is the _____ part, and b is the _____ part.

3. If $a = 0$ and $b \neq 0$ in the complex number $a + bi$, the number is an _____ number.

4. If $b = 0$ in the complex number $a + bi$, the number is a _____ number.

5. The complex conjugate of $2 + 5i$ is _____.

6. By definition, $|a + bi| = $ _____.

7. The absolute value of a complex number is a _____ number.

8. The product of two complex conjugates is a _____ number.

Practice
Simplify the imaginary numbers.

9. $\sqrt{-144}$

10. $-\sqrt{-225}$

11. $-2\sqrt{-24}$

12. $7\sqrt{-48}$

13. $\sqrt{-\dfrac{50}{9}}$

14. $-\sqrt{-\dfrac{72}{25}}$

15. $-7\sqrt{-\dfrac{3}{8}}$

16. $5\sqrt{-\dfrac{5}{27}}$

Find the values of x and y.

17. $x + (x + y)i = 3 + 8i$

18. $x + 5i = y - yi$

19. $3x - 2yi = 2 + (x + y)i$

20. $\begin{cases} 2 + (x + y)i = 2 - i \\ x + 3i = 2 + 3i \end{cases}$

Perform all operations. Give all answers in $a + bi$ form.

21. $(2 - 7i) + (3 + i)$

22. $(-7 + 2i) + (2 - 8i)$

23. $(5 - 6i) - (7 + 4i)$

24. $(11 + 2i) - (13 - 5i)$

25. $(14i + 2) + \left(2 - \sqrt{-16}\right)$

26. $\left(5 + \sqrt{-64}\right) - (23i - 32)$

27. $\left(3 + \sqrt{-4}\right) - \left(2 + \sqrt{-9}\right)$

28. $\left(7 - \sqrt{-25}\right) + \left(-8 + \sqrt{-1}\right)$

29. $-5(3 + 5i)$

30. $5(2 - i)$

31. $7i(4 - 8i)$

32. $-2i(3 - 7i)$

33. $(2 + 3i)(3 + 5i)$

34. $(5 - 7i)(2 + i)$

35. $(2 + 3i)^2$

36. $(3 - 4i)^2$

37. $\left(11 + \sqrt{-25}\right)\left(2 - \sqrt{-36}\right)$

38. $\left(6 + \sqrt{-49}\right)\left(6 - \sqrt{-49}\right)$

39. $\left(\sqrt{-16} + 3\right)\left(2 + \sqrt{-9}\right)$

40. $\left(12 - \sqrt{-4}\right)\left(-7 + \sqrt{-25}\right)$

41. $\dfrac{1}{-i}$

42. $\dfrac{3}{i}$

43. $\dfrac{-4}{3i}$

44. $\dfrac{10}{7i}$

45. $\dfrac{1}{2 + i}$

46. $\dfrac{-2}{3 - i}$

47. $\dfrac{2i}{7 + i}$

48. $\dfrac{-3i}{2 + 5i}$

49. $\dfrac{2 + i}{3 - i}$

50. $\dfrac{3 - i}{1 + i}$

51. $\dfrac{4 - 5i}{2 + 3i}$

52. $\dfrac{34 + 2i}{2 - 4i}$

53. $\dfrac{5 - \sqrt{-16}}{-8 + \sqrt{-4}}$

54. $\dfrac{3 - \sqrt{-9}}{2 - \sqrt{-1}}$

55. $\dfrac{2 + i\sqrt{3}}{3 + i}$

56. $\dfrac{3 + i}{4 - i\sqrt{2}}$

Simplify each expression.

57. i^9

58. i^{26}

59. i^{38}

60. i^{99}

61. i^{87}

62. i^{44}

63. i^{100}

64. i^{201}

65. i^{-6}

66. i^0

67. i^{-10}

68. i^{-31}

69. $\dfrac{1}{i^3}$

70. $\dfrac{3}{i^5}$

71. $\dfrac{-4}{i^{10}}$

72. $\dfrac{-10}{i^{24}}$

Write without absolute value symbols.

73. $|3 + 4i|$

74. $|5 + 12i|$

75. $|2 + 3i|$

76. $|5 - i|$

77. $\left|-7 + \sqrt{-49}\right|$

78. $\left|-2 - \sqrt{-16}\right|$

79. $\left|\dfrac{1}{2} + \dfrac{1}{2}i\right|$

80. $\left|\dfrac{1}{2} - \dfrac{1}{4}i\right|$

81. $|-6i|$

82. $|5i|$

83. $\left|\dfrac{2}{1 + i}\right|$

84. $\left|\dfrac{3}{3 + i}\right|$

85. $\left|\dfrac{-3i}{2 + i}\right|$

86. $\left|\dfrac{5i}{i - 2}\right|$

87. $\left|\dfrac{i + 2}{i - 2}\right|$

88. $\left|\dfrac{2 + i}{2 - i}\right|$

Solve each quadratic equation using the Square Root Property.

89. $x^2 = -169$

90. $x^2 = -81$

91. $y^2 + 54 = 0$

92. $x^2 + 125 = 0$

93. $2x^2 = -90$

94. $5x^2 = -400$

95. $9x^2 = -7$

96. $25x^2 = -11$

97. $2x^2 + 15 = 0$

98. $-5x^2 = 11$

99. $(x + 1)^2 + 12 = 0$

100. $(y + 2)^2 + 120 = 0$

101. $(5x + 1)^2 = -8$

102. $(7y + 2)^2 + 48 = 0$

Solve the following quadratic equations by completing the square. Simplify the solutions and write them in a + bi form.

103. $x^2 - 10x + 37 = 0$

104. $a^2 + 16a + 82 = 0$

105. $y^2 + 11y = -49$

106. $x^2 - 5x = -22$

107. $9x^2 = 18x - 14$

108. $7z^2 = -14z - 13$

109. $2x^2 = 14x - 30$

110. $5x^2 + x = -5$

Solve the following quadratic equations by the Quadratic Formula. Simplify the solutions and write them in a + bi form.

111. $x^2 + 2x + 2 = 0$

112. $a^2 + 4a + 8 = 0$

113. $y^2 + 4y + 5 = 0$

114. $x^2 + 2x + 5 = 0$

115. $x^2 - 2x = -5$

116. $z^2 - 3z = -8$

117. $x^2 - \dfrac{2}{3}x = -\dfrac{2}{9}$

118. $x^2 + \dfrac{5}{4} = x$

Factor each expression over the set of complex numbers.

119. $x^2 + 4$

120. $16a^2 + 9$

121. $25p^2 + 36q^2$

122. $100r^2 + 49s^2$

123. $2y^2 + 8z^2$

124. $12b^2 + 75c^2$

125. $50m^2 + 2n^2$

126. $64a^4 + 4b^2$

Applications

In electronics, the formula V = IR is called Ohm's Law. It gives the relationship in a circuit between the voltage V (in volts), the current I (in amperes), and the resistance R (in ohms).

127. Electronics Find V when $I = 3 - 2i$ amperes and $R = 3 + 6i$ ohms.

128. Electronics Find R when $I = 2 - 3i$ amperes and $V = 21 + i$ volts.

129. Electronics The impedance Z in an AC (alternating current) circuit is a measure of how much the circuit impedes (hinders) the flow of current through it. The impedance is related to the voltage V and the current I by the following formula.

$$V = IZ$$

If a circuit has a current of $(0.5 + 2.0i)$ amps and an impedance of $(0.4 - 3.0i)$ ohms, find the voltage.

130. Fractals Complex numbers are fundamental in the creation of the intricate geometric shape shown below, called a *fractal*. The process of creating this image is based on the following sequence of steps, which begins by picking any complex number, which we will call z.

1. Square z, and then add that result to z.

2. Square the result from step 1, and then add it to z.

3. Square the result from step 2, and then add it to z.

If we begin with the complex number i, what is the result after performing steps 1, 2, and 3?

Kostyantyn Ivanyshen/Shutterstock.com

Discovery and Writing

131. Show that the addition of two complex numbers is commutative by adding the complex numbers $a + bi$ and $c + di$ in both orders and observing that the sums are equal.

132. Show that the multiplication of two complex numbers is commutative by multiplying the complex numbers $a + bi$ and $c + di$ in both orders and observing that the products are equal.

133. Show that the addition of complex numbers is associative.

134. Find three examples of complex numbers that are reciprocals of their own conjugates.

135. Explain how to determine whether two complex numbers are equal.

136. Define the complex conjugate of a complex number.

Review

Simplify each expression. Assume that all variables represent nonnegative numbers.

137. $\sqrt{8x^3}\sqrt{4x}$

138. $\left(\sqrt{x} - 5\right)^2$

139. $\left(\sqrt{x+1} - 2\right)^2$

140. $\left(-3\sqrt{2x+1}\right)^2$

141. $\dfrac{4}{\sqrt{5} - 1}$

142. $\dfrac{x - 4}{\sqrt{x} + 2}$

1.6 Polynomial and Radical Equations

In this section, we will learn to

1. Solve polynomial equations by factoring.

2. Solve other equations by factoring.

3. Solve radical equations.

4. Solve applications of radical equations.

John Hoffman/Shutterstock.com

Pike's Peak is in the Rocky Mountain range, near Colorado Springs, Colorado. Standing at its summit, a person can see for miles.

The distance a person can see from the peak of the mountain is called the *horizon distance*. If this distance, d, is measured in miles and the height of the observer, h, is measured in feet, d and h are related by the formula $d = \sqrt{1.5h}$.

Since the height of Pike's Peak is approximately 14,000 feet, we can substitute 14,000 for h into the formula and simplify.

$$d = \sqrt{1.5h}$$

$$d = \sqrt{1.5(\mathbf{14{,}000})} \qquad \text{Substitute 14,000 for } h.$$

$$= \sqrt{21{,}000}$$

$$\approx 144.9137675$$

From the top of Pike's Peak, a person can see about 145 miles.

Since this equation contains a radical, it is called a *radical equation,* one of the topics of the section.

1. Solve Polynomial Equations by Factoring

The equation $ax^2 + bx + c = 0$ is a polynomial equation of second degree, because its left side contains a second-degree polynomial. Many polynomial equations of higher degree can be solved by factoring. A strategy for solving a polynomial equation is shown here.

Strategy for Solving Polynomial Equations	1. Write the polynomial equation in standard form. • Arrange the terms of the polynomial in descending order based on their degrees. • Set the polynomial equal to 0. 2. Use the Zero-Factor Theorem and solve by factoring.

EXAMPLE 1 **Solving Polynomial Equations by Factoring**

Solve: **a.** $6x^3 - x^2 - 2x = 0$ **b.** $x^4 - 5x^2 + 4 = 0$

SOLUTION We will solve each equation by factoring.

a.
$$6x^3 - x^2 - 2x = 0$$
$$x(6x^2 - x - 2) = 0 \qquad \text{Factor out } x.$$
$$x(3x - 2)(2x + 1) = 0 \qquad \text{Factor } 6x^2 - x - 2.$$

We set each factor equal to 0.

$$x = 0 \quad \text{or} \quad 3x - 2 = 0 \quad \text{or} \quad 2x + 1 = 0$$

$$x = \frac{2}{3} \qquad\qquad x = -\frac{1}{2}$$

Verify that each solution satisfies the original equation.

b.
$$x^4 - 5x^2 + 4 = 0$$
$$(x^2 - 4)(x^2 - 1) = 0 \qquad \text{Factor } x^4 - 5x^2 + 4.$$
$$(x + 2)(x - 2)(x + 1)(x - 1) = 0 \qquad \text{Factor each difference of two squares.}$$

We set each factor equal to 0.

$$x + 2 = 0 \quad \text{or} \quad x - 2 = 0 \quad \text{or} \quad x + 1 = 0 \quad \text{or} \quad x - 1 = 0$$
$$x = -2 \qquad\qquad x = 2 \qquad\qquad x = -1 \qquad\qquad x = 1$$

Verify that each solution satisfies the original equation.   ∎

Self Check 1   Solve: $2x^3 + 3x^2 - 2x = 0$.

Now Try Exercise 9.

2. Solve Other Equations by Factoring

To solve another type of equation by factoring, we use a property that states that equal powers of equal numbers are equal.

Power Property of Real Numbers

If a and b are numbers, n is an integer, and $a = b$, then

$$a^n = b^n$$

When we raise both sides of an equation to the same power, the resulting equation might not be equivalent to the original one. For example, if we raise both sides of

(1) $x = 4$ with a solution set of $\{4\}$

to the second power, we obtain

(2) $x^2 = 16$ with a solution set of $\{4, -4\}$

Equations 1 and 2 have different solution sets, and the solution -4 of Equation 2 does not satisfy Equation 1. Because raising both sides of an equation to the same power often introduces **extraneous solutions** (false solutions that don't satisfy the original equation), we must check all suspected roots to be certain that they satisfy the original equation.

The following equation has an extraneous solution.

$$x - x^{1/2} - 6 = 0$$
$$(x^{1/2} - 3)(x^{1/2} + 2) = 0 \qquad\qquad \text{Factor } x - x^{1/2} - 6.$$
$$x^{1/2} - 3 = 0 \quad \text{or} \quad x^{1/2} + 2 = 0 \qquad \text{Set each factor equal to 0.}$$
$$x^{1/2} = 3 \qquad\qquad x^{1/2} = -2$$

Because equal powers of equal numbers are equal, we can square both sides of the previous equations to get

$$(x^{1/2})^2 = (3)^2 \quad \text{or} \quad (x^{1/2})^2 = (-2)^2$$
$$x = 9 \qquad\qquad x = 4$$

The number 9 satisfies the equation $x - x^{1/2} - 6 = 0$ but 4 does not, as the following check shows:

If $x = 9$	**If $x = 4$**
$x - x^{1/2} - 6 = 0$	$x - x^{1/2} - 6 = 0$
$9 - 9^{1/2} - 6 \stackrel{?}{=} 0$	$4 - 4^{1/2} - 6 \stackrel{?}{=} 0$
$9 - 3 - 6 \stackrel{?}{=} 0$	$4 - 2 - 6 \stackrel{?}{=} 0$
$0 = 0$	$-4 \neq 0$

The number 9 is the only root.

EXAMPLE 2   **Solving Other Types of Equations by Factoring**

Solve: **a.** $2x^{2/5} - 5x^{1/5} - 3 = 0$ **b.** $3(3x - 2x^{1/2}) = -1$

SOLUTION   We will solve each equation by factoring.

a.
$$2x^{2/5} - 5x^{1/5} - 3 = 0$$
$$(2x^{1/5} + 1)(x^{1/5} - 3) = 0 \qquad \text{Factor } 2x^{2/5} - 5x^{1/5} - 3.$$
$$2x^{1/5} + 1 = 0 \quad \text{or} \quad x^{1/5} - 3 = 0 \qquad \text{Set each factor equal to 0.}$$
$$2x^{1/5} = -1 \qquad\qquad x^{1/5} = 3$$
$$x^{1/5} = -\frac{1}{2}$$

We can raise both sides of each of the previous equations to the fifth power to obtain

$$(x^{1/5})^5 = \left(-\frac{1}{2}\right)^5 \quad \text{or} \quad (x^{1/5})^5 = (3)^5$$
$$x = -\frac{1}{32} \qquad\qquad x = 243$$

Verify that each solution satisfies the original equation.

b.
$$3(3x - 2x^{1/2}) = -1$$
$$9x - 6x^{1/2} + 1 = 0 \qquad \text{Remove parentheses and add 1 to both sides.}$$
$$(3x^{1/2} - 1)(3x^{1/2} - 1) = 0 \qquad \text{Factor.}$$
$$3x^{1/2} - 1 = 0 \quad \text{or} \quad 3x^{1/2} - 1 = 0 \qquad \text{Set each factor equal to 0.}$$
$$x^{1/2} = \frac{1}{3} \qquad\qquad x^{1/2} = \frac{1}{3} \qquad \text{Solve each equation.}$$

We can square both sides of each of the previous equations to obtain

$$(x^{1/2})^2 = \left(\frac{1}{3}\right)^2 \quad \text{or} \quad (x^{1/2})^2 = \left(\frac{1}{3}\right)^2$$
$$x = \frac{1}{9} \qquad\qquad x = \frac{1}{9}$$

Here, the solutions are the same. Verify that $x = \frac{1}{9}$ satisfies the equation. ∎

Self Check 2   Solve: $x^{2/5} - x^{1/5} - 2 = 0$.

Now Try Exercise 19.

3. Solve Radical Equations

Radical equations are equations containing radicals with variables in the radicand. To solve such equations, we use the Power Property of Real Numbers. A strategy for solving radical equations with square roots or cube roots is stated here.

Strategy for Solving Radical Equations with Square Roots or Cube Roots

1. Isolate one radical on the left side of the equation.
2. Raise both sides of the equation to the same power (the index of the radical).
   - If the radical is a square root, square both sides.
   - If the radical is a cube root, cube both sides.
3. If a radical remains, repeat Steps 1 and 2.
4. Solve the resulting equation and check your answers.

We can extend the strategy stated above to solve radical equations containing fourth roots, fifth roots, ..., nth roots.

EXAMPLE 3 Solving an Equation with One Radical

Solve: $\sqrt{x + 3} - 4 = 7$.

SOLUTION We will isolate the radical on the left side and then square both sides.

$$\sqrt{x + 3} - 4 = 7$$

$$\sqrt{x + 3} = 11 \qquad \text{Add 4 to both sides to isolate the radical.}$$

$$\left(\sqrt{x + 3}\right)^2 = (11)^2 \qquad \text{Square both sides.}$$

$$x + 3 = 121 \qquad \text{Simplify.}$$

$$x = 118 \qquad \text{Subtract 3 from both sides.}$$

Since squaring both sides might introduce extraneous roots, we must check the result of 118.

$$\sqrt{x + 3} - 4 = 7$$

$$\sqrt{118 + 3} - 4 \stackrel{?}{=} 7 \qquad \text{Substitute 118 for } x.$$

$$\sqrt{121} - 4 \stackrel{?}{=} 7$$

$$11 - 4 \stackrel{?}{=} 7$$

$$7 = 7$$

Because it checks, 118 is a root of the equation. ∎

Comment

Remember to check all roots when solving radical equations, because raising both sides of an equation to a power can introduce extraneous roots.

Self Check 3 Solve: $\sqrt{x - 3} + 4 = 7$.

Now Try Exercise 25.

EXAMPLE 4 Solving an Equation with One Radical

Solve: $\sqrt{x + 3} = 3x - 1$.

SOLUTION We will square both sides of the equation to eliminate the radical and solve the resulting equations by factoring.

$$\sqrt{x + 3} = 3x - 1$$

$$\left(\sqrt{x + 3}\right)^2 = (3x - 1)^2 \qquad \text{Square both sides.}$$

$$x + 3 = 9x^2 - 6x + 1 \qquad \text{Remove parentheses.}$$

$$0 = 9x^2 - 7x - 2 \qquad \text{Add } -x - 3 \text{ to both sides.}$$

$$0 = (9x + 2)(x - 1) \qquad \text{Factor } 9x^2 - 7x - 2.$$

$$9x + 2 = 0 \quad \text{or} \quad x - 1 = 0 \qquad \text{Set each factor equal to 0.}$$

$$x = -\frac{2}{9} \qquad\qquad x = 1$$

Since squaring both sides can introduce extraneous roots, we must check each result.

$$\sqrt{x + 3} = 3x - 1 \qquad \text{or} \qquad \sqrt{x + 3} = 3x - 1$$

$$\sqrt{-\frac{2}{9} + 3} \overset{?}{=} 3\left(-\frac{2}{9}\right) - 1 \qquad \qquad \sqrt{1 + 3} \overset{?}{=} 3(1) - 1$$

$$\sqrt{\frac{25}{9}} \overset{?}{=} -\frac{2}{3} - 1 \qquad \qquad \sqrt{4} \overset{?}{=} 3 - 1$$

$$\frac{5}{3} \neq -\frac{5}{3} \qquad \qquad 2 = 2$$

Since $-\frac{2}{9}$ does not satisfy the equation, it is extraneous. Since 1 checks, it is the only solution.

Caution

> If we *forget* to check solution(s) to a radical equation, we risk having an *incorrect* solution set. *Failure* to check both $x = -\frac{2}{9}$ and $x = 1$ in Example 4 would have resulted in an *error*.

Self Check 4   Solve: $\sqrt{x - 2} = 2x - 10$.

Now Try Exercise 37.

EXAMPLE 5   **Solving a Radical Equation with a Cube Root**

Solve: $\sqrt[3]{x^3 + 56} = x + 2$.

SOLUTION   To eliminate the radical, we cube both sides of the equation.

$$\sqrt[3]{x^3 + 56} = x + 2$$

$$\left(\sqrt[3]{x^3 + 56}\right)^3 = (x + 2)^3 \qquad \qquad \text{Cube both sides.}$$

$$x^3 + 56 = x^3 + 6x^2 + 12x + 8 \qquad \text{Remove parentheses.}$$

$$0 = 6x^2 + 12x - 48 \qquad \qquad \text{Simplify.}$$

$$0 = x^2 + 2x - 8 \qquad \qquad \text{Divide both sides by 6.}$$

$$0 = (x + 4)(x - 2) \qquad \qquad \text{Factor } x^2 + 2x - 8.$$

$$x + 4 = 0 \quad \text{or} \quad x - 2 = 0 \qquad \text{Set each factor equal to 0.}$$

$$x = -4 \quad \bigm| \quad x = 2$$

We check each suspected solution to see whether either is extraneous.

$$\textit{For } x = -4 \qquad\qquad\qquad \textit{For } x = 2$$

$$\sqrt[3]{x^3 + 56} = x + 2 \qquad\qquad \sqrt[3]{x^3 + 56} = x + 2$$

$$\sqrt[3]{(-4)^3 + 56} \overset{?}{=} -4 + 2 \qquad \sqrt[3]{2^3 + 56} \overset{?}{=} 2 + 2$$

$$\sqrt[3]{-64 + 56} \overset{?}{=} -2 \qquad\qquad \sqrt[3]{8 + 56} \overset{?}{=} 4$$

$$\sqrt[3]{-8} \overset{?}{=} -2 \qquad\qquad\qquad \sqrt[3]{64} \overset{?}{=} 4$$

$$-2 = -2 \qquad\qquad\qquad\qquad 4 = 4$$

Since both values satisfy the equation, -4 and 2 are roots.

Self Check 5   Solve: $\sqrt[3]{x^3 + 7} = x + 1$.

Now Try Exercise 49.

EXAMPLE 6   **Solving an Equation with Two Radicals**

Solve: $\sqrt{2x + 3} + \sqrt{x - 2} = 4$.

SOLUTION   We can write the equation in the form

$$\sqrt{2x + 3} = 4 - \sqrt{x - 2} \qquad \text{Subtract } \sqrt{x - 2} \text{ from both sides.}$$

so that the left side contains one radical. We then square both sides to get

$$\left(\sqrt{2x + 3}\right)^2 = \left(4 - \sqrt{x - 2}\right)^2$$
$$2x + 3 = 16 - 8\sqrt{x - 2} + x - 2$$
$$2x + 3 = 14 - 8\sqrt{x - 2} + x \qquad \text{Combine like terms.}$$
$$x - 11 = -8\sqrt{x - 2} \qquad \text{Subtract 14 and } x \text{ from both sides.}$$

We then square both sides again to eliminate the radical.

$$(x - 11)^2 = \left(-8\sqrt{x - 2}\right)^2$$
$$x^2 - 22x + 121 = 64(x - 2)$$
$$x^2 - 22x + 121 = 64x - 128$$
$$x^2 - 86x + 249 = 0$$
$$(x - 3)(x - 83) = 0$$
$$x - 3 = 0 \quad \text{or} \quad x - 83 = 0 \qquad \text{Set each factor equal to 0.}$$
$$x = 3 \quad \mid \quad x = 83$$

Substituting these results into the equation will show that 83 doesn't check; it is extraneous. However, 3 does satisfy the equation and is a root. ∎

Self Check 6   Solve: $\sqrt{2x + 1} + \sqrt{x + 5} = 6$.

Now Try Exercise 53.

4. Solve Applications of Radical Equations

Many applications can be solved using radical equations.

EXAMPLE 7   **Solving an Application Problem**

A highway curve banked at 8° will accommodate traffic traveling s mph if the radius of the curve is r feet, according to the formula $s = 1.45\sqrt{r}$. Find what radius is necessary to accommodate 70-mph traffic. (See Figure 1-12.)

s mph = 70 mph

r ft

8°

FIGURE 1-12

SOLUTION   We can substitute 70 for s in the formula and solve for r.

$$s = 1.45\sqrt{r}$$

$$70 = 1.45\sqrt{r} \qquad \text{Substitute 70 for } s.$$

$$\frac{70}{1.45} = \sqrt{r} \qquad \text{Divide both sides by 1.45.}$$

$$\left(\frac{70}{1.45}\right)^2 = r \qquad \text{Square both sides.}$$

$$2330.558859 = r$$

We can use a calculator to find r. The radius of the curve is approximately 2,331 feet. ∎

Self Check 7   Find the radius necessary to accommodate 65-mph traffic.

Now Try Exercise 61.

Self Check Answers   **1.** $0, \frac{1}{2}, -2$ **2.** $-1, 32$ **3.** 12   **4.** 6   **5.** $1, -2$ **6.** 4
7. approximately 2,010 feet

Exercises **1.6**

Getting Ready
You should be able to complete these vocabulary and concept statements before you proceed to the practice exercises.

Fill in the blanks.

1. Equal powers of equal real numbers are _____.
2. If a and b are real numbers and $a = b$ then $a^2 = $ ____.
3. False solutions that don't satisfy the equation are called _____ solutions.
4. Radical equations contain radicals with variables in their _____.

Practice
Use factoring to solve each equation for real values of the variable.

5. $x^3 + 9x^2 + 20x = 0$

6. $x^3 + 4x^2 - 21x = 0$

7. $6a^3 - 5a^2 - 4a = 0$

8. $8b^3 - 10b^2 + 3b = 0$

9. $y^4 - 26y^2 + 25 = 0$

10. $y^4 - 13y^2 + 36 = 0$

11. $x^4 - 37x^2 + 36 = 0$

12. $x^4 - 50x^2 + 49 = 0$

13. $2y^4 - 46y^2 = -180$

14. $2x^4 - 102x^2 = -196$

15. $z^{3/2} - z^{1/2} = 0$

16. $r^{5/2} - r^{3/2} = 0$

17. $2m^{2/3} + 3m^{1/3} - 2 = 0$

18. $6t^{2/5} + 11t^{1/5} + 3 = 0$

19. $x - 13x^{1/2} + 12 = 0$

20. $p + p^{1/2} - 20 = 0$

21. $2t^{1/3} + 3t^{1/6} - 2 = 0$

22. $z^3 - 7z^{3/2} - 8 = 0$

23. $6p + p^{1/2} - 1 = 0$

24. $3r - r^{1/2} - 2 = 0$

Find all real solutions of each equation.

25. $\sqrt{x - 2} - 3 = 2$

26. $\sqrt{a - 3} - 5 = 0$

27. $3\sqrt{x + 1} = \sqrt{6}$

28. $\sqrt{x + 3} = 2\sqrt{x}$

29. $\sqrt{5a - 2} = \sqrt{a + 6}$

30. $\sqrt{16x + 4} = \sqrt{x + 4}$

31. $2\sqrt{x^2 + 3} = \sqrt{-16x - 3}$

32. $\sqrt{x^2 + 1} = \dfrac{\sqrt{-7x + 11}}{\sqrt{6}}$

33. $\sqrt[3]{7x + 1} = 4$

34. $\sqrt[3]{11a - 40} = 5$

35. $\sqrt[4]{30t + 25} = 5$

36. $\sqrt[4]{3z + 1} = 2$

37. $\sqrt{x^2 + 21} = x + 3$

38. $\sqrt{5 - x^2} = -(x + 1)$

39. $\sqrt{y + 2} = 4 - y$ **40.** $\sqrt{3z + 1} = z - 1$

41. $x - \sqrt{7x - 12} = 0$ **42.** $x - \sqrt{4x - 4} = 0$

43. $x + 4 = \sqrt{\dfrac{6x + 6}{5}} + 3$ **44.** $\sqrt{\dfrac{8x + 43}{3}} - 1 = x$

45. $\sqrt{\dfrac{x^2 - 1}{x - 2}} = 2\sqrt{2}$ **46.** $\dfrac{\sqrt{x^2 - 1}}{\sqrt{3x - 5}} = \sqrt{2}$

47. $\sqrt[3]{x^3 + 7} = x + 1$ **48.** $\sqrt[3]{x^3 - 7} + 1 = x$

49. $\sqrt[3]{8x^3 + 61} = 2x + 1$ **50.** $\sqrt[3]{8x^3 - 37} = 2x - 1$

51. $\sqrt{2p + 1} - 1 = \sqrt{p}$ **52.** $\sqrt{r} + \sqrt{r + 2} = 2$

53. $\sqrt{x + 3} = \sqrt{2x + 8} - 1$

54. $\sqrt{x + 2} + 1 = \sqrt{2x + 5}$

55. $\sqrt{y + 8} - \sqrt{y - 4} = -2$

56. $\sqrt{z + 5} - 2 = \sqrt{z - 3}$

57. $\sqrt{2b + 3} - \sqrt{b + 1} = \sqrt{b - 2}$

58. $\sqrt{a + 1} + \sqrt{3a} = \sqrt{5a + 1}$

59. $\sqrt{\sqrt{b} + \sqrt{b + 8}} = 2$

60. $\sqrt{\sqrt{x + 19} - \sqrt{x - 2}} = \sqrt{3}$

Applications

61. Height of a bridge The distance d (in feet) that an object will fall in t seconds is given by the following formula. To find the height of a bridge above a river, a man drops a stone into the water. (See the illustration.) If it takes the stone 5 seconds to hit the water, how high is the bridge?

$$t = \sqrt{\dfrac{d}{16}}$$

62. Horizon distance The higher a lookout tower, the farther an observer can see. (See the illustration.) The distance d (called the **horizon distance,** measured in miles) is related to the height h of the observer (measured in feet) by the following formula.

$$d = \sqrt{1.5h}$$

How tall must a tower be for the observer to see 30 miles?

63. Carpentry During construction, carpenters often brace walls, as shown in the illustration. The appropriate length of the brace is given by the following formula.

$$l = \sqrt{f^2 + h^2}$$

If a carpenter nails a 10-foot brace to the wall 6 feet above the floor, how far from the base of the wall should he nail the brace to the floor?

64. Windmills The power generated by a windmill is related to the velocity of the wind by the following formula where P is the power (in watts) and v is the velocity of the wind (in mph).

$$v = \sqrt[3]{\dfrac{P}{0.02}}$$

To the nearest 10 watts, find the power generated when the velocity of the wind is 31 mph.

65. Diamonds The *effective rate of interest r* earned by an investment is given by the following formula where P is the initial investment that grows to value A after n years.

$$r = \sqrt[n]{\frac{A}{P}} - 1$$

If a diamond buyer got \$4,000 for a 1.03-carat diamond that he had purchased 4 years earlier and earned an annual rate of return of 6.5% on the investment, what did he originally pay for the diamond?

66. Theater productions The ropes, pulleys, and sand-bags shown in the illustration are part of a mechanical system used to raise and lower scenery for a stage play. For the scenery to be in the proper position, the following formula must apply:

$$w_2 = \sqrt{w_1^2 + w_3^2}$$

If $w_2 = 12.5$ lb and $w_3 = 7.5$ lb, find w_1.

Discovery and Writing

67. Explain why squaring both sides of an equation might introduce extraneous roots.

68. Can cubing both sides of an equation introduce extraneous roots? Explain.

Review
Graph each subset of the real numbers on the number line.

69. The natural numbers between 0 and 4

70. The integers between -4 and 4

Write each inequality in interval notation and graph the interval.

71. $x \geq 3$ **72.** $x < -5$

73. $-2 \leq x < 1$ **74.** $-3 \leq x \leq 3$

75. $x < 1$ or $x \geq 2$ **76.** $x \leq 1$ or $x > 2$

1.7 Inequalities

In this section, we will learn to

1. Use the properties of inequalities.
2. Solve linear inequalities and applications.
3. Solve compound inequalities.
4. Solve quadratic inequalities.
5. Solve rational inequalities.

Studying abroad is a wonderful opportunity for students. Suppose you read about a program to study Spanish in Costa Rica for several weeks during the summer. The cost of the program includes \$900 for round-trip airfare plus \$350 per week, which covers tuition, meals per day, and living accommodations. If you have \$3,000, how many weeks can you afford to spend in Costa Rica?

If x represents the number of weeks you can spend in Costa Rica, we can write an inequality that represents the cost.

Airfare	plus	cost of \$350 per week for x weeks	is less than or equal to	\$3,000.
900	+	$350x$	$\leq$	3,000

To solve this inequality, we can proceed as follows:

$$900 + 350x \leq 3,000$$

$$350x \leq 2,100 \qquad \text{Subtract 900 from both sides.}$$

$$x \leq 6 \qquad \text{Divide both sides by 350.}$$

There is enough money to spend up to 6 weeks in Costa Rica.

In this section, we will review the inequality symbols, learn inequality properties, and learn strategies that can be applied to solve several types of inequalities. We previously introduced the following symbols.

Symbol	Read as	Examples
$\neq$	"is not equal to"	$8 \neq 10$ and $25 \neq 12$
$<$	"is less than"	$8 < 10$ and $12 < 25$
$>$	"is greater than"	$30 > 10$ and $100 > -5$
$\leq$	"is less than or equal to"	$-6 \leq 12$ and $-8 \leq -8$
$\geq$	"is greater than or equal to"	$12 \geq -5$ and $9 \geq 9$
$\approx$	"is approximately equal to"	$7.49 \approx 7.5$ and $\frac{1}{3} \approx 0.33$

Since the coordinates of points get larger as we move from left to right on the number line,

$a > b$ if point a lies to the right of point b on a number line.

$a < b$ if point a lies to the left of point b on a number line.

EXAMPLE 1 **Using Inequality Symbols**

a. $5 > -3$, because 5 lies to the right of -3 on the number line.

b. $-7 < -2$, because -7 lies to the left of -2 on the number line.

c. $3 \leq 3$, because $3 = 3$.

d. $2 \leq 3$, because $2 < 3$.

e. $x + 1 > x$, because $x + 1$ lies one unit to the right of x on the number line. ∎

Self Check 1 Write an inequality symbol to make a true statement:

a. 25 ☐ 12   **b.** -5 ☐ -5 **c.** -12 ☐ -20

Now Try Exercise 1.

1. Use the Properties of Inequalities

The Trichotomy Property   For any real numbers a and b, one of the following statements is true.

$$a < b, \qquad a = b, \qquad \text{or} \qquad a > b$$

The Trichotomy Property indicates that one of the following statements is true about two real numbers. Either the first is less than the second, or the first is equal to the second, or the first is greater than the second.

The Transitive Property

If a, b, and c are real numbers, then

if $a < b$ and $b < c$, then $a < c$.

if $a > b$ and $b > c$, then $a > c$.

The first part of the Transitive Property indicates that if a first number is less than a second and the second number is less than a third, then the first number is less than the third.

The second part of the Transitive Property is similar, with the words "is greater than" substituted for "is less than."

Addition and Subtraction Properties of Inequality

Let a, b, and c represent real numbers.

If $a < b$, then $a + c < b + c$.

If $a < b$, then $a - c < b - c$.

Similar properties exist for $>$, $\leq$, and $\geq$.

This property states that *any real number can be added to (or subtracted from) both sides of an inequality to obtain another inequality with the same order (direction)*. For example, if we add 4 to (or subtract 4 from) both sides of $8 < 12$, we get

$8 < 12$	$8 < 12$
$8 + 4 < 12 + 4$	$8 - 4 < 12 - 4$
$12 < 16$	$4 < 8$

and the $<$ symbol is unchanged.

Multiplication and Division Properties of Inequality

Let a, b, and c represent real numbers.

Part 1:   If $a < b$ and $c > 0$, then $ca < cb$.

If $a < b$ and $c > 0$, then $\frac{a}{c} < \frac{b}{c}$.

Part 2:   If $a < b$ and $c < 0$, then $ca > cb$.

If $a < b$ and $c < 0$, then $\frac{a}{c} > \frac{b}{c}$.

Similar properties exist for $>$, $\leq$, and $\geq$.

This property has two parts.

• Part 1 states that *both sides of an inequality can be multiplied (or divided) by the same positive number to obtain another inequality with the same order.*

For example, if we multiply (or divide) both sides of $8 < 12$ by 4, we get

$$8 < 12 \qquad\qquad\qquad 8 < 12$$

$$8(4) < 12(4) \qquad\qquad \frac{8}{4} < \frac{12}{4}$$

$$32 < 48 \qquad\qquad\qquad 2 < 3$$

and the $<$ symbol is unchanged.

- Part 2 states that *both sides of an inequality can be multiplied (or divided) by the same negative number to obtain another inequality with the opposite order.*

  For example, if we multiply (or divide) both sides of $8 < 12$ by -4, we get

$$8 < 12 \qquad\qquad\qquad 8 < 12$$

$$8(-4) > 12(-4) \qquad\qquad \frac{8}{-4} > \frac{12}{-4}$$

$$-32 > -48 \qquad\qquad\qquad -2 > -3$$

and the $<$ symbol is changed to a $>$ symbol.

Comment

The properties of inequalities are the same as the properties of equality, unless we are multiplying or dividing by a negative number.

2. Solve Linear Inequalities and Applications

Linear inequalities are inequalities such as $ax + c < 0$ or $ax - c \geq 0$ where $a \neq 0$. Numbers that make an inequality true when substituted for the variable are solutions of the inequality. Inequalities with the same solution set are called **equivalent inequalities.** Because of the previous properties, we can solve inequalities as we do equations. However, we must always remember to change the order of an inequality when multiplying (or dividing) both sides by a negative number.

EXAMPLE 2   **Solving a Linear Inequality**

Solve: $3(x + 2) < 8$.

SOLUTION   We proceed as with equations.

$$3(x + 2) < 8$$

$$3x + 6 < 8 \qquad \text{Remove parentheses.}$$

$$3x < 2 \qquad \text{Subtract 6 from both sides.}$$

$$x < \frac{2}{3} \qquad \text{Divide both sides by 3.}$$

All numbers that are less than $\frac{2}{3}$ are solutions of the inequality. The solution set can be expressed in interval notation as $\left(-\infty, \frac{2}{3}\right)$ and be graphed as in Figure 1-13.

FIGURE 1-13

Self Check 2   Solve: $5(p - 4) > 25$.

Now Try Exercise 15.

EXAMPLE 3	**Solving a Linear Inequality**

Solve: $-5(x - 2) \le 20 + x$.

SOLUTION   We proceed as with equations.

$$-5(x - 2) \le 20 + x$$

$$-5x + 10 \le 20 + x \qquad \text{Remove parentheses.}$$

$$-6x + 10 \le 20 \qquad \text{Subtract } x \text{ from both sides.}$$

$$-6x \le 10 \qquad \text{Subtract 10 from both sides.}$$

We now divide both sides of the inequality by -6, which changes the order of the inequality.

$$x \ge \frac{10}{-6} \qquad \text{Divide both sides by } -6.$$

$$x \ge -\frac{5}{3} \qquad \text{Simplify the fraction.}$$

The graph of the solution set is shown in Figure 1-14. It is the interval $\left[-\frac{5}{3}, \infty\right)$.

FIGURE 1-14

Self Check 3   Solve: $-4(x + 3) \ge 16$.

Now Try Exercise 19.

Caution

> The most common error made when solving inequalities is forgetting to reverse the inequality symbol when multiplying or dividing both sides by a negative number. In Example 3, both sides were divided by -6. If the order of the inequality isn't reversed, the solution will be incorrect.

EXAMPLE 4	**Solving an Application of a Linear Inequality**

An empty truck with driver weighs 4,350 pounds. It is loaded with feed corn weighing 31 pounds per bushel. Between farm and market is a bridge with a 10,000-pound load limit. How many bushels can the truck legally carry?

Robert Kyllo/Shutterstock.com

SOLUTION   The empty truck with driver weighs 4,350 pounds, and corn weighs 31 pounds per bushel. If we let b represent the number of bushels in a legal load, the weight of the corn will be $31b$ pounds. Since the combined weight of the truck, driver, and cargo cannot exceed 10,000 pounds, we can form the following inequality.

The weight of the empty truck with driver	plus	the weight of the corn	must be less than or equal to	10,000 pounds.
4,350	+	31b	≤	10,000

We can solve the inequality as follows.

$$4,350 + 31b \leq 10,000$$
$$31b \leq 5,650 \qquad \text{Subtract 4,350 from each side.}$$
$$b \leq 182.2580645 \qquad \text{Divide both sides by 31.}$$

The truck can legally carry $182\frac{1}{4}$ bushels or less.

Self Check 4   If the empty truck and driver in example 3 weigh 3,800 pounds, how many bushels can the truck legally carry?

Now Try Exercise 87.

3. Solve Compound Inequalities

The statement that x is between 2 and 5 implies two inequalities,

$$x > 2 \text{ and } x < 5$$

Comment

Remember that $2 < x < 5$ means that $x > 2$ and $x < 5$. The word *and* indicates that both inequalities must be true at the same time.

It is customary to write both inequalities as one **compound inequality:**

$$2 < x < 5 \qquad \text{Read as "2 is less than } x \text{ and } x \text{ is less than 5."}$$

To express that x is not between 2 and 5, we must convey the idea that either x is greater than or equal to 5, or that x is less than or equal to 2. This is equivalent to the statement

$$x \geq 5 \quad \text{or} \quad x \leq 2$$

This inequality is satisfied by all numbers x that satisfy one or both of its parts.

Caution

It is incorrect to write $x \geq 5$ or $x \leq 2$ as $2 \geq x \geq 5$ because this would means that $2 \geq 5$, which is false.

EXAMPLE 5   **Solving a Compound Inequality by Isolating x between the Inequality Symbols**

Solve: $5 < 3x - 7 \leq 8$.

SOLUTION   We can isolate x between the inequality symbols by adding 7 to each part of the inequality to get

$$5 + 7 < 3x - 7 + 7 \leq 8 + 7 \qquad \text{Add 7 to each part.}$$
$$12 < 3x \leq 15 \qquad \text{Do the additions.}$$

and dividing all parts by 3 to get

$$4 < x \leq 5$$

The solution set is the interval $(4, 5]$, whose graph appears in Figure 1-15.

FIGURE 1-15

Self Check 5   Solve: $-5 \leq 2x + 1 < 9$.

Now Try Exercise 33.

EXAMPLE 6   **Solving a Compound Inequality by Solving Each Inequality Separately**

Solve: $3 + x \leq 3x + 1 < 7x - 2$.

SOLUTION   Because it is impossible to isolate x between the inequality symbols, we must solve each inequality separately.

$$3 + x \le 3x + 1 \quad \text{and} \quad 3x + 1 < 7x - 2$$

$$
\begin{array}{c|c}
3 \le 2x + 1 & 1 < 4x - 2 \\
2 \le 2x & 3 < 4x \\
1 \le x & \dfrac{3}{4} < x \\
x \ge 1 & x > \dfrac{3}{4}
\end{array}
$$

Since the connective in this inequality is *and*, the solution set is the intersection (or overlap) of the intervals $[1, \infty)$ and $\left(\frac{3}{4}, \infty\right)$, which is $[1, \infty)$. The graph is shown in Figure 1-16.

FIGURE 1-16

Self Check 6   Solve: $x + 1 < 2x - 3 \le 3x - 5$.

Now Try Exercise 47.

Comment   It is possible for an inequality to be true for all values of its variable. It is also possible for an inequality to have no solutions.

For example,

- $x < x + 1$ is true for all numbers x.

- $x > x + 1$ is true for no numbers x.

4. Solve Quadratic Inequalities

If $a \neq 0$, inequalities like $ax^2 + bx + c < 0$ and $ax^2 + bx + c \ge 0$ are called **quadratic inequalities.** We will begin by giving two methods for solving quadratic inequalities.

Strategy for Solving Quadratic Inequalities

Method 1: Constructing a Table and Testing Numbers

- Solve the quadratic equation and use the roots of the equation to establish intervals on a number line.

- Construct a table. To do so, write down each interval, select a number to test from each interval, test the selected value to determine if it satisfies the inequality, and then write the result.

- Use the results from the table and write the solution of the quadratic inequality.

Method 2: Constructing a Sign Graph

- Solve the quadratic equation and use the roots of the equation to establish intervals on the number line.

- Construct a sign graph by determining the sign of each factor on each interval. Write these signs on the number line.

- Use these results to write the solution to the quadratic inequality.

The roots of the quadratic equation *will be included* in the solution if the quadratic inequality involves $\le$ or $\ge$. The roots *will not be included* in the solution if the quadratic inequality involves $<$ or $>$.

In our first example, we will solve the quadratic inequality using both of the strategies or methods outlined earlier.

EXAMPLE 7   Solving a Quadratic Inequality

Solve: $x^2 - x - 6 > 0$.

SOLUTION   **Method 1:**   First we solve the equation $x^2 - x - 6 = 0$.

$$x^2 - x - 6 = 0$$

$$(x + 2)(x - 3) = 0$$

$$x + 2 = 0 \quad \text{or} \quad x - 3 = 0$$

$$x = -2 \quad \quad \quad x = 3$$

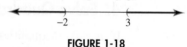

FIGURE 1-17

The graphs of these solutions establish the three intervals shown in Figure 1-17. To determine which intervals are solutions, we construct a table and test a number in each interval and see whether it satisfies the inequality.

Interval	Test Value	Inequality $x^2 - x - 6 > 0$		Result
$(-\infty, -2)$	-6	$(-6)^2 - (-6) - 6 \overset{?}{>} 0$ $36 > 0$	True	The numbers in this interval are solutions.
$(-2, 3)$	0	$0^2 - 0 - 6 \overset{?}{>} 0$ $-6 > 0$	False	The numbers in this interval are not solutions.
$(3, \infty)$	5	$5^2 - 5 - 6 \overset{?}{>} 0$ $14 > 0$	True	The numbers in this interval are solutions.

The solutions are in the intervals $(-\infty, -2)$ or $(3, \infty)$ as shown in Figure 1-18. Note that we write a parenthesis next to -2 and 3 because they do not satisfy the quadratic inequality. The quadratic inequality given contains $>$.

FIGURE 1-18

Method 2:   A second method relies on the number line and a notation that keeps track of the signs of the factors of $x^2 - x - 6$, which are $(x - 3)(x + 2)$.

- First, we consider the factor $x - 3$.
  If $x = 3$, then $x - 3 = 0$.
  If $x < 3$, then $x - 3$ is negative.
  If $x > 3$, then $x - 3$ is positive.

- Next, we consider the factor $x + 2$.
  If $x = -2$, then $x + 2 = 0$.
  If $x < -2$, then $x + 2$ is negative.
  If $x > -2$, then $x + 2$ is positive.

We construct a **sign graph** as shown in Figure 1-19 by using $+$ and $-$ signs and writing these above the number line.

$$
\begin{array}{ll}
x - 3 & \text{------} \; | \; \text{--------} \; 0{+}{+}{+}{+}{+}{+} \\
x + 2 & \text{------} \; 0{+}{+}{+}{+}{+}{+}{+}{+} \; | \; {+}{+}{+}{+}{+}{+}
\end{array}
$$

$$-5 \; -4 \; -3 \; -2 \; -1 \quad 0 \quad 1 \quad 2 \quad 3 \quad 4 \quad 5$$

FIGURE 1-19

Only to the left of -2 and to the right of 3 do the signs of both factors agree. Only there is the product positive. The solutions are in the intervals $(-\infty, -2)$ or $(3, \infty)$.

Self Check 7   Solve: $x(x + 1) - 6 \geq 0$.

Now Try Exercise 59.

EXAMPLE 8   **Solving a Quadratic Inequality**

Solve: $x(x + 3) \leq -2$.

SOLUTION   We remove parentheses and add 2 to both sides to make the right side of the equation equal to 0 and solve $x^2 + 3x + 2 \leq 0$.

Method 1:   First we solve the equation $x^2 + 3x + 2 = 0$.

$$x^2 + 3x + 2 = 0$$

$$(x + 2)(x + 1) = 0$$

$$x + 2 = 0 \quad \text{or} \quad x + 1 = 0$$

$$x = -2 \quad \bigg| \quad x = -1$$

These solutions establish the intervals shown in Figure 1-20.

$$\overline{(-\infty, -2)} \quad \big| \quad (-2, -1) \quad \big| \quad (-1, \infty)$$

$$\xleftarrow{\hspace{2cm}} \underset{-2}{\times} \quad \underset{-1}{\times} \xrightarrow{\hspace{2cm}}$$

FIGURE 1-20

The solutions of $x^2 + 3x + 2 \leq 0$ will be the numbers in one or more of these intervals. To determine which intervals are solutions, we test a number in each interval to see whether it satisfies the inequality.

Interval	Test Value	Inequality $x^2 + 3x + 2 \leq 0$		Result
$(-\infty, -2)$	-7	$(-7)^2 + 3(-7) + 2 \overset{?}{\leq} 0$ $30 \leq 0$	False	The numbers in this interval are not solutions.
$(-2, -1)$	$-\dfrac{3}{2}$	$\left(-\dfrac{3}{2}\right)^2 + 3\left(-\dfrac{3}{2}\right) + 2 \overset{?}{\leq} 0$ $-\dfrac{1}{4} \leq 0$	True	The numbers in this interval are solutions.
$(-1, \infty)$	0	$0^2 - 0 + 2 \overset{?}{\leq} 0$ $2 \leq 0$	False	The numbers in this interval are not solutions.

The solution is the interval $[-2, -1]$ whose graph appears in Figure 1-21. Note that we write a bracket next to -2 and -1 because they satisfy the quadratic inequality. The quadratic inequality given contains $\leq$.

$$\xleftarrow{\hspace{1cm}} \underset{-2}{[} \underset{}{\rule{3cm}{0.4pt}} \underset{-1}{]} \xrightarrow{\hspace{1cm}}$$

FIGURE 1-21

Method 2:   We construct a sign graph.

- First, we consider the factor $x + 1$.

    If $x = -1$, then $x + 1 = 0$.

    If $x < -1$, then $x + 1$ is negative.

    If $x > -1$, then $x + 1$ is positive.

- Next, we consider the factor $x + 2$.

  If $x = -2$ then $x + 2 = 0$.

  If $x < -2$ then $x + 2$ is negative.

  If $x > -2$ then $x + 2$ is positive.

The sign graph is shown in Figure 1-22.

FIGURE 1-22

Only between -2 and -1 do the factors have opposite signs. Here, the product is negative. The solution is the interval $[-2, -1]$. ∎

Self Check 8   Solve: $x^2 - 5x - 6 \leq 0$.

Now Try Exercise 61.

EXAMPLE 9   **Solving a Quadratic Inequality**

Solve: $x^2 - 5 \geq 0$.

SOLUTION   This equation will not factor using only integers. However, we can solve it by adding 5 to both sides and using the Square-Root Property. We will then use Method 1 and solve the inequality.

$$x^2 - 5 = 0$$

$$x^2 - 5 + 5 = 0 + 5 \qquad \text{Add 5 to both sides.}$$

$$x^2 = 5$$

$$x = \sqrt{5} \quad \text{or} \quad x = -\sqrt{5}$$

These solutions establish the intervals shown in the table and Figure 1-23. To decide which ones are solutions, we test a number in each interval to see whether it is a solution.

Interval	Test Value	Inequality $x^2 - 5 \geq 0$	Result
$\left(-\infty, -\sqrt{5}\right)$	-3	$(-3)^2 - 5 \overset{?}{\geq} 0$ $\quad 4 \geq 0 \quad$ True	The numbers in this interval are solutions.
$\left(-\sqrt{5}, \sqrt{5}\right)$	0	$(0)^2 - 5 \overset{?}{\geq} 0$ $\quad -5 \geq 0 \quad$ False	The numbers in this interval are not solutions.
$\left(\sqrt{5}, \infty\right)$	3	$(3)^2 - 5 \overset{?}{\geq} 0$ $\quad 4 \geq 0 \quad$ True	The numbers in this interval are solutions.

As shown in Figure 1-23, the solution is the union of two intervals:

$$\left(-\infty, -\sqrt{5}\right] \cup \left[\sqrt{5}, \infty\right).$$

FIGURE 1-23

Self Check 9   Solve $x^2 - 7 \leq 0$.

Now Try Exercise 67.

4. Solve Rational Inequalities

Inequalities that contain fractions with polynomial numerators and denominators are called **rational inequalities.** To solve them, we can use the same strategies that we use to solve quadratic inequalities.

EXAMPLE 10   **Solving a Rational Inequality**

Solve the rational inequality: $\dfrac{x^2 - x - 2}{x^2 - 4x + 3} \leq 0$.

SOLUTION   **Method 1:** The intervals are found by solving $x^2 - x - 2 = 0$ and $x^2 - 4x + 3 = 0$. The solutions of the first equation are -1 and 2, and the solutions of the second equation are 1 and 3. These solutions establish the five intervals shown in Figure 1-24.

FIGURE 1-24

The solutions of $\dfrac{x^2 - x - 2}{x^2 - 4x + 3} \leq 0$ will be the numbers in one or more of these intervals. To determine which intervals are solutions, we test a number in each interval to see whether it satisfies the inequality.

Interval	Test Value	Inequality $\dfrac{x^2 - x - 2}{x^2 - 4x + 3} \leq 0$	Result
$(-\infty, -1)$	-2	$\dfrac{(-2)^2 - (-2) - 2}{(-2)^2 - 4(-2) + 3} \leq 0$ $\dfrac{4}{15} \leq 0$ False	The numbers in this interval are not solutions.
$(-1, 1)$	0	$\dfrac{(0)^2 - (0) - 2}{(0)^2 - 4(0) + 3} \leq 0$ $-\dfrac{2}{3} \leq 0$ True	The numbers in this interval are solutions.
$(1, 2)$	$\dfrac{3}{2}$	$\dfrac{\left(\dfrac{3}{2}\right)^2 - \left(\dfrac{3}{2}\right) - 2}{\left(\dfrac{3}{2}\right)^2 - 4\left(\dfrac{3}{2}\right) + 3} \leq 0$ $\dfrac{5}{3} \leq 0$ False	The numbers in this interval are not solutions.
$(2, 3)$	$\dfrac{5}{2}$	$\dfrac{\left(\dfrac{5}{2}\right)^2 - \left(\dfrac{5}{2}\right) - 2}{\left(\dfrac{5}{2}\right)^2 - 4\left(\dfrac{5}{2}\right) + 3} \leq 0$ $-\dfrac{7}{3} \leq 0$ True	The numbers in this interval are solutions.
$(3, \infty)$	4	$\dfrac{(4)^2 - (4) - 2}{(4)^2 - 4(4) + 3} \leq 0$ $\dfrac{10}{3} \leq 0$ False	The numbers in this interval are not solutions.

The numbers in the intervals $(-1, 1)$ and $(2, 3)$ satisfy the inequality, but the numbers in the intervals $(-\infty, -1)$, $(1, 2)$, and $(3, \infty)$ do not. The solution set is $[-1, 1) \cup [2, 3)$. The graph of the solution set is shown in Figure 1-25.

FIGURE 1-25

Because $x = -1$ and $x = 2$ make the numerator 0, they satisfy the inequality. Thus, their graphs are drawn with brackets to show that -1 and 2 are included. Because 1 and 3 give 0's in the denominator, the parentheses at $x = 1$ and $x = 3$ show that 1 and 3 are not in the solution set.

Method 2: We factor each trinomial and write the inequality in the form

$$\frac{(x - 2)(x + 1)}{(x - 3)(x - 1)} \le 0$$

We then construct the sign graph shown in Figure 1-26. The value of the fraction will be 0 when $x = 2$ and $x = -1$. The value will be negative when there is an odd number of negative factors. This happens between -1 and 1 and between 2 and 3.

The graph of the solution set also appears in Figure 1-26. The brackets at -1 and 2 show that these numbers are in the solution set. The parentheses at 1 and 3 show that these numbers are not in the solution set.

Caution

A common error made when writing the solution set for a rational inequality that contains $\le$ or $\ge$ is to write a bracket next to each number in the solution set. The real numbers that make the denominator zero will *never* be included in the solution set, and we should always write a parenthesis next to them.

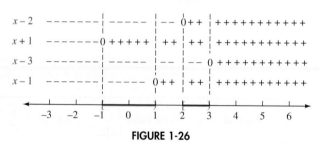

FIGURE 1-26

Self Check 10   Solve: $\dfrac{x^2 + 2x - 3}{x^2 + 4x + 3} > 0$.

Now Try Exercise 73.

EXAMPLE 11   **Solving a Rational Inequality**

Solve: $\dfrac{6}{x} > 2$.

SOLUTION   We will first rewrite the rational inequality and get a 0 on the right side. Then we can use either method to solve the inequality.

To get a 0 on the right side, we subtract 2 from both sides. We then combine like terms on the left side.

$$\frac{6}{x} > 2$$

$$\frac{6}{x} - 2 > 0 \qquad \text{Subtract 2 from both sides.}$$

$$\frac{6}{x} - \frac{2x}{x} > 0 \qquad \frac{x}{x} = 1$$

$$\frac{6 - 2x}{x} > 0 \qquad \text{Add the numerators and keep the common denominator.}$$

The inequality now has the form of a rational inequality. We can use either method to solve the inequality. The intervals are found by solving $6 - 2x = 0$ and $x = 0$. The solution of the first equation is 3, and the solution of the second equation is 0. This determines the intervals $(-\infty, 0)$, $(0, 3)$, and $(3, \infty)$. Because only the numbers in the interval $(0, 3)$ satisfy the original inequality, the solution set is $(0, 3)$. The graph is shown in Figure 1-27.

FIGURE 1-27

We could construct a sign graph as in Figure 1-28 and obtain the same solution set.

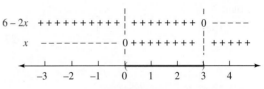

FIGURE 1-28

Self Check 11   Solve: $\dfrac{2}{x} < 4$.

Now Try Exercise 77.

Caution   It is tempting to solve Example 11 by multiplying both sides by x and solving the inequality $6 > 2x$. However, multiplying both sides by x gives $6 > 2x$ only when x is positive. If x is negative, multiplying both sides by x will reverse the direction of the $>$ symbol, and the inequality $\frac{6}{x} > 2$ will be equivalent to $6 < 2x$. If you fail to consider both cases, you will get a wrong answer.

Self Check Answers   **1. a.** $>$ or $\geq$ **b.** $\leq$ or $\geq$ **c.** $>$ or $\geq$ **2.** $(9, \infty)$

3. $(-\infty, -7]$ **4.** 200 bushels or less   **5.** $[-3, 4)$

6. $(4, \infty)$ **7.** $(-\infty, -3] \cup [2, \infty)$ **8.** $[-1, 6]$

9. $\left[-\sqrt{7}, \sqrt{7}\,\right]$ **10.** $(-\infty, -3) \cup (-3, -1) \cup (1, \infty)$

11. $(-\infty, 0) \cup \left(\dfrac{1}{2}, \infty\right)$

Exercises **1.7**

Getting Ready

You should be able to complete these vocabulary and concept statements before you proceed to the practice exercises.

Fill in the blanks.

1. If $x > y$, then x lies to the _____ of y on a number line.
2. $a < b$, _____, or $a > b$.
3. If $a < b$ and $b < c$, then _____.
4. If $a < b$ then $a + c <$ _____.
5. If $a < b$ then $a - c <$ _____.
6. If $a < b$ and $c > 0$, then ac _____ bc.
7. If $a < b$ and $c < 0$, then ac _____ bc.
8. If $a < b$ and $c < 0$, then $\frac{a}{c}$ _____ $\frac{b}{c}$.
9. $3x - 5 < 12$ and $ax + c > 0$ $(a \neq 0)$ are examples of _____ inequalities.
10. $ax^2 + bx - c \geq 0$ and $3x^2 - 6x < 0$ are examples of _____ inequalities.
11. If two inequalities have the same solution set, they are called _____ inequalities.
12. An inequality that contains a fraction with a polynomial numerator and denominator is called a _____ inequality.

Practice

Solve each inequality, graph the solution set, and write the answer in interval notation. Do not worry about drawing your graphs exactly to scale.

13. $3x + 2 < 5$

14. $-2x + 4 < 6$

15. $3x + 2 \geq 5$

16. $-2x + 4 \geq 6$

17. $-5x + 3 > -2$

18. $4x - 3 > -4$

19. $-5x + 3 \leq -2$

20. $4x - 3 \leq -4$

21. $2(x - 3) \leq -2(x - 3)$ 22. $3(x + 2) \leq 2(x + 5)$

23. $\frac{3}{5}x + 4 > 2$

24. $\frac{1}{4}x - 3 > 5$

25. $\frac{x + 3}{4} < \frac{2x - 4}{3}$

26. $\frac{x + 2}{5} > \frac{x - 1}{2}$

27. $\frac{6(x - 4)}{5} \geq \frac{3(x + 2)}{4}$

28. $\frac{3(x + 3)}{2} < \frac{2(x + 7)}{3}$

29. $\frac{5}{9}(a + 3) - a \geq \frac{4}{3}(a - 3) - 1$

30. $\frac{2}{3}y - y \leq -\frac{3}{2}(y - 5)$

31. $\frac{2}{3}a - \frac{3}{4}a < \frac{3}{5}\left(a + \frac{2}{3}\right) + \frac{1}{3}$

32. $\frac{1}{4}b + \frac{2}{3}b - \frac{1}{2} > \frac{1}{2}(b + 1) + b$

33. $4 < 2x - 8 \leq 10$

34. $3 \leq 2x + 2 < 6$

35. $9 \geq \frac{x - 4}{2} > 2$

36. $5 < \frac{x - 2}{6} < 6$

37. $0 \leq \frac{4 - x}{3} \leq 5$

38. $0 \geq \frac{5 - x}{2} \geq -10$

39. $-2 \geq \frac{1 - x}{2} \geq -10$

40. $-2 \leq \frac{1 - x}{2} < 10$

41. $-3x > -2x > -x$

42. $-3x < -2x < -x$

43. $x < 2x < 3x$ **44.** $x > 2x > 3x$

45. $2x + 1 < 3x - 2 < 12$ **46.** $2 - x < 3x + 5 < 18$

47. $2 + x < 3x - 2 < 5x + 2$

48. $x > 2x + 3 > 4x - 7$

49. $3 + x > 7x - 2 > 5x - 10$

50. $2 - x < 3x + 1 < 10x$

51. $x \le x + 1 \le 2x + 3$

52. $-x \ge -2x + 1 \ge -3x + 1$

53. $x^2 + 7x + 12 < 0$ **54.** $x^2 - 13x + 12 \le 0$

55. $x^2 - 5x + 6 \ge 0$ **56.** $6x^2 + 5x - 6 > 0$

57. $x^2 + 5x + 6 < 0$ **58.** $x^2 + 9x + 20 \ge 0$

59. $6x^2 + 5x + 1 \ge 0$ **60.** $x^2 + 9x + 20 < 0$

61. $6x^2 - 5x < -1$ **62.** $9x^2 + 24x > -16$

63. $2x^2 \ge 3 - x$ **64.** $9x^2 \le 24x - 16$

65. $x^2 - 3 \ge 0$ **66.** $x^2 - 7 \le 0$

67. $x^2 - 11 < 0$ **68.** $x^2 - 20 > 0$

69. $\dfrac{x + 3}{x - 2} < 0$ **70.** $\dfrac{x + 3}{x - 2} > 0$

71. $\dfrac{x^2 + x}{x^2 - 1} > 0$ **72.** $\dfrac{x^2 - 4}{x^2 - 9} < 0$

73. $\dfrac{x^2 + 5x + 6}{x^2 + x - 6} \ge 0$ **74.** $\dfrac{x^2 + 10x + 25}{x^2 - x - 12} \le 0$

75. $\dfrac{6x^2 - x - 1}{x^2 + 4x + 4} > 0$ **76.** $\dfrac{6x^2 - 3x - 3}{x^2 - 2x - 8} < 0$

77. $\dfrac{3}{x} > 2$ **78.** $\dfrac{3}{x} < 2$

79. $\dfrac{6}{x} < 4$ **80.** $\dfrac{6}{x} > 4$

81. $\dfrac{3}{x - 2} \le 5$ **82.** $\dfrac{3}{x + 2} \le 4$

83. $\dfrac{6}{x^2 - 1} < 1$ **84.** $\dfrac{6}{x^2 - 1} > 1$

Applications
Solve each problem.

85. Long distance A long-distance telephone call costs 40¢ for the first three minutes and 10¢ for each additional minute. At most how many minutes can a person talk and not exceed $2?

86. Buying a computer A student who can afford to spend up to $2,000 sees the ad shown in the illustration. If she buys a computer, how many games can she buy?

Big Sale!!!!

◀▉▉ $1,695.95

Games
$19.95

87. Buying albums Andy can spend up to $275 on an iPod and some albums. If he can buy an iPod for $150 and albums for $9.75, what is the greatest number of albums that he can buy?

88. Buying DVDs Mary wants to spend less than $600 for a DVD recorder and some DVDs. If the recorder of her choice costs $425 and DVDs cost $7.50 each, how many DVDs can she buy?

89. Buying a refrigerator A woman who has $1,200 to spend wants to buy a refrigerator. Refer to the following table and write an inequality that shows how much she can pay for the refrigerator.

State sales tax	6.5%
City sales tax	0.25%

90. Renting a rototiller The cost of renting a rototiller is $17.50 for the first hour and $8.95 for each additional hour. How long can a person have the rototiller if the cost must be less than $75?

Istockphoto.com/
Keith Webber Jr.

91. Real estate taxes A city council has proposed the following two methods of taxing real estate:

Method 1	$2,200 + 4% of assessed value
Method 2	$1,200 + 6% of assessed value

For what range of assessments *a* would the first method benefit the taxpayer?

92. Medical plans A college provides its employees with a choice of the two medical plans shown in the following table. For what size hospital bills is Plan 2 better for the employee than Plan 1? (*Hint:* The cost to the employee includes both the deductible payment and the employee's coinsurance payment.)

Plan 1	Plan 2
Employee pays $100	Employee pays $200
Plan pays 70% of the rest	Plan pays 80% of the rest

93. Medical plans To save costs, the college in Exercise 92 raised the employee deductible, as shown in the following table. For what size hospital bills is Plan 2 better for the employee than Plan 1? (*Hint:* The cost to the employee includes both the deductible payment and the employee's coinsurance payment.)

Plan 1	Plan 2
Employee pays $200	Employee pays $400
Plan pays 70% of the rest	Plan pays 80% of the rest

94. Geometry The perimeter of a rectangle is to be between 180 inches and 200 inches. Find the range of values for its length when its width is 40 inches.

95. Geometry The perimeter of an equilateral triangle is to be between 50 centimeters and 60 centimeters. Find the range of lengths of one side.

96. Geometry The perimeter of a square is to be from 25 meters to 60 meters. Find the range of values for its area.

Discovery and Writing

97. Express the relationship $20 < l < 30$ in terms of P, where $P = 2l + 2w$.

98. Express the relationship $10 < C < 20$ in terms of F, where $F = \frac{9}{5}C + 32$.

99. The techniques used for solving linear equations and linear inequalities are similar, yet different. Explain.

100. Explain why the relation $\geq$ is transitive.

Review

In Exercises 101–106,
$A = \left\{ -9, -\pi, -2, -\frac{1}{2}, 0, 1, 2, \sqrt{7}, \frac{21}{2} \right\}.$

101. Which numbers are even integers?

102. Which numbers are natural numbers?

103. Which numbers are prime numbers?

104. Which numbers are irrational numbers?

105. Which numbers are real numbers?

106. Which numbers are rational numbers?

1.8 Absolute Value

In this section, we will learn to

1. Define and use absolute value.

2. Solve equations of the form $|x| = k$.

3. Solve equations with two absolute values.

4. Solve inequalities of the forms $|x| < k$ and $|x| \leq k$.

5. Solve inequalities of the forms $|x| > k$ and $|x| \geq k$.

6. Solve compound inequalities with absolute value.

7. Solve inequalities with two absolute values.

Cancun, Mexico, is a popular spring-break destination for college students. The beautiful beaches, exciting nightlife, and tropical weather make it a pleasurable experience.

The average annual temperature in Cancun is 78°F with fluctuations of approximately 7 degrees. We can represent this temperature range using absolute value notation. If we let x represent the temperature at a given time, the absolute value of the difference between x and 78 is less than or equal to 7. We can write this as $|x - 78| \leq 7$.

In this section, we will review absolute value and examine its consequences in greater detail.

1. Define and Use Absolute Value

Absolute Value   The **absolute value** of the real number x, denoted by $|x|$, is defined as follows:

If $x \geq 0$, then $|x| = x$.

If $x < 0$, then $|x| = -x$.

This definition provides a way to associate a nonnegative real number with any real number.

• If $x \geq 0$, then x (which is positive or 0) is its own absolute value.
• If $x < 0$, then $-x$ (which is positive) is the absolute value.

Either way, $|x|$ is positive or 0:

$|x| \geq 0$ for all real numbers x

EXAMPLE 1   **Using the Definition of Absolute Value**

Write each expression without using absolute value symbols:

a. $|7|$ **b.** $|-3|$ **c.** $-|-7|$ **d.** $|x - 2|$

SOLUTION   In each case, we will apply the definition of absolute value.

a. Because 7 is positive, $|7| = 7$.

b. Because –3 is negative, $|-3| = -(-3) = 3$.

c. The expression $-|-7|$ means "the negative of the absolute value of -7." Thus, $-|-7| = -(7) = -7$.

d. To denote the absolute value of a variable quantity, we must give a conditional answer.

If $x - 2 \geq 0$, then $|x - 2| = x - 2$.

If $x - 2 < 0$, then $|x - 2| = -(x - 2) = -x + 2$.

Self Check 1   Write each expression without using absolute value symbols:

a. $|0|$ **b.** $|-17|$ **c.** $|x + 5|$

Now Try Exercise 13.

2. Solve Equations of the Form $|x| = k$

In the equation $|x| = 8$, x can be either 8 or -8, because $|8| = 8$ and $|-8| = 8$. In general, the following is true.

Absolute Value Equations

If $k \geq 0$, then

$|x| = k$ is equivalent to $x = k$ or $x = -k$

The absolute value of a number represents the distance on the number line from a point to the origin. The solutions of $|x|$ are the coordinates of the two points that lie exactly k units from the origin. (See Figure 1-29.)

FIGURE 1-29

The equation $|x - 3| = 7$ indicates that a point on the number line with a coordinate of $x - 3$ is 7 units from the origin. Thus, $x - 3$ can be 7 or -7.

$$x - 3 = 7 \quad \text{or} \quad x - 3 = -7$$
$$x = 10 \quad\quad x = -4$$

The solutions of 10 and -4 are shown in Figure 1-30. Both of these numbers satisfy the equation.

FIGURE 1-30

$$|x - 3| = 7 \quad \text{and} \quad |x - 3| = 7$$
$$|10 - 3| = 7 \quad\quad |-4 - 3| = 7$$
$$|7| = 7 \quad\quad |-7| = 7$$
$$7 = 7 \quad\quad 7 = 7$$

Comment   In general, absolute value equations will have two solutions. Consider these exceptions:

- Note that if $k < 0$, then $|x| = k$ has no solution.

  For example, the equation $|x| = -5$ has no solution.

- If $k = 0$, then $|x| = k$ has only one solution.

  For example, the equation $|x| = 0$ has one solution, $x = 0$.

EXAMPLE 2   **Solving an Absolute Value Equation**

Solve: $|3x - 5| + 3 = 10$.

SOLUTION   We will first write the equation in the form $|x| = k$. To do so, we will subtract 3 from both sides of the equation.

$$|3x - 5| + 3 = 10$$
$$|3x - 5| + 3 - 3 = 10 - 3$$
$$|3x - 5| = 7$$

The equation $|3x - 5| = 7$ is equivalent to two equations

$$3x - 5 = 7 \quad \text{or} \quad 3x - 5 = -7$$

which can be solved separately:

$$3x - 5 = 7 \quad \text{or} \quad 3x - 5 = -7$$
$$3x = 12 \qquad\qquad 3x = -2$$
$$x = 4 \qquad\qquad x = -\frac{2}{3}$$

The solution set consists of the points shown in Figure 1-31.

FIGURE 1-31

Self Check 2   Solve: $|2x + 3| = 7$.

Now Try Exercise 23.

3. Solve Equations with Two Absolute Values

The equation $|a| = |b|$ is true when $a = b$ or when $a = -b$. For example,

$$|3| = |3| \quad \text{or} \quad |3| = |-3|$$
$$3 = 3 \qquad\qquad 3 = 3$$

In general, the following is true.

Equations with Two Absolute Values   If a and b represent algebraic expressions, the equation $|a| = |b|$ is equivalent to

$$a = b \quad \text{or} \quad a = -b$$

EXAMPLE 3   **Solving an Equation with Two Absolute Values**

Solve: $|2x| = |x - 3|$.

SOLUTION   The equation $|2x| = |x - 3|$ will be true when $2x$ and $x - 3$ are equal or when they are negatives. This gives two equations, which can be solved separately:

$$2x = x - 3 \quad \text{or} \quad 2x = -(x - 3)$$

$$x = -3 \qquad\qquad 2x = -x + 3$$

$$3x = 3$$

$$x = 1$$

Verify that -3 and 1 satisfy the equation. ∎

Self Check 3   Solve: $|3x + 1| = |5x - 3|$.

Now Try Exercise 39.

We will now turn our attention to inequalities and solve inequalities containing absolute values.

4. Solve Inequalities of the Forms $|x| < k$ and $|x| \leq k$

The inequality $|x| < 5$ indicates that a point with coordinate x is less than 5 units from the origin. (See Figure 1-32.) Thus, x is between -5 and 5, and

$$|x| < 5 \quad \text{is equivalent to} \quad -5 < x < 5$$

FIGURE 1-32

In general, the inequality $|x| < k$ $(k > 0)$ indicates that a point with coordinate x is less than k units from the origin. (See Figure 1-33.)

FIGURE 1-33

Similarly, the inequality $|x| \leq k$ $(k > 0)$ indicates that a point with coordinate x is less than or equal to k units from the origin.

Inequalities of the Forms $|x| < k$ and $|x| \leq k$

- If $k > 0$, then $|x| < k$ is equivalent to $-k < x < k$.
- If $k > 0$, then $|x| \leq k$ is equivalent to $-k \leq x \leq k$.

EXAMPLE 4   **Solving an Absolute Value Inequality of the Form $|x| < k$**

Solve: $|x - 2| < 7$.

SOLUTION   The inequality $|x - 2| < 7$ is equivalent to

$$-7 < x - 2 < 7$$

We can add 2 to each part of this inequality to get

$$-5 < x < 9$$

The solution set is the interval $(-5, 9)$, shown in Figure 1-34.

FIGURE 1-34

Self Check 4   Solve: $|x + 3| < 9$.

Now Try Exercise 47.

5. Solve Inequalities of the Forms $|x| > k$ and $|x| \geq k$

The inequality $|x| > 5$ indicates that a point with coordinate x is more than 5 units from the origin. (See Figure 1-35.) Thus, $x < -5$ or $x > 5$.

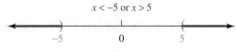

FIGURE 1-35

In general, the inequality $|x| > k$ $(k > 0)$ indicates that a point with coordinate x is more than k units from the origin. (See Figure 1-36.)

FIGURE 1-36

Similarly, the inequality $|x| \geq k$ $(k > 0)$ indicates that a point with coordinate x is k or more units from the origin and thus, $x \leq -5$ or $x \geq 5$.

Inequalities of the Forms $|x| > k$ and $|x| \geq k$	If $k > 0$, then • $|x| > k$ is equivalent to $x < -k$ or $x > k$ • $|x| \geq k$ is equivalent to $x \leq -k$ or $x \geq k$

EXAMPLE 5   **Solving an Absolute Value Inequality of the Form $|x| \geq k$**

Solve: $\left|\dfrac{2x + 3}{2}\right| + 7 \geq 12$.

SOLUTION   We begin by subtracting 7 from both sides of the inequality to isolate the absolute value on the left side.

$$\left|\frac{2x + 3}{2}\right| \geq 5$$

This result is equivalent to two inequalities that can be solved separately.

$$\frac{2x + 3}{2} \le -5 \quad \text{or} \quad \frac{2x + 3}{2} \ge 5$$

$$2x + 3 \le -10 \qquad\qquad 2x + 3 \ge 10$$

$$2x \le -13 \qquad\qquad\quad 2x \ge 7$$

$$x \le -\frac{13}{2} \qquad\qquad\quad x \ge \frac{7}{2}$$

The solution set is the union of the intervals $\left(-\infty, -\frac{13}{2}\right]$ and $\left[\frac{7}{2}, \infty\right)$. Its graph appears in Figure 1-37.

−13/2   0   7/2

FIGURE 1-37

Self Check 5   Solve: $\left|\dfrac{3x - 6}{3}\right| + 2 \ge 12$.

Now Try Exercise 59.

6. Solve Compound Inequalities with Absolute Value

EXAMPLE 6   **Solving a Compound Inequality with Absolute Value**

Solve: $0 < |x - 5| \le 3$.

SOLUTION   The inequality $0 < |x - 5| \le 3$ consists of two inequalities that can be solved separately. The solution will be the intersection of the inequalities

$$0 < |x - 5| \quad \text{and} \quad |x - 5| \le 3$$

The inequality $0 < |x - 5|$ is true for all x except 5. The inequality $|x - 5| \le 3$ is equivalent to the inequality

$$-3 \le x - 5 \le 3$$

$$2 \le x \le 8 \qquad \text{Add 5 to each part.}$$

The solution set is the intersection of these two solutions, which is the interval $[2, 8]$, except 5. This is the union of the intervals $[2, 5)$ and $(5, 8]$, as shown in Figure 1-38.

2   5   8

FIGURE 1-38

Self Check 6   Solve: $0 < |x + 2| \le 5$.

Now Try Exercise 63.

7. Solve Inequalities with Two Absolute Values

In Example 9b of Section 1.5, we saw that $|a|$ could be defined as

$$|a| = \sqrt{a^2}$$

We will use this fact in the next example.

EXAMPLE 7   **Solving an Inequality with Two Absolute Values**

Solve $|x + 2| > |x + 1|$ and give the result in interval notation.

SOLUTION $|x + 2| > |x + 1|$

$\sqrt{(x + 2)^2} > \sqrt{(x + 1)^2}$ Use $|a| = \sqrt{a^2}$.

$(x + 2)^2 > (x + 1)^2$ Square both sides.

$x^2 + 4x + 4 > x^2 + 2x + 1$ Expand each binomial.

$4x > 2x - 3$ Subtract x^2 and 4 from both sides.

$2x > -3$ Subtract $2x$ from both sides.

$x > -\dfrac{3}{2}$ Divide both sides by 2.

The solution set is the interval $\left(-\frac{3}{2}, \infty\right)$. Check several numbers in this interval to verify that this interval is the solution.

Self Check 7   Solve $|x - 3| \leq |x + 2|$ and give the result in interval notation.

Now Try Exercise 77.

Three other properties of absolute value are sometimes useful.

Properties of Absolute Value   If a and b are real numbers, then

1. $|ab| = |a||b|$ **2.** $\left|\dfrac{a}{b}\right| = \dfrac{|a|}{|b|}$ $(b \neq 0)$ **3.** $|a + b| \leq |a| + |b|$

Properties 1 and 2 above indicate that the absolute value of a product (or a quotient) is the product (or the quotient) of the absolute values.

Property 3 indicates that the absolute value of a sum is either equal to or less than the sum of the absolute values.

Self Check Answers   **1. a.** 0   **b.** 17   **c.** if $x + 5 \geq 0$, $|x + 5| = x + 5$; if $x + 5 < 0$,

$|x + 5| = -x - 5$ **2.** $-5, 2$ **3.** $2, \dfrac{1}{4}$

$-5 \qquad 0 \quad 2$

4. $(-12, 6)$ **5.** $(-\infty, -8] \cup [12, \infty)$ **6.** $[-7, -2) \cup (-2, 3]$ **7.** $\left[\dfrac{1}{2}, \infty\right)$

$-12 \qquad 6$

$-8 \quad 0 \qquad 12$

$-7 \qquad -2 \qquad 3$

Exercises **1.8**

Getting Ready
You should be able to complete these vocabulary and concept statements before you proceed to the practice exercises.

Fill in the blanks.

1. If $x \geq 0$, then $|x| =$ ____ .

2. If $x < 0$, then $|x| =$ ____ .

3. $|x| = k$ is equivalent to _____ .

4. $|a| = |b|$ is equivalent to $a = b$ or _____ .

5. $|x| < k$ is equivalent to _____ .

6. $|x| > k$ is equivalent to _____ .

7. $|x| \geq k$ is equivalent to _____ .

8. $\sqrt{a^2} =$ ____ .

Practice

Write each expression without absolute value symbols.

9. $|7|$

10. $|-9|$

11. $|0|$

12. $|3 - 5|$

13. $|5| - |-3|$

14. $|-3| + |5|$

15. $|\pi - 2|$

16. $|\pi - 4|$

17. $|x - 5|$ and $x \geq 5$

18. $|x - 5|$ and $x \leq 5$

19. $|x^3|$

20. $|2x|$

Solve each absolute value equation for x.

21. $|x + 2| = 2$

22. $|2x + 5| = 3$

23. $|3x - 1| - 7 = -2$

24. $|7x - 5| + 5 = 8$

25. $\left|\dfrac{3x - 4}{2}\right| = 5$

26. $\left|\dfrac{10x + 1}{2}\right| = \dfrac{9}{2}$

27. $\left|\dfrac{2x - 4}{5}\right| + 6 = 8$

28. $\left|\dfrac{3x + 11}{7}\right| - 15 = -14$

29. $\left|\dfrac{x - 3}{4}\right| = -2$

30. $\left|\dfrac{x + 5}{2}\right| + 3 = 2$

31. $\left|\dfrac{x - 5}{3}\right| = 0$

32. $\left|\dfrac{x + 7}{9}\right| = 0$

33. $\left|\dfrac{4x - 2}{x}\right| = 3$

34. $\left|\dfrac{2(x - 3)}{3x}\right| = 6$

35. $|x| = x$

36. $|x| + x = 2$

37. $|x + 3| = |x|$

38. $|x + 5| = |5 - x|$

39. $|x - 3| = |2x + 3|$

40. $|x - 2| = |3x + 8|$

41. $|x + 2| = |x - 2|$

42. $|2x - 3| = |3x - 5|$

43. $\left|\dfrac{x + 3}{2}\right| = |2x - 3|$

44. $\left|\dfrac{x - 2}{3}\right| = |6 - x|$

45. $\left|\dfrac{3x - 1}{2}\right| = \left|\dfrac{2x + 3}{3}\right|$

46. $\left|\dfrac{5x + 2}{3}\right| = \left|\dfrac{x - 1}{4}\right|$

Solve each absolute value inequality. Express the solution set in interval notation, and graph it.

47. $|x - 3| < 6$

48. $|x - 2| \geq 4$

49. $|x + 3| > 6$

50. $|x + 2| \leq 4$

51. $|2x + 4| \geq 10$

52. $|5x - 2| < 7$

53. $|3x + 5| + 1 \leq 9$

54. $|2x - 7| - 3 > 2$

55. $|x + 3| > 0$

56. $|x - 3| \leq 0$

57. $\left|\dfrac{5x + 2}{3}\right| < 1$

58. $\left|\dfrac{3x + 2}{4}\right| > 2$

59. $3\left|\dfrac{3x - 1}{2}\right| > 5$

60. $2\left|\dfrac{8x + 2}{5}\right| \leq 1$

61. $\dfrac{|x - 1|}{-2} > -3$

62. $\dfrac{|2x - 3|}{-3} < -1$

Solve each compound inequality with absolute value. Express the solution set in interval notation, and graph it.

63. $0 < |2x + 1| < 3$

64. $0 < |2x - 3| < 1$

65. $8 > |3x - 1| > 3$

66. $8 > |4x - 1| > 5$

67. $2 < \left|\dfrac{x - 5}{3}\right| < 4$

68. $3 < \left|\dfrac{x - 3}{2}\right| < 5$

69. $10 > \left|\dfrac{x - 2}{2}\right| > 4$

70. $5 \geq \left|\dfrac{x + 2}{3}\right| > 1$

71. $2 \le \left| \dfrac{x + 1}{3} \right| < 3$ **72.** $8 > \left| \dfrac{3x + 1}{2} \right| > 2$

Solve each inequality and express the solution using interval notation.

73. $|x + 1| \ge |x|$ **74.** $|x + 1| < |x + 2|$

75. $|2x + 1| < |2x - 1|$ **76.** $|3x - 2| \ge |3x + 1|$

77. $|x + 1| < |x|$ **78.** $|x + 2| \le |x + 1|$

79. $|2x + 1| \ge |2x - 1|$ **80.** $|3x - 2| < |3x + 1|$

Applications

81. Finding temperature ranges The temperatures on a summer day satisfy the inequality $|t - 78°| \le 8°$, where t is the temperature in degrees Fahrenheit. Express this range without using absolute value symbols.

82. Finding operating temperatures A car CD player has an operating temperature of $|t - 40°| < 80°$, where t is the temperature in degrees Fahrenheit. Express this range without using absolute value symbols.

83. Range of camber angles The specifications for a certain car state that the camber angle c of its wheels should be $0.6° \pm 0.5°$. Express this range with an inequality containing an absolute value.

84. Tolerance of a sheet of steel A sheet of steel is to be 0.25 inch thick, with a tolerance of 0.015 inch. Express this specification with an inequality containing an absolute value.

85. Humidity level A Steinway piano should be placed in an environment where the relative humidity h is between 38% and 72%. Express this range with an inequality containing an absolute value.

© istockphoto.com/iLexx

86. Light bulbs A light bulb is expected to last h hours, where $|h - 1,500| \le 200$. Express this range without using absolute value symbols.

87. Error analysis In a lab, students measured the percent of copper p in a sample of copper sulfate. The students know that copper sulfate is actually 25.46% copper by mass. They are to compare their results to the actual value and find the amount of *experimental error.*

   a. Which measurements shown in the illustration satisfy the absolute value inequality $|p - 25.46| \le 1.00$?

   b. What can be said about the amount of error for each of the trials listed in part a?

Lab 4	Section A
Title:	
"Percent copper (CU) in	
copper sulfate (CuSO$_4$·5H$_2$O)"	

Results

	% Copper
Trial #1:	22.91%
Trial #2:	26.45%
Trial #3	26.49%
Trial #4:	24.76%

88. Error analysis See Exercise 87.

   a. Which measurements satisfy the absolute value inequality $|p - 25.46| > 1.00$?

   b. What can be said about the amount of error for each of the trials listed in part a?

Discovery and Writing

89. Explain how to find the absolute value of a number.

90. Explain why the equation $|x| + 9 = 0$ has no solution.

91. Explain the use of parentheses and brackets when graphing inequalities.

92. If $k > 0$, explain the differences between the solution sets of $|x| < k$ and $|x| > k$.

93. If $k < 0$, explain why the solution set of $|x| < k$ has no solution.

94. If $k < 0$, explain why the solution set of of $|x| > k$ is all real numbers.

Review

Write each number in scientific notation.

95. 37,250   **96.** 0.0003725

Write each number in standard notation.

97. 5.23×10^5 **98.** 7.9×10^{-4}

Simplify each expression.

99. $(x - y)^2 - (x + y)^2$ **100.** $(p + q)^2 + (p - q)^2$

CHAPTER REVIEW

SECTION 1.1 Linear Equations and Rational Equations

Definitions and Concepts	Examples
An **equation** is a statement indicating that two quantities are equal. There can be restrictions on the variable in an equation.	**Equations:** $2x - 5 = 10$, $\dfrac{2(x-2)}{x-3} = \dfrac{7x+3}{x+2}$ In the equation $2x - 5 = 10$, x can be any real number. In the equation $\dfrac{2(x-2)}{x-3} = \dfrac{7x+3}{x+2}$, x cannot be 3 or -2, because this would give a 0 in the denominator.
Properties of equality: If $a = b$ and c is a number, then $a + c = b + c$ and $a - c = b - c$ $ac = bc$ and $\dfrac{a}{c} = \dfrac{b}{c}$ $(c \neq 0)$	If $a = b$, then $a + 7 = b + 7$ and $a - 7 = b - 7$ $7a = 7b$ and $\dfrac{a}{7} = \dfrac{b}{7}$
A **linear equation** is an equation that can be written in the form $ax + b = 0$ $(a \neq 0)$. To solve a linear equation, use the properties of equality to isolate x on one side of the equation.	Solve $3x - 5 = 4$. $3x - 5 = 4$ $3x - 5 + 5 = 4 + 5$ Add 5 to both sides. $3x = 9$ Combine like terms. $\dfrac{3x}{3} = \dfrac{9}{3}$ Divide both sides by 3. $x = 3$
An **identity** is an equation that is true for all acceptable replacements for its variable.	**Identities:** $x + x = 2x$, $2(x + 1) = 2x + 2$
A **contradiction** is an equation that is false for all acceptable replacements for its variable.	**Contradictions:** $x + 1 = x$, $2(x + 1) = 2x + 3$
Rational equations are equations that contain rational expressions. To solve rational equations, multiply both sides of the equation by an expression that will remove the denominators and solve the resulting equation. Be sure to check the answers to identify any **extraneous solutions.**	Solve $\dfrac{2x}{x-3} = \dfrac{6}{x-3}$. $\dfrac{2x}{x-3} = \dfrac{6}{x-3}$ $(x-3)\left(\dfrac{2x}{x-3}\right) = (x-3)\left(\dfrac{6}{x-3}\right)$ Multiply both sides by $x - 3$. $2x = 6$ Simplify. $x = 3$ Divide both sides by 2 and simplify. The result of 3 is extraneous because when you substitute 3 into the original equation, you get a denominator of 0.

Definitions and Concepts	Examples
Formulas can be solved for a specific variable.	Solve $A = \dfrac{1}{2}bh$ for h.

$$A = \frac{1}{2}bh$$

$2A = bh$ Multiply both sides by 2.

$\dfrac{2A}{b} = \dfrac{bh}{b}$ Divide both sides by b.

$\dfrac{2A}{b} = h$ Simplify.

EXERCISES

Find the restrictions on x, if any.

1. $3x + 7 = 4$

2. $x + \dfrac{1}{x} = 2$

3. $\dfrac{1}{x-1} = 4$

4. $\dfrac{1}{x-2} = \dfrac{2}{x-3}$

Solve each equation and classify it as an identity, a conditional equation, or a contradiction.

5. $3(9x + 4) = 28$

6. $\dfrac{3}{2}a = 7(a + 11)$

7. $8(3x - 5) - 4(x + 3) = 12$

8. $\dfrac{x+3}{x+4} + \dfrac{x+3}{x+2} = 2$

9. $\dfrac{3}{x-1} = \dfrac{1}{2}$

10. $\dfrac{8x^2 + 72x}{9 + x} = 8x$

11. $\dfrac{3x}{x-1} - \dfrac{5}{x+3} = 3$

12. $x + \dfrac{1}{2x-3} = \dfrac{2x^2}{2x-3}$

13. $\dfrac{4}{x^2 - 13x - 48} - \dfrac{1}{x^2 + x - 6} = \dfrac{2}{x^2 - 18x + 32}$

14. $\dfrac{a-1}{a+3} + \dfrac{2a-1}{3-a} = \dfrac{2-a}{a-3}$

Solve each formula for the indicated variable.

15. $C = \dfrac{5}{9}(F - 32); F$

16. $P_n = l + \dfrac{si}{f}; f$

17. $\dfrac{1}{f} = \dfrac{1}{f_1} + \dfrac{1}{f_2}; f_1$

18. $S = \dfrac{a - lr}{1 - r}; l$

SECTION 1.2   Application of Linear Equations

Definitions and Concepts	Examples
Use the following steps to solve an application problem:	Two students leave their dorm in two cars traveling in opposite directions. If one student drives at a rate of 55 mph and the other at a rate of 50 mph, how long will it take for them to be 210 miles apart?

1. Analyze the problem.

2. Pick a variable to represent the quantity to be found.

3. Form an equation.

4. Solve the equation.

5. Check the solution in the words of the problem.

Analyze the problem and pick a variable. We can organize the facts of the problem in the following chart. Since each student drives the same amount of time, let t represent that time.

	d	$=$	r	$\cdot$	t
Student 1	$55t$		55		t
Student 2	$50t$		50		t

Definitions and Concepts	Examples
	Form and solve an equation. Since the students are driving in opposite directions, the distance they are apart in t hours is the sum of the distances they drive, a total of 210 miles. We can form and solve the following equation:
	$55t + 50t = 210$
	$105t = 210$ Combine like terms.
	$t = 2$ Divide both sides by 105.
	Check. In 2 hours, student 1 drives 55(2) miles and student 2 drives 50(2) miles, or 110 miles plus 100 miles. At this time, they will be 210 miles apart.

EXERCISES

19. **Test scores** Carlos took four tests in an English class. On each successive test, his score improved by 4 points. If his mean score was 66%, what did he score on the first test?

20. **Fencing a garden** A homeowner has 100 ft of fencing to enclose a rectangular garden. If the garden is to be 5 ft longer than it is wide, find its dimensions.

21. **Travel** Two women leave a shopping center by car traveling in opposite directions. If one car averages 45 mph and the other 50 mph, how long will it take for the cars to be 285 miles apart?

22. **Travel** Two taxis leave an airport and travel in the same direction. If the average speed of one taxi is 40 mph and the average speed of the other taxi is 46 mph, how long will it take before the cars are 3 miles apart?

23. **Preparing a solution** A liter of fluid is 50% alcohol. How much water must be added to dilute it to a 20% solution?

24. **Washing windows** Scott can wash 37 windows in 3 hours, and Bill can wash 27 windows in 2 hours. How long will it take the two of them to wash 100 windows?

25. **Filling a tank** A tank can be filled in 9 hours by one pipe and in 12 hours by another. How long will it take both pipes to fill the empty tank?

26. **Producing brass** How many ounces of pure zinc must be alloyed with 20 ounces of brass that is 30% zinc and 70% copper to produce brass that is 40% zinc?

27. **Lending money** A bank lends $10,000, part of it at 11% annual interest and the rest at 14%. If the annual income is $1,265, how much was lent at each rate?

28. **Producing oriental rugs** An oriental rug manufacturer can use one loom with a setup cost of $750 that can weave a rug for $115. Another loom, with a setup cost of $950, can produce a rug for $95. How many rugs are produced if the costs are the same on each loom?

SECTION 1.3   Quadratic Equations

Definitions and Concepts	Examples
A **quadratic equation** is an equation that can be written in the form $ax^2 + bx + c = 0$, where a, b, and c are real numbers and $a \neq 0$.	$3x^2 - 5x - 7 = 0$, $5x^2 - 25 = 0$, $7x^2 + 14x = 0$

Definitions and Concepts	Examples
Zero-Factor Theorem:	Solve $x^2 - x - 6 = 0$ using the Zero-Factor Theorem.
If $ab = 0$, then $a = 0$ or $b = 0$.	$x^2 - x - 6 = 0$
	$(x + 2)(x - 3) = 0$ Factor $x^2 - x - 6$.
	$x + 2 = 0$ or $x - 3 = 0$
	$x = -2$ $\quad\vert\quad$ $x = 3$
Square Root Property:	If $x^2 = 32$, then
If $c > 0$, $x^2 = c$ has two real roots:	$x = \sqrt{32}$ $\quad$ or $\quad$ $x = -\sqrt{32}$
$x = \sqrt{c}$ $\ $ or $\ $ $x = -\sqrt{c}$	$= \sqrt{16 \cdot 2}$ $\quad\vert\quad$ $= -\sqrt{16 \cdot 2}$
	$= 4\sqrt{2}$ $\quad\vert\quad$ $= -4\sqrt{2}$
Steps to complete the square:	Solve $x^2 - x - 6 = 0$ by completing the square:
1. Make the coefficient of x^2 equal to 1.	**1.** Since the coefficient of $x^2 = 1$, we go to Step 2.
2. Get the constant on the right side of the equation.	**2.** Add 6 to both sides to get the constant on the right side: $x^2 - x = 6$.
3. Complete the square on x. Take one-half the coefficient of x, square it, and add it to both sides of the equation.	**3.** $x^2 - x + \left(-\dfrac{1}{2}\right)^2 = 6 + \left(-\dfrac{1}{2}\right)^2$
4. Factor the resulting perfect-square trinomial and combine like terms.	**4.** $\left(x - \dfrac{1}{2}\right)^2 = \dfrac{25}{4}$
5. Solve the resulting quadratic equation by using the Square Root Property.	**5.** $\qquad x - \dfrac{1}{2} = \pm\sqrt{\dfrac{25}{4}}$
	$x = \dfrac{1}{2} \pm \dfrac{5}{2}$
	$x = \dfrac{6}{2} = 3$ $\ $ or $\ $ $x = -\dfrac{4}{2} = -2$
Quadratic Formula:	If $3x^2 - 5x + 1 = 0$, then $a = 3$, $b = -5$, and $c = 1$. So
$x = \dfrac{-b \pm \sqrt{b^2 - 4ac}}{2a}$ $\quad (a \neq 0)$	$x = \dfrac{-b \pm \sqrt{b^2 - 4ac}}{2a} = \dfrac{-(-5) \pm \sqrt{(-5)^2 - 4(3)(1)}}{2(3)}$
	$= \dfrac{5 \pm \sqrt{25 - 12}}{6} = \dfrac{5 \pm \sqrt{13}}{6}$
Discriminant:	
The value $b^2 - 4ac$ is the **discriminant.**	
• If $b^2 - 4ac = 0$, the roots of $ax^2 + bx + c = 0$ are repeated rational numbers.	In $4x^2 - 12x + 9 = 0$, the discriminant is $b^2 - 4ac = (-12)^2 - 4(4)(9) = 0$. So the roots are repeated rational numbers.
• If $b^2 - 4ac > 0$ and a perfect square, the roots of $ax^2 + bx + c = 0$ are two different rational numbers.	In $x^2 - x - 6 = 0$, the discriminant is $b^2 - 4ac = (-1)^2 - 4(1)(-6) = 25$. Since 25 is positive and a perfect square, the roots are two different rational numbers.

Definitions and Concepts	Examples
• If $b^2 - 4ac > 0$ and not a perfect square, the roots of $ax^2 + bx + c = 0$ are two different irrational numbers.	In $x^2 - x - 5 = 0$, the discriminant is $b^2 - 4ac = (-1)^2 - 4(1)(-5) = 21$. Since 21 is positive and not a perfect square, the roots are two different irrational numbers.
• If $b^2 - 4ac < 0$, the roots of $ax^2 + bx + c = 0$ are two different nonreal numbers.	In $3x^2 - 2x + 1 = 0$, the discriminant is $b^2 - 4ac = (-2)^2 - 4(3)(1) = -8 < 0$. So the roots are two different nonreal numbers.

EXERCISES

Solve each equation by factoring.

29. $2x^2 - x - 6 = 0$

30. $12x^2 + 13x = 4$

31. $5x^2 - 8x = 0$

32. $27x^2 = 30x - 8$

Solve each equation by using the Square Root Property.

33. $2x^2 = 16$

34. $12x^2 = 60$

35. $(4z - 5)^2 = 32$

36. $(5x - 7)^2 = 45$

Solve each equation by completing the square.

37. $x^2 - 8x + 15 = 0$

38. $3x^2 + 18x = -24$

39. $5x^2 - x - 1 = 0$

40. $5x^2 - x = 0$

Use the Quadratic Formula to solve each equation.

41. $x^2 + 5x - 14 = 0$

42. $3x^2 - 25x = 18$

43. $5x^2 = 1 - x$

44. $5 = a^2 + 2a$

45. Calculate the discriminant associated with the equation $6x^2 + 5x + 1 = 0$.

46. Determine the number and nature of the roots of the equation in Exercise 45.

47. Find the value of k that will make the roots of
$kx^2 + 4x + 12 = 0$ equal.

48. Find the values of k that will make the roots of
$4y^2 + (k + 2)y = 1 - k$ equal.

49. Solve: $\dfrac{1}{a} - \dfrac{1}{5} = \dfrac{3}{2a}$.

50. Solve: $\dfrac{4}{a - 4} + \dfrac{4}{a - 1} = 5$.

SECTION **1.4**   Applications of Quadratic Equations

Definitions and Concepts	Examples
Many real-life problems are modeled by quadratic equations.	If a missile is launched straight up into the air with an initial velocity of 128 feet per second, its height will be given by the formula $h = -16t^2 + 128t$, where h represents its height (in feet) and t represents the time (in seconds) since it was launched. How long will it take the missile to return to its starting point?
	When the missile returns to its starting point, its height will again be 0. So we let $h = 0$ and solve for t.
	$$0 = -16t^2 + 128t$$ $$0 = -16t^2(t - 8)$$ $$-16t = 0 \quad \text{or} \quad t - 8 = 0$$ $$t = 0 \qquad \qquad t = 8$$
	The missile will leave its starting point at 0 seconds and return at 8 seconds.

EXERCISES

51. Fencing a field A farmer wishes to enclose a rectangular garden with 300 yards of fencing. A river runs along one side of the garden, so no fencing is needed there. Find the dimensions of the rectangle if the area is 10,450 square yards.

52. Flying rates A jet plane, flying 120 mph faster than a propeller-driven plane, travels 3,520 miles in 3 hours less time than the propeller plane requires to fly the same distance. How fast does each plane fly?

53. Flight of a ball A ball thrown into the air reaches a height h (in feet) according to the formula $h = -16t^2 + 64t$, where t is the time elapsed since the ball was thrown. Find the shortest time it will take the ball to reach a height of 48 feet.

54. Width of a walk A man built a walk of uniform width around a rectangular pool. If the area of the walk is 117 square feet and the dimensions of the pool are 16 feet by 20 feet, how wide is the walk?

SECTION 1.5   Complex Numbers

Definitions and Concepts	Examples
Complex numbers: Numbers that can be written in the form $a + bi$, where a and b are real numbers and $i = \sqrt{-1}$, are **complex numbers.**	$7 - 2i$, $9 + 5i$, and $2 + \sqrt{7}i$ are complex numbers. $\sqrt{-36} = \sqrt{(-1)(36)} = \sqrt{-1}\sqrt{36} = (i)(6) = 6i$
Equality of complex numbers: $a + bi = c + di$ if and only if $a = c$ and $b = d$	$3 + \sqrt{4}i = \frac{6}{2} + 2i$ because $3 = \frac{6}{2}$ and $\sqrt{4} = 2$.
Adding, subtracting, and multiplying complex numbers: • $(a + bi) + (c + di) = (a + c) + (b + d)i$ • $(a + bi) - (c + di) = (a - c) + (b - d)i$ • $(a + bi)(c + di) = (ac - bd) + (ad + bc)i$ or multiply them as if they were binomials.	$(-3 + 4i) + (2 + 7i) = (-3 + 2) + (4 + 7)i = -1 + 11i$ $(-3 + 4i) - (2 + 7i) = (-3 - 2) + (4 - 7)i = -5 - 3i$ $(-3 + 4i)(2 + 7i) = -3(2) - 3(7i) + 4i(2) + 4i(7i)$ $= -6 - 21i + 8i + 28i^2$ $= -6 - 21i + 8i - 28$ $= -34 - 13i$
The **complex conjugate** of $a + bi$ is $a - bi$.	$3 + 4i$ and $3 - 4i$ are complex conjugates.
Division of complex numbers: To divide complex numbers, rationalize the denominator.	Divide $2 + i$ by $2 - i$. $\dfrac{2 + i}{2 - i} = \dfrac{(2 + i)(2 + i)}{(2 - i)(2 + i)}$ $\dfrac{2 + i}{2 + i} = 1$ $= \dfrac{4 + 2i + 2i + i^2}{4 + 2i - 2i - i^2}$ $= \dfrac{4 + 4i - 1}{4 - (-1)}$ $= \dfrac{3 + 4i}{5}$ $= \dfrac{3}{5} + \dfrac{4}{5}i$

Definitions and Concepts	Examples
Powers of i: If n is a natural number that has a remainder of r when divided by 4, then $i^n = i^r$.	$i^2 = -1, i^3 = -i, i^4 = 1, i^5 = i, i^6 = -i, i^7 = -i,$ $i^8 = 1, \ldots$
Absolute value of a complex number: $\lvert a + bi \rvert = \sqrt{a^2 + b^2}$	$\lvert 5 - 7i \rvert = \sqrt{5^2 + (-7)^2} = \sqrt{25 + 49} = \sqrt{74}$

EXERCISES

Perform all operations and express all answers in $a + bi$ form.

55. $(2 - 3i) + (-4 + 2i)$ **56.** $(2 - 3i) - (4 + 2i)$

57. $(3 - \sqrt{-36}) + (\sqrt{-16} + 2)$

58. $(3 + \sqrt{-9})(2 - \sqrt{-25})$

59. $\dfrac{3}{i}$ **60.** $-\dfrac{2}{i^3}$

61. $\dfrac{3}{1 + i}$ **62.** $\dfrac{2i}{2 - i}$

63. $\dfrac{3 + i}{3 - i}$ **64.** $\dfrac{3 - 2i}{1 + i}$

65. Simplify: i^{53}.   **66.** Simplify: i^{103}.

67. $\lvert 3 - i \rvert$ **68.** $\left\lvert \dfrac{1 + i}{1 - i} \right\rvert$

69. Solve: $3x^2 - 2x + 1 = 0$.

70. Solve: $3x^2 + 4 = 2x$.

SECTION **1.6**   Polynomials and Radical Equations

Definitions and Concepts	Examples
Polynomial equations: Many polynomial equations of higher degree can be solved by factoring.	Solve $x^3 - 5x^2 + 6x = 0$. $x^3 - 5x^2 + 6x = 0$ $x(x^2 - 5x + 6) = 0$ Factor out x. $x(x - 2)(x - 3) = 0$ Factor $x^2 - 5x + 6$. $x = 0$ or $x - 2 = 0$ or $x - 3 = 0$ $x = 2$ $x = 3$ The solution set is $\{0, 2, 3\}$.
Power property of real numbers: If $a = b$, then $a^2 = b^2$.	If $x = 5$, then $x^2 = 5^2$ or $x^2 = 25$.
Factoring can be used to solve certain nonpolynomial equations. Check all solutions because extraneous roots can be introduced.	Solve $2x - 5x^{1/2} + 3 = 0$. $2x - 5x^{1/2} + 3 = 0$ $(2x^{1/2} - 3)(x^{1/2} - 1) = 0$ $2x^{1/2} - 3 = 0$ or $x^{1/2} - 1 = 0$ $x^{1/2} = \dfrac{3}{2}$ $x^{1/2} = 1$ $x = \dfrac{9}{4}$ $x = 1$ Both roots check.

Definitions and Concepts	Examples
Radical equations:	Solve $\sqrt{2x - 3} = x - 1$.
To solve radical equations, use the Power Property of Real Numbers.	$\sqrt{2x - 3} = x - 1$
	$\left(\sqrt{2x - 3}\right)^2 = (x - 1)^2$　　Square both sides.
	$2x - 3 = x^2 - 2x + 1$
	$0 = x^2 - 4x + 4$
	$0 = (x - 2)(x - 2)$
	$x - 2 = 0$　or　$x - 2 = 0$
	$x = 2$　$\mid$　$x = 2$
	Since 2 checks, it is a root.

EXERCISES

Solve each equation.

71. $\dfrac{3x}{2} - \dfrac{2x}{x - 1} = x - 3$　　**72.** $\dfrac{12}{x} - \dfrac{x}{2} = x - 3$

73. $x^4 - 2x^2 + 1 = 0$　　　**74.** $x^4 + 36 = 37x^2$

75. $a - a^{1/2} - 6 = 0$　　**76.** $x^{2/3} + x^{1/3} - 6 = 0$

77. $\sqrt{x - 1} + x = 7$　　**78.** $\sqrt{a + 9} - \sqrt{a} = 3$

79. $\sqrt{5 - x} + \sqrt{5 + x} = 4$　　**80.** $\sqrt{y + 5} + \sqrt{y} = 1$

SECTION **1.7**　　Inequalities

Definitions and Concepts	Examples
Addition, Subtraction, Multiplication, and Division Properties of Inequalities:	
If a, b, and c are real numbers:	
If $a < b$, $a + c < b + c$ and $a - c < b - c$.	If $x < 10$, then $x + 6 < 10 + 6$ and $x - 6 < 10 - 6$.
If $a < b$ and $c > 0$, $ac < bc$ and $\dfrac{a}{c} < \dfrac{b}{c}$.	If $x < 12$, then $3x < 3(12)$ and $\dfrac{x}{3} < \dfrac{12}{3}$.
If $a < b$ and $c < 0$, $ac > bc$ and $\dfrac{a}{c} > \dfrac{b}{c}$.	If $x \leq 12$, then $-3x \geq -3(12)$ and $\dfrac{x}{-3} \geq \dfrac{12}{-3}$.
Trichotomy Property:	
$a < b$, $a = b$, or $a > b$	Either $x < 3$, $x = 3$, or $x > 3$.
Transitive Property:	
If $a < b$ and $b < c$, then $a < c$.	If $x < 4$ and $4 < y$, then $x < y$.

Definitions and Concepts	Examples
Types of inequalities:	
• Linear inequality	$-4(x - 3) \geq 7$
• Compound inequality	$-5 \leq 2x + 1 < 3$
• Quadratic inequality	$x^2 - 2x + 3 \leq 0$
• Rational inequality	$\dfrac{x + 1}{x - 2} > 0$

Solving a linear inequality:

Use the same steps to solve a linear inequality as you would use to solve a linear equation. However, remember to reverse the order of the inequality when you multiply (or divide) both sides of an inequality by a negative number.

Solve the *linear* inequality: $-4(x - 3) \geq 7$.

$$-4(x - 3) \geq 7$$

$-4x + 12 \geq 7$ Remove parentheses.

$-4x \geq -5$ Subtract 12 from both sides.

$x \leq \dfrac{5}{4}$ Divide both sides by -4.

In interval notation, the solution is $\left(-\infty, \dfrac{5}{4}\right]$.

Solving a compound inequality:

For a compound inequality, isolate x in the middle, if possible. If not, solve each inequality separately. The intersection of the intervals is the solution.

Solve the *compound* inequality: $-5 \leq 2x + 1 < 3$.

$$-5 \leq 2x + 1 < 3$$

$-6 \leq 2x < 2$ Subtract 1 from all three parts.

$-3 \leq x < 1$ Divide each part by 2.

In interval notation, the solution is $[-3, 1)$.

Solving quadratic and rational inequalities:

Quadratic and rational inequalities can be solved by constructing a table and testing values or by constructing a sign graph.

Solve the *rational* inequality: $\frac{x + 1}{x - 2} > 0$.

First note that the solution of $x + 1 = 0$ ($x = -1$) and the solution of $x - 2 = 0$ ($x = 2$) form three intervals: $(-\infty, -1), (-1, 2),$ and $(2, \infty)$. To determine which intervals are solutions, we test a number in each interval to see whether it satisfies the inequality.

Definitions and Concepts

Examples

Interval	Test Value	Inequality $\dfrac{x+1}{x-2} > 0$	Result
$(-\infty, -1)$	-2	$\dfrac{-2+1}{-2-2} = \dfrac{1}{4} > 0$ True	The numbers in this interval are solutions.
$(-1, 2)$	0	$\dfrac{0+1}{0-2} = -\dfrac{1}{2} > 0$ False	The numbers in this interval are not solutions.
$(2, \infty)$	3	$\dfrac{3+1}{3-2} = 4 > 0$ True	The numbers in this interval are solutions.

The solution is the union of two intervals:

$(-\infty, -1) \cup (2, \infty)$

$-1 \qquad 2$

EXERCISES

Solve each inequality; graph the solution set and write the answer in interval notation.

81. $2x - 9 < 5$

82. $5x + 3 \geq 2$

83. $\dfrac{5(x-1)}{2} < x$

84. $\dfrac{1}{4}x + \dfrac{2}{3}x - x > \dfrac{1}{2} + \dfrac{1}{2}(x+1)$

85. $0 \leq \dfrac{3+x}{2} < 4$

86. $2 + a < 3a - 2 \leq 5a + 2$

87. $(x+2)(x-4) > 0$

88. $(x-1)(x+4) < 0$

89. $x^2 - 2x - 3 < 0$

90. $2x^2 + x - 3 > 0$

91. $\dfrac{x+2}{x-3} \geq 0$

92. $\dfrac{x-1}{x+4} \leq 0$

93. $\dfrac{x^2 + x - 2}{x - 3} \geq 0$

94. $\dfrac{5}{x} < 2$

SECTION **1.8** Absolute Value

Definitions and Concepts

Examples

Definition of absolute value of x:

$$|x| = \begin{cases} x \text{ when } x \geq 0 \\ -x \text{ when } x < 0 \end{cases}$$

$|5| = 5 \qquad |-7| = 7 \qquad -|-10| = -10$

Definitions and Concepts	Examples
Absolute value equations:	Solve: $\lvert x - 2 \rvert = 6$.
• If $k \geq 0$, then $\lvert x \rvert = k$ is equivalent to $x = k$ or $x = -k$.	$x - 2 = 6 \quad$ or $\quad x - 2 = -6$ $\qquad x = 8 \qquad \qquad x = -4$
• If a and b are algebraic expressions, $\lvert a \rvert = \lvert b \rvert$ is equivalent to $a = b$ or $a = -b$.	Solve: $\lvert 3x \rvert = \lvert x - 2 \rvert$. $3x = x - 2 \quad$ or $\quad 3x = -(x - 2)$ $2x = -2 \qquad \qquad 3x = -x + 2$ $\quad x = -1 \qquad \qquad 4x = 2$ $\qquad \qquad \qquad \qquad x = \dfrac{1}{2}$ Both solutions check.
Absolute value inequality properties:	Solve: $\lvert x - 2 \rvert < 6$.
• If $k > 0$, then $\lvert x \rvert < k$ is equivalent to $-k < x < k$.	$-6 < x - 2 < 6$
• If $k > 0$, then $\lvert x \rvert > k$ is equivalent to $x > k$ or $x < -k$.	$-4 < x < 8 \qquad$ Add 2 to all three parts.
These two properties also hold for $\leq$ and $\geq$.	The solution in interval notation is $(-4, 8)$. Solve: $\lvert x - 2 \rvert > 6$. $x - 2 > 6 \quad$ or $\quad x - 2 < -6$ $\quad x > 8 \qquad \qquad x < -4 \qquad$ Add 2 to both parts. Thus, $x < -4 \quad$ or $\quad x > 8$ The solution in interval notation is $(-\infty, -4) \cup (8, \infty)$.
Properties of absolute value:	
1. $\lvert ab \rvert = \lvert a \rvert \lvert b \rvert$	$\lvert -3x \rvert = \lvert -3 \rvert \lvert x \rvert = 3 \lvert x \rvert$
2. $\left\lvert \dfrac{a}{b} \right\rvert = \dfrac{\lvert a \rvert}{\lvert b \rvert} \quad (b \neq 0)$	$\left\lvert \dfrac{-3}{x} \right\rvert = \dfrac{\lvert -3 \rvert}{\lvert x \rvert} = \dfrac{3}{\lvert x \rvert} \ (x \neq 0)$
3. $\lvert a + b \rvert \leq \lvert a \rvert + \lvert b \rvert$	$\lvert x + 3 \rvert \leq \lvert x \rvert + \lvert 3 \rvert$

EXERCISES

Solve each equation or inequality.

95. $\lvert x + 1 \rvert = 6$

96. $\lvert 2x - 1 \rvert = \lvert 2x + 1 \rvert$

97. $\left\lvert \dfrac{3x + 11}{7} \right\rvert - 1 = 0$

98. $\left\lvert \dfrac{2a - 6}{3a} \right\rvert - 6 = 0$

99. $\lvert x + 3 \rvert < 3$

100. $\lvert 3x - 7 \rvert \geq 1$

101. $\left\lvert \dfrac{x + 2}{3} \right\rvert < 1$

102. $\left\lvert \dfrac{x - 3}{4} \right\rvert > 8$

103. $1 < \lvert 2x + 3 \rvert < 4$

104. $0 < \lvert 3x - 4 \rvert < 7$

CHAPTER TEST

Find all restrictions on x.

1. $\dfrac{x}{x(x-1)} = 2$

2. $\dfrac{4}{3x-2} + 3 = 7$

Solve each equation.

3. $7(2a+5) - 7 = 6(a+8)$

4. $\dfrac{3}{x^2 - 5x - 14} = \dfrac{4}{x^2 + 5x + 6}$

5. Solve for x: $z = \dfrac{x - \mu}{\sigma}$.

6. Solve for a: $\dfrac{1}{a} = \dfrac{1}{b} + \dfrac{1}{c}$.

7. Test scores A student's average on three tests is 75. If the final is to count as two one-hour tests, what grade must the student make to bring the average up to 80?

8. Investment A woman invested part of $20,000 at 6% interest and the rest at 7%. If her annual interest is $1,260, how much did she invest at 6%?

Solve each equation.

9. $4x^2 - 8x + 3 = 0$

10. $2b^2 - 12 = -5b$

11. Write the Quadratic Formula.

12. Use the Quadratic Formula to solve $3x^2 - 5x - 9 = 0$.

13. Find k such that $x^2 + (k+1)x + k + 4 = 0$ will have two equal roots.

14. Height of a projectile The height of a projectile shot up into the air is given by the formula $h = -16t^2 + 128t$. Find the time t required for the projectile to return to its starting point.

Perform each operation and write all answers in $a + bi$ form.

15. $(4 - 5i) - (-3 + 7i)$

16. $(4 - 5i)(3 - 7i)$

17. $\dfrac{2}{2 - i}$

18. $\dfrac{1 + i}{1 - i}$

Simplify each expression.

19. i^{13}

20. i^0

Find each absolute value.

21. $|5 - 12i|$

22. $\left| \dfrac{1}{3 + i} \right|$

Solve each equation.

23. $z^4 - 13z^2 + 36 = 0$

24. $2p^{2/5} - p^{1/5} - 1 = 0$

25. $\sqrt{x + 5} = 12$

26. $\sqrt{2z + 3} = 1 - \sqrt{z + 1}$

Solve each inequality; graph the solution set and write the answer using interval notation.

27. $5x - 3 \le 7$

28. $\dfrac{x + 3}{4} > \dfrac{2x - 4}{3}$

29. $5 \le 2x - 1 < 7$

30. $1 + x < 3x - 3 < 4x - 2$

31. $x^2 - 7x - 8 \ge 0$

32. $\dfrac{x + 2}{x - 1} \le 0$

Solve each equation.

33. $\left| \dfrac{3x + 2}{2} \right| = 4$

34. $|x + 3| = |x - 3|$

Solve each inequality; graph the solution set and write the answer using interval notation.

35. $|2x - 5| > 2$

36. $\left| \dfrac{2x + 3}{3} \right| \le 5$

CUMULATIVE REVIEW EXERCISES

Consider the set $\{-5, -3, -2, 0, 1, \sqrt{2}, 2, \frac{5}{2}, 5, 6, 11\}.$

1. Which numbers are even integers?

2. Which numbers are prime numbers?

Write each inequality as an interval and graph it.

3. $-4 \le x < 7$

4. $x \ge 2$ or $x < 0$

Determine which property of the real numbers justifies each expression.

5. $(a + b) + c = c + (a + b)$

6. If $x < 3$ and $3 < y$, then $x < y$.

Simplify each expression. Assume that all variables represent positive numbers. Give all answers with positive exponents.

7. $(81a^4)^{1/2}$

8. $81(a^4)^{1/2}$

9. $(a^{-3}b^{-2})^{-2}$

10. $\left(\dfrac{4x^4}{12x^2y}\right)^{-2}$

11. $\left(\dfrac{4x^0y^2}{x^2y}\right)^{-2}$

12. $\left(\dfrac{4x^{-5}y^2}{6x^{-2}y^{-3}}\right)^{2}$

13. $(a^{1/2}b)^2(ab^{1/2})^2$

14. $(a^{1/2}b^{1/2}c)^2$

Rationalize each denominator and simplify.

15. $\dfrac{3}{\sqrt{3}}$

16. $\dfrac{2}{\sqrt[3]{4x}}$

17. $\dfrac{3}{y - \sqrt{3}}$

18. $\dfrac{3x}{\sqrt{x} - 1}$

Simplify each expression and combine like terms.

19. $\sqrt{75} - 3\sqrt{5}$

20. $\sqrt{18} + \sqrt{8} - 2\sqrt{2}$

21. $\left(\sqrt{2} - \sqrt{3}\right)^2$

22. $\left(3 - \sqrt{5}\right)\left(3 + \sqrt{5}\right)$

Perform the operations and simplify when necessary.

23. $(3x^2 - 2x + 5) - 3(x^2 + 2x - 1)$

24. $5x^2(2x^2 - x) + x(x^2 - x^3)$

25. $(3x - 5)(2x + 7)$

26. $(z + 2)(z^2 - z + 2)$

27. $3x + 2\overline{)6x^3 + x^2 + x + 2}$

28. $x^2 + 2\overline{)3x^4 + 7x^2 - x + 2}$

Factor each polynomial.

29. $3t^2 - 6t$

30. $3x^2 - 10x - 8$

31. $x^8 - 2x^4 + 1$

32. $x^6 - 1$

Perform the operations and simplify.

33. $\dfrac{x^2 - 4}{x^2 + 5x + 6} \cdot \dfrac{x^2 - 2x - 15}{x^2 + 3x - 10}$

34. $\dfrac{6x^3 + x^2 - x}{x + 2} \div \dfrac{3x^2 - x}{x^2 + 4x + 4}$

35. $\dfrac{2}{x + 3} + \dfrac{5x}{x - 3}$

36. $\dfrac{x - 2}{x + 3}\left(\dfrac{x + 3}{x^2 - 4} - 1\right)$

37. $\dfrac{\dfrac{1}{a} + \dfrac{1}{b}}{\dfrac{1}{ab}}$

38. $\dfrac{x^{-1} - y^{-1}}{x - y}$

Solve each equation.

39. $\dfrac{3x}{x + 5} = \dfrac{x}{x - 5}$

40. $8(2x - 3) - 3(5x + 2) = 4$

Solve each formula for the indicated variable.

41. $\dfrac{1}{R} = \dfrac{1}{R_1} + \dfrac{1}{R_2}; R$

42. $S = \dfrac{a - lr}{1 - r}; r$

43. **Gardening** A gardener wishes to enclose her rectangular raspberry patch with 40 feet of fencing. The raspberry bushes are planted along the garage, so no fencing is needed on that side. Find the dimensions if the total area is to be 192 square feet.

44. **Financial planning** A college student invested part of a $25,000 inheritance at 7% interest and the rest at 6%. If his annual interest is $1,670, how much did he invest at 6%?

Perform the operations. If the result is not real, express the answer in a + bi form.

45. $\dfrac{2 + i}{2 - i}$

46. $\dfrac{i(3 - i)}{(1 + i)(1 + i)}$

47. $|3 + 4i|$

48. $\dfrac{5}{i^7} + 5i$

Solve each equation.

49. $\dfrac{x + 3}{x - 1} - \dfrac{6}{x} = 1$

50. $x^4 + 36 = 13x^2$

51. $\sqrt{y + 2} + \sqrt{11 - y} = 5$

52. $z^{2/3} - 13z^{1/3} + 36 = 0$

Graph the solution set of each inequality and write the answer using interval notation.

53. $5x - 7 \le 4$

54. $x^2 - 8x + 15 > 0$

55. $\dfrac{x^2 + 4x + 3}{x - 2} \ge 0$

56. $\dfrac{9}{x} > x$

57. $|2x - 3| \ge 5$

58. $\left| \dfrac{3x - 5}{2} \right| < 2$

The Rectangular Coordinate System and Graphs of Equations

2

CAREERS AND MATHEMATICS: Cartographer

© Stock Connection Blue/Alamy

Cartographers collect, analyze, interpret, and map geographic information about the earth's surface. Their work involves geographical research and compiling data to produce maps. They analyze latitude and longitude, elevation and distance, as well as population density, land-use patterns, precipitation levels, and demographic characteristics. Their maps are prepared in either digital or graphic form, using information provided by geodetic surveys, aerial cameras, satellites, light-imaging detection, and Geographic Information Systems (GIS).

Education and Mathematics Required
- Cartographers usually have a bachelor's degree in cartography, geography, surveying, engineering, forestry, computer science, or a physical science.
- College Algebra, Trigonometry, Calculus I and II, Elementary Statistics, and Spatial Statistics are usually required.

How Cartographers Use Math and Who Employs Them
- Math helps cartographers with map scale, coordinate systems, and map projection. Map scale is the relationship between distances on a map and the corresponding distances on the earth's surface. Coordinate systems are numeric methods of representing locations on the earth's surface. Map projection is a function or transformation that relates coordinates of points on a curved surface to coordinates of points on a plane.
- Most cartographers work with engineering, architectural, and surveying firms. Government agencies hire cartographers to work in highway departments and in areas such as land management, natural resources planning, and national defense.

Career Outlook and Salary
- Employment of cartographers is expected to grow 19 percent from 2008 to 2018.
- The median annual wage in May 2008 was $51,180.

For more information see: www.bls.gov/oco

Mathematical expressions often indicate relationships between two variables. To visualize these relationships, we draw graphs of their equations.

2.1 The Rectangular Coordinate System

In this section, we will learn to

1. Plot points in the rectangular coordinate system.
2. Graph linear equations.
3. Graph vertical and horizontal lines.
4. Solve applications using linear equations.
5. Find the distance between two points.
6. Find the midpoint of a line segment.

We often say that a picture is worth a thousand words. In fact, pictures and graphs are an effective way to present information. For this reason, they appear frequently in newspapers and magazines. For example, the graph shown in Figure 2-1 provides a visual representation of the manatee population in Florida after the year 2003.

From the graph we can note many facts about manatees. Among them are:

- The number of manatees in Florida declined from 2005 to 2007.
- In 2005, the population was about 3,100 animals.
- In this time period, the lowest population of manatees occurred in 2004.

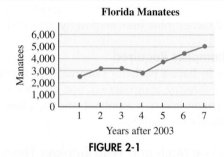

Florida Manatees

Years after 2003

FIGURE 2-1

In mathematics, graphs are also an effective way to present information. In this chapter, we will draw graphs of equations containing two variables and then discuss the information that we can derive from graphs.

The solutions of an equation with variables x and y such as $y = -\frac{1}{2}x + 4$ are ordered pairs of real numbers (x, y) that satisfy the equation. To find some ordered pairs that satisfy the equation, we substitute **input values** of x into the equation and find the corresponding **output values** of y. For example, if we substitute 2 for x, we obtain

$$y = -\frac{1}{2}x + 4$$

$$y = -\frac{1}{2}(2) + 4 \qquad \text{Substitute 2 for } x.$$

$$= -1 + 4$$

$$= 3$$

Since $y = 3$ when $x = 2$, the ordered pair $(2, 3)$ is a solution of the equation. The first coordinate, 2, of the ordered pair is usually called the **x-coordinate**. The second coordinate, 3, is usually called the **y-coordinate**. The solution $(2, 3)$ and several other solutions are listed in the table of values shown in Figure 2-2.

Comment

To complete the table of solutions, we first pick values for x. Next we compute each y-value. Then we write each solution as an ordered pair. Note that we choose x-values that are multiples of the denominator, 2. This makes the computations easier when multiplying the x-value by $-\frac{1}{2}$ to find the corresponding y-value.

$y = -\dfrac{1}{2}x + 4$		
x	y	(x, y)
-4	6	$(-4, 6)$
-2	5	$(-2, 5)$
0	4	$(0, 4)$
2	3	$(2, 3)$
4	2	$(4, 2)$

Pick values for x. ⟶

Compute each y-value.

⟵ Write each solution as an ordered pair.

FIGURE 2-2

ACCENT ON TECHNOLOGY   Generating Table Values

If an equation in x and y is solved for y, we can use a graphing calculator to generate a table of solutions. The instructions in this discussion are for a TI-84 Plus graphing calculator. For details about other brands, please consult the owner's manual.

To construct a table of solutions for $x + 2y = 8$, we first solve the equation for y.

$$x + 2y = 8$$

$$2y = -x + 8 \qquad \text{Subtract } x \text{ from both sides.}$$

$$y = -\frac{1}{2}x + 4 \qquad \text{Divide both sides by 2 and simplify.}$$

- To construct a table of values for $y = -\frac{1}{2}x + 4$, we first enter the equation. We press [Y=] and enter $-(1/2)x + 4$, as shown in Figure 2-3(a).
- Next, we press [2nd] [WINDOW] and enter one value for x on the line labeled TblStart=. In Figure 2-3(b), -4 has been entered on this line. Other values for x that will appear in the table are determined by setting an **increment value** on the line labeled ΔTbl=. In Figure 2-3(b), an increment value of 2 has been entered. This means that each x-value in the table will be 2 units larger than the previous one.
- Finally, we press [2nd] [GRAPH] to obtain the table of values shown in Figure 2-3(c). This table contains all of the solutions listed in Figure 2-2, plus the two additional solutions $(6, 1)$ and $(8, 0)$.

To see other values, we simply scroll up and down the screen by pressing the up and down arrow keys.

(a)   (b)   (c)

FIGURE 2-3

Before we can present the table of solutions shown in Figure 2-2 in graphical form, we need to discuss the rectangular coordinate system.

1. Plot Points in the Rectangular Coordinate System

The **rectangular coordinate system** consists of two perpendicular number lines that divide the plane into four **quadrants,** numbered as shown in Figure 2-4. The horizontal number line is called the **x-axis,** and the vertical number line is called the **y-axis.** These axes intersect at a point called the **origin,** which is 0 on each axis. The positive direction on the x-axis is to the right, the positive direction on the y-axis is upward, and the same unit distance is used on both axes, unless otherwise indicated.

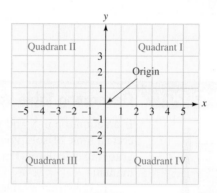

FIGURE 2-4

To plot (or graph) the point associated with the pair $x = 2$ and $y = 3$, denoted as (2, 3), we start at the origin, count 2 units to the right, and then count 3 units up. (See Figure 2-5.) Point P (which lies in the first quadrant) is the graph of the ordered pair (2, 3). The ordered pair (2, 3) gives the **coordinates** of point P.

To plot point Q with coordinates $(-4, 6)$, we start at the origin, count 4 units to the left, and then count 6 units up. Point Q lies in the second quadrant. Point R with coordinates $(6, -4)$ lies in the fourth quadrant.

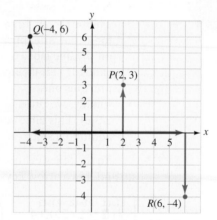

FIGURE 2-5

Caution

The ordered pairs $(-4, 6)$ and $(6, -4)$ represent **different** points. $(-4, 6)$ is in the second quadrant and $(6, -4)$ is in the fourth quadrant.

2. Graph Linear Equations

The **graph of the equation** $y = -\frac{1}{2}x + 4$ is the graph of all points (x, y) on the rectangular coordinate system whose coordinates satisfy the equation. To graph $y = -\frac{1}{2}x + 4$, we plot the pairs listed in the table of solutions shown in Figure 2-6. These points lie on the line shown in the figure. This line is the graph of the equation.

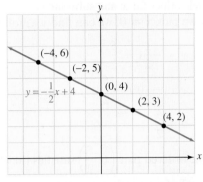

$y = -\dfrac{1}{2}x + 4$		
x	y	(x, y)
-4	6	$(-4, 6)$
-2	5	$(-2, 5)$
0	4	$(0, 4)$
2	3	$(2, 3)$
4	2	$(4, 2)$

FIGURE 2-6

Comment   When we say that the graph of an equation is a line, we imply two things:

1. Every point with coordinates that satisfy the equation will lie on the line.
2. Every point on the line will have coordinates that satisfy the equation.

When the graph of an equation is a line, we call the equation a **linear equation.** These equations are often written in **standard form** as $Ax + By = C$, where A, B, and C are specific numbers (called **constants**) and x and y are variables. Either A or B can be 0, but A and B cannot both be 0.

Standard Form of an Equation of a Line

The **standard form of an equation of a line** is

$$Ax + By = C$$

where A, B, and C are real numbers and A and B are not both 0.

Here are four examples of linear equations written in standard form.

Linear Equation	Values of A, B, and C
$3x + 2y = 6$	$A = 3, B = 2, C = 6$
$5x - 2y = -10$	$A = 5, B = -2, C = -10$
$2y = 7$	$A = 0, B = 2, C = 7$
$x = -4$	$A = 1, B = 0, C = -4$

EXAMPLE 1   Graphing a Linear Equation

Graph: $x + 2y = 5$.

SOLUTION   We will solve the equation for y and form a table of solutions by picking values for x, substituting them into the equation, and solving for the other variable y. We will plot the points represented in the table of solutions and draw a line through the points.

Solve the equation for y.

$$x + 2y = 5$$
$$x - x + 2y = 5 - x \qquad \text{Subtract } x \text{ from both sides.}$$
$$2y = -x + 5 \qquad \text{Simplify.}$$
$$y = -\frac{1}{2}x + \frac{5}{2} \qquad \text{Divide both sides by 2.}$$

Pick values for x and solve for y.

If we pick $x = 0$, we can find y as follows:

$$y = -\frac{1}{2}x + \frac{5}{2}$$

$$y = -\frac{1}{2}(0) + \frac{5}{2} \qquad \text{Substitute 0 in for } x.$$

$$y = \frac{5}{2} \qquad \text{Simplify.}$$

The ordered pair $\left(0, \frac{5}{2}\right)$ satisfies the equation.

To find another ordered pair, we pick $x = 1$ and find y.

$$y = -\frac{1}{2}x + \frac{5}{2}$$

$$y = -\frac{1}{2}(1) + \frac{5}{2} \qquad \text{Substitute 1 in for } x.$$

$$y = 2 \qquad \text{Simplify.}$$

The ordered pair $(1, 2)$ satisfies the equation.

These pairs and others that satisfy the equation are shown in Figure 2-7. We plot the points and join them with a line to get the graph of the equation.

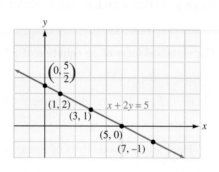

$x + 2y = 5$		
x	y	(x, y)
0	$\frac{5}{2}$	$\left(0, \frac{5}{2}\right)$
1	2	$(1, 2)$
3	1	$(3, 1)$
5	0	$(5, 0)$
7	-1	$(7, -1)$

FIGURE 2-7

Comment

Even though there are infinitely many points that lie on a line, only two are required to graph a line. However, it is a good idea to find a third point as a check.

Self Check 1   Graph: $3x - 2y = 6$.

Now Try Exercise 35.

EXAMPLE 2   Graphing a Linear Equation

Graph: $3(y + 2) = 2x - 3$.

SOLUTION   We will solve the equation for y and find ordered pairs (x, y) that satisfy the equation. Then, we will plot the points and graph the line.

Solve the equation for y.

$$3(y + 2) = 2x - 3$$

$$3y + 6 = 2x - 3 \qquad \text{Use the Distributive Property to remove parentheses.}$$

$$3y = 2x - 9 \qquad \text{Subtract 6 from both sides.}$$

$$y = \frac{2}{3}x - 3 \qquad \text{Divide both sides by 3.}$$

Pick values for x, solve for y.

We now substitute numbers for x to find the corresponding values of y. If we let $x = 0$ and find y, we get

$$y = \frac{2}{3}x - 3$$

$$y = \frac{2}{3}(0) - 3 \qquad \text{Substitute 0 for } x.$$

$$y = -3 \qquad \qquad \text{Simplify.}$$

The point $(0, -3)$ lies on the graph.

If we let $x = 3$, we get

$$y = \frac{2}{3}x - 3$$

$$y = \frac{2}{3}(3) - 3 \qquad \text{Substitute 3 for } x.$$

$$y = 2 - 3 \qquad \qquad \text{Simplify.}$$

$$y = -1$$

The point $(3, -1)$ lies on the graph.

We plot these points and others, as in Figure 2-8, and draw the line that passes through the points.

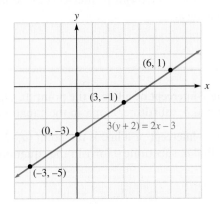

$3(y + 2) = 2x - 3$		
x	y	(x, y)
-3	-5	$(-3, -5)$
0	-3	$(0, -3)$
3	-1	$(3, -1)$
6	1	$(6, 1)$

FIGURE 2-8

Self Check 2   Graph: $2(x - 1) = 6 - 8y$.

Now Try Exercise 39.

ACCENT ON TECHNOLOGY   **Graphing Equations**

We can graph equations with a graphing calculator. To see a graph, we must choose the minimum and maximum values of the x- and y-coordinates that will appear on the calculator's window. A window with standard settings of

$$\text{Xmin} = -10 \qquad \text{Xmax} = 10 \qquad \text{Ymin} = -10 \qquad \text{Ymax} = 10$$

will produce a graph where the value of x is in the interval $[-10, 10]$, and the value of y is in the interval $[-10, 10]$.

- To use a graphing calculator to graph $3x + 2y = 12$, we first solve the equation for y.

$$2y = -3x + 12 \qquad \text{Subtract } 3x \text{ from both sides.}$$

$$y = -\frac{3}{2}x + 6 \qquad \text{Divide both sides by 2.}$$

- Next, we press ⟨ Y= ⟩ and enter the right side of the equation. The screen is shown in Figure 2-9(a).
- We then press ⟨GRAPH⟩ to obtain the graph shown in Figure 2-9(b).

(a)   (b)

FIGURE 2-9

In Figure 2-9, the graph intersects the y-axis at the point $(0, 6)$, which is called the **y-intercept.** It intersects the x-axis at the point $(4, 0)$, which is called the **x-intercept.**

Intercepts of a Line

The **y-intercept** of a line is the point $(0, b)$, where the line intersects the y-axis. To find b, substitute 0 for x in the equation of the line and solve for y.

The **x-intercept** of a line is the point $(a, 0)$, where the line intersects the x-axis. To find a, substitute 0 for y in the equation of the line and solve for x.

EXAMPLE 3   **Graphing a Line by Finding the Intercepts**

Use the x- and y-intercepts to graph the equation $3x + 2y = 12$.

SOLUTION   To find the y-intercept, we substitute 0 for x and solve for y. To find the x-intercept, we substitute 0 for y and solve for x. We will also find a third point as a check and then plot the points and draw the graph.

Find the y-intercept.

To find the y-intercept, we substitute 0 for x and solve for y.

$$3x + 2y = 12$$

$$3(0) + 2y = 12 \qquad \text{Substitute 0 for } x.$$

$$2y = 12 \qquad \text{Simplify.}$$

$$y = 6 \qquad \text{Divide both sides by 2.}$$

The y-intercept is the point $(0, 6)$.

Find the *x*-intercept.

To find the *x*-intercept, we substitute 0 for *y* and solve for *x*.

$$3x + 2y = 12$$

$$3x + 2(0) = 12 \qquad \text{Substitute 0 for } y.$$

$$3x = 12 \qquad \text{Simplify.}$$

$$x = 4 \qquad \text{Divide both sides by 3.}$$

The *x*-intercept is the point $(4, 0)$.

Find a third point as a check.

If we let $x = 2$, we will find that $y = 3$.

$$3x + 2y = 12$$

$$3(2) + 2y = 12 \qquad \text{Substitute 2 for } x.$$

$$6 + 2y = 12 \qquad \text{Simplify.}$$

$$2y = 6 \qquad \text{Subtract 6 from both sides.}$$

$$y = 3 \qquad \text{Divide both sides by 2.}$$

The point $(2, 3)$ satisfies the equation.

We plot each pair (as in Figure 2-10) and join them with a line to get the graph of the equation.

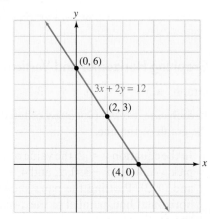

$3x + 2y = 12$		
x	y	(x, y)
0	6	$(0, 6)$
2	3	$(2, 3)$
4	0	$(4, 0)$

FIGURE 2-10

Self Check 3   Graph: $2x - 3y = 12$.

Now Try Exercise 47.

ACCENT ON TECHNOLOGY   **Finding Intercepts Using Zoom and Trace**

We can use the trace feature on a graphing calculator to find the approximate coordinates of any point on a graph. When we press TRACE, a flashing cursor will appear on the screen. The coordinates of the cursor will also appear at the bottom of the screen.

- To find the *y*-intercept of the graph of $2y = -5x - 7$ (or $y = -\frac{5}{2}x - \frac{7}{2}$), we graph the equation, using $[-10, 10]$ for *x* and $[-10, 10]$ for *y*, and press TRACE to get Figure 2-11(a). We see from the figure that the *y*-intercept is $(0, -3.5)$.

- We can approximate the x-intercept by using the left arrow key and moving the cursor toward the x-intercept until we arrive at a point with the coordinates shown in Figure 2-11(b). We see from the graph that the x-coordinate of the x-intercept is approximately -1.489362.

  To get better results, we can zoom in to get a magnified picture, trace again, and move the cursor to the point with coordinates shown in Figure 2-11(c). Since the y-coordinate is almost 0, we now have a good approximation for the x-intercept. The x-coordinate of the x-intercept is approximately -1.382979. We can achieve better results with repeated zooms.

(a)

(b)

(c)

FIGURE 2-11

3. Graph Horizontal and Vertical Lines

In the next example, we will graph a horizontal and a vertical line.

EXAMPLE 4   **Graphing Horizontal and Vertical Lines**

Graph: **a.** $y = 2$ **b.** $x = -3$

SOLUTION   In each case, we will plot a few ordered pairs that satisfy the equation and then draw the graph of the line.

a. In the equation $y = 2$, the value of y is always 2. Any value can be used for x. If we pick x-values of $-3, 0, 2,$ and 4, we get the ordered pairs: $(-3, 2)$, $(0, 2)$, $(2, 2)$, and $(4, 2)$. Plotting the pairs shown in Figure 2-12, we see that the graph is a horizontal line, parallel to the x-axis and having a y-intercept of $(0, 2)$. The line has no x-intercept.

b. In the equation $x = -3$, the value of x is always -3. Any value can be used for y. If we pick y-values of $-2, 0, 2$ and 3, we get the ordered pairs: $(-3, -2)$, $(-3, 0)$, $(-3, 2)$ and $(-3, 3)$. After plotting the pairs shown in Figure 2-12, we see that the graph is a vertical line, parallel to the y-axis and having an x-intercept of $(-3, 0)$. The line has no y-intercept.

$y = 2$		
x	y	(x, y)
-3	2	$(-3, 2)$
0	2	$(0, 2)$
2	2	$(2, 2)$
4	2	$(4, 2)$

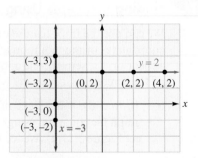

$x = -3$		
x	y	(x, y)
-3	-2	$(-3, -2)$
-3	0	$(-3, 0)$
-3	2	$(-3, 2)$
-3	3	$(-3, 3)$

FIGURE 2-12

Self Check 4   Graph: **a.** $x = 2$ **b.** $y = -3$

Now Try Exercise 51.

Example 4 suggests the following facts.

Equations of Vertical and Horizontal Lines   If a and b are real numbers, then

- The graph of the equation $x = a$ is a vertical line with x-intercept of $(a, 0)$. If $a = 0$, the line $x = 0$ is the y-axis.
- The graph of the equation $y = b$ is a horizontal line with y-intercept of $(0, b)$. If $b = 0$, the line $y = 0$ is the x-axis.

---

4. Solve Applications Using Linear Equations

EXAMPLE 5   **Solving an Application Problem**

A computer purchased for \$2,750 is expected to depreciate according to the formula $y = -550x + \$2{,}750$, where y is the value of the computer after x years. When will the computer be worth nothing?

SOLUTION   The computer will have no value when its value (y) is 0. To find x when $y = 0$, we substitute 0 for y and solve for x.

$$y = -550x + 2{,}750$$

$$0 = -550x + 2{,}750$$

$$-2{,}750 = -550x \qquad \text{Subtract 2,750 from both sides.}$$

$$5 = x \qquad \text{Divide both sides by } -550.$$

The computer will have no value in 5 years.

Self Check 5   When will the value of the computer be \$1,650?

Now Try Exercise 97.

5. Find the Distance between Two Points

To derive the formula used to find the distance between two points on a rectangular coordinate system, we use **subscript notation** and denote the points as

$P(x_1, y_1)$ Read as "point P with coordinates of x sub 1 and y sub 1."

$Q(x_2, y_2)$ Read as "point Q with coordinates of x sub 2 and y sub 2."

If $P(x_1, y_1)$ and $Q(x_2, y_2)$ are two points in Figure 2-13 and point R has coordinates (x_2, y_1), triangle PQR is a right triangle. By the Pythagorean Theorem, the square of the hypotenuse of right triangle PQR is equal to the sum of the squares of the two legs. Because leg RQ is vertical, the square of its length is $(y_2 - y_1)^2$. Since leg PR is horizontal, the square of its length is $(x_2 - x_1)^2$. Thus, we have

$$(1) \quad d^2 = (x_2 - x_1)^2 + (y_2 - y_1)^2$$

Because equal positive numbers have equal positive square roots, we can take the positive square root of both sides of Equation 1 to obtain the **Distance Formula**.

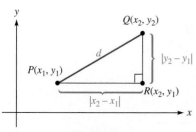

FIGURE 2-13

The Distance Formula   The distance d between points (x_1, y_1) and (x_2, y_2) is given by

$$d = \sqrt{(x_2 - x_1)^2 + (y_2 - y_1)^2}$$

EXAMPLE 6   **Finding the Distance between Two Points**

Find the distance between $P(-1, -2)$ and $Q(-7, 8)$.

SOLUTION   We use the Distance Formula, $d = \sqrt{(x_2 - x_1)^2 + (y_2 - y_1)^2}$, to find the distance between $P(-1, -2)$ and $Q(-7, 8)$.

If we let $P(-1, -2) = P(x_1, y_1)$ and $Q(-7, 8) = Q(x_2, y_2)$, we can substitute -1 for x_1, -2 for y_1, -7 for x_2, and 8 for y_2 into the formula and simplify.

$$d(PQ) = \sqrt{(x_2 - x_1)^2 + (y_2 - \mathbf{y_1})^2}$$ Read $d(PQ)$ as "the length of segment PQ."

$$d(PQ) = \sqrt{[-7 - (-1)]^2 + [8 - (\mathbf{-2})]^2}$$

$$= \sqrt{(-6)^2 + (10)^2}$$

$$= \sqrt{36 + 100}$$

$$= \sqrt{136}$$

$$= \sqrt{4 \cdot 34}$$

$$= 2\sqrt{34}$$ $\sqrt{4 \cdot 34} = \sqrt{4}\sqrt{34} = 2\sqrt{34}$

Self Check 6   Find the distance between $P(-2, -5)$ and $Q(3, 7)$.

Now Try Exercise 73.

6. Find the Midpoint of a Line Segment

If point M in Figure 2-14 lies midway between points $P(x_1, y_1)$ and $Q(x_2, y_2)$, point M is called the **midpoint** of segment PQ. To find the coordinates of M, we find the average of the x-coordinates and the average of the y-coordinates of P and Q.

The Midpoint Formula   The midpoint of the line segment with endpoints at $P(x_1, y_1)$ and $Q(x_2, y_2)$ is the point M with coordinates of

$$M = \left(\frac{x_1 + x_2}{2}, \frac{y_1 + y_2}{2} \right)$$

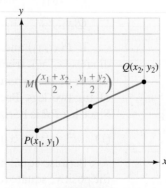

FIGURE 2-14

You will be asked to prove this formula in Exercise 107 by using the Distance Formula to show that $d(PM) + d(MQ) = d(PQ)$.

EXAMPLE 7 Finding the Midpoint of a Line Segment

Find the midpoint of the segment joining $P(-7, 2)$ and $Q(1, -4)$.

SOLUTION We use the Midpoint Formula, $M = \left(\dfrac{x_1 + x_2}{2}, \dfrac{y_1 + y_2}{2} \right)$ to find the midpoint of the line segment joining $P(-7, 2)$ and $Q(1, -4)$. To do so, we substitute $P(-7, 2)$ for $P(x_1, y_1)$ and $Q(1, -4)$ for $Q(x_2, y_2)$ into the Midpoint Formula to get

$$x_M = \frac{x_1 + x_2}{2} \quad \text{and} \quad y_M = \frac{y_1 + y_2}{2}$$
$$= \frac{-7 + 1}{2} \qquad\qquad = \frac{2 + (-4)}{2}$$
$$= \frac{-6}{2} \qquad\qquad\quad = \frac{-2}{2}$$
$$= -3 \qquad\qquad\qquad = -1$$

The midpoint is $M(-3, -1)$.

Self Check 7 Find the midpoint of the segment joining $P(-7, -8)$ and $Q(-2, 10)$.

Now Try Exercise 83.

EXAMPLE 8 Using Midpoint Formula to Find Coordinates

The midpoint of the segment joining $P(-3, 2)$ and $Q(x_2, y_2)$ is $M(1, 4)$. Find the coordinates of Q.

SOLUTION We can let $P(x_1, y_1) = P(-3, 2)$ and $M(x_M, y_M) = M(1, 4)$, and then find the coordinates x_2 and y_2 of point $Q(x_2, y_2)$.

$$x_M = \frac{x_1 + x_2}{2} \quad \text{and} \quad y_M = \frac{y_1 + y_2}{2}$$
$$1 = \frac{-3 + x_2}{2} \qquad\qquad 4 = \frac{2 + y_2}{2}$$
$$2 = -3 + x_2 \qquad\qquad 8 = 2 + y_2 \qquad \text{Multiply both sides by 2.}$$
$$5 = x_2 \qquad\qquad\qquad 6 = y_2$$

The coordinates of point Q are $(5, 6)$.

Self Check 8 If the midpoint of a segment PQ is $M(2, -5)$ and one endpoint is $Q(6, 9)$, find P.

Now Try Exercise 87.

Self Check Answers

1.

2.

3.

4.

5. 2 years   6. 13   7. $M\left(-\dfrac{9}{2}, 1 \right)$ 8. $(-2, -19)$

Exercises **2.1**

Getting Ready

You should be able to complete these vocabulary and concept statements before you proceed to the practice exercises.

Fill in the blanks.

1. The coordinate axes divide the plane into four _____.

2. The coordinate axes intersect at the _____.

3. The positive direction on the x-axis is _____.

4. The positive direction on the y-axis is _____.

5. The x-coordinate is the _____ coordinate in an ordered pair.

6. The y-coordinate is the _____ coordinate in an ordered pair.

7. A _____ equation is an equation whose graph is a line.

8. The point where a line intersects the _____ is called the y-intercept.

9. The point where a line intersects the x-axis is called the _____.

10. The graph of the equation $x = a$ will be a _____ line.

11. The graph of the equation $y = b$ will be a _____ line.

12. Complete the Distance Formula:

    $d = $ _____.

13. If a point divides a segment into two equal segments, the point is called the _____ of the segment.

14. The midpoint of the segment joining $P(x_1, y_1)$ and $Q(x_2, y_2)$ is _____.

Practice

Refer to the illustration and determine the coordinates of each point.

15. A 16. B

17. C 18. D

19. E 20. F

21. G 22. H

Graph each point. Indicate the quadrant in which the point lies, or the axis on which it lies.

23. $(2, 5)$ 24. $(-3, 4)$

25. $(-4, -5)$ 26. $(6, 2)$

27. $(5, 2)$ 28. $(3, -4)$

29. $(4, 0)$ 30. $(0, 2)$

Solve each equation for y and graph the equation. Then check your graph with a graphing calculator.

31. $y - 2x = 7$ 32. $y + 3 = -4x$

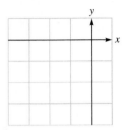

33. $y + 5x = 5$ 34. $y - 3x = 6$

35. $6x - 3y = 10$ 36. $4x + 8y - 1 = 0$

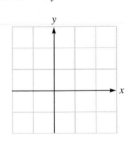

37. $3x = 6y - 1$ 38. $2x + 1 = 4y$

39. $2(x + y + 1) = x + 2$ **40.** $5(x + 2) = 3y - x$

Find the x- and y-intercepts and use them to graph each equation.

41. $x + y = 5$ **42.** $x - y = 3$

     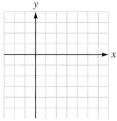

43. $2x - y = 4$ **44.** $3x + y = 9$

45. $3x + 2y = 6$ **46.** $2x - 3y = 6$

47. $4x - 5y = 20$ **48.** $3x - 5y = 15$

Graph each equation.

49. $y = 3$ **50.** $x = -4$

     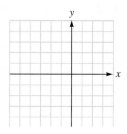

51. $3x + 5 = -1$ **52.** $7y - 1 = 6$

53. $3(y + 2) = y$ **54.** $4 + 3y = 3(x + y)$

55. $3(y + 2x) = 6x + y$ **56.** $5(y - x) = x + 5y$

Use a graphing calculator to graph each equation and then find the x-coordinate of the x-intercept to the nearest hundredth.

57. $y = 3.7x - 4.5$ **58.** $y = \dfrac{3}{5}x + \dfrac{5}{4}$

59. $1.5x - 3y = 7$ **60.** $0.3x + y = 7.5$

Find the distance between P and O(0, 0).

61. $P(4, -3)$ **62.** $P(-5, 12)$

63. $P(-3, 2)$ **64.** $P(5, 0)$

65. $P(1, 1)$ **66.** $P(6, -8)$

67. $P\left(\sqrt{3}, 1\right)$ **68.** $P\left(\sqrt{7}, \sqrt{2}\right)$

Find the distance between P and Q.

69. $P(3, 7)$; $Q(6, 3)$ **70.** $P(4, 9)$; $Q(9, 21)$

71. $P(4, -6)$; $Q(-1, 6)$ **72.** $P(0, 5)$; $Q(6, -3)$

73. $P(-2, -15)$; $Q(-6, -21)$ **74.** $P(-7, 11)$; $Q(-11, 7)$

75. $P(3, -3)$; $Q(-5, 5)$ **76.** $P(6, -3)$; $Q(-3, 2)$

77. $P(\pi, -2)$; $Q(\pi, 5)$ **78.** $P\left(\sqrt{5}, 0\right)$; $Q(0, 2)$

Find the midpoint of the line segment PQ.

79. $P(2, 4)$; $Q(6, 8)$ **80.** $P(3, -6)$; $Q(-1, -6)$

81. $P(2, -5)$; $Q(-2, 7)$ **82.** $P(0, 3)$; $Q(-10, -13)$

83. $P(-8, 5)$; $Q(6, -4)$ **84.** $P(3, -2)$; $Q(2, -3)$

85. $P(0, 0)$; $Q\left(\sqrt{5}, \sqrt{5}\right)$ **86.** $P\left(\sqrt{3}, 0\right)$; $Q\left(0, -\sqrt{5}\right)$

One endpoint P and the midpoint M of line segment PQ are given. Find the coordinates of the other endpoint, Q.

87. $P(1, 4)$; $M(3, 5)$ **88.** $P(2, -7)$; $M(-5, 6)$

89. $P(5, -5)$; $M(5, 5)$ **90.** $P(-7, 3)$; $M(0, 0)$

91. Show that a triangle with vertices at $(13, -2)$, $(9, -8)$, and $(5, -2)$ is isosceles.

92. Show that a triangle with vertices at $(-1, 2)$, $(3, 1)$, and $(4, 5)$ is isosceles.

93. In the illustration, points M and N are the midpoints of AC and BC, respectively. Find the length of MN.

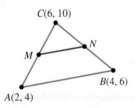

94. In the illustration, points M and N are the midpoints of AC and BC, respectively. Show that $d(MN) = \frac{1}{2}[d(AB)]$.

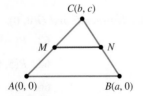

95. In the illustration, point M is the midpoint of the hypotenuse of right triangle AOB. Show that the area of rectangle $OLMN$ is one-half of the area of triangle AOB.

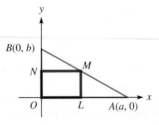

96. Rectangle $ABCD$ in the illustration is twice as long as it is wide, and its sides are parallel to the coordinate axes. If the perimeter is 42, find the coordinates of point C.

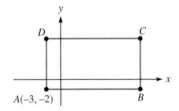

Applications

97. **House appreciation** A house purchased for \$225,000 is expected to appreciate according to the formula $y = 17{,}500x + 225{,}000$, where y is the value of the house after x years. Find the value of the house 5 years later.

98. **Car depreciation** A Chevy Cruze car purchased for \$17,000 is expected to depreciate according to the formula $y = -1{,}360x + 17{,}000$, where y is the value of the car after x years. When will the car be worthless?

99. Demand equations The number of photo scanners that consumers buy depends on price. The higher the price, the fewer photo scanners people will buy. The equation that relates price to the number of photo scanners sold at that price is called a **demand equation.** If the demand equation for a photo scanner is $p = -\frac{1}{10}q + 170$, where p is the price and q is the number of photo scanners sold at that price, how many photo scanners will be sold at a price of $150?

100. Supply equations The number of television sets that manufacturers produce depends on price. The higher the price, the more TVs manufacturers will produce. The equation that relates price to the number of TVs produced at that price is called a **supply equation.** If the supply equation for a 25-inch TV is $p = \frac{1}{10}q + 130$, where p is the price and q is the number of TVs produced for sale at that price, how many TVs will be produced if the price is $150?

101. Meshing gears The rotational speed V of a large gear (with N teeth) is related to the speed v of the smaller gear (with n teeth) by the equation $V = \frac{nv}{N}$. If the larger gear in the illustration is making 60 revolutions per minute, how fast is the smaller gear spinning?

102. Crime prevention The number n of incidents of family violence requiring police response appears to be related to d, the money spent on crisis intervention, by the equation $n = 430 - 0.005d$. What expenditure would reduce the number of incidents to 350?

103. Navigation See the illustration. An ocean liner is located 23 miles east and 72 miles north of Pigeon Cove Lighthouse, and its home port is 47 miles west and 84 miles south of the lighthouse. How far is the ship from port?

104. Engineering Two holes are to be drilled at locations specified by the engineering drawing shown in the illustration. Find the distance between the centers of the holes.

Discovery and Writing
105. Explain how to graph a line using the intercept method.

106. Explain how to determine the quadrant in which the point $P(a, b)$ lies.

107. In Figure 2-14, show that $d(PM) + d(MQ) = d(PQ)$.

108. Use the result of Exercise 107 to explain why point M is the midpoint of segment PQ.

Review
Graph each interval on the number line.

109. $[-3, 2) \cup (-2, 3]$

110. $(-1, 4) \cap [-2, 2]$

111. $[-3, -2) \cap (2, 3]$

112. $[-4, -3) \cup (2, 3]$

Solve each equation.

113. $\dfrac{3}{y + 6} = \dfrac{4}{y + 4}$

114. $\dfrac{z + 4}{z^2 + z} - \dfrac{z + 1}{z^2 + 2z} = \dfrac{8}{z^2 + 3z + 2}$

2.2 The Slope of a Nonvertical Line

In this section, we will learn to

1. Find the slope of a line.

2. Use slope to solve applications.

3. Find slopes of horizontal and vertical lines.

4. Find slopes of parallel and perpendicular lines.

© dk/Alamy

The world's steepest passenger railway is the Lookout Mountain Incline Railway in Chattanooga, Tennessee. Passengers experience breathtaking views of the city and surrounding mountains as the trolley-style railcars travel up Lookout Mountain. The grade or steepness of the track is 72.7% near the top.

Mathematicians use the term **slope** to represent the measure of the steepness of a line. We will explore the topic of slope in this section because it has many real-life applications.

1. Find the Slope of a Line

Suppose that a college student rents a room for $300 per month, plus a $200 nonrefundable deposit. The table shown in Figure 2-15(b) gives the cost (y) for different numbers of months (x). If we construct a graph from these data, we get the line shown in Figure 2-15(a).

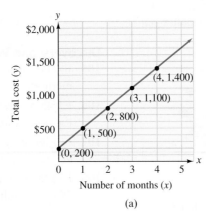

Time in Months	Total Cost
x	y
0	200
1	500
2	800
3	1,100
4	1,400

(a)   (b)

FIGURE 2-15

From the graph, we can see that if x changes from 0 to 1, y changes from 200 to 500. As x changes from 1 to 2, y changes from 500 to 800, and so on. The ratio of the change in y divided by the change in x is the constant 300.

$$\frac{\text{Change in } y}{\text{Change in } x} = \frac{500 - 200}{1 - 0} = \frac{800 - 500}{2 - 1} = \frac{1{,}100 - 800}{3 - 2} = \frac{1{,}400 - 1{,}100}{4 - 3} = \frac{300}{1} = 300$$

The ratio of the change in y divided by the change in x between any two points on any line is always a constant. This constant rate of change is called the **slope** of the line.

The Slope of a Nonvertical Line
The **slope of the nonvertical line** (see Figure 2-16) passing through points $P(x_1, y_1)$ and $Q(x_2, y_2)$ is

$$m = \frac{\text{change in } y}{\text{change in } x} = \frac{y_2 - y_1}{x_2 - x_1} \qquad (x_2 \neq x_1)$$

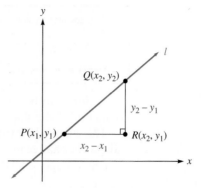

FIGURE 2-16

Comment

Slope is often considered to be a measure of the steepness or tilt of a line. Note that we can use the coordinates of any two points on a line to compute the slope of the line.

EXAMPLE 1   **Finding the Slope of a Line Given Two Points**

Find the slope of the line passing through $P(-1, -2)$ and $Q(7, 8)$.

SOLUTION   We will substitute the points $P(-1, -2)$ and $Q(7, 8)$ into the slope formula, $m = \dfrac{\text{change in } y}{\text{change in } x} = \dfrac{y_2 - y_1}{x_2 - x_1}$, to find the slope of the line.

Let $P(x_1, y_1) = P(-1, -2)$ and $Q(x_2, y_2) = Q(7, 8)$. Then we substitute -1 for x_1, -2 for y_1, 7 for x_2, and 8 for y_2 to get

$$m = \frac{\text{change in } y}{\text{change in } x}$$

$$m = \frac{y_2 - y_1}{x_2 - x_1}$$

$$= \frac{8 - (-2)}{7 - (-1)}$$

$$= \frac{10}{8}$$

$$= \frac{5}{4}$$

The slope of the line is $\frac{5}{4}$. See Figure 2-17.

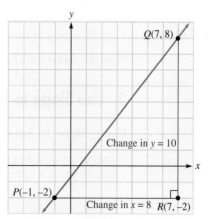

FIGURE 2-17

We would have obtained the same result if we had let $P(x_1, y_1) = P(7, 8)$ and $Q(x_2, y_2) = Q(-1, -2)$.

Self Check 1   Find the slope of the line passing through $P(-3, -4)$ and $Q(5, 9)$.

Now Try Exercise 13.

Caution

> When calculating slope, always subtract the y-values and the x-values in the same order.
>
> $$m = \frac{y_2 - y_1}{x_2 - x_1} \quad \text{or} \quad m = \frac{y_1 - y_2}{x_1 - x_2}$$
>
> Otherwise, we will obtain an *incorrect* result.

A slope can be a positive real number, 0, or a negative real number. If the denominator of the slope formula is 0, slope is not defined.

The change in y (often denoted as Δy) is the **rise** of the line between points P and Q. The change in x (often denoted as Δx) is the **run.** Using this terminology, we can define slope to be the ratio of the rise to the run:

$$m = \frac{y_2 - y_1}{x_2 - x_1} = \frac{\Delta y}{\Delta x} = \frac{\text{rise}}{\text{run}} \qquad (\Delta x \neq 0)$$

EXAMPLE 2   Finding the Slope of a Line Given Its Equation in Standard Form

Find the slope of the line determined by $5x + 2y = 10$. (See Figure 2-18.)

SOLUTION   We will find the coordinates of the x- and y-intercepts and substitute into slope formula, $m = \dfrac{\text{change in } y}{\text{change in } x} = \dfrac{y_2 - y_1}{x_2 - x_1}$, to find the slope of the line

- If $y = 0$, then $x = 2$, and the point $(2, 0)$ lies on the line.
- If $x = 0$, then $y = 5$, and the point $(0, 5)$ lies on the line.

We then find the slope of the line between $P(2, 0)$ and $Q(0, 5)$.

$$m = \frac{\text{change in } y}{\text{change in } x}$$

$$m = \frac{y_2 - y_1}{x_2 - x_1}$$

$$= \frac{5 - 0}{0 - 2}$$

$$= -\frac{5}{2}$$

The slope is $-\frac{5}{2}$.

$5x + 2y = 10$

FIGURE 2-18

Self Check 2   Find the slope of the line determined by $3x - 2y = 9$.

Now Try Exercise 27.

2. Use Slope to Solve Applications

EXAMPLE 3   Using Slope to Solve an Application Problem

If carpet costs $25 per square yard plus a delivery charge of $30, the total cost C of n square yards is given by the formula

Total cost	equals	cost per square yard	times	the number of square yards purchased	plus	the delivery charge.
C	=	25	·	n	+	30

Graph the equation $C = 25n + 30$ and interpret the slope of the line.

SOLUTION   We will complete a table of solutions and graph the equation on a coordinate system with a vertical C-axis and a horizontal n-axis. Figure 2-19 shows a table of ordered pairs and the graph.

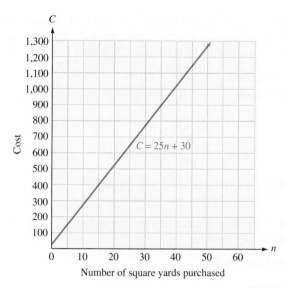

$C = 25n + 30$		
n	C	(n, C)
10	280	(10, 280)
20	530	(20, 530)
30	780	(30, 780)
40	1,030	(40, 1,030)
50	1,280	(50, 1,280)

FIGURE 2-19

If we pick the points (30, 780) and (50, 1,280) to find the slope, we have

$$m = \frac{\Delta C}{\Delta n}$$

$$= \frac{C_2 - C_1}{n_2 - n_1}$$

$$= \frac{1{,}280 - 780}{50 - 30} \qquad \text{Substitute 1,280 for } C_2\text{, 780 for } C_1\text{, 50 for } n_2\text{, and 30 for } n_1.$$

$$= \frac{500}{20}$$

$$= 25$$

The slope of 25 (in dollars/square yard) is the cost per square yard of the carpet. ■

Self Check 3   If the cost of the carpet in Example 3 increases to $35 per square yard, find the slope of the line.

Now Try Exercise 81.

EXAMPLE 4   **Solving an Application Problem**

It takes a skier 25 minutes to complete the course shown in Figure 2-20. Find his average rate of descent in feet per minute.

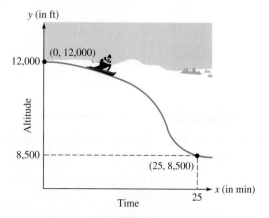

FIGURE 2-20

SOLUTION To find the average rate of descent, we will find the ratio of the change in altitude to the change in time. To find this ratio, we will calculate the slope of the line passing through the points (0, 12,000) and (25, 8,500).

$$\begin{array}{c}\text{Average rate}\\\text{of descent}\end{array} = \frac{12{,}000 - 8{,}500}{0 - 25}$$

$$= \frac{3{,}500}{-25}$$

$$= -140$$

The average rate of descent is 140 ft/min. ∎

Self Check 4 If it takes the skier 20 minutes to complete the course, find his average rate of descent in feet per minute.

Now Try Exercise 83.

3. Find Slopes of Horizontal and Vertical Lines

If $P(x_1, y_1)$ and $Q(x_2, y_2)$ are points on the horizontal line shown in Figure 2-21(a), then $y_1 = y_2$, and the numerator of the fraction is 0.

$$\frac{y_2 - y_1}{x_2 - x_1} \qquad \text{On a horizontal line, } x_2 \neq x_1.$$

Thus, the value of the fraction is 0, and the slope of the horizontal line is 0.

If $P(x_1, y_1)$ and $Q(x_2, y_2)$ are points on the vertical line shown in Figure 2-21(b), then $x_1 = x_2$, and the denominator of the fraction is 0.

$$\frac{y_2 - y_1}{x_2 - x_1} \qquad \text{On a vertical line, } y_2 \neq y_1.$$

Since the denominator of a fraction cannot be 0, the slope of a vertical line is not defined.

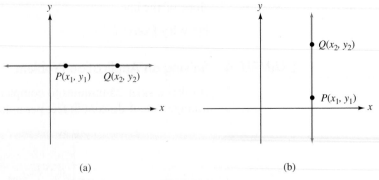

(a)   (b)

FIGURE 2-21

Slopes of Horizontal and Vertical Lines

The slope of a horizontal line (a line with an equation of the form $y = b$) is 0.

The slope of a vertical line (a line with an equation of the form $x = a$) is not defined.

Here are a few facts about slope. See Figure 2-22.

- If a line rises as we follow it from left to right, as in Figure 2-22(a), its slope is positive.
- If a line drops as we follow it from left to right, as in Figure 2-22(b), its slope is negative.
- If a line is horizontal, as in Figure 2-22(c), its slope is 0.
- If a line is vertical, as in Figure 2-22(d), it has no defined slope.

Slope Concepts

Positive slope | Negative slope | Zero slope | Undefined slope

(a)   (b)   (c)   (d)

FIGURE 2-22

4. Find Slopes of Parallel and Perpendicular Lines

To see a relationship between parallel lines and their slopes, we refer to the parallel lines l_1 and l_2 shown in Figure 2-23, with slopes of m_1 and m_2, respectively. Because right triangles ABC and DEF are similar, it follows that

$$m_1 = \frac{\Delta y \text{ of } l_1}{\Delta x \text{ of } l_1} = \frac{\Delta y \text{ of } l_2}{\Delta x \text{ of } l_2} = m_2$$

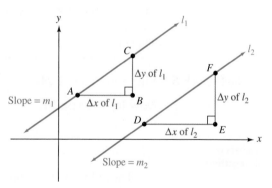

FIGURE 2-23

This shows that if two nonvertical lines are parallel, they have the same slope. It is also true that when two lines have the same slope, they are parallel.

Slopes of Parellel Lines   Nonvertical parallel lines have the same slope, and lines having the same slope are parallel.

Since vertical lines are parallel, lines with undefined slopes are parallel.

EXAMPLE 5   **Solving a Slope Problem Involving Parallel Lines**

The lines in Figure 2-24 are parallel. Find y.

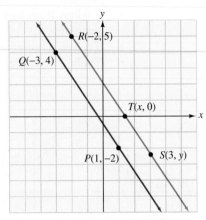

FIGURE 2-24

SOLUTION   Since the lines are parallel, their slopes are equal. To find y, we will find the slope of each line, set them equal, and solve the resulting equation.

Slope of PQ = slope of RS

$$\frac{-2 - 4}{1 - (-3)} = \frac{y - 5}{3 - (-2)}$$

$$\frac{-6}{4} = \frac{y - 5}{5} \qquad \text{Simplify.}$$

$$-30 = 4(y - 5) \qquad \text{Multiply both sides by 20.}$$

$$-30 = 4y - 20 \qquad \text{Remove parentheses and simplify.}$$

$$-10 = 4y \qquad \text{Add 20 to both sides.}$$

$$-\frac{5}{2} = y \qquad \text{Divide both sides by 4 and simplify.}$$

Thus, $y = -\frac{5}{2}$.   ∎

Self Check 5   Find x in Figure 2-24.

Now Try Exercise 59.

Comment

If the product of two numbers is -1, the numbers are called **negative reciprocals.**

The following theorem relates perpendicular lines and their slopes.

Slopes of Perpendicular Lines   If two nonvertical lines are perpendicular, the product of their slopes is -1.

If the product of the slopes of two lines is -1, the lines are perpendicular.

PROOF   Suppose l_1 and l_2 are lines with slopes of m_1 and m_2 that intersect at some point. See Figure 2-25. Then superimpose a coordinate system over the lines so that the intersection point is the origin. Let $P(a, b)$ be a point on l_1, and let $Q(c, d)$ be a point on l_2. Neither point P nor point Q can be the origin.

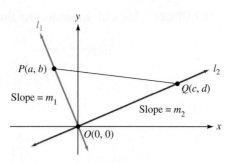

FIGURE 2-25

First, we suppose that l_1 and l_2 are perpendicular. Then triangle POQ is a right triangle with its right angle at O. By the Pythagorean Theorem,

$$d(OP)^2 + d(OQ)^2 = d(PQ)^2$$

$$(a - 0)^2 + (b - 0)^2 + (c - 0)^2 + (d - 0)^2 = (a - c)^2 + (b - d)^2$$

$$a^2 + b^2 + c^2 + d^2 = a^2 - 2ac + c^2 + b^2 - 2bd + d^2$$

$$0 = -2ac - 2bd$$

$$bd = -ac$$

(1) $$\frac{b}{a} \cdot \frac{d}{c} = -1$$ Divide both sides by ac.

The coordinates of P are (a, b), and the coordinates of O are $(0, 0)$. Using the definition of slope, we have

$$m_1 = \frac{b - 0}{a - 0} = \frac{b}{a}$$

Similarly, we have

$$m_2 = \frac{d}{c}$$

We substitute m_1 for $\frac{b}{a}$ and m_2 for $\frac{d}{c}$ in Equation 1 to obtain

$$m_1 m_2 = -1$$

Hence, if lines l_1 and l_2 are perpendicular, the product of their slopes is -1.

Conversely, we suppose that the product of the slopes of lines l_1 and l_2 is -1. Because the steps in the previous discussion are reversible, we have $d(OP)^2 + d(OQ)^2 = d(PQ)^2$. By the Pythagorean Theorem, triangle POQ is a right triangle. Thus, l_1 and l_2 are perpendicular.

Comment

It is also true that a horizontal line is perpendicular to a vertical line.

EXAMPLE 6   **Solving a Slope Problem Involving Perpendicular Lines**

Are the lines shown in Figure 2-26 perpendicular?

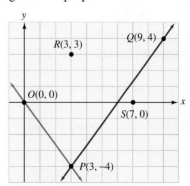

FIGURE 2-26

SOLUTION   We will determine the slopes of the lines and see whether their product is –1.

$$\text{Slope of } OP = \frac{\Delta y}{\Delta x} \qquad\qquad \text{Slope of } PQ = \frac{\Delta y}{\Delta x}$$

$$= \frac{y_2 - y_1}{x_2 - y_1} \qquad\qquad = \frac{y_2 - y_1}{x_2 - y_1}$$

$$= \frac{-4 - 0}{3 - 0} \qquad\qquad = \frac{4 - (-4)}{9 - 3}$$

$$= -\frac{4}{3} \qquad\qquad = \frac{8}{6}$$

$$\qquad\qquad\qquad\qquad = \frac{4}{3}$$

Since the product of the slopes is $-\frac{16}{9}$ and not -1, the lines are not perpendicular.

Self Check 6   Is either line in Figure 2-26 perpendicular to the line passing through R and S?

Now Try Exercise 55.

Self Check Answers   **1.** $\dfrac{13}{8}$ **2.** $\dfrac{3}{2}$ **3.** 35   **4.** 175 ft/min   **5.** $\dfrac{4}{3}$ **6.** yes

Exercises **2.2**

Getting Ready
You should be able to complete these vocabulary and concept statements before you proceed to the practice exercises.

Fill in the blanks.

1. The slope of a nonvertical line is defined to be the change in y _____ by the change in x.
2. The change in ___ is often called the rise.
3. The change in x is often called the ____.
4. When computing the slope from the coordinates of two points, always subtract the y-values and the x-values in the _____.
5. The symbol Δy means _____ y.
6. The slope of a _____ line is 0.
7. The slope of a _____ line is undefined.
8. If the slopes of two lines are equal, the lines are _____.
9. If the product of the slopes of two lines is -1, the lines are _____.
10. If two lines are perpendicular, the product of their slopes is ____.

Practice
Find the slope of the line passing through each pair of points, if possible.

11. $P(2, 2); Q(-1, -1)$

12. $P(3, -1); Q(5, 3)$

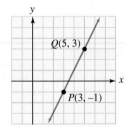

13. $P(-6, 3); Q(6, -2)$

14. $P(2, 5); Q(3, 10)$

15. $P(3, -2); Q(-1, 5)$

16. $P(3, 7); Q(6, 16)$

17. $P(8, -7); Q(4, 1)$

18. $P(5, 17)$; $Q(17, 17)$

19. $P(-4, 3)$; $Q(-4, -3)$

20. $P\left(2, \sqrt{7}\right)$; $Q\left(\sqrt{7}, 2\right)$

21. $P\left(\dfrac{3}{2}, \dfrac{2}{3}\right)$; $Q\left(\dfrac{5}{2}, \dfrac{7}{3}\right)$

22. $P\left(-\dfrac{2}{5}, \dfrac{1}{3}\right)$; $Q\left(\dfrac{3}{5}, -\dfrac{5}{3}\right)$

23. $P(a + b, c)$; $Q(b + c, a)$ assume $c \neq a$

24. $P(b, 0)$; $Q(a + b, a)$ assume $a \neq 0$

Find two points on the line and use slope formula to find the slope of the line.

25. $y = 3x + 2$

26. $y = 5x - 8$

27. $5x - 10y = 3$

28. $8y + 2x = 5$

29. $3(y + 2) = 2x - 3$

30. $4(x - 2) = 3y + 2$

31. $3(y + x) = 3(x - 1)$

32. $2x + 5 = 2(y + x)$

Find the slope of the line, if possible.

33. $y = 7$

34. $2y = 5$

35. $x = -\dfrac{1}{2}$

36. $x - 7 = 0$

Determine whether the slope of the line is positive, negative, 0, or undefined.

37.

38.

39.

40.

41.

42.

Determine whether the lines with the given slopes are parallel, perpendicular, or neither.

43. $m_1 = 3$; $m_2 = -\dfrac{1}{3}$

44. $m_1 = \dfrac{2}{3}$; $m_2 = \dfrac{3}{2}$

45. $m_1 = \sqrt{8}$; $m_2 = 2\sqrt{2}$

46. $m_1 = 1$; $m_2 = -1$

47. $m_1 = -\sqrt{2}$; $m_2 = \dfrac{\sqrt{2}}{2}$

48. $m_1 = 2\sqrt{7}$; $m_2 = \sqrt{28}$

49. $m_1 = -0.125$; $m_2 = 8$

50. $m_1 = 0.125$; $m_2 = \dfrac{1}{8}$

51. $m_1 = ab^{-1}$; $m_2 = -a^{-1}b$ $(a \neq 0, b \neq 0)$

52. $m_1 = \left(\dfrac{a}{b}\right)^{-1}$; $m_2 = -\dfrac{b}{a}$ $(a \neq 0, b \neq 0, a \neq b)$

Determine whether the line through the given points and the line through $R(-3, 5)$ and $S(2, 7)$ are parallel, perpendicular, or neither.

53. $P(2, 4)$; $Q(7, 6)$

54. $P(-3, 8)$; $Q(-13, 4)$

55. $P(-4, 6)$; $Q(-2, 1)$

56. $P(0, -9)$; $Q(4, 1)$

57. $P(a, a)$; $Q(3a, 6a)$ $(a \neq 0)$

58. $P(b, b)$; $Q(-b, 6b)$ $(b \neq 0)$

Lines PQ and RS are either parallel or perpendicular. Find x or y.

59. Parallel: $P(-3, 7)$; $Q(2, 9)$; $R(10, -4)$; $S(x, -6)$

60. Parallel: $P(2, -3)$; $Q(5, 7)$; $R(3, -1)$; $S(6, y)$

61. Perpendicular: $P(2, -7)$; $Q(1, 0)$; $R(-9, 5)$; $S(-2, y)$

62. Perpendicular: $P(1, -2)$; $Q(3, 4)$; $R(x, 6)$; $S(6, 5)$

Find the slopes of lines PQ and PR, and determine whether points P, Q, and R lie on the same line.

63. $P(-2, 8)$; $Q(-6, 9)$; $R(2, 5)$

64. $P(1, -1)$; $Q(3, -2)$; $R(-3, 0)$

65. $P(-a, a)$; $Q(0, 0)$; $R(a, -a)$

66. $P(a, a + b)$; $Q(a + b, b)$; $R(a - b, a)$

Determine which, if any, of the three lines PQ, PR, and QR are perpendicular.

67. $P(5, 4)$; $Q(2, -5)$; $R(8, -3)$

68. $P(8, -2)$; $Q(4, 6)$; $R(6, 7)$

69. $P(1, 3)$; $Q(1, 9)$; $R(7, 3)$

70. $P(2, -3)$; $Q(-3, 2)$; $R(3, 8)$

71. $P(0, 0)$; $Q(a, b)$; $R(-b, a)$

72. $P(a, b)$; $Q(-b, a)$; $R(a - b, a + b)$

73. **Right triangles** Show that the points $A(-1, -1)$, $B(-3, 4)$, and $C(4, 1)$ are the vertices of a right triangle.

74. **Right triangles** Show that the points $D(0, 1)$, $E(-1, 3)$, and $F(3, 5)$ are the vertices of a right triangle.

75. **Squares** Show that the points $A(1, -1)$, $B(3, 0)$, $C(2, 2)$, and $D(0, 1)$ are the vertices of a square.

76. Squares Show that the points $E(-1, -1)$, $F(3, 0)$, $G(2, 4)$, and $H(-2, 3)$ are the vertices of a square.

77. Parallelograms Show that the points $A(-2, -2)$, $B(3, 3)$, $C(2, 6)$, and $D(-3, 1)$ are the vertices of a parallelogram. (Show that both pairs of opposite sides are parallel.)

78. Trapezoids Show that points $E(1, -2)$, $F(5, 1)$, $G(3, 4)$, and $H(-3, 4)$ are the vertices of a trapezoid. (Show that only one pair of opposite sides is parallel.)

79. Geometry In the illustration, points M and N are midpoints of CB and BA, respectively. Show that MN is parallel to AC.

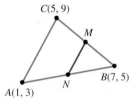

80. Geometry In the illustration, $d(AB) = d(AC)$. Show that AD is perpendicular to BC.

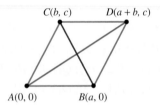

Applications

81. Rate of growth When a college started an aviation program, the administration agreed to predict enrollments using a straight-line method. If the enrollment during the first year was 12, and the enrollment during the fifth year was 26, find the rate of growth per year (the slope of the line). See the illustration.

82. Rate of growth A small business predicts sales according to a straight-line method. If sales were $50,000 in the first year and $110,000 in the third year, find the rate of growth in dollars per year (the slope of the line).

83. Rate of decrease The price of computers has been dropping steadily for the past ten years. If a desktop PC cost $6,700 ten years ago, and the same computing power cost $2,200 three years ago, find the rate of decrease per year. (Assume a straight-line model.)

84. Hospital costs The table shows the changing mean daily cost for a hospital room. For the ten-year period, find the rate of change per year of the portion of the room cost that is absorbed by the hospital.

Year	Total Cost to the Hospital	Amount Passed on to Patient
2000	$459	$212
2005	$670	$295
2010	$812	$307

85. Charting temperature changes The following Fahrenheit temperature readings were recorded over a four-hour period.

Time	12:00	1:00	2:00	3:00	4:00
Temperature	47°	53°	59°	65°	71°

Let t represent the time (in hours), with 12:00 corresponding to $t = 0$. Let T represent the temperature. Plot the points (t, T), and draw the line through those points. Explain the meaning of $\frac{\Delta T}{\Delta t}$.

86. Tracking the Dow The Dow Jones Industrial Averages at the close of trade on three consecutive days were as follows:

Day	Monday	Tuesday	Wednesday
Close	12,981	12,964	12,947

Let d represent the day, with $d = 0$ corresponding to Monday, and let D represent the Dow Jones average. Plot the points (d, D), and draw the graph. Explain the meaning of $\frac{\Delta D}{\Delta d}$.

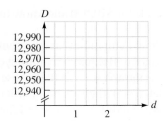

87. Speed of an airplane A pilot files a flight plan indicating her intention to fly at a constant speed of 590 mph. Write an equation that expresses the distance traveled in terms of the flying time. Then graph the equation and interpret the slope of the line. (*Hint: d = rt.*)

88. Growth of savings A student deposits $25 each month in a Holiday Club account at her bank. The account pays no interest. Write an equation that expresses the amount A in her account in terms of the number of deposits n. Then graph the line, and interpret the slope of the line.

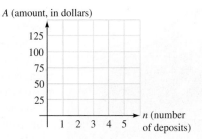

Discovery and Writing

89. Explain why the slope of a vertical line is undefined.

90. Explain how to determine whether two lines are parallel, perpendicular, or neither.

Review

Solve each equation for y and simplify.

91. $3x + 7y = 21$

92. $y - 3 = 5(x + 2)$

93. $\dfrac{x}{5} + \dfrac{y}{2} = 1$

94. $x - 5y = 15$

Factor each expression.

95. $6p^2 + p - 12$

96. $b^3 - 27$

97. $mp + mq + np + nq$

98. $x^4 + x^2 - 2$

2.3 Writing Equations of Lines

In this section, we will learn to

1. Use point-slope form to write an equation of a line.

2. Use slope-intercept form to write an equation of a line.

3. Graph linear equations using the slope and y-intercept.

4. Determine whether linear equations represent lines that are parallel, perpendicular, or neither.

5. Write equations of parallel and perpendicular lines.

6. Recognize and use the standard form of the equation of a line.

7. Write an equation of a line that models a real-life problem.

8. Use linear curve fitting to solve problems.

Suppose we purchase a Kawasaki motorcycle for $10,000 and know that it depreciates $1,200 in value each year.

We can use the facts given to write a linear equation that represents the value y of the motorcycle x years after it was purchased. Because the motorcycle's value decreases $1,200 each year, the slope of the line's graph is $-1,200$. Because the purchase price is $10,000, we know that when we let $x = 0$, the value of y will equal 10,000. A linear equation that satisfies these two conditions is $y = -1,200x + 10,000$. This equation represents the straight-line depreciation of the motorcycle.

In this section, we will write equations of lines given specific characteristics or features of the line.

1. Use Point-Slope Form to Write an Equation of a Line

Suppose that line l in Figure 2-27 has a slope of m and passes through the point $P(x_1, y_1)$. If $Q(x, y)$ is any other point on line l, we have

$$m = \frac{y - y_1}{x - x_1}$$

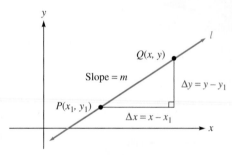

FIGURE 2-27

Comment

$y - y_1 = m(x - x_1)$ is often referred to as **point-slope formula** because we substitute a point and slope into it to write an equation of a line.

If we multiply both sides by $x - x_1$, we have

(1) $y - y_1 = m(x - x_1)$

Since Equation 1 displays the coordinates of the point (x_1, y_1) on the line and the slope m of the line, it is called the **point-slope form** of the equation of a line.

Point-Slope Form of an Equation of a Line

The equation of a line passing through $P(x_1, y_1)$ and with slope m is

$$y - y_1 = m(x - x_1).$$

EXAMPLE 1   **Writing an Equation of the Line with a Given Slope Passing through a Given Point**

Write an equation of the line with slope $-\frac{5}{3}$ and passing through $P(3, -1)$.

SOLUTION   We will substitute $-\frac{5}{3}$ for m, 3 for x_1, and -1 for y_1 in the point-slope form and simplify.

$$y - y_1 = \mathbf{m}(x - x_1) \qquad \text{This is the point-slope form.}$$

$$y - (-1) = -\frac{5}{3}(x - 3) \qquad \text{Substitute } -\frac{5}{3} \text{ for } m, 3 \text{ for } x_1, \text{ and } -1 \text{ for } y_1.$$

$$y + 1 = -\frac{5}{3}x + 5 \qquad \text{Remove parentheses.}$$

$$y = -\frac{5}{3}x + 4 \qquad \text{Subtract 1 from both sides.}$$

An equation of the line is $y = -\frac{5}{3}x + 4$.

Self Check 1   Write an equation of the line with slope $-\frac{2}{3}$ and passing through $P(-4, 5)$.

Now Try Exercise 11.

EXAMPLE 2   **Writing an Equation of the Line that Passes through Two Given Points**

Find an equation of the line passing through $P(3, 7)$ and $Q(-5, 3)$.

SOLUTION   We will find the slope of the line and then choose either point P or point Q and substitute both the slope and coordinates of the point into the point-slope form.

First we find the slope of the line.

$$m = \frac{y_2 - y_1}{x_2 - x_1} \qquad \text{This is the slope formula.}$$

$$= \frac{3 - 7}{-5 - 3} \qquad \text{Substitute 3 for } y_2, \text{7 for } y_1, -5 \text{ for } x_2, \text{and 3 for } x_1.$$

$$= \frac{-4}{-8}$$

$$= \frac{1}{2}$$

We can choose either point P or point Q and substitute its coordinates into the point-slope form. If we choose $P(3, 7)$, we substitute $\frac{1}{2}$ for m, 3 for x_1, and 7 for y_1.

$$y - y_1 = m(x - x_1) \qquad \text{This is the point-slope form.}$$

$$y - 7 = \frac{1}{2}(x - 3) \qquad \text{Substitute } \frac{1}{2} \text{ for } m, \text{3 for } x_1, \text{and 7 for } y_1.$$

$$y = \frac{1}{2}x - \frac{3}{2} + 7 \qquad \text{Remove parentheses and add 7 to both sides.}$$

$$y = \frac{1}{2}x + \frac{11}{2} \qquad -\frac{3}{2} + 7 = -\frac{3}{2} + \frac{14}{2} = \frac{11}{2}$$

An equation of the line is $y = \frac{1}{2}x + \frac{11}{2}$. ∎

Self Check 2   Find an equation of the line passing through $P(-5, 4)$ and $Q(8, -6)$.

Now Try Exercise 23.

2. Use Slope-Intercept Form to Write an Equation of a Line

FIGURE 2-28

Since the y-intercept of the line shown in Figure 2-28 is the point $P(0, b)$, we can write an equation of the line by substituting 0 for x_1 and b for y_1 into the point-slope form and simplifying.

$$y - y_1 = m(x - x_1) \qquad \text{This is the point-slope form.}$$

$$y - b = m(x - 0) \qquad \text{Substitute 0 for } x_1 \text{ and } b \text{ for } y_1.$$

$$y - b = mx \qquad x - 0 = x$$

$$(2) \qquad y = mx + b \qquad \text{Add } b \text{ to both sides.}$$

Because Equation 2 displays the slope m and the y-coordinate b of the y-intercept, it is called the **slope-intercept form** of the equation of a line.

Slope-Intercept Form of an Equation of a line   An equation of the line with slope m and y-intercept $(0, b)$ is

$$y = mx + b$$

Three examples of linear equations written in slope-intercept form are shown below.

Comment

Note that when a line is written in slope-intercept form the coefficient of x is the slope and the constant term is the y-coordinate of the y-intercept.

Example	Slope	y-Intercept
$y = 2x + 7$	$m = 2$	$b = 7;\ (0, 7)$
$y = \dfrac{2}{3}x - 5$	$m = \dfrac{2}{3}$	$b = -5;\ (0, -5)$
$y = -4x + \dfrac{1}{5}$	$m = -4$	$b = \dfrac{1}{5};\ \left(0, \dfrac{1}{5}\right)$

EXAMPLE 3

Using Slope-Intercept Form to Write an Equation of a Line

Use slope-intercept form to write an equation of the line with slope 4 that passes through $P(5, 9)$.

SOLUTION   Since we know that $m = 4$ and that the ordered pair $(5, 9)$ satisfies the equation, we substitute 4 for m, 5 for x, and 9 for y in the equation $y = mx + b$ and solve for b.

$$y = mx + b \qquad \text{This is the slope-intercept form.}$$

$$9 = 4(5) + b \qquad \text{Substitute 4 for } m, \text{ 5 for } x, \text{ and 9 for } y.$$

$$9 = 20 + b \qquad \text{Simplify.}$$

$$-11 = b \qquad \text{Subtract 20 from both sides.}$$

Comment

When we are given a point and slope we can determine an equation of the line by substituting into point-slope form or slope-intercept form.

Because $m = 4$ and $b = -11$, an equation is $y = 4x - 11$. ∎

Self Check 3   Use slope-intercept form to write an equation of the line with slope $\frac{7}{3}$ and passing through $(3, 1)$.

Now Try Exercise 37.

3. Graph Linear Equations Using the Slope and y-Intercept.

It is easy to graph a linear equation when it is written in slope-intercept form. For example, to graph $y = \frac{4}{3}x - 2$ we note that $b = -2$ and that the y-intercept is $(0, b) = (0, -2)$. (See Figure 2-29.)

Because the slope is $\frac{\Delta y}{\Delta x} = \frac{4}{3}$, we can locate another point Q on the line by starting at point P and counting 3 units to the right and 4 units up. The change in x from point P to point Q is $\Delta x = 3$, and the corresponding change in y is $\Delta y = 4$. The line joining points P and Q is the graph of the equation.

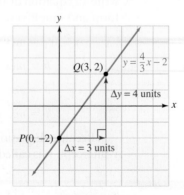

FIGURE 2-29

EXAMPLE 4   **Finding the Slope and y-Intercept of a Line and Graphing the Line**

Find the slope and the y-intercept of the line with equation $3(y + 2) = 6x - 1$ and graph it.

SOLUTION   We will write the equation in the form $y = mx + b$ to find the slope m and the y-intercept $(0, b)$. Then we will use m and b to graph the line.

$$3(y + 2) = 6x - 1$$

$$3y + 6 = 6x - 1 \qquad \text{Remove parentheses.}$$

$$3y = 6x - 7 \qquad \text{Subtract 6 from both sides.}$$

$$y = 2x - \frac{7}{3} \qquad \text{Divide both sides by 3.}$$

The slope of the graph is 2, and the y-intercept is $\left(0, -\frac{7}{3}\right)$. We plot the y-intercept. Then we find a second point on the line by moving 1 unit to the right and 2 units up to the point $\left(1, -\frac{1}{3}\right)$. To get the graph, we draw a line through the two points, as shown in Figure 2-30.

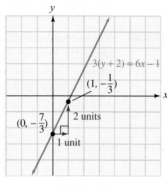

FIGURE 2-30

Self Check 4   Find the slope and the y-intercept of the line with equation $2(x - 3) = -3(y + 5)$. Then graph it.

Now Try Exercise 45.

4. Determine Whether Linear Equations Represent Lines that Are Parallel, Perpendicular, or Neither

EXAMPLE 5   **Determining Whether Lines are Parallel, Perpendicular, or Neither**

Determine whether the lines represented by $4x + 8y = 10$ and $2x = 12 - 4y$ are parallel, perpendicular, or neither.

SOLUTION   We will find the slope of each line and compare their slopes. If their slopes are the same, the lines are parallel. If the product of their slopes is -1, the lines are perpendicular. Otherwise, they are neither parallel nor perpendicular.

We solve each equation for y and write each equation in slope-intercept form.

$$4x + 8y = 10 \qquad\qquad\qquad 2x = 12 - 4y$$

$$8y = -4x + 10 \qquad\qquad\qquad 4y = -2x + 12$$

$$y = \frac{-4x}{8} + \frac{10}{8} \qquad\qquad\qquad y = \frac{-2x}{4} + \frac{12}{4}$$

$$y = -\frac{1}{2}x + \frac{5}{4} \qquad\qquad\qquad y = -\frac{1}{2}x + 3$$

Since the values of b are different, the lines are distinct. Since each slope is $-\frac{1}{2}$, the lines are parallel.

Self Check 5   Are the lines represented by $y = 3x + 2$ and $6x - 2y = 5$ parallel, perpendicular, or neither?

Now Try Exercise 57.

EXAMPLE 6   **Determining Whether Lines are Parallel, Perpendicular, or Neither**

Determine whether the lines represented by $4x + 8y = 10$ and $4x - 2y = 21$ are parallel, perpendicular, or neither.

SOLUTION   We will find the slope of each line and compare their slopes. If their slopes are the same, the lines are parallel. If the product of their slopes is -1, the lines are perpendicular. Otherwise, they are neither parallel nor perpendicular.

We solve each equation for y and write each equation in slope-intercept form.

$$4x + 8y = 10 \qquad\qquad\qquad 4x - 2y = 21$$

$$8y = -4x + 10 \qquad\qquad\qquad -2y = -4x + 21$$

$$y = \frac{-4x}{8} + \frac{10}{8} \qquad\qquad\qquad y = \frac{-4x}{-2} + \frac{21}{-2}$$

$$y = -\frac{1}{2}x + \frac{5}{4} \qquad\qquad\qquad y = 2x - \frac{21}{2}$$

Since the product of their slopes $\left(-\frac{1}{2}\text{ and }2\right)$ is -1, the lines are perpendicular.

Self Check 6   Are the lines represented by $3x + 2y = 7$ and $y = \frac{2}{3}x + 3$ parallel, perpendicular, or neither?

Now Try Exercise 59.

5. Write Equations of Parallel and Perpendicular Lines

EXAMPLE 7   **Writing an Equation of a Parallel Line**

Write an equation of the line passing through $P(-2, 5)$ and parallel to the line $y = 8x - 3$.

SOLUTION   We will substitute the coordinates of $P(-2, 5)$ and the slope of the line parallel to $y = 8x - 3$ into point-slope form and simplify the results to write an equation of the parallel line.

The slope of the line given by $y = 8x - 3$ is 8, the coefficient of x. Since the graph of the desired equation is to be parallel to the graph of $y = 8x - 3$, its slope must also be 8.

We will substitute -2 for x_1, 5 for y_1, and 8 for m into the point-slope form and simplify.

$$y - y_1 = m(x - x_1)$$

$$y - 5 = 8[x - (-2)] \qquad \text{Substitute 5 for } y_1, \text{8 for } m, \text{and } -2 \text{ for } x_1.$$

$$y - 5 = 8(x + 2) \qquad -(-2) = 2$$

$$y - 5 = 8x + 16 \qquad \text{Use the Distributive Property to remove parentheses.}$$

$$y = 8x + 21 \qquad \text{Add 5 to both sides.}$$

An equation of the desired line is $y = 8x + 21$.

Self Check 7   Write an equation of the line passing through $Q(1, 2)$ and parallel to the line $y = 8x - 3$.

Now Try Exercise 67.

EXAMPLE 8   **Writing an Equation of a Perpendicular Line**

Write an equation of the line passing through $P(-2, 5)$ and perpendicular to the line $y = 8x - 3$.

SOLUTION   We will substitute the coordinates of $P(-2, 5)$ and the slope of the line perpendicular to $y = 8x - 3$ into point-slope form and simplify to write an equation of the parallel line.

Because the slope of the given line is 8, the slope of the desired perpendicular line must be $-\frac{1}{8}$.

We substitute -2 for x_1, 5 for y_1, and $-\frac{1}{8}$ for m into the point-slope form and simplify.

$$y - y_1 = m(x - x_1)$$

$$y - 5 = -\frac{1}{8}[x - (-2)] \qquad \text{Substitute 5 for } y_1, -\frac{1}{8} \text{ for } m, \text{and } -2 \text{ for } x_1.$$

$$y - 5 = -\frac{1}{8}(x + 2) \qquad -(-2) = 2$$

$$y = -\frac{1}{8}x - \frac{1}{4} + 5 \qquad \text{Remove parentheses and add 5 to both sides.}$$

$$y = -\frac{1}{8}x + \frac{19}{4} \qquad -\frac{1}{4} + 5 = -\frac{1}{4} + \frac{20}{4} = \frac{19}{4}$$

An equation of the line is $y = -\frac{1}{8}x + \frac{19}{4}$.

Self Check 8   Write an equation of the line passing through $Q(1, 2)$ and perpendicular to $y = 8x - 3$.

Now Try Exercise 73.

6. Recognize and Use the Standard Form of the Equation of a Line

We have shown that the graph of any equation of the form $y = mx + b$ is a line with slope m and y-intercept $(0, b)$. In Section 2.1, we saw that the graph of any equation of the form $Ax + By = C$ (where A and B are not *both* zero) is also a line. We consider three possibilities.

- If $A \neq 0$ and $B \neq 0$, the equation $Ax + By = C$ can be written in slope-intercept form.

$$Ax + By = C$$

$$By = -Ax + C \qquad \text{Subtract } Ax \text{ from both sides.}$$

$$y = -\frac{A}{B}x + \frac{C}{B} \qquad \text{Divide both sides by } B.$$

This is an equation of a line with slope $-\frac{A}{B}$ and y-intercept $\left(0, \frac{C}{B}\right)$.

- If $A = 0$ and $B \neq 0$, the equation $Ax + By = C$ can be written in the form $y = \frac{C}{B}$. This is an equation of a horizontal line with y-intercept $\left(0, \frac{C}{B}\right)$.

- If $A \neq 0$ and $B = 0$, the equation $Ax + By = C$ can be written in the form $x = \frac{C}{A}$. This is an equation of a vertical line with x-intercept at $\left(\frac{C}{A}, 0\right)$.

Recall that $Ax + By = C$ is called the **standard form of the equation of a line.**

Standard Form of an Equation on a Line

The **standard form of an equation of a line** is

$$Ax + By = C$$

where A, B, and C are real numbers, and both A and B are not zero.

- If $B \neq 0$, the slope of the nonvertical line is $-\frac{A}{B}$ and the y-intercept is $\left(0, \frac{C}{B}\right)$.
- If $B = 0$ the graph is a vertical line with x-intercept of $\left(\frac{C}{A}, 0\right)$.

Comment   When writing equations in $Ax + By = C$ form, we usually clear the equation of fractions and make A positive. For example, the equation $-x + \frac{5}{2}y = 2$ can be changed to $2x - 5y = -4$ by multiplying both sides by -2. We will also divide out any common integer factors of A, B, and C. For example, we would write $4x + 8y = 12$ as $x + 2y = 3$.

Comment   Sometimes linear equations are written with a constant term of 0 on the right side of the equation. This form is referred to as *general form*. The line $2x - 5y + 3 = 0$ is written in general form.

EXAMPLE 9   **Using Formulas to Find the Slope and y-Intercept**

Find the slope and the y-intercept of the graph of $3x - 2y = 5$.

SOLUTION   The equation $3x - 2y = 5$ is in standard form, with $A = 3$, $B = -2$, and $C = 5$. We will use $-\frac{A}{B}$ to determine the slope of the line and $\left(0, \frac{C}{B}\right)$ to determine the y-intercept.

The slope of the graph is

$$m = -\frac{A}{B} = -\frac{3}{-2} = \frac{3}{2}$$

and the y-intercept is

$$\left(0, \frac{C}{B}\right) = \left(0, \frac{5}{-2}\right)$$

The slope is $\frac{3}{2}$ and the y-intercept is $\left(0, -\frac{5}{2}\right)$.

Self Check 9   Find the slope and the y-intercept of the graph of $3x - 4y = 12$.

Now Try Exercise 77.

We summarize the various forms of an equation of a line as follows.

Forms of an Equation of a Line	
Standard form	$Ax + By = C$ A and B cannot both be 0.
Slope-intercept form	$y = mx + b$ The slope is m, and the y-intercept is $(0, b)$.
Point-slope form	$y - y_1 = m(x - x_1)$ The slope is m, and the line passes through (x_1, y_1).
A horizontal line	$y = b$ The slope is 0, and the y-intercept is $(0, b)$.
A vertical line	$x = a$ There is no defined slope, and the x-intercept is $(a, 0)$.

7. Write an Equation of the Line that Models a Real-Life Problem

For tax purposes, many businesses use *straight-line depreciation* to find the declining value of aging equipment.

EXAMPLE 10   **Solving an Application Problem**

A business purchases a digital multimedia projector for $1,970 and expects it to last for ten years. It can then be sold as scrap for a *salvage value* of $270.

    If y is the value of the projector after x years of use, and y and x are related by the equation of a line,

a. Find an equation of the line.

b. Find the value of the projector after $2\frac{1}{2}$ years.

c. Find the economic meaning of the y-intercept of the line.

d. Find the economic meaning of the slope of the line.

mpanch/Shutterstock.com

SOLUTION   **a.** We will find the slope and use the point-slope form to write an equation of the line. (See Figure 2-31.)

FIGURE 2-31

When the projector is new, its age x is 0, and its value y is \$1,970. When the projector is 10 years old, $x = 10$ and $y = \$270$. Since the line passes through the points (0, 1,970) and (10, 270) the slope of the line is

$$m = \frac{y_2 - y_1}{x_2 - x_1} \qquad \text{This is the slope formula.}$$

$$= \frac{270 - 1,970}{10 - 0} \qquad \text{Substitute 270 for } y_2, \text{ 1,970 for } y_1, \text{ 10 for } x_2, \text{ and 0 for } x_1.$$

$$= \frac{-1,700}{10}$$

$$= -170$$

To find an equation of the line, we substitute -170 for m, 0 for x_1, and 1,970 for y_1 in the point-slope form and simplify.

$$y - y_1 = m(x - x_1)$$

$$y - 1,970 = -170(x - 0)$$

(3) $$y = -170x + 1,970$$

The value y of the projector is related to its age x by the equation $y = -170x + 1,970$.

b. To find the value after $2\frac{1}{2}$ years, we will substitute 2.5 for x in Equation 3 and solve for y.

$$y = -170x + 1,970$$

$$= -170(2.5) + 1,970 \qquad \text{Substitute 2.5 for } x.$$

$$= -425 + 1,970$$

$$= 1,545$$

In $2\frac{1}{2}$ years, the projector will be worth \$1,545.

c. The y-intercept of the graph is $(0, b)$, where b is the value of y when $x = 0$.

$$y = -170x + 1,970$$

$$y = -170(0) + 1,970 \qquad \text{Substitute 0 for } x.$$

$$y = 1,970$$

The y-coordinate b of the y-intercept is the value of a 0-year-old projector, which is the projector's original cost, \$1,970.

d. Each year, the value decreases by \$170, because the slope of the line is -170. The slope of the depreciation line is called the *annual depreciation rate*.

Problems that have an annual appreciation rate can be worked similarly.

Self Check 10   A business purchases a Canon copier for \$2,700 and expects it to last for ten years. It can then be sold for \$300. Write a straight-line depreciation line for the copier.

Now Try Exercise 91.

8. Use Linear Curve Fitting to Solve Problems

In statistics, the process of using one variable to predict another is called **regression.** For example, if we know a woman's height, we can make a good prediction about her weight, because taller women usually weigh more than shorter women.

Figure 2-32 shows the result of sampling ten women and finding their heights and weights. The graph of the ordered pairs (h, w) is called a **scattergram.**

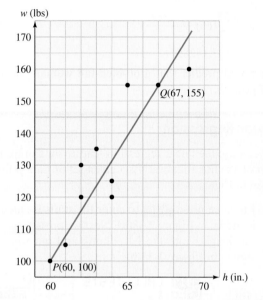

Woman	Height (h) in inches	Weight (w) in pounds
1	60	100
2	61	105
3	62	120
4	62	130
5	63	135
6	64	120
7	64	125
8	65	155
9	67	155
10	69	160

FIGURE 2-32

To write a **prediction equation** (sometimes called a **regression equation**), we must find an equation of the line that comes closer to all of the points in the scattergram than any other possible line. There are statistical methods to find this equation, but we can only approximate it here.

To write an approximation of the regression equation, we place a straightedge on the scattergram shown in Figure 2-32 and draw the line joining two points that seems to best fit all the points. In the figure, line PQ is drawn, where point P has coordinates of (60, 100) and point Q has coordinates of (67, 155).

Our approximation of the regression equation will be an equation of the line passing through points P and Q. To find an equation of this line, we first find its slope.

$$m = \frac{y_2 - y_1}{x_2 - x_1} \qquad \text{This is the slope formula.}$$

$$= \frac{155 - 100}{67 - 60} \qquad \text{Substitute 155 for } y_2\text{, 100 for } y_1\text{, 67 for } x_2\text{, and 60 for } x_1.$$

$$= \frac{55}{7}$$

We can then use point-slope form to find an equation of the line.

$$y - y_1 = m(x - x_1) \qquad \text{This is the point-slope form.}$$

$$y - 100 = \frac{55}{7}(x - 60) \qquad \text{Choose (60, 100) for } (x_1, y_1).$$

$$y = \frac{55}{7}x - \frac{3,300}{7} + 100 \qquad \text{Remove parentheses and add 100 to both sides.}$$

(4) $$y = \frac{55}{7}x - \frac{2,600}{7} \qquad \text{Simplify.}$$

Our approximation of the regression equation is $y = \frac{55}{7}x - \frac{2,600}{7}$.

To predict the weight of a woman who is 66 inches tall, for example, we substitute 66 for x in Equation 4 and simplify.

$$y = \frac{55}{7}x - \frac{2,600}{7}$$

$$y = \frac{55}{7}(66) - \frac{2,600}{7}$$

$$y \approx 147.1428571$$

We would predict that a 66-inch-tall woman chosen at random will weigh about 147 pounds.

ACCENT ON TECHNOLOGY / Linear Regression

We can use the linear regression feature on a graphing calculator to find an equation of the line that best fits a given set of data points. We will do that for the data given in Figure 2-32.

- First, we press **STAT** to enter the statistics menu on the calculator. This screen is shown in Figure 2-33(a). Next we press **ENTER** to input our data. We can input our heights into the L1 column and our weights into the L2 column. This is shown in Figure 2-33(b).

(a)   (b)

FIGURE 2-33

- To obtain an equation of the regression line, we press **STAT** and then the right-arrow key once to access the calculate menu. This screen is shown in Figure 2-34(a). To calculate a linear regression equation, we press **4** to select LinReg $(ax + b)$ and then **ENTER** to obtain an equation. The screen is shown in Figure 2-34(b).

(a)   (b)

FIGURE 2-34

Note that the regression line is of the form $y = ax + b$, where a is the slope and b is the y-coordinate of the y-intercept. If we substitute the values shown in Figure 2-34(b) for a and b and round to hundredths, we can write an equation of the line that best fits the data. The regression line is $y = 6.78x - 301.18$.

Self Check Answers **1.** $y = -\frac{2}{3}x + \frac{7}{3}$ **2.** $y = -\frac{10}{13}x + \frac{2}{13}$ **3.** $y = \frac{7}{3}x - 6$ **4.** $-\frac{2}{3}, (0, -3)$

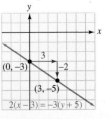

5. parallel   **6.** perpendicular   **7.** $y = 8x - 6$ **8.** $y = -\dfrac{1}{8}x + \dfrac{17}{8}$

9. $\dfrac{3}{4}$, $(0, -3)$ **10.** $y = -240x + 2{,}700$

Exercises **2.3**

Getting Ready

You should be able to complete these vocabulary and concept statements before you proceed to the practice exercises.

Fill in the blanks.

1. The formula for the point-slope form of a line is

_____ .

2. In the equation $y = mx + b$, ___ is the slope of the graph of the line, and $(0, b)$ is the _____ .

3. The equation $y = mx + b$ is called the _____ form of the equation of a line.

4. The standard form of an equation of a line is

_____ .

5. The slope of the graph of $Ax + By = C$ is ___ .

6. The y-intercept of the graph of $Ax + By = C$ is

___ .

Practice

Write an equation of the line with the given properties. Your answer should be written in standard form.

7. $m = 2$ passing through $P(2, 4)$

8. $m = -3$ passing through $P(3, 5)$

9. $m = 2$ passing through $P\left(-\dfrac{3}{2}, \dfrac{1}{2}\right)$

10. $m = -6$ passing through $P\left(\dfrac{1}{4}, -2\right)$

11. $m = \dfrac{2}{5}$ passing through $P(-1, 1)$

12. $m = -\dfrac{1}{5}$ passing through $P(-2, -3)$

13. $m = 0$ passing through $P(-6, -3)$

14. $m = 0$ passing through $P(7, 5)$

15. m is undefined passing through $P(-6, -3)$

16. m is undefined passing through $P(6, -1)$

17. $m = \pi$ passing through $P(\pi, 0)$

18. $m = \pi$ passing through $P(0, \pi)$

Find an equation of each line shown. Your answer should be written in standard form.

19.

$P(2, 5)$

20.

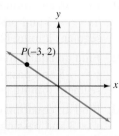

$P(-3, 2)$

Write an equation of a line that passes through the two given points. Your answer should be written in slope-intercept form.

21. $P(0, 0)$, $Q(4, 4)$ **22.** $P(-5, -5)$, $Q(0, 0)$

23. $P(3, 4)$, $Q(0, -3)$ **24.** $P(4, 0)$, $Q(6, -8)$

Write an equation in slope-intercept form of each line shown.

25.

26.

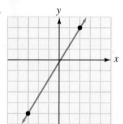

Use slope-intercept form to write an equation of the line with the given properties.

27. $m = 3$; $b = -2$ **28.** $m = -\dfrac{1}{3}$; $b = \dfrac{2}{3}$

29. $m = 5$; $b = -\dfrac{1}{5}$ **30.** $m = \sqrt{2}$; $b = \sqrt{2}$

31. $m = a$; $b = \dfrac{1}{a}$ **32.** $m = a$; $b = 2a$

33. $m = a$; $b = a$ **34.** $m = \dfrac{1}{a}$; $b = a$

Use slope-intercept form to write an equation of a line passing through the given point and having the given slope. Express the answer in standard form.

35. $P(0, 0)$; $m = \dfrac{3}{2}$ **36.** $P(-3, -7)$; $m = -\dfrac{2}{3}$

37. $P(-3, 5)$; $m = -3$ **38.** $P(-5, 1)$; $m = 1$

39. $P\left(0, \sqrt{2}\right)$; $m = \sqrt{2}$

40. $P\left(-\sqrt{3}, 0\right)$; $m = 2\sqrt{3}$

Write each equation in slope-intercept form to determine the slope and y-intercept. Then use the slope and y-intercept to graph the line.

41. $x - y = 1$

42. $x + y = 2$

43. $x = \dfrac{3}{2}y - 3$

44. $x = -\dfrac{4}{5}y + 2$

45. $3(y - 4) = -2(x - 3)$

46. $-4(2x + 3) = 3(3y + 8)$

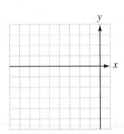

Find the slope and the y-intercept of the lines determined by the given equations.

47. $3x - 2y = 8$

48. $-2x + 4y = 12$

49. $-2(x + 3y) = 5$

50. $5(2x - 3y) = 4$

51. $x = \dfrac{2y - 4}{7}$

52. $3x + 4 = -\dfrac{2(y - 3)}{5}$

Determine whether the graphs of each pair of equations are parallel, perpendicular, or neither.

53. $y = 3x + 4, y = 3x - 7$

54. $y = 4x - 13, y = \dfrac{1}{4}x + 13$

55. $x + y = 2, y = x + 5$

56. $x = y + 2, y = x + 3$

57. $y = 3x + 7, 2y = 6x - 9$

58. $2x + 3y = 9, 3x - 2y = 5$

59. $x = 3y + 4, y = -3x + 7$

60. $3x + 6y = 1, y = \dfrac{1}{2}x$

61. $y = 3, x = 4$

62. $y = -3, y = -7$

63. $x = \dfrac{y - 2}{3}, 3(y - 3) + x = 0$

64. $2y = 8, 3(2 + x) = 3(y + 2)$

Write an equation of the line that passes through the given point and is parallel to the given line. Your answer should be written in slope-intercept form.

65. $P(0, 0), y = 4x - 7$

66. $P(0, 0), x = -3y - 12$

67. $P(2, 5), 4x - y = 7$

68. $P(-6, 3), y + 3x = -12$

69. $P(4, -2), x = \dfrac{5}{4}y - 2$

70. $P(1, -5), x = -\dfrac{3}{4}y + 5$

Write an equation of the line that passes through the given point and is perpendicular to the given line. Your answer should be written in slope-intercept form.

71. $P(0, 0), y = 4x - 7$

72. $P(0, 0), x = -3y - 12$

73. $P(2, 5), 4x - y = 7$

74. $P(-6, 3), y + 3x = -12$

75. $P(4, -2), x = \dfrac{5}{4}y - 2$

76. $P(1, -5), x = -\dfrac{3}{4}y + 5$

Use the method of Example 9 to find the slope and the y-intercept of the graph of each equation.

77. $4x + 5y = 20$ **78.** $9x - 12y = 17$

79. $2x + 3y = 12$ **80.** $5x + 6y = 30$

81. Find an equation of the line perpendicular to the line $y = 3$ and passing through the midpoint of the segment joining $(2, 4)$ and $(-6, 10)$.

82. Find an equation of the line parallel to the line $y = -8$ and passing through the midpoint of the segment joining $(-4, 2)$ and $(-2, 8)$.

83. Find an equation of the line parallel to the line $x = 3$ and passing through the midpoint of the segment joining $(2, -4)$ and $(8, 12)$.

84. Find an equation of the line perpendicular to the line $x = 3$ and passing through the midpoint of the segment joining $(-2, 2)$ and $(4, -8)$.

Applications

In Exercises 85-95, assume straight-line depreciation or straight-line appreciation.

85. Depreciation A Toyota Tundra truck was purchased for $24,300. Its salvage value at the end of its 7-year useful life is expected to be $1,900. Find a depreciation equation.

86. Depreciation A small business purchases the laptop computer shown. It will be depreciated over a 4-year period, when its salvage value will be $300. Find a depreciation equation.

$2,700

87. Appreciation A condominium in San Diego was purchased for $475,000. The owners expect the condominium to double in value in 10 years. Find an appreciation equation.

88. Appreciation A house purchased for $112,000 is expected to double in value in 12 years. Find an appreciation equation.

89. Depreciation Find a depreciation equation for the TV in the following want ad.

> *For Sale*: 3-year-old 54-inch TV, $1,900 new. Asking $1,190. Call 875-5555. Ask for Mike.

90. Depreciation A Bose Wave Radio cost $555 when new and is expected to be worth $80 after 5 years. What will it be worth after 3 years?

91. Salvage value A copier cost $1,050 when new and will be depreciated at the rate of $120 per year. If the useful life of the copier is 8 years, find its salvage value.

92. Rate of depreciation A ski boat that cost $27,600 when new will have no salvage value after 12 years. Find its annual rate of depreciation.

93. Value of an antique An antique table is expected to appreciate $40 each year. If the table will be worth $450 in 2 years, what will it be worth in 13 years?

94. Value of an antique An antique clock is expected to be worth $350 after 2 years and $530 after 5 years. What will the clock worth after 7 years?

95. Purchase price of real estate A cottage that was purchased 3 years ago is now appraised at $47,700. If the property has been appreciating $3,500 per year, find its original purchase price.

96. Computer repair A computer repair company charges a fixed amount, plus an hourly rate, for a service call. Use the information in the illustration to find the hourly rate

AAA Computer Repair

Typical Charges	
2 hours	$ 70
4 hours	$105

97. Automobile repair An auto repair shop charges an hourly rate, plus the cost of parts. If the cost of labor for a $1\frac{1}{2}$-hour radiator repair is $69, find the cost of labor for a 5-hour transmission overhaul.

98. Printer charges A printer charges a fixed setup cost, plus $1 for every 100 copies. If 700 copies cost $52, how much will it cost to print 1,000 copies?

99. Predicting fires A local fire department recognizes that city growth and the number of reported fires are related by a linear equation. City records show that 300 fires were reported in a year when the local population was 57,000 persons, and 325 fires were reported in a year when the population was 59,000 persons. How many fires can be expected in the year when the population reaches 100,000 persons?

100. Estimating the cost of rain gutter A neighbor tells you that an installer of rain gutter charges $60, plus a dollar amount per foot. If the neighbor paid $435 for the installation of 250 feet of gutter, how much will it cost you to have 300 feet installed?

101. Converting temperatures Water freezes at 32° F, or 0° C. Water boils at 212° F, or 100° C. Find a formula for converting a temperature from degrees Fahrenheit to degrees Celsius.

102. Converting units A speed of 1 mile per hour is equal to 88 feet per minute, and of course, 0 miles per hour is 0 feet per minute. Find an equation for converting a speed x, in miles per hour, to the corresponding speed y, in feet per minute.

103. Smoking The percent y of 18-to-25-year-old smokers in the United States has been declining at a constant rate since 1974. If about 47% of this group smoked in 1974 and about 29% smoked in 1994, find a linear equation that models this decline. If this trend continues, estimate what percent will smoke in 2014.

104. Forensic science Scientists believe there is a linear relationship between the height h (in centimeters) of a male and the length f (in centimeters) of his femur bone. Use the data in the table to find a linear equation that expresses the height h in terms of f. Round all constants to the nearest thousandth. How tall would you expect a man to be if his femur measures 50 cm? Round to the nearest centimeter.

Person	Length of femur (f)	Height (h)
A	62.5 cm	200 cm
B	40.2 cm	150 cm

105. Predicting stock prices The value of the stock of ABC Corporation has been increasing by the same fixed dollar amount each year. The pattern is expected to continue. Let 2010 be the base year corresponding to $x = 0$ with $x = 1, 2, 3, \ldots$ corresponding to later years. ABC stock was selling at $\$37\frac{1}{2}$ in 2010 and at $\$45$ in 2012. If y represents the price of ABC stock, find the equation $y = mx + b$ that relates x and y, and predict the price in the year 2014.

106. Estimating inventory Inventory of unsold goods showed a surplus of 375 units in January and 264 in April. Assume that the relationship between inventory and time is given by the equation of a line, and estimate the expected inventory in March. Because March lies between January and April, this estimation is called **interpolation.**

107. Oil depletion When a Petroland oil well was first brought on line, it produced 1,900 barrels of crude oil per day. In each later year, owners expect its daily production to drop by 70 barrels. Find the daily production after $3\frac{1}{2}$ years.

108. Waste management The corrosive waste in industrial sewage limits the useful life of the piping in a waste processing plant to 12 years. The piping system was originally worth $137,000, and it will cost the company $33,000 to remove it at the end of its 12-year useful life. Find a depreciation equation.

109. Crickets The table shows the approximate chirping rate at various temperatures for one type of cricket.

Temperature (° F)	Chirps per minute
50	20
60	80
70	115
80	150
100	250

a. Construct a scattergram below.

b. Assume a linear relationship and write a regression equation.

c. Estimate the chirping rate at a temperature of 90° F.

110. Fishing The table shows the lengths and weights of seven muskies captured by the Department of Natural Resources in Catfish Lake in Eagle River, Wisconsin.

Musky	Length (in.)	Weight (lb)
1	26	5
2	27	8
3	29	9
4	33	12
5	35	14
6	36	14
7	38	19

a. Construct a scattergram for the data.

b. Assume a linear relationship and write a regression equation.

c. Estimate the weight of a musky that is 32 inches long.

 111. Use the linear regression feature on a graphing calculator to determine an equation of the line that best fits the data given in Exercise 109. Round to the hundredths.

 112. Use the linear regression feature on a graphing calculator to determine an equation of the line that best fits the data given in Exercise 110. Round to the hundredths.

Discovery and Writing

113. Explain how to find an equation of a line passing through two given points.

114. In straight-line depreciation, explain why the slope of the line is called the *rate of depreciation*.

115. Prove that an equation of a line with x-intercept of $(a, 0)$ and y-intercept of $(0, b)$ can be written in the form

$$\frac{x}{a} + \frac{y}{b} = 1$$

116. Find the x- and y-intercepts of the line $bx + ay = ab$.

Investigate the properties of slope and the y-intercept by experimenting with the following problems.

117. Graph $y = mx + 2$ for several positive values of m. What do you notice?

118. Graph $y = mx + 2$ for several negative values of m. What do you notice?

119. Graph $y = 2x + b$ for several increasing positive values of b. What do you notice?

120. Graph $y = 2x + b$ for several decreasing negative values of b. What do you notice?

121. How will the graph of $y = \frac{1}{2}x + 5$ compare to the graph of $y = \frac{1}{2}x - 5$?

Using Excel to solve a linear regression problem.

122. The following table shows the length of a femur bone and the height for ten Caucasian males.

Length of femur bone (cm)	Height (cm)
x	y
49.3	180.8
47.4	176.7
47.1	176.1
48.5	176.5
45.2	170.6
47.8	176.8
49.4	178.6
49.6	179.6
50.9	185.2
47.8	176.2

a. Enter the data in an Excel spreadsheet. Enter the femur values in Column A and the height values in Column B.

b. To plot the data, click and drag to highlight the two columns, select Insert on the menu bar, and then select Chart. When a window pops up, select XY (Scatter) as the chart type. When you click Finish, a **scattergram** will appear on the spreadsheet.

c. Observe that the points are approximately linear. To draw the regression line, select Chart on the menu bar and select Add Trendline. When the dialog box appears, be sure that the Linear Regression type is selected, and then click OK. The regression line will appear.

d. To find an equation of the regression line, estimate the coordinates of two points on the regression line. Then use the two points to write an equation of the line.

e. Use the equation of the regression line to predict the height of a male whose femur bone measures 46 cm.

Review

Simplify each expression.

123. $x^7 x^3 x^{-5}$

124. $\dfrac{y^3 y^{-4}}{y^{-5}}$

125. $\left(\dfrac{81}{25}\right)^{-3/2}$

126. $\sqrt[3]{27x^7}$

127. $\sqrt{27} - 2\sqrt{12}$

128. $\dfrac{5}{\sqrt{5}}$

129. $\dfrac{5}{\sqrt{x} + 2}$

130. $\left(\sqrt{x} - 2\right)^2$

2.4 Graphs of Equations

In this section, we will learn to

1. Find the x- and y-intercepts of a graph.
2. Use symmetry to help graph equations.
3. Identify the center and radius of a circle.
4. Write equations of circles.
5. Graph circles.
6. Solve equations by using a graphing calculator.

The London Eye opened in 2000 and is one of the world's tallest and most beautiful observation wheels in the world.

It stands 443 feet high and was the vision of the architects David Marks and Julia Barfield. Its circular design was used as a metaphor for the turning of the century. The Eye has been described as a breathtaking feat of design and engineering.

The graphs of many equations are curves and circles. In this section, we will plot several points (x, y) that satisfy such an equation and join them with a smooth curve. Usually the shape of the graph will become evident.

1. Find the x- and y-Intercepts of a Graph

In Figure 2-35(a), the **x-intercepts** of the graph are $(a, 0)$ and $(b, 0)$, the points where the graph intersects the x-axis. In Figure 2-35(b), the **y-intercept** is $(0, c)$, the point where the graph intersects the y-axis.

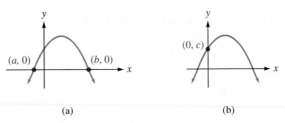

(a)   (b)

FIGURE 2-35

To graph the equation $y = x^2 - 4$, we first find the x- and y-intercepts. To find the x-intercepts, we let $y = 0$ and solve for x.

$$y = x^2 - 4$$

$$0 = x^2 - 4 \qquad \text{Substitute 0 for } y.$$

$$0 = (x + 2)(x - 2) \quad \text{Factor } x^2 - 4.$$

$$x + 2 = 0 \quad \text{or} \quad x - 2 = 0 \qquad \text{Set each factor equal to 0.}$$

$$x = -2 \qquad \qquad x = 2$$

Since $y = 0$ when $x = -2$ and $x = 2$, the x-intercepts are $(-2, 0)$ and $(2, 0)$. (See Figure 2-36.)

To find the y-intercept, we let $x = 0$ and solve for y.

$$y = x^2 - 4$$

$$y = 0^2 - 4 \qquad \text{Substitute 0 for } x.$$

$$y = -4$$

Since $y = -4$ when $x = 0$ the y-intercept is $(0, -4)$.

We can find other pairs (x, y) that satisfy the equation by substituting numbers for x and finding the corresponding values of y. For example, if $x = -3$, then $y = (-3)^2 - 4 = 5$ and the point $(-3, 5)$ lies on the graph.

The coordinates of the intercepts and other points appear in Figure 2-36. If we plot the points and draw a curve through them, we obtain the graph of the equation.

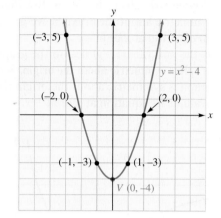

$y = x^2 - 4$		
x	y	(x, y)
-3	5	$(-3, 5)$
-2	0	$(-2, 0)$
-1	-3	$(-1, -3)$
0	-4	$(0, -4)$
1	-3	$(1, -3)$
2	0	$(2, 0)$
3	5	$(3, 5)$

FIGURE 2-36

This graph is called a **parabola.** Its lowest point, $V(0, -4)$, is called the **vertex.** Because the y-axis divides the parabola into two congruent halves, it is called an **axis of symmetry.** We say that the parabola is **symmetric about the y-axis.**

ACCENT ON TECHNOLOGY   **Graphing an Equation**

A graphing calculator can be used to draw the graph of the equation $y = x^2 - 4$. When using a graphing calculator, we must enter the equation and then set the window.

- To enter the equation, press ⟨ Y= ⟩, which opens the window shown in Figure 2-37(a) and enter the right side of the equation.
- To set the window, press ⟨WINDOW⟩ as shown in Figure 2-37(b). We can experiment with different windows, or we can use the ⟨ ZOOM ⟩ menu to select some default windows.
- Press ⟨ GRAPH ⟩, and the equation is graphed as shown in Figure 2-37(c).

(a)

(b)

(c)

FIGURE 2-37

2. Use Symmetry to Help Graph Equations

Symmetry is a tool that we can use to help graph equations. When we look at the McDonald's logo shown on the next page, we can see that the left and right sides of the logo are symmetric (mirror images of each other.)

There are several ways in which a graph can have symmetry.

1. If the point $(x, -y)$ lies on the graph whenever the point (x, y) does, the graph is **symmetric about the x-axis.** See Figure 2-38(a). This implies that a graph is symmetric about the x-axis if we get the same x-coordinate when we evaluate its equation at y or at $-y$.
2. If the point $(-x, y)$ lies on a graph whenever the point (x, y) does, the graph is **symmetric about the y-axis.** See Figure 2-38(b). This implies that a graph is symmetric about the y-axis if we get the same y-coordinate when we evaluate its equation at x or at $-x$.
3. If the point $(-x, -y)$ lies on the graph whenever the point (x, y) does, the graph is **symmetric about the origin.** See Figure 2-38(c). This implies that the graph is symmetric about the origin if we get opposite values of y when we evaluate its equation at x or at $-x$.

Comment

If a graph is symmetric with respect to the x-axis and y-axis, then it is symmetric about the origin.

(a)   (b)   (c)

FIGURE 2-38

Symmetry Tests

- **Test for x-Axis Symmetry** To test for x-axis symmetry, replace y with $-y$. If the resulting equation is equivalent to the original one, the graph is symmetric about the x-axis.
- **Test for y-Axis Symmetry** To test for y-axis symmetry, replace x with $-x$. If the resulting equation is equivalent to the original one, the graph is symmetric about the y-axis.
- **Test for Origin Symmetry** To test for symmetry about the origin, replace x with $-x$ and y with $-y$. If the resulting equation is equivalent to the original one, the graph is symmetric about the origin.

To graph various equations, we will use the following strategy.

Strategy for Graphing Equations

To graph various equations, we will use the following three steps:

1. Find the x- and y-intercepts.
2. Test for symmetries.
3. Graph the equation by plotting points, making use of symmetry, and joining the points with a smooth curve.

EXAMPLE 1

Graphing an Equation Using Intercepts and Symmetry

Graph: $y = |x|$.

SOLUTION

To graph $y = |x|$, we will find the x- and y-intercepts, test for symmetries, plot points, and join the points with a smooth curve.

Step 1: Find the x- and y-intercepts.   To find the x-intercepts, we let $y = 0$ and solve for x.

$$y = |x|$$

$$0 = |x| \qquad \text{Substitute 0 for } y.$$

$$|x| = 0$$

$$x = 0$$

The x-intercept is $(0, 0)$ (See Figure 2-39.)
    To find the y-intercepts, we let $x = 0$ and solve for y.

$$y = |x|$$

$$y = |0| \qquad \text{Substitute 0 for } x.$$

$$y = 0$$

The y-intercept is $(0, 0)$.

Step 2: Test for symmetries.   To test for x-axis symmetry, we replace y with $-y$.

(1) $y = |x|$ This is the original equation.

(2) $-y = |x|$ Replace y with $-y$.

Since Equations 1 and 2 are different, the graph is not symmetric about the x-axis.
    To test for y-axis symmetry, we replace x with $-x$.

(1) $y = |x|$ This is the original equation.

        $y = |-x|$ Replace x with $-x$.

(3) $y = |x|$ $|-x| = |x|$

Since Equations 1 and 3 are the same, the graph is symmetric about the y-axis.
    To test for symmetry about the origin, we replace x with $-x$ and y with $-y$.

(1) $y = |x|$ This is the original equation.

        $-y = |-x|$ Replace x with $-x$ and y with $-y$.

(4) $-y = |x|$ $|-x| = |x|$

Since Equations 1 and 4 are different, the graph is not symmetric about the origin.

Step 3: Graph the equation. To graph the equation, we plot the x- and y-intercepts and several other pairs (x, y) with positive values of x. We can use the y-axis symmetry to draw the graph for negative values of x. See Figure 2-39.

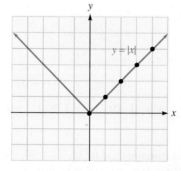

$y = |x|$		
x	y	(x, y)
0	0	$(0, 0)$
1	1	$(1, 1)$
2	2	$(2, 2)$
3	3	$(3, 3)$
4	4	$(4, 4)$

FIGURE 2-39

Self Check 1   Graph: $y = -|x|$.

Now Try Exercise 53.

ACCENT ON TECHNOLOGY   **Graphing an Absolute Value Equation**

A graphing calculator can be used to draw the graph of the equation $y = |0.5x|$.

- To enter the equation, press $\boxed{\text{Y=}}$, which opens the window shown in Figure 2-40(a). To enter the absolute value equation into Y_1, we need to access the absolute value function on our calculator. It is #1 in the $\boxed{\text{MATH}}$ NUM menu as shown in Figure 2-40(b). Press $\boxed{\text{ENTER}}$ and input $0.5x$, and the equation will appear in the graph window. Figure 2-40(c).
- To set the window, press $\boxed{\text{ZOOM}}$, scroll down to 6: [see Figure 2-40(d)], and then press $\boxed{\text{ENTER}}$.
- The equation is graphed as shown in Figure 2-40(e).

(a)   (b)   (c)

(d)   (e)

FIGURE 2-40

EXAMPLE 2   **Graphing an Equation Using Intercepts and Symmetry**

Graph: $y = x^3 - x$.

SOLUTION   To graph $y = x^3 - x$, we will find the x- and y-intercepts, test for symmetries, plot points, and join the points with a smooth curve.

Step 1: Find the x- and y-intercepts.   To find the x-intercepts, we let $y = 0$ and solve for x.

$$y = x^3 - x$$
$$0 = x^3 - x \qquad \text{Substitute 0 for } y.$$
$$0 = x(x^2 - 1) \qquad \text{Factor out } x.$$
$$0 = x(x + 1)(x - 1) \qquad \text{Factor } x^2 - 1.$$
$$x = 0 \quad \text{or} \quad x + 1 = 0 \quad \text{or} \quad x - 1 = 0 \qquad \text{Set each factor equal to 0.}$$
$$x = -1 \qquad x = 1$$

The x-intercepts are $(0, 0)$, $(-1, 0)$, and $(1, 0)$.

To find the y-intercepts, we let $x = 0$ and solve for y.

$$y = x^3 - x$$
$$y = 0^3 - 0 \qquad \text{Substitute 0 for } x.$$
$$y = 0$$

The y-intercept is $(0, 0)$.

Step 2: Test for symmetries.　We test for symmetry about the x-axis by replacing y with $-y$.

(1)　　　$y = x^3 - x$　　　This is the original equation.

　　　$-y = x^3 - x$　　　Replace y with $-y$.

(2)　　　$y = -x^3 + x$　　　Multiply both sides by -1.

Since Equations 1 and 2 are different, the graph is not symmetric about the x-axis.

　　To test for y-axis symmetry, we replace x with $-x$.

(1)　$y = x^3 - x$　　　This is the original equation.

　　$y = (-x)^3 - (-x)$　　Replace x with $-x$.

(3)　$y = -x^3 + x$　　　Simplify.

Since Equations 1 and 3 are different, the graph is not symmetric about the y-axis.
　　To test for symmetry about the origin, we replace x with $-x$ and y with $-y$.

(1)　　　$y = x^3 - x$　　　This is the original equation.

　　　$-y = (-x)^3 - (-x)$　　Replace x with $-x$ and y with $-y$.

　　　$-y = -x^3 + x$　　　Simplify.

(4)　　　$y = x^3 - x$　　　Multiply both sides by -1.

Since Equations 1 and 4 are the same, the graph is symmetric about the origin.

Step 3: Graph the equation.　To graph the equation, we plot the x- and y-intercepts and several other pairs (x, y) with positive values of x. We can use the property of symmetry about the origin to draw the graph for negative values of x. See Figure 2-41.

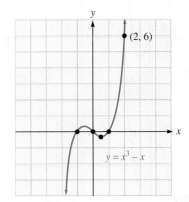

$y = x^3 - x$		
x	y	(x, y)
-1	0	$(-1, 0)$
0	0	$(0, 0)$
$\dfrac{1}{2}$	$-\dfrac{3}{8}$	$\left(\dfrac{1}{2}, -\dfrac{3}{8}\right)$
1	0	$(1, 0)$
2	6	$(2, 6)$

FIGURE 2-41

Self Check 2　Graph: $y = x^3 - 9x$.

Now Try Exercise 49.

ACCENT ON TECHNOLOGY　**Finding the Intercepts of a Graph Using the Zero Feature**

A graphing calculator can find the intercepts of an equation, such as $y = 2x^3 - 3x$. The easiest way to do this is to use the graph of the equation. The x-coordinate of the x-intercept is also called a **zero** of the equation.

- Enter the function into Y_1. See Figure 2-42(a).
- Set the window. Press [ZOOM], scroll down to 4:, and then then press [ENTER] for this graph. See Figures 2-42(a), (b), and (c).

- To find the zeros, we need to access the CALC menu, which is found by pressing 2nd TRACE. Select 2:ZERO. See Figure 2-42(d).
- Move the cursor until it is to the left of the zero we are trying to find and press ENTER. See Figure 2-42(e).
- Repeat the previous step by moving the cursor to the right of the zero. Press ENTER **two times**. Do not stop when the screen shows GUESS. See Figures 2-42 (f), (g), and (h).
- The zero is $x = -1.224745$.
- Repeat the steps to find the zero $x = 1.224745$. See Figures 2-42(i), (j), and (k).
- We can see that another zero is $x = 0$.

FIGURE 2-42

The x-intercepts are $(-1.224745, 0)$, $(1.224745, 0)$, and $(0, 0)$.

EXAMPLE 3   ### Graphing an Equation Using Intercepts and Symmetry

Graph: $y = \sqrt{x}$.

SOLUTION   To graph $y = \sqrt{x}$, we will find the x- and y-intercepts, test for symmetries, plot points, and join the points with a smooth curve.

Step 1: Find the x- and y-intercepts. We can see that the x- and y-intercepts of $y = \sqrt{x}$ are both $(0, 0)$. The graph passes through the origin.

Step 2: Test for symmetries.   We test for symmetry about the x-axis by replacing y with $-y$.

(1) $y = \sqrt{x}$ This is the original equation.

          $-y = \sqrt{x}$ Replace y with $-y$.

(2) $y = -\sqrt{x}$ Multiply both sides by -1.

Since Equations 1 and 2 are different, the graph is not symmetric about the x-axis. To test for y-axis symmetry, we replace x with $-x$.

(1) $y = \sqrt{x}$ This is the original equation.

(3) $y = \sqrt{-x}$ Replace x with $-x$.

Since Equations 1 and 3 are different, the graph is not symmetric about the y-axis. To test for symmetry about the origin, we replace x with $-x$ and y with $-y$.

(1) $y = \sqrt{x}$ This is the original equation.

          $-y = \sqrt{-x}$ Replace x with $-x$ and y with $-y$.

(4) $y = -\sqrt{-x}$ Multiply both sides by -1.

Since Equations 1 and 4 are different, the graph is not symmetric about the origin. The graph of this equation has no symmetries.

Step 3: Graph the equation.   We plot several points to obtain the graph in Figure 2-43.

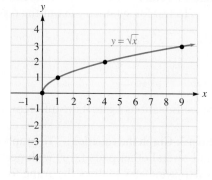

$y = \sqrt{x}$		
x	y	(x, y)
0	0	$(0, 0)$
1	1	$(1, 1)$
4	2	$(4, 2)$
9	3	$(9, 3)$

FIGURE 2-43

Self Check 3   Graph: $y = -\sqrt{x}$.

Now Try Exercise 59.

ACCENT ON TECHNOLOGY   **Graphing a Radical Equation.**

To draw the graph of $y = \sqrt{3.5x}$ using a graphing calculator, enter the equation into the graph menu. See Figure 2-44(a); set the window using the values shown in Figure 2-44(b), and press (GRAPH) to graph the equation. See Figure 2-44(c).

(a)

(b)

(c)

FIGURE 2-44

EXAMPLE 4   **Graphing an Equation Using Intercepts and Symmetry**

Graph: $y^2 = x$.

SOLUTION   To graph $y^2 = x$, we will find the x- and y-intercepts, test for symmetries, plot points, and join the points with a smooth curve.

Step 1: Find the x- and y-intercepts.   We can see that the x- and y-intercepts of $y^2 = x$ are both $(0, 0)$. The graph passes through the origin.

Step 2: Test for symmetries.   We test for symmetry about the x-axis by replacing y and $-y$.

(1) $y^2 = x$ This is the original equation.

          $(-y)^2 = x$ Replace y with $-y$.

(2) $y^2 = x$ Simplify.

Since Equations 1 and 2 are the same, the graph is symmetric about the x-axis. We test for symmetry about the y-axis by replacing x with $-x$.

(1) $y^2 = x$ This is the original equation.

(3) $y^2 = -x$ Replace x with $-x$.

Since Equations 1 and 3 are different, the graph is not symmetric about the y-axis. To test for symmetry about the origin, we replace x with $-x$ and y with $-y$.

(1) $y^2 = x$ This is the original equation.

          $(-y)^2 = -x$ Replace x with $-x$ and y with $-y$.

(4) $y^2 = -x$ Simplify.

Since Equations 1 and 4 are different, the graph is not symmetric about the origin.

Step 3: Graph the equation.   To graph the equation, we plot the x- and y-intercepts and several other pairs (x, y) with positive values of y. We can use the property of x-axis symmetry to draw the graph for negative values of y. See Figure 2-45.

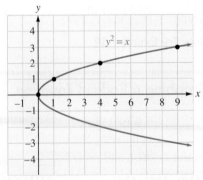

\multicolumn{3}{c}{$y^2 = x$}		
x	y	(x, y)
0	0	$(0, 0)$
1	1	$(1, 1)$
4	2	$(4, 2)$
9	3	$(9, 3)$

FIGURE 2-45

Self Check 4   Graph: $y^2 = -x$.

Now Try Exercise 57.

Graphing an Equation with a y^2 Term

A graphing calculator is programmed to graph equations with y defined in terms of x. To graph the equation $y^2 = 2x$, it is necessary to solve for y and then enter the resulting equations to see the graph.

$$y^2 = 2x$$

$$y = \pm\sqrt{2x}$$

$$y = \sqrt{2x} \quad \text{or} \quad y = -\sqrt{2x}$$

- We enter the two equations as shown in Figure 2-46(a).
- Next we set the [WINDOW] as shown in Figure 2-46(b).

Then we [GRAPH] the equation(s) as shown in Figure 2-46(c).

| (a) | (b) | (c) |

FIGURE 2-46

The graphs in Examples 3 and 4 are related. We have solved the equation $y^2 = x$ for y, and two equations resulted.

$$y = \sqrt{x} \quad \text{and} \quad y = -\sqrt{x}$$

The equation, $y = \sqrt{x}$ was graphed in Example 3. It is the top half of the parabola shown in Example 4. The equation, $y = -\sqrt{x}$ is the bottom half.

3. Identify the Center and Radius of a Circle

Circles   A **circle** is the set of all points in a plane that are a fixed distance from a point called its **center.** The fixed distance is the **radius** of the circle.

To find an equation of a circle with radius r and center at $C(h, k)$, we must find all points $P(x, y)$ in the xy-plane such that the length of line segment PC is r. (See Figure 2-47.)

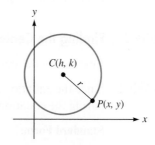

FIGURE 2-47

We can use the Distance Formula to find the length of CP, which is r:

$$r = \sqrt{(x - h)^2 + (y - k)^2}$$

After squaring both sides, we get

$$r^2 = (x - h)^2 + (y - k)^2$$

This equation is called the **standard form of an equation of a circle.**

The Standard Form of an Equation of a Circle with Center at (h, k) and Radius r

The graph of any equation that can be written in the standard form

$$(x - h)^2 + (y - k)^2 = r^2$$

is a circle with radius r and center at point (h, k).

If $r = 0$, the circle is a single point called a **point circle.** If the center of a circle is the origin, then $(h, k) = (0, 0)$ and we have the following result.

The Standard Form of an Equation of a Circle with Center at $(0, 0)$ and Radius r

The graph of any equation that can be written in the standard form

$$x^2 + y^2 = r^2$$

is a circle with radius r and center at the origin.

The equations of four circles written in standard form and their graphs are shown in Figure 2-48.

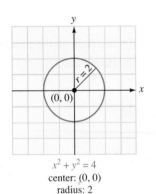

$x^2 + y^2 = 4$
center: $(0, 0)$
radius: 2
(a)

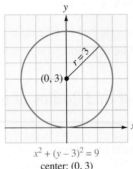

$x^2 + (y - 3)^2 = 9$
center: $(0, 3)$
radius: 3
(b)

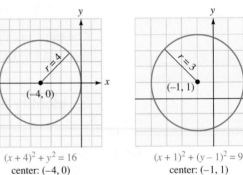

$(x + 4)^2 + y^2 = 16$
center: $(-4, 0)$
radius: 4
(c)

$(x + 1)^2 + (y - 1)^2 = 9$
center: $(-1, 1)$
radius: 3
(d)

FIGURE 2-48

If we are given an equation of a circle in standard form, we can easily determine the coordinates of its center and the length of its radius.

EXAMPLE 5   Finding the Center and Radius of a Circle in Standard Form

Find the center and radius of the circle with the equation $(x - 3)^2 + (y + 2)^2 = 36$.

SOLUTION   Since the equation is written in standard form, we can identify h, k, and r by comparing the equation to the equation $(x - h)^2 + (y - k)^2 = r^2$.

Standard Form: $(x - h)^2 + (y - k)^2 = r^2$

Given Form: $(x - 3)^2 + [y - (-2)]^2 = 6^2$

We see that $h = 3$, $k = -2$, and $r = 6$. The center (h, k) of the circle is at $(3, -2)$ and the radius is 6.

Self Check 5 Identify the center and radius of the circle with equation of $(x - 4)^2 + y^2 = 49$.

Now Try Exercise 69.

4. Write Equations of Circles

EXAMPLE 6 **Writing an Equation of a Circle Given the Center and Radius**

Write an equation of the circle with center at $(-2, 4)$ and radius 1.

SOLUTION We will substitute the coordinates of the center and the radius into the standard form $(x - h)^2 + (y - k)^2 = r^2$.

$$(x - h)^2 + (y - k)^2 = r^2$$

$$[x - (-2)]^2 + (y - 4)^2 = 1^2 \quad \text{Substitute } -2 \text{ for } h, 4 \text{ for } k, \text{ and } 1 \text{ for } r.$$

$$(x + 2)^2 + (y - 4)^2 = 1 \quad \text{Simplify.}$$

An equation of the circle with center at $(-2, 4)$ and radius 1 is $(x + 2)^2 + (y - 4)^2 = 1$.

Self Check 6 Write an equation in standard form of the circle with center $(2, -4)$ and radius $\sqrt{5}$.

Now Try Exercise 79.

If we square the binomials in the equation of the circle found in Example 6, we get another form of the equation, called the **general equation of a circle.**

$$(x + 2)^2 + (y - 4)^2 = 1 \quad \text{This is the equation of Example 6.}$$

$$x^2 + 4x + 4 + y^2 - 8y + 16 = 1 \quad \text{Remove parentheses.}$$

$$x^2 + y^2 + 4x - 8y + 19 = 0 \quad \text{Subtract 1 from both sides and simplify.}$$

The general form is $x^2 + y^2 + 4x - 8y + 19 = 0$.

Comment

We can easily recognize the equation of a circle. A circle's equation will always contain both x^2 and y^2 terms, and the coefficients of both terms will be equal.

The General Form of an Equation of a Circle

The **general form** of an equation of a circle is

$$x^2 + y^2 + cx + dy + e = 0$$

where c, d, and e are real numbers.

EXAMPLE 7 **Finding the General Form of an Equation of a Circle Given the Center and Radius**

Find the general form of an equation of the circle with radius 5 and center at $(3, 2)$.

SOLUTION We will substitute 5 for r, 3 for h, and 2 for k in the standard form of the equation of a circle and simplify.

$$(x - h)^2 + (y - k)^2 = r^2 \quad \text{This is the standard equation.}$$

$$(x - 3)^2 + (y - 2)^2 = 5^2 \quad \text{Substitute.}$$

$$x^2 - 6x + 9 + y^2 - 4y + 4 = 25 \quad \text{Remove parentheses.}$$

$$x^2 + y^2 - 6x - 4y - 12 = 0 \quad \text{Subtract 25 from both sides and simplify.}$$

The general form is $x^2 + y^2 - 6x - 4y - 12 = 0$.

ACCENT ON TECHNOLOGY   Graphing a Circle

When we graphed $y^2 = 2x$ using a graphing calculator, we saw that it is necessary to solve the equation for y in terms of x. The same is true when we graph a circle on a graphing calculator.

- To graph $(x - 2)^2 + (y + 1)^2 = 25$, we must solve the equation for y:

$$(x - 2)^2 + (y + 1)^2 = 25$$

$$(y + 1)^2 = 25 - (x - 2)^2$$

$$y + 1 = \pm\sqrt{25 - (x - 2)^2}$$

$$y = -1 \pm \sqrt{25 - (x - 2)^2}$$

This last expression represents two equations: $y = -1 + \sqrt{25 - (x - 2)^2}$ and $y = -1 - \sqrt{25 - (x - 2)^2}$.

- We graph both of these equations separately on the same coordinate axes by entering the first equation as Y_1 and the second as Y_2, as shown in Figure 2-50(a). Depending on the window setting of the maximum and minimum values of x and y, the graph may not appear to be a circle. However, if we use the ZOOM 5: ZSquare window, the graph will be circular. See Figures 2-50(b) and (c). If it appears that there are gaps in the graph, that is due to the way the calculator draws graphs by darkening pixels.

(a)   (b)   (c)

FIGURE 2-50

Note that in this example, it is easier to graph the circle by hand than with a calculator.

6. Solve Equations by Using a Graphing Calculator

We can solve many equations using the graphing concepts discussed in this chapter and a graphing calculator. For example, the solutions of $x^2 - x - 3 = 0$ will be the numbers x that will make $y = 0$ in the equation $y = x^2 - x - 3$. These numbers will be the x-coordinates of the x-intercepts of the graph of $y = x^2 - x - 3$.

ACCENT ON TECHNOLOGY   Solving Equations

To use a graphing calculator to solve $x^2 - x - 3 = 0$, we graph the equation $y = x^2 - x - 3$, and find the x-coordinates of the x-intercepts. These will be the solutions of the equation. The graph of $y = x^2 - x - 3$ is shown in Figure 2-51(c).

- Use the ZERO command shown earlier in this section to solve the equation. Notice the screen in Figures 2-51(h) and (i) looks different than in Figures 2-51(e) and (f). On some calculators we can just enter the value we want as the left and right bound rather than using the cursor to get to a bound. We see that the two solutions to the equation are $x \approx -1.302776$ and $x \approx 2.3027756$.

*   Every equation does not have a solution over the real numbers. For example, to try and solve the equation $x^2 + 2x + 2 = 0$, graph the equation $y = x^2 + 2x + 2$. We can see that it does not intersect the x-axis, and there is no solution to the equation. See Figure 2-51(k).

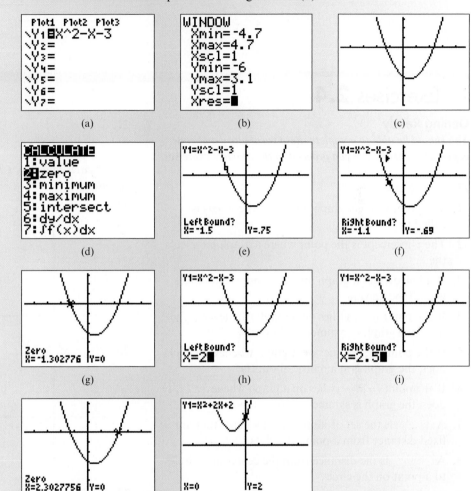

FIGURE 2-51

Self Check Answers

1.

2.

3.

4.
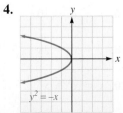

5. $(4, 0), 7$ **6.** $(x - 2)^2 + (y + 4)^2 = 5$ **7.** $x^2 + y^2 + 4x - 10y - 7 = 0$

8. $x^2 + y^2 - 4x - 10y + 4 = 0$ **9.**

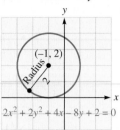

Exercises **2.4**

Getting Ready
You should be able to complete these vocabulary and concept statements before you proceed to the practice exercises.

Fill in the blanks.

1. The point where a graph intersects the x-axis is called the _____.

2. The y-intercept is the point where a graph intersects the _____.

3. If a line divides a graph into two congruent halves, we call the line an _____.

4. If the point $(-x, y)$ lies on a graph whenever (x, y) does, the graph is symmetric about the _____.

5. If the point $(x, -y)$ lies on a graph whenever (x, y) does, the graph is symmetric about the _____.

6. If the point $(-x, -y)$ lies on a graph whenever (x, y) does, the graph is symmetric about the _____.

7. A _____ is the set of all points in a plane that are fixed distance from a point called its _____.

8. A _____ is the distance from the center of a circle to a point on the circle.

9. The standard form of an equation of a circle with center at the origin and radius r is _____.

10. The standard form of an equation of a circle with center at (h, k) and radius r is _____.

Practice
Find the x- and y-intercepts of each graph. Do not graph the equation.

11. $y = x^2 - 4$ **12.** $y = x^2 - 9$

13. $y = 4x^2 - 2x$ **14.** $y = 2x - 4x^2$

15. $y = x^2 - 4x - 5$ **16.** $y = x^2 - 10x + 21$

17. $y = x^2 + x - 2$ **18.** $y = x^2 + 2x - 3$

19. $y = x^3 - 9x$ **20.** $y = x^3 + x$

21. $y = x^4 - 1$ **22.** $y = x^4 - 25x^2$

Graph each equation. Check your graph with a graphing calculator.

23. $y = x^2$

24. $y = -x^2$

25. $y = -x^2 + 2$

26. $y = x^2 - 1$

27. $y = x^2 - 4x$

28. $y = x^2 + 2x$

29. $y = \dfrac{1}{2}x^2 - 2x$

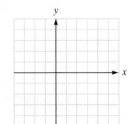

30. $y = \dfrac{1}{2}x^2 + 3$

Find the symmetries, if any, of the graph of each equation. Do not graph the equation.

31. $y = x^2 + 2$

32. $y = 3x + 2$

33. $y^2 + 1 = x$

34. $y^2 + y = x$

35. $y^2 = x^2$

36. $y = 3x + 7$

37. $y = 3x^2 + 7$

38. $x^2 + y^2 = 1$

39. $y = 3x^3 + 7$

40. $y = 3x^3 + 7x$

41. $y^2 = 3x$

42. $y = 3x^4 + 7$

43. $y = |x|$

44. $y = |x + 1|$

45. $|y| = x$

46. $|y| = |x|$

Graph each equation. Be sure to find any intercepts and symmetries. Check your graph with a graphing calculator.

47. $y = x^2 + 4x$

48. $y = x^2 - 6x$

49. $y = x^3$

50. $y = x^3 + x$

51. $y = |x - 2|$

52. $y = |x| - 2$

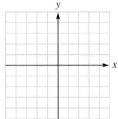

53. $y = 3 - |x|$

54. $y = 3|x|$

55. $y^2 = -x$

56. $y^2 = 4x$

57. $y^2 = 9x$

58. $y^2 = -4x$

59. $y = \sqrt{x} - 1$

60. $y = 1 - \sqrt{x}$

61. $xy = 4$

62. $xy = -9$

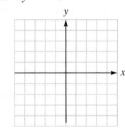

Identify the center and radius of each circle written in standard form.

63. $x^2 + y^2 = 100$

64. $x^2 + y^2 = 81$

65. $x^2 + (y - 5)^2 = 49$

66. $x^2 + (y + 3)^2 = 8$

67. $(x + 6)^2 + y^2 = \dfrac{1}{4}$

68. $(x - 5)^2 + y^2 = \dfrac{16}{25}$

69. $(x - 4)^2 + (y - 1)^2 = 9$

70. $(x + 11)^2 + (x + 7)^2 = 121$

71. $\left(x - \dfrac{1}{4}\right)^2 + (y + 2)^2 = 45$

72. $\left(x + \sqrt{5}\right)^2 + (y - 3)^2 = 1$

Write an equation in standard form of the circle with the given properties.

73. Center at the origin; $r = 5$

74. Center at the origin; $r = \sqrt{3}$

75. Center at $(0, -6)$; $r = 6$

76. Center at $(0, 7)$; $r = 9$

77. Center at $(8, 0)$; $r = \dfrac{1}{5}$

78. Center at $(-10, 0)$; $r = \sqrt{11}$

79. Center at $(-2, 12)$, $r = 13$

80. Center at $\left(\dfrac{2}{7}, -5\right)$; $r = 7$

Write an equation in general form of the circle with the given properties.

81. Center at the origin; $r = 1$

82. Center at the origin; $r = 4$

83. Center at $(6, 8)$; $r = 4$

84. Center at $(5, 3)$; $r = 2$

85. Center at $(3, -4)$; $r = \sqrt{2}$

86. Center at $(-9, 8)$; $r = 2\sqrt{3}$

87. Ends of diameter at $(3, -2)$ and $(3, 8)$

88. Ends of diameter at $(5, 9)$ and $(-5, -9)$

89. Center at $(-3, 4)$ and passing through the origin

90. Center at $(-2, 6)$ and passing through the origin

Convert the general form of each circle given into standard form.

91. $x^2 + y^2 - 6x + 4y + 4 = 0$

92. $x^2 + y^2 + 4x - 8y - 5 = 0$

93. $x^2 + y^2 - 10x - 12y + 57 = 0$

94. $x^2 + y^2 + 2x + 18y + 57 = 0$

95. $2x^2 + 2y^2 - 8x - 16y + 22 = 0$

96. $3x^2 + 3y^2 + 6x - 30y + 3 = 0$

Graph each circle.

97. $x^2 + y^2 - 25 = 0$

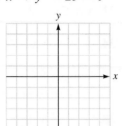

98. $x^2 + y^2 - 8 = 0$

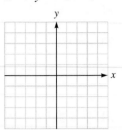

99. $(x - 1)^2 + (y + 2)^2 = 4$

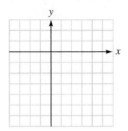

100. $(x + 1)^2 + (y - 2)^2 = 9$

101. $x^2 + y^2 + 2x - 24 = 0$

102. $x^2 + y^2 - 4y = 12$

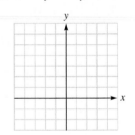

103. $x^2 + y^2 + 4x + 2y - 11 = 0$

104. $x^2 + y^2 - 6x + 2y + 1 = 0$

105. $9x^2 + 9y^2 - 12y = 5$ **106.** $4x^2 + 4y^2 + 4y = 15$

 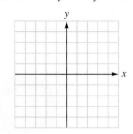

107. $4x^2 + 4y^2 - 4x + 8y + 1 = 0$

108. $9x^2 + 9y^2 - 6x + 18y + 1 = 0$

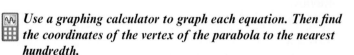
Use a graphing calculator to graph each equation. Then find the coordinates of the vertex of the parabola to the nearest hundredth.

109. $y = 2x^2 - x + 1$ **110.** $y = x^2 + 5x - 6$

111. $y = 7 + x - x^2$ **112.** $y = 2x^2 - 3x + 2$

Use a graphing calculator to solve each equation. Round to the nearest hundredth.

113. $x^2 - 7 = 0$ **114.** $x^2 - 3x + 2 = 0$

115. $x^3 - 3 = 0$ **116.** $3x^3 - x^2 - x = 0$

Applications

117. Golfing Phil Mickelson's tee shot follows a path given by $y = 64t - 16t^2$, where y is the height of the ball (in feet) after t seconds of flight. How long will it take for the ball to strike the ground?

118. Golfing Halfway through its flight, the golf ball of Exercise 117 reaches the highest point of its trajectory. How high is that?

119. Stopping distances The stopping distance D (in feet) for a Ford Fusion car moving V miles per hour is given by $D = 0.08V^2 + 0.9V$. Graph the equation for velocities between 0 and 60 mph.

120. Stopping distances See Exercise 119. How much farther does it take to stop at 60 mph than at 30 mph?

121. Basketball court The center circle of the Kansas Jayhawks basketball court is a circle with a 12-ft diameter. If the center of the circle is located at the origin, find an equation in standard form that models the circle.

ulisse/Shutterstock.com

122. Oil spill Oil spills from a tanker in the Gulf of Mexico and surfaces continuously at coordinates $(0, 0)$. If oil spreads in a circular pattern for ten hours and the circle's radius increases at a rate of 2 inches per hour, write an equation of the circle that models the range of the spill's effect.

123. **Super Loop** The Fire Ball Super Loop is a rollercoaster ride that is shaped like a circle. Find an equation of the loop in standard form if it is positioned 5 feet off of the ground, has a diameter of 60 feet, and its center is at coordinates (0, 35).

Kenneth William Caleno/Shutterstock.com

124. **Hurricane** As a hurricane strengthens an eye begins to form at the center of the storm. At a wind speed of 80 mph the eye of a hurricane is circular when viewed from above and is 30 miles in diameter. If the eye is located at map coordinates (5, 10), find an equation, in standard form, of the circle that models the eye of the hurricane.

125. **CB radios** The CB radio of a trucker covers the circular area shown in the illustration. Find an equation of that circle, in general form.

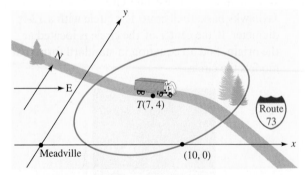

126. **Firestone tires** Two 24-inch-diameter Firestone tires stand against a wall, as shown in the illustration. Find equations in general form of the circular boundaries of the tires.

Discovery and Writing

The solution of the inequality $y < 0$ consists of those numbers x for which the graph of y lies below the x-axis. To solve $y < 0$, we graph y and trace to find numbers x that produce negative values of y. Solve each inequality.

127. $x^2 + x - 6 < 0$ 128. $x^2 - 3x - 10 > 0$

When converting a circle's equation from general to standard form, it is possible to obtain a constant term on the right side that is zero or negative. If the constant term is zero the graph is a single point. If the constant term is negative the graph is nonexistent. Determine whether the graph of the equation is a single point or nonexistent.

129. $x^2 - 4x + y^2 - 6y + 13 = 0$

130. $x^2 - 12x + y^2 + 4y + 43 = 0$

Review
Solve each equation.

131. $3(x + 2) + x = 5x$

132. $12b + 6(3 - b) = b + 3$

133. $\dfrac{5(2 - x)}{3} - 1 = x + 5$

134. $\dfrac{r - 1}{3} = \dfrac{r + 2}{6} + 2$

135. **Mixing an alloy** In 60 ounces of alloy for watch cases, there are 20 ounces of gold. How much copper must be added to the alloy so that a watch case weighing 4 ounces, made from the new alloy, will contain exactly 1 ounce of gold?

136. **Mixing coffee** To make a mixture of 80 pounds of coffee worth $272, a grocer mixes coffee worth $3.25 a pound with coffee worth $3.85 a pound. How many pounds of cheaper coffee should the grocer use?

CHAPTER REVIEW

SECTION **2.1**   The Rectangular Coordinate System

Definitions and Concepts	Examples
The rectangular coordinate system divides the plane into four quadrants.	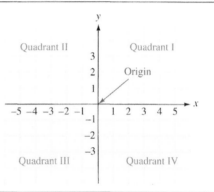

The **graph** of an equation in x and y is the set of all points (x, y) that satisfy the equation.

The **y-intercept** of a line is the point $(0, b)$, where the line intersects the y-axis. To find b, substitute 0 for x in the equation of the line and solve for y.

Use the x- and y-intercepts to graph the equation $6x + 4y = 24$.

Find the y-intercept. To find the y-intercept, we substitute 0 for x and solve for y.

$$6x + 4y = 24$$
$$6(0) + 4y = 24 \qquad \text{Substitute 0 in for } x.$$
$$4y = 24 \qquad \text{Simplify.}$$
$$y = 6 \qquad \text{Divide both sides by 4.}$$

The y-intercept is the point $(0, 6)$.

The **x-intercept** of a line is the point $(a, 0)$, where the line intersects the x-axis. To find a, substitute 0 for y in the equation of the line and solve for x.

Find the x-intercept. To find the x-intercept, we substitute 0 for y and solve for x.

$$6x + 4y = 24$$
$$6x + 4(0) = 24 \qquad \text{Substitute 0 for } y.$$
$$6x = 24 \qquad \text{Simplify.}$$
$$x = 4 \qquad \text{Divide both sides by 6.}$$

The x-intercept is the point $(4, 0)$.

Definitions and Concepts	Examples
	Find a third point as a check. If we let $x = 2$, we will find that $y = 3$.

$$6x + 4y = 24$$

$$6(2) + 4y = 24 \qquad \text{Substitute 2 for } x.$$

$$12 + 4y = 24 \qquad \text{Simplify.}$$

$$4y = 12 \qquad \text{Subtract 12 from both sides.}$$

$$y = 3 \qquad \text{Divide both sides by 4.}$$

The point $(2, 3)$ satisfies the equation.

We plot each pair and join them with a line to get the graph of the equation.

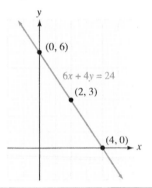

Equation of a vertical line through (a, b):

$$x = a$$

Equation of a horizontal line through (a, b):

$$y = b$$

The Distance Formula:

The distance d between points (x_1, y_1) and (x_2, y_2) is given by

$$d = \sqrt{(x_2 - x_1)^2 + (y_2 - y_1)^2}$$

Find the distance between $P(-5, 2)$ and $Q(-3, 4)$.

We can use the Distance Formula $d = \sqrt{(x_2 - x_1)^2 + (y_2 - y_1)^2}$ to find the distance between $P(-5, 2)$ and $Q(-3, 4)$. If we let $P(-5, 2) = P(x_1, y_1)$ and $Q(-3, 4) = Q(x_2, y_2)$, we can substitute -5 for x_1, 2 for y_1, -3 for x_2, and 4 for y_2 into the formula and simplify.

$$d(PQ) = \sqrt{(x_2 - x_1)^2 + (y_2 - y_1)^2}$$

$$d(PQ) = \sqrt{[-3 - (-5)]^2 + [4 - (2)]^2}$$

$$= \sqrt{(2)^2 + (2)^2}$$

$$= \sqrt{4 + 4} = \sqrt{8} = \sqrt{4 \cdot 2} = 2\sqrt{2}$$

The distance between the two points is $2\sqrt{2}$.

The Midpoint Formula:

The midpoint of the line segment joining (x_1, y_1) and (x_2, y_2) is the point M with coordinates

$$M = \left(\frac{x_1 + x_2}{2}, \frac{y_1 + y_2}{2} \right)$$

To find the midpoint of the segment with endpoints at $(-4, 5)$ and $(6, 7)$, average the x-coordinates and average the y-coordinates:

The midpoint is $\left(\frac{-4 + 6}{2}, \frac{5 + 7}{2} \right) = \left(\frac{2}{2}, \frac{12}{2} \right) = (1, 6)$.

EXERCISES

Refer to the illustration and find the coordinates of each point.

1. A 2. B

3. C 4. D

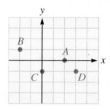

Graph each point. Indicate the quadrant in which the point lies or the axis on which it lies.

5. $(-3, 5)$ 6. $(5, -3)$

7. $(0, -7)$ 8. $\left(-\dfrac{1}{2}, 0\right)$

Solve each equation for y and graph the equation. Then check your graph with a graphing calculator.

9. $2x - y = 6$ 10. $2x + 5y = -10$

Use the x- and the y-intercepts to graph each equation.

11. $3x - 5y = 15$ 12. $x + y = 7$

13. $x + y = -7$ 14. $x - 5y = 5$

    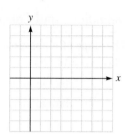

Graph each equation.

15. $y = 4$ 16. $x = -2$

17. **Depreciation** A Ford Mustang purchased for $18,750 is expected to depreciate according to the formula $y = -2,200x + 18,750$. Find its value after 3 years.

18. **House appreciation** A house purchased for $250,000 is expected to appreciate according to the formula $y = 16,500x + 250,000$, where y is the value of the house after x years. Find the value of the house 5 years later.

Find the length of the segment PQ.

19. $P(-3, 7)$; $Q(3, -1)$ 20. $P(-8, 6)$; $Q(-12, 10)$

21. $P\left(\sqrt{3}, 9\right)$; $Q\left(\sqrt{3}, 7\right)$ 22. $P(a, -a)$; $Q(-a, a)$

Find the midpoint of the segment PQ.

23. $P(-3, 7)$; $Q(3, -1)$ 24. $P(0, 5)$; $Q(-12, 10)$

25. $P\left(\sqrt{3}, 9\right)$; $Q\left(\sqrt{3}, 7\right)$ 26. $P(a, -a)$; $Q(-a, a)$

SECTION **2.2**   The Slope of a Nonvertical Line

Definitions and Concepts	Examples

The slope of a nonvertical line passing through points $P(x_1, y_1)$ and $Q(x_2, y_2)$ is
 	
$$m = \frac{\text{change in } y}{\text{change in } x} = \frac{y_2 - y_1}{x_2 - x_1} \quad (x_2 \neq x_1)$$
	Find the slope of the line passing through $P(-1, -3)$ and $Q(7, 9)$.
	    We will substitute the points $P(-1, -3)$ and $Q(7, 9)$ into the slope formula,
	
	$$m = \frac{\text{change in } y}{\text{change in } x} = \frac{y_2 - y_1}{x_2 - x_1}$$
	
	to find the slope of the line.
	    Let $P(x_1, y_1) = P(-1, -3)$ and $Q(x_2, y_2) = Q(7, 9)$. Then we substitute -1 for x_1, -3 for y_1, 7 for x_2, and 9 for y_2 to get
	
	$$m = \frac{\text{change in } y}{\text{change in } x}$$
	
	$$m = \frac{y_2 - y_1}{x_2 - x_1}$$
	
	$$= \frac{9 - (-3)}{7 - (-1)} = \frac{12}{8} = \frac{3}{2}$$
	
	The slope of the line is $\frac{3}{2}$.

Slopes of horizontal and vertical lines: The slope of a horizontal line (a line with an equation of the form $y = b$) is 0. The slope of a vertical line (a line with an equation of the form $x = a$) is not defined.	The slope of the graph of $y = 7$ is 0. The slope of the line $x = 6$ is not defined.
Slopes of parallel lines: Nonvertical parallel lines have the same slope. **Slopes of perpendicular lines:** The product of the slopes of two perpendicular lines is -1, provided neither line is vertical.	Determine whether the lines with the given slopes are parallel, perpendicular, or neither. $$m_1 = -6; m_2 = \frac{1}{6}$$ The product of the slopes $m_1 = -6$ and $m_2 = \frac{1}{6}$ is -1. The lines are perpendicular.

EXERCISES

Find the slope of the line PQ, if possible.

27. $P(3, -5)$; $Q(1, 7)$ **28.** $P(2,7)$; $Q(-5,-7)$

29. $P(b, a)$; $Q(a, b)$ **30.** $P(a + b, b)$; $Q(b, b - a)$

Find two points on the line and find the slope of the line.

31. $y = 3x + 6$ **32.** $y = 5x - 6$

Determine whether the slope of each line is 0 or undefined.

33.

34.

Determine whether the slope of each line is positive or negative.

35.

36.

Determine whether the lines with the given slopes are parallel, perpendicular, or neither.

37. $m_1 = 5; m_2 = -\dfrac{1}{5}$ **38.** $m_1 = \dfrac{2}{7}; m_2 = \dfrac{7}{2}$

39. A line passes through $(-2, 5)$ and $(6, 10)$. A line parallel to it passes through $(2, 2)$ and $(10, y)$. Find y.

40. A line passes through $(-2, 5)$ and $(6, 10)$. A line perpendicular to it passes through $(-2, 5)$ and $(x, -3)$. Find x.

41. Rate of descent If an airplane descends 3,000 feet in 15 minutes, what is the average rate of descent in feet per minute?

42. Rate of growth A small business predicts sales according to a straight-line method. If sales were $50,000 in the first year and $147,500 in the third year, find the rate of growth in dollars per year (the slope of the line).

SECTION **2.3**   Writing Equations of Lines

Definitions and Concepts	Examples
Point-slope form: An equation of the line passing through $P(x_1, y_1)$ and with slope m is $y - y_1 = m(x - x_1)$	Write an equation of the line with slope $-\frac{4}{3}$ and passing through $P(3, -2)$. We will substitute $-\frac{4}{3}$ for m, 3 for x_1, and -2 for y_1 in the point-slope form $y - y_1 = m(x - x_1)$ and simplify. $$y - y_1 = m(x - x_1)$$ $$y - (-2) = -\frac{4}{3}(x - 3) \quad \text{Substitute } -\frac{4}{3} \text{ for } m, 3 \text{ for } x_1, \text{ and } -2 \text{ for } y_1.$$ $$y + 2 = -\frac{4}{3}x + 4 \quad \text{Remove parentheses.}$$ $$y = -\frac{4}{3}x + 2 \quad \text{Subtract 2 from both sides.}$$
Slope-intercept form: An equation of the line with slope m and y-intercept $(0, b)$ is $y = mx + b$. **Standard form of an equation of a line:** $Ax + By = C$ Slope-intercept form can be used to find the slope and the y-intercept from the equation of a line.	The equation of the line $y = -\frac{5}{3}x + 4$ is written in slope-intercept form. The above equation written in standard form $Ax + By = C$ is $5x + 3y = 12$. Find the slope and the y-intercept of the line with equation $2x + 5y = -10$. We will write the equation in the form $y = mx + b$ to find the slope m and the y-intercept $(0, b)$. $$2x + 5y = -10$$ $$5y = -2x - 10 \quad \text{Subtract } 2x \text{ from both sides.}$$ $$y = -\frac{2}{5}x - 2 \quad \text{Divide both sides by 5.}$$ The slope of the graph is $-\frac{2}{5}$, and the y-intercept is $(0, -2)$.

Definitions and Concepts	Examples
Horizontal line: $y = b$ The slope is 0, and the y-intercept is $(0, b)$.	The equation of the horizontal line with slope 0 and y-intercept $(0, 7)$ is $y = 7$
Vertical line: $x = a$ There is no defined slope, and the x-intercept is $(a, 0)$.	The equation of the vertical line with no defined slope and the x-intercept $(-6, 0)$ is $x = -6$.

EXERCISES

Use point-slope form to write an equation of each line.
Write each equation in standard form.

43. The line passes through the origin and the point $(-5, 7)$.

44. The line passes through $(-2, 1)$ and has a slope of -4.

45. The line passes through $(2, -1)$ and has a slope of $-\frac{1}{5}$.

46. The line passes through $(7, -5)$ and $(4, 1)$.

Use slope-intercept form to write an equation of each line.

47. The line has a slope of $\frac{2}{3}$ and a y-intercept of 3.

48. The slope is $-\frac{3}{2}$ and the line passes through $(0, -5)$.

Use slope-intercept form to graph each equation.

49. $y = \dfrac{3}{5}x - 2$

50. $y = -\dfrac{4}{3}x + 3$

Find the slope and the y-intercept of the graph of each line.

51. $3x - 2y = 10$

52. $2x + 4y = -8$

53. $-2y = -3x + 10$

54. $2x = -4y - 8$

55. $5x + 2y = 7$

56. $3x - 4y = 14$

Write an equation of each line.

57. The line has a slope of 0 and passes through $(-5, 17)$.

58. The line has no defined slope and passes through $(-5, 17)$.

Write an equation of each line. Write the answer in slope-intercept form.

59. The line is parallel to $3x - 4y = 7$ and passes through $(2, 0)$.

60. The line passes through $(7, -2)$ and is parallel to the line segment joining $(2, 4)$ and $(4, -10)$.

61. The line passes through $(0, 5)$ and is perpendicular to the line $x + 3y = 4$.

62. The line passes through $(7, -2)$ and is perpendicular to the line segment joining $(2, 4)$ and $(4, -10)$.

Determine whether the graphs of each pair of equations are parallel, perpendicular, or neither.

63. $y = 3x + 8, 2y = 6x - 19$

64. $2x + 3y = 6, 3x - 2y = 15$

SECTION **2.4**   Graphs of Equations

Definitions and Concepts	Examples

Definitions and Concepts

To graph an equation:

1. Find the x- and y-intercepts.
2. Find the symmetries of the graph.
3. Plot some additional points, if necessary, and draw the graph.

Intercepts of a graph:
To find the x-intercepts, let $y = 0$ and solve for x.
To find the y-intercepts, let $x = 0$ and solve for y.

Examples

Graph: $y = x^3 - 4x$.

To graph $y = x^3 - 4x$, we will find the x- and y-intercepts, test for symmetries, plot points, and join the points with a smooth curve.

Step 1: Find the x- and y-intercepts.   To find the x-intercepts, we let $y = 0$ and solve for x.

$$y = x^3 - 4x$$
$$0 = x^3 - 4x \qquad \text{Substitute 0 for } y.$$
$$0 = x(x^2 - 4) \qquad \text{Factor out } x.$$
$$0 = x(x + 2)(x - 2) \qquad \text{Factor } x^2 - 4.$$
$$x = 0 \quad \text{or} \quad x + 2 = 0 \quad \text{or} \quad x - 2 = 0 \quad \text{Set each factor}$$
$$x = -2 \qquad\qquad x = 2 \qquad \text{equal to 0.}$$

The x-intercepts are $(0, 0)$, $(-2, 0)$, and $(2, 0)$.
    To find the y-intercepts, we let $x = 0$ and solve for y.

$$y = x^3 - 4x$$
$$y = 0^3 - 4(0) \qquad \text{Substitute 0 in for } x.$$
$$y = 0$$

The y-intercept is $(0, 0)$.

Test for x-axis symmetry:
To test for x-axis symmetry, replace y with $-y$. If the resulting equation is equivalent to the original one, the graph is symmetric about the x-axis.

Step 2: Test for symmetries.   We test for symmetry about the x-axis by replacing y with $-y$.

$(1) \quad y = x^3 - 4x \qquad$ This is the original equation.
$\quad\quad -y = x^3 - 4x \qquad$ Replace y with $-y$.
$(2) \quad y = -x^3 + 4x \qquad$ Multiply both sides by -1.

Since Equations 1 and 2 are different, the graph is not symmetric about the x-axis.
    To test for y-axis symmetry, we replace x with $-x$.

Test for y-axis symmetry:
To test for y-axis symmetry, replace x with $-x$. If the resulting equation is equivalent to the original one, the graph is symmetric about the y-axis.

$(1) \quad y = x^3 - 4x \qquad$ This is the original equation.
$\quad\quad y = (-x)^3 - 4(-x) \qquad$ Replace x with $-x$.
$(3) \quad y = -x^3 + 4x \qquad$ Simplify.

Since Equations 1 and 3 are different, the graph is not symmetric about the y-axis.

Definitions and Concepts	Examples

Test for origin symmetry:
To test for symmetry about the origin, replace x with $-x$ and y with $-y$. If the resulting equation is equivalent to the original one, the graph is symmetric about the origin.

To test for symmetry about the origin, we replace x with $-x$ and y with $-y$.

(1)	$y = x^3 - 4x$	This is the original equation.
	$-y = (-x)^3 - 4(-x)$	Replace x with $-x$ and y with $-y$.
	$-y = -x^3 + 4x$	Simplify.
(4)	$y = x^3 - 4x$	Multiply both sides by -1.

Since Equations 1 and 4 are the same, the graph is symmetric about the origin.

Plot some additional points and draw the graph.

Step 3: Graph the equation.   To graph the equation, we plot the x- and y-intercepts and several other pairs (x, y) with positive values of x. We can use the property of symmetry about the origin to draw the graph for negative values of x.

$y = x^3 - 4x$		
x	y	(x, y)
-2	0	$(-2, 0)$
0	0	$(0, 0)$
1	-3	$(1, -3)$
2	0	$(2, 0)$
3	15	$(3, 15)$

Circles:
A **circle** is the set of all points in a plane that are a fixed distance from a point called its **center.** The fixed distance is the **radius** of the circle.

The standard equation of a circle with center (h, k) and radius r:
The graph of any equation that can be written in the form

$$(x - h)^2 + (y - k)^2 = r^2$$

is a circle with radius r and center at point (h, k).

The standard equation of a circle with center $(0, 0)$ and radius r:
The graph of any equation that can be written in the form

$$x^2 + y^2 = r^2$$

is a circle with radius r and center at the origin.

Find the center and radius of the circle with the equation $(x - 6)^2 + (y + 5)^2 = 4$.

Standard Form: $(x - h)^2 + (y - k)^2 = r^2$

Given Form: $(x - 6)^2 + [y - (-5)]^2 = 2^2$

We see that $h = 6$, $k = -5$, and $r = 2$. The center (h, k) of the circle is at $(6, -5)$ and the radius is 2.

Definitions and Concepts	Examples
The general form of an equation of a circle: The general form of an equation of a circle is $$x^2 + y^2 + cd + dy + e = 0$$ where c, d, and e are real numbers.	To convert the general form of the equation of the circle $x^2 + y^2 + 4x - 2y - 20 = 0$ into standard form, we must find the coordinates of the center and the radius. To do so, we will complete the square on both x and y: $$x^2 + y^2 + 4x - 2y = 20$$ $$x^2 + 4x + y^2 - 2y = 20$$ $$x^2 + 4x + 4 + y^2 - 2y + 1 = 20 + 4 + 1 \quad \text{Add 4 and 1 to both sides to complete the square.}$$ $$(x + 2)^2 + (y - 1)^2 = 25 \quad \text{Factor } x^2 - 4x + 4 \text{ and } y^2 - 2y + 1.$$

EXERCISES

Find the x- and y-intercepts of each graph. Do not graph the equation.

65. $y = 4x - 8x^2$

66. $y = x^2 - 10x - 24$

Find the symmetries, if any, of the graph of each equation. Do not graph the equation.

67. $y^2 = 8x$

68. $y = 3y^4 + 6$

69. $y = -2|x|$

70. $y = |x + 2|$

Graph each equation. Find all intercepts and symmetries.

71. $y = x^2 + 2$

72. $y = x^3 - 2$

73. $y = \dfrac{1}{2}|x|$

74. $y = -\sqrt{x - 4}$

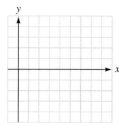

75. $y = \sqrt{x} + 2$

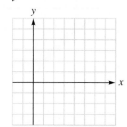

76. $y = |x + 1| + 2$

Use a graphing calculator to graph each equation.

77. $y = |x - 4| + 2$

78. $y = -\sqrt{x + 2} + 3$

79. $y = x + 2|x|$

80. $y^2 = x - 3$

Identify the center and radius of each circle written in standard form.

81. $x^2 + y^2 = 64$

82. $x^2 + (y - 6)^2 = 100$

83. $(x + 7)^2 + y^2 = \dfrac{1}{4}$

84. $(x - 5)^2 + (y + 1)^2 = 9$

Write an equation of each circle in standard form.

85. Center at $(0, 0)$; $r = 7$

86. Center at $(3, 0)$; $r = \dfrac{1}{5}$

87. Center at $(-2, 12)$, $r = 5$

88. Center at $\left(\dfrac{2}{7}, 5\right)$; $r = 9$

Write an equation of each circle in standard form and general form.

89. Center at $(-3, 4)$; radius 12

90. Ends of diameter at $(-6, -3)$ and $(5, 8)$

Convert the general form of each circle given into standard form.

91. $x^2 + y^2 + 6x - 4y + 4 = 0$

92. $2x^2 + 2y^2 - 8x - 16y - 10 = 0$

Graph each circle.

93. $x^2 + y^2 - 16 = 0$

94. $x^2 + y^2 - 4x = 5$

95. $x^2 + y^2 - 2y = 15$

96. $x^2 + y^2 - 4x + 2y = 4$

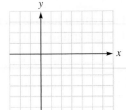

Use a graphing calculator to solve each equation. If an answer is not exact, round to the nearest hundredth.

97. $x^2 - 11 = 0$

98. $x^3 - x = 0$

99. $|x^2 - 2| - 1 = 0$

100. $x^2 - 3x = 5$

SECTION **2.5**   Proportion and Variation

Definitions and Concepts	Examples
Proportion: An equation indicating that two ratios are equal is called a **proportion.** In the proportion $\frac{a}{b} = \frac{c}{d}$, the numbers a and d are called the **extremes,** and the numbers b and c are called the **means.**	In the proportion $\frac{3}{5} = \frac{9}{15}$, 5 and 9 are called the means, and 3 and 15 are called the extremes.

Definitions and Concepts	Examples
Property of proportions: In any proportion, the product of the extremes is equal to the product of the means.	In the proportion on the previous page, the product of the means is equal to the product of the extremes: $$5(9) = 3(15) = 45$$
Use the property of proportions to solve a proportion for a variable.	Solve the proportion: $\dfrac{x}{6} = \dfrac{2}{x + 11}$ for x. We will use the property of proportions to solve the proportion. $$\frac{x}{6} = \frac{2}{x + 11}$$

$x(x + 11) = 6 \cdot 2$ — The product of the extremes equals the product of the means.

$x^2 + 11x = 12$ — Remove parentheses and simplify.

$x^2 + 11x - 12 = 0$ — Subtract 12 from both sides.

$(x + 12)(x - 1) = 0$ — Factor the trinomial.

$x + 12 = 0 \quad$ or $\quad x - 1 = 0$ — Set each factor equal to 0.

$x = -12 \qquad\qquad x = 1$

Thus, $x = -12$ or $x = 1$.

Direct variation: The words **"y varies directly with x,"** or **"y is directly proportional to x,"** mean that $y = kx$ for some real-number constant k. The number k is called the **constant of proportionality.**	In the direct variation formula, $y = 3x$, find y when $x = 5$. $$y = 3x = 3(5) = 15$$
Inverse variation: The words **"y varies inversely with x,"** or **"y is inversely proportional to x,"** mean that $y = \frac{k}{x}$ for some real-number constant k.	In the inverse variation formula $y = \frac{k}{x}$, find the constant of variation if $y = 5$ when $x = 20$. $$y = \frac{k}{x}$$ $$5 = \frac{k}{20} \quad \text{Substitute 5 for } y \text{ and 20 for } x.$$ $$100 = k$$

Definitions and Concepts	Examples
Joint variation: The words **"y varies jointly with w and x"** mean that $y = kwx$ for some real-number constant k.	Kinetic energy of an object varies jointly with its mass and the square of its velocity. A 50-gram mass moving at the rate of 20 centimeters per second has a kinetic energy of 40,000 dyne-centimeters. Find the kinetic energy of a 10-gram mass that is moving at 60 centimeters per second. We will use joint variation to solve the problem. If we let E, m, and v represent the kinetic energy, mass, and velocity, respectively, the phrase *energy varies jointly with the mass and the square of its velocity* translates into the formula $$E = kmv^2.$$ The constant k can be evaluated by substituting 40,000 for E, 50 for m, and 20 for v in the formula $$E = kmv^2$$ $$40{,}000 = k(50)(20)^2$$ $$40{,}000 = 20{,}000k$$ $$k = 2$$ We can now substitute 2 for k, 10 for m, and 60 for v in the formula and evaluate E. $$E = kmv^2$$ $$= 2(10)(60)^2$$ $$= 72{,}000$$ A 10-gram mass that is moving at 60 centimeters per second has a kinetic energy of 72,000 dyne-centimeters.

EXERCISES

Solve each proportion.

101. $\dfrac{x + 3}{10} = \dfrac{x - 1}{x}$

102. $\dfrac{x - 1}{2} = \dfrac{12}{x + 1}$

103. Hooke's Law The force required to stretch a spring is directly proportional to the amount of stretch. If a 3-pound force stretches a spring 5 inches, what force would stretch the spring 3 inches?

104. Kinetic energy A moving body has a kinetic energy directly proportional to the square of its velocity. By what factor does the kinetic energy of an automobile increase if its speed increases from 30 mph to 50 mph?

105. Gas laws The volume of gas in a balloon varies directly as the temperature and inversely as the pressure. If the volume is 400 cubic centimeters when the temperature is 300 K and the pressure is 25 dynes per square centimeter, find the volume when the temperature is 200 K and the pressure is 20 dynes per square centimeter.

106. The area of a rectangle varies jointly with its length and width. Find the constant of proportionality.

107. Electrical resistance The resistance of a wire varies directly as the length of the wire and inversely as the square of its diameter. A 1,000-foot length of wire, 0.05 inch in diameter, has a resistance of 200 ohms. What would be the resistance of a 1,500-foot length of wire that is 0.08 inch in diameter?

108. Billing for services Angie's Painting and Decorating Service charges a fixed amount for accepting a wallpapering job and adds a fixed dollar amount for each roll hung. If the company bills a customer $177 to hang 11 rolls and $294 to hang 20 rolls, find the cost to hang 27 rolls.

109. Paying for college Rolf must earn $5,040 for next semester's tuition. Assume he works x hours tutoring algebra at $14 per hour and y hours tutoring Spanish at $18 per hour and makes his goal. Write an equation expressing the relationship between x and y, and graph the equation. If Rolf tutors algebra for 180 hours, how long must he tutor Spanish?

CHAPTER TEST

Indicate the quadrant in which the point lies or the axis on which it lies.

1. $(-3, \pi)$

2. $(0, -8)$

Find the x- and y-intercepts and use them to graph the equation.

3. $x + 3y = 6$

4. $2x - 5y = 10$

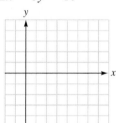

Graph each equation.

5. $2(x + y) = 3x + 5$

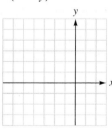

6. $3x - 5y = 3(x - 5)$

7. $\frac{1}{2}(x - 2y) = y - 1$

8. $\dfrac{x + y - 5}{7} = 3x$

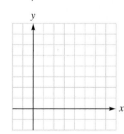

Find the distance between points P and Q.

9. $P(1, -1)$; $Q(-3, 4)$ **10.** $P(0, \pi)$; $Q(-\pi, 0)$

Find the midpoint of the line segment PQ.

11. $P(3, -7)$; $Q(-3, 7)$

12. $P\left(0, \sqrt{2}\right)$; $Q\left(\sqrt{8}, \sqrt{18}\right)$

Find the slope of the line PQ.

13. $P(3, -9)$; $Q(-5, 1)$

14. $P\left(\sqrt{3}, 3\right)$; $Q\left(-\sqrt{12}, 0\right)$

Determine whether the two lines are parallel, perpendicular, or neither.

15. $y = 3x - 2$; $y = 2x - 3$

16. $2x - 3y = 5$; $3x + 2y = 7$

Write an equation of the line with the given properties. Your answers should be written in slope-intercept form, if possible.

17. Passing through $(3, -5)$; $m = 2$

18. $m = 3$; $b = \dfrac{1}{2}$

19. Parallel to $2x - y = 3$; $b = 5$

20. Perpendicular to $2x - y = 3$; $b = 5$

21. Passing through $\left(2, -\dfrac{3}{2}\right)$ and $\left(3, \dfrac{1}{2}\right)$

22. Parallel to the y-axis and passing through $(3, -4)$

Find the x- and y-intercepts of each graph.

23. $y = x^3 - 16x$

24. $y = |x - 4|$

Find the symmetries of each graph.

25. $y^2 = x - 1$ **26.** $y = x^4 + 1$

Graph each equation. Find all intercepts and symmetries.

27. $y = x^2 - 9$ **28.** $x = |y|$

29. $y = 2\sqrt{x}$ **30.** $x = y^3$

Write an equation of each circle in standard form.

31. Center at $(5, 7)$; radius of 8

32. Center at $(2, 4)$; passing through $(6, 8)$

Graph each equation.

33. $x^2 + y^2 = 9$ **34.** $x^2 - 4x + y^2 + 3 = 0$

          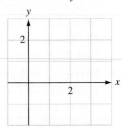

Write each statement as an equation.

35. y varies directly as the square of z.

36. w varies jointly with r and the square of s.

37. P varies directly with Q. $P = 7$ when $Q = 2$. Find P when $Q = 5$.

38. y is directly proportional to x and inversely proportional to the square of z, and $y = 16$ when $x = 3$ and $z = 2$. Find x when $y = 2$ and $z = 3$.

Use a graphing calculator to find the positive root of each equation. Round to two decimal places.

39. $x^2 - 7 = 0$ **40.** $x^2 - 5x - 5 = 0$

Functions

3

CAREERS AND MATHEMATICS: Computer Scientist

Benis Arapovic/Shutterstock.com

Computer scientists are highly trained innovative workers who design and invent new technology. They solve complex business, scientific, and general computing problems. Computer scientists conduct research on a variety of topics, including computer hardware, virtual reality, and robotics.

Education and Mathematics Required
- Most are required to possess a Ph.D. in computer science, computer engineering, or a closely related discipline. An aptitude for math is important.
- College Algebra, Trigonometry, Calculus, Linear Algebra, Ordinary Differential Equations, Theory of Analysis, Abstract Algebra, Graph Theory, Numerical Methods, and Combinatorics are math courses required.

How Computer Scientists Use Math and Who Employs Them
- Computer scientists use mathematics as they span a range of topics from theoretical studies of algorithms to the computation of implementing computing systems in hardware and software.
- Many computer scientists are employed by Internet service providers; Web search portals; and data processing, hosting, and related services firms. Others work for government, manufacturers of computer and electronic products, insurance companies, financial institutions, and universities.

Career Outlook and Earnings
- Employment of computer scientists is expected to grow by 24 percent through 2018, which is much faster than the average for all occupations.
- The median annual wages of computer and information scientists is approximately $98,000. Some earn more than $150,000 a year.

For more information see: www.bls.gov/oco

In this chapter, we will discuss one of the most important concepts in mathematics—the concept of a function.

3.1 Functions and Function Notation

In this section, we will learn to

1. Understand the concept of a function.
2. Determine whether an equation represents a function.
3. Find the domain of a function.
4. Evaluate a function.
5. Evaluate the difference quotient for a function.
6. Graph a function by plotting points.
7. Use the Vertical Line Test to identify functions.
8. Use linear functions to model applications.

Correspondences between the elements of two sets is a common occurrence in everyday life. For example,

- To every Motorola cell phone, there corresponds exactly one phone number.
- To every Honda Civic car, there corresponds exactly one vehicle identification number.
- To every case on the television show "Deal or No Deal," there corresponds exactly one amount of money.
- To every item's barcode at the Target store, there corresponds exactly one price.

This table shows the four highest-grossing movies of all time and the year each movie was released.

Movie	Year
Avatar	2009
The Lord of the Rings: The Return of the King	2003
Pirates of the Caribbean: Dead Man's Chest	2006
The Dark Knight	2008

The information shown in the table sets up a correspondence between a movie and the year it was released. Note that for each of the movies, there corresponds exactly one year in which it was released. The phase *there corresponds exactly one* is extremely important in mathematics, and we will use this idea to solve problems.

1. Understand the Concept of a Function

Correspondences in which exactly one quantity corresponds to (or depends on) another quantity according to some specific rule are called **functions.** Equations are frequently used in mathematics to represent functions. For example, the equation $y = x^2 - 1$ sets up a correspondence between two infinite sets of real numbers, x and y, according to the rule *square x and subtract 1.*

Equation: $y = x^2 - 1$

Correspondence: Each real number x determines exactly one real number y.

Rule: Square x and subtract 1.

Since the value of y depends on the number x, we call y the **dependent variable** and x the **independent variable.**

The equation $y = x^2 - 1$ determines what **output value** y will result from each **input value** x. This idea of inputs and outputs is shown in Figure 3-1(a). In the equation $y = x^2 - 1$, if the input x is 2, the output y is

$$y = 2^2 - 1 = 3$$

This is illustrated in Figure 3-1(b).

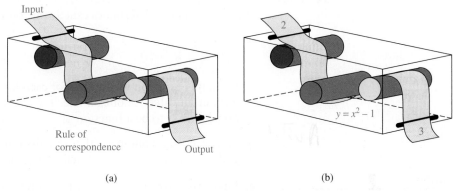

(a)   (b)

FIGURE 3-1

Comment

Correspondences can be set up by a verbal expression, by a table, by a set of ordered pairs, by an equation, and by a graph.

The equation $y = x^2 - 1$ also determines the table of ordered pairs, and the graph shown in Figure 3-2. To see how the table determines the correspondence, we find an input in the x-column and read across to find the corresponding output in the y-column. If we select $x = 2$ as an input, we get $y = 3$ for the output.

To see how the graph of $y = x^2 - 1$ determines the correspondence, we draw a vertical and horizontal line through any point (say, point P) on the graph shown in Figure 3-2. Because these lines intersect the x-axis at 2 and the y-axis at 3, the point $P(2, 3)$ associates 3 on the y-axis with 2 on the x-axis.

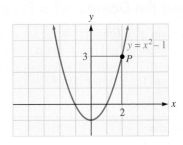

$y = x^2 - 1$		
x	y	(x, y)
-2	3	$(-2, 3)$
-1	0	$(-1, 0)$
0	-1	$(0, -1)$
1	0	$(1, 0)$
2	3	$(2, 3)$

FIGURE 3-2

Any correspondence that assigns exactly one value of y to each number x is called a **function**. We refer to the set of inputs as the **domain** of the function and the set of outputs as the **range** of the function.

Function	A **function** f is a correspondence between a set of input values x and a set of output values y, where to each x-value there corresponds exactly one y-value.
Domain	The set of input values x is called the **domain** of the function.
Range	The set of output values y is called the **range** of the function.

2. Determine Whether an Equation Represents a Function

EXAMPLE 1   **Determining Whether an Equation Represents a Function**

Determine whether the following equations define y to be a function of x.
a. $7x + y = 5$ **b.** $y = |x| + 1$ **c.** $y^2 = x + 2$

SOLUTION   In each case, we will solve each equation for y, if necessary, and determine whether each input value x determines exactly one output value y.

a. First, we solve $7x + y = 5$ for y to get

$$y = 5 - 7x$$

From this equation we see that for each input value x there corresponds exactly one output value y. For example, if $x = 3$, then $y = 5 - 7(3) = -16$. The equation defines y to be a function of x.

b. Since each input number x that we substitute for x determines exactly one output y, the equation $y = |x| + 1$ defines y to be a function of x.

c. First, we solve $y^2 = x + 2$ for y using the Square Root Property covered in Section 1.3 to get $y = \pm\sqrt{x + 2}$. Note that each input value x for which the function is defined (except -2) gives two outputs y. For example, if $x = 7$, then $y = \pm\sqrt{7 + 2} = \pm\sqrt{9} = \pm 3$. For this reason, the equation does not define y to be a function of x.   ■

Caution

> Some equations represent functions and some do not. If to some input x in an equation there corresponds more than one output y, the equation will not represent a function.

Self Check 1   Determine whether each equation defines y to be a function of x.
a. $y = |x|$ **b.** $y = \sqrt{x}$ **c.** $y^2 = 2x$

Now Try Exercise 17.

3. Find the Domain of a Function

The **domain** of a function is the set of all real numbers x for which the function is defined. Thus, to find the domain of a function we must find the set of numbers that are permissible inputs for x. It is often helpful to determine any restrictions on the input values for x. For example, we consider the information in the following table.

Equation	Restriction	Domain
$y = x^3 - x^2 + x - 5$	There are no restrictions on x because any real number can be cubed, squared and combined with constants.	all real numbers, $(-\infty, \infty)$
$y = \sqrt{x}$	The restriction that x cannot be a negative real number is placed on x because the square root of a negative number is an imaginary number.	$x \geq 0$, the interval $[0, \infty)$
$y = \dfrac{1}{x}$	The restriction that x cannot be 0 is placed on x because division by 0 isn't defined.	$x \neq 0$, $(-\infty, 0) \cup (0, \infty)$

EXAMPLE 2   **Finding the Domain of a Function**

Find the domain of the function defined by each equation:
a. $y = 2x - 5$ **b.** $y = \sqrt{3x - 2}$ **c.** $y = \dfrac{3}{x + 2}$

SOLUTION   We must determine what numbers are permissible inputs for x. This set of numbers is the domain.

a. Any real number that we input for x can be multiplied by 2 and then 5 can be subtracted from the result. Thus, the domain is the interval $(-\infty, \infty)$.

b. Since the radicand must be nonnegative, we have

$$3x - 2 \geq 0$$

$$3x \geq 2 \qquad \text{Add 2 to both sides.}$$

$$x \geq \frac{2}{3} \qquad \text{Divide both sides by 3.}$$

Thus, the domain is the interval $\left[\frac{2}{3}, \infty\right)$.

c. Since the fraction $\frac{3}{x+2}$ is undefined when $x = -2$, -2 is not a permissible input value. Since all other values of x are permissible inputs, the domain is $(-\infty, -2) \cup (-2, \infty)$.

Self Check 2   Find the domain of each function: **a.** $y = |x| + 2$ **b.** $y = \sqrt[3]{x + 2}$

Now Try Exercise 27.

EXAMPLE 3   **Finding the Domain of a Function**

Find the domain of the function defined by the equation $y = \dfrac{1}{x^2 - 5x - 6}$.

SOLUTION   We can factor the denominator to see what values of x will give 0's in the denominator. These values are not in the domain.

$$x^2 - 5x - 6 = 0$$

$$(x - 6)(x + 1) = 0$$

$$x - 6 = 0 \quad \text{or} \quad x + 1 = 0$$

$$x = 6 \quad \bigg| \quad x = -1$$

The domain is $(-\infty, -1) \cup (-1, 6) \cup (6, \infty)$.

Self Check 3   Find the domain of the function defined by the equation $y = \dfrac{2}{x^2 - 16}$.

Now Try Exercise 41.

4. Evaluate a Function

To indicate that y is a function of x, we often use **function notation** and write

$$y = f(x) \qquad \text{Read as ``} y \text{ is a function of } x \text{.''}$$

The notation $y = f(x)$ provides a way of denoting the value of y (the dependent variable) that corresponds to some input number x (the independent variable). For example, if $y = f(x)$, the value of y that is determined when $x = 2$ is denoted by $f(2)$, read as "f of 2." If $f(x) = 5 - 7x$, we can evaluate $f(2)$ by substituting 2 for x.

$$f(x) = 5 - 7x$$

$$f(2) = 5 - 7(2) \qquad \text{Substitute the input 2 for } x.$$

$$= -9$$

If $x = 2$, then $y = f(2) = -9$.

To evaluate $f(-5)$, we substitute -5 for x.

$$f(x) = 5 - 7x$$

$$f(-5) = 5 - 7(-5) \qquad \text{Substitute the input } -5 \text{ for } x.$$

$$= 40$$

If $x = -5$, then $y = f(-5) = 40$.

Comment   To see why function notation is helpful, consider the following sentences. Note that the second sentence is much more concise.

1. In the function $y = 3x^2 + x - 4$, find the value of y when $x = -3$.

2. In the function $f(x) = 3x^2 + x - 4$, find $f(-3)$.

In this context, the notations y and $f(x)$ both represent the output of a function and can be used interchangeably, but function notation is more concise.

Sometimes functions are denoted by letters other than f. The notations $y = g(x)$ and $y = h(x)$ also denote functions involving the independent variable x.

EXAMPLE 4   Evaluating a Function

Let $g(x) = 3x^2 + x - 4$. Find **a.** $g(-3)$ **b.** $g(k)$ **c.** $g(-t^3)$ **d.** $g(k + 1)$

SOLUTION   In each case, we will substitute the input value into the function and simplify.

a. $g(x) = 3x^2 + x - 4$ **b.** $g(x) = 3x^2 + x - 4$

$g(-3) = 3(-3)^2 + (-3) - 4$ $g(k) = 3k^2 + k - 4$

$= 3(9) - 3 - 4$

$= 20$

c. $g(x) = 3x^2 + x - 4$ **d.** $g(x) = 3x^2 + x - 4$

$g(-t^3) = 3(-t^3)^2 + (-t^3) - 4$ $g(k + 1) = 3(k + 1)^2 + (k + 1) - 4$

$= 3t^6 - t^3 - 4$ $= 3(k^2 + 2k + 1) + k + 1 - 4$

$= 3k^2 + 6k + 3 + k + 1 - 4$

$= 3k^2 + 7k$

■

Self Check 4   Evaluate: **a.** $g(0)$ **b.** $g(2)$ **c.** $g(k - 1)$

Now Try Exercise 49.

ACCENT ON TECHNOLOGY   **Evaluating a Function**

Functions can be easily evaluated on a graphing calculator. There are several ways to do this, but one of the easiest is to use the graph editor and the table. Press
[Y=] and input $3x^2 + x - 4$ in the graph editor. Next, press [2nd] [WINDOW] and use the table setup shown on the next page. Then press [2nd] [GRAPH] and enter values for x. The function values will appear in the table.

(a)   (b)   (c)

FIGURE 3-3

5. Evaluate the Difference Quotient for a Function

The fraction $\frac{f(x+h)-f(x)}{h}$ is called the **difference quotient** and is important in calculus. The difference quotient can be used to find quantities such as the velocity of a guided missile or the rate of change of a company's profit.

EXAMPLE 5   **Finding the Difference Quotient**

If $f(x) = x^2 - 2x - 5$, evaluate $\dfrac{f(x+h)-f(x)}{h}$.

SOLUTION   We will evaluate the difference quotient in three steps. Find $f(x+h)$. Then subtract $f(x)$. Then divide by h.

Step 1: Find $f(x+h)$.

$$f(x) = x^2 - 2x - 5$$

$$f(x+h) = (x+h)^2 - 2(x+h) - 5 \qquad \text{Substitute } x+h \text{ for } x.$$

$$= x^2 + 2xh + h^2 - 2x - 2h - 5$$

Step 2: Find $f(x+h) - f(x)$. We can use the result from Step 1.

$$f(x+h) - f(x) = x^2 + 2xh + h^2 - 2x - 2h - 5 - (x^2 - 2x - 5) \qquad \text{Subtract } f(x).$$

$$= x^2 + 2xh + h^2 - 2x - 2h - 5 - x^2 + 2x + 5 \qquad \text{Remove parentheses.}$$

$$= 2xh + h^2 - 2h \qquad \text{Combine like terms.}$$

Step 3: Find the difference quotient $\frac{f(x+h)-f(x)}{h}$. We can use the result from Step 2.

$$\frac{f(x+h)-f(x)}{h} = \frac{2xh + h^2 - 2h}{h} \qquad \text{Divide both sides by } h.$$

$$= \frac{h(2x + h - 2)}{h} \qquad \text{In the numerator, factor out } h.$$

$$= 2x + h - 2 \qquad \text{Divide out } h: \frac{h}{h} = 1.$$

Comment

After the completion of Step 2, in a polynomial function, when $f(x+h) - f(x)$ is simplified, each term will always include an h. Use that fact to check your work as you progress through the problem.

Self Check 5   If $f(x) = x^2 + 2$, evaluate $\dfrac{f(x+h)-f(x)}{h}$.

Now Try Exercise 65.

6. Graph a Function by Plotting Points

If f is a function whose domain and range are sets of real numbers, its graph is the set of all points $(x, f(x))$ in the xy-plane that satisfy the equation $y = f(x)$. For example, the graph of the function $y = f(x) = -7x + 5$ is a line with slope -7 and y-intercept $(0, 5)$. (See Figure 3-4.) If the graph of a function is a nonvertical line, the function is called a **linear function.**

FIGURE 3-4

| Graph of a Function | The **graph** of a function f in the xy-plane is the set of all points (x, y) where x is in the domain of f, y is in the range of f, and $y = f(x)$. |

EXAMPLE 6   **Graphing a Function by Plotting Points**

Graph the functions.   **a.** $f(x) = -2|x| + 3$ **b.** $f(x) = \sqrt{x - 2}$

SOLUTION   In each case, we will make a table of solutions and plot the points given by the table. Then we will connect the points by drawing a smooth curve through them and obtain the graph of the function.

a. $f(x) = -2|x| + 3$

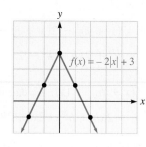

$f(x) = -2\|x\| + 3$		
x	$f(x)$	$(x, f(x))$
-2	-1	$(-2, -1)$
-1	1	$(-1, 1)$
0	3	$(0, 3)$
1	1	$(1, 1)$
2	-1	$(2, -1)$

FIGURE 3-5

b. $f(x) = \sqrt{x - 2}$

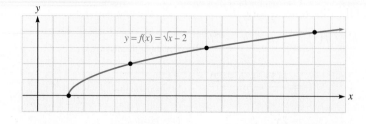

$f(x) = \sqrt{x - 2}$		
x	$f(x)$	$(x, f(x))$
2	0	$(2, 0)$
6	2	$(6, 2)$
11	3	$(11, 3)$
18	4	$(18, 4)$

FIGURE 3-6

Self Check 6   Graph: $f(x) = |x + 3|$.

Now Try Exercise 83.

Both the **domain** and the **range** of a function can be identified by viewing the graph of the function. The inputs or x-values that correspond to points on the graph of the function can be identified on the x-axis and used to state the domain of the function. The outputs or $f(x)$ values that correspond to points on the graph of the function can be identified on the y-axis and used to state the range of the function. (See Figure 3-7).

(a)   (b)

FIGURE 3-7

From Figure 3-6, we can see that the domain of the function $f(x) = -2|x| + 3$ is the set of all real numbers, and that the range is the set of real numbers that are less than or equal to 3.

From Figure 3-6, we can see that the domain of the function $f(x) = \sqrt{x - 2}$ is the set of all real numbers greater than or equal to 2, and that the range is the set of all real numbers greater than or equal to 0.

In Figure 3-8, we see the graphs of several basic functions.

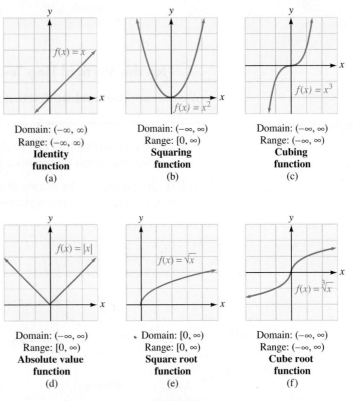

Domain: $(-\infty, \infty)$
Range: $(-\infty, \infty)$
**Identity
function**
(a)

Domain: $(-\infty, \infty)$
Range: $[0, \infty)$
**Squaring
function**
(b)

Domain: $(-\infty, \infty)$
Range: $(-\infty, \infty)$
**Cubing
function**
(c)

Domain: $(-\infty, \infty)$
Range: $[0, \infty)$
**Absolute value
function**
(d)

Domain: $[0, \infty)$
Range: $[0, \infty)$
**Square root
function**
(e)

Domain: $(-\infty, \infty)$
Range: $(-\infty, \infty)$
**Cube root
function**
(f)

FIGURE 3-8

ACCENT ON TECHNOLOGY   **Graphing the Absolute Value Function**

To graph the absolute value function on a graphing calculator, we must call up the function abs(into the graphing window. We press MATH , then scroll right to NUM as shown below in Figure 3-9.

Press Y= . Go to MATH NUM and press 1 . Input x and GRAPH . Use ZOOM 4 as the window.

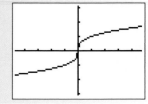

FIGURE 3-9

ACCENT ON TECHNOLOGY   **Graphing the Cube Root Function**

We can graph this function on a graphing calculator using the cube root key by selecting MATH 4 from the graph window as shown in Figure 3-10. Input x and GRAPH . Use ZOOM 4 as the window.

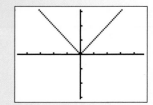

FIGURE 3-10

---

7. Use the Vertical Line Test to Identify Functions

We can use a **Vertical Line Test** to determine whether a graph represents a function.

Vertical Line Test
- If every vertical line that can be drawn intersects the graph in no more than one point, the graph represents a function. See Figure 3-11(a).

- If a vertical line can be drawn that intersects the graph at more than one point, the graph does not represent a function. See Figure 3-11(b).

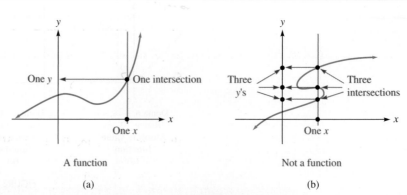

(a)   (b)

FIGURE 3-11

EXAMPLE 7   **Using the Vertical Line Test to Identify Functions**

Determine which of the following graphs represent functions.

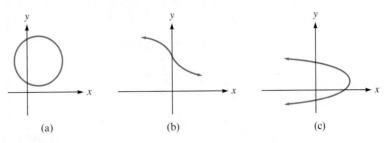

(a)   (b)   (c)

SOLUTION   We will use the Vertical Line Test by drawing several vertical lines through each graph. If every vertical line that intersects the graph does so exactly once, the graph represents a function. Otherwise, the graph does not represent a function.

a. This graph fails the Vertical Line Test, so it does not represent a function.

b. This graph passes the Vertical Line Test, so it does represent a function.

c. This graph fails the Vertical Line Test, so it does not represent a function.

Self Check 7   Does the graph shown in Figure 3-2 represent a function?

Now Try Exercise 97.

Comment

Some graphs represent functions and some do not. Graphs that pass the Vertical Line Test are functions.

Not all equations define functions. For example, the equation $x = |y|$ does not define a function, because two values of y can correspond to one number x. For example, if $x = 2$, then y can be either 2 or -2. The graph of the equation is shown in Figure 3-12. Since the graph does not pass the Vertical Line Test, it does not represent a function.

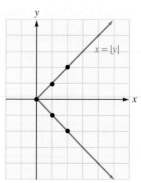

x = |y|		
x	y	(x, y)
2	−2	$(2, -2)$
1	−1	$(1, -1)$
0	0	$(0, 0)$
1	1	$(1, 1)$
2	2	$(2, 2)$

FIGURE 3-12

Correspondences between a set of input values x (called the domain) and a set of output values y (called the range), where to each x-value in the domain there corresponds one or more y-values in the range, are called **relations.** Although the graph in Figure 3-12 does not represent a function, it does represent a relation. We note that all functions are relations, but not all relations are functions.

Another way to visualize the definition of function is to consider the diagram shown in Figure 3-13(a). The function f that assigns the element y to the element x is represented by an arrow leaving x and pointing to y. The set of elements in **X** from which arrows originate is the domain of the function. The set of elements in **Y** to which arrows point is the range.

To constitute a function, each element of the domain must determine exactly one y-value in the range. However, the same value of y could correspond to several numbers x. In the function shown in Figure 3-13(b), the single value y corresponds to the three numbers x_1, x_2, and x_3 in the domain.

The correspondence shown in Figure 3-13(c) is not a function, because two values of y correspond to the same number x. However, it is still a relation.

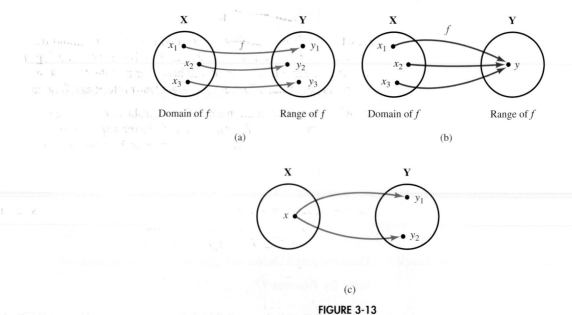

FIGURE 3-13

8. Use Linear Functions to Model Applications

We have seen that the equation of a nonvertical line defines a linear function—an important function in mathematics and its applications.

Linear Functions   A **linear function** is a function determined by an equation of the form

$$f(x) = mx + b \quad \text{or} \quad y = mx + b$$

EXAMPLE 8   **Using a Linear Function to Model an Application**

Cost of a Fraternity Dance   The cost associated with a fraternity dance is $300 for Country Club rental and $24 for each couple that attends.
a. Write the cost C of the dance in terms of the number of couples x attending.
b. Find the cost if 45 couples attend the dance.

SOLUTION   Use the information stated in the problem to write a linear function that models the application.

a. The cost C for the dance is $24 per couple plus the $300 rental fee. If x couples attend, the cost is $24x$ plus 300. Therefore, the linear cost function is

$$C(x) = 24x + 300$$

b. To find the cost when 45 couples attend, we find C(45).

$$C(x) = 24x + 300$$
$$C(45) = 24(45) + 300 \qquad \text{Substitute 45 for } x.$$
$$= 1,080 + 300$$
$$= 1,380$$

If 45 couples attend, the cost of the dance is $1,380.

Self Check 8   Find the cost when 60 couples attend.

Now Try Exercise 105.

EXAMPLE 9   **Writing a Linear Function that Models an Application**

Heart Rates   The target heart rate at which a person should train to get an effective workout is a linear function of his age. For a 20-year-old starting an exercise program, the target heart rate should be 120 beats per minute. For a 40-year-old, it should be 108 beats per minute. Express the target heart rate R as a function of age A.

SOLUTION   We will use the information stated in the problem to find the slope of the linear function and write a linear function that models the application.

Since the target heart rate (R) is given to be a linear function of age (A), there are constants m and b such that

$$R = mA + b$$

Since $R = 120$ when $A = 20$, the point $(A_1, R_1) = (20, 120)$ lies on the straight-line graph of this function. Since $R = 108$ when $A = 40$, the point $(A_2, R_2) = (40, 108)$ also lies on that line. The slope of the line is

$$m = \frac{R_2 - R_1}{A_2 - A_1}$$
$$= \frac{108 - 120}{40 - 20} \qquad \text{Substitute 108 for } R_2, 120 \text{ for } R_1, 40 \text{ for } A_2, \text{ and 20 for } A_1.$$
$$= -\frac{12}{20}$$
$$= -\frac{3}{5}$$
$$= -0.6$$

Thus, $m = -0.6$. To determine b, we can substitute -0.6 for m and the coordinates of one point, say $P(20, 120)$, in the equation $R = mA + b$ and solve for b.

$$R = mA + b$$

$$120 = -0.6(20) + b \qquad \text{Substitute 120 for } R, \text{ 20 for } b, \text{ and } -0.6 \text{ for } m.$$

$$120 = -12 + b$$

$$132 = b \qquad \text{Add 12 to both sides.}$$

If we substitute -0.6 for m and 132 for b in $R = mA + b$, we obtain $R = -0.6A + 132$.

Self Check 9   Find the target heart rate for a 30-year-old person.

Now Try Exercise 111.

Self Check Answers   **1. a.** a function   **b.** a function   **c.** not a function   **2. a.** $(-\infty, \infty)$
b. $(-\infty, \infty)$ **3.** $(-\infty, -4) \cup (-4, 4) \cup (4, \infty)$ **4. a.** -4 **b.** 10
c. $3k^2 - 5k - 2$ **5.** $2x + h$ **6.**   **7.** yes
8. \$1,740   **9.** 114 beats per minute

$f(x) = |x + 3|$

Exercises **3.1**

Getting Ready

You should be able to complete these vocabulary and concept statements before you proceed to the practice exercises.

Fill in the blanks.

1. A correspondence that assigns exactly one value of y to any number x is called a _____.

2. A correspondence that assigns one or more values of y to any number x is called a _____.

3. The set of input numbers x in a function is called the _____ of the function.

4. The set of all output values y in a function is called the _____ of the function.

5. The statement "y is a function of x" can be written as the equation _____.

6. The graph of a function $y = f(x)$ in the xy-plane is the set of all points _____ that satisfy the equation, where x is in the _____ of f and y is in the _____ of f.

7. In the function of Exercise 5, ___ is called the independent variable.

8. In the function of Exercise 5, y is called the _____ variable.

9. If every _____ line that intersects a graph does so _____, the graph represents a function.

10. A function that can be written in the form $y = mx + b$ is called a _____ function.

Practice

Assume that all variables represent real numbers. Determine whether each equation determines y to be a function of x.

11. $y = x$

12. $y - 2x = 0$

13. $y^2 = x$

14. $|y| = x$

15. $y = x^2$

16. $y - 7 = 7$

17. $y^2 - 4x = 1$

18. $|x - 2| = y$

19. $|x| = |y|$

20. $x = 7$

21. $y = 7$

22. $|x + y| = 7$

Let the function f be defined by the equation $y = f(x)$, where x and $f(x)$ are real numbers. Find the domain of each function.

23. $f(x) = 3x + 5$

24. $f(x) = -5x + 2$

25. $f(x) = x^2 - x + 1$

26. $f(x) = x^3 - 3x + 2$

27. $f(x) = \sqrt{x - 2}$

28. $f(x) = \sqrt{2x + 3}$

29. $f(x) = \sqrt{4 - x}$

30. $f(x) = 3\sqrt{2 - x}$

31. $f(x) = \sqrt{x^2 - 1}$

32. $f(x) = \sqrt{x^2 - 2x - 3}$

33. $f(x) = \sqrt[3]{x + 1}$

34. $f(x) = \sqrt[3]{5 - x}$

35. $f(x) = \dfrac{3}{x + 1}$

36. $f(x) = \dfrac{-7}{x + 3}$

37. $f(x) = \dfrac{x}{x - 3}$

38. $f(x) = \dfrac{x + 2}{x - 1}$

39. $f(x) = \dfrac{x}{x^2 - 4}$

40. $f(x) = \dfrac{2x}{x^2 - 9}$

41. $f(x) = \dfrac{1}{x^2 - 4x - 5}$

42. $f(x) = \dfrac{x}{2x^2 - 16x + 30}$

Let the function f be defined by $y = f(x)$, *where x and* $f(x)$ *are real numbers. Find* $f(2)$, $f(-3)$, $f(k)$, *and* $f(k^2 - 1)$.

43. $f(x) = 3x - 2$

44. $f(x) = 5x + 7$

45. $f(x) = \dfrac{1}{2}x + 3$

46. $f(x) = \dfrac{2}{3}x + 5$

47. $f(x) = x^2$

48. $f(x) = 3 - x^2$

49. $f(x) = x^2 + 3x - 1$

50. $f(x) = -x^2 - 2x + 1$

51. $f(x) = |x^2 + 1|$

52. $f(x) = |x^2 + x + 4|$

53. $f(x) = \dfrac{2}{x + 4}$

54. $f(x) = \dfrac{3}{x - 5}$

55. $f(x) = \dfrac{1}{x^2 - 1}$

56. $f(x) = \dfrac{3}{x^2 + 3}$

57. $f(x) = \sqrt{x^2 + 1}$

58. $f(x) = \sqrt{x^2 - 1}$

Evaluate the difference quotient for each function $f(x)$.

59. $f(x) = 3x + 1$

60. $f(x) = 5x - 1$

61. $f(x) = x^2 + 1$

62. $f(x) = x^2 - 3$

63. $f(x) = 4x^2 - 6$

64. $f(x) = 5x^2 + 3$

65. $f(x) = x^2 + 3x - 7$

66. $f(x) = x^2 - 5x + 1$

67. $f(x) = 2x^2 - 4x + 2$

68. $f(x) = 3x^2 + 2x - 3$

69. $f(x) = x^3$

70. $f(x) = \dfrac{1}{x}$

Graph each function. Use the graph to identify the domain and range of each function.

71. $f(x) = 2x + 3$

72. $f(x) = 3x + 2$

73. $f(x) = -\dfrac{3}{4}x + 4$

74. $f(x) = \dfrac{1}{2}x - 3$

75. $2x = 3y - 3$

76. $3x = 2(y + 1)$

77. $f(x) = x^2 - 4$

78. $f(x) = -x^2 + 3$

79. $f(x) = -x^3 + 2$

80. $f(x) = -x^3 + 1$

89. $f(x) = \sqrt{2x - 4}$

90. $f(x) = -\sqrt{2x - 4}$

81. $f(x) = -|x|$

82. $f(x) = -|x| - 3$

91. $f(x) = \sqrt[3]{x} + 2$

92. $f(x) = -\sqrt[3]{x} + 1$

83. $f(x) = |x - 2|$

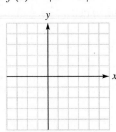

84. $f(x) = -|x - 2|$

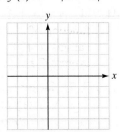

Draw lines to indicate the domain and range of each function as intervals on the x- and y-axes.

93.

94.

85. $f(x) = \left|\dfrac{1}{2}x + 3\right|$

86. $f(x) = -\left|\dfrac{1}{2}x + 3\right|$

Use the Vertical Line Test to determine whether each graph represents a function.

95.

96.

97.

98.

87. $f(x) = -\sqrt{x + 1}$

88. $f(x) = \sqrt{x} + 2$

99.

100.

📉 *Use a graphing calculator to graph each function. Then determine the domain and range of the function.*

101. $f(x) = |3x + 2|$

102. $f(x) = \sqrt{2x - 5}$

103. $f(x) = \sqrt[3]{5x - 1}$

104. $f(x) = -\sqrt[3]{3x + 2}$

Applications

105. Cost of *t*-shirts A chapter of Phi Theta Kappa, an honors society for two-year college students, is purchasing *t*-shirts for each of its members. A local company has agreed to make the shirts for $8 each plus a graphic arts fee of $75.

  a. Write a linear function that describes the cost C for the shirts in terms of x, the number of *t*-shirts ordered.

  b. Find the total cost of 85 *t*-shirts.

106. Service projects The Circle "K" Club is planning a service project for children at a local children's home. They plan to rent a "Dora the Explorer Moonwalk" for the event. The cost of the moonwalk will include a $60 delivery fee and $45 for each hour it is used. Express the total bill b in terms of the hours used h.

107. Cell phone plans A grandmother agrees to purchase a cell phone for emergency use only. AT&T now offers such a plan for $9.99 per month and $0.07 for each minute t the phone is used.

  a. Write a linear function that describes the monthly cost C in terms of the time in minutes t the phone is used.

  b. If the grandmother uses her phone for 20 minutes during the first month, what was her bill?

108. Concessions A concessionaire at a football game pays a vendor $40 per game for selling hot dogs at $2.50 each.

  a. Write a linear function that describes the income I the vendor earns for the concessionaire during the game if the vendor sells h hot dogs.

  b. Find the income if the vendor sells 175 hot dogs.

109. Home construction In a proposal to prospective clients, a contractor listed the following costs:

1. Fees, permits, site preparation	$14,000
2. Construction, per square foot	$95

  a. Write a linear function the clients can use to determine the cost C of building a house having f square feet.

  b. Find the cost to build a 2,600-square-foot house.

110. Temperature conversion The Fahrenheit temperature reading (F) is a linear function of the Celsius reading (C). If $C = 0$ when $F = 32$ and the readings are the same at $-40°$, express F as a function of C.

111. Cost of electricity The cost C of electricity in Eagle River is a linear function of x, the number of kilowatt-hours (kwh) used. If the cost of 100 kwh is $17 and the cost of 500 kwh is $57, find an equation that expresses C in terms of x.

112. Water billing The cost C of water is a linear function of n, the number of gallons used. If 1,000 gallons cost $4.70 and 9,000 gallons cost $14.30, express C as a function of n.

113. Coffee locations Suppose that in 2008 there were approximately 6,400 of your coffee company locations. Suppose that in 2012 this number had grown to approximately 13,168. Write a linear function that represents the number of coffee locations n as a function of time t. Let $t = 0$ represent 2008.

114. Cliff divers The cliff divers of Acapulco amaze tourists with their diving skills. The velocity v of a diver is a function of the time t the diver has fallen. If the initial velocity of the diver is 2 feet per second and $v = -66$ feet per second when $t = 2$ seconds, express v as a function t.

115. Exchange rates If fifty U.S. dollars can be exchanged for 69.5550 Euros and 125 U.S. dollars can be exchanged for 173.8875 Euros, write a linear function that represents the number of Euros E in terms of U.S. dollars D.

116. Exchange rates If fifty U.S. dollars can be exchanged for 600.1100 Mexican pesos and 125 U.S. dollars can be exchanged for 1500.275 Mexican pesos, write a linear function that represents the number of Mexican pesos P in terms of U.S. dollars D.

Discovery and Writing

Find all values of x that will make f(x) = 0.

117. $f(x) = 3x + 2$ **118.** $f(x) = -2x - 5$

119. Write a paragraph explaining how to find the domain of a function.

120. Write a paragraph explaining how to find the range of a function.

121. Explain why all functions are relations, but not all relations are functions.

122. Use a graphing calculator to graph the function $f(x) = \sqrt{x}$, and use $\boxed{\text{TRACE}}$ and $\boxed{\text{ZOOM}}$ to find $\sqrt{5}$ to three decimal places.

Review
Consider this set: $\{-3, -1, 0, 0.5, \frac{3}{4}, 1, \pi, 7, 8\}$

123. Which numbers are natural numbers?

124. Which numbers are rational numbers?

125. Which numbers are prime numbers?
126. Which numbers are even numbers?

Write each in interval notation.

127. ![interval from -4 to 7]   **128.** ![interval from -3 to 5]

Graph each union of two intervals.

129. $(-3, 5) \cup [6, \infty)$ **130.** $(-\infty, 0) \cup (0, \infty)$

Mayskyphoto/Shutterstock.com

3.2 Quadratic Functions

In this section, we will learn to

1. Recognize the characteristics of a quadratic function.
2. Find the vertex of a parabola whose equation is in standard form.
3. Graph a quadratic function.
4. Find the vertex of a parabola whose equation is in general form.
5. Use a quadratic function to solve maximum and minimum problems.

Quadratic functions are important because we can use them to model many real-life problems. For example, the path of a basketball jump shot by Shaquille O'Neal and the path of a guided missile can be modeled with quadratic functions. Businesses like Coca Cola and Best Buy can use quadratic functions to help maximize the profit and revenue for the products they produce and sell.

1. Recognize the Characteristics of a Quadratic Function

The linear function $f(x) = mx + b$ $(m \neq 0)$ is a first-degree polynomial function, because its right side is a first-degree polynomial in the variable x. A function defined by a polynomial of second degree is called a **quadratic function.**

Quadratic Function   A **quadratic function** is a second-degree polynomial function in one variable of the form

$$f(x) = ax^2 + bx + c \quad \text{or} \quad y = ax^2 + bx + c,$$

where a, b, and c are real numbers and $a \neq 0$.

Some examples of quadratic functions are

$$f(x) = x^2 - 2x - 3 \quad \text{and} \quad f(x) = -2x^2 - 8x - 3.$$

Quadratic functions can be graphed by plotting points. For example, to graph the function $f(x) = x^2 - 2x - 3$, we plot several points with coordinates that satisfy the equation. We then join them with a smooth curve to obtain the graph shown in Figure 3-14.

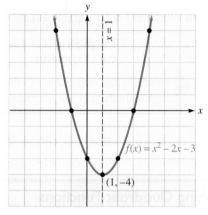

$f(x) = x^2 - 2x - 3$		
x	$f(x)$	$(x, f(x))$
-2	5	$(-2, 5)$
-1	0	$(-1, 0)$
0	-3	$(0, -3)$
1	-4	$(1, -4)$
2	-3	$(2, -3)$
3	0	$(3, 0)$
4	5	$(4, 5)$

Domain: $(-\infty, \infty)$, **Range:** $[-4, \infty)$

FIGURE 3-14

A table of values and the graph of $f(x) = -2x^2 - 8x - 3$ are shown in Figure 3-15.

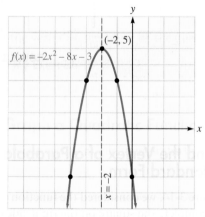

$f(x) = -2x^2 - 8x - 3$		
x	$f(x)$	$(x, f(x))$
-4	-3	$(-4, -3)$
-3	3	$(-3, 3)$
-2	5	$(-2, 5)$
-1	3	$(-1, 3)$
0	-3	$(0, -3)$

Domain: $(-\infty, \infty)$, **Range:** $(-\infty, 5]$

FIGURE 3-15

The graph of a quadratic function is called a **parabola**, a cup-shaped curve that either opens upward ∪ or downward ∩. The graphs in Figures 3-14 and 3-15 suggest that the graph of a quadratic function has the following characteristics.

Self Check 4 Graph the function: $f(x) = -3x^2 + 7x - 2$.

Now Try Exercise 53.

ACCENT ON TECHNOLOGY **Finding the Maximum Point or Minimum Point (Vertex) of a Parabola**

We can use a graphing calculator to find the maximum point or minimum point (vertex) of a parabola. Consider the $f(x) = -2x^2 - 5x + 3$ given in Example 4. We will apply the following steps to determine the maximum point or vertex of the parabola.

1. Enter the function.

2. Set a window that shows the function.

3. Graph the function.

4. Go to the CALC menu by pressing [2nd] [TRACE] and select maximum.

5. Use the [TRACE] key to get a left bound.

6. Use the [TRACE] key to get a right bound.

7. Use the [TRACE] key to make a guess.

8. Press [ENTER] and find the maximum point.

FIGURE 3-19

We see that the maximum point or the vertex is $(-1.250001, 6.125)$.

5. Use a Quadratic Function to Solve Maximum and Minimum Problems

EXAMPLE 5   **Using a Quadratic Function to Solve a Maximum Area Problem**

The Montana Dude Rancher's Association has 400 feet of fencing to enclose a rectangular corral. To save money and fencing, the association intends to use the bank of a river as one boundary of the corral, as in Figure 3-20. Find the dimensions that will enclose the largest area.

SOLUTION   We will represent the fenced area with a quadratic function. Since its parabolic graph opens downward, the largest or maximum area will occur at the vertex. We can use the vertex formula to find the vertex.

Step 1: Represent the area with a quadratic function.
Let x represent the width of the fenced area. Then $400 - 2x$ represents the length. Because the area A of a rectangle is the product of the length and the width, we have

$$A = (400 - 2x)x \quad \text{or} \quad A(x) = -2x^2 + 400x$$

FIGURE 3-20

The graph of this area function is a parabola. Since the coefficient of x^2 is negative, the parabola opens downward and its vertex is its highest point. The A-coordinate of the vertex (x, A) represents the maximum area, and the x-coordinate represents the width of the corral that will give the maximum area.

Step 2: Find the vertex of the parabola.
We compare the equations

$$A(x) = -2x^2 + 400x \quad \text{and} \quad y = ax^2 + bx + c$$

to see that $a = -2$, $b = 400$, and $c = 0$. Using the vertex formula, the vertex of the parabola is the point with coordinates

$$\left(-\frac{b}{2a}, c - \frac{b^2}{4a}\right) = \left(-\frac{400}{2(-2)}, 0 - \frac{400^2}{4(-2)}\right) = (100, 20{,}000)$$

Comment   Note that we could have determined the y-coordinate of 20,000 by finding $A(100)$.

$$A(x) = -2x^2 + 400x$$
$$A(100) = -2(100)^2 + 400(100) \qquad \text{Substitute 100 for } x.$$
$$= -2(10{,}000) + 40{,}000$$
$$= -20{,}000 + 40{,}000$$
$$= 20{,}000$$

If the fence runs 100 feet out from the river, 200 feet parallel to the river, and 100 feet back to the river, it will enclose the largest possible area, which is 20,000 square feet.   ■

Self Check 5   Find the largest area possible if the association has 1,200 feet of fencing available.

Now Try Exercise 55.

EXAMPLE 6   **Using a Quadratic Function to Solve a Minimum Cost Problem**

A company that makes and sells water skis has found that the total weekly cost C of producing x water skis is given by the function $C(x) = 0.5x^2 - 210x + 26{,}250$. Find the production level that minimizes the weekly cost and find that weekly minimum cost.

SOLUTION   The weekly cost function $C(x)$ is a quadratic function whose graph is a parabola that opens upward. The minumum value of $C(x)$ occurs at the vertex of the parabola. We will use the vertex formula to find the vertex of the parabola.

Since the coefficient of x^2 is 0.5 (a positive real number), the x-coordinate of the vertex is the production level that will minimize the cost, and the y-coordinate is that minimum cost. We compare the equations

$$C(x) = 0.5x^2 - 210x + 26{,}250 \quad \text{and} \quad y = ax^2 + bx + c$$

to see that $a = 0.5$, $b = -210$, and $c = 26{,}250$. Using the vertex formula, we see that the vertex of the parabola is the point with coordinates

$$\left(-\frac{b}{2a},\ c - \frac{b^2}{4a}\right) = \left(-\frac{-210}{2(0.5)},\ 26{,}250 - \frac{(-210)^2}{4(0.5)}\right) = (210,\ 4{,}200)$$

Comment   We can also determine the y-coordinate of 4,200 by finding $C(210)$.

$$C(x) = 0.5x^2 - 210x + 26{,}250$$

$$C(210) = 0.5(210)^2 - 210(210) + 26{,}250 \qquad \text{Substitute 210 for } x.$$

$$= 0.5(44{,}100) - 44{,}100 + 26{,}250$$

$$= 22{,}050 - 17{,}850$$

$$= 4{,}200$$

If the company makes 210 water skis each week, it will minimize its production cost. The minimum weekly cost will be $4,200.   ■

Self Check 6   A company that makes and sells baseball caps has found that the total monthly cost C of producing x caps is given by the function $C(x) = 0.2x^2 - 80x + 9{,}000$. Find the production level that will minimize the monthly cost and find the minimum cost.

Now Try Exercise 67.

Self Check Answers   1. $(-5, -4)$ 2.   3. $(2, 3)$ 4.
5. 180,000 square feet
6. 200, $1,000

$f(x) = -(x - 2)^2 + 4$

$f(x) = -3x^2 + 7x - 2$

Exercises **3.2**

Getting Ready
You should be able to complete these vocabulary and concept statements before you proceed to the practice exercises.

Fill in the blanks.

1. A quadratic function is defined by the equation
   _____ $(a \neq 0)$.

2. The standard form for the equation of a parabola is
   _____ $(a \neq 0)$.

3. The vertex of the parabolic graph of the equation
   $y = 2(x - 3)^2 + 5$ will be at _____.

4. The vertical line that intersects the parabola at its
   vertex is the _____.

5. If the parabola opens _____ the vertex will be a
   minimum point.

6. If the parabola opens _____ the vertex will be a
   maximum point.

7. The x-coordinate of the vertex of the parabolic graph
   of $f(x) = ax^2 + bx + c$ is _____.

8. The y-coordinate of the vertex of the parabolic
   graph of $f(x) = ax^2 + bx + c$ is _____.

Practice
Determine whether the graph of each quadratic function opens upward or downward. State whether a maximum or minimum point occurs at the vertex of the parabola.

9. $f(x) = \dfrac{1}{2}x^2 + 3$ 10. $f(x) = 2x^2 - 3x$

11. $f(x) = -3(x + 1)^2 + 2$ 12. $f(x) = -5(x - 1)^2 - 1$

13. $f(x) = -2x^2 + 5x - 1$ 14. $f(x) = 2x^2 - 3x + 1$

Find the vertex of each parabola.

15. $y = x^2 - 1$ 16. $y = -x^2 + 2$

17. $f(x) = (x - 3)^2 + 5$ 18. $f(x) = -2(x - 3)^2 + 4$

19. $f(x) = -2(x + 6)^2 - 4$ 20. $f(x) = \dfrac{1}{3}(x + 1)^2 - 5$

21. $f(x) = \dfrac{2}{3}(x - 3)^2$ 22. $f(x) = 7(x + 2)^2 + 8$

23. $f(x) = x^2 - 4x + 4$ 24. $y = x^2 - 10x + 25$

25. $y = x^2 + 6x - 3$ 26. $y = -x^2 + 9x - 2$

27. $y = -2x^2 + 12x - 17$ 28. $y = 2x^2 + 16x + 33$

29. $y = 3x^2 - 4x + 5$ 30. $y = -4x^2 + 3x + 4$

31. $y = \dfrac{1}{2}x^2 + 4x - 3$ 32. $y = -\dfrac{2}{3}x^2 + 3x - 5$

Graph each quadratic function given in standard form.

33. $f(x) = x^2 - 4$ 34. $f(x) = x^2 + 1$

35. $f(x) = -3x^2 + 6$ 36. $f(x) = -4x^2 + 4$

37. $f(x) = -\dfrac{1}{2}x^2 + 8$ 38. $f(x) = \dfrac{1}{2}x^2 - 2$

    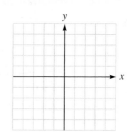

39. $f(x) = (x - 3)^2 - 1$ 40. $f(x) = (x + 3)^2 - 1$

    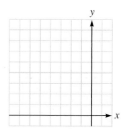

41. $f(x) = 2(x + 1)^2 - 2$

42. $f(x) = -\dfrac{3}{4}(x - 2)^2$

49. $f(x) = x^2 - 4x + 1$

50. $f(x) = x^2 - 6x - 7$

43. $f(x) = -(x + 4)^2 + 1$

44. $f(x) = -3(x - 4)^2 + 3$

51. $f(x) = 2x^2 - 12x + 10$

52. $f(x) = -x^2 - 4x + 1$

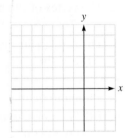

45. $f(x) = -3(x - 2)^2 + 6$

46. $f(x) = 2(x - 3)^2 - 4$

53. $f(x) = -3x^2 - 6x - 9$

54. $f(x) = -3x^2 - 3x + 18$

Graph each quadratic function given in general form.

47. $f(x) = x^2 + 2x$

48. $f(x) = x^2 - 6x$

Applications

55. Police investigations A police officer seals off the scene of an accident using a roll of yellow tape that is 300 feet long. What dimensions should be used to seal off the maximum rectangular area around the collision? Find the maximum area.

56. Maximizing area The rectangular garden shown has a width of x and a perimeter of 100 feet. Find x such that the area of the rectangle is maximum.

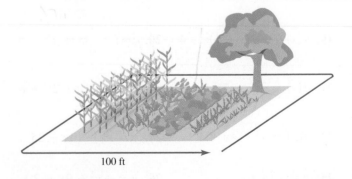

100 ft

57. Maximizing storage area A farmer wants to partition a rectangular feed storage area in a corner of his barn, as shown in the illustration. The barn walls form two sides of the stall, and the farmer has 50 feet of partition for the remaining two sides. What dimensions will maximize the area?

50 ft

58. Maximizing grazing area A rancher wishes to enclose a rectangular partitioned corral with 1,800 feet of fencing. (See the illustration.) What dimensions of the corral would enclose the largest possible area? Find the maximum area.

59. Sheet metal fabrication A 24-inch-wide sheet of metal is to be bent into a rectangular trough with the cross section shown in the illustration. Find the dimensions that will maximize the amount of water the trough can hold. That is, find the dimensions that will maximize the cross-sectional area.

Depth

24 in.

Width

60. Landscape design A gardener will use D feet of edging to border a rectangular plot of ground. Show that the maximum area will be enclosed if the rectangle is a square.

61. Architecture A parabolic arch has an equation of $x^2 + 20y - 400 = 0$, where x is measured in feet. Find the maximum height of the arch.

62. Path of a guided missile A guided missile is propelled from the origin of a coordinate system with the x-axis along the ground and the y-axis vertical. Its path, or **trajectory,** is given by the equation $y = 400x - 16x^2$. Find the object's maximum height.

63. Height of a basketball The path of a basketball thrown from the free throw line can be modeled by the quadratic function $f(x) = -0.06x^2 + 1.5x + 6$, where x is the horizontal distance (in feet) from the free throw line and $f(x)$ is the height (in feet) of the ball. Find the maximum height of the basketball.

64. Ballistics A child throws a ball up a hill that makes an angle of 45° with the horizontal. The ball lands 100 feet up the hill. Its trajectory is a parabola with equation $y = -x^2 + ax$ for some number a. Find a.

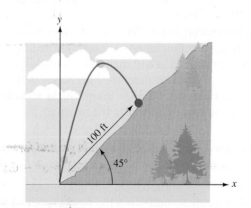

65. Maximizing height A ball is thrown straight up from the top of a building 144 ft. tall with an initial velocity of 64 ft per second. The distance $s(t)$ (in feet) of the ball from the ground is given by $s(t) = 144 + 64t - 16t^2$. Find the maximum height attained by the ball.

66. Flat-panel television sets A wholesaler of appliances finds that she can sell $(2,400 - p)$ flat-panel television sets each week when the price is p dollars. What price will maximize revenue?

67. Digital camera A company that produces and sells digital cameras has determined that the total weekly cost C of producing x digital cameras is given by the function $C(x) = 1.5x^2 - 144x + 5{,}856$. Determine the production level that minimizes the weekly cost for producing the digital cameras and find that weekly minimum cost.

68. Finding mass transit fares The Municipal Transit Authority serves 150,000 commuters daily when the fare is $1.80. Market research has determined that every penny decrease in the fare will result in 1,000 new riders. What fare will maximize revenue?

69. Finding hotel rates A 300-room hotel is two-thirds filled when the nightly room rate is $90. Experience has shown that each $5 increase in cost results in 10 fewer occupied rooms. Find the nightly rate that will maximize income.

70. Selling concert tickets Tickets for a concert are cheaper when purchased in quantity. The first 100 tickets are priced at $10 each, but each additional block of 100 tickets purchased decreases the cost of each ticket by 50¢. How many blocks of tickets should be sold to maximize the revenue?

Use this information: At a time t seconds after an object is tossed vertically upward, it reaches a height s in feet given by the equation $s = 80t - 16t^2$.

71. In how many seconds does the object reach its maximum height?

72. In how many seconds does the object return to the point from which it was thrown?

73. What is the maximum height reached by the object?

74. Show that it takes the same amount of time for the object to reach its maximum height as it does to return from that height to the point from which it was thrown.

Use a graphing calculator to determine the coordinates of the vertex of each parabola. You will have to select appropriate viewing windows.

75. $y = 2x^2 + 9x - 56$ **76.** $y = 14x - \dfrac{x^2}{5}$

77. $y = (x - 7)(5x + 2)$ **78.** $y = -x(0.2 + 0.1x)$

Discovery and Writing
Find all values of x that will make $f(x) = 0$.

79. $f(x) = x^2 - 5x + 6$ **80.** $f(x) = 6x^2 + x - 2$

81. Find the dimensions of the largest rectangle that can be inscribed in the right triangle ABC shown in the illustration.

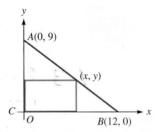

82. Point P lies in the first quadrant and on the line $x + y = 1$ in such a position that the area of triangle OPA is maximum. Find the coordinates of P. (See the illustration.)

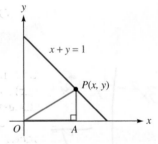

83. The sum of two numbers is 6, and the sum of the squares of those two numbers is as small as possible. What are the numbers?

84. What number most exceeds its square?

The maximum or minimum value of a quadratic function can be found automatically by using a computer program, such as Excel.

85. Find the minimum value of the function $f(x) = 2x^2 - 3x - 4$ by using the Solver in Excel. Give the value of x that minimizes the function as well as the minimum value of the function. See Problem 119 in Section 1.3.

86. Find the maximum value of the function $f(x) = -2x^2 + 3x + 4$ by using the Solver in Excel. Give the value of x that maximizes the function as well as the maximum value of the function. See Problem 119 in Section 1.3.

Review

Find $f(a)$ and $f(-a)$.

87. $f(x) = x^2 - 3x$

88. $f(x) = x^3 - 3x$

89. $f(x) = (5 - x)^2$

90. $f(x) = \dfrac{1}{x^2 - 4}$

91. $f(x) = 7$

92. $f(x) = -|x|$

3.3 Polynomial and Other Functions

In this section, we will learn to

1. Understand the characteristics of polynomial functions.
2. Graph polynomial functions.
3. Determine whether a function is even, odd, or neither.
4. Identify the open intervals on which a function is increasing, decreasing, or constant.
5. Graph piecewise-defined functions.
6. Evaluate and graph the greatest-integer function.

© Istockphoto.com/Steve Maehl

So far, we have discussed two types of polynomial functions—first-degree (or linear) functions, and second-degree (or quadratic) functions. In this section, we will discuss polynomial functions of higher degree.

Polynomial functions can be used to model the path of a roller coaster or to model the fluctuation of gasoline prices over the past few months. Goliath, a hypercoaster, is located in Atlanta at Six Flags over Georgia. It climbs to a height of 200 feet and reaches speeds of nearly 70 mph. It has over 4,400 feet of steel track. Portions of Goliath's tracks can be modeled with a polynomial function.

Polynomial Functions   A **polynomial function in one variable (say, x)** is a function of the form

$$f(x) = a_n x^n + a_{n-1} x^{n-1} + \cdots + a_1 x + a_0$$

where $a_n, a_{n-1}, \ldots, a_1,$ and a_0 are real numbers and n is a whole number.

The **degree of a polynomial function** is the largest power of x that appears in the polynomial.

The table shows three basic polynomial functions that we have already covered:

Name	Function	Degree	Graph
Constant function	$f(x) = 5$	0	Horizontal line
Linear function	$f(x) = 2x - 7$	1	Nonvertical line
Quadratic function	$f(x) = -2x^2 + 4x - 5$	2	Parabola

Here are two examples of higher-degree polynomial functions, along with their graphs.

FIGURE 3-21

$f(x) = 2x^3 - 2x^2 - 18x + 18$

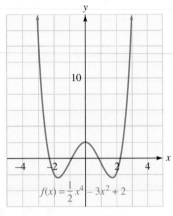

FIGURE 3-22

$f(x) = \frac{1}{2}x^4 - 3x^2 + 2$

1. Understand the Characteristics of Polynomial Functions

There are several basic characteristics common to all polynomial functions. We will list several of them.

1: The graphs of polynomial functions are smooth and continuous curves.

Like the graphs of linear and quadratic functions, the graphs of higher-degree polynomial functions are smooth continuous curves. Because their graphs are smooth, they have no cusps or corners. Because they are continuous, their graphs have no breaks or holes. They can always be drawn without lifting the pencil from the paper.

- The graph of a polynomial function

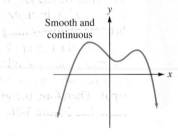

Graph of a polynomial function

FIGURE 3-23

- The graphs of two functions that are **not** polynomial functions

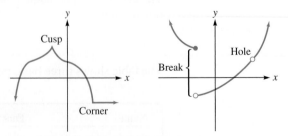

Not the graph of a polynomial function   Not the graph of a polynomial function

FIGURE 3-24

2: Many polynomial functions have graphs similar to the graphs of $f(x) = x$, $f(x) = x^2$, and $f(x) = x^3$.

Many polynomial functions are of the form $f(x) = x^n$, and several of their graphs are shown in Figure 3-25. Note that when n is even, the graph has the same general shape as $y = x^2$. When n is odd and greater than 1, the graph has the same general shape as $y = x^3$. However, the graphs are flatter at the origin and steeper as n becomes large.

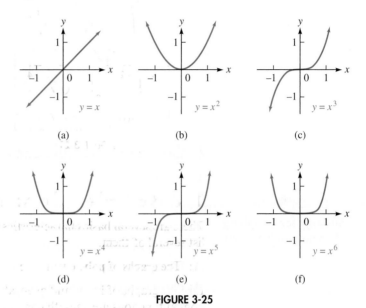

FIGURE 3-25

3: The end behavior of the graph of a polynomial function is similar to the graph of its term with highest degree.

The ends of the graph of any polynomial function will be similar to the graph of its term with the highest power of x, because when n becomes large, the other terms become relatively insignificant.

Consider the polynomial function $f(x) = x^3 + x^2 - 2x$. The end behavior of its graph will be similar to the ends of the graph of its leading term x^3. In Figure 3-25 (c), we see that the graph of $y = x^3$ falls on the far left and rises on the far right. Therefore, the graph of $f(x)$ will also fall on the far left and rise on the far right. See Figure 3-26.

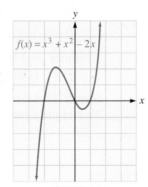

FIGURE 3-26

4: Polynomial functions can be symmetric about the y-axis or the origin.

In Section 2.4, we learned that a graph is symmetric about the y-axis if the graph of $y = f(x)$ has the same y-coordinate when the function is evaluated at x or at $-x$.

Thus, a function is symmetric about the y-axis if $f(x) = f(-x)$ for all values of x that are in the domain of the function. See Figure 3-27(a). Also recall that a graph is symmetric about the origin if the point $(-x, -f(x))$ lies on the graph whenever $(x, f(x))$ does. In this case, $f(-x) = -f(x)$. See Figure 3-27(b).

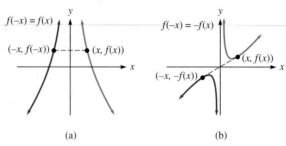

(a)   (b)

FIGURE 3-27

2. Graph Polynomial Functions

To graph polynomial functions, we can use the following steps.

Strategy for Graphing Polynomial Functions

1. Find any symmetries of the graph.
2. Find the x- and y-intercepts of the graph.
3. Determine where the graph is above and below the x-axis.
4. Plot a few points, if necessary, and draw the graph as a smooth continuous curve.

EXAMPLE 1   Graphing a Polynomial Function of Degree 3

Graph the function: $f(x) = x^3 - 4x$.

SOLUTION   We will use the four steps stated above to graph the polynomial function.

Step 1: Find any symmetries of the graph.
To test for symmetry about the y-axis, we check to see whether $f(x) = f(-x)$. To test for symmetry about the origin, we check to see whether $f(-x) = -f(x)$.

$$f(x) = x^3 - 4x$$

$$f(-x) = (-x)^3 - 4(-x) \qquad \text{Substitute } -x \text{ for } x.$$

$$f(-x) = -x^3 + 4x \qquad \qquad \text{Simplify.}$$

Since $f(x) \neq f(-x)$, there is no symmetry about the y-axis. However, since $f(-x) = -f(x)$, there is symmetry about the origin.

Step 2: Find the x- and y-intercepts of the graph.
To find the x-intercepts, we let $f(x) = 0$ and solve for x.

$$x^3 - 4x = 0$$

$$x(x^2 - 4) = 0 \qquad\qquad\qquad \text{Factor out } x.$$

$$x(x + 2)(x - 2) = 0 \qquad\qquad \text{Factor } x^2 - 4.$$

$$x = 0 \quad \text{or} \quad x + 2 = 0 \quad \text{or} \quad x - 2 = 0 \qquad \text{Set each factor equal to 0.}$$

$$x = -2 \qquad\qquad x = 2$$

The x-intercepts are $(0, 0)$, $(-2, 0)$, and $(2, 0)$. If we let $x = 0$ and solve for $f(x)$, we see that the y-intercept is also $(0, 0)$.

Step 3: Determine where the graph is above or below the *x*-axis.

To determine where the graph is above or below the *x*-axis, we plot the solutions of $x^3 - 4x = 0$ (the *x*-coordinates of the *x*-intercepts) on a number line and establish the four intervals shown in Figure 3-28. We then test a number from each interval to determine the sign of $f(x)$. (For a review of this process, see Example 7 in Section 1.7.)

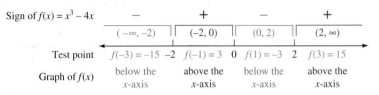

Sign of $f(x) = x^3 - 4x$	—	+	—	+
	$(-\infty, -2)$	$(-2, 0)$	$(0, 2)$	$(2, \infty)$
Test point	$f(-3) = -15$ -2	$f(-1) = 3$ 0	$f(1) = -3$ 2	$f(3) = 15$
Graph of $f(x)$	below the *x*-axis	above the *x*-axis	below the *x*-axis	above the *x*-axis

FIGURE 3-28

Comment

Note that the far right and far left ends of the graph are similar to the ends of the graph of $f(x) = x^3$, which is the leading term of the function $f(x) = x^3 - 4x$ or the term with highest degree. On the far right the graph rises and on the far left the graph falls.

Step 4: Plot a few points and draw the graph as a smooth continuous curve.

We now plot the intercepts and one additional point. In the previous step we found that $f(1) = -3$. This will be the additional point we plot $(1, -3)$. Making use of our knowledge of symmetry and where the graph is above and below the *x*-axis we now draw the graph as shown in Figure 3-29(a). A calculator graph, using the standard viewing window, is shown in Figure 3-29(b).

$f(x) = x^3 - 4x$		
x	$f(x)$	$(x, f(x))$
-2	0	$(-2, 0)$
0	0	$(0, 0)$
1	-3	$(1, -3)$
2	0	$(2, 0)$

(a)

(b)

FIGURE 3-29

Self Check 1   Graph: $f(x) = x^3 - 9x$.

Now Try Exercise 13.

The peak and valley of the graph shown in Figure 3-29 are called **turning points.** In calculus, such points are called **local minima** and **local maxima.** Although we cannot find these points without using calculus, we can approximate them by plotting points or by using the TRACE feature on a graphing calculator. We can also use the CALC Minimum and CALC Maximum features on a graphing calculator to find these local extrema.

Note that Figure 3-29 shows the graph of a third-degree polynomial and the graph has two turning points. This suggests the following result from calculus that helps us understand the shape of many polynomial graphs.

Number of Turning Points   If $f(x)$ is a polynomial function of *n*th degree, then the graph of $f(x)$ will have $n - 1$, or fewer, turning points.

EXAMPLE 2   **Graphing a Polynomial Function of Degree 4**

Graph the function: $f(x) = x^4 - 5x^2 + 4$.

SOLUTION   We will use the four steps for graphing a polynomial function.

Step 1: Find any symmetries of the graph.
Because x appears with only even exponents, $f(x) = f(-x)$, and the graph is symmetric about the y-axis. The graph is not symmetric about the origin.

Step 2: Find the x- and y-intercepts of the graph.
To find the x-intercepts, we let $f(x) = 0$ and solve for x.

$$x^4 - 5x^2 + 4 = 0$$

$$(x^2 - 4)(x^2 - 1) = 0$$

$$(x + 2)(x - 2)(x + 1)(x - 1) = 0$$

$$x + 2 = 0 \quad \text{or} \quad x - 2 = 0 \quad \text{or} \quad x + 1 = 0 \quad \text{or} \quad x - 1 = 0$$

$$x = -2 \quad | \quad x = 2 \quad | \quad x = -1 \quad | \quad x = 1$$

The x-intercepts are $(-2, 0), (2, 0), (-1, 0)$, and $(1, 0)$. To find the y-intercept, we let $x = 0$ and see that the y-intercept is $(0, 4)$.

Step 3: Determine where the graph is above or below the x-axis.
To determine where the graph is above or below the x-axis, we plot the x-coordinates of the x-intercepts on a number line and establish the five intervals shown in Figure 3-30. We then test a number from each interval to determine the sign of $f(x)$.

FIGURE 3-30

Comment

Note that the far right and far left ends of the graph are similar to the ends of the graph of $f(x) = x^4$, which is the leading term of the function $f(x) = x^4 - 5x^2 + 4$ or the term with highest degree. On the far right and far left the graph rises. Also note that the graph has three turning points.

Step 4: Plot a few points and draw the graph as a smooth continuous curve.
We can now plot the intercepts and use our knowledge of symmetry and where the graph is above and below the x-axis to draw the graph, as shown in Figure 3-31(a). A calculator graph, using the standard viewing window, is shown in Figure 3-31(b).

$f(x) = x^4 - 5x^2 + 4$		
x	$f(x)$	$(x, f(x))$
-2	0	$(-2, 0)$
-1	0	$(-1, 0)$
0	4	$(0, 4)$
1	0	$(1, 0)$
$\dfrac{3}{2}$	$-\dfrac{35}{16}$	$\left(\dfrac{3}{2}, -\dfrac{35}{16}\right)$
2	0	$(2, 0)$

(a)

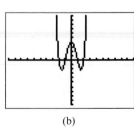

(b)

FIGURE 3-31

Self Check 2   Graph: $f(x) = x^4 - 10x^2 + 9$.

Now Try Exercise 19.

3. Determine Whether a Function Is Even, Odd, or Neither

Functions can be classified as being even, odd, or neither even nor odd. These definitions are given next.

| Even Function | A function is an **even function** if $f(-x) = f(x)$ for all x in the domain of f. |

Even functions are symmetric about the y-axis.

| Odd Function | A function is an **odd function** if $f(-x) = -f(x)$ for all x in the domain of f. |

Odd functions are symmetric about the origin.

Since the graph of the function $f(x) = x^3 - 4x$ in Example 1 is symmetric about the origin, it represents an odd function. Since the graph of the function $f(x) = x^4 - 5x + 4$ in Example 2 is symmetric about the y-axis, it represents an even function. If $f(x)$ does not have either of these symmetries, it is neither even nor odd.

EXAMPLE 3   **Determining Whether a Function Is Even, Odd, or Neither**

Determine whether each function is even, odd, or neither:
a. $f(x) = x^2 + 1$ **b.** $f(x) = x^3$

SOLUTION   To check whether the function is an even function, we find $f(-x)$ and see whether $f(-x) = f(x)$. To check whether the function is an odd function, we find $f(-x)$ and see whether $f(-x) = -f(x)$.

a. $f(-x) = (-x)^2 + 1 = x^2 + 1 = f(x)$

Since $f(-x) = f(x)$, the function is an even function.

The graph of $f(x) = x^2 + 1$ is shown in Figure 3-32. We see that the graph is symmetric about the y-axis.

b. $f(-x) = (-x)^3 = -x^3 = -f(x)$

Since $f(-x) \neq f(x)$, the function is not an even function.

However, the function is an odd function, because $f(-x) = -f(x)$.

The graph of $f(x) = x^3$ is shown in Figure 3-33. Note that the graph is symmetric about the origin.

FIGURE 3-32

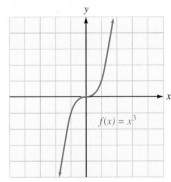

FIGURE 3-33

Self Check 3   Classify each function as even, odd, or neither: **a.** $f(x) = x^3 + x$
b. $f(x) = x^2 + 4$

Now Try Exercise 23.

4. Identify the Open Intervals on Which a Function Is Increasing, Decreasing, or Constant

If we trace the graph of a function from left to right and the values $f(x)$ increase as shown in Figure 3-34(a), we say that the function is an **increasing function.** If the values $f(x)$ decrease as in Figure 3-34(b), we say that the function is a **decreasing function.** If the values $f(x)$ remain unchanged as x increases, we say that the function is a **constant function.**

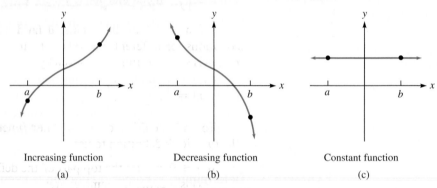

Increasing function
(a)

Decreasing function
(b)

Constant function
(c)

FIGURE 3-34

As we would expect, when we trace the graphs of some functions from left to right, there will be intervals where the function increases, intervals where the function decreases, and intervals where the function is constant. We will always state these intervals as open intervals because of the following definition.

Increasing on an Open Interval	A function f is **increasing on an open interval** (a, b) if for any x_1 and x_2 in (a, b), where $x_1 < x_2$, then $f(x_1) < f(x_2)$.
Decreasing on an Open Interval	A function f is **decreasing on an open interval** (a, b) if for any x_1 and x_2 in (a, b), where $x_1 < x_2$, then $f(x_1) > f(x_2)$.
Constant on an Open Interval	A function f is **constant on an open interval** (a, b) if for any x_1 and x_2 in (a, b), $f(x_1) = f(x_2)$.

EXAMPLE 4   **Identify the Open Intervals Where a Function Increases or Decreases**

Use the graph of the polynomial function shown to determine the intervals on which the function is increasing or decreasing.

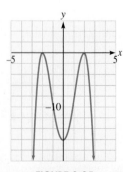

FIGURE 3-35

SOLUTION   We trace the graph of the function from left to right and identify the open intervals on which $f(x)$ values increase and where they decrease. We see from the graph shown in Figure 3-35 that the values of $f(x)$ increase on the open intervals $(-\infty, -2)$ and $(0, 2)$. They decrease on the open intervals $(-2, 0)$ and $(2, \infty)$. Hence, the function is increasing on $(-\infty, -2) \cup (0, 2)$ and is decreasing on $(-2, 0) \cup (2, \infty)$. ∎

Self Check 4   Use the graph shown in Figure 3-35 to identify the open intervals, if any, on which the function is constant.

Now Try Exercise 41.

Comment

Intervals on which a function is increasing, decreasing, or constant are open intervals. We use interval notation and x-values to write the open intervals. Note that y-values are not used.

5. Graph Piecewise-Defined Functions

Some functions, called **piecewise-defined functions,** are defined by using different equations for different intervals in their domains. To illustrate, we will graph the piecewise-defined function f given by

$$f(x) = \begin{cases} -2 & \text{if } x \le 0 \\ x + 1 & \text{if } x > 0 \end{cases}$$

To evaluate this piecewise-defined function, we must determine which part of the function's definition to use.

- If $x \le 0$, we use the top part of the definition and the corresponding value of $f(x)$ is -2. Some examples are:

  $$f(-2) = -2, \quad f(-1) = -2, \quad \text{and} \quad f(0) = -2$$

  In the interval $(-\infty, 0]$, the function value is always -2 and the graph is the horizontal line $y = -2$.

- If $x > 0$, we use the bottom part of the definition and the corresponding value of $f(x)$ is $x + 1$. Some examples are:

  $$f(1) = 1 + 1 = 2 \text{ and } f(2) = 2 + 1 = 3$$

  In the interval $(0, \infty)$, the graph of the function is the line $f(x) = x + 1$. This is a linear function with slope $m = 1$ and y-intercept $(0, b) = (0, 1)$.

The graph of this piecewise-defined function appears in Figure 3-36.

Comment

Note that when $x = 0$, we have $f(x) = -2$. For this reason, the point $(0, -2)$ is shown as a closed point and the point $(0, 1)$ is shown as an open point.

$$f(x) = \begin{cases} -2 & \text{if } x \le 0 \\ x + 1 & \text{if } x > 0 \end{cases}$$

FIGURE 3-36

EXAMPLE 5   **Graphing a Piecewise-Defined Function**

Graph the function: $f(x) = \begin{cases} -x & \text{if } x < 0 \\ x^2 & \text{if } 0 \le x \le 1. \\ 1 & \text{if } x > 1 \end{cases}$

SOLUTION   This piecewise-defined function is defined in three parts. We will graph each part of the function. That is, we will graph $f(x) = -x$ in the interval $(-\infty, 0)$, $f(x) = x^2$ in the interval $[0, 1]$, and $f(x) = 1$ in the interval $(1, \infty)$.

If $x < 0$, the value of $f(x)$ is determined by the equation $f(x) = -x$. We graph the line with slope $m = -1$ and y-intercept $(0, b) = (0, 0)$ in the interval $(-\infty, 0)$. In the interval $(-\infty, 0)$, the function is decreasing.

If $0 \leq x \leq 1$, the value of $f(x)$ is x^2. We graph the parabola in the interval $[0, 1]$. In the open interval $(0,1)$ the function is increasing.

If $x > 1$, the value of $f(x)$ is 1. In the open interval $(1, \infty)$, the function is constant and its graph is the same as the graph of $y = 1$.

The graph of the piecewise function appears in Figure 3-37.

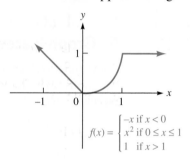

$$f(x) = \begin{cases} -x & \text{if } x < 0 \\ x^2 & \text{if } 0 \leq x \leq 1 \\ 1 & \text{if } x > 1 \end{cases}$$

FIGURE 3-37

Self Check 5   Graph: $f(x) = \begin{cases} 2x & \text{if } x \leq 0 \\ x - 1 & \text{if } x > 0 \end{cases}$.

Now Try Exercise 57.

ACCENT ON TECHNOLOGY   **Piecewise-Defined Functions**

Piecewise-defined functions can be graphed on a calculator. We will graph the piecewise-defined function $f(x) = \begin{cases} -x & \text{if } x < 0 \\ x^2 & \text{if } 0 \leq x \leq 1 \\ 1 & \text{if } x > 1 \end{cases}$ given in Example 5.

- The inequality symbols are found by pressing ⎡2nd⎤ ⎡MATH⎤ (TEST) shown in Figure 3-38(a).
- The "and" command is found in the LOGIC menu which is accessed via the TEST menu. See Figure 3-38(b).
- When graphing these functions, place the calculator in DOT mode. See Figure 3-38(c).
- Enter the function as shown in Figure 3-38(d). Note that the use of parentheses is essential. A viewing window of $[-5, 5]$ for x and $[-3, 3]$ for y is used here.

The graph of the function is shown in Figure 3-38(e).

(a)

(b)

(c)

FIGURE 3-38

(d)

(e)

FIGURE 3-38 (Continued)

6. Evaluate and Graph the Greatest-Integer Function

The **greatest-integer function** is important in many business applications and in the field of computer science. This function is determined by the equation $f(x) = [\![x]\!]$, where the value of $f(x)$ that corresponds to x is the greatest integer that is less than or equal to x.

Comment

Recall that the set of integers is $\{\ldots, -2, -1, 0, 1, 2, \ldots\}$.

For example,

$$f(2.71) = [\![2.71]\!] = 2$$
$$f(23.5) = [\![23.5]\!] = 23$$
$$f(10) = [\![10]\!] = 10$$
$$f(\pi) = [\![\pi]\!] = 3$$
$$f(-2.5) = [\![-2.5]\!] = -3$$

EXAMPLE 6   **Graphing the Greatest-Integer Function**

Graph: $f(x) = [\![x]\!]$.

SOLUTION   We will list several intervals and determine the corresponding values of the greatest-integer function. Then we will use these values to graph the function.

$[0, 1)$ $f(x) = [\![x]\!] = 0$ For numbers from 0 to 1 (not including 1), the greatest integer in the interval is 0.

$[1, 2)$ $f(x) = [\![x]\!] = 1$ For numbers from 1 to 2 (not including 2), the greatest integer in the interval is 1.

$[2, 3)$ $f(x) = [\![x]\!] = 2$ For numbers from 2 to 3 (not including 3), the greatest integer in the interval is 2.

Within each interval, the values of y are constant, but they jump by 1 at integer values of x. The graph is shown in Figure 3-39. From the graph, we can see that the domain of the greatest integer function is the interval $(-\infty, \infty)$. The range is the set of integers.

$$y = [\![x]\!]$$

FIGURE 3-39

Self Check 6   Find **a.** $[\![7.61]\!]$ and **b.** $[\![-3.75]\!]$.

Now Try Exercise 63.

Since the greatest-integer function is made up of a series of horizontal line segments, it is an example of a group of functions called **step functions.**

EXAMPLE 7   **Graphing a Step Function Occurring in an Application**

To print business forms, a printing company charges customers $10 for the order, plus $20 for each box containing 200 forms. The printing company counts any portion of a box as a full box. Graph this step function.

SOLUTION   To graph the step function, we will determine the cost for printing various amounts of boxes of forms. Then we will graph our result.

If we order the forms and then change our minds before the forms are printed, the cost will be $10. Thus, the ordered pair (0, 10) will be on the graph.

If we purchase up to one full box, the cost will be $10 for the order and $20 for the printing, for a total of $30. Thus, the ordered pair (1, 30) will be on the graph.

The cost for $1\frac{1}{2}$ boxes will be the same as the cost for 2 full boxes, or $50. Thus, the ordered pairs (1.5, 50) and (2, 50) are on the graph.

The complete graph is shown in Figure 3-40.

FIGURE 3-40

Self Check 7   Find the cost of $4\frac{1}{2}$ boxes.

Now Try Exercise 69.

Self Check Answers   **1.**

$f(x) = x^3 - 9x$

2.

$f(x) = x^4 - 10x^2 + 9$

3. a. odd   **b.** even

4. no intervals   **5.**

$f(x) = \begin{cases} 2x & \text{if } x \le 0 \\ x - 1 & \text{if } x > 0 \end{cases}$

6. a. 7   **b.** −4   **7.** $110

Exercises **3.3**

Getting Ready

You should be able to complete these vocabulary and concept statements before you proceed to the practice exercises.

Fill in the blanks.

1. The degree of the function $y = f(x) = x^4 - 3$ is ___.
2. Peaks and valleys on a polynomial graph are called _____ points.
3. The graph of a nth degree polynomial function can have at most _____ turning points.
4. If the graph of a function is symmetric about the _____, it is called an even function.
5. If the graph of a function is symmetric about the origin, it is called an ____ function.
6. If the values of $f(x)$ get larger as x increases on an interval, we say that the function is _____ on the open interval.
7. _____ functions are defined by different equations for different intervals in their domains.
8. If the values of $f(x)$ get smaller as x increases on an interval, we say that the function is _____ on the open interval.
9. $[\![3.69]\!] =$ ___.
10. If the values of $f(x)$ do not change as x increases on an interval, we say that the function is _____ on the open interval.

Practice

Graph each polynomial function.

11. $f(x) = x^3 - 9x$

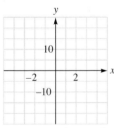

12. $f(x) = x^3 - 16x$

13. $f(x) = -x^3 - 4x^2$

14. $f(x) = x^3 - x$

15. $f(x) = x^3 + x^2$

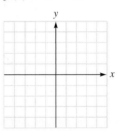

16. $f(x) = -x^3 + 1$

17. $f(x) = x^3 - x^2 - 4x + 4$

18. $f(x) = 4x^3 - 4x^2 - x + 1$

19. $f(x) = x^4 - 2x^2 + 1$

20. $f(x) = x^4 - 5x^2 + 4$

21. $f(x) = -x^4 + 5x^2 - 4$

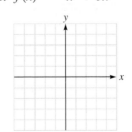

22. $f(x) = x(x - 3)(x - 2)(x + 1)$

Determine whether each function is even, odd, or neither.

23. $f(x) = x^4 + x^2$ **24.** $f(x) = x^3 - 2x$

25. $f(x) = x^3 + x^2$ **26.** $f(x) = x^6 - x^2$

27. $f(x) = x^5 + x^3$ **28.** $f(x) = x^3 - x^2$

29. $f(x) = 2x^3 - 3x$ **30.** $f(x) = 4x^2 - 5$

Determine whether each function is even, odd, or neither.

31.

32.

33.

34.

35.

36.

State the open intervals where each function is increasing, decreasing, or constant.

37.

38.

39.

40.

41.

42.

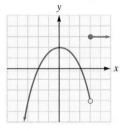

43. $f(x) = x^2 - 4x + 4$

44. $f(x) = 4 - x^2$

Evaluate each piecewise-defined function.

45. $f(x) = \begin{cases} 2x + 2 & \text{if } x < 0 \\ 3 & \text{if } x \geq 0 \end{cases}$

   a. $f(-2)$ **b.** $f(0)$

46. $f(x) = \begin{cases} x - 2 & \text{if } x < 1 \\ x^2 & \text{if } x \geq 1 \end{cases}$

   a. $f(1)$ **b.** $f(5)$

47. $f(x) = \begin{cases} 2 & \text{if } x < 0 \\ 2 - x & \text{if } 0 \leq x < 2 \\ x + 1 & \text{if } x \geq 2 \end{cases}$

   a. $f(-1)$ **b.** $f(1)$ **c.** $f(2)$

48. $f(x) = \begin{cases} 2x & \text{if } x < 0 \\ 3 - x & \text{if } 0 \leq x < 2 \\ |x| & \text{if } x \geq 2 \end{cases}$

   a. $f(-0.5)$ **b.** $f(0)$ **c.** $f(2)$

Graph each piecewise-defined function.

49. $f(x) = \begin{cases} x + 2 & \text{if } x < 0 \\ 2 & \text{if } x \geq 0 \end{cases}$

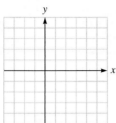

50. $f(x) = \begin{cases} 2x & \text{if } x < 0 \\ -2x & \text{if } x \geq 0 \end{cases}$

51. $f(x) = \begin{cases} x & \text{if } x \leq 0 \\ 2 & \text{if } x > 0 \end{cases}$

52. $f(x) = \begin{cases} -x & \text{if } x < 0 \\ \dfrac{1}{2}x & \text{if } x > 0 \end{cases}$

53. $f(x) = \begin{cases} -4 - x & \text{if } x < 1 \\ 3 & \text{if } x \geq 1 \end{cases}$

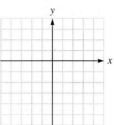

54. $f(x) = \begin{cases} -5 - x & \text{if } x < 1 \\ -3 & \text{if } x \geq 1 \end{cases}$

55. $f(x) = \begin{cases} -x & \text{if } x < 0 \\ x^2 & \text{if } x \geq 0 \end{cases}$

56. $f(x) = \begin{cases} |x| & \text{if } x < 0 \\ \sqrt{x} & \text{if } x \geq 0 \end{cases}$

57. $f(x) = \begin{cases} 0 & \text{if } x < 0 \\ x^2 & \text{if } 0 \le x \le 2 \\ 4 - 2x & \text{if } x > 2 \end{cases}$

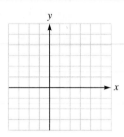

58. $f(x) = \begin{cases} 2 & \text{if } x < 0 \\ 2 - x & \text{if } 0 \le x < 2 \\ x & \text{if } x \ge 2 \end{cases}$

Evalute each function at the indicated x-values.

59. $f(x) = [\![x]\!]$　　**a.** $f(3)$　**b.** $f(-4)$　**c.** $f(-2.3)$

60. $f(x) = [\![3x]\!]$　　**a.** $f(4)$　**b.** $f(-2)$　**c.** $f(-1.2)$

61. $f(x) = [\![x + 3]\!]$　**a.** $f(-1)$　**b.** $f\left(\dfrac{2}{3}\right)$　**c.** $f(1.3)$

62. $f(x) = [\![4x]\!] - 1$　**a.** $f(-3)$　**b.** $f(0)$　**c.** $f(\pi)$

Graph each function.

63. $y = [\![2x]\!]$

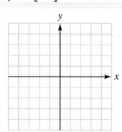

64. $y = \left[\!\left[\dfrac{1}{3}x + 3 \right]\!\right]$

65. $y = [\![x]\!] - 1$

66. $y = [\![x + 2]\!]$

Applications

67. Grading scales A mathematics instructor assigns letter grades according to the following scale.

From	Up to but less than	Grade
60%	70%	D
70%	80%	C
80%	90%	B
90%	100% (including 100%)	A

Graph the ordered pairs (p, g), where p represents the percent and g represents the grade. Find the final semester grade of a student who has test scores of 67%, 73%, 84%, 87%, and 93%.

68. Calculating grades See Exercise 67 and find the final semester grade of a student who has test scores of 53%, 65%, 64%, 73%, 89%, and 82%.

69. Renting a jeep A rental company charges $20 to rent a Jeep Wrangler for one day, plus $4 for every 100 miles (or portion of 100 miles) that it is driven. Graph the ordered pairs (m, C), where m represents the miles driven and C represents the cost. Find the cost if the Jeep is driven 275 miles in one day.

70. Riding in a taxi A taxicab company charges $3 for a trip up to 1 mile, and $2 for every extra mile (or portion of a mile). Graph the ordered pairs (m, C), where m represents the miles traveled and C represents the cost. Find the cost to ride $10\frac{1}{4}$ miles.

71. Computer communications An on-line information service charges for connect time at a rate of $12 per hour, computed for every minute or fraction of a minute. Graph the points (t, C), where C is the cost of t minutes of connect time. Find the cost of $7\frac{1}{2}$ minutes.

72. iPad repair There is a charge of $30, plus $40 per hour (or fraction of an hour), to repair an iPad. Graph the points (t, C), where t is the time it takes to do the job and C is the cost. If it takes 4 hours to repair the iPad, how much did it cost?

73. Rounding numbers Measurements are rarely exact; they are often *rounded* to an appropriate precision. Graph the points (x, y), where y is the result of rounding the number x to the nearest ten.

74. Signum function Computer programmers often use the following function, denoted by $y = \text{sgn } x$. Graph this function and find its domain and range.

$$y = \begin{cases} -1 & \text{if } x < 0 \\ 0 & \text{if } x = 0 \\ 1 & \text{if } x > 0 \end{cases}$$

75. Graph the function defined by $y = \frac{|x|}{x}$ and compare it to the graph in Exercise 74. Are the graphs the same?

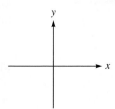

76. Graph: $y = x + |x|$.

Discovery and Writing

Use a graphing calculator to explore the properties of graphs of polynomial functions. Write a paragraph summarizing your observations.

77. Graph the function $y = x^2 + ax$ for several values of a. How does the graph change?

78. Graph the function $y = x^3 + ax$ for several values of a. How does the graph change?

79. Graph the function $y = (x - a)(x - b)$ for several values of a and b. What is the relationship between the x-intercepts and the equation?

80. Use the insight you gained in Exercise 79 to factor $x^3 - 3x^2 - 4x + 12$.

Review

81. If $f(x) = 3x + 2$, find $f(x + 1)$ and $f(x) + 1$.

82. If $f(x) = x^2$, find $f(x - 2)$ and $f(x) - 2$.

83. If $f(x) = \dfrac{3x + 1}{5}$, find $f(x - 3)$ and $f(x) - 3$.

84. If $f(x) = 8$, find $f(x + 8)$ and $f(x) + 8$.

85. Solve: $2x^2 - 3 = x$.

86. Solve: $4x^2 = 24x - 37$.

3.4 Transformations of the Graphs of Functions

In this section, we will learn to

1. Use vertical translations to graph functions.
2. Use horizontal translations to graph functions.
3. Graph functions using two translations.
4. Use reflections about the x- and y-axes to graph functions.
5. Use vertical stretching and shrinking to graph functions.
6. Use horizontal stretching and shrinking to graph functions.
7. Graph functions using a combination of transformations.

We can often transform the graph of a function into the graph of another function by shifting the graph vertically or horizontally. Also, we can reflect a graph about the x- or y-axis, and stretch or shrink a graph horizontally or vertically to transform the graph of a function into the graph of another function. In this section, we will graph new functions from known ones using these methods.

Consider a white water rafting trip on the Ocoee River in Tennessee. Suppose one company charges a group of students $20 for each hour on the river, plus $100 for a guide and equipment. The cost of the rafting trip can be represented by the function

$$C_1(t) = 20t + 100$$

where $C_1(t)$ represents the cost in dollars to raft t hours on the river.

If the company increases its charge for the guide and equipment to $150, the new cost function can be represented by

$$C_2(t) = 20t + 150$$

The graphs of the two cost functions are shown in Figure 3-41.

FIGURE 3-41

Note that if we shift the graph of $C_1(t)$ 50 units vertically, we obtain the graph of $C_2(t)$. This shift is called a *translation*.

As we continue our study of translations, it will be helpful to review the graphs of the basic functions that are shown in Figure 3-8 in Section 3.1. In this section, the graphs of $f(x) = x^2$, $f(x) = x^3$, $f(x) = |x|$, $f(x) = \sqrt{x}$, and $f(x) = \sqrt[3]{x}$ will be translated and stretched in various ways.

1. Use Vertical Translations to Graph Functions

Comment

The graphs of the functions shown in Figure 3-42 are exactly the graphs we would expect based on our previous study of quadratic functions.

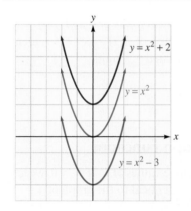

The graphs of functions can be identical except for their position in the xy-plane. For example, Figure 3-42 shows the graph of $y = x^2 + k$ for three values of k. If $k = 0$, we have the graph of $y = x^2$. The graph of $y = x^2 + 2$ is identical to the graph of $y = x^2$, except that it is shifted 2 units upward. The graph of $y = x^2 - 3$ is identical to the graph of $y = x^2$, except that it is shifted 3 units downward. These shifts are called **vertical translations.**

$y = x^2$		
x	y	(x, y)
-2	4	$(-2, 4)$
-1	1	$(-1, 1)$
0	0	$(0, 0)$
1	1	$(1, 1)$
2	4	$(2, 4)$

$y = x^2 + 2$		
x	y	(x, y)
-2	6	$(-2, 6)$
-1	3	$(-1, 3)$
0	2	$(0, 2)$
1	3	$(1, 3)$
2	6	$(2, 6)$

$y = x^2 - 3$		
x	y	(x, y)
-2	1	$(-2, 1)$
-1	-2	$(-1, -2)$
0	-3	$(0, -3)$
1	-2	$(1, -2)$
2	1	$(2, 1)$

FIGURE 3-42

In general, we can make the following observations:

Vertical Translations   If f is a function and k is a positive number, then

- The graph of $y = f(x) + k$ is identical to the graph of $y = f(x)$ except that it is translated k units upward.

- The graph of $y = f(x) - k$ is identical to the graph of $y = f(x)$ except that it is translated k units downward.

EXAMPLE 1   ## Using Vertical Translations to Graph Functions

Graph each function: **a.** $g(x) = |x| - 2$ **b.** $h(x) = |x| + 3$

SOLUTION   We will use vertical translations of $f(x) = |x|$ to graph each function.

a. The graph of $g(x) = |x| - 2$ is identical to the graph of $f(x) = |x|$, except that it is translated 2 units downward. It is translated downward because 2 is subtracted from $|x|$. The graph of $g(x)$ is shown in Figure 3-43(a).

b. The graph of $h(x) = |x| + 3$ is identical to the graph of $f(x) = |x|$, except that it is translated 3 units upward. It is translated upward because 3 is added to $|x|$. The graph of $h(x)$ is shown in Figure 3-43(b).

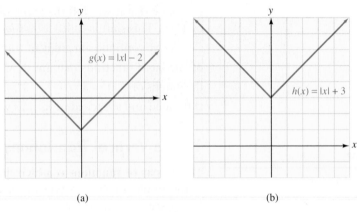

(a)   (b)

FIGURE 3-43

Self Check 1   *Fill in the blanks:* The graph of $g(x) = x^2 + 3$ is identical to the graph of $f(x) = x^2$, except that it is translated ___ units _____. The graph of $h(x) = x^2 - 4$ is identical to the graph of $f(x) = x^2$, except that it is translated ___ units _____.

Now Try Exercise 27.

2. Use Horizontal Translations to Graph Functions

Comment

The graphs of the functions shown in Figure 3-44 are exactly the graphs we would expect based on our previous knowledge of quadratic functions.

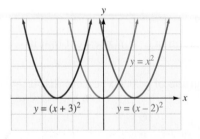

Figure 3-44 shows the graph of $y = (x + k)^2$ for three values of k. If $k = 0$, we have the graph of $y = x^2$. The graph of $y = (x - 2)^2$ is identical to the graph of $y = x^2$, except that it is shifted 2 units to the right. The graph of $y = (x + 3)^2$ is identical to the graph of $y = x^2$, except that it is shifted 3 units to the left. These shifts are called **horizontal translations.**

$y = x^2$		
x	y	(x, y)
-2	4	$(-2, 4)$
-1	1	$(-1, 1)$
0	0	$(0, 0)$
1	1	$(1, 1)$
2	4	$(2, 4)$

$y = (x - 2)^2$		
x	y	(x, y)
0	4	$(0, 4)$
1	1	$(1, 1)$
2	0	$(2, 0)$
3	1	$(3, 1)$
4	4	$(4, 4)$

$y = (x + 3)^2$		
x	y	(x, y)
-5	4	$(-5, 4)$
-4	1	$(-4, 1)$
-3	0	$(-3, 0)$
-2	1	$(-2, 1)$
-1	4	$(-1, 4)$

FIGURE 3-44

In general, we can make the following observations.

Horizontal Translations

If f is a function and k is a positive number, then

- The graph of $y = f(x - k)$ is identical to the graph of $y = f(x)$ except that it is translated k units to the right.

- The graph of $y = f(x + k)$ is identical to the graph of $y = f(x)$ except that it is translated k units to the left.

EXAMPLE 2   **Using Horizontal Translations to Graph Functions**

Graph each function: **a.** $g(x) = |x - 4|$ **b.** $h(x) = |x + 2|$

SOLUTION   We will use horizontal translations of the graph of $f(x) = |x|$ to graph each function.

a. The graph of $g(x) = |x - 4|$ is identical to the graph of $f(x) = |x|$, except that it is translated 4 units to the right. It is translated 4 units to the right because within the absolute value symbols 4 is subtracted from x. The graph of $g(x)$ is shown in Figure 3-45(a).

b. The graph of $h(x) = |x + 2|$ is identical to the graph of $f(x) = |x|$, except that it is translated 2 units to the left. It is translated 2 units to the left because within the absolute value symbols 2 is added to x. The graph of $h(x)$ is shown in Figure 3-45(b).

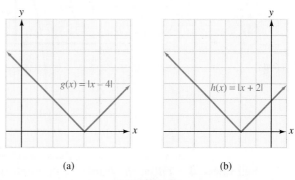

(a)   (b)

FIGURE 3-45

Self Check 2   *Fill in the blanks:* The graph of $g(x) = (x - 3)^2$ is identical to the graph of $f(x) = x^2$ except that it is translated ___ units to the _____. The graph of $h(x) = (x + 2)^2$ is identical to the graph of $f(x) = x^2$ except that it is translated ___ units to the

_____.

Now Try Exercise 29.

Caution

When using horizontal translations to graph a function, it is easy to shift the function in the *wrong* direction.

- If we see a positive constant subtracted from x, we have the tendency to shift the graph left. This is **incorrect.**

- If we see a positive constant added to x, we have the tendency to shift the graph right. This too is **incorrect.**

We should avoid making these common errors.

3. Graph Functions Using Two Translations

Sometimes we can obtain a graph by using both a horizontal and a vertical translation.

EXAMPLE 3   **Using a Horizontal and a Vertical Translation to Graph a Function**

Graph each function:
a. $g(x) = (x - 5)^3 + 4$ **b.** $h(x) = (x + 2)^2 - 2$

SOLUTION   By inspection, we see that the function in part **a** involves two translations of $f(x) = x^3$ and the function in part **b** involves two translations of $f(x) = x^2$. We will perform the horizontal translation first, followed by a vertical translation to obtain the graph of each function.

a. The graph of $g(x) = (x - 5)^3 + 4$ is identical to the graph of $f(x) = x^3$, except that it is translated 5 units to the right and 4 units upward, as shown in Figure 3-46(a).

b. The graph of $h(x) = (x + 2)^2 - 2$ is identical to the graph of $f(x) = x^2$, except that it is translated 2 units to the left and 2 units downward, as shown in Figure 3-46(b).

(a)

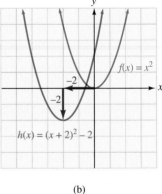
(b)

FIGURE 3-46

Self Check 3   *Fill in the blanks:* The graph of $g(x) = |x - 4| + 5$ is identical to the graph of $f(x) = |x|$, except that it is translated ___ units to the _____ and ___ units _____.

Now Try Exercise 31.

ACCENT ON TECHNOLOGY   **Translations of Functions**

We can use a graphing calculator to help understand translations of functions. Compare the graph of each function listed to the graph of $f(x) = \sqrt{x}$.

   a. $g(x) = \sqrt{x} - 4$ **b.** $h(x) = \sqrt{x + 2}$ **c.** $k(x) = \sqrt{x - 2} + 3$

a. Graph the functions $f(x) = \sqrt{x}$ and $g(x) = \sqrt{x} - 4$ on the same screen using the window shown in Figure 3-47(a). From these graphs, we can see that the graph of g is obtained by shifting the graph of f downward 4 units.

b. Graph the functions $f(x) = \sqrt{x}$ and $h(x) = \sqrt{x + 2}$ on the same screen using the window shown in Figure 3-47(b). From these graphs, we can see that the graph of h is obtained by shifting the graph of f to the left 2 units.

c. Graph the functions $f(x) = \sqrt{x}$ and $k(x) = \sqrt{x - 2} + 3$ on the same screen using the window shown in Figure 3-47(c). From these graphs, we can see that the graph of k is obtained by shifting the graph of f right 2 units and upward 3 units.

Comment

To make the graph of $f(x) = \sqrt{x}$ appear bold, scroll to the left of Y₁ and press ENTER.

(a) Vertical shift downward 4 units. The graph of $f(x) = \sqrt{x}$ is the bold graph.

  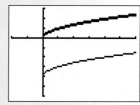

(b) Horizontal shift left 2 units. The graph of $f(x) = \sqrt{x}$ is the bold graph.

  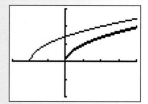

(c) Horizontal shift 2 units right and vertical shift 3 units upward. The graph of $f(x) = \sqrt{x}$ is the bold graph.

 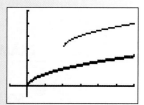

FIGURE 3-47

4. Use Reflections about the x- and y- Axes to Graph Functions

Figure 3-48(a) shows that the graph of $y = -\sqrt{x}$ is identical to the graph of $y = \sqrt{x}$ except that it is reflected about the x-axis. Figure 3-48(b) shows that the graph of $y = \sqrt{-x}$ is identical to the graph of $y = \sqrt{x}$ except that it is reflected about the y-axis.

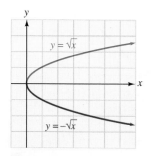

$y = -\sqrt{x}$		
x	y	(x, y)
0	0	$(0, 0)$
1	-1	$(1, -1)$
4	-2	$(4, -2)$

(a)

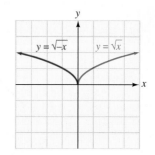

$y = \sqrt{-x}$		
x	y	(x, y)
0	0	$(0, 0)$
-1	1	$(-1, 1)$
-4	2	$(-4, 2)$

(b)

FIGURE 3-48

In general, we can make the following observations.

Reflections   If f is a function, then

- The graph of $y = -f(x)$ is identical to the graph of $f(x)$ except that it is reflected about the x-axis.

- The graph of $y = f(-x)$ is identical to the graph of $f(x)$ except that it is reflected about the y-axis.

EXAMPLE 4   **Using Reflections to Graph Functions**

Graph each function: **a.** $g(x) = -|x + 1|$ **b.** $h(x) = |-x + 1|$

SOLUTION   By inspection, we see that the function given in part **a** involves a reflection about the x-axis and the function given in part **b** involves a reflection about the y-axis. We will use reflections to draw the graph of each function.

a. The graph of $g(x) = -|x + 1|$ is identical to the graph of $f(x) = |x + 1|$, except that it is reflected about the x-axis. This is because $g(x) = -f(x)$. The graphs of both functions are shown in Figure 3-49(a).

b. The graph of $h(x) = |-x + 1|$ is identical to the graph of $f(x) = |x + 1|$, except that it is reflected about the y-axis. This is because $f(-x) = h(x)$. The graphs of both functions are shown in Figure 3-49(b).

Comment

It is often helpful to think of a reflection as a mirror image of the graph about the x- or y-axis.

(a)

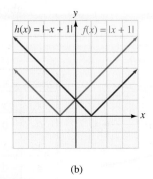

(b)

FIGURE 3-49

Self Check 4   *Fill in the blanks:* The graph of $g(x) = -\sqrt[3]{x}$ is identical to the graph of $f(x) = \sqrt[3]{x}$, except that it is reflected about the ____ axis. The graph of $h(x) = \sqrt{-x - 4}$ is identical to the graph of $f(x) = \sqrt{x - 4}$, except that it is reflected about the ____ axis.

Now Try Exercise 51.

5. Use Vertical Stretching and Shrinking to Graph Functions

Figure 3-50 shows the graphs of $y = x^2$, $y = 3x^2$, and $y = \frac{1}{3}x^2$.

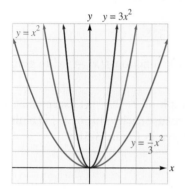

$y = x^2$		
x	y	(x, y)
-2	4	$(-2, 4)$
-1	1	$(-1, 1)$
0	0	$(0, 0)$
1	1	$(1, 1)$
2	4	$(2, 4)$

$y = 3x^2$		
x	y	(x, y)
-2	12	$(-2, 12)$
-1	3	$(-1, 3)$
0	0	$(0, 0)$
1	3	$(1, 3)$
2	12	$(2, 12)$

$y = \frac{1}{3}x^2$		
x	y	(x, y)
-2	$\frac{4}{3}$	$\left(-2, \frac{4}{3}\right)$
-1	$\frac{1}{3}$	$\left(-1, \frac{1}{3}\right)$
0	0	$(0, 0)$
1	$\frac{1}{3}$	$\left(1, \frac{1}{3}\right)$
2	$\frac{4}{3}$	$\left(2, \frac{4}{3}\right)$

FIGURE 3-50

Because each value of $y = 3x^2$ is 3 times greater than the corresponding value of $y = x^2$, its graph is stretched vertically by a factor of 3. Because each value of $y = \frac{1}{3}x^2$ is 3 times smaller than the corresponding value of $y = x^2$, its graph shrinks vertically by a factor of $\frac{1}{3}$.

In general, we can make the following observations.

Vertical Stretching and Shrinking   If f is a function and $k > 1$, then

- The graph of $y = kf(x)$ can be obtained by stretching the graph of $y = f(x)$ vertically by multiplying each value of $f(x)$ by k.

If f is a function and $0 < k < 1$, then

- The graph of $y = kf(x)$ can be obtained by shrinking the graph of $y = f(x)$ vertically by multiplying each value of $f(x)$ by k.

EXAMPLE 5 Graphing a Function by Vertical Stretching or Shrinking

Graph each function: **a.** $g(x) = 2|x|$ **b.** $h(x) = \dfrac{1}{2}|x|$

SOLUTION We will vertically stretch or vertically shrink the basic function $f(x) = |x|$ to graph each of the given functions.

a. The graph of $g(x) = 2|x|$ is identical to the graph of $f(x) = |x|$ except that it is vertically stretched by a factor of 2. This is because each value of $|x|$ is multiplied by 2. The graphs of both functions are shown in Figure 3-51.

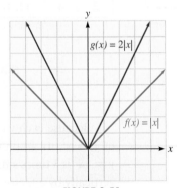

FIGURE 3-51

b. The graph of $g(x) = \frac{1}{2}|x|$ is identical to the graph of $f(x) = |x|$ except that it is vertically shrunk by a factor of $\frac{1}{2}$. This is because each value of $|x|$ is multiplied by $\frac{1}{2}$. The graphs of both functions are shown in Figure 3-52.

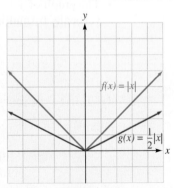

FIGURE 3-52

Comment

Note that vertically stretching the graph of a function narrows the graph of the function. Vertically shrinking the graph of a function widens the graph.

Self Check 5   *Fill in the blanks:* The graph of $g(x) = 5x^3$ is identical to the graph of $f(x) = x^3$, except that it is vertically _____ by a factor of __. The graph of $h(x) = \frac{1}{5}x^3$ is identical to the graph $f(x) = x^3$, except that it is vertically _____ by a factor of __.

Now Try Exercise 57.

6. Use Horizontal Stretching and Shrinking to Graph Functions

Functions can also be graphed by using horizontal stretchings and shrinkings.

Horizontal Stretching and Shrinking	If f is a function and $k > 1$, then

Horizontal Stretching and Shrinking   If f is a function and $k > 1$, then

- The graph of $y = f(kx)$ can be obtained by shrinking the graph of $y = f(x)$ horizontally by multiplying each x-value of $f(x)$ by $\frac{1}{k}$.

If f is a function and $0 < k < 1$, then

- The graph of $y = f(kx)$ can be obtained by stretching the graph of $y = f(x)$ horizontally by multiplying each x-value of $f(x)$ by $\frac{1}{k}$.

Because we multiply each x-value of $f(x)$ by k to obtain the graph of $y = f(kx)$, the graphs are horizontally stretched or shrunk by a factor of $\frac{1}{k}$.

EXAMPLE 6   **Graphing a Function by Horizontally Shrinking or Stretching**

Graph $y = (3x)^2 - 1$ using the graph of the function $y = x^2 - 1$.

SOLUTION   Since $3 > 1$, the graph of $y = (3x)^2 - 1$ can be obtained by shrinking the graph of $y = x^2 - 1$ horizontally by multiplying each x-coordinate of $y = x^2 - 1$ by $\frac{1}{3}$.

First, we complete the table of solutions for $y = x^2 - 1$, shown in Figure 3-53. Next, we multiply each x-value in the table by $\frac{1}{3}$ to obtain the table of solutions for $y = (3x)^2 - 1$, also shown in Figure 3-53.

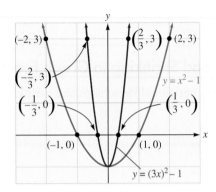

$y = x^2 - 1$		
x	y	(x, y)
-2	3	$(-2, 3)$
-1	0	$(-1, 0)$
0	-1	$(0, -1)$
1	0	$(1, 0)$
2	3	$(2, 3)$

$y = (3x)^2 - 1$		
x	y	(x, y)
$-\dfrac{2}{3}$	3	$\left(-\dfrac{2}{3}, 3\right)$
$-\dfrac{1}{3}$	0	$\left(-\dfrac{1}{3}, 0\right)$
0	-1	$(0, -1)$
$\dfrac{1}{3}$	0	$\left(\dfrac{1}{3}, 0\right)$
$\dfrac{2}{3}$	3	$\left(\dfrac{2}{3}, 3\right)$

FIGURE 3-53

We now draw each graph as shown in Figure 3-53.

Self Check 6   *Fill in the blank:* The graph of $g(x) = \left(\frac{1}{3}x\right)^2 - 1$ is identical to the graph of $f(x) = x^2 - 1$, except that it is horizontally _____ by a factor of ___.

Now Try Exercise 63.

We can summarize the ideas in this section as follows.

Summary of Transformations   If f is a function and k represents a positive number, then

The graph of	*can be obtained by graphing $y = f(x)$ and*
$y = f(x) + k$	translating the graph k units upward.
$y = f(x) - k$	translating the graph k units downward.
$y = f(x + k)$	translating the graph k units to the left.
$y = f(x - k)$	translating the graph k units to the right.
$y = -f(x)$	reflecting the graph about the x-axis.
$y = f(-x)$	reflecting the graph about the y-axis.
$y = kf(x) \quad k > 1$	stretching the graph vertically by multiplying each value of $f(x)$ by k.
$y = kf(x) \quad 0 < k < 1$	shrinking the graph vertically by multiplying each value $f(x)$ by k.
$y = f(kx) \quad k > 1$	shrinking the graph horizontally by multiplying each x-value of $f(x)$ by $\frac{1}{k}$.
$y = f(kx) \quad 0 < k < 1$	stretching the graph horizontally by multiplying each x-value of $f(x)$ by $\frac{1}{k}$.

EXAMPLE 7   **Applying Transformations of Graphs**

Figure 3-54 shows the graph of $y = f(x)$. Use this graph and a translation to sketch the graph of **a.** $y = f(x) + 2$ **b.** $y = f(x - 2)$ **c.** $y = 2f(x)$

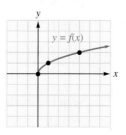

FIGURE 3-54

SOLUTION   We will use the summary of transformations in the section given earlier to graph each function.

a. The graph of $y = f(x) + 2$ is identical to the graph of $y = f(x)$, except that it is translated 2 units upward. See Figure 3-55(a).

b. The graph of $y = f(x - 2)$ is identical to the graph of $y = f(x)$, except that it is translated 2 units to the right. See Figure 3-55(b).

c. The graph of $y = 2f(x)$ is identical to the graph of $y = f(x)$, except that it is stretched vertically by multiplying each y-value of $f(x)$ by 2. See Figure 3-55(c).

(a)   (b)   (c)

FIGURE 3-55

Self Check 7   Use Figure 3-50 and a reflection to sketch the graph of **a.** $y = -f(x)$
b. $y = f(-x)$

Now Try Exercise 79.

7. Graph Functions Using a Combination of Transformations

To graph functions involving a combination of transformations, we must apply each translation or stretching to the function.

Strategy for Graphing Using a Sequence of Transformations   To graph a function using a combination of transformations, perform the transformations in the following order:

   1. horizontal translation

   2. stretching or shrinking

   3. reflection

   4. vertical translation

EXAMPLE 8   **Graphing a Function by Using a Combination of Transformations**

Use the function $f(x) = |x|$ to graph $g(x) = 3|x - 2| + 4$.

SOLUTION   We will graph $g(x) = 3|x - 2| + 4$ by applying three transformations to the basic function $f(x) = |x|$:

Step 1: Translate $f(x) = |x|$ horizontally 2 units to the right.

Step 2: Vertically stretch the graph by a factor of 3.

Step 3: Translate the graph vertically 4 units upward.

Step 1: Translate $f(x) = |x|$ horizontally 2 units to the right to obtain the graph of $y = |x - 2|$.

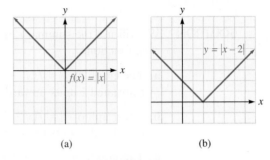

(a)   (b)

FIGURE 3-56

Step 2: Vertically stretch the graph of $y = |x - 2|$ by a factor of 3 to obtain the graph of $y = 3|x - 2|$.

FIGURE 3-57

Step 3: Translate the graph of $y = 3|x - 2|$ vertically 4 units upward to obtain the graph of $g(x) = 3|x - 2| + 4$.

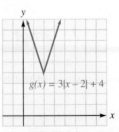

FIGURE 3-58

Self Check 8   Use the graph of the function $f(x) = x^3$ to graph $g(x) = \frac{1}{3}(x + 1)^3 - 2$.

Now Try Exercise 69.

37. h(

The g
f(x) =

39. g(

41. g(

43. h

The g
y = x
each f
45. f

Self Check Answers   **1.** 3, upward; 4, downward   **2.** 3, right; 2, left   **3.** 4, right; 5, upward

4. x; y **5.** stretched, 5; shrunk, $\frac{1}{5}$ **6.** stretched, 3

7. a.   **b.**   **8.**

Exercises **3.4**

Getting Ready

You should be able to complete these vocabulary and concept statements before you proceed to the practice exercises.

Fill in the blanks.

1. The graph of $y = f(x) + 5$ is identical to the graph of $y = f(x)$ except that it is translated 5 units _____ .

2. The graph of _____ is identical to the graph of $y = f(x)$ except that it is translated 7 units downward.

3. The graph of $y = f(x - 3)$ is identical to the graph of $y = f(x)$ except that it is translated 3 units _____ .

4. The graph of $y = f(x + 2)$ is identical to the graph of $y = f(x)$ except that it is translated 2 units _____ .

5. To draw the graph of $y = (x + 2)^2 - 3$, translate the graph of $y = x^2$ ___ units to the left and 3 units _____ .

6. To draw the graph of $y = (x - 3)^3 + 1$, translate the graph of $y = x^3$ 3 units to the _____ and 1 unit _____ .

7. The graph of $y = f(-x)$ is a reflection of the graph of $y = f(x)$ about the _____ .

8. The graph of _____ is a reflection of the graph of $y = f(x)$ about the x-axis.

9. The graph of $y = f(4x)$ shrinks the graph of $y = f(x)$ _____ by multiplying each x-value of $f(x)$ by $\frac{1}{4}$.

10. The graph of $y = 8f(x)$ stretches the graph of $y = f(x)$ _____ by a factor of 8.

Practice

The graph of each function is a translation of the graph of $f(x) = x^2$. Graph each function.

11. $g(x) = x^2 - 2$

12. $g(x) = (x - 2)^2$

13. $g(x) = (x + 3)^2$

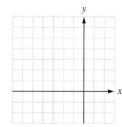

14. $g(x) = x^2 + 3$

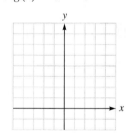

15. $h(x) = (x + 1)^2 + 2$

16. $h(x) = (x - 3)^2 - 1$

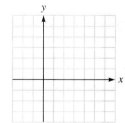

17. *h*

57. $f(x) = \frac{1}{2}x^3$

58. $g(x) = 2x^3$

The g
f(x)

19. *g*

59. $h(x) = -3|x|$

60. $f(x) = \frac{1}{3}|x|$

21. *g*

The graph of each function is a horizontal stretching or shrinking of the graph of y = x² or y = x³. Graph each function.

61. $f(x) = \left(\frac{1}{2}x\right)^3$

62. $f(x) = (2x)^3$

23. *h*

63. $f(x) = (2x)^2$

64. $f(x) = (-2x)^3$

25. *y*

Graph each function using a combination of transformations applied to the graph of a basic function.

65. $g(x) = 3(x + 2)^2 - 1$

66. $g(x) = -\frac{1}{3}(x + 1)^2 + 1$

67. $h(x) = -2|x| + 3$

68. $f(x) = -2|x + 3|$

69. $f(x) = 2|x - 2| + 1$

70. $f(x) = -3|x + 5| - 2$

71. $f(x) = 2\sqrt{x} + 3$
    $(x \geq 0)$

72. $g(x) = 2\sqrt{x + 3}$
    $(x \geq -3)$

73. $h(x) = 2\sqrt{x - 2} + 1$
    $(x \geq 2)$

74. $h(x) = \frac{1}{2}\sqrt{x + 5} - 2$
    $(x \geq -5)$

75. $g(x) = -2(x + 2)^3 - 1$

76. $g(x) = \frac{1}{3}(x + 1)^3 - 1$

77. $f(x) = 2\sqrt[3]{x} + 4$

78. $f(x) = -2\sqrt[3]{x} + 1$

85. $y = 2f(-x)$

86. $y = f(x + 1) - 2$

Use the following graph and a translation, stretching, or reflection to sketch the graph of each function.

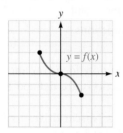

$y = f(x)$

79. $y = f(x) + 1$

80. $y = f(x + 1)$

81. $y = 2f(x)$

82. $y = f\left(\dfrac{x}{2}\right)$

83. $y = f(x - 2) + 1$

84. $y = -f(x)$

Discovery and Writing

Use a graphing calculator to perform each experiment. Write a brief paragraph describing your findings.

87. Investigate the translations of the graph of a function by graphing the parabola $y = (x - k)^2 + k$ for several values of k. What do you observe about successive positions of the vertex?

88. Investigate the translations of the graph of a function by graphing the parabola $y = (x - k)^2 + k^2$ for several values of k. What do you observe about successive positions of the vertex?

89. Investigate the horizontal stretching of the graph of a function by graphing $y = \sqrt{ax}$ for several values of a. What do you observe?

90. Investigate the vertical stretching of the graph of a function by graphing $y = b\sqrt{x}$ for several values of b. What do you observe? Are these graphs different from the graphs in Exercise 89?

Write a paragraph using your own words.

91. Explain why the effect of vertically stretching a graph by a factor of -1 is to reflect the graph about the x-axis.

92. Explain why the effect of horizontally stretching a graph by a factor of -1 is to reflect the graph about the y-axis.

Review

Simplify each function.

93. $\dfrac{x^2 + x - 6}{x^2 + 5x + 6}$

94. $\dfrac{2x^2 + 3x}{2x^2 + x - 3}$

Find the domain of each function. Use interval notation to write each answer.

95. $f(x) = \dfrac{x + 7}{x - 3}$

96. $f(x) = \dfrac{x^2 + 1}{x^2 + 3x + 2}$

Perform each division and write the answer in quotient $+ \frac{remainder}{divider}$ form.

97. $\dfrac{x^2 + 3x}{x + 1}$

98. $\dfrac{x^2 + 3}{x + 1}$

3.5 Rational Functions

In this section, we will learn to

1. Find the domain of a rational function.
2. Understand the characteristics of rational functions and their graphs.
3. Find vertical asymptotes of rational functions.
4. Find horizontal asymptotes of rational functions.
5. Identify slant asymptotes of rational functions.
6. Graph rational functions.
7. Understand when a graph has a missing point.
8. Solve problems modeled by rational functions.

Walter G Arce/Shutterstock.com

We have discussed polynomial functions and now focus on another class of functions called **rational functions.** Rational functions are defined by rational expressions that are quotients of polynomials.

For example, consider the time t it takes a Nascar driver to drive the 500 miles in the Daytona 500 race. The time t can be defined as a function of the average rate of the driver's speed r. That is

$$t = f(r) = \frac{500}{r}$$

If a driver averages a speed of 170 mph, we can evaluate $f(170)$ to determine the time in hours driven.

$$f(170) = \frac{500}{170} = \frac{50}{17} \qquad \text{This is approximately 2.94 hours.}$$

We will discuss this type of function in this section.

Rational Functions   A **rational function** is a function defined by an equation of the form

$$y = \frac{P(x)}{Q(x)}$$

where $P(x)$ and $Q(x)$ are polynomials and $Q(x) \neq 0$.

1. Find the Domain of a Rational Function

Because rational functions are quotients of polynomials and $Q(x)$ is the denominator of a fraction, $Q(x)$ cannot equal 0. Thus, the domain of a rational function must exclude all values of x for which $Q(x) = 0$.

Here are some examples of rational functions and their domains:

Function	Domain
$f(x) = \dfrac{3}{x + 7}$	$(-\infty, -7) \cup (-7, \infty)$, x cannot equal -7
$f(x) = \dfrac{5x + 2}{x^2 - 4}$	$(-\infty, -2) \cup (-2, 2) \cup (2, \infty)$, x cannot equal 2 or -2
$f(x) = \dfrac{2x}{x^2 + 3}$	$(-\infty, \infty)$, x can equal any real number

EXAMPLE 1 **Finding the Domain of a Rational Function**

Find the domain of $f(x) = \dfrac{3x + 2}{x^2 - 7x + 12}$.

SOLUTION We can factor the denominator to see what values of x will give 0's in the denominator. These values are not in the domain.

To find the numbers x that make the denominator 0, we set $x^2 - 7x - 12$ equal to 0 and solve for x.

$$x^2 - 7x + 12 = 0$$

$$(x - 4)(x - 3) = 0 \qquad \text{Factor } x^2 - 7x + 12.$$

$$x - 4 = 0 \quad \text{or} \quad x - 3 = 0 \qquad \text{Set each factor equal to 0.}$$

$$x = 4 \quad \bigg| \quad x = 3 \qquad \text{Solve each linear equation.}$$

Since 4 and 3 make the denominator 0, the domain is the set of all real numbers except $x = 4$ and $x = 3$. In interval notation, we have $(-\infty, 3) \cup (3, 4) \cup (4, \infty)$. ∎

Caution

Do not exclude values of the variable from the domain that make the numerator equal to zero, unless the denominator has the same factor. We will discuss this situation later in this section.

Self Check 1 Find the domain of $f(x) = \dfrac{2x - 3}{x^2 - x - 2}$.

Now Try Exercise 23.

ACCENT ON TECHNOLOGY **Domain and Range of a Rational Function**

FIGURE 3-59

We can use a graphing calculator to find domains and ranges of rational functions. If we use settings of $[-10, 10]$ for x and $[-10, 10]$ for y and graph $f(x) = \frac{2x + 1}{x - 1}$, we will obtain Figure 3-59.

From the graph, we can see that every real number x except 1 gives a value of y. Thus, the domain of the function is $(-\infty, 1) \cup (1, \infty)$. We can also see that y can be any value except 2. The range of the function is $(-\infty, 2) \cup (2, \infty)$.

Comment

When using a graphing calculator to graph a rational function, make sure that the function is entered properly. To avoid making an error, place both the numerator and denominator in parentheses.

2. Understand the Characteristics of Rational Functions and Their Graphs

Consider the rational function $t = f(r) = \frac{500}{r}$ given at the beginning of the section. A graph of this rational function is shown in Figure 3-60.

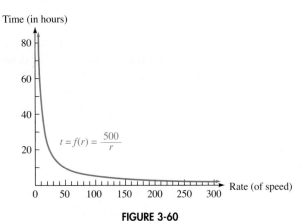

FIGURE 3-60

We see from the graph that as the rate of speed increases, the time it takes to complete the race decreases. In fact, if we drive at rocket speed, we will arrive in almost no time at all. We can express this by saying that "as the rate increases without bound (or approaches ∞), the time it takes to complete the race approaches 0 hours." When a graph approaches a line as shown in the figure, we call the line an **asymptote.** The horizontal line representing the rate axis shown in the graph is a **horizontal asymptote.**

We also see from the graph that as the rate of speed decreases, the time it takes to complete the race increases. In fact, if the car goes at turtle speed, it will take almost forever to finish the race. We can express this by saying that "as the rate gets slower and slower (or approaches 0 mph), the time approaches ∞." The vertical line representing the time axis shown on the graph is a **vertical asymptote.** A vertical asymptote is a vertical line that the graph approaches, but never touches.

One important characteristic of the graph of a rational function is that asymptotes often occur. We will first consider vertical and horizontal asymptotes. Later in the section, we will discuss slant asymptotes.

Vertical Asymptote	The line $x = a$ is a **vertical asymptote** of the graph of a function $y = f(x)$ if $f(x)$ either increases or decreases without bound (approaches ∞ or $-\infty$) as x approaches a.

Horizontal Asymptote	The line $y = b$ is a **horizontal asymptote** of the graph of a function $y = f(x)$ if $f(x)$ approaches b as x increases or decreases without bound (approaches ∞ or $-\infty$).

Figure 3-61 shows a typical vertical and typical horizontal asymptote.

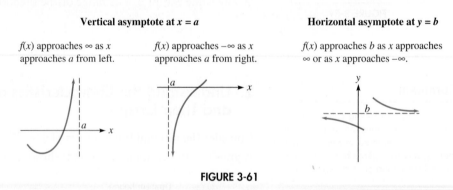

Vertical asymptote at $x = a$

$f(x)$ approaches ∞ as x approaches a from left.

$f(x)$ approaches $-\infty$ as x approaches a from right.

Horizontal asymptote at $y = b$

$f(x)$ approaches b as x approaches ∞ or as x approaches $-\infty$.

FIGURE 3-61

The graph of the rational function $f(x) = \frac{1}{x}$, called the **reciprocal function,** is shown in Figure 3-62. The domain of the function is $(-\infty, 0) \cup (0, \infty)$ and the range is $(-\infty, 0) \cup (0, \infty)$.

$f(x) = \frac{1}{x}$

FIGURE 3-62

The reciprocal function has a vertical asymptote of $x = 0$ because

- We see from the graph that as x approaches 0 from the right that y or $f(x)$ approaches ∞.
- We see from the graph that as x approaches 0 from the left that y or $f(x)$ approaches $-\infty$.

The reciprocal function has a horizontal asymptote of $y = 0$ because

- We see from the graph that as x approaches ∞ that y or $f(x)$ approaches 0.
- We see from the graph that as x approaches $-\infty$ that y or $f(x)$ approaches 0.

3. Find Vertical Asymptotes of Rational Functions

To find the vertical asymptotes of a rational function written in simplest form, we must find the values of x for which the denominator of the rational function is 0 and the function is undefined. For example, since the denominator of $f(x) = \frac{2x - 1}{x + 2}$ is 0 when $x = -2$, there are no corresponding values of y and the line $x = -2$ is a vertical asymptote. We note that when x approaches -2 from the right or from the left, $f(x)$ approaches $-\infty$ and ∞ respectively. A graph of the function appears in Figure 3-63.

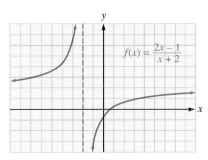

FIGURE 3-63

Strategy for Locating Vertical Asymptotes

To locate the vertical asymptotes of the rational function $f(x) = \frac{P(x)}{Q(x)}$, we follow these steps:

Step 1: Factor $P(x)$ and $Q(x)$ and remove any common factors.

Step 2: Set the denominator equal to 0 and solve the equation.

If a is a solution of the equation found in Step 2, $x = a$ is a vertical asymptote.

EXAMPLE 2

Finding Vertical Asymptotes of Rational Functions

Find the vertical asymptotes, if any, of each function:

a. $f(x) = \dfrac{2x}{x^2 - 16}$ **b.** $g(x) = \dfrac{x - 4}{x^2 - 16}$ **c.** $h(x) = \dfrac{5x}{x^2 + 16}$

SOLUTION

We will locate the vertical asymptotes of the graph of each function by factoring its numerator and/or denominator and removing any common factors. Then we will set the resulting denominator equal to zero, solve the equation, and identify the vertical asymptotes.

a. $f(x) = \dfrac{2x}{x^2 - 16}$

$f(x) = \dfrac{2x}{(x + 4)(x - 4)}$ Factor the denominator completely.

We then set the denominator equal to 0 and solve for x.

$$(x + 4)(x - 4) = 0$$

$$x + 4 = 0 \quad \text{or} \quad x - 4 = 0$$

$$x = -4 \quad \big| \quad x = 4$$

The vertical asymptotes are $x = 4$ and $x = -4$. See Figure 3-64.

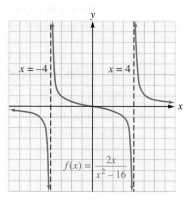

FIGURE 3-64

b. $g(x) = \dfrac{x - 4}{x^2 - 16}$

$$g(x) = \dfrac{x - 4}{(x + 4)(x - 4)} \qquad \text{Factor the denominator completely.}$$

$$g(x) = \dfrac{1}{x + 4} \qquad\qquad \text{Simplify: } \dfrac{x - 4}{x - 4} = 1.$$

We set the denominator equal to 0 and solve for x.

$$x + 4 = 0$$

$$x = -4$$

Comment

A rational function can have zero, one, or several vertical asymptotes.

The vertical asymptote is $x = -4$. See Figure 3-65.

FIGURE 3-65

c. $h(x) = \dfrac{5x}{x^2 + 16}$

Because the denominator is the sum of two squared quantities, it cannot be factored over the set of real numbers. Thus, no values of x will make the denominator equal to 0. Thus, the rational function has no vertical asymptotes. See Figure 3-66.

FIGURE 3-66

Self Check 2   Find the vertical asymptotes, if any, of each function.

a. $g(x) = \dfrac{x + 5}{x^2 - 25}$ **b.** $h(x) = \dfrac{5}{x^2 + 25}$

Now Try Exercise 31.

4. Find Horizontal Asymptotes of Rational Functions

To find the horizontal asymptote of a rational function, we must find the value of y that the function approaches as x approaches ∞ or $-\infty$. To illustrate, we will consider three functions and some given function values.

First we consider a function where the degree of the numerator is less than the degree of the denominator.

$$f(x) = \frac{x + 2}{x^2 - 1} \qquad f(999) \approx 0.001 \qquad f(-999) \approx -0.001$$

- The degree of the numerator is 1 and the degree of the denominator is 2. Since $1 < 2$, the degree of the numerator is less than the degree of the denominator.
- If f is evaluated at large x-values (in both the positive and negative directions) such as 999 and -999, we obtain y-values that are close to 0.
- **Conclusion:** The line $y = 0$ (the x-axis) is a horizontal asymptote. See Figure 3-67.

FIGURE 3-67

Second we consider a function where the degree of the numerator is equal to the degree of the denominator.

$$g(x) = \frac{2x}{x - 1} \qquad g(999) \approx 2.002 \qquad g(-999) \approx 1.998$$

- The degree of the numerator is 1 and the degree of the denominator is 1. Thus, the degrees of the numerator and denominator are equal.
- The leading coefficient of the numerator is 2 and the leading coefficient of the denominator is 1. Note that $2 \div 1$ is 2.
- If g is evaluated at large x-values (in both the positive and negative directions) such as 999 and -999, we obtain y-values that are close to 2.
- **Conclusion:** The line $y = 2$ is a horizontal asymptote. See Figure 3-68.

FIGURE 3-68

Finally we consider a function where the degree of the numerator is greater than the degree of the denominator.

$$h(x) = \frac{x^3}{x - 1} \qquad h(999) \approx 999{,}001 \qquad h(-999) \approx 997{,}003$$

- The degree of the numerator is 3 and the degree of the denominator is 1. Thus, the degree of the numerator is greater than the degree of the denominator.
- If h is evaluated at large x-values (in both the positive and negative directions) such as 999 and -999, we obtain y-values that are extremely large and do not seem to approach a finite number.
- **Conclusion:** There is no horizontal asymptote. See Figure 3-69.

FIGURE 3-69

We summarize the conclusions made in the previous examples.

Strategy for Locating Horizontal Asymptotes	To locate the horizontal asymptote of the rational function $f(x) = \frac{P(x)}{Q(x)}$, we consider three cases:

Case 1: If the degree of $P(x)$ *is less than* the degree of $Q(x)$, the line $y = 0$ is a horizontal asymptote.

Case 2: If the degree of $P(x)$ and $Q(x)$ are equal, the line $y = \frac{p}{q}$, where p and q are the leading coefficients of $P(x)$ and $Q(x)$, is a horizontal asymptote.

Case 3: If the degree of $P(x)$ is greater than the degree of $Q(x)$, there is no horizontal asymptote.

EXAMPLE 3 **Finding Horizontal Asymptotes of Rational Functions**

Find the horizontal asymptote, if any, of each function:

a. $f(x) = \dfrac{3x}{2x^2 - 1}$ **b.** $g(x) = \dfrac{3x^2 + 1}{x^2 - 2x + 1}$ **c.** $h(x) = \dfrac{x^3 + 2}{x - 5}$

SOLUTION In each part, we will locate the horizontal asymptote by comparing the degree of the numerator to the degree of the denominator. Then we will decide which case applies and identify the horizontal asymptote.

a. Because the degree of the numerator is 1, the degree of the denominator is 2, and $1 < 2$, Case 1 applies. The horizontal asymptote is the line $y = 0$.

b. The degree of the numerator is 2 and the degree of the denominator is 2. Since the degrees are the same, Case 2 applies. Because the leading coefficient of the numerator is 3 and the leading coefficient of the denominator is 1, we divide 3 by 1 to obtain $\frac{3}{1} = 3$. The horizontal asymptote is the line $y = 3$.

c. Because the degree of the numerator is 3, the degree of the denominator is 1, and $3 > 1$, Case 3 applies. There is no horizontal asymptote.

Self Check 3   Find the horizontal asymptotes, if any, of each function.

a. $g(x) = \dfrac{4x - 5}{5 - x}$ **b.** $h(x) = \dfrac{3x^2}{x^3 - 5}$

Now Try Exercise 39.

5. Identify Slant Asymptotes of Rational Functions

A third type of asymptote is called a **slant asymptote**. These asymptotes occur when the degree of the numerator of a rational function is one more than the degree of the denominator. As the name implies, it is a slanted line, neither vertical nor horizontal.

To illustrate a slant asymptote, we consider the graph of $f(x) = \dfrac{x^2}{x - 2}$ shown in Figure 3-70.

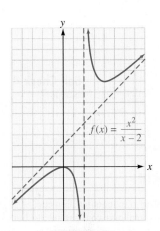

FIGURE 3-70   FIGURE 3-71

When x increases without bound to the right and to the left, the graph of the rational function approaches the slant asymptote shown in Figure 3-71. The equation of the slant asymptote is $y = x + 2$. To find this equation, we perform a long division, write the result in quotient $+ \frac{\text{remainder}}{\text{divisor}}$ form, and ignore the remainder.

$$
\begin{array}{r}
x + 2 \\
x - 2 \overline{\smash{)}x^2 + 0x + 0} \\
\underline{x^2 - 2x} \\
2x + 0 \\
\underline{2x - 4} \\
4
\end{array}
$$

Thus, $y = \dfrac{x^2}{x - 2} = x + 2 + \dfrac{4}{x - 2}$. Because the last fraction approaches 0 as x approaches ∞ and $-\infty$, the equation of the slant asymptote is $y = x + 2$.

Strategy for Locating Slant Asymptotes   If the degree of $P(x)$ is 1 greater than the degree of $Q(x)$ for the rational function $f(x) = \dfrac{P(x)}{Q(x)}$, there is a slant asymptote. To find it, divide $P(x)$ by $Q(x)$ and ignore the remainder.

EXAMPLE 4   **Finding a Slant Asymptote of a Rational Function**

Find the slant asymptote of $y = f(x) = \dfrac{3x^3 + 2x^2 + 2}{x^2 - 1}$.

SOLUTION   To find the slant asymptote, we divide the numerator by the denominator, write the result in quotient $+ \frac{\text{remainder}}{\text{divisor}}$ form, and ignore the remainder.

$$
\begin{array}{r}
3x + 2 \\
x^2 - 1 \overline{)3x^3 + 2x^2 + 2} \\
\underline{3x^3 - 3x } \\
2x^2 + 3x + 2 \\
\underline{2x^2 - 2} \\
3x + 4
\end{array}
$$

Thus,

$$
y = \frac{3x^3 + 2x^2 + 2}{x^2 - 1} = 3x + 2 + \frac{3x + 4}{x^2 - 1}
$$

The last fraction approaches 0 as x approaches ∞ and $-\infty$. Thus the graph of the rational function approaches the slant asymptote with equation of $y = 3x + 2$. ∎

Self Check 4   Find the slant asymptote of $f(x) = \dfrac{2x^3 - 3x + 1}{x^2 - 4}$.

Now Try Exercise 45.

6. Graph Rational Functions

Comment

The graph of a rational function can cross horizontal and slant asymptotes but can never cross a vertical asymptote.

We will use the following strategy to graph the rational function $f(x) = \frac{P(x)}{Q(x)}$, where $P(x)$ and $Q(x)$ are polynomials written in descending powers of x and $\frac{P(x)}{Q(x)}$ is in simplest form (no common factors).

Strategy for Graphing Rational Functions of the Form
$$f(x) = \frac{P(x)}{Q(x)}$$

Step 1: Check for symmetry.
•   If $f(-x) = f(x)$, the graph is symmetric about the y-axis.
•   If $f(-x) = -f(x)$, the graph is symmetric about the origin.

Step 2: Find the vertical asymptotes.
The real roots of $Q(x) = 0$, if any, determine the vertical asymptotes of the graph.

Step 3: Find the y- and x-intercepts, if any.
• $f(0)$ is the y-coordinate of the y-intercept of the graph.
•   Set $P(x) = 0$ and solve to find the x-intercepts of the graph.

Step 4: Find the horizontal asymptotes, if any.
•   If the degree of $P(x)$ is less than the degree of $Q(x)$, the line $y = 0$ is a horizontal asymptote.
•   If the degree of $P(x)$ is equal to the degree of $Q(x)$, the graph of $y = \frac{p}{q}$ is a horizontal asymptote, where p and q are the leading coefficients of $P(x)$ and $Q(x)$.

Step 5: Find the slant asymptotes, if any.
•   If the degree of $P(x)$ is 1 greater than the degree of $Q(x)$, there is a slant asymptote. To find it, divide $P(x)$ by $Q(x)$ and ignore the remainder.

Step 6: Draw the graph.
Find additional points (if necessary) near the asymptotes.

EXAMPLE 5 **Graphing a Rational Function**

Graph: $y = f(x) = \dfrac{x^2 - 4}{x^2 - 1}$.

SOLUTION We will use the steps outlined on the previous page to graph the rational function.

Step 1: Symmetry
Because x appears to even powers only, $f(-x) = f(x)$ and there is symmetry about the y-axis. There is no symmetry about the origin.

Step 2: Vertical asymptotes
To find the vertical asymptotes, we factor the numerator and denominator of $f(x)$ and simplify, if possible.

$$f(x) = \frac{x^2 - 4}{x^2 - 1} = \frac{(x + 2)(x - 2)}{(x + 1)(x - 1)} \qquad \text{There are no common factors.}$$

We then set the denominator equal to 0 and solve for x.

$$(x + 1)(x - 1) = 0$$

$$x + 1 = 0 \quad \text{or} \quad x - 1 = 0$$

$$x = -1 \quad \Big| \quad x = 1$$

There will be vertical asymptotes at $x = -1$ and $x = 1$.

Step 3: y- and x-intercepts
We can find the y-intercept by finding $f(0)$.

$$f(0) = \frac{0^2 - 4}{0^2 - 1} = \frac{-4}{-1} = 4$$

The y-intercept is $(0, 4)$.
We can find the x-intercepts by setting the numerator equal to 0 and solving for x:

$$x^2 - 4 = 0$$

$$(x + 2)(x - 2) = 0$$

$$x + 2 = 0 \quad \text{or} \quad x - 2 = 0$$

$$x = -2 \quad \Big| \quad x = 2$$

The x-intercepts are $(2, 0)$ and $(-2, 0)$.

Step 4: Horizontal asymptotes
Since the degrees of the numerator and denominator of the polynomials are the same, the line

$$y = \frac{1}{1} = 1 \qquad \begin{array}{l}\text{The leading coefficient of the numerator is 1.}\\ \text{The leading coefficient of the denominator is 1.}\end{array}$$

is a horizontal asymptote.

Step 5: Slant asymptotes
Since the degree of the numerator is not 1 greater than the degree of the denominator, there are no slant asymptotes.

Step 6: Graph
We plot the intercepts, draw the asymptotes, and make use of symmetry to graph the rational function. The graph is shown in Figure 3-72.

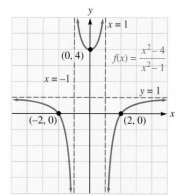

FIGURE 3-72

Self Check 5 Graph: $f(x) = \dfrac{x^2 - 9}{x^2 - 1}$.

Now Try Exercise 59.

Graphing a Rational Function

A graphing calculator can be very useful in helping us draw the graph of a rational function. However, certain precautions must be used or we will get a graph that is not going to give us a good idea of how the function looks. For example, in Figure 3-73 (a) the graph of the function from Example 5 is shown. Using the ZOOM Standard window, a good representation of the graph is shown. In Figure 3-73 (b) the ZOOM Decimal window is used, and part of the graph is not shown.

(a)　　　　　(b)

FIGURE 3-73

EXAMPLE 6　**Graphing a Rational Function**

Graph: $y = f(x) = \dfrac{3x}{x - 2}$.

SOLUTION　We will use the steps outlined earlier to graph the rational function.

Step 1: Symmetry
We find $f(-x)$.

$$f(-x) = \frac{3(-x)}{(-x) - 2} = \frac{-3x}{-x - 2} = \frac{3x}{x + 2}.$$

Because $f(-x) \neq f(x)$ and $f(-x) \neq -f(x)$, there is no symmetry about the y-axis or the origin.

Step 2: Vertical asymptotes
We first note that $f(x)$ is in simplest form. We then set the denominator equal to 0 and solve for x. Since the solution is 2, there will be a vertical asymptote at $x = 2$.

Step 3: y- and x-intercepts
We can find the y-intercept by finding $f(0)$.

$$f(0) = \frac{3(0)}{0 - 2} = \frac{0}{-2} = 0$$

The y-intercept is $(0, 0)$.
　　We can find the x-intercepts by setting the numerator equal to 0 and solving for x:

$3x = 0$

$x = 0$

The x-intercept is $(0, 0)$.

Step 4: Horizontal asymptotes
Since the degrees of the numerator and denominator of the polynomials are the same, the line

$$y = \frac{3}{1} = 3$$ 　　The leading coefficient of the numerator is 3.
　　　　　　　　　　　The leading coefficient of the denominator is 1.

is a horizontal asymptote.

Step 5: Slant asymptotes
Since the degree of the numerator is not 1 greater than the degree of the denominator, there are no slant asymptotes.

Step 6: Graph
First, we plot the intercept $(0, 0)$ and draw the asymptotes. We then find one additional point on our graph to see what happens when x is greater than 2. To do so, we choose 3, a value of x that is greater than 2, and evaluate $f(3)$.

$$f(3) = \frac{3(3)}{3 - 2} = \frac{9}{1} = 9$$

Since $f(3) = 9$, the point $(3, 9)$ lies on our graph. We sketch the graph as shown in Figure 3-74.

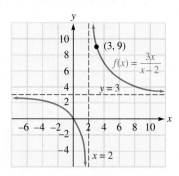

FIGURE 3-74

Self Check 6 Graph: $f(x) = \dfrac{3x}{x + 2}$.

Now Try Exercise 53.

EXAMPLE 7 **Graphing a Rational Function**

Graph the function: $y = \dfrac{1}{x(x - 1)^2}$.

SOLUTION We will use the steps outlined earlier to graph the rational function.

Step 1: Symmetry
We find $f(-x)$.

$$f(x) = \frac{1}{x(x - 1)^2}$$

$$f(-x) = \frac{1}{(-x)(-x - 1)^2} \qquad \text{Replace } x \text{ with } -x$$

$$= \frac{1}{(-x)[(-1)(x + 1)]^2} \qquad \text{Factor out } -1.$$

$$= \frac{1}{(-x)(-1)^2(x + 1)^2} \qquad \text{Square } -1 \text{ and } x + 1.$$

$$= \frac{1}{(-x)(x + 1)^2}$$

$$= \frac{-1}{x(x + 1)^2} \qquad \text{Simplify.}$$

Because $f(-x) \neq f(x)$ and $f(-x) \neq -f(x)$, there is no symmetry about the y-axis or origin.

Step 2: Vertical asymptotes

We set the denominator equal to 0 and solve for x. Since 0 and 1 make the denominator 0, the vertical asymptotes are $x = 0$ and $x = 1$.

Step 3: y- and x-intercepts

Since x cannot be 0, the graph has no y-intercept. Since the numerator cannot be 0, y cannot be 0, and the graph has no x-intercepts.

Step 4: Horizontal asymptotes

Since the degree of the numerator is 0 and the degree of the denominator is 3, and $0 < 3$, we conclude that the horizontal asymptote is the line $y = 0$.

Step 5: Slant asymptotes

There are no slant asymptotes because the degree of the numerator is not 1 greater than the degree of the denominator.

Step 6: Graph

Because there are no intercepts to plot, we draw the asymptotes and find a few additional points to plot. The table gives three points lying in different intervals separated by the asymptotes. We sketch the graph as shown in Figure 3-75.

$y = \dfrac{1}{x(x - 1)^2}$		
x	y	(x, y)
-1	$-\dfrac{1}{4}$	$\left(-1, -\dfrac{1}{4}\right)$
$\dfrac{1}{2}$	8	$\left(\dfrac{1}{2}, 8\right)$
2	$\dfrac{1}{2}$	$\left(2, \dfrac{1}{2}\right)$

FIGURE 3-75

Self Check 7   Graph the function: $f(x) = \dfrac{1}{x(x - 2)^2}$.

Now Try Exercise 69.

EXAMPLE 8   ## Graphing a Rational Function

Graph: $y = f(x) = \dfrac{1}{x^2 + 1}$.

SOLUTION   We will use the steps outlined earlier to graph the rational function.

Step 1: Symmetry

Because x appears to an even power and $f(-x) = f(x)$, there is symmetry about the y-axis. There is no symmetry about the origin.

Step 2: Vertical asymptotes

Since no number x makes the denominator 0, the graph has no vertical asymptotes.

Step 3: y- and x-intercepts

We can find the y-intercept by finding $f(0)$.

$$f(0) = \frac{1}{0^2 + 1} = \frac{1}{1} = 1$$

The y-intercept is $(0, 1)$.

Because the denominator is always positive, the fraction is always positive and the graph lies entirely above the x-axis. There are no x-intercepts. We also see that if we set the numerator equal to 0 there are no solutions for x.

Step 4: Horizontal asymptotes
Since the degree of the numerator is less than the degree of the denominator, the line $y = 0$ is a horizontal asymptote.

Step 5: Slant asymptotes
There are no slant asymptotes because the degree of the numerator is not 1 greater than the degree of the denominator.

Step 6: Graph
We first plot the y-intercept $(0, 1)$. Then, we make use of the fact that the graph has y-axis symmetry and a horizontal asymptote of $y = 0$ and sketch the graph. The graph is shown in Figure 3-76.

FIGURE 3-76

Self Check 8   Graph: $f(x) = \dfrac{4}{x^2 + 1}$.

Now Try Exercise 73.

EXAMPLE 9   **Graphing a Rational Function with a Slant Asymptote**

Graph: $y = f(x) = \dfrac{x^2 + x - 2}{x - 3}$.

SOLUTION   We first factor the numerator of the expression $y = \dfrac{(x - 1)(x + 2)}{x - 3}$ and use the steps outlined earlier to graph the rational function.

Step 1: Symmetry
We find $f(-x)$.

$$f(x) = \frac{x^2 + x - 2}{x - 3}$$

$$f(-x) = \frac{(-x)^2 + (-x) - 2}{(-x) - 3} \qquad \text{Replace } x \text{ with } -x.$$

$$= \frac{x^2 - x - 2}{-x - 3} \qquad \text{Simplify.}$$

$$= \frac{x^2 - x - 2}{(-1)(x + 3)} \qquad \text{Factor } -1 \text{ out of the denominator.}$$

$$= \frac{-x^2 + x + 2}{x + 3} \qquad \text{Divide by } -1.$$

Because $f(-x) \neq f(x)$ and $f(x) \neq -f(x)$, there is no symmetry about the y-axis or origin.

Step 2: Vertical asymptotes
We set the denominator equal to 0 and solve for x. Since 3 makes the denominator 0, the vertical asymptote is $x = 3$.

EXAMPLE 11 **Solving an Application Using a Rational Function**

Suppose the cost C of a no contract cell phone is $20 per month plus $0.15 per minute. Write a rational function that represents the average (mean) cost per minute, $\overline{C}$. Let n represent the number of minutes used per month. Find the mean cost per minute when the service is used for 180 minutes.

SOLUTION Because the mean cost is the total monthly cost divided by the number of minutes used, we can write a rational function that models the problem. We will then evaluate the mean cost function at 180 to find the mean cost for 180 minutes used.

We know that the mean cost $\overline{C}$ is total cost C divided by the number of access minutes n. That is,

$$\overline{C} = \frac{C}{n}$$

Since total cost C is $20 per month plus $0.15 for each minute n, we can write $C(n) = 0.15n + 20$.

Thus, the function

$$\overline{C}(n) = \frac{0.15n + 20}{n} \qquad (n > 0)$$

gives the mean cost per minute of using the service for n minutes per month.

To find the mean cost for 180 minutes of usage, we substitute 180 for n and simplify.

$$\overline{C}(180) = \frac{0.15(180) + 20}{180} \approx 0.26$$

The mean cost per minute for 180 minutes of usage is approximately $0.26 per minute. ∎

Self Check 11 Find the mean hourly cost when the cell phone described above is used for 240 minutes.

Now Try Exercise 87.

ACCENT ON TECHNOLOGY **Graphs of Rational Functions**

We can use a graphing calculator to graph the function $\overline{C}(n) = \frac{0.15n + 20}{n}$ in Example 11. We enter the function as shown in Figure 3-79(a) using the window settings as shown in Figure 3-79 (b). The graph of the rational function appears in Figure 3-79(c). Note the following characteristics:

- The graph of the function passes the Vertical Line Test, as expected.
- From the graph in Figure 3-79(c), we see that the mean cost per minute decreases as the number of minutes of usage increases.

Since the cost of each extra minute of usage of time is $0.15, the mean minute cost can approach $0.15 but will never drop below it. The graph of the function approaches the line $y = 0.15$ as n increases without bound. The line $y = 0.15$ is a horizontal asymptote of the graph.

- As n gets smaller and approaches 0, the graph approaches the y-axis. The y-axis is a vertical asymptote of the graph.

(a)

```
Plot1 Plot2 Plot3
\Y1■(.15X+20)/X
\Y2=
\Y3=
\Y4=
\Y5=
\Y6=
\Y7=
```

(b)

```
WINDOW
 Xmin=0
 Xmax=400
 Xscl=20
 Ymin=0
 Ymax=1
 Yscl=.1
 Xres=1■
```

(c)

FIGURE 3-79

Self Check Answers   **1.** $(-\infty, -1) \cup (-1, 2) \cup (2, \infty)$ **2. a.** $x = 5$ **b.** none   **3. a.** $y = -4$
b. $y = 0$ **4.** $y = 2x$ **5.**

6.

7.

8.

9.

10.

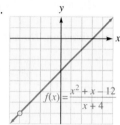

11. $0.23 per minute

Exercises **3.5**

Getting Ready
You should be able to complete these vocabulary and concept statements before you proceed to the practice exercises.

Fill in the blanks.

1. When a graph approaches a vertical line but never touches it, we call the line an _____.

2. A rational function is a function with a polynomial numerator and a _____ polynomial denominator.

3. To find a _____ asymptote of a rational function in simplest form, set the denominator polynomial equal to 0 and solve the equation.

4. To find the _____ of a rational function, let $x = 0$ and solve for y or find $f(0)$.

5. To find the _____ of a rational function, set the numerator equal to 0 and solve the equation.

6. In the function $\frac{P(x)}{Q(x)}$, if the degree of $P(x)$ is less than the degree of $Q(x)$, the horizontal asymptote is _____.

7. In the function $f(x) = \frac{P(x)}{Q(x)}$, if the degree of $P(x)$ and $Q(x)$ are the _____, the horizontal symptote is

$$y = \frac{\text{the leading coefficient of the numerator}}{\text{the leading coefficient of the denominator}}.$$

8. In a rational function, if the degree of the numerator is 1 greater than the degree of the denominator, the graph will have a _____.

9. A graph can cross a _____ asymptote but can never cross a _____ asymptote.

10. The graph of $f(x) = \frac{x^2 - 4}{x + 2}$ will have a _____ point.

Find the equations of the vertical and horizontal asymptotes of each graph. Find the domain and range.

11.

12.

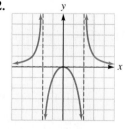

Practice

The time t it takes to travel 600 miles is a function of the mean rate of speed r:

$$t = f(r) = \frac{600}{r}$$

Find t for the given values of r.

13. 30 mph

14. 40 mph

15. 50 mph

16. 60 mph

Suppose the cost (in dollars) of removing p% of the pollution in a river is given by the function

$$C = f(p) = \frac{50{,}000p}{100 - p} \quad (0 \le p < 100)$$

Find the cost of removing each percent of pollution.

17. 10%

18. 30%

19. 50%

20. 80%

Find the domain of each rational function. Do not graph the function.

21. $f(x) = \dfrac{x^2}{x - 2}$

22. $f(x) = \dfrac{x^3 - 3x^2 + 1}{x + 3}$

23. $f(x) = \dfrac{2x^2 + 7x - 2}{x^2 - 25}$

24. $f(x) = \dfrac{5x^2 + 1}{x^2 + 5}$

25. $f(x) = \dfrac{x - 1}{x^3 - x}$

26. $f(x) = \dfrac{x + 2}{2x^2 - 9x + 9}$

27. $f(x) = \dfrac{3x^2 + 5}{x^2 + 1}$

28. $f(x) = \dfrac{7x^2 - x + 2}{x^4 + 4}$

Find the vertical asymptotes, if any, of each rational function. Do not graph the function.

29. $f(x) = \dfrac{x}{x - 3}$

30. $f(x) = \dfrac{2x}{2x + 5}$

31. $f(x) = \dfrac{x + 2}{x^2 - 1}$

32. $f(x) = \dfrac{x - 4}{x^2 - 16}$

33. $f(x) = \dfrac{1}{x^2 - x - 6}$

34. $f(x) = \dfrac{x + 2}{2x^2 - 6x - 8}$

35. $f(x) = \dfrac{x^2}{x^2 + 5}$

36. $f(x) = \dfrac{x^3 - 3x^2 + 1}{2x^2 + 3}$

Find the horizontal asymptotes, if any, of each rational function. Do not graph the function.

37. $f(x) = \dfrac{2x - 1}{x}$

38. $f(x) = \dfrac{x^2 + 1}{3x^2 - 5}$

39. $f(x) = \dfrac{x^2 + x - 2}{2x^2 - 4}$

40. $f(x) = \dfrac{5x^2 + 1}{5 - x^2}$

41. $f(x) = \dfrac{x + 1}{x^3 - 4x}$

42. $f(x) = \dfrac{x}{2x^2 - x + 11}$

43. $f(x) = \dfrac{x^2}{x - 2}$

44. $f(x) = \dfrac{x^4 + 1}{x - 3}$

Find the slant asymptote, if any, of each rational function. Do not graph the function.

45. $f(x) = \dfrac{x^2 - 5x - 6}{x - 2}$

46. $f(x) = \dfrac{x^2 - 2x + 11}{x + 3}$

47. $f(x) = \dfrac{2x^2 - 5x + 1}{x - 4}$

48. $f(x) = \dfrac{5x^3 + 1}{x + 5}$

49. $f(x) = \dfrac{x^3 + 2x^2 - x - 1}{x^2 - 1}$

50. $f(x) = \dfrac{-x^3 + 3x^2 - x + 1}{x^2 + 1}$

Find all vertical, horizontal, and slant asymptotes, x- and y-intercepts, and symmetries, and then graph each function. Check your work with a graphing calculator.

51. $y = \dfrac{1}{x - 2}$

52. $y = \dfrac{3}{x + 3}$

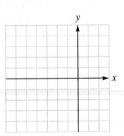

53. $y = \dfrac{x}{x - 1}$

54. $y = \dfrac{x}{x + 2}$

55. $f(x) = \dfrac{x+1}{x+2}$

56. $f(x) = \dfrac{x-1}{x-2}$

63. $y = \dfrac{x^2+2x-3}{x^3-4x}$

64. $y = \dfrac{3x^2-4x+1}{2x^3+3x^2+x}$

57. $f(x) = \dfrac{2x-1}{x-1}$

58. $f(x) = \dfrac{3x+2}{x^2-4}$

65. $y = \dfrac{x^2-9}{x^2}$

66. $y = \dfrac{3x^2-12}{x^2}$

59. $g(x) = \dfrac{x^2-9}{x^2-4}$

60. $g(x) = \dfrac{x^2-4}{x^2-9}$

67. $f(x) = \dfrac{x}{(x+3)^2}$

68. $f(x) = \dfrac{x}{(x-1)^2}$

61. $g(x) = \dfrac{x^2-x-2}{x^2-4x+3}$

62. $g(x) = \dfrac{x^2+7x+12}{x^2-7x+12}$

69. $f(x) = \dfrac{x+1}{x^2(x-2)}$

70. $f(x) = \dfrac{x-1}{x^2(x+2)^2}$

71. $y = \dfrac{x}{x^2+1}$

72. $y = \dfrac{x-1}{x^2+2}$

73. $y = \dfrac{3x^2}{x^2 + 1}$

74. $y = \dfrac{x^2 - 9}{2x^2 + 1}$

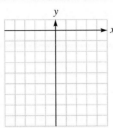

Graph each rational function. Note that the numerator and denominator of the fraction share a common factor.

79. $f(x) = \dfrac{x^2}{x}$

80. $f(x) = \dfrac{x^2 - 1}{x - 1}$

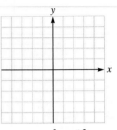

75. $h(x) = \dfrac{x^2 - 2x - 8}{x - 1}$

76. $h(x) = \dfrac{x^2 + x - 6}{x + 2}$

81. $f(x) = \dfrac{x^3 + x}{x}$

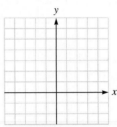

82. $f(x) = \dfrac{x^3 - x^2}{x - 1}$

77. $f(x) = \dfrac{x^3 + x^2 + 6x}{x^2 - 1}$

83. $f(x) = \dfrac{x^2 - 2x + 1}{x - 1}$

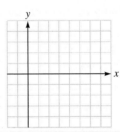

84. $f(x) = \dfrac{2x^2 + 3x - 2}{x + 2}$

78. $f(x) = \dfrac{x^3 - 2x^2 + x}{x^2 - 4}$

85. $f(x) = \dfrac{x^3 - 1}{x - 1}$

86. $f(x) = \dfrac{x^2 - x}{x^2}$

Applications

A service club wants to publish a directory of its members. Some investigation shows that the cost of typesetting and photography will be $700, and the cost of printing each directory will be $3.25.

87. a. Find a function that gives the total cost C of printing x directories.

b. Find the total cost of printing 500 directories.

c. Find a function that gives the mean cost per directory $\overline{C}$ of printing x directories.

d. Find the mean cost per directory if 500 directories are printed.

e. Find the mean cost per directory if 1,000 directories are printed.

f. Find the mean cost per directory if 2,000 directories are printed.

An electric company charges $10 per month plus 20¢ for each kilowatt-hour (kwh) of electricity used.

88. a. Find a function that gives the total cost C of n kwh of electricity.

b. Find the total cost for using 775 kwh.

c. Find a function that gives the mean cost per kwh, $\overline{C}$, when using n kwh.

d. Find the mean cost per kwh when 775 kwh are used. Round to the nearest hundredth.

e. Find the mean cost per kwh when 3,200 kwh are used. Round to the nearest hundredth.

89. Utility costs An overseas electric company charges $8.50 per month plus 9.5¢ for each kilowatt-hour (kwh) of electricity used.

a. Find a linear function that gives the total cost C of n kwh of electricity.

b. Find a rational function that gives the average cost per kwh when using n kwh.

c. Find the average cost per kwh when 850 kwh are used.

90. Scheduling work crews The following rational function gives the number of days it would take two construction crews, working together, to frame a house that crew 1 (working alone) could complete in t days and crew 2 (working alone) could complete in $(t + 3)$ days.

$$f(t) = \frac{t^2 + 3t}{2t + 3}$$

a. If crew 1 could frame a certain house in 21 days, how long would it take both crews working together?

b. If crew 2 could frame a certain house in 25 days, how long would it take both crews working together?

Discovery and Writing

91. Can a rational function have two horizontal asymptotes? Explain.

92. Can a rational function have two slant asymptotes? Explain.

In Exercises 93–96, a, b, c, and d are nonzero constants.

93. Show that $y = 0$ is a horizontal asymptote of the graph of $y = \frac{ax + b}{cx^2 + d}$.

94. Show that $y = \frac{a}{c}x$ is a slant asymptote of the graph of $y = \frac{ax^3 + b}{cx^2 + d}$.

95. Show that $y = \frac{a}{c}$ is a horizontal asymptote of the graph of $y = \frac{ax^2 + b}{cx^2 + d}$.

96. Graph the rational function $y = \frac{x^3 + 1}{x}$ and explain why the curve is said to have a *parabolic asymptote*.

Use a graphing calculator to perform each experiment. Write a brief paragraph describing your findings.

97. Investigate the positioning of the vertical asymptotes of a rational function by graphing $y = \frac{x}{x - k}$ for several values of k. What do you observe?

98. Investigate the positioning of the vertical asymptotes of a rational function by graphing $y = \frac{x}{x^2 - k}$ for $k = 4, 1, -1$, and 0. What do you observe?

99. Find the range of the rational function $y = \frac{kx^2}{x^2 + 1}$ for several values of k. What do you observe?

100. Investigate the positioning of the x-intercepts of a rational function by graphing $y = \frac{x^2 - k}{x}$ for $k = 1, -1$, and 0. What do you observe?

Review

Perform each operation.

101. $(2x^2 + 3x) + (x^2 - 2x)$ **102.** $(3x + 2) - (x^2 + 2)$

103. $(5x + 2)(2x + 5)$ **104.** $\dfrac{2x^2 + 3x + 1}{x + 1}$

105. If $f(x) = 3x + 2$, find $f(x + 1)$.

106. If $f(x) = x^2 + x$, find $f(2x + 1)$.

3.6 Operations on Functions

In this section, we will learn to

1. Add, subtract, multiply, and divide functions, specifying domains.
2. Write functions as sums, differences, products, or quotients of other functions.
3. Evaluate composite functions.
4. Determine domains for composite functions.
5. Write functions as compositions.
6. Use operations on functions to solve problems.

© Istockphoto.com/Ian McDonnell

Functions can be combined by addition, subtraction, multiplication, and division. In this section, we will explore these operations on functions and give careful attention to their domains and ranges.

Suppose that the functions $R(x) = 140x$ and $C(x) = 120{,}000 + 40x$ model a company's yearly revenue and cost for producing and selling surfboards. By subtracting the functions, $R(x) - C(x)$, we would arrive at a new function represented by

$$(R - C)(x) = 140x - (120{,}000 + 40x)$$

$$= 140x - 120{,}000 - 40x \qquad \text{Remove parentheses.}$$

$$= 100x - 120{,}000$$

This function represents the profit made by the company when it sells x surfboards. We will now discuss how to add, subtract, multiply, and divide functions.

1. Add, Subtract, Multiply, and Divide Functions, Specifying Domains

With the following definitions, it is possible to perform arithmetic operations on algebraic functions.

Adding, Subtracting, Multiplying, and Dividing Functions

If the ranges of functions f and g are subsets of the real numbers, then

1. The **sum** of f and g, denoted as $f + g$, is defined by

$$(f + g)(x) = f(x) + g(x)$$

2. The **difference** of f and g, denoted as $f - g$, is defined by

$$(f - g)(x) = f(x) - g(x)$$

3. The **product** of f and g, denoted as $f \cdot g$, is defined by

$$(f \cdot g)(x) = f(x)g(x)$$

4. The **quotient** of f and g, denoted as f/g, is defined by

$$(f/g)(x) = \frac{f(x)}{g(x)} \quad (g(x) \neq 0)$$

The **domain** of each function, unless otherwise restricted, is the set of real numbers x that are in the domains of both f and g. In the case of the quotient f/g, there is the restriction that $g(x) \neq 0$.

EXAMPLE 1   Finding the Sum and Difference of Two Functions and Specifying Domains

Let $f(x) = 3x + 1$ and $g(x) = 2x - 3$. Find each function and its domain:
a. $f + g$ **b.** $f - g$

SOLUTION   We will find the sum of f and g by using the definition

$$(f + g)(x) = f(x) + g(x)$$

We will find the difference of f and g by using the definition

$$(f - g)(x) = f(x) - g(x).$$

To find the domain of each result, we will consider the domains of both f and g.

a. $(f + g)(x) = f(x) + g(x)$

$$= (3x + 1) + (2x - 3)$$

$$= 5x - 2$$

Since the domain of both f and g is the set of real numbers, the domain of $f + g$ is the interval $(-\infty, \infty)$.

b. $(f - g)(x) = f(x) - g(x)$

$$= (3x + 1) - (2x - 3)$$

$$= 3x + 1 - 2x + 3 \qquad \text{Remove parentheses.}$$

$$= x + 4$$

Since the domain of both f and g is the set of real numbers, the domain of $f - g$ is the interval $(-\infty, \infty)$.

Self Check 1   Find $g - f$.

Now Try Exercise 15.

EXAMPLE 2   Finding the Product and Quotient of Two Functions and Specifying Domains

Let $f(x) = 3x + 1$ and $g(x) = 2x - 3$. Find each function and its domain:
a. $f \cdot g$ **b.** f/g

SOLUTION   We will multiply f and g by using the definition

$$(f \cdot g)(x) = f(x)g(x)$$

We will divide f by g by using the definition

$$(f/g)(x) = \frac{f(x)}{g(x)} \qquad (g(x) \neq 0)$$

We will find the domains of each result by considering the domains of both f and g.

a. $(f \cdot g)(x) = f(x) \cdot g(x)$

$$= (3x + 1)(2x - 3)$$

$$= 6x^2 - 7x - 3$$

Since the domain of both f and g is the set of real numbers, the domain of $f \cdot g$ is the interval $(-\infty, \infty)$.

b. $(f/g)(x) = \dfrac{f(x)}{g(x)}$ $(g(x) \neq 0)$

$\qquad = \dfrac{3x + 1}{2x - 3}$ $(2x - 3 \neq 0)$

Since $\frac{3}{2}$ will make $2x - 3$ equal to 0, the domain of f/g is the set of all real numbers except $\frac{3}{2}$. This is $\left(-\infty, \frac{3}{2}\right) \cup \left(\frac{3}{2}, \infty\right)$. ■

Self Check 2   Find g/f and its domain.

Now Try Exercise 17.

EXAMPLE 3   **Using Operations on Functions and Specifying Domains**

Let $f(x) = x^2 - 4$ and $g(x) = \sqrt{x}$. Find each function and its domain: **a.** $f + g$
b. $f \cdot g$ **c.** f/g **d.** g/f

SOLUTION   To determine each result, we use the definitions of the sum, product, and quotient of two functions. We will determine the domain of each result by considering the domains of both f and g.

First, we find the domains of f and g. Because 4 can be subtracted from any real number squared, the domain of f is the interval $(-\infty, \infty)$. Because $\sqrt{x}$ is to be a real number, the domain of g is the interval $[0, \infty)$.

a. $(f + g)(x) = f(x) + g(x)$

$\qquad = x^2 - 4 + \sqrt{x}$

The domain of $f + g$ consists of the numbers x that are in the domain of both f and g. This is $(-\infty, \infty) \cap [0, \infty)$, which is $[0, \infty)$. The domain of $f + g$ is $[0, \infty)$.

b. $(f \cdot g)(x) = f(x)g(x)$

$\qquad = (x^2 - 4)\sqrt{x}$

$\qquad = x^2\sqrt{x} - 4\sqrt{x}$ Distribute the multiplication of $\sqrt{x}$.

The domain of $f \cdot g$ consists of the numbers x that are in the domain of both f and g. The domain of $f \cdot g$ is $[0, \infty)$.

c. $(f/g)(x) = \dfrac{f(x)}{g(x)}$ $(g(x) \neq 0)$

$\qquad = \dfrac{x^2 - 4}{\sqrt{x}}$

The domain of f/g consists of the numbers x that are in the domain of both f and g, except 0 (because division by 0 is undefined). The domain of f/g is $(0, \infty)$.

To write $(f/g)(x)$ in a different form, we can rationalize the denominator of $\frac{x^2 - 4}{\sqrt{x}}$ and simplify.

$(f/g)(x) = \dfrac{x^2 - 4}{\sqrt{x}}$

$\qquad = \dfrac{(x^2 - 4)\sqrt{x}}{\sqrt{x} \cdot \sqrt{x}}$ Multiply numerator and denominator by $\sqrt{x}$.

$\qquad = \dfrac{x^2\sqrt{x} - 4\sqrt{x}}{x}$

d. $(g/f)(x) = \dfrac{g(x)}{f(x)}$ $(f(x) \neq 0)$

$$= \frac{\sqrt{x}}{x^2 - 4}$$

The domain of g/f consists of the numbers x that are in $[0, \infty)$, the domain of both f and g, except 2 (because division by 0 is undefined). The domain of g/f is $[0, 2) \cup (2, \infty)$. ∎

Self Check 3   Find $g - f$ and its domain.

Now Try Exercise 19.

We can perform these operations using a graphing calculator.

ACCENT ON TECHNOLOGY   **Operations on Functions**

A graphing calculator can be used to graph operations on function. Consider Example 3.

- We will use a bold setting to indicate the function $f + g$. In Figure 3-80, we see in the left graph that the graph of $f + g$ appears to be the same as f. However, if we zoom in to a small part of the graph as shown in the right graph, we can see that the functions are different. To input Y_1 and Y_2, press **VARS**, scroll right to Y-VARS, press **ENTER**, and select the desired function.

FIGURE 3-80

- We use the bold setting to indicate the function $f \cdot g$. Again, by zooming in to just part of the window, we can see the graphs are different. See Figure 3-81.

FIGURE 3-81

- We demonstrate the graph of f/g using a graphing calculator. See Figure 3-82. f/g appears bold.

FIGURE 3-82

•   We demonstrate the graph of g/f using a graphing calculator. See Figure 3-83. g/f appears bold.

FIGURE 3-83

EXAMPLE 4   **Evaluating the Sum of Two Functions**

Find $(f + g)(3)$ when $f(x) = x^2 + 1$ and $g(x) = 2x + 1$.

SOLUTION   We will first find $(f + g)(x)$ and then find $(f + g)(3)$. To find $(f + g)(x)$, we proceed as follows:

$$(f + g)(x) = f(x) + g(x)$$
$$= x^2 + 1 + 2x + 1$$
$$= x^2 + 2x + 2$$

To find $(f + g)(3)$, we proceed as follows:

$$(f + g)(x) = x^2 + 2(x) + 2$$
$$(f + g)(3) = 3^2 + 2(3) + 2 \qquad \text{Substitute 3 for } x.$$
$$= 9 + 6 + 2$$
$$= 17$$

Comment

We can also determine $(f + g)(3)$ by finding $f(3) + g(3)$. Note that $f(3) = 10$, $g(3) = 7$, and $f(3) + g(3) = 10 + 7 = 17$.

Self Check 4   Find $(f \cdot g)(-2)$.

Now Try Exercise 25.

2. Write Functions as Sums, Differences, Products, or Quotients of Other Functions

EXAMPLE 5   **Writing Functions as Combinations of Other Functions**

Let $h(x) = x^2 + 3x + 2$. Find two functions f and g such that
a. $f + g = h$ **b.** $f \cdot g = h$

SOLUTION   For part **a**, we must find two functions f and g whose sum is h. For part **b**, we must find two functions f and g whose product is h.

a. There are many possibilities. One is $f(x) = x^2$ and $g(x) = 3x + 2$, then

$$(f + g)(x) = f(x) + g(x)$$
$$= (x^2) + (3x + 2)$$
$$= x^2 + 3x + 2$$
$$= h(x)$$

Another possibility is $f(x) = x^2 + 2x$ and $g(x) = x + 2$.

b. Again, there are many possibilities. One is suggested by factoring $x^2 + 3x + 2$.

$x^2 + 3x + 2 = (x + 1)(x + 2)$

If we let $f(x) = x + 1$ and $g(x) = x + 2$, then

$(f \cdot g)(x) = f(x) \cdot g(x)$

$\qquad = (x + 1)(x + 2)$

$\qquad = x^2 + 3x + 2$

$\qquad = h(x)$

Another possibility is $f(x) = 3$ and $g(x) = \frac{x^2}{3} + x + \frac{2}{3}$.

Self Check 5   Find two functions f and g such that $f - g = h$.

Now Try Exercise 35.

3. Evaluate Composite Functions

Often one quantity is a function of a second quantity that depends, in turn, on a third quantity. For example, the cost of a car trip is a function of the gasoline consumed. The amount of gasoline consumed, in turn, is a function of the number of miles driven. Such chains of dependence are analyzed mathematically as *composition of functions.*

Suppose that $y = f(x)$ and $y = g(x)$ define two functions. Any number x in the domain of g will produce a corresponding value $g(x)$ in the range of g. If $g(x)$ is in the domain of function f, then $g(x)$ can be substituted into f, and a corresponding value $f(g(x))$ will be determined. This two-step process defines a new function, called a **composite function,** denoted by $f \circ g$. (See Figure 3-84.)

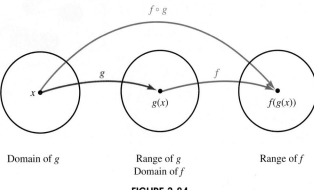

FIGURE 3-84

Composite Function   The **composite function** $f \circ g$ is defined by

$$(f \circ g)(x) = f(g(x))$$

The **domain** of $f \circ g$ consists of all those numbers in the domain of g for which $g(x)$ is in the domain of f.

To illustrate the previous definition, we consider the functions $f(x) = 5x + 1$ and $g(x) = 4x - 3$ and find $(f \circ g)(x)$ and $(g \circ f)(x)$.

$$\begin{aligned}
(f \circ g)(x) &= f(g(x)) & (g \circ f)(x) &= g(f(x)) \\
&= f(4x - 3) & &= g(5x + 1) \\
&= 5(4x - 3) + 1 & &= 4(5x + 1) - 3 \\
&= 20x - 14 & &= 20x + 1
\end{aligned}$$

Caution

Note that in the previous example $(f \circ g)(x) \neq (g \circ f)(x)$.

Since we get different results, the composition of functions is not commutative.

We have seen that a function can be represented by a machine. If we put a number from the domain into the machine (the input), a number from the range comes out (the output). For example, if we put 2 into the machine shown in Figure 3-85(a), the number $f(2) = 5(2) - 2 = 8$ comes out. In general, if we put x into the machine shown in Figure 3-85(b), the value $f(x)$ comes out.

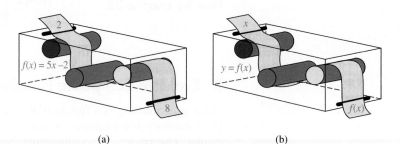

(a)   (b)

FIGURE 3-85

The function machines shown in Figure 3-86 illustrate the composition $f \circ g$. When we put a number x into the function g, the value $g(x)$ comes out. The value $g(x)$ then goes into function f, and $f(g(x))$ comes out.

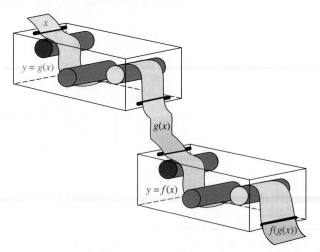

FIGURE 3-86

To further illustrate these ideas, we let $f(x) = 2x + 1$ and $g(x) = x - 4$.

- $(f \circ g)(9)$ means $f(g(9))$. In Figure 3-87(a), function g receives the number 9 and subtracts 4, and the number $g(x) = 5$ comes out. The 5 goes into the f function, which doubles it and adds 1. The final result, 11, is the output of the composite function $f \circ g$:

$$(f \circ g)(9) = f(g(9)) = f(5) = 2(5) + 1 = 11$$

- $(f \circ g)(x)$ means $f(g(x))$. In Figure 3-87(a), function g receives the number x and subtracts 4, and the number $x - 4$ comes out. The $x - 4$ goes into the f function, which doubles it and adds 1. The final result, $2x - 7$, is the output of the composite function $f \circ g$.

$$(f \circ g)(x) = f(g(x)) = f(x - 4) = 2(x - 4) + 1 = 2x - 7$$

- $(g \circ f)(-2)$ means $g(f(-2))$. In Figure 3-87(b), function f receives the number -2, doubles it and adds 1, and releases -3 into the g function. Function g subtracts 4 from -3 and releases a final output of -7. Thus,

$$(g \circ f)(-2) = g(f(-2)) = g(-3) = -3 - 4 = -7$$

(a)   (b)

FIGURE 3-87

EXAMPLE 6 **Finding the Composition of Two Functions**

If $f(x) = 2x + 7$ and $g(x) = x^2 - 1$, find **a.** $(f \circ g)(x)$ **b.** $(g \circ f)(x)$

SOLUTION In part **a**, because $(f \circ g)(x)$ means $f(g(x))$, we will replace x in $f(x) = 2x + 7$ with $g(x)$. In part **b**, because $(g \circ f)(x)$ means $g(f(x))$ we will replace x in $g(x) = x^2 - 1$ with $f(x)$.

a. $(f \circ g)(x) = f(g(x))$

$\qquad\qquad\quad = f(x^2 - 1)$ Substitute $x^2 - 1$ for $g(x)$.

$\qquad\qquad\quad = 2(x^2 - 1) + 7$ Evaluate $f(x^2 - 1)$.

$\qquad\qquad\quad = 2x^2 - 2 + 7$ Remove parentheses.

$\qquad\qquad\quad = 2x^2 + 5$

b. $(g \circ f)(x) = g(f(x))$

$\qquad\qquad\quad = g(2x + 7)$ Substitute $2x + 7$ for $f(x)$.

$\qquad\qquad\quad = (2x + 7)^2 - 1$ Evaluate $g(2x + 7)$.

$\qquad\qquad\quad = 4x^2 + 28x + 49 - 1$ Square the binomial.

$\qquad\qquad\quad = 4x^2 + 28x + 48$

Self Check 6   If $f(x) = 2x + 7$ and $h(x) = x + 1$, find $(f \circ h)(x)$.

Now Try Exercise 51.

EXAMPLE 7   **Evaluating the Composition of Two Functions**

If $f(x) = 3x - 2$ and $g(x) = 3x^2 + 6x - 5$, find $(f \circ g)(-2)$.

SOLUTION   Because $(f \circ g)(-2)$ means $f(g(-2))$, we first find $g(-2)$. We then find $f(g(-2))$.

$$g(x) = 3x^2 + 6x - 5$$
$$g(-2) = 3(-2)^2 + 6(-2) - 5$$
$$= 3(4) - 12 - 5$$
$$= -5$$
$$(f \circ g)(-2) = f(g(-2))$$
$$= f(-5)$$
$$= 3(-5) - 2$$
$$= -17$$

Self Check 7   Find $(g \circ f)(-1)$.

Now Try Exercise 43.

4. Determine Domains of Composite Functions

To be in the domain of the composite function $f \circ g$, a number x has to be in the domain of g, and the output of g must be in the domain of f. Thus, the domain of $f \circ g$ consists of those inputs x that are in the domain of g and for which $g(x)$ is in the domain of f.

Strategy to Determine the Domain of $f \circ g$ To determine the domain of $(f \circ g)(x) = f(g(x))$, apply the following restrictions to the composition:

1. If x is not in the domain of g, it will not be in the domain of $f \circ g$.
2. Any x that has an output $g(x)$ that is not in the domain of f will not be in the domain of $f \circ g$.

EXAMPLE 8   **Finding the Domain of Composite Functions**

Let $f(x) = \sqrt{x}$ and $g(x) = x - 3$. Find the domain of **a.** $f \circ g$ **b.** $g \circ f$

SOLUTION   We will first find the domains of $f(x)$ and $g(x)$. Then, we will find the domain of $f \circ g$ and $g \circ f$ by applying the restrictions stated above.

For $\sqrt{x}$ to be a real number, x must be a nonnegative real number. Thus, the domain of f is the interval $[0, \infty)$. Since any real number x can be an input into g, the domain of g is the interval $(-\infty, \infty)$.

a. The domain of $f \circ g$ is the set of real numbers x such that x is in the domain of g and $g(x)$ is in the domain of f. We have seen that all values of x are in the domain of g. However, $g(x)$ must be nonnegative, because $g(x)$ must be in the domain of f. So we must find the values of x such that $g(x)$ is greater than or equal to 0.

$$g(x) \geq 0 \qquad \text{\small $g(x)$ must be nonnegative.}$$

$$x - 3 \geq 0 \qquad \text{\small Substitute $x - 3$ for $g(x)$.}$$

$$x \geq 3 \qquad \text{\small Add 3 to both sides.}$$

Since $x \geq 3$, the domain of $f \circ g$ is the interval $[3, \infty)$.

b. The domain of $g \circ f$ is the set of real numbers x such that x is in the domain of f and $f(x)$ is in the domain of g. We have seen that only nonnegative values of x are in the domain of f. Because all values of $f(x)$ are in the domain of g, the domain of $g \circ f$ is the domain of f, which is the interval $[0, \infty)$. ∎

Self Check 8   Find the domain of $f \circ f$.

Now Try Exercise 55.

Composition of Functions and Domain

Consider the two functions given in Example 8(a). We can use a graphing calculator to graph the composite function $f \circ g$. To enter the composition, we enter $y_1(y_2)$ using ⬛VARS⬛. See Figure 3-88. From the graph, we can determine the domain of $f \circ g$. We see that the domain is $[3, \infty)$.

FIGURE 3-88

EXAMPLE 9   **Finding the Domain of Composite Functions**

Let $f(x) = \dfrac{x + 3}{x - 2}$ and $g(x) = \dfrac{1}{x}$.

a. Find the domain of $f \circ g$.   **b.** Find $f \circ g$.

SOLUTION   We will first find the domains of $f(x)$ and $g(x)$. Then, we will find the domain of $f \circ g$ and $g \circ f$ by applying the restrictions stated earlier.

Since any real number except 2 can be an input into f, the domain of f is $(-\infty, 2) \cup (2, \infty)$.

For $\frac{1}{x}$ to be a real number, x cannot be 0. Thus, the domain of g is $(-\infty, 0) \cup (0, \infty)$.

a. The domain of $f \circ g$ is the set of real numbers x such that x is in the domain of g and $g(x)$ is in the domain of f. We have seen that all values of x but 0 are in the domain of g and that all values of $g(x)$ but 2 are in the domain of f. So we must exclude 0 from the domain of $f \circ g$ and all values of x where $g(x) = 2$. To find the excluded values, we proceed as follows:

$$g(x) = 2$$

$$\frac{1}{x} = 2 \qquad \text{Substitute } \frac{1}{x} \text{ for } g(x).$$

$$1 = 2x \qquad \text{Since } x \neq 0, \text{ we can multiply both sides by } x.$$

$$x = \frac{1}{2} \qquad \text{Divide both sides by 2.}$$

The domain of $f \circ g$ is the set of all real numbers except 0 and $\frac{1}{2}$, which is $(-\infty, 0) \cup \left(0, \frac{1}{2}\right) \cup \left(\frac{1}{2}, \infty\right)$.

b. To find $f \circ g$, we proceed as follows.

$$(f \circ g)(x) = f(g(x))$$

$$= f\left(\frac{1}{x}\right) \qquad \text{Substitute } \frac{1}{x} \text{ for } g(x).$$

$$= \frac{\dfrac{1}{x} + 3}{\dfrac{1}{x} - 2} \qquad \text{Substitute } \frac{1}{x} \text{ for } x \text{ in } f.$$

$$= \frac{1 + 3x}{1 - 2x} \qquad \text{Multiply numerator and denominator by } x.$$

Thus, $(f \circ g)(x) = \frac{1 + 3x}{1 - 2x}$. ■

Self Check 9   Let $f(x) = \dfrac{x}{x - 1}$ and $g(x) = \dfrac{1}{x}$. **a.** Find the domain of $f \circ g$ **b.** Find $f \circ g$

Now Try Exercise 63.

Caution

> Example 9 illustrates that the domain of the composite function $f \circ g$ **cannot** always be found by finding $f \circ g$ and analyzing it. In the example, we found that the domain is all real numbers, except for 0 and $\frac{1}{2}$. If we only analyze the form $f \circ g$, we would state the domain incorrectly as all real numbers except $\frac{1}{2}$.

5. Write Functions as Compositions

Comment

The result of a decomposition is not unique. There are several possibilities. In the example to the right, another possibility is $f(x) = x^2$ and $g(x) = (2x^2 - 6x + 3)^2$.

When we form a composite function $f \circ g$, we obtain a function h. It is possible to reverse this composition process and begin with a function h and express it as a composition of two functions. This process is called **decomposition**.

For example, consider $h(x) = (2x^2 - 6x + 3)^4$. The function h takes $2x^2 - 6x + 3$ and raises it to the fourth power. To write the function h as a composition of functions f and g, we can let

$$f(x) = x^4 \quad \text{and} \quad g(x) = 2x^2 - 6x + 3$$

Then

$$(f \circ g)(x) = f(g(x))$$

$$= f(2x^2 - 6x + 3)$$

$$= (2x^2 - 6x + 3)^4$$

$$= h(x)$$

EXAMPLE 10   **Writing a Function as a Composition of Two Functions**

Let $h(x) = \sqrt{x + 1}$. Find two functions f and g such that $f \circ g = h$.

SOLUTION   Because h takes the square root of the algebraic function $x + 1$, we let $f(x) = \sqrt{x}$ and $g(x) = x + 1$.

$$f(x) = \sqrt{x} \quad \text{and} \quad g(x) = x + 1$$

We can check the composition $f \circ g$ to see that it gives the original function h.

$$(f \circ g)(x) = f(g(x))$$

$$= f(x + 1)$$

$$= \sqrt{x + 1}$$

$$= h(x)$$

■

Self Check 10   Let $h(x) = \sqrt[3]{x^2 - 5}$. Find functions f and g such that $f \circ g = h$.

Now Try Exercise 73.

6. Use Operations on Functions to Solve Problems

EXAMPLE 11   **Solving an Application Using Composition of Functions**

A laboratory sample is removed from a cooler at a temperature of $15°$ F. Technicians then warm the sample at the rate of $3°$F per hour. Express the sample's temperature in degrees Celsius as a function of the time t (in hours) since it was removed from the cooler.

SOLUTION   We first write a Fahrenheit temperature function that represents the warming of the sample. We then use composition of functions to write degrees Celsius as a function of degrees Fahrenheit.

The temperature of the sample is $15°$ F when $t = 0$. Because the sample warms at $3°$ F per hour, it warms $3t°$ after t hours. Thus, the Fahrenheit temperature after t hours is given by the function

$$F(t) = 3t + 15 \qquad \text{\small $F(t)$ is the Fahrenheit temperature and t represents the time in hours.}$$

The Celsius temperature is a function of the Fahrenheit temperature $F(t)$, given by the formula

$$C(F(t)) = \frac{5}{9}(F(t) - 32)$$

To express the sample's Celsius temperature as a function of time, we find the composition function $C \circ F$.

$$(C \circ F)(t) = C(F(t))$$

$$= C(3t + 15) \qquad \text{Substitute for } F(t).$$

$$= \frac{5}{9}[(3t + 15) - 32] \qquad \text{Substitute } 3t + 15 \text{ for } F(t) \text{ in } C(F(t)).$$

$$= \frac{5}{9}(3t - 17) \qquad \text{Simplify.}$$

$$= \frac{15}{9}t - \frac{85}{9}$$

$$= \frac{5}{3}t - \frac{85}{9}$$

■

Self Check 11   Find the $(C \circ F)(10)$.

Now Try Exercise 93.

Self Check Answers   **1.** $(g - f)(x) = -x - 4$ **2.** $(g/f)(x) = \dfrac{2x - 3}{3x + 1}, \left(-\infty, -\dfrac{1}{3}\right) \cup \left(-\dfrac{1}{3}, \infty\right)$

3. $(g - f)(x) = \sqrt{x} - x^2 + 4, [0, \infty)$ **4.** $(f \cdot g)(2) = -15$
5. One possibility is $f(x) = 2x^2$ and $g(x) = x^2 - 3x - 2$.
6. $(f \circ h)(x) = 2x + 9$ **7.** $(g \circ f)(-1) = 40$ **8.** $[0, \infty)$
9. $(-\infty, 0) \cup (0, 1) \cup (1, \infty)$; $(f \circ g)(x) = \dfrac{1}{1 - x}$
10. One possibility is $f(x) = \sqrt[3]{x}, g(x) = x^2 - 5$ **11.** approximately $7.2°C$

Exercises **3.6**

Getting Ready
You should be able to complete these vocabulary and concept statements before you proceed to the practice exercises.

Fill in the blanks.

1. $(f + g)(x) = $ _____
2. $(f - g)(x) = $ _____
3. $(f \cdot g)(x) = $ _____
4. $(f/g)(x) = $ _____, where $g(x) \neq 0$
5. The domain of $f + g$ is the _____ of the domains of f and g.
6. $(f \circ g)(x) = $ _____
7. $(g \circ f)(x) = $ _____
8. To determine $(f \circ g)(-5)$, first find _____.
9. Composition of functions is not _____.
10. To be in the domain of the composite function $f \circ g$, a number x has to be in the _____ of g, and the output of g must be in the _____ of f.

Practice
Let $f(x) = 2x + 1$ and $g(x) = 3x - 2$. Find each function and its domain.

11. $f + g$ 12. $f - g$

13. $f \cdot g$ 14. f/g

Let $f(x) = x^2 + x$ and $g(x) = x^2 - 1$. Find each function and its domain.

15. $f - g$ 16. $f + g$

17. f/g **18.** $f \cdot g$ **49.** $f \circ f$ **50.** $g \circ g$

Let $f(x) = x^2$ and $g(x) = 2x$. Determine the domain of each composite function and then find the composite function.

51. $g \circ f$ **52.** $f \circ g$

Let $f(x) = x^2 - 7$ and $g(x) = \sqrt{x}$. Find each function and its domain.

53. $g \circ g$ **54.** $f \circ f$

19. $f + g$ **20.** $f - g$

21. f/g **22.** $f \cdot g$

Let $f(x) = \sqrt{x}$ and $g(x) = x + 1$. Determine the domain of each composite function and then find the composite function.

55. $f \circ g$ **56.** $g \circ f$

Let $f(x) = x^2 - 1$ and $g(x) = 3x - 2$. Find each value, if possible.

57. $f \circ f$ **58.** $g \circ g$

23. $(f + g)(2)$ **24.** $(f + g)(-3)$
25. $(f - g)(0)$ **26.** $(f - g)(-5)$
27. $(f \cdot g)(2)$ **28.** $(f \cdot g)(-1)$
29. $(f/g)\left(\dfrac{2}{3}\right)$ **30.** $(f/g)(t)$

Let $f(x) = \sqrt{x + 1}$ and $g(x) = x^2 - 1$. Determine the domain of each composite function and then find the composite function.

59. $g \circ f$ **60.** $f \circ g$

Find two functions f and g such that $h(x)$ can be expressed as the function indicated. Several answers are possible.

31. $h(x) = 3x^2 + 2x;\ f + g$
32. $h(x) = 3x^2;\ f \cdot g$

61. $g \circ g$ **62.** $f \circ f$

33. $h(x) = \dfrac{3x^2}{x^2 - 1};\ f/g$
34. $h(x) = 5x + x^2;\ f - g$
35. $h(x) = x(3x^2 + 1);\ f - g$
36. $h(x) = (3x - 2)(3x + 2);\ f + g$
37. $h(x) = x^2 + 7x - 18;\ f \cdot g$
38. $h(x) = 5x^5;\ f/g$

Let $f(x) = \dfrac{1}{x - 1}$ and $g(x) = \dfrac{1}{x - 2}$. Determine the domain of each composite function and then find the composite function.

63. $f \circ g$ **64.** $g \circ f$

Let $f(x) = 2x - 5$ and $g(x) = 5x - 2$. Find each value.

39. $(f \circ g)(2)$ **40.** $(g \circ f)(-3)$
41. $(f \circ f)\left(-\dfrac{1}{2}\right)$ **42.** $(g \circ g)\left(\dfrac{3}{5}\right)$

65. $f \circ f$ **66.** $g \circ g$

Let $f(x) = 3x^2 - 2$ and $g(x) = 4x + 4$. Find each value.

43. $(f \circ g)(-3)$ **44.** $(g \circ f)(3)$
45. $(f \circ f)\left(\sqrt{3}\right)$ **46.** $(g \circ g)(-4)$

Find two functions f and g such that the composition $f \circ g = h$ expresses the given correspondence. Several answers are possible.

67. $h(x) = 3x - 2$ **68.** $h(x) = 7x - 5$

Let $f(x) = 3x$ and $g(x) = x + 1$. Determine the domain of each composite function and then find the composite function.

69. $h(x) = x^2 - 2$ **70.** $h(x) = x^3 - 3$

47. $f \circ g$ **48.** $g \circ f$

71. $h(x) = (x - 2)^2$ **72.** $h(x) = (x - 3)^3$

73. $h(x) = \sqrt{x + 2}$ **74.** $h(x) = \dfrac{1}{x - 5}$

75. $h(x) = \sqrt{x} + 2$ **76.** $h(x) = \dfrac{1}{x} - 5$

77. $h(x) = x$ **78.** $f(x) = 3$

Use the graphs of functions f and g to answer each problem.

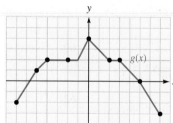

79. $(f + g)(-4)$ **80.** $(f - g)(1)$

81. $(f \cdot g)(5)$ **82.** $(f/g)(-1)$

83. $(f \circ g)(3)$ **84.** $(g \circ f)(2)$

85. $(f \circ f)(-2)$ **86.** $(g \circ g)(-5)$

Use the tables of values of f and g to answer each problem.

x	$f(x)$
2	4
4	9
6	13
13	17

x	$g(x)$
0	0
2	4
3	9
4	16

87. $(f + g)(2)$ **88.** $(f/g)(4)$

89. $(f \circ g)(2)$ **90.** $(g \circ f)(2)$

Applications

91. DVD camcorder Suppose that the functions $R(x) = 300x$ and $C(x) = 60,000 + 40x$ model a company's monthly revenue and cost for producing and selling DVD camcorders.

  a. Find $(R - C)(x)$, the function that models the monthly profit, $P(x)$.

  b. Find the company's profit if 500 camcorders are produced and sold in one month.

92. TV screen The height of the television screen shown is 13 inches.

  a. Write a formula to find the area of the viewing screen.

  b. Use the Pythagorean Theorem to write a formula to find the width w of the screen.

  c. Write a formula to find the area of the screen as a function of the diagonal d.

93. Area of an oil spill Suppose an oil spill from a tanker is spreading in the shape of a circular ripple. If the function $d(t) = 3t$ represents the diameter of the spill in inches at time t minutes, express the area, A, of the oil spill as a function of time. Find the area of the oil spill after 2 hours. Round to one decimal place.

94. Area of a square Write a formula for the area A of a square in terms of its perimeter P.

95. Perimeter of a square Write a formula for the perimeter P of a square in terms of its area A.

96. Ceramics When the temperature of a pot in a kiln is 1,200° F, an artist turns off the heat and leaves the pot to cool at a controlled rate of 81° F per hour. Express the temperature of the pot in degrees Celsius as a function of the time t (in hours) since the kiln was turned off.

Discovery and Writing

97. Let $f(x) = 3x$. Show that $(f + f)(x) = f(x + x)$.

98. Let $g(x) = x^2$. Show that $(g + g)(x) \neq g(x + x)$.

99. Let $f(x) = \frac{x-1}{x+1}$. Find $(f \circ f)(x)$.

100. Let $g(x) = \frac{x}{x-1}$. Find $(g \circ g)(x)$.

 Let $f(x) = x^2 - x$, $g(x) = x - 3$, and $h(x) = 3x$. Use a graphing calculator to graph both functions on the same axes. Write a brief paragraph summarizing your observations.

101. f and $f \circ g$

102. f and $g \circ f$

103. f and $f \circ h$

104. f and $h \circ f$

Review

Solve each equation for y.

105. $x = 3y - 7$

106. $x = \dfrac{7}{y}$

107. $x = \dfrac{y}{y+3}$

108. $x = \dfrac{y-1}{y}$

3.7 Inverse Functions

In this section, we will learn to

1. Understand the definition of a one-to-one function.

2. Determine whether a function is one-to-one.

3. Verify inverse functions.

4. Find the inverse of a one-to-one function.

5. Understand the relationship between the graphs of f and f^{-1}.

In this section, we will discuss inverse functions. A function and its inverse do opposite things.

Suppose we climb the Great Wall of China on a summer day when the temperature reaches a high of 35°C.

The linear function defined by $F = \frac{9}{5}C + 32$ gives a formula to convert degrees Celsius to degrees Fahrenheit. If we substitute a Celsius reading into the formula, a Fahrenheit reading comes out. For example, if we substitute 35 for C, we obtain a Fahrenheit reading of 95°:

$$F = \frac{9}{5}C + 32$$

$$= \frac{9}{5}(35) + 32$$

$$= 63 + 32$$

$$= 95$$

If we want to find a Celsius reading from a Fahrenheit reading, we need a formula into which we can substitute a Fahrenheit reading and have a Celsius reading come out. Such a formula is $C = \frac{5}{9}(F - 32)$, which takes the Fahrenheit reading of 95° and turns it back into a Celsius reading of 35°.

$$C = \frac{5}{9}(F - 32)$$

$$= \frac{5}{9}(95 - 32)$$

$$= \frac{5}{9}(63)$$

$$= 35$$

The functions defined by these two formulas do opposite things. The first turns $35°C$ into $95°$ Fahrenheit, and the second turns $95°$ Fahrenheit back into $35°C$. Such functions are called *inverse functions*.

Some functions have inverses that are functions and some do not. To guarantee that the inverse of a function will also be a function, we must know that the function is *one-to-one*.

1. Understand the Definition of a One-to-One Function

In this section, we will find inverses of functions that are one-to-one. *One-to-one functions* are functions whose inverses are also functions.

We now examine what it means for a function to be one-to-one. Consider the following two functions:

Function 1: To each student, there corresponds exactly one eye color

Function 2: To each student, there corresponds exactly one college identification number

Function 1 **is not a one-to-one function** because two different students can have the same eye color.

Function 2 **is a one-to-one function** because two different students will always have two different ID numbers.

Recall that each element x in the domain of a function has a single output y. For some functions, different numbers x in the domain can have the same output. See Figure 3-89(a). For other functions, called **one-to-one functions,** different numbers x have different outputs. See Figure 3-89(b).

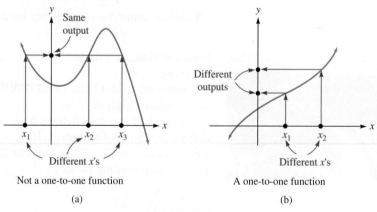

Not a one-to-one function

(a)

A one-to-one function

(b)

FIGURE 3-89

One-to-One Functions   A function f from a set **X** to a set **Y** is called a **one-to-one function** if and only if different numbers in the domain of f have different outputs in the range of f.

The previous definition implies that if x_1 and x_2 are two numbers in the domain of f and $x_1 \neq x_2$, then $f(x_1) \neq f(x_2)$.

2. Determine Whether a Function Is One-to-One

EXAMPLE 1   Determining Whether a Function Is One-to-One

Determine whether each function is one-to-one.
a. $f(x) = x^4 + x^2$ **b.** $f(x) = x^3$

SOLUTION   We will examine the functions and determine whether the definition of a one-to-one function applies. If different x-values always produce different y-values, the function is one-to-one.

a. The function $f(x) = x^4 + x^2$ is not one-to-one, because different numbers in the domain have the same output. For example, 2 and –2 have the same output: $f(2) = f(-2) = 20$.

b. The function $f(x) = x^3$ is one-to-one, because different numbers x produce different outputs $f(x)$. This is because different numbers have different cubes. ∎

Self Check 1   Determine whether $f(x) = \sqrt{x}$ is one-to-one.

Now Try Exercise 11.

A **Horizontal Line Test** can be used to determine whether the graph of a function represents a one-to-one function. If every horizontal line that intersects the graph of a function does so exactly once, the function passes the Horizontal Line Test and is one-to-one. See Figure 3-90(a). If any horizontal line intersects the graph of a function more than once, the function fails the Horizontal Line Test and is not one-to-one. See Figure 3-90(b).

Comment

A one-to-one function satisfies both the Horizontal and Vertical Line Tests.

A one-to-one function

(a)

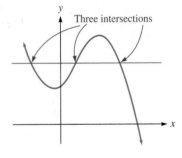

Not a one-to-one function

(b)

FIGURE 3-90

EXAMPLE 2   **Using the Horizontal Line Test**

Use the Horizontal Line Test to determine whether each graph represents a one-to-one function.

a.

b.

SOLUTION   We will use the Horizontal Line Test and draw many horizontal lines. If every horizontal line that intersects the graph does so exactly once, the function is one-to-one. If any horizontal line intersects the graph more than once, the function is not one-to-one.

a. Because the horizontal line drawn in Figure 3-91 intersects the graph in two places, we know that the function fails the Horizontal Line Test and is not a one-to-one function.

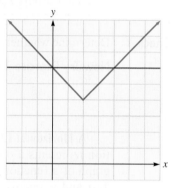

FIGURE 3-91

b. Several horizontal lines are drawn in Figure 3-92, and each one intersects the graph exactly once. We conclude that the graph passes the Horizontal Line Test and represents a one-to-one function.

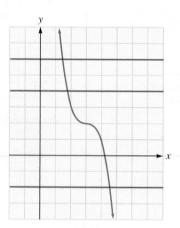

FIGURE 3-92

Self Check 2   Determine whether the graph in the margin represents a one-to-one function.

Now Try Exercise 19.

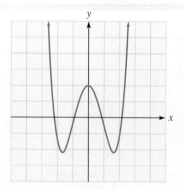

3. Verify Inverse Functions

Figure 3-93(a) illustrates a function f from set **X** to set **Y**. Since three arrows point to a single y, the function f is not one-to-one. If the arrows in Figure 3-93(a) were reversed, the diagram would not represent a function.

If the arrows of the one-to-one function f in Figure 3-93(b) were reversed, as in Figure 3-93(c), the diagram would represent a function. This function is called the **inverse of function f** and is denoted by the symbol f^{-1}.

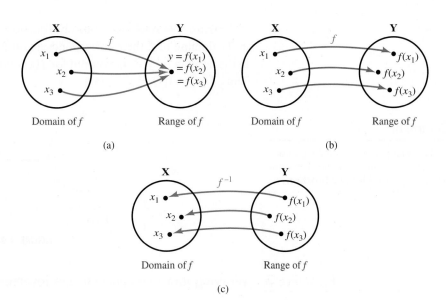

FIGURE 3-93

Caution

The -1 in the notation for inverse function is **not** an exponent. Remember that

$$f^{-1}(x) \neq \frac{1}{f(x)}$$

Consider the functions:

$$f(x) = 4x \quad \text{and} \quad g(x) = \frac{x}{4}$$

These functions are inverses of each other because f multiplies any input x by 4 and function g will take the result and divide it by 4. The final result will be the original input x.

We can show that the composition of these functions (in either order) is the identity function.

$$(f \circ g)(x) = f(g(x)) = f\left(\frac{x}{4}\right) = 4\left(\frac{x}{4}\right) = x \quad \text{and} \quad (g \circ f)(x) = g(f(x)) = g(4x) = \frac{4x}{4} = x$$

Since $g(x)$ is the inverse of $f(x)$, we can write $g(x)$ using inverse notation as $f^{-1}(x) = \frac{x}{4}$. Thus, $(f \circ f^{-1}) = x$ and $(f^{-1} \circ f)(x) = x$.

We can now define inverse functions.

Inverse Functions   If f and g are two one-to-one functions such that $(f \circ g)(x) = x$ for every x in the domain of g and $(g \circ f)(x) = x$ for every x in the domain of f, then f and g are **inverse functions**. Function g can be denoted as f^{-1} and is called the **inverse function of f.**

We can also list two important properties of one-to-one functions.

Properties of a One-to-One Function

Property 1: If f is a one-to-one function, there is a one-to-one function $f^{-1}(x)$ such that

$$(f^{-1} \circ f)(x) = x \quad \text{and} \quad (f \circ f^{-1})(x) = x.$$

Property 2: The domain of f is the range of f^{-1} and the range of f is the domain of f^{-1}.

Figure 3-94 shows a one-to-one function f and its inverse f^{-1}. To the number x in the domain of f, there corresponds an output $f(x)$ in the range of f. Since $f(x)$ is in the domain of f^{-1}, the output for $f(x)$ under the function f^{-1} is $f^{-1}(f(x)) = x$. Thus, $(f^{-1} \circ f)(x) = f^{-1}(f(x)) = x$.

Comment

To show that one function is the inverse of another, we must show that their compositions are the **identity function,** x.

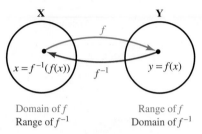

Domain of f
Range of f^{-1}

Range of f
Domain of f^{-1}

FIGURE 3-94

EXAMPLE 3   Verifying that Two Functions are Inverses

Verify that $f(x) = x^3$ and $g(x) = \sqrt[3]{x}$ are inverse functions.

SOLUTION   To show that f and g are inverse functions, we must show that $f \circ g$ and $g \circ f$ are x, the identity function.

$$(f \circ g)(x) = f(g(x)) = f(\sqrt[3]{x}) = (\sqrt[3]{x})^3 = x$$
$$(g \circ f)(x) = g(f(x)) = g(x^3) = \sqrt[3]{x^3} = x$$

Because g is the inverse of f, we can use inverse notation and write $g(x) = \sqrt[3]{x}$ as $f^{-1}(x) = \sqrt[3]{x}$. Because f is the inverse of g, we can use inverse notation and write $f(x) = x^3$ as $g^{-1}(x) = x^3$.

Self Check 3   If $x \geq 0$, are $f(x) = x^2$ and $g(x) = \sqrt{x}$ inverse functions?

Now Try Exercise 21.

4. Find the Inverse of a One-to-One Function

If f is the one-to-one function $y = f(x)$, then f^{-1} reverses the correspondence of f. That is, if $f(a) = b$, then $f^{-1}(b) = a$. To determine f^{-1}, we follow these steps.

Strategy for Finding f^{-1} from a Given Function $f(x)$

Step 1: Replace $f(x)$ with y.
Step 2: Interchange the variables x and y.
Step 3: Solve the resulting equation for y.
Step 4: Replace y with $f^{-1}(x)$.

Once $f^{-1}(x)$ is determined, it should be verified by showing that $(f \circ f^{-1})(x) = x$ and $(f^{-1} \circ f)(x) = x$.

EXAMPLE 4   Finding the Inverse of a One-to-One Function

Find the inverse of $f(x) = \dfrac{3}{2}x + 2$ and verify the result.

SOLUTION   We will use the strategy given above to find f^{-1}. We then will verify the result by showing that $(f \circ f^{-1})(x) = x$ and $(f^{-1} \circ f)(x) = x$.

Definitions and Concepts	Examples
Graphing polynomial functions:	Graph the function $f(x) = -x^3 + 9x$ and determine whether it is even, odd, or neither.
1. Find any symmetries of the graph.	
2. Find the x- and y-intercepts of the graph.	**Step 1: Find any symmetries of the graph.**
3. Determine where the graph is above and below the x-axis.	To test for symmetry about the y-axis, we check to see whether $f(x) = f(-x)$. To test for symmetry about the origin, we check to see whether $f(x) = -f(-x)$.
4. Plot a few points, if necessary, and draw the graph as a smooth continuous curve.	

If $f(-x) = f(x)$ for all x in the domain of f, the graph of the function is symmetric about the y-axis, and the function is called an **even function.**

If $f(-x) = -f(x)$ for all x in the domain of f, the function is symmetric about the origin, and the function is called an **odd function.**

Graph the function $f(x) = -x^3 + 9x$ and determine whether it is even, odd, or neither.

Step 1: Find any symmetries of the graph.
To test for symmetry about the y-axis, we check to see whether $f(x) = f(-x)$. To test for symmetry about the origin, we check to see whether $f(x) = -f(x)$.

$$f(x) = -x^3 + 9x$$
$$f(-x) = -(-x)^3 + 9(-x)$$
$$f(-x) = x^3 - 9x$$

Since $f(x) \neq f(-x)$, there is no symmetry about the y-axis. However, since $f(-x) = -f(x)$, there is symmetry about the origin.

Step 2: Find the x- and y-intercepts of the graph. To find the x-intercepts, we let $f(x) = 0$ and solve for x.

$$-x^3 + 9x = 0$$
$$-x(x^2 - 9) = 0$$
$$-x(x + 3)(x - 3) = 0$$

$$-x = 0 \quad \text{or} \quad x + 3 = 0 \quad \text{or} \quad x - 3 = 0$$
$$x = 0 \quad \quad x = -3 \quad \quad x = 3$$

The x-intercepts are $(0, 0)$, $(-3, 0)$, and $(3, 0)$.

If we let $x = 0$ and solve for $f(x)$, we see that the y-intercept is also $(0, 0)$.

Step 3: Determine where the graph is above or below the x-axis. To determine where the graph is above or below the x-axis, we plot the solutions of $-x^3 + 9x = 0$ on a number line and establish the four intervals shown in the figure. We then test a number from each interval to determine the sign of $f(x)$.

+	−	+	−
$(-\infty, -3)$	$(-3, 0)$	$(0, 3)$	$(3, \infty)$

$f(-4) = 28$ -3 $f(-1) = -8$ 0 $f(1) = 8$ 3 $f(4) = -28$

above the x-axis   below the x-axis   above the x-axis   below the x-axis

Definitions and Concepts	Examples
	Step 4: Plot a few points and draw the graph as a smooth continuous curve. We now plot the intercepts and one additional point. In the previous step we found that $f(1) = 8$. This will be the additional point we plot $(1, 8)$. Making use of our knowledge of symmetry about the origin and where the graph is above and below the x-axis, we now draw the graph as shown. 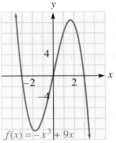 The function $f(x) = -x^3 + 9x$ is an odd function because the function is symmetric about the origin.
Some functions, called **piecewise-defined functions**, are defined by using different equations for different intervals in their domains.	$$f(x) = \begin{cases} x - 2 & \text{if } x < 3 \\ x^2 & \text{if } x \geq 3 \end{cases}$$ • $f(2) = 2 - 2 = 0$ • $f(4) = (4)^2 = 16$
The **greatest-integer function** is important in many business applications and in the field of computer science. This function is determined by the equation $f(x) = [x]$, where the value of $f(x)$ that corresponds to x is the greatest integer that is less than or equal to x.	Let $f(x) = [x - 3]$. Find $f(2.2)$. $$f(x) = [x - 3]$$ $$f(2.2) = [2.2 - 3] = [-0.8] = -1$$ -1 is the greatest integer less than or equal to -0.8.

EXERCISES

Graph each polynomial function and determine whether it is even, odd, or neither.

37. $y = x^3 - x$

38. $y = x^2 - 4x$

39. $y = x^3 - x^2$

40. $y = 1 - x^4$

Evaluate each piecewise-defined function.

41. $f(x) = \begin{cases} x - 2 & \text{if } x < 3 \\ x^2 & \text{if } x \geq 3 \end{cases}$

    a. $f(-2)$ **b.** $f(3)$

42. $f(x) = \begin{cases} 2 & \text{if } x < 0 \\ 2 - x & \text{if } 0 \le x < 2 \\ x + 1 & \text{if } x \ge 2 \end{cases}$

   a. $f\left(\dfrac{3}{2}\right)$ **b.** $f(2)$

Graph each piecewise-defined function and determine the open intervals on which it is increasing, decreasing, or constant.

43. $y = f(x) = \begin{cases} x + 5 & \text{if } x \le 0 \\ 5 - x & \text{if } x > 0 \end{cases}$

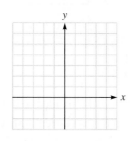

44. $y = f(x) = \begin{cases} x + 3 & \text{if } x \le 0 \\ 3 & \text{if } x > 0 \end{cases}$

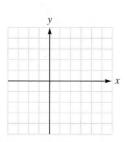

Evaluate each function at the indicated x-values.

45. $f(x) = [\![2x]\!]$ Find $f(1.7)$.

46. $f(x) = [\![x - 5]\!]$ Find $f(4.99)$.

Graph each function.

47. $f(x) = [\![x]\!] + 2$ 48. $f(x) = [\![x - 1]\!]$

49. **Renting a Jeep** A rental company charges $20 to rent a Jeep Wrangler for one day, plus $8 for every 100 miles (or portion of 100 miles) that it is driven. Find the cost if the Jeep is driven 295 miles in one day.

50. **Riding in a taxi** A taxicab company charges $4 for a trip up to 1 mile, and $2 for every extra mile (or portion of a mile). Find the cost to ride $11\frac{1}{2}$ miles.

SECTION **3.4**   Transformations of the Graphs of Functions

Definitions and Concepts	Examples
Vertical translations: If $k > 0$, the graph of $\begin{cases} y = f(x) + k \\ y = f(x) - k \end{cases}$ is identical to the graph of $y = f(x)$, except that it is translated k units $\begin{cases} \text{upward} \\ \text{downward} \end{cases}$.	The function $g(x) = \sqrt{x + 3} - 2$ is a translation of the graph of $f(x) = \sqrt{x}$. Graph both on one set of coordinate axes.

Definitions and Concepts	**Examples**

Horizontal translations:

If $k > 0$, the graph of $\begin{cases} y = f(x - k) \\ y = f(x + k) \end{cases}$

is identical to the graph of $y = f(x)$, except that it is

translated k units to the $\begin{cases} \text{right} \\ \text{left} \end{cases}$.

Vertical stretchings:

If f is a function and $k > 1$, then
- The graph of $y = kf(x)$ can be obtained by stretching the graph of $y = f(x)$ vertically by multiplying each value of $f(x)$ by k.

If f is a function and $0 < k < 1$, then
- The graph of $y = kf(x)$ can be obtained by shrinking the graph of $y = f(x)$ vertically by multiplying each value of $f(x)$ by k.

Horizontal stretchings:

If f is a function and $k > 1$, then
- The graph of $y = f(kx)$ can be obtained by shrinking the graph of $y = f(x)$ horizontally by multiplying each x-value of $f(x)$ by $\frac{1}{k}$.

If f is a function and $0 < k < 1$,
- The graph of $y = f(kx)$ can be obtained by stretching the graph of $y = f(x)$ horizontally by multiplying each x-value of $f(x)$ by $\frac{1}{k}$.

Reflections:

If f is a function, then
- The graph of $y = -f(x)$ is identical to the graph of $y = f(x)$ except that it is reflected about the x-axis.
- The graph of $y = f(-x)$ is identical to the graph of $y = f(x)$ except that it is reflected about the y-axis.

To graph functions involving a combination of transformations, we must apply each transformation to the basic function. We will apply these transformations in the following order:

1. Horizontal translation
2. Stretching or shrinking
3. Reflection
4. Vertical translation

By inspection, we see that the function $g(x) = \sqrt{x + 3} - 2$ involves two translations of $f(x) = \sqrt{x}$. The graph of $g(x) = \sqrt{x + 3} - 2$ is identical to the graph of $f(x) = \sqrt{x}$ except it is translated 3 units to the left and 2 units downward as shown in the figure.

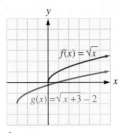

Graph: $g(x) = -\frac{1}{3}|x|$.

The graph of $g(x) = -\frac{1}{3}|x|$ is identical to the graph of $f(x) = |x|$ except that it is vertically shrunk by a factor of $\frac{1}{3}$ and reflected about the x-axis. This is because each value of $|x|$ is multiplied by $-\frac{1}{3}$. The graphs of both functions are shown in the figure.

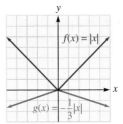

Graph $g(x) = 2(x - 4)^3 + 1$.

We will graph $g(x) = 2(x - 4)^3 + 1$ by applying three translations to the basic function $f(x) = x^3$: translate $f(x) = x^3$ horizontally 4 units to the right, stretch the graph by a factor of 2, and translate the graph vertically 1 unit upward. The graphs of both functions are shown in the figure.

EXERCISES

Each function is a translation of a basic function. Graph both on one set of coordinate axes.

51. $g(x) = x^2 + 5$

52. $g(x) = (x - 7)^3$

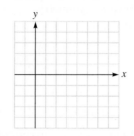

53. $g(x) = \sqrt{x + 2} + 3$

54. $g(x) = |x - 4| + 2$

Each function is a stretching of $f(x) = x^3$. Graph both on one set of coordinate axes.

55. $g(x) = \dfrac{1}{3}x^3$

56. $g(x) = (-5x)^3$

Graph each function using a combination of translations and stretchings.

57. $g(x) = -|x - 4| + 3$

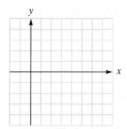

58. $g(x) = \dfrac{1}{4}|x - 4| + 1$

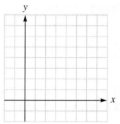

59. $g(x) = 3\sqrt{x + 3} + 2$

60. $g(x) = \dfrac{1}{3}(x + 3)^3 + 2$

61. $f(x) = \sqrt{-x} + 3$

62. $g(x) = 2\sqrt[3]{x} - 5$

SECTION **3.5** Rational Functions

Definitions and Concepts	Examples
A **rational function** is a function defined by an equation of the form $y = \frac{P(x)}{Q(x)}$, where $P(x)$ and $Q(x)$ are polynomials and $Q(x) \neq 0$.	$f(x) = \dfrac{3}{x + 2}$ $f(x) = \dfrac{3x + 4}{x^2 - 3x + 4}$

Definitions and Concepts	**Examples**
Locating vertical asymptotes:	Graph: $y = f(x) = \dfrac{4x}{x-2}$.

Locating vertical asymptotes:

To locate the vertical asymptotes of rational function $f(x) = \frac{P(x)}{Q(x)}$, we follow these steps:

Step 1: Factor $P(x)$ and $Q(x)$ and remove any common factors.

Step 2: Set the denominator equal to 0 and solve the equation.

If a is a solution of the equation found in Step 2, $x = a$ is a vertical asymptote.

Locating horizontal asymptotes:

To locate the horizontal asymptote of the rational function $f(x) = \frac{P(x)}{Q(x)}$, we consider three cases:

Case 1: If the degree of $P(x)$ *is less than* the degree of $Q(x)$, the line $y = 0$ is the horizontal asymptote.

Case 2: If the degree of $P(x)$ and $Q(x)$ are equal, the line $y = \frac{p}{q}$, where p and q are the leading coefficients of $P(x)$ and $Q(x)$, is the horizontal asymptote.

Case 3: If the degree of $P(x)$ is greater than the degree of $Q(x)$, there is no horizontal asymptote.

A third type of asymptote is called a **slant asymptote.** These asymptotes occur when the degree of the numerator of a rational function is 1 more than the degree of the denominator. As the name implies, it is a slanted line, neither vertical nor horizontal.

Locating slant asymptotes:

If the degree of $P(x)$ is 1 greater than the degree of $Q(x)$ for the rational function $f(x) = \frac{P(x)}{Q(x)}$, there is a slant asymptote. To find it, divide $P(x)$ by $Q(x)$ and ignore the remainder.

Graph: $y = f(x) = \dfrac{4x}{x-2}$.

We will use the steps outlined to graph the function.

Step 1: Symmetry

We find $f(-x)$.

$$f(-x) = \frac{4(-x)}{(-x)-2} = \frac{-4x}{-x-2} = \frac{4x}{x+2}$$

Because $f(-x) \neq f(x)$ and $f(-x) \neq -f(x)$, there is no symmetry about the y-axis or the origin.

Step 2: Vertical asymptotes

We first note that $f(x)$ is in simplest form. We then set the denominator equal to 0 and solve for x. Since the solution is 2, there will be a vertical asymptote at $x = 2$.

Step 3: y- and x-intercepts

We can find the y-intercept by finding $f(0)$.

$$f(0) = \frac{4(0)}{0-2} = \frac{0}{-2} = 0$$

The y-intercept is $(0, 0)$.

We can find the x-intercepts by setting the numerator equal to 0 and solving for x:

$$4x = 0$$
$$x = 0$$

The x-intercept is $(0, 0)$.

Step 4: Horizontal asymptotes

Since the degrees of the numerator and denominator of the polynomials are the same, the line

$$y = \frac{4}{1} = 4 \qquad \begin{array}{l}\text{The leading coefficient of the numerator is 4.}\\ \text{The leading coefficient of the denominator is 1.}\end{array}$$

is a horizontal asymptote.

Step 5: Slant asymptotes

Since the degree of the numerator is not 1 greater than the degree of the denominator, there are no slant asymptotes.

Definitions and Concepts	Examples
Steps to graph a rational function:	**Step 6: Graph**
We will use the following steps to graph the rational function $f(x) = \frac{P(x)}{Q(x)}$, where $\frac{P(x)}{Q(x)}$ is in simplest form (no common factors).	First, we plot the intercept $(0, 0)$ and draw the asymptotes. We then find one additional point on our graph to see what happens when x is greater than 2. To do so, we choose 3, a value of x that is greater than 2, and evaluate $f(3)$.
1. Check symmetries.	$$f(3) = \frac{4(3)}{3 - 2} = \frac{12}{1} = 12$$
2. Look for vertical asymptotes.	Since $f(3) = 12$, the point $(3, 12)$ lies on our graph. We sketch the graph as shown in the figure.
3. Look for the y- and x-intercepts.	
4. Look for horizontal asymptotes.	
5. Look for slant asymptotes.	
6. Graph the function.	

EXERCISES

Find the domain of each rational function.

63. $f(x) = \dfrac{3x^2 + x - 2}{x^2 - 25}$ **64.** $f(x) = \dfrac{2x^2 + 1}{x^2 + 7}$

Find the vertical asymptotes, if any, of each rational function.

65. $f(x) = \dfrac{x + 5}{x^2 - 1}$ **66.** $f(x) = \dfrac{x - 7}{x^2 - 49}$

67. $f(x) = \dfrac{x}{x^2 + x - 6}$ **68.** $f(x) = \dfrac{5x + 2}{2x^2 - 6x - 8}$

Find the horizontal asymptotes, if any, of each rational function.

69. $f(x) = \dfrac{2x^2 + x - 2}{4x^2 - 4}$ **70.** $f(x) = \dfrac{5x^2 + 4}{4 - x^2}$

71. $f(x) = \dfrac{x + 1}{x^3 - 4x}$ **72.** $f(x) = \dfrac{x^3}{2x^2 - x + 11}$

Find the slant asymptote, if any, for each rational function.

73. $f(x) = \dfrac{2x^2 - 5x + 1}{x - 4}$ **74.** $f(x) = \dfrac{5x^3 + 1}{x + 5}$

Graph each rational function.

75. $f(x) = \dfrac{2x}{x - 4}$ **76.** $f(x) = \dfrac{-4x}{x + 4}$

77. $f(x) = \dfrac{x}{(x - 1)^2}$ **78.** $f(x) = \dfrac{(x - 1)^2}{x}$

    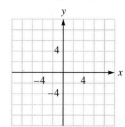

79. $f(x) = \dfrac{x^2 - x - 2}{x^2 + x - 2}$ **80.** $f(x) = \dfrac{x^3 + x}{x^2 - 4}$

    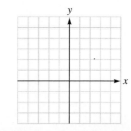

SECTION **3.6**   Operations on Functions

Definitions and Concepts	Examples
Adding, subtracting, multiplying, and dividing functions: If the ranges of functions f and g are subsets of the real numbers, then	Let $f(x) = 3x + 5$ and $g(x) = 4x - 7$. Find each function and its domain: **a.** $f + g$ **b.** $f - g$ **c.** $f \cdot g$ **d.** f/g

1. The **sum of f and g**, denoted as $f + g$, is defined by $(f + g)(x) = f(x) + g(x)$.

   a. $(f + g)(x) = f(x) + g(x)$

$$= (3x + 5) + (4x - 7)$$

$$= 7x - 2$$

   Since the domain of both f and g is the set of real numbers, the domain of $f + g$ is the interval $(-\infty, \infty)$.

2. The **difference of f and g**, denoted as $f - g$, is defined by $(f - g)(x) = f(x) - g(x)$.

   b. $(f - g)(x) = f(x) - g(x)$

$$= (3x + 5) - (4x - 7)$$

$$= 3x + 5 - 4x + 7$$

$$= -x + 12$$

   Since the domain of both f and g is the set of real numbers, the domain of $f - g$ is the interval $(-\infty, \infty)$.

3. The **product of f and g**, denoted as $f \cdot g$, is defined by $(f \cdot g)(x) = f(x) \cdot g(x)$.

   c. $(f \cdot g)(x) = f(x) \cdot g(x)$

$$= (3x + 5)(4x - 7)$$

$$= 12x^2 - x - 35$$

   Since the domain of both f and g is the set of real numbers, the domain of $f \cdot g$ is the interval $(-\infty, \infty)$.

4. The **quotient of f and g**, denoted as f/g, is defined by $(f/g)(x) = \frac{f(x)}{g(x)}, g(x) \neq 0$.

The domain of each function, unless otherwise restricted, is the set of real numbers x that are in the domains of both f and g. In the case of the quotient f/g, there is the restriction that $g(x) \neq 0$.

   d. $(f/g)(x) = \dfrac{f(x)}{g(x)}$

$$= \dfrac{3x + 5}{4x - 7} \quad (4x - 7 \neq 0)$$

   Since $\frac{7}{4}$ will make $4x - 7$ equal to 0, the domain of f/g is the set of all real numbers except $\frac{7}{4}$. This is $\left(-\infty, \frac{7}{4}\right) \cup \left(\frac{7}{4}, \infty\right)$.

The **composite function** $f \circ g$ is defined by $(f \circ g)(x) = f(g(x))$.

If $f(x) = 2x + 7$ and $g(x) = x^2 + 1$, find $(f \circ g)(x)$ and its domain.

Definitions and Concepts	Examples
The domain of $f \circ g$ consists of all those numbers in the domain of g for which $g(x)$ is in the domain of f.	Because $(f \circ g)(x)$ means $f(g(x))$, we will replace x in $f(x) = 2x + 7$ with $g(x)$. $$(f \circ g)(x) = f(g(x))$$ $$= f(x^2 + 1)$$ $$= 2(x^2 + 1) + 7$$ $$= 2x^2 + 9$$ The domain of $(f \circ g)(x)$ is the interval $(-\infty, \infty)$ because the domain of both f and g consists of all real numbers.

EXERCISES

Let $f(x) = x^2 - 1$ and $g(x) = 2x + 1$. Find each function and its domain.

81. $f + g$

82. $f \cdot g$

83. $f - g$

84. f/g

Let $f(x) = 2x^2 - 1$ and $g(x) = 2x - 1$. Find each value, if possible.

85. $(f + g)(-3)$

86. $(f - g)(-5)$

87. $(f \cdot g)(2)$

88. $(f/g)\left(\dfrac{1}{2}\right)$

Let $f(x) = x^2 - 1$ and $g(x) = 2x + 1$. Find each function and its domain.

89. $f \circ g$

90. $g \circ f$

Let $f(x) = x^2 - 5$ and $g(x) = 3x + 1$. Find each value.

91. $(f \circ g)(-2)$

92. $(g \circ f)(-2)$

Find two functions f and g such that the composition $f \circ g = h$ expresses the given correspondence. Several answers are possible.

93. $h(x) = (x - 5)^2$

94. $h(x) = (x + 6)^3$

SECTION **3.7**   Inverse Functions

Definitions and Concepts	Examples
A function f from a set **X** to a set **Y** is called a **one-to-one function** if and only if different numbers in the domain of f have different outputs in the range of f. A **Horizontal Line Test** can be used to determine whether the graph of a function represents a one-to-one function. If every horizontal line that intersects the graph of a function does so exactly once, the function passes the Horizontal Line Test and is one-to-one.	Determine whether the function $f(x) = x^4 - 2x^2$ is one-to-one. The function $f(x) = x^4 - 2x^2$ is not one-to-one, because different numbers in the domain have the same output. For example, 2 and –2 have the same output: $f(2) = f(-2) = 8$.

Definitions and Concepts	Examples
Inverse functions: If f and g are two one-to-one functions such that $(f \circ g)(x) = x$ for every x in the domain of g and $(g \circ f)(x) = x$ for every x in the domain of f, then f and g are **inverse functions.** Function g is denoted as f^{-1} and is called the **inverse function of f.**	Verify that $f(x) = x^5$ and $g(x) = \sqrt[5]{x}$ are inverse functions. To show that f and g are inverse functions, we must show that $f \circ g$ and $g \circ f$ are x, the identity function. $$(f \circ g)(x) = f(g(x)) = f\left(\sqrt[5]{x}\right) = \left(\sqrt[5]{x}\right)^5 = x$$ $$(g \circ f)(x) = g(f(x)) = g(x^5) = \sqrt[5]{x^5} = x$$
Properties of a one-to-one function: **Property 1:** If f is a one-to-one function, there is a one-to-one function $f^{-1}(x)$ such that $(f^{-1} \circ f)(x) = x$ and $(f \circ f^{-1})(x) = x$. **Property 2:** The domain of f is the range of f^{-1}, and the range of f is the domain of f^{-1}.	Because g is the inverse of f, we can use inverse notation and write $f(x) = x^5$ and $f^{-1}(x) = \sqrt[5]{x}$. Because f is the inverse of g, we can use inverse notation and write $g(x) = \sqrt[5]{x}$ and $g^{-1}(x) = x^5$.
Strategy for finding f^{-1}: **Step 1:** Replace $f(x)$ with y. **Step 2:** Interchange the variables x and y. **Step 3:** Solve the resulting equation for y. **Step 4:** Replace y with $f^{-1}(x)$. The graph of a function and its inverse are reflections of each other about the line $y = x$.	Find the inverse of $f(x) = x^3 + 5$. We will find the inverse of the function using the strategy given in the section. **Step 1:** Replace $f(x)$ with y. $$f(x) = x^3 + 5$$ $$y = x^3 + 5$$ **Step 2:** Interchange the variables x and y. $$x = y^3 + 5$$ **Step 3:** Solve the resulting equation for y. $$x - 5 = y^3$$ $$y = \sqrt[3]{x - 5}$$ **Step 4:** Replace y with $f^{-1}(x)$. $$f^{-1}(x) = \sqrt[3]{x - 5}$$

EXERCISES

Determine whether each function is one-to-one.

95. $f(x) = x^2 + 7$

96. $f(x) = x^3$

Use the Horizontal Line Test to determine whether each graph represents a one-to-one function.

97.

98.

Verify that the functions are inverses by showing that $f \circ g$ and $g \circ f$ are the identity function.

99. $f(x) = 8x - 3$

100. $f(x) = \dfrac{1}{2 - x}$

Each equation defines a one-to-one function. Find f^{-1} and verify that $f \circ f^{-1}$ and $f^{-1} \circ f$ are the identity function.

101. $y = 7x - 1$

102. $y = \dfrac{1}{2 - x}$

103. $y = \dfrac{x}{1 - x}$

104. $y = \dfrac{3}{x^3}$

105. Find the inverse of the one-to-one function $f(x) = 2x - 5$ and graph both the function and its inverse on the same set of coordinate axes.

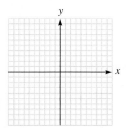

106. Find the range of $y = \frac{2x + 3}{5x - 10}$ by finding the domain of f^{-1}.

CHAPTER TEST

Find the domain of each function. Write each answer using interval notation.

1. $f(x) = \dfrac{3}{x - 5}$

2. $f(x) = \sqrt{x + 3}$

Find $f(-1)$ and $f(2)$.

3. $f(x) = \dfrac{x}{x - 1}$

4. $f(x) = \sqrt{x + 7}$

Find the vertex of each parabola.

5. $y = 3(x - 7)^2 - 3$

6. $y = x^2 - 2x - 3$

7. $f(x) = 3x^2 - 24x + 38$

8. $f(x) = 5 - 4x - x^2$

Graph each function.

9. $f(x) = x^4 - x^2$

10. $f(x) = x^5 - x^3$

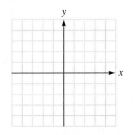

Assume that an object tossed vertically upward reaches a height of h feet after t seconds, where $h = 100t - 16t^2$.

11. In how many seconds does the object reach its maximum height?

12. What is that maximum height?

13. Suspension bridges The cable of a suspension bridge is in the shape of the parabola $x^2 - 2{,}500y + 25{,}000 = 0$ in the coordinate system shown in the illustration. (Distances are in feet.) How far above the roadway is the cable's lowest point?

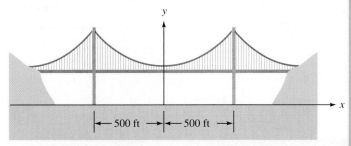

14. Refer to Question 13. How far above the roadway does the cable attach to the vertical pillars?

Graph each function.

15. $f(x) = (x - 3)^2 + 1$

16. $f(x) = \sqrt{x - 1} + 5$

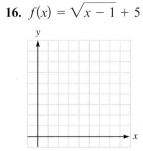

Find all asymptotes of the graph of each rational function. Do not graph the function.

17. $y = \dfrac{x - 1}{x^2 - 9}$

18. $y = \dfrac{x^2 - 5x - 14}{x - 3}$

Graph each rational function. Check for asymptotes, intercepts, and symmetry.

19. $y = \dfrac{x^2}{x^2 - 9}$

20. $y = \dfrac{x}{x^2 + 1}$

Graph each rational function. The numerator and denominator share a common factor.

21. $y = \dfrac{2x^2 - 3x - 2}{x - 2}$

22. $y = \dfrac{x}{x^2 - x}$

Let $f(x) = 3x$ and $g(x) = x^2 + 2$. Find each function.

23. $f + g$

24. $g \circ f$

25. f/g

26. $f \circ g$

Assume that $f(x)$ is one-to-one. Find f^{-1}.

27. $f(x) = \dfrac{x + 1}{x - 1}$

28. $f(x) = x^3 - 3$

Find the range of f by finding the domain of f^{-1}.

29. $y = \dfrac{3}{x} - 2$

30. $y = \dfrac{3x - 1}{x - 3}$

CUMULATIVE REVIEW EXERCISES

Use the x- and y-intercepts to graph each equation.

1. $5x - 3y = 15$

2. $3x + 2y = 12$

Find the length, the midpoint, and the slope of the line segment PQ.

3. $P\left(-2, \dfrac{7}{2}\right)$; $Q\left(3, -\dfrac{1}{2}\right)$

4. $P(3, 7)$; $Q(-7, 3)$

Write the equation of the line with the given properties. Give the answer in slope-intercept form.

5. The line passes through $(-3, 5)$ and $(3, -7)$.

6. The line passes through $\left(\dfrac{3}{2}, \dfrac{5}{2}\right)$ and has a slope of $\dfrac{7}{2}$.

7. The line is parallel to $3x - 5y = 7$ and passes through $(-5, 3)$.

8. The line is perpendicular to $x - 4y = 12$ and passes through the origin.

Graph each equation. Make use of intercepts and symmetries.

9. $x^2 = y - 2$

10. $y^2 = x - 2$

11. $x^2 + y^2 = 100$

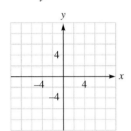

12. $x^2 - 2x + y^2 = 8$

Solve each proportion.

13. $\dfrac{x - 2}{x} = \dfrac{x - 6}{5}$

14. $\dfrac{x + 2}{x - 6} = \dfrac{3x + 1}{2x - 11}$

15. Dental billing The billing schedule for dental X-rays specifies a fixed amount for the office visit plus a fixed amount for each X-ray exposure. If 2 X-rays cost $37 and 4 cost $54, find the cost of 5 exposures.

16. Automobile collisions The energy dissipated in an automobile collision varies directly with the square of the speed. By what factor does the energy increase in a 50-mph collision compared with a 20-mph collision?

Determine whether each equation defines a function.

17. $y = 3x - 1$

18. $y = x^2 + 3$

19. $y = \dfrac{1}{x - 2}$

20. $y^2 = 4x$

Find the domain of each function.

21. $f(x) = x^2 + 5$

22. $f(x) = \dfrac{7}{x + 2}$

23. $y = -\sqrt{x - 2}$

24. $f(x) = \sqrt{x + 4}$

Find the vertex of each parabola.

25. $y = x^2 + 5x - 6$

26. $f(x) = -x^2 + 5x + 6$

Graph each function.

27. $f(x) = x^2 - 4$

28. $f(x) = -x^2 + 4$

29. $f(x) = x^3 + x$

30. $f(x) = -x^4 + 2x^2 + 1$

Graph each function. Show all asymptotes.

31. $f(x) = \dfrac{x}{x - 3}$

32. $f(x) = \dfrac{x^2 - 1}{x^2 - 9}$

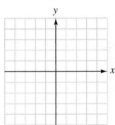

Let $f(x) = 3x - 4$ and $g(x) = x^2 + 1$. Find each function and its domain.

33. $(f + g)(x)$

34. $(f - g)(x)$

35. $(f \cdot g)(x)$

36. $(f/g)(x)$

Let $f(x) = 3x - 4$ and $g(x) = x^2 + 1$. Find each value.

37. $(f \circ g)(2)$

38. $(g \circ f)(2)$

39. $(f \circ g)(x)$

40. $(g \circ f)(x)$

Find the inverse of the function defined by each equation.

41. $y = 3x + 2$

42. $y = \dfrac{1}{x - 3}$

43. $y = x^2 + 5 \ (x \geq 0)$　　　**44.** $3x - y = 1$

Write each sentence as an equation.

45. y varies directly with the product of w and z.

46. y varies directly with x and inversely with the square of t.

Exponential and Logarithmic Functions

4

CAREERS AND MATHEMATICS: Epidemiologists

Kiselev Andrey Valerevich/Shutterstock.com

Epidemiologists investigate and describe the determinants and distribution of disease, disability, and other health outcomes. They also develop means for prevention and control. *Applied epidemiologists* typically work for state health agencies and are responsible for responding to disease outbreaks and determining the cause and method of containment. *Research epidemiologists* work in laboratories studying ways to prevent future outbreaks. This career can be quite rewarding, both mentally and financially. Epidemiologists spend a lot of time saving lives and finding solutions for better health.

Education and Mathematics Required
- Applied epidemiologists are generally required to have a master's degree from a school of public health. Research epidemiologists may need a Ph.D. or medical degree, depending on their area of work.
- College Algebra, Trigonometry, Calculus, Applied Data Analysis, Survey and Research Methods, Mathematical Statistics, and Biostatistics are required math courses.

How Epidemiologists Use Math and Who Employs Them
- Epidemiologists use mathematical models when they are tracking the progress of an infectious disease. The SIR model consists of three variables: S (for susceptible), I (for infectious), and R (for recovered). It is used for infectious diseases such as measles, mumps, and rubella.
- Government agencies employ 57%; hospitals employ 12%; colleges and universities employ 11%, and 9% are employed in areas of scientific research and developmental services like the American Cancer Society.

Career Outlook and Earnings
- Employment growth is projected to be 15% over the 2008–2018 decade, which is faster than average. This is due to an increased threat of bioterrorism and rare but infectious diseases, such as West Nile Virus or Avian flu.
- The median annual income is $61,700, with the top 10% of salaries at $92,610.

For more information see: www.bls.gov/oco

In this chapter, we will discuss exponential functions, which are often used in banking, ecology, and science. We will also discuss logarithmic functions, which are applied in chemistry, geology, and environmental science.

4.1 Exponential Functions and Their Graphs

In this section, we will learn to

1. Approximate and simplify exponential expressions.
2. Graph exponential functions.
3. Solve compound interest problems.
4. Define e and graph base-e exponential functions.
5. Use transformations to graph exponential functions.

Extreme water slides, called "plunge" or "plummet" slides, are fearsome water slides because of their heights. With near vertical drops, the slides are designed to allow riders to reach the greatest possible speeds. Summit Plummet at Blizzard Beach, a part of Walt Disney World Resort in Florida, stands 120 ft tall. On this slide, riders can achieve speeds up to 55 mph.

The shapes of extreme water slides can be modeled using *exponential functions*, the topic of this section.

Exponential functions are also important in business. Consider the graph shown in Figure 4-1. It shows the balance in a bank account in which $5,000 was invested in 1990 at 8%, compounded monthly. The graph shows that in the year 2015, the value of the account will be approximately $38,000, and in the year 2030, the value will be approximately $121,000.

The curve in Figure 4-1 is the graph of an exponential function. From the graph, we can see that the longer the money is kept on deposit, the more rapidly it will grow.

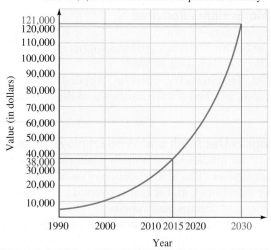

Value of $5,000 invested at 8% compounded monthly

FIGURE 4-1

Before we can discuss exponential functions, we must define irrational exponents.

1. Approximate and Simplify Exponential Expressions

We have discussed expressions of the form b^x, where x is a rational number.

- 5^2 means "the square of 5."
- $4^{1/3}$ means "the cube root of 4."
- $6^{-2/5} = \frac{1}{6^{2/5}}$ means "the reciprocal of the fifth root of 6^2."

To understand exponential functions and their graphs requires that we give meaning to b^x when x is an irrational number. Consider the expression

$3^{\sqrt{2}}$ where $\sqrt{2}$ is the irrational number 1.414213562 ...

We can use closer and closer approximations as shown below. Since $\sqrt{2}$ is an irrational number, we will use a calculator to find the approximations.

$$3^{\sqrt{2}} \approx 3^{1.4} \approx 4.655536722$$

$$3^{\sqrt{2}} \approx 3^{1.41} \approx 4.706965002$$

$$3^{\sqrt{2}} \approx 3^{1.414} \approx 4.727695035$$

$$3^{\sqrt{2}} \approx 3^{1.4142} \approx 4.72873393$$

Since the exponents of the expressions in the list are getting closer to $\sqrt{2}$, the values of the expressions are getting closer to the value of $3^{\sqrt{2}}$.

On a scientific calculator, there is an exponential key, usually y^x. On a graphing calculator, we can use the $\boxed{\;\wedge\;}$ key.

EXAMPLE 1 **Approximating Exponential Expressions**

Approximate each expression correct to 4 decimals.

a. $4^{2/3}$ **b.** $5^{-\sqrt{3}}$ **c.** $\left(\dfrac{4}{7}\right)^{\pi}$

SOLUTION   We will use a calculator.

a. $4^{\wedge}(2/3) \approx 2.5198$ Enter 2/3 in parentheses.

b. $5^{\wedge}\left(-\sqrt{3}\right) \approx 0.0616$ Enter $-\sqrt{3}$ in parentheses.

c. $(4/7)^{\wedge}\pi \approx 0.1724$ Enter the base, 4/7, in parentheses.

Figure 4-2 shows the graphing calculator screen that was used to find the values.

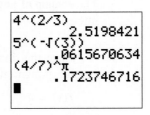

FIGURE 4-2

Self Check 1   Approximate each expression correct to 4 decimals.

a. $5^{3/5}$ **b.** $-3^{\sqrt{6}}$ **c.** $7^{-2.356}$

Now Try Exercise 15.

If b is a positive number and x is a real number, the expression b^x always represents a positive number. It is also true that the familiar properties of exponents hold for irrational exponents.

EXAMPLE 2   **Simplifying Expressions with Irrational Exponents**

Simplify each expression:

a. $\left(3^{\sqrt{2}}\right)^{\sqrt{2}}$

b. $a^{\sqrt{8}} \cdot a^{\sqrt{2}}$

SOLUTION   We will use properties of exponents to simplify each expression.

a. $\left(3^{\sqrt{2}}\right)^{\sqrt{2}} = 3^{\sqrt{2}\sqrt{2}}$ Keep the base and multiply the exponents.

$\qquad\qquad = 3^2$ $\sqrt{2}\sqrt{2} = \sqrt{4} = 2$

$\qquad\qquad = 9$

b. $a^{\sqrt{8}} \cdot a^{\sqrt{2}} = a^{\sqrt{8}+\sqrt{2}}$ Keep the base and add the exponents.

$\qquad\qquad = a^{2\sqrt{2}+\sqrt{2}}$ $\sqrt{8} = \sqrt{4}\sqrt{2} = 2\sqrt{2}$

$\qquad\qquad = a^{3\sqrt{2}}$ $2\sqrt{2} + \sqrt{2} = 3\sqrt{2}$

■

Self Check 2   Simplify: **a.** $\left(2^{\sqrt{3}}\right)^{\sqrt{12}}$ **b.** $x^{\sqrt{20}} \cdot x^{\sqrt{5}}$

Now Try Exercise 19.

2. Graph Exponential Functions

If $b > 0$ and $b \neq 1$, the function $y = b^x$ defines a function, because for each input x, there is exactly one output y. Since x can be any real number, the domain of the function is the set of real numbers. Since the base b of the expression b^x is positive, y is always positive, and the range is the set of positive numbers. Since b^x is an exponential expression, the function is called an **exponential function.**

We make the restriction that $b > 0$ to exclude any imaginary numbers that might result from taking even roots of negative numbers. The restriction that $b \neq 1$ excludes the constant function $f(x) = 1^x$, in which $f(x) = 1$ for every real number x.

Exponential Functions   An **exponential function with base b** is defined by the equation

$$f(x) = b^x \quad \text{or} \quad y = b^x \qquad (b > 0, b \neq 1, \text{ and } x \text{ is a real number})$$

The **domain of any exponential function** is the interval $(-\infty, \infty)$. The **range** is the interval $(0, \infty)$.

Since the domain and range of $f(x) = b^x$ are sets of real numbers, we can graph exponential functions. For example, to graph

$$f(x) = 2^x$$

we find several points $(x, f(x))$ whose coordinates satisfy the equation, plot the points, and join them with a smooth curve, as in Figure 4-3(a). To graph the function

$$f(x) = \left(\frac{1}{2}\right)^x$$

we find several points $(x, f(x))$ whose coordinates satisfy the equation, plot the points, and join them with a smooth curve, as shown in Figure 4-3(b) on the next page.

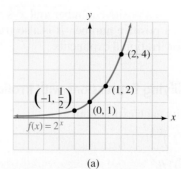

$f(x) = 2^x$		
x	$f(x)$	$(x, f(x))$
-1	$\dfrac{1}{2}$	$\left(-1, \dfrac{1}{2}\right)$
0	1	$(0, 1)$
1	2	$(1, 2)$
2	4	$(2, 4)$

(a)

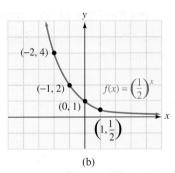

FIGURE 4-3

By looking at the graphs in Figure 4-3, we can see that the domain of each function is the interval $(-\infty, \infty)$ and that the range is the interval $(0, \infty)$.

EXAMPLE 3   **Graphing an Exponential Function**

Graph: $f(x) = 4^x$.

SOLUTION   We will find several points (x, y) that satisfy the equation, plot the points, and join them with a smooth curve, as in Figure 4-4.

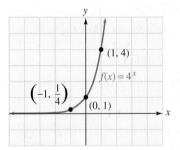

FIGURE 4-4

Self Check 3   Graph: $f(x) = \left(\dfrac{1}{4}\right)^x$.

Now Try Exercise 29.

The graph of $f(x) = 4^x$ in Example 3 has the following properties:

1. It passes through the point $(0, 1)$.
2. It passes through the point $(1, 4)$.
3. It approaches the x-axis. The x-axis is a horizontal asymptote.
4. The domain is the interval $(-\infty, \infty)$, and the range is the interval $(0, \infty)$.

This example illustrates the following properties of exponential functions.

Properties of Exponential Functions

- The **domain of the exponential function** $f(x) = b^x$ is $(-\infty, \infty)$, the set of real numbers.

- The **range** is $(0, \infty)$, the set of positive real numbers.

- The graph has a y-intercept at $(0, 1)$.

- The x-axis is a horizontal asymptote of the graph.

- The graph of $f(x) = b^x$ passes through the point $(1, b)$.

EXAMPLE 4   **Determining the Base of an Exponential Function**

The graph of an exponential function of the form $f(x) = b^x$ is shown in Figure 4-5. Find the value of b.

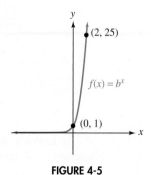

FIGURE 4-5

SOLUTION   We note that the graph passes through the point $(0, 1)$, a property of exponential functions of this form. Since the graph also passes through the point $(2, 25)$, we can find the base b by substituting 2 for x and 25 for $f(2)$ in the equation $f(x) = b^x$ and solving for b.

$$f(x) = b^x$$

$$f(2) = b^2$$

$$25 = b^2$$

$$5 = b \qquad \text{b must be positive.}$$

The base b is 5. Note that the points $(0, 1)$ and $(2, 25)$ satisfy the equation $f(x) = 5^x$.

Self Check 4   Can a graph passing through $(0, 2)$ and $\left(1, \dfrac{3}{2}\right)$ be the graph of $f(x) = b^x$?

Now Try Exercise 45.

In Figure 4-3(a) (where $b = 2$ and $2 > 1$), the values of y increase as the values of x increase. Since the graph rises as we move to the right, the function is an increasing function. Such a function is said to model *exponential growth*.

In Figure 4-3(b) where $\left(b = \frac{1}{2} \text{ and } 0 < \frac{1}{2} < 1\right)$, the values of y decrease as the values of x increase. Since the graph drops as we move to the right, the function is a decreasing function. Such a function is said to model *exponential decay*. Two additional properties are stated here.

Additional Properties of Exponential Functions   If $b > 1$, then $f(x) = b^x$ is an **increasing function.** This function models **exponential growth.**

Increasing function

If $0 < b < 1$, then $f(x) = b^x$ is a **decreasing function.** This function models **exponential decay.**

$f(x) = b^x$
$0 < b < 1$

$(0, 1)$ $(1, b)$

Decreasing function

Comment   Recall that $b^{-x} = \frac{1}{b^x} = \left(\frac{1}{b}\right)^x$. If $b > 1$, any function of the form $f(x) = b^{-x}$ models exponential decay, because $0 < \frac{1}{b} < 1$.

An exponential function $f(x) = b^x$ is either increasing (for $b > 1$) or decreasing (for $0 < b < 1$). Because different real numbers x always determine different values of b^x, an exponential function is one-to-one.

One-to-One Property of Exponential Functions   An exponential function defined by $f(x) = b^x$ or $y = b^x$, where $b > 0$ and $b \neq 1$, is one-to-one. This implies that

1. If $b^r = b^s$, then $r = s$.
2. If $r \neq s$, then $b^r \neq b^s$.

ACCENT ON TECHNOLOGY   Graphing Exponential Functions

When using a graphing calculator to draw the graphs of exponential functions, use care entering the function. Proper use of parentheses is critical to obtaining the correct graph. Since we know the shape of an exponential function, it is usually easy to find a good window for the graph. For any function in the form $f(x) = b^x$, where $b > 1$, the graph will be steeper as the base increases. The opposite is true if the base is between 0 and 1. Several graphs are shown below along with a window that works well with these basic functions.

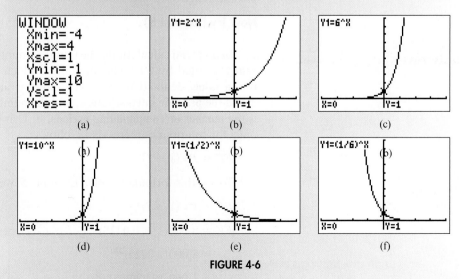

(a) (b) (c)

(d) (e) (f)

FIGURE 4-6

3. Solve Compound Interest Problems

Banks pay **interest** for using their customers' money. Interest is calculated as a percent of the amount on deposit in an account and is paid annually (once a year), quarterly (four times per year), monthly, or daily. Interest left on deposit in a bank account will also earn interest. Such accounts are said to earn **compound interest.**

Compound Interest Formula   If P dollars are deposited in an account earning interest at an annual rate r, compounded n times each year, the amount A in the account after t years is given by

$$A = P\left(1 + \frac{r}{n}\right)^{nt}$$

EXAMPLE 5   **Solving a Compound Interest Problem**

The parents of a newborn child invest $8,000 in a plan that earns 9% interest, compounded quarterly. If the money is left untouched, how much will the child have in the account in 55 years?

SOLUTION   We will substitute 8,000 for P, 0.09 for r, and 55 for t in the formula for compound interest. Because quarterly compounding means four times per year, we will substitute 4 for n.

$$A = P\left(1 + \frac{r}{n}\right)^{nt}$$

$$A = 8,000\left(1 + \frac{0.09}{4}\right)^{4 \cdot 55}$$

$$= 8,000(1.0225)^{220}$$

$$\approx 1,069,103.266 \qquad \text{Use a calculator.}$$

In 55 years, the account will be worth $1,069,103.27.

Self Check 5   Would $20,000 invested at 7% interest, compounded monthly, have provided more income at age 55?

Now Try Exercise 81.

In financial calculations, the initial amount deposited is often called the **present value,** denoted by PV. The amount to which the account will grow is called the **future value,** denoted by FV. The interest rate for each compounding period is called the **periodic interest rate,** i, and the number of times interest is compounded is the **number of compounding periods,** n. Using these definitions, an alternate formula for compound interest is as follows.

$$FV = PV(1 + i)^n$$

To use this formula to solve Example 5, we proceed as follows:

$$FV = PV(1 + i)^n$$

$$FV = 8,000(1 + 0.0225)^{220} \qquad i = \frac{0.09}{4} = 0.0225 \text{ and } n = 4(55) = 220.$$

$$= 8,000(1.0225)^{220}$$

$$\approx 1,069,103.266 \qquad \text{Use a calculator.}$$

4. Define e and Graph Base-e Exponential Functions

In mathematical models of natural events, the number

$$e = 2.71828182845904\ldots$$

often appears as the base of an exponential function. We can introduce this number by considering the compound interest formula

$$A = P\left(1 + \frac{r}{n}\right)^{nt}$$ A is the amount, P is the initial deposit, r is the annual rate, n is the number of compoundings per year, and t is the time in years.

and allowing n to become very large. To see what happens, we let $n = rx$, where x is another variable.

$$A = P\left(1 + \frac{r}{n}\right)^{nt}$$

$$A = P\left(1 + \frac{r}{rx}\right)^{rxt}$$ Substitute rx for n.

$$A = P\left(1 + \frac{1}{x}\right)^{rxt}$$ Simplify $\frac{r}{rx}$.

$$A = P\left[\left(1 + \frac{1}{x}\right)^{x}\right]^{rt}$$ Remember that $(a^m)^n = a^{mn}$.

Since all variables in this formula are positive, r is a constant rate, and $n = rx$, it follows that as n becomes large, so does x. What happens to the value of A as n becomes large will depend on the value of $\left(1 + \frac{1}{x}\right)^{x}$ as x becomes large. Some results calculated for increasing values of x appear in the table shown.

x	$\left(1 + \dfrac{1}{x}\right)^{x}$
1	2
10	2.5937425
100	2.7048138
1,000	2.7169239
1,000,000	2.7182805
1,000,000,000	2.7182818

From the table, we can see that as x increases, the value of $\left(1 + \frac{1}{x}\right)^{x}$ approaches the value of e, and the formula

$$A = P\left[\left(1 + \frac{1}{x}\right)^{x}\right]^{rt}$$

becomes

$$A = Pe^{rt}$$ Substitute e for $\left(1 + \frac{1}{x}\right)^{x}$.

When the amount invested grows exponentially according to the formula $A = Pe^{rt}$, we say that interest is **compounded continuously.**

Continuous Compound Interest Formula

If P dollars are deposited in an account earning interest at an annual rate r, compounded continuously, the amount A after t years is given by the formula

$$A = Pe^{rt}$$

EXAMPLE 6 **Solving a Continuous Compound Interest Problem**

If the parents of the newborn child in Example 5 had invested $8,000 at an annual rate of 9%, compounded continuously, how much would the child have in the account in 55 years?

SOLUTION We will substitute $8,000 for P, 0.09 for r, and 55 for t in the continuous compound interest formula $A = Pe^{rt}$.

$$A = Pe^{rt}$$

$$A = 8,000e^{(0.09)(55)}$$

$$= 8,000e^{4.95}$$

$$\approx 1,129,399.711 \qquad \text{Use a calculator.}$$

In 55 years, the balance will be $1,129,399.71, which is $60,296.44 more than the amount earned with quarterly compounding. ∎

Self Check 6 Find the balance in 60 years.

Now Try Exercise 89.

To graph the exponential function $f(x) = e^x$, we plot several points and join them with a smooth curve [as in Figure 4-7(a)] or use a graphing calculator [as in Figure 4-7(b)].

$f(x) = e^x$		
x	$f(x)$	$(x, f(x))$
-1	0.37	$(-1, 0.37)$
0	1	$(0, 1)$
1	2.72	$(1, 2.72)$
2	7.39	$(2, 7.39)$

(a)

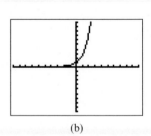

(b)

FIGURE 4-7

Comment The graph of $f(x) = e^x$ is very important in mathematics and should be memorized.

5. Use Transformations to Graph Exponential Functions

In Section 3.4, translations, reflections, and stretchings were applied to functions. These may also be applied to the graphs of exponential functions. A summary of these transformations, when $k > 0$, is shown in the table.

Equation	Transformations of the Graph of $f(x) = b^x$
$y = b^x + k$	Translates the graph of $f(x) = b^x$ upward k units
$y = b^x - k$	Translates the graph of $f(x) = b^x$ downward k units
$y = b^{x-k}$	Translates the graph of $f(x) = b^x$ to the right k units
$y = b^{x+k}$	Translates the graph of $f(x) = b^x$ to the left k units
$y = -b^x$	Reflects the graph of $f(x) = b^x$ about the x-axis
$y = b^{-x}$	Reflects the graph of $f(x) = b^x$ about the y-axis
$y = kb^x$	• Vertically stretches the graph of $f(x) = b^x$ if $k > 1$ • Vertically shrinks the graph of $f(x) = b^x$ if $0 < k < 1$
$y = b^{kx}$	• Horizontally stretches the graph of $f(x) = b^x$ if $0 < k < 1$ • Horizontally shrinks the graph of $f(x) = b^x$ if $k > 1$

EXAMPLE 7 **Using Translations to Graph an Exponential Function**

On one set of axes, graph $f(x) = 2^x$ and $g(x) = 2^x + 3$.

SOLUTION The graph of $g(x) = 2^x + 3$ is identical to the graph of $f(x) = 2^x$, except that it is translated 3 units upward. (See Figure 4-8.)

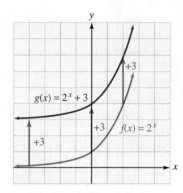

$f(x) = 2^x$		
x	$f(x)$	$(x, f(x))$
-4	$\dfrac{1}{16}$	$\left(-4, \dfrac{1}{16}\right)$
0	1	$(0, 1)$
2	4	$(2, 4)$

$g(x) = 2^x + 3$		
x	$g(x)$	$(x, g(x))$
-4	$3\dfrac{1}{16}$	$\left(-4, 3\dfrac{1}{16}\right)$
0	4	$(0, 4)$
2	7	$(2, 7)$

FIGURE 4-8

Self Check 7 On one set of axes, graph $f(x) = 2^x$ and $g(x) = 2^x - 2$.

Now Try Exercise 53.

EXAMPLE 8 **Using Translations to Graph an Exponential Function with Base e**

On one set of axes, graph $f(x) = e^x$ and $g(x) = e^{x-3}$.

SOLUTION The graph of $g(x) = e^{x-3}$ is identical to the graph of $f(x) = e^x$, except that it is translated 3 units to the right. (See Figure 4-9.)

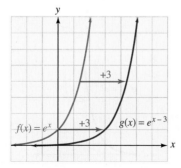

$f(x) = e^x$		
x	$f(x)$	$(x, f(x))$
-1	0.37	$(-1, 0.37)$
0	1	$(0, 1)$
1	2.72	$(1, 2.72)$
2	7.39	$(2, 7.39)$

$g(x) = e^{x-3}$		
x	$g(x)$	$(x, g(x))$
2	0.37	$(2, 0.37)$
3	1	$(3, 1)$
4	2.72	$(4, 2.72)$
5	7.39	$(5, 7.39)$

FIGURE 4-9

Self Check 8   On one set of axes, graph $f(x) = e^x$ and $g(x) = e^{x+2}$.

Now Try Exercise 61.

We can use a graphing calculator to graph exponential functions that are vertically or horizontally stretched or shrunk.

ACCENT ON TECHNOLOGY   **Graphing Exponential Functions**

Some exponential functions are very difficult to graph by hand. A graphing calculator can be used.

- To graph the exponential function $f(x) = 2(3^{x/2})$, we enter the right side of the equation after $Y_1 =$. The display will show the equation $Y_1 = 2(3\wedge(X/2))$. If we use [WINDOW] settings of $[-10, 10]$ for x and $[-2, 18]$ for y and press [GRAPH], we will obtain the graph shown in Figure 4-10.

FIGURE 4-10

- To graph the exponential function $f(x) = 3e^{-x/2}$, we enter the right side of the equation $Y_1 =$. The display will show the equation $Y_1 = 3e\wedge(-x/2)$. If we use [WINDOW] settings of $[-10, 10]$ for x and $[-2, 18]$ for y and press [GRAPH], we will obtain the graph shown in Figure 4-11.

FIGURE 4-11

Self Check Answers   **1. a.** 2.6265   **b.** -14.7470 **c.** 0.0102   **2. a.** 64   **b.** $x^{3\sqrt{5}}$
3.

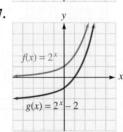

4. no   **5.** no   **6.** $1,771,251.33

7.

8.

Exercises **4.1**

Getting Ready

You should be able to complete these vocabulary and concept statements before you proceed to the practice exercises.

Fill in the blanks.

1. If $b > 0$ and $b \neq 1$, $y = b^x$ represents an _____ function.

2. If $f(x) = b^x$ represents an increasing function, then $b > $ ___.

3. In interval notation, the domain of the exponential function $f(x) = b^x$ is _____.

4. The number b is called the _____ of the exponential function $y = b^x$.

5. The range of the exponential function $f(x) = b^x$ is _____.

6. The graphs of all exponential functions $y = b^x$ have the same ___-intercept, the point _____.

7. If $b > 0$ and $b \neq 1$, the graph of $y = b^x$ approaches the x-axis, which is called a horizontal _____ of the curve.

8. If $f(x) = b^x$ represents a decreasing function, then ___ $< b <$ ___.

9. If $b > 1$, then $y = b^x$ defines a (an) _____ function.

10. The graph of an exponential function $y = b^x$ always passes through the points $(0, 1)$ and _____.

11. To two decimal places, the value of e is ____.

12. The continuous compound interest formula is $A = $ ____.

13. Since $e > 1$, the base-e exponential function is a (an) _____ function.

14. The graph of the exponential function $y = e^x$ passes through the points $(0, 1)$ and _____.

Practice

 Use a calculator to find each value to four decimal places.

15. $4^{\sqrt{3}}$

16. $5^{\sqrt{2}}$

17. 7^{π}

18. $3^{-\pi}$

Simplify each expression.

19. $5^{\sqrt{2}}5^{\sqrt{2}}$

20. $\left(5^{\sqrt{2}}\right)^{\sqrt{2}}$

21. $\left(a^{\sqrt{8}}\right)^{\sqrt{2}}$

22. $a^{\sqrt{12}}a^{\sqrt{3}}$

Find $f(0)$ and $f(2)$ for each of the given exponential functions.

23. $f(x) = 5^x$

24. $f(x) = 4^{-x}$

25. $f(x) = \left(\dfrac{1}{3}\right)^{-x}$

26. $f(x) = \left(\dfrac{1}{4}\right)^{x}$

Graph each exponential function.

27. $f(x) = 3^x$

28. $f(x) = 5^x$

29. $f(x) = \left(\dfrac{1}{5}\right)^{x}$

30. $f(x) = \left(\dfrac{1}{3}\right)^{x}$

31. $f(x) = \left(\dfrac{3}{4}\right)^{x}$

32. $f(x) = \left(\dfrac{4}{3}\right)^{x}$

33. $f(x) = (1.5)^x$

34. $f(x) = (0.3)^x$

35. $f(x) = 3^{-x}$

36. $f(x) = -5^x$

37. $f(x) = -\left(\dfrac{1}{5}\right)^x$

38. $f(x) = \left(\dfrac{1}{3}\right)^{-x}$

49.

50.

Determine whether the graph could represent an exponential function of the form $f(x) = b^x$.

39.

40.

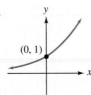

Graph each function by using transformations. Do not use a graphing calculator.

51. $f(x) = 3^x - 1$

52. $f(x) = 2^x + 3$

41.

42.

53. $f(x) = 2^x + 1$

54. $f(x) = 4^x - 4$

Find the value of b, if any, that would cause the graph of $y = b^x$ ***to look like the graph indicated.***

43.

44.

55. $f(x) = 3^{x-1}$

56. $f(x) = 2^{x+3}$

45.

46.

57. $f(x) = 3^{x+1}$

58. $f(x) = 2^{x-3}$

47.

48.

59. $f(x) = e^x - 4$

60. $f(x) = e^x + 2$

69. $f(x) = 2^{-x} - 3$

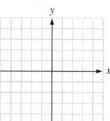

70. $f(x) = 4^{-x} + 4$

61. $f(x) = e^{x-2}$

62. $f(x) = e^{x+3}$

71. $f(x) = -e^x + 2$

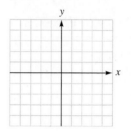

72. $f(x) = e^{-x} + 3$

63. $f(x) = 2^{x+1} - 2$

64. $f(x) = 3^{x-1} + 2$

 Use a graphing calculator to graph each function.

73. $f(x) = 5(2^x)$ **74.** $f(x) = 2(5^x)$

75. $f(x) = 3^{-x}$ **76.** $f(x) = 2^{-x}$

65. $y = 3^{x-2} + 1$

66. $y = 3^{x+2} - 1$

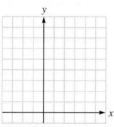

77. $f(x) = 2e^x$ **78.** $f(x) = 3e^{-x}$

79. $f(x) = 5e^{-0.5x}$ **80.** $f(x) = -3e^{2x}$

67. $f(x) = -3^x + 1$

68. $f(x) = -2^x - 3$

Applications

In Exercises 81–84, assume that there are no deposits or withdrawals.

81. Compound interest An initial deposit of $10,000 earns 8% interest, compounded quarterly. How much will be in the account in 10 years?

82. Compound interest An initial deposit of $1,000 earns 9% interest, compounded monthly. How much will be in the account in $4\frac{1}{2}$ years?

83. **Comparing interest rates** How much more interest could $500 earn in 5 years, compounded semiannually (two times a year), if the annual interest rate were $5\frac{1}{2}\%$ instead of 5%?

84. **Comparing savings plans** Which institution in the ads provides the better investment?

> ### *Fidelity Savings & Loan*
> Earn 5.25%
> compounded monthly

> ### **Union Trust**
> Money Market Account
> paying 5.35%
> compounded annually

85. **Compound interest** If $1 had been invested on July 4, 1776, at 5% interest, compounded annually, what would it be worth on July 4, 2076?

86. **360/365 method** Some financial institutions pay daily interest, compounded by the 360/365 method, using the following formula. Using this method, what will an initial investment of $1,000 be worth in 5 years, assuming a 7% annual interest rate?

$$A = A_0\left(1 + \frac{r}{360}\right)^{365t} \quad (t \text{ is in years})$$

87. **Carrying charges** A college student takes advantage of the ad shown and buys a bedroom set for $1,100. He plans to pay the $1,100 plus interest when his income tax refund comes in 8 months. At that time, what will he need to pay?

> ## BUY NOW, PAY LATER!
> Only $1\frac{3}{4}\%$ interest per month.

88. **Credit card interest** A bank credit card charges interest at the rate of 21% per year, compounded monthly. If a senior in college charges $1,500 to pay for college expenses and intends to pay it in one year, what will she have to pay?

Mark Stout Photography/Shutterstock.com

89. **Continuous compound interest** An initial investment of $5,000 earns 8.2% interest, compounded continuously. What will the investment be worth in 12 years?

90. **Continuous compound interest** An initial investment of $2,000 earns 8% interest, compounded continuously. What will the investment be worth in 15 years?

91. **Comparison of compounding methods** An initial deposit of $5,000 grows at an annual rate of 8.5% for 5 years. Compare the final balances resulting from continuous compounding and annual compounding.

92. **Comparison of compounding methods** An initial deposit of $30,000 grows at an annual rate of 8% for 20 years. Compare the final balances resulting from continuous compounding and annual compounding.

93. **Frequency of compounding** $10,000 is invested in each of two accounts, both paying 6% annual interest. In the first account, interest compounds quarterly, and in the second account, interest compounds daily. Find the difference between the accounts after 20 years.

94. **Determining an initial deposit** An account now contains $11,180 and has been accumulating interest at a 7% annual rate, compounded continuously, for 7 years. Find the initial deposit.

95. **Saving for college** In 20 years, a father wants to accumulate $40,000 to pay for his daughter's college expenses. If he can get 6% interest, compounded quarterly, how much must he invest now to achieve his goal?

96. **Saving for college** In Problem 95, how much should he invest to achieve his goal if he can get 6% interest, compounded continuously?

97. **Population of a city** The population $P(t)$ of a small city can be approximated by the exponential function, $P(t) = 1{,}200e^{0.2t}$, where t represents time in years. What will be the population of the city in 12 years? Round to a whole number.

98. **Amount of drug present** The amount of a drug $A(t)$, in mg, present in the bloodstream t hours after being intravenously administered can be approximated by the exponential function, $A(t) = -1{,}000e^{-0.3t} + 1{,}250$. How much of the drug is present in the bloodstream after 14 hours? Round to a whole number.

Discovery and Writing

99. Financial planning To have $P available in n years, $A can be invested now in an account paying interest at an annual rate r, compounded annually. Show that

$$A = P(1 + r)^{-n}$$

100. If $2^{t+4} = k2^t$, find k.

101. If $5^{3t} = k^t$, find k.

102. a. If $e^{t+3} = ke^t$, find k.

b. If $e^{3t} = k^t$, find k.

Review

Factor each expression completely.

103. $x^2 + 9x^4$

104. $x^2 - 9x^4$

105. $x^2 + x - 12$

106. $x^3 + 27$

4.2 Applications of Exponential Functions

In this section, we will learn to

1. Solve radioactive decay problems.

2. Solve oceanography problems.

3. Solve Malthusian population growth problems.

4. Solve epidemiology problems.

Flu kills an estimated 36,000 Americans each year and results is a much larger number of hospitalizations. The influenza virus replicates quickly and can rapidly infect a population. The most effective method of preventing the virus infection and its severe complications is a flu vaccination.

An event that changes with time, such as the spread of the influenza virus, can by modeled by an exponential function. In this section, we will see several important applications of these functions: radioactive decay, oceanography, population growth, and epidemiology.

A mathematical description of an observed event is called a **model** of that event. Many real-world occurrences change with time and can be modeled by exponential functions of the form

$$y = f(t) = ab^{kt} \qquad \text{Remember that } ab^{kt} \text{ means } a(b^{kt}).$$

where a, b, and k are constants and t represents time. If f is an increasing function, we say that y *grows exponentially.* If f is a decreasing function, we say that y *decays exponentially.*

1. Solve Radioactive Decay Problems

The atomic structure of a radioactive material changes as the material emits radiation. Uranium, for example, changes (decays) into thorium, then into radium, and eventually into lead.

Experiments have determined the time it takes for one-half of a sample of a given radioactive element to decompose. That time is a constant, called the element's **half-life.** The amount present decays exponentially according to this formula.

Radioactive Decay Formula

The amount A of radioactive material present at time t is given by

$$A = A_0 2^{-t/h}$$

where A_0 is the amount that was present initially (at $t = 0$) and h is the material's half-life.

EXAMPLE 1 **Solving a Radioactive Decay Problem**

The half-life of radium is approximately 1,600 years. How much of a 1-gram sample will remain after 1,000 years?

SOLUTION In this example, $A_0 = 1$, $h = 1,600$, and $t = 1,000$. We substitute these values into the formula for radioactive decay and simplify.

$$A = A_0 2^{-t/h}$$

$$A = 1 \cdot 2^{-1,000/1,600}$$

$$\approx 0.648419777 \qquad \text{Use a calculator.}$$

After 1,000 years, approximately 0.65 gram of radium will remain. ∎

Self Check 1 After 800 years, how much radium will remain?

Now Try Exercise 3.

2. Solve Oceanography Problems

Intensity of Light Formula

The intensity I of light (in lumens) at a distance x meters below the surface of a body of water decreases exponentially according to the formula

$$I = I_0 k^x$$

where I_0 is the intensity of light above the water and k is a constant that depends on the clarity of the water.

Comment A lumen is a unit of standard measurement that describes how much light is contained in a certain area. The lumen is part of the photometry group which measures different aspects of light.

EXAMPLE 2 **Solving an Intensity of Light Problem**

At one location in the Atlantic Ocean, the intensity of light above water I_0 is 12 lumens and $k = 0.6$. Find the intensity of light at a depth of 5 meters.

SOLUTION We will substitute 12 for I_0, 0.6 for k, and 5 for x into the formula for light intensity and then simplify.

$$I = I_0 k^x$$

$$I = 12(0.6)^5$$

$$I = 0.93312$$

At a depth of 5 meters, the intensity of the light is slightly less than 1 lumen. ∎

Self Check 2 Find the intensity at a depth of 10 meters.

Now Try Exercise 11.

3. Solve Malthusian Population Growth Problems

An equation based on the exponential function provides a model for **population growth.** One such model, called the **Malthusian model of population growth,** assumes a constant birth rate and a constant death rate. In this model, the population P grows exponentially according to the following formula.

Malthusian Model of Population Growth

If b is the annual birth rate, d is the annual death rate, t is the time (in years), P_0 is the initial population at $t = 0$, and P is the current population, then

$$P = P_0 e^{kt}$$

where $k = b - d$ is the **annual growth rate,** the difference between the annual birth rate and death rate.

EXAMPLE 3   **Using the Malthusian Model to Predict Population Growth**

The population of the United States is approximately 300 million people. Assuming that the annual birth rate is 19 per 1,000 and the annual death rate is 7 per 1,000, what does the Malthusian model predict the U.S. population will be in 50 years?

SOLUTION   We can use the stated information to write the Malthusian model for U.S. population. We will then substitute into the model to predict the population in 50 years.
Since k is the difference between the birth and death rates, we have

$$k = b - d$$

$$k = \frac{19}{1,000} - \frac{7}{1,000} \qquad \text{Substitute } \frac{19}{1,000} \text{ for } b \text{ and } \frac{7}{1,000} \text{ for } d.$$

$$k = 0.019 - 0.007$$

$$= 0.012$$

We can now substitute 300,000,000 for P_0, 50 for t, and 0.012 for k in the formula for the Malthusian model of population growth and simplify.

$$P = P_0 e^{kt}$$

$$P = (300,000,000)e^{(0.012)(50)}$$

$$= (300,000,000)e^{0.6}$$

$$\approx 546,635,640.1 \qquad \text{Use a calculator.}$$

After 50 years, the U.S. population will exceed 546 million people. ■

Self Check 3   Find the population in 100 years.

Now Try Exercise 23.

The English economist Thomas Robert Malthus (1766–1834) pioneered in population study. He believed that poverty and starvation were unavoidable, because the human population tends to grow exponentially, whereas the food supply tends to grow linearly.

EXAMPLE 4   **Using a Graphing Calculator to Solve a Population Problem**

Suppose that a country with a population of 1,000 people is growing exponentially according to the formula

$$P = 1,000e^{0.02t}$$

where t is in years. Furthermore, assume that the food supply, measured in adequate food per day per person, is growing linearly according to the formula

$$y = 30.625x + 2,000$$

In how many years will the population outstrip the food supply?

SOLUTION   We can use a graphing calculator with [WINDOW] settings of $[0,100]$ for x and $[0,10,000]$ for y. After graphing the functions as shown in Figure 4-12, we find the point where the two graphs intersect. We can see that the food supply will be adequate for about 72 years. At that time, the population of approximately 4,200 people will begin to have problems, assuming all conditions remain static.

FIGURE 4-12

Self Check 4   In 80 years, what is the approximate number of people per day that will not have adequate food?

Now Try Exercise 43.

4. Solve Epidemiology Problems

Many infectious diseases, including some caused by viruses, spread most rapidly when they first infect a population, but then more slowly as the number of uninfected individuals decreases. These situations are often modeled by a function, called a *logistic function*.

Logistic Epidemiology Model   The size P of an infected population at any time t in years is given by the logistic function

$$P = \frac{M}{1 + \left(\dfrac{M}{P_0} - 1\right)e^{-kt}}$$

where P_0 is the infected population size at $t = 0$, k is a constant determined by how contagious the virus is in a given environment, and M is the theoretical maximum size of the population P.

EXAMPLE 5   **Solving an Epidemiology Problem**

In a city with a population of 1,200,000, there are currently 1,000 cases of infection with HIV. If the spread of the disease is projected by the formula

$$P = \frac{1,200,000}{1 + (1,200 - 1)e^{-0.4t}}$$

how many people will be infected in 3 years?

SOLUTION   We can substitute 3 for t in the logistic formula and calculate P.

$$P = \frac{1,200,000}{1 + (1,200 - 1)e^{-0.4t}}$$

$$P = \frac{1,200,000}{1 + (1,199)e^{-0.4(3)}}$$

$$\approx 3,313.710094$$

In 3 years, approximately 3,300 people are expected to be infected. ∎

Self Check 5   How many will be infected in 10 years?

Now Try Exercise 35.

ACCENT ON TECHNOLOGY   **Exponential Regression**

The table below shows the cooling temperatures of a hot cup of coffee after it is made.

Time in minutes	Temperature °F
0	179.5
5	168.7
8	158.1
11	149.2
15	141.7
18	134.6
22	125.4
25	123.5
30	116.3
34	113.2
38	109.1
42	105.7
45	102.2
50	100.5

graphx/Shutterstock.com

We can use a graphing calculator to determine an exponential regression model function that best fits or represents the given data.

- **Step 1:** Enter the data into lists in the calculator. Press STAT and then choose 1:Edit to access the list window and then enter the values. Enter the *x*-values (time in minutes) into L1 and the *y*-values (temperature) into LIST 2. See Figure 4-13(a).
- **Step 2:** Set a window to fit the data. See Figure 4-13(b).
- **Step 3:** Create a scatter plot of the data. To do so, select STAT PLOT, located above the Y= button, and turn Plot 1 on. See Figure 4-14(c). Press GRAPH to see the scatter plot. See Figure 4-13(d).

| (a) | (b) |
| (c) | (d) |

FIGURE 4-13

- **Step 4:** To determine the exponential regression function, we Press STAT and scroll right to the CALC menu. We scroll downward to 0:ExpReg and press ENTER twice. This gives the equation. See Figure 4-14 (a) and (b). The function is $y = 171.4617283 \cdot (0.9882469577)^x$.
- **Step 5:** To graph the exponential function, we first press Y= , then we press VARS and scroll downward to 5: Statistics and press ENTER. Finally, we select EQ, then press ENTER and GRAPH. See Figure 4-14(c), (d), (e) and (f).

| (a) | (b) | (c) |
| (d) | (e) | (f) |

FIGURE 4-14

Self Check Answers   **1.** about 0.71 g   **2.** 0.073 lumen   **3.** over 996 million   **4.** About 503
5. about 52,000

Exercises **4.2**

Getting Ready

You should be able to complete these vocabulary and concept statements before you proceed to the practice exercises.

Fill in the blanks.

1. The Malthusian model assumes a constant _____ rate and a constant _____ rate.

2. The Malthusian prediction is pessimistic, because a _____ grows exponentially, but food supplies grow _____.

Applications

Use a calculator to help solve each problem.

3. **Tritium decay** Tritium, a radioactive isotope of hydrogen, has a half-life of 12.4 years. Of an initial sample of 50 grams, how much will remain after 100 years?

4. **Chernobyl** In April 1986, the world's worst nuclear power disaster occurred at Chernobyl in the former USSR. An explosion released about 1,000 kilograms of radioactive cesium-137 (^{137}Cs) into the atmosphere. If the half-life of ^{137}Cs is 30.17 years, how much will remain in the atmosphere in 100 years?

5. **Chernobyl** Refer to Exercise 4. How much ^{137}Cs will remain in 200 years?

6. **Carbon-14 decay** The half-life of radioactive carbon-14 is 5,700 years. How much of an initial sample will remain after 3,000 years?

7. **Plutonium decay** One of the isotopes of plutonium, ^{237}Pu, decays with a half-life of 40 days. How much of an initial sample will remain after 60 days?

8. **Comparing radioactive decay** One isotope of holmium, ^{162}Ho, has a half-life of 22 minutes. The half-life of a second isotope, ^{164}Ho, is 37 minutes. Starting with a sample containing equal amounts, find the ratio of the amounts of ^{162}Ho to ^{164}Ho after one hour.

9. **Drug absorption in smokers** The biological half-life of the asthma medication theophylline is 4.5 hours for smokers. Find the amount of the drug retained in a smoker's system 12 hours after a dose of 1 unit is taken.

10. **Drug absorption in nonsmokers** For a nonsmoker, the biological half-life of theophylline is 8 hours. Find the amount of the drug retained in a nonsmoker's system 12 hours after taking a one-unit dose.

11. **Oceanography** The intensity I of light (in lumens) at a distance x meters below the surface is given by $I = I_0 k^x$, where I_0 is the intensity at the surface and k depends on the clarity of the water. At one location in the Arctic Ocean, $I_0 = 8$ lumens and $k = 0.5$. Find the intensity at a depth of 2 meters.

12. **Oceanography** At one location in the Atlantic Ocean, $I_0 = 14$ lumens and $k = 0.7$. Find the intensity of light at a depth of 12 meters. (See Exercise 11.)

13. **Oceanography** At a depth of 3 meters at one location in the Pacific Ocean, the intensity I of light is 1 lumen and $k = 0.5$. Find the intensity I_0 of light at the surface.

14. **Oceanography** At a depth of 2 meters at one location off the coast of Belize, the intensity I of light is 2 lumens and $k = 0.2$. Find the intensity I_0 of light at the surface.

15. **Bluegill population** A Wisconsin lake is stocked with 10,000 bluegill. The population is expected to grow exponentially according to the model $P = P_0 2^{t/2}$. How many bluegill will be in the lake in 5 years?

© Istockphoto.com/Dirk Nelson

16. **Community growth** The population of Eagle River is growing exponentially according to the model $P = 375(1.3)^t$, where t is measured in years from the present date. Find the population in 3 years.

17. **Newton's Law of Cooling** Some hot water, initially at 100°C, is placed in a room with a temperature of 40°C. The temperature T of the water after t hours is given by $T = 40 + 60(0.75)^t$. Find the temperature in $3\frac{1}{2}$ hours.

18. **Bacterial cultures** A colony of 6 million bacteria is growing in a culture medium. The population P after t hours is given by the formula $P = (6 \times 10^6)(2.3)^t$. Find the population after 4 hours.

19. **Population growth** The growth of a town's population is modeled by $P = 173e^{0.03t}$. How large will the population be when $t = 20$?

20. **Population decline** The decline of a city's population is modeled by $P = 1.2 \times 10^6 e^{-0.008t}$. How large will the population be when $t = 30$?

21. **Epidemics** The spread of hoof and mouth disease through a herd of cattle can be modeled by the formula $P = P_0 e^{0.27t}$, where P is the size of the infected population, P_0 is the infected population size at $t = 0$, and t is in days. If a rancher does not act quickly to treat two cases, how many cattle will have the disease in one week?

22. **Alcohol absorption** In one individual, the percent of alcohol absorbed into the bloodstream after drinking two glasses of wine is given by the following formula. Find the percent of alcohol absorbed into the blood after $\frac{1}{2}$ hour.

$$P = 0.3(1 - e^{-0.05t}) \text{ where } t \text{ is in minutes}$$

23. **World population growth** The population of the Earth is approximately 6 billion people and is growing at an annual rate of 1.9%. Assuming a Malthusian growth model, find the world population in 30 years.

24. **World population growth** See Exercise 23. Assuming a Malthusian growth model, find the world population in 40 years.

25. **World population growth** See Exercise 23. By what factor will the current population of the Earth increase in 50 years?

26. **World population growth** See Exercise 23. By what factor will the current population of the Earth increase in 100 years?

27. **Drug absorption** The percent P of the drug triazolam (a drug for treating insomnia) remaining in a person's bloodstream after t hours is given by $P = e^{-0.3t}$. What percent will remain in the bloodstream after 24 hours?

28. **Medicine** The concentration x of a certain drug in an organ after t minutes is given by $x = 0.08(1 - e^{-0.1t})$. Find the concentration of the drug in $\frac{1}{2}$ hour.

29. **Medicine** Refer to Exercise 28. Find the initial concentration of the drug (*Hint:* when $t = 0$).

30. **Spreading the news** Suppose the function

$$N = P(1 - e^{-0.1t})$$

is used to model the length of time t (in hours) it takes for N people living in a town with population P to hear a news flash. How many people in a town of 50,000 will hear the news between 1 and 2 hours after it happened?

31. **Spreading the news** How many people in the town described in Problem 30 will not have heard the news after 10 hours?

32. **Epidemics** Refer to Example 5. How many people will be infected with HIV in 5 years?

33. **Epidemics** Refer to Example 5. How many people will be infected with HIV in 8 years?

34. **Epidemics** In a city with a population of 450,000, there are currently 1,000 cases of hepatitis. If the spread of the disease is projected by the following logistic function, how many people will contract the hepatitis virus after 6 years?

$$P = \frac{450,000}{1 + (450 - 1)e^{-0.2t}}$$

35. **Epidemics** In an Indonesian city with a population of 55,000, there are currently 100 cases of the avian bird flu. If the spread of the disease is projected by the following formula, how many people will contract the bird flu after 2 years?

$$P = \frac{55,000}{1 + (550 - 1)e^{-0.8t}}$$

36. **Life expectancy** The life expectancy l of white females can be estimated by using the function $l = 78.5(1.001)^x$, where x is the current age. Find the life expectancy of a white female who is currently 50 years old. Give the answer to the nearest tenth.

37. **Oceanography** The width w (in millimeters) of successive growth spirals of the sea shell *Catapulus voluto*, shown in the illustration, is given by the function $w = 1.54e^{0.503n}$, where n is the spiral number. To the nearest tenth of a millimeter, find the width of the fifth spiral.

38. **Skydiving** Before the parachute opens, the velocity v (in meters per second) of a skydiver is given by $v = 50(1 - e^{-0.2t})$. Find the initial velocity.

39. Skydiving Refer to Exercise 38 and find the velocity after 20 seconds.

40. Free-falling objects After t seconds, a certain falling object has a velocity v given by $v = 50(1 - e^{-0.3t})$. Which is falling faster after 2 seconds, this object or the skydiver in Exercise 38?

41. Population growth In 1999, the male population of the United States was about 133 million, and the female population was about 139 million. Assuming a Malthusian growth model with a 1% annual growth rate, how many more females than males will there be in 20 years?

42. Population growth See Exercise 41. How many more females than males will there be in 50 years?

 Use a graphing calculator to solve each problem.

43. In Example 4, suppose that better farming methods change the formula for food growth to $y = 31x + 2,000$. How long will the food supply be adequate?

44. In Example 4, suppose that a birth control program changed the formula for population growth to $P = 1,000e^{0.01t}$. How long will the food supply be adequate?

Discovery and Writing

 45. The value of e can be calculated to any degree of accuracy by adding the first several terms of the following list. The more terms that are added, the closer the sum will be to e. Add the first six numbers in the following list. To how many decimal places is the sum accurate?

$$1, 1, \frac{1}{2}, \frac{1}{2 \cdot 3}, \frac{1}{2 \cdot 3 \cdot 4}, \frac{1}{2 \cdot 3 \cdot 4 \cdot 5}, \ldots$$

 46. Graph the function defined by the equation $f(x) = \frac{e^x + e^{-x}}{2}$ from $x = -2$ to $x = 2$. The graph will look like a parabola, but it is not. The graph, called a **catenary,** is important in the design of power distribution networks, because it represents the shape of a uniform flexible cable whose ends are suspended from the same height. The function is called the **hyperbolic cosine function.**

 47. Graph the following logistic function, first discussed in Example 5. Use WINDOW settings of $[0, 20]$ for x and $[0, 1,500,000]$ for y.

$$P = \frac{1,200,000}{1 + (1,199)e^{-0.4t}}$$

48. Use the TRACE capabilities of your graphing calculator to explore the logistic function of Example 5 and Exercise 47. As time passes, what value does P approach? How many years does it take for 20% of the population to become infected? For 80%?

Review
Find the value of x that makes each statement true.

49. $2^3 = x$

50. $3^x = 9$

51. $x^3 = 27$

52. $3^{-2} = x$

53. $x^{-3} = \frac{1}{8}$

54. $3^x = \frac{1}{3} \quad -1$

55. $9^{1/2} = x$

56. $x^{1/3} = 3$

4.3 Logarithmic Functions and Their Graphs

In this section, we will learn to

1. Evaluate logarithms.

2. Evaluate common logarithms.

3. Evaluate natural logarithms.

4. Graph logarithmic functions.

5. Use transformations to graph logarithmic functions.

Guests aboard the Royal Caribbean's cruise ship *Freedom of the Seas* can now "hang ten" while out to sea. The flowrider surf simulator allows riders to body board surf against a wave-like water flow of 34,000 gallons per minute.

It is important that water in the flowrider has the proper pH value. For example, if it is too acidic, the water will make our eyes and nose burn, and it will make our skin get dry and itchy. The pH of the water is one of the most important factors in pool water balance and should be tested frequently. To calculate pH, we need to understand *logarithms*, the topic of this section. As we continue through this chapter, we will see several real-life applications of logarithms.

Since exponential functions are one-to-one functions, each one has an inverse. For example, to find the inverse of the function $y = 3^x$, we interchange the positions of x and y to obtain $x = 3^y$. The graphs of these two functions are shown in Figure 4-15(a).

To find the inverse of the function $y = \left(\frac{1}{3}\right)^x$, we again interchange the positions of x and y to obtain $x = \left(\frac{1}{3}\right)^y$. The graphs of these two functions are shown in Figure 4-15(b).

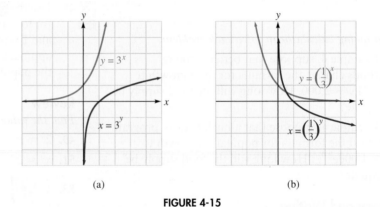

(a)   (b)

FIGURE 4-15

Comment   The graphs of the functions are inverses and therefore symmetric about the line $y = x$.

In general, the inverse of the function $y = b^x$ is $x = b^y$. When $b > 1$, their graphs appear as shown in Figure 4-16(a). When $0 < b < 1$, their graphs appear as shown in Figure 4-16(b).

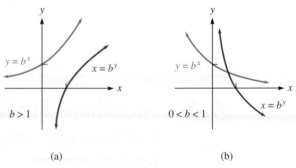

(a)   (b)

FIGURE 4-16

1. Evaluate Logarithms

Since an exponential function defined by $y = b^x$ is one-to-one, it has an inverse function that is defined by the equation $x = b^y$. To express this inverse function in the form $y = f^{-1}(x)$, we must solve the equation $x = b^y$ for y. To do this, we need the following definition.

Logarithmic Functions   If $b > 0$ and $b \neq 1$, the **logarithmic function with base b** is defined by

$$y = \log_b x \qquad \text{if and only if} \qquad x = b^y$$

The **domain of the logarithmic function** is the interval $(0, \infty)$. The **range** is the interval $(-\infty, \infty)$. The logarithmic function is also denoted as $f(x) = \log_b x$.

Caution

Since the domain of the logarithmic function is the set of positive numbers, the logarithm of 0 and the logarithm of a negative number are **undefined** in the set of real numbers.

The range of the logarithmic function is the set of real numbers, because the value of y in the equation $x = b^y$ can be any real number. The domain is the set of positive numbers, because the value of x in the equation $x = b^y$ $(b > 0)$ is always positive.

Since the function $y = \log_b x$ is the inverse of the one-to-one exponential function $y = b^x$, the logarithmic function is also one-to-one.

The expression $x = b^y$ is said to be written in *exponential form*. The equivalent expression $y = \log_b x$ is said to be written in *logarithmic form*. To translate from one form to the other, it is helpful to keep track of the base and the exponent.

Exponential Form	*Logarithmic Form*
$x = b^y$	$y = \log_b x$
Base Exponent	Exponent Base

Comment   In general, we usually write $b^y = x$ instead of writing $x = b^y$. Both are acceptable. Also, many students prefer writing $\log_b x = y$ instead of writing $y = \log_b x$. This too is acceptable.

EXAMPLE 1   **Converting from Exponential Form to Logarithmic Form**

Write each equation in logarithmic form.

a. $2^6 = 64$ **b.** $27^{\frac{1}{3}} = \sqrt[3]{27} = 3$ **c.** $6^{-2} = \dfrac{1}{36}$

SOLUTION   For each part, we can use the definition of the logarithm of a number.

a. $2^6 = 64$ is equivalent to $\log_2 64 = 6$

b. $27^{\frac{1}{3}} = \sqrt[3]{27} = 3$ is equivalent to $\log_{27} 3 = \frac{1}{3}$

c. $6^{-2} = \frac{1}{36}$ is equivalent to $\log_6 \frac{1}{36} = -2$

Self Check 1   Write $13^{-2} = \dfrac{1}{169}$ in logarithmic form.

Now Try Exercise 21.

EXAMPLE 2   **Converting from Logarithmic Form to Exponential Form**

Write each equation in exponential form.

a. $\log_5 125 = 3$ **b.** $\log_{64} 8 = \dfrac{1}{2}$ **c.** $\log_{\frac{1}{4}} 16 = -2$

SOLUTION   For each part, we can use the definition of the logarithm of a number.

a. $\log_5 125 = 3$ is equivalent to $5^3 = 125$

b. $\log_{64} 8 = \frac{1}{2}$ is equivalent to $64^{\frac{1}{2}} = 8$

c. $\log_{\frac{1}{4}} 16 = -2$ is equivalent to $\left(\dfrac{1}{4}\right)^{-2} = 16$

Self Check 2   Write $\log_5 625 = 4$ in exponential form.

Now Try Exercise 29.

The definition of a logarithm can be used to find the values of many logarithms. Several examples are shown in the table.

Examples of the Values of Logarithms
$\log_5 25 = 2$ because 2 is the exponent to which 5 is raised to get 25: $5^2 = 25$
$\log_7 1 = 0$ because 0 is the exponent to which 7 is raised to get 1: $7^0 = 1$
$\log_{16} 4 = \dfrac{1}{2}$ because $\dfrac{1}{2}$ is the exponent to which 16 is raised to get 4: $16^{1/2} = \sqrt{16} = 4$
$\log_2 \dfrac{1}{8} = -3$ because -3 is the exponent to which 2 is raised to get $\dfrac{1}{8}$: $2^{-3} = \dfrac{1}{8}$

In each of these examples, the logarithm of a number is an exponent. In fact,

$\log_b x$ *is the exponent to which b is raised to get x.*

To express this as an equation, we write $b^{\log_b x} = x$

EXAMPLE 3   **Finding an Unknown Term in a Logarithmic Equation**

Find y in each equation: **a.** $\log_2 8 = y$ **b.** $\log_5 1 = y$ **c.** $\log_7 \dfrac{1}{49} = y$

SOLUTION   For each part, we can use the definition of the logarithm of a number to find y.

a. $\log_2 8 = y$ is equivalent to $2^y = 8$. Since $2^3 = 8$, we have $2^y = 2^3$ and $y = 3$.

b. $\log_5 1 = y$ is equivalent to $5^y = 1$. Since $5^0 = 1$, we have $5^y = 5^0$ and $y = 0$.

c. $\log_7 \dfrac{1}{49} = y$ is equivalent to $7^y = \dfrac{1}{49}$. Since $7^{-2} = \dfrac{1}{49}$, we have $7^y = 7^{-2}$ and $y = -2$.

Self Check 3   Find y in each equation:

a. $\log_3 9 = y$ **b.** $\log_2 16 = y$ **c.** $\log_5 \dfrac{1}{25} = y$

Now Try Exercise 35.

EXAMPLE 4   **Finding an Unknown Term in a Logarithmic Equation**

Find a in each equation: **a.** $\log_a 32 = 5$ **b.** $\log_9 a = -\dfrac{1}{2}$ **c.** $\log_9 3 = a$.

SOLUTION   For each part, we will use the definition of the logarithm of a number to find a.

a. $\log_a 32 = 5$ is equivalent to $a^5 = 32$. Since $2^5 = 32$, we have $a^5 = 2^5$ and $a = 2$.

b. $\log_9 a = -\dfrac{1}{2}$ is equivalent to $9^{-1/2} = a$. Since $9^{-1/2} = \dfrac{1}{3}$, it follows that $a = \dfrac{1}{3}$.

c. $\log_9 3 = a$ is equivalent to $9^a = 3$. Since $3 = 9^{1/2}$, we have $9^a = 9^{1/2}$ and $a = \dfrac{1}{2}$.

Self Check 4   Find d in each equation:

a. $\log_4 \dfrac{1}{16} = d$ **b.** $\log_d 36 = 2$ **c.** $\log_8 d = -\dfrac{1}{3}$

Now Try Exercise 49.

2. Evaluate Common Logarithms

Many applications use base-10 logarithms (also called **common logarithms**). When the base b is not indicated in the notation $\log x$, we assume that $b = 10$:

$\log x$ means $\log_{10} x$

Because base-10 logarithms appear so often, you should become familiar with the following base-10 logarithms:

Examples of Common Logarithms		
$\log_{10} \dfrac{1}{100} = -2$	because	$10^{-2} = \dfrac{1}{100}$
$\log_{10} \dfrac{1}{10} = -1$	because	$10^{-1} = \dfrac{1}{10}$
$\log_{10} 1 = 0$	because	$10^{0} = 1$
$\log_{10} 10 = 1$	because	$10^{1} = 10$
$\log_{10} 100 = 2$	because	$10^{2} = 100$
$\log_{10} 1,000 = 3$	because	$10^{3} = 1,000$

In general, we have

$\log_{10} 10^x = x$

ACCENT ON TECHNOLOGY   **Approximating Base-10 Logarithms**

We can use the [LOG] key on a graphing calculator to evaluate base-10 logarithms. Figure 4-17 shows the evaluation of $\log 2.34$ and demonstrates that **a logarithm is an exponent**. Notice that the logarithm is evaluated, and then the answer is used as the exponent of 10 to get 2.34. Remember: $\log 2.34$ is the exponent of 10 that will yield 2.34.

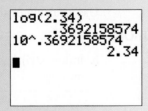

```
log(2.34)
       .3692158574
10^.3692158574
              2.34
■
```

FIGURE 4-17

EXAMPLE 5   **Using a Calculator to Solve a Common Logarithmic Equation**

Find x in the equation $\log x = 0.7482$ to four decimal places.

SOLUTION   We can use the definition of the common logarithm and a calculator to find x.

The equation $\log x = 0.7482$ is equivalent to $10^{0.7482} = x$.

Therefore we have $x = 10^{0.7482} \approx 5.6002$.   ■

Self Check 5   Solve: $\log x = 1.87737$. Give the result to four decimal places.

Now Try Exercise 81.

3. Evaluate Natural Logarithms

We have seen the importance of the number e in mathematical models of events in nature. Base-e logarithms are just as important. They are called **natural logarithms** or **Napierian logarithms** after John Napier (1550–1617). They are usually written as $\ln x$, rather than $\log_e x$:

$$\ln x \qquad \text{means} \qquad \log_e x$$

Like all logarithmic functions, the domain of $f(x) = \ln x$ is the interval $(0, \infty)$, and the range is the interval $(-\infty, \infty)$.

To estimate the base-e logarithms of numbers, we can use a calculator. Scientific and graphing calculators have a natural logarithm key [LN], which is used like the [LOG] key.

ACCENT ON TECHNOLOGY   **Approximating Natural Logarithms**

We can use the [LN] key on a graphing calculator to evaluate base-e logarithms. Figure 4-18 shows the evaluation of $\ln 2.34$ and demonstrates that **a logarithm is an exponent**. Notice that the logarithm is evaluated, and then the answer is used as the exponent of e to get 2.34. Remember: $\ln 2.34$ is the exponent of e that will yield 2.34.

```
ln(2.34)
            .8501509294
e^(.8501509294)
                   2.34
■
```

FIGURE 4-18

EXAMPLE 6   **Using a Calculator to Approximate Natural Logarithms**

Use a calculator to find   **a.** $\ln 17.32$ **b.** $\ln(\log 0.05)$

SOLUTION   **a.** $\ln 17.32 \approx 2.851861903$, which means $e^{2.851861903} \approx 17.32$

b. $\ln(\log 0.05)$ has no value because $\log(0.05) < 0$. Our calculator gives an error message.

Self Check 6   Find each value to four decimal places:

a. $\ln \pi$ **b.** $\ln\left(\log \dfrac{1}{3}\right)$

Now Try Exercise 75.

EXAMPLE 7   **Using a Calculator to Solve Natural Logarithmic Equations**

Solve each equation and give the result to four decimal places:

a. $\ln x = 1.335$ **b.** $\ln x = \log 5.5$

SOLUTION   We will write the equation in exponential form and use our calculator to find x.

a. The equation $\ln x = 1.335$ is equivalent to $e^{1.335} = x$. We will use a calculator to evaluate the expression. $x = e^{1.335} \approx 3.8000$.

b. The equation $\ln x = \log 5.5$ is equivalent to $e^{\log 5.5} = x$. Using a calculator, we find $x = e^{\log 5.5} \approx 2.0967$.

Self Check 7   Solve each equation and give each result to four decimal places:

a. $\ln x = 1.9344$ **b.** $\log x = \ln 3.2$

Now Try Exercise 85.

4. Graph Logarithmic Functions

To draw the graph of a logarithmic function, we will use the fact that a logarithmic function is the inverse of an exponential function.

To graph the logarithmic function $y = f(x) = \log_2 x$, we calculate and plot several points with coordinates (x, y) that satisfy the equivalent equation $x = 2^y$. After joining these points with a smooth curve, we have the graph shown in Figure 4-19.

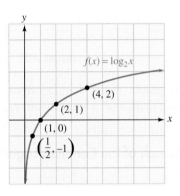

$f(x) = \log_2 x$		
x	$f(x)$	$(x, f(x))$
$\dfrac{1}{4}$	-2	$\left(\dfrac{1}{4}, -2\right)$
$\dfrac{1}{2}$	-1	$\left(\dfrac{1}{2}, -1\right)$
1	0	$(1, 0)$
2	1	$(2, 1)$
4	2	$(4, 2)$
8	3	$(8, 3)$

FIGURE 4-19

EXAMPLE 8   **Graphing a Logarithmic Function**

Graph: $y = f(x) = \log_{1/2} x$.

SOLUTION   To graph $y = f(x) = \log_{1/2} x$. we calculate and plot several points with coordinates (x, y) that satisfy the equation $x = \left(\dfrac{1}{2}\right)^y$. After joining these points with a smooth curve, we have the graph shown in Figure 4-20.

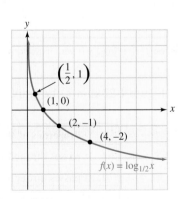

$f(x) = \log_{1/2} x$		
x	$f(x)$	$(x, f(x))$
$\dfrac{1}{4}$	2	$\left(\dfrac{1}{4}, 2\right)$
$\dfrac{1}{2}$	1	$\left(\dfrac{1}{2}, 1\right)$
1	0	$(1, 0)$
2	-1	$(2, -1)$
4	-2	$(4, -2)$
8	-3	$(8, -3)$

FIGURE 4-20

Self Check 8   Graph: $y = f(x) = \log_6 x$.

Now Try Exercise 105.

The graphs of all logarithmic functions are similar to those in Figure 4-21. If $b > 1$, the logarithmic function is an increasing function, as in Figure 4-21(a). If $0 < b < 1$, the logarithmic function is a decreasing function, as in Figure 4-21(b). We also know that the exponential function $f(x) = b^x$ and the logarithmic function $f(x) = \log_b x$ are inverse functions and therefore symmetric about the line $y = x$, as in Figure 4-21(c) and (d).

FIGURE 4-21

To graph, $f(x) = \log_{10} x$, we can plot points that satisfy the equation $x = 10^y$ and join them with a smooth curve, as shown in Figure 4-22.

The Graph of the Common Logarithm Function $f(x) = \log_{10} x$

$f(x) = \log x$		
x	$f(x)$	$(x, f(x))$
$\dfrac{1}{100}$	-2	$\left(\dfrac{1}{100}, -2\right)$
$\dfrac{1}{10}$	-1	$\left(\dfrac{1}{10}, -1\right)$
1	0	$(1, 0)$
10	1	$(10, 1)$
100	2	$(100, 2)$

FIGURE 4-22

Comment   The function $f(x) = \log_{10} x$ is very important and its graph should be memorized.

As Figure 4-22 shows, the graph of $f(x) = \log_b x$ has these properties:

Properties of the Graph of $f(x) = \log_b x$
1. It passes through the point $(1, 0)$.
2. It passes through the point $(b, 1)$.
3. The y-axis is a vertical asymptote.
4. The domain is $(0, \infty)$, and the range is $(-\infty, \infty)$.

To graph $f(x) = \ln x$, we can plot points that satisfy the equation $x = e^y$ and join them with a smooth curve, as shown in Figure 4-23.

The Graph of the Natural Logarithm Function $f(x) = \ln x$

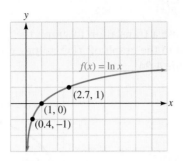

$f(x) = \ln x$		
x	$f(x)$	$(x, f(x))$
$\dfrac{1}{e} \approx 0.4$	-1	$(0.4, -1)$
1.0	0	$(1, 0)$
$e \approx 2.7$	1	$(2.7, 1)$
$e^2 \approx 7.4$	2	$(7.4, 2)$

FIGURE 4-23

Comment

The function $y = \ln x$ is very important and its graph should be memorized. The functions $y = e^x$ and $y = \ln x$ are inverses.

From the definition of logarithm, we know that

$$y = \ln x \quad \text{if and only if} \quad x = e^y \quad \text{Remember that } \ln x = \log_e x.$$

Thus, $\ln e = 1$ because $e^1 = e$. This is an important property of the natural logarithm function. Two other important properties follow from the fact that $y = \ln x$ and $y = e^x$ are inverses:

$$\ln e^x = x \quad \text{and} \quad e^{\ln x} = x.$$

These two properties and examples are shown in the table:

Properties Involving e and ln	Examples
$\ln e^x = x$	$\ln e^8 = 8$
	$\ln e^{-5x} = -5x$
	$\ln e^{3x+2} = 3x + 2$
$e^{\ln x} = x$	$e^{\ln 4} = 4$
	$e^{\ln(7x)} = 7x$
	$e^{\ln(9x-2)} = 9x - 2$

5. Use Transformations to Graph Logarithmic Functions

The graphs of many functions involving logarithms are transformations of the basic logarithmic graphs. A summary of these are shown in the table for $k > 0$.

Equation	Transformations of the Graph of $f(x) = \log_b x$
$y = \log_b x + k$	Translates the graph of $f(x) = \log_b x$ upward k units
$y = \log_b x - k$	Translates the graph of $f(x) = \log_b x$ downward k units
$y = \log_b(x - k)$	Translates the graph of $f(x) = \log_b x$ to the right k units
$y = \log_b(x + k)$	Translates the graph of $f(x) = \log_b x$ to the left k units
$y = -\log_b x$	Reflects the graph of $f(x) = \log_b x$ about the x-axis
$y = \log_b(-x)$	Reflects the graph of $f(x) = \log_b x$ about the y-axis
$y = k \log_b x$	• Vertically stretches the graph of $y = \log_b x$ if $k > 1$ • Vertically shrinks the graph of $y = \log_b x$ if $0 < k < 1$
$y = \log_b(kx)$	• Horizontally stretches the graph of $y = \log_b x$ if $0 < k < 1$ • Horizontally shrinks the graph of $y = \log_b x$ if $k > 1$

EXAMPLE 9   **Using a Translation to Graph a Logarithmic Function**

Graph: $g(x) = 3 + \log_2 x$.

SOLUTION   We can use a translation to graph the function. The graph of $g(x) = 3 + \log_2 x$ is identical to the graph of $f(x) = \log_2 x$, except that it is translated 3 units upward. See Figure 4-24.

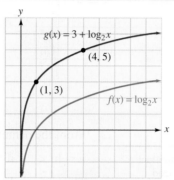

FIGURE 4-24

Self Check 9   Graph: $g(x) = -2 + \log_3 x$.

Now Try Exercise 111.

EXAMPLE 10   **Using a Translation to Graph a Logarithmic Function**

Graph: $g(x) = \log_{1/2}(x - 1)$.

SOLUTION   We can use a translation to graph the function. The graph of $g(x) = \log_{1/2}(x - 1)$ is identical to the graph of $f(x) = \log_{1/2} x$, except that it is translated 1 unit to the right. See Figure 4-25.

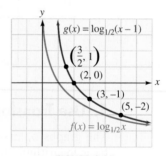

FIGURE 4-25

Self Check 10   Graph: $g(x) = \log_{1/3}(x + 2)$.

Now Try Exercise 113.

Many graphs of logarithmic functions involve translations of the graph of $f(x) = \ln x$. Consider the calculator graphs of the functions $f(x) = \ln x$, $g(x) = 2 + \ln x$, and $h(x) = -2 + \ln x$.

FIGURE 4-26

The graph of $f(x) = \ln x$ is the middle graph shown.

The graph of $g(x) = 2 + \ln x$ is 2 units above the graph of $f(x) = \ln x$.

The graph of $h(x) = -2 + \ln x$ is 2 units below the graph of $f(x) = \ln x$.

Figure 4-27 shows a calculator graph of the functions $f(x) = \ln x$, $g(x) = \ln(x + 2)$, and $h(x) = \ln(x - 2)$.

The graph of $f(x) = \ln x$ is the middle graph shown.

The graph of $g(x) = \ln(x + 2)$ is 2 units to the left of the graph of $f(x) = \ln x$.

The graph of $h(x) = \ln(x - 2)$ is 2 units to the right of the graph of $f(x) = \ln x$.

FIGURE 4-27

ACCENT ON TECHNOLOGY   **Graphing Logarithmic Functions**

Graphing calculators can be used to graph logarithmic functions. However, the only bases that are built in are 10 and e. There is a way to graph logarithmic functions in other bases, but it involves changing the base. We will cover that in Section 4.5. In most applications either common logarithms or natural logarithms are used. When we are graphing logarithmic functions on a graphing calculator, we need to be aware of the domain so that we can set a proper window.

• Graph: $f(x) = -2 + \log_{10}\left(\frac{1}{2}x\right)$.

To graph the function, we enter the right-hand side of the equation and use WINDOW settings of $[-1, 5]$ for x and $[-5, 1]$ for y. The graph is shown in Figure 4-28.

FIGURE 4-28

• Notice that the graph in Figure 4-28 appears to stop on the left and not continue toward negative infinity. That is a result of how the calculator plots points as it approaches the vertical asymptote.

Self Check Answers   **1.** $\log_{13} \dfrac{1}{169} = -2$ **2.** $5^4 = 625$ **3. a.** 2 **b.** 4 **c.** -2

4. a. -2 **b.** 6 **c.** $\dfrac{1}{2}$ **5.** 75.3998   **6. a.** 1.1447 **b.** no value

7. a. 6.9199 **b.** 14.5596

8.   **9.**   **10.**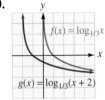

Exercises **4.3**

Getting Ready
You should be able to complete these vocabulary and concept statements before you proceed to the practice exercises.

Fill in the blanks.

1. The equation $y = \log_b x$ is equivalent to _____.
2. The domain of a logarithmic function is the interval _____.
3. The _____ of a logarithmic function is the interval $(-\infty, \infty)$.
4. $b^{\log_b x} = $ ___.
5. Because the exponential function is one-to-one, it has an _____ function.
6. The inverse of an exponential function is called a _____ function.
7. $\log_b x$ is the _____ to which b is raised to get x.
8. The y-axis is an _____ of a graph of $f(x) = \log_b x$.
9. The graph of $f(x) = \log_b x$ passes through the points _____ and _____.
10. $\log_{10} 10^x = $ ___.
11. $\ln x$ means _____.
12. The domain of the function $f(x) = \ln x$ is the interval _____.
13. The range of the function $f(x) = \ln x$ is the interval _____.
14. The graph of $f(x) = \ln x$ has the _____ as an asymptote
15. In the expression $\log x$, the base is understood to be ___.
16. In the expression $\ln x$, the base is understood to be ___.

Practice
Write each equation in logarithmic form.

17. $8^2 = 64$ 18. $10^3 = 1{,}000$

19. $4^{-2} = \dfrac{1}{16}$ 20. $3^{-4} = \dfrac{1}{81}$

21. $\left(\dfrac{1}{2}\right)^{-5} = 32$ 22. $\left(\dfrac{1}{3}\right)^{-3} = 27$

23. $x^y = z$ 24. $m^n = p$

Write each equation in exponential form.

25. $\log_3 81 = 4$ 26. $\log_7 7 = 1$

27. $\log_{1/2} \dfrac{1}{8} = 3$ 28. $\log_{1/5} 1 = 0$

29. $\log_4 \dfrac{1}{64} = -3$ 30. $\log_6 \dfrac{1}{36} = -2$

31. $\log_\pi \pi = 1$ 32. $\log_7 \dfrac{1}{49} = -2$

Find each value of x.

33. $\log_2 8 = x$ 34. $\log_3 9 = x$

35. $\log_4 \dfrac{1}{64} = x$ 36. $\log_6 216 = x$

37. $\log_{1/2} \dfrac{1}{8} = x$ 38. $\log_{1/3} \dfrac{1}{81} = x$

39. $\log_9 3 = x$ 40. $\log_{125} 5 = x$

41. $\log_{1/2} 8 = x$ 42. $\log_{1/2} 16 = x$

43. $\log_8 x = 2$ 44. $\log_7 x = 0$

45. $\log_7 x = 1$ 46. $\log_2 x = 8$

47. $\log_{25} x = \dfrac{1}{2}$ 48. $\log_4 x = \dfrac{1}{2}$

49. $\log_5 x = -2$ 50. $\log_3 x = -4$

51. $\log_{36} x = -\dfrac{1}{2}$ 52. $\log_{27} x = -\dfrac{1}{3}$

53. $\log_x 5^3 = 3$ 54. $\log_x 5 = 1$

55. $\log_x \dfrac{9}{4} = 2$ 56. $\log_x \dfrac{\sqrt{3}}{3} = \dfrac{1}{2}$

57. $\log_x \dfrac{1}{64} = -3$ 58. $\log_x \dfrac{1}{100} = -2$

59. $\log_x \dfrac{9}{4} = -2$ 60. $\log_x \dfrac{\sqrt{3}}{3} = -\dfrac{1}{2}$

61. $2^{\log_2 5} = x$ 62. $3^{\log_3 4} = x$

63. $x^{\log_4 6} = 6$ 64. $x^{\log_3 8} = 8$

Use a calculator to find each value to four decimal places.

65. $\log 3.25$ 66. $\log 0.57$

67. $\log 0.00467$ 68. $\log 375.876$

69. $\ln 45.7$ 70. $\ln 0.005$

71. $\ln \dfrac{2}{3}$ 72. $\ln \dfrac{12}{7}$

73. $\ln 35.15$ 74. $\ln 0.675$

75. $\ln 7.896$ 76. $\ln 0.00465$

77. $\log(\ln 1.7)$ 78. $\ln(\log 9.8)$

79. $\ln(\log 0.1)$ 80. $\log(\ln 0.01)$

Use a calculator to find y to four decimal places, if possible.

81. $\log y = 1.4023$ **82.** $\log y = 0.926$

83. $\log y = -3.71$ **84.** $\log y = \log \pi$

85. $\ln y = 1.4023$ **86.** $\ln y = 2.6490$

87. $\ln y = 4.24$ **88.** $\ln y = 0.926$

89. $\ln y = -3.71$ **90.** $\ln y = -0.28$

91. $\log y = \ln 8$ **92.** $\ln y = \log 7$

Find each value without using a calculator.

93. $\log 10,000$ **94.** $\log 1,000,000$

95. $\log 0.001$ **96.** $\log \dfrac{1}{100,000}$

97. $e^{(\ln 7)}$ **98.** $e^{(\ln 9)}$

99. $\ln(e^4)$ **100.** $\ln(e^{-6})$

Find the value of b, if any, that would cause the graph of $y = \log_b x$ *to look like the graph shown.*

101.

102.

103.

104.

Graph each function.

105. $f(x) = \log_3 x$ **106.** $f(x) = \log_4 x$

107. $f(x) = \log_{1/3} x$ **108.** $f(x) = \log_{1/4} x$

109. $f(x) = -\log_5 x$ **110.** $f(x) = -\log_2 x$

111. $f(x) = 2 + \log_2 x$ **112.** $f(x) = \log_2(x - 1)$

113. $f(x) = \log_3(x + 2)$ **114.** $f(x) = -3 + \log_3 x$

115. $f(x) = 3 + \log_3(x + 1)$

116. $f(x) = -3 + \log_3(x + 1)$

pop culture. Since many students prefer their music loud, the loudness of sound and its intensity are interesting concepts. In this section, we will see that loudness of sound and the intensity of sound are related by a formula involving the natural logarithmic function.

1. Use Properties of Logarithms to Simplify Expressions

Since logarithms are exponents, the properties of exponents have counterparts in the theory of logarithms. We begin with four basic properties.

Properties of Logarithms   If b is a positive number and $b \neq 1$, then

1. $\log_b 1 = 0$ 2. $\log_b b = 1$
3. $\log_b b^x = x$ 4. $b^{\log_b x} = x$ $(x > 0)$

Properties 1 through 4 follow directly from the definition of logarithm.

1. $\log_b 1 = 0$, because $b^0 = 1$.
2. $\log_b b = 1$, because $b^1 = b$.
3. $\log_b b^x = x$, because $b^x = b^x$.
4. $b^{\log_b x} = x$, because $\log_b x$ is the exponent to which b is raised to get x.

Properties 3 and 4 also indicate that the composition of the exponential and logarithmic functions (in both directions) is the identity function. This is expected, because the exponential and logarithmic functions with the same base are inverse functions.

EXAMPLE 1   **Using Properties of Logarithms to Simplify Expressions**

Simplify each expression: **a.** $\log_3 1$ **b.** $\log_4 4$ **c.** $\log_7 7^3$ **d.** $b^{\log_b 3}$

SOLUTION   We can simplify each expression using the properties of logariathms.

a. By Property 1, $\log_3 1 = 0$, because $3^0 = 1$.

b. By Property 2, $\log_4 4 = 1$, because $4^1 = 4$.

c. By Property 3, $\log_7 7^3 = 3$, because $7^3 = 7^3$.

d. By Property 4, $b^{\log_b 3} = 3$, because $\log_b 3$ is the power to which b is raised to get 3. ∎

Self Check 1   Simplify: **a.** $\log_4 1$ **b.** $\log_3 3$ **c.** $\log_2 2^4$ **d.** $5^{\log_5 2}$

Now Try Exercise 13.

The four properties also hold for natural logarithms.

1. $\ln 1 = 0$, because $e^0 = 1$.
2. $\ln e = 1$, because $e^1 = e$.
3. $\ln e^x = x$, because $e^x = e^x$.
4. $e^{\ln x} = x$, because $\ln x$ is the exponent to which e is raised to get x.

The next two properties state that

The logarithm of a product is the sum of the logarithms.
The logarithm of a quotient is the difference of the logarithms.

The Logarithm of a Product and a Difference	If M, N, and b are positive numbers and $b \neq 1$, then

5. $\log_b MN = \log_b M + \log_b N$ **6.** $\log_b \dfrac{M}{N} = \log_b M - \log_b N$

Property 5 is known as the **Product Rule**.
Property 6 is known as the **Quotient Rule**.

PROOF   To prove Property 5, we let $x = \log_b M$ and $y = \log_b N$ and use the definition of logarithm to write each equation in exponential form.

$$M = b^x \quad \text{and} \quad N = b^y$$

Then $MN = b^x b^y$ and a property of exponents gives

$$MN = b^{x+y} \qquad b^x b^y = b^{x+y}; \text{ keep the base and add the exponents.}$$

We write this exponential equation in logarithmic form as

$$\log_b MN = x + y$$

Substituting the values of x and y completes the proof.

$$\log_b MN = \log_b M + \log_b N$$

The proof of Property 6 is similar. You will be asked to do it in an Exercise 111. ∎

Caution

By Property 5 of logarithms, the logarithm of a *product* is equal to the *sum* of the logarithms. The logarithm of a product is **not** the product of the logarithms:

$$\log_b MN = (\log_b M)(\log_b N)$$

Caution

The logarithm of a sum or a difference usually does **not** simplify. In general,

$$\log_b(M + N) = \log_b M + \log_b N$$

and

$$\log_b(M - N) = \log_b M - \log_b N$$

Caution

By Property 6, the logarithm of a *quotient* is equal to the *difference* of the logarithms. The logarithm of a quotient is **not** the quotient of the logarithms:

$$\log_b \frac{M}{N} = \frac{\log_b M}{\log_b N}$$

Properties 5 and 6 also hold for natural logarithms.

5. $\ln MN = \ln M + \ln N$ Product Rule

6. $\ln \dfrac{M}{N} = \ln M - \ln N$ Quotient Rule

EXAMPLE 2   Using the Product and Quotient Rules

Assume that x, y, z, and b are positive numbers and $b \neq 1$. Write each expression in terms of the logarithms of x, y, and z: **a.** $\log_b xyz$ **b.** $\ln \dfrac{x}{yz}$

SOLUTION   We can use the properties of logarithms to write each logarithm as the sum or difference of several logarithms.

a. $\log_b xyz = \log_b(xy)z$

$\qquad\qquad = \log_b(xy) + \log_b z \qquad$ The log of a product is the sum of the logs.

$\qquad\qquad = \log_b x + \log_b y + \log_b z \qquad$ The log of a product is the sum of the logs.

b. $\ln \dfrac{x}{yz} = \ln x - \ln(yz) \qquad$ The ln of a quotient is the difference of the natural logs.

$\qquad\qquad = \ln x - (\ln y + \ln z) \qquad$ The ln of a product is the sum of the natural logs.

$\qquad\qquad = \ln x - \ln y - \ln z \qquad$ Remove parentheses.

Self Check 2   Write the expression in terms of the logarithms of x, y, and z: $\log_b \dfrac{xy}{z}$

Now Try Exercise 27.

ACCENT ON TECHNOLOGY   **Product and Quotient Rules**

A graphing calculator can be used to verify the Product and Quotient Rules.

• Using the Product Rule, we can write the expression

$\ln(75 \cdot 20) = \ln 75 + \ln 20$

Using a graphing calculator, we can verify that these two are equal as shown in Figure 4-29.

FIGURE 4-29

• Using the Quotient Rule, we can write the expression

$\log \dfrac{240}{13} = \log 240 - \log 13.$

Using a graphing calculator, we can verify that these two are equal as shown in Figure 4-30.

FIGURE 4-30

Two more properties state that

The logarithm of a power is the power times the logarithm.

If the logarithms of two numbers are equal, the numbers are equal.

More Properties of Logarithms   If M and b are positive numbers and $b \neq 1$, then

> **7.** $\log_b M^p = p \log_b M$ **8.** If $\log_b x = \log_b y$, then $x = y$.
>
> Property 7 is known as the **Power Rule**.
> Property 8 is known as the **One-to-One Property**.

PROOF   To prove Property 7, we let $x = \log_b M$, write the expression in exponential form, and raise both sides to the pth power:

$$M = b^x$$

$$(M)^p = (b^x)^p \qquad \text{Raise both sides to the } p\text{th power.}$$

$$M^p = b^{px} \qquad \text{Keep the base and multiply the exponents.}$$

Using the definition of logarithm gives

$$\log_b M^p = px$$

Substituting the value for x completes the proof.

$$\log_b M^p = p \log_b M$$

Property 8 follows from the fact that the logarithmic function is a one-to-one function. Property 8 will be important in the next section when we solve logarithmic equations.

Properties 7 and 8 also hold for natural logarithms.

7. $\ln M^p = p \ln M$ Power Rule
8. If $\ln x = \ln y$, then $x = y$.

We can use the properties of logarithms to write a logarithm as the sum or difference of several logarithms.

EXAMPLE 3   **Using the Power Rule and Expanding a Logarithmic Expression**

Assume that x, y, z, and b are positive numbers and $b \neq 1$. Write each expression in terms of the logarithms of x, y, and z:

a. $\log_b(x^3 y^2 z)$ **b.** $\ln \dfrac{y^2 \sqrt{z}}{x}$

SOLUTION   We can use the properties of logarithms to write each logarithm as the sum or difference of several logarithms.

a. $\log_b(x^3 y^2 z) = \log_b x^3 + \log_b y^2 + \log_b z$ The log of a product is the sum of the logs.

$$= 3 \log_b x + 2 \log_b y + \log_b z \qquad \text{The log of a power is the power times the log.}$$

b. $\ln \dfrac{y^2 \sqrt{z}}{x} = \ln\left(y^2 \sqrt{z}\right) - \ln x$ The ln of a quotient is the difference of the natural logs.

$$= \ln y^2 + \ln z^{1/2} - \ln z \qquad \text{The ln of a product is the sum of the natural logs: } \sqrt{z} = z^{1/2}.$$

$$= 2 \ln y + \frac{1}{2} \ln z - \ln z \qquad \text{The ln of a power is the power times the ln.}$$

Self Check 3   Write the expression in terms of the logarithms of x, y, and z: $\log_b \sqrt[3]{\dfrac{x^2 y}{z}}$.

Now Try Exercise 35.

ACCENT ON TECHNOLOGY   **Applying the Power Rule**

The development of calculators has made computations extremely easy and accurate, but hand-held calculators have a limit to the size of numbers they can display and evaluate.

- For example, if we were to try to calculate $\log 12^{1000}$, see Figure 4-31(a), we would most likely get an overflow error message as shown in Figure 4-31(b). However, by applying the Power Rule, the number can be evaluated with our calculator as shown in Figure 4-31(c).

| (a) | (b) | (c) |

FIGURE 4-31

We can use the properties of logarithms to combine several logarithms into one logarithm.

EXAMPLE 4   **Combining Logarithmic Expressions**

Assume that x, y, z, and b are positive numbers and $b \neq 1$. Write each expression as one logarithm:

a. $2 \log_b x + \dfrac{1}{3} \log_b y$ **b.** $\dfrac{1}{2} \log_b(x - 2) - \log_b y + 3 \log_b z$

SOLUTION   We can use the properties of logarithms to combine several logarithms into one logarithm.

a. $2 \log_b x + \dfrac{1}{3} \log_b y = \log_b x^2 + \log_b y^{1/3}$ A power times a log is the log of the power.

$\qquad\qquad\qquad = \log_b(x^2 y^{1/3})$ The sum of two logs is the log of the product.

$\qquad\qquad\qquad = \log_b\left(x^2 \sqrt[3]{y}\right)$

b. $\dfrac{1}{2} \log_b(x - 2) - \log_b y + 3 \log_b z$

$\qquad = \log_b(x - 2)^{1/2} - \log_b y + \log_b z^3$ A power times a log is the log of the power.

$\qquad = \log_b \dfrac{(x - 2)^{1/2}}{y} + \log_b z^3$ The difference of two logs is the log of the quotient.

$\qquad = \log_b \dfrac{z^3 \sqrt{x - 2}}{y}$ The sum of two logs is the log of the product.

Self Check 4   Write as one logarithm: $2 \ln x + \dfrac{1}{2} \ln y - 3 \ln(x - y)$.

Now Try Exercise 45.

We summarize the eight properties of logarithms and natural logarithms as follows.

Summary of the Properties of Logarithms

If b, M, and N are positive numbers and $b \neq 1$, then

1. $\log_b 1 = 0$
2. $\log_b b = 1$
3. $\log_b b^x = x$
4. $b^{\log_b x} = x$
5. $\log_b MN = \log_b M + \log_b N$
6. $\log_b \dfrac{M}{N} = \log_b M - \log_b N$
7. $\log_b M^p = p \log_b M$
8. If $\log_b x = \log_b y$, then $x = y$.

1. $\ln 1 = 0$
2. $\ln e = 1$
3. $\ln e^x = x$
4. $e^{\ln x} = x$
5. $\ln MN = \ln M + \ln N$
6. $\ln \dfrac{M}{N} = \ln M - \ln N$
7. $\ln M^p = p \ln M$
8. If $\ln x = \ln y$, then $x = y$.

EXAMPLE 5   Using Properties of Logarithms to Find Approximations

Given that $\log_{10} 2 \approx 0.3010$ and $\log_{10} 3 \approx 0.4771$, find approximations for

a. $\log_{10} 18$ **b.** $\log_{10} 2.5$

SOLUTION   We will use the properties of logarithms to write each expression in terms of known logarithms. Then, we can substitute the values of the known logarithms and simplify.

a. $\log_{10} 18 = \log_{10}(2 \cdot 3^2)$

$\qquad = \log_{10} 2 + \log_{10} 3^2$ The log of a product is the sum of the logs.

$\qquad = \log_{10} 2 + 2 \log_{10} 3$ The log of a power is the power times the log.

$\qquad \approx 0.3010 + 2(0.4771)$

$\qquad \approx 1.2552$

b. $\log_{10} 2.5 = \log_{10}\left(\dfrac{5}{2}\right)$

$\qquad = \log_{10} 5 - \log_{10} 2$ The log of a quotient is the difference of the logs.

$\qquad = \log_{10} \dfrac{10}{2} - \log_{10} 2$ Write 5 as $\dfrac{10}{2}$.

$\qquad = \log_{10} 10 - \log_{10} 2 - \log_{10} 2$ The log of a quotient is the difference of the logs.

$\qquad = 1 - 2 \log_{10} 2$ $\log_{10} 10 = 1$

$\qquad \approx 1 - 2(0.3010)$

$\qquad \approx 0.3980$

Self Check 5   Use the information given in Example 5 to find an approximation for $\log_{10} 0.75$.

Now Try Exercise 77.

Comment   In Example 5, it is important to note that we can use logarithmic values that are not stated in the problem. For example, $\log 10 = 1$, $\log 100 = 2$, and $\log 1000 = 3$.

2. Use the Change-of-Base Formula

We have seen how to use a calculator to find base-10 and base-e logarithms. To use a calculator to find logarithms with different bases, such as $\log_7 63$, we can divide the base-10 (or base-e) logarithm of 63 by the base-10 (or base-e) logarithm of 7.

$$\log_7 63 = \frac{\log 63}{\log 7} \qquad\qquad \log_7 63 = \frac{\ln 63}{\ln 7}$$

$$\approx 2.129150068 \qquad\qquad \approx 2.129150068$$

To check the result, we verify that $7^{2.129150063} \approx 63$. This example suggests that if we know the base-a logarithm of a number, we can find its logarithm to some other base b.

Change-of-Base Formula   If a, b, and x are positive numbers and $a \neq 1$ and $b \neq 1$, then

$$\log_b x = \frac{\log_a x}{\log_a b}$$

To prove this formula, we begin with the equation $\log_b x = y$.

$y = \log_b x$

$x = b^y$ \qquad\qquad Change the equation from logarithmic to exponential form.

$\log_a x = \log_a b^y$ \qquad\qquad Take the base-a logarithm of both sides.

$\log_a x = y \log_a b$ \qquad\qquad The log of a power is the power times the log.

$y = \dfrac{\log_a x}{\log_a b}$ \qquad\qquad Divide both sides by $\log_a b$.

$\log_b x = \dfrac{\log_a x}{\log_a b}$ \qquad\qquad Refer to the first equation and substitute $\log_b x$ for y.

Caution

$\dfrac{\log_a x}{\log_a b}$ means that one logarithm is to be divided by the other. They are **not** to be subtracted.

If we know logarithms to base a (for example, $a = 10$), we can find the logarithm of x to a new base b by dividing the base-a logarithm of x by the base-a logarithm of b.

EXAMPLE 6   **Using the Change-of-Base Formula**

Use the Change-of-Base Formula to find $\log_3 5$.

SOLUTION   We can substitute 3 for b, 10 for a, and 5 for x into the Change-of-Base Formula and simplify.

$$\log_b x = \frac{\log_a x}{\log_a b}$$

$$\log_3 5 = \frac{\log_{10} 5}{\log_{10} 3} \qquad\qquad \text{Divide the base-10 logarithm of 5 by the base-10 logarithm of 3.}$$

$$\approx 1.464973521$$

To four decimal places, $\log_3 5 = 1.4650$.   ∎

Self Check 6   Find $\log_5 3$ to four decimal places.

Now Try Exercise 89.

ACCENT ON TECHNOLOGY	**Using the Change-of-Base Formula to Graph a Logarithmic Function**

We can use the Change-of-Base Formula to graph logarithmic functions that do not have a base of 10. Consider the function

$$f(x) = \log_4(x + 1)$$

- Since the base of the function $f(x) = \log_4(x + 1)$ is 4, to graph this function on a calculator, we use the Change-of-Base Formula and rewrite the function as

$$f(x) = \log_4(x + 1) = \frac{\log(x + 1)}{\log 4}$$

We enter the function as shown in Figure 4-32(a). We can also use the natural logarithm function if we prefer.
- The domain of this function is $(-1, \infty)$, so there will be a vertical asymptote of $x = -1$. This will help us set our [WINDOW]. We then [GRAPH] the function. See Figures 4-32(b) and (c).
- Notice that the graph appears to "stop" at $x = -1$, but that is not the case. We can have the calculator evaluate the function at a value very close to $x = -1$ to verify this. Notice in Figure 4-32(d) that the point on the graph is not shown, but the value is indicated.

Enter the function.

Set the window.

(a)

(b)

Graph the function.

Calculate value close to $x = -1$.

(c)

(d)

FIGURE 4-32

We can use properties of logarithms to solve many problems.

3. Use Logarithms to Solve pH Problems

The more acidic a chemical solution, the greater the concentration of hydrogen ions. Chemists measure this concentration indirectly by the **pH scale,** or the **hydrogen ion index.**

pH of a Solution	If $[H^+]$ is the hydrogen ion concentration in gram-ions per liter, then

$$pH = -\log[H^+]$$

Since pure water has approximately 10^{-7} gram-ions per liter, its pH is

$$\text{pH} = -\log[\text{H}^+]$$
$$\text{pH} = -\log \mathbf{10^{-7}}$$
$$= -(-7)\log 10 \qquad \text{The log of a power is the power times the log.}$$
$$= -(-7) \cdot 1 \qquad \text{Use Property 2 of logarithms: } \log_b b = 1.$$
$$= 7$$

EXAMPLE 7   **Solving an Application Involving pH**

Seawater has a pH of approximately 8.5. Find its hydrogen ion concentration.

SOLUTION   We can substitute 8.5 for pH and solve the equation $\text{pH} = -\log[\text{H}^+]$ for $[\text{H}^+]$.

$$8.5 = -\log[\text{H}^+]$$
$$-8.5 = \log[\text{H}^+]$$
$$[\text{H}^+] = 10^{-8.5} \qquad \text{Change the equation from logarithmic form to exponential form.}$$

We can then use a calculator to find that $[\text{H}^+] \approx 3.2 \times 10^{-9}$ gram-ions per liter.

Self Check 7   The pH of a solution is 5.7. Find the hydrogen ion concentration.

Now Try Exercise 101.

4. Use Logarithms to Solve Problems in Electronics

Recall that if E_O is the output voltage of a device and E_I is the input voltage, the decibel voltage gain is given by

$$(1) \quad \textbf{dB gain} = 20 \log \frac{E_O}{E_I}$$

If input and output are measured in watts instead of volts, a different formula is needed.

EXAMPLE 8   **Finding an Alternate Formula for Voltage Gain**

Show that an alternate formula for dB voltage gain is

$$\text{dB gain} = 10 \log \frac{P_O}{P_I}$$

where P_I is the power input and P_O is the power output.

SOLUTION   Power is directly proportional to the square of the voltage. So for some constant k,

$$P_I = k(E_I)^2 \qquad \text{and} \qquad P_O = k(E_O)^2$$

and

$$\frac{P_O}{P_I} = \frac{k(E_O)^2}{k(E_I)^2} = \left(\frac{E_O}{E_I}\right)^2$$

We raise both sides to the $\frac{1}{2}$ power to get

$$\frac{E_O}{E_I} = \left(\frac{P_O}{P_I}\right)^{1/2}$$

which we substitute into Equation (1) for dB gain.

$$\text{dB gain} = 20 \log \frac{E_O}{E_I}$$

$$= 20 \log \left(\frac{P_O}{P_I} \right)^{1/2}$$

$$= 20 \cdot \frac{1}{2} \log \frac{P_O}{P_I} \qquad \text{The log of a power is the power times the log.}$$

$$\text{dB gain} = 10 \log \frac{P_O}{P_I} \qquad \text{Simplify.}$$

Self Check 8   Find the dB gain of a device to the nearest hundredth when $P_O = 30$ watts and $P_I = 2$ watts.

Now Try Exercise 103.

5. Use Logarithms to Solve Physiology Problems

In physiology, experiments suggest that the relationship between the loudness and the intensity of sound is a logarithmic one known as the Weber–Fechner Law.

Weber–Fechner Law   If L is the apparent loudness of a sound and I is the intensity, then

$$L = k \ln I$$

EXAMPLE 9   **Using the Weber-Fechner Law**

What increase in the intensity of a sound is necessary to cause a doubling of the apparent loudness?

SOLUTION   We use the formula $L = k \ln I$. To double the apparent loudness, we multiply both sides of the equation by 2 and use Property 7 of logarithms.

$$L = k \ln I$$

$$2L = 2k \ln I$$

$$= k \ln I^2$$

To double the apparent loudness, we must square the intensity.

Self Check 9   What increase is necessary to triple the apparent loudness?

Now Try Exercise 105.

Self Check Answers   **1. a.** 0   **b.** 1   **c.** 4   **d.** 2   **2.** $\log_b x + \log_b y - \log_b z$

3. $\dfrac{1}{3}(2 \log_b x + \log_b y - \log_b z)$ **4.** $\ln \dfrac{x^2 \sqrt{y}}{(x - y)^3}$

5. -0.1249 **6.** 0.6826 **7.** 2×10^{-6} **8.** 11.76 decibels
9. Cube the intensity.

Exercises **4.5**

Getting Ready
You should be able to complete these vocabulary and concept statements before you proceed to the practice exercises.

Fill in the blanks.

1. $\log_b 1 = \underline{\hphantom{xx}}$

2. $\log_b b = \underline{\hphantom{xx}}$

3. $\log_b MN = \log_b \underline{\hphantom{xx}} + \log_b \underline{\hphantom{xx}}$

4. $b^{\log_b x} = \underline{\hphantom{xx}}$

5. If $\log_b x = \log_b y$, then $\underline{\hphantom{xx}} = \underline{\hphantom{xx}}$.

6. $\log_b \dfrac{M}{N} = \log_b M \underline{\hphantom{xx}} \log_b N$

7. $\log_b x^p = p \cdot \log_b \underline{\hphantom{xx}}$

8. $\log_b b^x = \underline{\hphantom{xx}}$

9. $\log_b(A + B) \underline{\hphantom{xx}} \log_b A + \log_b B$

10. $\log_b A + \log_b B \underline{\hphantom{xx}} \log_b AB$

Simplify each expression.

11. $\log_4 1 = \underline{\hphantom{xx}}$

12. $\log_4 4 = \underline{\hphantom{xx}}$

13. $\log_4 4^7 = \underline{\hphantom{xx}}$

14. $4^{\log_4 8} = \underline{\hphantom{xx}}$

15. $5^{\log_5 10} = \underline{\hphantom{xx}}$

16. $\log_5 5^2 = \underline{\hphantom{xx}}$

17. $\log_5 5 = \underline{\hphantom{xx}}$

18. $\log_5 1 = \underline{\hphantom{xx}}$

Practice
 Use a calculator to verify each equation.

19. $\log[(3.7)(2.9)] = \log 3.7 + \log 2.9$

20. $\ln \dfrac{9.3}{2.1} = \ln 9.3 - \ln 2.1$

21. $\ln(3.7)^3 = 3 \ln 3.7$

22. $\log\sqrt{14.1} = \dfrac{1}{2} \log 14.1$

23. $\log 3.2 = \dfrac{\ln 3.2}{\ln 10}$

24. $\ln 9.7 = \dfrac{\log 9.7}{\log e}$

Assume that x, y, z, and b are positive numbers and $b \neq 1$. Use the properties of logarithms to write each expression in terms of the logarithms of x, y, and z.

25. $\log_b 2xy$

26. $\log_b 3xz$

27. $\log_b \dfrac{2x}{y}$

28. $\log_b \dfrac{x}{yz}$

29. $\log_b x^2 y^3$

30. $\log_b x^3 y^2 z$

31. $\log_b(xy)^{1/3}$

32. $\log_b x^{1/2} y^3$

33. $\log_b x\sqrt{z}$

34. $\log_b \sqrt{xy}$

35. $\log_b \dfrac{\sqrt[3]{x}}{\sqrt[3]{yz}}$

36. $\log_b \sqrt[4]{\dfrac{x^3 y^2}{z^4}}$

37. $\ln x^7 y^8$

38. $\ln \dfrac{4x}{y}$

39. $\ln \dfrac{x}{y^4 z}$

40. $\ln x\sqrt{y}$

Assume that x, y, z, and b are positive numbers and $b \neq 1$. Use the properties of logarithms to write each expression as the logarithm of one quantity.

41. $\log_b(x + 1) - \log_b x$

42. $\log_b x + \log_b(x + 2) - \log_b 8$

43. $2 \log_b x + \dfrac{1}{3} \log_b y$

44. $-2 \log_b x - 3 \log_b y + \log_b z$

45. $-3 \log_b x - 2 \log_b y + \dfrac{1}{2} \log_b z$

46. $3 \log_b(x + 1) - 2 \log_b(x + 2) + \log_b x$

47. $\log_b\left(\dfrac{x}{z} + x\right) - \log_b\left(\dfrac{y}{z} + y\right)$

48. $\log_b(xy + y^2) - \log_b(xz + yz) + \log_b z$

49. $\ln x + \ln(x + 5) - \ln 9$

50. $5 \ln x + \dfrac{1}{5} \ln y$

51. $-6 \ln x - 2 \ln y + \ln z$

52. $-2 \ln x - 3 \ln y + \dfrac{1}{3} \ln z$

Determine whether each statement is true or false.

53. $\log_b ab = \log_b a + 1$

54. $\log_b \dfrac{1}{a} = -\log_b a$

55. $\log_b 0 = 1$

56. $\log_b 2 = \log_2 b$

57. $\log_b(x + y) \neq \log_b x + \log_b y$

58. $\log_b xy = (\log_b x)(\log_b y)$

59. If $\log_a b = c$, then $\log_b a = c$.

60. If $\log_a b = c$, then $\log_b a = \dfrac{1}{c}$.

61. $\log_7 7^7 = 7$

62. $7^{\log_7 7} = 7$

63. $\log_b(-x) = -\log_b x$

64. If $\log_b a = c$, then $\log_b a^p = pc$.

65. $\dfrac{\log_b A}{\log_b B} = \log_b A - \log_b B$

66. $\log_b(A - B) = \dfrac{\log_b A}{\log_b B}$

67. $\log_b \dfrac{1}{5} = -\log_b 5$

68. $3 \log_b \sqrt[3]{a} = \log_b a$

69. $\dfrac{1}{3} \log_b a^3 = \log_b a$

70. $\log_{4/3} y = -\log_{3/4} y$

71. $\log_b y + \log_{1/b} y = 0$

72. $\log_{10} 10^3 = 3(10^{\log_{10} 3})$

73. $\ln xy = (\ln x)(\ln y)$

74. $\dfrac{\ln A}{\ln B} = \ln A - \ln B$

75. $\dfrac{1}{5} \ln a^5 = \ln a$

76. $\ln y = -\ln \dfrac{1}{y}$

Given that $\log_{10} 4 \approx 0.6021$, $\log_{10} 7 \approx 0.8451$, and $\log_{10} 9 \approx 0.9542$, use these values and the properties of logarithms to approximate each value. Do not use a calculator.

77. $\log_{10} 28$

78. $\log_{10} \dfrac{7}{4}$

79. $\log_{10} 2.25$

80. $\log_{10} 36$

81. $\log_{10} \dfrac{63}{4}$

82. $\log_{10} \dfrac{4}{63}$

83. $\log_{10} 252$

84. $\log_{10} 49$

85. $\log_{10} 112$

86. $\log_{10} 324$

87. $\log_{10} \dfrac{144}{49}$

88. $\log_{10} \dfrac{324}{63}$

Use a calculator and the Change-of-Base Formula to find each logarithm. Round to four decimal places.

89. $\log_3 7$

90. $\log_7 3$

91. $\log_\pi 3$

92. $\log_3 \pi$

93. $\log_3 8$

94. $\log_5 10$

95. $\log_{\sqrt{2}} \sqrt{5}$

96. $\log_\pi e$

Applications

97. pH of water slide The water in the Abyss, a water slide at the Atlantis Resort in the Bahamas, has a hydrogen ion concentration of 6.3×10^{-8} gram-ions per liter. Find the pH.

98. pH of swimming pool The ideal pH for a swimming pool is 7.2, the same pH as our eyes. The swimming pool at the local YMCA has a hydrogen ion concentration of 1.6×10^{-7} gram-ions per liter. Find the pH of the pool. Is this ideal?

99. pH of a solution Find the pH of a solution with a hydrogen ion concentration of 1.7×10^{-5} gram-ions per liter.

100. pH of calcium hydroxide Find the hydrogen ion concentration of a saturated solution of calcium hydroxide whose pH is 13.2.

101. pH of apples The pH of apples can range from 2.9 to 3.3. Find the range in the hydrogen ion concentration.

Mazzur/Shutterstock.com

102. pH of sour pickles The hydrogen ion concentration of sour pickles is 6.31×10^{-4}. Find the pH.

© Istockphoto.com/James McQuillan

103. dB gain An amplifier produces a 40-watt output with a $\frac{1}{2}$-watt input. Find the dB gain.

104. dB loss Losses in a long telephone line reduce a 12-watt input signal to an output of 3 watts. Find the dB gain. (Because it is a loss, the "gain" will be negative.)

105. Weber–Fechner Law What increase in intensity is necessary to quadruple the loudness?

106. Weber–Fechner Law What decrease in intensity is necessary to make a sound half as loud?

107. Isothermal expansion If a certain amount E of energy is added to one mole of a gas, it expands from an initial volume of 1 liter to a final volume V without changing its temperature according to the formula

$$E = 8,300 \ln V$$

Find the volume if twice that energy is added to the gas.

108. Richter scale By what factor must the amplitude of an earthquake change to increase its severity by 1 point on the Richter scale? Assume that the period remains constant. The Richter scale is given by

$$R = \log \frac{A}{P}$$

where A is the amplitude and P the period of the tremor.

Discovery and Writing

109. Simplify: $3^{4\log_3 2} + 5^{\frac{1}{2}\log_5 25}$

110. Find the value of $a - b$:

$$5 \log x + \frac{1}{3} \log y - \frac{1}{2} \log x - \frac{5}{6} \log y = \log(x^a y^b)$$

111. Prove Property 6 of logarithms:

$$\log_b \frac{M}{N} = \log_b M - \log_b N$$

112. Show that $-\log_b x = \log_{1/b} x$.

113. Show that $e^{x \ln a} = a^x$.

114. Show that $e^{\ln x} = x$.

115. Show that $\ln(e^x) = x$.

116. If $\log_b 3x = 1 + \log_b x$, find b.

117. Explain why $\ln(\log 0.9)$ is undefined.

118. Explain why $\log_b(\ln 1)$ is undefined.

In Exercises 119–120, A and B both are negative. Thus, AB and $\frac{A}{B}$ are positive, and $\log AB$ and $\log \frac{A}{B}$ are defined.

119. Is it still true that $\log AB = \log A + \log B$? Explain.

120. Is it still true that $\log \frac{A}{B} = \log A - \log B$? Explain.

Review
Determine whether each equation defines a function.

121. $y = 3x - 1$

122. $y = \dfrac{x + 3}{x - 1}$

123. $y^2 = 4x$

124. $y = 4x^2$

Find the domain of each function.

125. $f(x) = x^2 - 4$

126. $f(x) = \dfrac{1}{x^2 - 4}$

127. $f(x) = \sqrt{x^2 + 4}$

128. $f(x) = \sqrt{x^2 - 4}$

4.6 Exponential and Logarithmic Equations

In this section, we will learn to

1. Use like bases to solve exponential equations.
2. Use logarithms to solve exponential equations.
3. Solve logarithmic equations.
4. Solve carbon-14 dating problems.
5. Solve population growth problems.

Coffee is one of the most popular beverages worldwide. Suppose we visit a coffee shop and order a white chocolate mocha. After blending smooth white chocolate with rich espresso and steamed milk and topping it with whipped cream, the coffee is served to us at a temperature of 180°F.

Suppose the exponential function $T = 70 + 110e^{-0.2t}$ models the temperature T of the mocha after t minutes. If we are interested in determining how long it will take for the temperature of the coffee to reach 80°F, we would substitute 80 in for

T and solve the resulting equation $80 = 70 + 110e^{-0.2t}$ for t. This equation is called an *exponential equation* because the variable t occurs as an exponent.

In this section, we will learn to solve exponential equations. When we complete Exercise 105, we will see that it takes the mocha approximately 12 minutes to reach a temperature of 80°F. We will also learn to solve *logarithmic equations* in this section.

An **exponential equation** is an equation with a variable in one of its exponents. Some examples of exponential equations are

$$3^x = 5 \qquad e^{2x} = 7 \qquad 6^{x-3} = 2^x \qquad 3^{2x+1} - 10(3^x) + 3 = 0$$

A **logarithmic equation** is an equation with logarithmic expressions that contain a variable. Some examples of logarithmic equations are

$$\log 2x = 25 \qquad \ln x - \ln(x - 12) = 24 \qquad \log x = \log \frac{1}{x} + 4$$

1. Use Like Bases to Solve Exponential Equations

Some exponential equations can be solved by using like bases.

One-to-One Property of Exponents	If $b^x = b^y$ and $b \neq 1$, $b \neq 0$, then $x = y$. That is, equal quantities with like bases have equal exponents.

EXAMPLE 1   Using Like Bases to Solve an Exponential Equation

Solve: $4^{x+3} = 8^{2x}$.

SOLUTION   We will use like bases to solve the exponential equation.

$$4^{x+3} = 8^{2x}$$

$(2^2)^{x+3} = (2^3)^{2x}$ Write 4 as 2^2 and 8 as 2^3.

$2^{2(x+3)} = 2^{6x}$ Multiply exponents.

$2(x + 3) = 6x$ Equal quantities with like bases have equal exponents.

$2x + 6 = 6x$ Use the Distributive Property.

$-4x = -6$ Subtract 6 and $6x$ from both sides.

$x = \dfrac{3}{2}$ Divide both sides by -4 and simplify.

Self Check 1   Solve: $3^{3x-5} = 81$.

Now Try Exercise 13.

EXAMPLE 2   Using Like Bases to Solve an Exponential Equation

Solve: $2^{x^2+2x} = \dfrac{1}{2}$.

SOLUTION   Since $\frac{1}{2} = 2^{-1}$, we can write the equation in the form $2^{x^2+2x} = 2^{-1}$ and use like bases to solve the equation.

Because equal quantities with like bases have equal exponents, we have

$$x^2 + 2x = -1$$

$$x^2 + 2x + 1 = 0 \qquad \text{Add 1 to both sides.}$$

$$(x + 1)(x + 1) = 0 \qquad \text{Factor the trinomial.}$$

$$x + 1 = 0 \quad \text{or} \quad x + 1 = 0 \qquad \text{Set each factor equal to 0.}$$

$$x = -1 \quad \bigg| \quad x = -1$$

Verify that -1 satisfies the equation.

Self Check 2   Solve: $3^{x^2+2x} = 27$.

Now Try Exercise 19.

ACCENT ON TECHNOLOGY   **Verifying Solutions of an Exponential Equation**

We can verify that -1 satisfies the equation shown in Example 2 by using the TABLE feature on a graphing calculator.

- Enter each side of the equation as shown in Figure 4-33.
- Go to TABLE and enter $x = -1$. Notice in Figure 4-33 that the y-values are exactly the same. This confirms that $x = -1$ is a solution.

```
Plot1 Plot2 Plot3
\Y1🔲2^(X^2+2X)
\Y2🔲1/2
\Y3=
\Y4=
\Y5=
\Y6=
\Y7=
```

X	Y₁	Y₂
-1	.5	.5

X=

FIGURE 4-33

EXAMPLE 3   **Using Like Bases to Solve an Exponential Equation**

Solve: $e^{6x^2} = e^{-x+1}$.

SOLUTION   We can use like bases to solve the exponential equation.
Because equal quantities with like bases have equal exponents, we have

$$6x^2 = -x + 1$$

$$6x^2 + x - 1 = 0 \qquad \text{Add } x - 1 \text{ to both sides.}$$

$$(3x - 1)(2x + 1) = 0 \qquad \text{Factor the trinomial.}$$

$$3x - 1 = 0 \quad \text{or} \quad 2x + 1 = 0 \qquad \text{Set each factor equal to 0.}$$

$$x = \frac{1}{3} \quad \bigg| \quad x = -\frac{1}{2} \qquad \text{Solve each equation.}$$

Verify that $\frac{1}{3}$ and $-\frac{1}{2}$ satisfy the equation.

Self Check 3   Solve: $e^{4x^2} = e^{24}$.

Now Try Exercise 23.

2. Use Logarithms to Solve Exponential Equations

If the bases of the terms in an exponential equation are not equal, as is often the case, we use logarithms to solve the equation.

Since logarithmic functions are one-to-one, we can take the logarithm of both sides of an equation. This allows us to use the properties of logarithms to help solve the equation. A logarithm of any base may be used, but it is most efficient to use natural logarithms or common logarithms because a calculator is often needed to get an approximate answer. A strategy for solving exponential equations with different bases is given next.

Strategy for Solving Exponential Equations with Different Bases

To solve an exponential equation we can follow these steps:

Step 1: Isolate the exponential expression.

Step 2: Take the same logarithm of both sides.

Step 3: Simplify using the rules of logarithms.

Step 4: Solve for the variable.

When using the strategy given, please keep the following things in mind:

- If the equation contains base e, it is most efficient to use natural logarithms because

   $$\ln e^x = x$$

- If the equation contains base 10, it is most efficient to use common logarithms because

   $$\log 10^x = x$$

- If the equation contains exponential terms with bases other than base e or 10, use either natural logarithms or common logarithms.

EXAMPLE 4   **Using Logarithms to Solve an Exponential Equation with Different Bases**

Solve the exponential equation: $3^x = 5$.

SOLUTION   We will use the strategy outlined above to solve the exponential equation. First, we note that the exponential expression 3^x is isolated. Since logarithms of equal numbers are equal, we can take the common logarithm of each side of the equation. We can then use the Power Rule and move the variable x from its position as an exponent to a position as a coefficient and solve the equation.

$$3^x = 5$$

$$\log 3^x = \log 5 \qquad \text{Take the common logarithm of each side.}$$

$$x \log 3 = \log 5 \qquad \text{The log of a power is the power times the log.}$$

$$(1) \qquad x = \frac{\log 5}{\log 3} \qquad \text{Divide both sides by log 3.}$$

$$\approx 1.464973521 \qquad \text{Use a calculator.}$$

To four decimal places, $x = 1.4650$.

Self Check 4   Solve $5^x = 3$ to four decimal places.

Now Try Exercise 27.

Caution

A careless reading of Equation 1 leads to a common error. The right side of the equation calls for a division, **not** a subtraction.

$$\frac{\log 5}{\log 3} \quad \text{means} \quad (\log 5) \div (\log 3)$$

It is the expression $\log \frac{5}{3}$ that means $\log 5 - \log 3$.

EXAMPLE 5 **Using Logarithms to Solve an Exponential Equation with Different Bases**

Solve the exponential equation: $6^{x-3} = 2^x$.

SOLUTION We will use logarithms to solve the exponential equation and apply the strategy stated earlier.

$$6^{x-3} = 2^x$$

$\log 6^{x-3} = \log 2^x$ Take the common logarithm of each side.

$(x - 3)\log 6 = x \log 2$ The log of a power is the power times the log.

$x \log 6 - 3 \log 6 = x \log 2$ Use the Distributive Property.

$x \log 6 - x \log 2 = 3 \log 6$ Add 3 log 6 and subtract x log 2 from both sides.

$x(\log 6 - \log 2) = 3 \log 6$ Factor out x on the left-hand side.

$$x = \frac{3 \log 6}{\log 6 - \log 2}$$ Divide both sides by log 6 − log 2.

$x \approx 4.892789261$ Use a calculator.

To four decimal places, $x = 4.8928$.

Self Check 5 Solve: $5^{x+3} = 3^x$.

Now Try Exercise 29.

Comment We can use common logarithms or natural logarithms to solve many exponential equations. In Examples 4 and 5, we took the common logarithm of both sides of an equation to solve the equation. We could just as well have taken the natural logarithm of both sides and obtained the same decimal result.

In the next example, we will take the natural logarithm of both sides of an exponential equation. However, before we do, it is a good idea to review the following properties of natural logarithms.

Natural Logarithm Properties		
$\ln 1 = 0$ $\ln e = 1$ $\ln e^x = x$		
Product Rule: $\ln MN = \ln M + \ln N$		
Quotient Rule: $\ln \dfrac{M}{N} = \ln M - \ln N$		
Power Rule: $\ln M^p = p \ln M$		

EXAMPLE 6 **Using Natural Logarithms to Solve Exponential Equations**

Use natural logarithms to solve **a.** $e^x - 7 = 0$ **b.** $4^{x+3} = 8^{2x}$

SOLUTION For each problem, we will use the strategy stated earlier. We will isolate the exponential expression, take the natural logarithm of both sides, simplify using the natural logarithms properties, and solve for x.

a. $e^x - 7 = 0$

$$e^x - 7 + 7 = 0 + 7 \qquad \text{Isolate the exponential expression. Add 7 to both sides.}$$

$$e^x = 7$$

$$\ln e^x = \ln 7 \qquad \text{Take the natural logarithm of both sides.}$$

$$x = \ln 7 \qquad \text{Substitute } x \text{ for } \ln e^x : \ln e^x = x .$$

$$x \approx 1.95 \qquad \text{Use a calculator and round to two decimal places.}$$

b. $4^{x+3} = 8^{2x}$

$$\ln 4^{x+3} = \ln 8^{2x} \qquad \text{Take the natural logarithm of both sides.}$$

$$(x + 3)\ln 4 = (2x)\ln 8 \qquad \text{The log of a power is the power times the log.}$$

$$x \ln 4 + 3 \ln 4 = 2x \ln 8 \qquad \text{Use the Distributive Property on the left side.}$$

$$x \ln 4 - 2x \ln 8 = -3 \ln 4 \qquad \text{Subtract } 2x \ln 8 \text{ and } 3 \ln 4 \text{ from both sides.}$$

$$x(\ln 4 - 2 \ln 8) = -3 \ln 4 \qquad \text{Factor out } x \text{ on the left-hand side.}$$

$$x = \frac{-3 \ln 4}{\ln 4 - 2 \ln 8} \qquad \text{Divide both sides by } \ln 4 - 2 \ln 8 .$$

$$x = 1.5 \qquad \text{Use a calculator.}$$

Comment

As we see in Example 6a, if an exponential equation has a term with a base of e, then taking the natural logarithm of both sides is a good choice.

Comment

Note that the exponential equations in Examples 1 and 6b are identical and the answers are the same. As we see, sometimes we can use like bases or logarithms to solve the same equation.

Self Check 6 Use natural logarithms to solve: **a.** $3e^x = 12$ **b.** $8^{x+1} = 4^{2x}$

Now Try Exercise 39.

ACCENT ON TECHNOLOGY **Finding Approximate Solutions to an Exponential Equation**

If only a decimal approximation of a solution is needed, a graphing calculator can be used to solve exponential equations. Our strategy is to graph each side of the equation and then find the point of intersection.

We will use a graphing calculator to solve the exponential equation $\sqrt{3}^{\,-x} = 2^{\pi x - 3}$.

• Enter each side of the equation in the graph menu and find the point of intersection. We see in the figure below that the solution is $x \approx 1.2770786$.

(a) (b) (c)

(d) (e) (f)

FIGURE 4-34

3. Solve Logarithmic Equations

We can use the One-to-One Property of logarithms to change some logarithmic equations into algebraic equations that we can solve. Here's a reminder of that property.

One-to-One Property of Logarithms If $\log_b x = \log_b y$, then $x = y$. That is, logarithms of equal numbers are equal.

EXAMPLE 7 **Using the One-to-One Property of Logarithms to Solve a Logarithmic Equation**

Solve: $\log_5(3x + 2) = \log_5(2x - 3)$.

SOLUTION We will use the property of logarithms stated above to solve the equation. Then we will check our solutions.

$$\log_5(3x + 2) = \log_5(2x - 3)$$
$$3x + 2 = 2x - 3 \qquad \text{If the logs of two numbers are equal, the numbers are equal.}$$
$$x = -5 \qquad \text{Subtract } 2x \text{ and 2 from both sides.}$$

Check:
$$\log_5(3x + 2) = \log_5(2x - 3)$$
$$\log_5[3(-5) + 2] \stackrel{?}{=} \log_5[2(-5) - 3]$$
$$\log_5(-13) \stackrel{?}{=} \log_5(-13)$$

Since the logarithm of a negative number does not exist, -5 is extraneous and must be discarded. The equation has no roots. ∎

Self Check 7 Solve: $\log_3(5x + 2) = \log_3(6x + 1)$.

Now Try Exercise 57.

Comment It is incorrect to state that the logarithms in Example 7 are canceled. The logarithms aren't canceled; the One-to-One Property is used.

Caution Example 7 illustrates that we **must** check the solutions of a logarithmic equation. If we fail to do so, we risk having incorrect answers.

EXAMPLE 8 **Solving a Logarithmic Equation Using the Properties of Logarithms**

Solve: $\log x + \log(x - 3) = 1$.

SOLUTION We will first combine the two logarithms as a single logarithm. Next, we will use the definition of logarithm to write the equation in exponential form. Finally, we will solve the equation and check the solutions.

$$\log x + \log(x - 3) = 1$$
$$\log x(x - 3) = 1 \qquad \text{The sum of two logs is the log of a product.}$$
$$x(x - 3) = 10^1 \qquad \text{Use the definition of logarithms to change the equation to exponential form.}$$
$$x^2 - 3x - 10 = 0 \qquad \text{Remove parentheses and subtract 10 from both sides.}$$
$$(x + 2)(x - 5) = 0 \qquad \text{Factor the trinomial.}$$
$$x + 2 = 0 \quad \text{or} \quad x - 5 = 0$$
$$x = -2 \qquad\qquad x = 5$$

Check: The number -2 is not a solution, because it does not satisfy the equation (a negative number does not have a logarithm). We check the remaining number, 5.

$$\log x + \log(x - 3) = 1$$

$$\log 5 + \log(5 - 3) \stackrel{?}{=} 1 \qquad \text{Substitute 5 for } x.$$

$$\log 5 + \log 2 \stackrel{?}{=} 1$$

$$\log 10 \stackrel{?}{=} 1 \qquad \text{The sum of two logs is the log of a product.}$$

$$1 = 1 \qquad \log_b b = 1$$

Since 5 does check, it is a root.

Self Check 8   Solve: $\log x + \log(x - 15) = 2$.

Now Try Exercise 61.

EXAMPLE 9   **Solving Logarithmic Equations**

Solve: $\ln(2x + 5) - \ln(x + 5) = \ln \dfrac{5}{3}$.

SOLUTION   First, we combine the two logarithms on the left. Then we will use the One-to-One Property and solve for x.

$$\ln(2x + 5) - \ln(x + 5) = \ln \frac{5}{3}$$

$$\ln \frac{2x + 5}{x + 5} = \ln \frac{5}{3} \qquad \text{Use the Quotient Rule and combine logs.}$$

$$\frac{2x + 5}{x + 5} = \frac{5}{3} \qquad \text{Use the One-to-One Property of logs.}$$

$$3(2x + 5) = 5(x + 5) \qquad \text{Multiply both sides by } 3(x + 5).$$

$$6x + 15 = 5x + 25$$

$$x = 10$$

Check: The solution $x = 10$ checks as we see here.

$$\ln(2x + 5) - \ln(x + 5) \stackrel{?}{=} \ln \frac{5}{3}$$

$$\ln[2(10) + 5] - \ln[(10) + 5] \stackrel{?}{=} \ln \frac{5}{3} \qquad \text{Substitute 10 in for } x.$$

$$\ln 25 - \ln 15 \stackrel{?}{=} \ln \frac{5}{3}$$

$$\ln \frac{25}{15} \stackrel{?}{=} \ln \frac{5}{3} \qquad \text{Use the Quotient Rule.}$$

$$\ln \frac{5}{3} = \ln \frac{5}{3} \qquad \text{This is a true statement.}$$

Self Check 9   Solve: $\log_7(2x + 2) - \log_7(x + 6) = \log_7 \dfrac{4}{3}$.

Now Try Exercise 69.

EXAMPLE 10   **Solving Logarithmic Equations**

Solve **a.** $\ln x = 5$ **b.** $\dfrac{\ln(5x - 6)}{\ln x} = 2$

SOLUTION   For part (a), we will write the natural logarithm as $\log_e x = 5$ and use the definition of logarithm to solve the equation. For part (b), we will multiply both sides by $\ln x$ and then use properties of logarithms to write an algebraic equation. We will then solve the equation. We must verify the solutions to both parts.

a. $\ln x = 5$

   $\log_e x = 5$ Rewrite using the definition of natural logarithm.

   $x = e^5$ Write in exponential form.

Verify that e^5 satisfies the solution.

b. We multiply both sides of $\dfrac{\ln(5x - 6)}{\ln x} = 2$ by $\ln x$ to get

   $\ln(5x - 6) = 2 \ln x$

and apply the Power Rule of logarithms to get

   $\ln(5x - 6) = \ln x^2$

By the property of logarithms stated above $5x - 6 = x^2$, because they have equal logarithms. So

$$x^2 = 5x - 6$$

   $x^2 - 5x + 6 = 0$

   $(x - 3)(x - 2) = 0$

   $x - 3 = 0 \quad \text{or} \quad x - 2 = 0$

   $x = 3 \quad | \quad x = 2$

Verify that both 2 and 3 satisfy the equation.

Self Check 10   Solve: **a.** $6 \ln x = 12$ **b.** $\dfrac{\ln(8x - 15)}{\ln x} = 2$

Now Try Exercise 79.

The strategy we used to solve a logarithmic equation was dependent upon the nature of the equation. A summary of these strategies appears here.

Summary of Strategies Used to Solve Logarithmic Equations

1. For logarithmic equations containing one logarithm, we can use the definition of the logarithm. We write the logarithm in exponential form and then solve for the variable.

   Note: This strategy can be used to solve the following logarithmic equations.

   $$\log_3(x + 5) = 2, \ \log(x^2 - 4) = 5, \ \ln(4x) = 7$$

2. For more complicated logarithmic equations, we can combine and isolate the logarithmic expressions. We can then use the definition of the logarithm and write the logarithm in exponential form to solve for the variable.

Note: This strategy can be used to solve the following logarithmic equations.

$$\log(x) + \log(x - 1) = 3, \log_5(3x + 2) - \log_5(2x - 3) = 2,$$
$$\ln x - \ln(x + 3) = 4$$

3. We can use the One-to-One Property of logarithms for logarithmic equations of the form $\log_b x = \log_b y$.

Note: This strategy can be used to solve the following logarithmic equations.

$$\log(5x - 6) = \log x^2, \ln(2x - 7) = \ln(3x + 5)$$

4. For other types of logarithmic equations, we sometimes combine logarithms on one or both sides and then use the One-to-One Property of logarithms to solve the equations.

Note: This strategy can be used to solve the following logarithmic equations.

$$\ln(x^2) + \ln(x - 3) = \ln(x + 4), \log_4 x - \log_4(x + 2) = \log_4 5 + \log_4(3x)$$

ACCENT ON TECHNOLOGY | **Finding Approximate Solutions to a Logarithmic Equation**

We can use a graphing calculator to approximate the solutions of a logarithmic equation.

Consider the log equation $\ln x^2 + \ln(x - 3) = \ln(x + 4)$.

- Enter each side of the equation in the graph menu, and then find the point of intersection. We see that in Figure 4-35 that $x \approx 3.5891327$. Use [ZOOM] and select ZDecimal to graph.

FIGURE 4-35

4. Solve Carbon-14 Dating Problems

When a living organism dies, the oxygen/carbon dioxide cycle common to all living things ceases; then carbon-14, a radioactive isotope with a half-life of 5,700 years, is no longer absorbed. By measuring the amount of carbon-14 present in ancient objects, archaeologists can estimate the object's age.

The Shroud of Turin, the piece of linen long believed to have been wrapped around Jesus's body after the crucifixion, is much older than the date suggested by radiocarbon tests, according to new microchemical research. Published in the current issue of *Thermochimica Acta*, a chemistry peer-reviewed scientific journal, the study dismisses the results of the 1988 carbon-14 dating. At that time, three reputable laboratories in Oxford, Zurich, and Tucson, Ariz., concluded that the cloth on which the smudged outline of the body of a man is indelibly impressed was a medieval fake dating from 1260 to 1390 and not the burial cloth wrapped around the body of Christ.

The amount A of radioactive material present at time t is given by the model

$$A = A_0 2^{-t/h}$$

where A_0 is the amount present initially and h is the half-life of the material.

EXAMPLE 11   Solving a Carbon-14 Dating Problem

An archeologist finds a wooden statue in the tomb of an ancient Egyptian ruler. If the statue contains two-thirds of its original carbon-14 content, how old is it?

SOLUTION   To find the time t when $A = \frac{2}{3}A_0$, we substitute $\frac{2A_0}{3}$ for A and 5,700 for h in the radioactive decay formula and solve for t:

$$A = A_0 2^{-t/h}$$

$$\frac{2A_0}{3} = A_0 2^{-t/5,700}$$

$$1 = \frac{3}{2}\left(2^{-t/5,700}\right) \qquad \text{Divide both sides by } A_0 \text{ and multiply both sides by } \frac{3}{2}.$$

$$\log 1 = \log\frac{3}{2}\left(2^{-t/5,700}\right) \qquad \text{Take the common logarithm of each side.}$$

$$0 = \log\frac{3}{2} + \log 2^{-t/5,700} \qquad \text{The log of a product is the sum of the logs.}$$

$$-\log\frac{3}{2} = -\frac{t}{5,700}\log 2 \qquad \text{Subtract } \log\frac{3}{2} \text{ from both sides and use the Power Rule of logarithms.}$$

$$5,700\left(\frac{\log\frac{3}{2}}{\log 2}\right) = t \qquad \text{Multiply both sides by } -\frac{5,700}{\log 2}.$$

$$t \approx 3,334.286254 \qquad \text{Use a calculator.}$$

The wooden statue is approximately 3,300 years old.

Self Check 11　How old is an artifact that has 60% of its original carbon-14 content?

Now Try Exercise 95.

5. Solve Population Growth Problems

When there is sufficient food and space, populations of living organisms tend to increase exponentially according to the Malthusian growth model

$$P = P_0 e^{kt}$$

where P_0 is the initial population at $t = 0$ and k depends on the rate of growth.

EXAMPLE 12　**Solving a Population Growth Problem**

Streptococcus bacteria in a laboratory culture increased from an initial population of 500 to 1,500 in 3 hours. Find the time it will take for the population to reach 10,000.

SOLUTION　We will apply the following two steps to solve the problem:

Step 1: Substitute 1,500 for P, 500 for P_0, and 3 for t into the Malthusian growth model and find k.

Step 2: Substitute 10,000 for P, 500 for P_0, and the value of k found in Step 1 into the model and use logarithms to solve for t.

1. Substitute 1,500 for P, 500 for P_0, and 3 for t into the Malthusian growth model and find k:

$$P = P_0 e^{kt}$$

$1{,}500 = 500(e^{k3})$　　　Substitute 1,500 for P, 500 for P_0, and 3 for t.

$3 = e^{3k}$　　　Divide both sides by 500.

$3k = \ln 3$　　　Take the natural log of both sides.

$k = \dfrac{\ln 3}{3}$　　　Divide both sides by 3.

2. To find out when the population will reach 10,000, we substitute 10,000 for P, 500 for P_0, and $\frac{\ln 3}{3}$ for k in the equation $P = P_0 e^{kt}$, and solve for t:

$$P = P_0 e^{kt}$$

$10{,}000 = 500 e^{\left(\frac{\ln 3}{3}\right)t}$

$20 = e^{\left(\frac{\ln 3}{3}\right)t}$　　　Divide both sides by 500.

$\ln(20) = \ln\left[e^{\left(\frac{\ln 3}{3}\right)t}\right]$　　　Take the natural log of both sides.

$\ln(20) = \dfrac{\ln 3}{3}\, t$　　　Simplify the right side using the natural log property $\ln(e^x) = x$.

$t = \dfrac{3 \ln 20}{\ln 3}$　　　Multiply both sides by $\dfrac{3}{\ln 3}$.

≈ 8.180499084　　　Use a calculator.

The culture will reach 10,000 bacteria in a little more than 8 hours.

Self Check 12　If the population increases from 1,000 to 3,000 in 3 hours, how long will it take to reach 20,000?

Now Try Exercise 103.

Self Check Answers   **1.** 3   **2.** 1, -3 **3.** $\pm\sqrt{6}$ **4.** $x = 0.6826$ **5.** -9.4520
6. a. $\ln 4$ **b.** 3   **7.** 1   **8.** 20; -5 is extraneous   **9.** 9
10. a. e^2 **b.** 3, 5   **11.** about 4,200 years   **12.** about 8 hr

Exercises **4.6**

Getting Ready
You should be able to complete these vocabulary and concept statements before you proceed to the practice exercises.

Fill in the blanks.

1. An equation with a variable in its exponent is called a(n) _____ equation.
2. An equation with a logarithmic expression that contains a variable is a(n) _____ equation.
3. The formula for carbon dating is $A =$ _____.
4. The formula for population growth is $P =$ _____.

Practice
Solve each exponential equation using like bases.

5. $2^{3x+2} = 16^x$
6. $32^{x+2} = 2^{7x+12}$
7. $27^{x+1} = 3^{2x+1}$
8. $3^{x-1} = 9^{2x}$
9. $5^{4x+1} = 25^{-x-2}$
10. $5^{2x+1} = 125^x$
11. $4^{x-2} = 8^x$
12. $16^{x+1} = 8^{2x+1}$
13. $81^{2x} = 27^{2x-5}$
14. $625^{x-9} = 125^{x-12}$
15. $2^{x^2-2x} = 8$
16. $5^{x^2+3x} = 625$
17. $36^{x^2} = 216^{x^2-3}$
18. $25^{x^2-5x} = 3{,}125^{4x}$
19. $7^{x^2+3x} = \dfrac{1}{49}$
20. $3^{x^2+4x} = \dfrac{1}{81}$
21. $e^{-x+6} = e^x$
22. $e^{2x+1} = e^{3x-11}$
23. $e^{x^2-1} = e^{24}$
24. $e^{x^2+7x} = \dfrac{1}{e^{12}}$

Solve each exponential equation using logarithms. Give the answer in decimal form, rounding to four decimal places.

25. $4^x = 5$
26. $7^x = 12$
27. $13^{x-1} = 2$
28. $5^{x+1} = 3$
29. $2^{x+1} = 3^x$
30. $5^{x-3} = 3^{2x}$
31. $2^x = 3^x$
32. $3^{2x} = 4^x$
33. $7^{x^2} = 10$
34. $8^{x^2} = 11$
35. $8^{x^2} = 9^x$
36. $5^{x^2} = 2^{5x}$

Find the exact solution to each exponential equation.

37. $e^x = 10$
38. $8e^x = 16$
39. $4e^{2x} = 24$
40. $2e^{5x} = 18$

Solve each equation. If an answer is not exact, give the answer in decimal form. Round to four decimal places.

41. $4^{x+2} - 4^x = 15$ (*Hint:* $4^{x+2} = 4^x 4^2$.)
42. $3^{x+3} + 3^x = 84$ (*Hint:* $3^{x+3} = 3^x 3^3$.)
43. $2(3^x) = 6^{2x}$
44. $2(3^{x+1}) = 3(2^{x-1})$
45. $2^{2x} - 10(2^x) + 16 = 0$ (*Hint:* Let $y = 2^x$.)
46. $3^{2x} - 10(3^x) + 9 = 0$ (*Hint:* Let $y = 3^x$.)
47. $2^{2x+1} - 2^x = 1$ (*Hint:* $2^{a+b} = 2^a 2^b$.)
48. $3^{2x+1} - 10(3^x) + 3 = 0$ (*Hint:* $3^{a+b} = 3^a 3^b$.)

Solve each logarithmic equation. Use the definition of logarithm or the definition of natural logarithm.

49. $\log x^2 = 2$
50. $\log x^3 = 3$
51. $\log \dfrac{4x + 1}{2x + 9} = 0$
52. $\log \dfrac{5x + 2}{2(x + 7)} = 0$
53. $\ln x = 6$
54. $\ln x = 3$
55. $\ln(2x - 7) = 4$
56. $\ln(3x - 5) = 7$

Solve each logarithmic equation.

57. $\log(2x - 3) = \log(x + 4)$
58. $\log(3x + 5) - \log(2x + 6) = 0$
59. $\log x + \log(x - 48) = 2$
60. $\log x + \log(x + 9) = 1$
61. $\log x + \log(x - 15) = 2$
62. $\log x + \log(x + 21) = 2$
63. $\log(x + 90) = 3 - \log x$
64. $\log(x - 3) - \log(6) = 2$
65. $\log(5{,}000) - \log(x - 2) = 3$
66. $\log(2x - 3) - \log(x - 1) = 0$
67. $\log_7 x + \log_7(x - 5) = \log_7 6$
68. $\ln x + \ln(x - 2) = \ln 120$
69. $\ln 15 - \ln(x - 2) = \ln x$
70. $\ln 10 - \ln(x - 3) = \ln x$
71. $\log_6 8 - \log_6 x = \log_6(x - 2)$
72. $\log(x - 6) - \log(x - 2) = \log \dfrac{5}{x}$

73. $\log(x - 1) - \log 6 = \log(x - 2) - \log x$

74. $\log x^2 = (\log x)^2$

75. $\log(\log x) = 1$

76. $\log_3(\log_3 x) = 1$

77. $\dfrac{\log(3x - 4)}{\log x} = 2$

78. $\dfrac{\ln(8x - 7)}{\ln x} = 2$

79. $\dfrac{\ln(5x + 6)}{2} = \ln x$

80. $\dfrac{1}{2}\log(4x + 5) = \log x$

81. $\log_3 x = \log_3\left(\dfrac{1}{x}\right) + 4$

82. $\log_5(7 + x) + \log_5(8 - x) - \log_5 2 = 2$

83. $2\log_2 x = 3 + \log_2(x - 2)$

84. $2\log_3 x - \log_3(x - 4) = 2 + \log_3 2$

85. $\ln(7y + 1) = 2\ln(y + 3) - \ln 2$

86. $2\log(y + 2) = \log(y + 2) - \log 12$

Use a graphing calculator to solve each equation. If an answer is not exact, give the result to the nearest hundredth.

87. $\log x + \log(x - 15) = 2$

88. $\log x + \log(x + 3) = 1$

89. $2^{x+1} = 7$

90. $\ln(2x + 5) - \ln 3 = \ln(x - 1)$

Applications

Use a calculator to help solve each problem.

91. Tritium decay The half-life of tritium is 12.4 years. How long will it take for 25% of a sample of tritium to decompose?

92. Radioactive decay In 2 years, 20% of a radioactive element decays. Find its half-life.

93. Thorium decay An isotope of thorium, ^{227}Th, has a half-life of 18.4 days. How long will it take 80% of the sample to decompose?

94. Lead decay An isotope of lead, ^{201}Pb, has a half-life of 8.4 hours. How many hours ago was there 30% more of the substance?

95. Carbon-14 dating A cloth fragment is found in an ancient tomb. It contains 70% of the carbon-14 that it is assumed to have had initially. How old is the cloth?

96. Carbon-14 dating Only 25% of the carbon-14 in a wooden bowl remains. How old is the bowl?

97. Compound interest If $500 is deposited in an account paying 8.5% annual interest, compounded semiannually, how long will it take for the account to increase to $800?

98. Continuous compound interest In Exercise 97, how long will it take if the interest is compounded continuously?

99. Compound interest If $1,300 is deposited in a savings account paying 9% interest, compounded quarterly, how long will it take the account to increase to $2,100?

100. Compound interest A sum of $5,000 deposited in an account grows to $7,000 in 5 years. Assuming annual compounding, what interest rate is being paid?

101. Rule of Seventy A rule of thumb for finding how long it takes an investment to double is called the **Rule of Seventy.** To apply the rule, divide 70 by the interest rate (expressed as a percent). At 5%, it takes $\dfrac{70}{5} = 14$ years to double the investment. At 7%, it takes $\dfrac{70}{7} = 10$ years. Explain why this formula works.

102. Oceanography The intensity I of a light a distance x meters beneath the surface of a lake decreases exponentially. If the light intensity at 6 meters is 70% of the intensity at the surface, at what depth will the intensity be 20%?

103. Bacterial growth A staphylococcus bacterial culture grows according to the formula $P = P_0 a^t$. If it takes 5 days for the culture to triple in size, how long will it take to double in size?

104. Rodent control The rodent population in a city is currently estimated at 30,000. If it is expected to double every 5 years, when will the population reach 1 million?

105. Temperature of coffee Refer to the section opener and find the time it takes for the white chocolate mocha to reach a temperature of $80°F$.

106. Time of death The exponential function $T(t) = 17e^{-0.0626t} + 20$ models the temperature T in $°C$ of a person's body t hours after death. If a dead body is discovered at 8:30 a.m. and the body's temperature is $30°C$, what was the person's approximate time of death?

107. Newton's Law of Cooling Water whose temperature is at $100°C$ is left to cool in a room where the temperature is $60°C$. After 3 minutes, the water temperature is $90°$. If the water temperature T is a function of time t given by $T = 60 + 40e^{kt}$, find k.

108. Newton's Law of Cooling Refer to Exercise 107 and find the time for the water temperature to reach $70°C$.

109. Newton's Law of Cooling A block of steel, initially at $0°C$, is placed in an oven heated to $300°C$. After 5 minutes, the temperature of the steel is $100°C$. If the steel temperature T is a function of time t given by $T = 300 - 300e^{kt}$, find the value of k.

110. Newton's Law of Cooling Refer to Exercise 109 and find the time for the steel temperature to reach $200°C$.

Discovery and Writing
111. Explain why it is necessary to check the solutions of a logarithmic equation.

112. Use the population growth formula to show that the doubling time for population growth is given by $t = \frac{\ln 2}{r}$.

113. Use the population growth formula to show that the tripling time for population growth is given by $t = \frac{\ln 3}{r}$.

114. Can you solve $x = \log x$ algebraically? Can you find an approximate solution?

Find x.

115. $\log_2(\log_5(\log_7 x)) = 2$

116. $\log_8\left[16\sqrt[3]{4{,}096}\right]^{\frac{1}{6}} = x$

Review
Find the inverse of the function defined by each equation.

117. $y = 3x + 2$

118. $y = \dfrac{1}{x - 3}$

Let $f(x) = 5x - 1$ and $g(x) = x^2$. Find each value.

119. $(f \circ g)(2)$

120. $(g \circ f)(2)$

121. $(f \circ g)(x)$

122. $(g \circ f)(x)$

CHAPTER REVIEW

SECTION 4.1   Exponential Functions and Their Graphs

Definitions and Concepts

An **exponential function** with base b is defined by the equation

$$y = f(x) = b^x \qquad (b > 0, b \neq 1)$$

Examples

Graph: $f(x) = 6^x$.
We will find several points (x, y) that satisfy the equation, plot the points, and join them with a smooth curve, as shown in the figure.

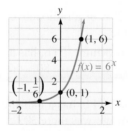

$f(x) = 6^x$		
x	$f(x)$	$(x, f(x))$
-1	$\dfrac{1}{6}$	$\left(-1, \dfrac{1}{6}\right)$
0	1	$(0, 1)$
1	6	$(1, 6)$

Definitions and Concepts	Examples
Compound interest formula: If P dollars are deposited in an account earning interest at an annual rate r, compounded n times each year, the amount A in the account after t years is given by $$A = P\left(1 + \frac{r}{n}\right)^{nt}$$	The grandparents of a newborn child invest \$10,000 in an educational savings plan that earns 8% interest, compounded quarterly. If the money is left untouched, how much will the child have in the account in 18 years? We will substitute 10,000 for P, 0.08 for r, and 18 for t in the formula for compound interest. Because quarterly compounding means four times per year, we will substitute 4 for n. $$A = P\left(1 + \frac{r}{n}\right)^{nt}$$ $$A = 10{,}000\left(1 + \frac{0.08}{4}\right)^{4 \cdot 18}$$ $$= 10{,}000(1.02)^{72}$$ $$\approx 41{,}611.40 \qquad \text{Use a calculator and round to two decimals.}$$ In 18 years, the account will be worth \$41,611.40.
The number $e \approx 2.718281828$. The graph of $f(x) = e^x$ is: 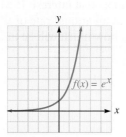 **Continuous compound interest formula:** If P dollars are deposited in an account earning interest at an annual rate r, compounded continuously, the amount A after t years is given by the formula $$A = Pe^{rt}$$	If the grandparents of the newborn child in the previous example had invested \$10,000 at an annual rate of 8%, compounded continuously, how much would the child have in the account in 18 years? We will substitute \$10,000 for P, 0.08 for r, and 18 in for t in the continuous compound interest formula $A = Pe^{rt}$. $$A = Pe^{rt}$$ $$A = 10{,}000e^{(0.08)(18)}$$ $$= 10{,}000e^{1.44}$$ $$\approx 42{,}206.96 \qquad \text{Use a calculator and round to two decimal places.}$$ In 18 years, the balance will be \$42,206.96.

EXERCISES

Use properties of exponents to simplify.

1. $5^{\sqrt{2}} \cdot 5^{\sqrt{2}}$

2. $\left(2^{\sqrt{5}}\right)^{\sqrt{2}}$

Graph the function defined by each equation.

3. $f(x) = 3^x$

4. $f(x) = \left(\dfrac{1}{3}\right)^x$

5. The graph of $f(x) = 7^x$ will pass through the points $(0, p)$ and $(1, q)$. Find p and q.

6. Give the domain and range of the function $f(x) = b^x$, with $b > 0$ and $b \neq 1$.

Use translations to help graph each function.

7. $g(x) = \left(\dfrac{1}{2}\right)^x - 2$

8. $g(x) = \left(\dfrac{1}{2}\right)^{x+2}$

Graph each function.

9. $f(x) = -5^x$

10. $f(x) = -5^x + 4$

11. $f(x) = e^x + 1$

12. $f(x) = e^{x-3}$

13. **Compound interest** How much will $10,500 become if it earns 9% per year for 60 years, compounded quarterly?

14. **Continuous compound interest** If $10,500 accumulates interest at an annual rate of 9%, compounded continuously, how much will be in the account in 60 years?

SECTION 4.2   Applications of Exponential Functions

Definitions and Concepts	Examples
Radioactive decay formula: The amount A of radioactive material present at time t is given by $\quad A = A_0 2^{-t/h}$ where A_0 is the amount that was present initially (at $t = 0$) and h is the material's half-life.	The half-life of radium is approximately 1,600 years. To find how much of a 1-gram sample will remain after 500 years, we will substitute $A_0 = 1$, $h = 1,600$, and $t = 500$ into the formula for radioactive decay and simplify. $\quad A = A_0 2^{-t/h}$ $\quad A = 1 \cdot 2^{-500/1,600}$ $\quad\quad \approx 0.81$ Use a calculator. Round to two decimal places. After 500 years, approximately 0.81 gram of radium will remain.

Definitions and Concepts	Examples
Intensity of light formula: The intensity I of light (in lumens) at a distance x meters below the surface of a body of water decreases exponentially according to the formula $$I = I_0 k^x$$ where I_0 is the intensity of light above the water and k is a constant that depends on the clarity of the water.	At one location in the Atlantic Ocean, the intensity of light above water I_0 is 10 lumens and $k = 0.4$. To find the intensity of light at a depth of 3 meters, we will substitute 10 for I_0, 0.4 for k, and 3 for x into the formula for light intensity and simplify. $$I = I_0 k^x$$ $$I = 10(0.4)^3$$ $$I = 0.64$$ At a depth of 3 meters, the intensity of the light is 0.64 lumen.
Malthusian model of population growth: If b is the annual birth rate, d is the annual death rate, t is the time (in years), P_0 is the initial population at $t = 0$, and P is the current population, then $$P = P_0 e^{kt}$$ where $k = b - d$ is the **annual growth rate,** the difference between the annual birth rate and death rate.	The population of the United States is approximately 300 million people. Assuming that the annual birth rate is 19 per 1,000 and the annual death rate is 7 per 1,000, what does the Malthusian model predict the U.S. population will be in 30 years? We can use the stated information to write the Malthusian model for U.S. population. We will then substitute into the model to predict the population in 30 years. Since k is the difference between the birth and death rates, we have $$k = b - d$$ $$k = \frac{19}{1,000} - \frac{7}{1,000} \quad \text{Substitute } \frac{19}{1,000} \text{ for } b \text{ and } \frac{7}{1,000} \text{ for } d.$$ $$k = 0.019 - 0.007$$ $$= 0.012$$ We can substitute 300,000,000 for P_0, 30 for t, and 0.012 for k in the formula for the Malthusian model of population growth and simplify. $$P = P_0 e^{kt}$$ $$P = (300,000,000)e^{(0.012)(30)}$$ $$= (300,000,000)e^{0.36}$$ $$\approx 429,998,824.4 \qquad \text{Use a calculator.}$$ After 30 years, the U.S. population will be approximately 430 million people.

EXERCISES

15. The half-life of a radioactive material is about 34.2 years. How much of the material is left after 20 years?

16. Find the intensity of light at a depth of 12 meters if $I_0 = 14$ and $k = 0.7$.

17. The population of the United States is approximately 300,000,000 people. Find the population in 50 years if $k = 0.015$.

18. Spread of hepatitis In a city with a population of 450,000, there are currently 1,000 cases of hepatitis. If the spread of the disease is projected by the following logistic function, how many people will contract the hepatitis virus after 5 years?

$$P = \frac{450,000}{1 + (450 - 1)e^{-0.2t}}$$

SECTION **4.3**   Logarithmic Functions and Their Graphs

Definitions and Concepts	Examples

Logarithmic functions:

If $b > 0$ and $b \neq 1$, the **logarithmic function with base b** is defined by $y = \log_b x$ if and only if $x = b^y$.

The **domain of the logarithmic function** is the interval $(0, \infty)$. The **range** is the interval $(-\infty, \infty)$.

Base-10 logarithms are called **common logarithms.** The notation $\log x$ represents $\log_{10} x$.

Examples

$\log_5 125 = 3 \quad$ because $\quad 5^3 = 125$

$\log_8 1 = 0 \quad$ because $\quad 8^0 = 1$

$\log_9 3 = \dfrac{1}{2} \quad$ because $\quad 9^{1/2} = \sqrt{9} = 3$

$\log_2 \dfrac{1}{16} = -4 \quad$ because $\quad 2^{-4} = \dfrac{1}{16}$

$\log 10{,}000 = 4 \quad$ because $\quad 10^4 = 10{,}000$

To find x in the equation $\log_8 \frac{1}{64} = x$, we note that $\log_8 \frac{1}{64} = x$ is equivalent to $8^x = \frac{1}{64}$. Since $8^{-2} = \frac{1}{64}$, we have $8^x = 8^{-2}$ and $x = -2$.

To graph $f(x) = \log_5 x$. We will find several points (x, y) that satisfy the equation, plot the points, and join them with a smooth curve, as shown in the figure.

$f(x) = \log_5 x$		
x	$f(x)$	$(x, f(x))$
$\dfrac{1}{25}$	-2	$\left(\dfrac{1}{25}, -2\right)$
$\dfrac{1}{5}$	-1	$\left(\dfrac{1}{5}, -1\right)$
1	0	$(1, 0)$
5	1	$(5, 1)$
25	2	$(25, 2)$

Natural logarithms:

Base-e logarithmms are called **natural logarithms**. The notation $\ln x$ means $\log_e x$.

The graph of $f(x) = \ln x$ is:

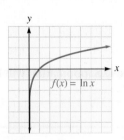

Since the functions $y = \ln x$ and $y = e^x$ are inverses

$\quad \ln e^x = x \quad$ and $\quad e^{\ln x} = x$

To graph $g(x) = \ln(x + 4)$, we will translate the graph of $f(x) = \ln x$ four units to the left as shown in the figure.

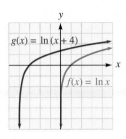

$\ln e^{-5x} = -5x \qquad e^{\ln(7x)} = 7x$

EXERCISES

19. Give the domain and range of the logarithmic function $f(x) = \log_3 x$.

20. Give the domain and range of the natural logarithm function, $f(x) = \ln x$.

Find each value.

21. $\log_3 9 =$

22. $\log_9 \dfrac{1}{3}$

23. $\log_x 1$

24. $\log_5 0.04$

25. $\log_a \sqrt{a}$

26. $\log_a \sqrt[3]{a}$

Find x.

27. $\log_2 x = 5$

28. $\log_{\sqrt{3}} x = 4$

29. $\log_{\sqrt{2}} x = 6$

30. $\log_{0.1} 10 = x$

31. $\log_x 2 = -\dfrac{1}{3}$

32. $\log_x 32 = 5$

33. $\log_{0.25} x = -1$

34. $\log_{0.125} x = -\dfrac{1}{3}$

35. $\log_{\sqrt{2}} 32 = x$

36. $\log_{\sqrt{5}} x = -4$

37. $\log_{\sqrt{3}} 9\sqrt{3} = x$

38. $\log_{\sqrt{5}} 5\sqrt{5} = x$

Graph each function.

39. $f(x) = \log(x - 2)$

40. $f(x) = 3 + \log x$

Graph each pair of equations on one set of coordinate axes.

41. $y = 4^x$ and $y = \log_4 x$

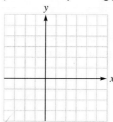

42. $y = \left(\dfrac{1}{3}\right)^x$ and $y = \log_{1/3} x$

 Use a calculator to find each value to four decimal places.

43. $\ln 452$

44. $\ln(\log 7.85)$

Use a calculator to solve each equation. Round each answer to four decimal places.

45. $\ln x = 2.336$

46. $\ln x = \log 8.8$

Graph each function.

47. $f(x) = 1 + \ln x$

48. $f(x) = \ln(x + 1)$

Simplify each expression.

49. $\ln(e^{12})$

50. $e^{\ln 14x}$

SECTION **4.4**   Applications of Logarithmic Functions

Definitions and Concepts	Examples
Decibel voltage gain: If E_O is the output voltage of a device and E_I is the input voltage, the **decibel voltage gain** is given by $$\text{dB gain} = 20 \log \frac{E_O}{E_I}$$	To find the dB gain of an amplifier with an input of 0.4 volt and an output of 50 volts, we can substitute the given values into the dB gain formula. $$\text{dB gain} = 20 \log \frac{E_O}{E_I}$$ $$\text{dB gain} = 20 \log \frac{50}{0.4} \qquad \text{Substitute 50 for } E_O \text{ and } 0.4 \text{ for } E_I.$$ $$= 20 \log 125$$ $$\approx 41.93820026 \qquad \text{Use a calculator.}$$ To the nearest decibel, the dB gain is 42 decibels.
Richter scale: If R is the intensity of an earthquake, A is the amplitude (measured in micrometers), and P is the period (the time of one oscillation of the Earth's surface, measured in seconds), then $$R = \log \frac{A}{P}$$	To find the intensity of an earthquake with amplitude of 5,000 micrometers $\left(\frac{1}{2} \text{ cm}\right)$ and a period of 0.08 second, we substitute 5,000 for A and 0.08 for P in the Richter scale formula and simplify. $$R = \log \frac{A}{P}$$ $$R = \log \frac{5{,}000}{0.08}$$ $$= \log 62{,}500$$ $$\approx 4.795880017 \qquad \text{Use a calculator}$$ To the nearest tenth, the earthquake measures 4.8 on the Richter scale.
Charging batteries: If M is the theoretical maximum charge that a battery can hold and k is a positive constant that depends on the battery and the charger, the length of time (in minutes) required to charge the battery to a given level C is given by $$t = -\frac{1}{k} \ln\left(1 - \frac{C}{M}\right)$$	To find how long will it take to bring a fully discharged battery to 80% of full charge, we will assume that $k = 0.02$ and that time is measured in minutes. Since 80% of full charge means 80% of M, we can substitute $0.80M$ for C and 0.02 for k in the formula for charging batteries and find t. $$t = -\frac{1}{k} \ln\left(1 - \frac{C}{M}\right)$$ $$t = -\frac{1}{0.02} \ln\left(1 - \frac{0.80M}{M}\right)$$ $$= -50 \ln(1 - 0.8)$$ $$= -50 \ln(0.2)$$ $$\approx 80.47189562 \qquad \text{Use a calculator.}$$ The battery will reach 80% charge in about 80 minutes.

Definitions and Concepts	Examples
Population doubling time: If r is the annual growth rate and t is the time (in years) required for a population to double, then $$t = \frac{\ln 2}{r}$$	The population of the Earth is growing at the approximate rate of 2.5% per year. If this rate continues, how long will it take the population to double? Because the population is growing at the rate of 2.5% per year, we can substitute 0.025 for r in the formula for doubling time and simplify. $$t = \frac{\ln 2}{r}$$ $$t = \frac{\ln 2}{0.025}$$ $$\approx 27.72588722$$ It will take about 28 years for the Earth's population to double.
Isothermal expansion: If the temperature T is constant, the energy E required to increase the volume of 1 mole of gas from an initial volume V_i to a final volume V_f is given by $$E = RT \ln\left(\frac{V_f}{V_i}\right)$$ E is measured in joules and T in Kelvins. R is the universal gas constant, which is 8.314 joules/mole/K.	To find the amount of energy that must be supplied to double the volume of 1 mole of gas at a constant temperature of 300 K, we substitute 8.314 for R and 300 for T in the formula. Since the final volume is to be two times the initial volume, we also substitute $2V_i$ for V_f. $$E = RT \ln\left(\frac{V_f}{V_i}\right)$$ $$E = (8.314)(300)\ln\left(\frac{2V_i}{V_i}\right)$$ $$= 2{,}494.2 \ln 2$$ $$\approx 1728.847698$$ Approximately 1,729 joules of energy must be added to double the volume.

EXERCISES

51. Decibel gain An amplifier has an output of 18 volts when the input is 0.04 volt. Find the dB gain.

52. Intensity of an earthquake An earthquake had a period of 0.3 second and an amplitude of 7,500 micrometers. Find its measure on the Richter scale.

53. Charging batteries How long will it take a dead battery to reach an 80% charge? (Assume $k = 0.17$.)

54. Doubling time How long will it take the population of the United States to double if the growth rate is 3% per year?

55. Isothermal energy Find the amount of energy that must be supplied to double the volume of 1 mole of gas at a constant temperature of 350K. (*Hint:* $R = 8.314$.)

SECTION **4.5** Properties of Logarithms

Definitions and Concepts	Examples
Properties of logarithms: If b is a positive number and $b \neq 1$,	
1. $\log_b 1 = 0$	By Property 1, $\log_9 1 = 0$, because $9^0 = 1$.
2. $\log_b b = 1$	By Property 2, $\log_{11} 11 = 1$, because $11^1 = 11$.
3. $\log_b b^x = x$	By Property 3, $\log_4 4^3 = 3$, because $4^3 = 4^3$.
4. $b^{\log_b x} = x$	By Property 4, $6^{\log_6 3} = 3$, because $\log_6 3$ is the power to which 6 is raised to get 3.
5. Product Rule: $\quad \log_b MN = \log_b M + \log_b N$	By Property 5, $\log(2 \cdot 3) = \log 2 + \log 3$
6. Quotient Rule: $\quad \log_b \dfrac{M}{N} = \log_b M - \log_b N$	By Property 6, $\log \dfrac{17}{5} = \log 17 - \log 5$
7. Power Rule: $\quad \log_b M^p = p \log_b M$	By Property 7, $\log 3^2 = 2 \log 3$
8. One-to-One Property: $\quad$ If $\log_b x = \log_b y$, then $x = y$.	By Property 8, if $\log 8 = \log y$, then $8 = y$.
The properties of logarithms also hold for natural logarithms.	
Properties of natural logarithms:	
1. $\ln 1 = 0$	By Property 1, $\ln 1 = 0$, because $e^0 = 1$.
2. $\ln e = 1$	By Property 2, $\ln e = 1$, because $e^1 = e$.
3. $\ln e^x = x$	By Property 3, $\ln(e^{13}) = 13$.
4. $e^{\ln x} = x$	By Property 4, $e^{\ln 23} = 23$.
5. Product Rule: $\quad \ln MN = \ln M + \ln N$	By Property 5, $\ln(2 \cdot 3) = \ln 2 + \ln 3$.
6. Quotient Rule: $\quad \ln \dfrac{M}{N} = \ln M - \ln N$	By Property 6, $\ln \dfrac{15}{5} = \ln 15 - \ln 5$.
7. Power Rule: $\quad \ln M^p = p \ln M$	By Property 7, $\ln 3^2 = 2 \ln 3$.
8. One-to-One Property: $\quad$ If $\ln x = \ln y$, then $x = y$.	By Property 8, if $\ln 8 = \ln y$, then $8 = y$.

Definitions and Concepts	Examples
Expanding or condensing logarithmic expressions: The properties of logarithms can be used to expand or condense logarithmic expressions.	Write the expression $\log_2 \dfrac{x^2}{y}$ in terms of logarithms of x and y. $\log_2 \dfrac{x^2}{y} = \log_2 x^2 - \log_2 y$ Use the Quotient Rule. $= 2\log_2 x - \log_2 y$ Use the Power Rule. Write $5\ln x + \dfrac{1}{2}\ln y$ as a single natural logarithm. $5\ln x + \dfrac{1}{2}\ln y = \ln x^5 + \ln y^{1/2}$ Use the Power Rule. $= \ln(x^5 y^{1/2})$ Use the Product Rule. $= \ln(x^5\sqrt{y})$
Change-of-Base Formula: $\log_b y = \dfrac{\log_a y}{\log_a b}$	Use the Change-of-Base Formula to find $\log_3 10$. We will substitute 3 for b and 10 for y in the Change-of-Base Formula. $\log_3 10 = \dfrac{\log_{10} 10}{\log_{10} 3} = \dfrac{1}{0.4771212547} = 2.095903274$
pH of a solution: If $[H^+]$ is the hydrogen ion concentration in gram-ions per liter, then $pH = -\log[H^+]$	Lemon juice in a bottle has a pH of approximately 4. To find its hydrogen ion concentration, we can substitute 4 for pH in the pH formula and solve it for $[H^+]$. $4 = -\log[H^+]$ $-4 = \log[H^+]$ $[H^+] = 10^{-4}$ Change the equation from logarithmic form to exponential form. We can then use a calculator to find that $[H^+] = 1 \times 10^{-4}$ gram-ions per liter.
Weber–Fechner Law: If L is the apparent loudness of a sound and I is the intensity, then $L = k\ln I$	To find what increase in the intensity of a sound is necessary to cause a quadrupling of the apparent loudness, we can use the formula $L = k\ln I$. To quadruple the apparent loudness, we multiply both sides of the equation by 4 and use Property 7 of natural logarithms. $L = k\ln I$ $4L = 4k\ln I$ $= k\ln I^4$ To quadruple the apparent loudness, we must raise the intensity to the fourth power.

EXERCISES

Simplify each expression.

56. $\log_7 1$

57. $\log_7 7$

58. $\log_7 7^3$

59. $7^{\log_7 4}$

60. $\ln e^4$

61. $\ln 1$

62. $10^{\log_{10} 7}$

63. $e^{\ln 3}$

64. $\log_b b^4$

65. $\ln e^9$

Write each expression in terms of the logarithms of x, y, and z.

66. $\log_b \dfrac{x^2 y^3}{z^4}$

67. $\log_8 \sqrt{\dfrac{x}{yz^2}}$

68. $\ln \dfrac{x^4}{y^5 z^6}$

69. $\ln \sqrt[3]{xyz}$

Write each expression as the logarithm of one quantity.

70. $3 \log_b x - 5 \log_b y + 7 \log_b z$

71. $\dfrac{1}{2}(\log_b x + 3 \log_b y) - 7 \log_b z$

72. $4 \ln x - 5 \ln y - 6 \ln z$

73. $\dfrac{1}{2} \ln x + 3 \ln y - \dfrac{1}{3} \ln z$

Given that log a ≈ 0.6, log b ≈ 0.36, and log c ≈ 2.4, approximate the value of each expression.

74. $\log abc$

75. $\log a^2 b$

76. $\log \dfrac{ac}{b}$

77. $\log \dfrac{a^2}{c^3 b^2}$

78. To four decimal places, find $\log_5 17$.

79. **pH of grapefruit** The pH of grapefruit juice is about 3.1. Find its hydrogen ion concentration.

80. **Loudness of sound** Find the decrease in loudness if the intensity is cut in half.

SECTION 4.6   Exponential and Logarithmic Equations

Definitions and Concepts	Examples
One-to-One Property of exponents: If $b^x = b^y$ then $x = y$. That is, equal quantities with like bases have equal exponents. The One-to-One Property of exponents can be used to solve exponential equations with like bases.	Solve using like bases: $5^{x^2 - 2x} = \dfrac{1}{5}$. Since $\frac{1}{5} = 5^{-1}$, we can write the equation in the form $5^{x^2 - 2x} = 5^{-1}$ and use like bases to solve the equation. Because equal quantities with like bases have equal exponents, we have

$$x^2 - 2x = -1$$

$$x^2 - 2x + 1 = 0 \qquad \text{Add 1 to both sides.}$$

$$(x - 1)(x - 1) = 0 \qquad \text{Factor the trinomial.}$$

$$x - 1 = 0 \quad \text{or} \quad x - 1 = 0 \qquad \text{Set each factor equal to 0.}$$

$$x = 1 \quad \bigm| \quad x = 1$$

Definitions and Concepts	Examples
Solving exponential equations with different bases: Exponential equations with different bases can be solve using logarithms.	Solve the exponential equation: $3^x = 15$. Since logarithms of equal numbers are equal, we can take the common logarithm of each side of the equation. We can then use the Power Rule and move the variable x from its position as an exponent to a position as a coefficient and solve the equation. $$3^x = 5$$ $$\log 3^x = \log 15 \qquad \text{Take the common logarithm of each side.}$$ $$x \log 3 = \log 15 \qquad \text{Use the Power Rule.}$$ $$x = \frac{\log 15}{\log 3} \qquad \text{Divide both sides by log 3.}$$ $$\approx 2.464973521 \qquad \text{Use a calculator.}$$ To four decimal places, $x = 2.4650$.
Solving exponential equations with e: Use natural logarithms to solve exponential equations with a base of e.	Solve $e^x = 19$. We will take the natural logarithm of both sides, simplify using the natural logarithms properties, and solve for x. $$e^x = 19$$ $$\ln e^x = \ln 19 \qquad \text{Take the natural logarithm of both sides.}$$ $$x = \ln 19 \qquad \text{Use the property } \ln(e^x) = x.$$ $$x \approx 2.94 \qquad \text{Use a calculator and round to two decimal places.}$$
Solving logarithmic equations: The One-to-One Property of logarithms can be used to solve some logarithmic equations. **One-to-One Property:** If $\log_b x = \log_b y$, then $x = y$. The solution(s) to a logarithmic equation must be checked.	Solve: $\log_4(5x + 3) = \log_4(-5x + 23)$. We will use the One-to-One Property to solve the equation. $$\log_4(5x + 3) = \log_4(-5x + 23)$$ $$5x + 3 = -5x + 23 \qquad \text{Use the log property stated above.}$$ $$10x = 20 \qquad \text{Add } 5x \text{ and subtract 3 from both sides.}$$ $$x = 2 \qquad \text{Divide both sides by 10.}$$ **Check:** $\log_4(5x + 3) = \log_4(-5x + 23)$ $$\log_4[5(2) + 3] \overset{?}{=} \log_4[-5(2) + 23]$$ $$\log_4(13) = \log_4(13)$$ Since $x = 2$ checks, it is the solution.

Definitions and Concepts	Examples
Solving logarithmic equations: Logarithmic properties can be used to solve many logarithmic equations.	Solve: $\log x + \log(x - 9) = 1$. $\log x + \log(x - 9) = 1$

$$\log x(x - 9) = 1 \qquad \text{Use the Product Rule.}$$

$$x(x - 9) = 10^1 \qquad \text{Use the definition of logarithm and write in exponential form.}$$

$$x^2 - 9x - 10 = 0 \qquad \text{Remove parentheses and subtract 10 from both sides.}$$

$$(x - 10)(x + 1) = 0 \qquad \text{Factor the trinomial.}$$

$$x - 10 = 0 \quad \text{or} \quad x + 1 = 0$$

$$x = 10 \quad | \quad x = -1$$

Check: The number -1 is not a solution, because it does not satisfy the equation (a negative number does not have a logarithm). We check the remaining number, 10.

$$\log x + \log(x - 9) = 1$$

$$\log 10 + \log(10 - 9) \overset{?}{=} 1 \qquad \text{Substitute 10 for } x.$$

$$\log 10 + \log 1 \overset{?}{=} 1$$

$$1 + 0 \overset{?}{=} 1 \qquad \log_{10} 10 = 1, \log_{10} 1 = 0$$

$$1 = 1$$

Since 10 does check, it is a root.

| **Carbon dating:**
The amount A of radioactive material present at time t is given by the model

$A = A_0 2^{-t/h}$

where A_0 is the amount present initially and h is the half-life of the material. | To find the age of an artifact that contains three-fourths of its original carbon-14 content, we substitute $\frac{3}{4}A_0$ for A and 5,700 for h in the formula for carbon dating and solve for t. |

$$A = A_0 2^{-t/h}$$

$$\frac{3}{4}A_0 = A_0 2^{-t/5,700}$$

$$\frac{3}{4} = 2^{-t/5,700} \qquad \text{Divide both sides by } A_0.$$

$$\log \frac{3}{4} = \log 2^{-t/5,700} \qquad \text{Take the base-10 log of both sides.}$$

$$-0.1249387366 = -\frac{t}{5,700}\log 2 \qquad \text{Use Property 7 of logarithms.}$$

$$t \approx 2,366 \qquad \text{Solve for } t.$$

The artifact is about 2,300 years old.

EXERCISES

Solve each equation for x.

81. $81^{x+2} = 27$

82. $2^{x^2+4x} = \dfrac{1}{8}$

83. $e^x = e^{-6x+14}$

84. $e^{2x^2} = e^{18}$

85. $3^x = 7$

86. $2^x = 3^{x-1}$

87. $2e^x = 16$

88. $-5e^x = -35$

Solve each equation for x.

89. $\log_7(-7x + 2) = \log_7(3x + 32)$

90. $\ln(x + 3) = \ln(-5x + 51)$

91. $\log x + \log(29 - x) = 2$

92. $\log_2 x + \log_2(x - 2) = 3$

93. $\log_2(x + 2) + \log_2(x - 1) = 2$

94. $\dfrac{\log(7x - 12)}{\log x} = 2$

95. $\ln x + \ln(x - 5) = \ln 6$

96. $\log 3 - \log(x - 1) = -1$

97. $e^{x \ln 2} = 9$

98. $\ln x = \ln(x - 1)$

99. $\ln x - 3 = 4$

100. $\ln x = \ln(x - 1) + 1$

101. $\ln x = \log_{10} x$ (*Hint:* Use the Change-of-Base Formula.)

102. **Carbon-14 dating** A wooden statue found in Egypt has a carbon-14 content that is two-thirds of that found in living wood. If the half-life of carbon-14 is 5,700 years, how old is the statue?

CHAPTER TEST

Graph each function.

1. $f(x) = 2^x + 1$

2. $f(x) = e^{x-2}$

Graph each function.

11. $f(x) = \log(x - 1)$

12. $f(x) = 2 + \ln x$

Solve each problem.

3. **Radioactive decay** A radioactive material decays according to the formula $A = A_0(2)^{-t}$. How much of a 3-gram sample will be left in 6 years?

4. **Compound interest** An initial deposit of $1,000 earns 6% interest, compounded twice a year. How much will be in the account in one year?

5. **Continuous compound interest** An account contains $2,000 and has been earning 8% interest, compounded continuously. How much will be in the account in 10 years?

Find each value.

6. $\log_7 343$

7. $\log_3 \dfrac{1}{27}$

8. $\log_{10} 10^{12} + 10^{\log_{10} 5}$

9. $\log_{3/2} \dfrac{9}{4}$

10. $\log_{2/3} \dfrac{27}{8}$

Write each expression in terms of the logarithms of a, b, and c.

13. $\log a^2bc^3$

14. $\ln\sqrt{\dfrac{a}{b^2c}}$

Write each expression as a logarithm of a single quantity.

15. $\dfrac{1}{2}\log(a + 2) + \log b - 2 \log c$

16. $\dfrac{1}{3}(\ln a - 2 \ln b) - \ln c$

Given that $\log 2 \approx 0.3010$ and $\log 3 \approx 0.4771$, approximate each value. Do not use a calculator.

17. $\log 24$

18. $\log \dfrac{8}{3}$

Use the Change-of-Base Formula to find each logarithm. Do not attempt to simplify the answer.

19. $\log_7 3$

20. $\log_\pi e$

Determine whether each statement is true or false.

21. $\log_a ab = 1 + \log_a b$

22. $\dfrac{\log a}{\log b} = \log a - \log b$

Find the solution.

23. pH of a solution   Find the pH of a solution with a hydrogen ion concentration of 3.7×10^{-7}. (*Hint:* $\mathrm{pH} = -\log[\mathrm{H}^+]$.)

24. Decibel gain   Find the dB gain of an amplifier when $E_O = 60$ volts and $E_I = 0.3$ volt. (*Hint:* dB gain $= 20 \log(E_O/E_I)$.)

Solve each equation.

25. $3^{x^2-2x} = 27$

26. $3^{x-1} = 100^x$

27. $5e^x = 45$

28. $\ln(5x + 2) = \ln(2x + 5)$

29. $\log x + \log(x - 9) = 1$

30. $\log_6 18 - \log_6(x - 3) = \log_6 3$

Solving Polynomial Equations

5

CAREERS AND MATHEMATICS: Teacher

AVAVA/Shutterstock.com

Teachers play an important role in fostering the intellectual and social development of students. Whether in elementary school, middle school, or high school, teachers provide the tools and the environment for their students to develop into responsible adults. Teaching is often cited as one of the most challenging, yet fulfilling careers.

Education and Mathematics Required
- Teachers begin their careers by earning a bachelor's degree. Some also earn a master's degree in education. Requirements for regular licenses to teach kindergarten through grade 12 vary by state.
- Elementary and middle school teachers are required to take College Algebra, Survey of the Real Number System, Concepts of Geometry, Measurement and Probability, and Problem Solving. Additional courses such as Trigonometry and Calculus I and II are often required for teachers who plan to concentrate in the mathematics area.
- High school math teachers are required to take Calculus I and II, Linear Algebra, Calculus of Several Variables, Ordinary Differential Equations, Theory of Analysis, Abstract Algebra, and Statistics.

How Teachers Use Math and Who Employs Them
- Teachers teach problem solving skills to students. Middle school math teachers and high school math teachers demonstrate sample math problems in class, create math assignments for students, and write and grade math tests.
- Most teachers work in public or private schools.

Career Outlook and Salary
- Employment of kindergarten, elementary, middle, and secondary school teachers is expected to grow by 13 percent between 2008 and 2018.
- Median annual wages of kindergarten, elementary, middle, and secondary school teachers ranged from $47,100 to $51,180 in May 2008.

For more information see: www.bls.gov/oco

A goal throughout all of algebra has been to solve equations. In this chapter, we will develop methods to solve polynomial equations of any degree.

5.1 The Remainder and Factor Theorems; Synthetic Division

In this section, we will learn to

1. Understand the definition of a zero of a polynomial function.
2. Use the Remainder Theorem.
3. Use the Factor Theorem.
4. Use synthetic division to divide polynomials.
5. Use synthetic division to evaluate polynomial functions.
6. Use synthetic division to solve polynomial equations.

Fuse/Jupiter Images

The cheetah is the fastest land animal and is known for its speed and stealth. Cheetahs can run at speeds between 70 mph and 75 mph. They have the ability to accelerate from 0 mph to 68 mph in three seconds. This acceleration is greater than that of most sports cars.

Although we will never run as fast as a cheetah, we do live in a society that wants convenience and speed. We demand fast service, fast food, fast communication, fast technology, and fast vehicles.

In this section, we will learn about synthetic division, a fast way to divide certain polynomials. Synthetic division can help us find the roots of many polynomial equations.

1. Understand the Definition of a Zero of a Polynomial Function

We have seen that many polynomial equations can be solved by factoring. For example, to solve the third-degree polynomial equation $x^3 - 3x^2 + 2x = 0$, we proceed as follows:

$$x^3 - 3x^2 + 2x = 0$$

$$x(x^2 - 3x + 2) = 0 \qquad \text{Factor out } x.$$

$$x(x - 1)(x - 2) = 0 \qquad \text{Factor } x^2 - 3x + 2.$$

$$x = 0 \quad \text{or} \quad x - 1 = 0 \quad \text{or} \quad x - 2 = 0 \qquad \text{Set each factor equal to 0.}$$
$$x = 1 \qquad\qquad x = 2$$

The solution set of this equation is $\{0, 1, 2\}$.

In this chapter, we will solve higher-degree polynomial equations. In general, an nth-degree polynomial equation is defined as follows:

Polynomial Equation   A **polynomial equation** is an equation that can be written in the form $P(x) = 0$, where

$$P(x) = a_n x^n + a_{n-1} x^{n-1} + a_{n-2} x^{n-2} + \cdots + a_1 x + a_0$$

and where n is a natural number and the polynomial is of degree n.

Any number that makes $P(x) = 0$ when substituted for x is called a *zero of the polynomial function.*

Zero of a Polynomial Function   A **zero of the polynomial function** $P(x)$ is any number r for which $P(r) = 0$.

The real numbers 0, 1, and 2 are zeros of the polynomial function

$$P(x) = x^3 - 3x^2 + 2x \text{ because}$$

$P(0) = 0^3 - 3(0)^2 + 2(0)$	$P(1) = 1^3 - 3(1)^2 + 2(1)$	$P(2) = 2^3 - 3(2)^2 + 2(2)$
$= 0 - 0 + 0$	$= 1 - 3 + 2$	$= 8 - 12 + 4$
$= 0$	$= 0$	$= 0$

As shown, the roots 0, 1, and 2 of the equation $x^3 - 3x^2 + 2x = 0$ are also zeros of the polynomial function $P(x) = x^3 - 3x^2 + 2x$. In general, the roots of the polynomial equation $P(x) = 0$ are the zeros of the polynomial function $P(x)$.

2. Use the Remainder Theorem

There is a relationship between a zero r of a polynomial function $P(x)$ and the results of a long division of $P(x)$ by $x - r$. We will examine this relationship in this section.

EXAMPLE 1   **Evaluating a Polynomial Function and Long Division**

Let $P(x) = 3x^3 - 5x^2 + 3x - 10$.
a. Find $P(1)$ **b.** Divide $P(x)$ by $x - 1$

SOLUTION   **a.** To find $P(1)$, we will substitute 1 for x in the polynomial function.

$$P(1) = 3(1)^3 - 5(1)^2 + 3(1) - 10$$
$$= 3 - 5 + 3 - 10$$
$$= -9$$

b. To divide $P(x)$ by $x - 1$, we proceed as follows:

$$
\begin{array}{r}
3x^2 - 2x + 1 \\
x - 1 \overline{\smash{)}\ 3x^3 - 5x^2 + 3x - 10} \\
\underline{3x^3 - 3x^2\phantom{{}+3x-10}} \\
-2x^2 + 3x\phantom{{}-10} \\
\underline{-2x^2 + 2x\phantom{{}-10}} \\
x - 10 \\
\underline{x - 1} \\
-9
\end{array}
$$

Note that the remainder is equal to $P(1)$. ∎

Self Check 1   Let $P(x) = 2x^2 - 3x + 5$. Find $P(2)$ and divide $P(x)$ by $x - 2$. What do you notice about the results?

Now Try Exercise 11.

EXAMPLE 2   **Evaluating a Polynomial Function and Long Division**

Let $P(x) = 3x^3 - 5x^2 + 3x - 10$.
a. Find $P(-2)$ **b.** Divide $P(x)$ by $x + 2$

SOLUTION   **a.** To find $P(-2)$, we will substitute -2 for x in the polynomial.

$$P(-2) = 3(-2)^3 - 5(-2)^2 + 3(-2) - 10$$
$$= 3(-8) - 5(4) + 3(-2) - 10$$
$$= -24 - 20 - 6 - 10$$
$$= -60$$

b. To divide $P(x)$ by $x + 2$, we proceed as follows:

$$
\begin{array}{r}
3x^2 - 11x + 25 \\
x+2\overline{\smash{)}3x^3 - 5x^2 + 3x - 10} \\
\underline{3x^3 + 6x^2} \\
-11x^2 + 3x \\
\underline{-11x^2 - 22x} \\
25x - 10 \\
\underline{25x + 50} \\
-60
\end{array}
$$

Note that the remainder is equal to $P(-2)$. ∎

Self Check 2   Let $P(x) = 2x^2 - 3x + 5$. Find $P(-3)$ and divide $P(x)$ by $x + 3$. What do you notice about the results?

Now Try Exercise 13.

When $P(x)$ was divided by $x - 1$ in Example 1, the remainder was $P(1) = -9$. When $P(x)$ was divided by $x + 2$, or $x - (-2)$, in Example 2, the remainder was $P(-2) = -60$. These results are not coincidental. The **Remainder Theorem** states that a division of any polynomial function $P(x)$ by $x - r$ gives $P(r)$ as the remainder.

The Remainder Theorem   If $P(x)$ is a polynomial function, r is any number, and $P(x)$ is divided by $x - r$, the remainder is $P(r)$.

⟨

PROOF   To divide $P(x)$ by $x - r$, we must find a quotient $Q(x)$ and a remainder $R(x)$ such that

$$
\begin{array}{ccccccc}
\text{Dividend} & = & \text{divisor} & \cdot & \text{quotient} & + & \text{remainder} \\
\downarrow & & \downarrow & & \downarrow & & \downarrow \\
P(x) & = & (x - r) & \cdot & Q(x) & + & R(x)
\end{array}
$$

Since the degree of the remainder $R(x)$ must be less than the degree of the divisor $x - r$, and the degree of $x - r$ is 1, $R(x)$ must be a constant R.

In the equation

$$P(x) = (x - r)Q(x) + R$$

the polynomial on the left side is the same as the polynomial on the right side, and the values that they assume for any number x are equal. If we replace x with r, we have

$$P(r) = (r - r)Q(r) + R$$
$$= (0)Q(r) + R$$
$$= R$$

Thus, $P(r) = R$. ∎

EXAMPLE 3   **Using the Remainder Theorem**

Use the Remainder Theorem to find the remainder that will occur when $P(x) = 2x^4 - 10x^3 + 17x^2 - 14x - 3$ is divided by $x - 3$.

SOLUTION   By the Remainder Theorem, the remainder will be $P(3)$.

$$P(x) = 2x^4 - 10x^3 + 17x^2 - 14x - 3$$

$$P(3) = 2(3)^4 - 10(3)^3 + 17(3)^2 - 14(3) - 3 \qquad \text{Substitute 3 for } x.$$

$$= 0$$

The remainder will be 0. Although this calculation is tedious, it is easy to do with a calculator.

Self Check 3   Find the remainder when $P(x)$ is divided by $x - 2$.

Now Try Exercise 17.

3. Use the Factor Theorem

If $R = P(r) = 0$ in the equation $P(x) = (x - r)Q(x) + R$, then $P(x)$ factors as $(x - r)Q(x)$. This fact can help us factor polynomials.

The Factor Theorem   If $P(x)$ is a polynomial function and r is any number, then

If $P(r) = 0$, then $x - r$ is a factor of $P(x)$.

If $x - r$ is a factor of $P(x)$, then $P(r) = 0$.

PROOF   **Part 1:** First, we assume that $P(r) = 0$ and prove that $x - r$ is a factor of $P(x)$. If $P(r) = 0$, then $R = 0$, and the equation $P(x) = (x - r)Q(x) + R$ becomes

$$P(x) = (x - r)Q(x) + 0$$

$$P(x) = (x - r)Q(x)$$

Therefore, $x - r$ divides $P(x)$ exactly, and $x - r$ is a factor of $P(x)$.

Part 2: Conversely, we assume that $x - r$ is a factor of $P(x)$ and prove that $P(r) = 0$. Because, by assumption, $x - r$ is a factor of $P(x)$, $x - r$ divides $P(x)$ exactly, and the division has a remainder of 0. By the Remainder Theorem, this remainder is $P(r)$. Hence, $P(r) = 0$.

Below, we state the Factor Theorem in a slightly different way.

Alternate Form of the Factor Theorem   If r is a zero of the polynomial function $P(x)$, then $x - r$ is a factor of $P(x)$.

If $x - r$ is a factor of $P(x)$, then r is a zero of the polynomial.

It is important to note that for each factor of a polynomial function, there corresponds a zero. Several possible factors of a polynomial function are shown next with their corresponding zeros.

Factor	Zero
$x - 5$	5
$x + 2$	-2
$x - \dfrac{1}{2}$	$\dfrac{1}{2}$
$x + \dfrac{2}{3}$	$-\dfrac{2}{3}$

EXAMPLE 4   **Using the Factor Theorem**

Determine whether $x + 2$ is a factor of $P(x) = x^4 - 7x^2 - 6x$.

SOLUTION   By the Factor Theorem, $x + 2$, or $x - (-2)$, is a factor of $P(x)$ if $P(-2) = 0$. So we find the value of $P(-2)$.

$$P(x) = x^4 - 7x^2 - 6x$$

$$P(-2) = (-2)^4 - 7(-2)^2 - 6(-2) \qquad \text{Substitute } -2 \text{ for } x.$$

$$= 16 - 28 + 12$$

$$= 0$$

Since $P(-2) = 0$, we know that $x - (-2)$, or $x + 2$, is a factor of $P(x)$.

Comment

In Example 4, $x + 2$ is a factor of the polynomial function $P(x) = x^4 - 7x^2 - 6x$. By the Factor Theorem, we know that -2 is a zero of the polynomial function.

Self Check 4   Determine whether $x + 3$ is a factor of $P(x)$.

Now Try Exercise 27.

4. Use Synthetic Division to Divide Polynomials

Synthetic division is an easy way to divide higher-degree polynomials by binomials of the form $x - r$, and it is much faster than long division. To see how it works, we consider the following long division. On the left is a complete division. On the right is a modified version in which the variables have been removed.

$$
\begin{array}{r}
2x^2 + 10x + 27 \\
x - 3 \overline{)2x^3 + 4x^2 - 3x + 10} \\
\underline{2x^3 - 6x^2} \\
10x^2 - 3x \\
\underline{10x^2 - 30x} \\
27x + 10 \\
\underline{27x - 81} \\
\text{(remainder) } 91
\end{array}
\qquad
\begin{array}{r}
2 + 10 + 27 \\
1 - 3 \overline{)2 + 4 - 3 + 10} \\
\underline{2 - 6} \\
10 - 3 \\
\underline{10 - 30} \\
27 + 10 \\
\underline{27 - 81} \\
\text{(remainder) } 91
\end{array}
$$

We can shorten the work even more by omitting the numbers printed in color.

$$
\begin{array}{r}
2 + 10 + 27 \\
-3 \overline{)2 + 4 - 3 + 10} \\
\underline{- 6} \\
10 - \\
\underline{- 30} \\
27 \\
\underline{- 81} \\
\text{(remainder) } 91
\end{array}
$$

We can then compress the work vertically to get

$$
\begin{array}{r}
2 + 10 + 27 \\
-3\overline{)2 + \ 4 - \ \ 3 + 10} \\
- \ 6 - 30 - 81 \\
\hline
10 \quad 27 \quad 91
\end{array}
$$

If we write the 2 in the quotient on the bottom line, the bottom line gives both the coefficients of the quotient and the remainder. The top line can now be eliminated, and the division appears as

$$
\begin{array}{r}
-3\,\underline{|\ 2 + \ 4 - \ \ 3 + 10\ } \\
- \ 6 - 30 - 81 \\
\hline
2 \quad 10 \quad 27 \quad 91
\end{array}
$$

The bottom line was obtained by subtracting the middle line from the top line. If we replace the -3 in the divisor with $+3$, the signs of each number in the middle line will be reversed in the division process. Then the bottom line can be obtained by addition, and we have the final form of the synthetic division.

$$
\begin{array}{r}
+3\,\underline{|\ 2 + \ 4 - \ \ 3 + 10\ } \\
+ \ 6 + 30 + 81 \\
\hline
2 \quad 10 \quad 27 \quad 91
\end{array}
$$

These are the coefficients of the dividend.

These are the coefficients of the quotient and the remainder.

Thus,

$$
\frac{2x^3 + 4x^2 - 3x + 10}{x - 3} = 2x^2 + 10x + 27 + \frac{91}{x - 3}
$$

EXAMPLE 5   **Using Synthetic Division to Divide Polynomials**

Use synthetic division to divide $10x + 3x^4 - 8x^3 + 3$ by $x - 2$.

SOLUTION   We will first write the terms in descending powers of x:

$$3x^4 - 8x^3 + 10x + 3$$

We then write the coefficients of the dividend, with its terms in descending powers of x, and the 2 from the divisor in the following form:

$$
2\,\underline{|\ 3 \ \ -8 \quad 0 \ \ 10 \ \ 3\ }
$$

Write 0 for the coefficient of the missing x^2 term.

Then we follow these steps:

$$
\begin{array}{c}
2\,\underline{|\ 3 \ \ -8 \quad 0 \ \ 10 \ \ 3\ } \\
\downarrow \qquad \qquad \qquad \\
\hline
3 \qquad \qquad \qquad
\end{array}
$$

Bring down the 3.

$$
\begin{array}{c}
2\,\underline{|\ 3 \ \ -8 \quad 0 \ \ 10 \ \ 3\ } \\
6 \qquad \qquad \\
\hline
3 \ \ -2 \qquad \qquad
\end{array}
$$

Multiply 2 and 3 together to get 6, and add 6 and -8 to get -2.

$$
\begin{array}{c}
2\,\underline{|\ 3 \ \ -8 \quad 0 \ \ 10 \ \ 3\ } \\
6 \ \ -4 \qquad \\
\hline
3 \ \ -2 \ \ -4 \qquad
\end{array}
$$

Multiply 2 and -2 together to get -4, and add -4 and 0 to get -4.

$$\begin{array}{r|rrrrr} 2 & 3 & -8 & 0 & 10 & 3 \\ & & 6 & -4 & -8 & \\ \hline & 3 & -2 & -4 & 2 & \end{array}$$

Multiply 2 and -4 together to get -8, and add -8 and 10 to get 2.

$$\begin{array}{r|rrrrr} 2 & 3 & -8 & 0 & 10 & 3 \\ & & 6 & -4 & -8 & 4 \\ \hline & 3 & -2 & -4 & 2 & 7 \end{array}$$

Multiply 2 and 2 together to get 4, and add 4 and 3 to get 7. These are the coefficients of the quotient and the remainder.

Thus,

$$\frac{10x + 3x^4 - 8x^3 + 3}{x - 2} = 3x^3 - 2x^2 - 4x + 2 + \frac{7}{x - 2}$$

Self Check 5   Divide $2x^3 - 4x^2 + 5x - 7$ by $x - 3$.

Now Try Exercise 43.

5. Use Synthetic Division to Evaluate Polynomial Functions

EXAMPLE 6   **Using Synthetic Division to Evaluate a Polynomial Function**

Use synthetic division to find $P(-2)$ when $P(x) = 5x^3 + 3x^2 - 21x - 1$.

SOLUTION   Because of the Remainder Theorem, $P(-2)$ is the remainder when $P(x)$ is divided by $x - (-2)$. Earlier in the section, we would find the remainder by using long division. We can now simplify the work and find the remainder by using synthetic division.

$$\begin{array}{r|rrrr} -2 & 5 & 3 & -21 & -1 \\ & & -10 & & \\ \hline & 5 & -7 & & \end{array}$$

$-2(5) = -10; 3 + (-10) = -7$

$$\begin{array}{r|rrrr} -2 & 5 & 3 & -21 & -1 \\ & & -10 & 14 & \\ \hline & 5 & -7 & -7 & \end{array}$$

$-2(-7) = 14; -21 + 14 = -7$

$$\begin{array}{r|rrrr} -2 & 5 & 3 & -21 & -1 \\ & & -10 & 14 & 14 \\ \hline & 5 & -7 & -7 & 13 \end{array}$$

$-2(-7) = 14; -1 + 14 = 13$

Because the remainder is 13, $P(-2) = 13$.

Self Check 6   Find $P(3)$.

Now Try Exercise 49.

EXAMPLE 7   **Using Synthetic Division to Evaluate a Polynomial Function at i**

If $P(x) = x^3 - x^2 + x - 1$, find $P(i)$, where $i = \sqrt{-1}$.

SOLUTION　We will use synthetic division and find the remainder.

$$\underline{i\,|}\ \ 1\quad -1\qquad\quad 1\quad -1$$
$$\qquad\quad i\quad -1-i\quad\ 1$$
$$\overline{\qquad 1\quad i-1\qquad -i\qquad 0}$$

Since the remainder is 0, $P(i) = 0$ and i is a zero of $P(x)$.

Comment

Example 7 illustrates that synthetic division can be used with complex numbers.

Self Check 7　Find $P(-i)$.

Now Try Exercise 53.

6. Use Synthetic Division to Solve Polynomial Equations

EXAMPLE 8　**Solving a Polynomial Equation When Given One Solution**

Let $P(x) = 3x^3 - 5x^2 + 3x - 10$. Completely solve the polynomial equation $P(x) = 0$ given that 2 is one solution.

SOLUTION　Since 2 is a solution of the equation $P(x) = 0$, we know that 2 is a zero of $P(x)$. We will use synthetic division and divide $P(x)$ by $x - 2$, obtaining a remainder of 0. Then, we will use the result of the synthetic division to help factor the polynomial and solve the equation.

1. We use synthetic division to divide $P(x)$ by $x - 2$.

$$\underline{2\,|}\ \ 3\quad -5\quad 3\quad -10$$
$$\qquad\qquad 6\quad 2\qquad 10$$
$$\overline{\qquad 3\quad\ \ 1\quad 5\qquad 0}$$

2. We then write the quotient and factor it.

$$3x^3 - 5x^2 + 3x - 10 = (x - 2)(3x^2 + x + 5)$$

3. Finally, we solve the polynomial equation $P(x) = 0$.

$$3x^3 - 5x^2 + 3x - 10 = 0$$
$$(x - 2)(3x^2 + x + 5) = 0$$

To solve for x, we set each factor equal to 0 and apply the Quadratic Formula to the equation $3x^2 + x + 5 = 0$.

$$x - 2 = 0 \quad \text{or} \quad 3x^2 + x + 5 = 0$$

$$x = 2 \qquad\qquad x = \frac{-1 \pm \sqrt{1^2 - 4(3)(5)}}{2(3)}$$

$$x = \frac{-1 \pm i\sqrt{59}}{6}$$

The solution set is $\left\{2,\ -\dfrac{1}{6} + \dfrac{\sqrt{59}}{6}i,\ -\dfrac{1}{6} - \dfrac{\sqrt{59}}{6}i\right\}$.

Self Check 8　Solve: $x^3 - 1 = 0$ given that 1 is one solution.

Now Try Exercise 75.

EXAMPLE 9   **Finding a Polynomial Function When Given the Zeros**

Find a third-degree polynomial function $P(x)$ with three zeros of 3, 3, and -5.

SOLUTION   We will use the Factor Theorem and write the three factors that correspond to the three zeros of 3, 3, and -5. We will then multiply the resulting binomials.

If 3, 3, and -5 are the three zeros of $P(x)$, then $x - 3$, $x - 3$, and $x - (-5)$ are the three factors of $P(x)$.

$$P(x) = (x - 3)(x - 3)(x + 5)$$

$$P(x) = (x^2 - 6x + 9)(x + 5) \qquad \text{Multiply } x - 3 \text{ and } x - 3.$$

$$P(x) = x^3 - x^2 - 21x + 45 \qquad \text{Multiply using the Distributive Property.}$$

The polynomial function $P(x) = x^3 - x^2 - 21x + 45$ has zeros of 3, 3, and -5. Because 3 occurs twice as a zero, we say that 3 is a **zero of multiplicity 2**.

Self Check 9   Find a polynomial function $P(x)$ with zeros of -2, 2, and 3.

Now Try Exercise 85.

Self Check Answers   **1.** $P(2)$ is the remainder.   **2.** $P(-3)$ is the remainder.   **3.** -11 **4.** no
5. $2x^2 + 2x + 11 + \dfrac{26}{x - 3}$ **6.** 98   **7.** 0   **8.** $1, -\dfrac{1}{2} + \dfrac{\sqrt{3}}{2}i, -\dfrac{1}{2} - \dfrac{\sqrt{3}}{2}i$
9. $P(x) = x^3 - 3x^2 - 4x + 12$

Exercises **5.1**

Getting Ready
You should be able to complete these vocabulary and concept statements before you proceed to the practice exercises.

Fill in the blanks.

1. The variables in a polynomial have _____ -number exponents.

2. A zero of $P(x)$ is any number r for which _____.

3. The Remainder Theorem holds when r is _____ number.

4. If $P(x)$ is a polynomial function and $P(x)$ is divided by _____, the remainder will be $P(r)$.

5. If $P(x)$ is a polynomial function, then $P(r) = 0$ if and only if $x - r$ is a _____ of $P(x)$.

6. A shortcut method for dividing a polynomial by a binomial of the form $x - r$ is called _____ division.

Practice
Use long division to perform each division.

7. $\dfrac{4x^3 - 2x^2 - x + 1}{x - 1}$

8. $\dfrac{2x^3 + 3x^2 - 5x + 1}{x + 3}$

9. $\dfrac{2x^4 + x^3 + 2x^2 + 15x - 5}{x + 2}$

10. $\dfrac{x^4 + 6x^3 - 2x^2 + x - 1}{x - 1}$

Find each value by substituting the given value of x into the polynomial and simplifying. Then find the value by performing long division and finding the remainder.

11. $P(x) = 3x^3 - 2x^2 - 5x - 7$; $P(2)$

12. $P(x) = 5x^3 + 4x^2 + x - 1$; $P(-2)$

13. $P(x) = 7x^4 + 2x^3 + 5x^2 - 1$; $P(-1)$

14. $P(x) = 2x^4 - 2x^3 + 5x^2 - 1$; $P(2)$

15. $P(x) = 2x^5 + x^4 - x^3 - 2x + 3$; $P(1)$

16. $P(x) = 3x^5 + x^4 - 3x^2 + 5x + 7$; $P(-2)$

Use the Remainder Theorem to find the remainder that occurs when $P(x) = 3x^4 + 5x^3 - 4x^2 - 2x + 1$ is divided by each binomial. Use a calculator on Exercises 21–24.

17. $x + 2$ 18. $x - 1$

19. $x - 2$ 20. $x + 1$

21. $x - 12$ 22. $x + 15$

23. $x + 3.25$ 24. $x - 7.12$

Use the Factor Theorem to determine whether each statement is true. If the statement is not true, so indicate.

25. $x - 1$ is a factor of $P(x) = x^7 - 1$.

26. $x - 2$ is a factor of $P(x) = x^3 - x^2 + 2x - 8$.

27. $x - 1$ is a factor of $P(x) = 3x^5 + 4x^2 - 7$.

28. $x + 1$ is a factor of $P(x) = 3x^5 + 4x^2 - 7$.

29. $x + 3$ is a factor of $P(x) = 2x^3 - 2x^2 + 1$.

30. $x - 3$ is a factor of
$P(x) = 3x^5 - 3x^4 + 5x^2 - 13x - 6$.

31. $x - 1$ is a factor of
$P(x) = x^{1,984} - x^{1,776} + x^{1,492} - x^{1,066}$.

32. $x + 1$ is a factor of
$P(x) = x^{1,984} + x^{1,776} - x^{1,492} - x^{1,066}$.

Use synthetic division to express the polynomial function $P(x) = 3x^3 - 2x^2 - 6x - 4$ in the form (divisor)(quotient) + remainder for each divisor.

33. $x - 1$

34. $x - 2$

35. $x - 3$

36. $x - 4$

37. $x + 1$

38. $x + 2$

39. $x + 3$

40. $x + 4$

Use synthetic division to perform each division.

41. $\dfrac{x^3 + x^2 + x - 3}{x - 1}$

42. $\dfrac{x^3 - x^2 - 5x + 6}{x - 2}$

43. $\dfrac{7x^3 - 3x^2 - 5x + 1}{x + 1}$

44. $\dfrac{2x^3 + 4x^2 - 3x + 8}{x - 3}$

45. $\dfrac{4x^4 - 3x^3 - x + 5}{x - 3}$

46. $\dfrac{x^4 + 5x^3 - 2x^2 + x - 1}{x + 1}$

47. $\dfrac{3x^5 - 768x}{x - 4}$

48. $\dfrac{x^5 - 4x^2 + 4x + 4}{x + 3}$

Let $P(x) = 5x^3 + 2x^2 - x + 1$. Use synthetic division to find each value.

49. $P(2)$ **50.** $P(-2)$

51. $P(-5)$ **52.** $P(3)$

53. $P(i)$ **54.** $P(-i)$

Let $P(x) = 2x^4 - x^2 + 2$. Use synthetic division to find each value.

55. $P\left(\dfrac{1}{2}\right)$ **56.** $P\left(\dfrac{1}{3}\right)$

57. $P(i)$ **58.** $P(-i)$

Let $P(x) = x^4 - 8x^3 + 8x + 14x^2 - 15$. Write the terms of $P(x)$ in descending powers of x and use synthetic division to find each value.

59. $P(1)$ **60.** $P(0)$

61. $P(-3)$ **62.** $P(-1)$

63. $P(-i)$ **64.** $P(i)$

Let $P(x) = 8 - 8x^2 + x^5 - x^3$. Write the terms of $P(x)$ in descending powers of x and use synthetic division to find each value.

65. $P(i)$ **66.** $P(-i)$

67. $P(-2i)$ **68.** $P(2i)$

A partial solution set is given for each polynomial equation. Find the complete solution set.

69. $x^3 + 3x^2 - 13x - 15 = 0$; $\{-1\}$

70. $x^3 + 6x^2 + 5x - 12 = 0$; $\{1\}$

71. $2x^3 + x^2 - 18x - 9 = 0$; $\left\{-\dfrac{1}{2}\right\}$

72. $2x^3 - 3x^2 - 11x + 6 = 0$; $\left\{\dfrac{1}{2}\right\}$

73. $x^3 - 6x^2 + 7x + 2$; $\{2\}$

74. $x^3 + x^2 - 8x - 6$; $\{-3\}$

75. $x^3 - 3x^2 + x + 57$; $\{-3\}$

76. $2x^3 - x^2 + x - 2$; $\{1\}$

77. $x^4 - 2x^3 - 2x^2 + 6x - 3 = 0$; $\{1, 1\}$

78. $x^5 + 4x^4 + 4x^3 - x^2 - 4x - 4 = 0$; $\{1, -2, -2\}$

79. $x^4 - 5x^3 + 7x^2 - 5x + 6 = 0$; $\{2, 3\}$

80. $x^4 + 2x^3 - 3x^2 - 4x + 4 = 0$; $\{1, -2\}$

Find a polynomial function $P(x)$ with the given zeros.

81. $4, 5$

82. $-3, 5$

83. $1, 1, 1$

84. $1, 0, -1$

85. $2, 4, 5$

86. $7, 6, 3$

87. $1, -1, \sqrt{2}, -\sqrt{2}$

88. $0, 0, 0, \sqrt{3}, -\sqrt{3}$

89. $\sqrt{2}, i, -i$

90. $i, i, 2$

91. $0, 1 + i, 1 - i$

92. $i, 2 + i, 2 - i$

Discovery and Writing

93. If 0 is a zero of
$P(x) = a_n x^n + a_{n-1} x^{n-1} + \cdots + a_1 x + a_0,$
find a_0.

94. If 0 occurs twice as a zero of
$P(x) = a_n x^n + a_{n-1} x^{n-1} + \cdots + a_1 x + a_0,$
find a_1.

95. If $P(2) = 0$ and $P(-2) = 0$, explain why $x^2 - 4$ is a factor of $P(x)$.

96. If $P(x) = x^4 - 3x^3 + kx^2 + 4x - 1$ and $P(2) = 11$, find k.

Review

Find the quadrant in which each point lies.

97. $P(3, -2)$

98. $Q(-2, -5)$

99. $R(8, \pi)$

100. $S(-9, 9)$

Find the distance between each pair of points.

101. $A(3, -3), B(-5, 3)$

102. $C(-8, 2), D(2, -22)$

Find the slope of the line passing through each pair of points.

103. $E(3, 5), F(-5, -3)$

104. $G\left(3, \dfrac{3}{5}\right), H\left(-\dfrac{3}{5}, 1\right)$

5.2 Descartes' Rule of Signs and Bounds on Roots

In this section, we will learn to

1. Understand the Fundamental Theorem of Algebra.

2. Use the Conjugate Pairs Theorem.

3. Use Descartes' Rule of Signs.

4. Find integer bounds on roots.

Englishman David Beckham currently plays major league soccer for the Los Angeles Galaxy. Beckham is one of the highest paid players in the world, and he has twice been runner-up for the *International Federation of Association Football*'s player of the year award.

In soccer, it is important for players to know the boundaries of the playing field. They need to know when it is advantageous to kick the ball out of bounds and when it is advantageous to keep the ball in bounds.

Knowing where the boundaries are can also be helpful in mathematics. Establishing integer bounds on roots can be an important aid in locating and finding the roots of polynomial equations. In this section, we will learn how to find integer bounds for the roots.

The Remainder Theorem and synthetic division provide a way of verifying that a particular number is a root of a polynomial equation, but they do not provide the roots. We need some guidelines that indicate how many roots to expect, what kind of roots to expect, and where they are located. This section develops several theorems that provide such guidelines.

1. Understand the Fundamental Theorem of Algebra

Before attempting to find the roots of a polynomial equation, it would be useful to know whether any roots exist. This question was answered by Carl Friedrich Gauss (1777–1855) when he proved the **Fundamental Theorem of Algebra.**

The Fundamental Theorem of Algebra	If $P(x)$ is a polynomial function with positive degree, then $P(x)$ has at least one zero.

The Fundamental Theorem of Algebra guarantees that polynomials such as

$$P(x) = 2x^3 - 2x^2 + 7x - 3 \text{ and } P(x) = 32x^{11} + x^3 - 2x - 5$$

all have zeros. Since all polynomials with positive degree have zeros, their corresponding polynomial equations all have roots. They are the zeros of the polynomial function.

The next theorem will help us show that every nth-degree polynomial equation $P(x) = 0$ has exactly n roots.

The Polynomial Factorization Theorem	If $n > 0$ and $P(x)$ is an nth-degree polynomial function, then $P(x)$ has exactly n linear factors: $$P(x) = a_n(x - r_1)(x - r_2)(x - r_3) \cdot \cdots \cdot (x - r_n)$$ where $r_1, r_2, r_3, \ldots, r_n$ are numbers and a_n is the leading coefficient of $P(x)$.

PROOF   Let $P(x)$ be a polynomial function of degree n $(n > 0)$. Because of the Fundamental Theorem of Algebra, we know that $P(x)$ has a zero r_1 and that the equation $P(x) = 0$ has r_1 for a root. By the Factor Theorem, we know that $x - r_1$ is a factor of $P(x)$. Thus,

$$P(x) = (x - r_1)Q_1(x)$$

If the leading coefficient of the nth-degree polynomial function $P(x)$ is a_n, then $Q_1(x)$ is a polynomial function of degree $n - 1$ whose leading coefficient is also a_n.

By the Fundamental Theorem of Algebra, we know that $Q_1(x)$ also has a zero, r_2. By the Factor Theorem, $x - r_2$ is a factor of $Q_1(x)$, and

$$P(x) = (x - r_1)(x - r_2)Q_2(x)$$

where $Q_2(x)$ is a polynomial function of degree $n - 2$ with leading coefficient a_n.

This process can continue only to n factors of the form $x - r_i$ until the final quotient $Q_n(x)$ is a polynomial function of degree $n - n$, or degree 0. Thus, the polynomial function $P(x)$ factors completely as

$$(1) \qquad P(x) = a_n(x - r_1)(x - r_2)(x - r_3) \cdot \cdots \cdot (x - r_n)$$

We can use the Polynomial Factorization Theorem and make the following conclusions:

1. If we substitute any one of the numbers $r_1, r_2, r_3, \ldots, r_n$ for x in Equation 1, $P(x)$ will equal 0. Thus, each value of r is a zero of $P(x)$ and a root of the equation $P(x) = 0$.

2. There can be no other roots, because no single factor in Equation 1 is 0 for any value of x not included in the list $r_1, r_2, r_3, \ldots, r_n$.

3. The values of r in the previous list need not be distinct. Any number r_i that occurs k times as a root of a polynomial equation is called a **root of multiplicity k**.

The following theorem summarizes the previous discussion.

Number of Roots Theorem If multiple roots are counted individually, the polynomial equation $P(x) = 0$ with degree n $(n > 0)$ has exactly n roots among the complex numbers.

The previous theorems are illustrated by the examples shown below.

Polynomial Function	Properties
$P(x) = x - 6$	**Degree:** First **Number of Linear Factors:** 1 **Linear Factor:** $x - 6$ **Number of Zeros:** 1 **Zero:** 6 **Multiplicity of Each Zero:** • 6 has a multiplicity of one.
$P(x) = x^2 - 8x + 16$ $= (x - 4)(x - 4)$	**Degree:** Second **Number of Linear Factors:** 2 **Linear Factors:** $x - 4$, $x - 4$ **Number of Zeros:** 2 **Zeros:** 4 and 4 **Multiplicity of Each Zero:** • 4 has a multiplicity of two.
$P(x) = x^3 + 100x$ $= x(x^2 + 100)$ $= x(x - 10i)(x + 10i)$	**Degree:** Third **Number of Linear Factors:** 3 **Linear Factors:** $x, x - 10i,$ and $x + 10i$ **Number of Zeros:** 3 **Zeros:** $0, 10i,$ and $-10i$ **Multiplicity of Each Zero:** • 0 has a multiplicity of one. • $10i$ has a multiplicity of one. • $-10i$ has a multiplicity of one.
$P(x) = x^4 - 7x^2$ $= x^2(x^2 - 7)$ $= x \cdot x\left(x + \sqrt{7}\right)\left(x - \sqrt{7}\right)$	**Degree:** Fourth **Number of Linear Factors:** 4 **Linear Factors:** $x, x, x + \sqrt{7}, x - \sqrt{7}$ **Number of Zeros:** 4 **Zeros:** $0, 0, -\sqrt{7},$ and $\sqrt{7}$ **Multiplicity of Each Zero:** • 0 has a multiplicity of two. • $-\sqrt{7}$ has a multiplicity of one. • $\sqrt{7}$ has a multiplicity of one.

Comment Remember that every nth degree polynomial function has exactly n linear factors and exactly n zeros. The n zeros are also the roots of the polynomial equation $P(x) = 0$.

2. Use the Conjugate Pairs Theorem

Recall that the complex numbers $a + bi$ and $a - bi$ are called **complex conjugates** of each other. The next theorem points out that *complex roots of polynomial equations with real coefficients occur in complex conjugate pairs.*

The Conjugate Pairs Theorem	If a polynomial equation $P(x) = 0$ with real-number coefficients has a complex root $a + bi$ with $b \neq 0$, then its conjugate $a - bi$ is also a root.

A strategy is given next for finding a polynomial equation.

Strategy for Finding a Polynomial Equation with Real Coefficients	To find a polynomial equation with real coefficients, apply the following two steps. **1.** Use the Conjugate Pairs Theorem to determine the roots of the polynomial equation. **2.** Write the linear factorization of the polynomial and form the equation. Then multiply.

EXAMPLE 1   **Finding a Polynomial Equation**

Find a second-degree polynomial equation with real coefficients that has a root of $2 + i$.

SOLUTION   We can use the Conjugate Pairs Theorem to determine the second root. Then, we will use the two roots to write the linear factorization and equation of the polynomial.

1. Determine the roots.
   Because $2 + i$ is a root, its complex conjugate $2 - i$ is also a root. The solution set is $\{2 + i, 2 - i\}$.

2. Write the linear factorization of the polynomial and form the equation. Then multiply.
   Because $2 + i$ is a root, $x - (2 + i)$ is a factor. Because $2 - i$ is a root, $x - (2 - i)$ is a factor. The polynomial equation is

$$[x - (2 + i)][x - (2 - i)] = 0$$

$$(x - 2 - i)(x - 2 + i) = 0$$

$$x^2 - 4x + 5 = 0 \qquad \text{Multiply.}$$

   The equation $x^2 - 4x + 5 = 0$ will have roots of $2 + i$ and $2 - i$.

Self Check 1   Find a second-degree polynomial equation with real coefficients that has a root of $1 - i$.

Now Try Exercise 23.

EXAMPLE 2   **Finding a Polynomial Equation**

Find a fourth-degree polynomial equation with real coefficients and i as a root of multiplicity 2.

SOLUTION   We can use the Conjugate Pairs Theorem to determine the other two roots. Then, we will use the four roots to write the linear factorization and equation of the polynomial.

1. **Determine the roots.**
   Because i is a root twice and a fourth-degree polynomial equation has four roots, we must find the other two roots. According to the Conjugate Pairs Theorem, the missing roots are the conjugates of the given roots. Thus, the complete solution set is

$$\{i, i, -i, -i\}$$

2. **Write the linear factorization of the polynomial and form the equation. Then multiply.**
   Because i is a root of multiplicity 2, the factor $x - i$ occurs twice. Because $-i$ is a root of multiplicity 2, the factor $x - (-i)$ occurs twice. The equation is

$$(x - i)(x - i)[x - (-i)][x - (-i)] = 0$$
$$(x - i)(x + i)(x - i)(x + i) = 0$$
$$(x^2 + 1)(x^2 + 1) = 0 \qquad \text{Multiply.}$$
$$x^4 + 2x^2 + 1 = 0 \qquad \text{Multiply.}$$

Comment

The Conjugate Pairs Theorem applies only to polynomials with real-number coefficients. In Examples 1 and 2, the theorem does apply and the results were polynomials with real-number coefficients.

Self Check 2   Find a fourth-degree polynomial equation with real coefficients and $-i$ as a root of multiplicity 2.

Now Try Exercise 29.

EXAMPLE 3   **Finding a Quadratic Equation with a Double Root**

Find a second-degree equation with a double root of i.

SOLUTION   We will use the two given roots of i to write the linear factorization of the polynomial and quadratic equation.

Because i is a root twice, the linear factorization of the polynomial and the quadratic equation are

$$(x - i)(x - i) = 0$$
$$x^2 - 2ix - 1 = 0 \qquad \text{Multiply.}$$

Caution

In Example 3, the Conjugate Pairs Theorem does **not** apply because the resulting polynomial equation does **not** have real-number coefficients.

In this equation, the coefficient of x is $-2i$, which is not a real number. Therefore, it is not surprising that the roots are not in complex conjugate pairs.

Self Check 3   Find a second-degree equation with a double root of $-i$.

Now Try Exercise 33.

2. Use Descartes' Rule of Signs

René Descartes (1596–1650) is credited with a theorem known as **Descartes' Rule of Signs,** which enables us to estimate the number of positive, negative, and nonreal roots of a polynomial equation.

If a polynomial is written in descending powers of x and we scan it from left to right, we say that a variation in sign occurs whenever successive terms have opposite signs. For example, the polynomial function

$$P(x) = \overbrace{3x^5}^{+ \text{ to } -} - 2x^4 \overbrace{- 5x^3}^{- \text{ to } +} \overbrace{+ x^2}^{+ \text{ to } -} - x - 9$$

has three variations in sign, and the polynomial function

$$P(-x) = 3(-x)^5 - 2(-x)^4 - 5(-x)^3 + (-x)^2 - (-x) - 9$$

$$= -3x^5 \overbrace{- 2x^4}^{- \text{ to } +} + 5x^3 + x^2 \overbrace{+ x}^{+ \text{ to } -} - 9$$

has two variations in sign.

Descartes' Rule of Signs   Let $P(x)$ be a polynomial function with real coefficients.

- The number of positive roots of $P(x) = 0$ is either equal to the number of variations in sign of $P(x)$ or less than that by an even number.

- The number of negative roots of $P(x) = 0$ is either equal to the number of variations in sign of $P(-x)$ or less than that by an even number.

EXAMPLE 4   **Using Descartes' Rule of Signs**

Find the number of possible positive, negative, and nonreal roots of $3x^3 - 2x^2 + x - 5 = 0$.

SOLUTION   We can use Descartes' Rule of Signs to determine the number of possible positive, negative, and nonreal roots.

1. **Determine the number of possible positive roots.**
   Let $P(x) = 3x^3 - 2x^2 + x - 5$. Since there are three variations of sign in $P(x) = 3x^3 - 2x^2 + x - 5$, there can be either 3 positive roots or only 1 (1 is less than 3 by the even number 2).

2. **Determine the number of possible negative roots.**
   Because

   $$P(-x) = 3(-x)^3 - 2(-x)^2 + (-x) - 5$$
   $$= -3x^3 - 2x^2 - x - 5$$

   has no variations in sign, there are 0 negative roots. Furthermore, 0 is not a root, because the terms of the polynomial do not have a common factor of x.

Comment

To obtain $P(-x)$ quickly, we can simply multiply each odd degree term of $P(x)$ by negative one.

3. **Determine the number of nonreal roots.**
   If there are 3 positive roots, then all of the roots are accounted for. If there is 1 positive root, the 2 remaining roots must be nonreal complex numbers. The following chart shows these possibilities.

Number of positive roots	Number of negative roots	Number of nonreal roots
3	0	0
1	0	2

The number of nonreal complex roots is the number needed to bring the total number of roots up to 3.

Self Check 4   Discuss the possibilities for the roots of $5x^3 + 2x^2 - x + 3 = 0$.

Now Try Exercise 37.

EXAMPLE 5   **Using Descartes' Rule of Signs**

Find the number of possible positive, negative, and nonreal roots of $5x^5 - 3x^3 - 2x^2 + x - 1 = 0$.

SOLUTION   We can use Descartes' Rule of Signs to determine the number of possible positive, negative, and nonreal roots.

1. **Determine the number of possible positive roots.**
   Let $P(x) = 5x^5 - 3x^3 - 2x^2 + x - 1$. Since there are three variations of sign in $P(x)$, there are either 3 or 1 positive roots.

2. **Determine the number of possible negative roots.**
   Because $P(-x) = -5x^5 + 3x^3 - 2x^2 - x - 1$ has two variations in sign, there are 2 or 0 negative roots.

3. **Determine the number of nonreal roots.**
   The possibilities are shown as follows:

Number of positive roots	Number of negative roots	Number of nonreal roots
1	0	4
3	0	2
1	2	2
3	2	0

In each case, the number of nonreal complex roots is an even number. This is expected, because this polynomial has real coefficients, and its nonreal complex roots will occur in conjugate pairs. ∎

Self Check 5   Discuss the possibilities for the roots of $5x^5 - 2x^2 - x - 1 = 0$.

Now Try Exercise 41.

3. Find Integer Bounds on Roots

A final theorem provides a way to find **bounds** on the roots of a polynomial equation, enabling us to look for roots where they can be found.

Upper and Lower Bounds on Roots

Let $P(x)$ be a polynomial function with real coefficients and a positive leading coefficient.

1. If $P(x)$ is synthetically divided by a positive number c and each term in the last row of the division is nonnegative, then no number greater than c can be a root of $P(x) = 0$. (c is called an **upper bound** of the real roots.)

2. If $P(x)$ is synthetically divided by a negative number d and the signs in the last row alternate,* no value less than d can be a root of $P(x) = 0$. (d is called a **lower bound** of the real roots.)

*If 0 appears in the third row, that 0 can be assigned either a + or a − sign to help the signs alternate.

EXAMPLE 6   **Finding Integer Bounds on Roots**

Establish integer bounds for the roots of $2x^3 + 3x^2 - 5x - 7 = 0$.

SOLUTION   We will use the upper and lower bound rules previously stated to establish the integer bounds for the roots.

1. We will perform several synthetic divisions by positive integers, looking for non-negative values in the last row.
   Trying 1 first gives

   $$\underline{1|}\quad \begin{array}{rrrr} 2 & 3 & -5 & -7 \\ & 2 & +5 & +0 \\ \hline +2 & +5 & 0 & -7 \end{array}$$

   Because one of the signs in the last row is negative, we cannot claim that 1 is an upper bound. We now try 2.

   $$\underline{2|}\quad \begin{array}{rrrr} 2 & 3 & -5 & -7 \\ & +4 & 14 & 18 \\ \hline +2 & +7 & +9 & +11 \end{array}$$

   Because the last row is entirely nonnegative, we can claim that 2 is an upper bound. That is, no number greater than 2 can be a root of the equation.

2. We perform several synthetic divisions by negative divisors, looking for alternating signs in the last row.
   We begin with -3.

   $$\underline{-3|}\quad \begin{array}{rrrr} 2 & 3 & -5 & -7 \\ & -6 & 9 & -12 \\ \hline +2 & -3 & +4 & -19 \end{array}$$

   Since the signs in the last row alternate, -3 is a lower bound. That is, no number less than -3 can be a root. To see whether there is a greater lower bound, we try -2.

   $$\underline{-2|}\quad \begin{array}{rrrr} 2 & 3 & -5 & -7 \\ & -4 & 2 & 6 \\ \hline +2 & -1 & -3 & -1 \end{array}$$

   Since the signs in the last row do not alternate, we cannot claim that -2 is a lower bound.
   Since -3 is a lower bound and 2 is an upper bound, then all of the real roots must be in the interval $(-3, 2)$.   ■

Self Check 6   Establish integer bounds for the roots of $2x^3 + 3x^2 - 11x - 7 = 0$.

Now Try Exercise 53.

It is important to understand what the theorem on the bounds of roots says and what it doesn't say. The following two explanations will help clarify that for us.

1. If we divide synthetically by a positive number c and the last row of the synthetic division is entirely nonnegative, the theorem guarantees that c is an upper bound of the roots. However, if the last row contains some negative values, c could still be an upper bound.
2. If we divide by a negative number d and the signs in the last row alternate, the theorem guarantees that d is a lower bound of the roots. However, if the signs in the last row do not alternate, d could still be a lower bound. This is illustrated in Example 6. It can be shown that the smallest negative root of the equation is

approximately -1.81. Thus, -2 is a lower bound for the roots of the equation. However, when we checked -2, the last row of the synthetic division did not have alternating signs. Unfortunately, the theorem does not always determine the best bounds for the roots of the equation.

Self Check Answers   1. $x^2 - 2x + 2 = 0$ 2. $x^4 + 2x^2 + 1 = 0$ 3. $x^2 + 2ix - 1 = 0$

4.

Num. of pos. roots	Num. of neg. roots	Num. of nonreal roots
2	1	0
0	1	2

5.

Num. of pos. roots	Num. of neg. roots	Num. of nonreal roots
1	2	2
1	0	4

6. Roots are in $(-4, 3)$.

Exercises 5.2

Getting Ready

You should be able to complete these vocabulary and concept statements before you proceed to the practice exercises.

Fill in the blanks.

1. If $P(x)$ is a polynomial function with positive degree, then $P(x)$ has at least one _____.

2. The statement in Exercise 1 is called the

   _____.

3. The _____ of $a + bi$ is $a - bi$.

4. The polynomial $6x^4 + 5x^3 - 2x^2 + 3$ has ___ variations in sign.

5. The polynomial $(-x)^3 - (-x)^2 - 4$ has ___ variations in sign.

6. The equation $7x^4 + 5x^3 - 2x + 1 = 0$ can have at most ___ positive roots.

7. The equation $7x^4 + 5x^3 - 2x + 1 = 0$ can have at most ___ negative roots.

8. Complex roots occur in complex _____ pairs. (Assume that the equation has real coefficients.)

9. If no number less than d can be a root of $P(x) = 0$, then d is called a(n) _____.

10. If no number greater than c can be a root of $P(x) = 0$, then c is called a(n) _____.

Practice

Determine how many roots each equation has.

11. $x^{10} = 1$

12. $x^{40} = 1$

13. $3x^4 - 4x^2 - 2x = -7$

14. $-32x^{111} - x^5 = 1$

15. One root of $x(3x^4 - 2) = 12x$ is 0. How many other roots are there?

16. Two roots of $3x^2(x^7 - 14x + 3) = 0$ are 0. How many other roots are there?

Determine how many linear factors and zeros each polynomial function has.

17. $P(x) = x^4 - 81$

18. $P(x) = x^{40} + x^{39}$

19. $P(x) = 4x^5 + 8x^3$

20. $P(x) = x^3 + 144x$

Write a second-degree polynomial equation with real coefficients and the given root.

21. $2i$

22. $-3i$

23. $3 - i$

24. $4 + 2i$

Write a third-degree polynomial equation with real coefficients and the given roots.

25. $3, -i$

26. $1, i$

27. $2, 2 + i$

28. $-2, 3 - i$

Write a fourth-degree polynomial equation with real coefficients and the given roots.

29. $3, 2, i$

30. $1, 2, 1 + i$

31. $i, 1 - i$

32. $i, 2 - i$

Write a second-degree equation with the given double root.

33. $2i$

34. $-2i$

Use Descartes' Rule of Signs to find the number of possible positive, negative, and nonreal roots of each equation.

35. $3x^3 + 5x^2 - 4x + 3 = 0$

36. $3x^3 - 5x^2 - 4x - 3 = 0$

37. $2x^3 + 7x^2 + 5x + 5 = 0$

38. $-2x^3 - 7x^2 - 5x - 4 = 0$

39. $8x^4 = -5$

40. $-3x^3 = -5$

41. $x^4 + 8x^2 - 5x - 10 = 0$

42. $5x^7 + 3x^6 - 2x^5 + 3x^4 + 9x^3 + x^2 + 1 = 0$

43. $-x^{10} - x^8 - x^6 - x^4 - x^2 - 1 = 0$

44. $x^{10} + x^8 + x^6 + x^4 + x^2 + 1 = 0$

45. $x^9 + x^7 + x^5 + x^3 + x = 0$ (Is 0 a root?)

46. $-x^9 - x^7 - x^5 - x^3 - x = 0$ (Is 0 a root?)

47. $-2x^4 - 3x^2 + 2x + 3 = 0$

48. $-7x^5 - 6x^4 + 3x^3 - 2x^2 + 7x - 4 = 0$

Find integer bounds for the roots of each equation. Answers can vary.

49. $x^2 - 2x - 4 = 0$ **50.** $9x^2 - 6x - 1 = 0$

51. $18x^2 - 6x - 1 = 0$ **52.** $2x^2 - 10x - 9 = 0$

53. $6x^3 - 13x^2 - 110x = 0$

54. $12x^3 + 20x^2 - x - 6 = 0$

55. $x^5 + x^4 - 8x^3 - 8x^2 + 15x + 15 = 0$

56. $3x^4 - 5x^3 - 9x^2 + 15x = 0$

57. $3x^5 - 11x^4 - 2x^3 + 38x^2 - 21x - 15 = 0$

58. $3x^6 - 4x^5 - 21x^4 + 4x^3 + 8x^2 + 8x + 32 = 0$

Discovery and Writing

59. Explain why the Fundamental Theorem of Algebra guarantees that every polynomial equation of positive degree has at least one root.

60. Explain why the Fundamental Theorem of Algebra and the Factor Theorem guarantee that an nth-degree polynomial equation has n roots.

61. Prove that any odd-degree polynomial equation with real coefficients must have at least one real root.

62. If a, b, c, and d are positive numbers, prove that $ax^4 + bx^2 + cx - d = 0$ has exactly two nonreal roots.

Review

Assume that k represents a positive real number, and complete each sentence.

63. The graph of $y = f(x - k)$ looks like the graph of $y = f(x)$, except that it has been translated

_____.

64. The graph of $y = f(x) - k$ looks like the graph of $y = f(x)$, except that it has been translated

_____.

65. The graph of $y = f(-x)$ looks like the graph of $y = f(x)$, except that it has been

_____.

66. The graph of $y = -f(x)$ looks like the graph of $y = f(x)$, except that it has been

_____.

67. If $k > 1$, the graph of $y = kf(x)$ looks like the graph of $y = f(x)$, except that it has been

_____.

68. If $0 < k < 1$, the graph of $y = kf(x)$ looks like the graph of $y = f(x)$, except that it has been

_____.

EXAMPLE 1 **Finding the Rational Roots of a Polynomial Equation**

Find the solution set of $2x^3 + 3x^2 - 8x + 3 = 0$.

SOLUTION We will use the steps previously outlined to solve the polynomial equation. Since the equation is of third degree, it has 3 roots.

1. To determine the number of possible positive, negative, and nonreal roots, we will use Descartes' Rule of Signs. We find that there are two possible combinations of positive, negative, and nonreal roots. They are as follows:

Number of positive roots	Number of negative roots	Number of nonreal roots
2	1	0
0	1	2

2. We then find the possible rational roots that have the form $\frac{\text{factor of the constant 3}}{\text{factor of the leading coefficient 2}}$. They are

$$\pm\frac{3}{1}, \quad \pm\frac{1}{1}, \quad \pm\frac{3}{2}, \quad \pm\frac{1}{2}$$

or, written in order of increasing size,

$$-3, \quad -\frac{3}{2}, \quad -1, \quad -\frac{1}{2}, \quad \frac{1}{2}, \quad 1, \quad \frac{3}{2}, \quad 3$$

3. We then use synthetic division and check each possibility to see whether it is a root. We can start with $\frac{3}{2}$.

$$\frac{3}{2} \Big| \begin{array}{rrrr} 2 & 3 & -8 & 3 \\ & 3 & 9 & \frac{3}{2} \\ \hline 2 & 6 & 1 & \frac{9}{2} \end{array}$$

Since the remainder is not 0, $\frac{3}{2}$ is not a root and we can cross it off the list. Since every number in the last row of the synthetic division is positive, $\frac{3}{2}$ is an upper bound. So 3 cannot be a root either and we can cross it off the list.

$$-3, \quad -\frac{3}{2}, \quad -1, \quad -\frac{1}{2}, \quad \frac{1}{2}, \quad 1, \quad \cancel{\frac{3}{2}}, \quad \cancel{3}$$

We now try $\frac{1}{2}$:

$$\frac{1}{2} \Big| \begin{array}{rrrr} 2 & 3 & -8 & 3 \\ & 1 & 2 & -3 \\ \hline 2 & 4 & -6 & 0 \end{array}$$ This row represents the quotient $2x^2 + 4x - 6$.

Since the remainder is 0, $\frac{1}{2}$ is a root and the binomial $x - \frac{1}{2}$ is a factor of $P(x)$.

4. The remaining roots must be supplied by the remaining factor, which is the quotient $2x^2 + 4x - 6$. We can find the other roots by solving the equation $2x^2 + 4x - 6 = 0$, called the **depressed equation.**

$$2x^2 + 4x - 6 = 0$$

$$x^2 + 2x - 3 = 0 \qquad \text{Divide both sides by 2.}$$

$$(x - 1)(x + 3) = 0 \qquad \text{Factor } x^2 + 2x - 3.$$

$$x - 1 = 0 \quad \text{or} \quad x + 3 = 0$$

$$x = 1 \qquad \qquad x = -3$$

Comment

Example 1 illustrates that the upper and lower bound theorem is helpful when the list of possible rational roots is long.

The solution set of the equation is $\left\{\frac{1}{2}, 1, -3\right\}$. Note that two positive roots and one negative root is a predicted possibility. ∎

Self Check 1   Find the solution set of $3x^3 - 10x^2 + 9x - 2 = 0$.

Now Try Exercise 19.

ACCENT ON TECHNOLOGY   ## Confirming Roots of a Polynomial Equation

We can confirm that the roots found in Example 1 are correct by graphing the function $P(x) = 2x^3 + 3x^2 - 8x + 3$ and locating the resulting x-intercepts of the graph. If we use a graphing WINDOW as shown in Figure 5-1(a) and GRAPH the function, we will obtain the graph shown in Figure 5-1(b). From the graph, we can see that the graph crosses the x-axis at $x = -3$, $x = \frac{1}{2}$, and $x = 1$. These are the roots of the polynomial equation.

(a)

(b)

FIGURE 5-1

---

3. Find Real and Nonreal Roots of Polynomial Equations

EXAMPLE 2   ### Finding All the Solutions of a Polynomial Equation

Find the solution set of $x^7 - 2x^6 - 5x^5 + 6x^4 - x^3 + 2x^2 + 5x - 6 = 0$.

SOLUTION   We will use the steps outlined above to find the roots of the polynomial equation. Because the equation is of seventh degree, it has 7 roots.

1. To determine the number of possible positive, negative, and nonreal roots, we will use Descartes' Rule of Signs. We find that there are several possible combinations of positive, negative, and nonreal roots. They are as follows:

Number of positive roots	Number of negative roots	Number of nonreal roots
5	2	0
3	2	2
1	2	4
5	0	2
3	0	4
1	0	6

2. We then find the possible rational roots that have the form $\frac{\text{factor of the constant } -6}{\text{factor of the leading coefficient } 1}$. They are as follows:

$$-6, \quad -3, \quad -2, \quad -1, \quad 1, \quad 2, \quad 3, \quad 6$$

3. We then use synthetic division and check each possibility to see whether it is a root. We can start with -3.

$$
\begin{array}{r|rrrrrrrr}
-3 & 1 & -2 & -5 & 6 & -1 & 2 & 5 & -6 \\
   &   & -3 & 15 & -30 & 72 & -213 & 633 & -1{,}914 \\
\hline
   & 1 & -5 & 10 & -24 & 71 & -211 & 638 & -1{,}920
\end{array}
$$

Since the last number in the synthetic division is not 0, -3 is not a root and can be crossed off the list. Since the signs in the last row alternate, -3 is a lower bound, and we can cross off -6 as well.

$$-\!\!\!6, \quad -3, \quad -2, \quad -1, \quad 1, \quad 2, \quad 3, \quad 6$$

We now try -2:

$$
\begin{array}{r|rrrrrrrr}
-2 & 1 & -2 & -5 & 6 & -1 & 2 & 5 & -6 \\
   &   & -2 & 8 & -6 & 0 & 2 & -8 & 6 \\
\hline
   & 1 & -4 & 3 & 0 & -1 & 4 & -3 & 0
\end{array}
$$

Since the remainder is 0, -2 is a root.

4. Because the root -2 is negative, we can revise the chart of possibilities to eliminate the possibility that there are 0 negative roots.

Number of positive roots	Number of negative roots	Number of nonreal roots
5	2	0
3	2	2
1	2	4

The remaining roots must be supplied by the remaining factor, which is the quotient in the synthetic division shown above: $x^6 - 4x^5 + 3x^4 - x^2 + 4x - 3 = 0$. We can find the other roots by repeating steps 1–3 and solving this equation, called the **depressed equation.**

Because the constant term of this depressed equation is different from the constant term of the original equation, we can cross off other possible rational roots. For example, the number -2 cannot be a root a second time, because it is not a factor of -3. The numbers 2 and 6 are no longer possible roots, because neither is a factor of -3.

The list of possible roots is now

$$-\!\!\!6, \quad -\!\!\!3, \quad -2, \quad -1, \quad 1, \quad 2, \quad 3, \quad 6\!\!\!\diagdown$$

Since we know that there is one more negative root, we will synthetically divide the coefficients of the depressed equation by -1.

$$
\begin{array}{r|rrrrrrr}
-1 & 1 & -4 & 3 & 0 & -1 & 4 & -3 \\
   &   & -1 & 5 & -8 & 8 & -7 & 3 \\
\hline
   & 1 & -5 & 8 & -8 & 7 & -3 & 0
\end{array}
$$

Since the remainder is 0, -1 is a root, and the solution set so far is $\{-2, -1, \ldots\}$. The number -1 cannot be a root again, because we have found both negative roots. When we cross off -1, we have only two possibilities left.

$$-\cancel{6}, \quad -\cancel{3}, \quad -2, \quad -\cancel{1}, \quad 1, \quad 2, \quad 3, \quad \cancel{6}$$

The depressed equation is now $x^5 - 5x^4 + 8x^3 - 8x^2 + 7x - 3 = 0$.
We can synthetically divide the coefficients of this equation by 1 to get

$$\underline{1|} \begin{array}{rrrrrr} 1 & -5 & 8 & -8 & 7 & -3 \\ & 1 & -4 & 4 & -4 & 3 \\ \hline 1 & -4 & 4 & -4 & 3 & 0 \end{array}$$

The depressed equation is now $x^4 - 4x^3 + 4x^2 - 4x + 3 = 0$.

Since the remainder is 0, 1 joins the solution set $\{-2, -1, 1, \ldots\}$. To see whether 1 is a root a second time, we synthetically divide the coefficients of the new depressed equation by 1.

$$\underline{1|} \begin{array}{rrrrr} 1 & -4 & 4 & -4 & 3 \\ & 1 & -3 & 1 & -3 \\ \hline 1 & -3 & 1 & -3 & 0 \end{array}$$

The depressed equation is now $x^3 - 3x^2 + x - 3 = 0$.

Again, 1 is a root, and the solution set is now $\{-2, -1, 1, 1, \ldots\}$.
To see whether 1 is a root a third time, we synthetically divide the coefficients of the new depressed equation by 1.

$$\underline{1|} \begin{array}{rrrr} 1 & -3 & 1 & -3 \\ & 1 & -2 & -1 \\ \hline 1 & -2 & -1 & -4 \end{array}$$

Since the remainder is not 0, the number 1 is not a root for a third time, and we can cross 1 off the list of possibilities, leaving only 3.

$$-\cancel{6}, \quad -\cancel{3}, \quad -2, \quad -\cancel{1}, \quad \cancel{1}, \quad 2, \quad 3, \quad \cancel{6}$$

To see whether 3 is a root, we synthetically divide the coefficients of $x^3 - 3x^2 + x - 3 = 0$ by 3.

$$\underline{3|} \begin{array}{rrrr} 1 & -3 & 1 & -3 \\ & 3 & 0 & 3 \\ \hline 1 & 0 & 1 & 0 \end{array}$$

Since the remainder is 0, 3 joins the solution set, which is now $\{-2, -1, 1, 1, 3 \ldots\}$.
The depressed equation is now $x^2 + 1 = 0$, which can be solved as a quadratic equation.

$$x^2 + 1 = 0$$
$$x^2 = -1$$
$$x = i \quad \text{or} \quad x = -i$$

The complete solution set is $\{-2, -1, 1, 1, 3, i, -i\}$. The solution set contains 3 positive roots, 2 negative roots, and 2 nonreal roots that are complex conjugates. This combination was one of the predicted possibilities. ■

Comment

Example 2 illustrates that finding the seven roots of a seventh-degree polynomial equation can be a lengthy process. In such cases, the four-step process for finding rational roots must be repeated.

Self Check 2   Find the solution set of $x^5 - x^4 + 3x^3 - 3x^2 - 4x + 4 = 0$.

Now Try Exercise 51.

ACCENT ON TECHNOLOGY / **Confirming Roots of a Polynomial Equation**

We can confirm that the roots found in Example 2 are correct by graphing the function

$$P(x) = x^7 - 2x^6 - 5x^5 + 6x^4 - x^3 + 2x^2 + 5x - 6$$

and locating the resulting x-intercepts of the graph. If we use the graphing WINDOW shown in Figure 5-2(a) and GRAPH the function, we will obtain the graph shown in Figure 5-2(b). From the graph, we can see that the graph crosses or touches the x-axis at $x = -2$, $x = -1$, $x = 1$, and $x = 3$. We cannot detect the complex roots from the graph.

(a)

(b)

FIGURE 5-2

4. Solve Applications

EXAMPLE 3 **Solving an Application**

To protect cranberry crops from the damage of early freezes, growers flood the cranberry bogs. Three irrigation sources, used together, can flood a cranberry bog in one day. If the sources are used one at a time, the second source requires one day longer to flood the bog than the first, and the third requires four days longer than the first. If the bog must be flooded before a freeze that is predicted in three days, can the water in the last two sources be diverted to other bogs?

© Istockphoto.com/YinYang

SOLUTION We can use the given information to write an equation that models the situation. We will then solve the equation.

We can let x represent the number of days it would take the first irrigation source to flood the bog. Then $x + 1$ and $x + 4$ represent the number of days it would take the second and third sources, respectively, to flood the bog.

Because the first source, alone, requires x days to flood the bog, that source could fill $\frac{1}{x}$ of the bog in one day. In one day's time, the remaining sources could flood $\frac{1}{x+1}$ and $\frac{1}{x+4}$ of the bog. This gives the equation

The part of the bog the first source can flood in one day	plus	the part the second source can flood in one day	plus	the part the third source can flood in one day	equals	one bog.
$\dfrac{1}{x}$	$+$	$\dfrac{1}{x+1}$	$+$	$\dfrac{1}{x+4}$	$=$	1

We multiply both sides of the equation by $x(x + 1)(x + 4)$ to clear it of fractions and then simplify to get

$$x(x + 1)(x + 4)\left(\frac{1}{x} + \frac{1}{x + 1} + \frac{1}{x + 4}\right) = 1 \cdot x(x + 1)(x + 4)$$

$$(x + 1)(x + 4) + x(x + 4) + x(x + 1) = x(x + 1)(x + 4)$$

$$x^2 + 5x + 4 + x^2 + 4x + x^2 + x = x^3 + 5x^2 + 4x$$

$$0 = x^3 + 2x^2 - 6x - 4$$

To solve the equation $x^3 + 2x^2 - 6x - 4 = 0$, we first list its possible rational roots, which are the factors of the constant term, -4.

$$-4, -2, -1, 1, 2, \text{ and } 4$$

One solution of this equation is $x = 2$, because when we synthetically divide by 2, the remainder is 0:

$$\underline{2|}\ \begin{array}{rrrr} 1 & 2 & -6 & -4 \\ & 2 & 8 & 4 \\ \hline 1 & 4 & 2 & 0 \end{array}$$ The depressed equation is $x^2 + 4x + 2 = 0$.

We can find the remaining solutions by using the Quadratic Formula to solve the depressed equation. The two solutions are $-2 + \sqrt{2}$ and $-2 - \sqrt{2}$. Since both of these numbers are negative and the time it takes to flood the bog cannot be negative, these roots must be discarded. The only meaningful solution is 2.

Since the first source, alone, can flood the bog in two days, and it is three days until the freeze, the other two water sources can be diverted to flood other bogs. ∎

Self Check 3   If a freeze is predicted in one day, can the water in the last two sources be diverted?

Now Try Exercise 65.

ACCENT ON TECHNOLOGY   **Using the Table Feature on a Graphing Calculator to Find Roots of a Polynomial Equation**

A graphing calculator can be used to reduce the amount of work involved in finding the roots of a polynomial equation. From a list of possible rational zeros, we can utilize the TABLE function and identify the rational roots. Consider the following example.

*   We will use the Rational Root Theorem, a calculator, and synthetic division, if necessary, to find all the rational zeros of the polynomial equation $2x^4 + x^3 - 9x^2 - 4x + 4 = 0$.
*   First, we list all the possible rational roots. For the polynomial, we see that

$$p = 4, q = 2 \rightarrow \frac{p}{q} = \frac{\text{all integer factors of 4}}{\text{all interger factors of 2}} = \frac{\pm 1, \pm 2, \pm 4}{\pm 1, \pm 2} = \pm 1, \pm 2, \pm 4, \pm \frac{1}{2}$$

*   Next, we evaluate the function at these values. The work is shown in Figure 5-3.

(a)   (b)

FIGURE 5-3

*   From the table, we see that the rational roots are $x = -1, 2, -2,$ and $\frac{1}{2}$. Because the polynomial is of fourth degree and we have identified four roots, our work is finished.

It wasn't necessary for us to use synthetic division to solve this equation. If, for example, we had only found two rational roots using the table feature, we could be able to finish the problem using synthetic division. The table feature simply saves us time.

Self Check Answers   1. $\left\{1, 2, \dfrac{1}{3}\right\}$ **2.** $\{-1, 1, 1, 2i, -2i\}$ **3.** no

Exercises **5.3**

Getting Ready

You should be able to complete these vocabulary and concept statements before you proceed to the practice exercises.

Fill in the blanks.

1. The rational roots of the equation $3x^3 + 4x - 7 = 0$ will have the form $\frac{p}{q}$, where p is a factor of _____ and q is a factor of 3.

2. The rational roots of the equation $5x^3 + 3x^2 - 4 = 0$ will have the form $\frac{p}{q}$, where p is a factor of -4 and q is a factor of ___.

3. Consider the synthetic division of $5x^3 - 7x^2 - 3x - 63 = 0$.

$$
\begin{array}{r|rrrr}
3 & 5 & -7 & -3 & -63 \\
  &   & 15 & 24 & 63 \\
\hline
  & 5 & 8 & 21 & 0
\end{array}
$$

Since the remainder is 0, 3 is a _____ of the equation.

4. In Exercise 3, the depressed equation is

_____.

Practice

Use the Rational Root Theorem to list all possible rational roots of the polynomial equation.

5. $x^3 + 10x^2 + 5x - 12 = 0$
6. $-x^3 + 3x^2 - 4x - 8 = 0$

7. $2x^4 - x^3 + 10x^2 + 5x - 6 = 0$

8. $3x^4 - x^3 + 7x^2 - 5x - 8 = 0$

9. $4x^5 - x^4 - x^3 + x^2 + 5x - 10 = 0$

10. $6x^4 - 2x^3 + x^2 - x + 3 = 0$

Find all rational roots of each equation.

11. $x^3 - 5x^2 - x + 5 = 0$
12. $x^3 + 7x^2 - x - 7 = 0$
13. $x^3 - 2x^2 - x + 2 = 0$

14. $x^3 + x^2 - 4x - 4 = 0$

15. $x^3 - x^2 - 4x + 4 = 0$

16. $x^3 + 2x^2 - x - 2 = 0$

17. $x^3 - 2x^2 - 9x + 18 = 0$

18. $x^3 + 3x^2 - 4x - 12 = 0$

19. $2x^3 - x^2 - 2x + 1 = 0$

20. $3x^3 + x^2 - 3x - 1 = 0$

21. $3x^3 + 5x^2 + x - 1 = 0$

22. $2x^3 - 3x^2 + 1 = 0$

23. $30x^3 - 47x^2 - 9x + 18 = 0$

24. $20x^3 - 53x^2 - 27x + 18 = 0$

25. $15x^3 - 61x^2 - 2x + 24 = 0$

26. $20x^3 - 44x^2 + 9x + 18 = 0$

27. $24x^3 - 82x^2 + 89x - 30 = 0$

28. $3x^3 - 2x^2 + 12x - 8 = 0$

29. $x^4 - 10x^3 + 35x^2 - 50x + 24 = 0$
30. $x^4 + 4x^3 + 6x^2 + 4x + 1 = 0$
31. $x^4 + 3x^3 - 13x^2 - 9x + 30 = 0$
32. $x^4 - 8x^3 + 14x^2 + 8x - 15 = 0$

33. $4x^4 - 8x^3 - x^2 + 8x - 3 = 0$

34. $3x^4 - 14x^3 + 11x^2 + 16x - 12 = 0$

35. $2x^4 - x^3 - 2x^2 - 4x - 40 = 0$

36. $12x^4 + 20x^3 - 41x^2 + 20x - 3 = 0$

37. $36x^4 - x^2 + 2x - 1 = 0$

38. $12x^4 + x^3 + 42x^2 + 4x - 24 = 0$

39. $x^5 + 3x^4 - 5x^3 - 15x^2 + 4x + 12 = 0$
40. $x^5 - 3x^4 - 5x^3 + 15x^2 + 4x - 12 = 0$

41. $4x^5 - 12x^4 + 15x^3 - 45x^2 - 4x + 12 = 0$

42. $6x^5 - 7x^4 - 48x^3 + 81x^2 - 4x - 12 = 0$

43. $x^7 - 12x^5 + 48x^3 - 64x = 0$

44. $x^7 + 7x^6 + 21x^5 + 35x^4 + 35x^3 + 21x^2 + 7x + 1 = 0$

Find all roots of each polynomial equation.

45. $x^3 - 3x^2 - 2x + 6 = 0$

46. $x^3 + 3x^2 - 3x - 9 = 0$

47. $2x^3 - x^2 + 2x - 1 = 0$

48. $3x^3 + x^2 + 3x + 1 = 0$

49. $x^4 - 2x^3 - 8x^2 + 8x + 16 = 0$

50. $x^4 - 2x^3 - 2x^2 + 2x + 1 = 0$

51. $2x^4 + x^3 + 17x^2 + 9x - 9 = 0$

52. $2x^4 - 4x^3 + 2x^2 + 4x - 4 = 0$

53. $x^5 - 3x^4 + 28x^3 - 76x^2 + 75x - 25 = 0$

54. $x^5 + 3x^4 - 2x^3 - 14x^2 - 15x - 5 = 0$

55. $2x^5 - 3x^4 + 6x^3 - 9x^2 - 8x + 12 = 0$

56. $3x^5 - x^4 + 36x^3 - 12x^2 - 192x + 64 = 0$

In Exercises 57–60, $1 + i$ is a root of each polynomial equation. Find the other roots.

57. $x^3 - 5x^2 + 8x - 6 = 0$

58. $x^3 - 2x + 4 = 0$

59. $x^4 - 2x^3 - 7x^2 + 18x - 18 = 0$

60. $x^4 - 2x^3 - 2x^2 + 8x - 8 = 0$

Solve each equation.

61. $x^3 - \frac{4}{3}x^2 - \frac{13}{3}x - 2 = 0$

62. $x^3 - \frac{19}{6}x^2 + \frac{1}{6}x + 1 = 0$

63. $x^{-5} - 8x^{-4} + 25x^{-3} - 38x^{-2} + 28x^{-1} - 8 = 0$

64. $1 - x^{-1} - x^{-2} - 2x^{-3} = 0$

Applications

65. Parallel resistance If three resistors with resistances of R_1, R_2, and R_3 are wired in parallel, their combined resistance R is given by the following formula. The design of a voltmeter requires that the resistance R_2 be 10 ohms greater than the resistance R_1, that the resistance R_3 be 50 ohms greater than R_1, and that their combined resistance be 6 ohms. Find the value of each resistance.

$$\frac{1}{R} = \frac{1}{R_1} + \frac{1}{R_2} + \frac{1}{R_3}$$

66. Fabricating sheet metal The open tray shown in the illustration is to be manufactured from a 12-by-14-inch rectangular sheet of metal by cutting squares from each corner and folding up the sides. If the volume of the tray is to be 160 cubic inches and x is to be an integer, what size squares should be cut from each corner?

67. FedEx box The length of a FedEx 25-kg box is 7 inches more than its height. The width of the box is 4 inches more than its height. If the volume of the box is 4,420 cubic inches, find the height of the box.

68. Mountain Dew can A Mountain Dew aluminum can is approximately the shape of a cylinder. If the height of the can is 9 centimeters more than its radius and the volume of the can is approximately 108π cubic centimeters, find the radius of the can. The formula for the volume of a cylinder is $V = \pi r^2 h$

69. Hilly terrain We are interested in the nature of some hilly terrain. Computer simulation has told us that for a cross-section from west to east, the height $h(x)$, in feet above sea level is related to the horizontal distance x (in miles) from a fixed point by the function,

$$h(x) = -x^4 + 5x^3 + 91x^2 - 545x + 550, \; x \in [0,9].$$

At what distances from the fixed point is the height 100 feet above sea level?

70. Velocity of a hot-air balloon A hot-air balloon is tethered to the ground and only moves up and down. You and a friend take a ride on the ballon for approximately 25 minutes. On this particular ride the velocity of the balloon, $v(t)$ in feet per minute, as a function of time, t in minutes, is represented by the function

$$v(t) = -t^3 + 34t^2 - 320t + 850$$

At what times is the velocity of the balloon 50 feet per minute?

Steve Bower/Shutterstock.com

Discovery and Writing

71. If n is an even integer and c is a positive constant, show that $x^n + c = 0$ has no real roots.

72. If n is an even positive integer and c is a positive constant, show that $x^n - c = 0$ has two real roots.

73. Precalculus A rectangle is inscribed in the parabola $y = 16 - x^2$, as shown in the illustration. Find the point (x, y) if the area of the rectangle is 42 square units.

74. Precalculus One corner of the rectangle shown is at the origin, and the opposite corner (x, y) lies in the first quadrant on the curve $y = x^3 - 2x^2$. Find the point (x,y) if the area of the rectangle is 27 square units.

Review

Simplify each radical expression. Assume that all variables represent positive numbers.

75. $\sqrt{72a^3b^5c}$

76. $\dfrac{5a}{\sqrt{5a}}$

77. $\sqrt{18a^2b} + a\sqrt{50b}$

78. $(\sqrt{3} + \sqrt{5b})(\sqrt{12} - \sqrt{45b})$

79. $\dfrac{2}{\sqrt{3} - 1}$

80. $\dfrac{\sqrt{11} + \sqrt{x}}{\sqrt{11} - \sqrt{x}}$

5.4 Approximating Irrational Roots of Polynomial Equations

In this section, we will learn to

1. Use the Intermediate Value Theorem.

2. Use the Bisection Method.

3. Approximate real roots with a graphing calculator.

Sometimes we find ourselves in a car wondering how to get somewhere. Fortunately, many cars are now equipped with a navigation system that can give us directions to a specific address or point of interest.

kaczor58/Shutterstock.com

A navigation system uses satellite signals to determine the exact location of our car. Once the system knows the location of the car, it can guide us to our destination.

When solving more complicated equations, there are several theorems that act like a navigation system and can tell us the location of the roots of the equation. Once we know their location, it is much easier to find them.

Before developing these theorems, we will review some facts about solving equations.

- All first-degree equations are easy to solve by using simple algebraic methods.
- All quadratic equations can be solved by using the Quadratic Formula.
- There are formulas for solving third- and fourth-degree polynomial equations. However, they are complicated.
- No formulas exist for solving polynomial equations of degree 5 or greater. This fact was proved by the Norwegian mathematician Niels Henrik Abel (1802−1829) and (for equations of degree greater than 5) by the French mathematician Evariste Galois (1811−1832).

To solve a higher-degree polynomial equation with integer coefficients, we can use the methods of the previous section to find its *rational roots*. To find any irrational or complex roots, the final depressed equation would have to be a first- or second-degree equation.

In this section, we will discuss ways of approximating *irrational roots* of higher-degree polynomial equations that may not have any rational roots.

EXAMPLE 1

Showing That an Equation Has Irrational Roots

Show that $\sqrt{3}$ is a root of $x^4 - 9 = 0$ and that it is irrational.

SOLUTION   We know that $\sqrt{3}$ is a root of the equation because

$$x^4 - 9 = 0$$
$$\left(\sqrt{3}\right)^4 - 9 \overset{?}{=} 0 \qquad \text{Substitute } \sqrt{3} \text{ for } x.$$
$$9 - 9 \overset{?}{=} 0 \qquad \left(\sqrt{3}\right)^4 = 9$$
$$0 = 0$$

If there were any rational roots of this equation, they must have the form $\frac{\text{factor of the constant } -9}{\text{factor of the leading coefficient } 1}$. Therefore, the only possible rational roots of the equation would be

$$\pm\frac{1}{1}, \qquad \pm\frac{3}{1}, \qquad \text{and} \qquad \pm\frac{9}{1}$$

Since none of the numbers $1, -1, 3, -3, 9$, or -9 satisfies the equation, no rational number can be a root. Thus, the root of $\sqrt{3}$ must be irrational. ∎

Self Check 1   Show that $-\sqrt{5}$ is a root of $x^4 - 25 = 0$ and that it is irrational.

Comment

Roots of polynomial equations can be rational numbers, irrational numbers, or complex numbers. In this section, we will restrict ourselves to roots that are real, that is, rational or irrational numbers.

Now Try Exercise 5.

1. Use the Intermediate Value Theorem

The following theorem, called the **Intermediate Value Theorem,** leads to a way of locating an interval that contains a root.

| **The Intermediate Value Theorem** | Let $P(x)$ be a polynomial function with real coefficients. If $P(a) \neq P(b)$ for $a < b$, then $P(x)$ takes on all values between $P(a)$ and $P(b)$ on the closed interval $[a, b]$. |

JUSTIFICATION   This theorem becomes clear when we consider the graph of the polynomial function $y = P(x)$, shown in Figure 5-4. We have seen that graphs of polynomials are *continuous* curves, a technical term that means, roughly, that they can be drawn without lifting the pencil from the paper. If $P(a) \neq P(b)$, the continuous curve joining the points $A(a, P(a))$ and $B(b, P(b))$ must take on all values between $P(a)$ and $P(b)$ in the interval $[a, b]$, because the curve has no gaps in it.

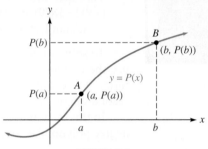

FIGURE 5-4

The next theorem follows from the Intermediate Value Theorem.

| **The Location Theorem** | Let $P(x)$ be a polynomial function with real coefficients. If $P(a)$ and $P(b)$ have opposite signs, there is at least one number r in the interval (a, b) for which $P(r) = 0$. |

PROOF   See Figure 5-5. By the Intermediate Value Theorem, $P(x)$ takes on all values between $P(a)$ and $P(b)$. Since $P(a)$ and $P(b)$ have opposite signs, the number 0 lies between them. Thus, there is a number r between a and b for which $P(r) = 0$. This number r is a zero of $P(x)$ and a root of the equation $P(x) = 0$.

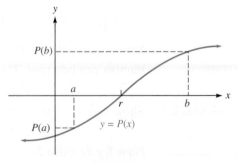

FIGURE 5-5

EXAMPLE 2   **Using the Intermediate Value Theorem and Location Theorem**

Show that $2x^3 - x^2 - 8x + 4 = 0$ has at least one real root between 0 and 1.

SOLUTION   Let $P(x) = 2x^3 - x^2 - 8x + 4$. We will evaluate the polynomial function at $x = 0$ and $x = 1$. If the resulting values have opposite signs, we know that the equation has a root that lies between 0 and 1.

Evaluate $P(0)$ and $P(1)$ as follows:

$$P(0) = 2(0)^3 - (0)^2 - 8(0) + 4 = 4$$

$$P(1) = 2(1)^3 - (1)^2 - 8(1) + 4 = -3$$

Because $P(0)$ and $P(1)$ have opposite signs, we know by the Location Theorem that there is at least one real root between 0 and 1, as shown in Figure 5-6. The root shown is $\frac{1}{2}$.

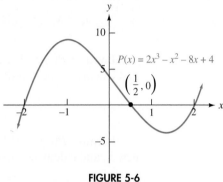

FIGURE 5-6

Self Check 2   Show that $2x^3 - 9x^2 + 7x + 6 = 0$ has at least one real root between -1 and 0.

Now Try Exercise 13.

2. Use the Bisection Method

The Location Theorem provides a method (called the **Bisection Method**) for finding the roots of $P(x) = 0$ to any desired degree of accuracy.

Suppose we find, by trial and error, that the numbers x_l and x_r (for left and right) straddle a root—that is, $x_l < x_r$ and $P(x_l)$ and $P(x_r)$ have opposite signs. (See Figure 5-7.) Further suppose that $P(x_l) < 0$ and $P(x_r) > 0$. We can compute the number c that is halfway between x_l and x_r and then compute $P(c)$. If $P(c) = 0$, we've found a root. However, if $P(c)$ is not 0, we proceed in one of two ways:

1. If $P(c) < 0$, the root r lies between c and x_r, as shown in Figure 5-7(a). In this case, we let c become a new x_l and repeat the procedure.
2. If $P(c) > 0$, the root r lies between x_l and c, as shown in Figure 5-7(b). In this case, we let c become a new x_r and repeat the procedure

FIGURE 5-7

At any stage in this procedure, the root is contained between the current values of x_l and x_r. If the original bounds were 1 unit apart, after 10 repetitions of this procedure, the root would be between bounds that were 2^{-10} units apart. This means that the zero of $P(x)$ would be within 0.0001 units of either x_l or x_r.

After 20 repetitions, the root would be between bounds that were 2^{-20} units apart. This means that the zero of $P(x)$ would be within 0.000001 of either x_l or x_r.

EXAMPLE 3 **Using the Bisection Method**

Use the Bisection Method to find the positive root of $x^2 - 2 = 0$ to the nearest tenth.

SOLUTION We will use the Location Theorem and the Bisection Method to find the positive root of the equation to the nearest tenth.

Since $P(1) = -1$ and $P(2) = 2$ have opposite signs, there is a root between 1 and 2. We can let $x_l = 1$ and $x_r = 2$ and compute the midpoint c:

$$c = \frac{x_l + x_r}{2} = \frac{1 + 2}{2} = 1.5$$

Because $P(c) = P(1.5) = 0.25$ is a positive number, we let c become a new x_r and calculate a new midpoint, which we will call c_1.

$$c_1 = \frac{x_l + x_r}{2} = \frac{1 + 1.5}{2} = 1.25$$

Because $P(c_1) = P(1.25) = -0.4375$ is a negative number, we let c_1 become a new x_l and calculate a new midpoint, which we will call c_2.

$$c_2 = \frac{x_l + x_r}{2} = \frac{1.25 + 1.5}{2} = 1.375$$

Because $P(c_2) = P(1.375) = -0.109375$ is a negative number, we let c_2 become a new x_l and calculate a new midpoint, which we will call c_3.

$$c_3 = \frac{x_l + x_r}{2} = \frac{1.375 + 1.5}{2} = 1.4375$$

Because $P(c_3) = P(1.4375) = 0.066406$ is a positive number, we let c_3 become a new x_r and calculate a new midpoint, which we will call c_4.

$$c_4 = \frac{x_l + x_r}{2} = \frac{1.375 + 1.4375}{2} = 1.40625$$

From here on, the first two digits of the midpoints will remain 1.4. The root r of the equation (to the nearest tenth) is 1.4.

Self Check 3 Find the negative root of $x^2 - 2 = 0$ to the nearest tenth.

Now Try Exercise 19.

3. Approximate Real Roots with a Graphing Calculator

We can approximate the real roots of an equation either by using the TRACE and ZOOM capabilities of a graphing calculator or by using the ZERO feature.

ACCENT ON TECHNOLOGY **Using a Graphing Calculator to Approximate Real Roots**

We will use the ZERO feature on a graphing calculator to approximate the real roots of the equation $x^4 - 6x^2 + 9 = 0$.

- We first enter the equation, using the WINDOW shown, and GRAPH the equation to obtain the graph shown in Figure 5-8.

FIGURE 5-8

- We then select ZERO under the CALC menu. To find the positive root, we guess a left bound and press ⌈ENTER⌋, guess a right bound and press ⌈ENTER⌋, and then press ⌈ENTER⌋ again. The root of the equation is approximately 1.7320511. See Figure 5-9.

FIGURE 5-9

Because of symmetry, we know that the negative solution is -1.7320511. The real roots are $x \approx \pm 1.7320511$.

The graph shown in Figure 5-9 illustrates a situation in which the Bisection Method does not work. Since the graph doesn't cross the x-axis, the values of the function on opposite sides of the intercepts do not have opposite signs. In this case, the Bisection Method would be useless.

Self Check Answers   **1.** $\pm\dfrac{1}{1}$, $\pm\dfrac{5}{1}$, or $\pm\dfrac{25}{1}$ do not satisfy $x^4 - 25 = 0$.   **2.** $P(-1) = -12$; $P(0) = 6$

They have opposite signs.   **3.** -1.4

Exercises **5.4**

Getting Ready

You should be able to complete these vocabulary and con-cept statements before you proceed to the practice exercises.

Fill in the blanks.

1. If $P(x)$ is a polynomial function with real coefficients and $P(a) \neq P(b)$ for $a < b$, then $P(x)$ takes on all values between _____ in the interval $[a, b]$.

2. If $P(x)$ has real coefficients and $P(a)$ and $P(b)$ have opposite signs, there is at least one number r in (a, b) for which _____.

3. In the Bisection Method, we find two numbers x_l and x_r that straddle a root. We then compute a new guess for the root (a number c) by finding the aver-age of _____.

4. A _____ curve has no gaps in it.

Practice

Show that the given number is a root of the equation and that it is irrational.

5. $x^4 - 4 = 0$; $\sqrt{2}$

6. $x^4 - 36 = 0$; $\sqrt{6}$

7. $x^4 - 49 = 0$; $-\sqrt{7}$

8. $x^4 - 64 = 0$; $-2\sqrt{2}$

Show that each equation has at least one real root between the specified numbers.

9. $2x^2 + x - 3 = 0$; -2 and -1

10. $2x^3 + 17x^2 + 31x - 20 = 0$; -1 and 2

11. $3x^3 - 11x^2 - 14x = 0$; 4 and 5

12. $2x^3 - 3x^2 + 2x - 3 = 0$; 1 and 2

13. $x^4 - 8x^2 + 15 = 0$; 1 and 2

14. $x^4 - 8x^2 + 15 = 0$; 2 and 3

15. $30x^3 + 10 = 61x^2 + 39x$; 2 and 3

16. $30x^3 + 10 = 61x^2 + 39x$; -1 and 0

17. $30x^3 + 10 = 61x^2 + 39x$; 0 and 1

18. $5x^3 - 9x^2 - 4x + 9 = 0$; -1 and 0

Use the Bisection Method to find the following values to the nearest tenth.

19. The positive root of $x^2 - 3 = 0$.

20. The negative root of $x^2 - 3 = 0$.

21. The negative root of $x^2 - 5 = 0$.

22. The positive root of $x^2 - 5 = 0$.

23. The positive root of $x^3 - x^2 - 2 = 0$.

24. The negative root of $x^3 - x + 2 = 0$.

25. The negative root of $3x^4 + 3x^3 - x^2 - 4x - 4 = 0$.

26. The positive root of
    $x^5 + x^4 - 4x^3 - 4x^2 - 5x - 5 = 0$.

Use a graphing calculator to find the distinct real solutions of each equation to the nearest tenth. Which roots, if any, would the Bisection Method fail to find?

27. $x^2 - 5 = 0$

28. $x^2 - 10x + 25 = 0$

29. $x^3 - 5x^2 + 8x - 4 = 0$

30. $x^3 - 5x^2 - 2x + 10 = 0$

Applications
31. **Containers** A box has a length of 16 inches, a width of 10 inches, and a height of between 4 inches and 8 inches. Can it have a volume of 1,000 in.^{3}? *Hint:* Model the volume of the box with a function of h.

32. **Lollipops** If a candy company makes spherical-shaped lollipops with radii between 1 and 4 cm, use the Intermediate Value Theorem to determine whether a lollipop can be made with a volume of 200 cubic centimeters. *Hint:* The volume formula for a sphere is $V = \frac{4}{3}\pi r^3$.

33. **Precalculus** Use the Bisection Method or a graphing calculator to find the coordinates of the two points on the graph of $y = x^3$ that lie 1 unit from the origin. (See the illustration.) Give the result to the nearest hundredth.

34. **Building crates** The width of the shipping crate shown is to be 2 feet greater than its height, the length is to be 5 feet greater than its width, and its volume is to be 170 cubic feet. Use the Bisection Method or a graphing calculator to find the height of the crate to the nearest tenth of a foot.

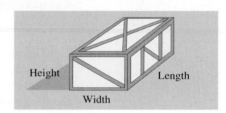

Discovery and Writing
35. Explain when the Bisection Method will not work.

36. Describe how you could tell from a graph that a polynomial equation has no real roots.

Review
Give the equations of all of the asymptotes of each rational function. Don't graph the functions.

37. $y = \dfrac{5x - 3}{x^2 - 4}$

38. $y = \dfrac{5x^2 - 3}{x^2 - 25}$

39. $y = \dfrac{x^2}{x - 2}$

40. $y = \dfrac{x + 1}{x^2 + 1}$

CHAPTER REVIEW

SECTION **5.1**   The Remainder and Factor Theorems; Synthetic Division

Definitions and Concepts	Examples
A **polynomial equation** is an equation that can be written in the form $P(x) = 0$, where $P(x) = a_n x^n + a_{n-1} x^{n-1} + a_{n-2} x^{n-2} + \cdots + a_1 x + a_0$ where n is a natural number and the polynomial is of degree n.	$3x - 10 = 0$; degree: 1 $7x^2 + 3x - 1 = 0$; degree: 2 $4x^3 + 7x^2 + 3x - 1 = 0$; degree: 3 $x^4 - 4x^3 + 7x^2 + 3x - 1 = 0$; degree: 4
Zero of a polynomial function: A **zero of the polynomial** $P(x)$ is any number r for which $P(r) = 0$.	The real number 1 is a zero of the polynomial function $P(x) = x^3 - 4x^2 + 3x$ because $$P(1) = 1^3 - 4(1)^2 + 3(1)$$ $$= 1 - 4 + 3$$ $$= 0$$
The Remainder Theorem: If $P(x)$ is a polynomial function, r is any number, and $P(x)$ is divided by $x - r$, the remainder is $P(r)$.	Let $P(x) = 3x^3 - 5x^2 + 3x - 10$ and use the Remainder Theorem and long division to find $P(2)$. We will divide $P(x)$ by $x - 2$ as follows: $$\begin{array}{r} 3x^2 + x + 5 \\ x - 2 \overline{)3x^3 - 5x^2 + 3x - 10} \\ \underline{3x^3 - 6x^2} \\ x^2 + 3x \\ \underline{x^2 - 2x} \\ 5x - 10 \\ \underline{5x - 10} \\ 0 \end{array}$$ The remainder is 0. $P(2) = 0$.
The Factor Theorem: If $P(x)$ is a polynomial function and r is any number, then if $P(r) = 0$, then $x - r$ is a factor of $P(x)$. If $x - r$ is a factor of $P(x)$, then $P(r) = 0$. **Alternate Form of the Factor Theorem:** If r is a zero of the polynomial function $P(x)$, then $x - r$ is a factor of $P(x)$. If $x - r$ is a factor of $P(x)$, then r is a zero of the polynomial function.	We see in the previous example that $P(2) = 0$. By the Factor Theorem, we know that $x - 2$ is a factor of the polynomial function $P(x) = 3x^3 - 5x^2 + 3x - 10$. We also know that 2 is a zero of the polynomial function.

Definitions and Concepts	Examples
Synthetic division is a fast way to divide higher-degree polynomials by binomials of the form $x - r$.	Divide $P(x) = 5x^3 + 3x^2 - 21x - 1$ by $x - 2$ using synthetic division.

We first write the coefficients of the dividend, with its terms in descending powers of x, and the 2 from the divisor in the following form:

$$\underline{2|}\ 5 \quad 3 \quad -21 \quad -1$$

$$\underline{2|}\ 5 \quad 3 \quad -21 \quad -1$$
$$5 \qquad\qquad\qquad\qquad\text{Bring down the 5.}$$

$$\underline{2|}\ 5 \quad 3 \quad -21 \quad -1$$
$$\qquad 10 \qquad\qquad 2(5) = 10; 3 + 10 = 13$$
$$5 \quad 13 \qquad\quad 9$$

$$\underline{2|}\ 5 \quad 3 \quad -21 \quad -1$$
$$\qquad 10 \quad 26 \qquad 2(13) = 26; -21 + 26 = 5$$
$$5 \quad 13 \quad 5 \quad 9$$

$$\underline{2|}\ 5 \quad 3 \quad -21 \quad -1$$
$$\qquad 10 \quad 26 \quad 10 \qquad 2(5) = 10; -1 + 10 = 9$$
$$5 \quad 13 \quad 5 \quad 9$$

The quotient is $5x^2 + 13x + 5$. The remainder is 9. Thus,

$$\frac{5x^3 - 3x^2 - 21x - 1}{x - 2} = 5x^2 + 13x + 5 + \frac{9}{x - 2}$$

Because the remainder is 9, we know by the Remainder Theorem that $P(2) = 9$. Because $P(2) \neq 0$, we know by the Factor Theorem that $x - 2$ is not a factor of $5x^3 + 3x^2 - 21x - 1$.

Definitions and Concepts	Examples
Synthetic division can be used to solve polynomial equations.	Let $P(x) = x^3 + x^2 - 3x - 3$. Completely solve the polynomial equation $P(x) = 0$ given that -1 is a root.

1. We use synthetic division to divide $P(x)$ by $x + 1$.

$$\underline{-1|}\ 1 \quad 1 \quad -3 \quad -3$$
$$\qquad\quad -1 \quad 0 \quad 3$$
$$\overline{\quad 1 \quad 0 \quad -3 \quad 0}$$

2. We then write the quotient and factor it.

$$x^3 + x^2 - 3x - 3 = (x + 1)(x^2 - 3).$$

Definitions and Concepts	Examples
	3. Finally, we solve the polynomial equation $P(x) = 0$. $$x^3 + x^2 - 3x - 3 = 0$$ $$(x + 1)(x^2 - 3) = 0$$ We then set each factor equal to 0 and solve for x. $$x + 1 = 0 \quad \text{or} \quad x^2 - 3 = 0$$ $$x = -1 \qquad\qquad x^2 = 3$$ $$x = \pm\sqrt{3}$$ The solution set is $\left\{-1, \sqrt{3}, -\sqrt{3}\right\}$.

EXERCISES

Let $P(x) = 4x^4 + 2x^3 - 3x^2 - 2$. Find the remainder when $P(x)$ is divided by each binomial.

1. $x - 1$

2. $x - 2$

3. $x + 3$

4. $x + 2$

Use the Factor Theorem to determine whether each statement is true.

5. $x - 2$ is a factor of $x^3 + 4x^2 - 2x + 4$.

6. $x + 3$ is a factor of $2x^4 + 10x^3 + 4x^2 + 7x + 21$.

7. $x - 5$ is a factor of $x^5 - 3{,}125$.

8. $x - 6$ is a factor of $x^5 - 6x^4 - 4x + 24$.

Use synthetic division to perform each division.

9. $3x^4 + 2x^2 + 3x + 7; \ x - 3$

10. $2x^4 - 3x^2 + 3x - 1; \ x - 2$

11. $5x^5 - 4x^4 + 3x^3 - 2x^2 + x - 1; \ x + 2$

12. $4x^5 + 2x^4 - x^3 + 3x^2 + 2x + 1; \ x + 1$

Let $P(x) = 5x^3 + 2x^2 - x + 1$. Use synthetic division to find each value.

13. $P(3)$

14. $P(-3)$

15. $P\left(\dfrac{1}{2}\right)$

16. $P(i)$

A partial solution set is given for each polynomial equation. Find the complete solution set.

17. $2x^3 - 3x^2 - 11x + 6 = 0; \ \{3\}$

18. $x^4 + 4x^3 - x^2 - 20x - 20 = 0; \ \{-2, -2\}$

Find the polynomial function of lowest degree with integer coefficients and the given zeros.

19. $-1, 2,$ and $\dfrac{3}{2}$

20. $1, -3,$ and $\dfrac{1}{2}$

21. $2, -5, i,$ and $-i$

22. $-3, 2, i,$ and $-i$

SECTION 5.2   Descartes' Rule of Signs and Bounds on Roots

Definitions and Concepts	Examples
The Fundamental Theorem of Algebra: If $P(x)$ is a polynomial function with positive degree, then $P(x)$ has at least one zero.	The Fundamental Theorem of Algebra guarantees that polynomial functions like $P(x) = 3x^3 - 5x^2 + 7x - 2$ and $P(x) = 4x^5 + x^3 - 6x - 15$ have zeros.

Definitions and Concepts	Examples
The Polynomial Factorization Theorem: If $n > 0$ and $P(x)$ is an nth-degree polynomial function, then $P(x)$ has exactly n linear factors: $$P(x) = a_n(x - r_1)(x - r_2)(x - r_3) \cdot \cdots \cdot (x - r_n)$$ where $r_1, r_2, r_3, \ldots, r_n$ are numbers and a_n is the leading coefficient of $P(x)$.	Consider the following polynomial function of degree $n = 3$. $$P(x) = x^3 + 144x$$ $$= x(x^2 + 144)$$ $$= x(x - 12i)(x + 12i)$$ The Polynomial Factorization Theorem guarantees that we have exactly 3 linear factors. They are $$x, \ x - 12i, \ \text{and} \ x + 12i$$
If multiple roots are counted individually, the polynomial equation $P(x) = 0$ with degree n $(n > 0)$ has exactly n roots among the complex numbers.	The polynomial equation $P(x) = x^3 + 144x = 0$ has exactly 3 roots. They are $$0, \ 12i, \ \text{and} \ -12i$$ Each root occurs once and has a multiplicity of one.
The Conjugate Pairs Theorem: If a polynomial equation $P(x) = 0$ with real-number coefficients has a complex root $a + bi$ with $b \neq 0$, then its conjugate $a - bi$ is also a root.	The Conjugate Pairs Theorem applies to $P(x) = x^3 + 144x = 0$ because the polynomial has real coefficients. The complex roots $12i$ and $-12i$ that occur are conjugate pairs.
Descartes' Rule of Signs: Let $P(x)$ be a polynomial function with real coefficients. • The number of positive roots of $P(x) = 0$ is either equal to the number of variations in sign of $P(x)$ or less than that by an even number. • The number of negative roots of $P(x) = 0$ is either equal to the number of variations in sign of $P(-x)$ or less than that by an even number.	Use Descartes' Rule of Signs to find the number of possible positive, negative, and nonreal roots of $P(x) = 5x^3 - 7x^2 + x - 6 = 0$. **1. Find the number of possible positive roots.** Since there are three variations of sign in $P(x) = 5x^3 - 7x^2 + x - 6 = 0$, there can be either 3 positive roots or only 1 (1 is less than 3 by the even number 2). **2. Find the number of possible negative roots.** Because $$P(-x) = 5(-x)^3 - 7(-x)^2 + (-x) - 6$$ $$= -5x^3 - 7x^2 - x - 6$$ has no variations in sign, there are 0 negative roots. Furthermore, 0 is not a root, because the terms of the polynomial do not have a common factor of x. **3. Find the number of nonreal roots.** If there are 3 positive roots, then all of the roots are accounted for. If there is 1 positive root, the 2 remaining roots must be nonreal complex numbers. The following chart shows these possibilities.

Number of positive roots	Number of negative roots	Number of nonreal roots
3	0	0
1	0	2

The number of nonreal complex roots is the number needed to bring the total number of roots up to 3.

Definitions and Concepts	Examples
Upper and lower bounds on roots: Let $P(x)$ be a polynomial function with real coefficients and a positive leading coefficient.	Use the upper and lower bound rules to establish bounds for the roots of $2x^3 + 2x^2 - 8x - 8 = 0$.

Upper and lower bounds on roots:

Let $P(x)$ be a polynomial function with real coefficients and a positive leading coefficient.

1. If $P(x)$ is synthetically divided by a positive number c and each term in the last row of the division is nonnegative, then no number greater than c can be a root of $P(x) = 0$. (c is called an **upper bound** of the real roots.)

2. If $P(x)$ is synthetically divided by a negative number d and the signs in the last row alternate,* no value less than d can be a root of $P(x) = 0$. (d is called a **lower bound** of the real roots.)

*If 0 appears in the third row, that 0 can be assigned either a + or a − sign to help the signs alternate.

Use the upper and lower bound rules to establish bounds for the roots of $2x^3 + 2x^2 - 8x - 8 = 0$.

1. We will perform several synthetic divisions by positive integers, looking for nonnegative values in the last row.

   Trying 1 first gives

$$\begin{array}{r|rrrr} 1 & 2 & 2 & -8 & -8 \\ & & 2 & 4 & -4 \\ \hline & +2 & +4 & -4 & -12 \end{array}$$

   Because at least one of the signs in the last row is negative, we cannot claim that 1 is an upper bound. We now try 2.

$$\begin{array}{r|rrrr} 2 & 2 & 2 & -8 & -8 \\ & & 4 & 12 & 8 \\ \hline & +2 & +6 & +4 & 0 \end{array}$$

   Because the last row is entirely nonnegative, we can claim that 2 is an upper bound. That is, no number greater than 2 can be a root of the equation.

2. We perform several synthetic divisions by negative divisors, looking for alternating signs in the last row. We begin with -3.

$$\begin{array}{r|rrrr} -3 & 2 & 2 & -8 & -8 \\ & & -6 & 12 & -12 \\ \hline & +2 & -4 & +4 & -20 \end{array}$$

   Since the signs in the last row alternate, -3 is a lower bound. That is, no number less than -3 can be a root. All of the real roots must be in the interval $(-3, 2)$.

EXERCISES

How many roots does each equation have?

23. $3x^6 - 4x^5 + 3x + 2 = 0$

24. $2x^6 - 5x^4 + 5x^3 - 4x^2 + x - 12 = 0$

25. $3x^{65} - 4x^{50} + 3x^{17} + 2x = 0$

26. $x^{1,984} - 12 = 0$

Determine how many linear factors and zeros each polynomial function has.

27. $P(x) = x^4 - 16$

28. $P(x) = x^{40} + x^{30}$

29. $P(x) = 4x^5 + 2x^3$

30. $P(x) = x^3 - 64x$

Find another root of a polynomial equation with real coefficients if the given quantity is one root.

31. $2 + i$ **32.** $-i$

Write a third-degree polynomial equation with real coefficients and the given roots.

33. $4, -i$ **34.** $-5, i$

Find the number of possible positive, negative, and nonreal roots for each equation. Do not attempt to solve the equation.

35. $3x^4 + 2x^3 - 4x + 2 = 0$

36. $2x^4 - 3x^3 + 5x^2 + x - 5 = 0$

37. $4x^5 + 3x^4 + 2x^3 + x^2 + x = 7$

38. $3x^7 - 4x^5 + 3x^3 + x - 4 = 0$

39. $x^4 + x^2 + 24{,}567 = 0$

40. $-x^7 - 5 = 0$

Find integer bounds for the roots of each equation. Answers can vary.

41. $5x^3 - 4x^2 - 2x + 4 = 0$

42. $x^4 + 3x^3 - 5x^2 - 9x + 1 = 0$

SECTION 5.3   Roots of Polynomial Equations

Definitions and Concepts	**Examples**
Rational Root Theorem: Let the polynomial function $$P(x) = a_nx^n + a_{n-1}x^{n-1} + a_{n-2}x^{n-2} + \cdots + a_1x + a_0$$ have integer coefficients. If the rational number $\frac{p}{q}$ (written in lowest terms) is a root of $P(x) = 0$, then p is a factor of the constant a_0, and q is a factor of the leading coefficient a_n.	Consider $2x^3 - 7x^2 - 17x + 10 = 0$ By the Rational Root Theorem, the only possible numerators for the rational roots of the equation are the factors of the constant term 10: $$\pm 1, \pm 2, \pm 5, \text{ and } \pm 10$$ The only possible denominators are the factors of the leading coefficient 2: $$\pm 1, \text{ and } \pm 2$$ We can form a list of all possible rational solutions by listing the combinations of possible numerators and denominators: $$\pm\frac{1}{1}, \pm\frac{2}{1}, \pm\frac{5}{1}, \pm\frac{10}{1}, \pm\frac{1}{2}, \pm\frac{2}{2}, \pm\frac{5}{2}, \pm\frac{10}{2}$$ Since several of these possibilities are duplicates, we can condense the list to get ***Possible Rational Roots*** $$\pm 1, \pm 2, \pm 5, \pm 10, \pm\frac{1}{2}, \text{ and } \pm\frac{5}{2}$$
Finding rational roots: 1. Use Descartes' Rule of Signs to determine the number of possible positive, negative, and nonreal roots. 2. Use the Rational Root Theorem to list possible rational roots. 3. Use synthetic division to find a root. 4. If there are more roots, repeat the previous steps. (Once the depressed equation is quadratic, synthetic division isn't required. It can be solved as a quadratic equation.)	Find the solution set of the polynomial equation $P(x) = 2x^3 - 7x^2 - 17x + 10 = 0$. 1. To determine the number of possible positive, negative, and nonreal roots, we will use Descartes' Rule of Signs. Since there are two variations in sign of $P(x)$, the number of positive roots is either 2 or 0. Next, we consider $P(-x)$. $$P(-x) = -2x^3 - 7x^2 + 17x + 10.$$ Since there is one variation in sign of $P(-x)$, the number of negative roots is 1. The following chart shows these possibilities:

Number of positive roots	Number of negative roots	Number of nonreal roots
2	1	0
0	1	2

Definitions and Concepts	Examples

	2. List the possible rational roots.
	    The possible rational roots were found in the previous example. They are:
	
	        Possible Rational Roots
	
	$$\pm 1,\ \pm 2,\ \pm 5,\ \pm 10,\ \pm\frac{1}{2},\ \text{and}\ \pm\frac{5}{2}$$
	
	3. Use synthetic division to find a root. We can start with -2.
	
	$$\begin{array}{r|rrrr} -2 & 2 & -7 & -17 & 10 \\ & & -4 & 22 & -10 \\ \hline & 2 & -11 & 5 & 0 \end{array}$$
	
	    Since the remainder is 0, -2 is a root and the binomial $x + 2$ is a factor of $P(x)$.
	
	4. The remaining roots must be supplied by the remaining factor, which is the quotient $2x^2 - 11x + 5$. We can find the other roots by solving the depressed equation $2x^2 - 11x + 5 = 0$.
	
	$$2x^2 - 11x + 5 = 0$$
	$$(2x - 1)(x - 5) = 0 \quad \text{Factor.}$$
	$$2x - 1 = 0 \quad \text{or} \quad x - 5 = 0$$
	$$2x = 1 \qquad\qquad x = 5$$
	$$x = \frac{1}{2}$$
	
	    The solution set of the equation is $\left\{-2, \frac{1}{2}, 5\right\}$.
	Note that two positive roots and one negative root is a predicted possibility.

EXERCISES

Use the Rational Root Theorem to list all possible rational roots of the polynomial equation.

43. $2x^4 + x^3 - 3x^2 - 5x - 6 = 0$

44. $4x^5 - 2x^4 + 3x^3 - 5x - 10 = 0$

Find all rational roots of each equation.

45. $x^3 - 10x^2 + 29x - 20 = 0$

46. $x^3 - 8x^2 - x + 8 = 0$

47. $2x^3 + 17x^2 + 41x + 30 = 0$

48. $3x^3 + 2x^2 + 2x - 1 = 0$

49. $4x^4 - 25x^2 + 36 = 0$

50. $2x^4 - 11x^3 - 6x^2 + 64x + 32 = 0$

Find all roots of each equation.

51. $3x^3 - x^2 + 48x - 16 = 0$

52. $x^4 - 2x^3 - 9x^2 + 8x + 20 = 0$

SECTION **5.4**   Approximating Irrational Roots of Polynomial Equations

Definitions and Concepts	**Examples**
The Intermediate Value Theorem: Let $P(x)$ be a polynomial function with real coefficients. If $P(a) \neq P(b)$ for $a < b$, then $P(x)$ takes on all values between $P(a)$ and $P(b)$ on the closed interval $[a, b]$.	Consider the polynomial function $P(x) = 4x^3 + 2x^2 - 12x + 3$ and note that $$P(0) = 4(0)^3 + 2(0)^2 - 12(0) + 3 = 3$$ $$P(1) = 4(1)^3 + 2(1)^2 - 12(1) + 3 = -3$$ Because $P(0) \neq P(1)$ and $0 < 1$, the Intermediate Value Theorem guarantees that $P(x)$ takes on all values between -3 and 3 on the closed interval $[0,1]$.
The Location Theorem: Let $P(x)$ be a polynomial function with real coefficients. If $P(a)$ and $P(b)$ have opposite signs, there is at least one number r in the interval (a, b) for which $P(r) = 0$.	To show that the polynomial equation, $4x^3 + 2x^2 - 12x + 3 = 0$ has at least one real root between 0 and 1, we see from above that $P(0) = 3$ and $P(1) = -3$ have opposite signs. Therefore, we know by the Location Theorem that there is at least one real root between 0 and 1, as shown in the figure. 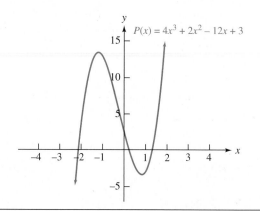

Bisection Method:
The Bisection Method is a method for finding the roots of $P(x) = 0$ to any desired degree of accuracy.
 	
   Suppose we find, by trial and error, that the numbers x_l and x_r (for left and right) straddle a root—that is, $x_l < x_r$ and $P(x_l)$ and $P(x_r)$ have opposite signs. Further suppose that $P(x_l) < 0$ and $P(x_r) > 0$. We can compute the number c that is halfway between x_l and x_r and then compute $P(c)$. If $P(c) = 0$, we've found a root. However, if $P(c)$ is not 0, we proceed in one of two ways:
 	
1. If $P(c) < 0$, the root r lies between c and x_r. In this case, we let c become a new x_l and repeat the procedure.
2. If $P(c) > 0$, the root r lies between x_l and c. In this case, we let c become a new x_r and repeat the procedure.
	Use the Bisection Method to find the positive root of $x^2 - 5 = 0$ to the nearest tenth.
	   We let $P(x) = x^2 - 5$. Since $P(2) = -1$ and $P(3) = 4$ have opposite signs, there is a root between 2 and 3. We can let $x_l = 2$ and $x_r = 3$ and compute the midpoint c:
	
	$$c = \frac{x_l + x_r}{2} = \frac{2 + 3}{2} = 2.5$$
	
	   Because $P(c) = P(2.5) = 1.25$ is a positive number, we let c become a new x_r and calculate a new midpoint, which we will call c_1.
	
	$$c_1 = \frac{x_l + x_r}{2} = \frac{2 + 2.5}{2} = 2.25$$
	
	   Because $P(c_1) = P(2.25) = 0.0625$ is a positive number, we let c_1 become a new x_r and calculate a new midpoint, which we will call c_2.
	
	$$c_2 = \frac{x_l + x_r}{2} = \frac{2 + 2.25}{2} = 2.125$$

Definitions and Concepts	Examples
	Because $P(c_2) = P(2.125) = -0.484375$ is a negative number, we let c_2 become a new x_l and calculate a new midpoint, which we will call c_3. $$c_3 = \frac{x_l + x_r}{2} = \frac{2.125 + 2.25}{2} = 2.1875$$ Because $P(c_3) = P(2.1875) = -0.21484375$ is a negative number, we let c_3 become a new x_l and calculate a new midpoint, which we will call c_4. $$c_4 = \frac{x_l + x_r}{2} = \frac{2.1875 + 2.25}{2} = 2.21875$$ Because $P(c_4) = P(2.21875) = -0.0771484375$ is a negative number, we calculate a new midpoint. From here on, the first two digits of the midpoints will remain 2.2. The root r of the equation (to the nearest tenth) is 2.2.
Graphing calculator usage: To approximate the roots of a polynomial equation using a graphing calculator, we can use the ZOOM and TRACE capabilities of the calculator or the ZERO feature of the calculator.	See Accent on Technology in Section 5.4.

EXERCISES

Show that each polynomial has a zero between the two given numbers.

53. $5x^3 + 37x^2 + 59x + 18 = 0$; -1 and 0

54. $6x^3 - x^2 - 10x - 3 = 0$; 1 and 2

 Use the Bisection Method to find the positive root of each equation to the nearest tenth.

55. $x^3 - 2x^2 - 9x - 2 = 0$

56. $6x^2 - 13x - 5 = 0$

 Use a graphing calculator to find the positive root of each equation to the nearest hundredth.

57. $6x^2 - 7x - 5 = 0$

58. $3x^2 + x - 2 = 0$

59. Designing solar collectors The space available for the installation of three solar collecting panels requires that their lengths differ by the amounts shown in the illustration, and that the total of their widths be 15 meters. To be equally effective, each panel must measure exactly 60 square meters. Find the dimensions of each panel.

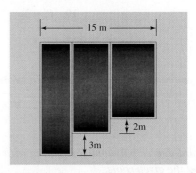

60. Designing a storage tank The design specifications for the cylindrical storage tank shown require that its height be 3 feet greater than the radius of its circular base and that the volume of the tank be 19,000 cubic feet. Use the Bisection Method or a graphing calculator to find the radius of the tank to the nearest hundredth of a foot.

CHAPTER TEST

1. Is $x = -2$ a zero of $P(x) = x^2 + 5x + 6$?

Use long division and the Remainder Theorem to find each value.

2. $P(x) = 3x^3 - 9x - 5$; $P(2)$

3. $P(x) = x^5 + 2$; $P(-2)$

4. Use the Factor Theorem to determine whether $x - 3$ is a factor of $2x^4 - 10x^3 + 4x^2 + 7x + 21$.

Use synthetic division to express $P(x) = 2x^3 - 3x^2 - 4x - 1$ in the form (divisor)(quotient) + remainder for each divisor.

5. $x - 2$

6. $x + 1$

Use synthetic division to perform each division.

7. $\dfrac{2x^2 - 7x - 15}{x - 5}$

8. $\dfrac{3x^3 + 7x^2 + 2x}{x + 2}$

Let $P(x) = 3x^3 - 2x^2 + 4$. Use synthetic division to find each value.

9. $P(1)$

10. $P(-2)$

11. $P\left(-\dfrac{1}{3}\right)$

12. $P(i)$

Find a polynomial function with the given zeros.

13. $5, -1, 0$

14. $i, -i, \sqrt{3}, -\sqrt{3}$

Write a third-degree polynomial equation with real coefficients and the given roots.

15. $2, i$

16. $1, 2 + i$

17. How many linear factors and zeros does $P(x) = 3x^3 + 2x^2 - 4x + 1$ have?

18. If $3 - 2i$ is a root of $P(x) = 0$ where $P(x)$ has real-number coefficients, find another root.

Use Descartes' Rule of Signs to find the number of possible positive, negative, and nonreal roots of each equation.

19. $3x^5 - 2x^4 + 2x^2 - x - 3 = 0$

20. $2x^3 - 5x^2 - 2x - 1 = 0$

Find integer bounds for the roots of each equation. Answers can vary.

21. $x^5 - x^4 - 5x^3 + 5x^2 + 4x - 5 = 0$

22. $2x^3 - 11x^2 + 10x + 3 = 0$

23. Use the Rational Root Theorem to list all possible rational roots of $x^3 + 4x^2 + 3x + 8 = 0$.

24. Use the Rational Root Theorem to list all possible rational roots of $5x^3 + 4x^2 + 3x + 2 = 0$.

25. Find all roots of the equation $2x^3 + 3x^2 - 11x - 6 = 0$.

26. Find all roots of the equation $x^3 - 2x^2 + x - 2 = 0$.

27. Find all roots of the equation $x^4 + x^3 + 3x^2 + 9x - 54 = 0$.

28. Find all roots of the equation $x^5 + 2x^4 + 3x^3 + 6x^2 - 4x - 8 = 0$.

29. Does the polynomial $P(x) = 3x^3 + 2x^2 - 4x + 4$ have a zero between the values $x = 1$ and $x = 2$?

Use the Bisection Method to find the positive root of the equation to the nearest tenth.

30. $x^2 - 11 = 0$

CUMULATIVE REVIEW EXERCISES

Graph the function defined by each equation.

1. $f(x) = 3^x - 2$

2. $f(x) = 2e^x$

3. $f(x) = \log_3 x$

4. $f(x) = \ln(x - 2)$

Find each value.

5. $\log_2 64$

6. $\log_{1/2} 8$

7. $\ln e^3$

8. $2^{\log_2 2}$

Write each expression in terms of the logarithms of a, b, and c.

9. $\log abc$

10. $\log \dfrac{a^2 b}{c}$

11. $\log \sqrt{\dfrac{ab}{c^3}}$

12. $\ln \dfrac{\sqrt{ab^2}}{c}$

Write each expression as the logarithm of a single quantity.

13. $3 \ln a - 3 \ln b$

14. $\dfrac{1}{2} \log a + 3 \log b - \dfrac{2}{3} \log c$

Solve each equation.

15. $3^{x+1} = 8$

16. $3^{x-1} = 3^{2x}$

17. $\log x + \log 2 = 3$

18. $\log (x + 1) + \log (x - 1) = 1$

Let $P(x) = 4x^3 + 3x + 2$. Use synthetic division to find each value.

19. $P(1)$

20. $P(-2)$

21. $P\left(\dfrac{1}{2}\right)$

22. $P(i)$

Determine whether each binomial is a factor of $P(x) = x^3 + 2x^2 - x - 2$. Use synthetic division.

23. $x + 1$

24. $x - 2$

25. $x - 1$

26. $x + 2$

Determine how many roots each equation has.

27. $x^{12} - 4x^8 + 2x^4 + 12 = 0$

28. $x^{2,000} - 1 = 0$

Determine the number of possible positive, negative, and nonreal roots of each equation.

29. $x^4 + 2x^3 - 3x^2 + x + 2 = 0$

30. $x^4 - 3x^3 - 2x^2 - 3x - 5 = 0$

Solve each equation.

31. $x^3 + x^2 - 9x - 9 = 0$

32. $x^3 - 2x^2 - x + 2 = 0$

Linear Systems

6

CAREERS AND MATHEMATICS: Cryptanalyst

© Istockphoto.com/nullplus

Cryptanalysts are essential to the implementation of protection systems employed by corporations and private citizens to keep hackers out of important data systems. They also play an important part in the safety of cities, states, and countries by analyzing and deciphering secret coding systems used by terrorists and other enemies. With increased reliance on the Internet to conduct business, store data, and pass information between groups, the job of a cryptanalyst is becoming increasingly more important to ensure both private and governmental security of data.

Education and Mathematics Required
- Most are required to have at least an undergraduate degree in mathematics or computer science. Many will also have a graduate degree in mathematics, with a Ph.D. being required for those wishing to be employed in a research facility or by a university.
- College Algebra, Trigonometry, Calculus I, II, and III, Linear Algebra, Differential and Partial Differential Equations, Elementary Number Theory, Introduction to Real Analysis, Analysis I and II, Methods of Complex Analysis, and Mathematical Cryptography are math courses required.

How Cyptanalysts Use Math and Who Employs Them
- Among the many ways that cryptanalysts use mathematics are the encoding and encrypting of systems and databases, devising systems used to prevent hackers from stealing consumer data, and consulting with business and industry to solve problems related to security.
- Cryptanalysts are employed in all levels of government, including intelligence agencies and special services, universities, financial institutions, insurance companies, telecommunications companies, computer design firms, consulting firms, and science and engineering firms.

Career Outlook and Earnings
- Employment of cryptanalysts is expected to grow by 22 percent through 2018, which is much faster than the average for all occupations.
- The median annual wages of cryptanalysts is approximately $101,645.

For more information see: www.bls.gov/oco

In this chapter, we will learn to solve systems of equations—sets of several equations, most with more than one variable. One method of solution uses matrices, an important tool in mathematics and its applications.

6.1 Systems of Linear Equations

In this section, we will learn to

1. Solve systems using the graphing method.
2. Solve systems using the substitution method.
3. Solve systems using the addition method
4. Solve systems with infinitely many solutions.
5. Solve inconsistent systems.
6. Solve systems involving three equations in three variables.
7. Solve applications involving systems of equations.

In economics we often talk about the law of supply and demand.

- As the illustration above shows, few units of a product will be in demand when the price is high. However, more units will be in demand when the price is low.
- As the illustration above also shows, few units of product will be supplied when the price is low. However, more product will be supplied when the price is high.

In a free economy, the intersection of the graph of the supply function and the demand function will be the market price of the product.

To see that this is true, suppose that the price of a product is $3. At this price, less than 30 units of product would be in demand, but over 40 units would be supplied. Since supply is greater than demand, the price would come down.

At a price of $2, a little less than 40 units would be in demand, but less than 30 units would be supplied. Since demand is greater than supply, the price would go up.

Only when the graphs cross would the demand and supply be in equilibrium.

In this section, we will begin to discuss how to find the common solution of two equations that occur simultaneously.

Equations with two variables have infinitely many solutions. For example, the tables shown give a few of the solutions of $x + y = 5$ and $x - y = 1$.

$x + y = 5$	
x	y
1	4
2	3
3	2
5	0

$x - y = 1$	
x	y
8	7
3	2
1	0
0	-1

Only the pair $x = 3$ and $y = 2$ satisfies both equations. The pair of equations

$$\begin{cases} x + y = 5 \\ x - y = 1 \end{cases}$$

is called a **system of equations,** and the solution $x = 3$, $y = 2$ is called its **simultaneous solution,** or just its **solution.** The process of finding the solution of a system of equations is called **solving the system.**

The graph of an equation in two variables displays the equation's infinitely many solutions. For example, the graph of one of the lines in Figure 6-1 represents the infinitely many solutions of the equation $5x - 2y = 1$. The other line in the figure is the graph of the infinitely many solutions of $2x + 3y = 8$.

Because only point $P(1, 2)$ lies on both lines, only its coordinates satisfy both equations. Thus, the simultaneous solution of the system of equations

$$\begin{cases} 5x - 2y = 1 \\ 2x + 3y = 8 \end{cases}$$

is the pair of numbers $x = 1$ and $y = 2$ or simply the pair $(1, 2)$.

This discussion suggests a graphical method of solving systems of equations in two variables.

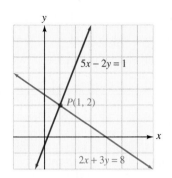

FIGURE 6-1

1. Solve Systems Using the Graphing Method

We can use the following steps to solve a system of two equations in two variables.

Strategy for Using the Graphing Method

1. On one coordinate grid, graph each equation.
2. Find the coordinates of the point or points where all of the graphs intersect. These coordinates give the solutions of the system.
3. If the graphs have no point in common, the system has no solution.

EXAMPLE 1   Using the Graphing Method to Solve a System of Equations

Use the graphing method to solve each system:

a. $\begin{cases} 3x + y = 1 \\ -x + 2y = 9 \end{cases}$ b. $\begin{cases} 2x - 3y = 4 \\ 4x = -4 + 6y \end{cases}$ c. $\begin{cases} y = 4 - x \\ 2x + 2y = 8 \end{cases}$

SOLUTION   a. The graphs of the equations are the lines shown in Figure 6-2(a). The solution of this system is given by the coordinates of the point $(-1, 4)$, where the lines intersect. By checking both values in both equations, we can verify that the solution is $x = -1$ and $y = 4$.

b. The graphs of the equations are the parallel lines shown in Figure 6-2(b). Since parallel lines do not intersect, the system has no solution.

c. The graphs of the equations are the lines shown in Figure 6-2(c). Since the lines are the same, they have infinitely many points in common, and the system has infinitely many solutions. All ordered pairs whose coordinates satisfy one of the equations satisfy the other also.

To find some solutions, we substitute numbers for x in the first equation and solve for y. If $x = 3$ for example, then $y = 1$. One solution is the pair $(3, 1)$. Other solutions are $(0, 4)$ and $(5, -1)$.

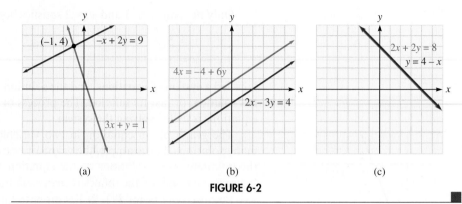

FIGURE 6-2

Self Check 1   Solve: $\begin{cases} y = 2x \\ x + y = 3 \end{cases}$.

Now Try Exercise 13.

Example 1 illustrates three possibilities that can occur when we solve systems of equations. If a system of equations has at least one solution, as in parts a and c of Example 1, the system is called **consistent.** If it has no solution, as in part b, it is called **inconsistent.**

If a system of two equations in two variables has exactly one solution as in part a, or no solution as in part b, the equations in the system are called **independent.** If a system of linear equations has infinitely many solutions, as in part c, the equations of the system are called **dependent.**

There are three possibilities that can occur when two equations, each with two variables, are graphed.

Possibilities		Conclusion
	The lines are distinct and intersect.	The equations are independent, and the system is consistent. The system has one solution.
	The lines are distinct and parallel.	The equations are independent, and the system is inconsistent. The system has no solution.
	The lines coincide.	The equations are dependent, and the system is consistent. The system has infinitely many solutions.

ACCENT ON TECHNOLOGY   **Solving a System of Linear Equations**

In order to use a graphing calculator to solve a system of equations, each equation must be written with y as a function of x. This will allow us to enter each equation into the graph editor. Let's solve the system $\begin{cases} x - 4y = 7 \\ x + 2y = 4 \end{cases}$.

Solving each equation for y gives us $\begin{cases} y = \dfrac{x - 7}{4} \\ y = \dfrac{4 - x}{2} \end{cases}$. Now we are ready to solve the system using the graphing calculator.

The point where the lines intersect is the solution for the system. We will use the INTERSECT function to solve this system.

1. Enter the equations. Make sure you put parentheses around the numerators.

2. Set a proper WINDOW.

3. GRAPH the lines. Select the intersect function by pressing 2nd TRACE : 5 . Move the cursor near the intersection. It doesn't have to be really close, just near.

4. Now press the ENTER key three times, and the intersection will be shown.

FIGURE 6-3

We now consider two algebraic methods to find solutions of systems containing any number of variables.

2. Solve Systems Using the Substitution Method

We use the following steps to solve a system of two equations in two variables by substitution.

Strategy for Using the Substitution Method

1. Solve one equation for a variable—say, y.
2. Substitute the expression obtained for y for every y in the second equation.
3. Solve the equation that results.
4. Substitute the solution found in Step 3 into the equation found in Step 1 and solve for y.

EXAMPLE 2   **Using the Substitution Method to Solve a System of Equations**

Use the substitution method to solve $\begin{cases} 3x + y = 1 \\ -x + 2y = 9 \end{cases}$.

Comment

We could solve either equation for x or y. However, it is easier to solve for a variable with a coefficient of 1 or -1. Then fractions will be avoided.

SOLUTION   We can solve the first equation for y and then substitute that result for y in the second equation.

$$\begin{cases} 3x + y = 1 \rightarrow y = \boxed{1 - 3x} \\ -x + 2y = 9 \end{cases}$$

The substitution gives one linear equation with one variable, which we can solve for x:

$$-x + 2(1 - 3x) = 9$$

$$-x + 2 - 6x = 9$$

$$-7x = 7 \qquad \text{Combine like terms and subtract 2 from both sides.}$$

$$x = -1 \qquad \text{Divide both sides by } -7.$$

To find y, we substitute -1 for x in the equation $y = 1 - 3x$ and simplify:

$$y = 1 - 3x$$

$$= 1 - 3(-1)$$

$$= 1 + 3$$

$$= 4$$

The solution is the pair $(-1, 4)$. ∎

Self Check 2   Solve: $\begin{cases} 2x + 3y = 1 \\ x - y = 3 \end{cases}$.

Now Try Exercise 29.

3. Solve Systems Using the Addition Method

As with substitution, the addition method combines the equations of a system to eliminate terms involving one of the variables.

Strategy for Using the Addition Method

1. Write the equations of the system in general form so that terms with the same variable are aligned vertically.
2. Multiply all the terms of one or both of the equations by constants chosen to make the coefficients of x (or y) differ only in sign.
3. Add the equations. Solve the equation that results, if possible.
4. Substitute the value obtained in Step 3 into either of the original equations, and solve for the remaining variable.
5. The results obtained in Steps 3 and 4 are the solution of the system.

EXAMPLE 3   **Using the Addition Method to Solve a System of Equations**

Use the addition method to solve $\begin{cases} 3x + 2y = 8 \\ 2x - 5y = 18 \end{cases}$.

SOLUTION   To eliminate y, we multiply the terms of the first equation by 5 and the terms of the second equation by 2, to obtain an equivalent system in which the coefficients of y differ only in sign. Then we add the equations to eliminate y.

Comment

To make the coefficients of y differ only in sign and be the smallest numbers possible, we multiply each equation by a number that makes the new coefficients of y the least common multiple of the original coefficients.

$$\begin{cases} 3x + 2y = 8 & \rightarrow & 15x + 10y = 40 & \quad \text{Multiply by 5.} \\ 2x - 5y = 18 & \rightarrow & \underline{4x - 10y = 36} & \quad \text{Multiply by 2.} \end{cases}$$

$$19x \qquad\quad = 76 \qquad \text{Add the equations.}$$

$$x = 4 \qquad\qquad\quad \text{Divide both sides by 19.}$$

We now substitute 4 for x into either of the original equations and solve for y. If we use the first equation,

$$3x + 2y = 8$$

$$3(4) + 2y = 8 \qquad \text{Substitute 4 for } x.$$

$$12 + 2y = 8 \qquad \text{Simplify.}$$

$$2y = -4 \qquad \text{Subtract 12 from both sides.}$$

$$y = -2 \qquad \text{Divide both sides by 2.}$$

The solution is $(4, -2)$.

Self Check 3   Solve: $\begin{cases} 2x + 5y = 8 \\ 2x - 4y = -10 \end{cases}$.

Now Try Exercise 37.

EXAMPLE 4   **Using the Addition Method to Solve a System of Equations**

Solve: $\begin{cases} \dfrac{x + 2y}{4} + \dfrac{x - y}{5} = \dfrac{6}{5} \\ \dfrac{x + y}{7} - \dfrac{x - y}{3} = -\dfrac{12}{7} \end{cases}$.

SOLUTION   To clear the first equation of fractions, we multiply both sides by the lowest common denominator, 20. To clear the second equation of fractions, we multiply both sides of the second equation by the LCD, which is 21.

$$\begin{cases} 20\left(\dfrac{x + 2y}{4} + \dfrac{x - y}{5}\right) = 20\left(\dfrac{6}{5}\right) \\ 21\left(\dfrac{x + y}{7} - \dfrac{x - y}{3}\right) = 21\left(-\dfrac{12}{7}\right) \end{cases}$$

$$\begin{cases} 5(x + 2y) + 4(x - y) = 24 \\ 3(x + y) - 7(x - y) = -36 \end{cases}$$

$$\begin{cases} 9x + 6y = 24 \\ -4x + 10y = -36 \end{cases} \qquad \text{Remove parentheses and combine like terms.}$$

$$\begin{cases} 3x + 2y = 8 \qquad \text{Divide both sides by 3.} \\ 2x - 5y = 18 \qquad \text{Divide both sides by } -2. \end{cases}$$

In Example 3, we saw that the solution to this final system is $(4, -2)$.

Self Check 4   Solve: $\begin{cases} \dfrac{x + y}{3} + \dfrac{x - y}{4} = \dfrac{3}{4} \\ \dfrac{x - y}{3} - \dfrac{2x - y}{2} = -\dfrac{1}{3} \end{cases}$.

Now Try Exercise 51.

4. Solve Systems with Infinitely Many Solutions

EXAMPLE 5   **Solving a System with Infinitely Many Solutions**

Use the addition method to solve $\begin{cases} x + 2y = 3 \\ 2x + 4y = 6 \end{cases}$.

SOLUTION   To eliminate the variable y, we can multiply both sides of the first equation by -2 and add the result to the second equation to get

$$\begin{array}{r} -2x - 4y = -6 \\ \underline{2x + 4y = 6} \\ 0 = 0 \end{array}$$

Although the result $0 = 0$ is true, it does not give the value of y.

Since the second equation in the original system is twice the first, the equations are equivalent. If we were to solve this system by graphing, the two lines would coincide. The (x, y) coordinates of points on that one line form the infinite set of solutions to the given system. The system is consistent, but the equations are dependent.

To find a general solution, we can solve either equation of the system for y. If we solve the first equation for y, we obtain

$$\begin{aligned} x + 2y &= 3 \\ 2y &= 3 - x \\ y &= \frac{3 - x}{2} \end{aligned}$$

All ordered pairs that are solutions will have the form $\left(x, \frac{3 - x}{2}\right)$. For example:

- If $x = 3$ then $y = 0$ and $(3, 0)$ is a solution.
- If $x = 0$ then $y = \frac{3}{2}$ and $\left(0, \frac{3}{2}\right)$ is a solution.
- If $x = -7$ then $y = 5$ and $(-7, 5)$ is a solution.

Self Check 5   Solve: $\begin{cases} 3x - y = 2 \\ 6x - 2y = 4 \end{cases}$.

Now Try Exercise 43.

5. Solve Inconsistent Systems

EXAMPLE 6   **Solving an Inconsistent System**

Solve: $\begin{cases} x + y = 3 \\ x + y = 2 \end{cases}$.

SOLUTION   We can multiply both sides of the second equation by -1 and add the results to the first equation to get

$$\begin{array}{r} x + y = 3 \\ \underline{-x - y = -2} \\ 0 = 1 \end{array}$$

Because $0 \neq 1$ the system has no solutions. If we graph each equation in this system, the graphs will be parallel lines. This system is inconsistent, and the equations are independent.

Self Check 6   Solve: $\begin{cases} 3x + 2y = 2 \\ 3x + 2y = 3 \end{cases}$.

Now Try Exercise 45.

6. Solve Systems Involving Three Equations in Three Variables

To solve three equations in three variables, we use addition to eliminate one variable. This will produce a system of two equations in two variables, which we can solve using the methods previously discussed.

EXAMPLE 7   **Solving a System Involving Three Equations in Three Variables**

Solve the system:

$$\begin{array}{ll} (1) \\ (2) \\ (3) \end{array} \begin{cases} x + 2y + z = 8 \\ 2x + y - z = 1 \\ x + y - 2z = -3 \end{cases}$$

SOLUTION   We can add Equations 1 and 2 to eliminate z

$$\begin{array}{ll} (1) & x + 2y + z = 8 \\ (2) & \underline{2x + y - z = 1} \\ (4) & 3x + 3y = 9 \end{array}$$

and divide both sides of Equation 4 by 3 to get

$(5) \quad x + y = 3$

We now choose a different pair of equations—say, Equations 1 and 3—and eliminate z again. If we multiply both sides of Equation 1 by 2 and add the result to Equation 3, we get

$$\begin{array}{ll} & 2x + 4y + 2z = 16 \\ (3) & \underline{x + y - 2z = -3} \\ (6) & 3x + 5y = 13 \end{array}$$

Equations 5 and 6 form the system $\begin{cases} x + y = 3 \\ 3x + 5y = 13 \end{cases}$, which we can solve by substitution.

$$\begin{array}{ll} (5) & x + y = 3 \rightarrow y = 3 - x \\ (6) & 3x + 5y = 13 \end{array}$$

$$\begin{array}{ll} 3x + 5(3 - x) = 13 & \text{Substitute } 3 - x \text{ for } y. \\ 3x + 15 - 5x = 13 & \text{Remove parentheses.} \\ -2x = -2 & \text{Combine like terms and subtract 15 from both sides.} \\ x = 1 & \text{Divide both sides by } -2. \end{array}$$

To find y, we substitute 1 for x in the equation $y = 3 - x$.

$$y = 3 - 1$$
$$y = 2$$

To find z, we substitute 1 for x and 2 for y in any one of the original equations that includes z, and we find that $z = 3$. The solution is the triple

$$(x, y, z) = (1, 2, 3)$$

Because there is one solution, the system is consistent, and its equations are independent.

Self Check 7   Solve: $\begin{cases} x - y + 2z = 2 \\ 2x + y + z = 4 \\ -x - 2y + 3z = 0 \end{cases}$.

Now Try Exercise 53.

EXAMPLE 8   **Solving a System Involving Three Equations in Three Variables**

Solve the system:

(1) $\begin{cases} x + 2y + z = 8 \\ 2x + y - z = 1 \\ x - y - 2z = -7 \end{cases}$
(2)
(3)

SOLUTION   We can add Equations 1 and 2 to eliminate z.

$$x + 2y + z = 8$$
$$\underline{2x + \ y - z = 1}$$
(4) $3x + 3y \qquad = 9$

We can now multiply Equation 1 by 2 and add it to Equation 3 to eliminate z again.

$$2x + 4y + 2z = \ 16$$
$$\underline{x - \ y - 2z = -7}$$
(5) $3x + 3y \qquad = \ 9$

Since Equations 4 and 5 are the same, the system is consistent, but the equations are dependent. There will be infinitely many solutions. To find a general solution, we can solve either Equation 4 or 5 for y to get

(6) $y = 3 - x$

We can find the value of z in terms of x by substituting the right side of Equation 6 into any of the first three equations—say Equation 1.

$$x + 2y + z = 8$$
$$x + 2(3 - x) + z = 8 \qquad \text{Substitute } 3 - x \text{ for } y.$$
$$x + 6 - 2x + z = 8 \qquad \text{Use the Distributive Property to remove parentheses.}$$
$$-x + 6 + z = 8 \qquad \text{Combine terms.}$$
$$z = x + 2 \qquad \text{Solve for } z.$$

A general solution to this system is $(x, y, z) = (x, 3 - x, x + 2)$. To find some specific solutions, we can substitute numbers for x and compute y and z. For example,

If $x = 1$, then $y = 2$ and $z = 3$. One possible solution is $(1, 2, 3)$.

If $x = 0$, then $y = 3$ and $z = 2$. Another possible solution is $(0, 3, 2)$.

Self Check 8   Solve: $\begin{cases} x + y + z = 3 \\ x - y + 3z = 4 \\ 2x + 2y + 2z = 5 \end{cases}$.

Now Try Exercise 61.

7. Solve Applications Involving Systems of Equations

EXAMPLE 9   Solving an Application Problem

An airplane flies 600 miles with the wind for 2 hours and returns against the wind in 3 hours. Find the speed of the wind and the air speed of the plane.

SOLUTION

If a represents the air speed and w represents wind speed, the ground speed of the plane with the wind is the combined speed $a + w$. On the return trip, against the wind, the ground speed is $a - w$. The information in this problem is organized in Figure 6-4 and can be used to give a system of two equations in the variables a and w.

	d	$=$	r	$\cdot$	t
Outbound trip	600		$a + w$		2
Return trip	600		$a - w$		3

FIGURE 6-4

Since $d = rt$ we have $\begin{cases} 600 = 2(a + w) \\ 600 = 3(a - w) \end{cases}$, which can be written as

(7) $\begin{cases} 300 = a + w \\ 200 = a - w \end{cases}$

We can add these equations to get

$500 = 2a$

$a = 250$ Divide both sides by 2.

To find w, we substitute 250 for a into either of the previous equations (we'll use Equation 7) and solve for w:

(7) $300 = a + w$

$300 = \mathbf{250} + w$

$w = 50$ Subtract 250 from both sides.

The air speed of the plane is 250 mph. With a 50-mph tailwind, the ground speed is $250 + 50$, or 300 mph. At 300 mph, the 600-mile trip will take 2 hours.

With a 50-mph headwind, the ground speed is $250 - 50$, or 200 mph. At 200 mph, the 600-mile trip will take 3 hours. The answers check. ∎

Self Check 9   An airplane flies 500 miles with the wind for 2 hours and returns against the wind in 3 hours. Find the speed of the wind and the air speed of the plane. Round to tenths.

Now Try Exercise 75.

Self Check Answers   **1.** $(1, 2)$ **2.** $(2, -1)$ **3.** $(-1, 2)$ **4.** $(1, 2)$ **5.** A general solution is $(x, 3x - 2)$.   **6.** The system is inconsistent; no solution.   **7.** $(1, 1, 1)$ **8.** no solution; inconsistent solution   **9.** speed of wind: 41.7 mph; air speed of the plane: 208.3 mph.

Exercises **6.1**

Getting Ready

You should be able to complete these vocabulary and concept statements before you proceed to the practice exercises.

Fill in the blanks.

1. A set of several equations with several variables is called a _____ of equations.

2. Any set of numbers that satisfies each equation of a system is called a _____ of the system.

3. If a system of equations has a solution, the system is _____ .

4. If a system of equations has no solution, the system is _____ .

5. If a system of equations has only one solution, the equations of the system are _____ .

6. If a system of equations has infinitely many solutions, the equations of the system are _____ .

7. The system $\begin{cases} x + y = 5 \\ x - y = 1 \end{cases}$ is _____ (consistent, inconsistent).

8. The system $\begin{cases} x + y = 5 \\ x + y = 1 \end{cases}$ is _____ (consistent, inconsistent).

9. The equations of the system $\begin{cases} x + y = 5 \\ 2x + 2y = 10 \end{cases}$ are _____ (dependent, independent).

10. The equations of the system $\begin{cases} x + y = 5 \\ x - y = 1 \end{cases}$ are _____ (dependent, independent).

11. The pair $(1, 3)$ ___ (is, is not) a solution of the system $\begin{cases} x + 2y = 7 \\ 2x - y = -1 \end{cases}$

12. The pair $(1, 3)$ ___ (is, is not) a solution of the system $\begin{cases} 3x + y = 6 \\ x - 3y = -8 \end{cases}$

Practice

Solve each system of equations by graphing.

13. $\begin{cases} y = -3x + 5 \\ x - 2y = -3 \end{cases}$

14. $\begin{cases} x - 2y = -3 \\ 3x + y = -9 \end{cases}$

15. $\begin{cases} 3x + 2y = 2 \\ -2x + 3y = 16 \end{cases}$

16. $\begin{cases} x + y = 0 \\ 5x - 2y = 14 \end{cases}$

17. $\begin{cases} y = -x + 5 \\ 3x + 3y = 30 \end{cases}$

18. $\begin{cases} x - 3y = -3 \\ 2x - 6y = 12 \end{cases}$

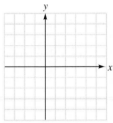

19. $\begin{cases} y = -x + 6 \\ 5x + 5y = 30 \end{cases}$

20. $\begin{cases} 2x - y = -3 \\ 8x - 4y = -12 \end{cases}$

Use a graphing calculator to approximate the solutions of each system. Give answers to the nearest tenth.

21. $\begin{cases} y = -5.7x + 7.8 \\ y = 37.2 - 19.1x \end{cases}$ **22.** $\begin{cases} y = 3.4x - 1 \\ y = -7.1x + 3.1 \end{cases}$

23. $\begin{cases} y = \dfrac{5.5 - 2.7x}{3.5} \\ 5.3x - 9.2y = 6.0 \end{cases}$ **24.** $\begin{cases} 29x + 17y = 7 \\ -17x + 23y = 19 \end{cases}$

Solve each system by substitution, if possible.

25. $\begin{cases} y = x - 1 \\ y = 2x \end{cases}$ **26.** $\begin{cases} y = 2x - 1 \\ x + y = 5 \end{cases}$

27. $\begin{cases} 2x + 3y = 0 \\ y = 3x - 11 \end{cases}$ **28.** $\begin{cases} 2x + y = 3 \\ y = 5x - 11 \end{cases}$

29. $\begin{cases} 4x + 3y = 3 \\ 2x - 6y = -1 \end{cases}$ **30.** $\begin{cases} 4x + 5y = 4 \\ 8x - 15y = 3 \end{cases}$

31. $\begin{cases} x + 3y = 1 \\ 2x + 6y = 3 \end{cases}$ **32.** $\begin{cases} x - 3y = 14 \\ 3(x - 12) = 9y \end{cases}$

33. $\begin{cases} y = 3x - 6 \\ x = \dfrac{1}{3}y + 2 \end{cases}$ **34.** $\begin{cases} 3x - y = 12 \\ y = 3x - 12 \end{cases}$

Solve each system by the addition method, if possible.

35. $\begin{cases} 5x - 3y = 12 \\ 2x - 3y = 3 \end{cases}$ **36.** $\begin{cases} 2x + 3y = 8 \\ -5x + y = -3 \end{cases}$

37. $\begin{cases} x - 7y = -11 \\ 8x + 2y = 28 \end{cases}$ **38.** $\begin{cases} 3x + 9y = 9 \\ -x + 5y = -3 \end{cases}$

39. $\begin{cases} 3(x - y) = y - 9 \\ 5(x + y) = -15 \end{cases}$ **40.** $\begin{cases} 2(x + y) = y + 1 \\ 3(x + 1) = y - 3 \end{cases}$

41. $\begin{cases} 2 = \dfrac{1}{x + y} \\ 2 = \dfrac{3}{x - y} \end{cases}$ **42.** $\begin{cases} \dfrac{1}{x + y} = 12 \\ \dfrac{3x}{y} = -4 \end{cases}$

43. $\begin{cases} y + 2x = 5 \\ 0.5y = 2.5 - x \end{cases}$

44. $\begin{cases} -0.3x + 0.1y = -0.1 \\ 6x - 2y = 2 \end{cases}$

45. $\begin{cases} x + 2(x - y) = 2 \\ 3(y - x) - y = 5 \end{cases}$ **46.** $\begin{cases} 3x = 4(2 - y) \\ 3(x - 2) + 4y = 0 \end{cases}$

47. $\begin{cases} x + \dfrac{y}{3} = \dfrac{5}{3} \\ \dfrac{x + y}{3} = 3 - x \end{cases}$ **48.** $\begin{cases} 3x - y = 0.25 \\ x + \dfrac{3}{2}y = 2.375 \end{cases}$

49. $\begin{cases} \dfrac{3}{2}x + \dfrac{1}{3}y = 2 \\ \dfrac{2}{3}x + \dfrac{1}{9}y = 1 \end{cases}$ **50.** $\begin{cases} \dfrac{x + y}{2} + \dfrac{x - y}{5} = 2 \\ x = \dfrac{y}{2} + 1 \end{cases}$

51. $\begin{cases} \dfrac{x - y}{5} + \dfrac{x + y}{2} = 6 \\ \dfrac{x - y}{2} - \dfrac{x + y}{4} = 3 \end{cases}$ **52.** $\begin{cases} \dfrac{x - 2}{5} + \dfrac{y + 3}{2} = 5 \\ \dfrac{x + 3}{2} + \dfrac{y - 2}{3} = 6 \end{cases}$

Solve each system, if possible.

53. $\begin{cases} x + y + z = 3 \\ 2x + y + z = 4 \\ 3x + y - z = 5 \end{cases}$ **54.** $\begin{cases} x - y - z = 0 \\ x + y - z = 0 \\ x - y + z = 2 \end{cases}$

55. $\begin{cases} x - y + z = 0 \\ x + y + 2z = -1 \\ -x - y + z = 0 \end{cases}$ **56.** $\begin{cases} 2x + y - z = 7 \\ x - y + z = 2 \\ x + y - 3z = 2 \end{cases}$

57. $\begin{cases} 2x + y = 4 \\ x - z = 2 \\ y + z = 1 \end{cases}$ **58.** $\begin{cases} 3x + y + z = 0 \\ 2x - y + z = 0 \\ 2x + y + z = 0 \end{cases}$

59. $\begin{cases} x + y + z = 6 \\ 2x + y + 3z = 17 \\ x + y + 2z = 11 \end{cases}$ **60.** $\begin{cases} x + y + z = 3 \\ 2x + y + z = 6 \\ x + 2y + 3z = 2 \end{cases}$

61. $\begin{cases} x + y + z = 3 \\ x + z = 2 \\ 2x + 2y + 2z = 3 \end{cases}$ **62.** $\begin{cases} x + y + z = 3 \\ x + z = 2 \\ 2x + y + 2z = 5 \end{cases}$

63. $\begin{cases} x + 2y - z = 2 \\ 2x - y = -1 \\ 3x + y + z = 1 \end{cases}$ **64.** $\begin{cases} x + y = 2 \\ y + z = 2 \\ 3x + 3y = 2 \end{cases}$

65. $\begin{cases} 3x + 4y + 2z = 4 \\ 6x - 2y + z = 4 \\ 3x - 8y - 6z = -3 \end{cases}$ **66.** $\begin{cases} x + y = 2 \\ y + z = 2 \\ x - z = 0 \end{cases}$

67. $\begin{cases} 2x - y - z = 0 \\ x - 2y - z = -1 \\ x - y - 2z = -1 \end{cases}$ **68.** $\begin{cases} x + 3y - z = 5 \\ 3x - y + z = 2 \\ 2x + y = 1 \end{cases}$

69. $\begin{cases} (x + y) + (y + z) + (z + x) = 6 \\ (x - y) + (y - z) + (z - x) = 0 \\ x + y + 2z = 4 \end{cases}$

70. $\begin{cases} (x + y) + (y + z) = 1 \\ (x + z) + (x + z) = 3 \\ (x - y) - (x - z) = -1 \end{cases}$

Applications
Use systems of equations to solve each problem.

71. Price of food items If Jonathan purchases two hamburgers and four orders of french fries for $8 and Hannah purchases 3 hamburgers and two orders of fries for $8, what is the price of each item?

72. Price of tennis equipment Hunter purchases two tennis rackets and four cans of tennis balls for $102. Jana purchases three tennis rackets and two cans of tennis balls for $141. What is the price of each item?

73. Planning for harvest A farmer raises corn and soybeans on 350 acres of land. Because of expected prices at harvest time, he thinks it would be wise to plant 100 more acres of corn than of soybeans. How many acres of each does he plant?

74. Club memberships There is an initiation fee to join the Pine River Country Club, as well as monthly dues. The total cost after 7 months' membership will be $3,025, and after $1\frac{1}{2}$ years, $3,850. Find both the initiation fee and the monthly dues.

75. Boating A Mississippi riverboat can travel 30 kilometers downstream in 3 hours and can make the return trip in 5 hours. Find the speed of the boat in still water.

76. Framing pictures A rectangular picture frame has a perimeter of 1,900 centimeters and a width that is 250 centimeters less than its length. Find the area of the picture.

77. Making an alloy A metallurgist wants to make 60 grams of an alloy that is to be 34% copper. She has samples that are 9% copper and 84% copper. How many grams of each must she use?

78. Archimedes' law of the lever The two weights shown will be in balance if the product of one weight and its distance from the fulcrum is equal to the product of the other weight and its distance from the fulcrum. Two weights are in balance when one is 2 meters and the other 3 meters from the fulcrum. If the fulcrum remained in the same spot and the weights were interchanged, the closer weight would need to be increased by 5 pounds to maintain balance. Find the weights.

79. Lifting weights A 112-pound force can lift the 448-pound load shown. If the fulcrum is moved 1 additional foot away from the load, a 192-pound force is required. Find the length of the lever.

80. Writing test questions For a test question, a mathematics teacher wants to find two constants a and b such that the test item "Simplify $a(x + 2y) - b(2x - y)$" will have an answer of $-3x + 9y$. What constants a and b should the teacher use?

81. Break-even point Rollowheel, Inc., can manufacture a pair of in-line skates for $43.53. Daily fixed costs of manufacturing in-line skates amount to $742.72. A pair of in-line skates can be sold for $89.95. Find equations expressing the expenses E and the revenue R as functions of x, the number of pairs manufactured and sold. At what production level will expenses equal revenues?

82. Choosing salary options For its sales staff, a company offers two salary options. One is $326 per week plus a commission of $3\frac{1}{2}\%$ of sales. The other is $200 per week plus $4\frac{1}{4}\%$ of sales. Find equations that express incomes as functions of sales, and find the weekly sales level that produces equal salaries.

Use systems of three equations in three variables to solve each problem.

83. Work schedules A college student earns $198.50 per week working three part-time jobs. Half of his 30-hour work week is spent cooking hamburgers at a fast-food chain, earning $5.70 per hour. In addition, the student earns $6.30 per hour working at a gas station and $10 per hour doing janitorial work. How many hours per week does the student work at each job?

84. Investment income A woman invested a $22,000 rollover IRA account in three banks paying 5%, 6%, and 7% annual interest. She invested $2,000 more at 6% than at 5%. The total annual interest she earned was $1,370. How much did she invest at each rate?

85. Age distribution Approximately 3 million people live in Costa Rica. 2.61 million are younger than 50 years, and 1.95 million are older than 14 years. How many people are in each of the categories 0–14 years, 15–49 years, and 50 years and older?

86. Designing arches The engineer designing a parabolic arch knows that its equation has the form $y = ax^2 + bx + c$. Use the information in the illustration to find a, b, and c. Assume that the distances are given in feet. (*Hint:* The coordinates of points on the parabola satisfy its equation.)

87. Geometry The sum of the angles of a triangle is 180°. In a certain triangle, the largest angle is 20° greater than the sum of the other two and is 10° greater than 3 times the smallest. How large is each angle?

88. Ballistics The path of a thrown object is a parabola with the equation $y = ax^2 + bx + c$. Use the information in the illustration to find a, b, and c. (Distances are in feet.)

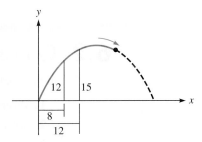

Discovery and Writing

89. Use a graphing calculator to attempt to find the solution of the system $\begin{cases} x - 8y = -51 \\ 3x - 25y = -160 \end{cases}$.

90. Solve the system of Exercise 89 algebraically. Which method is easier, and why?

91. Use a graphing calculator to attempt to find the solution of the system $\begin{cases} 17x - 23y = -76 \\ 29x + 19y = -278 \end{cases}$.

92. Solve the system of Exercise 91 algebraically. Which method is easier, and why?

93. Invent a system of two equations with the solution $x = 1$, $y = 2$ that is difficult to solve with a graphing calculator (as in Exercise 91).

94. Invent a system of two equations with the solution $x = 1$, $y = 2$ that is easier to solve graphically than algebraically.

Examples of Matrices in Reduced Row Echelon Form

The matrices

$$\begin{bmatrix} 1 & 0 & 0 \\ 0 & 1 & 0 \end{bmatrix}, \quad \begin{bmatrix} 1 & 0 & 0 & 7 \\ 0 & 1 & 0 & 8 \\ 0 & 0 & 1 & 3 \end{bmatrix}$$

are in reduced row echelon form, because each matrix is in row echelon form and the entries above each lead entry are 0's.

Examples of Matrices That Are Not in Reduced Row Echelon Form

$$\begin{bmatrix} 1 & 3 & 0 & 7 \\ 0 & 0 & 1 & 8 \\ 0 & 0 & 1 & 0 \end{bmatrix} \quad \text{The matrix is not in row echelon form.}$$

$$\begin{bmatrix} 0 & 3 & 5 \\ 0 & 1 & 1 \end{bmatrix} \quad \text{The number above the lead entry of 1 is not 0.}$$

In the next example, we solve a system by Gauss–Jordan elimination.

EXAMPLE 5 **Using Gauss–Jordan Elimination to Solve a System of Equations**

Use Gauss–Jordan elimination to solve $\begin{cases} w + 2x + 3y + z = 4 \\ x + 4y - z = 0 \\ w - x - y + 2z = 2 \end{cases}$.

SOLUTION We will use row operations to reduce the system matrix as follows. We first use the 1 in the upper left corner to zero out the rest of the first column:

$$\begin{bmatrix} 1 & 2 & 3 & 1 & \vdots & 4 \\ 0 & 1 & 4 & -1 & \vdots & 0 \\ 1 & -1 & -1 & 2 & \vdots & 2 \end{bmatrix} \begin{array}{c} \\ \\ (-1)R1 + R3 \to \end{array} \begin{bmatrix} 1 & 2 & 3 & 1 & \vdots & 4 \\ 0 & 1 & 4 & -1 & \vdots & 0 \\ 0 & -3 & -4 & 1 & \vdots & -2 \end{bmatrix}$$

The lead entry in the second row is already 1. We use it to zero out the rest of the second column.

$$\begin{array}{c} (-2)R2 + R1 \to \\ \\ (3)R2 + R3 \to \end{array} \begin{bmatrix} 1 & 0 & -5 & 3 & \vdots & 4 \\ 0 & 1 & 4 & -1 & \vdots & 0 \\ 0 & 0 & 8 & -2 & \vdots & -2 \end{bmatrix}$$

To make the lead entry in the third row equal to 1, we multiply the third row by $\frac{1}{8}$ and use it to zero out the rest of the third column.

$$\left(\tfrac{1}{8}\right)R3 \to \begin{bmatrix} 1 & 0 & -5 & 3 & \vdots & 4 \\ 0 & 1 & 4 & -1 & \vdots & 0 \\ 0 & 0 & 1 & -\dfrac{1}{4} & \vdots & -\dfrac{1}{4} \end{bmatrix}$$

$$\begin{array}{c} (5)R3 + R1 \to \\ \\ (-4)R3 + R2 \to \\ \\ \\ \end{array} \begin{bmatrix} 1 & 0 & 0 & \dfrac{7}{4} & \vdots & \dfrac{11}{4} \\ 0 & 1 & 0 & 0 & \vdots & 1 \\ 0 & 0 & 1 & -\dfrac{1}{4} & \vdots & -\dfrac{1}{4} \end{bmatrix}$$

The final matrix is in reduced row echelon form. Note that each lead entry is 1, and each is alone in its column. The matrix represents the system of equations

$$\begin{cases} w + \dfrac{7}{4}z = \dfrac{11}{4} \\ x = 1 \\ y - \dfrac{1}{4}z = -\dfrac{1}{4} \end{cases} \quad \text{or} \quad \begin{cases} w = \dfrac{11}{4} - \dfrac{7}{4}z \\ x = 1 \\ y = -\dfrac{1}{4} + \dfrac{1}{4}z \end{cases}$$

A general solution is $(w, x, y, z) = \left(\dfrac{11}{4} - \dfrac{7}{4}z, 1, -\dfrac{1}{4} + \dfrac{1}{4}z, z\right)$. To find some specific solutions, we choose values for z, and the corresponding values of w, x, and y will be determined. For example, if $z = 1$, then $w = 1$, $x = 1$, and $y = 0$. Thus, $(w, x, y, z) = (1, 1, 0, 1)$ is a solution. If $z = -1$, another solution is $(w, x, y, z) = \left(\dfrac{9}{2}, 1, -\dfrac{1}{2}, -1\right)$. ∎

Self Check 5   Solve: $\begin{cases} w + x + y - z = 2 \\ 2w + 2x + 2y - 2z = 3 \\ w + x - y + 3z = 4 \\ w + 3x + 2y - 2z = -1 \end{cases}$.

Now Try Exercise 59.

ACCENT ON TECHNOLOGY   **Reduce a Matrix to Row Reduced Echelon Form**

A graphing calculator can also reduce a matrix to a row reduced echelon form. If the matrix has been entered, then go to the home screen, and select the function shown.

FIGURE 6-6

In Example 5, there were more variables than equations. In the next example, there are more equations than variables.

EXAMPLE 6   **Using Gauss–Jordan Elimination to Solve a System of Equations**

Use Gauss–Jordan elimination to solve $\begin{cases} 2x + y = 4 \\ x - 3y = 9 \\ x + 4y = -5 \end{cases}$.

SOLUTION   To get a 1 in the top left corner, we could multiply the first row by $\frac{1}{2}$, but that would introduce fractions. Instead, we can exchange the first two rows and proceed as follows:

$$\begin{bmatrix} 2 & 1 & \vdots & 4 \\ 1 & -3 & \vdots & 9 \\ 1 & 4 & \vdots & -5 \end{bmatrix} \overset{R1 \leftrightarrow R2}{} \begin{bmatrix} 1 & -3 & \vdots & 9 \\ 2 & 1 & \vdots & 4 \\ 1 & 4 & \vdots & -5 \end{bmatrix}$$

$$\begin{matrix} \\ (-2)R1 + R2 \rightarrow \\ (-1)R1 + R3 \rightarrow \end{matrix} \begin{bmatrix} 1 & -3 & \vdots & 9 \\ 0 & 7 & \vdots & -14 \\ 0 & 7 & \vdots & -14 \end{bmatrix}$$

$$\left(\tfrac{1}{7}\right)R2 \to \begin{bmatrix} 1 & -3 & \vdots & 9 \\ 0 & 1 & \vdots & -2 \\ 0 & 1 & \vdots & -2 \end{bmatrix}$$
$$\left(\tfrac{1}{7}\right)R3 \to$$

$$(3)R2 + R1 \to \begin{bmatrix} 1 & 0 & \vdots & 3 \\ 0 & 1 & \vdots & -2 \\ 0 & 0 & \vdots & 0 \end{bmatrix}$$
$$(-1)R2 + R3 \to$$

This final matrix is in reduced echelon form. It represents the system

$$\begin{cases} x = 3 \\ y = -2 \end{cases}$$

Verify that $x = 3$ and $y = -2$ satisfy the equations of the original system.

Self Check 6   Solve: $\begin{cases} x + y = 5 \\ x - y = 1 \\ x + 2y = 7 \end{cases}$.

Now Try Exercise 67.

Self Check Answers   1. $(4, 1)$ 2. $(1, 2, 1)$ 3. The system is inconsistent.
4. $(x, y, z) = (2 + z, -z, z)$ 5. no solution; inconsistent system
6. $x = 3, y = 2$

Exercises 6.2

Getting Ready
You should be able to complete these vocabulary and concept statements before you proceed to the practice exercises.

Fill in the blanks.

1. A rectangular array of numbers is called a _____ .

2. A 3×5 matrix has ___ rows and ___ columns.

3. The matrix containing the coefficients of the variables is called the _____ matrix.

4. The coefficient matrix joined to the column of constants is called the _____ matrix or the _____ matrix.

5. Each row of a system matrix represents one _____ .

6. The rows of the system matrix are changed using elementary _____ .

7. If one system matrix is changed to another using row operations, the matrices are _____ .

8. If two system matrices are row equivalent, then the systems have the _____ .

9. In a type 1 row operation, two rows of a matrix can be _____ .

10. In a type 2 row operation, one entire row can be _____ by a nonzero constant.

11. In a type 3 row operation, any row can be changed by _____ to it any _____ of another row.

12. The first nonzero entry in a row is called that row's _____ .

Practice
Use Gaussian elimination to solve each system.

13. $\begin{cases} x + y = 5 \\ x - 2y = -4 \end{cases}$ 14. $\begin{cases} x + 3y = 8 \\ 2x - 5y = 5 \end{cases}$

15. $\begin{cases} x - y = 1 \\ 2x - y = 8 \end{cases}$ 16. $\begin{cases} x - 5y = 4 \\ 2x + 3y = 21 \end{cases}$

17. $\begin{cases} x + 2y - z = 2 \\ x - 3y + 2z = 1 \\ x + y - 3z = -6 \end{cases}$ 18. $\begin{cases} x + 5y - z = 2 \\ x + 2y + z = 3 \\ x + y + z = 2 \end{cases}$

19. $\begin{cases} x - y - z = -3 \\ 5x + y = 6 \\ y + z = 4 \end{cases}$ 20. $\begin{cases} x + y = 1 \\ x + z = 3 \\ y + z = 2 \end{cases}$

Determine whether each matrix is in row echelon form, reduced row echelon form, or neither.

21. $\begin{bmatrix} 1 & 3 & 0 & 5 \\ 0 & 1 & 2 & 7 \\ 0 & 0 & 1 & 0 \end{bmatrix}$ **22.** $\begin{bmatrix} 1 & 3 & 0 & 5 \\ 0 & 1 & 2 & 7 \\ 0 & 0 & 0 & 0 \end{bmatrix}$

23. $\begin{bmatrix} 1 & 0 & 1 \\ 0 & 1 & 5 \\ 0 & 0 & 0 \\ 0 & 0 & 0 \end{bmatrix}$ **24.** $\begin{bmatrix} 1 & 0 & 1 \\ 0 & 1 & 5 \\ 0 & 0 & 1 \\ 0 & 0 & 0 \end{bmatrix}$

Write each system as a matrix and solve it by Gaussian elimination. If a system has infinitely many solutions, show a general solution.

25. $\begin{cases} 2x + y = 3 \\ x - 3y = 5 \end{cases}$ **26.** $\begin{cases} x + 2y = -1 \\ 3x - 5y = 19 \end{cases}$

27. $\begin{cases} x - 7y = -2 \\ 5x - 2y = -10 \end{cases}$ **28.** $\begin{cases} 3x - y = 3 \\ 2x + y = -3 \end{cases}$

29. $\begin{cases} 2x - y = 5 \\ x + 3y = 6 \end{cases}$ **30.** $\begin{cases} 3x - 5y = -25 \\ 2x + y = 5 \end{cases}$

31. $\begin{cases} x - 2y = 3 \\ -2x + 4y = 6 \end{cases}$ **32.** $\begin{cases} 2(2y - x) = 6 \\ 4y = 2(x + 3) \end{cases}$

33. $\begin{cases} 2x - y = 7 \\ -x + \dfrac{1}{3}y = -\dfrac{7}{3} \end{cases}$ **34.** $\begin{cases} 45x - 6y = 60 \\ 30x + 15y = 63.75 \end{cases}$

35. $\begin{cases} x - y + z = 3 \\ 2x - y + z = 4 \\ x + 2y - z = -1 \end{cases}$ **36.** $\begin{cases} 2x + y - z = 1 \\ x + y - z = 0 \\ 3x + y + 2z = 2 \end{cases}$

37. $\begin{cases} x + y - z = -1 \\ 3x + y = 4 \\ y - 2z = -4 \end{cases}$ **38.** $\begin{cases} 3x + y = 7 \\ x - z = 0 \\ y - 2z = -8 \end{cases}$

39. $\begin{cases} x - y + z = 2 \\ 2x + y + z = 5 \\ 3x - 4z = -5 \end{cases}$ **40.** $\begin{cases} x + z = -1 \\ 3x + y = 2 \\ 2x + y + 5z = 3 \end{cases}$

41. $\begin{cases} x + y - z = 5 \\ x + y + z = 2 \\ 3x + 3y - z = 12 \end{cases}$ **42.** $\begin{cases} x + y + 2z = 4 \\ -x - y - 3z = -5 \\ 2x + y + z = 2 \end{cases}$

43. $\begin{cases} 2x - y + z = 6 \\ 3x + y - z = 2 \\ -x + 3y - 3z = 8 \end{cases}$ **44.** $\begin{cases} -x + 3y + 2z = -10 \\ 3x - 2y - 2z = 7 \\ -2x + y - z = -10 \end{cases}$

Write each system as a matrix and solve it by Gauss–Jordan elimination. If a system has infinitely many solutions, show a general solution.

45. $\begin{cases} x - 2y = 7 \\ y = 3 \end{cases}$ **46.** $\begin{cases} x - 2y = 7 \\ y = 8 \end{cases}$

47. $\begin{cases} x + 2y - z = 3 \\ y + 3z = 1 \\ z = -2 \end{cases}$ **48.** $\begin{cases} x - 3y + 2z = -1 \\ y - 2z = 3 \\ z = 5 \end{cases}$

49. $\begin{cases} x - y = 7 \\ x + y = 13 \end{cases}$ **50.** $\begin{cases} x + 2y = 7 \\ 2x - y = -1 \end{cases}$

51. $\begin{cases} x - \dfrac{1}{2}y = 0 \\ x + 2y = 0 \end{cases}$ **52.** $\begin{cases} x - y = 5 \\ -x + \dfrac{1}{5}y = -9 \end{cases}$

53. $\begin{cases} x + y + 2z = 0 \\ x + y + z = 2 \\ x + z = 1 \end{cases}$ **54.** $\begin{cases} x + 2y = -3 \\ x + 4y = -2 \\ 2x + z = -8 \end{cases}$

55. $\begin{cases} 2x + y - 2z = 1 \\ -x + y - 3z = 0 \\ 4x + 3y = 4 \end{cases}$ **56.** $\begin{cases} 3x + y = 3 \\ 3x + y - z = 2 \\ 6x + z = 5 \end{cases}$

57. $\begin{cases} 2x - 2y + 3z + t = 2 \\ x + y + z + t = 5 \\ -x + 2y - 3z + 2t = 2 \\ x + y + 2z - t = 4 \end{cases}$ **58.** $\begin{cases} x + y + 2z + t = 1 \\ x + 2y + z + t = 2 \\ 2x + y + z + t = 4 \\ x + y + z + 2t = 3 \end{cases}$

59. $\begin{cases} x + y + t = 4 \\ x + z + t = 2 \\ 2x + 2y + z + 2t = 8 \\ x - y + z - t = -2 \end{cases}$ **60.** $\begin{cases} x - y + 2z + t = 3 \\ 3x - 2y - z - t = 4 \\ 2x + y + 2z - t = 10 \\ x + 2y + z - 3t = 8 \end{cases}$

61. $\begin{cases} \dfrac{1}{3}x + \dfrac{3}{4}y - \dfrac{2}{3}z = -2 \\ x + \dfrac{1}{2}y + \dfrac{1}{3}z = 1 \\ \dfrac{1}{6}x - \dfrac{1}{8}y - z = 0 \end{cases}$ **62.** $\begin{cases} \dfrac{1}{4}x + y + 3z = 1 \\ \dfrac{1}{2}x - 4y + 6z = -1 \\ \dfrac{1}{3}x - 2y - 2z = -1 \end{cases}$

63. $\begin{cases} \dfrac{1}{2}x + \dfrac{1}{4}y - z = 2 \\ \dfrac{2}{3}x + \dfrac{1}{4}y + \dfrac{1}{2}z = \dfrac{3}{2} \\ \dfrac{2}{3}x + z = -\dfrac{1}{3} \end{cases}$

64. $\begin{cases} \dfrac{5}{7}x - \dfrac{1}{3}y + z = 0 \\ \dfrac{2}{7}x + y + \dfrac{1}{8}z = 9 \\ 6x + 4y - \dfrac{27}{4}z = 20 \end{cases}$

65. $\begin{cases} 3x - 6y + 9z = 18 \\ 2x - 4y + 3z = 12 \\ x - 2y + 3z = 6 \end{cases}$

66. $\begin{cases} x + 2y - z = 7 \\ 2x - y + z = 2 \\ 3x - 4y + 3z = -3 \end{cases}$

Each system contains a different number of equations than variables. Solve each system using Gauss–Jordan elimination. If a system has infinitely many solutions, show a general solution.

67. $\begin{cases} x + y = -2 \\ 3x - y = 6 \\ 2x + 2y = -4 \\ x - y = 4 \end{cases}$

68. $\begin{cases} x - y = -3 \\ 2x + y = -3 \\ 3x - y = -7 \\ 4x + y = -7 \end{cases}$

69. $\begin{cases} x + 2y + z = 4 \\ 3x - y - z = 2 \end{cases}$

70. $\begin{cases} x + 2y - 3z = 5 \\ 5x + y - z = -11 \end{cases}$

71. $\begin{cases} w + x = 1 \\ w + y = 0 \\ x + z = 0 \end{cases}$

72. $\begin{cases} w + x - y + z = 2 \\ 2w - x - 2y + z = 0 \\ w - 2x - y + z = -1 \end{cases}$

73. $\begin{cases} x + y = 3 \\ 2x + y = 1 \\ 3x + 2y = 2 \end{cases}$

74. $\begin{cases} x + 2y + z = 4 \\ x - y + z = 1 \\ 2x + y + 2z = 2 \\ 3x + 3z = 6 \end{cases}$

Applications

Use matrix methods to solve each problem.

75. Flight range The speed of an airplane with a tailwind is 300 miles per hour and with a headwind is 220 miles per hour. On a day with no wind, how far could the plane travel on a 5-hour fuel supply?

76. Resource allocation 120,000 gallons of fuel are to be divided between two airlines. Triple A Airways requires twice as much as UnityAir. How much fuel should be allocated to Triple A?

77. Library shelving To use space effectively, librarians like to fill shelves completely. One 35-inch shelf can hold 3 dictionaries, 5 atlases, and 1 thesaurus; or 6 dictionaries and 2 thesauruses; or 2 dictionaries, 4 atlases, and 3 thesauruses. How wide is one copy of each book?

78. Copying machine productivity When both copying machines A and B are working, secretaries can make 100 copies in one minute. In one minute's time, copiers A and C together produce 140 copies, and all three working together produce 180 copies. How many copies per minute can each machine produce separately?

© Istockphoto.com/Doug Sims

79. Nutritional planning One ounce of each of three foods has the vitamin and mineral content shown in the table. How many ounces of each must be used to provide exactly 22 milligrams (mg) of niacin, 12 mg of zinc, and 20 mg of vitamin C?

Food	Niacin	Zinc	Vitamin C
A	1 mg	1 mg	2 mg
B	2 mg	1 mg	1 mg
C	2 mg	1 mg	2 mg

80. Chainsaw sculpting A wood sculptor carves three types of statues with a chainsaw. The number of hours required for carving, sanding, and painting a totem pole, a bear, and a deer are shown in the table. How many of each should be produced to use all available labor hours?

	Totem pole	Bear	Deer	Time available
Carving	2 hr	2 hr	1 hr	14 hr
Sanding	1 hr	2 hr	2 hr	15 hr
Painting	3 hr	2 hr	2 hr	21 hr

Discovery and Writing

81. Explain the difference between the row echelon form and the reduced row echelon form of a matrix.

82. If the upper-left corner entry of a matrix is zero, what row operation might you do first?

83. What characteristics of a row reduced matrix would let you conclude that the system is inconsistent?

84. Explain the differences between Gaussian elimination and Gauss−Jordan elimination.

Use matrix methods to solve each system.

85. $\begin{cases} x^2 + y^2 + z^2 = 14 \\ 2x^2 + 3y^2 - 2z^2 = -7 \\ x^2 - 5y^2 + z^2 = 8 \end{cases}$
(*Hint:* Solve first as a system in x^2, y^2, and z^2.)

86. $\begin{cases} 5\sqrt{x} + 2\sqrt{x} + \sqrt{z} = 22 \\ \sqrt{x} + \sqrt{y} - \sqrt{z} = 5 \\ 3\sqrt{x} - 2\sqrt{y} - 3\sqrt{z} = 10 \end{cases}$

Review

Fill in the blanks.

87. The slope-intercept form of an equation of a line is _____.

88. The point-slope form of an equation of a line is _____.

89. The slopes of parallel lines are _____.

90. The slopes of _____ lines are negative reciprocals.

Write the equation of a line with the given properties.

91. The line has a slope of 2 and a y-intercept of 7.

92. The line has a slope of -3 and passes through the point $(2, -3)$.

93. The line is vertical and passes through $(2, -3)$.

94. The line is horizontal and passes through $(2, -3)$.

6.3 Matrix Algebra

In this section, we will learn to

1. Add and subtract matrices.
2. Multiply a matrix by a constant.
3. Multiply matrices.
4. Solve applications using matrices.
5. Recognize the identity matrix.

With certain restrictions, we can add, subtract, and multiply matrices. In fact, many problems can be solved using the arithmetic of matrices.

To illustrate the addition of matrices, suppose there are 108 police officers employed at two different locations:

Downtown Station	Male	Female
Day Shift	21	18
Night Shift	12	6

Suburban Station	Male	Female
Day Shift	14	12
Night Shift	15	10

The employment information about the police officers is contained in two matrices.

$$D = \begin{bmatrix} 21 & 18 \\ 12 & 6 \end{bmatrix} \quad \text{and} \quad S = \begin{bmatrix} 14 & 12 \\ 15 & 10 \end{bmatrix}$$

The entry 21 in matrix D indicates that 21 male officers work the day shift at the downtown station. The entry 10 in matrix S indicates that 10 female officers work the night shift at the suburban station.

To find the city-wide totals, we can add the corresponding entries of matrices D and S:

$$D + S = \begin{bmatrix} 21 & 18 \\ 12 & 6 \end{bmatrix} + \begin{bmatrix} 14 & 12 \\ 15 & 10 \end{bmatrix} = \begin{bmatrix} 35 & 30 \\ 27 & 16 \end{bmatrix}$$

We interpret the total to mean:

$$\begin{array}{c} \text{Male} \quad \text{Female} \\ \begin{array}{l} \text{Day Shift} \\ \text{Night Shift} \end{array} \begin{bmatrix} 35 & 30 \\ 27 & 16 \end{bmatrix} \end{array}$$

To illustrate how to multiply a matrix by a number, suppose that one-third of the officers at the downtown station retire. The downtown staff would then consist of $\frac{2}{3}D$ officers. We can compute $\frac{2}{3}D$ by multiplying each entry of matrix D by $\frac{2}{3}$.

$$\frac{2}{3}D = \frac{2}{3}\begin{bmatrix} 21 & 18 \\ 12 & 6 \end{bmatrix} = \begin{bmatrix} 14 & 12 \\ 8 & 4 \end{bmatrix}$$

After retirements, the downtown staff will be

$$\begin{array}{c} \text{Male} \quad \text{Female} \\ \begin{array}{l} \text{Day Shift} \\ \text{Night Shift} \end{array} \begin{bmatrix} 14 & 12 \\ 8 & 4 \end{bmatrix} \end{array}$$

These examples illustrate two calculations used in the algebra of matrices, which is the topic of this section. We begin by giving a formal definition of a matrix and defining when two matrices are equal.

Matrices An $m \times n$ **matrix** is a rectangular array of mn numbers arranged in m rows and n columns. We say that the matrix is of **size** (or **order**) $m \times n$.

Matrices are often denoted by letters such as A, B, and C. To denote the entries in an $m \times n$ matrix A, we use double-subscript notation: The entry in the first row, third column is a_{13}, and the entry in the ith row, jth column is a_{ij}. We can use any of the following notations to denote the $m \times n$ matrix A:

$$A, [a_{ij}], \underbrace{\begin{bmatrix} a_{11} & a_{12} & a_{13} & \cdots & a_{1n} \\ a_{21} & a_{22} & a_{23} & \cdots & a_{2n} \\ \vdots & \vdots & \vdots & \ddots & \vdots \\ a_{m1} & a_{m2} & a_{m3} & \cdots & a_{mn} \end{bmatrix}}_{n \text{ columns}} \left. \vphantom{\begin{bmatrix} a_{11} \\ a_{21} \\ \vdots \\ a_{m1} \end{bmatrix}} \right\} m \text{ rows}$$

Two matrices are equal if they are the same size, with the same entries in corresponding positions.

Equality of Matrices If $A = [a_{ij}]$ and $B = [b_{ij}]$ are both $m \times n$ matrices, then

$$A = B$$

provided that each entry a_{ij} in matrix A is equal to the corresponding entry b_{ij} in matrix B.

The following matrices are equal, because they are the same size and corresponding entries are equal.

$$\begin{bmatrix} \sqrt{9} & 0.5 \\ 1 & 4 \end{bmatrix} = \begin{bmatrix} 3 & \frac{1}{2} \\ 1 & 2^2 \end{bmatrix}$$

The following matrices are not equal, because they are not the same size.

$$\begin{bmatrix} 1 & 2 & 3 \\ 1 & 2 & 3 \end{bmatrix} \neq \begin{bmatrix} 1 & 2 & 3 \\ 1 & 2 & 3 \\ 1 & 2 & 3 \end{bmatrix}$$ The first matrix is 2×3, and the second is 3×3.

1. Add and Subtract Matrices

We can add matrices of the same size by adding the entries in corresponding positions.

Sum of Two Matrices   Let A and B be two $m \times n$ matrices. The **sum**, $A + B$, is the $m \times n$ matrix C found by adding the corresponding entries of matrices A and B:

$$A + B = C$$

where each entry c_{ij} in C is equal to the sum of a_{ij} in A and b_{ij} in B.

EXAMPLE 1   **Adding Matrices**

Add: $\begin{bmatrix} 2 & 1 & 3 \\ 1 & -1 & 0 \end{bmatrix} + \begin{bmatrix} 1 & -1 & 2 \\ -1 & 1 & 5 \end{bmatrix}$.

SOLUTION   Since each matrix is 2×3, we can find their sum by adding their corresponding entries.

$$\begin{bmatrix} 2 & 1 & 3 \\ 1 & -1 & 0 \end{bmatrix} + \begin{bmatrix} 1 & -1 & 2 \\ -1 & 1 & 5 \end{bmatrix} = \begin{bmatrix} 2+1 & 1-1 & 3+2 \\ 1-1 & -1+1 & 0+5 \end{bmatrix}$$

$$= \begin{bmatrix} 3 & 0 & 5 \\ 0 & 0 & 5 \end{bmatrix}$$

Self Check 1   Add: $\begin{bmatrix} 3 & -5 \\ 2 & 0 \\ -6 & 5 \end{bmatrix} + \begin{bmatrix} -3 & 4 \\ -1 & -3 \\ 7 & 0 \end{bmatrix}$.

Now Try Exercise 13.

Caution

Matrices that are not the same size cannot be added.

In arithmetic, 0 is the **additive identity,** because $a + 0 = 0 + a = a$ for any real number a. In matrix algebra, the matrix $\mathbf{0} = \begin{bmatrix} 0 & 0 \\ 0 & 0 \end{bmatrix}$ is called the **additive identity** for 2×2 matrices, because $A + \mathbf{0} = \mathbf{0} + A$. For example,

$$\begin{bmatrix} 1 & 2 \\ 3 & 4 \end{bmatrix} + \begin{bmatrix} 0 & 0 \\ 0 & 0 \end{bmatrix} = \begin{bmatrix} 0 & 0 \\ 0 & 0 \end{bmatrix} + \begin{bmatrix} 1 & 2 \\ 3 & 4 \end{bmatrix} = \begin{bmatrix} 1 & 2 \\ 3 & 4 \end{bmatrix}$$

The Additive Identity Matrix   Let A be any $m \times n$ matrix. There is an $m \times n$ matrix $\mathbf{0}$, called the **zero matrix** or the **additive identity matrix,** for which

$$A + \mathbf{0} = \mathbf{0} + A = A$$

The matrix $\mathbf{0}$ consists of m rows and n columns of 0's.

Every matrix also has an additive inverse.

The Additive Inverse of a Matrix

Any $m \times n$ matrix A has an **additive inverse,** an $m \times n$ matrix $-A$, with the property that the sum of A and $-A$ is the zero matrix:

$$A + (-A) = (-A) + A = \mathbf{0}$$

The entries of $-A$ are the negatives of the corresponding entries of A.

The additive inverse of $A = \begin{bmatrix} 1 & -3 & 2 \\ 0 & 1 & -5 \end{bmatrix}$ is the matrix

$$-A = \begin{bmatrix} -1 & 3 & -2 \\ 0 & -1 & 5 \end{bmatrix} \qquad \text{Each entry of } -A \text{ is the negative of the corresponding entry of } A.$$

because their sum is the zero matrix:

$$A + (-A) = \begin{bmatrix} 1 & -3 & 2 \\ 0 & 1 & -5 \end{bmatrix} + \begin{bmatrix} -1 & 3 & -2 \\ 0 & -1 & 5 \end{bmatrix}$$

$$= \begin{bmatrix} 1-1 & -3+3 & 2-2 \\ 0+0 & 1-1 & -5+5 \end{bmatrix}$$

$$= \begin{bmatrix} 0 & 0 & 0 \\ 0 & 0 & 0 \end{bmatrix}$$

Subtraction of matrices is similar to the subtraction of real numbers.

Difference of Two Matrices

If A and B are $m \times n$ matrices, their **difference** $A - B$ is the sum of A and the additive inverse of B:

$$A - B = A + (-B)$$

For example,

$$\begin{bmatrix} 3 & 7 \\ -4 & 0 \end{bmatrix} - \begin{bmatrix} -1 & 4 \\ -5 & 1 \end{bmatrix} = \begin{bmatrix} 3 & 7 \\ -4 & 0 \end{bmatrix} + \begin{bmatrix} 1 & -4 \\ 5 & -1 \end{bmatrix} = \begin{bmatrix} 4 & 3 \\ 1 & -1 \end{bmatrix}$$

2. Multiply a Matrix by a Constant

As we have seen in the police officers example at the beginning of the section, we can multiply a matrix by a constant by multiplying each of its entries by that constant. For example, if $A = \begin{bmatrix} 1 & -2 \\ 3 & 4 \end{bmatrix}$, then

$$5A = 5\begin{bmatrix} 1 & -2 \\ 3 & 4 \end{bmatrix} = \begin{bmatrix} 5 \cdot 1 & 5(-2) \\ 5 \cdot 3 & 5 \cdot 4 \end{bmatrix} = \begin{bmatrix} 5 & -10 \\ 15 & 20 \end{bmatrix}$$

$$-A = -1A = -1\begin{bmatrix} 1 & -2 \\ 3 & 4 \end{bmatrix} = \begin{bmatrix} -1 \cdot 1 & -1(-2) \\ -1 \cdot 3 & -1 \cdot 4 \end{bmatrix} = \begin{bmatrix} -1 & 2 \\ -3 & -4 \end{bmatrix}$$

The second example above illustrates that we can find the additive inverse of a matrix by multiplying the matrix by -1.

If A is a matrix, the real number k in the product kA is called a **scalar.**

Multiplying a Matrix by a Scalar If A and B are two $m \times n$ matrices and k is a scalar, then kA, the **scalar multiple of k times A,** is B where each entry b_{ij} in B is equal to k times the corresponding entry a_{ij} in A.

EXAMPLE 2 **Solving a Matrix Equation**

Let $\begin{bmatrix} 5 & y \\ 15 & z \end{bmatrix} = 5 \begin{bmatrix} x & 3 \\ 3 & y \end{bmatrix}$. Find y and z.

SOLUTION We simplify the right side of the expression by multiplying each entry of the matrix by 5.

$$\begin{bmatrix} 5 & y \\ 15 & z \end{bmatrix} = \begin{bmatrix} 5x & 15 \\ 15 & 5y \end{bmatrix}$$

Because the matrices are equal, their corresponding entries are equal. So $y = 15$, and $z = 5y$. We conclude that $y = 15$ and $z = 5 \cdot 15 = 75$. ∎

Self Check 2 Find x.

Now Try Exercise 11.

3. Multiply Matrices

To introduce multiplication of matrices, we consider the grading policy at a school where a student's final grade is based on a test score average and a homework average.

Shutterstock.com/Lisa F. Young

The grades for three students are shown below, along with how the test scores and the homework scores are weighted.

	Test score average	Homework average
Ann	83	95
Tonya	72	80
Carlos	85	92

	Weighting	
	System 1	System 2
Test average	0.5	0.3
Homework average	0.5	0.7

To calculate the students' final grades, we must use information from both tables. For example, if their teacher used weighting system 1, their final grades would be

- Ann's grade $= 83(0.5) + 95(0.5) = 41.5 + 47.5 = 89$
- Tonya's grade $= 72(0.5) + 80(0.5) = 36 + 40 = 76$
- Carlos' grade $= 85(0.5) + 92(0.5) = 42.5 + 46 = 88.5$

If we calculate their final grades using weighting system 2, we get

- Ann's grade $= 83(0.3) + 95(0.7) = 24.9 + 66.5 = 91.4$
- Tonya's grade $= 72(0.3) + 80(0.7) = 21.6 + 56 = 77.6$
- Carlos' grade $= 85(0.3) + 92(0.7) = 25.5 + 64.4 = 89.9$

The result of each grade calculation is the sum of the products of the elements in one row of the first matrix and one column of the second matrix. Each calculation is a part of the product of the matrices

$$A = \begin{bmatrix} 83 & 95 \\ 72 & 80 \\ 85 & 92 \end{bmatrix} \quad \text{and} \quad B = \begin{bmatrix} 0.5 & 0.3 \\ 0.5 & 0.7 \end{bmatrix}$$

To further illustrate how to find the product of two matrices, we will find the product of the 3×2 matrix A and the 2×2 matrix B. This product will exist because the number of columns in A is equal to the number of rows in B. The result will be a 3×2 matrix C.

$$AB = \begin{bmatrix} 83 & 95 \\ 72 & 80 \\ 85 & 92 \end{bmatrix} \begin{bmatrix} 0.5 & 0.3 \\ 0.5 & 0.7 \end{bmatrix} = \begin{bmatrix} ? & ? & ? \\ ? & ? & ? \\ ? & ? & ? \end{bmatrix} = C$$

Each entry of matrix C will be the result of multiplying the entries in one row of A and the entries in one column of B and adding the results. As shown below, the first-row, first-column entry of matrix C is the sum of the products of entries of the first row of A and the first column of B. The second-row, second-column entry of matrix C is the sum of the products of entries of the second row of A and the second column of B.

$$AB = \begin{bmatrix} 83 & 95 \\ 72 & 80 \\ 85 & 92 \end{bmatrix} \begin{bmatrix} 0.5 & 0.3 \\ 0.5 & 0.7 \end{bmatrix} = \begin{bmatrix} 83(0.5) + 95(0.5) & ? \\ ? & 72(0.3) + 80(0.7) \\ ? & ? \end{bmatrix} = \begin{bmatrix} 89 & ? \\ ? & 77.6 \\ ? & ? \end{bmatrix} = C$$

As shown below, the first-row, second-column entry of matrix C is the sum of the products of entries of the first row of A and the second column of B. The second-row, first-column entry of matrix C is the sum of the products of entries of the second row of A and the first column of B.

$$AB = \begin{bmatrix} 83 & 95 \\ 72 & 80 \\ 85 & 92 \end{bmatrix} \begin{bmatrix} 0.5 & 0.3 \\ 0.5 & 0.7 \end{bmatrix} = \begin{bmatrix} 83(0.5) + 95(0.5) & 83(0.3) + 95(0.7) \\ 72(0.5) + 80(0.5) & 72(0.3) + 80(0.7) \\ ? & ? \end{bmatrix} = \begin{bmatrix} 89 & 91.4 \\ 76 & 77.6 \\ ? & ? \end{bmatrix} = C$$

As shown below, the third-row, first-column entry of matrix C is the sum of the products of entries of the third row of A and the first column of B. The third-row, second-column entry of matrix C is the sum of the products of entries of the third row of A and the second column of B.

$$AB = \begin{bmatrix} 83 & 95 \\ 72 & 80 \\ 85 & 92 \end{bmatrix} \begin{bmatrix} 0.5 & 0.3 \\ 0.5 & 0.7 \end{bmatrix} = \begin{bmatrix} 83(0.5) + 95(0.5) & 83(0.3) + 95(0.7) \\ 72(0.5) + 80(0.5) & 72(0.3) + 80(0.7) \\ 85(0.5) + 92(0.5) & 85(0.3) + 92(0.7) \end{bmatrix} = \begin{bmatrix} 89 & 91.4 \\ 76 & 77.6 \\ 88.5 & 89.9 \end{bmatrix} = C$$

The resulting 3×2 matrix C is the product of matrix A and B, and gives the final grades of each student with respect to each weighting system.

	Weighting	
	System 1	System 2
Ann	89	91.4
Tonya	76	77.6
Carlos	88.5	89.9

For the product AB of two matrices to exist, the number of columns of A must equal the number of rows of B. If the product exists, it will have as many rows as A and as many columns as B:

$$
\begin{array}{ccccc}
A & \cdot & B & = & C \\
m \times n & & n \times p & & m \times p
\end{array}
$$

These must agree.

The product is of size $m \times p$.

We now formally define the product of two matrices.

Product of Two Matrices   Let A be an $m \times n$ matrix and B be an $n \times p$ matrix. The **product**, AB, is the $m \times p$ matrix C

$$AB = C$$

where each entry c_{ij} in C is the sum of the products of the corresponding entries in the ith row of A and the jth column of B, where $i = 1, 2, 3, \ldots, m$ and $j = 1, 2, 3, \ldots, p$.

EXAMPLE 3   **Multiplying Matrices**

Find $C = AB$ if $A = \begin{bmatrix} 1 & 2 & 4 \\ -2 & 1 & -1 \end{bmatrix}$ and $B = \begin{bmatrix} 1 & 5 \\ -2 & 4 \\ 1 & -3 \end{bmatrix}$.

SOLUTION   Because matrix A is 2×3 and B is 3×2, the number of columns of A is the same as the number of rows of B. Therefore, the product C exists and it will be a 2×2 matrix. To find entry c_{11} of C, we find the sum of the products of the entries in the first row of A and the first column of B:

$$c_{11} = 1 \cdot 1 + 2 \cdot (-2) + 4 \cdot (1) = 1$$

$$\begin{bmatrix} 1 & 2 & 4 \\ -2 & 1 & -1 \end{bmatrix} \begin{bmatrix} 1 & 5 \\ -2 & 4 \\ 1 & -3 \end{bmatrix} = \begin{bmatrix} 1 & ? \\ ? & ? \end{bmatrix}$$

To find entry c_{12}, we move across the first row of A and down the second column of B:

$$c_{12} = 1 \cdot 5 + 2 \cdot 4 + 4 \cdot (-3) = 1$$

$$\begin{bmatrix} 1 & 2 & 4 \\ -2 & 1 & -1 \end{bmatrix} \begin{bmatrix} 1 & 5 \\ -2 & 4 \\ 1 & -3 \end{bmatrix} = \begin{bmatrix} 1 & 1 \\ ? & ? \end{bmatrix}$$

To find entry c_{21}, we move across the second row of A and down the first column of B:

$$c_{21} = (-2) \cdot 1 + 1 \cdot (-2) + (-1) \cdot 1 = -5$$

$$\begin{bmatrix} 1 & 2 & 4 \\ -2 & 1 & -1 \end{bmatrix} \begin{bmatrix} 1 & 5 \\ -2 & 4 \\ 1 & -3 \end{bmatrix} = \begin{bmatrix} 1 & 1 \\ -5 & ? \end{bmatrix}$$

To find entry c_{22}, we move across the second row of A and down the second column of B:

$$c_{22} = (-2) \cdot 5 + 1 \cdot 4 + (-1) \cdot (-3) = -3$$

Caution

When we multiply matrices of the same size, keep in mind that we do not multiply corresponding entries.

$$\begin{bmatrix} 1 & 2 & 4 \\ -2 & 1 & -1 \end{bmatrix} \begin{bmatrix} 1 & 5 \\ -2 & 4 \\ 1 & -3 \end{bmatrix} = \begin{bmatrix} 1 & 1 \\ -5 & -3 \end{bmatrix}$$

Self Check 3   Find $D = EF$ if $E = \begin{bmatrix} 1 & -2 \\ 2 & 0 \end{bmatrix}$ and $F = \begin{bmatrix} 2 & 1 \\ 3 & 5 \end{bmatrix}$.

Now Try Exercise 27.

EXAMPLE 4   **Multiplying Matrices**

Find the product: $\begin{bmatrix} 1 & -1 & 2 \\ 1 & 3 & 0 \\ 0 & 1 & 1 \end{bmatrix} \begin{bmatrix} 2 & 1 \\ 1 & 3 \\ 0 & 1 \end{bmatrix}$.

SOLUTION   Because the matrices are 3×3 and 3×2, the number of columns of the first matrix is the same as the number of rows of the second matrix. The product will be a 3×2 matrix.

$$\begin{bmatrix} 1 & -1 & 2 \\ 1 & 3 & 0 \\ 0 & 1 & 1 \end{bmatrix} \begin{bmatrix} 2 & 1 \\ 1 & 3 \\ 0 & 1 \end{bmatrix} = \begin{bmatrix} 1 \cdot 2 + (-1) \cdot 1 + 2 \cdot 0 & 1 \cdot 1 + (-1) \cdot 3 + 2 \cdot 1 \\ 1 \cdot 2 + 3 \cdot 1 + 0 \cdot 0 & 1 \cdot 1 + 3 \cdot 3 + 0 \cdot 1 \\ 0 \cdot 2 + 1 \cdot 1 + 1 \cdot 0 & 0 \cdot 1 + 1 \cdot 3 + 1 \cdot 1 \end{bmatrix}$$

$$= \begin{bmatrix} 1 & 0 \\ 5 & 10 \\ 1 & 4 \end{bmatrix}$$

Self Check 4   Find the product: $\begin{bmatrix} 1 & -2 \\ 3 & 1 \\ -4 & 0 \end{bmatrix} \begin{bmatrix} 4 & -3 \\ 1 & -1 \end{bmatrix}$.

Now Try Exercise 29.

EXAMPLE 5   **Multiplying Matrices**

Find each product: **a.** $\begin{bmatrix} 1 & 2 & 3 \end{bmatrix} \begin{bmatrix} 4 \\ 5 \\ 6 \end{bmatrix}$ **b.** $\begin{bmatrix} 1 \\ 2 \\ 3 \end{bmatrix} \begin{bmatrix} 4 & 5 & 6 \end{bmatrix}$

SOLUTION   **a.** Since the first matrix is 1×3 and the second matrix is 3×1 the product is a 1×1 matrix:

$$\begin{bmatrix} 1 & 2 & 3 \end{bmatrix} \begin{bmatrix} 4 \\ 5 \\ 6 \end{bmatrix} = \begin{bmatrix} 1 \cdot 4 + 2 \cdot 5 + 3 \cdot 6 \end{bmatrix} = \begin{bmatrix} 32 \end{bmatrix}$$

b. Since the first matrix is 3×1 and the second matrix is 1×3 the product is a 3×3 matrix:

$$\begin{bmatrix} 1 \\ 2 \\ 3 \end{bmatrix} \begin{bmatrix} 4 & 5 & 6 \end{bmatrix} = \begin{bmatrix} 1 \cdot 4 & 1 \cdot 5 & 1 \cdot 6 \\ 2 \cdot 4 & 2 \cdot 5 & 2 \cdot 6 \\ 3 \cdot 4 & 3 \cdot 5 & 3 \cdot 6 \end{bmatrix} = \begin{bmatrix} 4 & 5 & 6 \\ 8 & 10 & 12 \\ 12 & 15 & 18 \end{bmatrix}$$

Self Check 5 Find each product:

a. $\begin{bmatrix} 1 & 3 & 5 \end{bmatrix} \begin{bmatrix} 1 \\ 0 \\ 1 \end{bmatrix}$ **b.** $\begin{bmatrix} 1 \\ 2 \end{bmatrix} \begin{bmatrix} 3 & 4 \end{bmatrix}$

Now Try Exercise 31.

Comment

There are cases where the product of two matrices is commutative, $AB = BA$, but, in general, the multiplication of matrices is not commutative.

The multiplication of matrices is not commutative. To show this, we compute AB and BA, where $A = \begin{bmatrix} 1 & 1 \\ 0 & 0 \end{bmatrix}$ and $B = \begin{bmatrix} 0 & 1 \\ 0 & 1 \end{bmatrix}$.

$$AB = \begin{bmatrix} 1 & 1 \\ 0 & 0 \end{bmatrix} \begin{bmatrix} 0 & 1 \\ 0 & 1 \end{bmatrix} = \begin{bmatrix} 0 & 2 \\ 0 & 0 \end{bmatrix}$$

$$BA = \begin{bmatrix} 0 & 1 \\ 0 & 1 \end{bmatrix} \begin{bmatrix} 1 & 1 \\ 0 & 0 \end{bmatrix} = \begin{bmatrix} 0 & 0 \\ 0 & 0 \end{bmatrix}$$

Since the products are not equal, matrix multiplication is not commutative.

ACCENT ON TECHNOLOGY

Add and Multiply Matrices

Most graphing calculators can perform numerous operations on matrices. We must always be mindful that the sizes of the matrices allow these operations. This example will demonstrate the operations of addition and multiplication.

Given the two matrices, $A = \begin{bmatrix} 2 & 3.7 \\ -2.1 & 3 \end{bmatrix}$ and $B = \begin{bmatrix} 2 & -1 \\ 0 & 0.3 \end{bmatrix}$, add and multiply the matrices using a graphing calculator.

Enter the values for the matrix by pressing [2nd] [x⁻¹] **and using the MATRIX menu. Then select EDIT. We can enter the values from this menu.**

```
MATRIX[A] 2 ×2          MATRIX[B] 2 ×2
[ 2      3.7    ]        [ 2      -1     ]
[ -2.1   3      ]        [ 0      .3     ]




2,2=3                    2,2=.3
```

On the home screen, enter the names of the matrices by using the MATRIX menu. Use the operations of addition and multiplication on the home screen.

```
[A]+[B]                  [A]*[B]
    [[4      2.7]            [[4      -.89]
     [-2.1   3.3]]            [-4.2   3   ]]
[A]+[B]▶Frac            ■
[[4       27/10]
 [-21/10  33/10]]
```

FIGURE 6-7

4. Solve Applications Using Matrices

EXAMPLE 6   **Solving an Application Problem**

Suppose that supplies must be purchased for the police officers discussed at the beginning of the section. The quantities and prices of each item required for each shift are as follows:

	Quantities				Unit Prices (in $)
	Uniforms	Badges	Whistles	Uniforms	47
Day Shift	17	13	19	Badges	7
Night Shift	14	24	27	Whistles	5

Find the cost of supplies of each shift.

SOLUTION   We can write the quantities Q and prices P in matrix form and multiply them to get a cost matrix.

$$C = QP$$

$$= \begin{bmatrix} 17 & 13 & 19 \\ 14 & 24 & 27 \end{bmatrix} \begin{bmatrix} 47 \\ 7 \\ 5 \end{bmatrix}$$

$$= \begin{bmatrix} 17 \cdot 47 & 13 \cdot 7 & 19 \cdot 5 \\ 14 \cdot 47 & 24 \cdot 7 & 27 \cdot 5 \end{bmatrix}$$

     (17 uniforms)($47) + (13 badges)($7) + (19 whistles)($5)
     (14 uniforms)($47) + (24 badges)($7) + (27 whistles)($5)

$$= \begin{bmatrix} 985 \\ 961 \end{bmatrix}$$

It will cost \$985 to buy supplies for the day shift and \$961 to buy supplies for the night shift. ∎

Self Check 6   If the unit prices (in $) in Example 6 increase and are \$50 for uniforms, \$10 for badges, and \$6 for whistles, how much will it cost to buy supplies for the day shift and the night shift?

Now Try Exercise 55.

5. Recognize the Identity Matrix

The number 1 is called the *identity for multiplication* because multiplying a number by 1 does not change the number: $a \cdot 1 = 1 \cdot a = a$. There is a **multiplicative identity matrix** with a similar property.

The Identity Matrix   Let A be an $n \times n$ matrix. There is an $n \times n$ **identity matrix I** for which

$$AI = IA = A$$

It is the matrix I consisting of 1's on its diagonal and 0's elsewhere.

Comment

An identity matrix is always a square matrix—a matrix that has the same number of rows and columns.

$$I = \begin{bmatrix} 1 & 0 & 0 & \cdots & 0 \\ 0 & 1 & 0 & \cdots & 0 \\ 0 & 0 & 1 & \cdots & 0 \\ \vdots & \vdots & \vdots & \ddots & \vdots \\ 0 & 0 & 0 & \cdots & 1 \end{bmatrix}$$

We illustrate the previous definition for the 3×3 identity matrix.

$$\begin{bmatrix} 1 & 0 & 0 \\ 0 & 1 & 0 \\ 0 & 0 & 1 \end{bmatrix} \begin{bmatrix} 1 & 2 & 3 \\ 4 & 5 & 6 \\ 7 & 8 & 9 \end{bmatrix} = \begin{bmatrix} 1 \cdot 1 + 0 \cdot 4 + 0 \cdot 7 & 1 \cdot 2 + 0 \cdot 5 + 0 \cdot 8 & 1 \cdot 3 + 0 \cdot 6 + 0 \cdot 9 \\ 0 \cdot 1 + 1 \cdot 4 + 0 \cdot 7 & 0 \cdot 2 + 1 \cdot 5 + 0 \cdot 8 & 0 \cdot 3 + 1 \cdot 6 + 0 \cdot 9 \\ 0 \cdot 1 + 0 \cdot 4 + 1 \cdot 7 & 0 \cdot 2 + 0 \cdot 5 + 1 \cdot 8 & 0 \cdot 3 + 0 \cdot 6 + 1 \cdot 9 \end{bmatrix}$$

$$= \begin{bmatrix} 1 & 2 & 3 \\ 4 & 5 & 6 \\ 7 & 8 & 9 \end{bmatrix}$$

$$\begin{bmatrix} 1 & 2 & 3 \\ 4 & 5 & 6 \\ 7 & 8 & 9 \end{bmatrix} \begin{bmatrix} 1 & 0 & 0 \\ 0 & 1 & 0 \\ 0 & 0 & 1 \end{bmatrix} = \begin{bmatrix} 1 & 2 & 3 \\ 4 & 5 & 6 \\ 7 & 8 & 9 \end{bmatrix}$$

The following properties of real numbers carry over to matrices. In the exercises, you will be asked to illustrate many of these properties.

Properties of Matrices

Let A, B, and C be matrices and a and b be scalars.

Commutative Property of Addition: $A + B = B + A$

Associative Property of Addition: $A + (B + C) = (A + B) + C$

Associative Properties of Scalar Multiplication: $\begin{cases} a(bA) = (ab)A \\ a(AB) = (aA)B \end{cases}$

Distributive Properties of Scalar Multiplication: $\begin{cases} (a + b)A = aA + bA \\ a(A + b) = aA + aB \end{cases}$

Associative Property of Multiplication: $A(BC) = (AB)C$

Distributive Properties of Matrix Multiplication: $\begin{cases} A(B + C) = AB + AC \\ (A + B)C = AC + BC \end{cases}$

EXAMPLE 7   **Verifying the Distributive Property of Matrix Multiplication**

Verify the Distributive Property $A(B + C) = AB + AC$ using the matrices

$$A = \begin{bmatrix} 2 & 1 \\ 3 & 1 \end{bmatrix}, \quad B = \begin{bmatrix} 3 & -4 \\ 1 & -1 \end{bmatrix}, \quad \text{and} \quad C = \begin{bmatrix} -1 & 3 \\ 0 & 1 \end{bmatrix}$$

SOLUTION   We do the operations on the left side and the right side separately and compare the results.

$$\begin{bmatrix} 2 & 1 \\ 3 & 1 \end{bmatrix} \left(\begin{bmatrix} 3 & -4 \\ 1 & -1 \end{bmatrix} + \begin{bmatrix} -1 & 3 \\ 0 & 1 \end{bmatrix} \right) = \begin{bmatrix} 2 & 1 \\ 3 & 1 \end{bmatrix} \left(\begin{bmatrix} 2 & -1 \\ 1 & 0 \end{bmatrix} \right)$$ Do the addition within the parentheses.

$$= \begin{bmatrix} 5 & -2 \\ 7 & -3 \end{bmatrix}$$ Multiply.

$$\begin{bmatrix} 2 & 1 \\ 3 & 1 \end{bmatrix} \begin{bmatrix} 3 & -4 \\ 1 & -1 \end{bmatrix} + \begin{bmatrix} 2 & 1 \\ 3 & 1 \end{bmatrix} \begin{bmatrix} -1 & 3 \\ 0 & 1 \end{bmatrix} = \begin{bmatrix} 7 & -9 \\ 10 & -13 \end{bmatrix} + \begin{bmatrix} -2 & 7 \\ -3 & 10 \end{bmatrix}$$ Do the multiplications.

$$= \begin{bmatrix} 5 & -2 \\ 7 & -3 \end{bmatrix}$$ Add.

Because the left and right sides agree, this example illustrates the Distributive Property.

Self Check 7   Verify the Distributive Property for Multiplication

$$(A + B)C = AC + BC$$

for the matrices given in Example 7.

Now Try Exercise 43.

Self Check Answers   **1.** $\begin{bmatrix} 0 & -1 \\ 1 & -3 \\ 1 & 5 \end{bmatrix}$ **2.** 1   **3.** $\begin{bmatrix} -4 & -9 \\ 4 & 2 \end{bmatrix}$ **4.** $\begin{bmatrix} 2 & -1 \\ 13 & -10 \\ -16 & 12 \end{bmatrix}$

5. a. $\begin{bmatrix} 6 \end{bmatrix}$ **b.** $\begin{bmatrix} 3 & 4 \\ 6 & 8 \end{bmatrix}$ **6.** day shift \$1,094 and night shift \$1,102

Exercises **6.3**

Getting Ready
You should be able to complete these vocabulary and concept statements before you proceed to the practice exercises.

Fill in the blanks.

1. In a matrix A, the symbol a_{ij} is the entry in row ___ and column ___.

2. For matrices A and B to be equal, they must be the same ____, and corresponding entries must be _____.

3. To find the sum of matrices A and B, we add the _____ entries.

4. To multiply a matrix by a scalar, we multiply _____ by that scalar.

5. The product of a 3×2 matrix A and a 2×4 matrix B will exist because the number of _____ of A is equal to the number of _____ of B.

6. The product of the matrices A and B in Exercise 5 will be a _____ matrix.

7. Among 2×2 matrices, $\begin{bmatrix} 0 & 0 \\ 0 & 0 \end{bmatrix}$ is the _____ or zero matrix.

8. Among 2×2 matrices, $\begin{bmatrix} 1 & 0 \\ 0 & 1 \end{bmatrix}$ is the _____ matrix.

Practice
Find values of x and y, if any, that will make the matrices equal.

9. $\begin{bmatrix} x & y \\ 1 & 3 \end{bmatrix} = \begin{bmatrix} 2 & 5 \\ 1 & 3 \end{bmatrix}$

10. $\begin{bmatrix} x & 5 \\ 3 & y \end{bmatrix} = \begin{bmatrix} 0 & 5 \\ 3 & 2 \end{bmatrix}$

11. $\begin{bmatrix} x + y & 3 + x \\ -2 & 5y \end{bmatrix} = \begin{bmatrix} 3 & 4 \\ -2 & 10 \end{bmatrix}$

12. $\begin{bmatrix} x + y & x - y \\ 2x & 3y \end{bmatrix} = \begin{bmatrix} -x & x - 2 \\ -y & 8 - y \end{bmatrix}$

Find A + B.

13. $A = \begin{bmatrix} 2 & 1 & -1 \\ -3 & 2 & 5 \end{bmatrix}$, $B = \begin{bmatrix} -3 & 1 & 2 \\ -3 & -2 & -5 \end{bmatrix}$

14. $A = \begin{bmatrix} 3 & 2 & 1 \\ -2 & 3 & -3 \\ -4 & -2 & -1 \end{bmatrix}$, $B = \begin{bmatrix} -2 & 6 & -2 \\ 5 & 7 & -1 \\ -4 & -6 & 7 \end{bmatrix}$

Find the additive inverse of each matrix.

15. $A = \begin{bmatrix} 5 & -2 & 7 \\ -5 & 0 & 3 \\ -2 & 3 & -5 \end{bmatrix}$

16. $A = \begin{bmatrix} 3 & -\dfrac{2}{3} & -5 & \dfrac{1}{2} \end{bmatrix}$

Find A − B.

17. $A = \begin{bmatrix} -3 & 2 & -2 \\ -1 & 4 & -5 \end{bmatrix}$, $B = \begin{bmatrix} 3 & -3 & -2 \\ -2 & 5 & -5 \end{bmatrix}$

18. $A = \begin{bmatrix} 2 & 2 & 0 \\ -2 & 8 & 1 \\ 3 & -3 & -8 \end{bmatrix}$, $B = \begin{bmatrix} -4 & 3 & 7 \\ -1 & 2 & 0 \\ 1 & 4 & -1 \end{bmatrix}$

Find 5A.

19. $A = \begin{bmatrix} 3 & -3 \\ 0 & -2 \end{bmatrix}$ **20.** $A = \begin{bmatrix} 3 & \frac{3}{5} \\ 0 & -1 \end{bmatrix}$

21. $A = \begin{bmatrix} 5 & 15 & -2 \\ -2 & -5 & 1 \end{bmatrix}$

22. $A = \begin{bmatrix} -3 & 1 & 2 \\ -8 & -2 & -5 \end{bmatrix}$

Find 5A + 3B.

23. $A = \begin{bmatrix} 3 & 1 & -2 \\ -4 & 3 & -2 \end{bmatrix}, B = \begin{bmatrix} 1 & -2 & 2 \\ -5 & -5 & 3 \end{bmatrix}$

24. $A = \begin{bmatrix} 2 & -5 \\ -5 & 2 \end{bmatrix}, B = \begin{bmatrix} 5 & -2 \\ 2 & -5 \end{bmatrix}$

Find each product, if possible.

25. $\begin{bmatrix} 2 & 3 \\ 3 & -2 \end{bmatrix}\begin{bmatrix} 1 & 2 \\ 0 & -2 \end{bmatrix}$

26. $\begin{bmatrix} -2 & 3 \\ 3 & -2 \end{bmatrix}\begin{bmatrix} 2 & 4 \\ -5 & 7 \end{bmatrix}$

27. $\begin{bmatrix} -4 & -2 \\ 21 & 0 \end{bmatrix}\begin{bmatrix} -5 & 6 \\ 21 & -1 \end{bmatrix}$

28. $\begin{bmatrix} -5 & 4 \\ 4 & -5 \end{bmatrix}\begin{bmatrix} 6 & -2 \\ 1 & 3 \end{bmatrix}$

29. $\begin{bmatrix} 2 & 1 & 3 \\ 1 & 2 & -1 \\ 0 & 1 & 0 \end{bmatrix}\begin{bmatrix} 1 & 2 & 3 \\ 2 & -2 & 1 \\ 0 & 0 & 1 \end{bmatrix}$

30. $\begin{bmatrix} 2 & 1 & 1 \\ 1 & 1 & 2 \\ 1 & -2 & -1 \end{bmatrix}\begin{bmatrix} 1 & 2 & 3 \\ 1 & 2 & -3 \\ -1 & -1 & 3 \end{bmatrix}$

31. $\begin{bmatrix} 1 \\ -2 \\ -3 \end{bmatrix}\begin{bmatrix} 4 & -5 & -6 \end{bmatrix}$

32. $\begin{bmatrix} 1 & -2 & -3 \\ 2 & 0 & 1 \end{bmatrix}\begin{bmatrix} 4 \\ -5 \\ -6 \end{bmatrix}$

33. $\begin{bmatrix} 1 & 2 & 3 \end{bmatrix}\begin{bmatrix} 4 & 5 & 6 \\ 7 & 8 & 9 \end{bmatrix}$

34. $\begin{bmatrix} 2 & 5 \\ -1 & 7 \end{bmatrix}\begin{bmatrix} 3 & 5 & -8 \\ -2 & 7 & 5 \\ 3 & -6 & 2 \end{bmatrix}$

35. $\begin{bmatrix} 2 & 3 & 4 \\ 1 & 2 & 3 \\ -2 & 2 & 2 \end{bmatrix}\begin{bmatrix} -1 \\ 2 \\ 3 \end{bmatrix}$

36. $\begin{bmatrix} 2 & 5 \\ -3 & 1 \\ 0 & -2 \\ 1 & -5 \end{bmatrix}\begin{bmatrix} 3 & -2 & 4 \\ -2 & -3 & 1 \end{bmatrix}$

37. $\begin{bmatrix} 1 & 2 & 3 \\ 4 & 5 & 6 \\ 7 & 8 & 9 \end{bmatrix}\begin{bmatrix} 1 & 2 \\ 3 & 4 \end{bmatrix}$

38. $\begin{bmatrix} 1 & 4 & 0 & 0 \\ -4 & 1 & 0 & -2 \\ 0 & 0 & 1 & 0 \\ 0 & 2 & 0 & 1 \end{bmatrix}\begin{bmatrix} 1 \\ 2 \\ -2 \\ -1 \end{bmatrix}$

Let $A = \begin{bmatrix} 2.3 & -1.7 & 3.1 \\ -2 & 3.5 & 1 \\ -8 & 4.7 & 9.1 \end{bmatrix}, B = \begin{bmatrix} -2.5 \\ 5.2 \\ -7 \end{bmatrix},$ *and*

$C = \begin{bmatrix} -5.8 \\ 2.9 \\ 4.1 \end{bmatrix}.$ *Use a graphing calculator to find each result.*

39. AB **40.** $B + C$

41. A^2 **42.** $AB + C$

Let $A = \begin{bmatrix} 2 & 3 \\ 1 & 3 \end{bmatrix}, B = \begin{bmatrix} 2 & 1 & -5 \\ 1 & 1 & 2 \end{bmatrix},$

$C = \begin{bmatrix} -2 & -1 & 6 \\ 0 & -1 & -1 \end{bmatrix}, D = \begin{bmatrix} 1 & 2 \\ 1 & 3 \end{bmatrix},$ *and*

$E = \begin{bmatrix} 1 & -2 \\ 2 & 3 \end{bmatrix}.$

Verify each property by doing the operations on each side of the equation and comparing the results.

43. Distributive Property: $A(B + C) = AB + AC$

44. Associative Property of Scalar Multiplication: $5(6A) = (5 \cdot 6)A$

45. Associative Property of Scalar Multiplication: $3(AB) = (3A)B$

46. Associative Property of Multiplication: $A(DE) = (AD)E$

Let $A = \begin{bmatrix} 1 & 3 \\ 2 & 5 \end{bmatrix}, B = \begin{bmatrix} -1 \\ 3 \end{bmatrix},$ *and* $C = \begin{bmatrix} 3 & 2 \end{bmatrix}.$ *Perform the operations, if possible.*

47. $A - BC$ **48.** $AB + B$

49. $CB - AB$ **50.** CAB

51. ABC

52. $CA + C$

53. A^2B

54. $(BC)^2$

Price	
Coffee	$0.75
Milk	$1.00
Cola	$1.25

Applications

Use a graphing calculator to help solve each problem.

55. Sporting goods Two suppliers manufactured footballs, baseballs, and basketballs in the quantities and costs given in the tables. Find matrices Q and C that represent the quantities and costs, find the product QC, and interpret the result.

	Quantities		
	Footballs	Baseballs	Basketballs
Supplier 1	200	300	100
Supplier 2	100	200	200

Unit costs	(in $)
Footballs	5
Baseballs	2
Basketballs	4

56. Retailing Three ice cream stores sold cones, sundaes, and milkshakes in the quantities and prices given in the tables. Find matrices Q and P that represent the quantities and prices, find the product QP, and interpret the results.

	Quantities		
	Cones	Sundaes	Shakes
Store 1	75	75	32
Store 2	80	69	27
Store 3	62	40	30

Unit price	
Cones	$1.50
Sundaes	$1.75
Shakes	$3.00

57. Beverage sales Beverages were sold to parents and children at a school basketball game in the quantities and prices given in the tables. Find matrices Q and P that represent the quantities and prices, find the product QP, and interpret the result.

	Quantities		
	Coffee	Milk	Cola
Adult males	217	23	319
Adult females	347	24	340
Children	3	97	750

58. Production costs Each of four factories manufactures three products in the daily quantities and unit costs given in the tables. Find a suitable matrix product to represent production costs.

	Production Quantities		
Factory	Product A	Product B	Product C
Ashtabula	19	23	27
Boston	17	21	22
Chicago	21	18	20
Denver	27	25	22

Unit Production Costs		
	Day shift	Night shift
Product A	$1.20	$1.35
Product B	$0.75	$0.85
Product C	$3.50	$3.70

59. Connectivity matrix An entry of 1 in the following **connectivity matrix** A indicates that the person associated with that row knows the address of the person associated with that column. For example, the 1 in Bill's row and Alan's column indicates that Bill can write to Alan. The 0 in Bill's row and Carl's column indicates that Bill cannot write to Carl. However, Bill could ask Alan to forward his letter to Carl. The matrix A^2 indicates the number of ways that one person can write to another with a letter that is forwarded exactly once. Find A^2.

$$\begin{array}{c} \\ \text{Alan} \\ \text{Bill} \\ \text{Carl} \end{array} \begin{array}{ccc} \text{Alan} & \text{Bill} & \text{Carl} \\ \left[\begin{array}{ccc} 0 & 1 & 1 \\ 1 & 0 & 0 \\ 0 & 1 & 0 \end{array}\right] \end{array} = A$$

60. Communication routing Refer to Exercise 59. Find the matrix $A + A^2$. Can everyone receive a letter from everyone else with at most one forwarding?

Discovery and Writing

61. Routing telephone calls A long-distance telephone carrier has established several direct microwave links among four cities. In the following connectivity matrix, entries a_{ij} and a_{ji} indicate the number of direct links between cities i and j. For example, cities 2 and 4 are not linked directly but could be connected through city 3. Find and interpret matrix A^2.

$$A = \begin{bmatrix} 0 & 2 & 1 & 0 \\ 2 & 0 & 1 & 0 \\ 1 & 1 & 0 & 2 \\ 0 & 0 & 2 & 0 \end{bmatrix}$$

62. Communication on one-way channels Three communication centers are linked as indicated in the illustration, with communication only in the direction of the arrows. Thus, location 1 can send a message directly to location 2 along two paths, but location 2 can return a message directly on only one path. Entry c_{ij} of matrix C indicates the number of channels from i to j. Find and interpret C^2.

$$C = \begin{bmatrix} 0 & 2 & 2 \\ 1 & 0 & 1 \\ 1 & 0 & 0 \end{bmatrix}$$

63. If A and B are 2×2 matrices, is $(AB)^2$ equal to A^2B^2? Support your answer.

64. Let a, b, and c be real numbers. If $ab = ac$ and $a \neq 0$, then $b = c$. Find 2×2 matrices A, B, and C, where $A \neq 0$ to show that such a law does not hold for all matrices.

65. Another property of the real numbers is that if $ab = 0$, then either $a = 0$ or $b = 0$. To show that this property is not true for matrices, find two nonzero 2×2 matrices A and B, such that $AB = 0$.

66. Find 2×2 matrices to show that
$$(A + B)(A - B) \neq A^2 - B^2.$$

Review
Perform the operations and simplify.

67. $(3x + 2)(2x - 3) - (2 - x)$

68. $\dfrac{x^2 + 3x - 4}{2x + 5 - (x + 1)}$

69. $\dfrac{1 + \dfrac{1}{x}}{1 - \dfrac{1}{x}}$

70. $\dfrac{1 - x^{-1}}{1 + x^{-1}}$

71. Solve the formula for a.
$$s = \frac{n(a + l)}{2}$$

72. Solve the formula for x_1.
$$y - y_1 = m(x - x_1)$$

6.4 Matrix Inversion

In this section, we will learn to

1. Find the inverse of a square matrix using row operations.

2. Solve a system of equations by matrix inversion.

3. Solve applications using matrix inversion.

Since the beginning of civilized society, governments and businesses have been interested in communicating in secret. This required the development of secret codes. Today, credit card information, bank account information, and even many e-mail messages are *encrypted*. Encryption is a process of converting ordinary text into unreadable text called *cipher text*.

BMCL/Shutterstock.com

Codes and code breaking have a long history in warfare. A very important event that helped the United States win WWII was the capture of German U-boat 110, which carried an Enigma encryption machine like the one shown. By breaking the code, the British and United States Navies knew the movements of German submarines.

Some of the most sophisticated codes we have today involve matrices. In Exercises 39 and 40, we must find the inverse of a matrix to decode a message.

Two real numbers are called **multiplicative inverses** if their product is the multiplicative identity 1. Some matrices have multiplicative inverses also.

Inverse of a Matrix   If A and B are $n \times n$ matrices, I is the $n \times n$ identity matrix, and

$$AB = BA = I,$$

then A and B are called **multiplicative inverses.** Matrix A is the **inverse** of B, and B is the **inverse** of A.

It can be shown that if a matrix A has an inverse, it only has one inverse. The inverse of A is written as A^{-1}.

$$AA^{-1} = A^{-1}A = I$$

EXAMPLE 1   **Showing that Two Matrices Are Inverses**

Show that A and B are inverses.

$$A = \begin{bmatrix} 1 & 1 & 0 \\ 4 & 3 & 0 \\ 2 & 1 & -1 \end{bmatrix} \qquad B = \begin{bmatrix} -3 & 1 & 0 \\ 4 & -1 & 0 \\ -2 & 1 & -1 \end{bmatrix}$$

SOLUTION   We must show that both AB and BA are equal to I.

$$AB = \begin{bmatrix} 1 & 1 & 0 \\ 4 & 3 & 0 \\ 2 & 1 & -1 \end{bmatrix}\begin{bmatrix} -3 & 1 & 0 \\ 4 & -1 & 0 \\ -2 & 1 & -1 \end{bmatrix}$$

$$= \begin{bmatrix} -3 + 4 + 0 & 1 - 1 + 0 & 0 + 0 + 0 \\ -12 + 12 + 0 & 4 - 3 + 0 & 0 + 0 + 0 \\ -6 + 4 + 2 & 2 - 1 - 1 & 0 + 0 + 1 \end{bmatrix}$$

$$= \begin{bmatrix} 1 & 0 & 0 \\ 0 & 1 & 0 \\ 0 & 0 & 1 \end{bmatrix}$$

$$BA = \begin{bmatrix} -3 & 1 & 0 \\ 4 & -1 & 0 \\ -2 & 1 & -1 \end{bmatrix}\begin{bmatrix} 1 & 1 & 0 \\ 4 & 3 & 0 \\ 2 & 1 & -1 \end{bmatrix} = \begin{bmatrix} 1 & 0 & 0 \\ 0 & 1 & 0 \\ 0 & 0 & 1 \end{bmatrix}$$

Self Check 1   Are C and D inverses? $C = \begin{bmatrix} 2 & 5 \\ 1 & 3 \end{bmatrix}$ $D = \begin{bmatrix} 3 & -5 \\ -1 & 2 \end{bmatrix}$

Now Try Exercise 1.

1. Find the Inverse of a Square Matrix Using Row Operations

A matrix that has an inverse is called a **nonsingular matrix** and is said to be **invertible.** If it does not have an inverse, it is a **singular matrix** and is not invertible. The following method provides a way to find the inverse of an invertible matrix.

Strategy for Finding the Inverse of a Matrix

If a sequence of row operations performed on the $n \times n$ matrix A reduces A to the $n \times n$ identity matrix I, then those same row operations, performed in the same order on I, will transform I into A^{-1}.

If no sequence of row operations will reduce A to I, then A is not invertible.

Comment

The row operations we use to change the matrix into the identity matrix are the same row operations we use in Gauss–Jordan elimination.

To use this method to find the inverse of an invertible matrix, we perform row operations on matrix A to change it to the identity matrix I. At the same time, we perform the same row operations on I. This changes I into A^{-1}.

A notation for this process uses an n-row-by-$2n$-column matrix, with matrix A as the left half and matrix I as the right half. If A is invertible, the proper row operations performed on $[A|I]$ will transform it into $[I|A^{-1}]$.

EXAMPLE 2   **Finding the Inverse of a 2 x 2 Matrix**

Find the inverse of matrix A if $A = \begin{bmatrix} 2 & -4 \\ 4 & -7 \end{bmatrix}$.

SOLUTION   We can set up a 2×4 matrix with A on the left and I on the right of the dashed line:

$$[A|I] = \begin{bmatrix} 2 & -4 & \vdots & 1 & 0 \\ 4 & -7 & \vdots & 0 & 1 \end{bmatrix}$$

We perform row operations on the entire matrix to transform the left half into I:

$$\begin{bmatrix} 2 & -4 & \vdots & 1 & 0 \\ 4 & -7 & \vdots & 0 & 1 \end{bmatrix} \begin{matrix} \left(\frac{1}{2}\right)R1 \to \\ (-2)R1 + R2 \to \end{matrix} \begin{bmatrix} 1 & -2 & \vdots & \frac{1}{2} & 0 \\ 0 & 1 & \vdots & -2 & 1 \end{bmatrix}$$

$$(2)R2 + R1 \to \begin{bmatrix} 1 & 0 & \vdots & -\frac{7}{2} & 2 \\ 0 & 1 & \vdots & -2 & 1 \end{bmatrix}$$

Since matrix A has been transformed into I, the right side of the previous matrix is A^{-1}. We can verify this by finding AA^{-1} and $A^{-1}A$ and showing that each product is I:

Caution

We do not find the inverse of a square matrix by finding the multiplicative inverse of each of its entries.

$$AA^{-1} = \begin{bmatrix} 2 & -4 \\ 4 & -7 \end{bmatrix}\begin{bmatrix} -\frac{7}{2} & 2 \\ -2 & 1 \end{bmatrix} = \begin{bmatrix} 1 & 0 \\ 0 & 1 \end{bmatrix}$$

$$A^{-1}A = \begin{bmatrix} -\frac{7}{2} & 2 \\ -2 & 1 \end{bmatrix}\begin{bmatrix} 2 & -4 \\ 4 & -7 \end{bmatrix} = \begin{bmatrix} 1 & 0 \\ 0 & 1 \end{bmatrix}$$

Self Check 2   Find the inverse of $A = \begin{bmatrix} 3 & 2 \\ 4 & 3 \end{bmatrix}$.

Now Try Exercise 5.

EXAMPLE 3   **Finding the Inverse of a 3 x 3 Matrix**

Find the inverse of matrix A if $A = \begin{bmatrix} 1 & 1 & 0 \\ 1 & 2 & 1 \\ 2 & 3 & 2 \end{bmatrix}$.

SOLUTION   We set up a 3×6 matrix with A on the left and I on the right of the dashed line.

$$[A|I] = \begin{bmatrix} 1 & 1 & 0 & 1 & 0 & 0 \\ 1 & 2 & 1 & 0 & 1 & 0 \\ 2 & 3 & 2 & 0 & 0 & 1 \end{bmatrix}$$

We then perform row operations on the matrix to transform the left half into I.

$$\begin{bmatrix} 1 & 1 & 0 & 1 & 0 & 0 \\ 1 & 2 & 1 & 0 & 1 & 0 \\ 2 & 3 & 2 & 0 & 0 & 1 \end{bmatrix} \begin{matrix} \\ (-1)R1 + R2 \rightarrow \\ (-2)R1 + R3 \rightarrow \end{matrix} \begin{bmatrix} 1 & 1 & 0 & 1 & 0 & 0 \\ 0 & 1 & 1 & -1 & 1 & 0 \\ 0 & 1 & 2 & -2 & 0 & 1 \end{bmatrix}$$

$$\begin{matrix} (-1)R2 + R1 \rightarrow \\ \\ (-1)R2 + R3 \rightarrow \end{matrix} \begin{bmatrix} 1 & 0 & -1 & 2 & -1 & 0 \\ 0 & 1 & 1 & -1 & 1 & 0 \\ 0 & 0 & 1 & -1 & -1 & 1 \end{bmatrix}$$

$$\begin{matrix} R3 + R1 \rightarrow \\ (-1)R3 + R2 \rightarrow \\ \end{matrix} \begin{bmatrix} 1 & 0 & 0 & 1 & -2 & 1 \\ 0 & 1 & 0 & 0 & 2 & -1 \\ 0 & 0 & 1 & -1 & -1 & 1 \end{bmatrix}$$

Since the left half of the matrix has been transformed into the identity matrix, the right half has become A^{-1}, and

$$A^{-1} = \begin{bmatrix} 1 & -2 & 1 \\ 0 & 2 & -1 \\ -1 & -1 & 1 \end{bmatrix}$$

Self Check 3   Find the inverse of $B = \begin{bmatrix} 1 & 1 & 1 \\ 2 & 1 & 4 \\ 2 & 2 & 3 \end{bmatrix}$.

Now Try Exercise 9.

EXAMPLE 4   **Finding the Inverse (if Possible) of a Square Matrix**

If possible, find the inverse of $A = \begin{bmatrix} 1 & 2 \\ 2 & 4 \end{bmatrix}$.

SOLUTION   We form the 2×4 matrix

$$[A|I] = \begin{bmatrix} 1 & 2 & 1 & 0 \\ 2 & 4 & 0 & 1 \end{bmatrix}$$

and begin to transform the left side of the matrix into the identity matrix I:

$$\begin{bmatrix} 1 & 2 & 1 & 0 \\ 2 & 4 & 0 & 1 \end{bmatrix} (-2)R1 + R2 \rightarrow \begin{bmatrix} 1 & 2 & 1 & 0 \\ 0 & 0 & -2 & 1 \end{bmatrix}$$

In obtaining the second-row, first-column position of A, the entire second row of A is zeroed out. Since we cannot transform matrix A to the identity matrix, A is not invertible.

Self Check 4   If possible, find the inverse of $B = \begin{bmatrix} 1 & -2 \\ -3 & 6 \end{bmatrix}$.

Now Try Exercise 13.

Caution

Do not attempt to find the inverse of a matrix that isn't square. It is not invertible.

The previous examples suggest the following facts:

*   Matrices that are not square matrices do not have inverses.
*   Some square matrices have inverses and others do not.

ACCENT ON TECHNOLOGY

Finding the Inverse of a Matrix

If a matrix is invertible, the inverse can be found using a graphing calculator.

1. Access the MATRIX menu; select EDIT, and enter the values of the matrix.

2. Go to the HOME screen, and press the key x^{-1}.

3. If we are going to use the inverse matrix, then we store (use STO▸ key) it in matrix B.

4. To verify that $AA^{-1} = I$, multiply matrix A by the inverse stored in B.

FIGURE 6-8

2. Solve a System of Equations by Matrix Inversion

If we multiply the matrices on the left side of the equation

$$\begin{bmatrix} 1 & 1 & 0 \\ 1 & 2 & 1 \\ 2 & 3 & 2 \end{bmatrix} \begin{bmatrix} x \\ y \\ z \end{bmatrix} = \begin{bmatrix} 20 \\ 30 \\ 55 \end{bmatrix}$$

and set the corresponding entries equal, we get the following system of equations:

$$\begin{cases} x + y = 20 \\ x + 2y + z = 30 \\ 2x + 3y + 2z = 55 \end{cases}$$

A system of equations can always be written as a matrix equation $AX = B$, where A is the coefficient matrix of the system, X is a column matrix of variables, and B is the column matrix of constants. If matrix A is invertible, the matrix equation $AX = B$ is easy to solve, as we will see in the next example.

EXAMPLE 5   **Using the Inverse of a Matrix to Solve a System of Equations**

Solve: $\begin{bmatrix} 1 & 1 & 0 \\ 1 & 2 & 1 \\ 2 & 3 & 2 \end{bmatrix} \begin{bmatrix} x \\ y \\ z \end{bmatrix} = \begin{bmatrix} 20 \\ 30 \\ 55 \end{bmatrix}$.

SOLUTION   The 3×3 matrix on the left is the matrix whose inverse was found in Example 3. We multiply both sides of the equation on the left by this inverse to obtain an equivalent system of equations.

$$\begin{bmatrix} 1 & -2 & 1 \\ 0 & 2 & -1 \\ -1 & -1 & 1 \end{bmatrix}\begin{bmatrix} 1 & 1 & 0 \\ 1 & 2 & 1 \\ 2 & 3 & 2 \end{bmatrix}\begin{bmatrix} x \\ y \\ z \end{bmatrix} = \begin{bmatrix} 1 & -2 & 1 \\ 0 & 2 & -1 \\ -1 & -1 & 1 \end{bmatrix}\begin{bmatrix} 20 \\ 30 \\ 55 \end{bmatrix}$$

$$\begin{bmatrix} 1 & 0 & 0 \\ 0 & 1 & 0 \\ 0 & 0 & 1 \end{bmatrix}\begin{bmatrix} x \\ y \\ z \end{bmatrix} = \begin{bmatrix} 15 \\ 5 \\ 5 \end{bmatrix}$$ Multiply the matrices. On the left, remember that $A^{-1}A = I$.

$$\begin{bmatrix} x \\ y \\ z \end{bmatrix} = \begin{bmatrix} 15 \\ 5 \\ 5 \end{bmatrix}$$ $IX = X$

The solution of this system can be read directly from the matrix on the right side. Verify that the values $x = 15$, $y = 5$, $z = 5$ satisfy the original equations. ∎

Self Check 5   Solve: $\begin{bmatrix} 2 & -4 \\ 4 & -7 \end{bmatrix}\begin{bmatrix} x \\ y \end{bmatrix} = \begin{bmatrix} -4 \\ 2 \end{bmatrix}$. (The inverse was found in Example 2.)

Now Try Exercise 29.

Example 5 suggests the following result.

Solving Systems of Equations   If A is invertible, the solution of the matrix equation $AX = B$ is

$$X = A^{-1}B$$

ACCENT ON TECHNOLOGY   **Solving a System of Equations Using Matrix Inversion**

To solve the system $\begin{cases} x - 2y + 3z = 9 \\ -x + 3y + z = -2 \\ 2x - 5y + 5z = 17 \end{cases}$ with a graphing calculator, follow the procedure shown.

Enter the coefficient matrix in A.   **Enter the column matrix in B.**   **Multiply $A^{-1}B$ and obtain the solution.**

FIGURE 6-9

The solution is $x = 1$, $y = -1$, and $z = 2$. Always check the results in the original equation.

This method is especially useful for finding solutions of several systems of equations that differ from each other only in the column matrix B. If the coefficient matrix A remains unchanged from one system of equations to the next, then A^{-1}

needs to be found only once. The solution of each system is found by a single matrix multiplication, $A^{-1}B$.

3. Solve Applications Involving Matrix Inversion

EXAMPLE 6   **Solving an Application Problem Using the Inverse of a Matrix**

A company that manufactures medical equipment spends time on paperwork, manufacture, and testing for each of three versions of a circuit board. The times spent on each and the total time available are given in the following tables.

Hours Required per Unit			
	Product A	Product B	Product C
Paperwork	1	1	0
Manufacture	1	2	1
Testing	2	3	2

Hours Available	
Paperwork	20
Manufacture	30
Testing	55

SOLUTION   We can let x, y, and z represent the number of units of products A, B, and C to be manufactured, respectively. We can then set up the following system of equations:

Paperwork: $x + y = 20$ One hour is needed for every A, and one hour for every B.

Manufacture: $x + 2y + z = 30$ One hour is needed for every A and C, and two hours for every B.

Testing: $2x + 3y + 2z = 55$ Two hours are needed for every A and C, and three hours for every B.

In matrix form, the system becomes

$$\begin{bmatrix} 1 & 1 & 0 \\ 1 & 2 & 1 \\ 2 & 3 & 2 \end{bmatrix} \begin{bmatrix} x \\ y \\ z \end{bmatrix} = \begin{bmatrix} 20 \\ 30 \\ 55 \end{bmatrix}$$

We solved this equation in Example 5 to get $x = 15$, $y = 5$, and $z = 5$. To use all of the available time, the company should manufacture 15 units of product A and 5 units each of products B and C.   ■

Self Check 6   In Example 6 if 18 hours are available for paperwork, 32 for manufacture, and 57 for testing, how many of each product should the company manufacture?

Now Try Exercise 37.

Self Check Answers   **1.** yes   **2.** $\begin{bmatrix} 3 & -2 \\ -4 & 3 \end{bmatrix}$ **3.** $\begin{bmatrix} 5 & 1 & -3 \\ -2 & -1 & 2 \\ -2 & 0 & 1 \end{bmatrix}$ **4.** no inverse

5. $\begin{bmatrix} x \\ y \end{bmatrix} = \begin{bmatrix} 18 \\ 10 \end{bmatrix}$ **6.** The company should manufacture 11 units of product A and 7 units each of products B and C.

Exercises **6.4**

Getting Ready

You should be able to complete these vocabulary and concept statements before you proceed to the practice exercises.

Fill in the blanks.

1. Matrices A and B are multiplicative inverses if _____.

2. A nonsingular matrix ___ (is, is not) invertible.

3. If A is invertible, elementary row operations can change $[A|I]$ into _____.

4. If A is invertible, the solution of $AX = B$ is _____.

Practice

Find the inverse of each matrix, if possible.

5. $\begin{bmatrix} 3 & -4 \\ -2 & 3 \end{bmatrix}$ 6. $\begin{bmatrix} 2 & 3 \\ 3 & 5 \end{bmatrix}$

7. $\begin{bmatrix} 3 & 7 \\ 2 & 5 \end{bmatrix}$ 8. $\begin{bmatrix} 1 & -2 \\ 2 & -5 \end{bmatrix}$

9. $\begin{bmatrix} 1 & 0 & 3 \\ -1 & 1 & 3 \\ -2 & 1 & 1 \end{bmatrix}$ 10. $\begin{bmatrix} 2 & 1 & -1 \\ 2 & 2 & -1 \\ -1 & -1 & 1 \end{bmatrix}$

11. $\begin{bmatrix} 3 & 2 & 1 \\ 1 & 1 & -1 \\ 4 & 3 & 1 \end{bmatrix}$ 12. $\begin{bmatrix} -2 & 1 & -3 \\ 2 & 3 & 0 \\ 1 & 0 & 1 \end{bmatrix}$

13. $\begin{bmatrix} 1 & 3 & 5 \\ 0 & 1 & 6 \\ 1 & 4 & 11 \end{bmatrix}$ 14. $\begin{bmatrix} 1 & 2 & 3 \\ 4 & 5 & 6 \\ 7 & 8 & 9 \end{bmatrix}$

15. $\begin{bmatrix} 1 & 2 & 3 \\ 0 & 1 & 2 \\ 0 & 0 & 1 \end{bmatrix}$ 16. $\begin{bmatrix} 1 & 2 & 3 \\ 0 & 1 & 1 \\ 0 & -1 & 0 \end{bmatrix}$

17. $\begin{bmatrix} 1 & 6 & 4 \\ 1 & -2 & -5 \\ 2 & 4 & -1 \end{bmatrix}$ 18. $\begin{bmatrix} 1 & 1 & 1 \\ 1 & 0 & -1 \\ 1 & 2 & 3 \end{bmatrix}$

Use a graphing calculator to find the inverse of each matrix.

19. $\begin{bmatrix} 1 & 2 & 3 & 4 \\ 0 & 1 & 2 & 3 \\ 0 & 0 & 1 & 2 \\ 0 & 0 & 0 & 1 \end{bmatrix}$

20. $\begin{bmatrix} 1 & 0 & 0 & 0 \\ 1 & 1 & 0 & 0 \\ 1 & 1 & 1 & 0 \\ 1 & 2 & 2 & 1 \end{bmatrix}$

21. $\begin{bmatrix} 1 & 1 & -1 \\ 0.5 & 1 & 0.5 \\ 1 & 1 & -1.5 \end{bmatrix}$

22. $\begin{bmatrix} -2 & -1 & 1 \\ 0.5 & -1.5 & -0.5 \\ 0 & 1 & 0.5 \end{bmatrix}$

23. $\begin{bmatrix} 3 & 3 & -3 & 2 \\ 1 & -4 & 3 & -5 \\ 3 & 0 & -2 & -1 \\ -1 & 5 & -3 & 6 \end{bmatrix}$

24. $\begin{bmatrix} 1 & 0 & 0 & 0 \\ 2 & 1 & 0 & 0 \\ 3 & 2 & 1 & 0 \\ 4 & 3 & 2 & 1 \end{bmatrix}$

Use matrix inversion to solve each system of equations. Note that several systems have the same coefficient matrix.

25. $\begin{cases} 3x - 4y = 1 \\ -2x + 3y = 5 \end{cases}$ 26. $\begin{cases} 3x - 4y = -1 \\ -2x + 3y = 3 \end{cases}$

27. $\begin{cases} 3x - 4y = 0 \\ -2x + 3y = 0 \end{cases}$ 28. $\begin{cases} 3x - 4y = -3 \\ -2x + 3y = -2 \end{cases}$

29. $\begin{cases} 2x + y - z = 2 \\ 2x + 2y - z = 4 \\ -x - y + z = -1 \end{cases}$ 30. $\begin{cases} 2x + y - z = 3 \\ 2x + 2y - z = -1 \\ -x - y + z = 4 \end{cases}$

31. $\begin{cases} -2x + y - 3z = 2 \\ 2x + 3y = -3 \\ x + z = 5 \end{cases}$ 32. $\begin{cases} -2x + y - 3z = 5 \\ 2x + 3y = 1 \\ x + z = -2 \end{cases}$

Use a graphing calculator to solve each system of equations. Use matrix inversion.

33. $\begin{cases} 5x + 3y = 13 \\ -7x + 5y = -9 \end{cases}$

34. $\begin{cases} 8x - 3y = 7 \\ -3x + 2y = 0 \end{cases}$

35. $\begin{cases} 5x + 2y + 3z = 12 \\ 2x + 5z = 7 \\ 3x + z = 4 \end{cases}$

36. $\begin{cases} 3x + 2y - z = 0 \\ 5x - 2y = 5 \\ 3x + y + z = 6 \end{cases}$

Applications

37. Manufacturing and testing The numbers of hours required to manufacture and test each of two models of heart monitor are given in the first table, and the numbers of hours available each week for manufacturing and testing are given in the second table.

	Hours Required per Unit	
	Model A	**Model B**
Manufacturing	23	27
Testing	21	22

Hours Available	
Manufacturing	127
Testing	108

How many of each model can be manufactured each week?

38. Making clothes A clothing manufacturer makes coats, shirts, and slacks. The times required for cutting, sewing, and packaging each item are shown in the table. How many of each should be made to use all available labor hours?

	Coats	Shirts	Slacks
Cutting	20 min	15 min	10 min
Sewing	60 min	30 min	24 min
Packaging	5 min	12 min	6 min

Time Available	
Cutting	115 hr
Sewing	280 hr
Packaging	65 hr

39. Cryptography The letters of a message, called **plain text,** are assigned values $1-26$ (for a$-$z) and are written in groups of 2 as 2×1 matrices. To write the message in **cipher text**, each 2×1 matrix B is multiplied by a matrix A, where

$$A = \begin{bmatrix} 1 & 1 \\ 2 & 3 \end{bmatrix}.$$

Find the plain text if the cipher text of one message is

$$AB = \begin{bmatrix} 17 \\ 43 \end{bmatrix}.$$

40. Cryptography The letters of a message, called **plain text,** are assigned values $1-26$ (for a$-$z) and are written in groups of 3 as 3×1 matrices. To write the message in **cipher text**, each 3×1 matrix Y is multiplied by matrix A, where

$$A = \begin{bmatrix} 1 & 1 & 0 \\ 2 & 3 & 3 \\ 1 & 1 & 1 \end{bmatrix}.$$

Find the plain text if the cipher text of one message is

$$AY = \begin{bmatrix} 30 \\ 122 \\ 49 \end{bmatrix}.$$

Discovery and Writing

Use examples chosen from 2×2 matrices to support each answer.

41. Does $(AB)^{-1} = A^{-1}B^{-1}$?

42. Does $(AB)^{-1} = B^{-1}A^{-1}$?

Let $A = \begin{bmatrix} -1 & -1 \\ 1 & 1 \end{bmatrix}$.

43. Show that $A^2 = \mathbf{0}$.

44. Show that the inverse of $I - A$ is $I + A$.

Let $A = \begin{bmatrix} 3 & 0 & 0 \\ -2 & -1 & -2 \\ 3 & 6 & 3 \end{bmatrix}$ and $X = \begin{bmatrix} x \\ y \\ z \end{bmatrix}$. **Solve each equation. Each solution is called an eigenvector of the matrix A.**

45. $(A - 2I)X = 0$

46. $(A - 3I)X = 0$

47. Suppose that A, B, and C are $n \times n$ matrices and A is invertible. If $AB = AC$, prove that $B = C$.

48. Prove that $\begin{bmatrix} a & b \\ c & d \end{bmatrix}$ has an inverse if and only if $ad - bc \neq 0$. (*Hint:* Try to find the inverse and see what happens.)

49. Suppose that B is any matrix for which $B^2 = 0$. Show that $I - B$ is invertible by showing that the inverse of $I - B$ is $I + B$.

50. Suppose that C is any matrix for which $C^3 = 0$. Show that $I - C$ is invertible by showing that the inverse of $I - C$ is $I + C + C^2$.

Review

Find the domain of each function. Use interval notation to write your answer.

51. $y = \dfrac{3x - 5}{x^2 - 4}$

52. $y = \dfrac{3x - 5}{x^2 + 4}$

53. $y = \dfrac{3x - 5}{\sqrt{x^2 + 4}}$

54. $y = \dfrac{3x - 5}{\sqrt{x^2 - 4}}$

Find the range of each function. Use interval notation to write your answer.

55. $y = x^2$

56. $y = x^3$

57. $y = \log x$

58. $y = 2^x$

6.5 Determinants

In this section, we will learn to

1. Evaluate determinants of higher-order matrices.
2. Understand and use properties of determinants.
3. Use determinants to solve systems of equations.
4. Write equations of lines.
5. Find areas of triangles.

There is a function, called the **determinant function**, that associates a number with every square matrix. The domain of this function is the set of all square matrices, and the range is the set of numbers. Historically, determinants were considered before matrices. They first appeared in the 3rd century BC when they were considered in a Chinese textbook, called *The Nine Chapters on the Mathematical Art*. Gerolamo Cardano, an Italian mathematician, considered two-by-two determinants toward the end of the 16th century. However, it was the great Swiss mathematician, Gabriel Cramer, who made them popular.

In this section, we will use determinants to solve systems of linear equations, and to find an equation of a line and the area of a triangle.

The determinant function is written as $\det(A)$ or as $|A|$.

Determinant of a 2 × 2 Matrix If $a, b, c,$ and d are numbers, the **determinant** of $A = \begin{bmatrix} a & b \\ c & d \end{bmatrix}$ is

$$\det(A) = \begin{vmatrix} a & b \\ c & d \end{vmatrix} = ad - bc$$

EXAMPLE 1 **Finding the Determinant of a 2 × 2 Matrix**

a. $\begin{vmatrix} 1 & 2 \\ 3 & 4 \end{vmatrix} = 1 \cdot 4 - 2 \cdot 3$ b. $\begin{vmatrix} -2 & 3 \\ -\pi & \frac{1}{2} \end{vmatrix} = (-2)\left(\frac{1}{2}\right) - (3)(-\pi)$

Caution

| Do not confuse the notation $|A|$ with absolute value symbols. |

$= 4 - 6$ $= -1 + 3\pi$

$= -2$

Self Check 1 Evaluate: $\begin{vmatrix} 3 & -2 \\ 5 & -4 \end{vmatrix}$.

Now Try Exercise 7.

1. Evaluate Determinants of Higher-Order Matrices

To evaluate determinants of higher-order matrices, we must define the **minor** and the **cofactor** of an element in a matrix.

Minor and Cofactor of a Matrix Let $A = [a_{ij}]$ be a square matrix of size (or order) $n \geq 2$.
1. The **minor** of a_{ij}, denoted as M_{ij}, is the determinant of the $n - 1 \times n - 1$ matrix formed by deleting the ith row and the jth column of A.
2. The **cofactor** of a_{ij}, denoted as C_{ij}, is $\begin{cases} M_{ij} \text{ when } i + j \text{ is even} \\ -M_{ij} \text{ when } i + j \text{ is odd} \end{cases}$.

EXAMPLE 2 **Finding Minors and Cofactors of a Matrix**

In $A = \begin{bmatrix} 1 & 2 & 3 \\ 4 & 5 & 6 \\ 7 & 8 & 9 \end{bmatrix}$ find the minor and cofactor of **a.** a_{31} **b.** a_{12}

SOLUTION **a.** The minor M_{31} is the minor of $a_{31} = 7$ appearing in row 3, column 1. It is found by deleting row 3 and column 1:

$$M_{31} = \begin{vmatrix} 1 & 2 & 3 \\ 4 & 5 & 6 \\ 7 & 8 & 9 \end{vmatrix} = \begin{vmatrix} 2 & 3 \\ 5 & 6 \end{vmatrix} = -3$$

Because $i + j$ is even $(3 + 1 = 4)$ the cofactor of the minor M_{31} is M_{31}:

$$C_{31} = M_{31} = \begin{vmatrix} 2 & 3 \\ 5 & 6 \end{vmatrix} = 2 \cdot 6 - 3 \cdot 5 = 12 - 15 = -3$$

b. The minor M_{12} is the minor of $a_{12} = 2$ appearing in row 1, column 2. It is found by deleting row 1 and column 2.

$$M_{12} = \begin{vmatrix} 1 & 2 & 3 \\ 4 & 5 & 6 \\ 7 & 8 & 9 \end{vmatrix} = \begin{vmatrix} 4 & 6 \\ 7 & 9 \end{vmatrix} = -6$$

Because $i + j$ is odd $(1 + 2 = 3)$ the cofactor of the minor M_{12} is $-M_{12}$:

$$C_{12} = -M_{12} = -\begin{vmatrix} 4 & 6 \\ 7 & 9 \end{vmatrix} = -(4 \cdot 9 - 6 \cdot 7) = -(36 - 42) = -(-6) = 6$$

Self Check 2   Find the cofactor of a_{23}.

Now Try Exercise 13.

We are now ready to evaluate determinants of higher-order matrices.

Determinant of a Higher-Order Matrix   If A is a square matrix of order $n \geq 2$, the **determinant of A, $|A|$,** is the sum of the products of the elements in any row (or column) and the cofactors of those elements.

In Example 3, we will evaluate a 3×3 determinant by expanding the determinant in three ways: along two different rows and along a column. This method is called **expanding a determinant by cofactors.**

EXAMPLE 3   **Finding the Determinant of a 3×3 Matrix**

Evaluate $\begin{vmatrix} 1 & 2 & -3 \\ -1 & 0 & 1 \\ -2 & 2 & 1 \end{vmatrix}$ by expanding by cofactors along the designated row or column.

Expanding on row 1:

$$\begin{vmatrix} 1 & 2 & -3 \\ -1 & 0 & 1 \\ -2 & 2 & 1 \end{vmatrix} = a_{11}C_{11} + a_{12}C_{12} + a_{13}C_{13}$$

$$= 1\begin{vmatrix} 0 & 1 \\ 2 & 1 \end{vmatrix} + 2\left(-\begin{vmatrix} -1 & 1 \\ -2 & 1 \end{vmatrix}\right) + (-3)\begin{vmatrix} -1 & 0 \\ -2 & 2 \end{vmatrix}$$

$$= 1(-2) + 2(-1) - 3(-2)$$

$$= -2 - 2 + 6$$

$$= 2$$

Expanding on row 3:

$$\begin{vmatrix} 1 & 2 & -3 \\ -1 & 0 & 1 \\ -2 & 2 & 1 \end{vmatrix} = a_{31}C_{31} + a_{32}C_{32} + a_{33}C_{33}$$

$$= -2\begin{vmatrix} 2 & -3 \\ 0 & 1 \end{vmatrix} + 2\left(-\begin{vmatrix} 1 & -3 \\ -1 & 1 \end{vmatrix}\right) + 1\begin{vmatrix} 1 & 2 \\ -1 & 0 \end{vmatrix}$$

$$= -2(2) + 2(+2) + 1(2)$$

$$= -4 + 4 + 2$$

$$= 2$$

Expanding on column 2:

$$\begin{vmatrix} 1 & 2 & -3 \\ -1 & 0 & 1 \\ -2 & 2 & 1 \end{vmatrix} = a_{12}C_{12} + a_{22}C_{22} + a_{32}C_{32}$$

$$= 2\left(-\begin{vmatrix} -1 & 1 \\ -2 & 1 \end{vmatrix}\right) + 0\begin{vmatrix} 1 & -3 \\ -2 & 1 \end{vmatrix} + 2\left(-\begin{vmatrix} 1 & -3 \\ -1 & 1 \end{vmatrix}\right)$$

$$= 2(-1) + 0(-5) + 2(+2)$$

$$= -2 + 4$$

$$= 2$$

In each case, the result is 2.

Comment

Note that we don't need to evaluate the determinant $\begin{vmatrix} 1 & -3 \\ -2 & 1 \end{vmatrix}$ because it has a coefficient of 0. When we expand by cofactors along a row or column containing some 0's, the work is easier because we have fewer determinants to evaluate.

Self Check 3   Evaluate $\begin{vmatrix} 1 & 0 & 1 \\ 2 & -1 & 0 \\ 3 & 1 & -1 \end{vmatrix}$ by expanding on its first row and second columns.

Now Try Exercise 19.

EXAMPLE 4   **Finding the Determinant of a 4 × 4 Matrix**

Evaluate: $\begin{vmatrix} 0 & 0 & 2 & 0 \\ 1 & 2 & 17 & -3 \\ -1 & 0 & 28 & 1 \\ -2 & 2 & -37 & 1 \end{vmatrix}$.

SOLUTION   Because row 1 contains three 0's, we expand the determinant along row 1. Then only one cofactor needs to be evaluated.

$$\begin{vmatrix} 0 & 0 & 2 & 0 \\ 1 & 2 & 17 & -3 \\ -1 & 0 & 28 & 1 \\ -2 & 2 & -37 & 1 \end{vmatrix} = 0|?| - 0|?| + 2\begin{vmatrix} 1 & 2 & -3 \\ -1 & 0 & 1 \\ -2 & 2 & 1 \end{vmatrix} - 0|?|$$

$$= 2(2) \qquad \text{See Example 3.}$$

$$= 4$$

Self Check 4   Evaluate: $\begin{vmatrix} 0 & 1 & 0 \\ 2 & 11 & -2 \\ 1 & 13 & 1 \end{vmatrix}$.

Now Try Exercise 27.

Example 4 suggests the following theorem.

Zero Row or Column Theorem   If every entry in a row or column of a square matrix A is 0, then $|A| = 0$.

 Evaluating Determinants

The MATRIX:MATH menu can be used to evaluate a determinant. For example, we will evaluate the determinant

$$\begin{vmatrix} 2 & 3 & 0.5 & 6 \\ 1 & 4 & -2 & -3 \\ 3 & 4 & -3 & -2 \\ -0.7 & 6 & 2 & 1 \end{vmatrix}.$$

Enter the values of the determinant into MATRIX A.

Go to the home screen; use the MATRIX menu, and select MATH 1:det(.

Enter the matrix name and press ENTER. The value of the determinant is 99.3.

FIGURE 6-10

2. Understand and Use Properties of Determinants

We have seen that there are row operations for transforming matrices. There are similar row and column operations for transforming determinants.

Row and Column Operations and Determinants

Let A be a square matrix and k be a real number.

1. If a matrix B is obtained from matrix A by interchanging two rows (or columns), then $|B| = -|A|$.

2. If B is obtained from A by multiplying every element in a row (or column) of A by k, then $|B| = k|A|$.

3. If B is obtained from A by adding k times any row (or column) of A to another row (or column) of A, then $|B| = |A|$.

We will illustrate each row operation by showing that the operation holds true for the 2×2 determinant.

$$(1) \quad |A| = \begin{vmatrix} 3 & 4 \\ 1 & 2 \end{vmatrix} = 3(2) - 4(1) = 6 - 4 = 2$$

- **Interchanging two rows**
  Let $|B|$ be the determinant obtained from $|A|$ by interchanging its two rows. Then

$$|B| = \begin{vmatrix} 1 & 2 \\ 3 & 4 \end{vmatrix} = 1(4) - 2(3) = 4 - 6 = -2$$

Since $-2 = -1(2)$, we have $|B| = -|A|$.
In general, if $|A|$ and $|B|$ are as follows, we have

$$|A| = \begin{vmatrix} a & b \\ c & d \end{vmatrix} = ad - bc$$

$$|B| = \begin{vmatrix} c & d \\ a & b \end{vmatrix} = cb - da = -(ad - bc) = -|A|$$

- **Multiplying every element in a row by k**

  Let $|B|$ be the determinant obtained from $|A|$ in Equation 1 by multiplying its second row by 3. Then

$$|B| = \begin{vmatrix} 3 & 4 \\ 3(1) & 3(2) \end{vmatrix} = \begin{vmatrix} 3 & 4 \\ 3 & 6 \end{vmatrix} = 3(6) - 4(3) = 18 - 12 = 6$$

  Since $6 = 3(2)$, we have $|B| = 3|A|$.

  In general, if $|A|$ and $|B|$ are as follows, we have

(2)
$$|A| = \begin{vmatrix} a & b \\ c & d \end{vmatrix} = ad - bc$$

$$|B| = \begin{vmatrix} a & b \\ kc & kd \end{vmatrix} = akd - bkc = k(ad - bc) = k|A|$$

- **Adding k times any row of A to another row of A**

  Let $|B|$ be the determinant obtained from $|A|$ in Equation 1 by adding 3 times its first row to its second row. Then

$$|B| = \begin{vmatrix} 3 & 4 \\ 3(3) + 1 & 3(4) + 2 \end{vmatrix} = 3(14) - 4(10) = 42 - 40 = 2$$

  Since $2 = 2$, we have $|A| = |B|$.

  In general, if $|B|$ is obtained from $|A|$ in Equation 2 by adding k times its first row to its second row, then

$$\begin{aligned} |B| = \begin{vmatrix} a & b \\ ka + c & kb + d \end{vmatrix} &= a(kb + d) - b(ka + c) \\ &= akb + ad - bka - bc \\ &= ad - bc \\ &= |A| \end{aligned}$$

Evaluating higher-order determinants can be very time consuming. However, as we have seen, if we use row and column operations to introduce as many 0's as possible in a row (or column) and then expand the determinant by cofactors along that row (or column), the work is much easier. In the next example, we will use several row and column operations to introduce 0's into the determinant.

EXAMPLE 5   **Using Row and Column Operations to Help Evaluate the Determinant**

Use row and column operations to evaluate: $\begin{vmatrix} 10 & 20 & -10 & 20 \\ 2 & 1 & 1 & 1 \\ 1 & 2 & -3 & 2 \\ 2 & -1 & -1 & 1 \end{vmatrix}$

SOLUTION   To get smaller numbers in the first row, we can use a type 2 row operation and multiply each entry in the first row by $\frac{1}{10}$. However, we must then multiply the resulting determinant by 10 to retain its original value.

(1)
$$\begin{vmatrix} 10 & 20 & -10 & 20 \\ 2 & 1 & 1 & 1 \\ 1 & 2 & -3 & 2 \\ 2 & -1 & -1 & 1 \end{vmatrix} \begin{array}{c} \left(\frac{1}{10}\right)R1 \to \\ = 10 \end{array} \begin{vmatrix} 1 & 2 & -1 & 2 \\ 2 & 1 & 1 & 1 \\ 1 & 2 & -3 & 2 \\ 2 & -1 & -1 & 1 \end{vmatrix}$$

EXAMPLE 9   **Using the Determinant to Find the Area of a Triangle**

Find the area of the triangle shown in Figure 6-11.

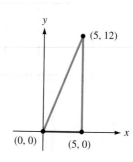

FIGURE 6-11

SOLUTION   We set up the equation

$$A = \pm \frac{1}{2} \begin{vmatrix} 0 & 0 & 1 \\ 5 & 0 & 1 \\ 5 & 12 & 1 \end{vmatrix}$$

and expand the determinant along the first row to get

$$= \pm \frac{1}{2} \left[1 \begin{vmatrix} 5 & 0 \\ 5 & 12 \end{vmatrix} \right]$$

$$= \pm \frac{1}{2}(60 - 0)$$

$$= 30$$

The area of the triangle is 30 square units.

Self Check 9   Find the area of the triangle with vertices at $(1, 2)$, $(2, 3)$, and $(-1, 4)$.

Now Try Exercise 57.

Self Check Answers   **1.** -2 **2.** 6   **3.** 6, 6   **4.** -4 **5.** 30   **6.** $(2, 1)$ **7.** $(1, 2, 3)$
8. $x - y = -2$ **9.** 2 sq. units

Exercises **6.5**

Getting Ready
You should be able to complete these vocabulary and concept statements before you proceed to the practice exercises.

Fill in the blanks.

1. The determinant of a square matrix A is written as
_____ or _____.

2. $\begin{vmatrix} a & b \\ c & d \end{vmatrix} =$ _____

3. If every entry in one row or one column of A is zero, then $|A| =$ ___.

4. If a matrix B is obtained from matrix A by adding one row to another, then $|B| =$ ____.

5. If two columns of A are identical, then $|A| =$ ___.

6. In Cramer's Rule, the denominator is the determinant of the _____.

Practice
Evaluate each determinant.

7. $\begin{vmatrix} 2 & 1 \\ -2 & 3 \end{vmatrix}$

8. $\begin{vmatrix} -3 & -6 \\ 2 & -5 \end{vmatrix}$

9. $\begin{vmatrix} 2 & -3 \\ -3 & 5 \end{vmatrix}$

10. $\begin{vmatrix} 5 & 8 \\ -6 & -2 \end{vmatrix}$

In Exercises 11–18, $A = \begin{vmatrix} 1 & -2 & 3 \\ 4 & 5 & -6 \\ -7 & 8 & 9 \end{vmatrix}$. Find each minor or cofactor.

11. M_{21} **12.** M_{13}

13. M_{33} **14.** M_{32}

15. C_{21} **16.** C_{13}

17. C_{33} **18.** C_{32}

Evaluate each determinant by expanding by cofactors.

19. $\begin{vmatrix} 2 & -3 & 5 \\ -2 & 1 & 3 \\ 1 & 3 & -2 \end{vmatrix}$ **20.** $\begin{vmatrix} 1 & 3 & 1 \\ -2 & 5 & 3 \\ 3 & -2 & -2 \end{vmatrix}$

21. $\begin{vmatrix} 1 & -1 & 2 \\ 2 & 1 & 3 \\ 1 & 1 & -1 \end{vmatrix}$ **22.** $\begin{vmatrix} 1 & 3 & 1 \\ 2 & 1 & -1 \\ 2 & -1 & 1 \end{vmatrix}$

23. $\begin{vmatrix} 2 & 1 & -1 \\ 1 & 3 & 5 \\ 2 & -5 & 3 \end{vmatrix}$ **24.** $\begin{vmatrix} 3 & 1 & -2 \\ -3 & 2 & 1 \\ 1 & 3 & 0 \end{vmatrix}$

25. $\begin{vmatrix} 0 & 1 & -3 \\ -3 & 5 & 2 \\ 2 & -5 & 3 \end{vmatrix}$ **26.** $\begin{vmatrix} 1 & -7 & -2 \\ -2 & 0 & 3 \\ -1 & 7 & 1 \end{vmatrix}$

27. $\begin{vmatrix} 0 & 0 & 1 & 0 \\ -2 & 1 & 0 & 1 \\ 1 & 0 & 1 & 2 \\ 2 & 0 & 1 & 2 \end{vmatrix}$ **28.** $\begin{vmatrix} 1 & 0 & -2 & 1 \\ 0 & 1 & 0 & 1 \\ 0 & 3 & -1 & 2 \\ 0 & -1 & 0 & 1 \end{vmatrix}$

29. $\begin{vmatrix} 10 & 20 & 10 & 30 \\ -2 & 1 & -3 & 1 \\ -1 & 0 & 1 & -2 \\ 2 & -1 & -1 & 3 \end{vmatrix}$ **30.** $\begin{vmatrix} -1 & 3 & -2 & 5 \\ 2 & 1 & 0 & 1 \\ 1 & 3 & -2 & 5 \\ 2 & -1 & 0 & -1 \end{vmatrix}$

Determine whether each statement is true. Do not evaluate the determinants.

31. $\begin{vmatrix} 1 & 3 & -4 \\ -2 & 1 & 3 \\ 1 & 3 & 2 \end{vmatrix} = -\begin{vmatrix} -2 & 1 & 3 \\ 1 & 3 & -4 \\ 1 & 3 & 2 \end{vmatrix}$

32. $\begin{vmatrix} 4 & 6 & 8 \\ 10 & 5 & 15 \\ 20 & 5 & 10 \end{vmatrix} = \begin{vmatrix} 2 & 3 & 4 \\ 10 & 5 & 15 \\ 20 & 5 & 10 \end{vmatrix}$

33. $\begin{vmatrix} -2 & -3 & -4 \\ 5 & -1 & 2 \\ 1 & 2 & 3 \end{vmatrix} = -\begin{vmatrix} 2 & 3 & 4 \\ -5 & 1 & -2 \\ 1 & 2 & 3 \end{vmatrix}$

34. $\begin{vmatrix} 1 & 2 & 3 \\ 4 & 5 & 6 \\ 7 & 8 & 9 \end{vmatrix} = \begin{vmatrix} 5 & 7 & 9 \\ 4 & 5 & 6 \\ 7 & 8 & 9 \end{vmatrix}$

If $\begin{vmatrix} a & b & c \\ d & e & f \\ g & h & i \end{vmatrix} = 3$, *find the value of each determinant.*

35. $\begin{vmatrix} d & e & f \\ a & b & c \\ -g & -h & -i \end{vmatrix}$ **36.** $\begin{vmatrix} 5a & 5b & 5c \\ -d & -e & -f \\ 3g & 3h & 3i \end{vmatrix}$

37. $\begin{vmatrix} a+g & b+h & c+i \\ d & e & f \\ g & h & i \end{vmatrix}$ **38.** $\begin{vmatrix} g & h & i \\ a & b & c \\ d & e & f \end{vmatrix}$

Use Cramer's Rule to find the solution of each system, if possible.

39. $\begin{cases} 3x + 2y = 7 \\ 2x - 3y = -4 \end{cases}$ **40.** $\begin{cases} x - 5y = -6 \\ 3x + 2y = -1 \end{cases}$

41. $\begin{cases} x - y = 3 \\ 3x - 7y = 9 \end{cases}$ **42.** $\begin{cases} 2x - y = -6 \\ x + y = 0 \end{cases}$

43. $\begin{cases} x + 2y + z = 2 \\ x - y + z = 2 \\ x + y + 3z = 4 \end{cases}$ **44.** $\begin{cases} x + 2y - z = -1 \\ 2x + y - z = 1 \\ x - 3y - 5z = 17 \end{cases}$

45. $\begin{cases} 2x - y + z = 5 \\ 3x - 3y + 2z = 10 \\ x + 3y + z = 0 \end{cases}$ **46.** $\begin{cases} x - y - z = 2 \\ x + y + z = 2 \\ -x - y + z = -4 \end{cases}$

47. $\begin{cases} \dfrac{x}{2} + \dfrac{y}{3} + \dfrac{z}{2} = 11 \\ \dfrac{x}{3} + y - \dfrac{z}{6} = 6 \\ \dfrac{x}{2} + \dfrac{y}{6} + z = 16 \end{cases}$ **48.** $\begin{cases} \dfrac{x}{2} + \dfrac{y}{5} + \dfrac{z}{3} = 17 \\ \dfrac{x}{5} + \dfrac{y}{2} + \dfrac{z}{5} = 32 \\ x + \dfrac{y}{3} + \dfrac{z}{2} = 30 \end{cases}$

49. $\begin{cases} 2p - q + 3r - s = 0 \\ p + q - s = -1 \\ 3p - r = 2 \\ p - 2q + 3s = 7 \end{cases}$ **50.** $\begin{cases} a + b + c + d = 8 \\ a + b + c + 2d = 7 \\ a + b + 2c + 3d = 3 \\ a + 2b + 3c + 4d = 4 \end{cases}$

Use determinants to write an equation of the line in standard form that passes through the given points.

51. $P(0, 0)$, $Q(4, 6)$ **52.** $P(2, 3)$, $Q(6, 8)$

53. $P(-2, 3)$, $Q(5, -3)$ **54.** $P(1, -2)$, $Q(-4, 3)$

Use determinants to find the area of each triangle with vertices at the given points.

55. $P(0, 0)$, $Q(12, 0)$, $R(12, 5)$

56. $P(0, 0)$, $Q(0, 5)$, $R(12, 5)$

57. $P(2, 3)$, $Q(10, 8)$, $R(0, 20)$

58. $P(1, 1)$, $Q(6, 6)$, $R(2, 10)$

In Exercises 59–61, illustrate each column operation by showing that it is true for the determinant $\begin{vmatrix} a & b \\ c & d \end{vmatrix}$.

59. Interchanging two columns

60. Multiplying each element in a column by k

61. Adding k times any column to another column

62. Use the method of addition to solve $\begin{cases} ax + by = e \\ cx + dy = f \end{cases}$

for y, and thereby show that $y = \dfrac{af - ec}{ad - bc}$.

Expand the determinants and solve for x.

63. $\begin{vmatrix} 3 & x \\ 1 & 2 \end{vmatrix} = \begin{vmatrix} 2 & -1 \\ x & -5 \end{vmatrix}$

64. $\begin{vmatrix} 4 & x^2 \\ 1 & -1 \end{vmatrix} = \begin{vmatrix} x & 4 \\ 2 & 3 \end{vmatrix}$

65. $\begin{vmatrix} 3 & x & 1 \\ x & 0 & -2 \\ 4 & 0 & 1 \end{vmatrix} = \begin{vmatrix} 2 & x \\ x & 4 \end{vmatrix}$

66. $\begin{vmatrix} x & -1 & 2 \\ -2 & x & 3 \\ 4 & -3 & -1 \end{vmatrix} = \begin{vmatrix} 2 & 2 \\ 5 & x \end{vmatrix}$

Applications

67. Investing A student wants to average a 6.6% return by investing $20,000 in the three stocks listed in the table. Because HiTech is a high-risk investment, he wants to invest three times as much in SaveTel and OilCo combined as he invests in HiTech. How much should he invest in each stock?

Stock	Rate of Return
HiTech	10%
SaveTel	5%
OilCo	6%

68. Ice skating The illustration shows three circles traced out by a figure skater during her performance. If the centers of the circles are the given distances apart, find the radius of each circle.

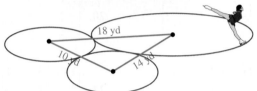

18 yd   10 yd   14 yd

testing/Shutterstock.com

Discovery and Writing

Evaluate each determinant. What do you discover?

69. $\begin{vmatrix} 1 & 3 & 4 \\ 0 & 5 & 2 \\ 0 & 0 & 2 \end{vmatrix}$ **70.** $\begin{vmatrix} 2 & 1 & -2 \\ 0 & 3 & 4 \\ 0 & 0 & -1 \end{vmatrix}$

71. $\begin{vmatrix} 1 & 2 & 4 & 3 \\ 0 & 2 & 2 & 1 \\ 0 & 0 & 3 & 2 \\ 0 & 0 & 0 & 4 \end{vmatrix}$ **72.** $\begin{vmatrix} 2 & 1 & -2 & 1 \\ 0 & 2 & 2 & -1 \\ 0 & 0 & 3 & 1 \\ 0 & 0 & 0 & 2 \end{vmatrix}$

73. Another way to evaluate a 3×3 determinant is to copy its first two columns to the right of the determinant as shown. Then find the product of the numbers on each red diagonal and find their sum. Then find the product of the numbers on each blue diagonal and find their sum. Then subtract the sum of the products on the blue diagonals from the sum of the products on the red diagonals. Find the value of the determinant.

74. Use the method of Exercise 73 to evaluate the

determinant $\begin{vmatrix} 0 & 1 & -3 \\ -3 & 5 & 2 \\ 2 & -5 & 3 \end{vmatrix}$.

75. Use an example chosen from 2×2 matrices to show that the determinant of the product of two matrices is the product of the determinants of those two matrices.

76. Find an example among 2×2 matrices to show that the determinant of a sum of two matrices is not equal to the sum of the determinants of those matrices.

77. A determinant is a function that associates a number with every square matrix. Give the domain and the range of that function.

78. Use an example chosen from 2×2 matrices to show that for $n \times n$ matrices A and B, $AB \neq BA$ but $|AB| = |BA|$.

79. If A and B are matrices and $|AB| = 0$, must $|A| = 0$ or $|B| = 0$? Explain.

80. If A and B are matrices and $|AB| = 0$, must $A = 0$ or $B = 0$? Explain.

Use a graphing calculator to evaluate each determinant.

81. $\begin{vmatrix} 2.3 & 5.7 & 6.1 \\ 3.4 & 6.2 & 8.3 \\ 5.8 & 8.2 & 9.2 \end{vmatrix}$

82. $\begin{vmatrix} 0.32 & -7.4 & -6.7 \\ 3.3 & 5.5 & -0.27 \\ -8 & -0.13 & 5.47 \end{vmatrix}$

Review

Factor each polynomial, if possible.

83. $x^2 + 3x - 4$

84. $2x^2 - 5x - 12$

85. $9x^3 - x$

86. $x^2 + 3x + 5$

Add the fractions.

87. $\dfrac{1}{x-2} + \dfrac{2}{2x-1}$

88. $\dfrac{2}{x} + \dfrac{3}{x^2} - \dfrac{1}{x-1}$

89. $\dfrac{2}{x^2+1} + \dfrac{1}{x}$

90. $\dfrac{2x}{x^2+1} + \dfrac{1}{x}$

CHAPTER REVIEW

SECTION **6.1**   Systems of Linear Equations

Definitions and Concepts	Examples
Solving a system by graphing: To solve a system of equations by graphing, graph each equation in the system and find the coordinates of the point where all of the graphs intersect. If the graphs have no point in common, the system has no solutions. If the graphs coincide, the system has infinitely many solutions.	Solve $\begin{cases} x - 2y = -9 \\ 3x + y = 1 \end{cases}$ by graphing. We graph each equation as shown in the illustration and find the coordinates of the point where the graphs intersect. From the illustration, we see that the solution is $(-1, 4)$.

Definitions and Concepts	Examples
	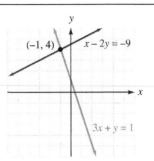
Solving a system by substitution: To solve a system by substitution, solve one equation for one variable, and substitute that result into the other equation. Then solve for the other variable.	Solve $\begin{cases} x - 2y = -9 \\ 3x + y = 1 \end{cases}$ by substitution. We can solve the first equation for x and substitute the result for x in the other equation. $$x - 2y = -9 \;\rightarrow\; x = 2y - 9$$ $$3(2y - 9) + y = 1 \qquad \text{Substitute } 2y - 9 \text{ for } x.$$ $$6y - 27 + y = 1$$ $$7y = 28$$ $$y = 4$$ To find x, we can substitute 4 for y in the equation $x = 2y - 9$ to get $x = -1$. The solution is $(-1, 4)$.
Solving a system by addition: To solve a system by addition, multiply one or both equations by suitable constants so that when the results are added, one variable will be eliminated. Then back substitute to find the other variable.	Solve $\begin{cases} x - 2y = -9 \\ 3x + y = 1 \end{cases}$ by addition. We can multiply the second equation by 2 and add the equations to eliminate y. $$\begin{cases} x - 2y = -9 \\ 3x + y = 1 \end{cases} \quad \rightarrow \quad \begin{aligned} x - 2y &= -9 \\ \underline{6x + 2y} &= \underline{2} \\ 7x &= -7 \\ x &= -1 \end{aligned}$$ We can substitute -1 for x in any equation and find that $y = 4$. The solution is $(-1, 4)$.

EXERCISES

Solve each system by graphing.

1. $\begin{cases} 2x - y = -1 \\ x + y = 7 \end{cases}$

2. $\begin{cases} 5x + 2y = 1 \\ 2x - y = -5 \end{cases}$

3. $\begin{cases} y = 5x + 7 \\ x = y - 7 \end{cases}$

4. $\begin{cases} 3x + 2y = 6 \\ y = -\dfrac{3}{2}x + 3 \end{cases}$

5. $\begin{cases} 4x - y = 4 \\ y = 4(x - 2) \end{cases}$

Solve by substitution.

6. $\begin{cases} 2y + x = 0 \\ x = y + 3 \end{cases}$

7. $\begin{cases} 2x + y = -3 \\ x - y = 3 \end{cases}$

8. $\begin{cases} \dfrac{x + y}{2} + \dfrac{x - y}{3} = 1 \\ y = 3x - 2 \end{cases}$

9. $\begin{cases} y = 3x - 4 \\ 9x - 3y = 12 \end{cases}$

10. $\begin{cases} x = -\dfrac{3}{2}y + 3 \\ 2x + 3y = 4 \end{cases}$

Solve by addition.

11. $\begin{cases} x + 5y = 7 \\ 3x + y = -7 \end{cases}$

12. $\begin{cases} 2x + 3y = 11 \\ 3x - 7y = -41 \end{cases}$

13. $\begin{cases} 2(x + y) - x = 0 \\ 3(x + y) + 2y = 1 \end{cases}$

14. $\begin{cases} 8x + 12y = 24 \\ 2x + 3y = 4 \end{cases}$

15. $\begin{cases} 3x - y = 4 \\ 9x - 3y = 12 \end{cases}$

Solve by any method.

16. $\begin{cases} 3x + 2y - z = 2 \\ x + y - z = 0 \\ 2x + 3y - z = 1 \end{cases}$

17. $\begin{cases} 5x - y + z = 3 \\ 3x + y + 2z = 2 \\ x + y = 2 \end{cases}$

18. $\begin{cases} 2x - y + z = 1 \\ x - y + 2z = 3 \\ x - y + z = 1 \end{cases}$

19. Department store order The buyer for a large department store must order 40 coats, some fake fur and some leather. He is unsure of the expected sales. He can buy 25 fur coats and the rest leather for $9,300, or 10 fur coats and the rest leather for $12,600. How much does he pay if he decides to split the order evenly?

20. Ticket sales Adult tickets for the championship game are usually $5, but on Seniors' Day, seniors paid $4. Children's tickets were $2.50. Sales of 1,800 tickets totaled $7,425, and children and seniors accounted for one-half of the tickets sold. How many of each were sold?

SECTION **6.2**   Gaussian Elimination and Matrix Methods

Definitions and Concepts	Examples
Three matrices associated with a system: There are three matrices associated with a system of equations, a *coefficient matrix*, a *matrix of constants*, and an *augmented* or *system matrix*.	There are three matrices associated with the following system of equations $\begin{cases} x + 3y + z = 2 \\ 3x - 2y - z = 5 \\ 4x + 2y + z = 9 \end{cases}$

Coefficient Matrix   **Constants**   **System Matrix**

$$\begin{bmatrix} 1 & 3 & 1 \\ 3 & -2 & -1 \\ 4 & 2 & 1 \end{bmatrix} \qquad \begin{bmatrix} 2 \\ 5 \\ 9 \end{bmatrix} \qquad \left[\begin{array}{ccc|c} 1 & 3 & 1 & 2 \\ 3 & -2 & -1 & 5 \\ 4 & 2 & 1 & 9 \end{array}\right]$$

Definitions and Concepts	Examples

Elementary row operations:
1. In a type 1 row operation, any two rows of a matrix can be interchanged.
2. In a type 2 row operation, the elements of any row of a matrix can be multiplied by any nonzero constant.
3. In a type 3 row operation, any row of a matrix can be changed by adding a multiple of another row to it.

Row echelon form of a matrix:
1. The first nonzero entry in each row is 1.
2. Lead entries appear farther to the right as you move down the rows of the matrix.
3. Any rows containing only 0's are at the bottom of the matrix.

To solve the previous system, we can use row operations to write the system matrix in row echelon form.

$$\begin{bmatrix} 1 & 3 & 1 & | & 2 \\ 3 & -2 & -1 & | & 5 \\ 4 & 2 & 1 & | & 9 \end{bmatrix} \begin{matrix} \\ (-3)R_1 + R_2 \rightarrow \\ (-4)R_1 + R_3 \rightarrow \end{matrix} \begin{bmatrix} 1 & 3 & 1 & | & 2 \\ 0 & -11 & -4 & | & -1 \\ 0 & -10 & -3 & | & 1 \end{bmatrix}$$

$$(-1)R_3 + R_2 \rightarrow \begin{bmatrix} 1 & 3 & 1 & | & 2 \\ 0 & -1 & -1 & | & -2 \\ 0 & -10 & -3 & | & 1 \end{bmatrix}$$

$$(-1)R_2 \rightarrow \begin{bmatrix} 1 & 3 & 1 & | & 2 \\ 0 & 1 & 1 & | & 2 \\ 0 & -10 & -3 & | & 1 \end{bmatrix}$$

$$(10)R_2 + R_3 \rightarrow \begin{bmatrix} 1 & 3 & 1 & | & 2 \\ 0 & 1 & 1 & | & 2 \\ 0 & 0 & 7 & | & 21 \end{bmatrix}$$

$$\left(\tfrac{1}{7}\right)R_3 \rightarrow \begin{bmatrix} 1 & 3 & 1 & | & 2 \\ 0 & 1 & 1 & | & 2 \\ 0 & 0 & 1 & | & 3 \end{bmatrix}$$

From the last line, we see that $z = 3$. From the middle line, we see that $y + z = 2$. Since $z = 3$, we know that $y = -1$. From the top equation, we know that $x + 3y + z = 2$. Substituting the values for y and z, we can determine that $x = 2$. The solution is $(2, -1, 3)$.

EXERCISES

Solve by matrix methods, if possible.

21. $\begin{cases} 2x + 5y = 7 \\ 3x - y = 2 \end{cases}$

22. $\begin{cases} 3x - y = -4 \\ -6x + 2y = 8 \end{cases}$

23. $\begin{cases} x + 3y - z = 8 \\ 2x + y - 2z = 11 \\ x - y + 5z = -8 \end{cases}$

24. $\begin{cases} x + 3y + z = 3 \\ 2x - y + z = -11 \\ 3x + 2y + 3z = 2 \end{cases}$

25. $\begin{cases} x + y + z = 4 \\ 3x - 2y - 2z = -3 \\ 4x - y - z = 0 \end{cases}$

SECTION **6.3** Matrix Algebra

Definitions and Concepts	Examples

Equality of matrices:
Matrices are equal if and only if they are the same size and have the same corresponding entries.

The following matrices are equal because they are the same size and their corresponding entries are equal.

$$\begin{bmatrix} 2 & \sqrt{9} \\ \tfrac{8}{4} & 7 \end{bmatrix} = \begin{bmatrix} \sqrt{4} & 3 \\ 2 & \sqrt{49} \end{bmatrix}$$

Definitions and Concepts	Examples
Matrix operations: • Two $m \times n$ matrices are added by adding the corresponding elements of those matrices. • Two $m \times n$ matrices are subtracted by the rule $A - B = A + (-B)$. • The product AB of the $m \times n$ matrix A and the $n \times p$ matrix B is the $m \times p$ matrix C. The ith-row, jth-column entry of C is found by keeping a running total of the products of the elements in the ith row of A with the corresponding elements in the jth column of B.	$\begin{bmatrix} 2 & -3 \\ -7 & 5 \end{bmatrix} + \begin{bmatrix} -3 & 4 \\ -2 & 2 \end{bmatrix} = \begin{bmatrix} -1 & 1 \\ -9 & 7 \end{bmatrix}$ Add the corresponding entries. $\begin{bmatrix} 2 & -3 \\ -7 & 5 \end{bmatrix} - \begin{bmatrix} -3 & 4 \\ -2 & 2 \end{bmatrix} = \begin{bmatrix} 5 & -7 \\ -5 & 3 \end{bmatrix}$ Subtract the corresponding entries. $\begin{bmatrix} 2 & -3 \\ -7 & 5 \end{bmatrix}\begin{bmatrix} -3 & 4 \\ -2 & 2 \end{bmatrix} = \begin{bmatrix} 2(-3)+(-3)(-2) & 2(4)+(-3)(2) \\ (-7)(-3)+5(-2) & -7(4)+(5)(2) \end{bmatrix}$ $= \begin{bmatrix} 0 & 2 \\ 11 & -18 \end{bmatrix}$

EXERCISES

Solve for x and y.

26. $\begin{bmatrix} 1 & -4 \\ x & 2 \\ 0 & x+7 \end{bmatrix} = \begin{bmatrix} 1 & x \\ -4 & 2 \\ x+4 & y \end{bmatrix}$

Perform the matrix operations, if possible.

27. $\begin{bmatrix} 3 & 2 & 1 \\ 3 & 2 & 1 \end{bmatrix} + \begin{bmatrix} -2 & 1 & 3 \\ 1 & -2 & 1 \end{bmatrix}$

28. $\begin{bmatrix} 2 & 3 & 5 \\ 1 & -2 & 4 \\ 2 & 1 & -2 \end{bmatrix} - \begin{bmatrix} 0 & -2 & 1 \\ 3 & 4 & -2 \\ 6 & -4 & 1 \end{bmatrix}$

29. $\begin{bmatrix} 1 & -2 \\ -3 & 1 \end{bmatrix}\begin{bmatrix} 2 & 3 \\ -1 & 2 \end{bmatrix}$

30. $\begin{bmatrix} -2 & 3 & 5 \\ 1 & -2 & -3 \end{bmatrix}\begin{bmatrix} 2 & 1 \\ -1 & 2 \\ -2 & 3 \end{bmatrix}$

31. $\begin{bmatrix} 1 & -3 & 2 \end{bmatrix}\begin{bmatrix} 2 \\ 1 \\ 3 \end{bmatrix}$

32. $\begin{bmatrix} 1 \\ 2 \\ 1 \\ 5 \end{bmatrix}\begin{bmatrix} 2 & -1 & 1 & 3 \end{bmatrix}$

33. $\begin{bmatrix} 1 & -5 & 3 \\ 2 & 1 & -1 \end{bmatrix}\begin{bmatrix} 2 \\ -2 \\ 3 \end{bmatrix}\begin{bmatrix} 1 & -1 \\ -1 & 3 \end{bmatrix}\begin{bmatrix} 1 \\ -2 \end{bmatrix}$

34. $\begin{bmatrix} 1 & -3 & 2 \end{bmatrix}\begin{bmatrix} 2 \\ 1 \\ -5 \end{bmatrix} + \begin{bmatrix} 1 & -3 \end{bmatrix}\begin{bmatrix} 2 \\ 5 \end{bmatrix}$

35. $\left(\begin{bmatrix} 1 & -3 \\ 3 & 1 \end{bmatrix} + \begin{bmatrix} -1 & 3 \\ 1 & 1 \end{bmatrix}\right)\begin{bmatrix} 1 \\ -5 \end{bmatrix}$

SECTION **6.4**   Matrix Inversion

Definitions and Concepts	Examples
The inverse of a matrix: The **inverse** of an $n \times n$ matrix A is A^{-1}, where $$AA^{-1} = A^{-1}A = I$$ Use elementary row operations to transform $[A\vert I]$ into $[I\vert A^{-1}]$, where I is an identity matrix. If A cannot be transformed into I, then A is singular.	To find the inverse of matrix $A = \begin{bmatrix} 1 & 4 \\ 3 & 2 \end{bmatrix}$, we form the matrix $\begin{bmatrix} 1 & 4 & \vert & 1 & 0 \\ 3 & 2 & \vert & 0 & 1 \end{bmatrix}$ and use row operations to transform matrix A to the left of the dashed line into the identity matrix. These row operations performed on the identity matrix to the right of the dashed line will transform it into the inverse.

Definitions and Concepts	Examples
If A is invertible, then the solution of $AX = B$ is $X = A^{-1}B$.	$\begin{bmatrix} 1 & 4 & \vdots & 1 & 0 \\ 3 & 2 & \vdots & 0 & 1 \end{bmatrix} (-3)R_1 + R_2 \to \begin{bmatrix} 1 & 4 & \vdots & 1 & 0 \\ 0 & -10 & \vdots & -3 & 1 \end{bmatrix}$

$$\left(-\tfrac{1}{10}\right)R_2 \to \begin{bmatrix} 1 & 4 & \vdots & 1 & 0 \\ 0 & 1 & \vdots & \dfrac{3}{10} & -\dfrac{1}{10} \end{bmatrix}$$

$$-4R_2 + R_1 \to \begin{bmatrix} 1 & 0 & \vdots & -\dfrac{1}{5} & \dfrac{2}{5} \\ 0 & 1 & \vdots & \dfrac{3}{10} & -\dfrac{1}{10} \end{bmatrix}$$

The inverse is $\begin{bmatrix} -\dfrac{1}{5} & \dfrac{2}{5} \\ \dfrac{3}{10} & -\dfrac{1}{10} \end{bmatrix}$. Check by showing that the product of matrix A and the inverse is the identity matrix.

EXERCISES

Find the inverse of each matrix, if possible.

36. $\begin{bmatrix} 2 & 3 \\ 3 & 5 \end{bmatrix}$

37. $\begin{bmatrix} 1 & 0 & 0 \\ 2 & 0 & -2 \\ 1 & 2 & 2 \end{bmatrix}$

38. $\begin{bmatrix} 1 & 0 & 8 \\ 3 & 7 & 6 \\ 1 & 2 & 3 \end{bmatrix}$

39. $\begin{bmatrix} -6 & 4 \\ -3 & 2 \end{bmatrix}$

40. $\begin{bmatrix} 4 & 4 & 1 \\ 1 & 1 & 1 \\ -1 & -1 & 0 \end{bmatrix}$

Use the inverse of the coefficient matrix to solve each system of equations.

41. $\begin{cases} 4x - y + 2z = 0 \\ x + y + 2z = 1 \\ x + z = 0 \end{cases}$

42. $\begin{cases} w + 3x + y + 3z = 1 \\ w + 4x + y + 3z = 2 \\ x + y = 1 \\ w + 2x - y + 2z = 1 \end{cases}$

SECTION 6.5   Determinants

Definitions and Concepts	Examples
The determinant: • The **determinant** of $A = \begin{bmatrix} a & b \\ c & d \end{bmatrix}$ is $\det(A) = \lvert A \rvert = \begin{vmatrix} a & b \\ c & d \end{vmatrix} = ad - bc.$	$\begin{vmatrix} 2 & -3 \\ -4 & 5 \end{vmatrix} = 2(5) - (-3)(-4) = 10 - 12 = -2$

Definitions and Concepts	Examples
• The **determinant** of an $n \times n$ matrix A is the sum of the products of the elements of any row (or column) and the cofactors of those elements.	Evaluate the following determinant by expanding along the first row.$$\begin{vmatrix} 2 & 3 & -4 \\ 3 & 2 & 1 \\ -2 & 5 & -1 \end{vmatrix} = 2\begin{vmatrix} 2 & 1 \\ 5 & -1 \end{vmatrix} - 3\begin{vmatrix} 3 & 1 \\ -2 & -1 \end{vmatrix} + (-4)\begin{vmatrix} 3 & 2 \\ -2 & 5 \end{vmatrix}$$ $$= 2(-2-5) - 3[-3-(-2)] - 4[15-(-4)]$$ $$= 2(-7) - 3(-1) - 4(19)$$ $$= -14 + 3 - 76$$ $$= -87$$
Properties of determinants: • If two rows (or columns) of a matrix are interchanged, the sign of its determinant is reversed.	$$\begin{vmatrix} 2 & 3 \\ 4 & 5 \end{vmatrix} = -\begin{vmatrix} 4 & 5 \\ 2 & 3 \end{vmatrix} \qquad \begin{vmatrix} 2 & 3 \\ 4 & 5 \end{vmatrix} = -\begin{vmatrix} 3 & 2 \\ 5 & 4 \end{vmatrix}$$
• If a row (or column) of a matrix is multiplied by a constant k, the value of its determinant is multiplied by k.	$$\begin{vmatrix} 3 & 4 \\ -2 & 1 \end{vmatrix} = 11, \text{ but}$$ $$5\begin{vmatrix} 3 & 4 \\ -2 & 1 \end{vmatrix} = \begin{vmatrix} 5(3) & 5(4) \\ -2 & 1 \end{vmatrix} = \begin{vmatrix} 15 & 20 \\ -2 & 1 \end{vmatrix} = 55 \text{ and } 55 = 5(11)$$
• If a row (or column) of a matrix is altered by adding to it a multiple of another row (or column), the value of its determinant is unchanged.	$$\begin{vmatrix} 3 & 4 \\ -2 & 1 \end{vmatrix} = 11 \text{ If we multiply row 2 by 5 and add it to row 1, the}$$ value of the determinant is still 11. $$\begin{vmatrix} 3 & 4 \\ -2 & 1 \end{vmatrix} = \begin{vmatrix} 3+5(-2) & 4+5(1) \\ -2 & 1 \end{vmatrix} = \begin{vmatrix} -7 & 9 \\ -2 & 1 \end{vmatrix} = 11$$
Cramer's Rule: Form quotients of two determinants. The denominator is the determinant of the coefficient matrix, A. The numerator is the determinant of a modified coefficient matrix. When solving for the ith variable, replace the ith column of A with a column of constants, B.	Use Cramer's Rule to solve the following system for x. $$\begin{cases} 2x + 3y - 4z = 1 \\ 3x + 2y + z = 6 \\ -2x + 5y - z = 2 \end{cases}$$ $$x = \frac{\begin{vmatrix} 1 & 3 & -4 \\ 6 & 2 & 1 \\ 2 & 5 & -1 \end{vmatrix}}{\begin{vmatrix} 2 & 3 & -4 \\ 3 & 2 & 1 \\ -2 & 5 & -1 \end{vmatrix}} = \frac{1\begin{vmatrix} 2 & 1 \\ 5 & -1 \end{vmatrix} - 3\begin{vmatrix} 6 & 1 \\ 2 & -1 \end{vmatrix} - 4\begin{vmatrix} 6 & 2 \\ 2 & 5 \end{vmatrix}}{-87 \text{ (See above.)}}$$ $$= \frac{1(-7) - 3(-8) - 4(26)}{-87}$$ $$= \frac{-87}{-87}$$ $$= 1$$

EXERCISES

Evaluate each determinant.

43. $\begin{vmatrix} 3 & -2 \\ 1 & -3 \end{vmatrix}$

44. $\begin{vmatrix} 1 & -2 & 3 \\ 2 & -1 & 3 \\ 1 & -1 & 0 \end{vmatrix}$

45. $\begin{vmatrix} 1 & 3 & -1 \\ 1 & 2 & 1 \\ 1 & 0 & 2 \end{vmatrix}$

46. $\begin{vmatrix} 1 & 2 & 3 & 4 \\ -1 & 3 & -3 & 2 \\ 0 & 0 & 0 & -1 \\ 3 & 3 & 4 & 3 \end{vmatrix}$

Use Cramer's Rule to solve each system.

47. $\begin{cases} x + 3y = -5 \\ -2x + y = -4 \end{cases}$

48. $\begin{cases} x - y + z = -1 \\ 2x - y + 3z = -4 \\ x - 3y + z = -1 \end{cases}$

49. $\begin{cases} x - 3y + z = 7 \\ x + y - 3z = -9 \\ x + y + z = 3 \end{cases}$

50. $\begin{cases} w + x - y + z = 4 \\ 2w + x + z = 4 \\ x + 2y + z = 0 \\ w + y + z = 2 \end{cases}$

If $\begin{vmatrix} a & b & c \\ d & e & f \\ g & h & i \end{vmatrix} = 7$*, evaluate each determinant.*

51. $\begin{vmatrix} 3a & 3b & 3c \\ d & e & f \\ g & h & i \end{vmatrix}$

52. $\begin{vmatrix} a & b & c \\ d+g & e+h & f+i \\ g & h & i \end{vmatrix}$

SECTION **6.6** Partial Fractions

Definitions and Concepts	Examples

Partial fraction decomposition:

The fraction $\frac{P(x)}{Q(x)}$ can be written as the sum of simpler fractions with denominators determined by the prime factors of $Q(x)$. For a review of all cases, see Section 6.6.

Decompose $\dfrac{4x - 1}{2x^2 + 3x + 1}$ into partial fractions.

We factor the denominator to get $\dfrac{4x - 1}{(2x + 1)(x + 1)}$.

Since each denominator is linear, there are constants A and B such that

$$\frac{4x - 1}{(2x + 1)(x + 1)} = \frac{A}{2x + 1} + \frac{B}{x + 1}$$

Adding the fractions on the right, we get

$$\frac{4x - 1}{(2x + 1)(x + 1)} = \frac{A(x + 1)}{(2x + 1)(x + 1)} + \frac{B(2x + 1)}{(x + 1)(2x + 1)}$$

$$= \frac{Ax + A + 2Bx + B}{(2x + 1)(x + 1)}$$

$$= \frac{(A + 2B)x + A + B}{(2x + 1)(x + 1)}$$

Setting the coefficients of the polynomial numerators equal, we have the following system of equations:

$$\begin{cases} A + 2B = 4 \\ A + B = -1 \end{cases}$$

whose solution is $A = -6$ and $B = 5$. Thus,

$$\frac{4x - 1}{(2x + 1)(x + 1)} = \frac{-6}{2x + 1} + \frac{5}{x + 1}$$

EXERCISES

Decompose into partial fractions.

53. $\dfrac{7x + 3}{x^2 + x}$

54. $\dfrac{4x^3 + 3x + x^2 + 2}{x^4 + x^2}$

55. $\dfrac{x^2 + 5}{x^3 + x^2 + 5x}$

56. $\dfrac{x^2 + 1}{(x + 1)^3}$

SECTION **6.7**   Graphs of Linear Inequalities

Definitions and Concepts	Examples
Solving a system of inequalities: Systems of inequalities in two variables can be solved by graphing. The solution is represented by a plane region with boundaries determined by graphing the inequalities as if they were equations.	To use graphing to solve the system $\begin{cases} y \le -x + 1 \\ 2x > y + 2 \end{cases}$, we graph each inequality on the same coordinate axes as shown below. The solution is the overlapping region shown in purple.

EXERCISES

57. Graph: $y \ge -2x - 1$.

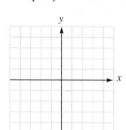

58. Graph: $x^2 + y^2 > 4$.

Solve each system by graphing.

59. $\begin{cases} 3x + 2y \le 6 \\ x - y > 3 \end{cases}$

60. $\begin{cases} y \le x^2 + 1 \\ y \ge x^2 - 1 \end{cases}$

SECTION **6.8**   Linear Programming

Definitions and Concepts	Examples
Solving linear programming problems: The maximum and the minimum values of a linear function in two variables, subject to the constraints of a system of linear inequalities, are attained at a corner or along an entire edge of the region determined by the system of inequalities.	See Example 1 in the text.

EXERCISES

Maximize P subject to the given conditions.

61. $P = 2x + y$

$$\begin{cases} x \geq 0 \\ y \geq 0 \\ x + y \leq 3 \end{cases}$$

62. $P = 2x - 3y$

$$\begin{cases} x \geq 0 \\ y \leq 3 \\ x - y \leq 4 \end{cases}$$

63. $P = 3x - y$

$$\begin{cases} y \geq 1 \\ y \leq 2 \\ y \leq 3x + 1 \\ x \leq 1 \end{cases}$$

64. $P = y - 2x$

$$\begin{cases} x + y \geq 1 \\ x \leq 1 \\ y \leq \dfrac{x}{2} + 2 \\ x + y \leq 2 \end{cases}$$

65. A company manufactures two fertilizers, x and y. Each 50-pound bag of fertilizer requires three ingredients, which are available in the limited quantities shown in the table. The profit on each bag of fertilizer x is \$6 and on each bag of y is \$5. How many bags of each product should be produced to maximize the profit?

Ingredient	Number of pounds in fertilizer x	Number of pounds in fertilizer y	Total number of pounds available
Nitrogen	6	10	20,000
Phosphorus	8	6	16,400
Potash	6	4	12,000

CHAPTER TEST

Solve each system of equations by the graphing method.

1. $\begin{cases} x - 3y = -5 \\ 2x - y = 0 \end{cases}$

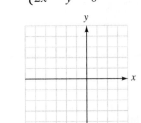

2. $\begin{cases} x = 2y + 5 \\ y = 2x - 4 \end{cases}$

Solve each system of equations by the substitution or addition method.

3. $\begin{cases} 3x + y = 0 \\ 2x - 5y = 17 \end{cases}$

4. $\begin{cases} \dfrac{x + y}{2} + x = 7 \\ \dfrac{x - y}{2} - y = -6 \end{cases}$

5. Mixing solutions A chemist has two solutions; one has a 20% concentration and the other a 45% concentration. How many liters of each must she mix to obtain 10 liters of 30% concentration?

6. Wholesale distribution Ace Electronics, Hi-Fi Stereo, and CD World buy a total of 175 DVD players from the same distributor each month. Because CD World buys 25 more units than the other two stores combined, CD World's cost is only \$160 per unit. The players cost Hi-Fi \$165 each and Ace \$170 each. How many players does each retailer buy each month if the distributor receives \$28,500 each month from the sale of the players to the three stores?

Write each system of equations as a matrix and solve it by Gaussian elimination.

7. $\begin{cases} 3x - 2y = 4 \\ 2x + 3y = 7 \end{cases}$

8. $\begin{cases} x + 3y - z = 6 \\ 2x - y - 2z = -2 \\ x + 2y + z = 6 \end{cases}$

Write each system of equations as a matrix and solve it by Gauss–Jordan elimination. If the system has infinitely many solutions, show how each can be determined.

9. $\begin{cases} x + 2y + 3z = -5 \\ 3x + y - 2z = 7 \\ y - z = 2 \end{cases}$

10. $\begin{cases} x + 2y + z = 0 \\ 3x - 2y - 2z = 7 \\ 4x - z = 7 \end{cases}$

Perform the operations.

11. $3\begin{bmatrix} 2 & -3 & 5 \\ 0 & 3 & -1 \end{bmatrix} - 5\begin{bmatrix} -2 & 1 & -1 \\ 0 & 3 & 2 \end{bmatrix}$

12. $\begin{bmatrix} 1 & 2 & 3 \end{bmatrix}\begin{bmatrix} 2 & -2 \\ -2 & 2 \\ 1 & 0 \end{bmatrix}\begin{bmatrix} 3 \\ -2 \end{bmatrix}$

Find the inverse of each matrix, if possible.

13. $\begin{bmatrix} 5 & 19 \\ 2 & 7 \end{bmatrix}$

14. $\begin{bmatrix} -1 & 3 & -2 \\ 4 & 1 & 4 \\ 0 & 3 & -1 \end{bmatrix}$

Use the inverses found in Questions 13 and 14 to solve each system.

15. $\begin{cases} 5x + 19y = 3 \\ 2x + 7y = 2 \end{cases}$

16. $\begin{cases} -x + 3y - 2z = 1 \\ 4x + y + 4z = 3 \\ 3y - z = -1 \end{cases}$

Evaluate each determinant.

17. $\begin{vmatrix} 3 & -5 \\ -3 & 1 \end{vmatrix}$

18. $\begin{vmatrix} 3 & 5 & -1 \\ -2 & 3 & -2 \\ 1 & 5 & -3 \end{vmatrix}$

Use Cramer's Rule to solve each system for y.

19. $\begin{cases} 3x - 5y = 3 \\ -3x + y = 2 \end{cases}$

20. $\begin{cases} 3x + 5y - z = 2 \\ -2x + 3y - 2z = 1 \\ x + 5y - 3z = 0 \end{cases}$

Decompose each fraction into partial fractions.

21. $\dfrac{5x}{2x^2 - x - 3}$

22. $\dfrac{3x^2 + x + 2}{x^3 + 2x}$

Graph the solution set of each system.

23. $\begin{cases} x - 3y \geq 3 \\ x + 3y \leq 3 \end{cases}$

24. $\begin{cases} 3x + 4y \leq 12 \\ 3x + 4y \geq 6 \\ x \geq 0 \\ y \geq 0 \end{cases}$

25. Maximize $P = 3x + 2y$ subject to

$$\begin{cases} y \geq 0 \\ x \geq 0 \\ 2x + y \leq 4 \\ y \leq 2 \end{cases}$$

26. Minimize $P = y - x$ subject to

$$\begin{cases} x \geq 0 \\ y \geq 0 \\ x + y \leq 8 \\ 2x + y \geq 2 \end{cases}$$

Conic Sections and Quadratic Systems

CAREERS AND MATHEMATICS: Engineer

Nomad_Soul/Shutterstock.com

Engineers are the link between a discovery in science and the practical application of that discovery to meet consumer demands. Engineers will often design and develop new products. They are also supervisors in manufacturing facilities. Most engineers have a specialty. Aerospace engineers, biological engineers, chemical engineers, electrical engineers, mechanical engineers, civil engineers, and petroleum engineers are a few of the specialists in engineering.

Education and Mathematics Required
- Engineers typically have a bachelor's degree in an engineering specialty. Research positions will often require a graduate degree.
- College Algebra, Geometry, Trigonometry, the Calculus sequence, Linear Algebra, Differential Equations, and Statistics are math courses required.

How Engineers Use Math and Who Employs Them
- Mathematics is important for all types of engineers. It is the language of engineering and physical science. Mathematics can develop the intellectual maturity to solve difficult problems. An understanding of mathematical analysis is essential to validate the work of computer programs and to write code that can make programs even more powerful.
- About 37% of engineers are employed in manufacturing industries, and 28% in professional, scientific, and technical services. Federal, state, and local government agencies employ engineers in highway and public works departments. Potential employers are determined by the engineering specialty.

Career Outlook and Earnings
- Employment of engineers is expected to grow about as fast as the average for all occupations, although growth will vary by specialty. Job opportunities are expected to be good.
- Earnings vary significantly among the specialties. Median salaries run from $108,020 for petroleum engineers to $68,730 for agricultural engineers. Highest salaries can be over $165,000.

For more information see: www.bls.gov/oco

In this chapter, we will study second-degree equations in x and y. They have many applications in fields such as navigation, astronomy, and satellite communications.

7.1 The Circle and the Parabola

In this section, we will learn to

1. Write an equation of a circle.
2. Graph circles.
3. Write an equation of a parabola in standard form.
4. Graph parabolas.
5. Solve applied problems involving parabolas.

The suspension bridge is one of the oldest types of bridges. An example is the Golden Gate Bridge that spans the opening of San Francisco Bay and the Pacific Ocean. Completed in 1937, it is currently the second longest suspension bridge in the United States. As the illustration shows, the main cables that hold up the bridge hang in the shape of a parabola. A parabola is an example of a *conic section.*

Second-degree equations in x and y have the general form

$$Ax^2 + Bxy + Cy^2 + Dx + Ey + F = 0$$

where at least one of the coefficients A, B, and C is not zero. The graphs of these equations fall into one of several categories: a point, a pair of lines, a circle, a parabola, an ellipse, a hyperbola, or no graph at all. These graphs are called **conic sections,** because each one is the intersection of a plane and a right-circular cone, as shown in Figure 7-1.

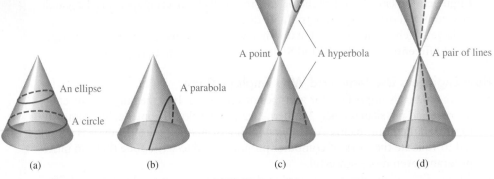

(a)	(b)	(c)	(d)

FIGURE 7-1

Although these shapes have been known since the time of the ancient Greeks, it wasn't until the 17th century that René Descartes (1596–1650) and Blaise Pascal (1623–1662) developed the mathematics needed to study them in detail.

In this section, we will consider two conic sections, the circle and the parabola.

1. Write an Equation of a Circle

In Section 2.4, we developed the following standard equations for circles:

The Standard Form of an Equation of a Circle with Center at (h, k)	The graph of any equation that can be written in the form $$(x - h)^2 + (y - k)^2 = r^2$$ is a circle with radius r and center at point (h, k).

If $h = 0$ and $k = 0$, we have this result.

The Standard Form of an Equation of a Circle with Center at $(0, 0)$	The graph of any equation that can be written in the form $$x^2 + y^2 = r^2$$ is a circle with radius r and center at the origin.

The graphs of two circles, one with center at (h, k) and one with center at $(0, 0)$ are shown in Figure 7-2.

FIGURE 7-2

EXAMPLE 1   Writing an Equation of a Circle

Find an equation of the circle shown in Figure 7-3. Write both the standard and general forms of the equation.

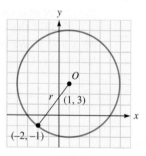

FIGURE 7-3

SOLUTION   We will use distance formula to find the radius of the circle and then substitute the coordinates of the center and radius into the standard equation of a circle.

To find the radius of the circle, we substitute the coordinates of the points $(1, 3)$ and $(-2, -1)$ into the distance formula and simplify:

$$r = \sqrt{(x_2 - x_1)^2 + (y_2 - y_1)^2}$$

$$r = \sqrt{(-2 - 1)^2 + (-1 - 3)^2}$$ Substitute 1 for x_1, 3 for y_1, -2 for x_2, and -1 for y_2.

$$= \sqrt{(-3)^2 + (-4)^2}$$

$$= \sqrt{9 + 16}$$

$$= \sqrt{25}$$

$$= 5$$

To find an equation of a circle with radius 5 and center at $(1, 3)$, we substitute 1 for h, 3 for k, and 5 for r in the standard form of the circle.

$$(x - h)^2 + (y - k)^2 = r^2$$

$$(x - 1)^2 + (y - 3)^2 = 5^2$$

To write the equation in general form, we square the binomials and simplify.

$$x^2 - 2x + 1 + y^2 - 6y + 9 = 25$$

$$x^2 + y^2 - 2x - 6y - 15 = 0 \qquad \text{Subtract 25 from both sides and simplify.}$$

Self Check 1   Find the general equation of a circle with center at $(-2, 1)$ and radius of 4.

Now Try Exercise 17.

The final equation in Example 1 can be written as

$$1x^2 + 0xy + 1y^2 - 2x - 6y - 15 = 0$$

which illustrates that the graph of

$$Ax^2 + Bxy + Cy^2 + Dx + Ey + F = 0$$

is a circle whenever $B = 0$ and $A = C$.

2. Graph Circles

EXAMPLE 2   Graphing a Circle

Graph the circle whose equation is $2x^2 + 2y^2 + 4x + 3y = 3$.

SOLUTION   We will convert the general form of the circle into standard form so we can identify the center and radius. Then we will graph the circle.

To find the coordinates of the center and the radius, we complete the square on x and y. We begin by dividing both sides of the equation by 2 and rearranging terms to get

$$x^2 + 2x + y^2 + \frac{3}{2}y = \frac{3}{2}$$

To complete the square on x and y, we add 1 and $\frac{9}{16}$ to both sides.

$$x^2 + 2x + 1 + y^2 + \frac{3}{2}y + \frac{9}{16} = \frac{3}{2} + 1 + \frac{9}{16}$$

We can factor $x^2 + 2x + 1$ and $y^2 + \frac{3}{2}y + \frac{9}{16}$ and simplify on the right side to get

$$(x + 1)^2 + \left(y + \frac{3}{4}\right)^2 = \frac{49}{16}$$

$$[x - (-1)]^2 + \left[y - \left(-\frac{3}{4}\right)\right]^2 = \left(\frac{7}{4}\right)^2$$

From the equation, we see that the coordinates of the center of the circle are $h = -1$ and $k = -\frac{3}{4}$ and that the radius of the circle is $\frac{7}{4}$. The graph is shown in Figure 7-4.

Comment

Since the graphs of circles fail the vertical line test, their equations do not represent functions. It is somewhat more difficult to use a graphing calculator to graph equations that are not functions. Please see the Accent on Technology, Graphing Circles, in Section 2.4. In many cases, it is easier to graph the circle by hand.

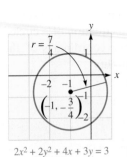

$2x^2 + 2y^2 + 4x + 3y = 3$

FIGURE 7-4

Self Check 2   Graph the circle whose equation is $x^2 + y^2 - 6x - 2y = -6$.

Now Try Exercise 23.

EXAMPLE 3   Solving an Application Problem

The effective broadcast area of a radio station is bounded by the circle

$$x^2 + y^2 = 2{,}500$$

where x and y are measured in miles. Another station's broadcast area is bounded by the circle

$$(x - 100)^2 + (y - 100)^2 = 900$$

Can any location receive both stations?

SOLUTION   It is possible to receive both stations only if their circular broadcast areas overlap. (See Figure 7-5.) This happens when the sum of the radii, r and r', of the two circles is greater than the distance, d, between their centers. That is, $r + r' > d$.

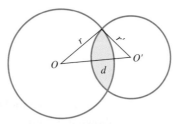

FIGURE 7-5

The center of the circle $x^2 + y^2 = 2{,}500$ is $(x_1, y_1) = (0, 0)$, and its radius r is 50 miles. The center of the circle $(x - 100)^2 + (y - 100)^2 = 900$ is $(x_2, y_2) = (100, 100)$, and its radius r' is 30 miles.

We can use the distance formula to find the distance d between the centers.

$$d = \sqrt{(x_2 - x_1)^2 + (y_2 - y_1)^2}$$

$$d = \sqrt{(100 - 0)^2 + (100 - 0)^2}$$

$$= \sqrt{100^2 + 100^2}$$

$$= \sqrt{100^2 \cdot 2}$$

$$= 100\sqrt{2}$$

$$\approx 141 \text{ miles}$$

The sum of the radii, $r + r'$, of the two circles is $(50 + 30)$ miles, or 80 miles. Since this is less than the distance d between their centers (141 miles), there is no location where both stations can be received.

Self Check 3   In Example 3, if the station at the origin boosted its power to cover the area within $x^2 + y^2 = 9{,}000$, would the coverage overlap?

Now Try Exercise 67.

2. Write an Equation of a Parabola in Standard Form

In Chapter 3, we saw that the graphs of quadratic functions of the forms

$$y = ax^2 + bx + c \quad \text{or} \quad y = a(x - h)^2 + k \ (a \neq 0)$$

were parabolas that open upward or downward. We now discuss parabolas that open to the left or to the right and examine the properties of all parabolas in greater detail.

The Parabola   A **parabola** is the set of all points in a plane equidistant from a line *l* (called the **directrix**) and a fixed point *F* (called the **focus**) that is not on line *l*. See Figure 7-6.

The point on the parabola that is closest to the directrix is called the **vertex,** and the line passing through the vertex and the focus is called the **axis of the parabola.**

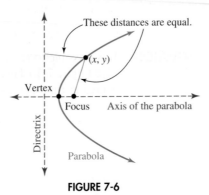

FIGURE 7-6

A basic parabola is one whose vertex occurs at the origin and opens upward, as shown in Figure 7-7. Consider such a parabola with the following characteristics:

FIGURE 7-7

To find the equation of the parabola, we will find the distance from point $P(x, y)$ on the parabola to the focus and find the distance from point $P(x, y)$ to the directrix and set the two distances equal. Using the distance formula, we can find that the distance from $P(x, y)$ to $F(0, p)$.

$$d(PF) = \sqrt{x^2 + (y - p)^2}$$

From the figure, we see that the distance from $P(x, y)$ to the directrix $y = -p$ is:

$$|y - (-p)| = |y + p|$$

We can equate these distances and simplify.

$$\sqrt{x^2 + (y - p)^2} = |y + p|$$

$$x^2 + (y - p)^2 = |y + p|^2 \qquad \text{Square both sides.}$$

$$x^2 + (y - p)^2 = (y + p)^2 \qquad |y + p|^2 = (y + p)^2$$

$$x^2 + y^2 - 2yp + p^2 = y^2 + 2py + p^2 \qquad \text{Expand the binomials.}$$

$$x^2 - 2py = 2py \qquad \text{Subtract } y^2 + p^2 \text{ from both sides.}$$

(1) $$x^2 = 4py \qquad \text{Add } 2py \text{ to both sides.}$$

Equation 1 is one of the **standard equations of a parabola** with vertex at the origin. If $p > 0$ as in Equation 1, the graph of the equation will be a parabola that opens upward. If $p < 0$, the graph of the equation will be a parabola that opens downward.

It can be shown that a parabola whose vertex is at the origin and opens to the left or to the right has an equation of the form $y^2 = 4px$.

The standard equations of a parabola with vertex $V(0, 0)$ and some of the characteristics of the parabola are summarized below.

Standard Form of an Equation of a Parabola with Vertex (0, 0)		
Equation	$x^2 = 4py$	$y^2 = 4px$
Focus	$(0, p)$	$(p, 0)$
Directrix	$y = -p$	$x = -p$
Axis of Symmetry	Vertical y-axis	Horizontal x-axis
$p > 0$	Opens upward	Opens right
$p < 0$	Opens downward	Opens left

Consider the parabola with equation $x^2 = 8y$, which is shown in Figure 7-8. Since the equation of the parabola is written in standard form, $x^2 = 4py$, we know that $4p = 8$ and $p = 2$. Thus, the focus of the parabola is $F(0, p) = F(0, 2)$ and the directrix is $y = -p$ or $y = -2$. Because $p = 2$ and $2 > 0$, the parabola opens upward. The axis of symmetry is a vertical line, which is the y-axis.

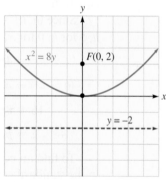

FIGURE 7-8

EXAMPLE 4   **Finding an Equation of a Parabola**

Find an equation of the parabola with vertex at the origin and focus at $(3, 0)$.

SOLUTION   A sketch of the parabola is shown in Figure 7-9. Because the focus is to the right of the vertex, the parabola opens to the right, and because the vertex is the origin, the standard equation is $y^2 = 4px$. The distance between the focus and the vertex is $p = 3$. We can substitute 3 for p in the standard equation to get

$$y^2 = 4px$$

$$y^2 = 4(3)x$$

$$y^2 = 12x$$

An equation of the parabola is $y^2 = 12x$.

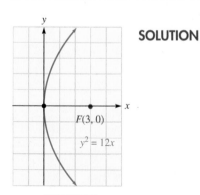

FIGURE 7-9

Self Check 4   Find an equation of the parabola with vertex at the origin and focus at $(-3, 0)$.

Now Try Exercise 31.

In Section 3.4 we used translations to sketch graphs of functions. Translations can also be applied to graphs that are parabolas. The following table summarizes the characteristics of parabolas with vertex at $V(h, k)$.

Standard Form of an Equation of a Parabola with Vertex (h, k)		
Equation	$(x - h)^2 = 4p(y - k)$	$(y - k)^2 = 4p(x - h)$
Focus	$(h, k + p)$	$(h + p, k)$
Directrix	$y = -p + k$	$x = -p + h$
Axis of Symmetry	Vertical $x = h$	Horizontal $y = k$
$p > 0$	Opens upward	Opens right
$p < 0$	Opens downward	Opens left

EXAMPLE 5　Finding an Equation of a Parabola

Find an equation of the parabola that opens upward, has vertex at the point $(4, 5)$, and passes through the point $(0, 7)$.

SOLUTION　Because the parabola opens upward, we will substitute the coordinates of the given vertex and the point into the equation $(x - h)^2 = 4p(y - k)$ and solve for p. Then we will substitute the coordinates of the vertex and the value of p into the previous equation.

Since $(h, k) = (4, 5)$ and the point $(0, 7)$ is on the curve, we can substitute 4 for h, 5 for k, 0 for x, and 7 for y in the standard equation and solve for p.

$$(x - h)^2 = 4p(y - k)$$
$$(0 - 4)^2 = 4p(7 - 5)$$
$$16 = 8p$$
$$2 = p$$

To find an equation of the parabola, we substitute 4 for h, 5 for k, and 2 for p in the standard equation and simplify:

$$(x - h)^2 = 4p(y - k)$$
$$(x - 4)^2 = 4(2)(y - 5)$$
$$(x - 4)^2 = 8(y - 5)$$

The graph of the equation appears in Figure 7-10.

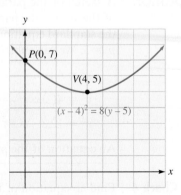

FIGURE 7-10

Self Check 5   Find an equation of the parabola that opens upward, has vertex at (4, 5), and passes through (0, 9).

Now Try Exercise 43.

EXAMPLE 6   **Finding Equations of Two Parabolas**

Find equations of two parabolas with a vertex at (2, 4) that pass through (0, 0).

SOLUTION   The two parabolas are shown in Figure 7-11.

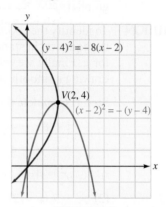

FIGURE 7-11

Part 1: To find the parabola that opens to the left, we use the equation $(y - k)^2 = 4p(x - h)$. Since the curve passes through the point $(x, y) = (0, 0)$ and the vertex $(h, k) = (2, 4)$, we substitute 0 for x, 0 for y, 2 for h, and 4 for k in the standard equation and solve for p:

$$(y - k)^2 = 4p(x - h)$$
$$(0 - 4)^2 = 4p(0 - 2)$$
$$16 = -8p$$
$$-2 = p$$

Since $h = 2$, $k = 4$, $p = -2$, and the parabola opens to the left, its equation is

$$(y - k)^2 = 4p(x - h)$$
$$(y - 4)^2 = 4(-2)(x - 2)$$
$$(y - 4)^2 = -8(x - 2)$$

Part 2: To find an equation of the parabola that opens downward, we use the equation $(x - h)^2 = 4p(y - k)$ and substitute 2 for h, 4 for k, 0 for x, and 0 for y and solve for p:

$$(x - h)^2 = 4p(y - k)$$
$$(0 - 2)^2 = 4p(0 - 4)$$
$$4 = -16p$$
$$p = -\frac{1}{4}$$

Since $h = 2$, $k = 4$, $p = -\frac{1}{4}$, the equation is

$$(x - h)^2 = 4p(y - k)$$
$$(x - 2)^2 = 4\left(-\frac{1}{4}\right)(y - 4) \qquad \text{Substitute 2 for } h, -\frac{1}{4} \text{ for } p, \text{ and 4 for } k.$$
$$(x - 2)^2 = -(y - 4)$$

Self Check 6   Find equations of two parabolas with vertex at $(2, 4)$ and that pass through $(0, 8)$.

Now Try Exercise 45.

4. Graph Parabolas

EXAMPLE 7   **Graphing a Parabola**

Find the vertex and y-intercepts of the parabola with the following equation and graph it: $y^2 + 8x - 4y = 28$.

SOLUTION   To identify the coordinates of the vertex, we will complete the square on y and write the equation in standard form. To find the y-intercepts, we will let $x = 0$ and solve for y. Finally, we will graph the parabola by plotting the vertex and y-intercepts and drawing a smooth curve through the points.

Step 1: Complete the square and write the equation in standard form.

$$y^2 + 8x - 4y = 28$$

$$y^2 - 4y = -8x + 28 \qquad \text{Subtract } 8x \text{ from both sides.}$$

$$y^2 - 4y + 4 = -8x + 28 + 4 \qquad \text{Add 4 to both sides.}$$

(2) $\qquad (y - 2)^2 = -8(x - 4) \qquad \text{Factor both sides.}$

Equation 2 represents a parabola opening to the left with vertex at $(4, 2)$.

Step 2: Find the y-intercept.

To find the y-intercepts, we substitute 0 for x in Equation 2 and solve for y.

$$(y - 2)^2 = -8(x - 4)$$

$$(y - 2)^2 = -8(0 - 4) \qquad \text{Substitute 0 for } x.$$

$$y^2 - 4y + 4 = 32 \qquad \text{Remove parentheses.}$$

(3) $\quad y^2 - 4y - 28 = 0$

We can use the quadratic formula to find that the roots of Equation 3 are $y \approx 7.7$ and $y \approx -3.7$. So the points with coordinates of approximately $(0, 7.7)$ and $(0, -3.7)$ lie on the graph of the parabola and are the y-intercepts.

Step 3: Graph the parabola.

We can use the information above and the knowledge that the graph opens to the left and has vertex at $(4, 2)$ to draw the graph, as shown in Figure 7-12.

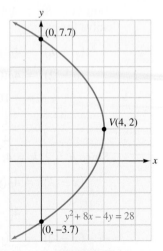

FIGURE 7-12

Self Check 7 Find the vertex and y-intercepts of the parabola with an equation of $y^2 - x + 2y = 3$. Then graph it.

Now Try Exercise 53.

ACCENT ON TECHNOLOGY **Graphing Parabolas**

Parabolas with a vertical axis, such as $y = x^2 - 3x + 5$, can be entered into a graphing calculator as it is written. However, a parabola with a horizontal axis, such as $y^2 = 4x - 4$, cannot be entered into a calculator in this form. To graph this parabola using a graphing calculator, we must first solve for y by taking the square root of both sides, getting the equations $y = \sqrt{4x - 4}$ and $y = -\sqrt{4x - 4}$.

Enter the equations.   Set an appropriate WINDOW.   GRAPH the equations.

FIGURE 7-13

5. Solve Applied Problems Involving Parabolas

Parabolas arise in many real world settings. A few examples are:

- As shown in the illustration, a bouncing ball travels in a series of parabolic paths. Air resistance causes the ball to deviate slightly from a perfect parabola shape.

- A satellite dish is a type of parabolic antenna designed with the specific purpose of transmitting signals to and/or receiving signals from satellites.

• Objects extended in space often follow parabolic paths, such as a diver jumping from a diving board or cliff. The diver may follow a complex motion, but his center of mass of the object forms a parabola.

EXAMPLE 8 Solving an Applied Problem

The Gateway Arch in St. Louis has a shape that approximates a parabola. (See Figure 7-14.) The vertex of the parabola is $V(0, 630)$ and the x-intercepts are $(315, 0)$ and $(-315, 0)$. Find an equation of the parabola that models the arch.

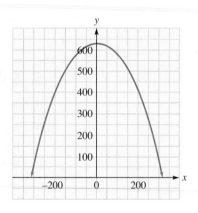

FIGURE 7-14

SOLUTION To find an equation of the parabola that opens downward, we use the equation $(x - h)^2 = 4p(y - k)$ and substitute the vertex $V(0, 630)$ and the x-intercept $(315, 0)$ and solve for p. Then, we write an equation of the parabola.

We substitute 0 for h, 630 for k, 315 for x, and 0 for y and solve for p:

$$(x - h)^2 = 4p(y - \boldsymbol{k})$$

$$(\boldsymbol{315} - 0)^2 = 4p(\boldsymbol{0} - \boldsymbol{630})$$

$$99{,}225 = -2{,}520p$$

$$p = -\frac{99{,}225}{2{,}520}$$

$$= -\frac{315}{8}$$

Since $h = 0$, $k = 630$, $p = -\frac{315}{8}$, an equation is

$$(x - h)^2 = 4p(y - k)$$

$$(x - 0)^2 = 4\left(-\frac{315}{8}\right)(y - 630) \qquad \text{Substitute 0 for } h, \ -\frac{315}{8} \text{ for } p, \text{ and 630 for } k.$$

$$x^2 = -\frac{315}{2}(y - 630) \qquad \text{Simplify.}$$

Self Check 8 What is the height of the arch 115 feet from the base?

Now Try Exercise 83.

EXAMPLE 9   **Solving an Applied Problem**

If water is propelled straight up by a "super nozzle" during a water fountain show in Las Vegas, the equation $s = 128 - 16t^2$ expresses the water's height s (in feet), t seconds after it is propelled. Find the maximum height reached by the water.

SOLUTION   The graph of $s = 128t - 16t^2$, which expresses the height s of the water t seconds after it is propelled, is the parabola shown in Figure 7-15. To find the maximum height reached by the water, we find the s-coordinate k of the vertex of the parabola. To find k, we write the equation of the parabola in standard form by completing the square on t.

$$s = 128t - 16t^2$$

$$16t^2 - 128t = -s \qquad \text{Multiply both sides by } -1.$$

$$t^2 - 8t = \frac{-s}{16} \qquad \text{Divide both sides by 16.}$$

$$t^2 - 8t + 16 = \frac{-s}{16} + 16 \qquad \text{Add 16 to both sides to complete the square.}$$

$$(t - 4)^2 = \frac{-s + 256}{16} \qquad \text{Factor } t^2 - 8t + 16 \text{ and combine terms.}$$

$$(t - 4)^2 = -\frac{1}{16}(s - 256) \qquad \text{Factor out } -\frac{1}{16}.$$

This equation indicates that the maximum height is 256 feet.

Caution

The parabola shown in Figure 7-15 is not the path of the water. The water goes straight up and straight down.

FIGURE 7-15

Self Check 9 At what time will the water strike the ground? (*Hint:* Find the t-intercept.)

Now Try Exercise 79.

Self Check Answers   **1.** $x^2 + y^2 + 4x - 2y - 11 = 0$ **2.**   **3.** no

4. $y^2 = -12x$ **5.** $(x - 4)^2 = 4(y - 5)$ **6.** $(y - 4)^2 = -8(x - 2)$ or
$(x - 2)^2 = y - 4$ **7.** vertex $(-4, -1)$; y-intercepts $(0, 1), (0, -3)$
8. approximately 376 feet
9. $t = 8$ seconds

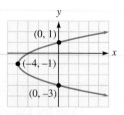

Exercises **7.1**

Getting Ready
You should be able to complete these vocabulary and concept statements before you proceed to the practice exercises.

Fill in the blanks.

1. $(x - 2)^2 + (y + 5)^2 = 9$: center (___, ___);
radius ___

2. $x^2 + y^2 - 36 = 0$: center (___, ___); radius ___

3. $x^2 + y^2 = 5$: center (___, ___); radius ____

4. $2(x - 9)^2 + 2y^2 = 7$: center (___, ___); radius

_____

Determine whether the parabolic graph of the equation opens upward, downward, to the left, or to the right.

5. $y^2 = -4x$: opens _____

6. $y^2 = 10x$: opens _____

7. $x^2 = -8(y - 3)$:
opens _____

8. $(x - 2)^2 = (y + 3)$:
opens _____

Fill in the blanks.

9. A parabola is the set of all points in a plane equidistant from a line, called the _____, and a fixed
point not on the line, called the _____.

10. The general form of a second-degree equation in the
variables x and y is
Ax^2 _____ $= 0$.

Identify the conic as a circle or parabola.

11. $x^2 - 5x + y^2 = 12$

12. $3x^2 + 3y^2 + 18x + 6y = 24$

13. $x^2 - 8y = 6x - 1$ **14.** $2y^2 + 4y - 6x = 4$

Practice
*Write an equation of each circle shown or described.
Write your answer in standard form and then general form.*

15.

16.

17.

18.

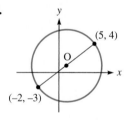

19. Radius of 6; center at the intersection of $3x + y = 1$
and $-2x - 3y = 4$

20. Radius of 8; center at the intersection of $x + 2y = 8$
and $2x - 3y = -5$

Graph each circle.

21. $x^2 + y^2 = 4$

22. $x^2 - 2x + y^2 = 15$

23. $3x^2 + 3y^2 - 12x - 6y = 12$

24. $2x^2 + 2y^2 + 4x - 8y + 2 = 0$

Find the vertex, focus, and directrix of each parabola.

25. $x^2 = 12y$

26. $y^2 = -12y$

27. $(y - 3)^2 = 20x$

28. $x^2 = -\dfrac{1}{2}(y + 5)$

29. $(x + 2)^2 = -24(y - 1)$

30. $(y + 1)^2 = 28(x - 2)$

Find an equation in standard form of each parabola described.

31. Vertex at $(0, 0)$; focus at $(0, 3)$

32. Vertex at $(0, 0)$; focus at $(0, -3)$

33. Vertex at $(0, 0)$; focus at $(-3, 0)$

34. Vertex at $(0, 0)$; focus at $(3, 0)$

35. Vertex at $(3, 5)$; focus at $(3, 2)$

36. Vertex at $(3, 5)$; focus at $(-3, 5)$

37. Vertex at $(3, 5)$; focus at $(3, -2)$

38. Vertex at $(3, 5)$; focus at $(6, 5)$

39. Vertex at $(0, 2)$; directrix at $y = 3$

40. Vertex at $(-3, 4)$; directrix at $y = 2$

41. Vertex at $(1, -5)$; directrix at $x = -1$

42. Vertex at $(3, 5)$; directrix at $x = 6$

43. Vertex at $(2, 2)$; passes through $(0, 0)$

44. Vertex at $(-2, -2)$; passes through $(0, 0)$

45. Vertex at $(-4, 6)$; passes through $(0, 3)$

46. Vertex at $(-2, 3)$; passes through $(0, -3)$

47. Vertex at $(6, 8)$; passes through $(5, 10)$ and $(5, 6)$

48. Vertex at $(2, 3)$; passes through $\left(1, \dfrac{13}{4}\right)$ and $\left(-1, \dfrac{21}{4}\right)$

49. Vertex at $(3, 1)$; passes through $(4, 3)$ and $(2, 3)$

50. Vertex at $(-4, -2)$; passes through $(-3, 0)$ and $\left(\dfrac{9}{4}, 3\right)$

Write each parabola in standard form and graph it.

51. $y = x^2 + 4x + 5$

52. $2x^2 - 12x - 7y = 10$

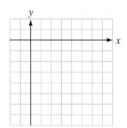

53. $y^2 + 4x - 6y = -1$

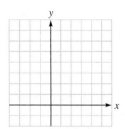

54. $x^2 - 2y - 2x = -7$

55. $y^2 - 4y = 4x - 8$

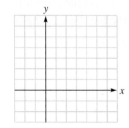

56. $y^2 + 2x - 2y = 5$

57. $y^2 - 4y = -8x + 20$

58. $y^2 - 2y = 9x + 17$

59. $x^2 - 6y + 22 = -4x$

60. $4y^2 - 4y + 16x = 7$

61. $4x^2 - 4x + 32y = 47$

62. $4y^2 - 16x + 17 = 20y$

63. Use a graphing calculator to graph the parabola $y^2 = 4x - 12$. Sketch the parabola by hand and compare the results.

64. Use a graphing calculator to graph the parabola $y^2 + 8x - 24 = 0$. Sketch the parabola by hand and compare the results.

Applications

65. Broadcast range A television tower broadcasts a signal with a circular range, as shown in the illustration. Can a city 50 miles east and 70 miles north of the tower receive the signal?

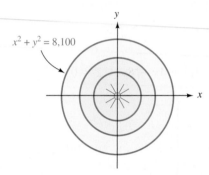

66. Warning sirens A tornado warning siren can be heard in the circular range shown in the illustration. Can a person 4 miles west and 5 miles south of the siren hear its sound?

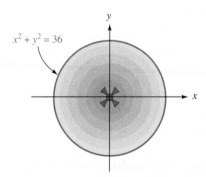

67. Radio translators Some radio stations extend their broadcast range by installing a translator—a remote device that receives the signal and retransmits it. A station with a broadcast range given by $x^2 + y^2 = 1,600$, where x and y are in miles, installs a translator with a broadcast area bounded by $x^2 + y^2 - 70y + 600 = 0$. Find the greatest distance from the main transmitter that the signal can be received.

68. Ripples in a pond When a stone is thrown into the center of a pond, the ripples spread out in a circular pattern, moving at a rate of 3 feet per second. If the stone is dropped at the point $(0, 0)$ in the illustration, when will the ripple reach the seagull floating at the point $(15, 36)$?

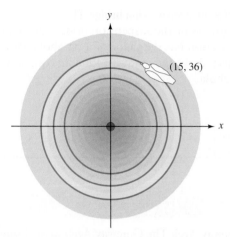

(15, 36)

69. Writing equations of circles Find an equation in standard form of the circle whose outer rim is the circular arch shown in the illustration.

8 feet

70. Writing equations of circles The shape of the window shown is a combination of a rectangle and a semicircle. Find an equation of the circle of which the semicircle is a part.

14 feet

10 feet

71. Meshing gears For design purposes, the large gear is described by the circle $x^2 + y^2 = 16$. The smaller gear is a circle centered at $(7, 0)$ and tangent to the larger circle. Find an equation in standard form of the smaller gear.

(7, 0)

72. Walkways The walkway shown is bounded by the two circles $x^2 + y^2 = 2{,}500$ and $(x - 10)^2 + y^2 = 900$, measured in feet. Find the largest and the smallest width of the walkway.

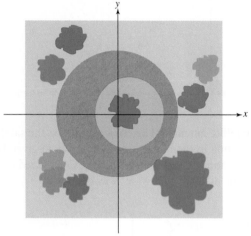

73. Solar furnaces A parabolic mirror collects rays of the sun and concentrates them at its focus. In the illustration, how far from the vertex of the parabolic mirror will it get the hottest? (All measurements are in feet.)

$y^2 = 8x$

74. Searchlight reflectors A parabolic mirror reflects light in a beam when the light source is placed at its focus. In the illustration, how far from the vertex of the parabolic reflector should the light source be placed? (All measurements are in feet.)

$y^2 = 12x$

75. Writing equations of parabolas Derive an equation of the parabolic arch shown.

10 meters

30 meters

76. Projectiles The cannonball in the illustration follows the parabolic trajectory $y = 30x - x^2$. How far short of the castle does it land?

77. Satellite antennas The cross section of the satellite antenna in the illustration is a parabola given by the equation $y = \frac{1}{16}x^2$, with distances measured in feet. If the dish is 8 feet wide, how deep is it?

78. Design of a satellite antenna The cross section of the satellite antenna shown is a parabola with the pickup at its focus. Find the distance d from the pickup to the center of the dish.

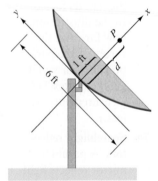

79. Toy rockets A toy rocket is s feet above the Earth at the end of t seconds, where $s = -16t^2 + 80\sqrt{3}t$. Find the maximum height of the rocket.

80. Operating a resort A resort owner plans to build and rent n cabins for d dollars per week. The price d that she can charge for each cabin depends on the number of cabins she builds, where $d = -45\left(\frac{n}{32} - \frac{1}{2}\right)$. Find the number of cabins she should build to maximize her weekly income.

81. Design of a parabolic reflector Find the outer diameter (the length $\overline{AB}$) of the parabolic reflector shown.

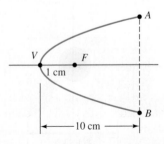

82. Design of a suspension bridge The cable between the towers of the suspension bridge shown in the illustration has the shape of a parabola with vertex 15 feet above the roadway. Find an equation of the parabola.

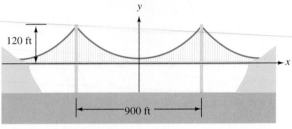

83. Gateway Arch The Gateway Arch in St. Louis has a shape that approximates a parabola. (See the illustration.) Find the width w of the arch 200 feet above the ground.

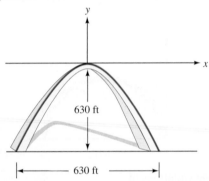

84. Building tunnels A construction firm plans to build a tunnel whose arch is in the shape of a parabola. (See the illustration.) The tunnel will span a two-lane highway 8 meters wide. To allow safe passage for vehicles, the tunnel must be 5 meters high at a distance of 1 meter from the tunnel's edge. Find the maximum height of the tunnel.

Discovery and Writing

85. Show that the standard form of the equation of a parabola $(y - 2)^2 = 8(x - 1)$ is a special case of the general form of a second-degree equation in two variables.

86. Show that the standard form of the equation of a circle $(x + 2)^2 + (y - 5)^2 = 36$ is a special case of the general form of a second-degree equation in two variables.

Find an equation, in the form $(x - h)^2 + (y - k)^2 = r^2$, of the circle passing through the given points.

87. $(0, 8)$, $(5, 3)$, and $(4, 6)$

88. $(-2, 0)$, $(2, 8)$, and $(5, -1)$

Find an equation of the parabola passing through the given points. Give the equation in the form $y = ax^2 + bx + c$.

89. $(1, 8)$, $(-2, -1)$, and $(2, 15)$

90. $(1, -3)$, $(-2, 12)$, and $(-1, 3)$

91. Ballistics A stone tossed upward is s feet above the Earth after t seconds, where $s = -16t^2 + 128t$. Show that the stone's height x seconds after it is thrown is equal to its height x seconds before it hits the ground.

92. Ballistics Show that the stone in Exercise 91 reaches its greatest height in one-half of the time it takes until it strikes the ground.

Review

Find the number that must be added to make each binomial a perfect square trinomial.

93. $x^2 + 4x + $ ___

94. $y^2 - 12y + $ ___

95. $x^2 - 7x + $ _____

96. $y^2 + 11y + $ _____

Solve each equation.

97. $x^2 + 4x = 5$

98. $y^2 - 12y = 13$

99. $x^2 - 7x - 18 = 0$

100. $y^2 + 11y = -18$

7.2   The Ellipse

In this section, we will learn to

1. Understand the definition of an ellipse.

2. Write an equation of an ellipse.

3. Graph ellipses.

4. Solve applied problems using ellipses.

Washington, D.C., has many historical sites. Many people touring the United States Capitol visit the National Statuary Hall, originally the chamber of the House of Representatives. It is said that because of the oval shape of the ceiling, politicians on one side of the hall could eavesdrop on politicians talking on the opposite side of the hall. Such rooms are often called *whispering galleries*. Problem 54 in the Exercises discusses some properties of whispering galleries.

Today, Statuary Hall houses a collection of statues donated by individual states. Sam Houston, Daniel Webster, and Will Rogers are among those honored with a statue.

A third important conic is an oval-shaped curve, called an *ellipse*.

1. Understand the Definition of an Ellipse

The Ellipse   An **ellipse** is the set of all points P in a plane such that the sum of the distances from P to two other fixed points F and F' is a positive constant.

We can illustrate this definition by showing how to construct an ellipse. To do so, we place two thumbtacks fairly close together, as in Figure 7-16. We then tie each end of a piece of string to a thumbtack, catch the loop with the point of a pencil, and (while keeping the string stretched tightly) draw the ellipse. Note that $d(F_1P) + d(PF_2)$ will be a positive constant.

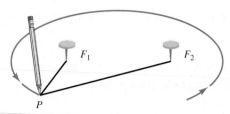

FIGURE 7-16

As we see in the figure, the graph of an ellipse is egg-shaped. The graphs of two ellipses are shown in Figure 7-17.

Ellipse with a horizontal axis   Ellipse with a vertical axis

(a)   (b)

FIGURE 7-17

Ellipses occur in many real-life settings.

- Rotating an ellipse about its axis produces a football.

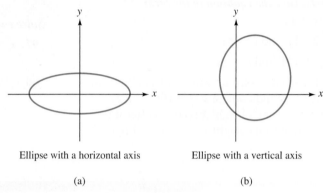

- Planets such as Mars revolve around the sun in an elliptical path.

- A workout machine, called an *elliptic trainer*, uses elliptical movements for exercise without causing damage to the joints.

- An ellipse has an interesting property. Any light or sound that starts at one focus will be reflected through the other. This property is the basis of a medical procedure for treating kidney stones, called **lithotripsy.** The patient is placed in an elliptical tank of water with the kidney stone at one focus. Shock waves from a controlled explosion at the other focus are concentrated on the stone, pulverizing it. See Figure 7-18. Though some machines are still in use today, most are being replaced and patients lie down on a soft water-filled cushion.

FIGURE 7-18

2. Write an Equation of an Ellipse

In the ellipse shown in Figure 7-19(a), the fixed points F and F' are called **foci** (each is a **focus**), the midpoint of the chord FF' is called the **center,** and the chord VV' is called the **major axis.** Each of the endpoints V and V' of the major axis is called a **vertex.** The chord BB', perpendicular to the major axis and passing through the center C of the ellipse, is called the **minor axis.**

Deriving the Standard Form for an Equation of an Ellipse

To derive an equation of the ellipse shown in Figure 7-19(b), we note that point O is the midpoint of chord FF' and let $d(OF) = d(OF') = c$, where $c > 0$. Then the coordinates of point F are $(c, 0)$, and the coordinates of F' are $(-c, 0)$. We also let $P(x, y)$ be any point on the ellipse.

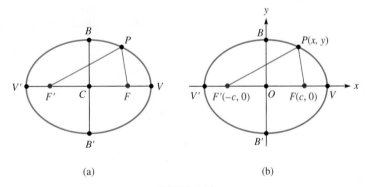

(a)   (b)

FIGURE 7-19

By the definition of an ellipse, $d(F'P) + d(PF)$ must be a positive constant, which we will call $2a$. Thus,

(1) $d(F'P) + d(PF) = 2a$

We can use the distance formula to compute the lengths of $F'P$ and PF,

$$d(F'P) = \sqrt{[x - (-c)]^2 + y^2} \quad \text{and} \quad d(PF) = \sqrt{(x - c)^2 + y^2}$$

and substitute these values into Equation 1 to obtain

$$\sqrt{[x - (-c)]^2 + y^2} + \sqrt{(x - c)^2 + y^2} = 2a$$

or

(2) $\sqrt{[x + c]^2 + y^2} = 2a - \sqrt{(x - c)^2 + y^2}$ Subtract $\sqrt{(x - c)^2 + y^2}$ from both sides.

We can square both sides of Equation 2 and simplify to get

$$(x + c)^2 + y^2 = 4a^2 - 4a\sqrt{(x - c)^2 + y^2} + [(x - c)^2 + y^2]$$

$$x^2 + 2cx + c^2 + y^2 = 4a^2 - 4a\sqrt{(x - c)^2 + y^2} + x^2 - 2cx + c^2 + y^2$$

$$4cx = 4a^2 - 4a\sqrt{(x - c)^2 + y^2}$$

$$cx = a^2 - a\sqrt{(x - c)^2 + y^2}$$

$$cx - a^2 = -a\sqrt{(x - c)^2 + y^2}$$

We square both sides again and simplify to get

$$c^2x^2 - 2a^2cx + a^4 = a^2[(x - c)^2 + y^2]$$

$$c^2x^2 - 2a^2cx + a^4 = a^2(x^2 - 2cx + c^2 + y^2)$$

$$c^2x^2 - 2a^2cx + a^4 = a^2x^2 - 2a^2cx + a^2c^2 + a^2y^2$$

$$c^2x^2 + a^4 = a^2x^2 + a^2c^2 + a^2y^2$$

$$a^4 - a^2c^2 = a^2x^2 - c^2x^2 + a^2y^2$$

(3) $$a^2(a^2 - c^2) = (a^2 - c^2)x^2 + a^2y^2$$

Because the shortest distance between two points is a line segment, $d(F'P) + d(PF) > d(F'F)$. Therefore, $2a > 2c$. Thus, $a > c$, and $a^2 - c^2$ is a positive number, which we will call b^2. Letting $b^2 = a^2 - c^2$ and substituting into Equation 3, we have

(4) $a^2b^2 = b^2x^2 + a^2y^2$

Dividing both sides of Equation 4 by a^2b^2 gives the equation

$$\frac{x^2}{a^2} + \frac{y^2}{b^2} = 1 \qquad \text{where } a > b > 0$$

This is the standard form of an equation of an ellipse centered at the origin and major axis on the x-axis.

To find the coordinates of the vertices V and V', we substitute 0 for y and solve for x:

$$\frac{x^2}{a^2} + \frac{y^2}{b^2} = 1$$

$$\frac{x^2}{a^2} + \frac{0^2}{b^2} = 1$$

$$\frac{x^2}{a^2} = 1$$

$$x^2 = a^2$$

$$x = a \quad \text{or} \quad x = -a$$

Since the coordinates of V are $(a, 0)$ and the coordinates of V' are $(-a, 0)$, a is the distance between the center of the ellipse and either of its vertices. Thus, the center of the ellipse is the midpoint of the major axis.

To find the coordinates of B and B', we substitute 0 for x and solve for y:

$$\frac{x^2}{a^2} + \frac{y^2}{b^2} = 1$$

$$\frac{0^2}{a^2} + \frac{y^2}{b^2} = 1$$

$$y^2 = b^2$$

$$y = b \quad \text{or} \quad y = -b$$

Since the coordinates of B are $(0, b)$ and the coordinates of B' are $(0, -b)$, the distance between the center of the ellipse and either endpoint of the minor axis is b. We have the following results.

The Ellipse: Major Axis on x-Axis, Center at (0, 0)

The standard form of an equation of an ellipse with center at the origin and the major axis (horizontal) on the x-axis is

$$\frac{x^2}{a^2} + \frac{y^2}{b^2} = 1 \quad \text{where} \quad a > b > 0$$

Vertices (ends of the major axis): $V(a, 0)$ and $V'(-a, 0)$

Length of major axis: $2a$

Ends of the minor axis: $B(0, b)$ and $B'(0, -b)$

Length of minor axis: $2b$

Foci: $F(c, 0)$ and $F'(-c, 0)$ where $c^2 = a^2 - b^2$

A similar equation results if the ellipse has a major axis on the y-axis and center at the origin.

The Ellipse: Major Axis on y-Axis, Center at (0, 0)

The standard form of an equation of an ellipse with center at the origin and the major axis (vertical) on the y-axis is

$$\frac{x^2}{b^2} + \frac{y^2}{a^2} = 1 \quad \text{where } a > b > 0$$

Vertices (ends of the major axis): $V(0, a)$ and $V'(0, -a)$

Length of major axis: $2a$

Ends of the minor axis: $B(b, 0)$ and $B'(-b, 0)$

Length of minor axis: $2b$

Foci: $F(0, c)$ and $F'(0, -c)$ where $c^2 = a^2 - b^2$

EXAMPLE 1   **Writing an Equation of an Ellipse**

Find an equation of the ellipse with center at the origin, major axis of length 6 units located on the x-axis, and minor axis of length 4 units.

SOLUTION   To find an equation, we determine a and b and substitute into the standard equation of an ellipse with center at the origin and major axis on the x-axis

$$\frac{x^2}{a^2} + \frac{y^2}{b^2} = 1$$

The center of the ellipse is given to be the origin and the length of the major axis is 6. Since the length of the major axis of an ellipse centered at the origin is $2a$, we have $2a = 6$ or $a = 3$. The coordinates of the vertices are $(3, 0)$ and $(-3, 0)$, as shown in Figure 7-20.

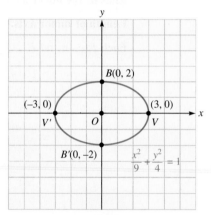

FIGURE 7-20

The length of the minor axis is given to be 4. Since the length of the minor axis of an ellipse centered at the origin is $2b$, we have $2b = 4$ or $b = 2$. The coordinates of B and B' are $(0, 2)$ and $(0, -2)$.

To find an equation of the ellipse, we substitute 3 for a and 2 for b in the standard equation of an ellipse with center at the origin and major axis on the x-axis.

$$\frac{x^2}{a^2} + \frac{y^2}{b^2} = 1$$

$$\frac{x^2}{3^2} + \frac{y^2}{2^2} = 1$$

$$\frac{x^2}{9} + \frac{y^2}{4} = 1$$

Self Check 1   Find an equation of the ellipse with center at the origin, major axis of length 10 on the y-axis, and minor axis of length 8.

Now Try Exercise 15.

EXAMPLE 2   **Writing an Equation of an Ellipse**

Find an equation of the ellipse with center at the origin, focus at $\left(2\sqrt{3}, 0\right)$, and vertex at $(4, 0)$.

SOLUTION   Because the vertex and focus are on the x-axis, the major axis of the ellipse is on the x-axis. (See Figure 7.21.) To find an equation of the ellipse, we will determine a^2 and b^2 and substitute into the standard equation

$$\frac{x^2}{a^2} + \frac{y^2}{b^2} = 1$$

The distance between the center of the ellipse and the vertex is $a = 4$. The distance between the focus and the center is $c = 2\sqrt{3}$.

Since $b^2 = a^2 - c^2$, we can substitute 4 for a and $2\sqrt{3}$ for c and solve for b^2:

$$b^2 = a^2 - c^2$$

$$b^2 = 4^2 - \left(2\sqrt{3}\right)^2$$

$$= 16 - 12$$

$$= 4$$

To find an equation of the ellipse, we substitute 16 for a^2, and 4 for b^2 in the standard equation.

$$\frac{x^2}{a^2} + \frac{y^2}{b^2} = 1$$

$$\frac{x^2}{16} + \frac{y^2}{4} = 1$$

The graph of the ellipse $\frac{x^2}{16} + \frac{y^2}{4} = 1$ is shown in the figure.

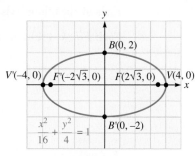

FIGURE 7-21

Self Check 2   Find an equation of the ellipse with center at the origin, focus at $\left(0, 2\sqrt{3}\right)$, and vertex at $(0, 4)$.

Now Try Exercise 17.

To translate an ellipse to a new position centered at the point (h, k) instead of the origin, we replace x and y in the standard equations with $x - h$ and $y - k$, respectively, to get the following results.

The Ellipse: Major Axis Horizontal, Center at (h, k)

The standard form of an equation of an ellipse with center at (h, k) and major axis horizontal is

$$\frac{(x - h)^2}{a^2} + \frac{(y - k)^2}{b^2} = 1 \quad \text{where } a > b > 0$$

Vertices (ends of the major axis): $V(a + h, k)$ and $V'(-a + h, k)$

Ends of the minor axis: $B(h, b + k)$ and $B'(h, -b + k)$

Foci: $F(h + c, k)$ and $F'(h - c, k)$ where $c^2 = a^2 - b^2$

There is a similar result when the major axis is vertical.

The Ellipse: Major Axis Vertical, Center at (h, k)

The standard form of an equation of an ellipse with center at (h, k) and major axis vertical is

$$\frac{(x - h)^2}{b^2} + \frac{(y - k)^2}{a^2} = 1 \quad \text{where } a > b > 0$$

Vertices (ends of the major axis): $V(h, a + k)$ and $V'(h, -a + k)$

Ends of the minor axis: $B(b + h, k)$ and $B'(-b + h, k)$

Foci: $F(h, k + c)$ and $F'(h, k - c)$ where $c^2 = a^2 - b^2$

In each case, the length of the major axis is $2a$, and the length of the minor axis is $2b$.

EXAMPLE 3   **Writing an Equation of an Ellipse**

Find an equation of the ellipse with focus at $(-1, 7)$ and vertices at $V(-1, 8)$ and $V'(-1, -2)$.

SOLUTION   We will use the coordinates of the focus and the vertices to determine the center of the ellipse and a and b. We will then substitute these coordinates into the appropriate standard equation of an ellipse. Because the major axis passes through points V and V', we see that the major axis is a vertical line that is parallel to the y-axis. So the standard equation to use is

$$\frac{(x - h)^2}{b^2} + \frac{(y - k)^2}{a^2} = 1 \quad \text{where } a > b > 0.$$

Since the midpoint of the major axis is the center of the ellipse, the coordinates of the center are $(-1, 3)$, as in Figure 7-22.

From Figure 7-22, we see that the distance between the center of the ellipse and either vertex is $a = 5$. We also see that the distance between the focus and the center is $c = 4$.

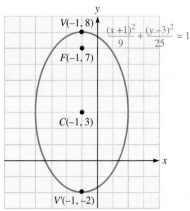

$$\frac{(x+1)^2}{9} + \frac{(y-3)^2}{25} = 1$$

FIGURE 7-22

Since $b^2 = a^2 - c^2$ is an ellipse, we can substitute 5 for a and 4 for c and solve for b^2:

$$b^2 = a^2 - c^2$$
$$= 5^2 - 4^2$$
$$= 9$$

To find an equation of the ellipse, we substitute -1 for h, 3 for k, 25 for a^2, and 9 for b^2 in the standard equation and simplify:

$$\frac{(x - h)^2}{b^2} + \frac{(y - k)^2}{a^2} = 1$$
$$\frac{[x - (-1)]^2}{9} + \frac{(y - 3)^2}{25} = 1$$
$$\frac{(x + 1)^2}{9} + \frac{(y - 3)^2}{25} = 1$$

Self Check 3 Find an equation of the ellipse with focus at $(3, 1)$ and vertices at $V(5, 1)$ and $V'(-5, 1)$.

Now Try Exercise 29.

3. Graph Ellipses

EXAMPLE 4   **Graphing an Ellipse**

Graph the ellipse $\dfrac{x^2}{49} + \dfrac{y^2}{4} = 1$.

SOLUTION   To graph the ellipse, we will first determine the coordinates of the vertices and end-points of the minor axis. We will then plot these points and draw an ellipse through them.

Because the equation is the standard form of an ellipse centered at the origin with major axis on the x-axis, we know that the center of the ellipse is at $(0, 0)$ and that the vertices lie on the x-axis. Because $a = 7$, the vertices are 7 units to the right and left of the origin at points $(7, 0)$ and $(-7, 0)$. Because $b^2 = 4$, $b = 2$, and the endpoints of the minor axis are 2 units above and below the origin at points $(0, 2)$ and $(0, -2)$. Using these points, we can sketch the ellipse shown in Figure 7-23.

Comment

In Example 4, note that $49 > 4$. Because 49 is the denominator of the x^2 term, the axis of the ellipse is horizontal and is the x-axis.

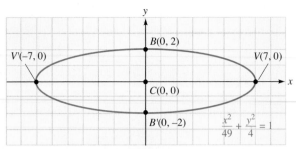

FIGURE 7-23

Self Check 4   Graph the ellipse $\dfrac{x^2}{4} + \dfrac{y^2}{9} = 1$.

Now Try Exercise 35.

EXAMPLE 5   Graphing an Ellipse

Graph the ellipse $\dfrac{(x + 2)^2}{4} + \dfrac{(y - 2)^2}{9} = 1$.

SOLUTION   The equation is the standard form of the equation of an ellipse whose major axis is vertical and whose center is at $(-2, 2)$. We will use translations to graph the ellipse.

Because $a^2 = 9$, we have $a = 3$ and the vertices are 3 units above and 3 units below the center at points $(-2, 5)$ and $(-2, -1)$. Because $b^2 = 4$, we have $b = 2$ and the endpoints of the minor axis are 2 units to the right and 2 units to the left of the center at points $(0, 2)$ and $(-4, 2)$. Using these points, we can sketch the ellipse as shown in Figure 7-24.

Comment

In Example 5, note that $9 < 4$. Because 9 is the denominator of the y^2 term, the axis of the ellipse is vertical.

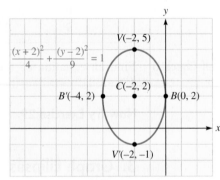

FIGURE 7-24

Self Check 5   Graph the ellipse $\dfrac{(x - 2)^2}{9} + \dfrac{(y + 1)^2}{25} = 1$.

Now Try Exercise 39.

EXAMPLE 6   Graphing an Ellipse

Graph: $4x^2 + 9y^2 - 16x - 18y = 11$.

SOLUTION   We write the equation in standard form by completing the square on x and y and then use translations to graph the ellipse.

$$4x^2 + 9y^2 - 16x - 18y = 11$$

$$4x^2 - 16x + 9y^2 - 18y = 11$$

$$4(x^2 - 4x) + 9(y^2 - 2y) = 11$$

$$4(x^2 - 4x + 4) + 9(y^2 - 2y + 1) = 11 + 16 + 9$$

$$4(x - 2)^2 + 9(y - 1)^2 = 36$$

$$\frac{(x - 2)^2}{9} + \frac{(y - 1)^2}{4} = 1$$

We can now see that the graph is an ellipse with center at (2, 1) and major axis parallel to the x-axis. Because $a^2 = 9$, we have $a = 3$ and the vertices are 3 units to the left and right of the center at (–1, 1) and (5, 1). Because $b^2 = 4$, we have $b = 2$ and the endpoints of the minor axis are 2 units above and below the center at (2, –1) and (2, 3). Using these points, we can sketch the ellipse as shown in Figure 7-25.

Caution

Circles are ellipses, but only some ellipses are circles. If the coefficients of x^2 and y^2 in an equation of an ellipse are equal, the ellipse is a circle. If the coefficients of x^2 and y^2 are not equal, the ellipse is not a circle.

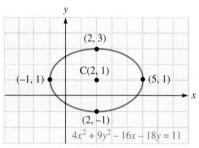

FIGURE 7-25

Self Check 6   Graph: $4x^2 + 9y^2 - 8x + 36y = -4$.

Now Try Exercise 47.

ACCENT ON TECHNOLOGY   **Graphing Ellipses**

To use a graphing calculator to graph $\frac{(x + 2)^2}{4} + \frac{(y - 2)^2}{25} = 1$, we must solve for y in terms of x.

$$25(x + 2)^2 + 4(y - 1)^2 = 100$$ Multiply both sides by 100.

$$4(y - 1)^2 = 100 - 25(x + 2)^2$$ Subtract $25(x + 2)^2$ from both sides.

$$(y - 1)^2 = \frac{100 - 25(x + 2)^2}{4}$$ Divide both sides by 4.

$$y - 1 = \pm\frac{\sqrt{100 - 25(x + 2)^2}}{2}$$ Take the square root of both sides.

$$y = 1 \pm \frac{\sqrt{100 - 25(x + 2)^2}}{2}$$ Add 1 to both sides.

$$y = 1 + \frac{\sqrt{100 - 25(x + 2)^2}}{2} \quad \text{or} \quad y = 1 - \frac{\sqrt{100 - 25(x + 2)^2}}{2}$$

Enter the equations.

Set a WINDOW.

GRAPH **the equations.**

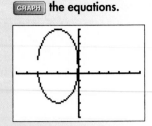

FIGURE 7-26

The eccentricity of an ellipse provides a measure of how much the curve resembles a true circle. Specifically, the eccentricity of a true circle equals 0.

4. Solve Applied Problems Using Ellipses

EXAMPLE 7   **Solving an Application Problem**

The orbit of the Earth is approximately an ellipse, with the sun at one focus. The ratio of c to a (called the **eccentricity** of the ellipse) is about $\frac{1}{62}$, and the length of the major axis is approximately 186,000,000 miles. How close does the Earth get to the sun?

SOLUTION   We will assume that the ellipse has its center at the origin and vertices V' and V at $(-93,000,000, 0)$ and $(93,000,000, 0)$, as shown in Figure 7-27.

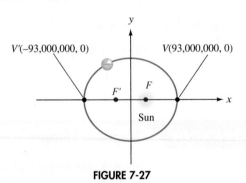

FIGURE 7-27

Because the eccentricity $\frac{c}{a}$ is given to be $\frac{1}{62}$ and $a = 93,000,000$, we have

$$\frac{c}{a} = \frac{1}{62}$$

$$c = \frac{1}{62}a$$

$$c = \frac{1}{62}(93,000,000)$$

$$= 1,500,000$$

The distance $d(FV)$ is the shortest distance between the Earth and the Sun. (You'll be asked to prove this in Exercise 62.) Thus,

$$d(FV) = a - c = 93,000,000 - 1,500,000 = 91,500,000 \text{ mi}$$

The Earth's point of closest approach to the Sun (called the **perihelion**) is approximately 91.5 million miles.

Self Check 7   Find the eccentricity of the ellipse $\dfrac{(x + 2)^2}{9} + \dfrac{(y - 5)^2}{25} = 1$.

Now Try Exercise 57.

The eccentricity of an ellipse provides a measure of how much the curve resembles a true circle. Specifically, the eccentricity of a true circle equals 0. We can use the eccentricity of an ellipse to judge its shape. If the eccentricity is close to 1, the ellipse is relatively flat, as in the ellipse shown.

If the eccentricity is close to 0, the ellipse is more circular, as shown.

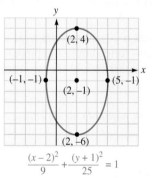

Since the eccentricity of the Earth's orbit is $\frac{1}{62}$, the Earth's orbit is almost a circle.

Self Check Answers   **1.** $\dfrac{x^2}{16} + \dfrac{y^2}{25} = 1$ **2.** $\dfrac{x^2}{4} + \dfrac{y^2}{16} = 1$ **3.** $\dfrac{x^2}{25} + \dfrac{(y - 1)^2}{16} = 1$

4.

5.

$\dfrac{(x - 2)^2}{9} + \dfrac{(y + 1)^2}{25} = 1$

6.
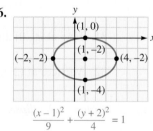

$\dfrac{(x - 1)^2}{9} + \dfrac{(y + 2)^2}{4} = 1$

7. $\dfrac{4}{5}$

Exercises **7.2**

Getting Ready

You should be able to complete these vocabulary and concept statements before you proceed to the practice exercises.

Fill in the blanks.

1. An ellipse is the set of all points in the plane such that the _____ of the distances from two fixed points is a positive _____.

2. Each of the two fixed points in the definition of an ellipse is called a _____ of the ellipse.

3. The chord that joins the _____ is called the major axis of the ellipse.

4. The chord through the center of an ellipse and perpendicular to the major axis is called the _____ axis.

5. In the ellipse $\frac{x^2}{a^2} + \frac{y^2}{b^2} = 1$ $(a > b > 0)$, the vertices are $V(\_\_, \_\_)$ and $V'(\_\_, \_\_)$.

6. In an ellipse, the relationship between a, b, and c is _____.

7. To draw an ellipse that is 26 inches wide and 10 inches tall, how long should the piece of string be, and how far apart should the two thumbtacks be?

8. To draw an ellipse that is 20 centimeters wide and 12 centimeters tall, how long should the piece of string be, and how far apart should the two thumbtacks be?

Identify the conic as a circle, parabola, or an ellipse.

9. $x^2 - 6x + y^2 = 7$

10. $5x^2 + 5y^2 + 10y - \frac{24}{5} = 0$

11. $x^2 - 4y + 5 = -2x$

12. $y^2 - 8y = -2x - 20$

13. $7x^2 + 5y^2 - 35 = 0$

14. $5x^2 + 2y^2 - 10x + 4y = 13$

Practice

Write an equation in standard form of the ellipse described. The center of each ellipse is the origin.

15. Major axis of length 8 units located on the x-axis and minor axis of length 6 units

16. Major axis of length 14 units located on the y-axis and minor axis of length 10 units

17. Focus at $(3, 0)$; vertex at $(5, 0)$

18. Focus at $(0, 4)$; vertex at $(0, 7)$

19. Focus at $(0, 1)$; $\frac{4}{3}$ is one-half the length of the minor axis

20. Focus at $(1, 0)$; $\frac{4}{3}$ is one-half the length of the minor axis

21. Focus at $(0, 3)$; major axis equal to 8

22. Focus at $(5, 0)$; major axis equal to 12

Write an equation in standard form of each ellipse described.

23. Center at $(3, 4)$; $a = 3$, $b = 2$; major axis parallel to the y-axis

24. Center at $(3, 4)$; passes through $(3, 10)$ and $(3, -2)$; $b = 2$

25. Center at $(3, 4)$; $a = 3$, $b = 2$; major axis parallel to the x-axis

26. Center at $(3, 4)$; passes through $(8, 4)$ and $(-2, 4)$; $b = 2$

27. Foci at $(-2, 4)$ and $(8, 4)$; $b = 4$

28. Foci at $(8, 5)$ and $(4, 5)$; $b = 3$

29. Vertex at $(6, 4)$; foci at $(-4, 4)$ and $(4, 4)$

30. Center at $(-4, 5)$; $\frac{c}{a} = \frac{1}{3}$; vertex at $(-4, -1)$

31. Foci at $(6, 0)$ and $(-6, 0)$; $\frac{c}{a} = \frac{3}{5}$

32. Vertices at $(2, 0)$ and $(-2, 0)$; $\frac{2b^2}{a} = 2$

Graph each ellipse.

33. $\frac{x^2}{25} + \frac{y^2}{9} = 1$

34. $\frac{x^2}{36} + \frac{y^2}{25} = 1$

35. $\dfrac{x^2}{25} + \dfrac{y^2}{49} = 1$ **36.** $4x^2 + y^2 = 4$

46. $x^2 + 4y^2 - 2x - 16y = -13$

37. $\dfrac{x^2}{16} + \dfrac{(y+2)^2}{36} = 1$ **38.** $(x-1)^2 + \dfrac{4y^2}{25} = 4$

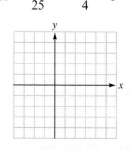

47. $16x^2 + 25y^2 - 160x - 200y + 400 = 0$

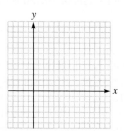

48. $3x^2 + 2y^2 + 7x - 6y = -1$

39. $\dfrac{(x-4)^2}{49} + \dfrac{(y-2)^2}{9} = 1$ **40.** $\dfrac{(x-1)^2}{25} + \dfrac{y^2}{4} = 1$

49. Use a graphing calculator to graph the ellipse $\dfrac{x^2}{4} + \dfrac{y^2}{36} = 1$. Sketch the ellipse by hand and compare the results.

Write each ellipse in standard form.

41. $4x^2 + y^2 - 2y = 15$

42. $4x^2 + 25y^2 + 8x - 96 = 0$

43. $9x^2 + 4y^2 + 18x + 16y - 11 = 0$

50. Use a graphing calculator to graph the ellipse $\dfrac{(x+3)^2}{4} + \dfrac{(y-2)^2}{25} = 1$. Sketch the ellipse by hand and compare the results.

44. $x^2 + 4y^2 - 10x - 8y = -13$

Graph each ellipse.

45. $x^2 + 4y^2 - 4x + 8y + 4 = 0$

Applications
51. Pool tables Find an equation of the outer edge of the elliptical pool table shown below.

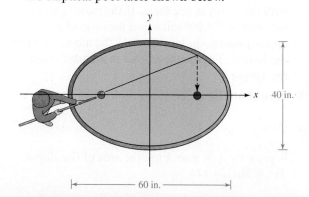

52. Equation of an arch An arch is a semiellipse 12 meters wide and 5 meters high. Write an equation of the ellipse if the ellipse is centered at the origin.

53. Design of a track A track is built in the shape of an ellipse with a maximum length of 100 meters and a maximum width of 60 meters. Write an equation of the ellipse and find its **focal width**. That is, find the length of a chord that is perpendicular to the major axis and passes through either focus of the ellipse.

54. Whispering galleries Any sound from one focus of an ellipse reflects off the ellipse directly back to the other focus. This property explains whispering galleries such as Statuary Hall in Washington, D.C. The ceiling of the whispering gallery shown has the shape of a semiellipse. Find the distance sound travels as it leaves focus F and returns to focus F'.

55. Finding the width of a mirror The oval mirror shown is in the shape of an ellipse. Find the width of the mirror 12 inches above its base.

56. Finding the height of a window The window shown has the shape of an ellipse. Find the height of the window 20 inches from one end.

57. Astronomy The moon has an orbit that is an ellipse, with the Earth at one focus. If the major axis of the orbit is 378,000 miles and the ratio of c to a is approximately $\frac{11}{200}$, how far does the moon get from the Earth? (This farthest point in an orbit is called the **apogee**.)

58. Area of an ellipse The area A of the ellipse

$$\frac{x^2}{a^2} + \frac{y^2}{b^2} = 1$$

is given by $A = \pi ab$. Find the area of the ellipse $9x^2 + 16y^2 = 144$.

Discovery and Writing

59. If F is a focus of the ellipse shown and B is an endpoint of the minor axis, use the distance formula to prove that the length of segment FB is a. (*Hint:* In an ellipse, $b^2 = a^2 - c^2$.)

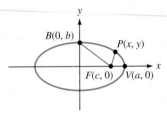

60. If F is a focus of the ellipse shown and P is any point on the ellipse, use the distance formula to show that the length of FP is $a - \frac{c}{a}x$. (*Hint:* In an ellipse, $b^2 = a^2 - c^2$.)

61. Finding the focal width In the ellipse shown, chord AA' passes through the focus F and is perpendicular to the major axis. Show that the length of AA' (called the **focal width**) is $\frac{2b^2}{a}$.

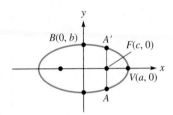

62. Prove that segment FV in Example 7 is the shortest distance between the Earth and the sun. (*Hint:* Refer to Exercise 60.)

63. Constructing an ellipse The ends of a piece of string 6 meters long are attached to two thumbtacks that are 2 meters apart. A pencil catches the loop and draws it tight. As the pencil is moved about the thumbtacks (always keeping the tension), an ellipse is produced, with the thumbtacks as foci. Write an equation of the ellipse. (*Hint:* You'll have to establish a coordinate system.)

64. The distance between point $P(x, y)$ and the point $(0, 2)$ is $\frac{1}{3}$ of the distance of point P from the line $y = 18$. Find an equation of the curve on which point P lies.

65. Prove that $a > b$ in the development of the standard equation of an ellipse.

66. Show that the expansion of the standard equation of an ellipse is a special case of the general second-degree equation in two variables.

67. The eccentricity of an ellipse provides a measure of how much the curve resembles a true circle. Specifically, the eccentricity of a true circle equals 0. Note that the semimajor axis is perpendicular to the axis containing the foci of an ellipse. When analyzing planetary orbits, astronomers plot the relationship between the length of the orbit's semimajor axis (measured in Astronomical Units, where 1 AU = 149,598,000 km) and the eccentricity of the orbit. Use the given data plot to estimate how many of the 75 planets shown follow orbits that are true circles.

Source for right panel: Eccentricity vs. semimajor axis for extrasolar planets. The 75 planets shown were found in a Doppler survey of 1,300 FGKM main sequence stars using the Lick, Keck, and AAT telescopes. The survey was carried out by the California-Carnegie planet search team. http://exoplanets.org/newsframe.html

Review

Let $A = \begin{bmatrix} 3 & -1 & 2 \\ 0 & 2 & -1 \\ 3 & 1 & 1 \end{bmatrix}$, $B = \begin{bmatrix} 1 & 2 \\ 2 & 0 \\ -1 & 1 \end{bmatrix}$, and

$C = \begin{bmatrix} 0 & 1 \\ -1 & 1 \\ -2 & 0 \end{bmatrix}$.

Find each of the following, if possible.

68. AB

69. $B + C$

70. $5B - 2C$

71. $AC + B$

72. The multiplicative inverse of A

7.3 The Hyperbola

In this section, we will learn to

1. Write equations of hyperbolas.

2. Graph hyperbolas.

When a military plane exceeds the speed of sound, it is said to break the sound barrier. When this happens, a visible vapor cloud appears and an explosion-like sound results that we call a *sonic boom*.

As the plane moves faster beyond the speed of sound, a cone shape intersects the ground forming one branch of a curve called a *hyperbola*, a fourth type of conic section. The sonic boom is heard at points inside this hyperbola.

Hyperbolas appear in many real-life applications.

- Hyperbolas are the basis of a navigational system known as LORAN (LOng RAnge Navigation). It is a radio navigation system that uses time intervals between radio signals to determine the location of a ship or aircraft.
- Hyperbolas are the basis for the design of hypoid and spiral bevel gears that are used in motor vehicles.
- Hyperbolas describe the orbits of some comets.

The definition of a hyperbola is similar to the definition of an ellipse, except that we require a constant difference of $2a$ instead of a constant sum.

The Hyperbola   A **hyperbola** is the set of all points P in a plane such that the absolute value of the difference of the distances from point P to two other points in the plane is a positive constant.

Although the definition of an ellipse and a hyperbola are quite similar, their graphs are very different. The graphs of two hyperbolas are shown in Figure 7-28.

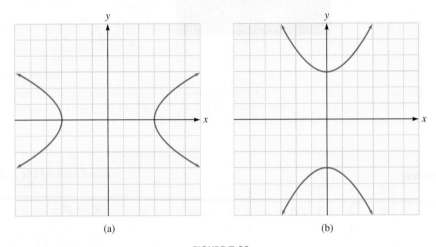

(a)   (b)

FIGURE 7-28

1. Write Equations of Hyperbolas

In the graph of the hyperbola shown in Figure 7-29, points F and F' are called the **foci** of the hyperbola and the midpoint of chord FF' is called the **center.** The points V and V', where the hyperbola intersects FF', are called **vertices.** The segment VV' is called the **transverse axis.**

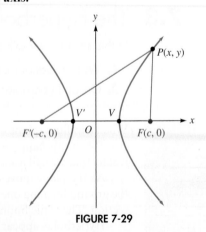

FIGURE 7-29

Deriving the Standard Form of an Equation of a Hyperbola

To develop the equation of the hyperbola centered at the origin, we note that the origin is the midpoint of chord FF', and we let $d(F'O) = d(OF) = c$, where $c > 0$. Then F is at $(c, 0)$, and F' is at $(-c, 0)$. The definition of a hyperbola requires that $d(F'P) - d(PF) = 2a$, where $2a$ is a positive constant. We use the distance formula to compute the lengths of $F'P$ and PF:

$$d(F'P) = \sqrt{[x - (-c)]^2 + y^2} \qquad d(PF) = \sqrt{(x - c)^2 + y^2}$$

Substituting these values into the equation $|d(F'P) - d(PF)| = 2a$ gives

$$\sqrt{(x + c)^2 + y^2} - \sqrt{(x - c)^2 + y^2} = 2a$$

or

$$\sqrt{(x + c)^2 + y^2} = 2a + \sqrt{(x - c)^2 + y^2}$$

After squaring, we have

$$(x + c)^2 + y^2 = 4a^2 + 4a\sqrt{(x - c)^2 + y^2} + (x - c)^2 + y^2$$

$$x^2 + 2cx + c^2 + y^2 = 4a^2 + 4a\sqrt{(x - c)^2 + y^2} + x^2 - 2cx + c^2 + y^2$$

$$4cx = 4a^2 + 4a\sqrt{(x - c)^2 + y^2}$$

$$cx - a^2 = a\sqrt{(x - c)^2 + y^2}$$

Squaring both sides again and simplifying gives

$$c^2x^2 - 2a^2cx + a^4 = a^2(x^2 - 2cx + c^2 + y^2)$$

$$c^2x^2 - 2a^2cx + a^4 = a^2x^2 - 2a^2cx + a^2c^2 + a^2y^2$$

$$c^2x^2 + a^4 = a^2x^2 + a^2c^2 + a^2y^2$$

(1) $(c^2 - a^2)x^2 - a^2y^2 = a^2(c^2 - a^2)$

Because $c > a$ (you will be asked to prove this in Exercise 65), $c^2 - a^2$ is a positive number. So we can let $b^2 = c^2 - a^2$ and substitute b^2 for $c^2 - a^2$ in Equation 1 to get

$$b^2x^2 - a^2y^2 = a^2b^2 \qquad \text{Substitute } b^2 \text{ for } c^2 - a^2.$$

If we divide both sides of the previous equation by a^2b^2, we will obtain the following equation.

$$\frac{x^2}{a^2} - \frac{y^2}{b^2} = 1$$

This equation is standard form of the equation of a hyperbola with center at the origin and horizontal axis the x-axis.

To find the x-intercepts of the graph, we let $y = 0$ and solve for x. We get

$$\frac{x^2}{a^2} = 1$$

$$x^2 = a^2$$

$$x = a \quad \text{or} \quad x = -a$$

We now know that the x-intercepts are the vertices $V(a, 0)$ and $V'(-a, 0)$. The distance between the center of the hyperbola and either vertex is a, and the center of the hyperbola is the midpoint of the segment $V'V$ as well as that of the segment FF'.

We attempt to find the y-intercepts by letting $x = 0$. Then the equation becomes

$$\frac{-y^2}{b^2} = 1 \quad \text{or} \quad y^2 = -b^2$$

Because $-b^2$ represents a negative number, and y^2 cannot be negative, the equation has no real solutions. Since there are no y-values corresponding to $x = 0$, the hyperbola does not intersect the y-axis.

This discussion suggests the following results.

Hyperbola: Foci on x-Axis, Center at (0, 0)   The standard form of an equation of a hyperbola with center at the origin and foci on the x-axis is

$$\frac{x^2}{a^2} - \frac{y^2}{b^2} = 1$$

where $a^2 + b^2 = c^2$.

Vertices: $V(a, 0)$ and $V'(-a, 0)$

Foci: $F(c, 0)$ and $F'(-c, 0)$

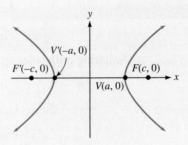

If the foci are on the y-axis, a similar equation results.

Hyperbola: Foci on y-Axis, Center at (0, 0)   The standard form of an equation of a hyperbola with center at the origin and foci on the y-axis is

$$\frac{y^2}{a^2} - \frac{x^2}{b^2} = 1$$

where $a^2 + b^2 = c^2$.

Vertices: $V(0, a)$ and $V'(0, -a)$

Foci: $F(0, c)$ and $F'(0, -c)$

EXAMPLE 1   Writing an Equation of a Hyperbola

Write an equation of the hyperbola with vertices $V(4, 0)$ and $V'(-4, 0)$ and a focus at $F(5, 0)$.

SOLUTION   Because the foci lie on the x-axis, we use the standard equation $\frac{x^2}{a^2} - \frac{y^2}{b^2} = 1$. We will find a^2 and b^2 and substitute the results into the standard equation.

The center of the hyperbola is midway between the vertices V and V'. Thus, the center is the origin $(0, 0)$. The distance between the vertex and the center is $a = 4$, and the distance between the focus and the center is $c = 5$. We can find b^2 by substituting 4 for a and 5 for c in the following equation to get

$b^2 = c^2 - a^2$ In a hyperbola, $b^2 = c^2 - a^2$.

$b^2 = 5^2 - 4^2$

$b^2 = 9$

Substituting the values for a^2 and b^2 in the standard equation gives an equation of the hyperbola:

$$\frac{x^2}{a^2} - \frac{y^2}{b^2} = 1$$

$$\frac{x^2}{16} - \frac{y^2}{9} = 1$$

The graph of $\frac{x^2}{16} - \frac{y^2}{9} = 1$ is shown in Figure 7-30.

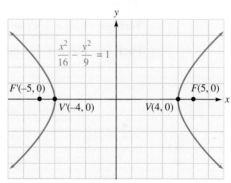

FIGURE 7-30

Self Check 1   Write an equation of the hyperbola with vertices $(0, 4)$ and $(0, -4)$ and a focus at $(0, 5)$.

Now Try Exercise 15.

To translate the hyperbola to a new position centered at the point (h, k) instead of the origin, we replace x and y with $x - h$ and $y - k$, respectively. We get the following results.

Hyperbola: Transverse Axis Horizontal, Center at (h, k)   The standard form of an equation of a hyperbola with center at the point (h, k) and foci on a line parallel to the x-axis is

$$\frac{(x - h)^2}{a^2} - \frac{(y - k)^2}{b^2} = 1$$

where $a^2 + b^2 = c^2$.

Vertices: $V(a + h, k)$ and $V'(-a + h, k)$

Foci: $F(c + h, k)$ and $F'(-c + h, k)$

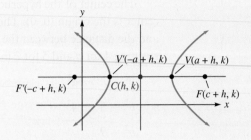

Hyperbola: Transverse Axis Vertical, Center at (h, k)

The standard form of an equation of a hyperbola with center at (h, k) and foci on a line parallel to the y-axis is

$$\frac{(y - k)^2}{a^2} - \frac{(x - h)^2}{b^2} = 1$$

where $a^2 + b^2 = c^2$.

Vertices: $V(h, a + k)$ and $V'(h, -a + k)$

Foci: $F(h, c + k)$ and $F'(h, -c + k)$

EXAMPLE 2   Writing an Equation of a Hyperbola

Write an equation of the hyperbola with vertices $(3, -3)$ and $(3, 3)$ and a focus at $(3, 5)$.

SOLUTION   Because the foci lie on a vertical line, as shown in Figure 7-31, we will use the standard form of the equation

$$\frac{(y - k)^2}{a^2} - \frac{(x - h)^2}{b^2} = 1$$

and determine h, k, a^2, and b^2, and substitute the results into the standard equation.

The center of the hyperbola is midway between the vertices V and V'. Thus, the center is point $(3, 0)$; $h = 3$; and $k = 0$. The distance between the vertex and the center is $a = 3$, and the distance between the focus and the center is $c = 5$. We can find b^2 by substituting 3 for a and 5 for c in the following equation to get

$b^2 = c^2 - a^2$ In a hyperbola, $b^2 = c^2 - a^2$.

$b^2 = 5^2 - 3^2$

$b^2 = 16$

Substituting the values for h, k, a^2, and b^2 in the standard equation gives an equation of the hyperbola:

$$\frac{(y-k)^2}{a^2} - \frac{(x-h)^2}{b^2} = 1$$

$$\frac{(y-0)^2}{9} - \frac{(x-3)^2}{16} = 1$$

$$\frac{y^2}{9} - \frac{(x-3)^2}{16} = 1$$

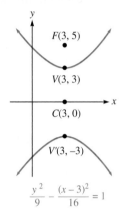

$$\frac{y^2}{9} - \frac{(x-3)^2}{16} = 1$$

FIGURE 7-31

Self Check 2   Write an equation of the hyperbola with vertices $(3, 1)$ and $(-3, 1)$ and a focus at $(5, 1)$.

Now Try Exercise 23.

2. Graph Hyperbolas

Consider the graph of the hyperbola with equation $\frac{x^2}{25} - \frac{y^2}{4} = 1$ shown in Figure 7-32. From the graph, we can see that

- The values of a and b are $a = 5$ and $b = 2$.
- The equations of the asymptotes of the graph are $y = \frac{2}{5}x$ and $y = -\frac{2}{5}x$.

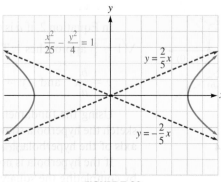

FIGURE 7-32

Exercises **7.3**

Getting Ready
You should be able to complete these vocabulary and concept statements before you proceed to the practice exercises.

Fill in the blanks.

1. A hyperbola is the set of all points in the plane such that the absolute value of the _____ of the distances from two fixed points is a positive _____.

2. Each of the two fixed points in the definition of a hyperbola is called a _____ of the hyperbola.

3. The vertices of the hyperbola $\frac{x^2}{a^2} - \frac{y^2}{b^2} = 1$ are $V(\_\_, \_\_)$ and $V'(\_\_, \_\_)$.

4. The vertices of the hyperbola $\frac{y^2}{a^2} - \frac{x^2}{b^2} = 1$ are $V(\_\_, \_\_)$ and $V'(\_\_, \_\_)$

5. The chord that joins the vertices is called the _____ of the hyperbola.

6. In a hyperbola, the relationship between a, b, and c is _____.

Identify the conic as a circle, parabola, ellipse, or hyperbola.

7. $x^2 + (y - 4)^2 = 12$

8. $7x^2 + 7y^2 + 70x - 14y = 119$

9. $y^2 - 2x + 23 = 5y$ 10. $(x - 8)^2 = 5(y + 6)$

11. $\dfrac{x^2}{35} + \dfrac{y^2}{9} = 1$

12. $2x^2 + 32y^2 + 4x - 30 = 0$

13. $x^2 - 2y^2 - 4y - 6 = 0$

14. $\dfrac{(x - 3)^2}{4} - \dfrac{y^2}{9} = 1$

Practice
Write an equation in standard form of each hyperbola described.

15. Vertices (5, 0) and (−5, 0); focus (7, 0)

16. Focus (3, 0); vertex (2, 0); center (0, 0)

17. Center (2, 4); $a = 2$, $b = 3$; transverse axis is horizontal

18. Center (−1, 3); vertex (1, 3); focus (2, 3)

19. Center (5, 3); vertex (5, 6); passes through (1, 8)

20. Foci (0, 10) and (0, −10); $\dfrac{c}{a} = \dfrac{5}{4}$

21. Vertices (0, 3) and (0, −3); $\dfrac{c}{a} = \dfrac{5}{3}$

22. Focus (4, 0); vertex (2, 0); center (0, 0)

23. Center (1, 4); focus (7, 4); vertex (3, 4)

24. Center (1, −3); $a^2 = 4$; $b^2 = 16$

25. Center at the origin; passes through (4, 2) and (8, −6)

26. Center (3, −1); y-intercept (0, −1); x-intercept $\left(3 + \dfrac{3\sqrt{5}}{2}, 0\right)$

Find the area of the fundamental rectangle of each hyperbola.

27. $4(x - 1)^2 - 9(y + 2)^2 = 36$

28. $x^2 - y^2 - 4x - 6y = 6$

29. $x^2 + 6x - y^2 + 2y = -11$

30. $9x^2 - 4y^2 = 18x + 24y + 63$

Write an equation in standard form of each hyperbola described.

31. Center (−2, −4); $a = 2$; area of fundamental rectangle is 36 square units

32. Center (3, −5); $b = 6$; area of fundamental rectangle is 24 square units

33. Vertex (6, 0); one end of conjugate axis at $\left(0, \dfrac{5}{4}\right)$

34. Vertex (3, 0); focus (−5, 0); center (0, 0)

Graph each hyperbola.

35. $\dfrac{x^2}{9} - \dfrac{y^2}{4} = 1$

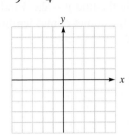

36. $\dfrac{y^2}{4} - \dfrac{x^2}{9} = 1$

37. $4x^2 - 3y^2 = 36$

38. $3x^2 - 4y^2 = 36$

39. $y^2 - x^2 = 1$

40. $x^2 - \dfrac{y^2}{4} = 1$

41. $\dfrac{(x+2)^2}{9} - \dfrac{y^2}{4} = 1$

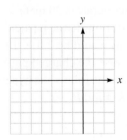

42. $\dfrac{y^2}{9} - \dfrac{(x-2)^2}{36} = 1$

43. $4(y-2)^2 - 9(x+1)^2 = 36$

44. $9(y+2)^2 - 4(x-1)^2 = 36$

45. $4x^2 - 2y^2 + 8x - 8y = 8$

46. $x^2 - y^2 - 4x - 6y = 6$

47. $y^2 - 4x^2 + 6y + 32x = 59$

48. $x^2 + 6x - y^2 + 2y = -11$

49. $-xy = 6$

50. $xy = 20$

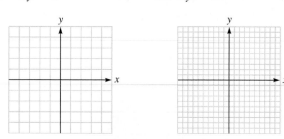

Find an equation of the curve on which point P lies.

51. The difference of the distances between $P(x, y)$ and the points $(-2, 1)$ and $(8, 1)$ is 6.

52. The difference of the distances between $P(x, y)$ and the points $(3, -1)$ and $(3, 5)$ is 5.

53. The distance between point $P(x, y)$ and the point $(0, 3)$ is $\frac{3}{2}$ of the distance between P and the line $y = -2$.

54. The distance between point $P(x, y)$ and the point $(5, 4)$ is $\frac{5}{3}$ of the distance between P and the line $x = -3$.

Use a graphing calculator to graph each hyperbola. Then sketch the hyperbola by hand and compare the results.

55. $x^2 - \dfrac{y^2}{4} = 1$

56. $\dfrac{(x + 3)^2}{4} - \dfrac{(y - 2)^2}{25} = 1$

Applications

57. Fluids See the illustration below. Two glass plates in contact at the left, and separated by about 5 millimeters on the right, are dipped in beet juice, which rises by capillary action to form a hyperbola. The hyperbola is modeled by an equation of the form $xy = k$. If the curve passes through the point $(12, 2)$, what is k?

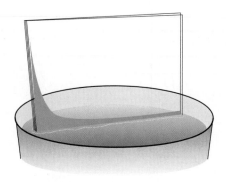

58. Astronomy Some comets have a hyperbolic orbit, with the sun as one focus. When the comet shown in the illustration is far away from Earth, it appears to be approaching Earth along the line $y = 2x$. Find the equation of its orbit if the comet comes within 100 million miles of Earth.

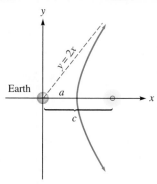

59. Alpha particles The particle in the illustration approaches the nucleus at the origin along the path $9y^2 - x^2 = 81$ in the coordinate system shown. How close does the particle come to the nucleus?

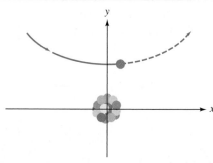

60. Physics Parallel beams of similarly charged particles are shot from two atomic accelerators 20 meters apart, as shown in the illustration. If the particles were not deflected, the beams would be 2.0×10^{-4} meters apart. However, because the charged particles repel each other, the beams follow the hyperbolic path $y = \frac{k}{x}$, for some k. Find k.

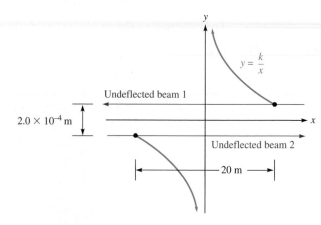

61. **Navigation** The LORAN (LOng RAnge Navigation) system in the illustration uses two radio transmitters 26 miles apart to send simultaneous signals. The navigator on a ship at $P(x, y)$ receives the closer signal first and determines that the difference of the distances between the ship and each transmitter is 24 miles. That places the ship on a certain curve. Identify the curve and find an equation in standard form.

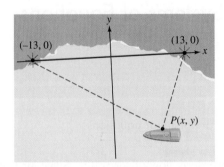

62. **Navigation** By determining the difference of the distances between the ship in the illustration and two radio transmitters, the LORAN navigation system places the ship on the hyperbola $x^2 - 4y^2 = 576$ in the coordinate system shown. If the ship is 5 miles out to sea, find its coordinates.

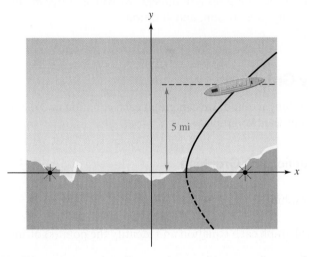

63. **Wave propagation** Stones dropped into a calm pond at points A and B create ripples that propagate in widening circles. In the illustration, points A and B are 20 feet apart, and the radii of the circles differ by 12 feet. The point $P(x, y)$ where the circles intersect moves along a curve. Identify the curve and find an equation in standard form.

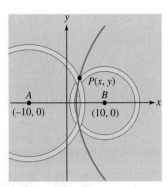

64. **Sonic boom** The position of a sonic boom caused by the faster-than-sound aircraft is one branch of the hyperbola $y^2 - x^2 = 25$ in the coordinate system shown. How wide is the hyperbola 5 miles from its vertex?

Discovery and Writing

65. Prove that $c > a$ for a hyperbola with center at $(0, 0)$ and line segment FF' on the x-axis.

66. Show that the extended diagonals of the fundamental rectangle of the hyperbola $\frac{x^2}{a^2} - \frac{y^2}{b^2} = 1$ are $y = \frac{b}{a}x$ and $y = -\frac{b}{a}x$.

67. Show that the expansion of the standard equation of a hyperbola is a special case of the general equation of second degree with $B = 0$.

68. Write a paragraph describing how you can tell from the equation of a hyperbola whether the transverse axis is vertical or horizontal.

Review

Find the inverse of each function. Write the answer using $f^{-1}(x)$.

69. $f(x) = 3x - 2$

70. $f(x) = \dfrac{x + 1}{x}$

71. $f(x) = \dfrac{5x}{x + 2}$

72. $f(x) = x$

Let $f(x) = x^2 + 1$ and $g(x) = (x + 1)^2$. Find each composite function.

73. $f(g(x))$ **74.** $g(f(x))$

75. $f(f(x))$

76. $g(g(x))$

7.4 Solving Nonlinear Systems of Equations

In this section, we will learn to

1. Solve systems by graphing.

2. Solve systems by substitution.

3. Solve systems by addition.

4. Solve problems using systems of nonlinear equations.

Air-traffic controllers maintain an orderly flow of air traffic. Since air-traffic controllers keep planes a safe distance apart, the paths of two planes will not intersect. This guarantees that there will be no mid-air collisions. Knowing where the graphs of two or more equations intersect can be very important. For example, the intersection point of the graphs of the flight paths of two planes will be a potential point of collision.

We will now discuss techniques for solving systems of two equations in two variables, where at least one of the equations is nonlinear. We will use three methods to solve such systems: graphing, substitution, and addition.

Comment

The solutions can be verified by substituting into the two equations and checking to see that both equations are satisfied.

1. Solve Systems by Graphing

To solve systems by the graphing method, we can graph each equation and identify the point(s) of intersection of the two graphs.

EXAMPLE 1   **Solving a System of Equations by Graphing**

Solve $\begin{cases} x^2 + y^2 = 25 \\ 2x + y = 10 \end{cases}$ by graphing.

SOLUTION   To solve this system, we will graph each equation and identify the point(s) of intersection of the two graphs.

The graph of $x^2 + y^2 = 25$ is a circle with center at the origin and radius of 5. The equation of $2x + y = 10$ is a line with x-intercept at $(5, 0)$ and y-intercept at $(0, 10)$.

After graphing the circle and the line, as shown in Figure 7-39, we see that there are two intersection points, $P(3, 4)$ and $P'(5, 0)$. The solutions to the system are

$$\begin{cases} x = 3 \\ y = 4 \end{cases} \quad \text{and} \quad \begin{cases} x = 5 \\ y = 0 \end{cases}$$

The line $2x + y = 10$ is a called a **secant line** because it intersects the graph of the circle at two points. In this case, the system has two solutions. If a line intersects the graph of a circle at one point, the line is called a **tangent line.** In this case, there is one solution. If the line does not intersect the circle, there is no solution.

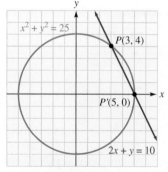

FIGURE 7-39

Self Check 1   Solve $\begin{cases} x^2 + y^2 = 25 \\ 2x - y = 5 \end{cases}$.

Now Try Exercise 9.

ACCENT ON TECHNOLOGY / **Solving Systems of Equations**

To solve the system of equations in Example 1 using a graphing calculator, we must solve each of the equations for y. From the equation $x^2 + y^2 = 25$, we get two equations to graph:

$$y_1 = \sqrt{25 - x^2} \quad \text{and} \quad y_2 = -\sqrt{25 - x^2}$$

From the equation $2x + y = 10$, we get a third equation to graph:

$$y_3 = 10 - 2x$$

1. Enter each equation.

2. Set a WINDOW.

3. GRAPH the equations.

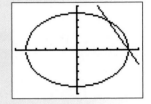

4. Press 2nd TRACE to access the CALCULATE menu.

5. Move the cursor close to the point of intersection.

6. Press ENTER and the cursor will move to Y2. This is not the curve that you need.

7. Press the DOWN CURSOR key to move the point to Y3.

8. Press ENTER twice to get to the point of intersection.

9. Repeat to find the other point of intersection.

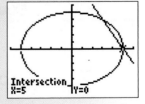

FIGURE 7-40

2. Solve Systems by Substitution

The substitution method can be used to find exact solutions. By making an appropriate substitution, we can convert a nonlinear system of two equations in two variables into one equation in one variable. We can then solve the resulting equation for one variable and back substitute to find the other variable.

EXAMPLE 2 **Solving a System of Equations Using Substitution**

Solve $\begin{cases} x^2 + y^2 = 25 \\ 2x + y = 10 \end{cases}$ by substitution.

SOLUTION We will solve the linear equation for y to obtain an equation called the **substitution equation.** We will then substitute the expression that represents y into the second-degree equation to obtain an equation in the one variable x. After solving the equation for x, we can find y by back substituting the resulting values of x into the substitution equation and simplifying.

We begin by solving the linear equation for y.

$$2x + y = 10 \qquad \text{This equation is linear.}$$

$$y = -2x + 10 \qquad \text{This is the substitution equation.}$$

We can now substitute $-2x + 10$ for y in the second-degree equation and solve the resulting quadratic equation for x:

$$x^2 + y^2 = 25 \qquad \text{This equation is nonlinear.}$$

$$x^2 + (-2x + 10)^2 = 25 \qquad \text{Substitute } -2x + 10 \text{ for } y.$$

$$x^2 + 4x^2 - 40x + 100 = 25 \qquad \text{Square the binomial.}$$

$$5x^2 - 40x + 75 = 0 \qquad \text{Subtract 25 from both sides and combine like terms.}$$

$$x^2 - 8x + 15 = 0 \qquad \text{Divide both sides by 5.}$$

$$(x - 5)(x - 3) = 0 \qquad \text{Factor } x^2 - 8x + 15.$$

$$x - 5 = 0 \quad \text{or} \quad x - 3 = 0$$

$$x = 5 \qquad \qquad x = 3$$

Because $y = -2x + 10$, if $x = 5$, then $y = 0$; and if $x = 3$, then $y = 4$. The two solutions are

$$\begin{cases} x = 5 \\ y = 0 \end{cases} \quad \text{and} \quad \begin{cases} x = 3 \\ y = 4 \end{cases}$$

Comment

Note that solutions we obtained by graphing and by substitution are the same.

Self Check 2 Solve $\begin{cases} x^2 + y^2 = 25 \\ 2x - y = 5 \end{cases}$ by substitution.

Now Try Exercise 21.

EXAMPLE 3 **Solving a System of Equations by Substitution**

Solve $\begin{cases} 4x^2 + 9y^2 = 5 \\ y = x^2 \end{cases}$ by substitution.

SOLUTION In this example, both equations are nonlinear. To solve it, we will substitute y for x^2 in the top equation to obtain one equation in the variable y. Then, we will solve the resulting equation for y and use back substitution to find x.

$$4x^2 + 9y^2 = 5$$

$$4y + 9y^2 = 5 \qquad \text{Substitute } y \text{ for } x^2.$$

$$9y^2 + 4y - 5 = 0 \qquad \text{Add } -5 \text{ to both sides.}$$

$$(9y - 5)(y + 1) = 0 \qquad \text{Factor } 9y^2 + 4y - 5.$$

$$9y - 5 = 0 \quad \text{or} \quad y + 1 = 0$$

$$y = \frac{5}{9} \qquad \qquad y = -1$$

Because $y = x^2$, we can find x by solving the equations

$$x^2 = \frac{5}{9} \quad \text{and} \quad x^2 = -1$$

The solutions of $x^2 = \frac{5}{9}$ are

$$x = \frac{\sqrt{5}}{3} \quad \text{or} \quad x = -\frac{\sqrt{5}}{3}$$

Since the equation $x^2 = -1$ has no real solutions, the only solutions of the system are

$$\left(\frac{\sqrt{5}}{3}, \frac{5}{9}\right) \quad \text{and} \quad \left(-\frac{\sqrt{5}}{3}, \frac{5}{9}\right)$$

Comment

The substitution method is a good choice when one variable in the system is raised to the first power.

Self Check 3 Solve $\begin{cases} x^2 + 3y^2 = 13 \\ x = y^2 - 1 \end{cases}$ by substitution.

Now Try Exercise 23.

3. Solve Systems by Addition

When we have two second-degree equations of the form $ax^2 + by^2 = c$, we can solve the system by using the addition method and eliminating one of the variables.

EXAMPLE 4 **Solving a System of Equations by Addition**

Solve $\begin{cases} 3x^2 + 2y^2 = 36 \\ 4x^2 - y^2 = 4 \end{cases}$ by addition.

SOLUTION In this example, we have two second-degree equations of the form $ax^2 + by^2 = c$. In such cases, we can solve the system by eliminating one of the variables by addition, solving the resulting equation, and using back substitution to solve for the second variable.

To eliminate the terms involving y^2, we copy the first equation and multiply the second equation by 2 to obtain the following equivalent system.

$$\begin{cases} 3x^2 + 2y^2 = 36 \\ 8x^2 - 2y^2 = 8 \end{cases}$$

We can then add the equations and solve the resulting equation for x:

$$11x^2 = 44$$

$$x^2 = 4$$

$$x = 2 \quad \text{or} \quad x = -2$$

To find y, we substitute 2 for x and then -2 for x in the first equation.

For $x = 2$	For $x = -2$
$3x^2 + 2y^2 = 36$	$3x^2 + 2y^2 = 36$
$3(2)^2 + 2y^2 = 36$	$3(-2)^2 + 2y^2 = 36$
$12 + 2y^2 = 36$	$12 + 2y^2 = 36$
$2y^2 = 24$	$2y^2 = 24$
$y^2 = 12$	$y^2 = 12$
$y = \sqrt{12} \quad \text{or} \quad y = -\sqrt{12}$	$y = \sqrt{12} \quad \text{or} \quad y = -\sqrt{12}$
$y = 2\sqrt{3} \quad \mid \quad y = -2\sqrt{3}$	$y = 2\sqrt{3} \quad \mid \quad y = -2\sqrt{3}$

The four solutions of this system are

$$\left(2, 2\sqrt{3}\right), \quad \left(2, -2\sqrt{3}\right), \quad \left(-2, 2\sqrt{3}\right), \quad \text{and} \quad \left(-2, -2\sqrt{3}\right)$$

∎

Self Check 4   Solve: $\begin{cases} 2x^2 + y^2 = 23 \\ 3x^2 - 2y^2 = 17 \end{cases}$ by addition.

Now Try Exercise 29.

4. Solve Problems Using Systems of Nonlinear Equations

EXAMPLE 5   **Solving an Application Problem**

The area of a tennis court for singles matches is 2,106 square feet, and the perimeter is 210 feet. Find the dimensions of the court.

SOLUTION   We will set up a system of two equations that models the problem and then use the substitution method to solve it.

Step 1: Write a system of two equations that models the problem. We let x represent the length of the tennis court and y represent its width as shown in Figure 7-41.

Arthur Ashe Tennis Stadium

FIGURE 7-41

Because the area of the tennis court (2,106 square feet) is the product of its length and width, we can form the equation $xy = 2{,}106$. Because the perimeter of the court (210 feet) is the sum of twice its length and twice its width, we can write the equation $2x + 2y = 210$, or $x + y = 105$. This gives the following system of equations that models the problem.

$$\begin{cases} xy = 2{,}106 & \text{This equation is nonlinear.} \\ x + y = 105 & \text{This equation is linear.} \end{cases}$$

Step 2: Use substitution to solve the system. First, we solve the linear equation for y.

$$x + y = 105$$
$$y = -x + 105 \qquad \text{This is the substitution equation.}$$

We can now substitute $-x + 105$ for y in the nonlinear equation and solve the resulting equation for x:

$$xy = 2{,}106$$
$$x(-x + 105) = 2{,}106 \qquad \text{Substitute } -x + 105 \text{ for } y.$$
$$-x^2 + 105x = 2{,}106 \qquad \text{Remove parentheses.}$$
$$-x^2 + 105x - 2{,}106 = 0 \qquad \text{Subtract 2,106 from both sides.}$$
$$x^2 - 105x + 2{,}106 = 0 \qquad \text{Multiply both sides by } -1.$$
$$(x - 78)(x - 27) = 0 \qquad \text{Factor } x^2 - 105x + 2{,}106.$$
$$x - 78 = 0 \quad \text{or} \quad x - 27 = 0$$
$$x = 78 \quad \mid \quad x = 27$$

Because $y = -x + 105$, if $x = 78$, then $y = 27$; and if $x = 27$, then $y = 78$. The two solutions are

$$\begin{cases} x = 78 \\ y = 27 \end{cases} \text{ and } \begin{cases} x = 27 \\ y = 78 \end{cases}$$

The dimensions of the tennis court are 78 feet by 27 feet.

Self Check 5   If the area of a tennis court for doubles matches is 2,808 square feet and the perimeter is 228 feet, find the dimensions of the court.

Now Try Exercise 45.

Self Check Answers   **1.** $\begin{cases} x = 4 \\ y = 3 \end{cases}$ and $\begin{cases} x = 0 \\ y = -5 \end{cases}$ **2.** $\begin{cases} x = 4 \\ y = 3 \end{cases}$ and $\begin{cases} x = 0 \\ y = -5 \end{cases}$ **3.** $\left(2, \sqrt{3}\right)$ and $\left(2, -\sqrt{3}\right)$

4. $\left(3, \sqrt{5}\right), \left(3, -\sqrt{5}\right), \left(-3, \sqrt{5}\right), \left(-3, -\sqrt{5}\right)$

5. 78 ft by 36 ft

Exercises **7.4**

Getting Ready
You should be able to complete these vocabulary and concept statements before you proceed to the practice exercises.

Fill in the blanks.

1. Solutions of nonlinear systems of equations are the points of intersection of the _____ of conic sections.

2. Approximate solutions of nonlinear systems can be found _____, and exact solutions can be found algebraically using the methods of _____ or _____.

Practice
Solve each system of equations by graphing.

3. $\begin{cases} 8x^2 + 32y^2 = 256 \\ x = 2y \end{cases}$

4. $\begin{cases} x^2 + y^2 = 2 \\ x + y = 2 \end{cases}$

5. $\begin{cases} x^2 + y^2 = 90 \\ y = x^2 \end{cases}$

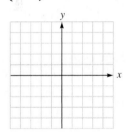

6. $\begin{cases} x^2 + y^2 = 5 \\ x + y = 3 \end{cases}$

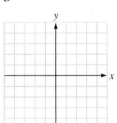

7. $\begin{cases} x^2 + y^2 = 25 \\ 12x^2 + 64y^2 = 768 \end{cases}$

8. $\begin{cases} x^2 + y^2 = 13 \\ y = x^2 - 1 \end{cases}$

9. $\begin{cases} x^2 - 13 = -y^2 \\ y = 2x - 4 \end{cases}$

10. $\begin{cases} x^2 + y^2 = 20 \\ y = x^2 \end{cases}$

11. $\begin{cases} x^2 - 6x - y = -5 \\ x^2 - 6x + y = -5 \end{cases}$

12. $\begin{cases} x^2 - y^2 = -5 \\ 3x^2 + 2y^2 = 30 \end{cases}$

Use a graphing calculator to solve each system of equations.

13. $\begin{cases} y = x + 1 \\ y = x^2 + x \end{cases}$

14. $\begin{cases} y = 6 - x^2 \\ y = x^2 - x \end{cases}$

15. $\begin{cases} 6x^2 + 9y^2 = 10 \\ 3y - 2x = 0 \end{cases}$

16. $\begin{cases} x^2 + y^2 = 68 \\ y^2 - 3x^2 = 4 \end{cases}$

Solve each system of equations using substitution or addition for real values of x and y.

17. $\begin{cases} 25x^2 + 9y^2 = 225 \\ 5x + 3y = 15 \end{cases}$

18. $\begin{cases} x^2 + y^2 = 20 \\ y = x^2 \end{cases}$

19. $\begin{cases} x^2 + y^2 = 2 \\ x + y = 2 \end{cases}$

20. $\begin{cases} x^2 + y^2 = 36 \\ 49x^2 + 36y^2 = 1,764 \end{cases}$

21. $\begin{cases} x^2 + y^2 = 5 \\ x + y = 3 \end{cases}$

22. $\begin{cases} x^2 - x - y = 2 \\ 4x - 3y = 0 \end{cases}$

23. $\begin{cases} x^2 + y^2 = 13 \\ y = x^2 - 1 \end{cases}$

24. $\begin{cases} x^2 + y^2 = 25 \\ 2x^2 - 3y^2 = 5 \end{cases}$

25. $\begin{cases} x^2 + y^2 = 30 \\ y = x^2 \end{cases}$

26. $\begin{cases} 9x^2 - 7y^2 = 81 \\ x^2 + y^2 = 9 \end{cases}$

27. $\begin{cases} 2x^2 + y^2 = 6 \\ x^2 - y^2 = 3 \end{cases}$

28. $\begin{cases} x^2 + y^2 = 13 \\ x^2 - y^2 = 5 \end{cases}$

29. $\begin{cases} x^2 + y^2 = 20 \\ x^2 - y^2 = -12 \end{cases}$

30. $\begin{cases} xy = -\dfrac{9}{2} \\ 3x + 2y = 6 \end{cases}$

31. $\begin{cases} y^2 = 40 - x^2 \\ y = x^2 - 10 \end{cases}$

32. $\begin{cases} x^2 - 6x - y = -5 \\ x^2 - 6x + y = -5 \end{cases}$

33. $\begin{cases} y = x^2 - 4 \\ x^2 - y^2 = -16 \end{cases}$

34. $\begin{cases} 6x^2 + 8y^2 = 182 \\ 8x^2 - 3y^2 = 24 \end{cases}$

35. $\begin{cases} x^2 - y^2 = -5 \\ 3x^2 + 2y^2 = 30 \end{cases}$

36. $\begin{cases} \dfrac{1}{x} + \dfrac{1}{y} = 5 \\ \dfrac{1}{x} - \dfrac{1}{y} = -3 \end{cases}$

37. $\begin{cases} \dfrac{1}{x} + \dfrac{2}{y} = 1 \\ \dfrac{2}{x} - \dfrac{1}{y} = \dfrac{1}{3} \end{cases}$

38. $\begin{cases} \dfrac{1}{x} + \dfrac{3}{y} = 4 \\ \dfrac{2}{x} - \dfrac{1}{y} = 7 \end{cases}$

39. $\begin{cases} 3y^2 = xy \\ 2x^2 + xy - 84 = 0 \end{cases}$

40. $\begin{cases} x^2 + y^2 = 10 \\ 2x^2 - 3y^2 = 5 \end{cases}$

41. $\begin{cases} xy = \dfrac{1}{6} \\ y + x = 5xy \end{cases}$

42. $\begin{cases} xy = \dfrac{1}{12} \\ y + x = 7xy \end{cases}$

Applications

43. Geometry The area of a rectangle is 63 square centimeters, and its perimeter is 32 centimeters. Find the dimensions of the rectangle.

44. Dimensions of a whiteboard The area of a SMART Board interactive whiteboard is 2,880 square inches, and its perimeter is 216 inches. Find the dimensions of the whiteboard.

45. Fencing pastures The rectangular pasture shown below is to be fenced in along a riverbank. If 260 feet of fencing is to enclose an area of 8,000 square feet, find the dimensions of the pasture.

46. Investments Grant receives $225 annual income from one investment. Jeff invested $500 more than Grant, but at an annual rate of 1% less. Jeff's annual income is $240. Find the amount and rate of Grant's investment.

47. Investments Carol receives $67.50 annual income from one investment. John invested $150 more than Carol at an annual rate of $1\frac{1}{2}$% more. John's annual income is $94.50. Find the amount and rate of Carol's investment. (*Hint:* There are two answers.)

48. Finding the rate and time Jim drove 306 miles. Jim's brother made the same trip at a speed 17 miles per hour slower than Jim did and required an extra $1\frac{1}{2}$ hours. Find Jim's rate and time.

49. Paintball See the illustration. A liquid-filled paintball is shot from the base of an incline and follows the parabolic path $y = -\frac{1}{300}x^2 + \frac{1}{5}x$, with distances measured in feet. The incline has a slope of $\frac{1}{10}$. Find the coordinates of the point of intersection of the paintball and the ground at impact.

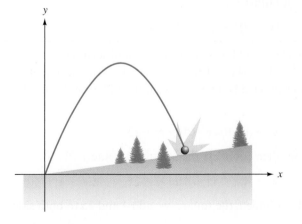

50. Artillery See the illustration for Exercise 49. A shell fired from the base of a hill follows the parabolic path $y = -\frac{1}{6}x^2 + 2x$, with distances measured in miles. The hill has a slope of $\frac{1}{3}$. How far from the base of the hill is the point of impact? (*Hint:* Find the coordinates of the point and then the distance.)

51. Air-traffic control A plane is flying over an airport on a path whose equation is $y = x^2$. If a second plane, flying at the same altitude, is traveling on a path whose equation is $x + y = 2$, is there any danger of a mid-air collision?

52. Ship traffic One ship is steaming on a path whose equation is $y = x^2 + 1$ and another is steaming on a path whose equation is $x + y = -4$. Is there any danger of collision?

53. Radio reception A radio station located 120 miles due east of Collinsville has a listening radius of 100 miles. A straight road joins Collinsville with Harmony, a town 200 miles to the east and 100 miles north. See the illustration. If a driver leaves Collinsville and heads toward Harmony, how far from Collinsville will the driver pick up the station?

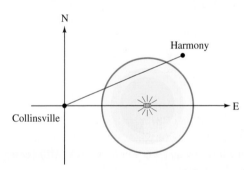

54. Listening ranges For how many miles will a driver in Exercise 53 continue to receive the signal?

Discovery and Writing

55. Is it possible for a system of second-degree equations to have no common solution? If so, sketch the graphs of the equations of such a system.

56. Can a system have exactly one solution? If so, sketch the graphs of the equations of such a system.

57. Can a system have exactly two solutions? If so, sketch possible graphs.

58. Can a system have three solutions? If so, sketch the graphs.

59. Can it have exactly four solutions? If so, sketch the graphs.

60. Can a system have more than four solutions? If so, sketch the graphs.

Review

Find the vertical, horizontal, or slant asymptotes of each of the following rational functions.

61. $f(x) = \dfrac{3x + 1}{x - 1}$

62. $f(x) = \dfrac{x^2 + 3}{x - 1}$

63. $f(x) = \dfrac{3x + 1}{x^2 - 1}$

64. $f(x) = \dfrac{x^2 + 3}{x^2 + 1}$

Determine whether the graph of each function has x-axis, y-axis, or origin symmetry, or none of these symmetries.

65. $f(x) = \dfrac{3x^2 + 5}{5x^2 + 3}$

66. $f(x) = \dfrac{3x^3 + 5}{5x^2 + 3}$

67. $f(x) = \dfrac{3x^3}{5x^2 + 3}$

68. $f(x) = \dfrac{3x^4 + 8}{2x^2 - 5}$

CHAPTER REVIEW

SECTION **7.1**   The Circle and the Parabola

Definitions and Concepts	Examples
Standard form of an equation of a circle with center at $(0, 0)$ and radius r: $$x^2 + y^2 = r^2$$	The standard equation of the circle with center $(0, 0)$ and radius 5 is: $x^2 + y^2 = 5^2$ or $x^2 + y^2 = 25$. The graph of the circle is: 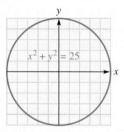
Standard form of an equation of a circle with center at (h, k) and radius r: $$(x - h)^2 + (y - k)^2 = r^2$$	The standard equation of the circle with center $(4, 6)$ and radius 3 is: $$(x - 4)^2 + (y - 6)^2 = 9$$
General form of a second-degree equation in x and y: $$Ax^2 + Bxy + Cy^2 + Dx + Ey + F = 0$$ The second degree equation is a circle if $A = C$ and $B = 0$.	The general form of an equation of a circle is $x^2 + y^2 + 4x - 10y + 25 = 0$. To write the equation in standard form, we first subtract 25 from both sides to obtain $$x^2 + y^2 + 4x - 10y = -25$$ and then complete the square on x and y. $$x^2 + 4x + y^2 - 10y = -25 \quad \text{Rearrange terms.}$$ To complete the square, we add 4 and 25 to both sides. $$x^2 + 4x + 4 + y^2 - 10y + 25 = -25 + 4 + 25$$

Definitions and Concepts	Examples
	We can factor and simplify on the right side to get $$(x + 2)^2 + (y - 5)^2 = 4$$ The circle is now written in standard form. From the equation, we can see that the coordinates of the center of the circle are $(-2, 5)$ and that the radius of the circle is 2.

Parabolas:

A **parabola** is the set of all points in a plane equidistant from a line l (called the **directrix**) and fixed point F (called the **focus**) that is not on line l.

Parabola opening	Vertex at origin	
Right	$y^2 = 4px$	$(p > 0)$
Left	$y^2 = 4px$	$(p < 0)$
Upward	$x^2 = 4py$	$(p > 0)$
Downward	$x^2 = 4py$	$(p < 0)$

For a parabola that opens right or left with vertex at the origin, the directrix is $x = -p$ and the focus is $(p, 0)$.

For a parabola that opens upward or downward with vertex at the origin, the directrix is $y = -p$ and the focus is $(0, p)$.

Parabola opening	Vertex at $V(h, k)$	
Right	$(y - k)^2 = 4p(x - h)$	$(p > 0)$
Left	$(y - k)^2 = 4p(x - h)$	$(p < 0)$
Upward	$(x - h)^2 = 4p(y - k)$	$(p > 0)$
Downward	$(x - h)^2 = 4p(y - k)$	$(p < 0)$

For a parabola that opens right or left with vertex at (h, k), the directrix is $x = -p + h$ and the focus is $(h + p, k)$.

For a parabola that opens upward or downward with vertex at (h, k), the directrix is $y = -p + k$ and the focus is $(h, k + p)$.

Find an equation of the parabola with vertex at the origin and focus at $(4, 0)$.

Because the focus is to the right of the vertex, the parabola opens to the right, and because the vertex is the origin, the standard equation is $y^2 = 4px$. Since the distance between the focus and the vertex is $p = 4$, we can substitute 4 for p in the standard equation to get

$$y^2 = 4px$$

$$y^2 = 4(4)x$$

$$y^2 = 16x$$

The graph of the parabola is shown in the figure.

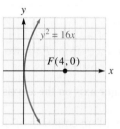

EXERCISES

Write an equation in standard form of each circle described.

1. Center $(0, 0)$; radius 4

2. Center $(0, 0)$; passes through $(6, 8)$

3. Center $(3, -2)$; radius 5

4. Center $(-2, 4)$; passes through $(1, 0)$

5. Endpoints of diameter $(-2, 4)$ and $(12, 16)$

6. Endpoints of diameter $(-3, -6)$ and $(7, 10)$

Write an equation of each circle in standard form and graph the circle.

7. $x^2 + y^2 - 6x + 4y = 3$

8. $x^2 + 4x + y^2 - 10y = -13$

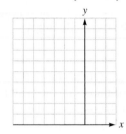

Write an equation in standard form of each parabola described.

9. Vertex $(0, 0)$; passes through $(-8, 4)$ and $(-8, -4)$

10. Vertex $(0, 0)$; passes through $(-8, 4)$ and $(8, 4)$

11. Find an equation of the parabola with vertex at $(-2, 3)$, curve passing through point $(-4, -8)$, and opening down.

Graph each parabola.

12. $x^2 - 4y - 2x + 9 = 0$

13. $y^2 - 6y = 4x - 13$

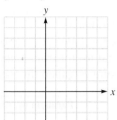

SECTION **7.2**   The Ellipse

Definitions and Concepts	**Examples**

Ellipse:
An **ellipse** is the set of all points P in a plane such that the sum of the distances from P to two other fixed points F and F' is a positive constant.

Ellipse with the major axis on the x-axis and center at $(0, 0)$:
The standard form of an equation of an ellipse with center at the origin and the major axis (horizontal) on the x-axis is

$$\frac{x^2}{a^2} + \frac{y^2}{b^2} = 1 \text{ where } a > b > 0$$

Vertices (ends of the major axis):

$$V(a, 0) \text{ and } V'(-a, 0)$$

Length of major axis: $2a$

Ends of the minor axis: $B(0, b)$ and $B'(0, -b)$

Length of minor axis: $2b$

Foci: $(c, 0)$ and $(-c, 0)$ where $c^2 = a^2 - b^2$

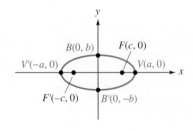

Find an equation of the ellipse with center at the origin, major axis of length 10 units located on the x-axis, and minor axis of length 4 units.

To find an equation, we determine a and b and substitute into the standard equation of an ellipse

$$\frac{x^2}{a^2} + \frac{y^2}{b^2} = 1$$

with center at the origin and major axis on the x-axis.

The center of the ellipse is given to be the origin and the length of the major axis is 10. Since the length of the major axis of an ellipse centered at the origin is $2a$, we have $2a = 10$ or $a = 5$ The coordinates of the vertices are $(5, 0)$ and $(-5, 0)$.

The length of the minor axis is given to be 4. Since the length of the minor axis of an ellipse centered at the origin is $2b$, we have $2b = 4$ or $b = 2$. The coordinates of B and B' are $(0, 2)$ and $(0, -2)$.

To find an equation of the ellipse, we substitute 5 for a and 2 for b in the standard equation of an ellipse with center at the origin and major axis on the x-axis.

$$\frac{x^2}{a^2} + \frac{y^2}{b^2} = 1$$

$$\frac{x^2}{5^2} + \frac{y^2}{2^2} = 1$$

$$\frac{x^2}{25} + \frac{y^2}{4} = 1$$

Definitions and Concepts	Examples
	The graph of the ellipse is shown below. 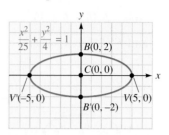

Ellipse with the major axis on the *y*-axis and center at (0, 0):

The standard form of an equation of an ellipse with center at the origin and the major axis (vertical) on the *y*-axis is

$$\frac{x^2}{b^2} + \frac{y^2}{a^2} = 1 \text{ where } a > b > 0$$

Vertices (ends of the major axis):

$V(0, a)$ and $V'(0, -a)$

Length of major axis: $2a$

Ends of the minor axis: $B(b, 0)$ and $B'(-b, 0)$

Length of minor axis: $2b$

Foci: $F(0, c)$ and $F'(0, -c)$ where $c^2 = a^2 - b^2$

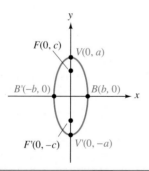

An example of an ellipse in standard form $\frac{x^2}{b^2} + \frac{y^2}{a^2} = 1$ with center at the origin and major axis (vertical) and on the *y*-axis is $\frac{x^2}{4} + \frac{y^2}{36} = 1$.

From the equation, we can see that $a = 6$ and the vertices of the ellipse are $V(0, 6)$ and $V'(0, -6)$. We can also see that $b = 2$ and the ends of the minor axis are $B(2, 0)$ and $B'(-2, 0)$.

Ellipse with the major axis horizontal and center at (*h*, *k*):

The standard form of an equation of an ellipse with center at (h, k) and major axis horizontal is

$$\frac{(x - h)^2}{a^2} + \frac{(y - k)^2}{b^2} = 1 \text{ where } a > b > 0$$

Vertices (ends of the major axis):

$V(a + h, k)$ and $V'(-a + h, k)$

Graph the ellipse $9x^2 + 4y^2 - 18x + 16y = 11$.

We first write the equation in standard form by completing the square on *x* and *y*.

$$9x^2 + 4y^2 - 18x + 16y = 11$$
$$9x^2 - 18x + 4y^2 + 16y = 11$$
$$9(x^2 - 2x) + 4(y^2 + 4y) = 11$$
$$9(x^2 - 2x + 1) + 4(y^2 + 4y + 4) = 11 + 9 + 16$$
$$9(x - 1)^2 + 4(y + 2)^2 = 36$$
$$\frac{(x - 1)^2}{4} + \frac{(y + 2)^2}{9} = 1$$

Definitions and Concepts	Examples
Ends of the minor axis: $$B(h, b + k) \quad \text{and} \quad B'(h, -b + k)$$ **Foci:** $F(h + c, k)$ and $F'(h - c, k)$ where $c^2 = a^2 - b^2$	The major axis of the ellipse is vertical and the center of the ellipse is $(1, -2)$. The graph of the ellipse is shown below. 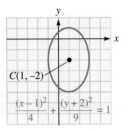 $$\frac{(x-1)^2}{4} + \frac{(y+2)^2}{9} = 1$$

Ellipse with the major axis vertical and center at (h, k):
The standard form of an equation of an ellipse with center at (h, k) and major axis vertical is

$$\frac{(x - h)^2}{b^2} + \frac{(y - k)^2}{a^2} = 1 \text{ where } a > b > 0$$

Vertices (ends of the major axis):

$$V(h, a + k) \text{ and } V'(h, -a + k)$$

Ends of the minor axis:

$$B(b + h, k) \text{ and } B'(-b + h, k)$$

Foci: $F(h, k + c)$ and $F'(h, k - c)$ where $c^2 = a^2 - b^2$

EXERCISES

14. Write an equation of the ellipse in standard form with center at the origin, major axis that is horizontal and 12 units long, and minor axis 8 units long.

15. Write an equation of the ellipse in standard form with center at the origin, major axis that is vertical and 10 units long, and minor axis 4 units long.

16. Write an equation of the ellipse in standard form with center at point $(-2, 3)$ and curve passing through points $(-2, 0)$ and $(2, 3)$.

17. Write the equation in standard form and graph it.
$$4x^2 + y^2 - 16x + 2y = -13$$

SECTION **7.3**   The Hyperbola

Definitions and Concepts	Examples

Definitions and Concepts

Hyperbola:
A **hyperbola** is the set of all points P in a plane such that the absolute value of the difference of the distances from point P to two other points in the plane is a positive constant.

Hyperbola with the foci on the x-axis and center at (0, 0):
The standard form of an equation of a hyperbola with center at the origin and foci on the x-axis is

$$\frac{x^2}{a^2} - \frac{y^2}{b^2} = 1 \text{ where } a^2 + b^2 = c^2$$

Vertices: $V(a, 0)$ and $V'(-a, 0)$

Foci: $F(c, 0)$ and $F'(-c, 0)$

Asymptotes: $y = \pm\dfrac{b}{a}x$

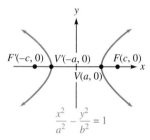

Hyperbola with the foci on the y-axis and center at (0, 0):
The standard form of an equation of a hyperbola with center at the origin and foci on the x-axis is

$$\frac{y^2}{a^2} - \frac{x^2}{b^2} = 1 \text{ where } a^2 + b^2 = c^2.$$

Vertices: $V(0, a)$ and $V'(0, -a)$

Foci: $F(0, c)$ and $F'(0, -c)$

Asymptotes: $y = \pm\dfrac{a}{b}x$

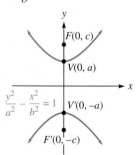

Examples

Write an equation of the hyperbola with vertices $V(3, 0)$ and $V'(-3, 0)$ and a focus at $F(5, 0)$.

Because the foci lie on the x-axis, we use the standard equation

$$\frac{x^2}{a^2} - \frac{y^2}{b^2} = 1.$$

We will find a^2 and b^2 and substitute the results into the standard equation.

The center of the hyperbola is midway between the vertices V and V'. Thus, the center is the origin $(0, 0)$. The distance between the vertex and the center is $a = 3$, and the distance between the focus and the center is $c = 5$. We can find b^2 by substituting 3 for a and 5 for c in the following equation to get

$$b^2 = c^2 - a^2 \qquad \text{In a hyperbola, } b^2 = c^2 - a^2.$$

$$b^2 = 5^2 - 3^2$$

$$b^2 = 16$$

Substituting the values for a^2 and b^2 in the standard equation gives an equation of the hyperbola:

$$\frac{x^2}{a^2} - \frac{y^2}{b^2} = 1$$

$$\frac{x^2}{9} - \frac{y^2}{16} = 1$$

Graph the hyperbola: $\dfrac{y^2}{4} - \dfrac{x^2}{25} = 1.$

Step 1: Write the hyperbola in standard form. The equation of the hyperbola $\frac{y^2}{4} - \frac{x^2}{25} = 1$ is already written in the standard form $\frac{y^2}{a^2} - \frac{x^2}{b^2} = 1$.

Step 2: Identify the center and a and b. From the standard equation of a hyperbola, we see that the center is $(0, 0)$, that $a = 2$ and $b = 5$, and that the vertices are on the y-axis.

Step 3: Draw the fundamental rectangle and asymptotes. The vertices V and V' are 2 units above and below the origin and have coordinates of $(0, 2)$ and $(0, -2)$. Points B and B' are 5 units right and left of the origin and have coordinates of $(5, 0)$ and $(-5, 0)$. We use the points V, V', B, and B' to construct the fundamental rectangle and extend the diagonals to graph the asymptotes as shown in the following figure.

Definitions and Concepts	Examples

Definitions and Concepts

Hyperbola with the transverse axis horizontal and center at (h, k):

The standard form of an equation of a hyperbola with center at the (h, k) and foci on a line parallel to the x-axis is

$$\frac{(x - h)^2}{a^2} - \frac{(y - k)^2}{b^2} = 1 \text{ where } a^2 + b^2 = c^2$$

Vertices: $V(a + h, k)$ and $V'(-a + h, k)$

Foci: $F(c + h, k)$ and $F'(-c + h, k)$

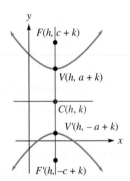

Hyperbola with the transverse axis vertical and center at (h, k):

The standard equation of a hyperbola with center at (h, k) and foci on a line parallel to the y-axis is

$$\frac{(y - k)^2}{a^2} - \frac{(x - h)^2}{b^2} = 1 \text{ where } a^2 + b^2 = c^2$$

Vertices: $V(h, a + k)$ and $V'(h, -a + k)$

Foci: $F(h, c + k)$ and $F'(h, -c + k)$

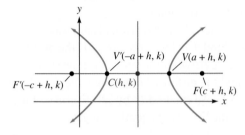

Graphing hyperbolas:
1. Write the hyperbola in standard form.
2. Identify the center and a and b.
3. Draw the fundamental rectangle and asymptotes.
4. Sketch the hyperbola beginning with the vertices and using the asymptotes as guides.

Examples

Step 4: Sketch the hyperbola. We begin with the vertices and sketch the graph of the hyperbola, as shown in the figure below using the asymptotes as guides.

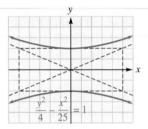

EXERCISES

18. Write an equation of the hyperbola in standard form with center at the origin, passing through points $(-2, 0)$ and $(2, 0)$, and having a focus at $(4, 0)$.

19. Write an equation of the hyperbola in standard form with center at the origin, one focus at $(0, 5)$, and one vertex at $(0, 3)$.

20. Write an equation of the hyperbola in standard form with vertices at points $(-3, 3)$ and $(3, 3)$ and a focus at point $(5, 3)$.

21. Write an equation of the hyperbola in standard form with vertices at points $(3, -3)$ and $(3, 3)$ and a focus at point $(3, 5)$.

22. Write equations of the asymptotes of the hyperbola $\frac{x^2}{25} - \frac{y^2}{16} = 1$.

23. Write the equation in standard form and graph it.
$$9x^2 - 4y^2 - 16y - 18x = 43$$

24. Graph: $4xy = 1$.

SECTION **7.4**   Solving Nonlinear Systems of Equations

Definitions and Concepts	**Examples**
There are three methods that can be used to solve nonlinear systems of equations: graphing, substitution, and addition.	**Solve by graphing:** $\begin{cases} x^2 + y^2 = 16 \\ x + y = 4 \end{cases}$.
Graphing method: Graph each equation and identify the point(s) of intersection of the graphs.	To solve the system, we will graph each equation and identify the point(s) of intersection of the two graphs. The graph of $x^2 + y^2 = 16$ is a circle with center at the origin and radius of 4. The equation of $x + y = 4$ is a line with x-intercept $(4, 0)$ and y-intercept $(0, 4)$. After graphing the circle and the line, as shown in the figure, we see that there are two intersection points or solutions, $P(0, 4)$ and $P'(4, 0)$.
	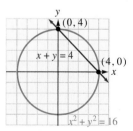

Definitions and Concepts	Examples

Substitution method:

We convert the two-variable, two-equation system into one equation and one variable using substitution.

To do so, solve one equation for one variable and then substitute into the second equation. Next, solve for the one variable. Finally, use back substitution to find the second variable.

This method is recommended when one of the equations is second degree and one equation is linear.

Solve by substitution: $\begin{cases} x^2 + y^2 = 2 \\ y = x \end{cases}$.

We will substitute y for x into the first equation and convert the system into one equation and one variable y. Then, we will solve for x and use back substitution to solve for the second variable.

$$x^2 + y^2 = 2$$
$$y^2 + y^2 = 2 \qquad \text{Substitute } y \text{ for } x.$$
$$2y^2 = 2$$
$$y^2 = 1$$
$$y = 1 \quad \text{or} \quad y = -1 \qquad \text{Solve by Square Root Property.}$$

Because $y = x$, the solutions are $(1, 1)$ and $(-1, -1)$.

Addition method:

We eliminate one of the variables by addition and then solve the system.

Use this method when a system consists of two second-degree equations of the form $ax^2 + by^2 = c$.

Solve by addition: $\begin{cases} x^2 + y^2 = 4 \\ 4x^2 + y^2 = 16 \end{cases}$.

To eliminate the terms involving y^2, we copy the first equation and multiply the second equation by -1 to obtain the following equivalent system.

$$\begin{cases} x^2 + y^2 = 4 \\ -4x^2 - y^2 = -16 \end{cases}$$

We can then add the equations and solve the resulting equation for x:

$$-3x^2 = -12$$
$$x^2 = 4$$
$$x = 2 \quad \text{or} \quad x = -2$$

To find y, we substitute 2 for x and then -2 for x in the first equation.

For $x = 2$	For $x = -2$
$x^2 + y^2 = 4$	$x^2 + y^2 = 4$
$(2)^2 + y^2 = 4$	$(-2)^2 + y^2 = 4$
$4 + y^2 = 4$	$4 + y^2 = 4$
$y^2 = 0$	$y^2 = 0$
$y = 0$	$y = 0$

The two solutions are $(2, 0)$ and $(-2, 0)$.

EXERCISES

25. Solve by graphing: $\begin{cases} x^2 + y^2 = 16 \\ y = x + 4 \end{cases}$.

26. Solve by graphing: $\begin{cases} 3x^2 + y^2 = 52 \\ x^2 - y^2 = 12 \end{cases}$.

27. Solve by graphing: $\begin{cases} \dfrac{x^2}{16} + \dfrac{y^2}{12} = 1 \\ x^2 - \dfrac{y^2}{3} = 1 \end{cases}$.

28. Solve by substitution or addition: $\begin{cases} 3x^2 + y^2 = 52 \\ x^2 - y^2 = 12 \end{cases}$.

29. Solve by substitution or addition:

$$\begin{cases} x^2 + y^2 = 16 \\ -\sqrt{3}y + 4\sqrt{3} = 3x \end{cases}.$$

30. Solve by substitution or addition: $\begin{cases} \dfrac{x^2}{16} + \dfrac{y^2}{12} = 1 \\ x^2 - \dfrac{y^2}{3} = 1 \end{cases}$.

CHAPTER TEST

Write an equation in standard form of each circle described.

1. Center (2, 3); $r = 3$

2. Ends of diameter at (–2, –2) and (6, 8)

3. Center (2, –5), passes through (7, 7)

4. Change the equation of the circle
$x^2 + y^2 - 4x + 6y + 4 = 0$ to standard form and graph it.

Find an equation in standard form of each parabola described.

5. Vertex (3, 2); focus at (3, 6)

6. Vertex (4, –6); passes through (3, –8) and (3, –4)

7. Vertex (2, –3); passes through (0, 0)

8. Change the equation of the parabola
$x^2 - 6x - 8y = 7$ into standard form and graph it.

Find an equation in standard form of each ellipse described.

9. Vertex $(10, 0)$, center at the origin, focus at $(6, 0)$

10. Minor axis 24, center at the origin, focus at $(5, 0)$

11. Center $(2, 3)$; passes through $(2, 9)$ and $(0, 3)$

12. Change the equation of the ellipse
$9x^2 + 4y^2 - 18x - 16y - 11 = 0$ into standard form and graph it.

Find an equation in standard form of each hyperbola described.

13. Center at the origin, focus at $(13, 0)$, vertex at $(5, 0)$

14. Vertices $(6, 0)$ and $(-6, 0)$; $\dfrac{c}{a} = \dfrac{13}{12}$

15. Center $(2, -1)$, major axis horizontal and of length 16, distance of 20 between foci

16. Change the equation of the hyperbola
$x^2 - 4y^2 + 16y = 8$ into standard form and graph it.

Solve each system using substitution or addition.

17. $\begin{cases} x^2 + y^2 = 23 \\ y = x^2 - 3 \end{cases}$

18. $\begin{cases} 2x^2 - 3y^2 = 9 \\ x^2 + y^2 = 27 \end{cases}$

Complete the square to write each equation in standard form, and identify the curve.

19. $y^2 - 4y - 6x - 14 = 0$

20. $2x^2 + 3y^2 - 4x + 12y + 8 = 0$

CUMULATIVE REVIEW EXERCISES

Simplify each expression. Assume that all variables represent positive numbers, and write answers without using negative exponents.

1. $64^{2/3}$

2. $8^{-1/3}$

3. $\dfrac{y^{2/3} y^{5/3}}{y^{1/3}}$

4. $\dfrac{(x^{5/3})(x^{1/2})}{x^{3/4}}$

5. $(x^{2/3} - x^{1/3})(x^{2/3} + x^{1/3})$

6. $(x^{-1/2} + x^{1/2})^2$

7. $\sqrt[3]{-27x^3}$

8. $\sqrt{48t^3}$

9. $\sqrt[3]{\dfrac{128x^4}{2x}}$

10. $\sqrt{x^2 + 6x + 9}$

11. $\sqrt{50} - \sqrt{8} + \sqrt{32}$

12. $-3\sqrt[4]{32} - 2\sqrt[4]{162} + 5\sqrt[4]{48}$

13. $3\sqrt{2}\left(2\sqrt{3} - 4\sqrt{12}\right)$

14. $\dfrac{5}{\sqrt[3]{x}}$

15. $\dfrac{\sqrt{x} + 2}{\sqrt{x} - 1}$

16. $\sqrt[6]{x^3 y^3}$

Solve each equation.

17. $5\sqrt{x + 2} = x + 8$

18. $\sqrt{x} + \sqrt{x + 2} = 2$

19. Use the method of completing the square to solve the equation $2x^2 + x - 3 = 0$.

20. Use the Quadratic Formula to solve the equation $3x^2 + 4x - 1 = 0$.

Perform each operation and write each complex number in a + bi form.

21. $(3 + 5i) + (4 - 3i)$

22. $(7 - 4i) - (12 + 3i)$

23. $(2 - 3i)(2 + 3i)$

24. $(3 + i)(3 - 3i)$

25. $(3 - 2i) - (4 + i)^2$

26. $\dfrac{5}{3 - i}$

Find each value.

27. $|3 + 2i|$

28. $|5 - 6i|$

29. For what values of k will the solutions of $2x^2 + 4x = k$ be equal?

30. Find the coordinates of the vertex of the graph of the equation $y = \frac{1}{2}x^2 - x + 1$.

Solve each inequality and give the result in interval notation.

31. Solve: $x^2 - x - 6 > 0$.

32. Solve: $x^2 - x - 6 \le 0$.

Let $f(x) = 3x^2 + 2$ and $g(x) = 2x - 1$.

Find each value or function.

33. $f(-1)$

34. $(g \circ f)(2)$

35. $(f \circ g)(x)$

36. $(g \circ f)(x)$

37. Write $y = \log_2 x$ in exponential notation.

38. Write $3^b = a$ in logarithmic notation.

Find x.

39. $\log_x 25 = 2$

40. $\log_5 125 = x$

41. $\log_3 x = -3$

42. $\log_5 x = 0$

43. Find the inverse of $y = \log_2 x$.

44. If $\log_{10} 10^x = y$, then y equals what quantity?

$\log 7 \approx 0.8451$ *and* $\log 14 \approx 1.1461$

Approximate each expression without using a calculator or tables.

45. $\log 98$

46. $\log 2$

47. $\log 49$

48. $\log \dfrac{7}{5}$ (*Hint:* $\log 10 = 1$.)

49. Solve: $2^{x+2} = 3^x$.

50. Solve: $2 \log 5 + \log x - \log 4 = 2$.

Use a calculator for Exercises 51 and 52.

51. **Boat depreciation** How much will a $9,000 boat be worth after 9 years if it depreciates 12% per year?

52. Find $\log_6 8$.

53. Use graphing to solve $\begin{cases} 2x + y = 5 \\ x - 2y = 0 \end{cases}$.

54. Use substitution to solve $\begin{cases} 3x + y = 4 \\ 2x - 3y = -1 \end{cases}$.

55. Use addition to solve $\begin{cases} x + 2y = -2 \\ 2x - y = 6 \end{cases}$.

56. Use any method to solve $\begin{cases} \dfrac{x}{10} + \dfrac{y}{5} = \dfrac{1}{2} \\ \dfrac{x}{2} - \dfrac{y}{5} = \dfrac{13}{10} \end{cases}$.

57. Evaluate: $\begin{vmatrix} 3 & -2 \\ 1 & -1 \end{vmatrix}$.

58. Use Cramer's Rule and solve for y only: $\begin{cases} 4x - 3y = -1 \\ 3x + 4y = -7 \end{cases}$.

59. Solve: $\begin{cases} x + y + z = 1 \\ 2x - y - z = -4 \\ x - 2y + z = 4 \end{cases}$.

60. Solve: $\begin{cases} x + 2y + 3z = 6 \\ 3x + 2y + z = 6 \\ 2x + 3y + z = 6 \end{cases}$.

Sequences, Series, and Probability

8

CAREERS AND MATHEMATICS: Actuary

Actuaries deal with the financial impact of risk and uncertainty. Actuaries are in high demand and are well paid for their services. They work for insurance companies and estimate the probability and likely cost of events such as death, sickness, injury, disability, or loss of property. They use this information to help design insurance policies. In the finance sector, they aid companies in how to invest their resources to maximize the return on investment and help ensure that pension plans are maintained on a sound financial basis.

Education and Mathematics Required
• Actuaries generally have a bachelor's degree and are required to pass a series of exams in order to become a certified actuary.
• College Algebra, Trigonometry, Calculus I and II, Linear Algebra, Probability and Mathematical Statistics, Applied Statistics, and Actuarial Mathematics are math courses required. Optional courses in numerical analysis, training in operations research, and substantial training in computer science are also necessary.

How Actuaries Use Math and Who Employs Them
• Actuaries estimate the probability and likely cost of an event, such as death, sickness, injury, or loss of property. To do this, they must gather and correctly analyze data. Actuaries also have a broad knowledge of statistics, finance, and business.
• About 55% of all actuaries are employed by insurance carriers. Another 16% work for management, scientific, and technical consulting services. A small number are employed by government agencies.

Career Outlook and Earnings
• Employment is expected to grow much faster than the average for all occupations. Employment of actuaries is expected to increase by 21% over the 2008–18 period. Greater job growth will occur in the financial and consulting areas than in the insurance sector.
• The median annual salary in 2008 was $84,810, with the top 10% earning more than $160,780.

For more information see: www.bls.gov/oco

In this chapter, we introduce a way to expand powers of binomials of the form $(x + y)^n$. This method leads to ideas needed when working with probability and statistics.

8.1 The Binomial Theorem

In this section, we will learn to

1. Use Pascal's Triangle to expand a binomial.
2. Define and use factorial notation.
3. Use the Binomial Theorem to expand binomials.
4. Find a specific term of a binomial expansion.

Needlepointed triangle by William H. Mitchell

We begin this chapter by discussing a triangle, called **Pascal's Triangle**, which is named after the French mathematician Blaise Pascal. Although the Western world gives credit for the triangle to Pascal, other mathematicians in other parts of the world studied it centuries before him. Around 1068, the Indian mathematician Bhattotpala presented the first seventeen rows of the triangle. Around the same time, the great Persian mathematician Omar Khayyám discussed the triangle. Today, in Iran, the triangle is referred to as the Khayyám Triangle. Around 1250, the Chinese mathematician Yang Hui developed the triangle, and in China, the triangle is known as Yang Hui's Triangle.

Over the years many people have searched the triangle for the many number patterns it contains. One such person, William H. Mitchell, was so impressed with the triangle that he created a needlepoint design of the triangle.

We introduce the triangle by discussing a way to expand binomials of the form $(x + y)^n$, where n is a natural number. Consider the following expansions.

$$(a + b)^0 = 1$$
$$(a + b)^1 = a + b$$
$$(a + b)^2 = a^2 + 2ab + b^2$$
$$(a + b)^3 = a^3 + 3a^2b + 3ab^2 + b^3$$
$$(a + b)^4 = a^4 + 4a^3b + 6a^2b^2 + 4ab^3 + b^4$$
$$(a + b)^5 = a^5 + 5a^4b + 10a^3b^2 + 10a^2b^3 + 5ab^4 + b^5$$
$$(a + b)^6 = a^6 + 6a^5b + 15a^4b^2 + 20a^3b^3 + 15a^2b^4 + 6ab^5 + b^6$$

Four patterns are apparent in the above expansions:

1. Each expansion has one more term than the power of the binomial.
2. The degree of each term in each expansion equals the exponent of the binomial.
3. The first term in each expansion is a raised to the power of the binomial.
4. The exponents of a decrease by 1 in each successive term, and the exponents on b, beginning with b^0 in the first term, increase by 1 in each successive term.

1. Use Pascal's Triangle to Expand a Binomial

To see another pattern, we write the coefficients of the above expansions in a triangular array:

$(a + b)^0 =$							1						**Row 0**
$(a + b)^1 =$						1		1					**Row 1**
$(a + b)^2 =$					1		2		1				**Row 2**
$(a + b)^3 =$				1		3		3		1			**Row 3**
$(a + b)^4 =$			1		4		6		4		1		**Row 4**
$(a + b)^5 =$		1		5		10		10		5		1	**Row 5**
$(a + b)^6 =$	1		6		15		20		15		6	1	**Row 6**

In this array, each entry other than the 1's is the sum of the closest pair of numbers in the line above it. For example, the first 3 in the third row is the sum of the 1 and 2 above it. The 20 in the sixth row is the sum of the 10's above it.

This array, called **Pascal's Triangle** after Blaise Pascal (1623–1662), continues with the same pattern forever. The next two lines are

| $(a + b)^7 =$ | 1 | 7 | 21 | 35 | 35 | 21 | 7 | 1 | | Row 7 |
| $(a + b)^8 =$ | 1 | 8 | 28 | 56 | 70 | 56 | 28 | 8 | 1 | Row 8 |

EXAMPLE 1   **Using Pascal's Triangle to Expand a Binomial**

Expand: $(x + y)^6$.

SOLUTION   The first term is x^6, and the exponents on x will decrease by 1 in each successive term. A y will appear in the second term, and the exponents on y will increase by 1 in each successive term, concluding when the term y^6 is reached. The variables in the expansion are

$$x^6 \quad x^5y \quad x^4y^2 \quad x^3y^3 \quad x^2y^4 \quad xy^5 \quad y^6$$

We can use Pascal's Triangle to find the coefficients of the variables. Because the binomial is raised to the sixth power, we choose Row 6 of Pascal's Triangle. The coefficients of the variables are the numbers in that row.

$$1 \quad 6 \quad 15 \quad 20 \quad 15 \quad 6 \quad 1$$

Putting this information together gives the expansion:

$$(x + y)^6 = x^6 + 6x^5y + 15x^4y^2 + 20x^3y^3 + 15x^2y^4 + 6xy^5 + y^6$$

Self Check 1   Expand: $(p + q)^3$.

Now Try Exercise 21.

EXAMPLE 2   **Expanding a Binomial**

Expand: $(x - y)^6$.

SOLUTION   We write the binomial as $[x + (-y)]^6$ and substitute $-y$ for y in the result of Example 1.

Comment

In general, the signs in the expansion of $(x - y)^n$ alternate. The sign of the first term is $+$, the sign of the second term is $-$, and so on.

$$[x + (-y)]^6$$
$$= x^6 + 6x^5(-y) + 15x^4(-y)^2 + 20x^3(-y)^3 + 15x^2(-y)^4 + 6x(-y)^5 + (-y)^6$$
$$= x^6 - 6x^5y + 15x^4y^2 - 20x^3y^3 + 15x^2y^4 - 6xy^5 + y^6$$

Self Check 2   Expand: $(p - q)^3$.

Now Try Exercise 23.

2. Define and Use Factorial Notation

To use the Binomial Theorem to expand a binomial, we will need **factorial notation.**

Factorial Notation   If n is a natural number, the symbol $n!$ (read either as "***n* factorial**" or as "**factorial *n***") is defined as

$$n! = n(n - 1)(n - 2)(n - 3) \cdot \cdots \cdot (3)(2)(1)$$

EXAMPLE 3   **Evaluating Factorials**

Evaluate: **a.** 3!   **b.** 6!   **c.** 10!

SOLUTION   We will apply the definition of factorial notation.

a. $3! = 3 \cdot 2 \cdot 1 = 6$

b. $6! = 6 \cdot 5 \cdot 4 \cdot 3 \cdot 2 \cdot 1 = 720$

c. $10! = 10 \cdot 9 \cdot 8 \cdot 7 \cdot 6 \cdot 5 \cdot 4 \cdot 3 \cdot 2 \cdot 1 = 3{,}628{,}800$

Self Check 3   Evaluate: **a.** 4!   **b.** 7!

Now Try Exercise 9.

ACCENT ON TECHNOLOGY   **Factorials**

A graphing calculator can be used to evaluate factorials. Consider 10!. The calculator operation that will be used is **!**

To find 10!, first enter 10 in your calculator.

Press **MATH** and move the cursor to PRB. Scroll down to **4:!**.

Press **ENTER** twice and obtain a value of 3,628,800 .

FIGURE 8-1

There are two fundamental properties of factorials.

Properties of Factorials   **1.** By definition, $0! = 1$.

2. If n is a natural number, $n(n - 1)! = n!$.

EXAMPLE 4   **Using Factorials**

Show that **a.** $6 \cdot 5! = 6!$ and   **b.** $8 \cdot 7! = 8!$.

SOLUTION   We will apply the definition of factorial notation.

a. $6 \cdot 5! = 6(5 \cdot 4 \cdot 3 \cdot 2 \cdot 1)$

$= 6 \cdot 5 \cdot 4 \cdot 3 \cdot 2 \cdot 1$

$= 6!$

b. $8 \cdot 7! = 8(7 \cdot 6 \cdot 5 \cdot 4 \cdot 3 \cdot 2 \cdot 1)$

$= 8 \cdot 7 \cdot 6 \cdot 5 \cdot 4 \cdot 3 \cdot 2 \cdot 1$

$= 8!$

Self Check 4   Show that $4 \cdot 3! = 4!$.

Now Try Exercise 7.

3. Use the Binomial Theorem to Expand Binomials

We can now state the Binomial Theorem.

The Binomial Theorem	If n is any positive number, then

$$(a + b)^n = a^n + \frac{n!}{1!(n-1)!} a^{n-1}b + \frac{n!}{2!(n-2)!} a^{n-2}b^2$$

$$+ \frac{n!}{3!(n-3)!} a^{n-3}b^3 + \cdots + \frac{n!}{r!(n-r)!} a^{n-r}b^r + \cdots + b^n$$

Comment

In the expansion of $(a + b)^n$, the term containing b^r is given by

$$\frac{n!}{r!(n-r)!}a^{n-r}b^r$$

A proof of the Binomial Theorem appears in Appendix I.

In the Binomial Theorem, the exponents on the variables in each term on the right side follow the familiar patterns:

1. The sum of the exponents on a and b in each term is n.
2. The exponents on a decrease by 1 in each successive term.
3. The exponents on b increase by 1 in each successive term.

However, the method of finding the coefficients is different. Except for the first and last terms, $n!$ is the numerator of each fractional coefficient. When the exponent on b is 2, the factors in the denominator of the fractional coefficient are $2!$ and $(n-2)!$. When the exponent on b is 3, the factors in the denominator are $3!$ and $(n-3)!$. When the exponent on b is r, the factors in the denominator are $r!$ and $(n-r)!$.

EXAMPLE 5   **Using the Binomial Theorem to Expand a Binomial**

Use the Binomial Theorem to expand $(a + b)^5$.

SOLUTION   We substitute directly into the Binomial Theorem.

$$(a + b)^5 = a^5 + \frac{5!}{1!(5-1)!} a^4b + \frac{5!}{2!(5-2)!} a^3b^2 + \frac{5!}{3!(5-3)!} a^2b^3 + \frac{5!}{4!(5-4)!} ab^4 + b^5$$

$$= a^5 + \frac{5 \cdot 4!}{1 \cdot 4!} a^4b + \frac{5 \cdot 4 \cdot 3!}{2 \cdot 1 \cdot 3!} a^3b^2 + \frac{5 \cdot 4 \cdot 3!}{3! \cdot 2 \cdot 1} a^2b^3 + \frac{5 \cdot 4!}{4! \cdot 1} ab^4 + b^5$$

$$= a^5 + 5a^4b + 10a^3b^2 + 10a^2b^3 + 5ab^4 + b^5$$

We note that the coefficients are the same numbers as in the fifth row of Pascal's Triangle. ∎

Self Check 5   Use the Binomial Theorem to expand $(p + q)^4$.

Now Try Exercise 25.

EXAMPLE 6   **Using the Binomial Theorem to Expand a Binomial**

Use the Binomial Theorem to expand $(2x - 3y)^4$.

SOLUTION   We first find the expansion of $(a + b)^4$.

$$(a + b)^4 = a^4 + \frac{4!}{1!(4-1)!} a^3b + \frac{4!}{2!(4-2)!} a^2b^2 + \frac{4!}{3!(4-3)!} ab^3 + b^4$$

$$= a^4 + \frac{4 \cdot 3!}{1 \cdot 3!} a^3b + \frac{4 \cdot 3 \cdot 2!}{2 \cdot 1 \cdot 2!} a^2b^2 + \frac{4 \cdot 3!}{3! \cdot 1} ab^3 + b^4$$

$$= a^4 + 4a^3b + 6a^2b^2 + 4ab^3 + b^4$$

We then substitute $2x$ for a and $-3y$ for b in the result.

$$(a + b)^4 = a^4 + 4a^3b + 6a^2b^2 + 4ab^3 + b^4$$

$$[2x + (-3y)]^4 = (2x)^4 + 4(2x)^3(-3y) + 6(2x)^2(-3y)^2 + 4(2x)(-3y)^3 + (-3y)^4$$

$$(2x - 3y)^4 = 16x^4 - 96x^3y + 216x^2y^2 - 216xy^3 + 81y^4$$

Self Check 6   Use the Binomial Theorem to expand $(3x - 2y)^4$.

Now Try Exercise 37.

4. Find a Specific Term of a Binomial Expansion

Suppose that we wish to find the fifth term of the expansion of $(a + b)^{11}$. It would be tedious to raise the binomial to the 11th power and then look at the fifth term. The Binomial Theorem provides an easier way.

EXAMPLE 7   **Finding a Specific Term of a Binomial Expansion**

Find the fifth term of the expansion of $(a + b)^{11}$.

SOLUTION   In the fifth term, the exponent on b is 4 (the exponent on b is always 1 less than the number of the term). Since the exponent on b added to the exponent on a equals 11, the exponent on a is 7. The variables of the fifth term are a^7b^4.

The number in the numerator of the fractional coefficient is $n!$, which in this case is $11!$. The factors in the denominator are $4!$ and $(11 - 4)!$. The complete fifth term is

$$\frac{11!}{4!(11 - 4)!} a^7b^4 = \frac{11!}{4!7!} a^7b^4$$

$$= \frac{11 \cdot 10 \cdot 9 \cdot 8 \cdot 7!}{4 \cdot 3 \cdot 2 \cdot 1 \cdot 7!} a^7b^4$$

$$= 330a^7b^4$$

Comment

We can also use the formula for the term containing b^r, where $r = 4$ and $n = 11$.

$$\frac{n!}{r!(n-r)!} a^{n-r}b^r = \frac{11!}{4!(11 - 4)!} a^{11-4}b^4$$

$$= \frac{11!}{4!7!} a^7b^4$$

$$= 330a^7b^4$$

Self Check 7   Find the sixth term of the expansion in Example 7.

Now Try Exercise 43.

EXAMPLE 8   **Finding a Specific Term of a Binomial Expansion**

Find the sixth term of the expansion of $(a + b)^9$.

SOLUTION   In the sixth term, the exponent on b is 5, and the exponent on a is $9 - 5$, or 4. The numerator of the fractional coefficient is $9!$, and the factors in the denominator are $5!$ and $(9 - 5)!$. The sixth term of the expansion is

$$\frac{9!}{5!(9 - 5)!} a^4b^5 = \frac{9 \cdot 8 \cdot 7 \cdot 6 \cdot 5!}{5! \cdot 4!} a^4b^5$$

$$= \frac{9 \cdot 8 \cdot 7 \cdot 6}{4 \cdot 3 \cdot 2 \cdot 1} a^4b^5$$

$$= 126a^4b^5$$

Comment

We can also use the formula for the term containing b^r, where $r = 5$ and $n = 9$.

$$\frac{n!}{r!(n - r)!} a^{n-r}b^r = \frac{9!}{5!(9 - 5)!} a^{9-5}b^5$$

$$= \frac{9!}{5!4!} a^4b^5$$

$$= 126a^4b^5$$

Self Check 8   Find the fifth term of the expansion in Example 8.

Now Try Exercise 47.

EXAMPLE 9 **Finding a Specific Term of a Binomial Expansion**

Find the third term of the expansion of $(3x - 2y)^6$.

SOLUTION We begin by finding the third term of the expansion of $(a + b)^6$.

(1) $\dfrac{6!}{2!(6 - 2)!} a^4 b^2 = \dfrac{6 \cdot 5 \cdot 4!}{2 \cdot 1 \cdot 4!} a^4 b^2 = 15a^4 b^2$

We can then substitute $3x$ for a and $-2y$ for b in Equation 1 to obtain the third term of the expansion of $(3x - 2y)^6$.

$15a^4 b^2 = 15(3x)^4(-2y)^2$

$= 15(3)^4(-2)^2 x^4 y^2$

$= 4{,}860 x^4 y^2$ ∎

Self Check 9 Find the fourth term of the expansion in Example 9.

Now Try Exercise 53.

Self Check Answers 1. $p^3 + 3p^2 q + 3pq^2 + q^3$ 2. $p^3 - 3p^2 q + 3pq^2 - q^3$ 3. **a.** 24
b. 5,040   4. $4 \cdot (3 \cdot 2 \cdot 1) = 4 \cdot 3 \cdot 2 \cdot 1 = 4!$
5. $p^4 + 4p^3 q + 6p^2 q^2 + 4pq^3 + q^4$
6. $81x^4 - 216x^3 y + 216x^2 y^2 - 96xy^3 + 16y^4$ 7. $462a^6 b^5$ 8. $126a^5 b^4$
9. $-4{,}320 x^3 y^3$

Exercises 8.1

Getting Ready

You should be able to complete these vocabulary and concept statements before you proceed to the practice exercises.

Fill in the blanks.

1. In the expansion of a binomial, there will be one more term than the _____ of the binomial.

2. The _____ of each term in a binomial expansion is the same as the exponent of the binomial.

3. The _____ term in a binomial expansion is the first term raised to the power of the binomial.

4. In the expansion of $(p + q)^n$, the _____ on p decrease by 1 in each successive term.

5. Expand 7!: _____

6. $0! =$ ___

7. $n \cdot$ _____ $= n!$

8. In the seventh term of $(a + b)^{11}$, the exponent on a is ___ .

Practice

Evaluate each expression.

9. $5!$

10. $-5!$

11. $3! \cdot 6!$

12. $0! \cdot 7!$

13. $6! + 6!$

14. $5! - 2!$

15. $\dfrac{9!}{12!}$

16. $\dfrac{8!}{5!}$

17. $\dfrac{5! \cdot 7!}{9!}$

18. $\dfrac{3! \cdot 5! \cdot 7!}{1!8!}$

19. $\dfrac{18!}{6!(18 - 6)!}$

20. $\dfrac{15!}{9!(15 - 9)!}$

Use Pascal's Triangle to expand each binomial.

21. $(a + b)^5$

22. $(a + b)^7$

23. $(x - y)^3$

24. $(x - y)^7$

Use the Binomial Theorem to expand each binomial.

25. $(a + b)^3$

26. $(a + b)^4$

27. $(a - b)^5$

28. $(x - y)^4$

29. $(2x + y)^3$

30. $(x + 2y)^3$

31. $(x - 2y)^3$

32. $(2x - y)^3$

33. $(2x + 3y)^4$

34. $(2x - 3y)^4$

35. $(x - 2y)^4$

36. $(x + 2y)^4$

37. $(x - 3y)^5$

38. $(3x - y)^5$

39. $\left(\dfrac{x}{2} + y\right)^4$

40. $\left(x + \dfrac{y}{2}\right)^4$

Find the required term in each binomial expansion.

41. $(a + b)^4$; 3rd term

42. $(a - b)^4$; 2nd term

43. $(a + b)^7$; 5th term

44. $(a + b)^5$; 4th term

45. $(a - b)^5$; 6th term

46. $(a - b)^8$; 7th term

47. $(a + b)^{17}$; 5th term

48. $(a - b)^{12}$; 3rd term

49. $\left(a - \sqrt{2}\right)^4$; 2nd term

50. $\left(a - \sqrt{3}\right)^8$; 3rd term

51. $\left(a + \sqrt{3}b\right)^9$; 5th term

52. $\left(\sqrt{2}a - b\right)^7$; 4th term

53. $\left(\dfrac{x}{2} + y\right)^4$; 3rd term

54. $\left(m + \dfrac{n}{2}\right)^8$; 3rd term

55. $\left(\dfrac{r}{2} - \dfrac{s}{2}\right)^{11}$; 10th term

56. $\left(\dfrac{p}{2} - \dfrac{q}{2}\right)^9$; 6th term

57. $(a + b)^n$; 4th term

58. $(a - b)^n$; 5th term

59. $(a + b)^n$; rth term

60. $(a + b)^n$; $(r + 1)$th term

Discovery and Writing

61. Find the sum of the numbers in each row of the first ten rows of Pascal's Triangle. Do you see a pattern?

62. Show that the sum of the coefficients in the binomial expansion of $(x + y)^n$ is 2^n. (*Hint:* Let $x = y = 1$.)

63. Find the constant term in the expansion of
$$\left(a - \dfrac{1}{a}\right)^{10}$$

64. Find the coefficient of x^5 in the expansion of
$$\left(x + \dfrac{1}{x}\right)^9$$

65. If we applied the pattern of coefficients to the coefficient of the first term in the Binomial Theorem, it would be $\dfrac{n!}{0!(n - 0)!}$. Show that this expression equals 1.

66. If we applied the pattern of coefficients to the coefficient of the last term in the Binomial Theorem, it would be $\dfrac{n!}{n!(n - n)!}$. Show that this expression equals 1.

67. Define factorial notation and explain how to evaluate 10!.

68. With a calculator, evaluate 69!. Explain why we cannot find 70! with a calculator.

69. Explain how the rth term of a binomial expansion is constructed.

70. Explain the four patterns apparent in a binomial expansion.

Review

Factor each expression.

71. $3x^3y^2z^4 - 6xyz^5 + 15x^2yz^2$

72. $3z^2 - 15tz + 12t^2$

73. $a^4 - b^4$

74. $3r^4 - 36r^3 - 135r^2$

Simplify each complex fraction.

75. $\dfrac{\dfrac{1}{x} + \dfrac{1}{3}}{\dfrac{1}{x} - \dfrac{1}{3}}$

76. $\dfrac{x - \dfrac{1}{y}}{y - \dfrac{1}{x}}$

8.2 Sequences, Series, and Summation Notation

In this section, we will learn to

1. Define and use sequences.
2. Define a sequence recursively.
3. Define series.
4. Define and use summation notation.

In this section, we will introduce a function whose domain is the set of natural numbers. This function, called a **sequence**, is a list of numbers in a specific order. Sequences are seen all around us. For example, we can unlock a digital lock by entering the correct sequence of numbers, a pilot performs the same sequence of checks before taking off, and our life is often changed by a sequence of events. We even use sequences for entertainment when we play the Sequence Game.

1. Define and Use Sequences

The meaning of the word *sequence* in mathematics is very similar to the meaning of the word in everyday English. It refers to a list of events in a particular order.

Sequences

An **infinite sequence** is a function whose domain is the set of natural numbers.

A **finite sequence** is a function whose domain is the set of the first n natural numbers.

Since a sequence is a function whose domain is the set of natural numbers, we can write its terms as a list of numbers. For example, if n is a natural number, the function defined by $f(n) = 2n - 1$ generates the following infinite sequence

$$f(1) = 2(1) - 1 = 1$$

$$f(2) = 2(2) - 1 = 3$$

$$f(3) = 2(3) - 1 = 5$$

$$f(n) = 2(n) - 1 = 2n - 1$$

Writing the results horizontally, we have

$$1, 3, 5, \ldots, 2n - 1, \ldots$$

The number 1 is the first term, 3 is the second term, 5 is the third term, and $2n - 1$ is the **general**, or **nth term**.

If n is a natural number, the function $f(n) = 3n^2 + 1$ generates the infinite sequence

$$4, 13, 28, \ldots, 3n^2 + 1, \ldots$$

The number 4 is the first term, 13 is the second term, 28 is the third term, and $3n^2 + 1$ is the general term.

If n is one of the first four natural numbers, the function defined by $f(n) = n^2 + 1$ generates the following finite sequence

$$2, 5, 10, 17$$

A constant function such as $g(n) = 1$ is a sequence, because it generates the infinite sequence

$$1, 1, 1, \ldots$$

Comment We seldom use function notation to denote a sequence, because it is often difficult or even impossible to write the general term. In such cases, if there is a pattern that is assumed to be continued, we simply list several terms of the sequence.

Some additional examples of infinite sequences are:

- $1^2, 2^2, 3^2, \ldots, n^2, \ldots$
- $3, 9, 19, 33, \ldots, 2n^2 + 1, \ldots$
- $1, 3, 6, 10, 15, 21, \ldots, \dfrac{n(n + 1)}{2}, \ldots$
- $2, 3, 5, 7, 11, 13, 17, 19, 23, \ldots$ **(prime numbers)**
- $1, 1, 2, 3, 5, 8, 13, 21, \ldots$ **(Fibonacci Sequence)**

The **Fibonacci Sequence** is named after the 12th-century mathematician Leonardo of Pisa, also known as Fibonacci. After the two 1's in the Fibonacci Sequence, each term is the sum of the two terms that immediately precede it. The Fibonacci Sequence occurs in many fields, such as music, the growth patterns of plants, and the reproductive habits of bees. For example, in one octave of a piano keyboard, there are 2 black keys followed by 3 black keys for a total of 5 black keys. In one octave, there are 8 white keys and a total of 13 black and white keys. These are numbers in the Fibonacci Sequence.

C D E F G A B C D E F G A B C D E F G A B

The fruitlets of a pineapple are arranged in interlocking spirals, 8 spirals in one direction and 13 in the other.

2. Define a Sequence Recursively

A sequence can be defined **recursively** by giving its first term and a rule showing how to obtain the $(n + 1)$th term from the nth term. For example, the information

$a_1 = 5$ (the first term)   and $a_{n+1} = 3a_n - 2$ (the rule showing how to get the $(n + 1)$th term from the nth term)

defines a sequence recursively. To find the first five terms of this sequence, we proceed as follows:

$$a_1 = 5$$

$$a_2 = 3(a_1) - 2 = 3(5) - 2 = 13 \qquad \text{Substitute 5 for } a_1 \text{ and simplify to get } a_2.$$

$$a_3 = 3(a_2) - 2 = 3(13) - 2 = 37 \qquad \text{Substitute 13 for } a_2 \text{ and simplify to get } a_3.$$

$$a_4 = 3(a_3) - 2 = 3(37) - 2 = 109 \qquad \text{Substitute 37 for } a_3 \text{ and simplify to get } a_4.$$

$$a_5 = 3(a_4) - 2 = 3(109) - 2 = 325 \qquad \text{Substitute 109 for } a_4 \text{ and simplify to get } a_5.$$

3. Define Series

To add the terms of a sequence, we replace each comma between its terms with a + sign to form a **series**. If a sequence is infinite, the number of terms in the series associated with it is infinite also. Two examples of infinite series are

$$1^2 + 2^2 + 3^2 + \cdots + n^2 + \cdots$$

and

$$1 + 2 + 3 + 5 + 8 + 13 + 21 + \cdots$$

If a sequence is finite, the number of terms in the series associated with it is finite also. An example of a finite series is

$$3 + 7 + 11 + 15$$

If the signs between successive terms of a series alternate, the series is called an **alternating series**. Two examples of alternating infinite series are

$$-3 + 6 - 9 + 12 - 15 + 18 - \cdots + (-1)^n 3n + \cdots$$

and

$$2 - 4 + 8 - 16 + \cdots + (-1)^{n+1} 2^n + \cdots$$

Comment

The series $1 + \frac{1}{2} + \frac{1}{3} + \cdots$ is called a **harmonic series** and is important in calculus. The series $1 - \frac{1}{2} + \frac{1}{3} - \cdots$ is an alternating harmonic series.

4. Define and Use Summation Notation

Summation notation is a shorthand way to indicate the sum of the first n terms, or the **nth partial sum**, of a sequence. For example, the expression

$$\sum_{n=1}^{4} n \qquad \text{The symbol } \Sigma \text{ is the capital letter sigma in the Greek alphabet.}$$

indicates the sum of the four terms obtained when we successively substitute 1, 2, 3, and 4 for n.

$$\sum_{n=1}^{4} n = 1 + 2 + 3 + 4 = 10$$

The expression

$$\sum_{n=2}^{4} n^2$$

indicates the sum of the three terms obtained when we successively substitute 2, 3, and 4 for n.

$$\sum_{n=2}^{4} n^2 = (2)^2 + (3)^2 + (4)^2$$

$$= 4 + 9 + 16$$

$$= 29$$

The expression

$$\sum_{n=1}^{3} (2n^2 + 1)$$

indicates the sum of the three terms obtained if we successively substitute 1, 2, and 3 for n in the expression $2n^2 + 1$.

$$\sum_{n=1}^{3} (2n^2 + 1) = [2(1)^2 + 1] + [2(2)^2 + 1] + [2(3)^2 + 1]$$
$$= 3 + 9 + 19$$
$$= 31$$

EXAMPLE 1   **Evaluating a Sum**

Evaluate: $\displaystyle\sum_{n=1}^{4} (n^2 - 1)$.

SOLUTION   Since n runs from 1 to 4, we substitute 1, 2, 3, and 4 for n in the expression $n^2 + 1$ and find the sum of the resulting terms:

$$\sum_{n=1}^{4} (n^2 - 1) = (1^2 - 1) + (2^2 - 1) + (3^2 - 1) + (4^2 - 1)$$
$$= 0 + 3 + 8 + 15$$
$$= 26$$

Self Check 1   Evaluate: $\displaystyle\sum_{n=1}^{5} (n^2 - 1)$.

Now Try Exercise 27.

EXAMPLE 2   **Evaluating a Sum**

Evaluate: $\displaystyle\sum_{n=3}^{5} (3n + 2)$.

SOLUTION   Since n runs from 3 to 5, we substitute 3, 4, and 5 for n in the expression $3n + 2$ and find the sum of the resulting terms:

$$\sum_{n=3}^{5} (3n + 2) = [3(3) + 2] + [3(4) + 2] + [3(5) + 2]$$
$$= 11 + 14 + 17$$
$$= 42$$

Self Check 2   Evaluate: $\displaystyle\sum_{n=2}^{5} (3n + 2)$.

Now Try Exercise 49.

We can use summation notation to state the Binomial Theorem concisely. In Exercise 58, you will be asked to explain why the Binomial Theorem can be stated as

$$\sum_{r=0}^{n} \frac{n!}{r!(n-r)!} a^{n-r}b^r$$

There are three basic properties of summations. The first states that *the summation of a constant as k runs from 1 to n is n times the constant.*

Summation of a Constant   If c is a constant, then $\displaystyle\sum_{k=1}^{n} c = nc$.

PROOF   Because c is a constant, each term is c for each value of k as k runs from 1 to n.

$$\sum_{k=1}^{n} c = \overbrace{c + c + c + c + \cdots + c}^{n \text{ number of } c\text{'s}} = nc$$

EXAMPLE 3   **Using the Summation of a Constant Property**

Evaluate: $\displaystyle\sum_{n=1}^{5} 13$.

SOLUTION $\displaystyle\sum_{n=1}^{5} 13 = 13 + 13 + 13 + 13 + 13$

$= 5(13)$

$= 65$

Self Check 3   Evaluate: $\displaystyle\sum_{n=1}^{6} 12$.

Now Try Exercise 47.

A second property states that *a constant factor can be brought outside a summation sign.*

Summation of a Product   If c is a constant, then $\displaystyle\sum_{k=1}^{n} cf(k) = c\sum_{k=1}^{n} f(k)$.

PROOF $\displaystyle\sum_{k=1}^{n} cf(k) = cf(1) + cf(2) + cf(3) + \cdots + cf(n)$

$= c[f(1) + f(2) + f(3) + \cdots + f(n)]$ Factor out c.

$= c\displaystyle\sum_{k=1}^{n} f(k)$

EXAMPLE 4   **Using the Summation of a Product Property**

Show that $\displaystyle\sum_{k=1}^{3} 5k^2 = 5\sum_{k=1}^{3} k^2$.

SOLUTION $\displaystyle\sum_{k=1}^{3} 5k^2 = 5(1)^2 + 5(2)^2 + 5(3)^2$ $\quad 5\displaystyle\sum_{k=1}^{3} k^2 = 5[(1)^2 + (2)^2 + (3)^2]$

$= 5 + 20 + 45$ $\qquad\qquad\qquad = 5[1 + 4 + 9]$

$= 70$ $\qquad\qquad\qquad\qquad\quad = 5(14)$

$\qquad\qquad\qquad\qquad\qquad\qquad\qquad\qquad = 70$

The quantities are equal.

Self Check 4   Evaluate: $\displaystyle\sum_{k=1}^{4} 3k$.

Now Try Exercise 43.

The third property states that *the summation of a sum is equal to the sum of the summations.*

Summation of a Sum	$\displaystyle\sum_{k=1}^{n}[f(k) + g(k)] = \sum_{k=1}^{n} f(k) + \sum_{k=1}^{n} g(k)$

PROOF

$$\sum_{k=1}^{n}[f(k) + g(k)] = [f(1) + g(1)] + [f(2) + g(2)] + [f(3) + g(3)] + \cdots + [f(n) + g(n)]$$
$$= [f(1) + f(2) + f(3) + \cdots + f(n)] + [g(1) + g(2) + g(3) + \cdots + g(n)]$$
$$= \sum_{k=1}^{n} f(k) + \sum_{k=1}^{n} g(k) \qquad\blacksquare$$

EXAMPLE 5 **Using the Summation of a Sum Property**

Show that $\displaystyle\sum_{k=1}^{3}(k + k^2) = \sum_{k=1}^{3} k + \sum_{k=1}^{3} k^2$.

SOLUTION

$$\sum_{k=1}^{3}(k + k^2) = (1 + 1^2) + (2 + 2^2) + (3 + 3^2)$$
$$= 2 + 6 + 12$$
$$= 20$$

$$\sum_{k=1}^{3} k + \sum_{k=1}^{3} k^2 = (1 + 2 + 3) + (1^2 + 2^2 + 3^2)$$
$$= 6 + 14$$
$$= 20 \qquad\blacksquare$$

Self Check 5 Evaluate: $\displaystyle\sum_{k=1}^{3}(k^2 + 2k)$.

Now Try Exercise 45.

EXAMPLE 6 **Evaluating a Sum Directly and by Using Properties**

Evaluate $\displaystyle\sum_{k=1}^{5}(2k - 1)^2$ directly. Then expand the binomial, apply the previous properties, and evaluate the expression again.

SOLUTION **Part 1:** $\displaystyle\sum_{k=1}^{5}(2k - 1)^2 = 1 + 9 + 25 + 49 + 81 = 165$

Part 2: $\displaystyle\sum_{k=1}^{5}(2k - 1)^2 = \sum_{k=1}^{5}(4k^2 - 4k + 1)$

$$= \sum_{k=1}^{5} 4k^2 + \sum_{k=1}^{5}(-4k) + \sum_{k=1}^{5} 1 \qquad \text{The summation of a sum is the sum of the summations.}$$

$$= 4\sum_{k=1}^{5} k^2 - 4\sum_{k=1}^{5} k + \sum_{k=1}^{5} 1 \qquad \text{Bring the constant factors outside the summation signs.}$$

$$= 4 \sum_{k=1}^{5} k^2 - 4 \sum_{k=1}^{5} k + 5$$

The summation of a constant as k runs from 1 to 5 is 5 times that constant.

$$= 4(1 + 4 + 9 + 16 + 25) - 4(1 + 2 + 3 + 4 + 5) + 5$$

$$= 4(55) - 4(15) + 5$$

$$= 220 - 60 + 5$$

$$= 165$$

Either way, the sum is 165.

Self Check 6   Evaluate: $\displaystyle\sum_{k=1}^{4} (2k - 1)^2$.

Now Try Exercise 51.

ACCENT ON TECHNOLOGY   **Sequences, Series, and Summation**

A graphing calculator will list a designated number of terms in a sequence as well as add a designated number of terms in a series. For example, let's find the first six terms of the sequence defined by the function

$$f(n) = 3n(n + 2) \text{ and then find } \sum_{n=1}^{6} 3n(n + 2).$$

The calculator operation that will be used is **seq(**, and the order for this operation is *seq(function,variable,start,end,increment)*. The default increment is 1, and it is not necessary to enter the 1. If we want the numbers listed in an increment other than 1, then we will have to put that value in the operation.

Step 1

- Press [2nd] [STAT] to access LIST.
- Move the cursor to OPS and then scroll down to 5:seq(.

Step 2

- Press [ENTER], and type the function, variable, starting value, and ending value.
- Press [ENTER] again to see the values.

Step 3

- Scroll to the right to see all the values.

Step 4

To evaluate $\displaystyle\sum_{n=1}^{6} 3n(n + 2)$, we need to store the list of values in the sequence to a list.

- Press [STO▸], then [2nd] [STAT] to access the LIST menu.
- Press [ENTER] twice to store the values in List 1.

```
NAMES OPS MATH
1:SortA(
2:SortD(
3:dim(
4:Fill(
5▮seq(
6:cumSum(
7↓ΔList(
```

```
seq(3X(X+2),X,1,
6)
{9 24 45 72 105…
▮
```

```
seq(3X(X+2),X,1,
6)
… 45 72 105 144}
▮
```

```
seq(3X(X+2),X,1,
6)
… 45 72 105 144}
Ans→L₁
{9 24 45 72 105…
▮
```

FIGURE 8-2

Step 5

Now we will access the operation cumSum(, which is located directly below the seq(operation.

- Press [2nd] [STAT].
- Scroll right to OPS.
- Scroll down to 6:cumSum(.

Step 6

- Put L₁ into the operation by pressing [2nd] [STAT] [1].
- Close the parentheses and press [ENTER]. The second number is the sum of the first two numbers in the sequence; the third number is the sum of the first 3 terms in the sequence, etc.

Step 7

- Move the cursor to the right until the last number is shown and you will see 399.

The sum of the first 6 terms in the sequence is 399.

$$\sum_{n=1}^{6} 3n(n + 2) = 399$$

```
NAMES OPS MATH
1:SortA(
2:SortD(
3:dim(
4:Fill(
5:seq(
6:cumSum(
7↓∆List(
```

```
seq(3X(X+2),X,1,
6)
 45 72 105 144)
Ans→L₁
{9 24 45 72 105…
cumSum(L₁)
{9 33 78 150 25…
```

```
seq(3X(X+2),X,1,
6)
 45 72 105 144)
Ans→L₁
{9 24 45 72 105…
cumSum(L₁)
…78 150 255 399)
```

FIGURE 8-2 (Continued)

Self Check Answers   **1.** 50   **2.** 50   **3.** 72   **4.** 30   **5.** 26   **6.** 84

Exercises 8.2

Getting Ready
You should be able to complete these vocabulary and concept statements before you proceed to the practice exercises.

Fill in the blanks.

1. An infinite sequence is a function whose _____ is the set of natural numbers.

2. A finite sequence is a function whose _____ is the set of the first n natural numbers.

3. A _____ is formed when we add the terms of a sequence.

4. A series associated with a finite sequence is a _____ series.

5. A series associated with a infinite sequence is an _____ series.

6. If the signs between successive terms of a series alternate, the series is called an _____ series.

7. _____ is a shorthand way to indicate the sum of the first n terms of a sequence.

8. The symbol $\sum_{k=1}^{5}(k^2 - 3)$ indicates the ____ of the five terms obtained when we successively substitute 1, 2, 3, 4, and 5 for k.

9. $\sum_{k=1}^{5} 6k^2 = \underline{\quad} \sum_{k=1}^{5} k^2$

10. $\sum_{k=1}^{5}(k^2 + 3k) = \sum_{k=1}^{5} k^2 + \underline{\quad}$

11. $\sum_{k=1}^{5} c$, where c is a constant, equals ___.

12. The summation of a sum is equal to the _____ of the summations.

Practice
Write the first six terms of the sequence defined by each function.

13. $f(n) = 5n(n - 1)$

14. $f(n) = n\left(\dfrac{n - 1}{2}\right)\left(\dfrac{n - 2}{3}\right)$

Find the next term of each sequence.

15. 1, 6, 11, 16, . . .

16. 1, 8, 27, 64, . . .

17. $a, a + d, a + 2d, a + 3d, . . .$

18. $a, ar, ar^2, ar^3, . . .$

19. 1, 3, 6, 10, . . .

20. 20, 17, 13, 8, . . .

Find the sum of the first five terms of the sequence with the given general term.

21. n

22. $2k$

23. 3

24. $4k^0$

25. $2\left(\dfrac{1}{3}\right)^n$

26. $(-1)^n$

27. $3n - 2$

28. $2k + 1$

Assume that each sequence is defined recursively. Find the first four terms of each sequence.

29. $a_1 = 3$ and $a_{n+1} = 2a_n + 1$

30. $a_1 = -5$ and $a_{n+1} = -a_n - 3$

31. $a_1 = -4$ and $a_{n+1} = \dfrac{a_n}{2}$

32. $a_1 = 0$ and $a_{n+1} = 2a_n^2$

33. $a_1 = k$ and $a_{n+1} = a_n^2$

34. $a_1 = 3$ and $a_{n+1} = ka_n$

35. $a_1 = 8$ and $a_{n+1} = \dfrac{2a_n}{k}$

36. $a_1 = m$ and $a_{n+1} = \dfrac{a_n^2}{m}$

Determine whether each series is an alternating infinite series.

37. $-1 + 2 - 3 + \cdots + (-1)^n n + \cdots$

38. $a + \dfrac{a}{b} + \dfrac{a}{b^2} + \cdots + a\left(\dfrac{1}{b}\right)^{n-1} + \cdots ; b = 4$

39. $a + a^2 + a^3 + \cdots + a^n + \cdots ; a = 3$

40. $a + a^2 + a^3 + \cdots + a^n + \cdots ; a = -2$

Evaluate each sum.

41. $\displaystyle\sum_{k=1}^{5} 2k$

42. $\displaystyle\sum_{k=3}^{6} 3k$

43. $\displaystyle\sum_{k=3}^{4} (-2k^2)$

44. $\displaystyle\sum_{k=1}^{100} 5$

45. $\displaystyle\sum_{k=1}^{5} (3k - 1)$

46. $\displaystyle\sum_{n=2}^{5} (n^2 + 3n)$

47. $\displaystyle\sum_{k=1}^{1{,}000} \dfrac{1}{2}$

48. $\displaystyle\sum_{x=4}^{5} \dfrac{2}{x}$

49. $\displaystyle\sum_{x=3}^{4} \dfrac{1}{x}$

50. $\displaystyle\sum_{x=2}^{6} (3k^2 + 2x) - 3\sum_{x=2}^{6} x^2$

51. $\displaystyle\sum_{x=1}^{4} (4x + 1)^2 - \sum_{x=1}^{4} (4x - 1)^2$

52. $\displaystyle\sum_{x=0}^{10} (2x - 1)^2 + 4\sum_{x=0}^{10} x(1 - x)$

53. $\displaystyle\sum_{x=6}^{8} (5x - 1)^2 + \sum_{x=6}^{8} (10x - 1)$

54. $\displaystyle\sum_{x=2}^{7} (3x + 1)^2 - 3\sum_{x=2}^{7} x(3x + 2)$

Discovery and Writing

55. Find a counterexample to disprove the proposition that the summation of a product is the product of the summations. In other words, prove that

$$\sum_{k=1}^{n} f(k)g(k) \neq \sum_{k=1}^{n} f(k) \sum_{k=1}^{n} g(k)$$

56. Find a counterexample to disprove the proposition that the summation of a quotient is the quotient of the summations. In other words, prove that

$$\sum_{k=1}^{n} \dfrac{f(k)}{g(k)} \neq \dfrac{\displaystyle\sum_{k=1}^{n} f(k)}{\displaystyle\sum_{k=1}^{n} g(k)}$$

57. Explain what it means to define something recursively.

58. Explain why the Binomial Theorem can be stated as

$$\sum_{r=0}^{n} \dfrac{n!}{r!(n - r)!} a^{n-r} b^r$$

Review

The triangles are similar. Find the value of x.

59.

60.

Find the third side of each right triangle.

61.

$AB = 24$ ft
$BC = 10$ ft

62.

8.3 Arithmetic Sequences and Series

In this section, we will learn to

1. Define and use arithmetic sequences.

2. Find arithmetic means.

3. Find the sum of the first n terms of an arithmetic series.

4. Solve problems involving sequences and series.

The German mathematician Carl Friedrich Gauss (1777–1855) was once a student in the class of a strict teacher. One day, the teacher asked the students to add together all of the natural numbers from 1 through 100. Gauss recognized that in the sum

$$1 + 2 + 3 + \cdots + 98 + 99 + 100$$

the first number (1) added to the last number (100) is 101, the second number (2) added to the second from the last number (99) is 101, and the third number (3) added to the third from the last number (98) is 101. He reasoned that there would be fifty pairs of such numbers, and that there would be fifty sums of 101. He multiplied 101 by 50 to get the correct answer of 5,050.

This story illustrates a problem involving the sum of the terms of a sequence, called an **arithmetic sequence**, in which each term except the first is found by adding a constant to the preceding term.

1. Define and Use Arithmetic Sequences

Arithmetic Sequences   An **arithmetic sequence** is a sequence of the form

$$a, \quad a + d, \quad a + 2d, \quad a + 3d, \quad \ldots, \quad a + (n - 1)d, \ldots$$

where a is the **first term**, $a + (n - 1)d$ is the **nth term**, and d is the **common difference.**

In this definition, the second term has an addend of d, the third term has an addend of $2d$, the fourth term has an addend of $3d$, and so on. This is why the nth term has an addend of $(n - 1)d$.

If an arithmetic sequence has infinitely many terms, it is called an **infinite arithmetic sequence**. If it has a finite number of terms, it is called a **finite arithmetic sequence**.

EXAMPLE 1   **Writing Terms of an Arithmetic Sequence**

Write the first six terms and the 21st term of an arithmetic sequence with a first term of 7 and a common difference of 5.

SOLUTION   Since the first term a is 7 and the common difference d is 5, the first six terms are

$$7, \quad 7 + 5, \quad 7 + 2(5), \quad 7 + 3(5), \quad 7 + 4(5), \quad 7 + 5(5)$$

or

$$7, \quad 12, \quad 17, \quad 22, \quad 27, \quad 32$$

To find the 21st term, we substitute 21 for n in the formula for the nth term:

$$n\text{th term} = a + (n - 1)d$$
$$21\text{st term} = 7 + (21 - 1)5$$
$$= 7 + (20)5$$
$$= 107$$

The 21st term is 107.

Self Check 1   Write the first five terms and the 18th term of an arithmetic sequence with a first term of 3 and a common difference of 6.

Now Try Exercise 9.

EXAMPLE 2   **Determining a Specific Term of an Arithmetic Sequence**

Find the 98th term of an arithmetic sequence whose first three terms are 2, 6, and 10.

SOLUTION   Here $a = 2$, $n = 98$, and $d = 6 - 2 = 10 - 6 = 4$. Because we want to find the 98th term, we substitute these numbers into the formula for the nth term:

$$n\text{th term} = a + (n - 1)d$$
$$98\text{th term} = 2 + (98 - 1)4$$
$$= 2 + (97)4$$
$$= 390$$

Self Check 2   Write the 50th term of the arithmetic sequence whose first three terms are 3, 8, and 13.

Now Try Exercise 19.

2. Find Arithmetic Means

Numbers inserted between a first and last term to form a segment of an arithmetic sequence are called **arithmetic means**. When finding arithmetic means, we consider the last term, a_n, to be the nth term:

$$a_n = a + (n - 1)d$$

EXAMPLE 3   **Inserting Arithmetic Means between Real Numbers**

Insert three arithmetic means between -3 and 12.

SOLUTION Since we are inserting three arithmetic means between -3 and 12, the total number of terms is five. Thus, $a = -3$, $a_n = 12$, and $n = 5$. To find the common difference, we substitute -3 for a, 12 for a_n, and 5 for n in the formula for the last term and solve for d:

$$a_n = a + (n - 1)d$$

$$12 = -3 + (5 - 1)d$$

$$15 = 4d \qquad \text{Add 3 to both sides and simplify.}$$

$$\frac{15}{4} = d \qquad \text{Divide both sides by 4.}$$

Once we know d, we can find the other terms of the sequence:

$$a + d = -3 + \frac{15}{4} = \frac{3}{4}$$

$$a + 2d = -3 + 2\left(\frac{15}{4}\right) = -3 + \frac{30}{4} = 4\frac{1}{2}$$

$$a + 3d = -3 + 3\left(\frac{15}{4}\right) = -3 + \frac{45}{4} = 8\frac{1}{4}$$

The three arithmetic means are $\frac{3}{4}$, $4\frac{1}{2}$, and $8\frac{1}{4}$. ∎

Self Check 3 Find three arithmetic means between -5 and 23.

Now Try Exercise 23.

3. Find the Sum of the First n Terms of an Arithmetic Series

If we replace the commas in an infinite arithmetic sequence with $+$ signs, we form an **infinite arithmetic series**.

$$a + (a + d) + (a + 2d) + (a + 3d) + \cdots + [a + (n - 1)d] + \cdots$$

If we replace the commas in a finite arithmetic sequence with $+$ signs, we form a **finite arithmetic series**.

$$a + (a + d) + (a + 2d) + (a + 3d) + \cdots + [a + (n - 1)d]$$

To find the sum of the first n terms of an arithmetic series, we use the following formula.

Sum of the First n Terms of an Arithmetic Series	The formula $$S_n = \frac{n(a + a_n)}{2}$$ gives the sum of the first n terms of an arithmetic series. In this formula, a is the first term, a_n is the last (or nth) term, and n is the number of terms.

PROOF We write the first n terms of an arithmetic series (letting S_n represent their sum). Then we write the same sum in reverse order and add the equations term by term:

$$
\begin{aligned}
S_n &= a + (a + d) + \cdots + [a + (n - 2)d] + [a + (n - 1)d] \\
S_n &= [a + (n - 1)d] + [a + (n - 2)d] + \cdots + (a + d) + a \\
\hline
2S_n &= [2a + (n - 1)d] + [2a + (n - 1)d] + \cdots + [2a + (n - 1)d] + [2a + (n - 1)d]
\end{aligned}
$$

Because there are n equal terms on the right side of the previous equation,

$$2S_n = n[2a + (n - 1)d]$$

or

(1) $2S_n = n\{a + [a + (n - 1)d]\}$ Write $2a$ as $a + a$.

We can substitute a_n for $a + (n - 1)d$ on the right side of Equation 1 and divide both sides by 2 to get

$$S_n = \frac{n(a + a_n)}{2}$$

EXAMPLE 4   **Finding the Sum of the Terms of an Arithmetic Series**

Find the sum of the first 30 terms of the arithmetic series $5 + 8 + 11 + \cdots$.

SOLUTION   Here $a = 5$, $n = 30$, $d = 3$, and $a_n = a_{30} = 5 + 29(3) = 92$.
Substituting these values into the formula for the sum of the first n terms of an arithmetic series gives

$$S_n = \frac{n(a + a_n)}{2}$$

$$S_{30} = \frac{30(5 + 92)}{2}$$

$$= 15(97)$$

$$= 1,455$$

The sum of the first 30 terms is 1,455.

Self Check 4   Find the sum of the first 50 terms of the arithmetic series $-2 + 5 + 12 + \cdots$.

Now Try Exercise 27.

4. Solve Problems Involving Sequences and Series

EXAMPLE 5   **Solving an Applied Problem**

A student deposits $50 in a non-interest-bearing account and plans to add $7 a week. How much will she have in the account one year after her first deposit?

SOLUTION   Her weekly balances form an arithmetic sequence:

$50, 57, 64, 71, 78, \ldots$

with a first term of 50 and a common difference of 7. To find her balance in one year (52 weeks), we substitute 50 for a, 7 for d, and 52 for n in the formula for the last term.

$$a_n = a + (n - 1)d$$

$$a_{52} = 50 + (52 - 1)7$$

$$= 50 + (51)7$$

$$= 407$$

After one year, the balance will be $407.

Self Check 5   How much will she have in the account after 60 weeks?

Now Try Exercise 37.

EXAMPLE 6   **Solving an Applied Problem**

The equation $s = 16t^2$ represents the distance s (in feet) that an object will fall in t seconds.

- In 1 second, the object will fall 16 feet.
- In 2 seconds, the object will fall 64 feet.
- In 3 seconds, the object will fall 144 feet.

The object fell 16 feet during the first second, 48 feet during the next second, and 80 feet during the third second. Find the distance the object will fall during the 12th second.

SOLUTION   The sequence 16, 48, 80, . . . is an arithmetic sequence with $a = 16$ and $d = 32$. To find the 12th term, we substitute these values into the formula for the last term.

$$a_n = a + (n - 1)d$$

$$a_{12} = 16 + (12 - 1)32$$

$$= 16 + 11(32)$$

$$= 368$$

During the 12th second, the object falls 368 feet.

Self Check 6   How far will the object fall during the 20th second?

Now Try Exercise 41.

Self Check Answers   **1.** 3, 9, 15, 21, 27; 105   **2.** 248   **3.** 2, 9, 16   **4.** 8,475   **5.** $463
6. 624 ft

Exercises **8.3**

Getting Ready
You should be able to complete these vocabulary and concept statements before you proceed to the practice exercises.

Fill in the blanks.

1. An arithmetic sequence is a sequence of the form

$a, a + d, a + 2d, a + 3d, \ldots, a +$ _____ $d, \ldots$

2. An arithmetic series is a series of the form

$a + (a + d) + (a + 2d) + (a + 3d) + \cdots$
$\qquad\qquad + [a + (n - 1)$ ___$] + \cdots$

3. If an arithmetic series has infinitely many terms, it is called an _____ arithmetic series.

4. In an arithmetic sequence, a is the _____ term, d is the common _____, and n is the _____ of terms.

5. The last term of an arithmetic sequence is given by the formula _____.

6. The formula for the sum of the first n terms of an arithmetic series is given by the formula

_____ .

7. _____ are numbers inserted between a first and last term of a sequence to form an arithmetic sequence.

8. The formula _____ gives the distance (in feet) that an object will fall in t seconds.

Practice
Write the first six terms of the arithmetic sequences with the given properties.

9. $a = 1; d = 2$

10. $a = -12; d = -5$

11. $a = 5$; 3rd term is 2

12. $a = 4$; 5th term is 12

13. 7th term is 24; common difference is $\frac{5}{2}$

14. 20th term is -49; common difference is -3

Find the missing term in each arithmetic sequence.

15. Find the 40th term of an arithmetic sequence with a first term of 6 and a common difference of 8.

16. Find the 35th term of an arithmetic sequence with a first term of 50 and a common difference of -6.

17. The 6th term of an arithmetic sequence is 28, and the first term is -2. Find the common difference.

18. The 7th term of an arithmetic sequence is -42, and the common difference is -6. Find the first term.

19. Find the 55th term of an arithmetic sequence whose first three terms are -8, -1, and 6.

20. Find the 37th term of an arithmetic sequence whose second and third terms are -4 and 6.

21. If the fifth term of an arithmetic sequence is 14 and the second term is 5, find the 15th term.

22. If the fourth term of an arithmetic sequence is 13 and the second term is 3, find the 24th term.

Find the required means.

23. Insert three arithmetic means between 10 and 20.

24. Insert five arithmetic means between 5 and 15.

25. Insert four arithmetic means between -7 and $\frac{2}{3}$.

26. Insert three arithmetic means between -11 and -2.

Find the sum of the first n terms of each arithmetic series.

27. $5 + 7 + 9 + \cdots$ (to 15 terms)

28. $-3 + (-4) + (-5) + \cdots$ (to 10 terms)

29. $\sum\limits_{n=1}^{20}\left(\dfrac{3}{2}n + 12\right)$ **30.** $\sum\limits_{n=1}^{10}\left(\dfrac{2}{3}n + \dfrac{1}{3}\right)$

Solve each problem.

31. Find the sum of the first 30 terms of an arithmetic sequence with 25th term of 10 and a common difference of $\frac{1}{2}$.

32. Find the sum of the first 100 terms of an arithmetic sequence with 15th term of 86 and first term of 2.

33. Find the sum of the first 200 natural numbers.

34. Find the sum of the first 1,000 natural numbers.

Applications

35. **Interior angles** The sums of the angles of several polygons are given in the table. Assuming that the pattern continues, complete the table.

Figure	Number of sides	Sum of angles
Triangle	3	180°
Quadrilateral	4	360°
Pentagon	5	540°
Hexagon	6	720°
Octagon	8	
Dodecagon	12	

36. **Borrowing money** To pay for college, a student borrows $5,000 interest-free from his father. If he pays his father back at the rate of $200 per month, how much will he still owe after 12 months?

37. **Borrowing money** If Juanita borrows $5,500 interest-free from her mother to buy a new car and agrees to pay her mother back at the rate of $105 per month, how much will she still owe after 4 years?

38. **Jogging** One day, some students jogged $\frac{1}{2}$ mile. Because it was fun, they decided to increase the jogging distance each day by a certain amount. If they jogged $6\frac{3}{4}$ miles on the 51st day, how much was the distance increased each day?

Tyler Olson/Shutterstock.com

39. **Sales** The year it incorporated, a company had sales of $237,500. Its sales were expected to increase by $150,000 annually for the next several years. If the forecast was correct, what will sales be in 10 years?

40. **Falling objects** Find how many feet a brick will travel during the 10th second of its fall.

41. Falling objects If a rock is dropped from the Golden Gate Bridge, how far will it fall in the third second?

42. Designing patios Each row of bricks in the following triangular patio is to have one more brick than the previous row, ending with the longest row of 150 bricks. How many bricks will be needed?

43. Pile of logs Several logs are stored in a pile with 20 logs on the bottom layer, 19 on the second layer, 18 on the third layer, and so on. If the top layer has one log, how many logs are in the pile?

44. Theater seating The first row in a movie theater contains 24 seats. As you move toward the back, each row has 1 additional seat. If there are 30 rows, what is the capacity of the theater?

Discovery and Writing

45. Can an arithmetic sequence have a first term of 4, a 25th term of 126, and a common difference of $4\frac{1}{4}$? Explain.

46. In an arithmetic sequence, can a and d be negative, but a_n positive?

47. Can an arithmetic sequence be an alternating sequence? Explain.

48. Between 5 and $10\frac{1}{3}$ are three arithmetic means. One of them is 9. Find the other two.

Review
Solve each equation.

49. $x + \sqrt{x + 3} = 9$

50. $\dfrac{x + 3}{x} + \dfrac{x - 3}{5} = 2$

51. $\dfrac{1}{x} + \dfrac{2}{x^2} + \dfrac{1}{x^3} = 0$

52. $x + 3\sqrt{x} - 10 = 0$

53. $x^4 - 1 = 0$

54. $x^4 - 29x^2 + 100 = 0$

8.4 Geometric Sequences and Series

In this section, we will learn to

1. Define and use geometric sequences.
2. Find geometric means.
3. Find the sum of the first n terms of a geometric series.
4. Define and find the sum of infinite geometric series.
5. Solve problems involving geometric sequences and series.

Bungee jumping is a sport invented by daredevil A. J. Hackett. His first jump was off the 43-meter high Kawarau Bridge in New Zealand. Since he was attached to a long rubber cord, he bounced up and down for a considerable time giving him a thrilling ride. Today, this sport is gaining in popularity. But it is not for the faint of heart.

Suppose a jumper is attached to a cord that stretches to a length of 100 feet. Also suppose that on each bounce, he rebounds to a height that is 60% of the distance from which he fell. If we list the distances that he falls, we will get the following sequence:

$100, 60, 36, \ldots$ Each number in the list is 60% of the number before it.

If we list the distances that he rebounds, we will get the following sequence:

$60, 36, 21.6, \ldots$ Each number in the list is 60% of the number before it.

Each of these sequences is an example of a common sequence called a *geometric sequence.*

1. Define and Use Geometric Sequences

A **geometric sequence** is a sequence in which each term, except the first, is found by multiplying the preceding term by a constant.

Geometric Sequence   A **geometric sequence** is a sequence of the form

$$a, \quad ar, \quad ar^2, \quad ar^3, \ldots, \quad ar^{n-1}, \ldots$$

where a is the **first term**, ar^{n-1} is the **nth term**, and r is the **common ratio**.

Caution

> Please note that the nth term of a geometric sequence is not $a_n = ar^n$. The nth term is $a_n = ar^{n-1}$.

In this definition, the second term of the sequence has a factor of r^1, the third term has a factor of r^2, the fourth term has a factor of r^3, and so on. This explains why the nth term has a factor of r^{n-1}.

If a geometric sequence has infinitely many terms, it is called an **infinite geometric sequence**. If it has a finite number of terms, it is called a **finite geometric sequence**.

EXAMPLE 1   **Writing the Terms of a Geometric Sequence**

Write the first six terms and the 15th term of the geometric sequence whose first term is 3 and whose common ratio is 2.

SOLUTION   We first write the first six terms of the geometric sequence:

$$3, \quad 3(2), \quad 3(2)^2, \quad 3(2)^3, \quad 3(2)^4, \quad 3(2)^5$$

or

$$3, \quad 6, \quad 12, \quad 24, \quad 48, \quad 96$$

To find the 15th term, we substitute 15 for n, 3 for a, and 2 for r in the formula for the nth term:

$$n\text{th term} = ar^{n-1}$$
$$15\text{th term} = 3(2)^{15-1}$$
$$= 3(2)^{14}$$
$$= 3(16,384)$$
$$= 49,152$$

Self Check 1   Write the first five terms of the geometric sequence whose first term is 2 and whose common ratio is 3. Find the 10th term.

Now Try Exercise 11.

EXAMPLE 2   **Finding a Specific Term of a Geometric Sequence**

Find the eighth term of a geometric sequence whose first three terms are 9, 3, and 1.

SOLUTION Here $a = 9$, $r = \frac{1}{3}$, and $n = 8$. To find the eighth term, we substitute these values into the formula for the nth term.

$$n\text{th term} = ar^{n-1}$$

$$8\text{th term} = 9\left(\frac{1}{3}\right)^{8-1}$$

$$= 9\left(\frac{1}{3}\right)^{7}$$

$$= \frac{1}{243}$$

Self Check 2 Find the eighth term of a geometric sequence whose first three terms are $\frac{1}{3}$, 1, and 3.

Now Try Exercise 17.

2. Find Geometric Means

Numbers inserted between a first and last term to form a segment of a geometric sequence are called **geometric means**. When finding geometric means, we consider the last term, a_n, to be the nth term.

EXAMPLE 3 **Inserting Geometric Means between Two Integers**

Insert two geometric means between 4 and 256.

SOLUTION The first term is $a = 4$, and because 256 is the fourth term, $n = 4$ and $a_n = a_4 = 256$. To find the common ratio, we substitute these values into the formula for the nth term and solve for r:

$$ar^{n-1} = a_n$$

$$4r^{4-1} = 256$$

$$r^3 = 64$$

$$r = 4$$

The common ratio is 4. The two geometric means are the second and third terms of the geometric sequence:

$$ar = 4 \cdot 4 = 16$$

$$ar^2 = 4 \cdot 4^2 = 4 \cdot 16 = 64$$

The first four terms of the geometric sequence are 4, 16, 64, and 256. The two geometric means between 4 and 256 are 16 and 64.

Self Check 3 Insert two geometric means between -3 and 192.

Now Try Exercise 23.

3. Find the Sum of the First n Terms of a Geometric Series

If we replace the commas in an infinite geometric sequence with $+$ signs, we form an **infinite geometric series**.

$$a + ar + ar^2 + ar^3 + \cdots + ar^{n-1} + \cdots$$

If we replace the commas in a finite geometric sequence with $+$ signs, we form a **finite geometric series**.

$$a + ar + ar^2 + ar^3 + \cdots + ar^{n-1}$$

To find the sum of the first n terms of a geometric series, we can use the following formula.

Sum of the First n Terms of a Geometric Series   The formula

$$S_n = \frac{a - ar^n}{1 - r} \qquad (r \neq 1)$$

gives the sum of the first n terms of a geometric series. In the formula, S_n is the sum, a is the first term, r is the common ratio, and n is the number of terms.

PROOF   We write the sum of the first n terms of the geometric series:

(1) $S_n = a + ar + ar^2 + \cdots + ar^{n-3} + ar^{n-2} + ar^{n-1}$

Multiplying both sides of this equation by r gives

(2) $S_n r = ar + ar^2 + \cdots + ar^{n-2} + ar^{n-1} + ar^n$

We now subtract Equation 2 from Equation 1 and solve for S_n:

$$S_n - S_n r = a - ar^n$$

$$S_n(1 - r) = a - ar^n \qquad \text{Factor out } S_n.$$

$$S_n = \frac{a - ar^n}{1 - r} \qquad \text{Divide both sides by } 1 - r.$$

EXAMPLE 4   **Finding the Sum of the Terms of a Geometric Series**

Find the sum of the first six terms of the geometric series $8 + 4 + 2 + \cdots$

SOLUTION   Here $a = 8$, $n = 6$, and $r = \frac{1}{2}$. Substituting these values in the formula for the sum of the first n terms of a geometric series gives

$$S_n = \frac{a - ar^n}{1 - r}$$

$$S_6 = \frac{8 - 8\left(\dfrac{1}{2}\right)^6}{1 - \dfrac{1}{2}}$$

$$= 2\left(\frac{63}{8}\right)$$

$$= \frac{63}{4}$$

The sum of the first six terms is $\frac{63}{4}$.

Self Check 4   Find the sum of the first eight terms of the geometric series $81, 27, 9, \ldots$.

Now Try Exercise 25.

4. Define and Find the Sum of Infinite Geometric Series

Under certain conditions, we can find the sum of all of the terms in an **infinite geometric series**. To define this sum, we consider the infinite geometric series

$$a + ar + ar^2 + \cdots$$

- The first partial sum, S_1, of the series is $S_1 = a$.
- The second partial sum, S_2, of the series is $S_2 = a + ar$.
- The nth partial sum, S_n, of the series is $S_n = a + ar + ar^2 + \cdots + ar^{n-1}$.

If the nth partial sum, S_n, of an infinite geometric series approaches some number S as n approaches ∞, then S is called the **sum of the infinite geometric series**. The following symbol denotes the sum, S, of an infinite geometric series, provided the sum exists.

n	$1\left(\dfrac{1}{2}\right)^n$
1	$\dfrac{1}{2}$
2	$\dfrac{1}{4}$
3	$\dfrac{1}{8}$
4	$\dfrac{1}{16}$
10	$\dfrac{1}{1,024}$

$$S = \sum_{n=1}^{\infty} ar^{n-1}$$

To develop a formula for finding the sum of all the terms in an infinite geometric series, we consider the formula

$$(3) \quad S_n = \frac{a - ar^n}{1 - r} \quad (r \neq 1)$$

If $|r| < 1$ and a is a constant, then as n approaches ∞, ar^n approaches 0, and the term ar^n in Equation 3 can be dropped. As an illustration, suppose that $a = 1$ and $r = \frac{1}{2}$. We can see from the table on the left that as n increases without bound, $ar^n = 1\left(\dfrac{1}{2}\right)^n$ approaches 0.

This argument gives the following formula.

Sum of the Terms of an Infinite Geometric Series   If $|r| < 1$, the sum of the terms of an infinite geometric series is given by

$$S_\infty = \frac{a}{1 - r}$$

where a is the first term and r is the common ratio.

Caution

If $|r| \geq 1$, the terms get larger and larger, and the sum does not approach a number. In this case, the previous theorem does not apply.

EXAMPLE 5   Changing a Repeating Decimal to a Fraction

Change $0.\overline{4}$ to a common fraction.

SOLUTION   We write the decimal as an infinite geometric series and find its sum:

$$S_\infty = \frac{4}{10} + \frac{4}{100} + \frac{4}{1,000} + \frac{4}{10,000} + \cdots$$

$$= \frac{4}{10} + \frac{4}{10}\left(\frac{1}{10}\right) + \frac{4}{10}\left(\frac{1}{10}\right)^2 + \frac{4}{10}\left(\frac{1}{10}\right)^3 + \cdots$$

Since the common ratio r equals $\frac{1}{10}$ and $\left|\frac{1}{10}\right| < 1$, we can use the formula for the sum of an infinite geometric series:

$$S_\infty = \frac{a}{1 - r} = \frac{\dfrac{4}{10}}{1 - \dfrac{1}{10}} = \frac{\dfrac{4}{10}}{\dfrac{9}{10}} = \frac{4}{9}$$

Long division will verify that $\frac{4}{9} = 0.\overline{4}$.

Comment

Using a generalization of the method used in Example 5, we can write any repeating decimal as a fraction.

Self Check 5   Change $0.\overline{7}$ to a common fraction.

Now Try Exercise 35.

5. Solve Problems Involving Geometric Sequences and Series

Many of the exponential growth problems discussed in Chapter 4 can be solved using the concepts of geometric sequences.

EXAMPLE 6   **Solving an Application Problem**

A statistician knows that a town with a population of 3,500 people has a predicted growth rate of 6% per year for the next 20 years. What should she predict the population to be 20 years from now?

© Istockphoto.com/Denis Jr. Tangney

SOLUTION   Let p_0 be the initial population of the town. After 1 year, the population p_1 will be the initial population (p_0) plus the growth (the product of p_0 and the rate of growth, r).

$$p_1 = p_0 + p_0 r$$
$$= p_0(1 + r) \qquad \text{Factor out } p_0.$$

The population p_2 at the end of 2 years will be

$$p_2 = p_1 + p_1 r$$
$$= p_1(1 + r) \qquad \text{Factor out } p_1.$$
$$= p_0(1 + r)(1 + r) \qquad \text{Substitute } p_0(1 + r) \text{ for } p_1.$$
$$= p_0(1 + r)^2$$

The population at the end of the third year will be $p_3 = p_0(1 + r)^3$. Writing the terms as a sequence gives

$$p_0, \qquad p_0(1 + r), \qquad p_0(1 + r)^2, \qquad p_0(1 + r)^3, \qquad p_0(1 + r)^4, \ldots$$

This is a geometric sequence with p_0 as the first term and $1 + r$ as the common ratio. In this example, $p_0 = 3,500$, $1 + r = 1.06$, and (since the population after 20 years will be the value of the 21st term of the geometric sequence) $n = 21$. We can substitute these values into the formula for the last term of a geometric sequence to get

$$a_n = ar^{n-1}$$

$$a_{21} = 3{,}500(1.06)^{21-1}$$

$$= 3{,}500(1.06)^{20}$$

$$\approx 11{,}224.97415 \qquad \text{Use a calculator.}$$

The population after 20 years will be approximately 11,225.

Self Check 6   After 30 years, what will be the approximate population?

Now Try Exercise 39.

EXAMPLE 7   Solving an Application Problem

A student deposits \$2,500 in a bank at 7% annual interest, compounded daily. If the investment is left untouched for 60 years, how much money will be in the account?

SOLUTION   We let the initial amount in the account be a_0 and r be the rate. At the end of the first day, the account is worth

$$a_1 = a_0 + a_0\left(\frac{r}{365}\right) = a_0\left(1 + \frac{r}{365}\right)$$

After the second day, the account is worth

$$a_2 = a_1 + a_1\left(\frac{r}{365}\right) = a_1\left(1 + \frac{r}{365}\right) = a_0\left(1 + \frac{r}{365}\right)^2$$

The daily amounts form the following geometric sequence

$$a_0, \quad a_0\left(1 + \frac{r}{365}\right), \quad a_0\left(1 + \frac{r}{365}\right)^2, \quad a_0\left(1 + \frac{r}{365}\right)^3, \ldots$$

where a_0 is the initial deposit and r is the annual rate of interest.

Because interest is compounded daily for 60 years (21,900 days), the amount at the end of 60 years will be the 21,901st term of the sequence.

$$a_{21{,}901} = 2{,}500\left(1 + \frac{0.07}{365}\right)^{21{,}900}$$

We can use a calculator to find that $a_{21{,}901} \approx \$166{,}648.71$.

Self Check 7   After 40 years, how much money was in the account?

Now Try Exercise 45.

EXAMPLE 8   Solving an Application Problem

A pump can remove 20% of the gas in a container with each stroke. Find the percentage of gas that remains in the container after six strokes.

SOLUTION   We let V represent the volume of the container. Because each stroke of the pump removes 20% of the gas, 80% remains after each stroke, and we have the geometric sequence

$$V, \quad 0.80V, \quad 0.80(0.80V), \quad 0.80[0.80(0.80V)], \ldots$$

or

$$V, \quad 0.8V, \quad (0.8)^2V, \quad (0.8)^3V, \ldots$$

The amount of gas remaining after six strokes is the seventh term, a_n, of the sequence:

$$a_n = ar^{n-1}$$
$$a_7 = V(0.8)^{7-1}$$
$$= V(0.8)^6$$

We can use a calculator to find that approximately 26% of the gas remains after six strokes. ■

Self Check 8   What approximate percentage would remain after seven strokes?

Now Try Exercise 47.

Self Check Answers   **1.** 2, 6, 18, 54, 162; 39,366   **2.** 729   **3.** 12, −48   **4.** $\dfrac{3,280}{27}$ **5.** $\dfrac{7}{9}$ **6.** approximately 20,102   **7.** $41,100.58   **8.** 21%

Exercises **8.4**

Getting Ready
You should be able to complete these vocabulary and concept statements before you proceed to the practice exercises.

Fill in the blanks.

1. A geometric sequence is a sequence of the form a, ar, ar^2, ar^3, ... The nth term is $a(\underline{\quad})$.
2. In a geometric sequence, a is the _____ term, r is the common _____, and n is the _____ of terms.
3. The last term of a geometric sequence is given by the formula $a_n = \underline{\quad}$.
4. A geometric _____ is the sum of the terms of a geometric sequence.
5. A geometric series with infinitely many terms is called an _____ geometric series.
6. The formula for the sum of the first n terms of a geometric series is given by _____.
7. _____ are numbers inserted between a first and a last term to form a geometric sequence.
8. If $|r| < 1$, the formula _____ gives the sum of the terms of an infinite geometric series.

Practice
Write the first four terms of each geometric sequence with the given properties.

9. $a = 10; r = 2$
10. $a = -3; r = 2$
11. $a = -2$ and $r = 3$
12. $a = 64; r = \frac{1}{2}$
13. $a = 3; r = \sqrt{2}$
14. $a = 2; r = \sqrt{3}$
15. $a = 2$; 4th term is 54
16. 3rd term is 4; $r = \frac{1}{2}$

Find the requested term of each geometric sequence.

17. Find the sixth term of the geometric sequence whose first three terms are $\frac{1}{4}$, 1, and 4.
18. Find the eighth term of the geometric sequence whose second and fourth terms are 0.2 and 5.
19. Find the fifth term of a geometric sequence whose second term is 6 and whose third term is −18.
20. Find the sixth term of a geometric sequence whose second term is 3 and whose fourth term is $\frac{1}{3}$.

Solve each problem.

21. Insert three positive geometric means between 10 and 20.
22. Insert five geometric means between −5 and 5, if possible.
23. Insert four geometric means between 2 and 2,048.
24. Insert three geometric means between 162 and 2. (There are two possibilities.)

Find the sum of the indicated terms of each geometric series.

25. $4 + 8 + 16 + \cdots$ (to 5 terms)
26. $9 + 27 + 81 + \cdots$ (to 6 terms)
27. $2 + (-6) + 18 + \cdots$ (to 10 terms)
28. $\dfrac{1}{8} + \dfrac{1}{4} + \dfrac{1}{2} + \cdots$ (to 12 terms)
29. $\displaystyle\sum_{n=1}^{6} 3\left(\frac{3}{2}\right)^{n-1}$
30. $\displaystyle\sum_{n=1}^{6} 12\left(-\frac{1}{2}\right)^{n-1}$

Find the sum of each infinite geometric series.

31. $6 + 4 + \dfrac{8}{3} + \cdots$ **32.** $8 + 4 + 2 + 1 + \cdots$

33. $\displaystyle\sum_{n=1}^{\infty} 12\left(-\dfrac{1}{2}\right)^{n-1}$ **34.** $\displaystyle\sum_{n=1}^{\infty} \left(\dfrac{1}{3}\right)^{n-1}$

Change each repeating decimal to a common fraction.

35. $0.\overline{5}$ **36.** $0.\overline{6}$

37. $0.\overline{25}$ **38.** $0.\overline{37}$

Applications

Use a calculator to help solve each problem.

39. Staffing a department The number of students studying algebra at State College is 623. The department chair expects enrollment to increase 10% each year. How many professors will be needed in 8 years to teach algebra if one professor can handle 60 students?

40. Bouncing balls On each bounce, the rubber ball in the illustration rebounds to a height one-half of that from which it fell. Find the total vertical distance the ball travels.

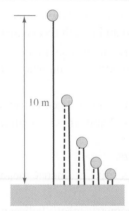

10 m

41. Bungee jumping A bungee jumper is attached to a cord that stretches to a length of 100 feet. If he rebounds to 60% of the height jumped, how far will he fall on his fifth descent? How far will he travel when he comes to rest?

42. Bungee jumping A bungee jumper is attached to a cord that stretches to a length of 100 feet. If he rebounds to 70% of the height jumped, how far will he travel upward on the fifth rebound? How far will he have traveled when he comes to rest?

43. Bouncing balls A SuperBall rebounds to approximately 95% of the height from which it is dropped. If the ball is dropped from a height of 10 meters, how high will it rebound after the 13th bounce?

44. Genealogy The following family tree spans 3 generations and lists 7 people. How many names would be listed in a family tree that spans 10 generations?

45. Investing money If a married couple invests $1,000 in a 1-year certificate of deposit at $6\frac{3}{4}\%$ annual interest, compounded daily, how much interest will be earned during the year?

46. Biology If a single cell divides into two cells every 30 minutes, how many cells will there be at the end of 10 hours?

47. Depreciation A lawn tractor, costing C dollars when new, depreciates 20% of the previous year's value each year. How much is the lawn tractor worth after 5 years?

48. Financial planning Maria can invest $1,000 at $7\frac{1}{2}\%$, compounded annually, or at $7\frac{1}{4}\%$, compounded daily. If she invests the money for a year, which is the better investment?

49. Population study If the population of the Earth were to double every 30 years, approximately how many people would there be in the year 3020? (Consider the population in 2000 to be 5 billion and use 2000 as the base year.)

50. Investing money If Linda deposits $1,300 in a bank at 7% interest, compounded annually, how much will be in the bank 17 years later? (Assume that there are no other transactions on the account.)

51. Real estate appreciation If a house purchased for $50,000 in 1998 appreciates in value by 6% each year, how much will the house be worth in the year 2020?

52. Compound interest Find the value of $1,000 left on deposit for 10 years at an annual rate of 7%, compounded annually.

53. Compound interest Find the value of $1,000 left on deposit for 10 years at an annual rate of 7%, compounded quarterly.

54. Compound interest Find the value of $1,000 left on deposit for 10 years at an annual rate of 7%, compounded monthly.

55. Compound interest Find the value of $1,000 left on deposit for 10 years at an annual rate of 7%, compounded daily.

56. Compound interest Find the value of $1,000 left on deposit for 10 years at an annual rate of 7%, compounded hourly.

57. Saving for retirement When John was 20 years old, he opened an individual retirement account by investing $2,000 at 11% interest, compounded quarterly. How much will his investment be worth when he is 65 years old?

58. Biology One bacterium divides into two bacteria every 5 minutes. If two bacteria multiply enough to completely fill a petri dish in 2 hours, how long will it take one bacterium to fill the dish?

59. Pest control To reduce the population of a destructive moth, biologists release 1,000 sterilized male moths each day into the environment. If 80% of these moths alive one day survive until the next, then after a long time the population of sterile males is the sum of the infinite geometric series

$$1,000 + 1,000(0.8) + 1,000(0.8)^2 + 1,000(0.8)^3 + \cdots$$

Find the long-term population.

60. Pest control If mild weather increases the day-to-day survival rate of the sterile male moths in Exercise 59 to 90%, find the long-term population.

61. Mathematical myth A legend tells of a king who offered to grant the inventor of the game of chess any request. The inventor said, "Simply place one grain of wheat on the first square of a chessboard, two grains on the second, four on the third, and so on, until the board is full. Then give me the wheat." The king agreed. How many grains did the king need to fill the chessboard?

62. Mathematical myth Estimate the size of the wheat pile in Exercise 61. (*Hint:* There are about one-half million grains of wheat in a bushel.)

Discovery and Writing

63. Does $0.999999 = 1$? Explain.

64. Does $0.999 \ldots = 1$? Explain.

Review
Perform each operation. $\left(i = \sqrt{-1}.\right)$ *Write the result in* $a + bi$ *form.*

65. $(3 + 2i) + (2 - 5i)$

66. $(7 + 8i) - (2 - 5i)$

67. $(3 + i)(3 - i)$

68. $\left(3 + \sqrt{3i}\right)\left(3 - \sqrt{3i}\right)$

69. $\dfrac{2 + 3i}{2 - i}$

70. $(7 + 3i)^2$

71. i^{127}

72. i^{-127}

8.5 Mathematical Induction

In this section, we will learn to

1. State the Principle of Mathematical Induction.

2. Use mathematical induction to prove formulas.

Suppose you are waiting in line to get into a movie and are wondering if you will be admitted. Even if the first person in line gets in, your worries will still be justified. Perhaps there is room in the theater for only a few more people.

It would be good news to hear the manager say, "If anyone gets in, the next person in line will also get in." However, this promise does not guarantee that anyone will be admitted. Perhaps the theater is full, and no one will get in.

However, when you see the first person in line walk in, you know that everyone will be admitted because you know two things:

• The first person was admitted.
• Because of the promise, if the first person is admitted, then so is the second, and when the second person is admitted, then so is the third, and so on until everyone gets in.

FIGURE 8-3

This situation is similar to a game played with dominoes. Suppose that some dominoes are placed on end, as in Figure 8-3. When the first domino is knocked over, it knocks over the second. The second domino, in turn, knocks over the third, which knocks over the fourth and so on until all of the dominoes fall. Two things must happen to guarantee that all of the dominoes will fall:

- The first domino must be knocked over.
- Every domino that falls must knock over the next one.

When both conditions are met, it is certain that all of the dominoes will fall.

These two examples illustrate the basic Principle of Mathematical Induction.

1. State the Principle of Mathematical Induction

In Section 8.3, we developed the following formula for the sum of the first n terms of an arithmetic series:

$$S_n = \frac{n(a + a_n)}{2}$$

If we apply this formula to the arithmetic series $1 + 2 + 3 + \cdots + n$, we have

$$S_n = 1 + 2 + 3 + \cdots + n = \frac{n(1 + n)}{2}$$

To see that this formula is true, we can check it for some positive numbers n:

For $n = 1$: $1 = \dfrac{1(1 + 1)}{2}$ is a true statement, because $1 = 1$.

For $n = 2$: $1 + 2 = \dfrac{2(1 + 2)}{2}$ is a true statement, because $3 = 3$.

For $n = 3$: $1 + 2 + 3 = \dfrac{3(1 + 3)}{2}$ is a true statement, because $6 = 6$.

For $n = 6$: $1 + 2 + 3 + 4 + 5 + 6 = \dfrac{6(1 + 6)}{2}$ is a true statement, because $21 = 21$.

Because the set of positive numbers is infinite, it is impossible to prove the formula by verifying it for all positive numbers. To verify this sequence formula for all positive numbers n, we must have a method of proof called **mathematical induction**, a method first used extensively by Giuseppe Peano (1858–1932).

Principle of Mathematical Induction

If a statement involving the natural number n has the following two properties

1. The statement is true for $n = 1$, and
2. If the statement is true for $n = k$, then it is true for $n = k + 1$,

then the statement is true for all natural numbers.

Mathematical induction provides a way to prove many formulas. Any proof by induction involves two parts. First, we must show that the formula is true for the number 1. Second, we must show that if the formula is true for any natural number k, then it also is true for the natural number $k + 1$. A proof by induction is complete only when both of these properties are established.

2. Use Mathematical Induction to Prove Formulas

EXAMPLE 1   **Using Mathematical Induction to Prove a Formula**

Use induction to prove that the following formula is true for every natural number n.

$$1 + 2 + 3 + \cdots + n = \frac{n(n+1)}{2}$$

SOLUTION   **Proof by induction:**

Part 1: Verify that the formula is true for $n = 1$. When $n = 1$, there is a single term, the number 1, on the left side of the equation. Substituting 1 for n on the right side, we have

$$1 = \frac{n(n+1)}{2}$$

$$1 = \frac{(1)(1+1)}{2}$$

$$1 = 1$$

The formula is true when $n = 1$. Part 1 of the proof is complete.

Part 2: We assume that the given formula is true when $n = k$. By this assumption, called the **induction hypothesis**, we accept that

$$(1) \quad 1 + 2 + 3 + \cdots + k = \frac{k(k+1)}{2}$$

is a true statement. We must show that the induction hypothesis forces the given formula to be true when $n = k + 1$. We can show this by verifying the statement

$$(2) \quad 1 + 2 + 3 + \cdots + k + (k+1) = \frac{(k+1)[(k+1)+1]}{2}$$

which is obtained from the given formula by replacing n with $k + 1$.

Comparing the left sides of Equations 1 and 2 shows that the left side of Equation 2 contains an extra term of $k + 1$. Thus, we add $k + 1$ to both sides of Equation 1 (which was assumed to be true) to obtain the equation

$$1 + 2 + 3 + \cdots + k + (k+1) = \frac{k(k+1)}{2} + (k+1)$$

Because both terms on the right side of this equation have a common factor of $k + 1$, the right side factors, and the equation can be written as follows:

$$1 + 2 + 3 + \cdots + k + (k+1) = (k+1)\left(\frac{k}{2} + 1\right)$$

$$= (k+1)\left(\frac{k+2}{2}\right)$$

$$= \frac{(k+1)(k+2)}{2}$$

$$= \frac{(k+1)[(k+1)+1]}{2}$$

This final result is Equation 2. Because the truth of Equation 1 implies the truth of Equation 2, part 2 of the proof is complete. Parts 1 and 2 together establish that the formula is true for any natural number n. ∎

Self Check 1   Verify that the formula holds for $n = 4$.

Now Try Exercise 9.

EXAMPLE 2   Using Mathematical Induction to Prove a Formula

Use induction to prove the following formula for all natural numbers n.

$$1 + 5 + 9 + \cdots + (4n - 3) = n(2n - 1)$$

SOLUTION   **Proof by induction:**

Part 1: First we verify the formula for $n = 1$. When $n = 1$, there is a single term, the number 1, on the left side of the equation. Substituting 1 for n on the right side, we have

$$1 = 1[2(1) - 1]$$

$$1 = 1$$

The formula is true for $n = 1$. Part 1 of the proof is complete.

Part 2: We assume that the formula is true for $n = k$. Hence,

(3) $1 + 5 + 9 + \cdots + (4k - 3) = k(2k - 1)$

is a true statement. To show that the induction hypothesis guarantees the truth of the formula for $k + 1$ terms, we add the $(k + 1)$th term to both sides of Equation 3. Because the terms on the left side increase by 4, the $(k + 1)$th term is $(4k - 3) + 4$, or $4k + 1$. Adding $4k + 1$ to both sides of Equation 3 gives

$$1 + 5 + 9 + \cdots + (4k - 3) + (4k + 1) = k(2k - 1) + (4k + 1)$$

We can simplify the right side and write the previous equation as follows:

$$1 + 5 + 9 + \cdots + (4k - 3) + [4(k + 1) - 3] = 2k^2 + 3k + 1$$
$$= (k + 1)(2k + 1)$$
$$= (k + 1)[2(k + 1) - 1]$$

Since this result has the same form as the given formula, except that $k + 1$ replaces n, the truth of the formula for $n = k$ implies the truth of the formula for $n = k + 1$. Part 2 of the proof is complete.

Because both of the induction requirements are true, the formula is true for all natural numbers n. ∎

Self Check 2   Verify that the formula holds for $n = 6$.

Now Try Exercise 11.

EXAMPLE 3   Using Mathematical Induction

Prove that $\dfrac{1}{2} + \dfrac{1}{4} + \dfrac{1}{8} + \cdots + \dfrac{1}{2^n} < 1$.

SOLUTION   **Proof by induction:**

Part 1: We verify the formula for $n = 1$. When $n = 1$, there is a single term, the fraction $\frac{1}{2}$, on the left side of the equation. On the right side, there is the single term of 1. We have the following true statement:

$$\frac{1}{2} < 1$$

The formula is therefore true for $n = 1$. Part 1 of the proof is complete.

Part 2: We assume that the inequality is true for $n = k$. Thus,

$$\frac{1}{2} + \frac{1}{4} + \frac{1}{8} + \cdots + \frac{1}{2^k} < 1$$

We can multiply both sides of the above inequality by $\frac{1}{2}$ to get

$$\frac{1}{2}\left(\frac{1}{2} + \frac{1}{4} + \frac{1}{8} + \cdots + \frac{1}{2^k}\right) < 1\left(\frac{1}{2}\right)$$

or

$$\frac{1}{4} + \frac{1}{8} + \frac{1}{16} + \cdots + \frac{1}{2^{k+1}} < \frac{1}{2}$$

We now add $\frac{1}{2}$ to both sides of this inequality to get

$$\frac{1}{2} + \frac{1}{4} + \frac{1}{8} + \frac{1}{16} + \cdots + \frac{1}{2^{k+1}} < \frac{1}{2} + \frac{1}{2}$$

or

$$\frac{1}{2} + \frac{1}{4} + \frac{1}{8} + \frac{1}{16} + \cdots + \frac{1}{2^{k+1}} < 1$$

The resulting inequality is the same as the original inequality, except that $k + 1$ appears in place of n. Thus, the truth of the inequality for $n = k$ implies the truth of the inequality for $n = k + 1$. Part 2 of the proof is complete.

Because both of the induction requirements have been verified, this inequality is true for all natural numbers.

Self Check 3   Verify that the formula holds for $n = 8$.

Now Try Exercise 21.

Some statements are not true when $n = 1$ but are true for all natural numbers equal to or greater than some given natural number (say, q). In these cases, we verify the given statements for $n = q$ in part 1 of the induction proof. After establishing part 2 of the induction proof, the given statement is proved for all natural numbers that are greater than q.

Self Check Answers   **1.** $10 = 10$ **2.** $66 = 66$ **3.** $\dfrac{255}{256} < 1$

Exercises **8.5**

Getting Ready
You should be able to complete these vocabulary and con-cept statements before you proceed to the practice exercises.

Fill in the blanks.

1. Any proof by induction requires ____ parts.
2. Part 1 is to show that the statement is true for

____.
3. Part 2 is to show that the statement is true for _____ whenever it is true for $n = k$.
4. When we assume that a formula is true for $n = k$, we call the assumption the induction _____.

Practice
Verify each formula for $n = 1, 2, 3,$ and 4.

5. $5 + 10 + 15 + \cdots + 5n = \dfrac{5n(n + 1)}{2}$

6. $1^2 + 2^2 + 3^2 + \cdots + n^2 = \dfrac{n(n + 1)(2n + 1)}{6}$

7. $7 + 10 + 13 + \cdots + (3n + 4) = \dfrac{n(3n + 11)}{2}$

8. $1(3) + 2(4) + 3(5) + \cdots + n(n + 2) =$
$\dfrac{n}{6}(n + 1)(2n + 7)$

Prove each formula by induction, if possible.

9. $2 + 4 + 6 + \cdots + 2n = n(n + 1)$

10. $1 + 3 + 5 + \cdots + (2n - 1) = n^2$

11. $3 + 7 + 11 + \cdots + (4n - 1) = n(2n + 1)$

12. $4 + 8 + 12 + \cdots + 4n = 2n(n + 1)$

13. $10 + 6 + 2 + \cdots + (14 - 4n) = 12n - 2n^2$

14. $8 + 6 + 4 + \cdots + (10 - 2n) = 9n - n^2$

15. $2 + 5 + 8 + \cdots + (3n - 1) = \dfrac{n(3n + 1)}{2}$

16. $3 + 6 + 9 + \cdots + 3n = \dfrac{3n(n + 1)}{2}$

17. $1^2 + 2^2 + 3^2 + \cdots + n^2 = \dfrac{n(n + 1)(2n + 1)}{6}$

18. $1 + 2 + 3 + \cdots + (n - 1) + n + (n - 1) + \cdots$
$+ 3 + 2 + 1 = n^2$

19. $\dfrac{1}{3} + 2 + \dfrac{11}{3} + \cdots + \left(\dfrac{5}{3}n - \dfrac{4}{3}\right) = n\left(\dfrac{5}{6}n - \dfrac{1}{2}\right)$

20. $\dfrac{1}{1 \cdot 2} + \dfrac{1}{2 \cdot 3} + \dfrac{1}{3 \cdot 4} + \cdots + \dfrac{1}{n(n + 1)} = \dfrac{n}{n + 1}$

21. $\dfrac{1}{2} + \dfrac{1}{4} + \dfrac{1}{8} + \cdots + \left(\dfrac{1}{2}\right)^n = 1 - \left(\dfrac{1}{2}\right)^n$

22. $\dfrac{1}{3} + \dfrac{2}{9} + \dfrac{4}{27} + \cdots + \dfrac{1}{3}\left(\dfrac{2}{3}\right)^{n-1} = 1 - \left(\dfrac{2}{3}\right)^n$

23. $2^0 + 2^1 + 2^2 + 2^3 + \cdots + 2^{n-1} = 2^n - 1$

24. $1^3 + 2^3 + 3^3 + \cdots + n^3 = \left[\dfrac{n(n + 1)}{2}\right]^2$

25. Prove that $x - y$ is a factor of $x^n - y^n$. (*Hint:* Consider subtracting and adding xy^k to the binomial $x^{k+1} - y^{k+1}$.)

26. Prove that $n < 2^n$.

27. There are 180° in the sum of the angles of any triangle. Prove that $(n - 2)180°$ is the sum of the angles of any simple polygon when n is its number of sides. (*Hint:* If a polygon has $k + 1$ sides, it has $k - 2$ sides plus three more sides.)

28. Consider the equation

$$1 + 3 + 5 + \cdots + 2n - 1 = 3n - 2$$

a. Is the equation true for $n = 1$?

b. Is the equation true for $n = 2$?

c. Is the equation true for all natural numbers n?

29. If $1 + 2 + 3 + \cdots + n = \frac{n}{2}(n + 1) + 1$ were true for $n = k$, show that it would be true for $n = k + 1$. Is it true for $n = 1$?

30. Prove that $n + 1 = 1 + n$ for each natural number n.

31. If n is any natural number, prove that $7^n - 1$ is divisible by 6.

32. Prove that $1 + 2n < 3^n$ for $n > 1$.

33. Prove that, if r is a real number where $r \neq 1$, then

$$1 + r + r^2 + \cdots + r^n = \dfrac{1 - r^{n+1}}{1 - r}.$$

34. Prove the formula for the sum of the first n terms of an arithmetic series:

$$a + [a + d] + [a + 2d] + [a + (n - 1)d] = \dfrac{n(a + a_n)}{2}$$

where $a_n = a + (n - 1)d$.

Discovery and Writing

35. The expression a^m, where m is a natural number, was defined in Section 0.2. An alternative definition of a^m is (part 1) $a^1 = a$ and (part 2) $a^{m+1} = a^m \cdot a$. Use induction on n to prove the Product Rule for Exponents, $a^m a^n = a^{m+n}$.

36. Use induction on n to prove the Power Rule for Exponents, $(a^m)^n = a^{mn}$. (See Exercise 35.)

37. **Tower of Hanoi** A well-known problem in mathematics is "The Tower of Hanoi," first attributed to Edouard Lucas in 1883. In this problem, several disks, each of a different size and with a hole in the center, are placed on a board, with progressively smaller disks going up the stack. The object is to transfer the stack of disks to another peg by moving only one disk at a time and never placing a disk over a smaller one.

a. Find the minimum number of moves required if there is only one disk.

b. Find the minimum number of moves required if there are two disks.

c. Find the minimum number of moves required if there are three disks.

d. Find the minimum number of moves required if there are four disks.

38. Tower of Hanoi The results in Exercise 37 suggest that the minimum number of moves required to transfer n disks from one peg to another is given by the formula $2^n - 1$. Use the following outline to prove that this result is correct using mathematical induction.

a. Verify the formula for $n = 1$.

b. Write the induction hypothesis.

c. How many moves are needed to transfer all but the largest of $k + 1$ disks to another peg?

d. How many moves are needed to transfer the largest disk to an empty peg?

e. How many moves are needed to transfer the first k disks back onto the largest one?

f. How many moves are needed to accomplish steps **c, d,** and **e**?

g. Show that part **f** can be written in the form $2^{(k+1)} - 1$.

h. Write the conclusion of the proof.

Review
Graph each inequality.

39. $3x + 4y \le 12$

40. $4x - 3y < 12$

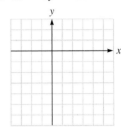

41. $2x + y > 5$

42. $x + 3y \ge 7$

8.6 Permutations and Combinations

In this section, we will learn to

1. Use the Multiplication Principle for Events.

2. Solve permutation problems.

3. Solve combination problems.

4. Use combination notation to write the Binomial Theorem.

5. Find the number of permutations of like things.

1. Use the Multiplication Principle for Events

Lydia plans to go to dinner and attend a movie. If she has a choice of four restaurants and three movies, in how many ways can she spend her evening? There are four choices of restaurants and, for any one of these choices, there are three choices of movies, as shown in the tree diagram in Figure 8-4.

FIGURE 8-4

The diagram shows that Lydia has 12 ways to spend her evening. One possibility is to eat at the Cheesecake Factory and watch True Grit. Another is to eat at the Olive Garden and watch Black Swan.

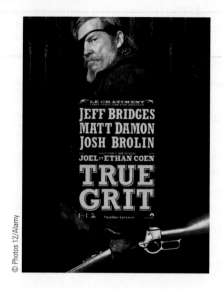

Any situation that has several outcomes is called an **event**. Lydia's first event (choosing a restaurant) can occur in 4 ways. Her second event (choosing a movie) can occur in 3 ways. Thus, she has $4 \cdot 3$, or 12, ways to spend her evening. This example illustrates the **Multiplication Principle for Events**.

Multiplication Principle for Events	Let E_1 and E_2 be two events. If E_1 can be done in a_1 ways, and if—after E_1 has occurred—E_2 can be done in a_2 ways, then the event "E_1 followed by E_2" can be done in $a_1 \cdot a_2$ ways.

The Multiplication Principle can be extended to n events.

EXAMPLE 1   Using the Multiplication Principle for Events

If a traveler has 4 ways to go from New York to Chicago, 3 ways to go from Chicago to Denver, and 6 ways to go from Denver to San Francisco, in how many ways can she go from New York to San Francisco?

SOLUTION   We can let E_1 be the event "going from New York to Chicago," E_2 the event "going from Chicago to Denver," and E_3 the event "going from Denver to San Francisco." Since there are 4 ways to accomplish E_1, 3 ways to accomplish E_2, and 6 ways to accomplish E_3, the number of routes available is

$$4 \cdot 3 \cdot 6 = 72$$

Self Check 1   If a man has 4 sweaters and 5 pairs of slacks, how many different outfits can he wear?

Now Try Exercise 29.

2. Solve Permutation Problems

Suppose we want to arrange 7 books in order on a shelf. We can fill the first space with any one of the 7 books, the second space with any of the remaining 6 books, the third space with any of the remaining 5 books, and so on, until there is only one space left to fill with the last book. According to the Multiplication Principle, the number of ordered arrangements of the books is

$$7 \cdot 6 \cdot 5 \cdot 4 \cdot 3 \cdot 2 \cdot 1 = 5,040$$

When finding the number of possible ordered arrangements of books on a shelf, we are finding the number of **permutations**. The number of permutations of 7 books, using all the books, is 5,040. The symbol $P(n, r)$ is read as "the number of permutations of n things r at a time." Thus, $P(7, 7) = 5,040$.

EXAMPLE 2   **Finding the Number of Permutations**

Assume that there are 7 signal flags of 7 different colors to hang on a mast. How many different signals can be sent when 3 flags are used?

SOLUTION   We are asked to find $P(7, 3)$, the number of permutations (ordered arrangements) of 7 things using 3 of them. Any one of the 7 flags can hang in the top position on the mast. Any one of the 6 remaining flags can hang in the middle position, and any one of the remaining 5 flags can hang in the bottom position. By the Multiplication Principle, we have

$$P(7, 3) = 7 \cdot 6 \cdot 5 = 210$$

It is possible to send 210 different signals.

Self Check 2   How many signals can be sent if two of the 7 flags are missing?

Now Try Exercise 37.

Although it is correct to write $P(7, 3) = 7 \cdot 6 \cdot 5$, we will change the form of the answer to obtain a convenient formula. To derive this formula, we proceed as follows:

$$P(7, 3) = 7 \cdot 6 \cdot 5$$

$$= \frac{7 \cdot 6 \cdot 5 \cdot 4 \cdot 3 \cdot 2 \cdot 1}{4 \cdot 3 \cdot 2 \cdot 1} \qquad \text{Multiply numerator and denominator by } 4 \cdot 3 \cdot 2 \cdot 1.$$

$$= \frac{7!}{4!}$$

$$= \frac{7!}{(7 - 3)!}$$

The generalization of this idea gives the following formula.

Formula for $P(n, r)$ The number of permutations of n things r at a time is given by

$$P(n, r) = \frac{n!}{(n - r)!}$$

EXAMPLE 3   **Using the Permutation Formula**

Find: **a.** $P(8, 4)$ **b.** $P(n, n)$ **c.** $P(n, 0)$

SOLUTION   We will substitute into the formula for $P(n, r)$ and simplify.

a. $P(8, 4) = \dfrac{8!}{(8 - 4)!} = \dfrac{8 \cdot 7 \cdot 6 \cdot 5 \cdot 4!}{4!} = 1,680$

b. $P(n, n) = \dfrac{n!}{(n - n)!} = \dfrac{n!}{0!} = \dfrac{n!}{1} = n!$

c. $P(n, 0) = \dfrac{n!}{(n - 0)!} = \dfrac{n!}{n!} = 1$

Self Check 3   Find: **a.** $P(7, 5)$ **b.** $P(6, 0)$

Now Try Exercise 13.

Parts (b) and (c) of Example 3 establish the following formulas.

Formulas for $P(n, n)$ and $P(n, 0)$

The number of permutations of n things n at a time and n things 0 at a time are given by the formulas

$$P(n, n) = n! \qquad \text{and} \qquad P(n, 0) = 1$$

EXAMPLE 4   **Solving a Permutation Problem**

In how many ways can a baseball manager arrange a batting order of 9 players if there are 25 players on the team?

SOLUTION   To find the number of permutations of 25 things 9 at a time, we substitute 25 for n and 9 for r in the formula for finding $P(n, r)$.

$$P(n, r) = \dfrac{n!}{(n - r)!}$$

$$P(25, 9) = \dfrac{25!}{(25 - 9)!}$$

$$= \dfrac{25!}{16!}$$

$$= \dfrac{25 \cdot 24 \cdot 23 \cdot 22 \cdot 21 \cdot 20 \cdot 19 \cdot 18 \cdot 17 \cdot \cancel{16!}}{\cancel{16!}}$$

$$= 741,354,768,000$$

The number of permutations is 741,354,768,000.

Self Check 4   In how many ways can the manager arrange a batting order if 2 players can't play?

Now Try Exercise 41.

Permutations

A graphing calculator can be used to find $P(n, r)$. For example, let's consider the permutation in Example 4 and determine $P(25, 9)$. The calculator operation that will be used is nPr.

To find $P(25, 9)$, first enter 25 in your calculator.

Press MATH and move the cursor to PRB. Scroll down to 2:nPr and press ENTER.

Enter 9 on your calculator and press ENTER. We see that $P(25, 9)$ is equal to 741,354,768,000.

FIGURE 8-5

EXAMPLE 5 Solving a Permutation Problem

In how many ways can 5 people stand in a line if 2 people refuse to stand next to each other?

SOLUTION The total number of ways that 5 people can stand in line is

$$P(5, 5) = 5! = 5 \cdot 4 \cdot 3 \cdot 2 \cdot 1 = 120$$

To find the number of ways that 5 people can stand in line if 2 people insist on standing together, we consider the two people as one person. Then there are 4 people to stand in line, and this can be done in $P(4, 4) = 4! = 24$ ways. However, because either of the two who are paired could be first, there are two arrangements for the pair who insist on standing together. Thus, there are $2 \cdot 4!$, or 48 ways that 5 people can stand in line if 2 people insist on standing together.

The number of ways that 5 people can stand in line if 2 people refuse to stand together is $5! = 120$ (the total number of ways to line up 5 people) minus $2 \cdot 4! = 48$ (the number of ways to line up the 5 people if 2 do stand together):

$$120 - 48 = 72$$

There are 72 ways to line up the people.

Self Check 5 In how many ways can 5 people stand in a line if one person demands to be first?

Now Try Exercise 39.

EXAMPLE 6 Solving a Permutation Problem

In how many ways can 5 people be seated at a round table?

SOLUTION If we were to seat 5 people in a row, there would be 5! possible arrangements. However, at a round table, each person has a neighbor to the left and to the right. If each person moves one, two, three, four, or five places to the left, everyone has the same neighbors and the arrangement has not changed. Thus, we must divide 5! by 5 to get rid of these duplications. The number of ways that 5 people can be seated at a round table is

$$\frac{5!}{5} = \frac{5 \cdot 4!}{5} = 4! = 4 \cdot 3 \cdot 2 \cdot 1 = 24$$

Self Check 6   In how many ways can 6 people be seated at a round table?

Now Try Exercise 43.

The results of Example 6 suggest the following fact.

Circular Arrangements   There are $(n - 1)!$ ways to arrange n things in a circle.

3. Solve Combination Problems

Suppose that a class of 12 students selects a committee of 3 persons to plan a party. With committees, order is not important. A committee of John, Maria, and Raul is the same as a committee of Maria, Raul, and John. However, if we assume for the moment that order is important, we can find the number of permutations of 12 things 3 at a time.

$$P(12, 3) = \frac{12!}{(12 - 3)!} = \frac{12 \cdot 11 \cdot 10 \cdot 9!}{9!} = 1{,}320$$

However, since we do not care about order, this result of 1,320 ways is too large. Because there are 6 ways $(3! = 6)$ of ordering every committee of 3 students, the result of $P(12, 3) = 1{,}320$ is exactly 6 times too big. To get the correct number of committees, we must divide $P(12, 3)$ by 6:

$$\frac{P(12, 3)}{6} = \frac{1{,}320}{6} = 220$$

In cases of selection where order is not important, we are interested in **combinations**, not permutations. The symbols $C(n, r)$ and $\binom{n}{r}$ both mean the number of combinations of n things r at a time.

If a committee of r people is chosen from a total of n people, the number of possible committees is $C(n, r)$, and there will be $r!$ arrangements of each committee. If we consider the committee as an ordered grouping, the number of orderings is $P(n, r)$. Thus, we have

(1) $r! C(n, r) = P(n, r)$

Comment

When discussing permutations, order counts. When discussing combinations, order doesn't count.

We can divide both sides of Equation 1 by $r!$ to obtain the formula for finding $C(n, r)$.

$$C(n, r) = \binom{n}{r} = \frac{P(n, r)}{r!} = \frac{n!}{r!(n - r)!}$$

Formula for $C(n, r)$ The number of combinations of n things r at a time is given by

$$C(n, r) = \binom{n}{r} = \frac{n!}{r!(n - r)!}$$

In Exercises 77 and 78, you will be asked to prove the following formulas.

Formulas for $C(n, n)$ and $C(n, 0)$ If n is a whole number, then

$$C(n, n) = 1 \quad \text{and} \quad C(n, 0) = 1$$

EXAMPLE 7   Solving a Combination Problem

If Carla must read 4 books from a reading list of 10 books, how many choices does she have?

SOLUTION   Because the order in which the books are read is not important, we find the number of combinations of 10 things 4 at a time:

$$C(10, 4) = \frac{10!}{4!(10-4)!} = \frac{10 \cdot 9 \cdot 8 \cdot 7 \cdot 6!}{4 \cdot 3 \cdot 2 \cdot 1 \cdot 6!}$$

$$= \frac{10 \cdot 9 \cdot 8 \cdot 7}{4 \cdot 3 \cdot 2}$$

$$= 210$$

Carla has 210 choices. ∎

Self Check 7   How many choices would Carla have if she had to read 5 books?

Now Try Exercise 49.

ACCENT ON TECHNOLOGY   Combinations

A graphing calculator can be used to find $C(n, r)$. For example, let's consider the permutation in Example 7 and determine $C(10, 4)$. The calculator operation that will be used is nCr.

To find $C(10, 4)$, first enter 10 in your calculator.

```
10█
```

Press MATH and move the cursor to PRB. Scroll down to 3:nCr and press ENTER.

```
MATH NUM CPX PRB
1:rand
2:nPr
3:nCr
4:!
5:randInt(
6:randNorm(
7:randBin(
```

Enter 4 on your calculator and press ENTER. We see that $C(10, 4)$ is equal to 210.

```
10 nCr 4
              210
█
```

FIGURE 8-6

EXAMPLE 8   Solving a Combination Problem

A class consists of 15 men and 8 women. In how many ways can a debate team be chosen with 3 men and 3 women?

SOLUTION   There are $C(15, 3)$ ways of choosing 3 men and $C(8, 3)$ ways of choosing 3 women. By the Multiplication Principle, there are $C(15, 3) \cdot C(8, 3)$ ways of choosing members of the debate team:

$$C(15, 3) \cdot C(8, 3) = \frac{15!}{3!(15-3)!} \cdot \frac{8!}{3!(8-3)!}$$

$$= \frac{15 \cdot 14 \cdot 13}{6} \cdot \frac{8 \cdot 7 \cdot 6}{6}$$

$$= 25,480$$

There are 25,480 ways to choose the debate team. ∎

Self Check 8   In how many ways can the debate team be chosen if it is to have 4 men and 2 women?

Now Try Exercise 59.

4. Use Combination Notation to Write the Binomial Theorem

The formula

$$C(n, r) = \frac{n!}{r!(n - r)!}$$

gives the coefficient of the $(r + 1)$th term of the binomial expansion of $(a + b)^n$. This implies that the coefficients of a binomial expansion can be used to solve problems involving combinations. The Binomial Theorem is restated below—this time listing the $(r + 1)$th term and using combination notation.

Binomial Theorem   If n is any positive integer, then

$$(a + b)^n = \binom{n}{0}a^n + \binom{n}{1}a^{n-1}b + \binom{n}{2}a^{n-2}b^2 + \cdots + \binom{n}{r}a^{n-r}b^r + \cdots + \binom{n}{n}b^n$$

Comment   In the expansion of $(a + b)^n$, the term containing b^r is given by

$$\binom{n}{r}a^{n-r}b^r$$

EXAMPLE 9   **Using Pascal's Triangle to Compute a Combination**

Use Pascal's Triangle to compute $C(7, 5)$.

SOLUTION   Consider the eighth row of Pascal's Triangle and the corresponding combinations:

$$\begin{array}{cccccccc} 1 & 7 & 21 & 35 & 35 & 21 & 7 & 1 \\ \binom{7}{0} & \binom{7}{1} & \binom{7}{2} & \binom{7}{3} & \binom{7}{4} & \binom{7}{5} & \binom{7}{6} & \binom{7}{7} \end{array}$$

$$C(7, 5) = \binom{7}{5} = 21.$$

Self Check 9   Use Pascal's Triangle to compute $C(6, 5)$.

Now Try Exercise 75.

5. Find the Number of Permutations of Like Things

A *word* is a distinguishable arrangement of letters. For example, six words can be formed with the letters a, b, and c if each letter is used exactly once. The six words are

$$\text{abc,} \quad \text{acb,} \quad \text{bac,} \quad \text{bca,} \quad \text{cab,} \quad \text{and} \quad \text{cba}$$

If there are n distinct letters and each letter is used once, the number of distinct words that can be formed is $n! = P(n, n)$. It is more complicated to compute the number of distinguishable words that can be formed with n letters when some of the letters are duplicates.

EXAMPLE 10   **Finding the Number of Permutations of Like Things**

Find the number of "words" that can be formed if each of the 6 letters of the word *little* is used once.

SOLUTION   For the moment, we assume that the letters of the word *little* are distinguishable: "LitTle." The number of words that can be formed using each letter once is $6! = P(6, 6)$. However, in reality we cannot tell the *l*'s or the *t*'s apart. Therefore, we must divide by a number to get rid of these duplications. Because there are 2! orderings of the two *l*'s and 2! orderings of the two *t*'s, we divide by $2! \cdot 2!$. The number of words that can be formed using each letter of the word *little* is

$$\frac{P(6, 6)}{2! \cdot 2!} = \frac{6!}{2! \cdot 2!} = \frac{6 \cdot 5 \cdot \overset{2}{4} \cdot 3 \cdot 2 \cdot 1}{2 \cdot 1 \cdot 2 \cdot 1} = 180$$

Self Check 10   How many words can be formed if each letter of the word *balloon* is used once?

Now Try Exercise 55.

Example 10 illustrates the following general principle.

Permutations of Like Things   The number of permutations of n things with a things alike, b things alike, and so on, is

$$\frac{n!}{a!b! \cdots}$$

Self Check Answers   **1.** 20   **2.** 60   **3. a.** 2,520   **b.** 1   **4.** 296,541,907,200   **5.** 24
6. 120   **7.** 252   **8.** 38,220   **9.** 6   **10.** 1,260

Exercises **8.6**

Getting Ready

You should be able to complete these vocabulary and concept statements before you proceed to the practice exercises.

Fill in the blanks.

1. If E_1 and E_2 are two events and E_1 can be done in 4 ways and E_2 can be done in 6 ways, then the event E_1 followed by E_2 can be done in ___ ways.

2. An arrangement of n objects is called a _____.

3. $P(n, r) = $ _____

4. $P(n, n) = $ ___

5. $P(n, 0) = $ ___

6. There are _____ ways to arrange n things in a circle.

7. $C(n, r) = $ _____

8. Using combination notation, $C(n, r) = $ ____.

9. $C(n, n) = $ ___

10. $C(n, 0) = $ ___

11. If a word with n letters has a of one letter, b of another letter, and so on, the number of different words that can be formed is _____.

12. Where the order of selection is not important, we are interested in _____, not _____.

Practice

Evaluate each expression.

13. $P(7, 4)$

14. $P(8, 3)$

15. $C(7, 4)$

16. $C(8, 3)$

17. $P(5, 5)$

18. $P(5, 0)$

19. $\dbinom{5}{4}$

20. $\dbinom{8}{4}$

21. $\dbinom{5}{0}$

22. $\dbinom{5}{5}$

23. $P(5, 4) \cdot C(5, 3)$

24. $P(3, 2) \cdot C(4, 3)$

25. $\binom{5}{3}\binom{4}{3}\binom{3}{3}$ **26.** $\binom{5}{5}\binom{6}{6}\binom{7}{7}\binom{8}{8}$

27. $\binom{68}{66}$ **28.** $\binom{100}{99}$

Applications

29. Choosing lunch A lunchroom has a machine with eight kinds of sandwiches, a machine with four kinds of soda, a machine with both white and chocolate milk, and a machine with three kinds of ice cream. How many different lunches can be chosen? (Consider a lunch to be one sandwich, one drink, and one ice cream.)

30. Manufacturing license plates How many six-digit license plates can be manufactured if no license plate number begins with 0?

31. Available phone numbers How many different seven-digit phone numbers can be used in one area code if no phone number begins with 0 or 1?

32. Arranging letters In how many ways can the letters of the word *number* be arranged?

33. Arranging letters with restrictions In how many ways can the letters of the word *number* be arranged if the e and r must remain next to each other?

34. Arranging letters with restrictions In how many ways can the letters of the word *number* be arranged if the e and r cannot be side by side?

35. Arranging letters with repetitions How many ways can five Scrabble tiles bearing the letters, F, F, F, L, and U be arranged to spell the word *fluff*?

36. Arranging letters with repetitions How many ways can six Scrabble tiles bearing the letters B, E, E, E, F, and L be arranged to spell the word *feeble*?

37. Placing people in line In how many arrangements can 8 women be placed in a line?

38. Placing people in line In how many arrangements can 5 women and 5 men be placed in a line if the women and men alternate?

39. Placing people in line In how many arrangements can 5 women and 5 men be placed in a line if all the men line up first?

40. Placing people in line In how many arrangements can 5 women and 5 men be placed in a line if all the women line up first?

41. Combination locks How many permutations does a combination lock have if each combination has 3 numbers, no two numbers of the combination are the same, and the lock dial has 30 notches?

42. Combination locks How many permutations does a combination lock have if each combination has 3 numbers, no two numbers of the combination are the same, and the lock dial has 100 notches?

43. Seating at a table In how many ways can 8 people be seated at a round table?

44. Seating at a table In how many ways can 7 people be seated at a round table?

45. Seating at a table In how many ways can 6 people be seated at a round table if 2 of the people insist on sitting together?

46. Seating arrangements with conditions In how many ways can 6 people be seated at a round table if 2 of the people refuse to sit together?

47. Arrangements in a circle In how many ways can 7 children be arranged in a circle if Sally and John want to sit together and Martha and Peter want to sit together?

48. Arrangements in a circle In how many ways can 8 children be arranged in a circle if Laura, Scott, and Paula want to sit together?

49. Selecting candy bars In how many ways can 4 candy bars be selected from 10 different candy bars?

50. Selecting birthday cards In how many ways can 6 birthday cards be selected from 24 different cards?

51. Circuit wiring A wiring harness containing a red, a green, a white, and a black wire must be attached to a control panel. In how many different orders can the wires be attached?

52. Grading homework A professor grades homework by randomly checking 7 of the 20 problems assigned. In how many different ways can this be done?

53. Forming words with distinct letters How many words can be formed from the letters of the word *plastic* if each letter is to be used once?

54. Forming words with distinct letters How many words can be formed from the letters of the word *computer* if each letter is to be used once?

55. Forming words with repeated letters How many words can be formed from the letters of the word *banana* if each letter is to be used once?

56. Forming words with repeated letters How many words can be formed from the letters of the word *laptop* if each letter is to be used once?

57. Manufacturing license plates How many license plates can be made using two different letters followed by four different digits if the first digit cannot be 0 and the letter O is not used?

58. Planning class schedules If there are 7 class periods in a school day, and a typical student takes 5 classes, how many different time patterns are possible for the student?

59. Selecting golf balls From a bucket containing 6 red and 8 white golf balls, in how many ways can we draw 6 golf balls of which 3 are red and 3 are white?

60. Selecting a committee In how many ways can you select a committee of 3 Republicans and 3 Democrats from a group containing 18 Democrats and 11 Republicans?

61. Selecting a committee In how many ways can you select a committee of 4 Democrats and 3 Republicans from a group containing 12 Democrats and 10 Republicans?

KamiGami/
Shutterstock.com

62. Drawing cards In how many ways can you select a group of 5 red cards and 2 black cards from a deck containing 10 red cards and 8 black cards?

63. Planning dinner In how many ways can a husband and wife choose 2 different dinners from a menu of 17 dinners?

64. Placing people in line In how many ways can 7 people stand in a row if 2 of the people refuse to stand together?

65. Geometry How many lines are determined by 8 points if no 3 points lie on a straight line?

66. Geometry How many lines are determined by 10 points if no 3 points lie on a straight line?

67. Coaching basketball How many different teams can a basketball coach start if the entire squad consists of 10 players? (Assume that a starting team has 5 players and each player can play all positions.)

68. Managing baseball How many different teams can a manager start if the entire squad consists of 25 players? (Assume that a starting team has 9 players and each player can play all positions.)

69. Selecting job applicants There are 30 qualified applicants for 5 openings in the sales department. In how many different ways can the group of 5 be selected?

70. Sales promotions If a customer purchases a new stereo system during the spring sale, he may choose any 6 CDs from 20 classical and 30 jazz selections. In how many ways can the customer choose 3 of each?

71. Guessing on matching questions Ten words are to be paired with the correct 10 out of 12 possible definitions. How many ways are there of guessing?

72. Guessing on true-false exams How many possible ways are there of guessing on a 10-question true-false exam, if it is known that the instructor will have 5 true and 5 false responses?

73. Number of Wendy's® hamburgers Wendy's® Old Fashioned Hamburgers offers eight toppings for their single hamburger. How many different single hamburgers can be ordered?

74. Number of ice cream sundaes A restaurant offers ten toppings for their ice cream sundaes. How many different sundaes can be ordered?

Practice
Use Pascal's Triangle to compute each combination.

75. $C(8, 3)$ **76.** $C(7, 4)$

Discovery and Writing
77. Prove that $C(n, n) = 1$.

78. Prove that $C(n, 0) = 1$.

79. Prove that $\dbinom{n}{r} = \dbinom{n}{n - r}$.

80. Show that the Binomial Theorem can be expressed in the form
$$(a + b)^n = \sum_{k=0}^{n} \binom{n}{k} a^{n-k} b^k$$

81. Explain how to use Pascal's Triangle to find $C(8, 5)$.

82. Explain how to use Pascal's Triangle to find $C(10, 8)$.

Review
Find the value of x.

83. $\log_x 16 = 4$ **84.** $\log_\pi x = \dfrac{1}{2}$

85. $\log_{\sqrt{7}} 49 = x$ **86.** $\log_x \dfrac{1}{2} = -\dfrac{1}{3}$

Determine whether the statement is true or false.

87. $\log_{17} 1 = 0$ **88.** $\log_5 0 = 1$

89. $\log_b b^b = b$

90. $\dfrac{\log_7 A}{\log_7 B} = \log_7 \dfrac{A}{B}$

8.7 Probability

In this section, we will learn to

1. Compute probabilities.

2. Use the Multiplication Property of Probabilities.

In some parts of the United States, casinos are a big part of the entertainment industry. Casinos design their games using the laws of probability to ensure they make huge amounts of money at their customers' expense.

Gerolamo Cardano, an Italian doctor and mathematician, was an accomplished gambler who developed much of the theory of probability in the casino. His book *Liber de Ludo Aleae* (published after his death in 1663) was the first book to develop the topics of probability. Cardano predicted the day of his death. On that day, when it looked like he would live, it is said that he committed suicide to make his prediction come true.

1. Compute Probabilities

The probability that an event will occur is a measure of the likelihood of that event. A tossed coin, for example, can land in two ways, either heads or tails. Because one of these two equally likely outcomes is heads, we expect that out of several tosses, about half will be heads. We say that the probability of obtaining heads in a single toss of the coin is $\frac{1}{2}$.

If records show that out of 100 days with weather conditions like today's, 30 have received rain, the weather service will report, "There is a $\frac{30}{100}$ or 30% probability of rain today."

An **experiment** is a process for which the outcome is uncertain. Tossing a coin, rolling a die, drawing a card, and predicting rain are examples of experiments. For any experiment, the set of all possible outcomes is called a **sample space**.

The sample space, S, for the experiment of tossing two coins is the set

$$S = \{(H, H), (H, T), (T, H), (T, T)\}$$

where the ordered pair (H, T) represents the outcome "heads on the first coin and tails on the second coin." Because there are two possible outcomes for the first coin and two for the second coin, we know (by the Multiplication Principle for Events) that there are $2 \cdot 2 = 4$ possible outcomes. Since there are 4 elements in the sample space S, we write

$n(S) = 4$ Read as "The number of elements in set S is 4."

An **event** associated with an experiment is any subset of the sample space of that experiment. For example, if E is the event "getting at least one heads" in the experiment of tossing two coins, then

$$E = \{(H, H), (H, T), (T, H)\}$$

and $n(E) = 3$. Because the outcome of getting at least one heads can occur in 3 out of 4 possible ways, we say that the **probability** of a favorable outcome is $\frac{3}{4}$.

$$P(E) = P(\text{at least one heads}) = \frac{3}{4}$$

We define the probability of an event as follows.

Probability of an Event   If S is the sample space of an experiment with n distinct and equally likely outcomes, and E is an event that occurs in s of those ways, then the **probability of E** is

$$P(E) = \frac{n(E)}{n(S)} = \frac{s}{n}$$

Because $0 \le s \le n$, it follows that $0 \le \frac{s}{n} \le 1$. This implies that all probabilities have values from 0 to 1. An event that cannot happen has probability 0. An event that is certain to happen has probability 1.

To say that the probability of tossing heads on one toss of a coin is $\frac{1}{2}$ means that if a fair coin is tossed a large number of times, the ratio of the number of heads to the total number of tosses is nearly $\frac{1}{2}$.

To say that the probability of rolling 5 on one roll of a die is $\frac{1}{6}$ means that as the number of rolls approaches infinity, the ratio of the number of favorable outcomes (rolling a 5) to the total number of outcomes (rolling a 1, 2, 3, 4, 5, or 6) approaches $\frac{1}{6}$.

EXAMPLE 1   **Showing the Sample Space of an Experiment**

Show the sample space of the experiment "rolling two dice a single time."

Sergey Mironov/Shutterstock.com

SOLUTION   We can list ordered pairs and let the first number be the result on the first die and the second number the result on the second die. The sample space, S, is the set with the following elements:

(1, 1)	(1, 2)	(1, 3)	(1, 4)	(1, 5)	(1, 6)
(2, 1)	(2, 2)	(2, 3)	(2, 4)	(2, 5)	(2, 6)
(3, 1)	(3, 2)	(3, 3)	(3, 4)	(3, 5)	(3, 6)
(4, 1)	(4, 2)	(4, 3)	(4, 4)	(4, 5)	(4, 6)
(5, 1)	(5, 2)	(5, 3)	(5, 4)	(5, 5)	(5, 6)
(6, 1)	(6, 2)	(6, 3)	(6, 4)	(6, 5)	(6, 6)

Since there are 6 possible outcomes with the first die and 6 possible outcomes with the second die, we expect $6 \cdot 6 = 36$ equally likely possible outcomes, and we have $n(S) = 36$.   ■

Self Check 1   How many pairs in the above sample space have a sum of 7?

Now Try Exercise 5.

EXAMPLE 2   **Finding the Probability of an Event**

Find the probability of the event "rolling a sum of 7 on one roll of two dice."

SOLUTION   The sample space is listed in Example 1. We let E be the set of favorable outcomes, those that give a sum of 7:

$$E = \{(1, 6), (2, 5), (3, 4), (4, 3), (5, 2), (6, 1)\}$$

Since there are 6 favorable outcomes among the 36 equally likely outcomes, $n(E) = 6$, and

$$P(E) = P(\text{rolling a 7}) = \frac{n(E)}{n(S)} = \frac{6}{36} = \frac{1}{6}$$

Self Check 2   Find the probability of rolling a sum of 10.

Now Try Exercise 21.

A standard playing deck of 52 cards has two red suits, hearts and diamonds, and two black suits, clubs and spades. Each suit has 13 cards, including an ace, a king, a queen, a jack, and cards numbered from 2 to 10. We will refer to a standard deck of cards in many examples and exercises.

EXAMPLE 3   **Finding the Probability of an Event**

Find the probability of drawing 5 cards, all hearts, from a standard deck of cards.

SOLUTION   Since the number of ways to draw 5 hearts from the 13 hearts is $C(13, 5)$, we have $n(E) = C(13, 5)$. Since the number of ways to draw 5 cards from the deck is $C(52, 5)$, we have $n(S) = C(52, 5)$. The probability of drawing 5 hearts is the ratio of the number of favorable outcomes to the number of possible outcomes.

$$P(\text{5 hearts}) = \frac{C(13, 5)}{C(52, 5)}$$

$$P(\text{5 hearts}) = \frac{\dfrac{13!}{5!8!}}{\dfrac{52!}{5!47!}}$$

$$= \frac{13!}{5!8!} \cdot \frac{5!47!}{52!}$$

$$= \frac{13 \cdot 12 \cdot 11 \cdot 10 \cdot 9 \cdot 8!}{8!} \cdot \frac{47!}{52 \cdot 51 \cdot 50 \cdot 49 \cdot 48 \cdot 47!}$$

$$= \frac{13 \cdot 12 \cdot 11 \cdot 10 \cdot 9}{52 \cdot 51 \cdot 50 \cdot 49 \cdot 48}$$

$$= \frac{33}{66,640}$$

The probability of drawing 5 hearts is $\frac{33}{66,640}$.

Self Check 3   Find the probability of drawing 6 cards, all hearts, from the deck.

Now Try Exercise 30.

2. Use the Multiplication Property of Probabilities

There is a property of probabilities that is similar to the Multiplication Principle for Events. In the following theorem, we read $P(A \cap B)$ as "the probability of A and B" and $P(B|A)$ as "the probability of B given A." If A and B are events, the set $A \cap B$ contains the outcomes that are in both A and B.

Multiplication Property of Probabilities	If $P(A)$ represents the probability of event A, and $P(B\|A)$ represents the probability that event B will occur after event A, then

$$P(A \cap B) = P(A) \cdot P(B|A)$$

EXAMPLE 4   Finding the Probability of an Event

A box contains 40 cubes of the same size. Of these cubes, 17 are red, 13 are blue, and the rest are yellow. If 2 cubes are drawn at random, without replacement, find the probability that 2 yellow cubes will be drawn.

SOLUTION   Of the 40 cubes in the box, 10 are yellow. The probability of getting a yellow cube on the first draw is

$$P(\text{yellow cube on the first draw}) = \frac{10}{40} = \frac{1}{4}$$

Because there is no replacement after the first draw, 39 cubes remain in the box, and 9 of these are yellow. The probability of drawing a yellow cube on the second draw is

$$P(\text{yellow cube on the second draw}) = \frac{9}{39} = \frac{3}{13}$$

The probability of drawing 2 yellow cubes in succession is the product of the probability of drawing a yellow cube on the first draw and the probability of drawing a yellow cube on the second draw.

$$P(\text{drawing two yellow cubes}) = \frac{1}{4} \cdot \frac{3}{13} = \frac{3}{52}$$

Self Check 4   Find the probability that 2 blue cubes will be drawn.

Now Try Exercise 23.

EXAMPLE 5   Using the Multiplication Property to Determine the Probability of an Event

Repeat Example 3 using the Multiplication Property of Probabilities.

SOLUTION   The probability of drawing a heart on the first draw is $\frac{13}{52}$. The probability of drawing a heart on the second draw *given that we got a heart on the first draw* is $\frac{12}{51}$. The probability is $\frac{11}{50}$ on the third draw, $\frac{10}{49}$ on the fourth draw, and $\frac{9}{48}$ on the fifth draw. By the Multiplication Property of Probabilities,

$$P(\text{5 hearts in a row}) = \frac{13}{52} \cdot \frac{12}{51} \cdot \frac{11}{50} \cdot \frac{10}{49} \cdot \frac{9}{48}$$

$$= \frac{33}{66,640}$$

Self Check 5   Use the Multiplication Property of Probabilities to find the probability of drawing 6 cards, all hearts, from the deck.

Now Try Exercise 25.

EXAMPLE 6   Finding the Probability of an Event

In a school, 30% of the students are gifted in mathematics and 10% are gifted in art and mathematics. If a student is gifted in mathematics, find the probability that the student is also gifted in art.

SOLUTION Let $P(M)$ be the probability that a randomly chosen student is gifted in mathematics, and let $P(M \cap A)$ be the probability that the student is gifted in both art and mathematics. We must find $P(A|M)$, the probability that the student is gifted in art, given that he or she is gifted in mathematics. To do so, we substitute the given values

$$P(M) = 0.3 \quad \text{and} \quad P(M \cap A) = 0.1$$

in the formula for multiplication of probabilities and solve for $P(A|M)$:

$$P(M \cap A) = P(M) \cdot P(A|M)$$

$$0.1 = (0.3)P(A|M)$$

$$P(A|M) = \frac{0.1}{0.3}$$

$$= \frac{1}{3}$$

If a student is gifted in mathematics, there is a probability of $\frac{1}{3}$ that he or she is also gifted in art.

Self Check 6 If 40% of the students are gifted in art, find the probability that a student gifted in art is also gifted in mathematics.

Now Try Exercise 55.

Self Check Answers **1.** 6 **2.** $\dfrac{1}{12}$ **3.** $\dfrac{33}{391,510}$ **4.** $\dfrac{1}{10}$ **5.** $\dfrac{33}{391,510}$ **6.** $\dfrac{1}{4}$

Exercises **8.7**

Getting Ready
You should be able to complete these vocabulary and concept statements before you proceed to the practice exercises.

Fill in the blanks.
1. An _____ is any process for which the outcome is uncertain.
2. A list of all possible outcomes for an experiment is called a _____.
3. The probability of an event E is defined as

$$P(E) = \frac{}{\underline{\quad}} = \frac{s}{n}$$

4. $P(A \cap B) = $ _____

Practice
List the sample space of each experiment.
5. Rolling one die and tossing one coin

6. Tossing three coins

7. Selecting a letter of the alphabet

8. Picking a one-digit number

An ordinary die is rolled. Find the probability of each event.

Holly Kuchera/Shutterstock.com

9. Rolling a 2

10. Rolling a number greater than 4

11. Rolling a number greater than 1 but less than 6

12. Rolling an odd number

Balls numbered from 1 to 42 are placed in a container and stirred. If one is drawn at random, find the probability of each result.

13. The number is less than 20.

14. The number is less than 50.

15. The number is a prime number.

16. The number is less than 10 or greater than 40.

If the spinner shown below is spun, find the probability of each event. Assume that the spinner never stops on a line.

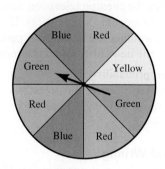

17. The spinner stops on red.

18. The spinner stops on green.

19. The spinner stops on orange.

20. The spinner stops on yellow.

Find the probability of each event.

21. Rolling a sum of 4 on one roll of two dice

22. Drawing a diamond on one draw from a card deck

23. Drawing two aces in succession from a card deck if the card is replaced and the deck is shuffled after the first draw

24. Drawing two aces from a card deck without replacing the card after the first draw

25. Drawing a red egg from a basket containing 5 red eggs and 7 blue eggs

26. Getting 2 red eggs in a single scoop from a bucket containing 5 red eggs and 7 yellow eggs

27. Drawing a bridge hand of 13 cards, all of one suit

28. Drawing 6 diamonds from a card deck without replacing the cards after each draw

29. Drawing 5 aces from a card deck without replacing the cards after each draw

30. Drawing 5 clubs from the black cards in a card deck

31. Drawing a face card (king, queen, or jack) from a card deck

32. Drawing 6 face cards in a row from a card deck without replacing the cards after each draw

33. Drawing 5 orange cubes from a bowl containing 5 orange cubes and 1 beige cube

34. Rolling a sum of 4 with one roll of three dice

35. Rolling a sum of 11 with one roll of three dice

36. Picking, at random, 5 Republicans from a group containing 8 Republicans and 10 Democrats

37. Tossing 3 heads in 5 tosses of a fair coin

38. Tossing 5 heads in 5 tosses of a fair coin

Assume that the probability that an airplane engine will fail during a torture test is $\frac{1}{2}$ and that the aircraft in question has 4 engines.

39. Construct a sample space for the torture test. Use S for survive and F for fail.

40. Find the probability that all engines will survive the test.

41. Find the probability that exactly 1 engine will survive.

42. Find the probability that exactly 2 engines will survive.

43. Find the probability that exactly 3 engines will survive.

44. Find the probability that no engines will survive.

45. Find the sum of the probabilities in Exercises 40 through 44.

Assume that a survey of 282 people is taken to determine the opinions of doctors, teachers, and lawyers on a proposed piece of legislation, with the results as shown in the table. A person is chosen at random from those surveyed. Refer to the table to find each probability.

	Number that favor	Number that oppose	Number with no opinion	Total
Doctors	70	32	17	119
Teachers	83	24	10	117
Lawyers	23	15	8	46
Total	176	71	35	282

46. The person favors the legislation.

47. A doctor opposes the legislation.

48. A person who opposes the legislation is a lawyer.

49. **Quality control** In a batch of 10 tires, 2 are known to be defective. If 4 tires are chosen at random, find the probability that all 4 tires are good.

50. **Medicine** Out of a group of 9 patients treated with a new drug, 4 suffered a relapse. Find the probability that 3 patients of this group, chosen at random, will remain disease-free.

Use the Multiplication Property of Probabilities.

51. If $P(A) = 0.3$ and $P(B|A) = 0.6$, find $P(A \cap B)$.

52. If $P(A \cap B) = 0.3$ and $P(B|A) = 0.6$, find $P(A)$.

53. **Conditional probability** The probability that a person owns a luxury car is 0.2, and the probability that the owner of such a car also owns a personal computer is 0.7. Find the probability that a person, chosen at random, owns both a luxury car and a computer.

54. **Conditional probability** If 40% of the population have completed college, and 85% of college graduates are registered to vote, what percent of the population are both college graduates and registered voters?

55. **Conditional probability** About 25% of the population watches the evening television news coverage as well as the morning soap operas. If 75% of the population watches the news, what percent of those who watch the news also watch the soaps?

56. **Conditional probability** The probability of rain today is 0.40. If it rains, the probability that Bill will forget his raincoat is 0.70. Find the probability that Bill will get wet.

Discovery and Writing

57. If $P(A \cap B) = 0.7$, is it possible that $P(B|A) = 0.6$? Explain.

58. Is it possible that $P(A \cap B) = P(A)$? Explain.

Review

Solve each equation.

59. $|x + 3| = 7$

60. $|3x - 2| = |2x - 3|$

Solve each inequality. Write the answer using interval notation.

61. $|x - 3| < 7$

62. $|3x - 2| \geq |2x - 3|$

CHAPTER REVIEW

SECTION 8.1   The Binomial Theorem

Definitions and Concepts

Pascal's Triangle:
Pascal's Triangle is a triangular array of numbers showing the coefficients of the expansion of $(a + b)^n$. The example shows the first several rows of Pascal's triangle. Except for the 1's, each number in the triangle is the sum of the two numbers above it.

Examples

			1				Row 0
		1		1			Row 1
	1		2		1		Row 2
1		3		3		1	Row 3
1	4		6		4	1	Row 4
1	5	10		10	5	1	Row 5

Definitions and Concepts	Examples
Factorial notation:	
$n! = n(n-1)(n-2) \cdot \cdots \cdot 3 \cdot 2 \cdot 1$	$7! = 7 \cdot 6 \cdot 5 \cdot 4 \cdot 3 \cdot 2 \cdot 1 = 5{,}040$
$0! = 1 \qquad n(n-1)! = n!$	$7 \cdot 6! = 7 \cdot 6 \cdot 5 \cdot 4 \cdot 3 \cdot 2 \cdot 1 = 7!$

Definitions and Concepts	Examples
The Binomial Theorem: If n is any positive integer, then $(a+b)^n = a^n + \dfrac{n!}{1!(n-1)!}\, a^{n-1}b$ $+ \dfrac{n!}{2!(n-2)!}\, a^{n-2}b^2 + \dfrac{n!}{3!(n-3)!}\, a^{n-3}b^3 + \cdots$ $+ \dfrac{n!}{r!(n-r)!}\, a^{n-r}b^r + \cdots + b^n$	$(a+b)^3 = a^3 + \dfrac{3!}{1!(3-1)!}\, a^{3-1}b + \dfrac{3!}{2!(3-2)!}\, a^{3-2}b^2 + b^3$ $= a^3 + \dfrac{3 \cdot 2!}{1 \cdot 2!}\, a^2b + \dfrac{3 \cdot 2 \cdot 1}{2 \cdot 1 \cdot 1}\, ab^2 + b^3$ $= a^3 + 3a^2b + 3ab^2 + b^3$ Note that the coefficients 1, 3, 3, and 1 are the numbers in the third row of Pascal's Triangle. Find the fourth term of $(a+b)^9$. In the 4th term, the exponent on b is 3, and the exponent on a is $9-3$ or 6. The numerator of the fractional coefficient is $9!$ and the factors of the denominator are $3!$ and $(9-3)!$. Thus the 4th term is $\dfrac{9!}{3!(9-3)!}\, a^6b^3 = 84a^6b^2$

EXERCISES

Find each value.

1. $6!$

2. $7! \cdot 0! \cdot 1! \cdot 3!$

3. $\dfrac{8!}{7!}$

4. $\dfrac{5! \cdot 7! \cdot 8!}{6! \cdot 9!}$

Expand each expression.

5. $(x+y)^3$

6. $(p+q)^4$

7. $(a-b)^5$

8. $(2a-b)^3$

Find the required term of each expansion.

9. $(a+b)^8$; 4th term

10. $(2x-y)^5$; 3rd term

11. $(x-y)^9$; 7th term

12. $(4x+7)^6$; 4th term

SECTION 8.2   Sequences, Series, and Summation Notation

Definitions and Concepts	Examples
Sequences and series: An **infinite sequence** is a function whose domain is the set of natural numbers.	$2, 5, 8, 11, 14, 17, 20, \ldots$
A **finite sequence** is a function whose domain is the set of the first n natural numbers.	$2, 5, 8, 11, 14, 17, 20$
If the commas in a sequence are replaced with $+$ signs, the result is called a **series**.	**Infinite series:** $2 + 5 + 8 + 11 + 14 + 17 + 20 + \cdots$ **Finite series:** $2 + 5 + 8 + 11 + 14 + 17 + 20$

Definitions and Concepts	Examples
Define a sequence recursively: A sequence can be defined **recursively** by giving its first term and a rule showing how to obtain the $(n + 1)$th term from the nth term.	Write the first 4 terms of the sequence with a first term of 3 and a general term of $a_{n+1} = 2a_n + 1$. $a_1 = 3$ $a_2 = 2(3) + 1 = 7$ $a_3 = 2(7) + 1 = 15$ $a_4 = 2(15) + 1 = 31$ The first four terms are 3, 7, 15, and 31.
Summation notation: $\sum\limits_{k=1}^{4} n^3$ indicates the sum of the four terms obtained when 1, 2, 3, and 4 are substituted for n. • If c is a constant, then $\quad \sum\limits_{k=1}^{n} c = nc$ • If c is a constant, then $\quad \sum\limits_{k=1}^{n} cf(k) = c \sum\limits_{k=1}^{n} f(k)$ • $\sum\limits_{k=1}^{n} [f(k) + g(k)] = \sum\limits_{k=1}^{n} f(k) + \sum\limits_{k=1}^{n} g(k)$	$\sum\limits_{k=1}^{4} n^3 = 1^3 + 2^3 + 3^3 + 4^3 = 1 + 8 + 27 + 64 = 100$ $\sum\limits_{k=1}^{5} 9 = 5 \cdot 9 = 45$ $\sum\limits_{k=1}^{8} 4k^2 = 4 \sum\limits_{k=1}^{8} k^2$ $\sum\limits_{k=1}^{5} (k + k^2) = \sum\limits_{k=1}^{5} k + \sum\limits_{k=1}^{5} k^2$

EXERCISES

Write the fourth term in each sequence.

13. $0, 7, 26, \ldots, n^3 - 1, \ldots$

14. $\dfrac{3}{2}, 3, \dfrac{11}{2}, \ldots, \dfrac{n^2 + 2}{2}, \ldots$

Find the first four terms of each sequence.

15. $a_1 = 5$ and $a_{n+1} = 3a_n + 2$

16. $a_1 = -2$ and $a_{n+1} = 2a_n^2$

Evaluate each expression.

17. $\sum\limits_{k=1}^{4} 3k^2$

18. $\sum\limits_{k=1}^{10} 6$

19. $\sum\limits_{k=5}^{8} (k^3 + 3k^2)$

20. $\sum\limits_{k=1}^{30} \left(\dfrac{3}{2} k - 12 \right) - \dfrac{3}{2} \sum\limits_{k=1}^{30} k$

SECTION 8.3   Arithmetic Sequences

Definitions and Concepts	Examples
Arithmetic sequence: An **arithmetic sequence** is of the form $\quad a, a + d, a + 2d, \ldots, a + (n - 1)d$ where a is the first term, d is the common difference, and $a_n = a + (n - 1)d$ is the n term.	In the arithmetic sequence 2, 5, 8, 11, 14, 17, $\ldots$, 2 is the first term, 3 is the common difference, and the sixth term is 17. The twentieth term of the sequence above is given by $\quad a_n = a + (n - 1)d$ $\quad a_{20} = 2 + (20 - 1)3$ $\quad\quad\; = 2 + (19)3$ $\quad\quad\; = 59$

Definitions and Concepts	Examples
Arithmetic means: Numbers inserted between a first and last term to form an arithmetic sequence are called **arithmetic means**.	To insert three arithmetic means between -4 and 16, we first determine the common difference d by substituting -4 for a, 16 for a_n, and 5 for n in the formula $a_n = a + (n - 1)d$ and solving for d. $$a_n = a + (n - 1)d$$ $$16 = -4 + (5 - 1)d$$ $$20 = 4d$$ $$5 = d$$ Since the common difference is 5, the three arithmetic means are $$-4 + 5, -4 + 2(5), -4 + 3(5) \quad \text{or} \quad 1, 6, 11$$
Sum of the first n terms of an arithmetic series: The formula $$S_n = \frac{n(a + a_n)}{2}$$ gives the sum of the first n terms of an arithmetic series, where S_n is the sum, a is the first term, a_n is the last (or nth) term, and n is the number of terms.	The sum of the first 20 terms of the series $$2 + 5 + 8 + 11 + 14 + 17 + 20 + \cdots$$ is given by $$S_n = \frac{n(a + a_n)}{2}$$ $$S_{20} = \frac{20(2 + 59)}{2} \qquad a_n = 59 \text{ was found earlier.}$$ $$= 610$$

EXERCISES

Find the required term of each arithmetic sequence.

21. $5, 9, 13, \ldots$; 29th term

22. $8, 15, 22, \ldots$; 40th term

23. $6, -1, -8, \ldots$; 15th term

24. $\dfrac{1}{2}, -\dfrac{3}{2}, -\dfrac{7}{2}, \ldots$; 35th term

25. Find three arithmetic means between 2 and 8.

26. Find five arithmetic means between 10 and 100.

Find the sum of the first 40 terms in each sequence.

27. $5, 9, 13, \ldots$

28. $8, 15, 22$

29. $6, -1, -8, \ldots$

30. $\dfrac{1}{2}, -\dfrac{3}{2}, -\dfrac{7}{2}, \ldots$

SECTION 8.4   Geometric Sequences

Definitions and Concepts	Examples
Geometric sequence: A **geometric sequence** is of the form $$a, ar, ar^2, ar^3, \ldots, ar^{n-1}, \ldots$$ where a is the first term and r is the common ratio. The formula $a_n = ar^{n-1}$ gives the nth term of the sequence.	In the geometric sequence $2, 6, 18, 54, 162, \ldots$, 2 is the first term, 3 is the common ratio, and the fifth term is 162. The tenth term of the sequence above is given by $$a_n = ar^{n-1}$$ $$a_{10} = 2 \cdot 3^{10-1}$$ $$= 2 \cdot 3^9$$ $$= 39{,}366$$

Definitions and Concepts	Examples
Formulas for permutations and combinations: $P(n, r) = \dfrac{n!}{(n-r)!}$ $P(n, n) = n!$ $P(n, 0) = 1$ $C(n, r) = \dbinom{n}{r} = \dfrac{n!}{r!(n-r)!}$ $C(n, n) = 1$ $C(n, 0) = 1$	$P(7, 2) = \dfrac{7!}{(7-2)!} = \dfrac{7 \cdot 6 \cdot 5!}{5!} = 42$ $P(7, 7) = \dfrac{7!}{(7-7)!} = \dfrac{7!}{0!} = \dfrac{7!}{1} = 7!$ $P(7, 0) = \dfrac{7!}{(7-0)!} = \dfrac{7!}{7!} = 1$ $C(7, 2) = \dfrac{7!}{2!(7-2)!} = \dfrac{7 \cdot 6 \cdot 5!}{2 \cdot 5!} = 7 \cdot 3 = 21$ $C(7, 7) = \dfrac{7!}{7!(7-7)!} = \dfrac{7!}{7! \cdot 0!} = \dfrac{7!}{7! \cdot 1} = 1$ $C(7, 0) = \dfrac{7!}{0!(7-0)!} = \dfrac{7!}{1 \cdot 7!} = \dfrac{7!}{1 \cdot 7!} = 1$
Circular arrangements: There are $(n-1)!$ ways to place n things in a circle.	There are $(6-1)! = 5! = 120$ ways to seat 6 people at a round table.
Permutations of like objects: The number of permutations of n things with a things alike, b things alike, and so on, is $$\dfrac{n!}{a!b! \cdots}$$	The number of distinguishable words that can be formed from the letters of the word *happy* is $\dfrac{5!}{1! \cdot 1! \cdot 2! \cdot 1!}$ There are 5 letters. *h, a,* and *y* occur once; *p* occurs twice. $= \dfrac{5 \cdot 4 \cdot 3 \cdot 2!}{2!} = 60$

EXERCISES

Evaluate each expression.

57. $P(8, 5)$ **58.** $C(7, 4)$

59. $0! \cdot 1!$ **60.** $P(10, 2) \cdot C(10, 2)$

61. $P(8, 6) \cdot C(8, 6)$ **62.** $C(8, 5) \cdot C(6, 2)$

63. $C(7, 5) \cdot P(4, 0)$ **64.** $C(12, 10) \cdot C(11, 0)$

65. $\dfrac{P(8, 5)}{C(8, 5)}$ **66.** $\dfrac{C(8, 5)}{C(13, 5)}$

67. $\dfrac{C(6, 3)}{C(10, 3)}$ **68.** $\dfrac{C(13, 5)}{C(52, 5)}$

69. In how many ways can 10 teenagers be seated at a round table if 2 girls wish to sit with their boyfriends?

70. How many distinguishable words can be formed from the letters of the word *casserole* if each letter is used exactly once?

SECTION 8.7   Probability

Definitions and Concepts	Examples
Probability of an event: An event that cannot happen has a probability of 0. An event that is certain to happen has a probability of 1. All other events have probabilities between 0 and 1.	The probability that pigs fly is 0. The probability that every pig will die is 1.

Definitions and Concepts	Examples
If S is the sample space of an experiment with n distinct and equally likely outcomes, and if E is an event that occurs in s of those ways, then the **probability of E** is $$P(E) = \frac{n(E)}{n(S)} = \frac{s}{n}$$	Since there are 28 days and 4 Fridays in February, the probability that a day chosen at random in February will be a Friday is $$P(\text{Friday}) = \frac{4}{28} \quad \begin{array}{l}\text{the number of Fridays}\\ \text{the number of days}\end{array}$$ $$= \frac{1}{7}$$
Multiplication Property of Probabilities: $$P(A \cap B) = P(A) \cdot P(B|A)$$	A jar contains 25 marbles of the same size. Of these marbles, 10 are red, 10 are blue, and 5 are yellow. If 2 marbles are drawn (without replacement), find the probability that both marbles will be red. Of the 25 marbles in the jar, 10 are red. The probability of getting a red marble on the first draw is $$P(\text{red marble on the first draw}) = \frac{10}{25} = \frac{2}{5}$$ Because there is no replacement after the first draw, 24 marbles remain in the jar and 9 of these are red. The probability of drawing a red marble on the second draw is $$P(\text{red marble on the second draw}) = \frac{9}{24} = \frac{3}{8}$$ The probability of drawing 2 red marbles in a row is the product of the probabilities: $$P(\text{drawing 2 red marbles}) = \frac{2}{5} \cdot \frac{3}{8} = \frac{3}{20}$$

EXERCISES

71. Make a tree diagram (like Figure 8-4 on page 761) to illustrate the possible results of tossing a coin four times.

72. In how many ways can you draw a 5-card poker hand of 3 aces and 2 kings?

73. Find the probability of drawing the hand described in Exercise 72.

74. Find the probability of not drawing the hand described in Exercise 72.

75. Find the probability of having a 13-card bridge hand consisting of 4 aces, 4 kings, 4 queens, and 1 jack.

76. Find the probability of choosing a committee of 3 men and 2 women from a group of 8 men and 6 women.

77. Find the probability of drawing a club or a spade on one draw from a card deck.

78. Find the probability of drawing a black card or a king on one draw from a card deck.

79. Find the probability of getting an ace-high royal flush in hearts (ace, king, queen, jack, and ten of hearts) in poker.

80. Find the probability of being dealt 5 cards of one suit in a poker hand.

81. Find the probability of getting 3 heads or fewer on 4 tosses of a fair coin.

CHAPTER TEST

Find each value.

1. $3! \cdot 0! \cdot 4! \cdot 1!$

2. $\dfrac{2! \cdot 4! \cdot 6! \cdot 8!}{3! \cdot 5! \cdot 7!}$

Find the required term in each expansion.

3. $(x + 2y)^5$; 2nd term

4. $(2a - b)^8$; 7th term

Find each sum.

5. $\displaystyle\sum_{k=1}^{3} (4k + 1)$

6. $\displaystyle\sum_{k=2}^{4} (3k - 21)$

Find the sum of the first ten terms of each sequence.

7. $2, 5, 8, \ldots$

8. $5, 1, -3, \ldots$

9. Find three arithmetic means between 4 and 24.

10. Find two geometric means between -2 and -54.

Find the sum of the first ten terms of each sequence.

11. $\dfrac{1}{4}, \dfrac{1}{2}, 1, \ldots$

12. $6, 2, \dfrac{2}{3}, \ldots$

13. A car costing $\$C$ when new depreciates 25% of the previous year's value each year. How much is the car worth after 3 years?

14. A house costing $\$C$ when new appreciates 10% of the previous year's value each year. How much will the house be worth after 4 years?

15. Prove by induction:

$$3 + 4 + 5 + \cdots + (n + 2) = \frac{1}{2}n(n + 5)$$

16. How many six-digit license plates can be made if no plate begins with 0 or 1?

Find each value.

17. $P(7, 2)$

18. $P(4, 4)$

19. $C(8, 2)$

20. $C(12, 0)$

21. How many ways can 4 men and 4 women stand in line if all the women are first?

22. How many different ways can 6 people be seated at a round table?

23. How many different words can be formed from the letters of the word *bluff* if each letter is used once?

24. Show the sample space of the experiment: toss a fair coin three times.

Find each probability.

25. Rolling a 5 on one roll of a die

26. Drawing a jack or a queen from a standard card deck

27. Receiving 5 hearts for a 5-card poker hand

28. Rolling a sum of 9 on one roll of two dice.

29. A box contains 50 cubes of the same size. Of these cubes, 20 are red, and 30 are blue. If 2 cubes are drawn at random, without replacement, find the probability that 2 blue cubes are drawn.

30. In a batch of 20 tires, 2 are known to be defective. If 4 tires are chosen at random, find the probability that all 4 tires are good.

Appendix I: A Proof of the Binomial Theorem

The Binomial Theorem can be proved for positive-integer exponents using mathematical induction.

The Binomial Theorem If n is a positive integer, then

$$(a + b)^n = a^n + \frac{n!}{1!(n-1)!}a^{n-1}b^1 + \frac{n!}{2!(n-2)!}a^{n-2}b^2 + \cdots$$

$$+ \frac{n!}{r!(n-r)!}a^{n-r}b^r + \cdots + b^n$$

PROOF As in all induction proofs, there are two parts.

Part 1: Substituting the number 1 for n on both sides of the equation, we have

$$(a + b)^1 = a^1 + \frac{1!}{1!(1-1)!}a^{1-1}b^1$$

$$a + b = a + a^0 b$$

$$a + b = a + b$$

and the theorem is true when $n = 1$. Part 1 is complete.

Part 2: We write expressions for two general terms in the statement of the induction hypothesis. We assume that the theorem is true for $n = k$:

$$(a + b)^k = a^k + \frac{k!}{1!(k-1)!}a^{k-1}b + \frac{k!}{2!(k-2)!}a^{k-2}b^2 + \cdots$$

$$+ \frac{k!}{(r-1)!(k-r+1)!}a^{k-r+1}b^{r-1}$$

$$+ \frac{k!}{r!(k-r)!}a^{k-r}b^r + \cdots + b^k$$

We multiply both sides of this equation by $a + b$ and hope to obtain a similar equation in which the quantity $k + 1$ replaces all of the n values in the Binomial Theorem:

$$(a + b)^k(a + b)$$

$$= (a + b)\left[a^k + \frac{k!}{1!(k-1)!}a^{k-1}b + \frac{k!}{2!(k-2)!}a^{k-2}b^2 + \cdots \right.$$

$$\left. + \frac{k!}{(r-1)!(k-r+1)!}a^{k-r+1}b^{r-1} + \frac{k!}{r!(k-r)!}a^{k-r}b^r + \cdots + b^k \right]$$

We distribute the multiplication first by a and then by b:

$$(a + b)^{k+1} = \left[a^{k+1} + \frac{k!}{1!(k-1)!}a^k b + \frac{k!}{2!(k-2)!}a^{k-1}b^2 + \cdots \right.$$

$$\left. + \frac{k!}{(r-1)!(k-r+1)!}a^{k-r+2}b^{r-1} + \frac{k!}{r!(k-r)!}a^{k-r+1}b^r + \cdots + ab^k \right]$$

$$+ \left[a^k b + \frac{k!}{1!(k-1)!}a^{k-1}b^2 + \frac{k!}{2!(k-2)!}a^{k-2}b^3 + \cdots \right.$$

$$\left. + \frac{k!}{(r-1)!(k-r+1)!}a^{k-r+1}b^r + \frac{k!}{r!(k-r)!}a^{k-r}b^{r+1} + \cdots + b^{k+1} \right]$$

Combining like terms, we have

$$(a + b)^{k+1} = a^{k+1} + \left[\frac{k!}{1!(k-1)!} + 1 \right] a^k b$$

$$+ \left[\frac{k!}{2!(k-2)!} + \frac{k!}{1!(k-1)!} \right] a^{k-1} b^2 + \cdots$$

$$+ \left[\frac{k!}{r!(k-r)!} + \frac{k!}{(r-1)!(k-r+1)!} \right] a^{k-r+1} b^r + \cdots + b^{k+1}$$

These results may be written as

$$(a + b)^{k+1} = a^{k+1} + \frac{(k+1)!}{1!(k+1-1)!} a^{(k+1)-1} b + \frac{(k+1)!}{2!(k+1-2)!} a^{(k+1)-2} b^2$$

$$+ \cdots + \frac{(k+1)!}{r!(k+1-r)!} a^{(k+1)-r} b^r + \cdots + b^{k+1}$$

This formula has precisely the same form as the Binomial Theorem, with the quantity $k + 1$ replacing all of the original n values. Therefore, the truth of the theorem for $n = k$ implies the truth of the theorem for $n = k + 1$. Because both parts of the axiom of mathematical induction are verified, the theorem is proved.

Appendix II: Tables

Table A Powers and Roots

n	n^2	$\sqrt{n}$	n^3	$\sqrt[3]{n}$	n	n^2	$\sqrt{n}$	n^3	$\sqrt[3]{n}$
1	1	1.000	1	1.000	51	2,601	7.141	132,651	3.708
2	4	1.414	8	1.260	52	2,704	7.211	140,608	3.733
3	9	1.732	27	1.442	53	2,809	7.280	148,877	3.756
4	16	2.000	64	1.587	54	2,916	7.348	157,464	3.780
5	25	2.236	125	1.710	55	3,025	7.416	166,375	3.803
6	36	2.449	216	1.817	56	3,136	7.483	175,616	3.826
7	49	2.646	343	1.913	57	3,249	7.550	185,193	3.849
8	64	2.828	512	2.000	58	3,364	7.616	195,112	3.871
9	81	3.000	729	2.080	59	3,481	7.681	205,379	3.893
10	100	3.162	1,000	2.154	60	3,600	7.746	216,000	3.915
11	121	3.317	1,331	2.224	61	3,721	7.810	226,981	3.936
12	144	3.464	1,728	2.289	62	3,844	7.874	238,328	3.958
13	169	3.606	2,197	2.351	63	3,969	7.937	250,047	3.979
14	196	3.742	2,744	2.410	64	4,096	8.000	262,144	4.000
15	225	3.873	3,375	2.466	65	4,225	8.062	274,625	4.021
16	256	4.000	4,096	2.520	66	4,356	8.124	287,496	4.041
17	289	4.123	4,913	2.571	67	4,489	8.185	300,763	4.062
18	324	4.243	5,832	2.621	68	4,624	8.246	314,432	4.082
19	361	4.359	6,859	2.668	69	4,761	8.307	328,509	4.102
20	400	4.472	8,000	2.714	70	4,900	8.367	343,000	4.121
21	441	4.583	9,261	2.759	71	5,041	8.426	357,911	4.141
22	484	4.690	10,648	2.802	72	5,184	8.485	373,248	4.160
23	529	4.796	12,167	2.844	73	5,329	8.544	389,017	4.179
24	576	4.899	13,824	2.884	74	5,476	8.602	405,224	4.198
25	625	5.000	15,625	2.924	75	5,625	8.660	421,875	4.217
26	676	5.099	17,576	2.962	76	5,776	8.718	438,976	4.236
27	729	5.196	19,683	3.000	77	5,929	8.775	456,533	4.254
28	784	5.292	21,952	3.037	78	6,084	8.832	474,552	4.273
29	841	5.385	24,389	3.072	79	6,241	8.888	493,039	4.291
30	900	5.477	27,000	3.107	80	6,400	8.944	512,000	4.309
31	961	5.568	29,791	3.141	81	6,561	9.000	531,441	4.327
32	1,024	5.657	32,768	3.175	82	6,724	9.055	551,368	4.344
33	1,089	5.745	35,937	3.208	83	6,889	9.110	571,787	4.362
34	1,156	5.831	39,304	3.240	84	7,056	9.165	592,704	4.380
35	1,225	5.916	42,875	3.271	85	7,225	9.220	614,125	4.397
36	1,296	6.000	46,656	3.302	86	7,396	9.274	636,056	4.414
37	1,369	6.083	50,653	3.332	87	7,569	9.327	658,503	4.431
38	1,444	6.164	54,872	3.362	88	7,744	9.381	681,472	4.448
39	1,521	6.245	59,319	3.391	89	7,921	9.434	704,969	4.465
40	1,600	6.325	64,000	3.420	90	8,100	9.487	729,000	4.481
41	1,681	6.403	68,921	3.448	91	8,281	9.539	753,571	4.498
42	1,764	6.481	74,088	3.476	92	8,464	9.592	778,688	4.514
43	1,849	6.557	79,507	3.503	93	8,649	9.644	804,357	4.531
44	1,936	6.633	85,184	3.530	94	8,836	9.695	830,584	4.547
45	2,025	6.708	91,125	3.557	95	9,025	9.747	857,375	4.563
46	2,116	6.782	97,336	3.583	96	9,216	9.798	884,736	4.579
47	2,209	6.856	103,823	3.609	97	9,409	9.849	912,673	4.595
48	2,304	6.928	110,592	3.634	98	9,604	9.899	941,192	4.610
49	2,401	7.000	117,649	3.659	99	9,801	9.950	970,299	4.626
50	2,500	7.071	125,000	3.684	100	10,000	10.000	1,000,000	4.642

Table B (continued)

N	0	1	2	3	4	5	6	7	8	9
5.5	7404	7412	7419	7427	7435	7443	7451	7459	7466	7474
5.6	7482	7490	7497	7505	7513	7520	7528	7536	7543	7551
5.7	7559	7566	7574	7582	7589	7597	7604	7612	7619	7627
5.8	7634	7642	7649	7657	7664	7672	7679	7686	7694	7701
5.9	7709	7716	7723	7731	7738	7745	7752	7760	7767	7774
6.0	7782	7789	7796	7803	7810	7818	7825	7832	7839	7846
6.1	7853	7860	7868	7875	7882	7889	7896	7903	7910	7917
6.2	7924	7931	7938	7945	7952	7959	7966	7973	7980	7987
6.3	7993	8000	8007	8014	8021	8028	8035	8041	8048	8055
6.4	8062	8069	8075	8082	8089	8096	8102	8109	8116	8122
6.5	8129	8136	8142	8149	8156	8162	8169	8176	8182	8189
6.6	8195	8202	8209	8215	8222	8228	8235	8241	8248	8254
6.7	8261	8267	8274	8280	8287	8293	8299	8306	8312	8319
6.8	8325	8331	8338	8344	8351	8357	8363	8370	8376	8382
6.9	8388	8395	8401	8407	8414	8420	8426	8432	8439	8445
7.0	8451	8457	8463	8470	8476	8482	8488	8494	8500	8506
7.1	8513	8519	8525	8531	8537	8543	8549	8555	8561	8567
7.2	8573	8579	8585	8591	8597	8603	8609	8615	8621	8627
7.3	8633	8639	8645	8651	8657	8663	8669	8675	8681	8686
7.4	8692	8698	8704	8710	8716	8722	8727	8733	8739	8745
7.5	8751	8756	8762	8768	8774	8779	8785	8791	8797	8802
7.6	8808	8814	8820	8825	8831	8837	8842	8848	8854	8859
7.7	8865	8871	8876	8882	8887	8893	8899	8904	8910	8915
7.8	8921	8927	8932	8938	8943	8949	8954	8960	8965	8971
7.9	8976	8982	8987	8993	8998	9004	9009	9015	9020	9025
8.0	9031	9036	9042	9047	9053	9058	9063	9069	9074	9079
8.1	9085	9090	9096	9101	9106	9112	9117	9122	9128	9133
8.2	9138	9143	9149	9154	9159	9165	9170	9175	9180	9186
8.3	9191	9196	9201	9206	9212	9217	9222	9227	9232	9238
8.4	9243	9248	9253	9258	9263	9269	9274	9279	9284	9289
8.5	9294	9299	9304	9309	9315	9320	9325	9330	9335	9340
8.6	9345	9350	9355	9360	9365	9370	9375	9380	9385	9390
8.7	9395	9400	9405	9410	9415	9420	9425	9430	9435	9440
8.8	9445	9450	9455	9460	9465	9469	9474	9479	9484	9489
8.9	9494	9499	9504	9509	9513	9518	9523	9528	9533	9538
9.0	9542	9547	9552	9557	9562	9566	9571	9576	9581	9586
9.1	9590	9595	9600	9605	9609	9614	9619	9624	9628	9633
9.2	9638	9643	9647	9652	9657	9661	9666	9671	9675	9680
9.3	9685	9689	9694	9699	9703	9708	9713	9717	9722	9727
9.4	9731	9736	9741	9745	9750	9754	9759	9763	9768	9773
9.5	9777	9782	9786	9791	9795	9800	9805	9809	9814	9818
9.6	9823	9827	9832	9836	9841	9845	9850	9854	9859	9863
9.7	9868	9872	9877	9881	9886	9890	9894	9899	9903	9908
9.8	9912	9917	9921	9926	9930	9934	9939	9943	9948	9952
9.9	9956	9961	9965	9969	9974	9978	9983	9987	9991	9996

Table B Base-10 Logarithms

N	0	1	2	3	4	5	6	7	8	9
1.0	.0000	.0043	.0086	.0128	.0170	.0212	.0253	.0294	.0334	.0374
1.1	.0414	.0453	.0492	.0531	.0569	.0607	.0645	.0682	.0719	.0755
1.2	.0792	.0828	.0864	.0899	.0934	.0969	.1004	.1038	.1072	.1106
1.3	.1139	.1173	.1206	.1239	.1271	.1303	.1335	.1367	.1399	.1430
1.4	.1461	.1492	.1523	.1553	.1584	.1614	.1644	.1673	.1703	.1732
1.5	.1761	.1790	.1818	.1847	.1875	.1903	.1931	.1959	.1987	.2014
1.6	.2041	.2068	.2095	.2122	.2148	.2175	.2201	.2227	.2253	.2279
1.7	.2304	.2330	.2355	.2380	.2405	.2430	.2455	.2480	.2504	.2529
1.8	.2553	.2577	.2601	.2625	.2648	.2672	.2695	.2718	.2742	.2765
1.9	.2788	.2810	.2833	.2856	.2878	.2900	.2923	.2945	.2967	.2989
2.0	.3010	.3032	.3054	.3075	.3096	.3118	.3139	.3160	.3181	.3201
2.1	.3222	.3243	.3263	.3284	.3304	.3324	.3345	.3365	.3385	.3404
2.2	.3424	.3444	.3464	.3483	.3502	.3522	.3541	.3560	.3579	.3598
2.3	.3617	.3636	.3655	.3674	.3692	.3711	.3729	.3747	.3766	.3784
2.4	.3802	.3820	.3838	.3856	.3874	.3892	.3909	.3927	.3945	.3962
2.5	.3979	.3997	.4014	.4031	.4048	.4065	.4082	.4099	.4116	.4133
2.6	.4150	.4166	.4183	.4200	.4216	.4232	.4249	.4265	.4281	.4298
2.7	.4314	.4330	.4346	.4362	.4378	.4393	.4409	.4425	.4440	.4456
2.8	.4472	.4487	.4502	.4518	.4533	.4548	.4564	.4579	.4594	.4609
2.9	.4624	.4639	.4654	.4669	.4683	.4698	.4713	.4728	.4742	.4757
3.0	.4771	.4786	.4800	.4814	.4829	.4843	.4857	.4871	.4886	.4900
3.1	.4914	.4928	.4942	.4955	.4969	.4983	.4997	.5011	.5024	.5038
3.2	.5051	.5065	.5079	.5092	.5105	.5119	.5132	.5145	.5159	.5172
3.3	.5185	.5198	.5211	.5224	.5237	.5250	.5263	.5276	.5289	.5302
3.4	.5315	.5328	.5340	.5353	.5366	.5378	.5391	.5403	.5416	.5428
3.5	.5441	.5453	.5465	.5478	.5490	.5502	.5514	.5527	.5539	.5551
3.6	.5563	.5575	.5587	.5599	.5611	.5623	.5635	.5647	.5658	.5670
3.7	.5682	.5694	.5705	.5717	.5729	.5740	.5752	.5763	.5775	.5786
3.8	.5798	.5809	.5821	.5832	.5843	.5855	.5866	.5877	.5888	.5899
3.9	.5911	.5922	.5933	.5944	.5955	.5966	.5977	.5988	.5999	.6010
4.0	.6021	.6031	.6042	.6053	.6064	.6075	.6085	.6096	.6107	.6117
4.1	.6128	.6138	.6149	.6160	.6170	.6180	.6191	.6201	.6212	.6222
4.2	.6232	.6243	.6253	.6263	.6274	.6284	.6294	.6304	.6314	.6325
4.3	.6335	.6345	.6355	.6365	.6375	.6385	.6395	.6405	.6415	.6425
4.4	.6435	.6444	.6454	.6464	.6474	.6484	.6493	.6503	.6513	.6522
4.5	.6532	.6542	.6551	.6561	.6571	.6580	.6590	.6599	.6609	.6618
4.6	.6628	.6637	.6646	.6656	.6665	.6675	.6684	.6693	.6702	.6712
4.7	.6721	.6730	.6739	.6749	.6758	.6767	.6776	.6785	.6794	.6803
4.8	.6812	.6821	.6830	.6839	.6848	.6857	.6866	.6875	.6884	.6893
4.9	.6902	.6911	.6920	.6928	.6937	.6946	.6955	.6964	.6972	.6981
5.0	.6990	.6998	.7007	.7016	.7024	.7033	.7042	.7050	.7059	.7067
5.1	.7076	.7084	.7093	.7101	.7110	.7118	.7126	.7135	.7143	.7152
5.2	.7160	.7168	.7177	.7185	.7193	.7202	.7210	.7218	.7226	.7235
5.3	.7243	.7251	.7259	.7267	.7275	.7284	.7292	.7300	.7308	.7316
5.4	.7324	.7332	.7340	.7348	.7356	.7364	.7372	.7380	.7388	.7396

Table C Base-e Logarithms

N	0	1	2	3	4	5	6	7	8	9
1.0	.0000	.0100	.0198	.0296	.0392	.0488	.0583	.0677	.0770	.0862
1.1	.0953	.1044	.1133	.1222	.1310	.1398	.1484	.1570	.1655	.1740
1.2	.1823	.1906	.1989	.2070	.2151	.2231	.2311	.2390	.2469	.2546
1.3	.2624	.2700	.2776	.2852	.2927	.3001	.3075	.3148	.3221	.3293
1.4	.3365	.3436	.3507	.3577	.3646	.3716	.3784	.3853	.3920	.3988
1.5	.4055	.4121	.4187	.4253	.4318	.4383	.4447	.4511	.4574	.4637
1.6	.4700	.4762	.4824	.4886	.4947	.5008	.5068	.5128	.5188	.5247
1.7	.5306	.5365	.5423	.5481	.5539	.5596	.5653	.5710	.5766	.5822
1.8	.5878	.5933	.5988	.6043	.6098	.6152	.6206	.6259	.6313	.6366
1.9	.6419	.6471	.6523	.6575	.6627	.6678	.6729	.6780	.6831	.6881
2.0	.6931	.6981	.7031	.7080	.7129	.7178	.7227	.7275	.7324	.7372
2.1	.7419	.7467	.7514	.7561	.7608	.7655	.7701	.7747	.7793	.7839
2.2	.7885	.7930	.7975	.8020	.8065	.8109	.8154	.8198	.8242	.8286
2.3	.8329	.8372	.8416	.8459	.8502	.8544	.8587	.8629	.8671	.8713
2.4	.8755	.8796	.8838	.8879	.8920	.8961	.9002	.9042	.9083	.9123
2.5	.9163	.9203	.9243	.9282	.9322	.9361	.9400	.9439	.9478	.9517
2.6	.9555	.9594	.9632	.9670	.9708	.9746	.9783	.9821	.9858	.9895
2.7	.9933	.9969	1.0006	.0043	.0080	.0116	.0152	.0188	.0225	.0260
2.8	1.0296	.0332	.0367	.0403	.0438	.0473	.0508	.0543	.0578	.0613
2.9	.0647	.0682	.0716	.0750	.0784	.0818	.0852	.0886	.0919	.0953
3.0	1.0986	.1019	.1053	.1086	.1119	.1151	.1184	.1217	.1249	.1282
3.1	.1314	.1346	.1378	.1410	.1442	.1474	.1506	.1537	.1569	.1600
3.2	.1632	.1663	.1694	.1725	.1756	.1787	.1817	.1848	.1878	.1909
3.3	.1939	.1969	.2000	.2030	.2060	.2090	.2119	.2149	.2179	.2208
3.4	.2238	.2267	.2296	.2326	.2355	.2384	.2413	.2442	.2470	.2499
3.5	1.2528	.2556	.2585	.2613	.2641	.2669	.2698	.2726	.2754	.2782
3.6	.2809	.2837	.2865	.2892	.2920	.2947	.2975	.3002	.3029	.3056
3.7	.3083	.3110	.3137	.3164	.3191	.3218	.3244	.3271	.3297	.3324
3.8	.3350	.3376	.3403	.3429	.3455	.3481	.3507	.3533	.3558	.3584
3.9	.3610	.3635	.3661	.3686	.3712	.3737	.3762	.3788	.3813	.3838
4.0	1.3863	.3888	.3913	.3938	.3962	.3987	.4012	.4036	.4061	.4085
4.1	.4110	.4134	.4159	.4183	.4207	.4231	.4255	.4279	.4303	.4327
4.2	.4351	.4375	.4398	.4422	.4446	.4469	.4493	.4516	.4540	.4563
4.3	.4586	.4609	.4633	.4656	.4679	.4702	.4725	.4748	.4770	.4793
4.4	.4816	.4839	.4861	.4884	.4907	.4929	.4951	.4974	.4996	.5019
4.5	1.5041	.5063	.5085	.5107	.5129	.5151	.5173	.5195	.5217	.5239
4.6	.5261	.5282	.5304	.5326	.5347	.5369	.5390	.5412	.5433	.5454
4.7	.5476	.5497	.5518	.5539	.5560	.5581	.5602	.5623	.5644	.5665
4.8	.5686	.5707	.5728	.5748	.5769	.5790	.5810	.5831	.5851	.5872
4.9	.5892	.5913	.5933	.5953	.5974	.5994	.6014	.6034	.6054	.6074
5.0	1.6094	.6114	.6134	.6154	.6174	.6194	.6214	.6233	.6253	.6273
5.1	.6292	.6312	.6332	.6351	.6371	.6390	.6409	.6429	.6448	.6467
5.2	.6487	.6506	.6525	.6544	.6563	.6582	.6601	.6620	.6639	.6658
5.3	.6677	.6696	.6715	.6734	.6752	.6771	.6790	.6808	.6827	.6845
5.4	.6864	.6882	.6901	.6919	.6938	.6956	.6974	.6993	.7011	.7029

Table C (continued)

N	0	1	2	3	4	5	6	7	8	9
5.5	1.7047	.7066	.7084	.7102	.7120	.7138	.7156	.7174	.7192	.7210
5.6	.7228	.7246	.7263	.7281	.7299	.7317	.7334	.7352	.7370	.7387
5.7	.7405	.7422	.7440	.7457	.7475	.7492	.7509	.7527	.7544	.7561
5.8	.7579	.7596	.7613	.7630	.7647	.7664	.7681	.7699	.7716	.7733
5.9	.7750	.7766	.7783	.7800	.7817	.7834	.7851	.7867	.7884	.7901
6.0	1.7918	.7934	.7951	.7967	.7984	.8001	.8017	.8034	.8050	.8066
6.1	.8083	.8099	.8116	.8132	.8148	.8165	.8181	.8197	.8213	.8229
6.2	.8245	.8262	.8278	.8294	.8310	.8326	.8342	.8358	.8374	.8390
6.3	.8405	.8421	.8437	.8453	.8469	.8485	.8500	.8516	.8532	.8547
6.4	.8563	.8579	.8594	.8610	.8625	.8641	.8656	.8672	.8687	.8703
6.5	1.8718	.8733	.8749	.8764	.8779	.8795	.8810	.8825	.8840	.8856
6.6	.8871	.8886	.8901	.8916	.8931	.8946	.8961	.8976	.8991	.9006
6.7	.9021	.9036	.9051	.9066	.9081	.9095	.9110	.9125	.9140	.9155
6.8	.9169	.9184	.9199	.9213	.9228	.9242	.9257	.9272	.9286	.9301
6.9	.9315	.9330	.9344	.9359	.9373	.9387	.9402	.9416	.9430	.9445
7.0	1.9459	.9473	.9488	.9502	.9516	.9530	.9544	.9559	.9573	.9587
7.1	.9601	.9615	.9629	.9643	.9657	.9671	.9685	.9699	.9713	.9727
7.2	.9741	.9755	.9769	.9782	.9796	.9810	.9824	.9838	.9851	.9865
7.3	.9879	.9892	.9906	.9920	.9933	.9947	.9961	.9974	.9988	2.0001
7.4	2.0015	.0028	.0042	.0055	.0069	.0082	.0096	.0109	.0122	.0136
7.5	2.0149	.0162	.0176	.0189	.0202	.0215	.0229	.0242	.0255	.0268
7.6	.0281	.0295	.0308	.0321	.0334	.0347	.0360	.0373	.0386	.0399
7.7	.0412	.0425	.0438	.0451	.0464	.0477	.0490	.0503	.0516	.0528
7.8	.0541	.0554	.0567	.0580	.0592	.0605	.0618	.0631	.0643	.0656
7.9	.0669	.0681	.0694	.0707	.0719	.0732	.0744	.0757	.0769	.0782
8.0	2.0794	.0807	.0819	.0832	.0844	.0857	.0869	.0882	.0894	.0906
8.1	.0919	.0931	.0943	.0956	.0968	.0980	.0992	.1005	.1017	.1029
8.2	.1041	.1054	.1066	.1078	.1090	.1102	.1114	.1126	.1138	.1150
8.3	.1163	.1175	.1187	.1199	.1211	.1223	.1235	.1247	.1258	.1270
8.4	.1282	.1294	.1306	.1318	.1330	.1342	.1353	.1365	.1377	.1389
8.5	2.1401	.1412	.1424	.1436	.1448	.1459	.1471	.1483	.1494	.1506
8.6	.1518	.1529	.1541	.1552	.1564	.1576	.1587	.1599	.1610	.1622
8.7	.1633	.1645	.1656	.1668	.1679	.1691	.1702	.1713	.1725	.1736
8.8	.1748	.1759	.1770	.1782	.1793	.1804	.1815	.1827	.1838	.1849
8.9	.1861	.1872	.1883	.1894	.1905	.1917	.1928	.1939	.1950	.1961
9.0	2.1972	.1983	.1994	.2006	.2017	.2028	.2039	.2050	.2061	.2072
9.1	.2083	.2094	.2105	.2116	.2127	.2138	.2148	.2159	.2170	.2181
9.2	.2192	.2203	.2214	.2225	.2235	.2246	.2257	.2268	.2279	.2289
9.3	.2300	.2311	.2322	.2332	.2343	.2354	.2364	.2375	.2386	.2396
9.4	.2407	.2418	.2428	.2439	.2450	.2460	.2471	.2481	.2492	.2502
9.5	2.2513	.2523	.2534	.2544	.2555	.2565	.2576	.2586	.2597	.2607
9.6	.2618	.2628	.2638	.2649	.2659	.2670	.2680	.2690	.2701	.2711
9.7	.2721	.2732	.2742	.2752	.2762	.2773	.2783	.2793	.2803	.2814
9.8	.2824	.2834	.2844	.2854	.2865	.2875	.2885	.2895	.2905	.2915
9.9	.2925	.2935	.2946	.2956	.2966	.2976	.2986	.2996	.3006	.3016

Answers to Selected Exercises

Section 0.1
1. set   **3.** union   **5.** decimal   **7.** 2   **9.** composite
11. decimals   **13.** negative   **5.** $x + (y + z)$
17. $5m + 5 \cdot 2$ **19.** interval   **21.** two   **23.** positive
25. true   **27.** false   **29.** true   **31.** $\{a, b, c, d, e, f, g\}$
33. $\{a, c, e\}$ **35.** terminates   **37.** repeats
39. 1, 2, 6, 7   **41.** $-5, -4, 0, 1, 2, 6, 7$ **43.** $\sqrt{2}$
45. 6   **47.** $-5, 1, 7$

49.

51.

53.

55.

57. $(2, \infty)$

59. $(0, 5)$

61. $(-4, \infty)$

63. $[-2, 2)$

65. $(-\infty, 5]$

67. $(-5, 0]$

69. $[-2, 3]$

71. $[2, 6]$

73. $(-5, \infty) \cap (-\infty, 4)$

75. $[-8, \infty) \cap (-\infty, -3]$

77. $(-\infty, -2) \cup (2, \infty)$

79. $(-\infty, -1] \cup [3, \infty)$

81. 13   **83.** 0   **85.** -8 **87.** -32 **89.** $5 - \pi$
91. 0   **93.** $x + 1$ **95.** $-(x - 4)$ **97.** 5   **99.** 5
101. natural numbers   **103.** integers

Section 0.2
1. factor   **3.** $3, 2x$ **5.** scientific, integer   **7.** x^{m+n}
9. $x^n y^n$ **11.** 1   **13.** 169   **15.** -25
17. $4 \cdot x \cdot x \cdot x$ **19.** $(-5x)(-5x)(-5x)(-5x)$
21. $-8 \cdot x \cdot x \cdot x \cdot x$ **23.** $7x^3$ **25.** x^2 **27.** $-27t^3$
29. $x^3 y^2$ **31.** 10.648   **33.** -0.0625 **35.** x^5 **37.** z^6
39. y^{21} **41.** z^{26} **43.** a^{14} **45.** $27x^3$ **47.** $x^6 y^3$
49. $\dfrac{a^6}{b^3}$ **51.** 1   **53.** 1   **55.** $\dfrac{1}{z^4}$ **57.** $\dfrac{1}{y^5}$ **59.** x^2

61. x^4 **63.** a^4 **65.** x **67.** $\dfrac{m^9}{n^6}$ **69.** $\dfrac{1}{a^9}$ **71.** $\dfrac{a^{12}}{b^4}$
73. $\dfrac{1}{r^4}$ **75.** $\dfrac{x^{32}}{y^{16}}$ **77.** $\dfrac{9x^{10}}{25y^2}$ **79.** $\dfrac{4y^{12}}{x^{20}}$ **81.** $\dfrac{64z^7}{25y^6}$
83. -50 **85.** 4   **87.** -8 **89.** 216   **91.** -12
93. 20   **95.** $\dfrac{3}{64}$ **97.** 3.72×10^5 **99.** -1.77×10^8
101. 7×10^{-3} **103.** -6.93×10^{-7} **105.** 1×10^{12}
107. 937,000   **109.** 0.0000221   **111.** 3.2
113. -0.0032 **115.** 1.17×10^4 **117.** 7×10^4
119. 5.3×10^{19} **121.** 1.986×10^4 meters per min
123. 1.67248×10^{-15} g   **125.** 9.3×10^7 mi, 1.48×10^8 mi
127. polar radius: 6.356750×10^3 km;
equatorial radius: 6.378135×10^3 km
129. x^{n+2} **131.** x^{m-1} **133.** x^{m+4}
137.   **139.** $5 - \pi$

Section 0.3
1. 0   **3.** not   **5.** $a^{1/n}$ **7.** $\sqrt[n]{ab}$ **9.** $\neq$ **11.** 3
13. $\dfrac{1}{5}$ **15.** -3 **17.** 10   **19.** $-\dfrac{3}{2}$
21. not a real number   **23.** $4|a|$ **25.** $2|a|$
27. $-2a$ **29.** $-6b^2$ **31.** $\dfrac{4a^2}{5|b|}$ **33.** $-\dfrac{10x^2}{3y}$
35. 8   **37.** -64 **39.** -100 **41.** $\dfrac{1}{8}$ **43.** $\dfrac{1}{512}$
45. $-\dfrac{1}{27}$ **47.** $\dfrac{32}{243}$ **49.** $\dfrac{16}{9}$ **51.** $10s^2$ **53.** $\dfrac{1}{2y^2 z}$
55. $x^6 y^3$ **57.** $\dfrac{1}{r^6 s^{12}}$ **59.** $\dfrac{4a^4}{25b^6}$ **61.** $\dfrac{100s^8}{9r^4}$ **63.** a
65. 7   **67.** 5   **69.** -5 **71.** $-\dfrac{1}{5}$ **73.** $6|x|$
75. $3y^2$ **77.** $2y$ **79.** $\dfrac{|x|y^2}{|z^3|}$ **81.** $\sqrt{2}$ **83.** $17x\sqrt{2}$
85. $2y^2\sqrt{3y}$ **87.** $12\sqrt[3]{3}$ **89.** $6z\sqrt[4]{3z}$ **91.** $6x\sqrt{2y}$
93. 0   **95.** $\sqrt{3}$ **97.** $\dfrac{2\sqrt{x}}{x}$ **99.** $\sqrt[3]{4}$ **101.** $\sqrt[3]{5a^2}$
103. $\dfrac{2b\sqrt[4]{27a^2}}{3a}$ **105.** $\dfrac{u\sqrt[3]{6uv^2}}{3v}$ **107.** $\dfrac{1}{2\sqrt{5}}$ **109.** $\dfrac{1}{\sqrt[3]{3}}$
111. $\dfrac{b}{32a\sqrt[5]{2b^2}}$ **113.** $\dfrac{2\sqrt{3}}{9}$ **115.** $-\dfrac{\sqrt{2x}}{8}$ **117.** $\sqrt{3}$
119. $\sqrt[5]{4x^3}$ **121.** $\sqrt[6]{32}$ **123.** $\dfrac{\sqrt[4]{12}}{2}$ **129.** $(-2, 5]$
131. -5 **133.** 6.17×10^8

Section 0.4
1. monomial, variables   **3.** trinomial   **5.** one   **7.** like
9. coefficients, variables   **11.** yes, trinomial, 2nd degree

A1

13. no   **15.** yes, binomial, 3rd degree   **17.** yes, monomial, 0th degree   **19.** yes, monomial, no defined degree
21. $6x^3 - 3x^2 - 8x$ **23.** $4y^3 + 14$ **25.** $-x^2 + 14$
27. $-28t + 96$ **29.** $-4y^2 + y$ **31.** $2x^2y - 4xy^2$
33. $8x^3y^7$ **35.** $\dfrac{m^4n^4}{2}$ **37.** $-4r^3s - 4rs^3$
39. $12a^2b^2c^2 + 18ab^3c^3 - 24a^2b^4c^2$ **41.** $a^2 + 4a + 4$
43. $a^2 - 12a + 36$ **45.** $x^2 - 16$ **47.** $x^2 + 2x - 15$
49. $3u^2 + 4u - 4$ **51.** $10x^2 + 13x - 3$
53. $9a^2 - 12ab + 4b^2$ **55.** $9m^2 - 16n^2$
57. $6y^2 - 16xy + 8x^2$ **59.** $9x^3 - x^2y - 27xy + 3y^2$
61. $5z^3 - 5tz + 2tz^2 - 2t^2$ **63.** $-3\sqrt{5}x^2 + x + 2\sqrt{5}$
65. $27x^3 - 27x^2 + 9x - 1$ **67.** $6x^3 + 14x^2 - 5x - 3$
69. $6x^3 - 5x^2y + 6xy^2 + 8y^3$ **71.** $6y^{2n} + 2$
73. $-10x^{4n} - 15y^{2n}$ **75.** $x^{2n} - x^n - 12$
77. $6r^{2n} - 25r^n + 14$ **79.** $xy + x^{3/2}y^{1/2}$
81. $a - b$ **83.** $\sqrt{3} + 1$ **85.** $x\left(\sqrt{7} - 2\right)$
87. $\dfrac{x\left(x + \sqrt{3}\right)}{x^2 - 3}$ **89.** $\dfrac{\left(y + \sqrt{2}\right)^2}{y^2 - 2}$
91. $\dfrac{\sqrt{3} + 3 - \sqrt{2} - \sqrt{6}}{2}$ **93.** $\dfrac{x - 2\sqrt{xy} + y}{x - y}$
95. $\dfrac{1}{2\left(\sqrt{2} - 1\right)}$ **97.** $\dfrac{y^2 - 3}{y^2 + 2y\sqrt{3} + 3}$
99. $\dfrac{1}{\sqrt{x + 3} + \sqrt{x}}$ **101.** $\dfrac{2a}{b^3}$ **103.** $-\dfrac{2z^9}{3x^3y^2}$
105. $\dfrac{x}{2y} + \dfrac{3xy}{2}$ **107.** $\dfrac{2y^3}{5} - \dfrac{3y}{5x^3} + \dfrac{1}{5x^4y^3}$ **109.** $3x + 2$
111. $x - 7 + \dfrac{2}{2x - 5}$ **113.** $2x^2 + 2x + 2 + \dfrac{3}{x - 1}$
115. $x - 3$ **117.** $x^2 - 2 + \dfrac{-x^2 + 5}{x^3 - 2}$
119. $x^4 + 2x^3 + 4x^2 + 8x + 16$ **121.** $6x^2 + x - 12$
123. $(x^2 + 3x - 10)$ ft^2 **125.** $(4x^3 - 48x^2 + 144x)$ in.^{3}
133. 27   **135.** $\dfrac{125x^3}{8y^6}$ **137.** $-b\sqrt[3]{2ab}$

Section 0.5
1. factor   **3.** $x(a + b)$ **5.** $(x + y)^2$
7. $(x + y)(x^2 - xy + y^2)$ **9.** $3(x - 2)$ **11.** $4x^2(2 + x)$
13. $7x^2y^2(1 + 2x)$ **15.** $(x + y)(a + b)$
17. $(4a + b)(1 - 3a)$ **19.** $(2x + 3)(2x - 3)$
21. $(2 + 3r)(2 - 3r)$ **23.** $(9x^2 + 1)(3x + 1)(3x - 1)$
25. $(x + z + 5)(x + z - 5)$ **27.** $(x + 4)^2$
29. $(b - 5)^2$ **31.** $(m + 2n)^2$
33. $(4x - 3y)(3x + 2y)$ **35.** $(x + 7)(x + 3)$
37. $(x - 6)(x + 2)$ **39.** $(2p + 3)(3p - 1)$
41. $(t + 7)(t^2 - 7t + 49)$ **43.** $(2z - 3)(4z^2 + 6z + 9)$
45. $3abc(a + 2b + 3c)$ **47.** $(x + 1)(3x^2 - 1)$
49. $t(y + c)(2x - 3)$ **51.** $(a + b)(x + y + z)$
53. $(x + y - z)(x - y + z)$ **55.** $-4xy$
57. $(x^2 + y^2)(x + y)(x - y)$ **59.** $3(x + 2)(x - 2)$
61. $2x(3y + 2)(3y - 2)$ **63.** prime
65. $(6a + 5)(4a - 3)$ **67.** $(3x + 7y)(2x + 5y)$
69. $2(6p - 35q)(p + q)$ **71.** $-(6m - 5n)(m - 7n)$
73. $-x(6x + 7)(x - 5)$ **75.** $x^2(2x - 7)(3x + 5)$
77. $(x^2 + 5)(x^2 - 3)$ **79.** $(a^n - 3)(a^n + 1)$

81. $(3x^n - 2)(2x^n - 1)$ **83.** $(2x^n + 3y^n)(2x^n - 3y^n)$
85. $(5y^n + 2)(2y^n - 3)$ **87.** $2(x + 10)(x^2 - 10x + 100)$
89. $(x + y - 4)(x^2 + 2xy + y^2 + 4x + 4y + 16)$
91. $(2a + y)(2a - y)(4a^2 - 2ay + y^2)(4a^2 + 2ay + y^2)$
93. $(a - b)(a^2 + ab + b^2 + 1)$
95. $(4x^2 + y^2)(16x^4 - 4x^2y^2 + y^4)$
97. $(x - 3 + 12y)(x - 3 - 12y)$
99. $(a + b - 5)(a + b + 2)$
101. $(x + 2)(x^2 - 2x + 4)(x - 1)(x^2 + x + 1)$
103. $(x^2 + 1 + x)(x^2 + 1 - x)$
105. $(x^2 + x + 4)(x^2 - x + 4)$
107. $(2a^2 + a + 1)(2a^2 - a + 1)$
109. $\dfrac{4}{3}\pi(r_1 - r_2)(r_1^2 + r_1r_2 + r_2^2)$ **115.** $2\left(\dfrac{3}{2}x + 1\right)$
117. $2\left(\dfrac{1}{2}x^2 + x + 2\right)$ **119.** $a\left(1 + \dfrac{b}{a}\right)$ **121.** $x^{1/2}(x^{1/2} + 1)$
123. $\sqrt{2}\left(\sqrt{2}x + y\right)$ **125.** $ab(b^{1/2} - a^{1/2})$
127. $(x - 2)(x + 3 + y)$ **129.** $(a + 1)(a^3 + a^2 + 1)$
131. 1   **133.** x^{20} **135.** 1   **137.** $-3\sqrt{5}x$

Section 0.6
1. numerator   **3.** $ad = bc$ **5.** $\dfrac{ac}{bd}$ **7.** $\dfrac{a + c}{b}$
9. equal   **11.** not equal   **13.** $\dfrac{a}{3b}$ **15.** $\dfrac{8x}{35a}$
17. $\dfrac{16}{3}$ **19.** $\dfrac{z}{c}$ **21.** $\dfrac{2x^2y}{a^2b^3}$ **23.** $\dfrac{2}{x + 2}$
25. $-\dfrac{x + 2}{x - 3}$ **27.** $\dfrac{3x - 4}{2x - 1}$ **29.** $\dfrac{x^2 + 2x + 4}{x + a}$
31. $\dfrac{x(x - 1)}{x + 1}$ **33.** $\dfrac{x - 1}{x}$ **35.** $\dfrac{x(x + 1)^2}{x + 2}$
37. $\dfrac{1}{2}$ **39.** $\dfrac{z - 4}{(z + 2)(z - 2)}$ **41.** 1   **43.** 1
45. $\dfrac{x - 5}{x + 5}$ **47.** $\dfrac{x + 5}{x + 3}$ **49.** 4   **51.** $\dfrac{-1}{x - 5}$
53. $\dfrac{5x - 1}{(x + 1)(x - 1)}$ **55.** $\dfrac{2(a - 2)}{(a + 4)(a - 4)}$
57. $\dfrac{2}{(x + 2)(x - 2)}$ **59.** $\dfrac{2(x^2 - 3x + 1)}{(x + 1)^2(x - 1)}$
61. $\dfrac{3y - 2}{y - 1}$ **63.** $\dfrac{1}{x + 2}$ **65.** $\dfrac{2x - 5}{2x(x - 2)}$
67. $\dfrac{2x^2 + 19x + 1}{(x + 4)(x - 4)}$ **69.** 0
71. $\dfrac{-x^4 + 3x^3 - 43x^2 - 58x + 697}{(x + 5)(x - 5)(x + 4)(x - 4)}$ **73.** $\dfrac{b}{2c}$
75. $81a$ **77.** -1 **79.** $\dfrac{y + x}{x^2y^2}$ **81.** $\dfrac{y + x}{y - x}$
83. $\dfrac{a^2(3x - 4ab)}{ax + b}$ **85.** $\dfrac{x - 2}{x + 2}$ **87.** $\dfrac{3x^2y^2}{xy - 1}$
89. $\dfrac{3x^2}{x^2 + 1}$ **91.** $\dfrac{x^2 - 3x - 4}{x^2 + 5x - 3}$ **93.** $\dfrac{x}{x + 1}$
95. $\dfrac{5x + 1}{x - 1}$ **97.** $\dfrac{k_1k_2}{k_2 + k_1}$ **99.** $\dfrac{3x}{3 + x}$
101. $\dfrac{x + 1}{2x + 1}$ **107.** 6   **109.** $\dfrac{y^9}{x^{12}}$ **111.** $-\sqrt{5}$

Chapter Review

1. 3, 6, 8   **2.** 0, 3, 6, 8   **3.** $-6, -3, 0, 3, 6, 8$

4. $-6, -3, 0, \frac{1}{2}, 3, 6, 8$ **5.** $\pi, \sqrt{5}$

6. $-6, -3, 0, \frac{1}{2}, 3, \pi, \sqrt{5}, 6, 8$ **7.** 3   **8.** 6, 8

9. $-6, 0, 6, 8$ **10.** $-3, 3$

11. Associative Property of Addition
12. Commutative Property of Addition
13. Associative Property of Multiplication
14. Distributive Property
15. Commutative Property of Multiplication
16. Commutative Property of Addition
17. Double Negative Rule

18.

19.

20.   **21.**

22.   **23.**

24.

25. 6   **26.** 25   **27.** $\sqrt{2} - 1$ **28.** $\sqrt{3} - 1$

29. 12   **30.** $-5aaa$ **31.** $(-5a)(-5a)$ **32.** $3t^3$

33. $-6b^2$ **34.** n^6 **35.** p^6 **36.** $x^{12}y^8$

37. $\dfrac{a^{12}}{b^6}$ **38.** $\dfrac{1}{m^6}$ **39.** $\dfrac{q^6}{8p^6}$ **40.** $\dfrac{1}{a^3}$ **41.** $\dfrac{b^6}{a^4}$

42. $\dfrac{y^8}{9}$ **43.** $\dfrac{a^8}{b^{10}}$ **44.** $\dfrac{y^4}{9x^4}$ **45.** $-\dfrac{8m^{12}}{n^3}$

46. 18   **47.** 6.75×10^3 **48.** 2.3×10^{-4}

49. 480   **50.** 0.00025   **51.** 1.5×10^{14} **52.** 11

53. $\dfrac{3}{5}$ **54.** $2x$ **55.** $3|a|$ **56.** $-10x^2$

57. not a real number   **58.** $x^6|y|$ **59.** $\dfrac{y^2}{x^6}$

60. $-c$ **61.** a^2 **62.** 16   **63.** $\dfrac{1}{8}$ **64.** $\dfrac{8}{27}$ **65.** $\dfrac{4}{9}$

66. $\dfrac{9}{4}$ **67.** $\dfrac{125}{8}$ **68.** $36x^2$ **69.** $p^{2a/3}$ **70.** 6

71. -7 **72.** $\dfrac{3}{5}$ **73.** $\dfrac{3}{5}$ **74.** $|x|y^2$ **75.** x

76. $\dfrac{m^2|n|}{p^4}$ **77.** $\dfrac{a^3b^2}{c}$ **78.** $7\sqrt{2}$ **79.** 0   **80.** $x\sqrt[3]{3x}$

81. $\dfrac{\sqrt{35}}{5}$ **82.** $2\sqrt{2}$ **83.** $\dfrac{\sqrt[3]{4}}{2}$ **84.** $\dfrac{2\sqrt[3]{5}}{5}$

85. $\dfrac{2}{5\sqrt{2}}$ **86.** $\dfrac{1}{\sqrt{5}}$ **87.** $\dfrac{2x}{3\sqrt{2x}}$ **88.** $\dfrac{21x}{2\sqrt[3]{49x^2}}$

89. 3rd degree, binomial   **90.** 2nd degree, trinomial
91. 2nd degree, monomial   **92.** 4th degree, trinomial
93. $5x - 6$ **94.** $2x^3 - 7x^2 - 6x$ **95.** $9x^2 + 12x + 4$
96. $6x^2 - 7xy - 3y^2$ **97.** $8a^2 - 8ab - 6b^2$
98. $3z^3 + 10z^2 + 2z - 3$ **99.** $a^{2n} + a^n - 2$
100. $2 + 2x\sqrt{2} + x^2$ **101.** $\sqrt{6} + \sqrt{2} + \sqrt{3} + 1$
102. -5 **103.** $\sqrt{3} + 1$ **104.** $-2\left(\sqrt{3} + \sqrt{2}\right)$

105. $\dfrac{2x\left(\sqrt{x} + 2\right)}{x - 4}$ **106.** $\dfrac{x - 2\sqrt{xy} + y}{x - y}$

107. $\dfrac{x - 4}{5\left(\sqrt{x} - 2\right)}$ **108.** $\dfrac{1 - a}{a\left(1 + \sqrt{a}\right)}$ **109.** $\dfrac{y}{2x}$

110. $2a^2b + 3ab^2$ **111.** $x^2 + 2x + 1$

112. $x^3 + 2x - 3 - \dfrac{6}{x^2 - 1}$ **113.** $3t(t + 1)(t - 1)$

114. $5(r - 1)(r^2 + r + 1)$ **115.** $(3x + 8)(2x - 3)$
116. $(3a + x)(a - 1)$ **117.** $(2x - 5)(4x^2 + 10x + 25)$
118. $2(3x + 2)(x - 4)$ **119.** $(x + 3 + t)(x + 3 - t)$
120. prime   **121.** $(2z + 7)(4z^2 - 14z + 49)$
122. $(7b + 1)^2$ **123.** $(11z - 2)^2$
124. $8(2y - 5)(4y^2 + 10y + 25)$ **125.** $(y - 2z)(2x - w)$
126. $(x^2 + 1 + x)(x^2 + 1 - x)(x^4 + 1 - x^2)$

127. $\dfrac{-1}{x - 2}$ **128.** $\dfrac{a + 3}{a - 3}$ **129.** $(x - 2)(x + 3)$

130. $\dfrac{2y - 5}{y - 2}$ **131.** $\dfrac{t + 1}{5}$ **132.** $\dfrac{p(p + 4)}{(p^2 + 8p + 4)(p - 3)}$

133. $\dfrac{(x - 2)(x + 3)(x - 3)}{(x - 1)(x + 2)^2}$ **134.** 1

135. $\dfrac{3x^2 - 10x + 10}{(x - 4)(x + 5)}$ **136.** $\dfrac{2(2x^2 + 3x + 6)}{(x + 2)(x - 2)}$

137. $\dfrac{3x^3 - 12x^2 + 11x}{(x - 1)(x - 2)(x - 3)}$ **138.** $\dfrac{-5x - 6}{(x + 1)(x + 2)}$

139. $\dfrac{-x^3 + x^2 - 12x - 15}{x^2(x + 1)}$ **140.** $\dfrac{3x}{x + 1}$

141. $\dfrac{20}{3x}$ **142.** $\dfrac{y}{2}$ **143.** $\dfrac{y + x}{xy(x - y)}$ **144.** $\dfrac{y + x}{x - y}$

Chapter Test

1. $-7, 1, 3$ **2.** 3   **3.** Commutative Property of Addition   **4.** Distributive Property

5.   **6.**

7. 17   **8.** $-(x - 7)$ **9.** 16   **10.** 8   **11.** x^{11}

12. $\dfrac{r}{s}$ **13.** a **14.** x^{24} **15.** 4.5×10^5

16. 3.45×10^{-4} **17.** 3,700   **18.** 0.0012

19. $5a^2$ **20.** $\dfrac{216}{729}$ **21.** $\dfrac{9s^6}{4t^4}$ **22.** $3a^2$

23. $5\sqrt{3}$ **24.** $-4x\sqrt[3]{3x}$ **25.** $\dfrac{x\left(\sqrt{x} + 2\right)}{x - 4}$

26. $\dfrac{x - y}{x + 2\sqrt{xy} + y}$ **27.** $-a^2 + 7$ **28.** $-6a^6b^6$

29. $6x^2 + 13x - 28$ **30.** $a^{2n} - a^n - 6$ **31.** $x^4 - 16$

32. $2x^3 - 5x^2 + 7x - 6$ **33.** $6x + 19 + \dfrac{34}{x - 3}$

34. $x^2 + 2x + 1$ **35.** $3(x + 2y)$ **36.** $(x + 10)(x - 10)$
37. $(5t - 2w)(2t - 3w)$ **38.** $3(a - 6)(a^2 + 6a + 36)$
39. $(x + 2)(x - 2)(x^2 + 3)$ **40.** $(3x^2 - 2)(2x^2 + 5)$

41. 1   **42.** $\dfrac{-2x}{(x + 1)(x - 1)}$ **43.** $\dfrac{(x + 5)^2}{x + 4}$

44. $\dfrac{1}{(x + 1)(x - 2)}$ **45.** $\dfrac{b + a}{a}$ **46.** $\dfrac{y}{y + x}$

Section 1.1

1. root; solution   **3.** no   **5.** linear   **7.** one   **9.** no restrictions   **11.** $x \neq 0$ **13.** $x \neq 3$ or -2

15. $x \neq 3, 4,$ or -4 **17.** 5; conditional equation

19. no solution; contradiction   **21.** 7; conditional equation

23. no solution; contradiction   **25.** all real numbers; identity

27. 6; conditional equation   **29.** all real numbers; identity

31. 1   **33.** 6   **35.** $\dfrac{5}{2}$ **37.** 9   **39.** 10   **41.** -3

43. 3   **45.** $\dfrac{21}{19}$ **47.** $-\dfrac{14}{11}$ **49.** 2   **51.** all real numbers

53. 4   **55.** -4 **57.** no solution   **59.** 17

61. $-\dfrac{2}{5}$ **63.** $\dfrac{2}{3}$ **65.** 3   **67.** 5   **69.** no solution

71. 2   **73.** $p = \dfrac{k}{2.2}$ **75.** $w = \dfrac{P - 2l}{2}$ **77.** $r^2 = \dfrac{3V}{\pi h}$

79. $s = \dfrac{f(P_n - L)}{i}$ **81.** $m = \dfrac{r^2 F}{Mg}$ **83.** $y = b\left(1 - \dfrac{x}{a}\right)$

85. $r = \dfrac{r_1 r_2}{r_1 + r_2}$ **87.** $n = \dfrac{l - a + d}{d}$ **89.** $n = \dfrac{360}{180 - a}$

91. $r_1 = \dfrac{-Rr_2 r_3}{Rr_3 + Rr_2 - r_2 r_3}$ **95.** $5|x|$ **97.** $\dfrac{4y^4}{25x^2}$

99. $5|y|$ **101.** $\dfrac{|ab^3|}{z^2}$

47. 5, 3   **49.** $-6 \pm 2\sqrt{7}$ **51.** $\dfrac{-5 \pm \sqrt{5}}{2}$

53. $\dfrac{10 \pm \sqrt{2}}{2}$ **55.** $\dfrac{-2 \pm \sqrt{7}}{3}$ **57.** $\dfrac{3 \pm \sqrt{17}}{4}$

59. $\pm 2\sqrt{3}$ **61.** 0, 25   **63.** 3, $-\dfrac{5}{2}$ **65.** $\dfrac{-5 \pm \sqrt{13}}{6}$

67. $\dfrac{-7 \pm 3\sqrt{5}}{2}$ **69.** $\dfrac{-3 \pm \sqrt{6}}{3}$ **71.** $\dfrac{-1 \pm \sqrt{61}}{10}$

73. $t = \pm\dfrac{\sqrt{2hg}}{g}$ **75.** $t = \dfrac{8 \pm \sqrt{64 - h}}{4}$

77. $y = \pm\dfrac{b\sqrt{a^2 - x^2}}{a}$ **79.** $a = \pm\dfrac{bx\sqrt{b^2 + y^2}}{b^2 + y^2}$

81. $x = \dfrac{-y \pm y\sqrt{5}}{2}$ **83.** one repeated rational root

85. no real roots   **87.** two different rational roots

89. two different irrational roots   **91.** yes   **93.** 2, 10

95. 3, -4 **97.** $\dfrac{3}{2}, -\dfrac{1}{4}$ **99.** $\dfrac{1}{2}, -\dfrac{4}{3}$ **101.** $\dfrac{5}{6}, -\dfrac{2}{5}$

103. 1, -1 **105.** $-\dfrac{1}{2}, 5$ **107.** -2 **109.** 3, $-\dfrac{8}{11}$

111. $\dfrac{7 \pm \sqrt{145}}{4}$ **121.** $2x^2 - 8x$ **123.** 12m

125. $3x\sqrt{2x}$

Section 1.2

1. add   **3.** amount   **5.** rate; time   **7.** 84   **9.** 94

11. 7   **13.** 10 ft by 36 ft   **15.** $2\dfrac{1}{2}$ ft   **17.** 20 ft by 8 ft

19. 20 ft   **21.** $10,000 at 7%, $12,000 at 6%

23. $29,100   **25.** 327   **27.** $79.95   **29.** 200 units

31. 21   **33.** $2\dfrac{6}{11}$ days   **35.** $1\dfrac{1}{3}$ hr   **37.** $21\dfrac{1}{9}$ hr

39. 10 oz   **41.** 1 liter   **43.** $\dfrac{1}{15}$ liter   **45.** about 4.5 gal

47. 4 liters   **49.** 50 lb   **51.** 30 gal   **53.** 39 mph going; 65

mph returning   **55.** $2\dfrac{1}{2}$ hr   **57.** 50 sec   **59.** 12 mph

61. 600 lb barley; 1,637 lb oats; 163 lb soybean meal

63. about 11.2 mm   **67.** $(x + 7)(x - 9)$

69. $(3x - 5)(3x + 1)$ **71.** $(x + 3)^2$

73. $(x + 2)(x^2 - 2x + 4)$

Section 1.3

1. $ax^2 + bx + c = 0$ **3.** $\sqrt{c}; -\sqrt{c}$

5. rational numbers   **7.** 3, -2 **9.** 12, -12

11. 2, $-\dfrac{5}{2}$ **13.** 2, $\dfrac{3}{5}$ **15.** $\dfrac{3}{5}, -\dfrac{5}{3}$ **17.** $\dfrac{3}{2}, \dfrac{1}{2}$

19. 3, -3 **21.** $5\sqrt{2}, -5\sqrt{2}$ **23.** $2\sqrt{5}, -2\sqrt{5}$

25. $\dfrac{\sqrt{7}}{2}, -\dfrac{\sqrt{7}}{2}$ **27.** $\dfrac{\sqrt{26}}{2}, -\dfrac{\sqrt{26}}{2}$ **29.** 3, -1

31. $-1 + 2\sqrt{2}, -1 - 2\sqrt{2}$ **33.** $\dfrac{-1 + 3\sqrt{3}}{2}, \dfrac{-1 - 3\sqrt{3}}{2}$

35. $x^2 + 6x + 9$ **37.** $x^2 - 4x + 4$ **39.** $a^2 + 5a + \dfrac{25}{4}$

41. $r^2 - 11r + \dfrac{121}{4}$ **43.** $y^2 + \dfrac{3}{4}y + \dfrac{9}{64}$ **45.** $q^2 - \dfrac{1}{5}q + \dfrac{1}{100}$

Section 1.4

1. $A = lw$ **3.** 4 ft by 8 ft   **5.** 72 ft by 160 ft   **7.** 9 cm

9. width: $7\dfrac{1}{4}$ ft; length: $13\dfrac{3}{4}$ ft   **11.** 2 in.   **13.** 4 m

15. 10 m and 24 m   **17.** 40.1 in. by 22.6 in.

19. 20 mph going and 10 mph returning   **21.** 7 hr

23. 25 sec   **25.** about 9.5 sec   **27.** 1.6 sec   **29.** 10¢

31. 1,440   **33.** Morgan at 7%; Chloe at 8%   **35.** 10

37. 4 hr   **39.** about 9.5 hr   **41.** 221   **43.** 24.3 ft

45. 1.70 in.   **47.** No   **49.** $\dfrac{x - 6}{x(x - 3)}$ **51.** $\dfrac{x + 3}{x(x + 2)}$

53. $\dfrac{y + x}{y - x}$

Section 1.5

1. imaginary   **3.** imaginary   **5.** $2 - 5i$ **7.** real

9. $12i$ **11.** $-4\sqrt{6}i$ **13.** $\dfrac{5\sqrt{2}}{3}i$ **15.** $-\dfrac{7\sqrt{6}}{4}i$

17. $x = 3; y = 5$ **19.** $x = \dfrac{2}{3}; y = -\dfrac{2}{9}$ **21.** $5 - 6i$

23. $-2 - 10i$ **25.** $4 + 10i$ **27.** $1 - i$

29. $-15 - 25i$ **31.** $56 + 28i$ **33.** $-9 + 19i$

35. $-5 + 12i$ **37.** $52 - 56i$ **39.** $-6 + 17i$

41. $0 + i$ **43.** $0 + \dfrac{4}{3}i$ **45.** $\dfrac{2}{5} - \dfrac{1}{5}i$ **47.** $\dfrac{1}{25} + \dfrac{7}{25}i$

49. $\dfrac{1}{2} + \dfrac{1}{2}i$ **51.** $-\dfrac{7}{13} - \dfrac{22}{13}i$ **53.** $-\dfrac{12}{17} + \dfrac{11}{34}i$

55. $\dfrac{6 + \sqrt{3}}{10} + \dfrac{3\sqrt{3} - 2}{10}i$ **57.** i **59.** -1

61. $-i$ **63.** 1   **65.** -1 **67.** -1 **69.** i **71.** 4

73. 5   **75.** $\sqrt{13}$ **77.** $7\sqrt{2}$ **79.** $\dfrac{\sqrt{2}}{2}$ **81.** 6

83. $\sqrt{2}$ **85.** $\dfrac{3\sqrt{5}}{5}$ **87.** 1   **89.** $\pm 13i$

91. $\pm 3\sqrt{6}i$ **93.** $\pm 3\sqrt{5}i$ **95.** $\pm\dfrac{\sqrt{7}}{3}i$

97. $\pm\dfrac{\sqrt{30}}{2}i$ **99.** $-1 \pm 2\sqrt{3}i$ **101.** $-\dfrac{1}{5} \pm \dfrac{2\sqrt{2}}{5}i$

103. $-5 \pm 2\sqrt{3}i$ **105.** $-\dfrac{11}{2} \pm \dfrac{5\sqrt{3}}{2}i$

107. $1 \pm \dfrac{\sqrt{5}}{3}i$ **109.** $\dfrac{7}{2} \pm \dfrac{\sqrt{11}}{2}i$ **111.** $-1 \pm i$

113. $-2 \pm i$ **115.** $1 \pm 2i$ **117.** $\dfrac{1}{3} \pm \dfrac{1}{3}i$

119. $(x + 2i)(x - 2i)$ **121.** $(5p + 6qi)(5p - 6qi)$
123. $2(y + 2zi)(y - 2zi)$ **125.** $2(5m + ni)(5m - ni)$
127. $21 + 12i$ **129.** $6.2 - 0.7i$ **137.** $4x^2\sqrt{2}$
139. $x - 4\sqrt{x + 1} + 5$ **141.** $\sqrt{5} + 1$

Section 1.6

1. equal   **3.** extraneous   **5.** $0, -5, -4$ **7.** $0, \dfrac{4}{3}, -\dfrac{1}{2}$

9. $5, -5, 1, -1$ **11.** $6, -6, 1, -1$

13. $3\sqrt{2}, -3\sqrt{2}, \sqrt{5}, -\sqrt{5}$ **15.** $0, 1$ **17.** $\dfrac{1}{8}, -8$

19. $1, 144$ **21.** $\dfrac{1}{64}$ **23.** $\dfrac{1}{9}$ **25.** 27   **27.** $-\dfrac{1}{3}$

29. 2   **31.** $-\dfrac{3}{2}, -\dfrac{5}{2}$ **33.** 9   **35.** 20   **37.** 2

39. 2   **41.** 3, 4   **43.** $\dfrac{1}{5}, -1$ **45.** 3, 5   **47.** $-2, 1$

49. $2, -\dfrac{5}{2}$ **51.** 0, 4   **53.** -2 **55.** no solution

57. 3   **59.** 1   **61.** 400 ft   **63.** 8 ft
65. about \$3,109
69.

71. $[3, \infty)$ **73.** $[-2, 1)$

75. $(-\infty, 1) \cup [2, \infty)$

Section 1.7

1. right   **3.** $a < c$ **5.** $b - c$ **7.** $>$ **9.** linear
11. equivalent
13. $(-\infty, 1)$ **15.** $[1, \infty)$

17. $(-\infty, 1)$ **19.** $[1, \infty)$

21. $(-\infty, 3]$ **23.** $(-10/3, \infty)$

25. $(5, \infty)$ **27.** $[14, \infty)$

29. $(-\infty, 15/4]$ **31.** $(-44/41, \infty)$

33. $(6, 9]$ **35.** $(8, 22]$

37. $[-11, 4]$ **39.** $[5, 21]$

41. $(-\infty, 0)$ **43.** $(0, \infty)$

45. $(3, 14/3)$ **47.** $(2, \infty)$

49. $(-4, 5/6)$ **51.** $[-2, \infty)$

53. $(-4, -3)$ **55.** $(-\infty, 2] \cup [3, \infty)$

57. $(-3, -2)$ **59.** $(-\infty, -1/2] \cup [-1/3, \infty)$

61. $(1/3, 1/2)$ **63.** $(-\infty, -3/2] \cup [1, \infty)$

65. $(-\infty, -\sqrt{3}] \cup [\sqrt{3}, \infty)$ **67.** $(-\sqrt{11}, \sqrt{11})$

69. $(-3, 2)$ **71.** $(-\infty, -1) \cup (-1, 0) \cup (1, \infty)$

73. $(-\infty, -3) \cup (-3, -2] \cup (2, \infty)$

75. $(-\infty, -2) \cup (-2, -1/3) \cup (1/2, \infty)$ **77.** $(0, 3/2)$

79. $(-\infty, 0) \cup (3/2, \infty)$ **81.** $(-\infty, 2) \cup [13/5, \infty)$

83. $(-\infty, -\sqrt{7}) \cup (-1, 1) \cup (\sqrt{7}, \infty)$ **85.** 19 min   **87.** 12

89. $p \le \$1,124.12$ **91.** $a > \$50,000$
93. anything over \$1,800   **95.** $16\dfrac{2}{3}$ cm $< s <$ 20 cm
97. $40 + 2w < P < 60 + 2w$ **101.** $0, -2, 2$ **103.** 2
105. All are real.

Section 1.8
1. x **3.** $x = k$ or $x = -k$ **5.** $-k < x < k$
7. $x \le -k$ or $x \ge k$ **9.** 7   **11.** 0   **13.** 2
15. $\pi - 2$ **17.** $x - 5$ **19.** x^3 if $x \ge 0$; $-x^3$ if $x < 0$
21. $0, -4$ **23.** $2, -\dfrac{4}{3}$ **25.** $\dfrac{14}{3}, -2$ **27.** $7, -3$

29. no solution   **31.** 5   **33.** $\dfrac{2}{7}, 2$ **35.** $x \ge 0$
37. $-\dfrac{3}{2}$ **39.** $0, -6$ **41.** 0   **43.** $\dfrac{3}{5}, 3$

45. $-\dfrac{3}{13}, \dfrac{9}{5}$

47. $(-3, 9)$

49. $(-\infty, -9) \cup (3, \infty)$ -9 3

51. $(-\infty, -7] \cup [3, \infty)$ -7 3

53. $[-13/3, 1]$ $-13/3$ 1

55. $(-\infty, -3) \cup (-3, \infty)$ -3

57. $(-1, 1/5)$ -1 $1/5$

59. $(-\infty, -7/9) \cup (13/9, \infty)$ $-7/9$ $13/9$

61. $(-5, 7)$ -5 7

63. $(-2, -1/2) \cup (-1/2, 1)$ -2 $-1/2$ 1

65. $(-7/3, -2/3) \cup (4/3, 3)$ $-7/3$ $-2/3$ $4/3$ 3

67. $(-7, -1) \cup (11, 17)$ -7 -1 11 17

69. $(-18, -6) \cup (10, 22)$ -18 -6 10 22

71. $(-10, -7] \cup [5, 8)$ -10 -7 5 8

73. $\left[-\dfrac{1}{2}, \infty\right)$ **75.** $(-\infty, 0)$ **77.** $\left(-\infty, -\dfrac{1}{2}\right)$

79. $[0, \infty)$ **81.** $70° \le t \le 86°$ **83.** $|c - 0.6°| \le 0.5°$

85. $|h - 55| < 17$ **87. a.** $26.45\%, 24.76\%$
b. It is less than or equal to 1%.   **95.** 3.725×10^4
97. $523{,}000$ **99.** $-4xy$

Chapter Review
1. no restrictions   **2.** $x \ne 0$ **3.** $x \ne 1$

4. $x \ne 2, x \ne 3$ **5.** $\dfrac{16}{27}$; conditional equation

6. -14; conditional equation   **7.** $\dfrac{16}{5}$; conditional equation

8. no solution; contradiction   **9.** 7; conditional equation

10. all real numbers except -9; identity

11. 7; conditional equation   **12.** $\dfrac{1}{3}$; conditional equation

13. -2; conditional equation   **14.** 0; conditional equation

15. $F = \dfrac{9}{5}C + 32$ **16.** $f = \dfrac{is}{P_n - l}$ **17.** $f_1 = \dfrac{ff_2}{f_2 - f}$

18. $l = \dfrac{a - S + Sr}{r}$ **19.** 60% **20.** 22.5 ft by 27.5 ft

21. 3 hr   **22.** 0.5 hr   **23.** 1.5 liters   **24.** about 3.9 hr

25. $5\dfrac{1}{7}$ hr   **26.** $3\dfrac{3}{3}$ oz   **27.** \$4,500 at 11%; \$5,500 at 14%

28. 10   **29.** $2, -\dfrac{3}{2}$ **30.** $\dfrac{1}{4}, -\dfrac{4}{3}$ **31.** $0, \dfrac{8}{5}$

32. $\dfrac{2}{3}, \dfrac{4}{9}$ **33.** $\pm 2\sqrt{2}$ **34.** $\pm\sqrt{5}$

35. $\dfrac{5 \pm 4\sqrt{2}}{4}$ **36.** $\dfrac{7 \pm 3\sqrt{5}}{5}$ **37.** $3, 5$

38. $-4, -2$ **39.** $\dfrac{1 \pm \sqrt{21}}{10}$ **40.** $0, \dfrac{1}{5}$ **41.** $2, -7$

42. $9, -\dfrac{2}{3}$ **43.** $\dfrac{-1 \pm \sqrt{21}}{10}$ **44.** $-1 \pm \sqrt{6}$ **45.** 1

46. two different rational numbers   **47.** $\dfrac{1}{3}$ **48.** $10, 2$

49. $-\dfrac{5}{2}$ **50.** $\dfrac{8}{5}, 5$ **51.** either 95 by 110 yd or 55 by 190 yd   **52.** 320 mph for prop plane; 440 mph for jet plane

53. 1 sec   **54.** $1\dfrac{1}{2}$ ft   **55.** $-2 - i$ **56.** $-2 - 5i$

57. $5 - 2i$ **58.** $21 - 9i$ **59.** $0 - 3i$ **60.** $0 - 2i$

61. $\dfrac{3}{2} - \dfrac{3}{2}i$ **62.** $-\dfrac{2}{5} + \dfrac{4}{5}i$ **63.** $\dfrac{4}{5} + \dfrac{3}{5}i$ **64.** $\dfrac{1}{2} - \dfrac{5}{2}i$

65. $0 + i$ **66.** $0 - i$ **67.** $\sqrt{10} + 0i$ **68.** $1 + 0i$

69. $\dfrac{1}{3} \pm \dfrac{\sqrt{2}}{3}i$ **70.** $\dfrac{1}{3} \pm \dfrac{\sqrt{11}}{3}i$ **71.** $2, -3$

72. $4, -2$ **73.** $1, 1, -1, -1$ **74.** $1, -1, 6, -6$ **75.** 9

76. $8, -27$ **77.** 5   **78.** 0   **79.** $4, -4$

80. no solution   **81.** $(-\infty, 7)$ 7

82. $[-1/5, \infty)$ $-1/5$

83. $(-\infty, 5/3)$ $5/3$

84. $(-\infty, -12/7)$ $-12/7$

85. $[-3, 5)$ -3 5

86. $(2, \infty)$ 2

87. $(-\infty, -2) \cup (4, \infty)$ -2 4

88. $(-4, 1)$ -4 1

89. $(-1, 3)$ -1 3

90. $(-\infty, -3/2) \cup (1, \infty)$ $-3/2$ 1

91. $(-\infty, -2] \cup (3, \infty)$ -2 3

92. $(-4, 1]$ -4 1

93. $[-2, 1] \cup (3, \infty)$ -2 1 3

94. $(-\infty, 0) \cup (5/2, \infty)$ 0 $5/2$

95. $5, -7$ **96.** 0   **97.** $-\dfrac{4}{3}, -6$ **98.** $-\dfrac{3}{8}, \dfrac{3}{10}$

99. $(-6, 0)$ -6 0

100. $(-\infty, 2] \cup [8/3, \infty)$ 2 $8/3$

101. $(-5, 1)$ -5 1

102. $(-\infty, -29) \cup (35, \infty)$ -29 35

103. $(-7/2, -2) \cup (-1, 1/2)$ $-7/2$ -2 -1 $1/2$

104. $(-1, 4/3) \cup (4/3, 11/3)$ -1 $4/3$ $11/3$

Chapter Test
1. $x \ne 0, x \ne 1$ **2.** $x \ne \dfrac{2}{3}$ **3.** $\dfrac{5}{2}$ **4.** 37

5. $x = \mu + z\sigma$ **6.** $a = \dfrac{bc}{c + b}$ **7.** 87.5   **8.** \$14,000

9. $\dfrac{1}{2}, \dfrac{3}{2}$　　**10.** $\dfrac{3}{2}, -4$　　**11.** $x = \dfrac{-b \pm \sqrt{b^2 - 4ac}}{2a}$

12. $\dfrac{5 \pm \sqrt{133}}{6}$　　**13.** $5, -3$　　**14.** 8 sec　　**15.** $7 - 12i$

16. $-23 - 43i$　　**17.** $\dfrac{4}{5} + \dfrac{2}{5}i$　　**18.** $0 + i$　　**19.** i

20. 1　　**21.** 13　　**22.** $\dfrac{\sqrt{10}}{10}$　　**23.** $2, -2, 3, -3$

24. $1, -\dfrac{1}{32}$　　**25.** 139　　**26.** -1

27.
$(-\infty, 2]$
2

28.
$(-\infty, 5)$
5

29.
$[3, 4)$
3　4

30.
$(2, \infty)$
2

31.
$(-\infty, -1] \cup [8, \infty)$
−1　8

32.
$[-2, 1)$
−2　1

33. $2, -\dfrac{10}{3}$　　**34.** 0

35.
$(-\infty, 3/2) \cup (7/2, \infty)$
3/2　7/2

36.
$[-9, 6]$
−9　6

Cumulative Review
1. $-2, 0, 2, 6$　　**2.** $2, 5, 11$

3.
$[-4, 7)$
−4　7

4.
$(-\infty, 0) \cup [2, \infty)$
0　2

5. Comm. Prop. of Addition　　**6.** Transitive Prop.　　**7.** $9a^2$

8. $81a^2$　　**9.** a^6b^4　　**10.** $\dfrac{9y^2}{x^4}$　　**11.** $\dfrac{x^4}{16y^2}$　　**12.** $\dfrac{4y^{10}}{9x^6}$

13. a^3b^3　　**14.** abc^2　　**15.** $\sqrt{3}$　　**16.** $\dfrac{\sqrt[3]{2x^2}}{x}$

17. $\dfrac{3(y + \sqrt{3})}{y^2 - 3}$　　**18.** $\dfrac{3x(\sqrt{x} + 1)}{x - 1}$　　**19.** $5\sqrt{3} - 3\sqrt{5}$

20. $3\sqrt{2}$　　**21.** $5 - 2\sqrt{6}$　　**22.** 4　　**23.** $-8x + 8$

24. $9x^4 - 4x^3$　　**25.** $6x^2 + 11x - 35$　　**26.** $z^3 + z^2 + 4$

27. $2x^2 - x + 1$　　**28.** $3x^2 + 1 - \dfrac{x}{x^2 + 2}$　　**29.** $3t(t - 2)$

30. $(3x + 2)(x - 4)$　　**31.** $(x + 1)^2(x - 1)^2(x^2 + 1)^2$

32. $(x + 1)(x^2 - x + 1)(x - 1)(x^2 + x + 1)$　　**33.** $\dfrac{x - 5}{x + 5}$

34. $(2x + 1)(x + 2)$　　**35.** $\dfrac{5x^2 + 17x - 6}{(x + 3)(x - 3)}$

36. $\dfrac{-x^2 + x + 7}{(x + 2)(x + 3)}$　　**37.** $b + a$　　**38.** $-\dfrac{1}{xy}$

39. $0, 10$　　**40.** 34　　**41.** $R = \dfrac{R_1 R_2}{R_1 + R_2}$

42. $r = \dfrac{a - S}{l - S}$ or $r = \dfrac{S - a}{S - l}$

43. either 8 ft by 24 ft or 12 ft by 16 ft　　**44.** \$8,000

45. $\dfrac{3}{5} + \dfrac{4}{5}i$　　**46.** $\dfrac{3}{2} - \dfrac{1}{2}i$　　**47.** 5　　**48.** $0 + 10i$

49. 3　　**50.** $2, -2, 3, -3$　　**51.** $2, 7$　　**52.** $64, 729$

53. $\left(-\infty, \dfrac{11}{5}\right]$　　　**54.** $(-\infty, 3) \cup (5, \infty)$

11/5

3　5

55. $[-3, -1] \cup (2, \infty)$　　**56.** $(-\infty, -3) \cup (0, 3)$

−3　−1　2

−3　0　3

57. $(-\infty, -1] \cup [4, \infty)$　　**58.** $\left(\dfrac{1}{3}, 3\right)$

−1　4

1/3　3

Section 2.1
1. quadrants　　**3.** to the right　　**5.** first　　**7.** linear
9. x-intercept　　**11.** horizontal　　**13.** midpoint
15. $A(2, 3)$　　**17.** $C(-2, -3)$　　**19.** $E(0, 0)$
21. $G(-5, -5)$　　**23.** QI　　**25.** QIII　　**27.** QI
29. x-axis

31.

$y = 2x + 7$　$\left(-\dfrac{7}{2}, 0\right)$

33.

$y = -5x + 5$

35.

$y = 2x - \dfrac{10}{3}$　$\left(\dfrac{5}{3}, 0\right)$　$\left(0, -\dfrac{10}{3}\right)$

37.
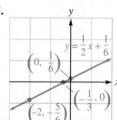
$y = \dfrac{1}{2}x + \dfrac{1}{6}$　$\left(0, \dfrac{1}{6}\right)$　$\left(-\dfrac{1}{3}, 0\right)$　$\left(-2, -\dfrac{5}{6}\right)$

39.

$y = -\dfrac{1}{2}x$

41.
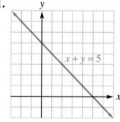
$x + y = 5$

43.

$2x - y = 4$

45.
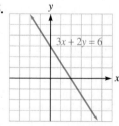
$3x + 2y = 6$

47.

$4x - 5y = 20$

49.

$y = 3$

51.

$3x + 5 = -1$

53.

$3(y + 2) = y$

55.

$3(y + 2x) = 6x + y$

57. 1.22   **59.** 4.67   **61.** 5   **63.** $\sqrt{13}$ **65.** $\sqrt{2}$
67. 2   **69.** 5   **71.** 13   **73.** $2\sqrt{13}$ **75.** $8\sqrt{2}$
77. 7   **79.** (4, 6)   **81.** (0, 1)   **83.** $\left(-1, \frac{1}{2}\right)$
85. $\left(\frac{\sqrt{5}}{2}, \frac{\sqrt{5}}{2}\right)$ **87.** (5, 6)   **89.** (5, 15)
93. $\sqrt{2}$ units   **97.** \$312,500   **99.** 200   **101.** 100 rpm
103. approx. 171 mi   **109.** ← ─[──────]─ → $-3 \quad 3$
111. no graph; the intersection is the empty set   **113.** -12

Section 2.2
1. divided   **3.** run   **5.** the change in   **7.** vertical
9. perpendicular   **11.** 1   **13.** $-\frac{5}{12}$ **15.** $-\frac{7}{4}$
17. -2 **19.** undefined   **21.** $\frac{5}{3}$ **23.** -1 **25.** 3
27. $\frac{1}{2}$ **29.** $\frac{2}{3}$ **31.** 0   **33.** 0   **35.** undefined
37. negative   **39.** positive   **41.** undefined
43. perpendicular   **45.** parallel   **47.** perpendicular
49. perpendicular   **51.** perpendicular   **53.** parallel
55. perpendicular   **57.** neither   **59.** 5   **61.** 6
63. not on same line   **65.** on same line
67. No two are perpendicular.   **69.** PQ and PR are
perpendicular.   **71.** PQ and PR are perpendicular.
81. 3.5 students per yr   **83.** \$642.86 per year

85. $\frac{\Delta T}{\Delta t}$ is the hourly rate of change in temperature.

(graph: T vs t, values 45, 50, 55, 60, 65, 70, 75 on T axis; 1, 2, 3, 4 on t axis)

87. The slope is the speed of the plane.

(graph: d (mi) vs t (hr); $d = 590t$; point (1, 590); 600 and 1,200 marked)

91. $y = -\frac{3}{7}x + 3$ **93.** $y = -\frac{2}{5}x + 2$
95. $(2p + 3)(3p - 4)$ **97.** $(m + n)(p + q)$

Section 2.3
1. $y - y_1 = m(x - x_1)$ **3.** slope-intercept   **5.** $-\frac{A}{B}$
7. $2x - y = 0$ **9.** $4x - 2y = -7$ **11.** $2x - 5y = -7$
13. $y = -3$ **15.** $x = -6$ **17.** $\pi x - y = \pi^2$
19. $2x - 3y = -11$ **21.** $y = x$ **23.** $y = \frac{7}{3}x - 3$
25. $y = -\frac{9}{5}x + \frac{2}{5}$ **27.** $y = 3x - 2$ **29.** $y = 5x - \frac{1}{5}$
31. $y = ax + \frac{1}{a}$ **33.** $y = ax + a$ **35.** $3x - 2y = 0$
37. $3x + y = -4$ **39.** $\sqrt{2}x - y = -\sqrt{2}$
41. 1, $(0, -1)$ **43.** $\frac{2}{3}$, $(0, 2)$

(graph: $y = x - 1$, with rise/run marks 1, 1)

(graph: $y = \frac{2}{3}x + 2$, with +2 and +3 marks)

45. $-\frac{2}{3}$, $(0, 6)$ **47.** $\frac{3}{2}$, $(0, -4)$

(graph: $y = -\frac{2}{3}x + 6$, with +3 and -2 marks)

49. $-\frac{1}{3}$, $\left(0, -\frac{5}{6}\right)$ **51.** $\frac{7}{2}$, $(0, 2)$ **53.** parallel
55. perpendicular   **57.** parallel   **59.** perpendicular
61. perpendicular   **63.** perpendicular   **65.** $y = 4x$

67. $y = 4x - 3$ **69.** $y = \dfrac{4}{5}x - \dfrac{26}{5}$ **71.** $y = -\dfrac{1}{4}x$

73. $y = -\dfrac{1}{4}x + \dfrac{11}{2}$ **75.** $y = -\dfrac{5}{4}x + 3$

77. $m = -\dfrac{4}{5}; (0, 4)$ **79.** $m = -\dfrac{2}{3}; (0, 4)$ **81.** $x = -2$

83. $x = 5$ **85.** $y = -3{,}200x + 24{,}300$

87. $y = 47{,}500x + 475{,}000$ **89.** $y = -\dfrac{710}{3}x + 1{,}900$

91. \$90   **93.** \$890   **95.** \$37,200   **97.** \$230

99. about 838   **101.** $C = \dfrac{5}{9}(F - 32)$

103. $y = -\dfrac{9}{10}x + 47; 11\%$ **105.** $y = 3.75x + 37.5; \$52\dfrac{1}{2}$

107. 1,655 barrels per day
109. a. Chirps/min

b. $y = \dfrac{23}{5}x - 210$ (answers may vary)

c. 204 (answers may vary)   **111.** $y = 4.44x - 196.62$

123. x^5 **125.** $\dfrac{125}{729}$ **127.** $-\sqrt{3}$ **129.** $\dfrac{5\left(\sqrt{x} - 2\right)}{x - 4}$

Section 2.4
1. x-intercept   **3.** axis of symmetry   **5.** x-axis
7. circle; center   **9.** $x^2 + y^2 = r^2$

11. $(-2, 0), (2, 0); (0, -4)$ **13.** $(0, 0), \left(\dfrac{1}{2}, 0\right); (0, 0)$

15. $(-1, 0), (5, 0); (0, -5)$ **17.** $(1, 0), (-2, 0); (0, -2)$
19. $(-3, 0), (0, 0), (3, 0); (0, 0)$ **21.** $(-1, 0), (1, 0); (0, -1)$
23.

25.

27.

29.

31. about the y-axis   **33.** about the x-axis
35. about the x-axis, the y-axis, and the origin
37. about the y-axis   **39.** none   **41.** about the x-axis
43. about the y-axis   **45.** about the x-axis
47.

49.

51.

53.

55.

57.

59.

61.

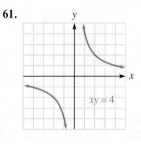

63. $(0, 0); 10$ **65.** $(0, 5); 7$ **67.** $(-6, 0); \dfrac{1}{2}$

69. $(4, 1); 3$ **71.** $\left(\dfrac{1}{4}, -2\right); 3\sqrt{5}$ **73.** $x^2 + y^2 = 25$

75. $x^2 + (y + 6)^2 = 36$ **77.** $(x - 8)^2 + y^2 = \dfrac{1}{25}$

79. $(x + 2)^2 + (y - 12)^2 = 169$ **81.** $x^2 + y^2 - 1 = 0$
83. $x^2 + y^2 - 12x - 16y + 84 = 0$
85. $x^2 + y^2 - 6x + 8y + 23 = 0$
87. $x^2 + y^2 - 6x - 6y - 7 = 0$
89. $x^2 + y^2 + 6x - 8y = 0$ **91.** $(x - 3)^2 + (y + 2)^2 = 9$
93. $(x - 5)^2 + (y - 6)^2 = 4$ **95.** $(x - 2)^2 + (y - 4)^2 = 9$
97.

99.

101.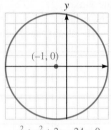
$x^2 + y^2 + 2x - 24 = 0$

103.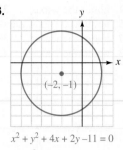
$x^2 + y^2 + 4x + 2y - 11 = 0$

5-8.

105.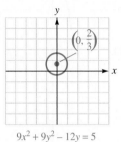
$9x^2 + 9y^2 - 12y = 5$

107.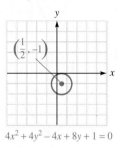
$4x^2 + 4y^2 - 4x + 8y + 1 = 0$

9.

10.

109. (0.25, 0.88)

111. (0.50, 7.25)

113. ±2.65

115. 1.44

11.

12.

117. 4 sec   **119.**

13.

14.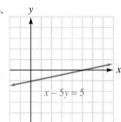

121. $x^2 + y^2 = 36$ **123.** $x^2 + (y - 35)^2 = 900$
125. $x^2 + y^2 - 14x - 8y + 40 = 0$ **127.** $(-3, 2)$
129. a single point   **131.** 6   **133.** -1 **135.** 20 oz

Section 2.5
1. quotient   **3.** means   **5.** extremes; means
7. inverse   **9.** joint   **11.** 14   **13.** 2, -3 **15.** 18
17. $\frac{1}{2}$ **19.** 1,000   **21.** 1   **23.** $\frac{21}{4}$ **25.** 6   **27.** -8
29. direct variation   **31.** neither   **33.** 202, 172, 136
35. about 2 gal   **37.** $14\frac{6}{11}$ ft^3 **39.** 3 sec   **41.** $\sqrt{2}$ m
43. 15 lumens   **45.** It is multiplied by 18.
47. The force is multiplied by $\frac{9}{4}$.   **49.** $\frac{\sqrt{3}}{4}$
57. $\frac{3x + 5}{(x + 2)(x + 1)}$ **59.** $\frac{(x + 4)(x + 1)}{x - 1}$ **61.** $-\frac{1}{x}$

15.

16.

17. \$12,150   **18.** \$332,500   **19.** 10   **20.** $4\sqrt{2}$
21. 2   **22.** $2\sqrt{2}|a|$ **23.** (0, 3)   **24.** $\left(-6, \frac{15}{2}\right)$
25. $\left(\sqrt{3}, 8\right)$ **26.** (0, 0)   **27.** -6 **28.** 2   **29.** -1
30. 1   **31.** 3   **32.** 5   **33.** 0   **34.** undefined
35. negative   **36.** positive   **37.** perpendicular
38. neither   **39.** $y = 7$ **40.** $x = 3$ **41.** 200 ft/min
42. \$48,750 per year   **43.** $7x + 5y = 0$
44. $4x + y = -7$ **45.** $x + 5y = -3$ **46.** $2x + y = 9$
47. $y = \frac{2}{3}x + 3$ **48.** $y = -\frac{3}{2}x - 5$

Chapter Review
1. (2, 0)   **2.** $(-2, 1)$ **3.** $(0, -1)$ **4.** $(3, -1)$

49.

50.

51. $\dfrac{3}{2}$, $(0, -5)$ **52.** $-\dfrac{1}{2}$, $(0, -2)$ **53.** $\dfrac{3}{2}$, $(0, -5)$

54. $-\dfrac{1}{2}$, $(0, -2)$ **55.** $-\dfrac{5}{2}$, $\left(0, \dfrac{7}{2}\right)$ **56.** $\dfrac{3}{4}$, $\left(0, -\dfrac{7}{2}\right)$

57. $y = 17$ **58.** $x = -5$ **59.** $y = \dfrac{3}{4}x - \dfrac{3}{2}$

60. $y = -7x + 47$ **61.** $y = 3x + 5$

62. $y = \dfrac{1}{7}x - 3$ **63.** parallel   **64.** perpendicular

65. $(0, 0)$, $\left(\dfrac{1}{2}, 0\right)$; $(0, 0)$ **66.** $(12, 0)$, $(-2, 0)$; $(0, -24)$

67. about the x-axis   **68.** about the y-axis
69. about the y-axis   **70.** none
71.
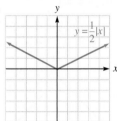
72. $y = x^3 - 2$

73.

74.

75.

76.

77.

78.

79.

80.

81. $(0, 0)$; 8 **82.** $(0, 6)$; 10 **83.** $(-7, 0)$; $\dfrac{1}{2}$

84. $(5, -1)$; 3 **85.** $x^2 + y^2 = 49$ **86.** $(x - 3)^2 + y^2 = \dfrac{1}{25}$

87. $(x + 2)^2 + (y - 12)^2 = 25$ **88.** $\left(x - \dfrac{2}{7}\right)^2 + (y - 5)^2 = 81$

89. $(x + 3)^2 + (y - 4)^2 = 144$ or $x^2 + y^2 + 6x - 8y - 119 = 0$

90. $\left(x + \dfrac{1}{2}\right)^2 + \left(y - \dfrac{5}{2}\right)^2 = \dfrac{121}{2}$ or $x^2 + y^2 + x - 5y - 54 = 0$

91. $(x + 3)^2 + (y - 2)^2 = 9$
92. $(x - 2)^2 + (y - 4)^2 = 25$
93.

94.

95.

96.

97. $3.32, -3.32$ **98.** $-1, 0, 1$ **99.** $1.73, -1.73, 1, -1$
100. $4.19, -1.19$ **101.** $x = 2, x = 5$ **102.** $x = -5, x = 5$
103. $\dfrac{9}{5}$ lb   **104.** $\dfrac{25}{9}$ **105.** $333\dfrac{1}{3}$ cc   **106.** 1
107. about 117 ohms   **108.** \$385
109. 140 hr

Chapter Test
1. QII   **2.** y-axis
3.

4.

5.

6.

7.

8.

9. $\sqrt{41}$ **10.** approximately 4.44   **11.** $(0, 0)$

12. $\left(\sqrt{2}, 2\sqrt{2}\right)$ **13.** $-\dfrac{5}{4}$ **14.** $\dfrac{\sqrt{3}}{3}$ **15.** neither

16. perpendicular   **17.** $y = 2x - 11$ **18.** $y = 3x + \dfrac{1}{2}$

19. $y = 2x + 5$ **20.** $y = -\dfrac{1}{2}x + 5$ **21.** $y = 2x - \dfrac{11}{2}$

22. $x = 3$ **23.** $(-4, 0), (0, 0), (4, 0); (0, 0)$

24. $(4, 0); (0, 4)$ **25.** about the x-axis

26. about the y-axis

27.

28.

29.

30.

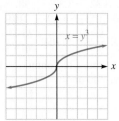

31. $(x - 5)^2 + (y - 7)^2 = 64$ **32.** $(x - 2)^2 + (y - 4)^2 = 32$

33.

34.

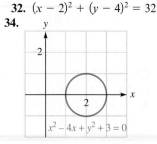

35. $y = kz^2$ **36.** $w = krs^2$ **37.** $P = \dfrac{35}{2}$ **38.** $x = \dfrac{27}{32}$

39. $x = 2.65$ **40.** $x = 5.85$

Section 3.1

1. function   **3.** domain   **5.** $y = f(x)$ **7.** x
9. vertical; once   **11.** function   **13.** not a function
15. function   **17.** not a function   **19.** not a function
21. function   **23.** domain: $(-\infty, \infty)$ **25.** domain: $(-\infty, \infty)$
27. domain: $[2, \infty)$ **29.** domain: $(-\infty, 4]$
31. domain: $(-\infty, -1] \cup [1, \infty)$ **33.** domain: $(-\infty, \infty)$
35. domain: $(-\infty, -1) \cup (-1, \infty)$

37. domain: $(-\infty, 3) \cup (3, \infty)$
39. domain: $(-\infty, -2) \cup (-2, 2) \cup (2, \infty)$
41. domain: $(-\infty, -1) \cup (-1, 5) \cup (5, \infty)$

43. $4; -11; 3k - 2; 3k^2 - 5$ **45.** $4; \dfrac{3}{2}; \dfrac{1}{2}k + 3; \dfrac{1}{2}k^2 + \dfrac{5}{2}$

47. $4; 9; k^2; k^4 - 2k^2 + 1$ **49.** $9; -1; k^2 + 3k - 1;$
$k^4 + k^2 - 3$ **51.** $5; 10; k^2 + 1; k^4 - 2k^2 + 2$

53. $\dfrac{1}{3}; 2; \dfrac{2}{k + 4}; \dfrac{2}{k^2 + 3}$ **55.** $\dfrac{1}{3}; \dfrac{1}{8}; \dfrac{1}{k^2 - 1}; \dfrac{1}{k^4 - 2k^2}$

57. $\sqrt{5}; \sqrt{10}; \sqrt{k^2 + 1}; \sqrt{k^4 - 2k^2 + 2}$ **59.** 3

61. $2x + h$ **63.** $8x + 4h$ **65.** $2x + h + 3$
67. $4x + 2h - 4$ **69.** $3x^2 + 3xh + h^2$

71.

domain: $(-\infty, \infty)$
range: $(-\infty, \infty)$

73.

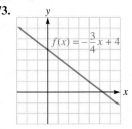

domain: $(-\infty, \infty)$
range: $(-\infty, \infty)$

75.

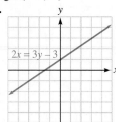

domain: $(-\infty, \infty)$
range: $(-\infty, \infty)$

77.

domain: $(-\infty, \infty)$
range: $[-4, \infty]$

79.

domain: $(-\infty, \infty)$
range: $(-\infty, \infty)$

81.

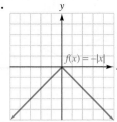

domain: $(-\infty, \infty)$
range: $(-\infty, 0]$

83.

domain: $(-\infty, \infty)$
range: $[0, \infty)$

85.

domain: $(-\infty, \infty)$
range: $[0, \infty)$

87.

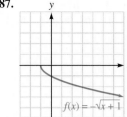

domain: $[-1, \infty)$
range: $(-\infty, 0]$

89.

$f(x) = \sqrt{2x - 4}$

domain: $[2, \infty)$
range: $[0, \infty)$

91.

$f(x) = \sqrt[3]{x} + 2$

domain: $(-\infty, \infty)$
range: $(-\infty, \infty)$

93.

Range

f

Domain

95. function   **97.** function   **99.** function

101.

domain: $(-\infty, \infty)$;
range: $[0, \infty)$

103.

domain: $(-\infty, \infty)$;
range: $(-\infty, \infty)$

105. a. $C(x) = 8x + 75$ **b.** $755

107. a. $C(t) = 0.07t + 9.99$ **b.** $11.39

109. a. $C(f) = 95f + 14,000$ **b.** $261,000

111. $C(x) = 0.10x + 7$ **113.** $n(t) = 1,692t + 6,400$

115. $E(D) = 1.3911D$ **117.** $-\dfrac{2}{3}$ **123.** 1, 7, 8   **125.** 7

127. $(-4, 7]$ **129.**

-3 5 6

Section 3.2

1. $f(x) = ax^2 + bx + c$ **3.** $(3, 5)$ **5.** upward

7. $-\dfrac{b}{2a}$ **9.** upward; minimum

11. downward; maximum   **13.** downward; maximum

15. $(0, -1)$ **17.** $(3, 5)$ **19.** $(-6, -4)$ **21.** $(3, 0)$

23. $(2, 0)$ **25.** $(-3, -12)$ **27.** $(3, 1)$

29. $\left(\dfrac{2}{3}, \dfrac{11}{3}\right)$ **31.** $(-4, -11)$

33.

$f(x) = x^2 - 4$

35.

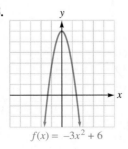

$f(x) = -3x^2 + 6$

37.

$f(x) = -\dfrac{1}{2}x^2 + 8$

39.

$f(x) = (x - 3)^2 - 1$

41.

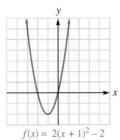

$f(x) = 2(x + 1)^2 - 2$

43.

$f(x) = -(x + 4)^2 + 1$

45.

$f(x) = -3(x - 2)^2 + 6$

47.

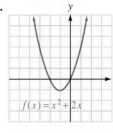

$f(x) = x^2 + 2x$

49.

$f(x) = x^2 - 4x + 1$

51.

$f(x) = 2x^2 - 12x + 10$

53.

$f(x) = -3x^2 - 6x - 9$

55. 75 ft by 75 ft, 5,625 ft^2

57. 25 ft by 25 ft   **59.** $w = 12$ in.; $d = 6$ in.   **61.** 20 ft

63. 15.4 ft   **65.** 208 ft

67. 48 digital cameras; minimum cost $2,400   **69.** $95

71. $\dfrac{5}{2}$ sec   **73.** 100 ft   **75.** $(-2.25, -66.13)$

77. $(3.3, -68.5)$ **79.** 2, 3   **81.** 6 by $4\dfrac{1}{2}$ units

83. Both numbers are 3.   **87.** $a^2 - 3a; a^2 + 3a$

89. $(5 - a)^2; (5 + a)^2$ **91.** 7; 7

Section 3.3

1. 4   **3.** $n - 1$ **5.** odd   **7.** piecewise-defined   **9.** 3

11.

13.

57.

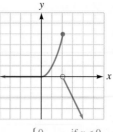

$$f(x) = \begin{cases} 0 & \text{if } x < 0 \\ x^2 & \text{if } 0 \le x \le 2 \\ 4 - 2x & \text{if } x > 2 \end{cases}$$

59. a. 3   **b.** −4
c. −3   **61. a.** 2   **b.** 3
c. 4

15.

17.

63.

65.

19.

21.

67. B

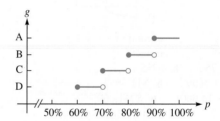

23. even   **25.** neither   **27.** odd   **29.** odd
31. even   **33.** odd   **35.** neither
37. decreasing on $(-\infty, 0)$; increasing on $(0, \infty)$
39. increasing on $(-\infty, 0)$; decreasing for $(0, \infty)$
41. decreasing on $(-\infty, -2)$; constant on $(-2, 2)$; increasing on
$(2, \infty)$ **43.** decreasing on $(-\infty, 2)$; increasing on $(2, \infty)$
45. a. −2   **b.** 3   **47. a.** 2   **b.** 1   **c.** 3

69. $32

49.

51.

53.

55.

71. $1.60

73.

75. no; this is not defined at $x = 0$

81. $3x + 5$; $3x + 3$ **83.** $\dfrac{3x - 8}{5}$; $\dfrac{3x + 1}{5} - 3$ or $\dfrac{3x - 14}{5}$

85. $-1, \dfrac{3}{2}$

Section 3.4

1. upward   **3.** to the right   **5.** 2; downward   **7.** y-axis
9. horizontally

11.

13.

15.

17.

19.

21.

23.

25.

27.

29.

31.

33.

35.

37.

39.

41.

43.

45.

47.

49.

51.

53.

55.

57.

83.

85.

93. $\dfrac{x-2}{x+2}$ **95.** $(-\infty, 3) \cup (3, \infty)$ **97.** $x + 2 + \dfrac{-2}{x+1}$

59.

61.

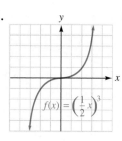

Section 3.5

1. asymptote   **3.** vertical   **5.** x-intercept   **7.** same
9. horizontal; vertical   **11.** vertical asymptote: $x = 2$;
horizontal asymptote: $y = 1$; domain: $(-\infty, 2) \cup (2, \infty)$; range:
$(-\infty, 1) \cup (1, \infty)$ **13.** 20 hr   **15.** 12 hr   **17.** \$5,555.56
19. \$50,000   **21.** $(-\infty, 2) \cup (2, \infty)$
23. $(-\infty, -5) \cup (-5, 5) \cup (5, \infty)$
25. $(-\infty, -1) \cup (-1, 0) \cup (0, 1) \cup (1, \infty)$ **27.** $(-\infty, \infty)$
29. $x = 3$ **31.** $x = 1, x = -1$ **33.** $x = -2, x = 3$

35. none   **37.** $y = 2$ **39.** $y = \dfrac{1}{2}$ **41.** $y = 0$

43. none   **45.** $y = x - 3$ **47.** $y = 2x + 3$
49. $y = x + 2$

63.

65.

51.

53.

67.

69.

55.

57.

71.

73.

59.

61.

75.

77.

79.

81.

63.

$$y = \frac{x^2 + 2x - 3}{x^3 - 4x}$$

65.

$$y = \frac{x^2 - 9}{x^2}$$

67.

$$f(x) = \frac{x}{(x+3)^2}$$

69.

$$f(x) = \frac{x+1}{x^2(x-2)}$$

71.

$$y = \frac{x}{x^2 + 1}$$

73.

$$y = \frac{3x^2}{x^2 + 1}$$

75.

$$h(x) = \frac{x^2 - 2x - 8}{x - 1}$$

77.

(2,8)

$$f(x) = \frac{x^3 + x^2 + 6x}{x^2 - 1}$$

79.

$$f(x) = \frac{x^2}{x}$$

81.

$$f(x) = \frac{x^3 + x}{x}$$

83.

$$f(x) = \frac{x^2 - 2x + 1}{x - 1}$$

85.

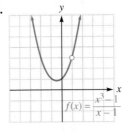

$$f(x) = \frac{x^3 - 1}{x - 1}$$

87. a. $C(x) = 3.25x + 700$ **b.** $2,325

c. $\overline{C}(x) = \dfrac{3.25x + 700}{x}$ **d.** $4.65   **e.** $3.95   **f.** $3.60

89. a. $C(n) = 0.095n + 8.50$ **b.** $\overline{C}(n) = \dfrac{0.095n + 8.50}{n}$

c. 10.5¢   **101.** $3x^2 + x$ **103.** $10x^2 + 29x + 10$

105. $3x + 5$

Section 3.6

1. $f(x) + g(x)$ **3.** $f(x)g(x)$ **5.** intersection

7. $g(f(x))$ **9.** commutative

11. $(f + g)(x) = 5x - 1; (-\infty, \infty)$

13. $(f \cdot g)(x) = 6x^2 - x - 2; (-\infty, \infty)$

15. $(f - g)(x) = x + 1; (-\infty, \infty)$

17. $(f/g)(x) = \dfrac{x^2 + x}{x^2 - 1} = \dfrac{x}{x - 1}; (-\infty, -1) \cup (-1, 1) \cup (1, \infty)$

19. $(f + g)(x) = x^2 + \sqrt{x} - 7; [0, \infty)$

21. $(f/g)(x) = \dfrac{x^2 - 7}{\sqrt{x}}; (0, \infty)$ **23.** 7   **25.** 1   **27.** 12

29. undefined   **31.** $f(x) = 3x^2; g(x) = 2x$

33. $f(x) = 3x^2; g(x) = x^2 - 1$ **35.** $f(x) = 3x^3; g(x) = -x$

37. $f(x) = x + 9; g(x) = x - 2$ **39.** 11   **41.** -17

43. 190   **45.** 145   **47.** $(-\infty, \infty); (f \circ g)(x) = 3x + 3$

49. $(-\infty, \infty); (f \circ f)(x) = 9x$ **51.** $(-\infty, \infty); (g \circ f)(x) = 2x^2$

53. $(-\infty, \infty); (g \circ g)(x) = 4x$

55. $[-1, \infty); (f \circ g)(x) = \sqrt{x + 1}$

57. $[0, \infty); (f \circ f)(x) = \sqrt[4]{x}$ **59.** $[-1, \infty); (g \circ f)(x) = x$

61. $(-\infty, \infty); (g \circ g)(x) = x^4 - 2x^2$

63. $(-\infty, 2) \cup (2, 3) \cup (3, \infty); (f \circ g)(x) = \dfrac{x - 2}{3 - x}$

65. $(-\infty, 1) \cup (1, 2) \cup (2, \infty); (f \circ f)(x) = \dfrac{x - 1}{2 - x}$

67. $f(x) = x - 2; g(x) = 3x$

69. $f(x) = x - 2; g(x) = x^2$

71. $f(x) = x^2; g(x) = x - 2$

73. $f(x) = \sqrt{x}; g(x) = x + 2$

75. $f(x) = x + 2; g(x) = \sqrt{x}$

77. $f(x) = x; g(x) = x$ **79.** 0   **81.** 0   **83.** 1

85. 1   **87.** 8   **89.** 9

91. a. $(R - C)(x) = 260x - 60,000$ **b.** $70,000

93. $A(t) = \dfrac{9}{4}\pi t^2$; 101,787.6 square inches   **95.** $P = 4\sqrt{A}$

105. $y = \dfrac{x + 7}{3}$ **107.** $y = \dfrac{3x}{1 - x}$

Section 3.7

1. one-to-one   **3.** identity   **5.** one-to-one

7. not one-to-one   **9.** not one-to-one

11. not one-to-one   **13.** not one-to-one   **15.** one-to-one

17. one-to-one   **19.** not a function

25. $f^{-1}(x) = \dfrac{1}{3}x$ **27.** $f^{-1}(x) = \dfrac{x - 2}{3}$

29. $f^{-1}(x) = \sqrt[3]{x - 2}$ **31.** $f^{-1}(x) = x^5$

33. $f^{-1}(x) = \dfrac{1}{x} - 3$ **35.** $f^{-1}(x) = \dfrac{1}{2x}$

37.

$$f(x) = 5x$$
$$f^{-1}(x) = \frac{1}{5}x$$

39.

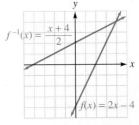

$$f^{-1}(x) = \frac{x + 4}{2}$$
$$f(x) = 2x - 4$$

41.

43.

45.

47.

49.

51.

53. $f^{-1}(x) = -\sqrt{x+3}$ $(x \ge -3)$
55. $f^{-1}(x) = \sqrt[4]{x+8}$ $(x \ge -8)$
57. $f^{-1}(x) = \sqrt{4-x^2}$ $(0 \le x \le 2)$
59. domain: $(-\infty, 2) \cup (2, \infty)$; range: $(-\infty, 1) \cup (1, \infty)$
61. domain: $(-\infty, 0) \cup (0, \infty)$; range: $(-\infty, -2) \cup (-2, \infty)$
63. a. $f(x) = 0.75x + 8.50$ **b.** $11.50

c. $f^{-1}(x) = \dfrac{x - 8.50}{0.75}$ **d.** 2   **67.** 0   **69.** $a \ge 0$

71. 8   **73.** 4   **75.** $\dfrac{5}{4}$ **77.** $\dfrac{1}{7}$

Chapter Review

1. function   **2.** function   **3.** not a function   **4.** function
5. domain: $(-\infty, \infty)$ **6.** domain: $(-\infty, 5] \cup [5, \infty)$
7. domain: $[1, \infty)$ **8.** domain: $(-\infty, \infty)$ **9.** $8; -17; 5k - 2$
10. $-2; -\dfrac{3}{4}; \dfrac{6}{k-5}$ **11.** $0; 5; |k - 2|$ **12.** $\dfrac{1}{7}; \dfrac{1}{2}; \dfrac{k^2-3}{k^2+3}$
13. 5   **14.** $4x + 2h - 7$

15.

domain: $(-\infty, \infty)$
range: $(-\infty, 4]$

16.
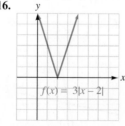
domain: $(-\infty, \infty)$
range: $[0, \infty)$

17. function   **18.** not a function   **19. a.** $I(h) = 3.5h - 50$
b. $650   **20.** $C(x) = 0.15x + 5$ **21.** upward; minimum
22. downward; maximum   **23.** $(1, 6)$ **24.** $(-4, -5)$
25. $(-3, -13)$ **26.** $\left(\dfrac{1}{2}, -8\right)$

27.

28.

29.

30.

31.

32.

33. 300 units   **34.** Both numbers are $\dfrac{1}{2}$.
35. 350 ft by 350 ft; 122,500 ft^2
36. 50 digital cameras; minimum cost $1,100

37.

odd function

38.

neither even nor odd

39.

neither even nor odd

40.

even function

41. a. 2   **b.** 9   **42. a.** $\dfrac{1}{2}$ **b.** 3

43.

$$y = f(x) = \begin{cases} x+5 & \text{if } x \le 0 \\ 5-x & \text{if } x > 0 \end{cases}$$

increasing on $(-\infty, 0)$;
decreasing on $(0, \infty)$

44.

$$y = f(x) = \begin{cases} x+3 & \text{if } x \le 0 \\ 3 & \text{if } x > 0 \end{cases}$$

increasing on $(-\infty, 0)$;
constant on $(0, \infty)$

45. 3   **46.** -1

47.

$f(x) = [\![x]\!] + 2$

48.

$f(x) = [\![x - 1]\!]$

49. \$44   **50.** \$26

51.

$g(x) = x^2 + 5$

$f(x) = x^2$

52.

$f(x) = x^3$

$g(x) = (x - 7)^3$

53.

$g(x) = \sqrt{x + 2} + 3$

$(-2, 3)$

$f(x) = \sqrt{x}$

54.

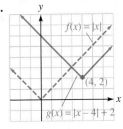

$f(x) = |x|$

$(4, 2)$

$g(x) = |x - 4| + 2$

55.

$f(x) = x^3$ $g(x) = \frac{1}{3} x^3$

56.

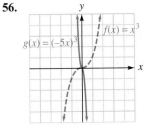

$g(x) = (-5x)^3$ $f(x) = x^3$

57.

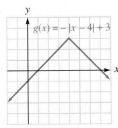

$g(x) = -|x - 4| + 3$

58.

$g(x) = \frac{1}{4}|x - 4| + 1$

59.

$g(x) = 3\sqrt{x + 3} + 2$

60.

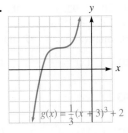

$g(x) = \frac{1}{3}(x + 3)^3 + 2$

61.

$f(x) = \sqrt{-x} + 3$

62.

$g(x) = 2\sqrt[3]{x} - 5$

63. $(-\infty, -5) \cup (-5, 5) \cup (5, \infty)$ **64.** $(-\infty, \infty)$
65. $x = 1, x = -1$ **66.** $x = -7$ **67.** $x = 2, x = -3$
68. $x = 4, x = -1$ **69.** $y = \dfrac{1}{2}$ **70.** $y = -5$
71. $y = 0$ **72.** none   **73.** $y = 2x + 3$ **74.** none

75.

$f(x) = \dfrac{2x}{x - 4}$

76.

$f(x) = \dfrac{-4x}{x + 4}$

77.

$f(x) = \dfrac{x}{(x-1)^2}$

78.

$f(x) = \dfrac{(x-1)^2}{x}$

79.

$f(x) = \dfrac{x^2 - x - 2}{x^2 + x - 2}$

80.

$f(x) = \dfrac{x^3 + x}{x^2 - 4}$

81. $(f + g)(x) = x^2 + 2x$; domain: $(-\infty, \infty)$
82. $(f \cdot g)(x) = 2x^3 + x^2 - 2x - 1$; domain: $(-\infty, \infty)$
83. $(f - g)(x) = x^2 - 2x - 2$; domain: $(-\infty, \infty)$
84. $(f/g)(x) = \dfrac{f(x)}{g(x)} = \dfrac{x^2 - 1}{2x + 1}$; domain: $\left(-\infty, -\dfrac{1}{2}\right) \cup \left(-\dfrac{1}{2}, \infty\right)$
85. 10   **86.** 60   **87.** 21   **88.** undefined
89. $(f \circ g)(x) = f(g(x)) = 4x^2 + 4x$; domain: $(-\infty, \infty)$
90. $(g \circ f)(x) = g(f(x)) = 2x^2 - 1$; domain: $(-\infty, \infty)$

91. 20   **92.** -2 **93.** $f(x) = x^2$; $g(x) = x - 5$
94. $f(x) = x^3$; $g(x) = x + 6$ **95.** not one-to-one
96. one-to-one   **97.** one-to-one   **98.** not one-to-one

101. $f^{-1}(x) = \dfrac{x + 1}{7}$ **102.** $f^{-1}(x) = 2 - \dfrac{1}{x}$

103. $f^{-1}(x) = \dfrac{x}{x + 1}$ **104.** $f^{-1}(x) = \sqrt[3]{\dfrac{3}{x}} = \dfrac{\sqrt[3]{3x^2}}{x}$

105. $f^{-1}(x) = \dfrac{x + 5}{2}$ **106.** $\left(-\infty, \dfrac{2}{5}\right) \cup \left(\dfrac{2}{5}, \infty\right)$

21.

22.

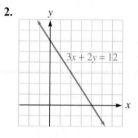

23. $(f + g)(x) = f(x) + g(x) = x^2 + 3x + 2$
24. $(g \circ f)(x) = g(f(x)) = 9x^2 + 2$
25. $(f/g)(x) = \dfrac{f(x)}{g(x)} = \dfrac{3x}{x^2 + 2}$
26. $(f \circ g)(x) = f(g(x)) = 3x^2 + 6$
27. $f^{-1}(x) = \dfrac{x + 1}{x - 1}$ **28.** $f^{-1}(x) = \sqrt[3]{x + 3}$
29. range: $(-\infty, -2) \cup (-2, \infty)$
30. range: $(-\infty, 3) \cup (3, \infty)$

Chapter Test
1. domain: $(-\infty, 5) \cup (5, \infty)$ **2.** domain: $[-3, \infty)$
3. $\dfrac{1}{2}, 2$ **4.** $\sqrt{6}, 3$ **5.** $(7, -3)$ **6.** $(1, -4)$
7. $(4, -10)$ **8.** $(-2, 9)$
9.

10.

11. $\dfrac{25}{8}$ sec   **12.** $\dfrac{625}{4}$ ft   **13.** 10 ft   **14.** 110 ft
15.

16.

17. vertical asymptotes: $x = -3$ and $x = 3$; horizontal asymptote: $y = 0$
18. vertical asymptote: $x = 3$; horizontal asymptote: none; slant asymptote: $y = x - 2$
19.

20.

Cumulative Review
1.

2.

3. $\sqrt{41}; \left(\dfrac{1}{2}, \dfrac{3}{2}\right); -\dfrac{4}{5}$ **4.** $2\sqrt{29}; (-2, 5); \dfrac{2}{5}$
5. $y = -2x - 1$ **6.** $y = \dfrac{7}{2}x - \dfrac{11}{4}$ **7.** $y = \dfrac{3}{5}x + 6$
8. $y = -4x$
9.

10.

11.

12.

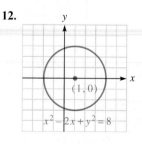

13. $x = 1, x = 10$ **14.** $x = 2, x = 8$ **15.** $62.50
16. $\dfrac{25}{4}$ **17.** function   **18.** function   **19.** function
20. not a function   **21.** domain: $(-\infty, \infty)$
22. domain: $(-\infty, -2) \cup (-2, \infty)$ **23.** domain: $[2, \infty)$

24. domain: $[-4, \infty)$ **25.** $\left(-\dfrac{5}{2}, -\dfrac{49}{4}\right)$ **26.** $\left(\dfrac{5}{2}, \dfrac{49}{4}\right)$

27.

28.

29.

30.

31.

32. $f(x) = \dfrac{x^2 - 1}{x^2 - 9}$

33. $(f + g)(x) = f(x) + g(x) = x^2 + 3x - 3$
domain: $(-\infty, \infty)$
34. $(f - g)(x) = f(x) - g(x) = -x^2 + 3x - 5$
domain: $(-\infty, \infty)$
35. $(f \cdot g)(x) = f(x) \cdot g(x) = 3x^3 - 4x^2 + 3x - 4$
domain: $(-\infty, \infty)$
36. $(f/g)(x) = \dfrac{f(x)}{g(x)} = \dfrac{3x - 4}{x^2 + 1}$ domain: $(-\infty, \infty)$
37. $(f \circ g)(2) = 11$ **38.** $(g \circ f)(2) = 5$
39. $(f \circ g)(x) = 3x^2 - 1$ **40.** $(g \circ f)(x) = 9x^2 - 24x + 17$
41. $f^{-1}(x) = \dfrac{x - 2}{3}$ **42.** $f^{-1}(x) = \dfrac{1}{x} + 3$
43. $f^{-1}(x) = \sqrt{x - 5}$ **44.** $f^{-1}(x) = \dfrac{x + 1}{3}$
45. $y = kwz$ **46.** $y = \dfrac{kx}{t^2}$

Section 4.1
1. exponential   **3.** $(-\infty, \infty)$ **5.** $(0, \infty)$ **7.** asymptote
9. increasing   **11.** 2.72   **13.** increasing   **15.** 11.0357
17. 451.8079   **19.** $5^{2\sqrt{2}} = 25^{\sqrt{2}}$ **21.** a^4 **23.** 1, 25
25. 1, 9

27.

29.

31.

33.

35.

37.

39. yes   **41.** no   **43.** $b = \dfrac{1}{2}$ **45.** no value of b
47. $b = 2$ **49.** $b = e$

51.

53.

55.

57.

59.

61.

63.

65.

67.

69.

103. $b = 2$

105.

107.

71.

73.

109.

111.

75.

77.

113.

115.

79.

117.

119.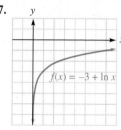

81. $22,080.40   **83.** $15.79   **85.** $2,273,996.13
87. $1,263.77   **89.** $13,375.68   **91.** $7,647.95
from continuous compounding, $7,518.28 from annual
compounding   **93.** $291.27   **95.** $12,155.61
97. 13,228   **101.** 125   **103.** $x^2(1 + 9x^2)$
105. $(x + 4)(x - 3)$

Section 4.2
1. birth; death   **3.** 0.1868 g   **5.** about 10 kg
7. about 35.4%   **9.** 0.1575 unit   **11.** 2 lumens
13. 8 lumens   **15.** about 56,570   **17.** $61.9°C$
19. 315   **21.** 13   **23.** 10.6 billion   **25.** 2.6
27. about 0.07%   **29.** 0   **31.** 18,394
33. about 24,060   **35.** about 492   **37.** 19.0 mm
39. 49 mps   **41.** about 7 million   **43.** about 72.2 years
49. 8   **51.** 3   **53.** 2   **55.** 3

121.

123.

Section 4.3
1. $x = b^y$ **3.** range   **5.** inverse   **7.** exponent
9. $(b, 1); (1, 0)$ **11.** $\log_e x$ **13.** $(-\infty, \infty)$ **15.** 10
17. $\log_8 64 = 2$ **19.** $\log_4 \frac{1}{16} = -2$ **21.** $\log_{1/2} 32 = -5$

23. $\log_x z = y$ **25.** $3^4 = 81$ **27.** $\left(\frac{1}{2}\right)^3 = \frac{1}{8}$

29. $4^{-3} = \frac{1}{64}$ **31.** $\pi^1 = \pi$ **33.** 3   **35.** -3 **37.** 3

39. $\frac{1}{2}$ **41.** -3 **43.** 64   **45.** 7   **47.** 5   **49.** $\frac{1}{25}$

125.

127.

51. $\frac{1}{6}$ **53.** 5   **55.** $\frac{3}{2}$ **57.** 4   **59.** $\frac{2}{3}$ **61.** 5

129.

63. 4   **65.** 0.5119   **67.** -2.3307 **69.** 3.8221
71. -0.4055 **73.** 3.5596   **75.** 2.0664   **77.** -0.2752
79. undefined   **81.** 25.2522   **83.** 1.9498×10^{-4}
85. 4.0645   **87.** 69.4079   **89.** 0.0245   **91.** 120.0719
93. 4   **95.** -3 **97.** 7   **99.** 4   **101.** $b = 2$

131. b is larger.   **135.** $\left(-\frac{7}{2}, -\frac{37}{4}\right)$
137. 425 ft by 850 ft   **139.** $y = 5x$

Section 4.4
1. $20 \log \frac{E_0}{E_I}$ **3.** $t = -\frac{1}{k} \ln\left(1 - \frac{C}{M}\right)$

5. $E = RT \ln\left(\frac{V_f}{V_i}\right)$ **7.** 55 dB   **9.** 29 dB   **11.** 49.5 dB

13. 4.4   **15.** 4   **17.** no   **19.** 19.8 min
21. about 5.8 yr   **23.** about 9.2 yr
25. about 3,654 joules   **27.** about 99% per year
29. 3 yr old   **31.** about 10.8 yr   **33.** about 208,000 V
35. 1 mi   **39.** $y = 7x + 3$ **41.** $x = 2$
43. $\dfrac{1}{2x - 3}$ **45.** $\dfrac{x + 1}{3(x - 2)}$

Section 4.5

1. 0   **3.** $M; N$ **5.** $x; y$ **7.** x **9.** $\neq$ **11.** 0
13. 7   **15.** 10   **17.** 1   **25.** $\log_b 2 + \log_b x + \log_b y$
27. $\log_b 2 + \log_b x - \log_b y$ **29.** $2 \log_b x + 3 \log_b y$
31. $\dfrac{1}{3}(\log_b x + \log_b y)$ **33.** $\log_b x + \dfrac{1}{2} \log_b z$
35. $\dfrac{1}{3} \log_b x - \dfrac{1}{3} \log_b y - \dfrac{1}{3} \log_b z$ **37.** $7 \ln x + 8 \ln y$
39. $\ln x - 4 \ln y - \ln z$ **41.** $\log_b \dfrac{x + 1}{x}$
43. $\log_b x^2 \sqrt[3]{y}$ **45.** $\log_b \dfrac{\sqrt{z}}{x^3 y^2}$ **47.** $\log_b \dfrac{\dfrac{x}{z} + x}{\dfrac{y}{z} + y} = \log_b \dfrac{x}{y}$
49. $\ln \dfrac{x(x + 5)}{9}$ **51.** $\ln \dfrac{z}{x^6 y^2}$ **53.** true   **55.** false
57. true   **59.** false   **61.** true   **63.** false   **65.** false
67. true   **69.** true   **71.** true   **73.** false   **75.** true
77. 1.4472   **79.** 0.3521   **81.** 1.1972   **83.** 2.4014
85. 2.0493   **87.** 0.4682   **89.** 1.7712   **91.** 0.9597
93. 1.8928   **95.** 2.3219   **97.** 7.20   **99.** 4.77
101. from 5.01×10^{-4} to 1.26×10^{-3} **103.** 19 dB
105. The original intensity must be raised to the 4th power.
107. The volume V is squared.   **121.** yes   **123.** no
125. $(-\infty, \infty)$ **127.** $(-\infty, \infty)$

Section 4.6

1. exponential   **3.** $A_0 2^{-t/h}$ **5.** 2   **7.** -2 **9.** $-\dfrac{5}{6}$
11. -4 **13.** $-\dfrac{15}{2}$ **15.** 3, -1 **17.** ± 3
19. $-2, -1$ **21.** 3   **23.** ± 5 **25.** 1.1610
27. 1.2702   **29.** 1.7095   **31.** 0   **33.** ± 1.0878
35. 0, 1.0566   **37.** $\ln 10$ **39.** $\dfrac{1}{2} \ln 6$ **41.** 0
43. 0.2789   **45.** 1, 3   **47.** 0   **49.** 10, -10 **51.** 4
53. e^6 **55.** $\dfrac{1}{2}(e^4 + 7)$ **57.** 7   **59.** 50   **61.** 20
63. 10   **65.** 7   **67.** 6   **69.** 5   **71.** 4   **73.** 3, 4
75. 10^{10} **77.** no solution   **79.** 6   **81.** 9   **83.** 4
85. 7, 1   **87.** 20   **89.** 1.81   **91.** about 5.1 yr
93. about 42.7 days   **95.** about 2,900 yr
97. about 5.6 yr   **99.** about 5.4 yr
101. because $\ln 2 \approx 0.70$ **103.** about 3.2 days
105. about 12 min   **107.** $k = \dfrac{\ln 0.75}{3}$ **109.** $\dfrac{\ln\left(\dfrac{2}{3}\right)}{5}$
117. $f^{-1}(x) = \dfrac{x - 2}{3}$ **119.** 19   **121.** $5x^2 - 1$

Chapter Review

1. $5^{2\sqrt{2}}$ **2.** $2^{\sqrt{10}}$
3.

4.
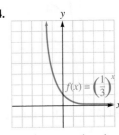
5. $p = 1, q = 7$ **6.** domain: $(-\infty, \infty)$; range: $(0, \infty)$
7.

8.

9.

10.

11.
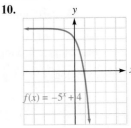
12.

13. \$2,189,703.45   **14.** \$2,324,767.37   **15.** $\dfrac{2}{3}$
16. 0.19 lumen   **17.** about 635,000,000   **18.** about 2,708
19. $(0, \infty)$; $(-\infty, \infty)$ **20.** $(0, \infty)$; $(-\infty, \infty)$ **21.** 2
22. $-\dfrac{1}{2}$ **23.** 0   **24.** -2 **25.** $\dfrac{1}{2}$ **26.** $\dfrac{1}{3}$ **27.** 32
28. 9   **29.** 8   **30.** -1 **31.** $\dfrac{1}{8}$ **32.** 2   **33.** 4
34. 2   **35.** 10   **36.** $\dfrac{1}{25}$ **37.** 5   **38.** 3
39.

40.

41.

42.

43. 6.1137   **44.** -0.1111 **45.** 10.3398   **46.** 2.5715

47.

48.

49. 12   **50.** $14x$ **51.** 53 dB   **52.** 4.4   **53.** $9\frac{1}{2}$ min

54. 23 yr   **55.** 2,017 joules   **56.** 0   **57.** 1   **58.** 3

59. 4   **60.** 4   **61.** 0   **62.** 7   **63.** 3   **64.** 4

65. 9   **66.** $2 \log_b x + 3 \log_b y - 4 \log_b z$

67. $\frac{1}{2}(\log_8 x - \log_8 y - 2 \log_8 z)$

68. $4 \ln x - 5 \ln y - 6 \ln z$ **69.** $\frac{1}{3}(\ln x + \ln y + \ln z)$

70. $\log_b \dfrac{x^3 z^7}{y^5}$ **71.** $\log_b \dfrac{\sqrt{xy^3}}{z^7}$ **72.** $\ln \dfrac{x^4}{y^5 z^6}$

73. $\ln \dfrac{y^3 \sqrt{x}}{\sqrt[5]{z}}$ **74.** 3.36   **75.** 1.56   **76.** 2.64

77. -6.72 **78.** 1.7604

79. about 7.94×10^{-4} gram-ions per liter   **80.** $k \ln 2$ less

81. $-\dfrac{5}{4}$ **82.** $-1, -3$ **83.** 2   **84.** $3, -3$

85. $\dfrac{\log 7}{\log 3} \approx 1.7712$ **86.** $\dfrac{\log 3}{\log 3 - \log 2} \approx 2.7095$

87. $\ln 8 \approx 2.0794$ **88.** $\ln 7 \approx 1.9459$ **89.** -3

90. 8   **91.** 25, 4   **92.** 4   **93.** 2   **94.** 4, 3   **95.** 6

96. 31   **97.** $\dfrac{\ln 9}{\ln 2} \approx 3.1699$ **98.** no solution

99. $e^7 \approx 1,096.6332$ **100.** $\dfrac{e}{e-1} \approx 1.5820$ **101.** 1

102. about 3,300 yr

Chapter Test

1.

2.

3. $\dfrac{3}{64}$ g   **4.** \$1,060.90   **5.** \$4,451.08   **6.** 3

7. -3 **8.** 17   **9.** 2   **10.** -3

11.

12.

13. $2 \log a + \log b + 3 \log c$ **14.** $\frac{1}{2}(\ln a - 2 \ln b - \ln c)$

15. $\log \dfrac{b\sqrt{a+2}}{c^2}$ **16.** $\ln \dfrac{\sqrt[3]{\dfrac{a}{b^2}}}{c}$ **17.** 1.3801

18. 0.4259   **19.** $\dfrac{\log 3}{\log 7}$ or $\dfrac{\ln 3}{\ln 7}$ **20.** $\dfrac{\log e}{\log \pi}$ or $\dfrac{1}{\ln \pi}$

21. true   **22.** false   **23.** 6.4   **24.** 46 dB   **25.** $-1, 3$

26. $\dfrac{\log 3}{\log 3 - 2} \approx -0.3133$ **27.** $\ln 9 \approx 2.1972$ **28.** 1

29. 10   **30.** 9

Section 5.1

1. whole   **3.** any   **5.** factor

7. $4x^2 + 2x + 1 + \dfrac{2}{x-1}$

9. $2x^3 - 3x^2 + 8x - 1 + \dfrac{-3}{x+2}$

11. -1 **13.** 9   **15.** 3   **17.** -3 **19.** 69

21. 70,249   **23.** 128.3085938   **25.** true   **27.** true

29. false   **31.** true   **33.** $(x-1)(3x^2 + x - 5) - 9$

35. $(x-3)(3x^2 + 7x + 15) + 41$

37. $(x+1)(3x^2 - 5x - 1) - 3$

39. $(x+3)(3x^2 - 11x + 27) - 85$

41. $x^2 + 2x + 3$ **43.** $7x^2 - 10x + 5 + \dfrac{-4}{x+1}$

45. $4x^3 + 9x^2 + 27x + 80 + \dfrac{245}{x-3}$

47. $3x^4 + 12x^3 + 48x^2 + 192x$ **49.** 47   **51.** -569

53. $-1 - 6i$ **55.** $\dfrac{15}{8}$ **57.** 5   **59.** 0   **61.** 384

63. $-28 - 16i$ **65.** $16 + 2i$ **67.** $40 - 40i$

69. $\{-1, -5, 3\}$ **71.** $\left\{-\dfrac{1}{2}, 3, -3\right\}$

73. $\left\{2, 2 + \sqrt{5}, 2 - \sqrt{5}\right\}$

75. $\left\{-3, 3 + \sqrt{10}i, 3 - \sqrt{10}i\right\}$

77. $\left\{1, 1, \sqrt{3}, -\sqrt{3}\right\}$ **79.** $\{2, 3, i, -i\}$

81. $P(x) = x^2 - 9x + 20$ **83.** $P(x) = x^3 - 3x^2 + 3x - 1$

85. $P(x) = x^3 - 11x^2 + 38x - 40$

87. $P(x) = x^4 - 3x^2 + 2$

89. $P(x) = x^3 - \sqrt{2}x^2 + x - \sqrt{2}$

91. $P(x) = x^3 - 2x^2 + 2x$ **93.** 0   **97.** QIV   **99.** QI

101. 10   **103.** 1

Section 5.2

1. zero   **3.** conjugate   **5.** 0   **7.** 2
9. lower bound   **11.** 10   **13.** 4   **15.** 4   **17.** 4, 4
19. 5, 5   **21.** $x^2 + 4 = 0$ **23.** $x^2 - 6x + 10 = 0$
25. $x^3 - 3x^2 + x - 3 = 0$
27. $x^3 - 6x^2 + 13x - 10 = 0$
29. $x^4 - 5x^3 + 7x^2 - 5x + 6 = 0$
31. $x^4 - 2x^3 + 3x^2 - 2x + 2 = 0$
33. $x^2 - 4xi - 4 = 0$
35. 0 or 2 positive; 1 negative; 0 or 2 nonreal
37. 0 positive; 1 or 3 negative; 0 or 2 nonreal
39. 0 positive; 0 negative; 4 nonreal
41. 1 positive; 1 negative; 2 nonreal
43. 0 positive; 0 negative; 10 nonreal
45. 0 positive; 0 negative; 8 nonreal; yes
47. 1 positive; 1 negative; 2 nonreal   **49.** $(-2, 4)$
51. $(-1, 1)$ **53.** $(-4, 6)$ **55.** $(-4, 3)$ **57.** $(-2, 4)$
63. k units to the right   **65.** reflected about the y-axis
67. stretched vertically by a factor of k

Section 5.3

1. -7 **3.** root   **5.** $\pm 1, \pm 2, \pm 3, \pm 4, \pm 6, \pm 12$
7. $\pm 1, \pm 2, \pm 3, \pm 6, \pm \dfrac{1}{2}, \pm \dfrac{3}{2}$
9. $\pm 1, \pm 2, \pm 5, \pm 10, \pm \dfrac{1}{2}, \pm \dfrac{5}{2}, \pm \dfrac{1}{4}, \pm \dfrac{5}{4}$
11. $1, -1, 5$ **13.** $1, 2, -1$ **15.** $1, 2, -2$ **17.** $3, -3, 2$
19. $1, -1, \dfrac{1}{2}$ **21.** $-1, -1, \dfrac{1}{3}$ **23.** $\dfrac{3}{2}, \dfrac{2}{3}, -\dfrac{3}{5}$
25. $\dfrac{2}{3}, -\dfrac{3}{5}, 4$ **27.** $\dfrac{3}{2}, \dfrac{2}{3}, \dfrac{5}{4}$ **29.** $1, 2, 3, 4$ **31.** $2, -5$
33. $1, -1, \dfrac{1}{2}, \dfrac{3}{2}$ **35.** $-2, \dfrac{5}{2}$ **37.** $\dfrac{1}{3}, -\dfrac{1}{2}$
39. $1, -1, 2, -2, -3$ **41.** $3, \dfrac{1}{2}, -\dfrac{1}{2}$
43. $0, 2, 2, 2, -2, -2, -2$ **45.** $3, \sqrt{2}, -\sqrt{2}$
47. $\dfrac{1}{2}, i, -i$ **49.** $2, -2, 1 + \sqrt{5}, 1 - \sqrt{5}$
51. $\dfrac{1}{2}, -1, 3i, -3i$ **53.** $1, 1, 1, 5i, -5i$
55. $\dfrac{3}{2}, 1, -1, 2i, -2i$ **57.** $3, 1 - i$ **59.** $3, -3, 1 - i$
61. $-\dfrac{2}{3}, 3, -1$ **63.** $\dfrac{1}{2}, \dfrac{1}{2}, \dfrac{1}{2}, 1, 1$ **65.** 10, 20, 60 ohms
67. 13 in.   **69.** 1, 5, and 9 miles
73. $(3, 7)$ or approx. $(1.54, 13.63)$ **75.** $6ab^2\sqrt{2abc}$
77. $8a\sqrt{2b}$ **79.** $\sqrt{3} + 1$

Section 5.4

1. $P(a)$ and $P(b)$ **3.** x_l and x_r
9. $P(-2) = 3$; $P(-1) = -2$ The signs of the results are opposites.
11. $P(4) = -40$; $P(5) = 30$ The signs of the results are opposites.
13. $P(1) = 8$; $P(2) = -1$ The signs of the results are opposites.

15. $P(2) = -72$; $P(3) = 154$ The signs of the results are opposites.
17. $P(0) = 10$; $P(1) = -60$ The signs of the results are opposites.
19. 1.7   **21.** -2.2 **23.** 1.7   **25.** -1.2 **27.** $-2.2, 2.2$
29. 1, 2; The Bisection Method fails to find the solution 2.
31. yes   **33.** $(0.83, 0.56), (-0.83, -0.56)$
37. vertical: $x = 2, x = -2$; horizontal: $y = 0$; slant: none
39. vertical: $x = 2$; horizontal: none; slant: $y = x + 2$

Chapter Review

1. 1   **2.** 66   **3.** 241   **4.** 34   **5.** false   **6.** false
7. true   **8.** true   **9.** $3x^3 + 9x^2 + 29x + 90 + \dfrac{277}{x - 3}$
10. $2x^3 + 4x^2 + 5x + 13 + \dfrac{25}{x - 2}$
11. $5x^4 - 14x^3 + 31x^2 - 64x + 129 + \dfrac{-259}{x + 2}$
12. $4x^4 - 2x^3 + x^2 + 2x + \dfrac{1}{x + 1}$ **13.** 151   **14.** -113
15. $\dfrac{13}{8}$ **16.** $-1 - 6i$ **17.** $\left\{3, \dfrac{1}{2}, -2\right\}$
18. $\left\{-2, -2, \sqrt{5}, -\sqrt{5}\right\}$
19. $P(x) = 2x^3 - 5x^2 - x + 6$
20. $P(x) = 2x^3 + 3x^2 - 8x + 3$
21. $P(x) = x^4 + 3x^3 - 9x^2 + 3x - 10$
22. $P(x) = x^4 + x^3 - 5x^2 + x - 6$ **23.** 6   **24.** 6
25. 65   **26.** 1,984   **27.** 4, 4   **28.** 40, 40   **29.** 5, 5
30. 3, 3   **31.** $2 - i$ **32.** i
33. $x^3 - 4x^2 + x - 4 = 0$ **34.** $x^3 + 5x^2 + x + 5 = 0$
35. 0 or 2 positive; 0 or 2 negative; 0, 2, or 4 nonreal
36. 1 or 3 positive; 1 negative; 0 or 2 nonreal
37. 1 positive; 0, 2, or 4 negative; 0, 2, or 4 nonreal
38. 1 or 3 positive; 0 or 2 negative; 2, 4, or 6 nonreal
39. 0 positive; 0 negative; 4 nonreal
40. 0 positive; 1 negative; 6 nonreal
41. $(-1, 2)$ **42.** $(-5, 2)$ **43.** $\pm 1, \pm 2, \pm 3, \pm 6, \pm \dfrac{1}{2}, \pm \dfrac{3}{2}$
44. $\pm 1, \pm 2, \pm 5, \pm 10, \pm \dfrac{1}{2}, \pm \dfrac{5}{2}, \pm \dfrac{1}{4}, \pm \dfrac{5}{4}$ **45.** 1, 4, 5
46. $1, -1, 8$ **47.** $-5, -\dfrac{3}{2}, -2$ **48.** $\dfrac{1}{3}$
49. $2, -2, \dfrac{3}{2}, -\dfrac{3}{2}$ **50.** $4, 4, -2, -\dfrac{1}{2}$ **51.** $\dfrac{1}{3}, 4i, -4i$
52. $2, -2, 1 + \sqrt{6}, 1 - \sqrt{6}$ **53.** $P(-1) = -9$; $P(0) = 18$
54. $P(1) = -8$; $P(2) = 21$ **55.** 4.2   **56.** 2.5
57. 1.67   **58.** 0.67
59. 10 m by 6 m; 12 m by 5 m; 15 m by 4 m   **60.** 17.27 ft

Chapter Test

1. yes   **2.** 1   **3.** -30 **4.** no
5. $(x - 2)(2x^2 + x - 2) - 5$
6. $(x + 1)(2x^2 - 5x + 1) - 2$ **7.** $2x + 3$ **8.** $3x^2 + x$
9. 5   **10.** -28 **11.** $\dfrac{11}{3}$ **12.** $6 - 3i$
13. $P(x) = x^3 - 4x^2 - 5x$ **14.** $P(x) = x^4 - 2x^2 - 3$
15. $x^3 - 2x^2 + x - 2 = 0$ **16.** $x^3 - 5x^2 + 9x - 5 = 0$
17. 3, 3   **18.** $3 + 2i$

19. 1 or 3 positive; 0 or 2 negative; 0, 2, or 4 nonreal
20. 1 positive; 0 or 2 negative; 0 or 2 nonreal   **21.** $(-3, 3)$
22. $(-1, 6)$

23. $\pm 1, \pm 2, \pm 4, \pm 8$ **24.** $\pm 1, \pm 2, \pm\frac{1}{5}, \pm\frac{2}{5}$

25. $2, -3, -\frac{1}{2}$ **26.** $2, i, -i$ **27.** $2, -3, 3i, -3i$

28. $1, -1, -2, 2i, -2i$ **29.** no   **30.** 3.3

Cumulative Review

1.

2.

$f(x) = 3^x - 2$

$f(x) = 2e^x$

3.

4.

$f(x) = \log_3 x$

$f(x) = \ln(x - 2)$

5. 6   **6.** -3 **7.** 3   **8.** 2
9. $\log a + \log b + \log c$ **10.** $2\log a + \log b - \log c$
11. $\frac{1}{2}(\log a + \log b - 3\log c)$ **12.** $\frac{1}{2}\ln a + \ln b - \ln c$
13. $\ln\dfrac{a^3}{b^3}$ **14.** $\log\dfrac{\sqrt{ab^3}}{\sqrt[3]{c^2}}$ **15.** $x = \dfrac{\log 8}{\log 3} - 1$
16. $x = -1$ **17.** $x = 500$ **18.** $x = \sqrt{11}$ **19.** 9
20. -36 **21.** 4   **22.** $2 - i$ **23.** a factor
24. not a factor   **25.** a factor   **26.** a factor   **27.** 12
28. 2,000   **29.** 2 or 0 positive; 2 or 0 negative; 4, 2, or 0
nonreal   **30.** 1 positive; 3 or 1 negative; 2 or 0 nonreal
31. $-1, -3, 3$ **32.** $-1, 1, 2$

Section 6.1

1. system   **3.** consistent   **5.** independent
7. consistent   **9.** dependent   **11.** is
13.

$x = 1$
$y = -3x + 5$
$y = 2$
$(1, 2)$
$x - 2y = -3$

15.

$x = -2$
$y = 4$
$(-2, 4)$
$3x + 2y = 2$
$-2x + 3y = 16$

17.

no solution;
inconsistent system
$\begin{cases} y = -x + 5 \\ 3x + 3y = 30 \end{cases}$

19.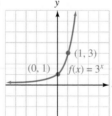

dependent equations;
infinite number
of solutions
$\begin{cases} y = -x + 6 \\ 5x + 5y = 30 \end{cases}$

21. $(2.2, -4.7)$ **23.** $(1.7, 0.3)$ **25.** $(-1, -2)$
27. $(3, -2)$ **29.** $\left(\frac{1}{2}, \frac{1}{3}\right)$ **31.** no solution; inconsistent
system   **33.** dependent equations; a general solution is
$(x, 3x - 6)$ **35.** $(3, 1)$ **37.** $(3, 2)$ **39.** $(-3, 0)$
41. $\left(1, -\frac{1}{2}\right)$ **43.** dependent equations; a general solution
is $(x, 5 - 2x)$ **45.** no solution; inconsistent system
47. $(4, -7)$ **49.** $(2, -3)$ **51.** $(9, -1)$ **53.** $(1, 2, 0)$
55. $\left(0, -\frac{1}{3}, -\frac{1}{3}\right)$ **57.** $(1, 2, -1)$ **59.** $(1, 0, 5)$
61. no solution; inconsistent system   **63.** $(0, 1, 0)$
65. $\left(\frac{2}{3}, \frac{1}{4}, \frac{1}{2}\right)$ **67.** $\left(\frac{1}{2}, \frac{1}{2}, \frac{1}{2}\right)$
69. dependent equations; a general solution is $(x, 2 - x, 1)$
71. hamburger \$2; fries \$1
73. 225 acres of corn; 125 acres of soybeans   **75.** 8 kph
77. 40 g and 20 g   **79.** 10 ft
81. $E(x) = 43.53x + 742.72$, $R(x) = 89.95x$; 16 pairs/day
83. 15 hr cooking hamburgers, 10 hr pumping gas, 5 hr
janitorial   **85.** 1.05 million in 0−14 group, 1.56 million in
15−49 group, 0.39 million in 50-and-older group
87. 30°, 50°, 100°
95.

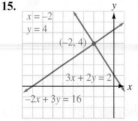

$(1, 3)$
$(0, 1)$ $f(x) = 3^x$

97. 8   **99.** $\log x - 2\log y - \log z$ **101.** $\log\dfrac{xy^3}{\sqrt{z}}$

Section 6.2

1. matrix   **3.** coefficient   **5.** equation
7. row equivalent   **9.** interchanged
11. adding, multiple   **13.** $(2, 3)$ **15.** $(7, 6)$
17. $(1, 2, 3)$ **19.** $(1, 1, 3)$ **21.** row echelon form
23. reduced row echelon form   **25.** $(2, -1)$
27. $(-2, 0)$ **29.** $(3, 1)$
31. no solution; inconsistent system   **33.** $(0, -7)$
35. $(1, 0, 2)$ **37.** $(2, -2, 1)$ **39.** $(1, 1, 2)$
41. dependent equations; a general solution is
$\left(x, -x + \frac{7}{2}, -\frac{3}{2}\right)$ **43.** no solution; inconsistent system
45. $(13, 3)$ **47.** $(-13, 7, -2)$ **49.** $(10, 3)$
51. $(0, 0)$ **53.** $(3, 1, -2)$ **55.** $\left(\frac{1}{4}, 1, \frac{1}{4}\right)$

57. $(1, 2, 1, 1)$ **59.** $(1, 2, 0, 1)$ **61.** $\left(\dfrac{9}{4}, -3, \dfrac{3}{4}\right)$

63. $\left(0, \dfrac{20}{3}, -\dfrac{1}{3}\right)$ **65.** dependent equations; a general

solution is $\left(x, \dfrac{1}{2}x - 3, 0\right)$ **67.** $(1, -3)$

69. dependent equations; a general solution is

$\left(\dfrac{8}{7} + \dfrac{1}{7}z, \dfrac{10}{7} - \dfrac{4}{7}z, z\right)$ **71.** dependent equations; a general

solution is $(1 + z, -z, -1 - z, z)$

73. no solution; inconsistent system   **75.** 1,300 mi
77. Dictionaries 4.5 in; atlases 3.5 in; thesauruses 4 in
79. 2 niacin, 4 zinc, 6 vitamin C
85. $x = \pm 2; y = \pm 1; z = \pm 3$ **87.** $y = mx + b$
89. equal   **91.** $y = 2x + 7$ **93.** $x = 2$

Section 6.3

1. i, j **3.** corresponding   **5.** columns, rows
7. additive identity   **9.** $x = 2, y = 5$ **11.** $x = 1, y = 2$

13. $\begin{bmatrix} -1 & 2 & 1 \\ -6 & 0 & 0 \end{bmatrix}$ **15.** $\begin{bmatrix} -5 & 2 & -7 \\ 5 & 0 & -3 \\ 2 & -3 & 5 \end{bmatrix}$

17. $\begin{bmatrix} -6 & 5 & 0 \\ 1 & -1 & 0 \end{bmatrix}$ **19.** $\begin{bmatrix} 15 & -15 \\ 0 & -10 \end{bmatrix}$

21. $\begin{bmatrix} 25 & 75 & -10 \\ -10 & -25 & 5 \end{bmatrix}$ **23.** $\begin{bmatrix} 18 & -1 & -4 \\ -35 & 0 & -1 \end{bmatrix}$

25. $\begin{bmatrix} 2 & -2 \\ 3 & 10 \end{bmatrix}$ **27.** $\begin{bmatrix} -22 & -22 \\ -105 & 126 \end{bmatrix}$

29. $\begin{bmatrix} 4 & 2 & 10 \\ 5 & -2 & 4 \\ 2 & -2 & 1 \end{bmatrix}$ **31.** $\begin{bmatrix} 4 & -5 & -6 \\ -8 & 10 & 12 \\ -12 & 15 & 18 \end{bmatrix}$

33. not possible   **35.** $\begin{bmatrix} 16 \\ 12 \\ 12 \end{bmatrix}$ **37.** not possible

39. $\begin{bmatrix} -36.29 \\ 16.2 \\ -19.26 \end{bmatrix}$ **41.** $\begin{bmatrix} -16.11 & 4.71 & 33.64 \\ -19.6 & 20.35 & 6.4 \\ -100.6 & 72.82 & 62.71 \end{bmatrix}$

47. $\begin{bmatrix} 4 & 5 \\ -7 & -1 \end{bmatrix}$ **49.** not possible

51. $\begin{bmatrix} 24 & 16 \\ 39 & 26 \end{bmatrix}$ **53.** $\begin{bmatrix} 47 \\ 81 \end{bmatrix}$

55. $QC = \begin{bmatrix} 2,000 \\ 1,700 \end{bmatrix}$ The cost to Supplier 1 is $2,000. The cost to Supplier 2 is $1,700.

57. $QP = \begin{bmatrix} 584.50 \\ 709.25 \\ 1,036.75 \end{bmatrix}$ Adult males spent $584.50. Adult females spent $709.25. Children spent $1,036.75.

59. $\begin{bmatrix} 1 & 1 & 0 \\ 0 & 1 & 1 \\ 1 & 0 & 0 \end{bmatrix}$

61. $A^2 = \begin{bmatrix} 5 & 1 & 2 & 2 \\ 1 & 5 & 2 & 2 \\ 2 & 2 & 6 & 0 \\ 2 & 2 & 0 & 4 \end{bmatrix}$ indicates the number of ways two cities can be linked with exactly one intermediate city to relay messages.

63. No; if $A = \begin{bmatrix} 1 & 1 \\ 1 & 1 \end{bmatrix}$ and $B = \begin{bmatrix} 1 & 0 \\ 0 & 0 \end{bmatrix}$, then $(AB)^2 \neq A^2B^2$.

65. Let $A = \begin{bmatrix} 1 & 2 \\ 1 & 2 \end{bmatrix}$ and $B = \begin{bmatrix} 2 & 2 \\ -1 & -1 \end{bmatrix}$. Neither is the zero matrix, yet $AB = 0$.

67. $6x^2 - 4x - 8$ **69.** $\dfrac{x+1}{x-1}$ **71.** $a = \dfrac{2s}{n} - l$

Section 6.4

1. $AB = BA = I$ **3.** $[I \mid A^{-1}]$ **5.** $\begin{bmatrix} 3 & 4 \\ 2 & 3 \end{bmatrix}$

7. $\begin{bmatrix} 5 & -7 \\ -2 & 3 \end{bmatrix}$ **9.** $\begin{bmatrix} -2 & 3 & -3 \\ -5 & 7 & -6 \\ 1 & -1 & 1 \end{bmatrix}$

11. $\begin{bmatrix} 4 & 1 & -3 \\ -5 & -1 & 4 \\ -1 & -1 & 1 \end{bmatrix}$ **13.** no inverse

15. $\begin{bmatrix} 1 & -2 & 1 \\ 0 & 1 & -2 \\ 0 & 0 & 1 \end{bmatrix}$ **17.** no inverse

19. $\begin{bmatrix} 1 & -2 & 1 & 0 \\ 0 & 1 & -2 & 1 \\ 0 & 0 & 1 & -2 \\ 0 & 0 & 0 & 1 \end{bmatrix}$ **21.** $\begin{bmatrix} 8 & -2 & -6 \\ -5 & 2 & 4 \\ 2 & 0 & -2 \end{bmatrix}$

23. $\begin{bmatrix} -2.5 & 5 & 3 & 5.5 \\ 5.5 & -8 & -6 & -9.5 \\ -1 & 3 & 1 & 3 \\ -5.5 & 9 & 6 & 10.5 \end{bmatrix}$

25. $x = 23, y = 17$ **27.** $x = 0, y = 0$
29. $x = 1, y = 2, z = 2$ **31.** $x = 54, y = -37, z = -49$
33. $x = 2, y = 1$ **35.** $x = 1, y = 2, z = 1$
37. 2 of model A, 3 of model B   **39.** hi   **41.** no

45. $X = \begin{bmatrix} 0 \\ 0 \\ 0 \\ 0 \end{bmatrix}$ **51.** $(-\infty, -2) \cup (-2, 2) \cup (2, \infty)$

53. $(-\infty, \infty)$ **55.** $[0, \infty)$ **57.** $(-\infty, \infty)$

Section 6.5

1. $|A|$, $\det(A)$ **3.** 0   **5.** 0   **7.** 8   **9.** 1
11. -42 **13.** 13   **15.** 42   **17.** 13   **19.** -54
21. -7 **23.** 86   **25.** -2 **27.** 2   **29.** 120
31. true   **33.** false   **35.** 3   **37.** 3   **39.** $(1, 2)$
41. $(3, 0)$ **43.** $(1, 0, 1)$ **45.** $(1, -1, 2)$ **47.** $(6, 6, 12)$
49. $\left(\dfrac{5}{6}, \dfrac{2}{3}, \dfrac{1}{2}, \dfrac{5}{2}\right)$ **51.** $3x - 2y = 0$ **53.** $6x + 7y = 9$
55. 30 sq. units   **57.** 73 sq. units   **63.** 8   **65.** -1
67. $5,000 in HiTech, $8,000 in SaveTel, $7,000 in OilCo
69. 10   **71.** 24   **73.** 8
77. domain: $n \times n$ matrices; range: all real numbers
79. yes   **81.** 21.468   **83.** $(x - 1)(x + 4)$

85. $x(3x + 1)(3x - 1)$ **87.** $\dfrac{4x - 5}{(x - 2)(2x - 1)}$

89. $\dfrac{x^2 + 2x + 1}{x(x^2 + 1)}$

Section 6.6

1. first-degree; second-degree   **3.** $\dfrac{1}{x} + \dfrac{2}{x - 1}$

5. $\dfrac{5}{x} - \dfrac{3}{x - 3}$ **7.** $\dfrac{1}{x + 1} + \dfrac{2}{x - 1}$ **9.** $\dfrac{2}{x} - \dfrac{2}{x - 2}$

11. $\dfrac{1}{x - 3} - \dfrac{3}{x + 2}$ **13.** $\dfrac{8}{x + 3} - \dfrac{5}{x - 1}$

15. $\dfrac{5}{2x - 3} + \dfrac{2}{x - 5}$ **17.** $\dfrac{2}{x} + \dfrac{3}{x - 1} - \dfrac{1}{x + 1}$

19. $\dfrac{1}{x} + \dfrac{1}{x^2 + 3}$ **21.** $\dfrac{3}{x + 1} + \dfrac{2}{x^2 + 2x + 3}$

23. $\dfrac{3}{x} + \dfrac{2}{x + 1} + \dfrac{1}{(x + 1)^2}$ **25.** $\dfrac{1}{x} + \dfrac{2}{x^2} - \dfrac{3}{x - 1}$

27. $\dfrac{2}{x} + \dfrac{1}{x - 3} + \dfrac{2}{(x - 3)^2}$ **29.** $\dfrac{1}{x - 1} - \dfrac{4}{(x - 1)^3}$

31. $\dfrac{1}{x} + \dfrac{1}{x^2} + \dfrac{2}{x^2 + x + 1}$ **33.** $\dfrac{3}{x} + \dfrac{4}{x^2} + \dfrac{x + 1}{x^2 + 1}$

35. $-\dfrac{1}{x + 1} - \dfrac{3}{x^2 + 2}$ **37.** $\dfrac{x + 1}{x^2 + 2} + \dfrac{2}{x^2 + x + 2}$

39. $\dfrac{1}{x} + \dfrac{x}{x^2 + 2x + 5} + \dfrac{x + 2}{(x^2 + 2x + 5)^2}$

41. $x - 3 - \dfrac{1}{x + 1} + \dfrac{8}{x + 2}$ **43.** $1 + \dfrac{2}{3x + 1} + \dfrac{1}{x^2 + 1}$

45. $1 + \dfrac{1}{x} + \dfrac{x}{x^2 + x + 1}$ **47.** $2 + \dfrac{1}{x} + \dfrac{3}{x - 1} + \dfrac{2}{x^2 + 1}$

49. No, it's the sum of two cubes.   **51.** $2|a|\sqrt{2ab}$

53. $3x^2\sqrt{2x}$ **55.** $x = 9$

Section 6.7

1. half-plane; boundary   **3.** is not

5.

7.

9.

11.

13.

15.

17.

19.

21.

23.

25.

27.

29.

31.

33.

35.

37.

39.

41.

43.
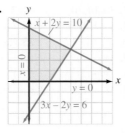

45. $\begin{cases} 6s + 4l \le 60 \\ s \ge 0 \\ l \ge 0 \end{cases}$ **53.** one; one   **55.** 0

Section 6.8
1. constraints   **3.** objective   **5.** $P = 12$ at $(0, 4)$
7. $P = \dfrac{13}{6}$ at $\left(\dfrac{5}{3}, \dfrac{4}{3}\right)$ **9.** $P = \dfrac{18}{7}$ at $\left(\dfrac{3}{7}, \dfrac{12}{7}\right)$
11. $P = 3$ at $(1, 0)$ **13.** $P = 0$ at $(0, 0)$
15. $P = 0$ at $(0, 0)$ **17.** $P = -12$ at $(-2, 0)$
19. $P = -2$ at the edge joining $(1, 2)$ and $(-1, 0)$
21. 3 tables, 12 chairs; $1,260
23. 30 IBMs, 30 Apple; $2,700
25. 15 DVRs, 30 TVs; $1,560
27. $150,000 in stocks, $50,000 in bonds; $17,000
29. 2 buses, 2 trucks; $1,100
33. $\begin{bmatrix} 1 & 0 & 0 \\ 0 & 1 & 0 \\ 0 & 0 & 1 \\ 0 & 0 & 0 \end{bmatrix}$ **35.** $\left(\dfrac{1}{3} - 3y, y, -\dfrac{1}{3}\right)$

Chapter Review
1.

2.

3.

4.

dependent equations; infinite number of solutions
$\begin{cases} 3x + 2y = 6 \\ y = -\dfrac{3}{2}x + 3 \end{cases}$
a general solution is $\left(x, -\dfrac{3}{2}x + 3\right)$

5.

no solution; inconsistent system
$\begin{cases} 4x - y = 4 \\ y = 4(x - 2) \end{cases}$

6. $x = 2, y = -1$ **7.** $x = 0, y = -3$ **8.** $x = 1, y = 1$
9. dependent equations; a general solution is $(x, 3x - 4)$
10. no solution; inconsistent system   **11.** $x = -3, y = 2$
12. $x = -2, y = 5$ **13.** $x = 2, y = -1$
14. no solution; inconsistent system   **15.** dependent
equations; a general solution is $(x, 3x - 4)$
16. $x = 1, y = 0, z = 1$ **17.** $x = 1, y = 1, z = -1$
18. $x = 0, y = 1, z = 2$ **19.** $10,400
20. 900 adult tickets, 450 senior tickets, 450 children's tickets
21. $x = 1, y = 1$ **22.** dependent equations; a general
solution is $(x, 3x + 4)$ **23.** $x = 3, y = 1, z = -2$
24. $x = -10, y = 1, z = 10$
25. no solution; inconsistent system
26. $x = -4, y = 3$ **27.** $\begin{bmatrix} 1 & 3 & 4 \\ 4 & 0 & 2 \end{bmatrix}$
28. $\begin{bmatrix} 2 & 5 & 4 \\ -2 & -6 & 6 \\ -4 & 5 & -3 \end{bmatrix}$ **29.** $\begin{bmatrix} 4 & -1 \\ -7 & -7 \end{bmatrix}$
30. $\begin{bmatrix} -17 & 19 \\ 10 & -12 \end{bmatrix}$ **31.** $[5]$ **32.** $\begin{bmatrix} 2 & -1 & 1 & 3 \\ 4 & -2 & 2 & 6 \\ 2 & -1 & 1 & 3 \\ 10 & -5 & 5 & 15 \end{bmatrix}$
33. not possible   **34.** $[-24]$ **35.** $\begin{bmatrix} 0 \\ -6 \end{bmatrix}$
36. $\begin{bmatrix} 5 & -3 \\ -3 & 2 \end{bmatrix}$ **37.** $\begin{bmatrix} 1 & 0 & 0 \\ -\dfrac{3}{2} & \dfrac{1}{2} & \dfrac{1}{2} \\ 1 & -\dfrac{1}{2} & 0 \end{bmatrix}$
38. $\begin{bmatrix} 9 & 16 & -56 \\ -3 & -5 & 18 \\ -1 & -2 & 7 \end{bmatrix}$ **39.** No inverse exists.
40. No inverse exists.   **41.** $x = 1, y = 2, z = -1$
42. $w = 1, x = 1, y = 0, z = -1$ **43.** -7 **44.** -6
45. 3   **46.** -25 **47.** $x = 1, y = -2$
48. $x = 1, y = 0, z = -2$ **49.** $x = 1, y = -1, z = 3$
50. $w = 1, x = 0, y = -1, z = 2$ **51.** 21   **52.** 7
53. $\dfrac{3}{x} + \dfrac{4}{x + 1}$ **54.** $\dfrac{3}{x} + \dfrac{2}{x^2} + \dfrac{x - 1}{x^2 + 1}$
55. $\dfrac{1}{x} - \dfrac{1}{x^2 + x + 5}$ **56.** $\dfrac{1}{x + 1} - \dfrac{2}{(x + 1)^2} + \dfrac{2}{(x + 1)^3}$
57.

58.

59.
(image)

60.
(image)

61. $P = 6$ at $(3,0)$ **62.** $P = 12$ at $(0, -4)$

63. $P = 2$ at $(1,1)$ **64.** $P = 3$ at $\left(-\dfrac{2}{3}, \dfrac{5}{3}\right)$

65. 1,000 bags of x, 1,400 bags of y

Chapter Test

1.

2.

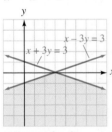

3. $x = 1, y = -3$ **4.** $x = 3, y = 5$
5. 6 liters of 20% solution, 4 liters of 45% solution
6. CD World 100 units, Ace 25 units, Hi-Fi 50 units
7. $x = 2, y = 1$ **8.** $x = 1, y = 2, z = 1$
9. $x = 1, y = 0, z = -2$

10. $x = -\dfrac{2}{5}y + \dfrac{7}{5}$, $z = -\dfrac{8}{5}y - \dfrac{7}{5}$, $y = $ any number

11. $\begin{bmatrix} 16 & -14 & 20 \\ 0 & -6 & -13 \end{bmatrix}$ **12.** $[-1]$ **13.** $\begin{bmatrix} -\dfrac{7}{3} & \dfrac{19}{3} \\ \dfrac{2}{3} & -\dfrac{5}{3} \end{bmatrix}$

14. $\begin{bmatrix} -13 & -3 & 14 \\ 4 & 1 & -4 \\ 12 & 3 & -13 \end{bmatrix}$ **15.** $x = \dfrac{17}{3}, y = -\dfrac{4}{3}$

16. $x = -36, y = 11, z = 34$ **17.** -12 **18.** -24

19. $-\dfrac{5}{4}$ **20.** 1   **21.** $\dfrac{3}{2x - 3} + \dfrac{1}{x + 1}$

22. $\dfrac{1}{x} + \dfrac{2x + 1}{x^2 + 2}$

23.

24.

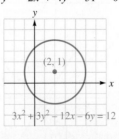

25. $P = 7$ at $(1, 2)$ **26.** $P = -8$ at $(8, 0)$

Section 7.1
1. $2, -5, 3$ **3.** $0, 0, \sqrt{5}$ **5.** to the left
7. downward   **9.** directrix, focus   **11.** circle
13. parabola   **15.** $x^2 + y^2 = 49, x^2 + y^2 - 49 = 0$
17. $(x - 2)^2 + (y + 2)^2 = 17, x^2 + y^2 - 4x + 4y - 9 = 0$
19. $(x - 1)^2 + (y + 2)^2 = 36, x^2 + y^2 - 2x + 4y - 31 = 0$
21.

23.

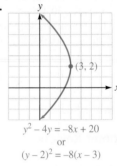

25. $(0, 0), (0, 3), y = -3$ **27.** $(0, 3), (5, 3), x = -5$
29. $(-2, 1), (-2, -5), y = 7$ **31.** $x^2 = 12y$
33. $y^2 = -12x$ **35.** $(x - 3)^2 = -12(y - 5)$
37. $(x - 3)^2 = -28(y - 5)$ **39.** $x^2 = -4(y - 2)$
41. $(y + 5)^2 = 8(x - 1)$
43. $(y - 2)^2 = -2(x - 2)$ or $(x - 2)^2 = -2(y - 2)$
45. $(x + 4)^2 = -\dfrac{16}{3}(y - 6)$ or $(y - 6)^2 = \dfrac{9}{4}(x + 4)$
47. $(y - 8)^2 = -4(x - 6)$ **49.** $(x - 3)^2 = \dfrac{1}{2}(y - 1)$
51.

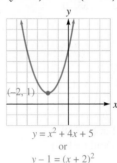

$y = x^2 + 4x + 5$
or
$y - 1 = (x + 2)^2$

53.

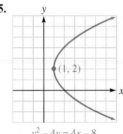

$y^2 + 4x - 6y = -1$
or
$(y - 3)^2 = -4(x - 2)$

55.

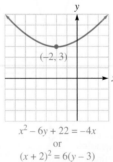

$y^2 - 4y = 4x - 8$
or
$(y - 2)^2 = 4(x - 1)$

57.

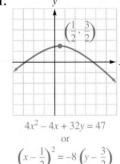

$y^2 - 4y = -8x + 20$
or
$(y - 2)^2 = -8(x - 3)$

59.

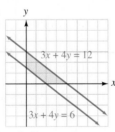

$x^2 - 6y + 22 = -4x$
or
$(x + 2)^2 = 6(y - 3)$

61.

$4x^2 - 4x + 32y = 47$
or
$\left(x - \dfrac{1}{2}\right)^2 = -8\left(y - \dfrac{3}{2}\right)$

63.

65. yes   **67.** 60 mi   **69.** $(x - 4)^2 + y^2 = 16$

71. $(x - 7)^2 + y^2 = 9$ **73.** 2 ft   **75.** $x^2 = -\dfrac{45}{2}y$

77. 1 ft   **79.** 300 ft   **81.** about 12.6 cm
83. about 520 ft   **85.** $0x^2 + 0xy + y^2 - 8x - 4y + 12 = 0$
87. $x^2 + (y - 3)^2 = 25$ **89.** $y = x^2 + 4x + 3$ **93.** 4

95. $\dfrac{49}{4}$ **97.** $x = 1, -5$ **99.** $x = -2, 9$

Section 7.2

1. sum, constant   **3.** vertices   **5.** $a, 0; -a, 0$

7. 26-in string; thumbtacks 24 in. apart   **9.** circle

11. parabola   **13.** ellipse   **15.** $\dfrac{x^2}{16} + \dfrac{y^2}{9} = 1$

17. $\dfrac{x^2}{25} + \dfrac{y^2}{16} = 1$ **19.** $\dfrac{9x^2}{16} + \dfrac{9y^2}{25} = 1$

21. $\dfrac{x^2}{7} + \dfrac{y^2}{16} = 1$ **23.** $\dfrac{(x-3)^2}{4} + \dfrac{(y-4)^2}{9} = 1$

25. $\dfrac{(x-3)^2}{9} + \dfrac{(y-4)^2}{4} = 1$

27. $\dfrac{(x-3)^2}{41} + \dfrac{(y-4)^2}{16} = 1$ **29.** $\dfrac{x^2}{36} + \dfrac{(y-4)^2}{20} = 1$

31. $\dfrac{x^2}{100} + \dfrac{y^2}{64} = 1$

33.   **35.**

37.   **39.**

41. $\dfrac{x^2}{4} + \dfrac{(y-1)^2}{16} = 1$ **43.** $\dfrac{(x+1)^2}{4} + \dfrac{(y+2)^2}{9} = 1$

45.   **47.**

49.   **51.** $\dfrac{x^2}{900} + \dfrac{y^2}{400} = 1$

53. $\dfrac{x^2}{2,500} + \dfrac{y^2}{900} = 1$; 36 m   **55.** about 20.8 in.

57. 199,395 mi   **63.** $\dfrac{x^2}{9} + \dfrac{y^2}{8} = 1$

67. 4 of the 75 planets shown have eccentricity 0.

69. $\begin{bmatrix} 1 & 3 \\ 1 & 1 \\ -3 & 1 \end{bmatrix}$ **71.** $\begin{bmatrix} -2 & 4 \\ 2 & 2 \\ -4 & 5 \end{bmatrix}$

Section 7.3

1. difference, constant   **3.** $a, 0; -a, 0$ **5.** transverse axis

7. circle   **9.** parabola   **11.** ellipse   **13.** hyperbola

15. $\dfrac{x^2}{25} - \dfrac{y^2}{24} = 1$ **17.** $\dfrac{(x-2)^2}{4} - \dfrac{(y-4)^2}{9} = 1$

19. $\dfrac{(y-3)^2}{9} - \dfrac{(x-5)^2}{9} = 1$ **21.** $\dfrac{y^2}{9} - \dfrac{x^2}{16} = 1$

23. $\dfrac{(x-1)^2}{4} - \dfrac{(y-4)^2}{32} = 1$ **25.** $\dfrac{x^2}{10} - \dfrac{3y^2}{20} = 1$

27. 24 sq. units   **29.** 12 sq. units

31. $\dfrac{(x+2)^2}{4} - \dfrac{4(y+4)^2}{81} = 1$ or $\dfrac{(y+4)^2}{4} - \dfrac{4(x+2)^2}{81} = 1$

33. $\dfrac{x^2}{36} - \dfrac{16y^2}{25} = 1$

35.   **37.**

39.   **41.**

43.   **45.**

47.   **49.**

51. $\dfrac{(x-3)^2}{9} - \dfrac{(y-1)^2}{16} = 1$ **53.** $4x^2 - 5y^2 - 60y = 0$

55.   **57.** 24   **59.** 3 units

61. hyperbola; $\dfrac{x^2}{144} - \dfrac{y^2}{25} = 1$

63. hyperbola; $\dfrac{x^2}{36} - \dfrac{y^2}{64} = 1$

69. $f^{-1}(x) = \dfrac{x+2}{3}$ **71.** $f^{-1}(x) = \dfrac{2x}{5-x}$

73. $f(g(x)) = (x+1)^4 + 1$

75. $f(f(x)) = (x^2+1)^2 + 1$

Section 7.4

1. graphs

3.

5.

7.

9.

11.

13. $(1, 2), (-1, 0)$ **15.** $(1, 0.67), (-1, -0.67)$

17. $(3, 0), (0, 5)$ **19.** $(1, 1)$ **21.** $(1, 2), (2, 1)$

23. $(-2, 3), (2, 3)$ **25.** $\left(\sqrt{5}, 5\right), \left(-\sqrt{5}, 5\right)$

27. $\left(\sqrt{3}, 0\right), \left(-\sqrt{3}, 0\right)$

29. $(2, 4), (2, -4), (-2, 4), (-2, -4)$

31. $\left(-\sqrt{15}, 5\right), \left(\sqrt{15}, 5\right), (-2, -6), (2, -6)$

33. $(0, -4), (-3, 5), (3, 5)$

35. $(-2, 3), (2, 3), (-2, -3), (2, -3)$

37. $(3, 3)$ **39.** $(6, 2), (-6, -2), \left(\sqrt{42}, 0\right), \left(-\sqrt{42}, 0\right)$

41. $\left(\dfrac{1}{2}, \dfrac{1}{3}\right), \left(\dfrac{1}{3}, \dfrac{1}{2}\right)$ **43.** 7 cm by 9 cm

45. 80 ft by 100 ft or 50 ft by 160 ft

47. either \$750 at 9% or \$900 at 7.5%

49. $(30, 3)$ **51.** yes at $(-2, 4)$ and $(1, 1)$

53. about 23 mi

61. vertical: $x = 1$; horizontal: $y = 3$

63. vertical: $x = 1, x = -1$; horizontal: $y = 0$

65. y-axis   **67.** origin

Chapter Review

1. $x^2 + y^2 = 16$ **2.** $x^2 + y^2 = 100$

3. $(x - 3)^2 + (y + 2)^2 = 25$ **4.** $(x + 2)^2 + (y - 4)^2 = 25$

5. $(x - 5)^2 + (y - 10)^2 = 85$

6. $(x - 2)^2 + (y - 2)^2 = 89$ **7.** $(x - 3)^2 + (y + 2)^2 = 16$

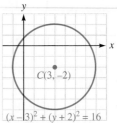

8. $(x + 2)^2 + (y - 5)^2 = 16$ **9.** $y^2 = -2x$

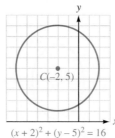

10. $x^2 = 16y$ **11.** $(x + 2)^2 = -\dfrac{4}{11}(y - 3)$

12.

13.

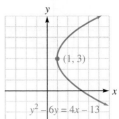

14. $\dfrac{x^2}{36} + \dfrac{y^2}{16} = 1$ **15.** $\dfrac{x^2}{4} + \dfrac{y^2}{25} = 1$

16. $\dfrac{(x + 2)^2}{16} + \dfrac{(y - 3)^2}{9} = 1$

17. $(x - 2)^2 + \dfrac{(y + 1)^2}{4} = 1$

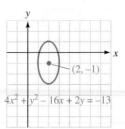

18. $\dfrac{x^2}{4} - \dfrac{y^2}{12} = 1$ **19.** $\dfrac{y^2}{9} - \dfrac{x^2}{16} = 1$ **20.** $\dfrac{x^2}{9} - \dfrac{(y - 3)^2}{16} = 1$

21. $\dfrac{y^2}{9} - \dfrac{(x - 3)^2}{16} = 1$ **22.** $y = \pm\dfrac{4}{5}x$

23. $\dfrac{(x-1)^2}{4} - \dfrac{(y+2)^2}{9} = 1$

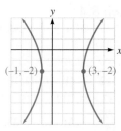

$9x^2 - 4y^2 - 16y - 18x = 43$

24.

$4xy = 1$

25.

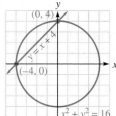

$y = x + 4$

$(0, 4)$

$(-4, 0)$

$x^2 + y^2 = 16$

26.

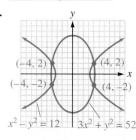

$(-4, 2)$ $(4, 2)$

$(-4, -2)$ $(4, -2)$

$x^2 - y^2 = 12$ $3x^2 + y^2 = 52$

27.

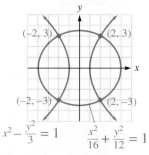

$(-2, 3)$ $(2, 3)$

$(-2, -3)$ $(2, -3)$

$x^2 - \dfrac{y^2}{3} = 1$ $\dfrac{x^2}{16} + \dfrac{y^2}{12} = 1$

28. $(-4, 2), (-4, -2), (4, 2), (4, -2)$

29. $(0, 4), \left(2\sqrt{3}, -2\right)$ **30.** $(-2, 3), (-2, -3), (2, 3), (2, -3)$

Chapter Test

1. $(x-2)^2 + (y-3)^2 = 9$ **2.** $(x-2)^2 + (y-3)^2 = 41$

3. $(x-2)^2 + (y+5)^2 = 169$

4.

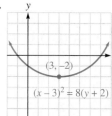

$(2, -3)$

$(x-2)^2 + (y+3)^2 = 9$

5. $(x-3)^2 = 16(y-2)$ **6.** $(y+6)^2 = -4(x-4)$

7. $(x-2)^2 = \dfrac{4}{3}(y+3)$ or $(y+3)^2 = -\dfrac{9}{2}(x-2)$

8.

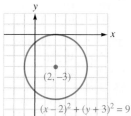

$(3, -2)$

$(x-3)^2 = 8(y+2)$

9. $\dfrac{x^2}{100} + \dfrac{y^2}{64} = 1$ **10.** $\dfrac{x^2}{169} + \dfrac{y^2}{144} = 1$

11. $\dfrac{(x-2)^2}{4} + \dfrac{(y-3)^2}{36} = 1$ **12.**

$(1, 2)$

$\dfrac{(x-1)^2}{4} + \dfrac{(y-2)^2}{9} = 1$

13. $\dfrac{x^2}{25} - \dfrac{y^2}{144} = 1$ **14.** $\dfrac{x^2}{36} - \dfrac{4y^2}{25} = 1$

15. $\dfrac{(x-2)^2}{64} - \dfrac{(y+1)^2}{36} = 1$

16.

$\dfrac{(y-2)^2}{2} - \dfrac{x^2}{8} = 1$

17. $\left(\sqrt{7}, 4\right), \left(-\sqrt{7}, 4\right)$

18. $\left(3\sqrt{2}, 3\right), \left(-3\sqrt{2}, 3\right), \left(3\sqrt{2}, -3\right), \left(-3\sqrt{2}, -3\right)$

19. $(y-2)^2 = 6(x+3)$; parabola

20. $\dfrac{(x-1)^2}{3} + \dfrac{(y+2)^2}{2} = 1$; ellipse

Cumulative Review

1. 16   **2.** $\dfrac{1}{2}$ **3.** y^2 **4.** $x^{17/12}$ **5.** $x^{4/3} - x^{2/3}$

6. $\dfrac{1}{x} + 2 + x$ **7.** $-3x$ **8.** $4t\sqrt{3t}$ **9.** $4x$

10. $x + 3$ **11.** $7\sqrt{2}$ **12.** $-12\sqrt[4]{2} + 10\sqrt[4]{3}$

13. $-18\sqrt{6}$ **14.** $\dfrac{5\sqrt[3]{x^2}}{x}$ **15.** $\dfrac{x + 3\sqrt{x} + 2}{x - 1}$

16. $\sqrt{xy}$ **17.** 2, 7   **18.** $\dfrac{1}{4}$ **19.** $1, -\dfrac{3}{2}$

20. $\dfrac{-2 \pm \sqrt{7}}{3}$ **21.** $7 + 2i$ **22.** $-5 - 7i$

23. $13 + 0i$ **24.** $12 - 6i$ **25.** $-12 - 10i$

26. $\dfrac{3}{2} + \dfrac{1}{2}i$ **27.** $\sqrt{13}$ **28.** $\sqrt{61}$ **29.** -2

30. $\left(1, \dfrac{1}{2}\right)$ **31.** $(-\infty, -2) \cup (3, \infty)$ **32.** $[-2, 3]$

33. 5   **34.** 27   **35.** $12x^2 - 12x + 5$ **36.** $6x^2 + 3$

37. $2^y = x$ **38.** $\log_3 a = b$ **39.** 5   **40.** 3

41. $\dfrac{1}{27}$ **42.** 1   **43.** $y = 2^x$ **44.** x

45. 1.9912   **46.** 0.301   **47.** 1.6902   **48.** 0.1461

49. $\dfrac{2\log 2}{\log 3 - \log 2}$ **50.** 16   **51.** \$2,848.31

52. 1.16056   **53.** (2, 1)   **54.** (1, 1)   **55.** (2, −2)
56. (3, 1)   **57.** −1   **58.** −1   **59.** (−1, −1, 3)
60. (1, 1, 1)

Section 8.1

1. power   **3.** first   **5.** $7 \cdot 6 \cdot 5 \cdot 4 \cdot 3 \cdot 2 \cdot 1$
7. $(n - 1)!$ **9.** 120   **11.** 4,320   **13.** 1,440
15. $\dfrac{1}{1,320}$ **17.** $\dfrac{5}{3}$ **19.** 18,564
21. $a^5 + 5a^4b + 10a^3b^2 + 10a^2b^3 + 5ab^4 + b^5$
23. $x^3 - 3x^2y + 3xy^2 - y^3$ **25.** $a^3 + 3a^2b + 3ab^2 + b^3$
27. $a^5 - 5a^4b + 10a^3b^2 - 10a^2b^3 + 5ab^4 - b^5$
29. $8x^3 + 12x^2y + 6xy^2 + y^3$
31. $x^3 - 6x^2y + 12xy^2 - 8y^3$
33. $16x^4 + 96x^3y + 216x^2y^2 + 216xy^3 + 81y^4$
35. $x^4 - 8x^3y + 24x^2y^2 - 32xy^3 + 16y^4$
37. $x^5 - 15x^4y + 90x^3y^2 - 270x^2y^3 + 405xy^4 - 243y^5$
39. $\dfrac{x^4}{16} + \dfrac{x^3y}{2} + \dfrac{3x^2y^2}{2} + 2xy^3 + y^4$ **41.** $6a^2b^2$
43. $35a^3b^4$ **45.** $-b^5$ **47.** $2,380a^{13}b^4$ **49.** $-4\sqrt{2}a^3$
51. $1,134a^5b^4$ **53.** $\dfrac{3x^2y^2}{2}$ **55.** $-\dfrac{55r^2s^9}{2,048}$
57. $\dfrac{n!}{3!(n-3)!}a^{n-3}b^3$ **59.** $\dfrac{n!}{(r-1)!(n-r+1)!}a^{n-r+1}b^{r-1}$
63. −252   **71.** $3xyz^2(x^2yz^2 - 2z^3 + 5x)$
73. $(a^2 + b^2)(a + b)(a - b)$ **75.** $\dfrac{3 + x}{3 - x}$

Section 8.2

1. domain   **3.** series   **5.** infinite
7. Summation notation   **9.** 6   **11.** $5c$
13. 0, 10, 30, 60, 100, 150   **15.** 21   **17.** $a + 4d$
19. 15   **21.** 15   **23.** 15   **25.** $\dfrac{242}{243}$ **27.** 35
29. 3, 7, 15, 31   **31.** $-4, -2, -1, -\dfrac{1}{2}$ **33.** k, k^2, k^4, k^8
35. $8, \dfrac{16}{k}, \dfrac{32}{k^2}, \dfrac{64}{k^3}$ **37.** an alternating infinite series
39. not an alternating infinite series   **41.** 30   **43.** −50
45. 40   **47.** 500   **49.** $\dfrac{7}{12}$ **51.** 160   **53.** 3,725
59. 6 cm   **61.** 26 ft

Section 8.3

1. $(n - 1)$ **3.** infinite   **5.** $a_n = a + (n - 1)d$
7. Arithmetic means   **9.** 1, 3, 5, 7, 9, 11
11. $5, \dfrac{7}{2}, 2, \dfrac{1}{2}, -1, -\dfrac{5}{2}$ **13.** $9, \dfrac{23}{2}, 14, \dfrac{33}{2}, 19, \dfrac{43}{2}$
15. 318   **17.** 6   **19.** 370   **21.** 44   **23.** $\dfrac{25}{2}, 15, \dfrac{35}{2}$
25. $-\dfrac{82}{15}, -\dfrac{59}{15}, -\dfrac{12}{5}, -\dfrac{13}{15}$ **27.** 285   **29.** 555
31. $157\dfrac{1}{2}$ **33.** 20,100   **35.** 1080°; 1800°   **37.** $460
39. $1,587,500   **41.** 80 ft   **43.** 210   **49.** 6   **51.** −1
53. $1, -1, i, -i$

Section 8.4

1. r^{n-1} **3.** ar^{n-1} **5.** infinite   **7.** Geometric means
9. 10, 20, 40, 80   **11.** −2, −6, −18, −54
13. $3, 3\sqrt{2}, 6, 6\sqrt{2}$ **15.** 2, 6, 18, 54   **17.** 256
19. −162   **21.** $10\sqrt[4]{2}, 10\sqrt[4]{4}$ or $10\sqrt{2}, 10\sqrt[4]{8}$
23. 8, 32, 128, 512   **25.** 124   **27.** −29,524
29. $\dfrac{1,995}{32}$ **31.** 18   **33.** 8   **35.** $\dfrac{5}{9}$ **37.** $\dfrac{25}{99}$
39. 23   **41.** 12.96 ft, 400 ft   **43.** 5.13 m
45. $69.82   **47.** about $\dfrac{1}{3}C$ **49.** about 1.03×10^{20}
51. $180,176.87   **53.** $2,001.60   **55.** $2,013.62
57. $264,094.58   **59.** 5,000   **61.** 1.8447×10^{19} grains
63. no   **65.** $5 - 3i$ **67.** $10 + 0i$ **69.** $\dfrac{1}{5} + \dfrac{8}{5}i$
71. $0 - i$

Section 8.5

1. two   **3.** $n = k + 1$
5. $5 = 5; 15 = 15; 30 = 30; 50 = 50$
7. $7 = 7; 17 = 17; 30 = 30; 46 = 46$
29. no
37. a. 1   **b.** 3   **c.** 7   **d.** 15
39.   **41.**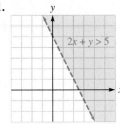

Section 8.6

1. 24   **3.** $\dfrac{n!}{(n - r)!}$ **5.** 1   **7.** $\dfrac{n!}{r!(n - r)!}$ **9.** 1
11. $\dfrac{n!}{a!b!\cdots}$ **13.** 840   **15.** 35   **17.** 120   **19.** 5
21. 1   **23.** 1,200   **25.** 40   **27.** 2,278   **29.** 144
31. 8,000,000   **33.** 240   **35.** 6   **37.** 40,320
39. 14,400   **41.** 24,360   **43.** 5,040   **45.** 48
47. 96   **49.** 210   **51.** 24   **53.** 5,040   **55.** 60
57. 2,721,600   **59.** 1,120   **61.** 59,400   **63.** 272
65. 28   **67.** 252   **69.** 142,506   **71.** 66   **73.** 256
75. 56   **83.** 2   **85.** 4   **87.** true   **89.** true

Section 8.7

1. experiment   **3.** $\dfrac{n(E)}{n(S)}$

5. {(1, H), (2, H), (3, H), (4, H), (5, H), (6, H), (1, T), (2, T), (3, T), (4, T), (5, T), (6, T)}   **7.** {a, b, c, d, e, f, g, h, i, j, k, l, m, n, o, p, q, r, s, t, u, v, w, x, y, z}   **9.** $\dfrac{1}{6}$ **11.** $\dfrac{2}{3}$
13. $\dfrac{19}{42}$ **15.** $\dfrac{13}{42}$ **17.** $\dfrac{3}{8}$ **19.** 0   **21.** $\dfrac{1}{12}$
23. $\dfrac{1}{169}$ **25.** $\dfrac{5}{12}$ **27.** about 6.3×10^{-12} **29.** 0
31. $\dfrac{3}{13}$ **33.** $\dfrac{1}{6}$ **35.** $\dfrac{1}{8}$ **37.** $\dfrac{5}{16}$

39. {SSSS, SSSF, SSFS, SFSS, FSSS, SSFF, SFSF, FSSF, SFFS, FSFS, FFSS, SFFF, FSFF, FFSF, FFFS, FFFF}

41. $\dfrac{1}{4}$ **43.** $\dfrac{1}{4}$ **45.** 1 **47.** $\dfrac{32}{119}$ **49.** $\dfrac{1}{3}$

51. 0.18 **53.** 0.14 **55.** about 33% **57.** no

59. $-10, 4$ **61.** $(-4, 10)$

Chapter Review

1. 720 **2.** 30,240 **3.** 8 **4.** $\dfrac{280}{3}$

5. $x^3 + 3x^2y + 3xy^2 + y^3$

6. $p^4 + 4p^3q + 6p^2q^2 + 4pq^3 + q^4$

7. $a^5 - 5a^4b + 10a^3b^2 - 10a^2b^3 + 5ab^4 - b^5$

8. $8a^3 - 12a^2b + 6ab^2 - b^3$ **9.** $56a^5b^3$ **10.** $80x^3y^2$

11. $84x^3y^6$ **12.** $439,040x^3$ **13.** 63 **14.** 9

15. 5, 17, 53, 161 **16.** $-2, 8, 128, 32,768$ **17.** 90

18. 60 **19.** 1,718 **20.** -360 **21.** 117 **22.** 281

23. -92 **24.** $-\dfrac{135}{2}$ **25.** $\dfrac{7}{2}, 5, \dfrac{13}{2}$

26. 25, 40, 55, 70, 85 **27.** 3,320 **28.** 5,780

29. $-5,220$ **30.** $-1,540$ **31.** $\dfrac{1}{729}$ **32.** 13,122

33. $\dfrac{9}{16,384}$ **34.** $\dfrac{8}{15,625}$ **35.** $2\sqrt{2}, 4, 4\sqrt{2}$

36. $4, -8, 16, -32$ **37.** 16 **38.** $\dfrac{3,280}{27}$ **39.** 6,560

40. $\dfrac{2,295}{128}$ **41.** $\dfrac{520,832}{78,125}$ **42.** $\dfrac{3,280}{3}$ **43.** $16\sqrt{2}$

44. $\dfrac{2}{3}$ **45.** $\dfrac{3}{25}$ **46.** no sum **47.** 1 **48.** $\dfrac{1}{3}$

49. 1 **50.** $\dfrac{17}{99}$ **51.** $\dfrac{5}{11}$ **52.** $4,775.81

53. 6,516; 3,134 **54.** $3,486.78

55. $1 = 1$; $9 = 9$; $36 = 36$; $100 = 100$

57. 6,720 **58.** 35 **59.** 1 **60.** 4,050 **61.** 564,480

62. 840 **63.** 21 **64.** 66 **65.** 120 **66.** $\dfrac{56}{1,287}$

67. $\dfrac{1}{6}$ **68.** $\dfrac{33}{66,640}$ **69.** 20,160 **70.** 90,720

72. 24 **73.** $\dfrac{1}{108,290}$ **74.** $\dfrac{108,289}{108,290}$

75. about 6.3×10^{-12} **76.** $\dfrac{60}{143}$ **77.** $\dfrac{1}{2}$ **78.** $\dfrac{7}{13}$

79. $\dfrac{1}{2,598,960}$ **80.** $\dfrac{33}{16,660}$ **81.** $\dfrac{15}{16}$

Chapter Test

1. 144 **2.** 384 **3.** $10x^4y$ **4.** $112a^2b^6$ **5.** 27

6. -36 **7.** 155 **8.** -130 **9.** 9, 14, 19

10. $-6, -18$ **11.** 255.75 **12.** about 9

13. about $0.42C$ **14.** about $1.46C$ **16.** 800,000

17. 42 **18.** 24 **19.** 28 **20.** 1 **21.** 576

22. 120 **23.** 60 **24.** {(H, H, H), (H, H, T), (H, T, H), (H, T, T), (T, H, H), (T, H, T), (T, T, H), (T, T, T)}

25. $\dfrac{1}{6}$ **26.** $\dfrac{2}{13}$ **27.** $\dfrac{33}{66,640}$ **28.** $\dfrac{1}{9}$ **29.** $\dfrac{87}{245}$

30. $\dfrac{12}{19}$

Index